Sports Law and Regulation

ASPEN CASEBOOK SERIES

Sports Law and Regulation

Cases, Materials, and Problems

Fifth Edition

Matthew J. Mitten

Professor of Law and Executive Director
National Sports Law Institute
Marquette University Law School

Timothy Davis

John W. & Ruth H. Turnage Professor of Law
Wake Forest University School of Law

N. Jeremi Duru

Professor of Law
Washington College of Law
American University

Barbara Osborne

Professor, Exercise and Sport Science
Adjunct Professor, School of Law
University of North Carolina

 Wolters Kluwer

Printed in the United States of America.

1 2 3 4 5 6 7 8 9 0

ISBN 978-1-5438-1081-3

Library of Congress Cataloging-in-Publication Data

Names: Mitten, Matthew J., 1959- author. | Davis, Timothy, 1954- author. | Duru, N. Jeremi, author. | Osborne, Barbara (Writer on sports law), author.
Title: Sports law and regulation : cases, materials, and problems / Matthew J. Mitten, Professor of Law and Executive Director, National Sports Law Institute, Marquette University Law School; Timothy Davis, John W. & Ruth H. Turnage Professor of Law, Wake Forest University School of Law; N. Jeremi Duru, Professor of Law, Washington College of Law, American University; Barbara Osborne, Professor, Exercise and Sport Science Adjunct Professor, School of Law University of North Carolina.
Description: Fifth edition. | New York : Wolters Kluwer, [2020] | Series: Aspen casebook series | Includes bibliographical references and index. | Summary: "Casebook for use in upper level Sports Law course"– Provided by publisher.
Identifiers: LCCN 2019040081 | ISBN 9781543810813 (hardcover) | ISBN 9781543817133 (ebook)
Subjects: LCSH: Sports–Law and legislation–United States. | LCGFT: Casebooks (Law)
Classification: LCC KF3989 .S6775 2020 | DDC 344.73/099–dc23
LC record available at https://lccn.loc.gov/2019040081

About Wolters Kluwer Legal & Regulatory U.S.

Wolters Kluwer Legal & Regulatory U.S. delivers expert content and solutions in the areas of law, corporate compliance, health compliance, reimbursement, and legal education. Its practical solutions help customers successfully navigate the demands of a changing environment to drive their daily activities, enhance decision quality and inspire confident outcomes.

Serving customers worldwide, its legal and regulatory portfolio includes products under the Aspen Publishers, CCH Incorporated, Kluwer Law International, ftwilliam.com and MediRegs names. They are regarded as exceptional and trusted resources for general legal and practice-specific knowledge, compliance and risk management, dynamic workflow solutions, and expert commentary.

To my wife Brenda for her love, patience,
and support in connection with our fifth edition
and the four prior editions.

—Matthew J. Mitten

To my wife, Ida,
and my daughter, Adia,
for their love and support.

—Timothy Davis

To my wife, Mellissa, and my sons,
Kanayo, Anikwe, and Nnaji for
their constant love and support.

—N. Jeremi Duru

To my parents for absolutely everything,
and to my family for their love,
patience, and support.

—Barbara Osborne

Summary of Contents

Contents

Preface

Fifth Edition

Our fifth edition has the same general organization and 12 chapters as our fourth edition and provides a comprehensive and timely discussion of youth, high school, college, Olympic, and professional sports legal issues, including gender and racial equity, health, safety, risk management, and intellectual property law issues. Significant additions include: revised NCAA bylaws relating to the cancelation or reduction of student-athlete scholarships, student-athlete transfer eligibility, student-athlete and agent interactions, the addition of independent members in the governance structure, and the new enforcement and penalties structure; discussion of NCAA infractions decisions applying the NCAA's post-2013 penalty structure; antitrust cases challenging NCAA eligibility rules; an updated comment on concussions that includes recent cases, state legislation seeking to reduce the incidence of concussions, and settlements of concussion-related disputes between claimants and the NCAA, NFL, and NHL; discussion of coaches' involvement in the college admissions and basketball scandals and a revised coaching contract negotiation exercise; provisions of the NFL, NBA, MLB, and NHL collective bargaining agreements; a revised problem analyzing the NBA uniform player contract; updated player association regulations governing sports agents; proposed revisions to the Uniform Athlete Agents Act; updated league drug and personal conduct policies; discussion of U.S. Safe Sport legislation and the obligations of sports organizations to protect athletes from sexual misconduct; significantly revised Olympic and international sports law materials, including recent CAS awards interpreting and applying the 2015 World Anti-doping Code as well as summaries of national court and European Court of Human Rights cases recognizing the independence of the CAS and the validity of its awards; a reorganized gender equity chapter that includes new and expanded discussion of Title IX regulations and pregnancy and sexual harassment, sexual orientation discrimination in sports, the participation rights of transgender and intersex athletes (including the Castor Semenya CAS award), the NCAA's 2018 sexual violence policy, and major professional sports leagues' domestic violence policies; new commentary questioning the baseball rule and the limited duty rule as applied to absolve stadium owners of liability to spectators; and revised or new problems relating to antitrust, labor relations, and intellectual property issues. Like past editions, the fifth edition has an accompanying extensive Teacher's Manual with sample syllabi, explanations, and suggestions for effectively teaching the materials in each chapter and detailed discussion of all problems. We miss the friendship and contributions of Rodney Smith. We are happy, however, to welcome Barbara Osborne to our team. As always, you are welcome to contact any of us with your comments and suggestions for improving our book: Matt (matt.mitten@marquette.edu), Tim (davistx@wfu.edu), Jeremi (duru@wcl.american.edu), or Barbara (sportlaw@unc.edu).

Matthew J. Mitten
Timothy Davis
N. Jeremi Duru
Barbara Osborne

October 2019

First Edition

This book facilitates study and analysis of the significant legal, historical, economic, and sociological issues affecting the development of both the amateur and professional sports industries in the twenty-first century. It provides sports law professors and students with a comprehensive, multipurpose text of cases, materials, and problems that gives a balanced perspective on how some of America's largest and most popular industries are regulated by our legal system. The book takes an in-depth look at the legal regulation of interscholastic athletics, intercollegiate athletics, Olympic and international sports, and professional sports.

In our experience, law students most effectively learn about legal regulation of the sports industries by understanding the underlying historical, economic, and sociological factors influencing the developing nature of the various legal relationships that exist therein (e.g., athlete and team, university and NCAA, professional team and league, etc.). To accomplish this objective, this book initially covers the respective internal regulatory mechanisms for the different levels of athletic competition (e.g., high school, college, Olympic, and professional sports); then it considers the primary bodies of public law that shape and constrain them. Individual chapters of this book focus on racial and gender equity issues in sports and facilitate multidisciplinary consideration of these important, contemporary topics. The book considers economic policy and consumer welfare issues as part of its coverage of how courts have applied antitrust law to the sports industries. This interdisciplinary examination of sports and law also is intended to appeal to upper-division undergraduate and graduate students.

This book provides a vehicle for applying general principles typically covered in first-year courses, such as contracts, torts, constitutional law, criminal law, and civil procedure, to sports-related legal issues and problems. For example, it includes coverage of the following issues: the nature of a university's contractual obligations to its student-athletes, tort liability of an athletic event participant to another participant, a state high school athletic association's status as a state actor and high school students' federal constitutional rights, criminal liability for on-field violence, and the implications of American courts' lack of personal jurisdiction over international sports governing bodies.

A sports law course also provides a means of initially exposing students to specialized areas of law such as antitrust, labor, intellectual property, and workers compensation laws as well as relatively new legislation such as the Americans with Disabilities Act. Our book considers how each of these areas of law (and others) regulates the sports industries. It also provides introductory materials and hypothetical problems to facilitate students' understanding of these legal principles and their application to the sports industries and society in general.

This book incorporates the strengths of existing casebooks while also providing broader coverage of contemporary sports law issues. It includes the leading historical and recent sports law cases and provides detailed explanatory material, notes, and questions to facilitate students' understanding of complex legal doctrines. It also raises some of the deeper philosophical, sociological, psychological, and economic policy issues that arise in the sports context. This approach both mirrors the practice of law in the twenty-first century generally and heightens students' understanding of sports-related legal issues. In addition, this book includes some negotiation exercises and problems designed to develop students' client counseling and transactional skills. These unique features combine both theoretical and practical components to provide sports law students with a well-rounded learning experience.

The breadth and depth of this book provide the flexibility necessary to achieve a wide range of teaching and learning objectives. It is suitable for use as a primary text in either a two- or three-credit-hour general sports law course covering individually selected amateur and sports law topics as well as issues common to both industries. It also can be used in separate two-hour or three-hour courses focusing primarily on either amateur or professional sports law issues. Alternatively, it can be used for two separate one-semester courses designated Sports Law I and Sports Law II. In addition, this book provides a suitable text for use in sports management programs and other academic disciplines studying sports law.

A sports law course provides several important educational benefits in addition to providing students with an understanding of the legal framework governing the amateur and professional sports industries. Perhaps the most important one is that the study of sports law provides students with a package of readily transferable knowledge and skills applicable to a wide variety of legal and non-legal careers. It is one of the relatively few law school courses not limited to consideration of a single, discrete area of substantive law. This book enables thoughtful study of how several different bodies of law combine to regulate the amateur and professional sports industries. It also facilitates students' ability to synthesize several different discrete bodies of law, to recognize how they combine to govern sports, and to understand how laws that conflict are harmonized. In doing so, the book also encourages student examination of the role of sport in our culture and how law responds to serious cultural and moral questions.

In whatever form this book is used, we trust that students and faculty alike will enjoy their engagement with the material as much as we have. We have found that sports law deals with issues that merit deep study and reflection. We hope that this book encourages such study.

Matthew J. Mitten
Timothy Davis
Rodney K. Smith
Robert C. Berry

March 2005

Acknowledgments

Matt expresses his gratitude to Brent J. Nowicki, Managing Counsel, Court of Arbitration for Sport (Lausanne, Switzerland) for his review and helpful comments regarding Chapter 4 (Regulating Olympic and International Athletics).

Tim expresses his gratitude to Wake Forest law students Maurice Goldston and Ryan Madden for their research assistance.

Jeremi wishes to thank Alexandria Adkins, Aaron Levitats, and Erin Winkfield for their valuable research assistance.

Barbara expresses her appreciation to her predecessors, Robert Berry and Rod Smith, and to her coauthors for their assistance and support.

We also thank the following authors, publishers, and copyright holders for permitting us to include excerpts from these works:

Athlete Graduation Rates Continue to Climb, NCAA News, Sept. 1, 2003. Copyright © 2003 National Collegiate Athletic Association. 2013. All rights reserved.

Collective Bargaining Agreement between The NFL Management Council and the NFL Players Association, 2002-2008, as amended Jan. 28, 2002. Copyright © 2002 by The NFL Management Council and the NFL Players Association. Reprinted with permission.

Davis, Timothy, *The Myth of the Superspade: The Persistence of Racism in College Athletics*, 22 Fordham Urban Law Journal 615 (1995). Copyright © 1995 Fordham Urban Law Journal. Reprinted with permission.

Davis, Timothy, *What Is Sports Law?*, 11 Marq. Sports L.J. 211 (2001). Copyright © 2001 Marquette Sports Law Journal. Reprinted with permission.

Gould, William B. IV, The Cambridge Lectures, Queens College, University of Cambridge, England, 1995. Copyright © 1995 by University of Cambridge. Reprinted with permission.

National Collegiate Athletic Association, 2012-13 NCAA Division I Manual (2012). Copyright © 2012 National Collegiate Athletic Association. All rights reserved.

National Collegiate Athletic Association, National Letter of Intent. Copyright © 2013 National Collegiate Athletic Association. All rights reserved.

National Conference of Commissioners on Uniform State Laws, Uniform Athlete Agents Act. Copyright © 2000 by National Conference of Commissioners on Uniform State Laws. Material here was reprinted with the permission of the National Conference of Commissioners on Uniform State Laws, 676 North St. Clair Street, Suite 1700, Chicago, Illinois 60611.

CHAPTER

1

An Introduction to the Study of Sports Law

A. WHAT IS SPORTS LAW?[1]

Should sports law be recognized as an independent substantive area of the law like torts, contracts, or employment law? Scholars have debated this question.

1. The Traditional View: "Sports Law" Does Not Exist

The traditional view is that sports law represents nothing more than an amalgamation of various substantive areas of the law that are relevant in the sports context. According to this perspective, the term *sports law* is a misnomer given that sport represents a form of activity and entertainment that is governed by the legal system in its entirety. Adherents to the traditional perspective argue that "sports law simply entails the application of basic legal precepts to a specific industry" that are drawn from other substantive areas of the law. Michael J. Cozzillio and Mark S. Levinstein, Sports Law 7 (1997). Consequently, no separately identifiable body of law exists that can be characterized as sports law.

2. The Moderate Position: "Sports Law" May Develop into a Field of Law

Other commentators have begun increasingly to question the traditional view that no corpus of law exists that can be characterized as an independent field of law called sports law. Some have staked out what represents a middle ground. Professor Kenneth Shropshire acknowledges that developments such as state and federal legislation impacting sports (for example, state statutes regulating sports agents and federal statutes such as Title IX) suggest a "growing sports-only corpus" of law. Kenneth L. Shropshire, *Introduction: Sports Law?*, 35 Am. Bus. L.J. 181, 182 (1998).

---

1. This section is adapted from Timothy Davis, *What Is Sports Law?*, 11 Marq. Sports L. Rev. 211 (2001).

Professor Burlette Carter argues that sports law is in the midst of an exciting, yet challenging, transformative process. According to Professor Carter, this process parallels the increased focus by law schools on sports and the growing significance of sports regulation to participants, organizations, and communities. She believes that these developments will better shape the contours of this emerging field of study. This in turn, will eventually transform sports law from "a course without a corpus" to a widely recognized independent substantive area of law. Burlette Carter, *Introduction: What Makes a "Field" a Field?*, 1 Va. J. Sports & L. 235, 245 (1999).

3. "Sports Law": A Separate Field of Law

Others argue that sports law currently exists as a field of law. Adherents to this view emphasize the growing body of case and statutory law specific to the sports industry as evidence of the existence of a separately identifiable body of law. Pointing to the increasing body of judicial and legislative law specific to sports, Professor Simone Gardiner argues:

> [I]t is true to say that [sports law] is largely an amalgam of interrelated legal disciplines involving such areas as contract, taxation, employment, competition and criminal law but dedicated legislation and case law has developed and will continue to do so. As an area of academic study and extensive practitioner involvement, the time is right to accept that a new legal area has been born—sports law.

Simon Gardiner et al., Sports Law 74 (1998).

Commentators also propose that references to sports law as merely an amalgamation of various other substantive areas of the law ignore an important present-day reality—very few substantive areas of the law fit into separate categories that are divorced from and independent of other substantive areas of the law. Doctrinal overlap exists not only within sports law, but within other areas of law as well. According to Professor Carter, "the field of sports law has moved beyond the traditional antitrust and labor law boundaries into sports representation and legal ethics, sports and corporate structure, sports and disability, sports and race, sports and gender, sports and taxation, international issues in sports law and numerous other permutations." Carter, *supra*, at 239-240.

Proponents of the sports law designation and those sympathetic to the view also argue that reticence to recognize sports law as a specific body of law may reflect attitudes regarding the intellectual seriousness of sports. In this regard, they emphasize the tendency to marginalize the study of sports rather than treat it as any other form of business. The intellectual marginalization of sport has been attributed, in part, to the belief that social relations extant in sports were not deemed proper subjects for reconstruction into legal relationships. Thus, private and public law were considered "inappropriate [mechanisms for] controlling the social norms of sport." Gardiner, *supra* at 45. The competing and increasingly predominant view, however, casts sports as a significant economic activity suitable, like other big businesses, to regulation, whether it be internal or external.

In the end, whether sports law is recognized as an independent field of law may turn on the perceptions of those who practice, teach, and engage in scholarship related to sports law. Professor Carter asks that we consider the following:

> But what makes a field a field? The answer is that a field becomes a field not because it is inherently so but because in our public legal dealings we shape it

as such, defining the concepts and legal norms that will prevail uniquely in that context. It becomes a field because enough people with power on all sides are so affected by it to require some special treatment of it in the law.

Carter, *supra* at 244-245.

––––––––––––––––

Regardless of the position that is adopted regarding the "what is sports law" debate, most would agree that matters arising in the sports law context implicate diverse substantive areas of law. Moreover, sports-related cases are sculpting a body of law particularly applicable in the sports context and influencing the development of general legal principles. According to Professor Daniel Lazaroff:

> On both the federal and state levels, sports related cases have not only had a profound impact on the narrow questions raised by the facts of particular disputes, but have also significantly influenced more general jurisprudential trends. . . . The growing body of sports-based legal authority has shaped the face of general legal doctrine in several important areas. In federal law, antitrust and labor doctrine have been significantly shaped by cases originating in the sports industries. In addition, constitutional principles involving drug testing and search and seizure have been influenced by sports law cases. On the state level, important tort doctrine has been and will continue to be affected by disputes arising in the context of sports. Undoubtedly, other areas of the law will be similarly influenced by sports litigation.

Daniel E. Lazaroff, *The Influence of Sports Law on American Jurisprudence*, 1 Va. Sports & Ent. L.J. 1, 2 (2001).

As sport evolves at the national and global levels, its impact on the development of a special and influential body of law is evident. An article that examines the development of international, comparative, and national sports law proposes that sport is an important contributor to the global economy and culture, which has resulted in the development of a body of sports law that is globally significant. Matthew J. Mitten and Hayden Opie, *"Sports Law": Implications for the Development of International, Comparative, and National Law and Dispute Resolution*, 85 Tul. L. Rev. 269 (2010).

NOTE AND QUESTION

Scholars have identified several factors that provide indicia that an area of law has matured to the point of common acceptance. Among them are: (1) the unique application by courts of law from other disciplines to a specific context; (2) factual peculiarities within a specific context that produce problems that require specialized analysis; (3) "within the proposed discipline, [the] elements of its subject matter must connect, interact, or interrelate"; (4) the proposed discipline significantly affects "the nation's (or the world's) business, economy, culture, or society"; (5) the development of interventionist legislation to regulate specific relationships; (6) the development and publication of legal casebooks, law journals, and other publications that specifically focus on the proposed discipline; and (7) acceptance of the proposed field as a separate substantive area by law schools and legal associations, such as bar associations. Timothy Davis, *What Is Sports Law?*, 11 Marq. Sports L.J. 211 (2001). As you continue your studies this semester, consider which of the foregoing factors support designating sports law as a separate corpus of law.

For further discussion of whether sports law is a separately identifiable substantive area of the law, see Simone Gardiner et al., Sports Law (4th ed. 2011); John C. Weistart and Cym H. Lowell, The Law of Sports xviii (1979); Carter, *supra*; Kenneth L. Shropshire, *Introduction: Sports Law?*, 35 Am. Bus. L.J. 181, 182 (1998). See also Todd S. Aagaard, *Environmental Law as a Legal Field: An Inquiry in Legal Taxonomy*, 95 Cornell L. Rev. 221 (2010).

B.   IS THE STUDY OF SPORTS LAW MARGINALIZED?

Notwithstanding its widespread influence, only recently has sport become recognized as a "legitimate" subject of intellectual inquiry. What accounts for the historical and continued marginalization of sport? Given our preoccupation with sports, it is remarkable, as Professors Gorn and Oriard note, "that athletics have remained so far beyond the boundary of intellectual discourse, [despite the fact that the] study of sport can take us to the very heart of critical issues in the study of culture and society." Elliott J. Gorn and Michael Oriard, *Taking Sports Seriously*, Chron. Higher Educ., Mar. 24, 1995, at A52.

Professor Drew Hyland agrees, stating: "[The] social phenomenon in American life which has the biggest impact on our culture, yet which receives the least serious attention from our intellectual standard-bearers, is sport and athletics. There seems to be a longstanding prejudice of professorial philosophy." Drew A. Hyland, Philosophy of Sport xiii (1990). Professor Scott Krechmar states that "college sport, given its centrality and influence in American culture and higher education, has been given less attention than it is due." R. Scott Krechmar, *Research, Sport, and Higher Education: An Introduction to the Journal of Intercollegiate Sport*, 1 J. Intercollegiate Sport 1, 1 (2008).

In a forthcoming article, Professor Robert Illig comments on the value of teaching sports law. He states that "[w]hether or not it constitutes a distinct field or a promising career opportunity, sports law has significant pedagogical value. It can serve as a vehicle for teaching how to navigate intersecting and conflicting areas of law. . . ." Robert C. Illig, *The Case for Teaching Sports Law*, at *17. See also David S. Caudill, *The Sports Law Course as Advanced Legal Skills Training*, 1 Va. J. Sports & L. 246, 246 (1999).

NOTE AND QUESTIONS

Why has sports been marginalized as an area of serious academic study?

Despite the continuing discussion in American studies of "the body" (of how human beings conceive of themselves physically), athletes' bodies remain curiously off-limits. . . . Is "the body" as conceived in cultural studies a rhetorical construction, while the bodies of athletes are too palpably real? Are we, as intellectuals, just uncomfortable with physicality, because our own bailiwick is the life of the mind?

Could it be that professors are creatures of words while the language of athletics is fundamentally non-verbal? Or are we simply playing out the long-standing faculty antagonism to the distorted priorities of universities with multimillion-dollar athletics programs?

Elliott J. Gorn and Michael Oriard, *Taking Sport Seriously*, Chron. Higher Educ., Mar. 24, 1995, A52. Academics' treatment of sport as a marginal social and cultural phenomenon transcends national boundaries. Hans Ulrich Gumbrecht, In Praise of Athletic Beauty 21 (2006). Gumbrecht offers several explanations for the global academic devaluation of sport, including intellectuals' preference to attach a higher status to those things that are metaphysical in contrast to those things deemed "material (or merely corporeal)." *Id.* at 30.

Do the views expressed by these scholars hold true today? If so, does the treatment of sport stem from the perception that sport is more a matter of entertainment than business, and therefore not worthy of serious academic interest? Will a failure to seriously study sport "distort our view of culture," as suggested by Professors Gorn and Oriard?

C.   THE SIGNIFICANCE OF SPORT AND SPORTS LAW

1.   *The Role of Sport in Society*

In commenting on the role of sport in society, Professor Matthew Mitten states:

> There is a reciprocal relationship between sports and societal values. Sport incorporates society's existing values and reinforces these values on the playing field, in its rules, and through its established institutions. Sport also exports its principles and the lessons learned from participating in athletics and its governance to society in general.

Matthew J. Mitten, *Foreword* to *Symposium: Sports Law as a Reflection of Society's Law and Values*, 38 S. Tex. L. Rev. 999 (1997). The following discussion initially analyzes the significance of sport in relation to its role in shaping and reflecting societal values. The discussion then provides specific illustrations of how sport intersects with other important aspects of American society.

As a predicate to this discussion, we attempt to define sports. Although definitions vary, we adopt one offered by a leading sociologist. "[S]ports are physical activities that involve challenges or competitive contests." Jay Coakley, Sport in Society: Issues and Controversies 6 (12th ed. 2017). See also D. Stanley Eitzen and George H. Sage, Sociology of North American Sport 15 (8th ed. 2008) (defining sport as "any competitive physical activity that is guided by established rules"). The SportsAccord, formerly known as the General Assembly of International Sports Federations, states that in considering new membership applications, it defines sport as follows:

1. The sport proposed should include an element of competition.
2. The sport should not rely on any element of "luck" specifically integrated into the sport.

3. The sport should not be judged to pose an undue risk to the health and
safety of its athletes or participants.
4. The sport proposed should in no way be harmful to any living creature.
5. The sport should not rely on equipment that is provided by a single
supplier.

Sports Accord, *Definition of Sport,* http://www.sportaccord.com/about/
membership/definition-of-sport.php.

These definitions inevitably lead to additional questions, including why some
activities are considered sports and others are not. Is an activity a sport merely
because it possesses the unique features suggested in the preceding definitions,
such as formalized structures (i.e., informal and formal rules enforced by regulatory bodies), off-field cooperation necessary to produce on-field competition,
and uncertain outcomes? Consider whether the Oxford and Cambridge Varsity
Wine Tasting Competition, featured in a segment on *Real Sports with Bryant
Gumbel* (HBO Episode 265 April 2019), meets the definition of sport. Oxford
and Cambridge universities have been competing in wine tasting for decades. It
is a timed competition lasting 80 minutes. Each team consists of six tasters. Each
taster has to taste six wines blindly to determine type of grape, nation of origin,
region of origin, vintage, and other categories. The competitors physically train
their olfactory senses and taste buds. They also train for stamina. Additionally,
there are concerns about performance-enhancing drugs: should nasal spray be
permitted before or during competition?

Is whether an activity is considered a sport more a function of other variables,
including cultural and historical tradition, the amount of television coverage
an activity garners, and political processes (e.g., the ability of particular countries to export their values and traditions to other nations, as the English did
with soccer)? See Stefan Szymanski and Andrew Zimbalist, National Pastime
48-83 (2006). Given these factors, could Nathan's Famous Hot Dog Eating
Contest, which occurs every Fourth of July, be considered a sport? See https://
nathansfamous.com/hot-dog-eating-contest/.

The designation of an activity as a sport is not merely a matter of intellectual
curiosity, since the resolution of disputes may hinge on such a designation. In
Biediger v. Quinnipiac University, 691 F.3d 85 (2d Cir. 2012), the court found that
cheerleading was not a sport for Title IX purposes. In reaching that conclusion, the court looked at the characteristics of athletic competition and concluded that cheerleading, as then constituted at Quinnipiac University, was an
activity and not a sport. See also *Fontes v. Irvine Unified Sch. Dist.,* 30 Cal. Rptr.
2d 521 (Cal. App. 1994) (noting characteristics of a sport). Looking ahead to
our discussion of gender equity in Chapter 10, the significance of designating
cheerleading and dance as sports is controversial, particularly given the Title IX
implications of such a characterization.

The importance of examining definitions of sport has taken on increased
significance as other activities, in addition to cheerleading, seek legitimacy as
sports. Among the most significant is esports, which involves video game competitions. In 2014, esports took a major step toward recognition as sport when
Robert Morris University-Illinois incorporated esports into its athletics program
and announced it would allocate athletic scholarships to esports players. As more
schools added esports programs, the National Association of Collegiate Esports
(NACE), a voluntary membership, non-profit organization was established in
2016 to advance varsity collegiate esports. The organization currently serves 130

member institutions that are granting $15 million in esports scholarships to student-gamers. See NAC Esports, https://nacesports.org/about/. Harrisburg University (PA) offers full scholarships to 20 student-gamers enrolled in their esports academic program. Student-gamers try out, practice several hours each day, work with coaches, and are expected to maintain a high GPA. The university has invested in facilities and secured sponsors to defray the costs. Their Overwatch team went undefeated in the 2019 season, and Harrisburg believes their investment in esports will build their institutional identity. Commercialism also impacts collegiate esports, with Blizzard Entertainment owning a collegiate program called TESPA and sponsoring "gaming clubs" at 270 North American colleges. Steven Asarch, *Esports College Scholarships Create a League of Their Own,* Newsweek, May 30, 2019. https://www.newsweek.com/esports-college-teams-scholarship-overwatch-lol-1439554. Professional esports is a rapidly growing at a rate of 41% per year, with an estimated 300 million spectators in a $1.5 billion market by 2020. John Koetsier, *Esports: The New Football Scholarship? Gaming Scholarships for College Grew 480% Last Year,* Forbes, May 12, 2018. https://www.forbes.com/sites/johnkoetsier/2018/05/12/esports-the-new-football-scholarship-gaming-scholarships-grew-480-last-year/#2625eb1322a1 The NCAA Board of Governors voted in April 2019 to table discussions on the possibility of offering esports championships. Is NCAA governance a good fit for esports? What would be the advantages and disadvantages?

In 2012, the Court of Arbitration for Sports (CAS), whose jurisdiction is limited to the resolution of "sports-related disputes," accepted jurisdiction in a case involving chess. In October 2017, however, the European Court of Justice (ECJ) ruled that bridge is not a sport. Determining that a sport must involve "a not negligible physical element," it concluded that bridge, which involves only mental exercises, does not satisfy this requirement. Its ruling rejected the English Bridge Union's request for an exemption from value-added tax (VAT) on entry fees to its competitions based on its contention that bridge is a sport. ESPN televises the World Series of Poker — are card games "sport"?

a.   Positive Values Associated with Sport

Some sociologists argue that sport "is infused with themes consistent with the American Dream." Howard L. Nixon II and James H. Frey, A Sociology of Sport 41 (1996). These themes include "competition, individualism, [and] achievement." Eitzen and Sage, *supra,* at 10. Sport has also been viewed as holding the potential to instill within its participants values of teamwork, perseverance, sacrifice, and hard work. What has been called the "American Sports Creed" stands for the proposition that "sport builds character, teaches discipline, develops competitiveness, prepares participants to compete in life, enhances physical and mental fitness, and contributes to a belief in (Christian) religion and a patriotic belief in America." Nixon and Frey, *supra,* at 41.

Similarly, academics argue that sport is premised on doctrines of equality of opportunity, sportsmanship, and fair play. This premise comports with a liberal jurisprudential approach that "conceives meritocracy as a system in which benefits and burdens are distributed in accord with one's deeds—presumably the products of rational choice—rather than characteristics over which one has no apparent control." Timothy Davis, *The Myth of the Superspade: The Persistence of Racism in College Athletics,* 22 Fordham Urb. L.J. 615, 639-640 (1995).

Judicial opinions also express notions of meritocracy that are central to the traditional vision of sport. "It must also be made clear that the mandate of equality of opportunity does not dictate a disregard of differences in talents and abilities among individuals. There is no right to a position on an athletic team. There is a right to compete for it on equal terms." *Hoover v. Meiklejohn*, 430 F. Supp. 164, 171 (D. Colo. 1977).

The judiciary has been influenced by positive values associated with sports. A California appellate court's resolution of an issue—the availability of assumption of the risk as a defense to a negligence claim—was influenced by the court's vision of the values associated with sport:

> For many, sports are part of the school learning experience, among other things teaching students how to deal properly with both success and failure, and instilling in them an understanding of the importance of teamwork, good sportsmanship, discipline, and respect for coaches, teammates and opposing players. Another important part of the experience is that students and their parents learn about accepting responsibility for the consequences of one's choices and actions. By choosing to participate in a sport that poses the obvious possibility of injury, the student athlete must learn to accept an adverse result of the risks inherent in the sport.

Lilley v. Elk Grove Unified Sch. Dist., 68 Cal. App. 4th 939, 946, 80 Cal. Rptr. 2d 638, 643 (1998).

Scholars contend that significant benefits arise from sports participation:

> Significant educational and physical benefits have been identified as arising from athletic participation at competitive and recreational levels. For example, some academics maintain that participation in competitive athletics is analogous to participation on the part of many students in a basic biology class, teaching the student memorization and basic analytical skills. . . . The same concept can be applied to a complex football playbook—the athlete learns to analyze how to respond to a unique set of complex situations by memorizing and applying an elaborate set of fundamental rules or plays that are designed to respond to certain situations as they arise.

Rodney K. Smith, *When Ignorance Is Not Bliss: In Search of Racial and Gender Equity in Intercollegiate Athletics*, 61 Mo. L. Rev. 329, 335-336, 339 (1996). For an elaboration of the benefits derived from participation in sports, see Matthew J. Mitten et al., *Targeted Reform of Commercialized Intercollegiate Athletics*, 47 San Diego L. Rev. 779, 797-798 (2010).

Some proponents of increased athletic participation by women assert that sport assists in the development of qualities and skills such as self-esteem, strategic thinking, team building, leadership, and the willingness to take risks. Mindy Bingham and Sandy Stryker, Things Will Be Different for My Daughter 271-276 (1995). In the landmark gender equity case, *Cohen v. Brown University*, 991 F.2d 888 (1st Cir. 1993), the court commented on short- and long-term benefits associated with participating in college sports:

> For college students, athletics offers an opportunity to [develop] leadership skills, learn teamwork, build self-confidence, and perfect self-discipline. In addition, for many student-athletes, physical skills are a passport to college admissions and scholarships, allowing them to attend otherwise inaccessible schools. These

opportunities, and the lessons learned on the playing fields, are invaluable in attaining career and life successes in and out of professional sports.

Id.

Sport has also been identified as a unifying mechanism that provides a sense of community among increasingly sizeable and diverse constituents:

> In our diverse culture, characterized by a wide variety of ethnic, religious, socio-economic and other groups, there may well be no other force quite like sport, in terms of bringing people of diverse backgrounds together in pursuit of a common purpose. People from all walks of life are able to sense some unity of purpose as they gather to participate in or watch competitive athletics. With growing divisiveness on the basis of ethnic, religious and cultural differences, the capacity of sport to unify may be of increasing significance, particularly if teams are not divided on the basis of race, religion or culture. Deep friendships that transcend such difference are often forged in the crucible of athletic competition. The need for such a sense of connection or community is significant, although the capacity of sport to contribute to connectedness may be discounted by those who refuse to embrace sport as anything more than mere fun and games.

Smith, *supra* at 341.

b. Negative Values Associated with Sport

In contrast to the vision of sport just discussed, certain aspects of sport mirror negative societal qualities. Such values include "selfishness, envy, conceit, [and] hostility," and a heightened level of competitiveness that may produce a winning-at-all-costs mentality. D. Stanley Eitzen, *Ethical Dilemmas in American Sport*, 62 Vital Speeches of the Day 182, 185 (1996). Notes Professor Eitzen, the winning-at-all-costs philosophy "leads to dehumanization of athletes and to their alienation from themselves and from their competitors." *Id.*

Illustrations abound of the negative consequences of the winning-at-all-costs mentality that is pervasive in sport and often leads to questionable strategies aimed at attempting to gain a competitive advantage. As discussed in Chapter 10, *infra*, some argue that the desire to win has led some colleges to prioritize winning over the safety of women students physically assaulted by student-athletes. Others argue that academic and other improprieties committed at colleges and universities, as discussed in Chapter 3, *infra*, are yet another manifestation of the win-at-all-cost mentality. A desire to secure a starting position on the University of Northern Colorado's football team resulted in Mitch Cozad's conviction and sentence of seven years in prison for the 2007 stabbing of his teammate Rafael Mendoza. In 1999, Ben Christensen, a pitcher for Wichita State University, threw a fastball that seriously injured Anthony Molina, a player for the University of Evansville. *Molina v. Christensen*, 44 P. 3d 1274, 1276 (Kan. App. 2001). In attempting to justify his throwing at Molina, who was in the on-deck circle, Christensen claimed that his coach instructed him to throw the pitch as a warning to dissuade Molina from standing too close to home plate when he came to bat, in an effort to time Christensen's pitches. *Id.*

In 2002, the NCAA imposed penalties on the University of Alabama (Tuscaloosa) for infractions of NCAA rules involving, among other things, prohibited recruiting inducements, such as providing cash to a prospect if he agreed to play for the university, and offering money to a high school coach who would seek to secure a recruit's commitment to play for the university. The NCAA Infractions Committee stated:

> The ingrained culture of non-compliance evident among certain of the university's athletics representatives was particularly troubling to the committee. While rogue athletics representatives are new neither to infractions cases generally nor to the infractions history of this university, their level of involvement and spending is an increasingly visible and major problem in intercollegiate athletics. . . . Even if sincere, their claimed motivation for cheating—helping a university to recruit blue-chip athletes—betrays a lack of integrity and a "win-at-all-costs" attitude that undermines and cheapens athletics competition and corrupts the ethics and maturation process of the young people they claim to be "helping."

NCAA Committee on Infractions, University of Alabama, Tuscaloosa, Public Infraction Report 2 (Feb. 2, 2002).

Youth sports provide an excellent context within which to view the negative consequences of placing undue emphasis on winning. In 2019, coaches and parents rushed the field at a Little League game in Colorado and engaged in an all-out brawl while their 7-year-old children ran away screaming. Apparently the 13-year-old umpire issued a warning to parents for using foul language: "I thought maybe by issuing a warning everyone would just chill, take a step back and realize how stupid they were acting . . . but [I] guess not." Multiple adults were injured, one seriously, and five were cited for public fighting and disorderly conduct. Jeremy Gotlieb, *Teenage Umpire Warned Coaches and Spectators to Calm Down Before Brawl at Youth Baseball Game*, The Washington Post, June 22, 2019. https://www.washingtonpost.com/sports/2019/06/22/teenage-umpire-warned-coaches-spectators-calm-down-before-brawl-youth-baseball-game/?utm_term=.5d4f38e384bb. In 2015, a former assistant coach pled guilty to misdemeanor assault for having ordered two players to hit a referee during a high school football game. A 2005 study published in the *Journal of Research in Character Education* documented ethical problems in youth sports that included athletes cheating, arguing with officials, and intentionally attempting to injure opponents and coaches encouraging athletes to cheat.

One of the more notorious instances of parental violence in youth sports occurred in 2001, when Thomas Junta was convicted of involuntary manslaughter and sentenced to six to ten years in prison. Junta beat another father, Michael Costin, to death following a hockey practice in which their sons participated. Although Junta's conduct may be an aberration, parents engage in improper behavior at youth games and practices that often manifests as physical and verbal assaults on officials, other parents, and children. The desire to be number one in our competitive society is one of the social and psychological factors that contribute to such behaviors. One commentator notes, "Whether it's a reflection of our confrontational, win-at-all-costs society or the desperate desire some parents have to see their kids earn a college scholarship or get their names in the papers, this is a problem that is not only very real but also very threatening to the purity of youth and high school sports." Patricia Babcock McGraw, *Games Kids Play Can Make Parents Behave in a Bad Way*, Chi. Daily Herald, Feb. 1, 2002, at 1. See Kevin P. Polansky, Note, *Parental Violence at Youth Sporting Events: Should*

Landowners Be Liable?, 39 Suffolk U.L. Rev. 561 (2006) (advocating landowner liability as a means of attempting to curb parental violence in sports). For one referee's attempt to curb parental violence in youth sport, see Bill Pennington, *Parents Behaving Badly: A Youth Sport Crisis Caught on Video*, The New York Times, July 18, 2018. https://www.nytimes.com/2018/07/18/sports/referee-parents-abuse-videos.html.

The role of money in sports also cannot be ignored. Money becomes the bait that not only lures individuals and entities into sports, but also becomes an impediment to sports' regulation. Parents push children to excel in sports as a means of increasing a child's chances of obtaining a college athletic scholarship or a lucrative contract with a professional sports team. See Fiore, *supra*. As discussed later in this chapter, the quest for financial rewards nurtures the win-at-all-cost mentality evident in big-time intercollegiate athletics. Communications, athletic apparel, and merchandising companies invest billions of dollars into amateur and professional sports. The real and perceived financial interests of the various participants in the sports industry influence their openness to regulation, particularly if regulation may lead to changes that will upset the financial status quo.

Thus, sport produces a fundamental dichotomy: the inherent conflict between values associated with competition, individualism, and the unrelenting pursuit of self-interest and those associated with teamwork, fair play, moral responsibility, and interdependence. As such, sport reproduces the tension between values that favor unrestricted personal autonomy and those that favor external regulation as a means of inserting community norms into the sports realm.

This tension leads to a concern about how sport should be regulated. When sport conflicts with other values, should sport or the other values prevail? What is different about sport as an object of regulation? Too much regulation reduces our freedom. Too little, arguably, does the same by giving sport leeway that would not be granted in other aspects of society.

Finally, sport reflects the group struggles of the larger society. Does sport encourage diversity? Does sport provide a forum within which barriers based on gender, race, or disability have been removed? Is sport a forum within which discrimination and power undermine the very ideas of meritocracy commonly associated with sport? These issues are addressed in Chapters 9, 10, and 11.

As stated by Nelson Mandela: "Sport has the power to change the world. It has the power to inspire. It has the power to unite people in a way that little else does. . . . It is more powerful than governments in breaking down . . . barriers."

2. Sport and Its Various Intersections

Any serious effort to study sport must begin from the premise that sport interfaces with other important cultural institutions. Commenting on the relevance of studying the intersection of sport and other social institutions, one sociologist notes that "there exist numerous *institutional interconnections* among the basic institutions of a society, and changes in one sphere reverberate into others because of their systemic connections." Wilbert M. Leonard II, A Sociological Perspective of Sport IX (5th ed. 1998). Professor Burlette Carter's observations concerning the importance of recognizing the interdisciplinary nature of sports law are equally applicable to sport generally. "[I]n the real world, there is no contracts case that does not bump into some other legal field—at the very least evidence, civil procedure and legal ethics, but possibly too corporations, anti-trust, labor law, securities law and others." Carter, *supra* at 243. Just as with sports law, sport cannot be critically assessed apart from its cultural, economic, political, and philosophical dimensions.

a.   Sport, Culture, and Metaphors

Sport's influence intrudes into various aspects of our culture. We make decisions regarding clothing and other products that we purchase based on the attire that is worn and the products that are used and endorsed by sports heroes. In 2015, NBA superstar LeBron James entered into a lifetime endorsement contract with Nike estimated to be worth as much as $1 billion. Forbes publishes a list of the highest-paid one hundred athletes annually. In 2019, Lionel Messi (soccer) earned the top spot at $127 million total, with salary of $92 million and endorsements of $35 million. The athlete with the most earnings in endorsements was Roger Federer (tennis), with $86 million. The only woman to make the list is Serena Williams, with earnings and endorsements of $25 million. Top U.S. athletes in earnings and endorsements by league are provided in Table 1. Companies seeking these and other athletes' endorsements want to persuade consumers that their affiliations with various products and services warrant their purchase of them.

Table 1
2019 Highest-Earning Athletes by Sport (in millions of U.S. dollars)

Rank	Athlete	Sport	Earnings	Endorsements	Total
1	Lionel Messi	Soccer	$92M	$35M	$127M
2	Cristiano Ronaldo	Soccer	$65M	$44M	$109M
4	Canelo Alvarez	Boxing	$92M	$2M	$94M
5	Roger Federer	Tennis	$7.4M	$86M	$93.4M
6	Russell Wilson	Football	$80.5M	$9M	$89.5M
8	Lebron James	Basketball	$36M	$53M	$89M
11	Tiger Woods	Golf	$9.9M	$54M	$63.9M
13	Lewis Hamilton	Auto Racing	$45M	$10M	$55M
17	Mike Trout	Baseball	$47.6M	$3M	$50.6M
21	Conor McGregor	Mixed Martial Arts	$32M	$15M	$47M
27	Drew Brees	Football	$26.4M	$16M	$42.4M
63	Serena Williams	Tennis	$4.2M	$25M	$29.2
100	Virat Kohli	Cricket	$4M	$21M	$25M

See Kurt Badenhausen, *The World's Highest Paid Athletes*, Forbes, June 11, 2019. https://www.forbes.com/athletes/#63729c2055ae.

i.   *Metaphors*

Expressions used in sport filter into popular culture. Terms and figures of speech that had their genesis in sport, such as cheap shot, pinch-hit, go to bat, and ballpark figure, are commonly used in nonsport contexts. Professor Elizabeth Thornburg argues that sport-, war-, and love-related metaphors, and the values that underlie them, influence the development of rules that foster competition rather than cooperation in our litigation system.

> Some sports metaphors . . . have to do with roles. They portray trial lawyers as game players, boxers, team members, or forensic athletes. Judges, not surprisingly, are referees or umpires.

Other metaphors compare lawsuits to particular sports or games: blind man's bluff, hide and seek, chess, a game of chance, a game of wits and strategy, a cat and mouse game, a poker game, a football game, a boxing match, tennis, fishing, a tug of war, dice, [and] a race. Metaphors using sports as a reference for litigation activities are also common. For example, litigants sometimes play with one hand tied behind their backs, skate close to the edge, strike a blow, lay their cards on the table, go close to the line, bluff, coach witnesses, ask for an extra inning, or get an elbow in the eye.

Sports metaphors also illustrate litigation strategy. As in war, the goal is to win. The players must know the rules of the game. Lawyers employ stratagems and devices; they need gamesmanship and game plans. As in chess, successful litigators make moves and need defensive gambits; as in cards, they need a poker face; as in wrestling they "go to the mat." Litigators can be hard hitting, play rough, or play tough but fair. It is currently extremely popular, despite frequent criticism, to play hardball. . . .

The complex use of game metaphors also reinforces competitive values and behaviors. The sin here is not playing too hard, but failing to take the game seriously. Many judges state that litigation is not a game because the game image fails to recognize the seriousness of the competition or suggest that the outcome might be somewhat random. Nevertheless, metaphors describing game activities are frequently used to describe what goes on in litigation, and are used approvingly to describe the strategic and competitive aspects of lawsuits.

Elizabeth G. Thornburg, *Metaphors Matter: How Images of Battle, Sports, and Sex Shape the Adversary System*, 10 Wis. Women's L.J. 225, 239, 242 (1995).

Professor Thornburg concludes that sport and game metaphors can be used to emphasize values such as teamwork, but rarely are. Consequently, sport metaphors stress "winning at all costs rather than fair play and rules."

ii.   Shaping Gender Identity

Some sociologists argue that sport as a social institution has historically contributed to shaping gender identity. Specifically, sport has traditionally amounted to an external dynamic that socialized boys and helped them to sculpt their developing gender identities. Some feminist scholars go further and argue that sport has significantly contributed to the construction of a male identity that is often harmful to women. For example, Professor Michael Messner argues:

> Sport is a social institution, that, in its dominant forms, was created by and for men. . . . [T]he gendered values of the institution of sport [make] it extremely unlikely that [young men will] construct anything but the kinds of personalities and relationships that [are] consistent with the dominant values and power relations of the larger gender order. . . . The fact that winning was premised on physical power, strength, discipline, and willingness to take, ignore, or deaden pain inclined men to experience their bodies as machines, instruments of power and domination — and to see other peoples' bodies as objects of their power and domination.

Michael A. Messner, Power at Play 54 (1992).

iii. Sport and Religion: The Ultimate Metaphor or Something More?

Considerable controversy revolves around the relationship, if any, between sport and religion. Some argue that sport and religion constitute unique cultural practices because the nature of religion and the nature of sport are essentially different. According to this view, "Religious beliefs, meanings, rituals, and events are fundamentally mystical and sacred, whereas sport beliefs, meanings, rituals, and events are fundamentally clear-cut and secular." Coakley, *supra*, at 512.

Other scholars argue that sport is a "new form" of religion. This view is based on the notion that sport involves expressions of beliefs and meanings that take on greater relevance in people's lives than those associated with traditional religions. According to one scholar, "Sport constitutes the primary lived world of the vast majority of Americans. The holy trinity—baseball, basketball, and football . . . are not simply interludes but the basic substratum of our intellectual and emotional lives. Play provides the fundamental metaphors and the paradigmatic experiences for understanding the other elements of life." Michael Novak, *The Natural Religion*, in Sport Inside Out 353, 363 (David L. Vanderwerken and Spencer K. Wertz eds., 1985).

An intermediate perspective suggests a connection between sport and religion, but it stops short of identifying sport as a "new form of religion." Proponents of this view propose that sport and religion share common characteristics, including the presence of gods in both sport and religion (e.g., saints, priests, and superstars); places of worship and communal gathering; a desire to achieve "perfection in body, mind, and spirit"; structured organizations with hierarchical systems of authority; and organized events that celebrate and reflect core values. Coakley, *supra*, at 511. Notwithstanding such parallels, these academics argue that sport fails to fulfil key functions of traditional religion, such as exploring the purpose of human existence on earth and life after death. Eitzen and Sage, *supra*, at 171.

Several questions emerge from efforts exploring the relationship between sport and religion. For example, does it demean religion to attempt to equate sport with religion? Does the willingness of some to equate sport with religion itself say something about sport's role in society? If so, what?

Sport and religion have on occasion intersected in a pragmatic context. For example, former NBA basketball player Chris Jackson changed his name to Mahmoud Abdul-Rauf after he converted to Islam. During the 1995-1996 NBA season, Abdul-Rauf decided that his religious beliefs precluded him from demonstrating respect for the American flag or the national anthem. Abdul-Rauf's stance conflicted with NBA rules that require players to stand respectfully during the playing of the national anthem before each game. After unsuccessful efforts to reach a compromise, NBA commissioner David Stern suspended Abdul-Rauf for his failure to comply with league rules. Abdul-Rauf promised, after a one-game suspension, that he would stand for the playing of the national anthem but with his eyes closed and his face cupped in his hands while he prayed to Allah. In response to his promise, the NBA ended the suspension, and Abdul-Rauf completed the season.

Adherence to religious belief also impacts organizations. Brigham Young University has maintained a decades-long stance against competing on Sundays. The NCAA has attempted to accommodate the university, which is the only major sports team that refuses to compete on Sundays. In May 2016, the NCAA made schedule adjustments to prevent BYU's women's golf team from having to compete during a tournament on Sundays. Ultimately, BYU's policy reflects a conflict between the institution's desire to have its teams compete at the highest levels and its commitment to observing its Sabbath. *Jeff Call, BYU Won't Budge on Sunday Games,* AthleticBusiness.com, June 26, 2016, http://www .athleticbusiness.com/college/byu-won-t-budge-on-sunday-games.html.

b. Sport and Economics

The pervasiveness of sport has had profound economic effect domestically and internationally. According to Plunkett Research, during 2015, an estimated $498 billion was spent on sports in the United States, and $1.5 trillion was spent globally. In 2018, U.S. sporting goods manufacturers earned $92.26 billion in wholesale revenues. In 2017, spectator sports, including professional sports teams, race tracks, and motorsports generated an estimated $44.25 billion in revenue. The major four professional sports leagues in the United States—the National Football League ($13 billion), Major League Baseball ($10 billion), National Basketball Association ($7.4 billion), and National Hockey League ($4.4 billion)—had combined annual revenues of over $34.8 billion. Recent naming-rights deals include: Scotiabank Arena (21 years/$639 million), MetLife Stadium (26 years/$425-$625 million), Citi Field (22 years/$400 million), Mercedes-Benz Stadium (27 years/$325 million), and Chase Center (20 years/ $300-400 million).

The foregoing numbers present an impressive picture of the extent of the economic influence of sport in the United States. Yet they tell only part of the story. The "athletic arms race" in college sports results in most university athletic departments operating at a loss due to the payment of high salaries to many coaches in men's basketball and football and pressure to win that produces for many a win-at-all-cost attitude. Between 2000 and 2015, public universities allocated $10.3 billion in mandatory student fees and other subsidies into their athletic programs. Student fees accounted for half of the subsidies. Brad Wolverton, et al., *The $10-Billion Sports Tab: How College Students Are Funding the Athletics Arms Race*, Chron. Higher Educ., Nov. 17, 2015. Large disparities exist in the NCAA Division I Football Bowl Subdivision (FBS), with total revenues ranging from $14.7 million to $194.4 million and expenses ranging from $14.7 million to $171.4 million, resulting in a net loss of $47.8 million to a gain of $57.3 million. Between 2004 and 2016, FBS revenues increased by 143.2%, while total expenditures increased by 147.3%. In 2016, only 24 FBS athletics programs had revenues that exceeded expenses, in amounts ranging from $129,000 to $57.3 million. NCAA, *Thirteen-Year Trends in Division I Athletics Finances*, Sept. 2017. The facilities arms race continues to escalate, with Northwestern University opening a $270 million indoor football practice facility. With respect to the "athletic arms race," as early as 2001, the Knight Foundation Commission on Intercollegiate Athletics foretold of the move toward excess:

> Too much in major college sports is geared to accommodating excess. Too many athletic directors and conference commissioners serve principally as money managers, ever alert to maximizing revenues. And too many have looked to their stadiums and arenas to generate more money. In the last seven years, capital expenditures at Division I-A institutions (e.g., construction or remodeling of athletics facilities, capital equipment, etc.) increased 250 percent. From east to west,

north to south, the test becomes who can build the biggest stadiums, the most luxurious skyboxes. Every one of the 12 schools in one major conference has built a new football stadium or refurbished its old one in recent years. All seem to have assumed they could not afford to do otherwise.

Knight Foundation Commission on Intercollegiate Athletics, A Call to Action: Reconnecting College Sports and Higher Education 17 (June 2001). See also Knight Commission on Intercollegiate Athletics, Athletic and Academic Spending Database for NCAA Division I Institutions (2016).

Another long-debated economic concern is public financing of sports stadiums. While research finds little evidence of tangible economic benefits (increased income, wages, or employment or tax revenues), communities have been willing to invest public funds in building stadiums as a means of attracting or retaining a professional sports franchise. What prompts community leaders to defy economic logic? Victor Matheson concludes that stadiums are public goods that can serve as an anchor for local economic development, increasing real estate prices as well as commercial and residential real estate development and improvements in nearby infrastructure. Victor Matheson, *Is there a Case for Subsidizing Sports Stadiums?*, J. Policy Analysis and Management (2018). https://onlinelibary.wiley.com/doi/full/10.1002/pam.22096.

In discussing the economics of sports franchises, Professor Kenneth Shropshire strikes a discordant note:

> Direct and indirect economic benefits such as increased tourism, arena or stadium income, sports franchise expenditures in the city, taxes, and employment are often mythically thought to be guaranteed by the acquisition of a professional sports franchise. Such is the proverbial carrot at the end of the stick that cities chase. In reality, the only reward a city that successfully attracts a sports franchise may receive is the public perception that their metropolis has been thrust into that class of cities nebulously described as "big-league."

Kenneth L. Shropshire, The Sports Franchise: Cities in Pursuit of Sports Franchises, Events, Stadiums, and Arenas 8 (1995). For economic analyses of professional sports franchises and events, see Garrett Johnson, *The Economic Impact of New Stadiums and Arenas on Cities*, 2011 Den. U. Sports & Ent. L.J. 1; Robert A. Baade, Robert Baumann, and Victor A. Matheson, *Selling the Game: Estimating the Economic Impact of Professional Sports through Taxable Sales*, 74 S. Econ. J. 794 (2008); Andrew Zimbalist, The Economics of Sport 287 (2001); Roger G. Noll and Andrew Zimbalist, Sports, Jobs, and Taxes: The Economic Impact of Sports Teams and Stadiums (1997).

c.   Sport and Politics

According to one scholar, organized competitive sports long have been connected with politics, government, and the global political processes:

> **Politics** *refers to the processes of organizing social power and making decisions that affect people's lives in social world. . . .* **Governments** *are formal organizations with the power to make and enforce rules in a particular territory or collection of people.*

Coakley, *supra*, at 430 (emphasis in the original).

Sociologists Stanley Eitzen and George Sage address the characteristics inherent in sport that make politics endemic to it. They first note that sport participants hold allegiances to particular ideologies that manifest in slogans, insignias, and music. In addition, as sports became organized, teams, regulatory bodies, and other organizations emerged. Political conflict arises when the interests of these groups diverge. Finally, Eitzen and Sage argue that a systemic entwinement between sport and politics arises because sport as a social institution typically reinforces societal values, including those of a political nature. Consequently, sport "serves as a preserver and a legitimator of the existing order." Eitzen and Sage, *supra*, at 194. Helpful discussions of the interconnectedness of sport and politics include John M. Hoberman, Sport and Political Ideology 20 (1984); Leonard II, *supra*; and Martin B. Vinokur, More Than a Game: Sports and Politics (1988).

The intersection of sport and politics to which these scholars refer is multidimensional. It plays out at local, national, and international levels. Title IX and efforts by sports leagues to stymie athletes' use of performance-enhancing drugs illustrate how issues in sports can become highly politicized. The politics surrounding public support for sports facilities, and laws such as "no-pass, no-play" legislation provide illustrations of the relationship between sport and politics at the local level. The politics of sport also involves diverse players, including governmental authorities, multinational corporations, other institutional entities, and individuals. Governmental involvement in sport may cover a broad range of activities, including enacting laws regulating sport-related activities, expending public funds to promote physical fitness among citizens, using sport to heighten national prestige, and using sport to forge a sense of national identity among a diverse populace. Governments have also used sport to promote particular values or ideologies and to take political positions on controversial issues. See Coakley, *supra*, at 438.

Reflecting on the politics of the Olympics, Professor Alfred Senn states:

> Although many sports fans consider "politics" an unwelcome intruder in the Olympic Games, politics are in fact an integral part of the Games. The glamour and attractiveness of the Olympic Games and the fact people care give Olympic performances great political significance and weight. Lord Killanin, the head of the IOC in the 1970s, confirmed this, writing, "[n]inety-five percent of my problems as president of the IOC involved national and international politics." In practice, the political dimensions of the Games are diverse and complicated, ranging from the certification of national teams, through the interplay and intrigues of the various international sports organizations, to the infighting of the IOC. Governments have tried to exploit the Games for their own ends, and at times the IOC has itself put pressure on governments. It is no surprise, then, that the Games have served as a focus for national rivalries and ideological rivalries between states.

Alfred E. Senn, Power, Politics, and the Olympic Games X (1999).

Specific illustrations of the Olympic politics to which Professor Senn refers include Nazi Germany's efforts to use the 1936 Olympic Games to promote its political ideology of Aryan supremacy, the United States and Canada's boycott of the 1980 Games to protest Soviet actions in Afghanistan, and the retaliatory boycott of the 1984 Games by the USSR and its allies in protest of commercialization. At the 1968 Olympics, when a proposed boycott did not materialize, some African American athletes developed a list of demands that focused on racial discrimination in athletics. Two African Americans, John Carlos and

Tommie Smith, who finished first and third in the 200-meter dash, raised black-gloved fists and wore black socks and bowed their heads as they stood on the medal stand while "The Star-Spangled Banner" played. Alfred D. Mathewson, *Grooming Crossovers*, 4 J. Gender Race & Just. 225, 236 (2001).

Sport has also been a vehicle for protest internationally and domestically. The organized boycott of sports competitions involving teams from South Africa that began in the 1960s contributed to the end of apartheid by focusing international attention on racial oppression in that country. A recent illustration of the complexity of the politics of sports involves athletes', principally African Americans, support for the Black Lives Matter movement. Another is the refusal of Colin Kaepernick, San Francisco 49ers quarterback, to stand for the playing of the national anthem during NFL games in protest of police brutality and racial oppression in the United States. Expressing their support for Kaepernick, other NFL players engaged in demonstrations during the playing of the national anthem. Although NFL players verbally expressed their support for Kaepernick, the number of player demonstrations during the anthem had dwindled considerably by the beginning of the fall 2017 NFL season. Politics and sports collided, however, when President Donald Trump on September 30, 2017, criticized NFL players for not standing during the playing of the national anthem and NFL owners for not requiring players to stand. President Trump stated that players who refused to stand for the anthem should be fired. The weekend following President Trump's comments saw widespread demonstrations by NFL players and a few owners as a means of showing their solidarity in response to President Trump's statements. Subsequent meetings were held between NFL players, owners, and the NFL commissioner in efforts to address player protests during the playing of the anthem. In October 2017, Kaepernick filed a grievance against the NFL and NFL team owners alleging they "colluded to deprive [him] of employment rights in retaliation for [his] leadership and advocacy for equality and social justice and his bringing social awareness to peculiar institutions still undermining racial equality in the United States." Kaepernick also alleged that the remarks and "public relations stunts" by President Trump as well as Vice President Mike Pence contributed to the NFL and its team owners retaliating against him by keeping him out of the league. *Claimant Colin Kaepernick's Demand for Arbitration in the Matter of Arbitration of Colin Kaepernick v. NFL et. al.*, Oct. 15, 2017, http://a.espncdn.com/pdf/2017/1015/KaepernickGrievance_r.pdf. In late November 2017, a group of players and the NFL agreed that the NFL would contribute $89 million over seven years to projects "dealing with criminal justice reform, law enforcement/community relations and education." Jim Trotter and Jason Reid, *Sources: NFL agrees to commit $89M over seven years to social justice causes*, ESPN.com, Nov. 30, 2017, http://www.espn.com/nfl/story/_/id/21614673/nfl-agrees-commit-nearly-100m-seven-years-charities-important-african-american-communities. Kaepernick agreed to a confidential settlement with the NFL in February 2019.

NFL fans have come out on different sides of this issue, with some criticizing the league for not disciplining the protesters and others criticizing the league for what they believe is a conspiracy to keep Kaepernick unsigned. One such fan in the latter category sued the NFL and Commissioner Goodell, as well as sports commentators Stephen A. Smith and Max Kellerman, for conspiring to mislead the public on "'the black ball[ing] of Colin Kaepernick for refusing to stand during the national anthem. . . .'" The U.S District Court for the Southern District of New York dismissed the lawsuit for lack of standing. See

Miller v. National Football League, 2017 U.S. Dist. LEXIS 162964 (S.D.N.Y. Sept. 27, 2017).

Another dimension of the endemic political nature of sport is its use by politicians. Apart from trumpeting their own personal past involvement in sport, politicians use the sporting venue for political purposes. It is very common for politicians to promote ties between themselves and athletes or sports teams. Presidents of the United States extend "White House" invitations to championship professional and amateur teams in the more popular sports. Such high-profile events attract considerable favorable media for presidents. Politicians also actively seek the support of athletes who, because of their popularity, are effective in getting the vote for candidates whom they support. See Eitzen and Sage, *supra*, at 199-200.

Sports teams and associations are also politically active. Athletic associations and individual clubs or institutions expend significant sums to increase their political influence. Finally, some commentators propose that sport has become transformed at the international level. According to this view, the increased significance of nongovernmental groups and organizations, such as multinational corporations that operate independently of national governments, redefines the politics of sports as transnational rather than international. Some argue that one consequence of such emerging relationships is the redefinition of the politics of sports. For example, messages promoting the interests of corporate entities may become more prevalent than themes that focus on patriotism or nationalism. See Coakley, *supra*, at 451-52; Senn, *supra*, at xii.

NOTES AND QUESTIONS

1. *The Value of Sports Participation.* This chapter introduced you to the idea that sport reflects and reinforces cultural themes, both empowering and harmful, that pervade our society. See, e.g., Eitzen and Sage, *supra*, at 13 (stating that sport provides a useful institution for examining the complexities of larger society because it represents a microcosm of the society in which it is embedded). In justifying the need to expand sports-related opportunities, one commentator opined that "values we learn from participation in sports [include] teamwork, standards, leadership, discipline, work ethics, self-sacrifice, pride in accomplishment [and] strength of character." Smith, *supra* at 340 (quoting Norma Cantu). Do you agree?

2. *Sport and the Construction of Gender Identity.* Does sport contribute to the construction of male identity in ways that are potentially harmful to women? What variables shape male and female identity? Is sport a critical variable? Will increased opportunities for women to participate in organized sport alter the way in which sport influences the shaping of male and female identity? How women view themselves?

   For thoughtful discussions of these issues, see Lois Bryson, *Sport and Maintenance of Masculine Hegemony, in* Women, Sport, and Culture 47, 60 (Susan Birrell and Cheryl L. Cole eds., 1994) (arguing that sport supports male hegemony, in part, because of the public's exposure to position-sanctioned use of aggression and violence by men); Mary Jo Kane and Lisa J. Disch, *Sexual Violence and the Reproduction of Male Power in the Locker Room: The "Lisa Olson Incident,"* Soc. Sport J., Dec. 1993, at 331, 334 (citations omitted) ("[s]port is an institution that creates and reproduces male power and domination in this culture"). See also Suzanne Janusz, *The NFL's Strict Enforcement of its Personal Conduct Policy for Crimes Against Women: A Useful Tool for Combating Violence or an Attempt to Punish Morality?*, 22 Seton Hall J. Sports & Ent. L. 93 (2012) (analyzing the use of the NFL's personal conduct policy for crimes against women); and Dionne L. Koller, *Not Just One of the Boys: A Post-Feminist Critique of Title IX's Vision for Gender Equity in Sports*, 43 Conn. L. Rev. 401 (2010) (critiquing the vision and role of Title IX from a "post-feminist" viewpoint).

3. *Sport and Religion.* One sociologist describes the relationship between sport and religion as follows: "The purpose of religion is to transcend the circumstances and conditions of the material world in the pursuit of eternal life, whereas the purpose of sport is to embrace material reality and seek victories through physical performance." Coakley, *supra*, at 512. Does the foregoing accurately cast the relationship between sport and religion?

4. *Sport and Religious Organizations.* The evangelistic activities of Athletes in Action, the Fellowship of Christian Athletes, and similar organizations have prompted some to coin the phrase "Sportianity" to identify this movement. Eitzen and Sage, *supra*, at 176 (noting that the effectiveness of athletes as evangelists is in part because of the prestige, visibility, and access that allows them to reach people, particularly the young, who a preacher or priest might not be able to reach). What are the consequences of organizations using athletes to evangelize? Should such organizations focus on matters other than religion that arise in sports? See Coakley, *supra*, at 523-27 (critically assessing the evangelistic activities of such groups).

3. *The Study of Sports Law*

In the next several chapters, you will be introduced to issues related to the regulation of sports primarily in four areas of athletic competition: the interscholastic (high school), intercollegiate, Olympic, and professional levels. During your studies, note the similarities and differences in the levels of competition and consider how these and other similarities and differences in the levels of athletic competition impact their legal regulation. For example, at all levels of sports competition, monolithic sports leagues and governing bodies (e.g., the National Football League, the International Olympic Committee, the National Collegiate Athletic Association, and state interscholastic athletic associations) establish eligibility requirements and conditions that must be satisfied for an individual to participate in athletics:

> Most governing bodies have broad, exclusive authority to regulate a single sport or group of sports on either an international, national, or state-wide basis, which provides the corresponding power to exclude or limit athletic participation opportunities. In some instances, unilaterally established eligibility rules either completely preclude an individual from athletic participation, or condition his or her right to participate upon compliance with several requirements.

Matthew J. Mitten and Timothy Davis, *Athlete Eligibility Requirements and Legal Protection of Sports Participation Opportunities*, 8 Va. Sports & Ent. L.J. 71, 73 (2009). You will also have the opportunity, however, to consider whether differences between the levels of competition help to explain the greater process and substantive protections afforded athlete participation rights at the professional and Olympic levels of competition, in contrast with the paucity of such protections afforded athletes at the high school and collegiate levels.

We begin our study of sports law by examining legal regulation of interscholastic and youth sports (Chapter 2) and intercollegiate sports (Chapter 3), two levels of athletic competition that are prevalent in North America but not in Europe or the rest of the world.

CHAPTER
2

Regulating Interscholastic
and Youth Athletics

A. ORIGIN, EVOLUTION, AND INTERNAL GOVERNANCE
OF INTERSCHOLASTIC AND YOUTH ATHLETICS

1. Interscholastic Sports

In 1851, the state superintendent of schools for Minnesota requested that an acre or more of land to be "set aside for the physical development of [students]." Mabel Lee, A History of Physical Education and Sports in the U.S.A. 34 (1983). In 1852, Massachusetts became the first state to require young boys and girls to attend school. During the mid-to-late nineteenth century, high schools were established throughout the United States and began providing organized athletic competitions for their students. For example, a Detroit high school football team was formed in 1888. In 1891, James Naismith, who taught at the School for Christian Workers in Springfield, Massachusetts, invented basketball. In 1892, the first interscholastic basketball game was played between his school and another local high school. In 1892, a Detroit high school baseball team travelled to Ann Arbor for an interscholastic game.

In 1895, a group of high schools gathered in Wisconsin and formed the Wisconsin Interscholastic Athletic Association, the nation's first state high school sports governing body. Following Wisconsin's lead, other states established a central body that provides statewide governance of high school athletics. In 1920, the National Federation of State Athletic Associations (NFHS) was formed to establish a national leadership organization for high school sports and performing arts activities (e.g., music, speech and debate, theater). Through its 50 member state associations and the District of Columbia, the NFHS promotes high school sports participation and athletics programs. Although it does not exercise governing, rules enforcement, or sanctioning authority, the NFHS provides leadership in the field of high school athletics administration, establishes rules and regulations for the sanctioning of high school athletics/activities events, and formulates model rationales for high school eligibility rules for use by high school athletics/activities administrators.

Interscholastic athletics is primarily governed at the state level under a variety of rules (e.g., student-athlete eligibility requirements) formulated by public and private high schools that are members of a state athletic association, which sponsors state championship competitions in each of its recognized female and male sports. The presence of public schools in state athletic associations requires consideration of whether the association is a state actor whose rules and decisions must comply with the requirements of the federal constitution, which is addressed in *Brentwood I* and *II, infra.* High schools usually form local or regional athletic conferences, primarily for scheduling games and sports events among its members as well as for organizing individual and team sport conference championship competitions. High school athletic conferences also may have rule-making and enforcement authority. Local school boards and officials generally adopt rules regarding participation in interscholastic athletics (e.g., conduct requirements).

Participation in interscholastic athletics has increased significantly over the years. Historically, girls' opportunities to participate in interscholastic athletics (as they were in other levels of sports participation) were significantly limited (see the detailed discussion in Chapter 10A). High school athletics participation had steady growth for 30 years, with a record high of 7,980,886 participants in 2017-18. However, there was a decline of 43,395 participants in 2018-19. Football remains the most popular boys sport, but participation has dropped for the past 5 years to 1,006,013 participants, the lowest number since 1999-2000. Outdoor track and field is the most popular girls sport with 488,267 participants. Girls outnumber boys in basketball participation (13,340 girls compared to 10,604 boys), but girls' participation is at its lowest level since 1992-93. See NFSH, 2018-19 High School Athletics Participation Survey, available at https://www.nfhs.org/media/1020406/2018-19-participation-survey.pdf.

2.   *Youth Sports*

In 1888, the Amateur Athletic Union (AAU) was formed to provide youth sports opportunities outside of and in addition to high school athletic competitions. Today it is one of the largest non-profit, volunteer, and multisport organizations in the world, which is dedicated to the promotion and development of grass roots amateur sports and physical fitness programs in 41 sports. Other youth athletics organizations were established and began to flourish during the early twentieth century. American Legion baseball, which was designed primarily to serve teenage youth, was formed in 1925. In 1939, the first Little League baseball game was played, giving birth to a highly successful youth program that now hosts a world series that includes mixed sex teams from all over the world. Youth football soon followed. Joseph Tomlin was hired by a factory in Philadelphia to solve a troubling problem—hundreds of windows had been broken by youths who could not resist the urge to throw a rock at a window. Tomlin encouraged business owners in the area to get together and fund youth athletics, which resulted in the founding of Pop Warner football, getting its name and a major boost in its popularity in 1933 from enlisting a legendary college football coach, Glenn Scobie ("Pop") Warner, to help promote this sport. Other youth club sports such as soccer and hockey were established during the twentieth century and continue to flourish today. The National Council of Youth Sports reports that 60 million children currently participate in youth sports programs, including national youth sport organizations affiliated with national governing bodies in Olympic sports (e.g., United States Youth Soccer Association, USA Volleyball clubs) and other national entities such as Little League Baseball and Pop Warner football. National Council of Youth Sports, https://www.ncys.org/.

Youth athletics other than school sponsored sports competition is generally governed by national entities (e.g., Little League baseball, Pop Warner football, USA Volleyball) that promulgate the rules of the game and participant eligibility requirements along with their respective state and local affiliates, all of which are private entities. Therefore, there generally are no state action or substantive federal constitutional law issues to consider in any legal disputes that arise. Because of their status as private sports governing bodies, courts generally provide only very deferential judicial review of their challenged rules and decisions in litigation.

For example, in *Aussmus v. Little League Baseball, Inc.*, 70 Misc.2d 1038, 1041-1041 (N.Y. Sup. Ct. 1972), a New York court dismissed a lawsuit by five players challenging their team's disqualification from a tournament for permitting other ineligible players to participate in violation of Little League rules:

> Plaintiffs' first cause of action seeks to have a declaration that they are entitled to due process hearing as to the charges made. There is no law, statute or otherwise, which prescribes a due process hearing in this respect. We cannot inject governmental due process requirements into private actions or disputes.
>
> The plaintiffs by joining Merrick-North Merrick Little League Baseball, Inc. voluntarily agreed to abide by Article V(d) of the Merrick-North Merrick Little League constitution that "any boy accepted to play ball . . . may not participate with any other organized baseball team in any league during the Little League season" and they also accepted the mandate of Article X(a) that the rules and regulations of the defendant Little League were binding upon them. Thus, they agreed to accept the rules and regulations of the defendant Little League, including the rules and regulations in respect to eligibility. . . .
>
> Plaintiffs' contention in its second cause of action that Regulation IV(a) is invalid because it prohibits plaintiffs from engaging in any form of organized baseball except under the control of defendant Little League and thereby deprives plaintiffs of their constitutional right of freedom to act is spurious. Regulation IV(a) does not prohibit plaintiffs from engaging in any form of organized baseball. They are free to engage in whatever form of baseball they want. Regulation IV(a) merely prohibits plaintiffs from participating in the defendant Little League baseball program and simultaneously engaging in another organized baseball program except during the regulation periods prescribed by the school systems.

In *The Atlantic*, Hillary Levey Friedman explores the increase in competitive youth sports. Hillary Levy Friedman, "When Did Competitive Sports Take Over American Childhood," http://www.theatlantic.com/education/archive/2013/09/when-did-competitive-sports-take-over-american-childhood/279868/. Has this development been a good one? If there are benefits related to participating in competitive sport at an early age, should the government intervene to make sure every child has an opportunity to participate?

B. JUDICIAL REGULATION OF INTERSCHOLASTIC ATHLETICS

1. State Action

As a prerequisite to bringing a claim alleging infringement of a federal constitutional right, it must be established that the deprivation of the right occurred as the result of state action. Nationwide, most interscholastic athletics programs are operated by public high schools generally under the auspices of a state board of education, which is a part of the state's government (usually the executive branch). Because it is an educational institution operated by a state government entity, a public high school must respect (i.e., not violate) the federal constitutional rights of its employees and student-athletes. However, in most jurisdictions, the state high school athletic association is a voluntary private membership association of both private and public high schools, which exercises governing authority over interscholastic athletics.

Brentwood I establishes and applies the legal standard for determining whether an ostensibly private state high school athletic association is a "state actor" for federal constitutional law purposes because its operation and conduct is so closely related to state government action. If so, *Brentwood II* illustrates that the association's conduct, decisions, and rules must comply with federal constitutional law requirements and not violate the rights of its private or public member schools or their student-athletes, employees, and others.

BRENTWOOD ACADEMY v. TENNESSEE SECONDARY SCHOOL ATHLETIC ASSN. (BRENTWOOD I)

531 U.S. 288 (2001)

Justice SOUTER delivered the opinion of the Court.

The issue is whether a statewide association incorporated to regulate interscholastic athletic competition among public and private secondary schools may be regarded as engaging in state action when it enforces a rule against a member school. The association in question here includes most public schools located within the State, acts through their representatives, draws its officers from them, is largely funded by their dues and income received in their stead, and has historically been seen to regulate in lieu of the State Board of Education's exercise of its own authority. We hold that the association's regulatory activity may and should be treated as state action owing to the pervasive entwinement of state school officials in the structure of the association, there being no offsetting reason to see the association's acts in any other way.

I

. . . [The District Court relied on language in the *Tarkanian* case, excerpted in Chapter 3, implying that state athletic associations might be state actors, even though the NCAA was not, in holding that the Tennessee Secondary School Athletic Association was a state actor.] The United States Court of Appeals for the Sixth Circuit reversed. . . . It said the District Court was mistaken in seeing a symbiotic relationship between the State and the Association, it emphasized that the Association was neither engaging in a traditional and exclusive public function nor responding to state compulsion, and it gave short shrift to the language from *Tarkanian* on which the District Court relied. . . .

We granted certiorari to resolve the conflict and now reverse.

A

. . . If the Fourteenth Amendment is not to be displaced . . . its ambit cannot be a simple line between States and people operating outside formally governmental organizations, and the deed of an ostensibly private organization or individual is to be treated sometimes as if a State had caused it to be performed. Thus, we say that state action may be found if, though only if, there is such a "close nexus between the State and the challenged action" that seemingly private behavior "may be fairly treated as that of the State itself." *Jackson, supra,* at 351, 95 S. Ct. 449.

To be sure, it is not the strict holding in *Tarkanian* that points to our view of this case, for we found no state action on the part of the NCAA. We could see, on the one hand, that the university had some part in setting the NCAA's rules, and the Supreme Court of Nevada had gone so far as to hold that the NCAA had been delegated the university's traditionally exclusive public authority over personnel. *Id.,* at 190, 109 S. Ct. 454. But on the other side, the NCAA's policies were shaped not by the University of Nevada alone, but by several hundred member institutions, most of them having no connection with Nevada, and exhibiting no color of Nevada law. *Id.,* at 193, 109 S. Ct. 454. Since it was difficult to see the NCAA, not as a collective membership, but as surrogate for the one State, we held the organization's connection with Nevada too insubstantial to ground a state action claim. *Id.,* at 193, 196, 109 S. Ct. 454.

But dictum in *Tarkanian* pointed to a contrary result on facts like ours, with an organization whose member public schools are all within a single State. "The situation would, of course, be different if the [Association's] membership consisted entirely of institutions located within the same State, many of them public institutions created by the same sovereign." *Id.,* at 193, n. 13, 109 S. Ct. 454. . . .

B

Just as we foresaw in *Tarkanian,* the "necessarily fact-bound inquiry," *Lugar,* 457 U.S., at 939, 102 S. Ct. 2744, leads to the conclusion of state action here. The nominally private character of the Association is overborne by the pervasive entwinement of public institutions and public officials in its composition and workings, and there is no substantial reason to claim unfairness in applying constitutional standards to it.

The Association is not an organization of natural persons acting on their own, but of schools, and of public schools to the extent of 84% of the total. Under the Association's bylaws, each member school is represented by its principal or a faculty member, who has a vote in selecting members of the governing legislative council and board of control from eligible principals, assistant principals and superintendents.

[T]o the extent of 84% of its membership, the Association is an organization of public schools represented by their officials acting in their official capacity to provide an integral element of secondary public schooling. There would be no recognizable Association, legal or tangible, without the public school officials, who do not merely control but overwhelmingly perform all but the purely ministerial acts by which the Association exists and functions in practical terms. Only the 16% minority of private school memberships prevents this entwinement of the Association and the public school system from being total and their identities totally indistinguishable.

To complement the entwinement of public school officials with the Association from the bottom up, the State of Tennessee has provided for entwinement from top down. State Board members are assigned ex officio to serve as members of the board of control and legislative council, and the Association's ministerial employees are treated as state employees to the extent of being eligible for membership in the state retirement system.

It is, of course, true that the time is long past when the close relationship between the surrogate association and its public members and public officials acting as such was attested frankly. As mentioned, the terms of the State Board's Rule expressly designating the Association as regulator of interscholastic athletics in public schools was deleted in 1996, the year after a Federal District Court held that the Association was a state actor because its rules were "caused, directed and controlled by the Tennessee Board of Education," *Graham v. TSSAA*, No. 1:95-CV-044, 1995 WL 115890, (E.D. Tenn., Feb. 20, 1995).

But the removal of the designation language from Rule 0520-1-2-.08 affected nothing but words. Today the State Board's member-designees continue to sit on the Association's committees as nonvoting members, and the State continues to welcome Association employees in its retirement scheme. The close relationship is confirmed by the Association's enforcement of the same preamendment rules and regulations reviewed and approved by the State Board (including the recruiting Rule challenged by Brentwood), and by the State Board's continued willingness to allow students to satisfy its physical education requirement by taking part in interscholastic athletics sponsored by the Association. The most one can say on the evidence is that the State Board once freely acknowledged the Association's official character but now does it by winks and nods. . . .

The entwinement down from the State Board is therefore unmistakable, just as the entwinement up from the member public schools is overwhelming. Entwinement will support a conclusion that an ostensibly private organization ought to be charged with a public character and judged by constitutional standards; entwinement to the degree shown here requires it.

Save for the Sixth Circuit, every Court of Appeals to consider a statewide athletic association like the one here has found it a state actor. . . . A reversal of the judgment here portends nothing more than the harmony of an outlying Circuit with precedent otherwise uniform.

Nor do we think there is anything to be said for the Association's contention that there is no need to treat it as a state actor since any public school applying the Association's rules is itself subject to suit under § 1983 or Title IX of the Education Amendments of 1972, 86 Stat. 373, 20 U.S.C. §§ 1681-1688. Brief for Respondents 30. . . . Its position boils down to saying that the Association should not be dressed in state clothes because other, concededly public actors are; that Brentwood should be kept out of court because a different plaintiff raising a different claim in a different case may find the courthouse open. Pleas for special treatment are hard to sell, although saying that does not, of course, imply anything about the merits of Brentwood's complaint; the issue here is merely whether Brentwood properly names the Association as a § 1983 defendant, not whether it should win on its claim.

The judgment of the Court of Appeals for the Sixth Circuit is reversed, and the case is remanded for further proceedings consistent with this opinion.

It is so ordered.

Justice THOMAS, with whom THE CHIEF JUSTICE, Justice SCALIA, and Justice KENNEDY join, dissenting.

We have never found state action based upon mere "entwinement." Until today, we have found a private organization's acts to constitute state action only when the organization performed a public function; was created, coerced, or encouraged by the government; or acted in a symbiotic relationship with the government. The majority's holding—that the Tennessee Secondary School

Athletic Association's (TSSAA) enforcement of its recruiting rule is state action—not only extends state-action doctrine beyond its permissible limits but also encroaches upon the realm of individual freedom that the doctrine was meant to protect. I respectfully dissent.

Regardless of these various tests for state action, common sense dictates that the TSSAA's actions cannot fairly be attributed to the State, and thus cannot constitute state action. The TSSAA was formed in 1925 as a private corporation to organize interscholastic athletics and to sponsor tournaments among its member schools. Any private or public secondary school may join the TSSAA by signing a contract agreeing to comply with its rules and decisions. Although public schools currently compose 84% of the TSSAA's membership, the TSSAA does not require that public schools constitute a set percentage of its membership, and, indeed, no public school need join the TSSAA. The TSSAA's rules are enforced not by a state agency but by its own board of control, which comprises high school principals, assistant principals, and superintendents, none of whom must work at a public school. . . .

The State of Tennessee did not create the TSSAA. The State does not fund the TSSAA and does not pay its employees. In fact, only 4% of the TSSAA's revenue comes from the dues paid by member schools; the bulk of its operating budget is derived from gate receipts at tournaments it sponsors. The State does not permit the TSSAA to use state-owned facilities for a discounted fee, and it does not exempt the TSSAA from state taxation. No Tennessee law authorizes the State to coordinate interscholastic athletics or empowers another entity to organize interscholastic athletics on behalf of the State. The only state pronouncement acknowledging the TSSAA's existence is a rule providing that the State Board of Education permits public schools to maintain membership in the TSSAA if they so choose.

Moreover, the State of Tennessee has never had any involvement in the particular action taken by the TSSAA in this case: the enforcement of the TSSAA's recruiting rule prohibiting members from using "undue influence" on students or their parents or guardians "to secure or to retain a student for athletic purposes." App. 115. There is no indication that the State has ever had any interest in how schools choose to regulate recruiting. In fact, the TSSAA's authority to enforce its recruiting rule arises solely from the voluntary membership contract that each member school signs, agreeing to conduct its athletics in accordance with the rules and decisions of the TSSAA.

B

Even approaching the issue in terms of any of the Court's specific state-action tests, the conclusion is the same: The TSSAA's enforcement of its recruiting rule against Brentwood Academy is not state action.

The TSSAA has not performed a function that has been "traditionally exclusively reserved to the State." *Jackson v. Metropolitan Edison Co.*, 419 U.S. 34-5 352, 95 S. Ct. 449, 42 L. Ed. 2d 477 (1974). The organization of interscholastic sports is neither a traditional nor an exclusive public function of the States. . . . Certainly, in Tennessee, the State did not even show an interest in interscholastic athletics until 47 years after the TSSAA had been in existence and had been orchestrating athletic contests throughout the State. Even then, the State Board of Education merely acquiesced in the TSSAA's actions and did not assume the role of regulating interscholastic athletics. . . .

It is also obvious that the TSSAA is not an entity created and controlled by the government for the purpose of fulfilling a government objective. . . . No one claims that the State of Tennessee played any role in the creation of the TSSAA as a private corporation in 1925. The TSSAA was designed to fulfill an objective—the organization of interscholastic athletic tournaments—that the government had not contemplated, much less pursued. And although the board of control currently is composed of public school officials, and although public schools currently account for the majority of the TSSAA's membership, this is not required by the TSSAA's constitution.

In addition, the State of Tennessee has not "exercised coercive power or . . . provided such significant encouragement [to the TSSAA], either overt or covert," *Blum*, 457 U.S., at 1004, 102 S. Ct. 2777, that the TSSAA's regulatory activities must in law be deemed to be those of the State. The State has not promulgated any regulations of interscholastic sports, and nothing in the record suggests that the State has encouraged or coerced the TSSAA in enforcing its recruiting rule. . . . Finally, there is no "symbiotic relationship" between the State and the TSSAA. *Moose Lodge, supra,* at 175, 92 S. Ct. 1965; cf. *Burton v. Wilmington Parking Authority*, 365 U.S. 715, 81 S. Ct. 856, 6 L. Ed. 2d 45 (1961). Contrary to the majority's assertion, *see ante,* at 932-933, the TSSAA's "fiscal relationship with the State is not different from that of many contractors performing services for the government." *Rendell-Baker, supra,* at 843, 102 S. Ct. 2764. The TSSAA provides a service—the organization of athletic tournaments—in exchange for membership dues and gate fees, just as a vendor could contract with public schools to sell refreshments at school events. Certainly the public school could sell its own refreshments, yet the existence of that option does not transform the service performed by the contractor into a state action. Also, there is no suggestion in this case that, as was the case in Burton, the State profits from the TSSAA's decision to enforce its recruiting rule.

Because I do not believe that the TSSAA's action of enforcing its recruiting rule is fairly attributable to the State of Tennessee, I would affirm.

NOTES AND QUESTIONS

1. *Analysis of* Brentwood I. In the *Tarkanian* case, 488 U.S. 179 (1988), included in Chapter 3E, the Supreme Court held in a 5-4 decision that the National Collegiate Athletic Association is *not* a state actor. In *Brentwood I*, another 5-4 decision rendered 12 years later, the Court holds that the Tennessee Secondary School Athletic Association (TSSAA) *is* a state actor. How does Justice Souter justify the Court's conclusion that the TSSAA is a state actor, but the NCAA is not? What is the legal standard the majority adopts to determine whether a state high school athletic association is a state actor? What factors are relevant in determining whether this standard is satisfied? If a state athletic association asked you, as its legal counsel, to minimize the likelihood that it would be found to be a state actor after *Brentwood I*, what would you suggest that it do and not do?

   The four dissenting justices strongly disagree with the majority's view. Why do they argue that the TSSAA is not a state actor? Do you agree with the dissent or the majority?

2. *Lower Courts' Application of* Brentwood I. In *Communities for Equity v. Michigan High School Athletic Assn.*, 377 F.3d 504 (6th Cir. 2004), the Sixth Circuit

relied on *Brentwood I* and held that the Michigan High School Athletic Association is a state actor: "MHSAA's stated purpose, '[t]o create, establish and provide for, supervise and conduct interscholastic athletic programs throughout the state,' is virtually identical to that of its Tennessee counterpart. Like TSSAA, MHSAA's membership is composed primarily of public schools. And, similar to TSSAA, public school teachers, administrators, and officials dominate MHSAA's leadership. Another common feature is that the bulk of MHSAA's revenue comes from ticket sales for state championship tournaments. Finally, MHSAA employees who had state teaching certificates were, until January of 1988, considered state employees and were therefore eligible to participate in the state's retirement system. Employees who started working for MHSAA before January of 1988 continue to be members of the state employees' retirement system. We therefore conclude that MHSAA is so entwined with the public schools and the state of Michigan, and that there is 'such a close nexus between the State and the challenged action,' that MHSAA should be considered a state actor." *Id.* at 511-512. See also *Holzmueller v. Illinois High Sch. Assoc.*, 263 F.Supp.3d 705, 719-720 (N.D. Ill. 2017), *aff'd*, 881 F.3d 587 (7th Cir. 2018) (holding that Illinois High School Association is a state actor "by virtue of its entwinement with the public school system"). But see *Bukowski v. Wisconsin Interscholastic Athletic Assn.*, 726 N.W.2d 356 (Wis. Ct. App. 2006) (in contrast to *Brentwood I*, plaintiff "failed to produce any evidence, by affidavit or otherwise, that the WIAA is a state actor"); *Mayo v. West Virginia Secondary Schools Activities Comm'n*, 672 S.E.2d 224, 229 (W. Va. 2008) (West Virginia state high school governing body is not a "state agency;" court's analysis suggests it is not a state actor).

2. Constitutional Rights Issues

a. Member Schools

In *Brentwood II*, which made its way back to the Supreme Court in 2007, the Court considered the merits of the plaintiff high school's federal constitutional law challenges to the TSSAA's anti-recruiting rule on free speech and due process grounds.

TENNESSEE SECONDARY SCHOOL ATHLETIC ASSOCIATION v. BRENTWOOD ACADEMY (BRENTWOOD II)

551 U.S. 291 (2007)

Justice STEVENS delivered the opinion of the Court with respect to Parts I, II-B, III, and IV, concluding:

The principal issue before us is whether the enforcement of a rule prohibiting high school coaches from recruiting middle school athletes violates the First Amendment. We also must decide whether the sanction imposed on respondent for violating that rule was preceded by a fair hearing.

I

Although this case has had a long history, the relevant facts may be stated briefly. The Tennessee Secondary School Athletic Association (TSSAA) is a not-for-profit membership corporation organized to regulate interscholastic sports among its members, which include some 290 public and 55 private high schools in Tennessee. Brentwood Academy is one of those private schools.

Since the early 1950's, TSSAA has prohibited high schools from using "undue influence" in recruiting middle school students for their athletic programs. In April 1997, Brentwood's football coach sent a letter to a group of eighth-grade boys inviting them to attend spring practice sessions. The letter explained that football equipment would be distributed and that "getting involved as soon as possible would definitely be to your advantage." It was signed "Your Coach." While the boys who received the letter had signed a contract signaling their intent to attend Brentwood, none had enrolled within the meaning of TSSAA rules [which defined "enrolled" as having "attended 3 days of school"]. All of the boys attended at least some of the spring practice sessions. As the case comes to us, it is settled that the coach's pre-enrollment solicitation violated the TSSAA's antirecruiting rule and that he had ample notice that his conduct was prohibited.

TSSAA accordingly sanctioned Brentwood. After proceeding through two layers of internal TSSAA review, Brentwood brought this action against TSSAA and its executive director in federal court under Rev.Stat. § 1979, 42 U.S.C. § 1983. As relevant here, Brentwood made two claims: first, that enforcement of the rule was state action in violation of the First and Fourteenth Amendments; and second, that TSSAA's flawed adjudication of its appeal had deprived the school of due process of law. . . .

II

The First Amendment protects Brentwood's right to publish truthful information about the school and its athletic programs. It likewise protects the school's right to try to persuade prospective students and their parents that its excellence in sports is a reason for enrolling. But Brentwood's speech rights are not absolute. It chose to join TSSAA, an athletic league [association] and a state actor invested with a three-fold obligation to prevent the exploitation of children, to ensure that high school athletics remain secondary to academics, and to promote fair competition among its members. TSSAA submits that these interests adequately support the enforcement against its member schools of a rule prohibiting coaches from trying to recruit impressionable middle school athletes. Brentwood disagrees, and maintains that TSSAA's asserted interests are too flimsy and its rule too broad to support what the school views as a serious curtailment of its constitutional rights. Two aspects of the case taken together persuade us that TSSAA should prevail.

A

The anti-recruiting rule strikes nowhere near the heart of the First Amendment. TSSAA has not banned the dissemination of truthful information relating to sports, nor has it claimed that it could.

[Relying on *Ohralik v. Ohio State Bar Assn.*, 436 U.S. 447 (1978), in which the Court held the First Amendment did not prevent a state bar association from disciplining a lawyer for in-person solicitation of clients, and other examples, the Court opined that] the dangers of undue influence and overreaching that exist when a lawyer chases an ambulance are also present when a high school coach contacts an eighth grader. . . . After all, it is a heady thing for an eighth-grade student to be contacted directly by a coach — here, "Your Coach" — and invited to join a high school sports team. In too many cases, the invitation will come accompanied with a suggestion, subtle or otherwise, that failure to accept will hurt the student's chances to play high school sports and diminish the odds that she could continue on to college or (dream of dreams) professional sports. Such a potent entreaty, playing as it does on youthful hopes and fears, could well exert the kind of undue pressure that "disserve[s] the individual and societal interest . . . in facilitation 'informed and reliable decisionmaking.' " Given that TSSAA member schools remain free to send brochures, post billboards, and otherwise advertise their athletic programs, TSSAA's limited regulation of recruiting conduct poses no significant First Amendment concerns.

B

Brentwood made a voluntary decision to join TSSAA and to abide by its anti-recruiting rule. Just as the government's interest in running an effective workplace can in some circumstances outweigh employee speech rights, so too can an athletic league's interest in enforcing its rules sometimes warrant curtailing the speech of its voluntary participants. . . . This is not to say that TSSAA has unbounded authority to condition membership on the relinquishment of any and all constitutional rights. As we recently emphasized in the employment context, "[s]o long as employees are speaking as citizens about matters of public concern, they must face only those speech restrictions that are necessary for their employers to operate efficiently and effectively." Assuming, without deciding, that the coach in this case was "speaking as [a] citize[n] about matters of public concern," TSSAA can similarly impose only those conditions on such speech that are necessary to managing an efficient and effective state-sponsored high school athletic league.

That necessity is obviously present here. We need no empirical data to credit TSSAA's common-sense conclusion that hard-sell tactics directed at middle school students could lead to exploitation, distort competition between high school teams, and foster an environment in which athletics are prized more highly than academics. . . . [T]he First Amendment does not excuse Brentwood from abiding by the same anti-recruiting rule that governs the conduct of its sister schools. To hold otherwise would undermine the principle, succinctly articulated by the dissenting judge at the Court of Appeals, that "[h]igh school football is a game. Games have rules."

III

The decision to sanction Brentwood for engaging in prohibited recruiting was preceded by an investigation, several meetings, exchanges of correspondence, an adverse written determination from TSSAA's executive director, a hearing before the director and an advisory panel composed of three members of TSSAA's Board of Directors. During the investigation, Brentwood was notified of all the charges against it. At each of the two hearings, Brentwood was represented by counsel and given the opportunity to adduce evidence. No evidence offered by Brentwood was excluded.

Even accepting the questionable holding [of the Sixth Circuit] that TSSAA's closed-door deliberations were unconstitutional, we can safely conclude that any due process violation was harmless beyond a reasonable doubt. . . . Brentwood's claim of prejudice rests on the unsupported premise that it would have adopted a different and more effective strategy at the board hearing had it been given an opportunity to cross-examine the investigators and review their notes. Despite having had nearly a decade since the hearing to undertake that cross-examination and review, Brentwood has identified nothing the investigators shared with the board that Brentwood did not already know.

Justice KENNEDY, with whom THE CHIEF JUSTICE, Justice SCALIA, and Justice ALITO join, concurring in part and concurring in the judgment.

Although I have little difficulty concluding that the regulation at issue does not contravene the First Amendment, I do not agree with the principal opinion's reliance on *Ohralik*. . . . In my view it is both unnecessary and ill advised to rely upon *Ohralik* in the instant matter. By doing so, the principal opinion, at a minimum, is open to the implication that the speech at issue is subject to state regulation whether or not the school has entered a voluntary contract with a state-sponsored association in order to promote a code of conduct affecting solicitation. To allow free-standing state regulation of speech by coaches and other representatives of nonmember schools would be a dramatic expansion of *Ohralik* to a whole new field of endeavor. Yet by relying on *Ohralik* the principal opinion undermines the argument that, in the absence of Brentwood Academy's consensual membership in the [TSSAA], the speech by the head coach would be entitled to First Amendment protection.

Justice THOMAS, concurring in the judgment.

Until today, *Pickering* governed limitations on the speech rights of government employees and contractors. The Court uproots *Pickering* from its context and applies it to speech by a private school that is a member of a private athletic association. The need to stretch *Pickering* to fit this case was occasioned by the Court when it held that TSSAA, a private organization, was a state actor. Because *Brentwood I* departed so dramatically from our earlier state-action cases, it is unsurprising that no First Amendment framework readily applies to this case. Rather than going through the bizarre exercise of extending obviously inapplicable First Amendment doctrine to these circumstances, I would simply overrule *Brentwood I.*

NOTES AND QUESTIONS

1. *Analysis of First Amendment Issues.* Although a majority of the Court does not agree with his reasoning in Part II-A of his opinion, Justice Stevens asserts that recruiting eighth graders is like ambulance chasing. Does recruiting young student-athletes necessarily result in exploitation? Should impressionable young people be shielded from recruiting efforts of this sort by state high school athletic associations? Is the age and impressionability of the student-athletes critical to the decision (i.e., if the letter came from a college coach, might it be protected speech)?

   In *Rottman v. PIAA*, 349 F. Supp. 2d 922 (W.D. Pa. 2004), the Pennsylvania Interscholastic Athletic Association's "anti-recruiting rule" was upheld against a claim that it was an impermissible content-based ban on protected speech. In finding the rule to be constitutional, the court applied an intermediate scrutiny test and found that the rule served the substantial governmental interests of prioritizing academics over athletics and protecting young student-athletes from exploitation.

2. *Analysis of Procedural Due Process Issues.* What argument was raised regarding due process? Why did Brentwood Academy assert that its hearing before the TSSAA was deficient? On what ground did the Court reject this argument?

In *Isler v. New Mexico Activities Assn.*, 2010 WL 8522978 (D.N.M. Feb. 19, 2010), a case involving the termination of a high school basketball coach for his alleged violation of a New Mexico state governing body rule prohibiting "undue influence," in connection with school transfers by student-athletes, the court distinguished *Brentwood II* and held that this rule was unconstitutionally vague. The rule prohibited communications between school personnel and students or parents that "might be construed as an inducement for them to attend a particular school." The court concluded that:

> [The rule] provides no guidance whatsoever as to the meaning of the phrase "might be construed as an inducement" and thus no guidance as to what conduct is actually prohibited. . . . While the NMAA does point out that the term "undue influence" is defined in the appendices of the NMAA Handbook as "[i]nappropriate, unethical, and prohibited acts by which [a] coach, sponsor or agent of the school persuades or attempts to persuade a potential athlete to transfer into his/her school," this definition does little to clarify the ambiguity embodied in Bylaw 6.1.3(K). No examples of what would be considered "inappropriate" or "unethical" are provided and nothing in this definition would put Mr. Isler on notice that the conduct at issue here would be prohibited by the NMAA; clearly his supervisor, Mr. Stacy, was not put on notice either. Moreover, apart from this vague definition, the NMAA has failed to provide any written guidance whatsoever.

Id. at *8-9.

3. *Equal Protection Issues.* In *Christian Heritage Academy v. Oklahoma Secondary School Activities Assn.*, 483 F.3d 1025 (10th Cir. 2007), the Tenth Circuit held that the Oklahoma Secondary School Activity Association's (OSSAA) discriminatory membership requirements for nonpublic schools violated the Equal Protection Clause of the Fourteenth Amendment. The court held that although OSSAA had offered a number of legitimate purposes supporting a rule that distinguished between nonpublic and public schools, its rule requiring majority approval for only nonpublic schools to be admitted to membership was not rationally related to any of those legitimate purposes. The court found that the only remaining reason for the decision to deny membership to Christian Heritage Academy (the plaintiff) was a growing animus against nonpublic schools because they were often more successful athletics teams than their public counterparts, which was not a legitimate ground for subjecting them to different membership requirements. A third judge concurred in the judgment, but disagreed with the majority's reasoning, concluding that Christian Heritage Academy was discriminated against because other similarly situated schools, both public and nonpublic, had been granted membership. The judges were also concerned that there were no voting standards or guidelines tied to the proffered rational bases, which made for a "complete disconnect" between the legitimate purposes behind the rule and its application.

b.   Student-Athletes

This section focuses on interscholastic student-athletes' First Amendment rights of speech, association, and religion as well as their Fourth Amendment right not to be subject to unreasonable personal searches or seizures in the context of mandatory suspicionless drug testing. Some coverage of corresponding state constitutional law issues, as well as religion-affiliated educational institutions' free exercise rights, are briefly considered.

i.   First Amendment Freedom of Speech and Association

In the following case, the Eighth Circuit considers whether a student's free speech rights were violated when her continued participation on the sophomore basketball team was conditioned on her issuing an apology for a letter she wrote regarding her coach.

WILDMAN v. MARSHALLTOWN SCHOOL DISTRICT
249 F.3d 768 (8th Cir. 2001)

BRIGHT, Circuit Judge.

Rebecca Wildman appeals from the district court's summary judgment dismissal of her action. Wildman filed this action under 42 U.S.C. § 1983 and § 1988 as a high school student against the school principal, school athletic director, varsity girls' basketball coach, as well as the school district, alleging that they violated her rights under the Free Speech Clause of the First Amendment when they conditioned her continued participation on the sophomore basketball team on her apologizing to her teammates for writing a letter which criticized the varsity coach. We affirm.

I.   BACKGROUND

We take the facts in the light most favorable to Wildman. In January 1998, Wildman was a sophomore student at Marshalltown High School in Marshalltown, Iowa, and a member of the school's basketball team. Wildman hoped to play on the varsity team and she testified that Coach Rowles, the high school girls' varsity basketball coach, promised in conversations with her before the season that he would promote her to the varsity team. When the promotion never materialized, Wildman testified that she "became frustrated and decided to write a letter to [her] teammates" and that her "purpose was to find out what they thought of the situation and Coach Rowles." She composed a letter on her home computer and distributed it to her teammates in the school's locker room on Saturday, January 24, 1998. The letter stated:

> To all of my teammates:
>   Everyone has done a great job this year and now is the time that we need to make ourselves stronger and pull together. It was a tough loss last night but we will get it back. We have had some bumps in the road to success but every team does and the time is here for us to smoothen it out. Everyone on this team is important

whether they think so or not. After watching last nights [*sic*] Varsity game and seeing their sophomores play up I think and I think [*sic*] that some of you are think [*sic*] the same thing. I think that we have to fight for our position. Am I the only one who thinks that some of us should be playing Varsity or even JV? We as a team have to do something about this. I want to say something to Coach Rowles. I will not say anything to him without the whole teams [*sic*] support. He needs us next year and the year after and what if we aren't there for him? It is time to give him back some of the bullshit that he has given us. We are a really great team and by the time we are seniors and we ALL have worked hard we are going to have an AWESOME season. We deserve better then [*sic*] what we have gotten. We now need to stand up for what we believe in!!!

She included below her statement a poem about geese in flight titled "We Makes Me Stronger."

The following week, Wildman's sophomore team coach received a telephone call from Charlotte Baltes, a parent of one of Wildman's teammates, who expressed concern about the letter her daughter brought home from the locker room. Coach Rowles received a copy of the letter from another player's parent, Diana Swanson, who worked as the attendance secretary at the high school. Both coaches, who stated in their depositions that they were alarmed by the letter's tone and language, met with athletic director Funk and principal Stephens to discuss how to handle the matter. On January 29, 1998, the coaches met with Wildman alone to discuss the letter with her. They told her the letter was disrespectful and demanded that she apologize to her teammates. Wildman claims that they did not ask her to explain what she hoped to accomplish with her letter. She contends that she did not advocate a strike or boycott but that the school did not give her a chance to explain herself before setting the condition for her continued participation in the basketball program. The coaches gave her twenty-four hours to apologize, and, if she did not, she would not be allowed to return to the team. Wildman refused to apologize and did not practice with the team or play in the season's remaining six games. She also complains that she was not invited to attend the postseason awards banquet and that Coach Rowles declined to give her a participation award because "she did not finish the season." Following the school year, Wildman and her family moved to another school district where she enrolled in high school.

On September 2, 1999, Wildman brought this suit for damages. On November 2, 1999, the defendants filed a motion for summary judgment. On April 6, 2000, the district court granted defendants' motion for summary judgment, holding that Wildman's letter materially interfered or substantially disrupted a school activity. . . . Wildman appeals the summary judgment dismissal of her action.

II.   Discussion

. . . For reversal, Wildman argues that the First Amendment prevents the school from disciplining her for distributing a letter which was a personal communication to other students containing her personal expression. Both parties agree that, as the Supreme Court acknowledged in *Tinker v. Des Moines Indep. Cnty. Sch. Dist.*, 393 U.S. 503, 506, 89 S. Ct. 733, 21 L. Ed. 2d 731 (1969), students do not "shed their constitutional rights to freedom of speech or expression at the schoolhouse gate." *Tinker* involved an attempt by high school students to wear black armbands on school property to symbolize their protest against the

Vietnam War. The Supreme Court struck down school authorities' efforts to discipline this expression of opinion (suspending the students from school until they would come back without their armbands) and stated that "undifferentiated fear or apprehension of disturbance is not enough to overcome the right to freedom of expression." *Tinker*, 393 U.S. at 508, 89 S. Ct. 733.

However, this right to express opinions on school premises is not absolute. It is well within the parameters of school officials' authority to prohibit the public expression of vulgar and offensive comments and to teach civility and sensitivity in the expression of opinions. . . .

Marshalltown had in place a handbook for student conduct in 1997-1998, as well as a Marshalltown Bobcat Basketball Handbook, drafted by Coach Rowles and distributed to Wildman and her teammates at the start of the season. Both handbooks indicated that disrespect and insubordination will result in disciplinary action at the coach's discretion. Appellees argue that they acted properly and lawfully in their reaction to Wildman's letter. They point to their interest in affording Wildman's teammates an educational environment conducive to learning team unity and sportsmanship and free from disruptions and distractions that could hurt or stray the cohesiveness of the team.

Wildman admits that her speech contained one profane word but contends that because there was no specific evidence of a material disruption of a school activity, her speech is protected. We disagree with the claim of protection.

The parties perhaps could have achieved with minimal creativity and flexibility a solution more amicable or less humiliating to the student. However, the school sanction only required an apology. The school did not interfere with Wildman's regular education. A difference exists between being in the classroom, which was not affected here, and playing on an athletic team when the requirement is that the player only apologize to her teammates and her coach for circulating an insubordinate letter. We agree with the district court's conclusions that the letter did suggest, at the least, that the team unite in defiance of the coach (where Wildman wrote that the coach "needs us next year and the year after and what if we aren't there for him?" and "[i]t is time to give him back some of the bullshit that he has given us" and "[w]e now need to stand up for what we believe in" and "I think that we have to fight for our position") and that the actions taken by the coaches in response were reasonable. Moreover, coaches deserve a modicum of respect from athletes, particularly in an academic setting.

This suit does not present a case like *Seamons v. Snow*, 206 F.3d 1021 (10th Cir. 2000), cited by Wildman for the proposition that dismissal of a high school player from an athletic team for refusing to apologize for the exercise of free speech rights amounts to an unconstitutional action. In that case, the Tenth Circuit Court of Appeals reversed the district court's summary judgment dismissal and remanded because of disputed issues of fact. The student athlete in *Seamons* asserted that the football coach asked the player to apologize to the football team for reporting to the police and to school authorities a hazing incident in which the player was assaulted in the high school locker room by a group of his teammates, forcibly restrained, and bound to a towel rack with adhesive athletic tape. *Id.* at 1027. The coach presented a different version, claiming that the player's ultimate failure to be involved with the football team was unrelated to his speech or refusal to speak. *Id.* The court determined that "[t]here [were] ample facts in the record to indicate that Brian's suspension and dismissal from the football team were directly related to his failure to apologize for reporting the assault." *Seamons*, 206 F.3d at 1028. Implicitly the court acknowledged that Brian's report of the assault was protected free expression.

In contrast, Wildman's letter, containing the word "bullshit" in relation to other language in it and motivated by her disappointment at not playing on the varsity team, constitutes insubordinate speech toward her coaches. Here, in an athletic context void of the egregious conduct which spurred the football play- er's speech about the hazing incident in *Seamons* and where Wildman's speech called for an apology, no basis exists for a claim of a violation of free speech.

III. Conclusion

Accordingly, we affirm the summary judgment of dismissal of Wildman's claim of alleged violation of her rights under the Free Speech Clause of the First Amendment.

NOTES AND QUESTIONS

1. *Student's Free Speech Rights.* Why did the court reject the student-athlete's free speech claim? If the student-athlete had not included the word "bullshit" in her letter, would the court have rendered a different decision? What kinds of comments by a student-athlete about her coach are or should be consti- tutionally protected? If a group of student-athletes decided to wear black headbands as a way of protesting poor coaching, would this be protected speech?

    The *Wildman* court states that "[t]he parties could have achieved with minimal creativity and flexibility a solution more amicable or less humiliat- ing to the student." What would you have recommended?

    In *Pinard v. Clatskanine School District 6J*, 446 F.3d 964 (9th Cir. 2006), a group of student-athletes alleged that the school's decision to remove them from the basketball team was in retaliation against their speaking out in opposition to the coach and expressing their desire that he be removed because of his abusive and intimidating behavior. The court found that the players' written, signed petition requesting that the school remove the coach was protected speech, but that the players' decision to refuse to board the bus to an away game was not protected, since it "[disrupted or inter- fered] with the [scheduled] activity." The court remanded the retaliation claim on the ground that there was an insufficient factual record presented on appeal, but in doing so, the court added, "[I]f the plaintiffs can show that their protected speech was a 'substantial or motivating factor' in the defendant's decision to suspend them from the team permanently, and the defendants fail to show that they 'would have taken the same action even in the absence' of that speech, then the defendants violated plaintiffs' First Amendment rights."

    On remand, the district court held that there was sufficient evidence to survive summary judgment. With regard to the timing issue, there was evi- dence that the players may have been suspended in part for retaliatory pur- poses, and the boycott was not enough to cut off the possible link between the petition and suspension. The court noted that there was no serious dis- pute with regard to the defendants having opposed the speech of the play- ers, and there was sufficient evidence to support the theory that a school official withheld information that could have averted the boycott. The court also noted that there was not an identifiable school policy requiring permanent suspension in such a case. *Pinard v. Clatskanie School District 6J,* 2008 WL 410097 (D. Or.). What facts in this case distinguish it from *Wildman,* and the cases cited as precedent in that case, for the court to conclude the student-athletes' criticism of the coach was protected speech?

In *Doe v. Silsbee Independent School District,* 402 Fed. Appx. 852 (5th Cir. 2010), *cert. denied,* 563 U.S. 974 (2011), a cheerleader cheered with her teammates throughout the game but refused to cheer, preferring to stand still with her arms crossed, when a young man who had pleaded guilty to sexual assault against her was shooting a free throw. After refusing to cheer for the young man, she was expelled from the cheerleading squad. She then filed suit claiming that her dismissal from the cheer squad for refusing to cheer under these circumstances constituted a violation of her First Amendment right of free speech. The district court dismissed her suit on the ground that a cheerleader agrees to represent the school and therefore waives her right of free speech in that capacity. The court also upheld her dismissal from the cheer squad and ordered her to reimburse the school $45,000 for costs associated with the litigation. The Fifth Circuit affirmed and the Supreme Court refused to grant certiorari. What would you have done as superintendent? Would you have permitted the young man to play? Would you require the young woman to cheer for the young man?

New Jersey has also limited expression by adopting a limit on "trash talking" and other offensive or negative language by players and fans, in the high school athletic context. As of July 5, 2018, all officials are required to read the "Officials Bias Statement" to coaches and team captains before each interscholastic game in New Jersey:

> There will be no tolerance for negative statements or actions between opposing players and coaches. This includes taunting, baiting, berating opponents, trash-talking or actions which ridicule or cause embarrassment to them. Any verbal, written or physical conduct related to race, gender, ethnicity, disability, sexual orientation or religion shall NOT be tolerated, could subject the violator to ejection, and may result in penalties being assessed against your team. If such comments are heard a penalty will be assessed immediately. We have been instructed not to issue warnings. It is your responsibility (Coaches and Captains) to remind your team of this policy.

Does this rule violate student-athletes' freedom of speech and expression rights? Should other states adopt a similar rule?

The pervasiveness of social media creates significant free speech challenges for public schools. In *Bell v. Itawamba Cnty. Sch. Bd.,* 799 F.3d 379 (5th Cir. 2015), the Fifth Circuit heard a free speech case involving off campus speech regarding coaches and others that was broadcast through social media. The lower court held that a school board in Mississippi violated a student's First Amendment free speech rights when it suspended the student for posting a rap song on social media accusing two coaches of sexual harassment with graphic language, without providing any evidence that the posting was in fact disruptive. On appeal, the court upheld the board's decision. Ultimately, the case was heard en banc. Writing for the majority of judges in the Fifth Circuit, Judge Rhesa Hawkins opined:

Put succinctly, "with near-constant student access to social networking sites on and off campus, when offensive and malicious speech is directed at school officials and disseminated online to the student body, it is reasonable to anticipate an impact on the classroom environment." . . . As stated, the school board reasonably could have forecast a substantial disruption at school, based on the threatening, intimidating, and harassing language in Bell's rap recording.

Id. at 400.

In a lengthy dissent, Judge Dennis strongly disagreed:

Bell's song was not a disruption of school activities but rather was an effort to participate as a citizen in our unique constitutional democracy by raising awareness of a serious matter of public concern. Yet, rather than commending Bell's efforts, the Itawamba County School Board punished him for the content of his speech, in effect teaching Bell that the First Amendment does not protect students who challenge those in power.

Id. at 432. In separate dissent Judge Prado added that he agreed with Judge Dennis' dissent but cautioned:

I share the majority opinion's concern about the potentially harmful impact of off-campus online speech on the on-campus lives of students. The ever-increasing encroachment of off-campus online and social-media speech into the campus, classroom, and lives of school students cannot be overstated. See Kowalski, 652 F.3d at 567-69, 571 (confronting a situation in which one high-school student created a webpage dedicated to spreading rumors about the sexually transmitted disease of another student and her supposed sexual promiscuity, thereby "singl[ing] out [that student] for harassment, bullying and intimidation"). Ultimately, the difficult issues of off campus online speech will need to be addressed by the Supreme Court.

Id. at 435. In another dissent, Judge Graves fashioned a new standard for off campus speech by students shared widely on social media and concluded that the school district had exceeded its powers. The Supreme Court denied the plaintiff's petition for certiorari so, for the present, Judge Hawkins' opinion for a majority of judges stands.

Which rationale is more compelling in the *Bell* case, the majority or the dissent? Does the use of social media to broadcast speech by a student-athlete raise new issues in such cases? Does the availability of social media to broadcast or share one's speech warrant a change in the *Tinker* standard that has been applied by courts since 1969?

The national anthem protests inspired by Colin Kaepernick in 2016 have been imitated by high school athletes across the country. Community backlash (often through social media) can be harsh, and school administrators are in the difficult position of choosing to support students' free speech rights versus sanctioning the players based on the *Tinker* disruption standard. Some schools have exercised the "teachable moment" approach to discuss the free exchange of ideas embodied in the First Amendment. Others have banned student-athletes from kneeling during the anthem and suspended them for their protest. If you were the general counsel for the school district, what would you recommend to school administrators? Is a one-rule-fits-all approach legally defensible or does the administration have to consider the totality of the circumstances to avoid legal liability?

2. *Parent's Free Speech Rights.* In *Parker v. The Waldron, Arkansas, School District,* 2006 WL 663401 (W.D. Ark. 2006), the district court held that a parent who published a letter in a local newspaper concerning the poor treatment of students on the school's sports teams had sufficiently alleged that he was being retaliated against by the school system for exercising his First Amendment right of free speech. The court held that evidence establishing that the school had penalized children following parental criticism of the coaching staff further implied that the school remained indifferent to or tacitly authorized such retaliation against the students. See also *Besler v. Board of Educ. of West-Windsor-Plainsboro Reg'l Sch. Dist.,* 993 A.2d 805 (N.J. 2010) (parent's free speech rights violated when he was denied the opportunity to complete his statement alleging that a high school coach verbally abused students, including his daughter). On the other hand, schools have the right to restrict persons, including parents, from entering campuses when their speech or conduct poses a threat to the safety of others. In *Cunningham v. Lenape Regional High Dist. Bd. of Educ.,* 2007 WL 1821010 (D. N.J.), the father of a high school wrestler brought suit against his son's school district after he was banished from the school's premises and instructed not to communicate with any coach or member of the wrestling team on the ground that the district's action violated his right of assembly under the First Amendment. The school district asserted that its decision was made to ensure public safety because the parent in question had engaged in behavior on six occasions that gave rise to complaints that he was aggressive and belittling and made people feel unsafe. Agreeing with the school district, the court ruled that schools have the right to impose restrictions to protect public safety and observed that a school district does not have to wait until such harm actually occurs, but does need to have evidence of inappropriate and hostile behavior that could result in public harm.

PROBLEM 2-1

A high school football player and wrestler was suspended indefinitely from participation in athletics for sending the following message to a fellow student regarding an upcoming football practice on his Twitter account: "Im boutta drill my 'teammates' on Monday." The school believed the message to be a threat. The student argued it was just his way of saying that he would be aggressive in football practice. The student was not permitted to participate in football and initially was not permitted to wrestle either. The student has a strong chance of obtaining a wrestling scholarship at the collegiate level but will lose all scholarship opportunities if he is not allowed to compete this season, his junior year. He wants to sue the school for violating his rights. As his attorney, what do you recommend? As general counsel for the school district, what policies and procedures would you want instituted at the school to avoid litigation?

ii. First Amendment Freedom of Religion Rights and Establishment Clause Limits

Free exercise and establishment of religion issues may arise in the context of interscholastic sports, implicating federal and/or state constitutional law issues. The Free Exercise Clause protects the rights of students, coaches, and other individuals to act on their religious beliefs. The Establishment Clause limits the power of a state actor (e.g., a public school) to engage in or permit activities that could be considered state endorsement or approval of particular religious activities, such as organized prayers before athletic events.

In his article, *Religious Freedom and the Interscholastic Athlete*, 12 Marq. Sports L. Rev. 295 (2001), Professor Scott Idleman observes:

> [A]thletic participation and religious observance appear to be two of Americans' most cherished endeavors. When these endeavors collide, and when the collision is due partly to a governmental regulation or policy, the Free Exercise Clause may very well dictate how this conflict between competition and conscience is resolved. The First Amendment's principal message in this regard is that regulations must be religiously neutral and generally applicable, and that religious requests for accommodation must be treated with at least the same solicitude that administrators display towards nonreligious requests (although more favorable treatment is in many instances permissible as well). The government may also have to bend its regulations where the athlete's predicament implicates not only free exercise, but also a conjunctive constitutional claim such as free speech or the right of parents to direct their children's education. To the extent that governments abide by these norms, the First Amendment otherwise permits them generally to regulate in any rational manner, and pursue any legitimate objectives, which they deem appropriate.

Id. at 344-345.

Professor Idleman also notes the role of other federal and state laws, including state constitutional provisions:

> [O]ther federal and especially state laws . . . might also be implicated . . ., depending on the jurisdiction, the legal status of the educational institution, the nature of the athletic regulation, and the particular circumstances of the alleged religious infringement. In some states, for example, strict scrutiny may apply to government regulations even if they are neutral and generally applicable. In others, the rights of students or student-athletes may be specifically protected. While in others, or in certain interscholastic venues, the regulations themselves may provide for certain forms of religious accommodation.

Id. at 345.

Some early cases evidence the propensity of courts to defer to institutions and interscholastic associations even when they act in a manner that clearly limits the free exercise of religion rights of a student-athlete (or coach). In *Walsh v. Louisiana High School Athletic Assn.*, 616 F.2d 152 (5th Cir. 1980), the court upheld a transfer rule against a claim that it burdened a student's free exercise of religious rights. The parents sought to have their children educated in Lutheran schools, as a matter of faith, and argued that the transfer rule prohibiting their children from participating for a period of time in interscholastic athletics infringed their free exercise rights. Similarly, in *Menora v. Illinois High School Assn.*, 683 F.2d 1030 (7th Cir. 1982), the court upheld a rule that forbade student-athletes from wearing hats or other headwear (with the sole exception of a headband no wider than two inches) while playing basketball, against a claim that this rule infringed on the religious freedom of Orthodox Jews who sought to wear yarmulkes during play. The court accepted the association's assertion that the rule preserved the safety of players by insuring that a player would not trip over a yarmulke that had fallen from a player's head.

The likelihood that a court will provide such a significant degree of deference, even when the challenged conduct implicates First Amendment free exercise of religion rights, is even greater today. In *Employment Division v. Smith*, 494 U.S. 872 (1990), the Supreme Court held that neutral laws of general applicability—laws that do not intentionally discriminate against religion or religious exercise—do not violate the Free Exercise Clause. It should be noted, however, that statutory or regulatory accommodations of religious exercise are permissible. Athletic associations may create rules or grant waivers that accommodate the free exercise of religion. For example, some state high school athletic associations have promulgated rules that enable their religious school members to refrain from participating in interscholastic competitions on their Sabbath. Thus, it is now clear that the Louisiana High School Athletic Association in the *Walsh* case noted above could have permitted the student-athlete's transfer on religious grounds without any loss of eligibility to participate in sports. That is one of the lessons of *Employment Division v. Smith*, which leaves such matters largely to the democratic or regulatory process at the state and federal levels.

Many states (approximately half of them) responded to *Employment Division v. Smith* by passing religious freedom restoration acts. These state constitutional provisions provide stronger support for free exercise rights, but they have not been invoked with any regularity in the interscholastic athletics context. Lawyers, however, need to remember that the best legal recourse for their clients is at the state constitutional level, not under the U.S. Constitution. Thus, they may be able to successfully argue that a religious accommodation or exemption is required under a state constitutional right of free exercise provision, which may be interpreted to provide broader rights than the U.S. Constitution's Free Exercise Clause.

NOTES AND QUESTIONS

1. *Student-Athlete's Free Exercise Rights.* The First Amendment offers little protection to student-athletes (or their parents or coaches) unless they can establish that they are actually being discriminated against on religious grounds (a difficult burden of proof to satisfy) or they can persuade an educational institution or governing body to provide them with an accommodation to avoid infringing their free exercise of religion rights. Is it reasonable to expect students to waive constitutional rights in exchange for the privilege of participating in interscholastic athletics?

   In *Hadley v. Rush Henrietta Central School District*, 409 F. Supp. 2d 164 (W.D.N.Y. 2006), the court granted an injunction allowing a high school lacrosse player to participate in the sport despite his refusal to get a required tetanus vaccination for religious reasons. The court acknowledged that participation in interscholastic athletics is not a constitutionally protected right but concluded that the school district's failure to extend a vaccination waiver granted to students generally to students desiring to participate in athletics likely constituted illegal discrimination on the basis of religion. However, in *Kunkel v. NKY Ind. Health Dept.*, Case No. 19-CI-00357 (April 2, 2019), a Kentucky state court held that barring a student from attending school and athletics participation for failing to have a chicken pox vaccination did not violate his First Amendment free exercise of religion rights. After an outbreak of 32 cases of chicken pox in the city, the health department banned all students who were not vaccinated from attending school for 21 days after the onset of rash for the last ill student or staff member in the community. Kunkel refused to be vaccinated based on his religious beliefs, was barred from school, and missed the last three games of the season. Do the circumstances in the two cases justify different legal conclusions?

2. *School's Free Exercise Rights.* In *Cornerstone Christian Schools v. University Interscholastic League*, 563 F.3d 127 (5th Cir. 2009), the Fifth Circuit ruled that a state high school athletic association's refusal to admit a Christian school did not constitute an infringement of federal free exercise rights. The challenged association rule, which rendered students who receive more than 25% of their tuition from merit-based financial aid ineligible for athletics participation, was religiously neutral, generally applicable, and did not, by its terms, distinguish between private and parochial schools. See also *Evans v. Kentucky High Sch. Athletic Assn.*, 2010 WL 1643758 (W.D. Ky.), *affirmed*, 2011 WL 6415055 (6th Cir.) (applying a rational basis test to bylaw that applies to all non-public schools equally, court rejects claim that it discriminates against Roman Catholic schools by rendering students who receive more than 25% of their tuition from merit-based financial aid ineligible to participate in KHSAA-sponsored interscholastic athletics).

On the other hand, in *Nakashima v. Board of Education*, 185 P.3d 429 (Or. 2008), the Oregon Supreme Court ruled that the state school board violated a state law prohibiting discrimination based on religion when it approved the Oregon School Activities Association's refusal to accommodate an Adventist school's request that it adjust a basketball tournament schedule to enable students to avoid having to choose between participating in athletics on their Sabbath or refusing to play. It also awarded attorney fees to the ACLU chapter that represented the Adventist school.

The First Amendment provides that "Congress shall make no law respecting an establishment of religion." The Establishment Clause prohibits state actors from engaging in activities that have the effect of establishing a religion by a governmental entity or state actor. One issue that regularly arises is the question of whether prayers may be offered prior to, or as a part of, interscholastic athletic events sponsored by public schools. In *Santa Fe Independent School District v. Doe*, 530 U.S. 290 (2000), the Court held that the school's policy permitting student-led prayer at football games was unconstitutional. Writing for the majority, Justice Stevens held that pregame prayers delivered "on school property, at school-sponsored events, over the school's public address system, by a speaker representing the student body, under the supervision of school faculty, and pursuant to a school policy that explicitly and implicitly encourages public prayer" are public speech and therefore prohibited. Justice Stevens and the majority applied an objective test and found that students in the district "will unquestionably perceive the inevitable pregame prayer as stamped with her school's seal of approval." Chief Justice Rehnquist, joined by Justices Scalia and Thomas, believed the Court was acting prematurely because the policy had not been put into practice. The dissenters were not convinced that speech (a prayer) under the policy would necessarily violate the Establishment Clause, because the speaker would be a private individual (not a public official) and the prayer, therefore, would be private rather than school-sponsored speech.

NOTES AND QUESTIONS

1. *What Religious Expression May Be Permitted?* The majority in the *Santa Fe* case indicated that religious activities in the interscholastic athletics context are permissible if a public school or state high school's athletics association determined to be a state actor is not viewed as sponsoring or endorsing the religious activity. What activities might be appropriate? If the captain of a public high school team led his team in prayer without the participation or knowledge of the coach, would that be permissible? If the coach learned that the captain did so and planned to do so in the future, would he need to prevent the captain from leading the team in a prayer in the future (i.e., would the coach's acquiescence be sufficient reason to find undue state involvement)? What if an athlete was injured and his teammates spontaneously knelt in prayer around him? If a school's mascot is the crusaders or the saints, should the school be prohibited from using that name on establishment of religion grounds?

2. *Relationship of Establishment of Religion Prohibitions to Freedom of Speech and Free Exercise of Religion Rights.* Cases involving prayer by public high school student-athletes and coaches often raise both free speech and free exercise issues in addition to establishment of religion issues, as was the case in *Santa Fe Independent School District.* In *Borden v. School District of the Township of East Brunswick,* 523 F.3d 153 (3d Cir. 2008), the Third Circuit ruled that a public school's refusal to permit a coach to silently bow his head during premeal grace and kneel with his team during a student-initiated locker room prayer did not constitute a violation of the coach's right of free speech and that the coach's doing so violated the Establishment Clause. Similarly, the Ninth Circuit held a football coach at a public high school had no First Amendment right to pray on the field during or immediately after games because communicating with students and fans was part of his normal job responsibilities and therefore was public speech conveying a preference for religion. See *Kennedy v. Bremerton Sch. Dist.,* 880 F.3d 1097 (9th Cir. 2018). On the other hand, in *Matthews v. Kountze Independent School District,* 2017 Tex. App. LEXIS 9165, the Texas Court of Appeals held that high school cheerleaders who displayed religious messages on run-through banners at football games were exercising private speech rights. Although the cheerleaders were a school-sponsored organization and the run-through banners were prominently displayed on the football field just before the start of the game, the court held the banners were not school-sponsored speech that violated the Establishment Clause. Are these cases consistent with *Santa Fe,* and can they be reconciled based on this precedent?

PROBLEM 2-2

A coach at a public high school has been bringing players together regularly for a prayer prior to practices and games. Does the coach have a free exercise right to offer a prayer for his or her team? Does such a prayer constitute an establishment of religion violation? If the coach learned that the prayer was constitutionally questionable and came to you with the following possible recommendations (in descending order of attractiveness to him), which ones, if any, do you believe may be constitutionally acceptable? (1) The coach selects a team chaplain. (2) The team elects a person to pray prior to practices and competition. (3) The coach invites a member of the team, on a noncompulsory basis, to join a representative of the Fellowship of Christian Athletes or some other religious group for a prayer prior to practice or competition. (4) The members of the team take turns offering a prayer or inspirational thought prior to practice or competition. (5) The coach asks the team members to join in a moment of silent reflection or prayer prior to practice and competition. Are there other possible ways in which religious interests of public school coaches and students are constitutionally permissible? If you were an attorney representing a public school district that wanted to recognize prayer in some form in the athletics context, what would you advise the district to do?

iii.   *Fourth Amendment Protection Against Unreasonable
       Search and Seizure*

Like society at large, drug use pervades all levels of athletic competition, including among high school athletes. The National Federation of State High Schools does not require that high schools develop a drug-testing program for athletes. Nevertheless, high school districts throughout the country have implemented random drug-testing programs that require students to consent to testing as a condition of being eligible to participate in interscholastic athletics. These policies vary by individual school district, with testing done for illegal recreational drugs such as marijuana and for performance-enhancing drugs such as anabolic steroids. A 2016 study found that fewer children and adolescents are using performance-enhancing substances to improve athletics performance and for appearance-related reasons than a decade ago. Michele LaBotz, Bernard A. Griesemer, *Use of Performance-Enhancing Substances,* 138(1) Pediatrics 1 (2016).

Prior to 1995, lower federal courts were split on whether drug testing of high school athletes by public schools violates the Fourth or Fourteenth Amendments, as unreasonable searches or violations of due process, respectively. See, e.g., *Schaill v. Tippecanoe County Sch. Corp.,* 864 F.2d 1309 (7th Cir. 1988); *Moule by & Through Moule v. Paradise Valley Unified Sch. Dist.,* 863 F. Supp. 1098 (D. Ariz. 1994). See also Diane Heckman, *The Evolution of Drug Testing of Interscholastic Athletes,* 9 Vill. Sports & Ent. L.J. 209 (2002) (presenting an overview of the testing of interscholastic athletes pre-and post-*Vernonia* and the impact of the *Earls* case).

In the following case, the United States Supreme Court considered whether suspicionless random drug testing of high school athletes for recreational drugs is constitutional.

VERNONIA SCHOOL DISTRICT 47J v. ACTON
515 U.S. 646 (1995)

Justice SCALIA delivered the opinion of the Court.

[EDS. The Student Athlete Drug Policy adopted by School District 47J in the town of Vernonia, Oregon, authorizes random urinalysis drug testing of students who participate in the district's school athletics programs. Drugs had not been a major problem in Vernonia schools. In the mid-to late 1980s, however, teachers and administrators observed a sharp increase in drug use. Students began to speak out about their attraction to the drug culture, and to boast that there was nothing the school could do about it. Along with more drugs came more disciplinary problems.

Not only were student athletes included among the drug users, athletes were also the leaders of the drug culture. This caused the district's administrators particular concern, since drug use increases the risk of sports-related injury. Expert testimony at the trial confirmed the deleterious effects of drugs on motivation, memory, judgment, reaction, coordination, and performance. The high school football and wrestling coach witnessed a severe sternum injury suffered by a wrestler and various omissions of safety procedures and misexecutions by football players, all attributable, in his belief, to the effects of drug use.

Initially, the district responded to the drug problem by offering special classes, speakers, and presentations designed to deter drug use. However, the drug problem persisted. Ultimately, the district adopted the Student Athlete Drug Policy (Policy) at a meeting, to which parents in attendance gave their unanimous approval.

The school board approved the Policy for implementation in the fall of 1989. Its expressed purpose was to prevent student-athletes from using drugs, to protect their health and safety, and to provide drug users with assistance programs.

The Policy applied to all students participating in interscholastic athletics. Students wishing to play sports must sign a form consenting to the testing and must obtain the written consent of their parents. Athletes are tested at the beginning of the season for their sport. In addition, once each week of the season the names of the athletes are placed in a "pool" from which a student, with the supervision of two adults, blindly draws the names of 10 percent of the athletes for random testing. Those selected are notified and tested that same day, if possible. Students to be tested enter an empty locker room accompanied by an adult monitor of the same sex and provide a urine sample. After the sample is produced, it is given to the monitor, who checks it for temperature and tampering and then transfers it to a vial.

The samples are sent to an independent laboratory, which routinely tests them for amphetamines, cocaine, and marijuana. Other drugs, such as LSD, may be screened at the request of the district, but the identity of a particular student does not determine which drugs will be tested. The laboratory's procedures are 99.94 percent accurate. The district follows strict procedures regarding the chain of custody and access to test results. The laboratory does not know the identity of the students whose samples it tests. It is authorized to mail written test reports only to the superintendent and to provide test results to district personnel by telephone only after the requesting official recites a code confirming his authority. Only the superintendent, principals, vice principals, and athletic directors have access to test results, and the results are not kept for more than one year.

If a sample tests positive, a second test is administered as soon as possible to confirm the result. If the second test is negative, no further action is taken. If the second test is positive, the athlete's parents are notified, and the school principal convenes a meeting with the student and the parents, at which the student is given the option of (1) participating for six weeks in an assistance program that includes weekly urinalysis or (2) suffering suspension from athletics for the remainder of the current season and the next athletic season. The student is then retested prior to the start of the next athletic season for which he or she is eligible. The Policy states that a second offense results in automatic imposition of option (2); a third offense results in suspension for the remainder of the current season and the next two athletic seasons.

In the fall of 1991, respondent James Acton, then a seventh grader, signed up to play football at one of the district's grade schools. He was denied participation, however, because he and his parents refused to sign the testing consent forms. The Actons filed suit, seeking declaratory and injunctive relief from enforcement of the Policy on the grounds that it violated the Fourth and Fourteenth Amendments to the United States Constitution and Article I, §9, of the Oregon Constitution. The District Court entered an order denying the claims on the merits and dismissing the action, but the Ninth Circuit reversed, holding that the Policy violated both the Fourth and Fourteenth Amendments and Article I, §9, of the Oregon Constitution. 23 F.3d 1514 (1994).]

II

. . . In *Skinner v. Railway Labor Executives' Assn.*, 489 U.S. 602, 617, 109 S. Ct. 1402, 1413, 103 L. Ed. 2d 639 (1989), we held that state-compelled collection and testing of urine, such as that required by the Policy, constitutes a "search" subject to the demands of the Fourth Amendment. See also *Treasury Employees v. Von Raab*, 489 U.S. 656, 665, 109 S. Ct. 1384, 1390, 103 L. Ed. 2d 685 (1989).

As the text of the Fourth Amendment indicates, the ultimate measure of the constitutionality of a governmental search is "reasonableness." At least in a case such as this, where there was no clear practice, either approving or disapproving the type of search at issue, at the time the constitutional provision was enacted, whether a particular search meets the reasonableness standard " 'is judged by balancing its intrusion on the individual's Fourth Amendment interests against its promotion of legitimate governmental interests.' " (Citation omitted.) Where a search is undertaken by law enforcement officials to discover evidence of criminal wrongdoing, this Court has said that reasonableness generally requires the obtaining of a judicial warrant, *Skinner, supra*, at 619, 109 S. Ct., at 1414. Warrants cannot be issued, of course, without the showing of probable cause required by the Warrant Clause. But a warrant is not required to establish the reasonableness of *all* government searches; and when a warrant is not required (and the Warrant Clause therefore not applicable), probable cause is not invariably required either. A search unsupported by probable cause can be constitutional, we have said, "when special needs, beyond the normal need for law enforcement, make the warrant and probable-cause requirement impracticable." (Citation omitted.)

We have found such "special needs" to exist in the public school context. There, the warrant requirement "would unduly interfere with the maintenance of the swift and informal disciplinary procedures [that are] needed," and "strict adherence to the requirement that searches be based upon probable cause" would undercut "the substantial need of teachers and administrators for freedom to maintain order in the schools." *T.L.O.*, 469 U.S., at 340, 341, 105 S. Ct., at 742. The school search we approved in *T.L.O.*, while not based on probable cause, *was* based on individualized *suspicion* of wrongdoing. As we explicitly acknowledged, however, " 'the Fourth Amendment imposes no irreducible requirement of such suspicion,' " (citation omitted). We have upheld suspicionless searches and seizures to conduct drug testing of railroad personnel involved in train accidents, see *Skinner, supra;* to conduct random drug testing of federal customs officers who carry arms or are involved in drug interdiction, see *Von Raab, supra;* and to maintain automobile checkpoints looking for illegal immigrants and contraband, *Martinez-Fuerte, supra,* and drunk drivers, *Michigan Dept. of State Police v. Sitz,* 496 U.S. 444, 110 S. Ct. 2481, 110 L. Ed. 2d 412 (1990).

III

The first factor to be considered is the nature of the privacy interest upon which the search here at issue intrudes. . . . Central, in our view, to the present case is the fact that the subjects of the Policy are (1) children, who (2) have been committed to the temporary custody of the State as schoolmaster.

Traditionally at common law, and still today, unemancipated minors lack some of the most fundamental rights of self-determination — including even the right of liberty in its narrow sense, *i.e.,* the right to come and go at will. They are subject, even as to their physical freedom, to the control of their parents or guardians. See 59 Am. Jur. 2d, Parent and Child § 10 (1987). When parents place minor children in private schools for their education, the teachers and administrators of those schools stand *in loco parentis* over the children entrusted to them. In fact, the tutor or schoolmaster is the very prototype of that status. . . .

Fourth Amendment rights, no less than First and Fourteenth Amendment rights, are different in public schools than elsewhere; the "reasonableness" inquiry cannot disregard the schools' custodial and tutelary responsibility for children. For their own good and that of their classmates, public school children are routinely required to submit to various physical examinations, and to be vaccinated against various diseases. . . . Particularly with regard to medical examinations and procedures, therefore, "students within the school environment have a lesser expectation of privacy than members of the population generally." [Citation omitted.]

Legitimate privacy expectations are even less with regard to student athletes. School sports are not for the bashful. They require "suiting up" before each practice or event, and showering and changing afterwards. Public school locker rooms, the usual sites for these activities, are not notable for the privacy they afford. The locker rooms in Vernonia are typical: No individual dressing rooms are provided; shower heads are lined up along a wall, unseparated by any sort of partition or curtain; not even all the toilet stalls have doors. As the United States Court of Appeals for the Seventh Circuit has noted, there is "an element of 'communal undress' inherent in athletic participation," *Schaill by Kross v. Tippecanoe County School Corp.,* 864 F.2d 1309, 1318 (1988).

There is an additional respect in which school athletes have a reduced expectation of privacy. By choosing to "go out for the team," they voluntarily subject themselves to a degree of regulation even higher than that imposed on students generally. In Vernonia's public schools, they must submit to a preseason physical exam (James testified that his included the giving of a urine sample, App. 17), they must acquire adequate insurance coverage or sign an insurance waiver, maintain a minimum grade point average, and comply with any "rules of conduct, dress, training hours and related matters as may be established for each sport by the head coach and athletic director with the principal's approval." Record, Exh. 2, p. 30, ¶8. Somewhat like adults who choose to participate in a "closely regulated industry," students who voluntarily participate in school athletics have reason to expect intrusions upon normal rights and privileges, including privacy. (Citation omitted.)

IV

Having considered the scope of the legitimate expectation of privacy at issue here, we turn next to the character of the intrusion that is complained of. . . . Under the District's Policy, male students produce samples at a urinal along a wall. They remain fully clothed and are only observed from behind, if at all. Female students produce samples in an enclosed stall, with a female monitor standing outside listening only for sounds of tampering. These conditions are nearly identical to those typically encountered in public restrooms, which men, women, and especially schoolchildren use daily. Under such conditions, the privacy interests compromised by the process of obtaining the urine sample are in our view negligible.

The other privacy-invasive aspect of urinalysis is, of course, the information it discloses concerning the state of the subject's body, and the materials he has ingested. In this regard it is significant that the tests at issue here look only for drugs, and not for whether the student is, for example, epileptic, pregnant, or diabetic. Moreover, the drugs for which the samples are screened are standard, and do not vary according to the identity of the student. And finally, the results of the tests are disclosed only to a limited class of school personnel who have a need to know; and they are not turned over to law enforcement authorities or used for any internal disciplinary function.

V

Finally, we turn to consider the nature and immediacy of the governmental concern at issue here, and the efficacy of this means for meeting it. In both *Skinner* and *Von Raab*, we characterized the government interest motivating the search as "compelling." [Citations omitted.] Relying on these cases, the District Court held that because the District's program also called for drug testing in the absence of individualized suspicion, the District "must demonstrate a 'compelling need' for the program." 796 F. Supp., at 1363. The Court of Appeals appears to have agreed with this view. See 23 F.3d, at 1526. It is a mistake, however, to think that the phrase "compelling state interest," in the Fourth Amendment context, describes a fixed, minimum quantum of governmental concern, so that one can dispose of a case by answering in isolation the question: Is there a compelling state interest here? Rather, the phrase describes an interest that appears *important enough* to justify the particular search at hand, in light of other factors that show the search to be relatively intrusive upon a genuine expectation of privacy. Whether that relatively high degree of government concern is necessary in this case or not, we think it is met.

That the nature of the concern is important—indeed, perhaps compelling—can hardly be doubted. Deterring drug use by our Nation's schoolchildren is at least as important as enhancing efficient enforcement of the Nation's laws against the importation of drugs, which was the governmental concern in *Von Raab, supra,* 489 U.S., at 668, 109 S. Ct., at 1392, or deterring drug use by engineers and trainmen, which was the governmental concern in *Skinner, supra,* at 628, 109

S. Ct., at 1419. School years are the time when the physical, psychological, and addictive effects of drugs are most severe. . . . And of course the effects of a drug-infested school are visited not just upon the users, but upon the entire student body and faculty, as the educational process is disrupted. In the present case, moreover, the necessity for the State to act is magnified by the fact that this evil is being visited not just upon individuals at large, but upon children for whom it has undertaken a special responsibility of care and direction. Finally, it must not be lost sight of that this program is directed more narrowly to drug use by school athletes, where the risk of immediate physical harm to the drug user or those with whom he is playing his sport is particularly high. Apart from psychological effects, which include impairment of judgment, slow reaction time, and a less-ening of the perception of pain, the particular drugs screened by the District's Policy have been demonstrated to pose substantial physical risks to athletes. Amphetamines produce an "artificially induced heart rate increase, [p]eriph-eral vasoconstriction, [b]lood pressure increase, and [m]asking of the normal fatigue response," making them a "very dangerous drug when used during exer-cise of any type." Hawkins, *Drugs and Other Ingesta: Effects on Athletic Performance,* in H. Appenzeller, Managing Sports and Risk Management Strategies 90, 90-91 (1993). Marijuana causes "[i]rregular blood pressure responses during changes in body position," "[r]eduction in the oxygen-carrying capacity of the blood," and "[i]nhibition of the normal sweating responses resulting in increased body temperature." *Id.,* at 94. Cocaine produces "[v]asoconstriction[,] [e]levated blood pressure," and "[p]ossible coronary artery spasms and myocardial infarction." *Ibid.*

As for the immediacy of the District's concerns: We are not inclined to question—indeed, we could not possibly find clearly erroneous—the District Court's con-clusion that "a large segment of the student body, particularly those involved in interscholastic athletics, was in a state of rebellion," that "[d]isciplinary actions had reached 'epidemic proportions,'" and that "the rebellion was being fueled by alcohol and drug abuse as well as by the student's misperceptions about the drug culture." . . .

VI

Taking into account all the factors we have considered above—the decreased expectation of privacy, the relative unobtrusiveness of the search, and the sever-ity of the need met by the search—we conclude Vernonia's Policy is reasonable and hence constitutional.

We caution against the assumption that suspicionless drug testing will readily pass constitutional muster in other contexts. The most significant element in this case is the first we discussed: that the Policy was undertaken in furtherance of the government's responsibilities, under a public school system, as guardian and tutor of children entrusted to its care. . . .

We may note that the primary guardians of Vernonia's schoolchildren appear to agree. The record shows no objection to this districtwide program by any par-ents other than the couple before us here—even though, as we have described, a public meeting was held to obtain parents' views. We find insufficient basis to contradict the judgment of Vernonia's parents, its school board, and the District Court, as to what was reasonably in the interest of these children under the circumstances.

The Ninth Circuit held that Vernonia's Policy not only violated the Fourth Amendment, but also, by reason of that violation, contravened Article I, § 9, of the Oregon Constitution. Our conclusion that the former holding was in error means that the latter holding rested on a flawed premise. We therefore vacate the judgment, and remand the case to the Court of Appeals for further proceedings consistent with this opinion.

Justice O'CONNOR, with whom Justice STEVENS and Justice SOUTER join, dissenting.

The population of our Nation's public schools, grades 7 through 12, numbers around 18 million. *See U.S. Dept. of Education, National Center for Education Statistics, Digest of Education Statistics* 58 (1994) (Table 43). By the reasoning of today's decision, the millions of these students who participate in interscholastic sports, an overwhelming majority of whom have given school officials no reason whatsoever to suspect they use drugs at school, are open to an intrusive bodily search. . . .

As an initial matter, I have serious doubts whether the Court is right that the District reasonably found that the lesser intrusion of a suspicion-based testing program outweighed its genuine concerns for the adversarial nature of such a program, and for its abuses. For one thing, there are significant safeguards against abuses. The fear that a suspicion-based regime will lead to the testing of "troublesome but not drug-likely" students, for example, ignores that the required level of suspicion in the school context is objectively *reasonable* suspicion. . . . Moreover, any distress arising from what turns out to be a false accusation can be minimized by keeping the entire process confidential. . . .

The record here indicates that the Vernonia schools are no exception. The great irony of this case is that most (though not all) of the evidence the District introduced to justify its suspicionless drug testing program consisted of first- or second-hand stories of particular, identifiable students acting in ways that plainly gave rise to reasonable suspicion of in-school drug use—and thus that would have justified a drug-related search under our *T.L.O.* decision. . . .

In light of all this evidence of drug use by particular students, there is a substantial basis for concluding that a vigorous regime of suspicion-based testing would have gone a long way toward solving Vernonia's school drug problem while preserving the Fourth Amendment rights of James Acton and others like him. And were there any doubt about such a conclusion, it is removed by indications in the record that suspicion-based testing could have been supplemented by an equally vigorous campaign to have Vernonia's parents encourage their children to submit to the District's *voluntary* drug testing program. In these circumstances, the Fourth Amendment dictates that a mass, suspicionless search regime is categorically unreasonable. . . .

I find unpersuasive the Court's reliance on the widespread practice of physical examinations and vaccinations, which are both blanket searches of a sort. . . .

It might also be noted that physical exams (and of course vaccinations) are not searches for conditions that reflect wrongdoing on the part of the student, and so are *wholly* nonaccusatory and have no consequences that can be regarded as punitive. . . .

. . . I find unreasonable the school's choice of student athletes as the class to subject to suspicionless testing—a choice that appears to have been driven more by a belief in what would pass constitutional muster (indicating that the original program was targeted at students involved in any extracurricular activity) than by a belief in what was required to meet the District's principal disciplinary concern. . . . [I]t seems quite obvious that the true driving force behind the District's adoption of its drug testing program was the need to combat the rise in drug-related disorder and disruption in its classrooms and around campus. I mean no criticism of the strength of that interest. On the contrary, where the record demonstrates the existence of such a problem, that interest seems self-evidently compelling. . . . And the record in this case surely demonstrates there was a drug-related discipline problem in Vernonia of " 'epidemic proportions.' " 796 F. Supp., at 1357. The evidence of a drug-related sports injury problem at Vernonia, by contrast, was considerably weaker. . . .

Having reviewed the record here, I cannot avoid the conclusion that the District's suspicionless policy of testing all student athletes sweeps too broadly, and too imprecisely, to be reasonable under the Fourth Amendment.

NOTES AND QUESTIONS

1. What is the legal standard for determining whether drug testing of interscholastic athletes by a public high school violates the Fourth Amendment? Why does the *Acton* majority uphold suspicionless testing of high school athletes for recreational drug use? Would suspicion-based drug testing accomplish high school administrators' legitimate objectives equally well without intruding on students' privacy rights?

2. In *Board of Education of Indep. Sch. Dist. No. 92 of Pottawatomie County v. Earls*, 536 U.S. 822 (2002), the Supreme Court upheld the constitutionality of mandatory suspicionless drug testing of all students participating in high school extracurricular activities such as the Academic Team, Future Farmers of America, band, choir, pom-pom, cheerleading, and athletics. The only consequence of a positive test for illegal drugs was to limit the student's privilege of participating in extracurricular activities; it did not result in the imposition of any other discipline or have any academic consequences.

   Writing for a narrow majority of five justices, Justice Thomas concluded that "the safety interest furthered by drug testing is undoubtedly substantial for all children, athletes and nonathletes alike." *Id.* at 837. The majority held that "testing students who participate in extracurricular activities is a reasonably effective means of addressing the School District's legitimate concerns in preventing, deterring, and detecting drug use." *Id.* The four dissenting justices asserted that "[i]nterscholastic athletics similarly require close safety and health regulation; a school's choir, band, and academic team do not." *Id.* at 846.

   Given that protection of high school students' health and safety is a legitimate reason for drug testing, would testing for performance-enhancing drugs such as anabolic steroids (instead of recreational drugs) be constitutional? See Thomas Proctor, Comment, *Constitutionality of Testing High School Male Athletes for Steroids Under* Vernonia School District v. Acton *and* Board of Education v. Earls, 2005 BYU L. Rev. 1335 (2005) (analyzing random, suspicionless testing of male high school athletes for steroid use under the *Acton* and *Earls* cases).

3. *State Constitutional Protections.* Although *Earls* gives broad approval under the Fourth Amendment of the United States Constitution to mandatory drug testing of all students wishing to participate in extracurricular activities, such policies may still face challenges under state constitutional provisions. In *York v. Wahkiakum*, 178 P.3d 995 (Wash. 2008), the Washington Supreme

Court considered the constitutionality of a school district's blanket suspicionless random drug testing program for student-athletes. Although the court acknowledged that the district's drug testing policy did not violate the Fourth Amendment of the U.S. Constitution, it concluded that the Washington state constitution provided a higher level of protection. It held that the district's drug testing policy violated a provision of the state constitution that provides, "No person shall be disturbed in his private affairs, or his home invaded, without authority of law." *Id.* at 306. See also *Theodore v. Delaware Valley Sch. Dist.*, 836 A.2d 76 (Pa. 2003) (invalidating suspicionless drug-testing of all middle and high school students desiring to participate in extracurricular activities because it violates Pennsylvania's constitution).

But see *Hageman v. Goshen County School Dist. No. 1*, 256 P.3d 487 (Wyo. 2011), in which the Supreme Court of Wyoming was not persuaded by *York* and held that a public school system's policy requiring all students who participate in extracurricular activities to submit to random drug and alcohol testing does not violate the Wyoming constitution, which the court declared to be more like the federal constitution than the Washington state constitution. The Wyoming Supreme Court examined both equal protection and due process issues under their state constitution, which makes it clear that advocates supporting the rights of student-athletes in such cases should invoke state constitutions rather than relying solely on the federal Constitution.

3. Athlete Eligibility Issues

This section considers a variety of federal constitutional and state law issues that have been raised by student-athletes and their parents challenging the nature and scope of associational (state athletic association) and institutional (high school) governance of interscholastic athletics. The principal cases consider student-athlete eligibility issues arising out of the application and enforcement of rules on transfer, "outside competition," age, academics, homeschooling, good conduct, personal appearance, and grooming. These principal cases are organized according to the specific rule or its application because multiple federal and state legal claims frequently are considered in the same judicial opinion.

When reading these cases, it is important to distinguish and separately consider these claims, while identifying their differing elements and judicial standard of review (e.g., *de novo*, strict, intermediate, rational basis, or arbitrary or capricious). State athletic associations, whether deemed to be "state actors" or not, as well as both public and private high schools must comply with their own substantive rules and internal procedural processes for resolving student-athlete eligibility disputes and with applicable state laws (e.g., contract, law of private associations). Public high schools and state athletic associations judicially characterized as state actors also must respect student-athletes' federal constitutional due process, equal protection, and other rights.

Federal due process claims raise the threshold issue of whether a constitutionally protected property or liberty interest is being deprived. As you are reading these cases, consider whether participation in interscholastic athletics (with or without the prospect of earning a future college athletic scholarship) is sufficiently important to be constitutionally protected and how courts have resolved this issue. Procedural due process typically requires consideration of whether fair notice and an opportunity to be heard have been provided by a state athletic association or high school before a student-athlete is denied eligibility to participate in interscholastic athletics. On occasion, substantive due process claims alleging that an eligibility rule, its application to a student-athlete's particular circumstances, or disciplinary action resulting in a loss of athletic eligibility is arbitrary or capricious or violates a protected property or liberty interest (e.g., privacy rights), regardless of the level of procedural process provided, have been raised in cases such as *Brands, infra.* Some student-athletes have argued, with little success, that substantive due process protects an independent right to participate in athletics or similar activities that are arguably of great value in his or her life. As a growing body of judicial precedent is created in these various contexts, think about whether participation in athletics should trigger either procedural or substantive due process protection.

Federal equal protection requires that similarly situated parties be treated alike, with a heightened level of judicial scrutiny applicable if there is discrimination denying an individual fundamental right or based on innate characteristics such as race, ethnicity, national origin, or gender. Otherwise, the validity of differing treatment is decided based on a less stringent and very deferential standard; if there is any rational basis for the challenged decision or rule, the court probably will not find a denial of equal protection of the law.

Regarding the extent to which an opportunity to participate in interscholastic athletics is worthy of legal protection, consider the following:

> In our increasingly technology-driven, isolated society, participation in interscholastic athletics provides a means of establishing social networks with one's peers and developing a community-based identity with corresponding positive academic effects. Finding a link between high school students' sense of identity, patterns of extracurricular involvement, and indicators of successful and risky adolescent development, a 1999 study found that female and male students who participate in high school team sports through the 12th grade have a school-based identity that correlates to positive academic performance (e.g., an increased 12th-grade GPA and an increased probability of being enrolled in college full-time at age 21). This highly positive finding is consistent with prior research evidencing that sports participation, relative to participation in other extracurricular activities such as student government and academic clubs, is "linked to lower likelihood of school dropout and higher rates of college attendance."

Matthew J. Mitten and Timothy Davis, *Athlete Eligibility Requirements and Legal Protection of Sports Participation Opportunities,* 8 Va. Sports & Ent. L.J. 71, 113 (2008).

a.   Transfer Rules

Student-athletes often challenge state interscholastic athletic association transfer rules that limit their ability to participate immediately in interscholastic competition after moving from one school to another. A common type of transfer rule renders a student-athlete who transfers from one high school to another without a corresponding change in his or her parents' residence ineligible to engage in interscholastic varsity competition for a period of time (generally one calendar year). These rules typically permit exceptions in exceptional circumstances.

PROBLEM 2-3

On June 25, 2009, the California Interscholastic Federation (CIF) issued *Understanding the Transfer Eligibility Procedure: A Parent Guideline Handbook.* In an effort to limit transfers between schools for athletic purposes, the CIF generally limits eligibility for students transferring from one school to another and establishes a procedure permitting the waiver of ineligibility when a student-athlete's transfer was not for athletic purposes:

HARDSHIP WAIVERS

The CIF [recognizes] that, in certain circumstances, students may transfer from one school to another due to a compelling need or situation beyond a student's control. In such cases . . . the transfer limitation [may be waived] when the case meets the definition of a hardship. (See "A" below.)

Consideration of any hardship request . . . requires documented proof of the hardship circumstance, and all facts to be considered must be submitted at the time of the application. Consideration will be given to those situations in which there is no evidence of athletic motivation, undue influence, pending disciplinary action or falsification of information.

A. A hardship is defined as an unforeseeable, unavoidable and uncorrectable act, condition or event that causes the imposition of a severe and non-athletic burden upon the student and his/her family. [The CIF] may only waive the transfer limitation if the conditions of hardship are met, and there is sufficient documentation to support the hardship claim. Sections may not waive the applicable rule if the conditions of hardship are not met.

B. Consideration of any hardship request . . . requires documentation. Such documents may include, but not be limited to copies of current transcripts, financial documents, medical statements and/or supportive statements from the previous school attended.

How should the following situations be resolved based on the foregoing provisions: (1) An all-state student-athlete, who has been living with his single mother, moves to live with his sister in another community because his mother has to work full time, and she feels that she lacks the discipline in her home necessary for her son's welfare. (2) Would it make a difference in question 1 if the parent was sick and named her daughter as the guardian of her son? (3) A student-athlete's parents, who live on a military base that has a weak music program, want their daughter, who is an accomplished violinist and has also competed in softball at the varsity level during the past 12 months, to transfer to live with her grandparents, who are in a school district with a nationally acclaimed music program and symphony. (4) Would it make a difference in question 3 if the base was in a dangerous area and the parents wanted their child to move to a safer area? As a lawyer, how would you counsel your clients in each of the cases noted in these four scenarios? What problems do you foresee? What kind of record or proof would you want to develop? How important is a letter from the school that the student is transferring from? Should such cases be decided on a case-by-case basis under a broad waiver provision, or should associations strongly enforce rules that limit transfers?

Carlberg provides an illustration of how courts have resolved a variety of federal and state law legal challenges to transfer rules and their application in individual cases. While reading this case, consider the purposes for which transfer rules are promulgated (e.g., protecting student-athletes from the pressure and harassment of zealous coaches and fans that might ensue from unregulated recruiting; affording academics a higher priority than athletics). See *Parker v. Ariz. Interscholastic Assn.*, 59 P.3d 806, 813 (Ariz. Ct. App. 2002) ("The purpose of the AIA transfer rule is to deter athletically motivated transfers and recruitment of students and promote 'the educational philosophy that participation in athletics is a privilege which should not take a dominant role over academics.'"). As you read *Carlberg* and the cases that follow, you will note that courts provide a much narrower scope of review in disputes between a member school and a state governing body than for actions by student-athletes against a state governing body.

INDIANA HIGH SCHOOL ATHLETIC ASSOCIATION v. CARLBERG

694 N.E.2d 222 (Ind. 1997)

SULLIVAN, Justice.

[EDS. After attending Brebeuf Preparatory School as a freshman (where he swam on the varsity swim team), Jason Carlberg, who lives with his parents near Indianapolis, transferred to Carmel High School for academic reasons. The Indiana High School Athletic Association (IHSAA) is a voluntary association of public and private high schools that adopts and enforces rules regarding eligibility and similar matters related to interscholastic athletic competition. Applying Rule 19 (the "Transfer Rule"), the IHSAA determined that Carlberg transferred for nonathletic reasons without a change of permanent residence by his parents or guardians. Therefore, he had only limited athletic eligibility for 365 days following enrollment (i.e., he was immediately eligible to participate in all interscholastic sports except as a member of a varsity athletic team).

After exhausting available administrative remedies, including a hearing before the IHSAA Executive Committee, which denied his appeal, Carlberg alleged, *inter alia*, that application of the Transfer Rule violated his constitutional rights under the due process and equal protection clauses of the Fourteenth Amendment of the U.S. Constitution, and was arbitrary and capricious in violation of Indiana common law. Agreeing with his contentions, the trial court enjoined the IHSAA from enforcing the Transfer Rule and ordered that Carlberg be allowed to participate on the Carmel High School varsity swimming team, which ruling was affirmed by an intermediate appellate court.

In its appeal to the Indiana Supreme Court, the IHSAA argued that the Transfer Rule is subject to the rule of limited judicial interference in the affairs of private voluntary membership associations, and that the trial court wrongly interfered with its internal affairs.

The Indiana Supreme Court held that "decisions of the IHSAA with respect to student-athletes constitute 'state action.'" It observed that the IHSAA's "very existence is entirely dependent upon the absolute cooperation and support of the public school systems of the State of Indiana" that "is derived from the lawful delegation from public schools to the IHSAA of authority conferred upon public schools by the legislature." The court added:

> [There are three other important reasons why the IHSAA is a state actor]: (i) the salaries of most the principals and coaches involved in interscholastic athletics are derived from tax funds; (ii) most of the athletic contests are held in, or on, athletic facilities which have been constructed and maintained with tax funds; and (iii) IHSAA rules are adopted by tax-supported schools and their enforcement may have a substantial impact upon the rights of students enrolled in these tax supported institutions.

Regarding his due process claim, the court ruled that Carlberg has no constitutional right to participate in interscholastic athletics and was not entitled to procedural due process before the IHSAA's adverse eligibility determination. Moreover, Carlberg was granted a hearing before the IHSAA Executive Committee and did not contend that this procedure was inadequate or denied him a fair opportunity to be heard.

Regarding his equal protection claim, the court held that "[a]bsent a burden upon the exercise of a constitutionally protected right (none is at stake here) or creation of a suspect class (none is alleged here), the general standard of review of state action challenged under the equal protection clause is the rational basis test." It found that the Transfer Rule's objectives of preserving the integrity of interscholastic athletics and preventing recruiting and school transfers for athletic reasons are legitimate, and concluded that the Transfer Rule is rationally related to achieving these goals.]

. . . We find resolution of challenges to IHSAA rules and enforcement actions well within the ambit of Indiana common law. Our state constitution specifically recognizes that "knowledge and learning" are "essential to the preservation of a free government" and so mandates a statewide system of free public education. Ind. Const. art. VIII, § 1. We believe athletics are an integral part of this constitutionally-mandated process of education. . . .

The substantial educational benefits derived from interscholastic athletics, together with the rationale that underlies the determination that IHSAA decisions constitute "state action," help explain why Indiana courts have been so willing to adjudicate disputes between the IHSAA and parties aggrieved by the association's decisions. We reaffirm our common law jurisdiction in this regard today and turn to an examination of the common law principles applicable in IHSAA cases. . . .

The rule in Indiana is that courts exercise limited interference with the internal affairs and rules of a voluntary membership association: A voluntary association may, without direction or interference by the courts, for its government, adopt a constitution, by-laws, rules and regulations which will control as to all questions of discipline, or internal policy and management, and its right to interpret and administer the same is as sacred as the right to make them. . . .

. . . Although we will continue to review for arbitrariness and capriciousness IHSAA decisions affecting students, we see little justification for such review when it comes to the IHSAA's member schools. As to its member schools, the IHSAA is a voluntary membership association. Those members have the internal procedures of their own association available to them to adjudicate disputes and, if necessary, change rules or leadership; there is no need for courts to micro-manage these matters. We hold in [*IHSAA v. Reyes*, 694 N.E.2d 249 (Ind. 1997)] and reiterate here, that judicial review of IHSAA decisions with respect to its member schools will be limited to those circumstances under which courts review the decisions of voluntary membership associations-fraud, other illegality, or abuse of civil or property rights having their origin elsewhere.

When it comes to student challenges, however, we reach a different result. Perhaps Judge Cummings said it best when he observed that "for a student athlete in public school, membership in IHSAA is not voluntary, and actions of the IHSAA arguably should be held to a stricter standard of judicial review." *Freeman*, 51 F.3d at 1363. Therein lies what is for us a crucial distinction between this case and *Reyes*: as a student, Carlberg has not voluntarily subjected himself to the rules of the IHSAA; he has no voice in its rules or leadership. We note as well the relatively short span of time a student spends in high school compared to the amount of time often required for institutional policies to change. These factors all point to the propriety of judicial scrutiny of IHSAA decisions with respect to student challenges.

But what should be the standard of review? This Court has never applied *de novo* review to IHSAA decisions and emphatically rejects it here. Rather than *de novo* review, . . . the appellate courts of this state have applied an "arbitrary and capricious" standard in reviewing the decisions of the IHSAA. (Citations omitted.)

While the doctrinal basis for judicial review of IHSAA decisions for arbitrariness and capriciousness is not clear from the cases, we believe that it is similar to that which justifies the conclusion that IHSAA decisions constitute "state action." The facts that make IHSAA decisions "state action" for purposes of federal and state constitutional analysis also suggest an analogy with government agency decisions: if IHSAA decisions are "state action," then they are like government agency decisions. We conclude that the "arbitrary and capricious" standard of review probably grows out of this similarity. That is, just as courts review IHSAA decisions in approximately the same way as those of government agencies for purposes of constitutional law, courts review IHSAA decisions in approximately the same way as those of government agencies for purposes of common law. . . .

In summary, as a matter of state common law, the courts of Indiana have jurisdiction to review challenges to IHSAA rules and enforcement decisions applicable to a particular student, assuming those challenges are brought by non-IHSAA members with standing. Such rules and decisions will not be reviewed *de novo* but in a manner analogous to judicial review of government agency action, recognizing, however, that the IHSAA is not a government agency and the common law will have to accommodate that difference.

The provisions of the IHSAA Transfer Rule at issue in this case apply to a student who changes schools without a corresponding change of residence by the student's parents. Such a student may participate as a member of a junior varsity or freshman team at his or her new school unless the transfer was either primarily for athletic reasons or as a result of undue influence. However, such a student may not participate in interscholastic athletics as a member of a *varsity* athletic team during the first 365 days after enrollment unless (i) the student meets one of the special criteria set forth in Rule 19-6.1 or (ii) is declared eligible under the IHSAA "Hardship Rule."

Carlberg agrees that he changed schools without a corresponding change of residence by his parents and that none of the special criteria of Rule 19-6.1 nor the Hardship Rule apply. For its part, the IHSAA acknowledges that the transfer was neither for primarily athletic reasons nor as a result of undue influence. Carlberg argues that the IHSAA acted arbitrarily and capriciously when it enforced the Transfer Rule against him where it was undisputed that his transfer was neither primarily for athletic reasons nor as a result of undue influence.

[W]e review the challenged IHSAA decision for arbitrariness or capriciousness. "Arbitrary and capricious" is a narrow standard of review and the reviewing court may not substitute its judgment for the judgment of the IHSAA. The rule or decision will be found to be arbitrary and capricious "only where it is willful and unreasonable, without consideration and in disregard of the facts or circumstances in the case, or without some basis which would lead a reasonable and honest person to the same conclusion." *Dep't of Natural Resources v. Indiana Coal Council, Inc.*, 542 N.E.2d 1000, 1007 (Ind. 1989) (citation omitted).

We do not find the IHSAA decision that Carlberg was ineligible for varsity athletics for 365 days following his transfer to be "willful and unreasonable, without consideration and in disregard of the facts or circumstances in the case, or without some basis which would lead a reasonable and honest person to the same conclusion." First, . . . there is no contention that the IHSAA failed to publicize its interpretation of the rule or failed to apply consistently its interpretation of the rule.

Second, by establishing objective standards for eligibility "governing residence and transfer," including the provision allowing for only limited eligibility upon a transfer not accompanied by a parental change of residence, Rule 19(c) acts as a deterrent to athletically motivated transfers. . . .

Third, the operation of the rule does not sweep too broadly in its proscription. While it is true that some students who change schools neither primarily for athletic reasons nor as a result of undue influence are denied varsity eligibility for one year, conducting a factual inquiry into the motivation for every transfer would impose a considerable burden on both the IHSAA and its member schools. IHSAA Commissioner Gardner testified that to the effect that the IHSAA could not afford to investigate individually each transfer: "Regular detailed investigations by the IHSAA are cost prohibitive, could not be staffed by the current IHSAA personnel, and would have limited success in identifying those athletic transfers thinly disguised as nonathletic transfers." The IHSAA has balanced these competing interests by (i) creating the thirteen special criteria for immediate eligibility under Rule 19-6.1, (ii) granting immediate eligibility under the Hardship Rule, and (iii) permitting students immediate eligibility at the junior varsity and freshman level.

While we do not find the IHSAA's application of the Transfer Rule to Carlberg to be either arbitrary or capricious, we believe fairness to Carlberg's position requires that we give additional consideration to his common law claim. That is, Carlberg's claim might fairly be categorized as a challenge to the validity of the Transfer Rule itself, asking whether the IHSAA has the authority to enforce a rule denying varsity athletic eligibility to a student who transfers schools whether the transfer is neither primarily for athletic reasons nor as a result of undue influence. To put the distinction in administrative law terms, Carlberg may be seen to argue that the IHSAA has abused its rulemaking authority rather than its adjudicatory authority.

Judicial review of whether a governmental agency has abused its rulemaking authority is highly deferential. But government agency rulemaking is not exempt from judicial review. Among the factors analyzed are whether the challenged agency rule (i) falls within the scope of the agency's enabling legislation,

(ii) is arbitrary or unreasonable, (iii) is consistent and harmonious with the legislative pronouncement under which it operates, and (iv) does not expand or vary the legislature's enactment.

We have already found that this rule is not arbitrary or unreasonable. [T]he IHSAA does not derive its authority directly from the legislature but instead from a delegation of authority from member schools. As such, the analysis with respect to the three factors that concern authorizing legislation is conducted best by examining the challenged rule's consistency with the IHSAA's purpose in general and the purpose of the Transfer Rule in particular.

The IHSAA exists "to encourage, regulate, and give direction to wholesome amateur interschool athletic competition between schools who are members." IHSAA Articles of Incorporation, art. II; IHSAA By-Laws, art. II. To further this purpose, the IHSAA Articles and By-Laws mandate that it "determine qualifications of individual contestants . . . and provide written communications to establish standards for eligibility." *Id.* We find authority to take such action, and to delegate that authority to the IHSAA, to be within the powers granted Indiana public school corporations by the legislature. We further find Rule 19-6.2 to fall within the scope of, to be consistent and harmonious with, and not to expand or vary this authority. . . .

[W]e vacate the opinion of the Court of Appeals and reverse the decision of the trial court.

DICKSON, Justice, concurring and dissenting.

I agree with the majority that the Indiana State High School Athletics Association ("IHSAA") is subject to common law oversight in Indiana's courts and that IHSAA action is equivalent to "state action" subjecting it to judicial enforcement for violations of the federal or state constitutions. . . . I am convinced that the trial court was correct in finding the IHSAA's attempts to apply its Transfer Rule . . . to be arbitrary and capricious and thus improper. . . .

Jason Carlberg attended Brebeuf Preparatory School, a private school, his ninth-grade year and also participated in their swimming program. However, Jason did not thrive academically in the environment at Brebeuf. Because Jason's parents, James and Donna Carlberg, believed that he would do better in a more structured environment, they transferred Jason to the public school in their area for the tenth grade. The parents' choice of schools proved to be well-founded, as Jason's grades improved significantly. . . .

The choices faced by the Carlbergs are choices all parents face: what school and type of education is best for their children. For some, one facet of that education is athletics. As noted by the majority, "athletics are an integral part of this constitutionally-mandated process of education." Physical fitness lowers mortality rates, promotes cardiovascular and muscular fitness, generates a general feeling of well-being, and reduces the symptoms of depression and anxiety. U.S. Dep't of Health and Human Servs., Physical Activity and Health: a Report of the Surgeon General 85-136 (1996). The "potentially positive outcomes of organized sport competition" have been documented. Wilbert Marcellus Leonard II, A Sociolgical Perspective of Sport 124 (1993). Among these outcomes are enhanced decision-making skills, self-image, character, morality, independence, and opportunities for youth to experience a sense of achievement. *Id.* Witnesses for both sides also testified that athletics provided several benefits, including "learning how to be part of a team, the process of goal setting and working hard, individually and within a team, to achieve goals, and how to deal with successes and overcome the failures provided in sports."

In addition, for the student who is not academically inclined, participation in sports requires a certain amount of academic progress and provides motivation for the athlete to meet those standards in order to compete. . . .

The IHSAA's action against Jason is blatantly contrary to the expressed purpose of the IHSAA Transfer Rule. The IHSAA rules provide that, "Standards governing residence and transfer are a necessary prerequisite to participation in interschool activities because: . . . (5) *they keep the focus of students* and educators *on the fact that they attend school to receive an education first* and participate in athletics second." The trial court found that the Carlbergs have always put Jason's education first and the IHSAA officials "indicated they had no reason to believe Jason Carlberg's transfer was athletically motivated." Thus, the arbitrariness of the IHSAA's application of its rule becomes apparent in the present case: A rule purporting to limit athletically-motivated transfers and promote education as the primary value of school in fact punishes a student whom the IHSAA found did *not* transfer for an athletic reason and where the uncontradicted evidence points only to academic reasons for the transfer. Common sense instructs that application of the Transfer Rule to limit Jason's opportunities for participation would be blatantly arbitrary and capricious. The trial court was correct in making such a finding.

NOTES AND QUESTIONS

1. *Analysis of* Carlberg. What standard of judicial review did *Carlberg* adopt regarding a student's law of private associations challenge to state governing body rules and decisions, and why did the court adopt that standard? By comparison, what standard of review applies in the case of an institutional member's challenge to such rules or decisions? Do you agree with the court's distinction and its far more deferential standard of review of an educational institution's claims against a state high school athletic association?

   There was no evidence that Jason Carlberg changed schools primarily for reasons related to participation in interscholastic athletics. What reasons warrant strict enforcement of the transfer rule against him? Do these reasons justify rendering him ineligible to participate in varsity athletics for one year? The association argues that the transaction costs of investigating individual cases warrant enforcement of a general rule that may prohibit student-athletes from participating even though the transfer is not primarily made for athletic reasons. Do you agree with this reasoning? What is the countervailing student-athlete interest, and is it being given sufficient weight by the majority? What are the advantages and disadvantages of the dissent's view?

2. *Judicial Deference in Applying Law of Private Associations.* Courts generally are very deferential to state athletic association eligibility determinations for transfer students. In *Art Gaines Baseball Camp, Inc. v. Houston*, 500 S.W.2d 735, 740-41 (Mo. Ct. App. 1973), the Missouri court of appeals provided the following reasons why judicial intervention should be minimal:

   > Along with entrusting the education of our children to teachers and administrators, we also entrust the control and supervision of the extracurricular activities incident to that education. Implicit in the responsibility for these activities is the power to make reasonable rules and regulations. . . . As members of this association, [schools] may, by majority vote, enact rules to govern

their interaction. It is obvious that chaos would result without such rules. It is also obvious that the members are in the most advantageous position to appreciate the regulations under which they must act to achieve desired goals.

In *Indiana High School Athletic Assn. v. Watson*, 938 N.E.2d 672 (Ind. 2010), the Indiana Supreme Court explained, "[A]n IHSAA determination is arbitrary and capricious 'only where it is willful and unreasonable, without consideration and in disregard of the facts or circumstances in the case, or without some basis which would lead a reasonable and honest person to the same conclusion.'" *Id.* at 680. Concluding that the evidence failed to establish that the defendant had acted arbitrarily and capriciously, the court stated, "While the IHSAA may not enforce its rules with arbitrary inconsistency, it must possess a level of discretion in sanctioning schools and athletes based on the language in the rules, the evidence available, and the overall justice of the situation." *Id.* at 682. Commenting on the trial court's ruling, the court stated that rather than inquiring into whether there was substantial evidence to support the athletic association's determination, the trial court had substituted its own judgment for that of the IHSAA.

What arguments favor judicial deference to decisions made by state high school athletic associations? Is a court competent to resolve these disputes fairly and effectively? Should courts defer because these cases involve education and athletics? On the other hand, given the importance of athletic participation opportunities to student-athletes, is such deference warranted?

3. *A Less Deferential Approach.* In *Scott v. Oklahoma Secondary School Activities Association,* 313 P.3d 891 (Okla. 2013), the Oklahoma Supreme Court found that the Oklahoma high school athletics association had acted in an arbitrary and capricious manner in sanctioning a student athlete without clearly indicating which rules the student athlete had violated, particularly because those sanctions involved monetary penalties. The sobering closing paragraphs in the seven-justice majority decision are indicative of a far less deferential view toward high school sports governing bodies than has prevailed in most jurisdictions, including Oklahoma, in the past:

> This Court has permitted the OSSAA, in the guise of a voluntary association, to govern the affairs of secondary school athletics in Oklahoma with near impunity. No more. An organization interwoven so tightly with the public school system and the statutes of Oklahoma, in which membership is functionally required to participate in nearly all extra-curricular activities, is not truly voluntary. We will, when necessary, examine its actions with the same careful depth we use in examining the decisions of state agencies. This examination should not be withheld from the prevailing party - nor should similarly situated litigants who have preserved the issue on appeal be bypassed, and left unaffected and unprotected in the appellate pipeline. To that end, our decision shall apply to this case, to cases now pending before judicial or administrative tribunals or in the appellate litigation process, as well as to all judicial review of OSSAA actions after this opinion is promulgated.
>
> However, under any standard of review, the OSSAA has never been permitted to act in an arbitrary and capricious manner in interpreting and enforcing its own rules. We are left in this instance with little doubt that it has done so. While it is true that the events for which Scott sought the permanent injunction have passed, and that while this type of conduct has up until now been capable of repetition, we trust this will be the last time. To the extent any monetary penalties were leveled, such as the demand to repay the costs for camps

allegedly attended in violation of the OSSAA's policies or for reimbursement of attorney fees, those penalties are reversed.

Competition in sports is more than a mere passing enjoyment for students. Particularly in rural areas, athletic teams are the glue which holds the community together. The college and post-college careers of student athletes often have their genesis at the secondary school level, and for some provide the only path to higher education. The OSSAA wields too much control over their future to be allowed to act in an arbitrary and capricious manner in applying its rules. It must be reasonable, it must be conscientious, and it must be fair. From now on, we trust, it will be.

Id. at 908-09.

It is uncertain whether this far less deferential judicial approach will be followed by other jurisdictions. The Oklahoma Supreme Court's recognition of the importance of athletics to communities and student-athletes is noteworthy and may be a step in the direction of recognizing that participation in sport is more than a mere privilege; a view that, it seems, motivates substantial judicial deference to association and institutional decisions that implicate student athletes and coaches.

State high school athletic associations differ regarding the degree to which transfers should be permitted without adverse effects on a student-athlete's immediate eligibility to compete in interscholastic athletics. There are essentially three options: (1) permitting transfers for any non-athletic reason (this approach is based on the belief that parents should have broad latitude in their child's choice of schools); (2) permitting school districts to fashion rules that meet their needs (deference to local school districts, giving them authority to decide how strict they should be with regard to transfers); and (3) strict rules designed to ensure that students not participate when they transfer unless they can establish the rule should be waived. How strict should transfer rules be? If they are too weak, will talented student-athletes simply find a way to transfer for athletic reasons? If students may transfer and still participate in a highly regarded music program, why shouldn't they be permitted to transfer for athletic purposes?

4. *Federal Constitutional Claims.* In *In re: United States ex rel. MSHSAA*, 682 F.2d 147 (8th Cir. 1982), the Eighth Circuit held that a Missouri State High School Activities Association rule barring a student's participation in interscholastic athletics for a period of one year after the student transfers from one high school to another did not violate the student's federal constitutional rights to travel or association. Rejecting the right to travel claim, the court stated:

> Plaintiffs argue that the transfer rule burdens their exercise of the fundamental right to travel interstate. . . . When a student alters his or her place of residence from one state to another without an accompanying change by his or her parents . . . the rule prohibits the student from participating in interscholastic athletics for one year. Classifications which penalize the exercise of the right to travel are subject to strict scrutiny. But most cases which implicate the rule's sanction do not involve interstate travel and, those which do, implicate the sanction because they involve school transfers and not because they involve interstate travel. The rule's minimal impact on interstate travel does not require strict scrutiny.

Id. at 151-52.

The court also rejected the student's right of association argument:

> Plaintiffs also argue the rule burdens the right to freely associate by penalizing students' choice to change schools and thus to alter the body of people with which they associate. Students have no indefeasible right to associate through choice of school. Mandatory assignment to public schools based on place of residence or other factors is clearly permissible. The transfer rule does not prevent association through private schooling nor discriminate against any such association. Thus no right is burdened and the rule is not thereby subject to strict scrutiny.

Id. at 152.

5. *State Constitutional Claims.* In *Indiana High School Athletic Assn., Inc. v. Avant,* 650 N.E.2d 1164 (Ind. Ct. App. 1995), an Indiana intermediate appellate court determined that the Indiana state constitution's equal protection clause provides a higher level of protection to a student-athlete challenging a transfer rule than is afforded under the federal equal protection clause. The court explained:

> [Our state constitution requires that]: 1. The classification must be based upon distinctive, inherent characteristics which rationally distinguish the unequally treated class [transfer students], and the disparate treatment accorded by the [rule] must be reasonably related to such distinguishing characteristics; and 2. The classification must be open to any and all persons who share the inherent characteristics which distinguish and justify the classification, with any special treatment accorded to any particular classification extended equally to all such persons.

Id. at 1170. It is important to heed the lesson that ought to be learned from reading cases like *Avant:* state constitutional provisions may provide a student-athlete with more legal protection than the corresponding federal constitutional provisions in terms of equal protection, due process, and other protected rights (e.g., freedom of association, educational opportunity, free exercise of religion, free speech, privacy).

b.   "Outside Competition" Rules

In the following case, the court considered whether a state athletic association rule rendering student-athletes eligible to compete in a high school sport if they compete in the same youth club sport at the same time is enforceable.

LETENDRE v. MISSOURI STATE HIGH SCHOOL ACTIVITIES ASSN.

86 S.W.3d 63 (Mo. App. 2002)

Claire Letendre seeks to enjoin the Missouri State High School Activities Association (MSHSAA) from enforcing by-law 235, which prohibits students from competing on both a school and a non-school team in the same sport during the school team's season. . . .

The MSHSAA is a voluntary association of 750 secondary public, private and parochial schools in Missouri. It is charged with developing uniform and equitable standards of eligibility for students and schools to participate in interscholastic activities. The rules ostensibly work to avoid interference with the educational program of the school by outside activities; to prevent exploitation of high school youth and the programs of member schools by special interest groups; and to provide a means of evaluating and controlling local, state, and national contests affecting secondary schools. The association is governed by a Constitution and by-laws adopted by its members. Claire's high school, St. Joseph's Academy, is a member of the MSHSAA.

At the time of trial, Claire was a 15-year-old sophomore earning good grades. She did not participate in any school-sponsored sports, clubs, student government, or organized activities, other than a prayer group, because she "loves to swim." Claire has been a member of the private Parkway Swim Club since the age of three, swimming in competitive meets since the age of five. She practices and competes with the private swim club team all year long, participating in regional and national meets that require out-of-state travel. Her swim club's practice schedule is Monday through Friday from 4:30 to 7:30 p.m. and on Saturdays from 6:15 to 9:30 a.m., swimming from 5,000 to 9,000 yards daily. Claire testified that her coach at the Parkway Swim Club enters her in every single event offered during her swim club seasons. Claire claimed her short-term goal is to qualify for the Senior Nationals and, ultimately, the Olympics.

On January 31, 2001, Claire attended a meeting for students interested in joining the school swim team. They discussed health forms, practice times, the season schedule and MSHSAA eligibility rules. On February 12, 2001, Claire attended another school swim team meeting held immediately prior to the first practice. Claire testified that after this meeting she knew she would become ineligible for school swimming if she chose to swim with the club team.

By-law 235(1)(a) provides that "during the sport season a student . . . shall neither practice nor compete as a member of a non-school team nor as an individual participant in organized non-school competition in that same sport."

. . . Unlike other St. Joseph Academy students who also swam for Parkway Swim Club, Claire chose to practice with her swim club team rather than her school team. . . .

The power of a court to review the quasi-judicial actions of a voluntary association is limited to determining: (1) whether there are inconsistencies between the association's charter and by-laws and any action taken in respect to them; (2) whether the member has been treated unfairly, i.e., denied notice, hearing, or an opportunity to defend; (3) whether the association undertakings were prompted by malice, fraud or collusion; and (4) whether the charter or by-laws contravene public policy or law.

Courts have no power to usurp the function of the tribunals of [voluntary] associations, [like the MSHSAA] and can interfere only when those tribunals proceed without evidence or in bad faith or violate a valid part of the constitution and rules in dealing with a member, or attempt to enforce against him, to his injury, invalid provisions thereof. It is only upon the clearest showing that the rules have been violated by a decision of the association's tribunal that courts should intercede.

Claire agrees that the Association has acted consistently with its rules, given her due process and did not act out of malice. But instead argues that by-law 235 is against public policy because it is arbitrary, capricious and violates her Constitutional rights to equal protection and free association as guaranteed by the Fourteenth Amendment of the United States Constitution.

The specific inequity she claims is that by-law 235 is internally inconsistent in that it does not affect those who wish to participate in non-athletic activities both in and outside of school; it does not affect those who participate in one sport in school and another sport outside of school; and it does not apply to athletes who participate in national or Olympic development competitions during a sport season. She maintains that the prohibition of simultaneous same-sport competition is irrational and unrelated to any legitimate goal of the association and asks us to declare by-law 235 unconstitutional as applied to her.

The Fourteenth Amendment guarantees that no person shall be denied equal protection of the law. It assures all individuals fair treatment if fundamental rights are at stake. It also eliminates distinctions based on impermissible criteria such as race, age, religion, or gender. Where there is no suspect classification or impingement on a fundamental right explicitly or implicitly protected by the U.S. Constitution, Equal Protection claims are reviewed by this Court under the "rational relationship" standard. . . .

Claire's claim is not based upon a suspect classification, such as race, religion, national origin, or gender. Nor is it based upon a claim that her fundamental rights were violated, because she recognizes there is no fundamental right to play high school athletics. Accordingly, our inquiry is confined to whether there is a "rational relationship" between by-law 235 and any legitimate interest of the MSHSAA. . . .

We have reviewed the history of the MSHSAA non-school competition standard. Since 1959 the rule has been reconsidered and modified fifteen times. The express purpose of these reconsiderations and modifications is to create standards that purport to serve the largest number of students. At trial the Executive Director of the MSHSAA identified several reasons for the adoption of by-law 235, including: (1) preventing or reducing interference with a school's academic program; (2) preventing interference with athletic programs by organized non-school athletics; (3) promoting and protecting competitive equity; (4) avoiding conflicts in coaching philosophy and scheduling; and (5) encouraging students not to overemphasize athletic competition.

The director of the MSHSAA testified that the association's 76 years of experience allowed them to conclude that the potential for harm is not as great in activities such as music, speech, debate and academics as in extracurricular sports. The Association has made, however, an exception for Olympic competitors because it is required by federal law. 36 U.S.C. 220501 et seq. The Amateur Sports Act of 1978 allows Olympic competitors to participate in interscholastic competitions, but gives organizations such as MSHSAA exclusive jurisdiction over such competitions. 36 U.S.C. 220526(a). The Amateur Sports Act also requires that national sports organizations minimize conflicts in scheduling of all practices and competitions through coordination with organizations such as the MSHSAA. 36 U.S.C. 220524(2). The National Federation of State High School Associations, including the MSHSAA, pledged to enact limited exceptions to their non-school participation restrictions to accommodate the national objectives reflected in The Amateur Sports Act. All state associations have an exception similar to this.

The issue for us, then, is not whether we agree with the Association, but whether the challenged rule bears a rational relationship to a reasonable goal of the MSHSAA. A rule of a quasi-judicial voluntary association "will not be set aside if any state of facts reasonably may be conceived to justify it." (Citation omitted.)

If the classification has some "reasonable basis" it does not offend the Constitution simply because "in practice it results in some inequality." (Citation omitted.) We conclude that there are reasonable grounds for by-law 235 because a reasonable person could believe that a legitimate goal of the Association is furthered by the rule.

In *Schoenlaub*, the Missouri Supreme Court adopted the following test for reasonableness:

> the court must determine if the board's action is so willful and unreasoning, without consideration of the facts and circumstances, and in such disregard of them as to be arbitrary and capricious. Where there is room for two opinions on the matter, such action is not "arbitrary and capricious," even though it may be believed that an erroneous conclusion has been reached.

507 S.W.2d at 359.

Since its inception 75 years ago, the MSHSAA has received a mandate to value the best interests of all student athletes. In 1975, the Association identified outside competition during the school year as one of the "principal areas of problems facing high schools and state associations." A reasonable person could conclude that it is not in the best interest of the majority of high school students to compete in the same sport at the same time on two different teams, with different coaches, different rules, different practice schedules, and different competition schedules. The Executive Director of MSHSAA explained that one purpose of the Association is to have standards that will be in the best interest of the larger number of high school students. Here there is substantial evidence to conclude that by-law 235 is rationally related to the legitimate goal of protecting that interest. Claire's Equal Protection argument must fail.

Claire's second argument is that by preventing her from simultaneously competing on her school and swim club teams the MSHSAA has violated her right to free association. The First Amendment assures the freedom of expression, including the implied right of association. The Supreme Court first recognized this right in *NAACP v. Alabama*, 357 U.S. 449, 460-61, 78 S. Ct. 1163, 2 L. Ed. 2d 1488 (1958), declaring that freedom to engage in association for the advancement of beliefs and ideas is an inseparable aspect of liberty.

The Court has made clear that the right of association encompasses only two distinct cases: (1) those involving "intimate" human relationships fundamental to personal liberty and (2) those involving activities expressly protected by the First Amendment such as speech, assembly, petitioning for redress of grievances and the exercise of religion. (citation omitted.) By-law 235 does not impinge upon intimate human relationships nor core First Amendment freedoms. There is, consequently, no First Amendment right for a high school student to associate simultaneously with both a school and a non-school swim team. . . .

While we might personally believe that a better rule could be drafted, one that would allow a student athlete who is getting good grades, such as Claire, to compete simultaneously on both her school and non-school swim teams, the law does not permit us to interject our personal beliefs in the name of the Constitution. Claire's constitutional challenges must fail because by-law 235 is rationally related to the MSHSAA's purpose of drafting rules that protect the welfare of the greatest number of high school athletes possible. The judgment of the trial court is, therefore, affirmed.

NOTE AND QUESTIONS

Letendre provides another example of judicial reluctance to second-guess an athletic governing body's judgment in formulating eligibility rules for high school students. Courts have uniformly rejected legal challenges to "outside competition" rules, even if the rule only applies to certain sports and prohibits participation in the same sport outside the time period for interscholastic competition in that sport. See, e.g., *Burrows v. Ohio High School Athletic Assn.*, 891 F.2d 122 (6th Cir. 1989); *Zuments v. Colo. High School Activities Assn.*, 737 P.2d 1113 (Colo. Ct. App. 1987); *Eastern New York Youth Soccer Assn. v. New York State Public High School Athletic Assn.*, 108 A.D.2d 39 (N.Y. App. Div. 1985); *University Interscholastic League v. North Dallas Chamber of Commerce Soccer Assn.*, 693 S.W.2d 513 (Tex. App. 1985); *Caso v. New York State Public High School Athletic Assn.*, 78 A.D.2d 41 60 (N.Y. App. Div. 1980). To comply with the Amateur Sports Act of 1978's objective of furthering the development of Olympic sports, "outside competition" rules generally provide waivers to enable high school students to try out and qualify for spots on American Olympic teams.

By generally upholding "outside competition" rules, the prevailing judicial view is that "all students are free to compete, or otherwise participate in any or all non-school events. Rather than impinging upon their right of free association, the rule merely delineates under what terms and conditions they may participate in interscholastic athletics." *Zuments*, 737 P.2d at 1115. As one court explained:

> Petitioners urge that the outside competition rule, either as originally written or as amended, unconstitutionally interferes with parental rights to control the upbringing of children, including the right to determine whether the children can physically and academically contend with participation in school and non-school athletic competition. While parents have a right to bring up their children as they see fit, the right is not free from legislative restrictions. . . . The instant rule does not interfere with parental privacy rights. The choice of whether to participate in school or nonschool teams remains with the parents and their children.
>
>   The other aspect of the issue, however, has to do with the obligation of public school officials to protect the well-being of their students. (Citation omitted.) Respondent's concern that students not overtax themselves is a legitimate interest and the outside competition rule is rationally related to that concern.

Eastern New York Youth Soccer Assn. v. New York State Public High School Athletic Ass'n, 488 N.Y.S.2d 293, 294-295 (N.Y. Sup. 1985).

Organized youth club sports programs also often prohibit club members from participating in school-based sports programs or other sports during the club season. The reasons for the outside competition ban include athletes' health and safety — i.e., protecting athletes from overtraining, which can cause injury and burn out. Should high school athletic governing bodies, or private youth club sport programs, have broad authority to effectively prohibit students' participation in outside sports as a condition of participation?

c. Age Rules

Most state interscholastic sports associations impose rules that prohibit student-athletes from engaging in interscholastic competition if they reach the age of 19 by a certain date. One commentator summarizes the underlying reasons:

> This rule serves a variety of purposes, including reducing the competitive advantage of teams with older athletes, protecting younger students from injury, discouraging students from delaying their education to enhance athletic performance, and preventing coaches from red-shirting athletes. The age nineteen rule also

aims to prevent older students from preempting participation by younger students, maintain uniformity of standards regarding participant's age, and retain a level playing field.

Brooke A. Fredrickson, *The Age Nineteen Rule and Students with Disabilities: Discrimination Against Disabled Students with Athletic Ability*, 25 T. Jefferson L. Rev. 635, 640 (2003). Which if either of these rationales are valid? If valid, should courts uphold general uniform enforcement of a maximum age rule even if none of these rationales are furthered by refusing to grant a waiver in an individual case?

The following case explores the legality of a state high school governing body's rule prohibiting 19-year-old students from participating in interscholastic athletics. As you read *Tiffany*, consider the reasons that underlie the imposition of age limits on athletic participation and which of them are furthered by categorically excluding 19-year-old students.

TIFFANY v. ARIZONA INTERSCHOLASTIC ASSN., INC.

726 P.2d 231 (Ariz. Ct. App. 1986)

MEYERSON, Judge.

Does a high school student have a constitutional right to participate in interscholastic athletic competition during his senior year in high school? This is the primary question raised in this appeal. As explained more fully herein, we hold that defendant-appellant Arizona Interscholastic Association, Inc. (AIA) did not violate the due process clause of the fourteenth amendment when it refused to grant plaintiff-appellee John Tiffany a hardship waiver from its nineteen-year-old eligibility rule. We concur with the trial court, however, that AIA acted unlawfully by failing to follow its own bylaws in considering the request for the waiver.

I. FACTS

Tiffany began his senior year at St. Mary's High School in Phoenix during the 1983-84 school term. He had been held back in kindergarten and first grade because of a learning disability. Thus, he turned nineteen years of age on August 5, 1983, the month before his senior year would begin. Tiffany had participated in athletics throughout grade school and during high school. He wanted to participate in athletic competition during his senior year.

AIA is a voluntary association composed of all public and most private high schools in Arizona. AIA formulates and promulgates rules and regulations pertaining to, among other things, interscholastic athletic competition among its members. Under AIA's bylaws, if a student turns nineteen before September 1 of the school year, he is not eligible to participate in interscholastic athletics. AIA bylaws provide, however, that:

> The Executive Board in individual cases may, at its discretion and upon such terms and conditions as it may impose, waive or modify any eligibility rule when in its opinion there are circumstances beyond the control of the student or parent whereby enforcement of the rule would work an undue hardship on the student. . . .

The parties have stipulated that the decision to hold Tiffany back in the early grades was made by his teachers and school administrators with his parents' approval. AIA does not contest that these circumstances were beyond the control of Tiffany and his parents.

At a hearing before the Executive Board of AIA, Tiffany presented evidence that he very much enjoyed his participation in interscholastic athletics, the friendship of those with whom he would compete, and the benefits from the discipline and regulation involved in playing varsity athletics. Tiffany indicated to the Executive Board that his motivation in studying came from the fact that in order to be eligible for interscholastic athletics a certain grade point average must be maintained. The Executive Board denied the request for the waiver. It is agreed by the parties that AIA has a policy of not making any exceptions to the nineteen-year-old eligibility rule.

Tiffany subsequently filed a complaint requesting that AIA be enjoined from disqualifying him from interscholastic athletic competition. He requested that AIA's actions be declared unconstitutional as a denial of due process. The trial court granted a preliminary injunction allowing Tiffany to play during the 1983-84 school year. Final judgment was entered in 1985. Because Tiffany requested attorney's fees, the trial court determined that the controversy was not moot.

The trial court held that AIA's Executive Board acted "unreasonably, capriciously and arbitrarily" when it failed to exercise its discretion in considering Tiffany's request for a waiver. The trial court also ruled that Tiffany possessed a "sufficient liberty or property interest or personal stake in participating in high school athletics" such that AIA's actions violated his constitutional rights. Tiffany was awarded attorney's fees in the amount of $2,500 pursuant to 42 U.S.C. § 1988. AIA has filed this appeal from that judgment. In order to determine whether the trial court could properly award attorney's fees to Tiffany pursuant to 42 U.S.C. § 1988, we must first decide whether the trial court correctly found that AIA violated Tiffany's constitutional rights.

II. CONSTITUTIONAL CLAIMS

. . . In order to decide whether Tiffany's exclusion from interscholastic athletics during his senior year in high school violated due process (and therefore 42 U.S.C. § 1983), it first must be determined whether Tiffany had any property or liberty interest in participating in high school sports during the 1983-84 school year. The beginning point in analyzing this constitutional issue is the decision of the United States Supreme Court in *Goss v. Lopez*, 419 U.S. 565, 95 S. Ct. 729, 42 L. Ed. 2d 725 (1975). In *Goss*, the Supreme Court held that a school could not suspend a student for ten days without insuring due process safeguards. The Court reasoned that a "State is constrained to recognize a student's legitimate entitlement to a public education as a property interest which is protected by the Due Process Clause and which may not be taken away for misconduct without adherence to the minimum procedures required by that Clause." *Id.* at 574, 95 S. Ct. at 736.

> [E]ducation is perhaps the most important function of state and local governments, and the total exclusion from the educational process for more than a trivial period, and certainly if the suspension is for ten days, is a serious event in the life of the suspended child. Neither the property interest in educational benefits temporarily denied nor the liberty interest in reputation, which is also implicated, is so insubstantial that suspensions may constitutionally be imposed by any procedure the school chooses, no matter how arbitrary.

Id. at 576, 95 S. Ct. at 737 (citation omitted). We now proceed to apply the ruling of *Goss* to the case before us. . . .

Most courts which have considered this issue have declined to hold that participation in a single year of high school athletic competition rises to the level of a constitutionally protectable property interest. . . . For example, in *Albach v. Odle*, 531 F.2d 983 (10th Cir. 1976), the plaintiff challenged a rule automatically barring from interscholastic high school athletic competition for one year any student who transferred from his home district to a boarding school or from a boarding school to his home district. The court found that the ruling in *Goss v. Lopez* was limited to the "educational process." In language which has been cited repeatedly by other courts, the court declared:

> The educational process is a broad and comprehensive concept with a variable and indefinite meaning. It is not limited to classroom attendance but includes innumerable separate components, such as participation in athletic activity and participation in school clubs and social groups, which combine to provide an atmosphere of intellectual and moral advancement. We do not read *Goss* to establish a property interest subject to constitutional protection in each of these separate components.

Id. at 985. In *Karmanos v. Baker*, 617 F. Supp. 809 (E.D. Mich. 1985), the court concluded that the plaintiff had not demonstrated that he had a property interest in participating in intercollegiate hockey. The court noted that the plaintiff had not alleged any acts which deprived him of educational or vocational opportunities other than the opportunity to play hockey.

Finally, in *Kulovitz v. Illinois High School Ass'n*, 462 F. Supp. 875 (N.D. Ill. 1978), the court rejected the plaintiff's constitutional claim arising out of his exclusion from participation in high school athletics during a single school year. The court held that "participation in interscholastic athletics is not a constitutionally protected civil right." *Id.* at 877. . . .

Under certain limited circumstances, however, courts have found that participation in interscholastic sports rises to the level of a constitutionally protected property interest. For example, in *Boyd v. Board of Directors*, 612 F. Supp. 86 (E.D. Ark. 1985), the court held that a student could not be suspended from the high school football team without procedural due process of law protections. The court found that the plaintiff-student was an outstanding athlete and that the 1983 season was his last opportunity to participate in football at the high school level. The testimony indicated that participation in high school sports was "vital and indispensable to a college scholarship and, in essence, a college education." *Id.* at 93. The court found that the plaintiff's continued status on the team was "very important" to his "development educationally and economically in the future." *Id.* Accordingly, the court found that his participation in interscholastic athletics must be deemed a property interest protected by the due process clause of the fourteenth amendment. . . .

In *Florida High School Activities Ass'n, Inc. v. Bryant*, 313 So. 2d 57 (Fla. Dist. Ct. App. 1975), the court affirmed the trial court which ordered the defendant to allow the plaintiff to participate in athletics during the 1974-75 school year. Although the court did not express its ruling in due process terms, it accepted the trial court's finding that basketball was an important and vital part of the plaintiff's life "'providing an impetus to his general scholastic and social development and rehabilitation from his prior problems as a juvenile delinquent.'" *Id.* at 57.

As the above cases demonstrate, in the realm of constitutional law, there are very few absolutes. We are persuaded that under certain circumstances a high school student can properly establish an entitlement to due process protection in connection with a suspension or exclusion from high school athletics. We believe that an appropriate extension of the holding in *Goss v. Lopez* was expressed by the court in *Pegram v. Nelson*, 469 F. Supp. 1134 (M.D.N.C. 1979). In that case, a high school student was suspended from school for ten days and was also excluded from after-school activities for a period of four months. The court acknowledged that the "opportunity to participate in extracurricular activities is not, by and in itself, a property interest." *Id.* at 1139. The court recognized, however, that:

> *Total exclusion* from participation in that part of the educational process designated as extracurricular activities for a *lengthy period of time* could, depending upon the particular circumstances, be a sufficient deprivation to implicate due process.

Id. at 1140.

It is not necessary in this case to define the precise parameters of the circumstances under which due process must be afforded to a student excluded from high school athletics. This is so because Tiffany has not asserted any cognizable interest beyond his claim to mere participation in one year of interscholastic sports. Tiffany argues that he very much enjoys his participation in athletics, the friendship of those that he competes with and the benefit he derives from the discipline and regulation involved in playing varsity sports. Such interests, albeit important to him, simply do not rise to the level of constitutional magnitude necessary to invoke the protection of the due process clause. We likewise conclude that the scholastic benefit derived from the incentive to maintain a certain grade point average to remain eligible for athletic competition is also an interest which is outside the scope of constitutional protection. Unlike the "deprivation of a previously granted scholarship [which] would invoke the protections of procedural due process," *Colorado Seminary v. National Collegiate Athletic Ass'n*, 417 F. Supp. 885, 895 (D. Colo. 1976), *aff'd*, 570 F.2d 320 (10th Cir. 1978), the educational stimulus Tiffany claims to derive from athletic participation is, in constitutional terms, a "mere subjective 'expectation,'" *Perry v. Sindermann*, 408 U.S. 593, 603 (1972) and not protected by procedural due process. In short, Tiffany has failed to demonstrate the type of serious damage to his "later opportunities for higher education and employment," *Goss v. Lopez*, 419 U.S. at 575, which would raise his interest in interscholastic athletics to a level warranting the safeguards of the due process clause.

III.   [EDS. LAW OF PRIVATE ASSOCIATIONS CLAIM]

Although we reject Tiffany's constitutional claim, we sustain the trial court's ruling that the Executive Board of AIA acted unlawfully when it failed to exercise its discretion at the eligibility hearing. As noted above, despite the fact that AIA's bylaws specifically provide that its Executive Board will exercise discretion in considering hardship waivers to its eligibility rules, it is undisputed that the Executive Board has adopted a policy of not making any exceptions to the nineteen-year-old eligibility requirement.

It is hornbook law that an administrative board must follow its own rules and regulations. . . . An administrative agency's failure to follow its own rules and regulations does not create a constitutional due process right on behalf of a party who suffers some wrong at the hands of the administrative body. . . .

Rather, the obligation of such a body to follow its own rules and regulations is founded in principles of administrative law. . . .

In Arizona, the procedure by which one can compel an administrative board to exercise its discretion is through the filing of a mandamus, *Eastman v. Southworth*, 87 Ariz. 394, 351 P.2d 992 (1960), now a special action. Rule 1, Rules of Procedure for Special Actions; *see* A.R.S. § 12-2021. Although Tiffany's complaint was not denominated a special action, the record of the trial court proceedings reflects that the mandamus issue was implicitly tried by the parties. We hold that the trial court was correct in concluding that the Executive Board of AIA acted "unreasonably, capriciously and arbitrarily" when it failed to exercise its discretion in considering Tiffany's request for a waiver.

Affirmed in part, reversed in part.

NOTES AND QUESTIONS

1. *Analysis of* Tiffany. Although the court rejected Tiffany's federal constitutional law claims, why did it hold that the defendant's failure to grant him a waiver of its maximum age rule unlawful? Do you agree with the court's conclusion regarding each of his legal claims?

2. *Federal and State Disability Discrimination Claims.* State governing body rules prohibiting 19-year-olds from participating in high school sports are increasingly the subject of challenges by learning and physically impaired student-athletes, who allege that such age rules violate federal legislation such as the Americans with Disabilities Act (see *Cruz v. Pennsylvania Interscholastic Athletic Association, Inc., infra* in Chapter 11) and similar state laws.

   In *Baisden v. West Virginia Secondary Schools Activities Commission,* 568 S.E.2d 32 (W. Va. 2002), the defendant's regulations rendered students who reach the age of 19 prior to a certain date ineligible to participate in interscholastic competition. The plaintiff sought a permanent injunction prohibiting the defendant from enforcing its age rule against him based on Virginia's Human Rights Act, which requires reasonable accommodations for persons with disabilities. The lower court ruled that the age rule was unenforceable against the plaintiff. Its decision was based on evidence that the plaintiff's learning disability with respect to math and reading required him to repeat two years of education. According to the lower court, enforcing the ban would constitute discrimination against the plaintiff on the basis of his learning disability.

   In addressing this question, the West Virginia Supreme Court first noted that the issue of the plaintiff's eligibility to participate in interscholastic sports was moot because he had graduated from high school. Nevertheless, because of the importance of the substantive issue and the probability that it would affect the rights of students under similar circumstances, the court elected to address it. In reversing the lower court, the appellate court observed that age limitations "are typically strictly enforced, based upon safety issues raised by permitting older, larger, more experienced players to compete against younger students." *Id.* at 37.

   The court held:

   > While we decide . . . that individualized assessments are required in cases of this nature and that reasonable accommodations may be made through waiver of the nineteen age rule under certain circumstances, we do not believe that the facts

of this case justify waiver as an accommodation. Mr. Baisden turned nineteen on July 27, 2001. He is six feet four inches tall and weighs 280 pounds. He runs the forty-yard-dash in 5.3 seconds. His participation in high school football would permit him to compete in this contact sport against students approximately five years younger. The safety of younger, smaller, more inexperienced students would be unreasonably compromised. In our view, this would fundamentally alter the structure of the interscholastic athletic program, a result which is not required by reasonable accommodation standards in anti-discrimination law.

Id. at 44.

3. *Fifth-Year Student Rule.* In *Mancuson v. Massachusetts Interscholastic Athletic Ass'n.*, 900 N.E.2d 518 (Mass. 2009), the Massachusetts Supreme Court upheld the MIAA's "fifth-year student rule" in a case involving a student who had repeated the ninth grade. The court rejected the student's argument that her federal constitutional due process rights were deprived because she had a property right in participation in athletics as part of her right to education. It found that there was no such right because athletics were "by their very nature" separate from the curriculum and were not, therefore, an outgrowth of the student's right to education. Do you agree?

PROBLEM 2-4

You represent a 12 year old girl and her family. The student has been promoted, because of high academic performance, to the twelfth grade. As such, this will be the last year in which she will be able to participate in varsity athletics at the interscholastic level. She is 5 feet 5 inches tall, weighs 123 pounds, and wants to participate in varsity lacrosse. The coach refused to permit her to try out for the varsity team, suggesting that she would be at risk if she were to play at the varsity level because of her age. He suggested that she try out for the freshman or middle school team. However, she wants to play at the varsity level. What advice would you give her and her family?

What if your client were 19 and just returned to finish her senior year after being overseas with her family (her father was serving in a diplomatic capacity in a foreign country) for two years? The coach wants her to play, but the rule limits participation by a 19-year-old. What advice would you give?

d. Academic Eligibility Requirements

No-pass, no-play rules have been controversial, and questions have been raised regarding whether they achieve their ultimate objective — better academic performance. One commentator describes the debate as follows:

> Proponents of the rules argue that they advance education by giving the student who fails to meet minimum academic standards an incentive to do better, and more free time to devote to studies. However, opponents of the rules question this logic. They contend that the rules may in fact lead more students to either drop out of school altogether, or to pursue academic course work which does not present any substantial challenge.

David J. Shannon, *No Pass, No Play: Equal Protection Analysis Under the Federal and State Constitutions*, 63 Ind. L.J. 161, 161-162 (1987/1988).

Students deemed ineligible to participate in interscholastic sports have challenged the legality of no-pass, no-play rules on federal equal protection and due process grounds. Starting from the premise that participation in extracurricular activities is neither a fundamental right nor an infringement on the rights of a suspect class, courts have applied a rational basis test in addressing equal protection challenges. The application of such a standard invariably leads them to conclude that no-pass, no-play rules are rationally related to their intended goal of ensuring student-athletes' academic achievement. Similarly, courts have rejected due process challenges to no-pass, no-play rules because a student's interest in participating in extracurricular activities is not a protected property or liberty interest protected by the federal constitution.

Bailey v. Truby, 321 S.E.2d 302 (W. Va. 1984) illustrates the prevailing judicial approach in these cases. A West Virginia State Board of Education policy required that students maintain a 2.0 or "C" grade point average and not receive a failing grade in any subject to participate in extracurricular activities. The plaintiff student-athlete maintained a 2.0 grade point average but was declared academically ineligible to play basketball after he failed an English class. Agreeing with the majority of courts refusing to recognize a federally protected property or liberty interest in interscholastic athletics participation (much less a fundamental right to participate in extracurricular activities), the court rejected his due process claim. On the question of whether the no-pass, no-play rule is rationally related to a legitimate governmental purpose, the court stated:

> Unquestionably, the encouragement of academic excellence is a legitimate concern of the . . . Board of Education. The regulation of nonacademic extracurricular activity is a common method of achieving this fundamental goal. Part of this regulatory activity traditionally includes academic achievement standards as a prerequisite to participation in nonacademic extracurricular activities, particularly in the area of interscholastic sports.

As one commentator has noted:

> Since amateur athletics are ordinarily conducted as a part of the educational activities of high schools and colleges, it is also common for there to be rules which limit eligibility of those who maintain a required grade average. Such a rule will ordinarily be a proper exercise of institutional authority, because it is normally both authorized and reasonable. It will be authorized because the fostering of scholastic, not athletic, achievement is the primary objective of the academic institution, and denying participation in extracurricular activities to those who are unable to render satisfactory performance is directly related to that objective. (Quoting W. Lowell, The Law of Sports §1.21 (1979)).

321 S.E.2d at 316.

PROBLEM 2-5

You represent a school district with three high schools and have been asked by the board to respond to the following questions: Can the school district legally adopt a minimum grade point average in a set of core courses for students participating in interscholastic sports that is higher than the 2.0 GPA required by the state athletic association rules? Would doing so be good policy? One member of the board supports raising the grade point average to 2.2, believing that a higher required GPA will cause students who desire to participate to take their core academic subjects seriously so that they can maximize their opportunities to pursue higher education. Another member disagrees, believing that a higher required GPA would cause more students to drop out or to lose interest in school. Can a district adopt a more lenient requirement than that required at the state level? In responding to the board, think about the impact such requirements have had in other contexts.

Eligibility rules commonly referred to as "no-pass, no-play" rules were initially promulgated in the early 1980s as state legislatures and athletic associations sought to strike an appropriate balance between academics and athletics. No-pass, no-play rules condition participation in extracurricular activities, including sports, on students maintaining a certain academic performance. The first no-pass, no-play statute, which was enacted in Texas, provided that:

> [a] student, other than a mentally retarded student, enrolled in a school district in this state shall be suspended from participation in any extracurricular activity sponsored or sanctioned by the school district during the grade reporting period after a grade reporting period in which the student received a grade lower than the equivalent of 70 on a scale of 100 in any academic class.

Spring Branch I.S.D. v. Stamos, 695 S.W.2d 556, 560 (Tex. 1985).

e. Exclusion of Homeschooled Students from Athletic Participation

In 1993, all 50 states made homeschooling of children by their parents or guardians a legal option. Since that time, homeschooling has continued to grow, with approximately 1.7 million school-age children (i.e., 3.4% of the school-age population) being homeschooled in 2016. As homeschool families continue to seek extracurricular options for their children, the issue of the eligibility of homeschooled students to participate in extracurricular sporting activities has required judicial consideration.

In *Jones v. West Virginia State Board of Education*, 622 S.E.2d 289 (W. Va. 2005), plaintiffs sought to have their 11-year-old child, whom they homeschooled, try out for the Mannington Middle School wrestling team. The West Virginia Secondary School Activities Commission (WVSSAC) denied their request on the ground that only full-time students were permitted to participate in interscholastic athletics. Plaintiffs filed a complaint, seeking declaratory, equitable, and injunctive relief. The trial court found in favor of plaintiffs and entered the injunction.

On appeal, the West Virginia Supreme Court addressed three issues: (1) Did the WVSSAC breach a statutory duty by not allowing homeschoolers to participate in interscholastic athletics? (2) Did the WVSSAC violate the West Virginia equal protection rights of homeschooled children by prohibiting them from participating in interscholastic athletics? (3) Did the WVSSAC breach its duty to promulgate reasonable rules and regulations by implementing a total ban on allowing homeschooled children to participate in interscholastic athletics?

The court held in favor of the WVSSAC on all three issues. With respect to the alleged breach of a statutory duty, the court held that the plain language of the relevant statute imposed an obligation on the school superintendent to provide assistance and resources to the person providing the homeschool instruction (here, the student's mother). The statute did not, however, require that resources, including interscholastic athletics, be provided to the homeschooled student himself.

The court also held that the WVSSAC did not violate plaintiffs' equal protection rights. In reaching this conclusion, the court first found that participation in interscholastic athletics is neither a fundamental nor a constitutional right under the West Virginia constitution. Consequently, any classification affecting participation in interscholastic athletics will be upheld as long as it is rationally related to a legitimate state interest. Among the several grounds offered by defendant as providing a rational basis for excluding homeschooled children, the court focused on two as offering sufficient justification: "(a) promoting academics over athletics, and (2) protecting the economic interests of the county school systems." *Id.* at 295. With respect to the former, the court examined the grade requirements for participating in extracurricular activities. It found that homeschooled children are graded on different standards than public school children and converting such grades would impose a burden on the school district. Moreover, the different grading standards would impede the ability of school officials to maintain the academic standards required for participation in interscholastic sports. The court noted that a parent could withdraw an underperforming student from the public school system and homeschool him or her in order to retain the student athlete's eligibility.

Regarding protection of the economic interests of the county school system, the court emphasized that money is apportioned to schools based on attendance in class. According to the court, requiring counties to spend limited funds to support the athletic participation of homeschooled students (from whom no funds are allocated) would create a financial burden. Finally, the court held that the WVSSAC did not breach its duty to promulgate reasonable rules and regulations. Even though homeschooled students are totally banned from interscholastic athletics participation, the court held that it is not arbitrary and capricious because it is rationally related to the two legitimate state purposes discussed above.

In *Reid v. Kenowa Hills Public Schools*, 680 N.W.2d 62 (Mich. Ct. App. 2004), the court similarly resolved a homeschooled student's challenge to a rule of the MHSAA providing that only students enrolled in school for at least 20 hours may participate in its athletic program. The court held that non-enrolled, homeschooled children have no right to participate in interscholastic sports.

More recently, in *Chapman v. Pennsylvania Interscholastic Athletic Association*, 2014 WL 580212 (N.D. Pa., Feb 12, 2014), a Pennsylvania district court ruled that a homeschooled student who was ineligible to play interscholastic sports for a year did not suffer irreparable harm. The plaintiff, a homeschooled student who enrolled in two classes at a private school, sought to participate on its soccer and basketball teams. Although the private high school was willing to allow him to play these sports, the state high school association ruled him ineligible to compete as a homeschooled student with less than full-time enrollment is only eligible to play sports at the public school he would otherwise attend based on residence. The court cited to numerous cases holding that ineligibility for sport participation alone does not constitute irreparable harm.

Many states now have laws permitting homeschooled students to participate in interscholastic sports. See HSLDA, *State Laws Concerning Participation of Homeschool Students in Public School Activities*, Sept. 6, 2018, http://www.hslda. org/docs/nche/issues/e/equal_eccess.pdf for an extensive discussion of a variety of approaches taken by states in determining the degree to which homeschoolers may participate in public school activities. Rules permitting participation by homeschoolers have been dubbed "Tim Tebow" laws, after Tim Tebow, who had been homeschooled, gained notoriety on the football field at the collegiate and professional levels. Not surprisingly, success on the part of homeschooled students has been primarily legislative in nature and not the result of litigation. Given the growth of the homeschool movement in the United States and its lobbying power, it is likely that legislative success at the state level will continue. Should homeschooled students be permitted to participate in interscholastic sports sponsored by a state athletic association as a matter of public policy? If you were a lawyer for a homeschool association what would you argue and what counterarguments would you anticipate? Paul J. Batista and Lance C. Hatfield, *Learn at Home, Play at School: A State-by-State Examination of Legislation, Litigation and Athletic Association Rules Governing Public School Athletic Participation by Homeschool Students*, 15 J. Legal Aspects Sport 213 (2005) (surveying the different legal, judicial, and athletic association responses to the issue of homeschooled students' participation in public school sports).

Homeschooled students' interests in high school sports participation may also intersect with First Amendment free exercise of religion rights. In *Trefelner v. Burrelle School District*, 655 F. Supp. 2d 581 (2009), the court held that a public school district must permit a private school student to participate in its jazz and marching bands. Consistent with state law, the school district's policy permitted homeschool, charter school, and cyber-school students to participate in extra-curricular activities. The law did not expressly require the district to permit private school students to participate, but the student argued successfully that he had been denied his free exercise of religion (and equal protection) rights as a result of the district's refusal to permit him to participate because his parents had elected to enroll him in a private religious school. The court found no justification for differentiating between religiously motivated homeschool programs and a religious private school for such purposes, and it held that the student's right to participate was protected by his right of free exercise of religion.

f. Good Conduct Rules

Individual high schools generally have broad authority to discipline and impose sanctions (such as the loss of their athletic eligibility) on student-athletes who engage in conduct that is considered inappropriate. Good conduct rules vary and prohibit a range of in-school and outside-of-school activities, including the consumption and use of drugs, tobacco, and alcohol; violations of the law; and conduct that violates community norms of appropriate behavior. Larry D. Bartlett, *The Courts' View of Good Conduct Rules for High School Student Athletes*, 82 Educ. L. Rep. 1087 (1993). Student-athletes who are punished for violating good conduct rules have asserted various legal challenges, including claims that such rules violate their federal constitutionally protected interests. However, *Brands, infra,* illustrates that such challenges have met with only limited success because courts provide considerable deference to schools (and interscholastic sports governing bodies) to use good conduct rules and disciplinary sanctions to regulate student-athlete behavior. One particularly interesting legal issue is the nature and scope of their authority to promulgate rules governing student-athletes' off-campus behavior and their legitimate interests in regulating such conduct.

PROBLEM 2-6

David Craig, a 17-year-old senior at Valley High School, is an outstanding wrestler. Although a "C" student, Craig planned to attend college and major in nursing and physical therapy. Because his parents cannot fund his college education, Craig hoped to obtain a wrestling scholarship. Craig is the defending state champion in his weight class and has not lost a match this season. He was expected to successfully defend his title at the state championship finals in March, where college coaches assess talent for offering wrestling scholarships.

At the beginning of the school year, parents and students were provided with a handbook, which includes the following student "eligibility policy" and "good conduct rules" for participation in extracurricular activities:

> To retain eligibility for participation in Valley High School extracurricular activities, students must conduct themselves as good citizens both in and out of school 24 hours a day and 365 days a year. Students who represent the school in an activity are expected to serve as role models to other students and to the members of the community. Students who wish to have the *privilege* of participating in extracurricular activities must conduct themselves in accordance with all school and athletic department conduct prohibitions and requirements rules as well as the rules established by the individual coaches for each sport or other activity. All students who participate in any extracurricular activities must refrain from engaging in any conduct that is illegal, immoral, unhealthy, or highly inappropriate for a Valley High School student.
>
> Specific violations of the good conduct rules include:
>
> 1. Possession, use or purchase of alcoholic beverages, including beer or wine (use includes having the odor of alcohol on one's breath); and/or
> 2. Being in attendance at a function or party where alcohol or other illegal drugs are being consumed by minors.

Under the policy, violators were subject to punishment ranging from a two-week period of ineligibility to participate in one sport or extracurricular activity to permanent ineligibility to participate in any sports or extracurricular activities. Students were required to admit a violation within 48 hours of the time at which the violation occurred, otherwise their punishment would be doubled.

The handbook states that Valley could take disciplinary action against a student only after completion of a "thorough investigation of the alleged violation."

On a Saturday in mid-February, a number of Valley students attended a party where alcohol was served to minors. According to the school rumor mill, David Craig was one of the students who attended the party. On the following Wednesday during girls' volleyball practice, the coaches informed the girls that they knew about the party and wanted any team members who had attended to come forward and admit their conduct. There was no response. The coaches then said that everyone on the team would run laps until those who attended the party admitted to it. After about ten minutes, three members of the volleyball team approached the coaches and admitted to having attended the party. Although the "admission" by the three girls occurred after the expiration of the 48-hour period, they were suspended from the volleyball team for only two weeks. None of these girls had their punishment doubled; they were all treated as if their good conduct code violations had been admitted within the required 48-hour period.

During Thursday's wrestling practice, the coaches tried a similar approach with the boys. None of them admitted to having attended the party. Thereafter, an assistant coach individually met with each wrestler, including Craig. Craig was asked several times if he had attended the party; each time he responded no. The next day, Valley's principal called Craig into his office and informed him that he had evidence that Craig had attended the party and that his failure to admit to being there would result in a doubling of his punishment to a one-month suspension from wrestling.

The principal had no evidence that Craig had attended the party. He suspended Craig from participating in wrestling for one month based on information that the principal had received from a police officer who had stopped Craig the night of the party and given him an alcohol sobriety test that tested positive. Craig and the three female volleyball players were the only Valley students who were disciplined for violating Valley's good conduct rules. Craig's one-month suspension will prevent him from participating in the state wrestling tournament and defending his championship.

Craig and his parents appealed his suspension to the Valley's superintendent, who upheld it after a 15-minute meeting with them. Valley's school board also upheld his suspension after a one-hour hearing. Craig's parents have filed a lawsuit seeking a court order that will allow him to continue wrestling and to participate in the upcoming state wrestling tournament.

Consider Craig's potential legal claims and their likely success based on *Brands* (which provides a legal framework for analyzing the validity of disciplinary sanctions imposed on student-athletes for misconduct occurring off campus during non-school hours) and the cases in its accompanying notes.

BRANDS v. SHELDON COMMUNITY SCHOOL

671 F. Supp. 627 (N.D. Iowa 1987)

O'BRIEN, Chief Judge.

This matter comes to the Court on plaintiff's motions for temporary restraining order or preliminary injunction. . . .

FINDINGS OF FACT

The plaintiff is a student at Sheldon Community High School. As a member of his school's wrestling team, he has amassed a nearly perfect record in four years of competition, and is a defending state champion. His performance and the equally outstanding performance of his twin brother have attracted the attention of the state media and college coaches . . ., and each brother hopes to attend college on a wrestling scholarship.

The events leading to this decision began on January 25, 1987. The plaintiff has been understandably reluctant to give his account of what took place at his home that day, but the Sheldon Community School Board ultimately concluded that the plaintiff "as well as three other male youths engaged in multiple acts of sexual intercourse with a sixteen-year-old female student of the Sheldon Community School District. . . ." The Court makes no judgment as to whether a preponderance of the evidence, clear and convincing evidence, or evidence beyond a reasonable doubt supports this finding.

As rumors about this incident spread throughout Sheldon Community High School, Principal David Kapfer began an investigation and interviewed the plaintiff and other parties rumored to have been involved. On February 4, the plaintiff and his mother were sent letters from Kapfer declaring the plaintiff ineligible for the remainder of the wrestling season. . . . These letters stated that he "committed a breach of discipline by engaging in conduct which interfered with the maintenance of school discipline and by engaging in behavior which was antagonistic to the rights of (name redacted) to attain her education." The letters further stated that he violated Section III of the Discipline Policy because his conduct on January 25 was "detrimental to the best interests of the Sheldon Community School District." In a section of the letter to the plaintiff, Kapfer stated that the plaintiff's conduct "was a breach of discipline in that you: (1) engaged in bullying behavior; (2) committed an assault on (same name) in that you took acts against her resulting in physical contact which was insulting and offensive and which caused her emotional injury; (3) willfully injured (same name) by doing an unjustified act causing her serious emotional and mental injury; and (4) participated in multiple acts of sexual intercourse involving (same name) which took place on January 25, 1987. . . . The Court makes no judgment as to whether a preponderance of the evidence, clear and convincing evidence, or evidence beyond a reasonable doubt supports these charges.

The period of ineligibility declared by the principal included the dates of the sectional, district and state wrestling tournaments. Thus, any reinstatement which would preserve the plaintiff's chance to again become a state champion would have to occur before 8:30 a.m. on February 14, when weigh-ins would take place for the sectional tournament.

Following an appeal to Superintendent Jerry Peterson on February 5 . . . , Peterson sent letters to the plaintiff and his mother affirming the principal's decision which were nearly identical to the February 4 letters. These letters were dated February 9. . . . On February 10, the plaintiff and his mother requested a closed hearing before the School Board . . . which began Thursday morning, February 12, and ended late that night. The Board deliberated for several hours on February 12 and 13 before reaching a decision which affirmed the administration's decision. Extensive findings of fact were made by the Board. . . . The complaint and motions presently before this Court were filed within three hours of the Board's decision.

It became clear at this Court's February 13 hearing that the Court could not fairly consider all of the evidence admitted in time to fully resolve this matter prior to weigh-ins. This dilemma significantly increased the risk of irreparable harm, and for this reason, the Court entered a temporary restraining order which permitted the plaintiff to compete and advance in the sectional tournament. The TRO expired at the beginning of the February 16 hearing.

CONCLUSIONS OF LAW

Whether a temporary restraining order or preliminary injunction should issue involves consideration of (1) the threat of irreparable harm to the movant;

(2) the state of the balance between this harm and the injury that granting the injunction will inflict upon other parties litigant; (3) the probability that movant will succeed on the merits; and (4) the public interest. *Dataphase Systems, Inc. v. C L Systems, Inc.*, 640 F.2d 109, 113 (8th Cir. 1981) (en banc). For the reasons stated below, the Court finds that the probability that the plaintiff will succeed on the merits is not great enough to satisfy that element of the *Dataphase* test, even if the plaintiff's allegations of irreparable harm, a favorable balance of interests and the public interest were accepted as true. Such relief is therefore improper.

The plaintiff asserts that he has been deprived of five constitutional rights—his Fourteenth Amendment rights to equal protection, substantive due process and procedural due process, his Eighth Amendment right to be free from cruel and unusual punishment, and his Sixth Amendment right to counsel. The equal protection claim must be rejected because the plaintiff has not alleged that he was treated differently because of his race, ethnicity, gender, or any other suspect classification, and his interests in wrestling or receiving a college scholarship are not among the small set of rights fundamental enough to warrant separate protection under the equal protection clause. *San Antonio Ind. School District v. Rodriguez*, 411 U.S. 1, 29-39, 93 S. Ct. 1278, 1294-1300, 36 L. Ed. 2d 16 (1973). Likewise, the Eighth Amendment claim must be rejected because school discipline does not implicate Eighth Amendment concerns, as the Supreme Court held in *Ingraham v. Wright*, 430 U.S. 651, 668, 97 S. Ct. 1401, 1410, 51 L. Ed. 2d 711 (1977). Because the Constitution limits the scope of Sixth Amendment rights to "all criminal prosecutions," U.S. Const. Amend. VI, that argument must be rejected. If any rights were violated, they can only be substantive or procedural due process rights.

PROCEDURAL DUE PROCESS

The majority of the plaintiff's complaints—including those concerning the vagueness of the school's standard of conduct, the School Board's reliance upon hearsay, the timing of his hearing, and the sufficiency of the evidence—are most relevant to his right to procedural due process. To consider those complaints, however, the Court must first find that the plaintiff is being deprived of liberty or property by the defendant. If not, no procedural protections were "due" to the plaintiff under the Constitution. *Board of Regents v. Roth*, 408 U.S. 564, 92 S. Ct. 2701, 33 L. Ed. 2d 548 (1972).

The Supreme Court has consistently held that the existence of a protected liberty or property interest does not depend upon the seriousness of the loss the plaintiff would suffer as a result of the government's action. "[T]o determine whether due process requirements apply in the first place, we must look not to the 'weight' but to the *nature* of the interest at stake." *Smith v. Organization of Foster Families*, 431 U.S. 816, 841, 97 S. Ct. 2094, 2107, 53 L. Ed. 2d 14 (1977). . . .

A clear majority of courts addressing this question in the context of interscholastic or intercollegiate athletics has found that athletes have no legitimate entitlement to participate. (Citations omitted.) In *In re U.S. Ex. Rel. Missouri State High School Activities Association*, 682 F.2d 147 (8th Cir. 1982), the Eighth Circuit stated that "a student's interest in participating in a single year of interscholastic athletics amounts to a mere expectation rather than a constitutionally protected claim of entitlement." *Id.* at 153 n. 8. . . .

In *Boyd v. Bd. of Directors of McGehee School District*, 612 F. Supp. 86 (E.D. Ark. 1985), a court recognized a property interest where the plaintiff's interest "was something more than a desire to participate in a single season of interscholastic athletics without the belief and desire to realizing any tangential benefits accruing to him in the future." *Id.* at 93. That court found that the plaintiff's "continued status as a member of the McGehee High School football team during his last year was very important to [his] development educationally and economically in the future." *Id.* Yet the fact that this plaintiff's performance in the tournament may help him receive a college scholarship does not change the nature of the interest at stake; it merely raises its value while leaving the degree of entitlement unchanged.

Once awarded, a college scholarship may give rise to a property interest in its continuation. *Hall v. University of Minnesota*, 530 F. Supp. 104 (D. Minn. 1982). "But there is not automatic entitlement to a college education." *Fluitt v. University of Nebraska*, 489 F. Supp. 1194, 1203 (D. Neb. 1980). When scholarships are awarded at the discretion of a college coach, and such discretion has not yet been exercised, no property interest in the receipt of a scholarship can exist, and the plaintiff cannot invoke his expectation that he would earn a scholarship at the state tournament in order to claim a property interest in wrestling there.

If any property interest of the plaintiff is involved in this case, it is a property right created by the defendant's own Disciplinary Policy and Administrative Rules. When a government must follow mandatory laws or regulations which limit its discretion to make a decision in any way or for any reason, those laws or regulations can create a property right which is deprived if those regulations are not followed. However, the plaintiff was not deprived of this right because (1) the basis for the defendant's action was a permissible basis for this sanction under Sections III and V(E) of the Disciplinary Policy, (2) the procedures in part IV of the Administrative Rules were followed, and (3) the sanction chosen was authorized in § 9.14(5) of Board Policy 503.6.

Even if this Court were to recognize a protected interest in participation, the Court is satisfied that the plaintiff received all process due to him. The plaintiff and his mother were notified of the charges against him and were told of opportunities for appeal. . . . The plaintiff was given an opportunity to explain his side of the story to the principal prior to the suspension. . . . He was given a five-to six-hour evidentiary hearing within ten days of the initial suspension, which was also early enough to permit the Board to reverse the administration's decision before the plaintiff would be precluded from participating in the state tournament. Evidence was presented on the administration's behalf by an independent attorney. The plaintiff was represented by legal counsel, who called several witnesses and rigorously cross-examined the administration's witnesses. All witnesses were sworn prior to their testimony.

The plaintiff objects that the description of the incident presented to the Board was based upon hearsay, and that the administration did not present testimony from anyone who was present when it took place. This claim is supported in the hearing record. However, the Due Process Clause does not require courtroom standards of evidence to be used in administrative hearings.

As long as a decision rests upon "some evidence," due process may have been satisfied. *Superintendent v. Hill*, 472 U.S. 445, 105 S. Ct. 2768, 2770, 86 L. Ed. 2d 356 (1985). . . . Hearsay which has a "rational probative force" can constitute substantial evidence, which is a higher standard than "some evidence." . . .

In this case there appears to be little or no evidence in the hearing record directly contradicting the Board's hearsay-based finding that the plaintiff "as well as three other male youths engaged in multiple acts of sexual intercourse with a sixteen year old female student of the Sheldon Community School District on or about January 25, 1987. . . ." The factual disagreement primarily concerned the effect of that incident upon the school and the female. Reliable and credible evidence was presented by Instructor Patti Thayer about the disruptive effect upon the school, and expert testimony was presented concerning the potential effect of such acts upon the female involved and upon student attitudes concerning sexuality, women and rape. While the Board was required to speculate about whether the female involved would react in the same way as the hypothetical female in the expert's answer . . . , that is not enough to prevent the testimony from constituting "some evidence." Further, it does not require experts to clearly demonstrate that such acts would, as it has in Sheldon, disrupt a good portion of the town and not just the school. . . .

For all of these reasons, the Court finds that the plaintiff's procedural due process rights were respected.

SUBSTANTIVE DUE PROCESS

The plaintiff can show that his right to substantive due process was denied if the Board's decision was arbitrary or capricious, *Littlefield v. City of Afton*, 785 F.2d 596, 607 (8th Cir. 1986); or if it violated one of the substantive due process rights such as the right to privacy, which cannot be deprived no matter how much procedural protection is used. *Griswold v. Connecticut*, 381 U.S. 479, 85 S. Ct. 1678, 14 L. Ed. 2d 510 (1965).

The Court is persuaded that the Board's decision was not arbitrary or capricious. The Board's objectives were legitimate. The Iowa Supreme Court has described the set of permissible school board objectives in this area in broad, sweeping terms. *Bunger v. Iowa High School Athletic Association*, 197 N.W.2d 555, 564-65 (Iowa 1972). "To some extent at least, school authorities may base disciplinary measures on immoral acts or acts definitely contrary to current mores." *Id.* at 565. The *Bunger* court also held that:

> The present case involves the advantages and enjoyment of an extracurricular activity provided by the school, a consideration which we believe extends the authority of a school board somewhat as to participation in that activity. The influence of the students involved is an additional consideration. Standout students, whether in athletics, forensics, dramatics, or other interscholastic activities, play a somewhat different role from the rank and file. Leadership brings additional responsibility. These student leaders are looked up to and emulated. They represent the school and depict its character. We cannot fault a school board for expecting somewhat more of them as to eligibility for their particular extracurricular activities.

Id. at 564.

The means chosen to achieve their objectives were not arbitrary or capricious. As the Nebraska Supreme Court found in a similar case involving alcohol use by athletes who were then suspended from a team:

> The rule involved in this case, even though the penalty of expulsion for the season might be deemed severe by some persons, clearly serves a legitimate rational interest and directly affects the discipline of student athletes. It cannot be said that the prescribed penalty was an arbitrary and unreasonable means to attain the legitimate end of deterrence of the use of alcoholic liquor by student athletes.

Braesch v. DePasquale, 200 Neb. 726, 265 N.W.2d 842, 846 (1978).

The plaintiff argues that he should not have been given a penalty more severe than penalties allegedly given in the past to other students for conduct the plaintiff considers to be more serious than his own. The record adequately demonstrates that the school's treatment of those students involved to the same degree in this incident could hardly have been more consistent; even the female involved was suspended from extracurricular activities. To go further and evaluate the Board's "consistency" across different times and different factual settings would require the Court to substitute its judgment concerning the relative seriousness of different acts for that of the School Board; the "arbitrary or capricious" standard of review is too narrow to authorize this kind of analysis.

During the February 16 hearing, the plaintiff sought to introduce a statement one member of the School Board made after the Board's hearing but before the end of deliberations which purported to show a predisposition to affirm the suspension. However probative this statement may be, the Court cannot consider it. When a board has made formal findings, a court may not look beyond those findings to question the integrity of decision-makers or the decision-making process without a "strong showing of bad faith or improper behavior." *Overton Park*, 401 U.S. at 420, 91 S. Ct. at 825; *United States v. Morgan*, 313 U.S. 409, 422, 61 S. Ct. 999, 1004, 85 L. Ed. 1429 (1941). No such showing has been made here. In his testimony before the School Board, the plaintiff would not admit or deny that the incident took place because he believed it was a private matter. . . .[5] A limited right to privacy is protected by the Due Process Clause. *Griswold v. Connecticut*, 381 U.S. 479, 85 S. Ct. 1678, 14 L. Ed. 2d 510 (1965). However, that right does not keep the state and its instrumentalities from regulating private sexual conduct. *Bowers v. Hardwick*, 478 U.S. 186, 106 S. Ct. 2841, 92 L. Ed. 2d 140 (1986); Note, *Fornication, Cohabitation and the Constitution*, 77 Mich. L. Rev. 252 (1978).[6] The Board's findings indicate that it was not merely trying to impose its moral standard upon the plaintiff; the Board found that his acts injured another student and disrupted the school. These are legitimate school board concerns. Moreover, the school has not regulated the plaintiff as a student; by revoking his eligibility without suspending or expelling him, it has regulated him as a representative of the school, and has chosen a sanction which limits his ability to represent the school without limiting his basic rights as a student. For these reasons, the Court finds that whatever right the plaintiff has to sexual privacy after *Bowers* was not violated in this case, and the last possible ground for finding a likelihood that his substantive due process rights were violated is rejected.

CONCLUSION

The Court finds that the likelihood the plaintiff can prove that his constitutional rights were violated is not great enough to warrant a temporary restraining

---

5. It should be noted that the plaintiff admits that a fellow wrestler was present when the incident took place, and this individual has admitted that he "was involved in an incident with (female's name redacted) on Sunday night Jan. 25, 1987. . . ."

6. *Bowers* may not have undermined all earlier decisions recognizing privacy rights of consenting adults engaged in private sexual conduct. *See, e.g., State v. Pilcher*, 242 N.W.2d 348 (Iowa 1976); *Erb v. Iowa State Board of Public Instruction*, 216 N.W.2d 339 (Iowa 1974). But in light of the public school system's responsibility to "inculcate the habits and manners of civility" in students, *Bethel School District v. Fraser*, 478 U.S. 675, 106 S. Ct. 3159, 3162, 92 L. Ed. 2d 549 (1986), the Court is hesitant to grant high school students the same degree of protection afforded adults.

order or preliminary injunction—nothing more and nothing less. The Court neither approves nor disapproves of the defendant's action, for that particular question has never been before it. However, it is the fervent hope of this judge that if or when this legal dispute is over, the parties and their respective supporters in the community have not burned so many bridges that a mutually beneficial reconciliation cannot be reached.

IT IS HEREBY ORDERED that the plaintiff's motions for a temporary restraining order or preliminary injunction are denied.

NOTES AND QUESTIONS

1. *Procedural Due Process Rights.* Procedural due process deals with the amount of procedural process that is due—what degree or amount of notice and hearing should be offered. As the *Brands* court observes, most courts have held that student-athletes do not possess a constitutionally protected property interest in interscholastic sports participation that requires procedural due process before being limited or denied by public school officials. See, e.g., *Mayo v. West Virginia Secondary Schools Activities Comm'n*, 672 S.E.2d 224, 229 (W. Va. 2008) ("Because there is no property or liberty interest that attaches to extracurricular activities, 'procedural due process protections' do not apply.").

Although courts generally rule that no property interest in athletic participation exists, *Brands* holds that a school's student disciplinary rules and procedures may create a property right for student-athletes. Similarly, in *Butler v. Oak Creek-Franklin Sch. Dist.*, 172 F. Supp. 2d 1102 (E.D. Wis. 2001), a high school football player received a 12-month athletic suspension for allegedly violating municipal ordinances prohibiting possession of intoxicants by a minor and possession of fireworks. He appealed his suspension alleging, *inter alia*, that it violated his due process rights. He had previously been suspended for violating good-conduct rules prohibiting smoking, drinking alcohol, and using marijuana. The court held that several documents, including the rules of the Wisconsin Interscholastic Athletic Association and the high school student/parent handbook, combined to grant student-athletes a property right in continued participation in interscholastic athletics, which is sufficient to trigger procedural due process protections. *Id.* at 1110. Having found the requisite property interest, the court identified the necessary due process as including a pre-deprivation hearing, notice of charges, an impartial decision, and a decision that rests on evidence presented at a hearing. See also Larry D. Bartlett, *The Courts' View of Good Conduct Rules for High School Student Athletes*, 82 Educ. L. Rep. 1087, 1098 (1993) ("A property interest exists because students may participate under those policies and rules until they are acted upon by school officials to deprive the students of those expectations.").

In *Brands*, the student-athlete was punished by being declared ineligible to participate in the state wrestling tournament because his conduct was "detrimental to the best interests of the school district." Courts tend to be unreceptive to claims that good conduct rules are unconstitutionally vague and do not provide sufficient notice for procedural due process purposes. In *Bush v. Dassel-Cokato Bd. of Educ.*, 745 F. Supp. 562 (D. Minn.

1990), a member of an interscholastic swim team was prohibited from participating in a swim meet because of a violation of a good conduct rule that imposed sanctions for "attending parties where alcohol and/or illegal drugs as defined by state law are *present*." *Id.* at 572 (italics included). Taking a common sense approach, the court rejected the student's arguments that the term *present* rendered this portion of the rule unconstitutionally vague. "[P]ersons of common intelligence would not need to guess at the meaning of the language in order to determine that it applied to the situation involved in this case." *Id.* at 572-573.

2. *Substantive Due Process Rights.* Consistent with the prevailing judicial view regarding procedural due process, courts generally have refused to recognize a separate property right or liberty interest to participate in interscholastic athletics for purposes of substantive due process. In *A.C. v. Board of Education for the Cambridge Community Unit District #227*, 2005 WL 3560658 (C.D. Ill. 2005), the court refused to reinstate a high school student-athlete's eligibility after he discharged a look-alike weapon in the school parking lot after class hours. In doing so, the court reaffirmed that playing high school sports is not a liberty or property interest giving rise to a substantive due process claim if it is denied. It noted that participation in athletics is not an "integral" part of education and should not be protected as an educational right. Do you agree? If it is not an integral part of education, why do school districts spend so many resources and so much time fostering competitive athletic programs? If interscholastic athletics were considered to be an integral part of a student's education, what would the implications be for students seeking to participate?

On the other hand, *Brands* recognizes that even minor student-athletes have privacy rights (e.g., sexual conduct) that constitute an independent liberty interest, which is protected from infringement by substantive due process. The court, however, found this right to be limited and not infringed by his high school's disciplinary suspension based on then-existing Supreme Court precedent and facts suggesting this was coerced sexual activity involving a female student. Perhaps the court's determination of this specific issue would have been different if the involved students were 18-years old and engaged in consensual sex. *Lawrence v. Texas*, 539 U.S. 558, 572 (2003) (constitutionally protected right to liberty "gives substantial protection to adult persons in deciding how to conduct their private life in matters pertaining to sex"). It is unlikely that courts would broadly construe the scope of recognized individual privacy rights or liberty interests to generally preclude a public high school from regulating student-athletes' illegal or other inappropriate off-campus conduct during non-school hours. For example, courts generally have rejected claims that discipline imposed on student-athletes by public schools for violating rules prohibiting drinking alcoholic beverages off campus violates their constitutionally protected property or liberty interests. See, e.g., *L.P.M. v. Sch. Bd. of Seminole County*, 753 So. 2d 130 (Fla. Dist. Ct. App. 2000), and *Farver v. Bd. of Educ. of Carroll County*, 40 F. Supp. 2d 323 (D. Md. 1999).

In *Brands*, the Eighth Circuit holds that a student-athlete has a liberty interest in not being treated in an arbitrary or capricious manner and that, if a school does so, it violates his or her substantive due process rights. When courts refer to substantive due process rights in this context, they generally are referring to arbitrary and capricious acts depriving students of the opportunity to participate in interscholastic sports, not merely the failure to provide them with fair notice and a hearing as required by procedural due process.

3.   *Other Constitutional Law Claims.* In *Brands*, the court summarily rejected three of the student-athlete's five constitutional challenges to his high school's good conduct rules—alleged violations of the Eighth Amendment prohibition against cruel and unusual punishment, Sixth Amendment right to counsel, and Fourteenth Amendment right to equal protection claims. Courts have rejected claims that good conduct rules violate other constitutional rights as well. See, e.g., *Bush v. Dassel-Cokato Bd. of Educ.*, 745 F. Supp. 562 (D. Minn. 1990) (suspension from interscholastic athletics for the violation of a rule prohibiting a student-athlete's presence at parties where alcohol was being served does not violate her alleged First Amendment right to associate socially with her friends); *Farver v. Bd. of Educ. of Carroll County*, 40 F. Supp. 2d 323 (D. Md. 1999) (same).

5.   *Policy Questions.* As the attorney for a state interscholastic athletic association or an educational institution, how would you answer the following questions: What kind of rules should be promulgated at the association-wide level regarding good conduct? What kind of rules should be promulgated at the institutional level? Can and should student-athletes be treated differently than other students generally, or other students involved in extracurricular activities, for good conduct purposes?

g.   Personal Appearance and Grooming Cases

Most cases involving the validity of personal appearance and grooming rules arose during 1965 to 1975, a very turbulent period in the United States. In a case not involving interscholastic sports, *Tinker v. Des Moines Independent Community Sch. Dist.*, 393 U.S. 503 (1969), a public school dress code prohibited students from wearing black armbands. Finding that the prohibition violated the students' First Amendment rights, the Supreme Court concluded:

> The problem posed by the present case does not relate to regulation of the length of skirts or the type of clothing, to hair style, or deportment. . . . It does not concern aggressive, disruptive action or even group demonstrations. Our problem involves direct, primary First Amendment rights akin to "pure speech." . . .
>
> The school officials banned and sought to punish petitioners for a silent, passive expression of opinion, unaccompanied by any disorder or disturbance on the part of petitioners. There is here no evidence whatever of petitioners' interference, actual or nascent, with the schools' work or of collision with the rights of other students to be secure and to be let alone. Accordingly, this case does not concern speech or action that intrudes upon the work of the schools or the rights of other students.

Id. at 514.

The following two federal appellate cases involve a "clean shaving" and a hair length policy, respectively, in which the courts seem to apply a different legal standard and reach conflicting conclusions.

DAVENPORT v. RANDOLPH COUNTY BOARD OF EDUCATION
730 F.2d 1395 (11th Cir. 1984)

KRAVITCH, Circuit Judge.

The plaintiffs, Jonathan Davenport and Micky Lazar O'Neal, are high school students who brought suit to challenge the "clean shaven" policy of defendant Ronald Watters, coach of the football and basketball teams at Randolph County High School (RCHS). Defendant Watters suspended Davenport from the RCHS basketball team in December 1981 for refusing to shave and barred both plaintiffs from participating on the football team for the 1982 season because of their refusal to abide by his grooming policy.

Defendant Watters' grooming policy prohibited team members from having beards, wearing mustaches extending beyond the corners of their mouths, or growing sideburns below the ear lobes. The plaintiffs' fathers approved of their sons' decisions not to abide by the coach's policy because they had suffered skin problems when shaving as youths and thus did not want their sons to shave. Defendant Randolph County School Board first considered the issue in March 1982 and recommended that coaches not require a minor to shave if the parents objected. At a later meeting, however, the Board reversed its position and endorsed Coach Watters' "clean shaven" policy. Plaintiffs proceeded to institute this suit pursuant to 42 U.S.C. § 1983 and the fourteenth amendment, requesting declaratory judgment and issuance of an injunction to prevent the defendants from refusing to allow the plaintiffs to participate in athletics at RCHS.

The plaintiffs contend that the "clean shaven" policy is unconstitutional because it is arbitrary and unreasonable to require fourteen and fifteen year-old adolescents to shave in order to participate in high school athletics. This court has previously ruled that in the high school environment there is "a per se rule that [grooming regulations] are constitutionally valid." *Karr v. Schmidt*, 460 F.2d 609, 617 (5th Cir. 1972) (en banc); *see also, Stevenson v. Board of Education of Wheeler County, Georgia*, 426 F.2d 1154 (5th Cir.), *cert. denied*, 400 U.S. 957, 91 S. Ct. 355, 27 L. Ed. 2d 265 (1970) ("clean shaven" policy not irrational). The rule announced in *Karr* is founded on the premise that "grooming regulations are a reasonable means of furthering the school board's undeniable interest in teaching hygiene, instilling discipline, asserting authority, and compelling uniformity." *Domico v. Rapides Parish School Board*, 675 F.2d 100, 102 (5th Cir. 1982) (discussing holding in *Karr*).

This case falls squarely within the holdings of *Karr* and *Stevenson*. The district court found that the policy was "adopted to accomplish the legitimate objective of presenting the school in the light deemed most favorable to the school by the students and coaches at the school." The court further found, and the plaintiffs do not disagree, that there was no evidence that the policy was racially motivated.

The plaintiffs attempt to distinguish the above cases primarily on the ground that their objections to the grooming code are based on a concern that shaving will cause them skin problems. The plaintiffs' fathers testified that they had suffered such problems as youths, and the district court recognized that blacks are prone to such medical problems. No evidence, however, was presented to the court or the school board that the plaintiffs themselves would be likely to suffer from such problems, and defendant Watters testified that he would not enforce the policy if it would have injurious results. Without such medical evidence, we find it unnecessary to decide whether enforcement of the "clean shaven" policy in such a context would amount to a constitutional violation outside the holding of *Karr's* per se rule. *Cf. Karr*, 460 F.2d at 617 n. 26 (per se rule does not apply if grooming policy has arbitrary effect or is discriminatorily enforced).

Finally, the plaintiffs argue that the "clean shaven" policy deprives them of property without due process of law because their inability to participate in high school athletics diminishes their chances of receiving athletic scholarships to college. This court has held that "[t]he privilege of participating in interscholastic activities must be deemed to fall . . . outside the protection of due process." *Mitchell v. Louisiana High School Athletic Association*, 430 F.2d 1155, 1158 (5th Cir. 1970); *see also Walsh v. Louisiana High School Athletic Association*, 616 F.2d 152, 159 (5th Cir. 1980). . . . We fail to perceive any principled distinction for due process purposes between the effect of the eligibility rides in *Mitchell* and *Walsh* in barring athletic participation and the plaintiffs' refusal to abide by the grooming regulations resulting in their ineligibility to compete in high school sports.

Having found that the disputed policy is within the school board's power to regulate grooming and that the plaintiffs have not proven unique circumstances that would render the policy arbitrary or unreasonable, the district court's denial of relief is AFFIRMED.

HAYDEN v. GREENSBURG COMMUNITY SCHOOL CORPORATION
743 F.3d 569 (7th Cir. 2014)

ROVNER, *Circuit Judge.*

[The parents of A.H., a boy desiring to play interscholastic basketball] challenge a policy which requires boys playing interscholastic basketball at the public high school in Greensburg, Indiana, to keep their hair cut short. The Haydens make two principal arguments: (1) the hair-length policy arbitrarily intrudes upon their son's liberty interest in choosing his own hair length, and thus violates his right to substantive due process, and (2) because the policy applies only to boys and not girls wishing to play basketball, the policy constitutes sex discrimination. The district court rejected both claims and granted judgment to the defendants. . . . We reverse in part. . . .

The board of trustees [in Greensburg, Indiana where A.H. plays, adopted] Policy 5511, entitled "Dress and Grooming"—which in relevant part directs the district superintendent to "establish such grooming guidelines as are necessary to promote discipline, maintain order, secure the safety of students, and provide a healthy environment conducive to academic purposes." . . . The district guidelines implementing this directive leave it to the individual principal of each school, in consultation with staff, parents, and/or students, to develop and enforce appropriate dress and grooming policies.

Greensburg Junior High School (which serves students in the sixth through eighth grades) has established an athletic code of conduct which includes the following provision regarding hair styles:

> Hair Styles which create problems of health and sanitation, obstruct vision, or call undue attention to the athlete are not acceptable. Athletes may not wear haircuts that include insignias, numbers, initials, or extremes in differing lengths. Mohawks are not acceptable, and hair coloring is not permitted. Each varsity head coach will be responsible for determining acceptable length of hair for a particular sport. Ask a coach before trying out for a team if you have a question regarding hair styles.

[The court assumed that there was a similar provision for athletes at the senior high school level].

Stacy Meyer, the head varsity basketball coach at Greensburg High School, has established an unwritten hair-length policy which applies to the boys basketball teams. That policy provides that each player's hair must be cut above the ears, eyebrows, and collar. Coach Meyer has explained the policy as one that promotes team unity and projects a "clean cut" image. The boys baseball teams have a similar hair-length policy, whereas the boys track and football teams do not. No girls athletic team is subject to a hair-length policy. . . .

A.H. . . . currently is a junior in high school. He wishes to play basketball, but he also wishes to wear his hair longer than the hair-length policy permits. During the 2009-2010 school year, when he was in the seventh grade, A.H. cut his hair in compliance with the policy so that he could play for the junior high school boys team, but he "didn't feel like himself" with the short haircut. The following year, he declined to cut his hair and his parents protested the hair-length policy as unconstitutional. He was permitted to practice with the boys team while the school and district entertained the objection. But the school principal and district superintendent ultimately sustained the policy and, when A.H. refused to cut his hair, he was removed from the team. . . .

In the Fall of 2012, when A.H. again tried out for the boys team, his hair was longer than the hair-length policy allowed, and he was reminded that he would have to comply with the policy in order to practice with the team. . . .

After A.H. refused to cut his hair and was removed from the boys junior high school basketball team in the Fall of 2010, his parents sued the Greensburg Community School Corporation, its governing school board, and various district and school officials, alleging that the hair-length policy violated multiple state and federal constitutional and statutory provisions. . . .

II.

A. SUBSTANTIVE DUE PROCESS

The Haydens contend that A.H. has a fundamental liberty interest in wearing his hair at the length of his choosing and that the hair-length policy, by compelling him to forgo that liberty and keep his hair short if he wishes to play interscholastic basketball at Greensburg High School, violates his Fourteenth Amendment right to substantive due process. . . .

The notion that one's hair length is an aspect of personal liberty so important that it constitutes a fundamental right is hard to square with the Supreme Court's . . . opinion in *Glucksberg*, which describes fundamental rights as those which are "deeply rooted in this Nation's history and tradition, and implicit in the concept of ordered liberty, such that neither liberty nor justice would exist if they were sacrificed." 521 U.S. at 720-21, 117 S. Ct. at 2268 (internal quotation marks and citations omitted). The Court in *Glucksberg* noted that in addition to the freedoms expressly protected by the Bill of Rights, it had held the due process clause to protect such non-enumerated rights as "the rights to marry, to have children, to direct the education and upbringing of one's children, to marital privacy, to use contraception, to bodily integrity, and to abortion." Id. at 720, 117 S. Ct. at 2267 (citations omitted). The Court called for the "utmost care" in adding to this short list of fundamental rights, "lest the liberty protected by the Due Process Clause be subtly transformed into the policy preferences of the Members of this Court."

Although hair length is not a fundamental right, there is a residual substantive limit on government action which prohibits arbitrary deprivations of liberty by government. . . . (Citations omitted.) This rational-basis variant of substantive due process differs little, if at all, from the most deferential form of equal protection review. . . . (Citations omitted.)

The Haydens have made no genuine attempt to demonstrate that the hair-length policy fails rational-basis review. . . . It is the Haydens who must demonstrate that the hair-length policy lacks a rational relationship with a legitimate government interest; it is not the school district's obligation to prove rationality with evidence. The Haydens' burden in this respect is a heavy one: So long as there is any conceivable state of facts that supports the policy, it passes muster under the due process clause; put another way, only if the policy is patently arbitrary would it fail. We therefore express no opinion on whether the policy would survive rational basis review. Apart from that, it is not our place to pass judgment on the wisdom of the policy.

B.   EQUAL PROTECTION

A more meritorious contention is that the hair-length policy deprives A.H. of equal protection because it discriminates against him on the basis of his sex. Because A.H. is a boy, he must cut his hair in order to play interscholastic basketball at Greensburg; were he a girl, he would not be subject to that requirement, as the girls team has no hair-length policy. . . . The equal protection clause of the Fourteenth Amendment protects individuals against intentional, arbitrary discrimination by government officials. . . . Gender is a quasi-suspect class that triggers intermediate scrutiny in the equal protection context; the justification for a gender-based classification thus must be exceedingly persuasive.

Whether and when the adoption of differential grooming standards for males and females amounts to sex discrimination is the subject of a discrete subset of judicial and scholarly analysis. This line of authority—much of it pre-dating the Supreme Court's decision in *Price Waterhouse v. Hopkins,* 490 U.S. 228, 250-51, 109 S. Ct. 1775, 1790-91 (1989) (plurality) (employer may not demand that employee's appearance and deportment match sex stereotype associated with her gender) . . . developed in the employment context, but it has a parallel in the school context as well. . . . The relevant and dispositive point here is that this line of precedent has been ignored entirely in this appeal.

The parties have litigated the hair-length policy in isolation rather than as an aspect of any broader grooming standards applied to boys and girls basketball teams. We were told, when we raised the subject at oral argument, that male and female athletes alike are subject to grooming standards; and indeed the parties jointly stipulated below for purposes of the preliminary injunction hearing that whereas only the boys basketball and baseball teams have hair-length policies, the other school athletic teams do have grooming policies. R. 34. But the content of those grooming policies has never been established, and the fact that there are grooming standards for both girls and boys teams was not even mentioned in the stipulated facts submitted to the district court for purposes of resolving the case. The stipulated facts reveal only that there is a hair-length policy for the boys basketball team but for not for the girls basketball team (or, for that matter, any other girls team). [T]he stipulated facts indicate that a boy wishing to play basketball at Greensburg is subject to a requirement, impinging upon a recognized liberty interest, [but] a girl is not.

The defendants argue that this is not sex-based discrimination because the hair-length policy applies to only two of the boys athletic teams. Boys wishing to compete on the football or track teams, for example, would be free to do so without having to keep their hair cut short. [Defendants argue] that the policy does not apply to all boys teams demonstrates that the policy does not categorically discriminate against boys. The district court agreed.

The argument is untenable. That the policy is not universally applied to boys does not negate the fact that it is based on sex: Again, boys wishing to play basketball (or baseball) are subject to a requirement that girls are not. . . . The equal protection clause protects the individual rather than the group, and the individual plaintiff in this case wishes to play basketball. . . . He is subject to a burden that a girl in the same position is not.

Equally problematic is the school district's alternative contention that the sex discrimination claim fails for lack of proof that any such discrimination is intentional. . . . This is a case of disparate treatment rather than disparate impact; the hair-length policy, being applicable only to boys teams, draws an explicit gender line. The intent to treat boys differently from girls is therefore evident from the one-sided nature of the policy. . . .

The problem for the defendants is that this case was jointly submitted to the district court for final judgment based on a set of stipulated facts. Those facts, if they are read to include the parties' prior stipulation that both male and female athletes are subject to grooming standards, reveal nothing that would permit a court to assess whether the standards are comparable, notwithstanding the disparity in the hair-length component of the grooming standards.

The Haydens plainly have made out a prima facie case of discrimination. The hair-length policy applies only to male athletes, and there is no facially apparent reason why that should be so. Girls playing interscholastic basketball have the same need as boys do to keep their hair out of their eyes, to subordinate individuality to team unity, and to project a positive image. Why, then, must only members of the boys team wear their hair short? Given the obvious disparity, the policy itself gives rise to an inference of discrimination. To defeat that inference, it was up to the school district to show that the hair-length policy is just one component of a comprehensive grooming code that imposes comparable although not identical demands on both male and female athletes. . . . [A]bsent any evidence as to the content of the grooming standards that are applicable to female athletes, we are not prepared to simply assume that an otherwise facially-discriminatory rule is justified.

The dissent looks to the parties' stipulation that there are grooming standards for all teams, coupled with the hair-style provision of the athletic code of conduct . . . as proof that male and female athletes are in fact subject to comparable grooming standards. . . . Yet, the mere stipulation that there are grooming standards applicable to girls as well as boys teams does not establish the content of those standards. Nor does the hair-style provision fill that void. . . . [T]he policy delegates to each varsity head coach the responsibility to determine "acceptable" hair lengths for his or her respective sport, which does not explain why short hair may be thought necessary for boys who play basketball but not girls.

[W]e know virtually nothing about the grooming standards to which female athletes at Greensburg are subject. May they wear earrings or other types of jewelry, for example, and if so, what if any restrictions are imposed on these items? If the goal for all interscholastic athletes is a neat, clean-cut appearance, which is one of the reasons that Coach Meyer gave for the hair-length policy, are girls required to maintain their hair to particular standards? Beyond the limits on mohawks and other extreme hairdos set forth in the hair-style provision, are there any limits on the manner in which girls may style their hair? Although girls can evidently wear their hair as long as they wish, could a female basketball player wear her hair in an extremely short "buzz-cut," which might literally qualify as "clean cut" but perhaps not in the sense that Coach Meyer means it and perhaps not in synch with local norms? . . .

[With regard to community standards], a principle that emerges from the Title VII and other cases we have cited is that sex-differentiated standards consistent with community norms may be permissible to the extent they are part of a comprehensive, evenly-enforced grooming code that imposes comparable burdens on both males and females alike. As our colleague's dissent points out, some of the cases in that line sustained workplace hair-length restrictions on male but not female employees . . . [citations omitted]. We would reiterate that each of those cases relied on the fact that female employees, although not subject to hair-length restrictions, were subject to comparable grooming requirements. . . . But it is worth noting that the community standards which may account for the differences in standards applied to men and women, girls and boys, do not remain fixed in perpetuity. See Jespersen, 444 F.3d at 1118 (Kozinski, J., dissenting). It is also worth reiterating that Coach Meyer's policy prohibits far more than an Age-of-Aquarius, Tiny-Tim, hair-crawling-past-the-shoulders sort of hair style—it compels all male basketball players to wear genuinely short hair. In 2014, it is not obvious that any and all hair worn over the ears, collar, or eyebrows would be out of the mainstream among males in the Greensburg community at large, among the student body, or among school athletes. (Even one or two men on this court might find themselves in trouble with Coach Meyer for hair over the ears.) We certainly agree that the pedagogical and caretaking responsibilities of schools give school officials substantial leeway in establishing grooming codes for their students generally and for their interscholastic athletes in particular. . . . But that leeway does not permit them to impose non-equivalent burdens on school athletes based on their sex. So far as this record reveals, that is exactly what the school district has done. . . .

What we have before us is a policy that draws an explicit distinction between male and female athletes and imposes a burden on male athletes alone, and a limited record that does not supply a legally sufficient justification for the sex-based classification. . . . But there is no suggestion that A.H. wishes to wear his hair in an extreme fashion, let alone that hair worn over a boy's ears or collar or eyebrows is invariably problematic. The record also tells us that Coach Meyer offered two reasons for the policy: promoting team unity, by having team members wear their hair in a uniform length, and projecting a "clean-cut" image. . . . What is noteworthy, for purposes of the Haydens' equal protection claim, is that the interests in team unity and projecting a favorable image are not unique to male interscholastic teams, and yet, so far as the record reveals, those interests are articulated and pursued solely with respect to members of the boys basketball team. If there is an argument that the goals of team unity and a "clean-cut" image are served through comparable, albeit different, grooming standards for female athletes, it has neither been advanced nor supported in this case. And the fact that other boys teams are not subject to a hair-length policy casts doubt on whether such an argument could be made.

The parties consented to the entry of final judgment on the record as it stands, and that record entitles the Haydens to judgment on the equal protection claim. The policy imposes a burden on only male athletes. There has been no showing that it does so pursuant to grooming standards for both male and female athletes that, although not identical, are comparable. Finally, no rational, let alone exceedingly persuasive, justification has been articulated for restricting the hair length of male athletes alone. . . .

III.

For the reasons discussed in this opinion, the district court's judgment in favor of the defendants on the Haydens' substantive due process claim is affirmed. However, the judgment in favor of the defendants on the equal protection and Title IX claims is reversed. . . . The case is remanded to the district court to determine appropriate relief on these claims. The parties shall bear their own costs of appeal. . . .

MANION, Circuit Judge, concurring in part and dissenting in part.

Having ruled against A.H.'s primary argument, the court decides this case on equal protection arguments that A.H. did not make, rooted in authority he did not cite. However, the court does not actually tell us why the policies here are not comparable under the correct standard. Rather, the court decides that the school loses by default because the record is missing some of the grooming provisions that are applicable to female athletes. But there is enough in the record to compare the grooming policies applicable to male and female athletes, and if anything that is missing were included, it would only make the burden of the grooming policy applicable to male athletes even more clearly balanced out by the burden on female athletes. Although I agree with the court's general summary of the law of equal protection, I write separately because the record does not establish any violation of the Equal Protection clause . . . .

As the court recognizes, sex-based equal protection analysis is much more nuanced than a simple "but for" test. . . . Discrimination based on sex violates the Equal Protection clause unless the state has an exceedingly persuasive justification. United States v. Virginia, 518 U.S. 515, 533 (1996). However, maintaining different grooming standards for men and women is not usually discrimination. As the court points out, there is a line of authority which addresses differing grooming standards for men and women in the workplace. . . . From that line of authority, a rule emerges that differing grooming standards are not discrimination if they are comparable; for the standards to be comparable, they must "find some justification in commonly accepted social norms" or "generally accepted community standards," be reasonably related to a legitimate interest, and be applied evenhandedly, not imposing an unequal burden. . . .

With this context, the grooming decisions reveal a common thread: as long as a grooming or appearance policy applies to both men and women, the fact that it has different provisions based on different social norms or community standards for men and women (or based on different athletic traditions) is acceptable. Distinction is not discrimination. The court and I agree that the rule permits a policy that is different for men and women so long as it is comparable. . . .

Accordingly, the record indicates that the policies for the boys and girls basketball teams are the same except for hair length. Only the hair length component is delegated to the coaches, and the stipulation indicates that only the boys baseball and basketball teams have imposed a hair-length requirement. . . .

But A.H.'s only argument—only allegation—is that the hair length standard is unfair, and the school has produced the hair style provision of the athletic code, and the coaches' decisions that the boys basketball team has to cut its hair to a certain length and the girls basketball team does not (the only decisions delegated to the coaches). Yet the court says the school has not produced enough, while leaving the school guessing about what is enough content. Must the school produce every provision tangentially related to female grooming? Perhaps it would have been better had the school done this. But the only thing the content of any other female grooming provision could provide is evidence of more burdens for female athletes, which would make the policies more comparable. The omission of any grooming provisions applicable to female athletes is, at worst, immaterial.

With enough of the policy to compare, the school's burden to produce is satisfied and we continue with the normal routine. The burden of persuasion rests always with the plaintiff, who must now show that a comparison of the policies reveals disparities that amount to sex discrimination. If he does so, then it is the school's burden to prove a justification. . . .

The stipulations in this case indicate that there is an athletic "hair style" policy that applies to both male and female athletes, with a "cut" requirement that applies only to (some) male athletes (and there may be other provisions applicable to female athletes, but we assume there are not to A.H.'s favor). Even with no additional grooming provisions applicable to female athletes, and therefore no additional burdens on females athletes (besides the athletic code's hairstyle provision), the policies are comparably burdensome. . . .

The main controversy throughout this case . . . has been whether there is a fundamental right to choose the length of one's hair. I agree with the court that there is not, so a student challenging a school rule regarding hair length bears the burden of proving it is not rationally related to a legitimate state interest—something A.H. has not done. . . . However, if we do address equal protection on the current record of stipulations, we should still affirm. The parties have stipulated that a grooming policy applies to both boys and girls. They have supplied an example in the junior-high grooming policy, which is identical for boys and girls. A.H. has only pointed out a single difference—hair length—which precedent says is a legitimate, nondiscriminatory distinction. A.H. has only argued that the policies are not identical, but that is not enough. On the record we have, A.H. cannot meet the burden of proving an argument he has not made—that the policies are not comparable. Based on the stipulations, the policies are comparable. Because A.H. has failed to either argue or prove sex discrimination, his equal protection claims should fail. . . .

NOTES AND QUESTIONS

1. *Constitutionality and Validity of Grooming Regulations.* The courts in *Davenport* and *Hayden* came to differing conclusions regarding the constitutionality of grooming regulations. Which court do you think is right and why? Courts are generally deferential to school districts in such matters. Should they

defer in grooming cases? What kinds of grooming differences, if any, should be acceptable between male and female athletes?

2. *Requisite Justification.* Some cases hold that for the grooming regulations to be constitutionally valid, the justification must be compelling, whereas, others require only that the justification have a reasonable or rational basis. Regulations required to meet the compelling standard generally fail. *Long v. Zopp*, 476 F.2d 180 (4th Cir. 1973) (holding that awards could not be used to enforce compliance with a "hair code," for the enforcement of which there was no compelling necessity); *Dunham v. Pulsifer*, 312 F. Supp. 411 (D. Vt. 1970) (finding the asserted justifications of preventing dissension, improving performance, aiding team discipline, and promoting conformity/uniformity were not compelling or necessary and not served by the grooming code, which was therefore invalid). Cases applying the lower reasonable or rational basis standard are much more likely to be upheld. *Humphries v. Lincoln Parish Sch. Bd.*, 467 So. 2d 870 (2d Cir. 1985) (finding a grooming policy that was a part of a "total discipline program" promoted athletic and academic excellence, both constitutionally permissible objectives and reasonably intended to accomplish their goals).

PROBLEM 2-7

The Salem Board of Education recently adopted a written "Hair and Dress" policy for Salem Public Schools. The policy prohibits male students whose hair and dress do not conform to certain guidelines from taking part in the public performances of extracurricular activities such as sports. For example, a boy's hair cannot extend below the top of his collar. In addition, the top of a boy's pants cannot fall more than an inch below his waistline. Boys are also prohibited from wearing bandanas of any type whether on their head or any other part of their body or attire.

Marcus Williams, a 16-year-old, is a star member of Salem High School's football team. Marcus is very proud of his braids, which fall several inches below the top of his shirt collar, and which have taken him several months to grow. He also wears popular fashions such as baggy pants that hang several inches below his waistline. In addition, Marcus will often style his hair into a ponytail, holding it in place with the type of blue bandana worn by members of a gang in the part of the city where he resides.

After the implementation of the Hair and Dress Code, Salem High's head football coach informed Marcus that he would have to cut his hair, discontinue wearing the bandana, and make certain that his pants do not fall more than an inch below his waistline, because he is in violation of the written policy. Marcus objected, arguing that none of these things have negatively affected his performance in the classroom or on the athletic field. Shortly after an assembly at which the Hair and Dress policy was announced, Marcus played in an interscholastic football game. Following the game, the football coach informed Marcus that he would not be able to play in another football game until he conformed to the Hair and Dress policy. He would be permitted, however, to practice with the team.

If Marcus challenges the dress policy, what is the likelihood he will prevail on his potential legal claims?

C. REVIEW OF GAME RESULTS

With the increasing use of instant replay to confirm or overrule on-the-field decisions by referees, judicial reconsideration of on-the-field decisions by referees, where instant replay is not in use, may become more common. While it is likely that courts will continue to be deferential to state athletic associations in their handling of such incidents, cases of this sort raise interesting legal and moral issues, as evidenced by a recent case in Oklahoma. With 64 seconds remaining in an Oklahoma high school football playoff game in November of 2014, Douglass High School took a 25-20 lead over Locust Grove. The receiver for Douglass caught a short pass and ran for over 50 yards to the end zone. Video depicted a Douglass coach running excitedly along the sideline, appearing to unintentionally bump one of the referees. The referee threw a flag and invalidated the touchdown. Under Oklahoma Secondary School Activities Association rules, this is a minor violation, calling for a five-yard penalty to be assessed on the extra-point attempt or the ensuing kickoff. Locust Grove went on to win the game.

The Association later apologized to Douglass, labeling the referees' mistake "inexcusable." Nevertheless, the Association found that state and national bylaws do not permit protesting the outcome of a game because of an official's error on the field. Questions of racism were raised by fans from Douglass, an Oklahoma City inner-city public school with a team made up of predominantly players of color.

In support of Douglass, the Oklahoma City School District sought a court order requiring that some or all of the game be replayed, arguing that fairness justified overruling a correctable mistake. It argued this is a unique case because it was not questioning the referee's judgment regarding a field of play decision. Rather, this was an instance in which the referee made a clear mistake based on his misunderstanding of the penalty prescribed by the rule, which justified the requested relief.

Judge Bernard M. Jones II, an African-American jurist, initially issued a temporary restraining order that prohibited Locust Grove from playing its scheduled state semifinal playoff game. But he ultimately denied the District's request to have all or part of the game replayed because there was no precedent allowing a court to order the replay of a high school football game. He also expressed concern that there was no way to ensure that a replay would be fair to both teams because the conditions of the disputed contest could not be replicated. The judge expressed concern that a "slippery slope of solving athletic contests in court instead of on campus will inevitably usher in a new era of robed referees and merit-less litigation due to disagreement with or disdain for decisions of gaming officials." Judge Jones added that the referee's error "could be considered by many as a tragedy," but he deferred to the Association's resolution of the matter because both teams agreed to be bound by the rules of the state high school activities association. Douglass High School officials declined to appeal the decision. See Cliff Brunt, *Oklahoma judge says disputed high school football game won't be replayed,* http://www.varsitykansas.com/2014/12/11/74398/oklahoma-judge-says-disputed-high.html. See also Nancy Loo and Mike Lowe, *Judge rules against Fenwick High School over football referee mistake* (Nov. 23, 2016), http://wgntv.com/2016/11/23/fenwick-high-school-lawsuit-semifinal-football-game/

(based on Illinois High School Association (IHSHA) bylaws stating that all game officials' decisions are final, Illinois court refuses to overturn game results despite IHSHA admission that high school football official made a mistaken call). Arbitral review of game official or referee field of play decisions are discussed in Chapter 4 B 2 and D 3.

NOTE AND QUESTIONS

When an obvious officiating mistake is made, does fairness dictate that the game be replayed? Or is this a slippery slope that would lead to litigation and judicial oversight of referees' decisions? Professor Paul Cassell concluded that Judge Jones made the correct judicial decision but argued that, in the interests of sportsmanship, Locust Grove should have agreed to replay the game. In doing so, Locust Grove would teach its coaches and players an important lesson—that sportsmanship matters and that they should do the right thing. In supporting this position, Cassell referred to the following statement by Berry Tramel, a reporter for the *Oklahoman*:

> This isn't about who's right. This is about what's right. This is about freeing the Locust Grove players from a lifetime of what-ifs. Freeing them from the gnawing feeling of ill-gotten gain. Giving them the precious gift that there are more important things than finishing first and having the most toys. What an opportunity to show, instead of tell. What an opportunity to instill those life lessons. . . . [W]hile winning a state championship would be great for Locust Grove, even greater would be teaching a bunch of teen-agers that doing the right thing is never a wrong way to go.

See Paul Cassell, *Should an Oklahoma judge order a high school football game replayed?*, http://www.washingtonpost.com/news/volokh-conspiracy/wp/2014/12/10/should-an-oklahoma-judge-order-a-high-school-football-game-replayed/.

If you represented Locust Grove, what would you recommend be done? If it were proven that the referee acted out of racial bias, should his erroneous call be judicially overruled?

CHAPTER

3

Regulating Intercollegiate Athletics

A. INTRODUCTION

This chapter initially provides a general overview and history of the governance of intercollegiate athletics, particularly by the National Collegiate Athletic Association (NCAA). Consideration of the nature of the legal relationship between a university and its student-athletes as well as First Amendment rights issues arising in connection with intercollegiate athletics follow. Finally, the NCAA's legal status as a private regulatory body, its internal rules enforcement process, and external legal limits on its regulatory authority, particularly federal antitrust law, are examined.

The NCAA is an association of over 1,100 private and public colleges and universities (including Simon Fraser University in Canada) organized into three divisions based on the nature of their intercollegiate athletic programs. Division I (D-I) offers full or partial athletic scholarships to many of its athletes and is the highest level of competition in most sports; Division II (D-II) also offers athletic scholarships and competes at an intermediate competitive level; Division III (D-III) does not offer athletic scholarships and is the most student-centered competitive level. Most NCAA member schools are members of regional athletic conferences throughout the U.S. With the NCAA's passage of legislation in 2015, five particularly powerful and competitive conferences were given autonomy within the NCAA governance structure in the form of additional legislative authority, effectively creating another decision-making tier. These conferences, known as the Power Five Conferences or the Autonomy Five Conferences, are the Atlantic Coast Conference ("ACC"), the Big Ten Conference, the Big 12 Conference, the Pac-12 Conference, and the Southeastern Conference ("SEC").

Although the NCAA is the most well-known and high-profile national regulator of intercollegiate athletics, there are others. The National Association of Intercollegiate Athletics (NAIA), which includes approximately 250 colleges and universities, is divided into two divisions and conducts numerous national championships. It has also developed innovative programs designed to enhance the experience of student-athletes, including its Champions of Character program that encourages schools to take actions designed to develop character traits among student-athletes. The National Christian College Athletic Association (NCCAA), with more than 90 members divided into two divisions, was established to provide an association for Christ-centered collegiate institutions that are committed to athletic competition as an integral component of education, evangelism, and encouragement. The United States Collegiate Athletic Association (USCAA), another smaller national organization comprised of approximately 80 schools and two divisions, was organized for the purpose of holding national championships in a number of sports for very small colleges. The National Junior College Athletic Association (NJCAA) consists of more than 500 junior and community colleges throughout 24 regions in the United States that sponsor men's and women's intercollegiate athletic teams, which compete for national championships in three divisions based on levels of competitiveness. California also has a community college athletic association made up of approximately 100 member schools that governs athletics within California.

Although the rules and governance structures differ among the various national membership associations that govern intercollegiate athletics, this chapter focuses on the rules regulating NCAA D-I intercollegiate athletics, which share some similarities with NCAA Division D-II and III, as well other college sports governing bodies.

B.   BRIEF HISTORY OF THE NCAA

Students, with some faculty oversight, initially were the major force in running intercollegiate athletics. After the deaths of 18 intercollegiate football players in 1905, President Theodore Roosevelt invited university officials to participate in a White House Conference to review football rules. These efforts to reform football rules led to the formation of a Rules Committee and gave birth to the Intercollegiate Athletic Association, which in 1910, was renamed the NCAA. Interest in intercollegiate sports and attendant increases in commercialization led the highly respected Carnegie Foundation for the Advancement of Education to issue, in 1929, a significant report regarding intercollegiate athletics, which concluded:

> [A] change of values is needed in a field that is sodden with the commercial and the material and the vested interests that these forces have created. Commercialism in college athletics must be diminished and college sport must rise to a point where it is esteemed primarily and sincerely for the opportunities it affords to mature youth. Such concerns have been expressed continually for nearly a century.

After the Great Depression and World War II, with a dramatic increase in access to higher education on the part of all segments of society, largely through government support for returning military personnel to cover the costs of attending college, public interest in intercollegiate athletics expanded significantly. Commercial pressures, which were already present, intensified with the advent of television, the presence of radio in the vast majority of homes in the United States, and the broadcasting of major sporting events. These factors, coupled with a series of gambling scandals and recruiting excesses, caused the NCAA to adopt additional rules, resulting in a significant expansion of its governance authority. In 1948, the NCAA enacted the so-called Sanity Code, which was designed to "alleviate the proliferation of exploitive practices in the recruitment of student-athletes." To enforce the rules in the Sanity Code, the

NCAA created the Constitutional Compliance Committee. Neither the Sanity Code with its rules nor the Constitutional Compliance Committee with its enforcement responsibility was particularly successful, because the only possible sanction was expulsion, which was so severe that enforcement of the rules was ineffectual. Two other developments in the 1950s, however, contributed to the transformation of the NCAA into a major regulatory body: (1) Walter Byers became executive director of the NCAA and strengthened the NCAA and its enforcement division; and (2) the NCAA negotiated its first contract to televise intercollegiate football, valued in excess of $1 million, opening the door to increasingly lucrative future television contracts.

In the following decades, the NCAA assumed even broader enforcement power, but found itself caught between two persistent critiques. On the one hand, it was criticized for responding inadequately to the increased commercialization and competitiveness of intercollegiate athletics, with all its attendant excesses. On the other hand, the NCAA was criticized for unfairly—directly and indirectly—exercising its disciplinary authority over member institutions, coaches, and others for violations of its rules, which had evolved significantly over the years to the system still in use today, of four levels of infractions and a series of guidelines for imposing disciplinary sanctions.

In difficult economic times for higher education in the 1980s, college and university presidents increasingly found themselves caught between the pressures applied by influential members of boards of trustees and alumni, who often demanded winning athletic programs (particularly football and men's basketball teams), and faculty, who were concerned about the rising commercialization of intercollegiate athletics and its impact on academic values and their institutions' budgets. In the mid-1980s, the presidents became increasingly involved in the governance of intercollegiate athletics through the NCAA, taking away some of the extensive power of athletics directors and faculty representatives, groups that had previously largely controlled intercollegiate athletics. In 1984, in *NCAA v. Board of Regents of the University of Oklahoma*, 468 U.S. 85 (1984), the U.S Supreme Court held that the NCAA's exclusive control and sale of college football television broadcasting rights violated federal antitrust law. This very important ruling limited NCAA member institutions' collective governing authority and ability to respond to the increasing commercialism of intercollegiate athletics, while also leading to the increasing economic and internal political strength of the Power Five Conferences.

In 1989, the Knight Commission, with support in the form of a $2 million grant from the Knight-Ridder newspaper chain, recommended a series of significant reforms that included more presidential involvement and control over NCAA athletics. The presidents, with nudging from groups like the Knight Commission, became increasingly concerned with cost containment and ensuring that academic values were given priority over intercollegiate athletics objectives. However, the pressure to produce more income from intercollegiate athletics programs, largely through the net revenue-generating sports of football and men's basketball, conflicted with academic values. With the challenge of budgetary issues created by difficult economic times, efforts to improve gender equity in intercollegiate athletics, and proliferating expenses for athletics facilities, coaches' salaries, student-athlete recruitment, and other athletic department efforts to produce winning teams, the presidents' efforts to gain more control of the NCAA's governance process intensified and resulted in their assuming a more significant role.

Presidential involvement in the governance of the NCAA increased during the 1990s and has continued throughout the twenty-first century, as evidenced by the successive hiring of former university presidents Myles Brand and Mark Emmert to serve as NCAA president. However, other university constituents (particularly athletics directors and faculty) have demanded and achieved an increasing role in the centralized governance of intercollegiate athletics; for example, Oliver Luck, a former athletic director at West Virginia University, was appointed in 2014 as NCAA executive vice president of regulatory affairs, reporting directly to President Emmert. There is also a Student-Athlete Advisory Committee for each of the three NCAA Divisions, and their members serve on many NCAA committees, which provide student-athletes with both a voice and a vote. University faculty representatives also play a significant role in the governance of intercollegiate athletics at the institutional, conference, and NCAA levels.

After being named NCAA President, Emmert emphasized his priorities would be to protect "student-athlete well-being and the collegiate model." Emmert has supported increasing financial aid for student-athletes, worked to develop a commercially successful playoff structure for Division I Football Bowl Series (FBS) football (the only sport for which the NCAA does not sponsor a championship), raised concerns regarding graduation rates, and has drawn increased attention to health and safety for student-athletes. His tenure has been marked by significant scandals, including the failure of former head coach Joe Paterno and other university officials, including Penn State University's former president, to address sexual abuse accusations against former assistant football coach Jerry Sandusky and the academic fraud scandal at the University of North Carolina. He is currently dealing with: a scandal in college basketball involving a FBI investigation and federal criminal indictments and convictions of several individuals, including coaches, agents, and a prominent Adidas executive; unfavorable court rulings in antitrust cases that erode the NCAA's vision of amateurism; and a college admissions scandal that has engulfed coaches at prominent colleges and universities. Each of these scandals is discussed in detail in the materials that follow.

In July of 2014, the NCAA Division I steering committee released a proposal for a new governance structure that would give the ACC, Big Ten, Big 12, Pac 12, and SEC conferences more autonomy. The new model was adopted and sets forth two ways in which autonomous legislation (legislation that applies only to the five conferences) can be passed: 1) When 60% of all member institutions in the power conferences (48 votes) and a majority of institutions in three of the power five conferences vote for the proposal; or 2) When a simple majority of all member institutions vote for the proposal and a simple majority of institutions in four of the power five conferences vote for the proposal. The autonomy movement is having a significant impact on the development and internal governance of the NCAA, including providing greater student-athlete engagement and increased governing authority for the major conferences.

Antitrust and labor law litigation as well as an effort by student-athlete advocates to unionize Northwestern University football players have challenged the traditional NCAA amateur/education model of intercollegiate athletics. There also are several pending lawsuits alleging NCAA and/or institutional tort liability for student-athlete head injuries, particularly those suffered by men's football players, as well as cases raising other college sports health and safety issues. The outcome of this litigation, combined with the application of Title IX gender equity laws and the resolution of other ethical and legal issues regarding student-athlete welfare and liability for conduct that injures third parties, may significantly change the traditional nature of intercollegiate athletics. These complex issues arise in a national environment in which NCAA D-I FBS football and men's basketball are increasingly commercialized sports that generate billions of dollars of annual revenues. At this level, a majority of participants in these revenue-generating sports are persons of color. These highly commercialized sports coexist with numerous other NCAA D-I, D-II, and D-III sports whose costs of production exceed their revenues and in which the majority of participants are not persons of color. Nevertheless, virtually all of the NCAA's 1,100-plus member universities have to subsidize their respective athletic departments (each year only 20 to 25 Division D-I intercollegiate sports programs generate net revenues).

When studying the existing legal framework and evaluating whether it effectively regulates intercollegiate athletics, it is important to consider the closely-intertwined issues regarding academics, competitive balance, economics, equity, health and safety, and other public policy concerns that are generated by the production and governance of intercollegiate sports by a national association of institutions of higher education. These considerations are discussed in the following material.

NOTES AND QUESTIONS

1. *Importance of Historical Context.* Why is it important for a lawyer working in intercollegiate athletics to have a sense of the historical development of regulation in that area? In their thoughtful book, *College Sports and Educational Values: The Game of Life* (Princeton University Press, 2002), James L. Shulman and William G. Bowen assert that "[d]evising ways of regulating recruitment of athletes . . . depends on detailed knowledge of differences in the circumstances and needs of individual schools within [a given league or conference], the predilections of various presidents and boards of trustees, the requirements associated with managing specific sports, and the implications of broader NCAA developments." *Id.* at 288. Are they correct? Calls for regulatory reform within intercollegiate athletics regularly appear in the media. If those calls are not grounded in a sense of the historical development of the regulatory rubric governing intercollegiate athletics, are they likely to be successful? How can history be of assistance in litigation about athletics? See W. Burlette Carter, *Student-Athlete Welfare in a Restructured NCAA*, 2 Va. J. of Sports & L. 1, 9 (2000) (providing a detailed discussion of the history of the NCAA and the multiple concerns that led to its creation).

    Shulman and Bowen also raise the following question:

    > In embracing intercollegiate athletics, colleges and universities gambled on their ability to "control the beast"—to harness the energies and many good qualities of sports to their own purposes, rather than to be subverted by them. The open question is whether the gamble was a good one: whether colleges and universities can rise to the challenge of re-balancing objectives and strengthening what we regard as the purer values of athletic competition.

    Shulman at 277. In retrospect, do you think that the gamble of "embracing intercollegiate athletics" was a good one?

2. *Commercialization and Academic Values.* Many have argued that intercollegiate athletics have become too commercialized, and that such commercialization will continue to compromise educational values. Can highly commercialized athletics programs be consistent with academic values? If so, what kinds of regulation can best assure adherence to academic values? Is President Emmert being realistic when he asserts that the NCAA must reclaim academic values and focus on the welfare of student-athletes?

A persistent tension in intercollegiate athletics, particularly at the Division I level, involves whether student-athlete academic opportunities are compromised by the goal of maintaining athletes' academic eligibility so that they can play sports. In 2018, such concerns led the Ohio University Chapter of the American Association of University Professors (AAUP) to propose that student-athlete academic services be placed under the control of an institution's academic unit (e.g., provost), rather than the athletic department. Eric Kelderman, *Who Should Oversee Athletes' Academic Progress?*, Chron. Higher Educ., Jan. 28, 2018. The proposal's goal was stated as "prevent[ing] coaches or others from trying to pressure academic support-support staff and faculty members to bend the rules to keep athletes eligible to play." *Id.* At this time, approximately one quarter of the NCAA's 350 Division I institutions, including two-thirds of the 130 FBS universities, grant control of student-athlete academic services to an administrator outside of athletics. *Id.* As you review the following materials, consider whether academic control of student-athlete academic services adequately protects the academic well-being of student-athletes.

3. *Changing the Intercollegiate Model for Commercialized Intercollegiate Sports.* As you study developments in intercollegiate athletics, think about how the present model could be changed. As you do so, think about the legal (e.g., Title IX, antitrust), economic, and policy impediments that will influence any such change. Professor Josephine Potuto, who has served as chair of the NCAA Committee on Infractions, as the Faculty Athletic Representative (FAR) at the University of Nebraska, and as a member of the NCAA Management Committee, argues that "[t]he NCAA has three choices: 1. Do nothing. Hope the noise goes away. Bet that neither college athlete unions nor Congress will step in to fill the void. 2. Give up on the collegiate model, go pro, and pay college athletes. 3. Recalibrate the collegiate model to get closer to what colleges and campuses are all about while finding ways to enhance services and benefits to college athletes." Josephine Potuto, *Professors Need Not Apply,* Inside Higher Educ., May 19, 2014. It is generally conceded by those who work in this field that the NCAA is likely to take the third approach. Is that the right one? Are there other forces at work that directly or indirectly impact who controls intercollegiate athletics? See Will Jarvis, *Florida Universities Have Turned Athletics Departments into Quasi-Private Arms. What Does that Mean for Public Accountability?* Chron. Higher Educ., June 17, 2019 (discussing the consequences of university athletic departments becoming entities that are direct-support organizations).

4. *Governance Roles.* What is the proper role for presidents, athletics personnel, student-athletes, and faculty in the governance of intercollegiate athletics? Should Congress and the courts play a greater role in regulating intercollegiate athletics? See Arne Duncan & Carol Cartwright, *The NCAA Is Too Far Gone for Incremental Reform,* Chronicle Higher Educ., June 7, 2018 (arguing that scandals such as the recent one involving college basketball underscore

the need for a radical transformation of the NCAA's governance structure, including taking control from university presidents and vesting it in independent appointees).

C. DEFINING THE STUDENT-ATHLETE AND UNIVERSITY RELATIONSHIP

1. *Contractual and Related Aspects*

The express contractual relationship between a student-athlete and his or her institution arises out of the Statement of Financial Assistance, the National Letter of Intent, and policies and procedures governing student-athletes (e.g., team and athletic department rules). These documents largely define the nature of the obligations that student-athletes owe to their colleges or universities and the obligations these educational institutions owe to their student-athletes.

Student-athletes who obtain athletic scholarships sign a form document commonly referred to as a *Statement of Financial Assistance.* Pursuant to a Statement of Financial Assistance, a college agrees to extend financial aid to student-athletes, which may include tuition, fees, room, board, books, and other education-related expenses up to the cost of attendance. The purpose of the financial aid award is to assist and enable a student-athlete to pursue a program of study and to participate in the educational process of the institution. In exchange for the university's commitment, a student-athlete promises to attend a particular college and to participate in athletics. A student-athlete's right to continue to receive financial assistance is contingent on the athlete remaining academically eligible to participate in the institution's athletic program and participating in his or her sport. Student-athletes also promise to comply with the rules and regulations of their teams, institutions, respective athletic conferences (e.g., ACC), and their athletic governing association or body (e.g., NCAA). As discussed below, a student-athlete's right to continue to receive financial assistance is also contingent on the annual renewal of their institution's financial commitment, unless the student-athlete has negotiated a multi-year scholarship.

The other key document that defines the student-athlete and university relationship is the *National Letter of Intent* (NLI). By signing an NLI, a prospective student-athlete agrees for a period of one year to attend the institution named in the Letter of Intent (hereinafter referred to as "named institution"). Thereafter, other institutions must cease all recruiting contacts with the student-athlete. Conversely, the named institution may freely contact the student-athlete. The NLI is not effective unless the student-athlete has received a promise in writing from the named institution to provide financial aid for at least an entire academic year. If the student-athlete complies with NCAA financial aid eligibility requirements and is admitted to the named institution, the student-athlete is entitled to a scholarship for a minimum of one full academic year from the named institution. A student-athlete who fails to attend the named institution will be penalized by having to serve one academic year in residence and losing one year of athletic eligibility to compete in all sports at the new institution in which he or she enrolls.

Notwithstanding the documents that create the express terms of their contract, litigation has ensued over the scope of the respective obligations that arise out of the parties' relationship, which generally has revolved around efforts by student-athletes to broaden the scope of the obligations their institutions owe to them. Student-athletes argue that gaps in the contractual relationship, occasioned by the failure of the express contract documents to clearly and specifically state colleges' obligations to them, support the implication of terms into the agreement. It also has been asserted that the Letter of Intent component of this contractual relationship constitutes an adhesion contract.

The text of the NLI may be found at http://www.nationalletter.org/nliProvisions/index.html. The following excerpts represent the NLI's key provisions.

THE NATIONAL LETTER OF INTENT

* * *

1. Initial Enrollment in Four-Year Institution. This NLI applies only to prospective student-athletes who will be entering four-year institutions for the first time as full-time students. It is also permissible for 4-2-4 transfer student-athletes to sign the NLI provided a previous valid NLI does not apply. The terms of the previous NLI are satisfied if a student-athlete graduates from the two-year college.

2. Financial Aid Requirement. At the time I sign this NLI, I must receive a written offer of athletics financial aid for the entire academic year from the institution named in this document. The offer must list the terms, conditions and amount of the athletics aid award. . . . In order for this NLI to be valid, my parent/legal guardian and I must sign the NLI and I must also sign the offer of athletics aid . . . prior to submission to the institution named in this document, and any other stated conditions must also be met. If the conditions stated on the financial aid offer are not met, this NLI shall be declared null and void.

- **Professional Sports Contract.** If I sign a professional sports contract in the sport in which I signed the NLI, I remain bound by the NLI in all other sports, even if NCAA rules prohibit the institution named in this document from providing me with athletics financial aid for the sport in which I signed the NLI.

3. Provisions of Letter Satisfied

  a. One-Year Attendance Requirement. The terms of this NLI shall be satisfied if I attend the institution named in this document for one academic year (two semesters or three quarters) as a full-time student.

  b. Two-Year College Graduation. After signing this NLI while in high school and if I later attend a two-year college, the terms of this NLI will be satisfied if I graduate from the two-year college.

4. Basic Penalty. I understand that if I do not attend the institution named in this document for one full academic year and I enroll in another institution participating in the NLI program, I may not compete in intercollegiate athletics until I have completed one full academic year in residence at the latter institution. Further, I understand I shall be charged with the loss of one season of intercollegiate athletics competition in all sports. This is in addition to any seasons of competition used at any institution. . . .

7. Letter Becomes Null and Void. This NLI shall be declared null and void if any of the following occur:

a. Admissions Requirement. This NLI shall be declared null and void if the institution named in this document notifies me in writing that I have been denied admission or, by the opening day of classes in the fall . . . , has failed to provide me with written notice of admission, provided I have submitted a complete admission application. . . .

If I am eligible for admission, but the institution named in this document defers my admission to a subsequent term, the NLI will be declared null and void; however, this NLI remains binding if I defer my admission.

b. Eligibility Requirements. This NLI shall be declared null and void if, by the opening day of classes in the fall . . . , I have not met NCAA initial eligibility requirements; NCAA, conference or institution's requirements for athletics financial aid; or two-year college transfer requirements. . . .
(1) This NLI shall be rendered null and void if I become a nonqualifier per the NCAA Eligibility Center. This NLI remains valid if I am a partial qualifier per NCAA Division II rules unless I do not meet the institution's polices for receipt of athletics aid. . . .

c. One-Year Absence. This NLI shall be declared null and void if I have not attended any institution (two-year or four-year) for at least one academic year, provided my request for athletics financial aid for a subsequent fall term is denied by the signing institution. *Service in active duty with the U.S. armed forces or an official church mission for at least 12 months can use the One-Year Absence to null and void this NLI.* I may still apply this provision if I initially enrolled in an NLI member institution but have been absent for at least one academic year. . . .

d. Discontinued Sport. This NLI shall be null and void if the institution named in the document discontinues my sport.

e. Recruiting Rules Violation. If eligibility reinstatement by the NCAA student-athlete reinstatement staff is necessary due to NCAA and/or conference recruiting rules violations, the institution must notify me that I have an option to have the NLI declared null and void due to the rules violation. It is my decision to have the NLI remain valid or to have the NLI declared null and void, permitting me to be recruited and not be subject to NLI penalties.

8. Recruiting Ban After Signing. I understand all participating conferences and institutions are obligated to respect my signing and shall cease contact with me and family members after my signing this NLI which includes me and my family members not initiating contact with athletic staffs at other institutions. Any conract in excess of an exchange of a greeting is not permitted regardless of the conversation. The conversation does not have to result in recruiting discussion for a recruiting ban to occur. I shall notify any coach who contacts me that I have signed an NLI. Once I enroll in the institution named in this document, the NLI Recruiting Ban is no longer in effect and I shall be governed by applicable NCAA bylaws.

9. 7-Day Signing Deadline. If my parent/legal guardian and I do not sign this NLI and accompanying offer of athletics financial aid . . . within 7 days after the date of issuance . . . , it will be invalid. The 7-day signing deadline does not apply if the NLI is received on the last day of a signing period. In this case, the 7-day signing deadline only applies if there are 7 days remaining for the signing period. Additionally, the institution must file the NLI with its conference within 14 days of the date of the final signature; otherwise, the NLI is invalid.

10. Statute of Limitations. I am subject to the NLI penalty if I do not fulfill the agreement; however, if I do not attend an NLI member institution to fulfill the agreement or penalty and four years has elapsed since my signing date, the NLI is no longer binding. Therefore, this NLI is in full force and effect for a period of four years, commencing with the date I sign this NLI, if I do not attend an NLI member institution during the period of four years.

11. Coaching Changes. I understand I have signed this NLI with the institution and not for a particular sport or coach. If a coach leaves the institution or the sports program (e.g., not retained, resigns), I remain bound by the provisions of this NLI. I understand it is not uncommon for a coach to leave his or her coaching position.

12. Coaching Contact Prohibited at Time of Signing. A coach or an institutional representative may not hand deliver this NLI off the institution's campus or be present off campus at the time I sign the NLI per NCAA rules. This NLI may be delivered by express mail, courier service, regular mail, email or facsimile. An NLI submitted to an institution electronically is permissible.

NOTES AND QUESTIONS

1. *National Letter of Intent Program.* The National Letter of Intent Program, which began in 1964 with seven conferences and eight independent institutions as its members, now includes "657 Division I and II participating institutions." National Letter of Intent, *About the National Letter of Intent (NLI)*, http://www .nationalletter.org/aboutTheNli/index.html. For a detailed discussion of the contractual relationship between student-athletes and their institutions, and of the National Letter of Intent, see Michael Cozzillio, *The Athletic Scholarship and the College National Letter of Intent: A Contract by Any Other Name*, 35 Wayne L. Rev. 1275 (1989). See also Stacey Meyer, *Unequal Bargaining Power: Making the National Letter of Intent More Equitable*, 15 Marq. Sports L. Rev. 227 (2004) (proposing changes to the National Letter of Intent Program in order to equalize the balance of power in the recruiting process).

2. *Conduct of Coaches.* The propriety of conduct engaged in by coaches during the recruiting process (e.g., revocation of scholarship offers and over-signing) has been subject to increased scrutiny. For helpful discussions of the legal and ethical dimensions of such conduct, see Alfred C. Yen, *Early Scholarship Offers and the NCAA*, 52 Boston Col. L. Rev. 585 (2011) (addressing the revocation of scholarship offers); Jonathan D. Bateman, *When the Numbers Don't Add Up: Oversigning in College Football*, 22 Marq. Sports L. Rev. 7 (2011) (discussing over-signing).

PROBLEM 3-1

Consider the following questions regarding the NLI:

a.   What conditions must be met before the NLI effectively commits a student-athlete to a particular institution?

b. A college coach provides a prospective student-athlete with extra benefits totaling $110.00, in violation of NCAA regulations. Will the coach's conduct invalidate the NLI? What factors must be considered?

c. A student-athlete is recruited to participate in a college's intercollegiate wrestling program. After the athlete signs an NLI, but before he arrives on campus, the wrestling program is discontinued. Does the discontinuance of the program affect the enforceability of the NLI?

d. You are a student-athlete whose decision to sign an NLI with a college is influenced by your desire to play for a certain coach. After you sign an NLI, and before you arrive on campus, the coach leaves to work at another college. Can you follow the coach to the new institution? What are the consequences of your doing so?

As the following cases illustrate, despite legal theories such as the implied duty of good faith when exercising discretion in connection with the performance of a contract, the judiciary has been reluctant to impose obligations on institutions different from or in addition to those expressly delineated in the contract documents.

TAYLOR v. WAKE FOREST UNIVERSITY

191 S.E.2d 379 (N.C. App. 1972)

CAMPBELL, Judge.

[EDS. Gregg Taylor, a student-athlete at Wake Forest University, and his father alleged that the university wrongfully terminated the athlete's football scholarship after he refused to participate in football because of his poor academic performance. Taylor's grade point average for the first semester of his freshman year was 1.0 on a 4.0 scale. As a result of this poor academic showing, Taylor refused, and in fact was ineligible, to play football during the spring term of his freshman year. Taylor's second semester grade point average improved to 1.9, which restored his academic eligibility to participate (at that time, Wake Forest required a 1.35 grade point average after freshman year). He refused, however, to play football during his sophomore year. Following a hearing before the university's Faculty Athletic Committee, Wake Forest terminated Taylor's scholarship after his sophomore year because of his failure to participate in the football program. Taylor, who ultimately received a degree from Wake Forest, sought to recover expenses that he incurred in completing his junior and senior years at the university.]

Plaintiffs contend that there was a genuine issue as to a material fact and that a jury should determine whether Gregg Taylor acted reasonably and in good faith in refusing to participate in the football program at Wake Forest when such participation interfered with reasonable academic progress.

The plaintiffs' position depends upon a construction of the contractual agreement between plaintiffs and Wake Forest. As stated in the affidavit of George J. Taylor, the position of the plaintiffs is that it was orally agreed between plaintiffs and the representative of Wake Forest that: "[I]n the event of any conflict between educational achievement and athletic involvement, participation in athletic activities could be limited or eliminated to the extent necessary to assure reasonable academic progress." And plaintiffs were to be the judge as to what "reasonable academic progress" constituted.

We do not agree with the position taken by plaintiffs. The scholarship application filed by Gregg Taylor provided: "I agree to maintain eligibility for intercollegiate athletics under both Conference and Institutional rules. Training rules for intercollegiate athletics are considered rules of the Institution, and I agree to abide by them."

Both Gregg Taylor and his father knew that the application was for "Football Grant-In-Aid or A Scholarship," and that the scholarship was "awarded for academic and athletic achievement." It would be a strained construction of the contract that would enable the plaintiffs to determine the "reasonable academic progress" of Gregg Taylor. Gregg Taylor, in consideration of the scholarship award, agreed to maintain his athletic eligibility and this meant both physically and scholastically. As long as his grade average equaled or exceeded the requirements of Wake Forest, he was maintaining his scholastic eligibility for athletics. Participation in and attendance at practice were required to maintain his physical eligibility. When he refused to do so in the absence of any injury or excuse other than to devote more time to studies, he was not complying with his contractual obligations.

The record disclosed that Wake Forest fully complied with its agreement and that Gregg Taylor failed to do so. There was no "genuine issue as to any material fact" and summary judgment was proper.

In determining the terms of the athletic scholarship between a university and its student-athletes, it is important to consider current NCAA rules governing this contractual relationship.

NCAA BYLAW, ARTICLE 15

FINANCIAL AID

15.3   TERMS AND CONDITIONS OF AWARDING INSTITUTIONAL FINANCIAL AID

15.3.3   Period of Institutional Financial Aid Award

15.3.3.1   **Period of Award.** If a student's athletics ability is considered in any degree in awarding financial aid, such aid shall neither be awarded for a period less than one academic year nor for a period that would exceed the student-athletes five-year period of eligibility. . . .

15.3.3.1.1   **One-Year Period.** An institution may award athletically related financial aid to a student athlete for a period of less than one academic year only under the following circumstances [Eds. The Manual lists six circumstances including when a student enrolls mid-year and when a student is in his or her final semester.]

[EDS. The following provisions of Bylaw 15.3.5 are mandatory for Autonomy Conference schools and discretionary for all other conference schools. Similar but not identical bylaws apply to nonautonomy institutions that have opted not to adopt the following bylaws.]

15.3.5 Reduction, Cancellation or Nonrenewal of Institutional Financial Aid.

15.3.5.1 Reduction, Cancellation or Nonrenewal Permitted. Institutional financial aid based in any degree on athletics ability may be reduced or canceled during the period of the award or reduced or not renewed for the following academic year or years of the student-athletes' five-year period of eligibility if the recipient:

(a) Renders himself or herself ineligible for intercollegiate competition;

(b) Fraudulently misrepresents any information on an application, letter of intent or financial aid agreement (see Bylaw 15.3.5.1.2);

(c) Engages in serious misconduct warranting substantial disciplinary penalty as determined by the institution's regular student disciplinary authority; (d) Voluntarily (on his or her own initiative) withdraws from a sport at any time for personal reasons; however, the recipient's financial aid may not be awarded to another student-athlete in the academic term in which the aid was reduced or canceled. A student-athlete's request for written permission to contact another four-year collegiate institution regarding a possible transfer does not constitute a voluntary withdrawal;

(e) Violates a nonathletically related condition outlined in the financial aid agreement or violates a documented institutional rule of policy (e.g., academic policies or standards, athletics department or team rules or policies); or

(f) Provides written notification of transfer (see Bylaw 13.1.1.3) to the institution; however, the student-athlete's financial aid may not be reduced or canceled until the end of the regular academic term in which written notification of transfer is received. If a student-athlete provides written notification of transfer to the institution between regular academic terms (winter break, summer break) the institution may reduce or cancel the financial aid immediately.

15.3.5.1.1 Timing of Reduction or Cancellation. Any reduction or cancellation of aid during the period of the award may occur only after the student-athlete has been provided an opportunity for a hearing per Bylaw 15.3.2.3 (other than as permitted in Bylaws 15.5.6.4.1 and 15.5.6.4.2).

* * *

15.3.5.2 Reduction or Cancellation Not Permitted—During the Period of the Award. Institutional financial aid based in any degree on athletics ability may not be reduced or canceled during the period of its award:

(a) On the basis of a student-athlete's athletics ability, performance or contribution to a team's success;

(b) Because of an injury, illness, or physical or mental medical condition (except as permitted pursuant to Bylaw 15.3.5.1); or

(c) For any other athletics reason.

15.3.5.2.1 Athletically Related Condition Prohibition. An institution may not set forth an athletically related condition (e.g., financial aid contingent upon specified performance or playing a specific position) that would permit the institution to reduce or cancel the student-athlete's financial aid during the period of the award if the conditions are not satisfied.

15.3.5.2.2 Decrease Not Permitted. An institution may not decrease a prospective student-athlete's or a student-athlete's financial aid from the time the prospective student-athlete or student-athlete signs the financial aid award letter until the conclusion of the period set forth in the financial aid agreement, except under the conditions set forth in Bylaw 15.3.5.1.

15.3.5.3 Reduction of Cancellation Not Permitted—After the Period of the Award. If a student-athlete receives athletically related financial aid in the academic year of his or her initial full-time enrollment at the certifying institution, the following factors shall not be considered in the reduction or nonrenewal of such aid for the following year or years of the student's five-year period of eligibility:

(a) A student-athlete's athletics ability, performance or contribution to a team's success (e.g., financial aid contingent upon specified performance or playing a specific position);

(b) An injury, illness, or physical or mental medical condition (except as permitted pursuant to Bylaw 15.3.4.2); or

(c) For any other athletics reason.

15.3.6 Increase Permitted. Institutional financial aid may be increased for any reason at any time.

15.3.7 Renewals and Nonrenewals

15.3.7.1 Institutional Obligation. The renewal of institutional financial aid based in any degree on athletics ability shall be made on or before July 1 prior to the academic year in which it is to be effective. The institution shall promptly notify in writing each student-athlete who received an award the previous academic year and who has eligibility remaining in the sport in which financial aid was awarded the previous academic year (under Bylaw 12.8) whether the grant has been renewed or not renewed for the ensuing academic year or multiple academic years within the student-athlete's five-year period of eligibility. Notification of financial aid renewals and nonrenewals must come from the institution's regular financial aid authority and not from the institution's athletics department.

15.3.7.2 Reconsideration of Nonrenewal. It is permissible for an institution that has notified a student-athlete that he or she will not be provided institutional financial aid for the next academic year subsequently to award financial aid to that student-athlete.

The 2018-19 NCAA Division I Manual can be accessed at: http://www .ncaapublications.com/p-4547-2018-2019-ncaa-division-i-manual-august-version-available-august-2018.aspx.

NOTES AND QUESTIONS

1. *Duration of Scholarship.* What is the minimum duration of a student-athlete's contract with his or her college or university? Pursuant to legislation the NCAA adopted in 1973, its rules restricted institutions to awarding to student-athletes one-year renewable athletic scholarships. Effective August 2012, however, NCAA-amended legislation permits institutions to award multiyear scholarships of up to five years. 2018-2019 NCAA Division I Manual §15.02.7. See Ray Yasser, *The Case for Reviving the Four-Year Deal,* 86 Tul. L. Rev. 987 (2012) (arguing for awarding multiyear scholarships to student-athletes); Louis Hakim, Note, *The Student-Athlete vs. the Athlete Student: Has the Time Arrived for an Extended-Term Scholarship Contract?,* 2 Va. J. Sports & L. 145 (2000) (arguing the same).

2. *Limiting Discretion in Renewing Scholarships.* What limitations, if any, are imposed on the discretion afforded institutions to refuse to renew a student-athlete's scholarship? Are these limitations sufficient? Does the discretion afforded institutions encourage particular forms of conduct by coaches? See *Milo v. University of Vermont*, 2013 WL 4647782 (D. Vt., Aug. 29, 2013) (recognizing the contractual nature of the student-athlete and university relationship, the court rejects various theories asserted by an athlete (e.g., duty of good faith and deprivation of due process) in upholding a coach's discretion not to renew the athlete's one-year scholarship).

3. *Incorporation by Reference.* It is important to note that NCAA and university athletic conference rules are incorporated as terms of a student-athlete's financial aid agreement with a university. For example, a student-athlete must comply with the NCAA's drug testing program and its amateurism rules (which, among other things, prohibit the receipt of any "extra benefits" from university employees or representatives of its athletics interests (NCAA Bylaw 16.02.3), or any "preferential treatment" because of one's athletics reputation or skill (NCAA Bylaw 12.1.2.1.6)). Student-athletes who violate NCAA (or conference) rules risk losing their eligibility to participate in intercollegiate athletes and athletic scholarships.

   With the advent of multi-year scholarships, coaches have tried to retain a modicum of discretion allowing them to reduce, cancel, or refuse to renew a scholarship. One such discretion-enhancing mechanism is expanding the list of team and institutional rules with which a student-athlete must comply. Reasons for canceling or not renewing a scholarship include: excessive violations of university parking regulations, failure to report a teammate's dangerous or harmful conduct (e.g., extreme risk taking, alcohol abuse, and abusive relationships) to athletics department personnel, not representing the university in a positive manner at all times, and failure to adhere to the university honor code.

Comment: Expanding Student-Athlete Benefits

Through autonomy legislation the Power Five Conferences have adopted initiatives that enhance student-athlete benefits. At the NCAA's January 2015 Convention, universities that are members of the ACC, SEC, Pac 12, Big Ten and Big-12 adopted legislation that expands the contractual benefits available to student-athletes. The following NCAA rules changes took effect beginning in August 2015.

True-Cost-of-Attendance. The centerpiece of this legislation is the redefinition of permissible financial aid. Previously, a student-athlete could receive athletically-related financial aid limited to tuition and fees, room and board, and required course-related books. An athletic scholarship is now redefined to encompass not only tuition, room, board, books, and fees, but also the incidental costs of attending college, such as transportation and miscellaneous personal expenses. The legislation provides in part: "A student-athlete may receive institutional financial aid based on athletics ability . . . and any other financial aid up to the value of his or her cost of attendance." 2018–19 NCAA DIVISION I MANUAL Article 15.1 (2018). The cost of attendance legislation is mandatory for autonomy schools but permissive for non-autonomy schools. Due to competitive pressures, certain non-autonomy schools have announced that they will also offer full-cost financial aid. These include non-autonomy schools within Conference USA, as well as the Mountain West and Mid-American Conferences. The cost of awarding the full cost of attendance has been estimated as increasing the annual costs to colleges from $500,000 to $2 million per institution. Jon Solomon, *Cost of Attendance Results: The Chase to Pay Players*, https://www.cbssports.com/college-football/news/cost-of-attendance-results-the-chase-to-pay-college-players/.

Multi-Year Scholarships. NCAA legislation permits (but does not require) its member institutions to award scholarships of more than a year. 2018-19 NCAA Division I Manual §15.02.8. Because of the legislation's permissive nature, institutions have the discretion to award scholarships from one year to up to four or five years. Three of the five autonomy conferences have adopted conference legislation pursuant to which their institutions will offer multi-year scholarships. The Big-Ten led the way when it announced in October 2014 that its institutions would offer multi-year scholarships in all sports. The Big-Ten policy also permits its institutions, consistent with NCAA financial aid rules, to award athletic aid to a student-athlete who returns to the school to complete his/her degree if his/her education was interrupted for a legitimate reason. 2018-19 NCAA Manual § 15.01.5.2. Thereafter, the Pac-12 and Big-12 adopted policies to award multi-year scholarships in all sports. The Pac-12 also followed the Big Ten in adopting a policy permitting a student-athlete to return to the institution and receive athletics aid under certain circumstances. Pac-12 Conference, *Pac-12 Universities Adopt Sweeping Reforms for Student-Athletes, Guaranteeing Scholarships, Improving Health Care and More*, https://pac-12.com/article/2014/10/27/pac-12-universities-adopt-sweeping-reforms-student-athletes-guaranteeing. As it relates to athletic scholarships, the Big 12 has adopted conference legislation that is substantively the same as that of the Pac-12 and Big Ten.

Consistent with these policies, autonomy schools adopted legislation at the NCAA's 2015 Convention seeking to protect the integrity of multi-year scholarships. In short, the 2015 NCAA legislation prevents colleges and universities from reducing a student-athlete's multi-year scholarship for athletic reasons, injury, or illness. 2018-19 NCAA Manual §15.3.4.3.

Loss-of-Value Insurance. The autonomy schools adopted legislation that permits a student-athlete to "borrow against future earnings to purchase so-called-loss of value insurance—policies that can help athletes if an injury while playing college sports results in an athlete getting less money from a professional contract." The legislation provides in part as follows:

> Exception for Insurance Against Disabling Injury or Illness, **or Loss of Value**. An individual may borrow against his or her future earnings potential from an established, accredited commercial lending institution exclusively for the purpose of purchasing insurance (with no cash surrender value) against a disabling injury or illness that would prevent the individual from pursuing a chosen career **or for the purpose of purchasing loss-of-value insurance**, provided a third party (including a representative of an institution's athletics interests) is not involved in arrangements for securing the loan. . . .

Id. at 12.1.2.4.4.

Insurance policies issued to student-athletes have spawned litigation. On March 9, 2018, former University of Arkansas defensive lineman, Deatrich Wise, Jr., sued Lloyd's of London and other insurers alleging they improperly denied his claim. Wise contends that a covered injury resulted in his slipping from a projected first-round draft pick to a fourth-round pick and the defendants failed to pay the corresponding salary differential pursuant to the terms of his loss-in-value policy. The case is pending. Another former University of Arkansas football player sued Lloyd's and other insurers on a disability policy that covered loss of future earnings. In his 2018 lawsuit, former running back Rawleigh Williams III alleged that defendants wrongfully denied his claim under a $1 million disability policy. See *Frost v. North American Capacity Ins. Co.*, 2018 WL 2210439 (M.D. Ala. April 20, 2018) (refusing to dismiss, on jurisdictional grounds, lawsuit by a former college football player seeking to collect on injury insurance policy). The parties settled in August of 2019.

Easing of Transfer Restrictions: In June 2018, the NCAA changed its Division I transfer rules effective October 2018. Under pre-June 2018 bylaws, student-athletes had to obtain the permission of their coaches before contacting other schools to discuss the possibility of transferring. Similarly, institutions wishing to recruit student-athletes interested in transferring had to seek the permission of athletes' schools. Under the new rule, student-athletes will be permitted to initiate the transfer process and seek a scholarship at a different school by notifying their coaches of their desire to transfer. Within two business days of such notification, coaches must enter the athletes' names in an NCAA-managed database identifying athletes who may be recruited by another college or university. Other schools may thereafter recruit the athletes. Notwithstanding the new rule, athletic conferences are permitted to impose more restrictive transfer policies for intra-conference transfers. 2018-19 NCAA Manual, art. 13.1.1.3.1.

Subsequent to the adoption of the new transfer policy, the five autonomy conferences adopted what has been characterized as "companion legislation" that permits an institution to cancel a student-athlete's scholarship at the end of a term upon a student-athlete's notification of an intention to transfer. See Christopher J. Gerace, Note, *The NCAA's Transfer Conundrum*, 94 Notre Dame L. Rev. 1819 (2019) (providing an overview of NCAA transfer legislation).

Revised Red-Shirt Policy: The NCAA has revised its medical red-shirt policy to allow Division I football players to participate in up to four games in a season without losing the ability to be red-shirted. Thus, a football player who suffers an early season injury will not have used a full season of competition and will not be required to seek a medical waiver from the NCAA.

Other Legislation and Resolutions. The autonomy schools also adopted legislation and a resolution relating to the following:

a. Concussion Protocol: Key elements of legislation that strengthens concussion management protocols include: Requiring colleges and universities to have a concussion management plan for their student-athletes that include the following elements: educating student-athletes regarding concussion symptoms; requiring the removal from athletic activity and evaluation of student-athletes who exhibit concussion symptoms; and incorporating policies precluding athletes diagnosed with a concussion from returning to athletic activity for at least the remainder of that calendar day, and requiring that a concussed athlete receive medical clearance by a physician before the athlete can return.

b. Playoff Expenses: In 2015, the NCAA granted a waiver that permitted the College Football Playoff to cover travel expenses to facilitate players' family members to attend the national championship game between The Ohio State University and the University of Oregon. The waiver permitted the College Football Playoff to reimburse families up to $3,000 per athlete for travel, hotel, and meals expenses for a maximum of two parents or legal guardians. Expenses were capped at $1,500 per parent or guardian. Marc Tracy, *NCAA to Allow Family Travel Aid for Top Title Games,* N.Y. Times (Jan. 6, 2015). The NCAA also established a pilot program that will allow it to cover the expenses of the families of players who participate in the men's and women's basketball Final Four games. The NCAA also established a pilot program that allows it to cover up to $3,000 in expenses for travel, hotel, and meals for family members of each player who advances to the Final Four and up to $4,000 for families of each player who advances to the title game. *Id.* In 2019, the NCAA codified the pilot program, making the playoff expense payment permanent. Michelle B. Hosick, *Council adopts Final Four family travel proposal,* Chronicle Higher Educ., Jan. 23, 2019.

c.   Increased Aid: In 2016, the NCAA Board of Governors approved a one-time supplemental distribution of $200 million to Division I schools. Institutions that received the funds in spring 2017 were required to use the money for programs beneficial to student-athletes. Permissible means of using the funds included: "creation of endowments that directly support students, to launch financial literacy and mental health programs, or to expand academic advising and tutoring resources." Other examples included: "funding for scholarships up to the full cost of attendance, four-year guaranteed scholarships and unlimited meals and snacks for athletes. . . ." Brian Hendrickson, *Board of Governors approves $200 million distribution to DI members: Funds earmarked for programs that benefit student-athletes,* http://www.ncaa.org/about/resources/media-center/news/board-governors-approves-200-million-distribution-di-members.

ROSS v. CREIGHTON UNIVERSITY

957 F.2d 410 (7th Cir. 1992)

RIPPLE, Circuit Judge.

Kevin Ross filed suit against Creighton University (Creighton or the University) for negligence and breach of contract arising from Creighton's alleged failure to educate him. The district court dismissed Mr. Ross' complaint for failure to state a claim. For the following reasons we affirm in part and reverse in part the judgment of the district court.

I.   BACKGROUND

A.   FACTS

In the spring of 1978, Mr. Ross was a promising senior basketball player at Wyandotte High School in Kansas City, Kansas. Sometime during his senior year in high school, he accepted an athletic scholarship to attend Creighton and to play on its varsity basketball team.

Creighton is an academically superior university. Mr. Ross comes from an academically disadvantaged background. At the time of his enrollment at Creighton, Mr. Ross was at an academic level far below that of the average Creighton student. For example, he scored in the bottom fifth percentile of college-bound seniors taking the American College Test, while the average freshman admitted to Creighton with him scored in the upper twenty-seven percent. According to the complaint, Creighton realized Mr. Ross' academic limitations when it admitted him, and, to induce him to attend and play basketball, Creighton assured Mr. Ross that he would receive sufficient tutoring so that he "would receive a meaningful education while at CREIGHTON." . . .

Mr. Ross attended Creighton from 1978 until 1982. During that time, he maintained a D average and acquired 96 of the 128 credits needed to graduate. However, many of these credits were in courses such as Marksmanship and Theory of Basketball, and did not count towards a university degree. Mr. Ross alleges that he took these courses on the advice of Creighton's Athletic Department, and that the department also employed a secretary to read his assignments and prepare and type his papers. Mr. Ross also asserts that Creighton failed to provide him with sufficient and competent tutoring that it had promised.

When he left Creighton, Mr. Ross had the overall language skills of a fourth grader and the reading skills of a seventh grader. Consequently, Mr. Ross enrolled, at Creighton's expense, for a year of remedial education at the Westside Preparatory School in Chicago. At Westside, Mr. Ross attended classes with grade school children. He later entered Roosevelt University in Chicago, but was forced to withdraw because of a lack of funds. In July 1987, Mr. Ross suffered what he terms a "major depressive episode," during which he barricaded himself in a Chicago motel room and threw furniture out the window. . . . To Mr. Ross, this furniture "symbolized" Creighton employees who had wronged him. . . .

B. DISTRICT COURT PROCEEDINGS

Creighton moved to dismiss the complaint under Federal Rule of Civil Procedure 12(b)(6), and the district court granted this motion. . . .

II. ANALYSIS

B. THE NEGLIGENCE CLAIMS

Mr. Ross advances three separate theories of how Creighton was negligent towards him: educational malpractice for not educating him, a new tort of "negligent admission" to an educational institution, and negligent infliction of emotional distress. We believe that, on the facts of this case, Illinois law would deny Mr. Ross recovery on all three theories.

1. Educational Malpractice

Illinois courts have never ruled on whether a tort cause of action exists against an institution for educational malpractice. However, the overwhelming majority of states that have considered this type of claim have rejected it. (citation omitted.) Only Montana allows these claims to go forward, and its decision was based on state statutes that place a duty of care on educators, a circumstance not present here. *B.M. v. State,* 200 Mont. 58, 649 P.2d 425, 427-28 (Mont. 1982).

Courts have identified several policy concerns that counsel against allowing claims for educational malpractice. First, there is the lack of a satisfactory standard of care by which to evaluate an educator. . . . Theories of education are not uniform, and "different but acceptable scientific methods of academic training [make] it unfeasible to formulate a standard by which to judge the conduct of those delivering the services." *Swidryk v. St. Michael's Medical Center*, 201 N.J. Super. 601, 493 A.2d 641, 643 (N.J. Super. Ct. Law Div. 1985) (citing *Peter W. v. San Francisco Unified School Dist.*, 60 Cal. App. 3d 814, 131 Cal. Rptr. 854, 859 (Ct. App. 1976)). Second, inherent uncertainties exist in this type of case about the cause and nature of damages. . . . "Factors such as the student's attitude, motivation, temperament, past experience and home environment may all play an essential and immeasurable role in learning." *Donohue v. Copiague Union Free School Dist.*, 47 N.Y.2d 440, 418 N.Y.S.2d 375, 391 N.E.2d 1352, 1355 (N.Y. 1979) (Wachtler, J., concurring). Consequently, it may be a "practical impossibility [to] prov[e] that the alleged malpractice of the teacher proximately caused the learning deficiency of the plaintiff student." *Id.* A third reason for denying this cause of action is the potential it presents for a flood of litigation against schools. . . . As the district court noted, "education is a service rendered on an immensely greater scale than other professional services." *Ross v. Creighton Univ.*, 740 F. Supp. 1319, 1329 (N.D. Ill. 1990). The sheer number of claims that could arise if this cause of action were allowed might overburden schools. *Id.* This consideration also suggests that a common-law tort remedy may not be the best way to deal with the problem of inadequate education. *Id.* A final reason courts have cited for denying this cause of action is that it threatens to embroil the courts into overseeing the day-to-day operations of schools. . . . This oversight might be particularly troubling in the university setting where it necessarily implicates considerations of academic freedom and autonomy. . . .

We believe that the Illinois Supreme Court would find the experience of other jurisdictions persuasive and, consequently, that these policy considerations are compelling. Consequently, the Illinois Supreme Court would refuse to recognize the tort of educational malpractice. We therefore affirm the district court's dismissal of Mr. Ross' claim based on that theory.

2.   "Negligent Admission"

In his complaint, Mr. Ross alleges that Creighton owed him a duty "to recruit and enroll only those students reasonably qualified and able to academically perform at CREIGHTON." . . . He then contends that Creighton breached this duty by admitting him, not informing him of how unprepared he was for studies there, and then not providing tutoring services or otherwise enabling him to receive a meaningful education. As a result, Mr. Ross underwent undue stress, which brought about, among other things, the incident at the motel.

We believe that Illinois would reject this claim for "negligent admission" for many of the same policy reasons that counsel against recognizing a claim for educational malpractice. First, this cause of action would present difficult, if not insuperable, problems to a court attempting to define a workable duty of care. . . . Mr. Ross suggests that the University has a duty to admit only students who are "reasonably qualified" and able to perform academically. However, determining who is a "reasonably qualified student" necessarily requires subjective assessments of such things as the nature and quality of the defendant institution and the intelligence and educability of the plaintiff. Such decisions are not open to ready determination in the judicial process. Second, such a cause of action might unduly interfere with a university's admissions decisions, to the detriment of students and society as a whole. *Ross*, 740 F. Supp. at 1330. As the district court noted, if universities and colleges faced tort liability for admitting an unprepared student, schools would be encouraged to admit only those students who were certain to succeed in the institution. The opportunities of marginal students to receive an education therefore would likely be lessened. *Id.* Also, the academic practice of promoting diversity by admitting students from disadvantaged backgrounds might also be jeopardized. . . .

C.   THE CONTRACT CLAIMS

In counts two and three of his complaint, Mr. Ross alleges that Creighton breached an oral or a written contract that it had with him. When read as a totality, these allegations fairly allege that Creighton agreed, in exchange for Mr. Ross' promise to play on its basketball team, to allow him an opportunity to participate, in a meaningful way, in the academic program of the University despite his deficient academic background. The complaint further alleges, when read as a totality, that Creighton breached this contract and denied Mr. Ross any real opportunity to participate in and benefit from the University's academic program when it failed to perform five commitments made to Ross: (1) "to provide adequate and competent tutoring services," (2) "to require [Mr. Ross] to attend tutoring sessions," (3) to afford Mr. Ross "a reasonable opportunity to take full advantage of tutoring services," (4) to allow Mr. Ross to red-shirt, and (5) to provide funds to allow Mr. Ross to complete his college education. . . .

It is held generally in the United States that the "basic legal relation between a student and a private university or college is contractual in nature. The catalogues, bulletins, circulars, and regulations of the institution made available to the matriculant become a part of the contract." *Zumbrun v. University of Southern California*, 25 Cal. App. 3d 1, 101 Cal. Rptr. 499, 504 (Ct. App. 1972) (collecting cases from numerous states). Indeed, there seems to be "no dissent" from this proposition. *Wickstrom v. North Idaho College*, 111 Idaho 450, 452, 725 P.2d 155, 157 (Idaho 1986) (quoting *Peretti v. Montana*, 464 F. Supp. 784, 786 (D. Mont. 1979), *rev'd on other grounds*, 661 F.2d 756 (9th Cir. 1981)). As the district court correctly noted, Illinois recognizes that the relationship between a student and an educational institution is, in some of its aspects, contractual. *See Steinberg v. Chicago Medical School*, 69 Ill. 2d 320, 13 Ill. Dec. 699, 371 N.E.2d 634 (Ill. 1977) (agreement that medical school application would be evaluated according to the criteria described by the medical school in its literature). . . . It is quite clear, however, that Illinois would not recognize all aspects of a university-student relationship as subject to remedy through a contract action. *DeMarco* makes the point quite clearly. "A contract between a private institution and a student confers duties upon both parties which cannot be arbitrarily disregarded and may be judicially enforced." *DeMarco*, 352 N.E.2d at 361-62. However, "a decision of the school authorities relating to the academic qualification of the students will not be reviewed. . . . Courts are not qualified to pass an opinion as to the attainments of a student . . . and . . . courts will not review a decision of the school authorities relating to academic qualifications of the students." *Id.*

There is no question, we believe, that Illinois would adhere to the great weight of authority and bar any attempt to repackage an educational malpractice claim as a contract claim. As several courts have noted, the policy concerns that preclude a cause of action for educational malpractice apply with equal force to bar a breach of contract claim attacking the general quality of an education. . . .

To state a claim for breach of contract, the plaintiff must do more than simply allege that the education was not good enough. Instead, he must point to an identifiable contractual promise that the defendant failed to honor. Thus, as was suggested in *Paladino*, if the defendant took tuition money and then provided no education, or alternately, promised a set number of hours of instruction and then failed to deliver, a breach of contract action may be available. *Paladino*, 454 N.Y.S.2d at 873; *see also Zumbrun*, 25 Cal. App. 3d 1, 101 Cal. Rptr. 499 (breach of contract action allowed against university when professor declined to give lectures and final exam, and all students received a grade of "B"). Similarly, a breach of contract action might exist if a student enrolled in a course explicitly promising instruction that would qualify him as a journeyman, but in which the fundamentals necessary to attain that skill were not even presented. *See Wickstrom*, 725 P.2d at 156-58. In these cases, the essence of the plaintiff's complaint would not be that the institution failed to perform adequately a promised educational service, but rather that it failed to perform that service at all. Ruling on this issue would not require an inquiry into the nuances of educational processes and theories, but rather an objective assessment of whether the institution made a good faith effort to perform on its promise.

We read Mr. Ross' complaint to allege more than a failure of the University to provide him with an education of a certain quality. Rather, he alleges that the University knew that he was not qualified academically to participate in its curriculum. Nevertheless, it made a specific promise that he would be able to participate in a meaningful way in that program because it would provide certain specific services to him. Finally, he alleges that the University breached its promise by reneging on its commitment to provide those services and, consequently, effectively cutting him off from any participation in and benefit from the University's academic program. To adjudicate such a claim, the court would not be required to determine whether Creighton had breached its contract with Mr. Ross by providing deficient academic services. Rather, its inquiry would be limited to whether the University had provided any real access to its academic curriculum at all.

Accordingly, we must disagree respectfully with our colleague in the district court as to whether the contract counts of the complaint can be dismissed at the pleadings stage. In our view, the allegations of the complaint are sufficient to warrant further proceedings. We emphasize, however, the narrow ground of our disagreement. We agree—indeed we emphasize—that courts should not "take on the job of supervising the relationship between colleges and student-athletes or creating in effect a new relationship between them." *Ross*, 740 F. Supp. at 1332. We also recognize a formal university-student contract is rarely employed and, consequently, "the general nature and terms of the agreement are usually implied, with specific terms to be found in the university bulletin and other publications; custom and usages can also become specific terms by implication." *Wickstrom*, 725 P.2d at 157 (quoting *Peretti*, 464 F. Supp. at 786). Nevertheless, we believe that the district court can adjudicate Mr. Ross' specific and narrow claim that he was barred from *any* participation in and benefit from the University's academic program without second-guessing the professional judgment of the University faculty on academic matters. . . .

Accordingly, the judgment of the district court is affirmed in part and reversed and remanded in part for proceedings consistent with this opinion.

AFFIRMED in part, REVERSED in part and REMANDED.

[EDS. Ross eventually settled his lawsuit for $30,000.]

PROBLEM 3-2

Rogers, a high school student-athlete, and his parents were considering athletic scholarship offers from several major universities for Rogers to play intercollegiate basketball when they arrived at Big-Time University for an official recruiting visit. Big-Time's head men's basketball coach, Blum, gave Rogers and his parents a tour of the Big-Time campus during their visit. As Blum drove them by Big-Time's law school, Rogers stated, "I want to be a lawyer." In response, Blum stated, "I can get you into Big-Time's law school; I can also make certain that your law school tuition is paid for." Blum's statements sold Rogers on attending Big-Time. At the beginning of his senior year, Rogers applied to Big-Time's law school as well as others. Rogers requested that Blum deliver on his promise to get him into Big-Time's highly competitive law school. Blum informed Rogers that there was nothing he could do. Does Rogers have any cause of action against Blum?

NOTES AND QUESTIONS

1. *Analysis of* Ross. In rejecting Ross's educational malpractice claim, the district and appellate courts relied on the reasoning adopted in cases in which courts have uniformly rejected such suits by non-athlete students against colleges and universities. See, e.g., *Vurimindi v. Fuqua Sch. of Bus.*, 435 Fed. Appx. 129, 133 (3d Cir. 2011) (refusing to recognize contract claims based on general complaints regarding the quality of the education a student received). But see Hazel G. Beh, *Student Versus University: The University's Implied Obligations of Good Faith and Fair Dealing*, 59 Md. L. Rev. 183, 184 (2000) (arguing that all students, under limited circumstances, should be able to sue their institutions for educational malpractice).

   Was the *Ross* court's reliance on such cases justified? Is the student-athlete's relationship with his or her university distinguishable from the non-athlete student's relationship with his or her university? Commentators disagree as to whether student-athletes should be able to sue their institutions for educational malpractice, based on the unique character of their relationships with colleges and universities. Harold B. Hilborn, *Student Athletes and Judicial Inconsistency: Establishing a Duty to Educate as a Means of Fostering Meaningful Reform of Intercollegiate Athletics*, 89 Nw. U. L. Rev. 741 (1995); Timothy Davis, *Examining Educational Malpractice Jurisprudence: Should a Cause of Action Be Created for Student-Athletes?*, 69 Denv. U. L. Rev. 57 (1992).

   Some authors argue that an imbalance exists in the student-athlete/university relationship that results in an unfair advantage to the institutions. Do you agree? See Rodney K. Smith & Neil Millhiser, *The BCS and Big-Time Intercollegiate Football Receive an "F": Reforming A Failed System*, 2 Wake Forest J.L. & Pol'y 45 (2012); Amy C. McCormick & Robert A. McCormick, *Race and Interest Convergence in NCAA Sports*, 2 Wake Forest J.L. & Pol'y 17 (2012); Michael J. Riella, Notes, *Leveling the Playing Field: Applying the Doctrine of Unconscionability and Condition Precedent to Effectuate Student-Athlete Intent Under the National Letter of Intent*, 43 Wm. & Mary L. Rev. 2181 (2002); Rodney K. Smith & Robert D. Walker, *From Inequity to Opportunity: Keeping the Promises Made to Big-Time Intercollegiate Student Athletes*, 1 Nev. L.J. 160 (2001).

For a comprehensive economic analysis of the student-athlete/university relationship, see Ahmed E. Taha, *Are College Athletes Economically Exploited?*, 2 Wake Forest J.L. & Pol'y 69 (2012).

2. *Student-Athlete Stipends.* The issue of whether student-athletes should be paid stipends often arises in discussions of whether equity resides in the relationship. Is allowing such a payment sound public policy? What problems might flow from instituting such a policy? For differing perspectives on whether student-athletes should receive cash payments for their services, see Jeffrey Standen, *The Next Labor Market in College Sports*, 92 Or. L. Rev. 1093 (2104); Mary Grace Miller, *The NCAA and the Student Athlete: Reform Is on the Horizon*, 46 U. Rich. L. Rev. 1141 (2012); Taylor Branch, *The Shame of College Sports*, Atlantic Magazine, (Oct. 2011); Barbara Osborne, *The Myth of the Exploited Student-Athlete*, J. Intercollegiate Sport, 7(2), 143-152 (2014).

3. *Disclosure Laws.* Student-athletes and their parents are often unaware of the terms and conditions of athletes' contracts with their schools. For example, many athletes and their parents incorrectly assume that scholarships are guaranteed for a four-year period as long as the athlete remains academically and athletically eligible. On September 30, 2010, former Governor Schwarzenegger signed into law the California Student-Athletes' Right to Know Act that requires university coaches who recruit athletes in California to disclose institutional and NCAA policies regarding payment of student-athlete medical expenses, scholarship renewals, and transfers to other institutions. The goal of this act is to provide increased disclosure to student-athletes to help them make wise choices. West's Ann. Cal. Educ. Code §67365 (West, Westlaw through Ch. 22 of 2012 Reg. Sess.). Connecticut has adopted similar legislation. Conn. Gen. Stat. Ann. §10a-55k (West, Westlaw through Public Acts approved on or before May 14, 2012).

Is the adoption of disclosure laws by individual states wise public policy? Is a national law with uniform requirements needed?

4. *Express Promises to Provide Academic Support.* Although the court rejected Ross's breach-of-contract claim, to the extent that it merely restated a tort claim for educational malpractice, what did the court recognize as the narrow exception to the general rule of no institutional liability for a student-athlete's substandard or failing academic performance? Related to this exception, what factual issue was to be determined on remand? See Timothy Davis, *Absence of Good Faith: Defining a University's Educational Obligation to Student-Athletes*, 28 Hous. L. Rev. 743, 783 (1991) (questioning judicial reliance on the academic abstention doctrine in the university/student-athlete context).

5. *Implied Contract Terms.* Another leading case, *Jackson v. Drake University*, 778 F. Supp. 1490 (S.D. Iowa 1991), reveals the reluctance of courts to imply terms into the agreement as a means of expanding the obligations that a university owes to student-athletes. In *Jackson*, a basketball player alleged that the coaching staff of the men's basketball team engaged in improper conduct, such as failing to provide adequate tutoring and counseling and requiring him to turn in plagiarized work, which undermined the athlete's ability to play basketball and to succeed academically. According to Jackson, the coaching staff's conduct amounted to a breach of contract because "the express contract between him and Drake implicitly granted him the right to an educational opportunity and the right to play basketball for a Division I school." *Id.* at 1493. The court held that "the financial aid agreements do

not implicitly contain a right to play basketball." *Id.* The court also refused to impose an implied obligation on Drake to provide Jackson with an educational opportunity. Do athletes have a reasonable expectation that, as long as they follow team rules and remain academically eligible, they will be allowed to participate on the intercollegiate athletic team for which they were recruited? Does judicial reticence to imply terms into the contractual relationship as a means of policing the relationship perpetuate an imbalance in the student-athlete/university relationship? What conceptualization of contract law is reflected by judicial refusal to imply terms into the student-athlete/university relationship?

In a case arising out of the University of North Carolina at Chapel Hill's academic scandal, the court ruled that the NCAA assumed neither a duty of reasonable care to safeguard student-athletes' educational opportunity nor a fiduciary duty to protect student-athletes' access to educational opportunities. *McCants v. NCAA*, 201 F.Supp.3d 732 (M.D. N.C. 2016).

6. *Discontinuation of Sports.* Student-athletes also have been unsuccessful in their attempts to imply into their agreement limitations on an institution's discretion to discontinue a particular sport. See e.g., *Equity in Athletics, Inc. v. Dep't of Educ.*, 675 F. Supp. 2d 660 (W.D. Va. 2009) (the discontinuance of seven men's sports and three women's sports in an effort to bring an athletic program into compliance with Title IX did not impinge on the substantive and procedural due process rights of the student-athletes). The question presented in these cases implicates the broader topic of whether student-athletes possess a property interest in participating in intercollegiate athletics, which is discussed *infra.*

7. *Oral Promises.* In *Fortay v. University of Miami*, 1994 WL 62319 (D. N.J. Feb. 17, 1994), a student-athlete maintained that his contract with the University of Miami (UM) impliedly obligated the university to provide the guidance necessary to allow him to develop his football talents. He asserted that oral promises by then-outgoing head coach Jimmy Johnson, his successor coach, and other UM officials supported a breach of contract claim. These promises allegedly included representations that UM would provide guidance that would enable Fortay to develop his football skills, that UM would not recruit other quarterbacks, and that Fortay would be UM's starting quarterback by his third year. Adhering to precedent from other jurisdictions, a federal district court ruled that the Letter of Intent and other contract documents did not give rise to the alleged implied obligations. Accord *Lesser v. Neosho Cty. Cmty. Coll.*, 741 F. Supp. 854, 865 (D. Kan. 1990) (refusing to imply the promise that plaintiff would have a position on a baseball team). The district court ruled, however, that Fortay alleged facts sufficient to support a breach of an oral contract claim. The district court also refused to dismiss Fortay's negligent hiring and supervision claims stemming from the conduct of a Miami athletic official that pertained to Fortay and other athletes' involvement in a Pell Grant scandal.

What impediments may confront a student-athlete who seeks to recover for breach of an oral promise? In *Searles v. Trustees of St. Joseph's College*, 695 A.2d 1206 (Me. 1997), a student-athlete allegedly suffered permanent injuries while playing basketball for his college. Searles sought to recover, among other things, reimbursement for medical expenses. He alleged that St. Joseph's orally agreed to pay his medical bills if he continued to play on the school's basketball team. In granting defendant summary judgment on this contract claim, the court concluded: "In order to be legally operative and to create a power of acceptance, it is necessary that the offer shall contain all the terms of the contract to be made. It is not enough for one party to promise to do something." *Id.* at 1211. See also *Eppley v. Univ. of Del.*, 2015 WL 156754 (D. Del. Jan. 12, 2015) (in dismissing plaintiff's negligent misrepresentation claim against the university, the court held that, assuming a coach promised a student-athlete an athletic scholarship for four years, the athlete's reliance was unjustified given the terms of the grant in aid and the National Letter of Intent, and the athlete's awareness that at the time the promise was made, multi-year scholarships were prohibited; the court also held that there was no fiduciary relationship between a student-athlete and coach); *Giuliani v. Duke Univ.*, 2010 WL 1292321 (M.D.N.C. Mar. 30, 2010) (holding that neither a coach's oral statements nor the provisions of the university's policy manuals were enforceable as binding contracts).

8. *Promissory Estoppel.* In *Hall v. NCAA*, 985 F. Supp. 782 (N.D. Ill. 1997), the court did not reject the viability of promissory estoppel in the student-athlete/university context. It rejected plaintiff's claim, however, based on his failure to offer evidence sufficient to establish the elements of promissory estoppel, which the court stated consists of (1) an unambiguous promise, (2) a reliance on that promise by the promisee (3) of a type that was expected and foreseeable to the promisor, and (4) on which the promisee actually relied to his or her detriment. *Id.* at 796. See *Williams v. University of Cincinnati*, 752 N.E. 2d 367, 377 (Ohio Misc. 2001) (without rejecting promissory estoppel as a viable theory, the court ruled that evidence established that an athlete was ineligible "because of his own failures, not because of any . . . unfulfilled promises"). See also Jamie U. Nomura, *Refereeing the Recruiting Game: Applying Contract Law to Make the Inter-Collegiate Recruiting Process Fair*, 32 U. Haw. L. Rev. 275 (2009) (arguing in favor of promissory estoppel as a basis for enforcing oral promises made by coaches to prospective student-athletes).

9. *Alleged Characterizations of the University/Student-Athlete Relationship.*
   a. *Fiduciary Relationship.* Is the student-athlete relationship with his or her institution imbued with the characteristics of a fiduciary relationship? Illustrations of fiduciary relationships that arise as a matter of law include those between a husband and wife and a minister and parishioner. An example of such a relationship that is the product of express agreement is the principal/agent relationship. The key characteristics of a fiduciary relationship are trust, confidence, and dominance by one party over the other. Thus, a "fiduciary relation arises where 'one person reposes trust or confidence or reliance in another' and where 'there is established an inequality of footing between the parties.' In these situations, courts feel justified in holding the more powerful party to a higher standard of care." Alvin L. Goldman, *The University and the Liberty of Its Students—a Fiduciary Theory*, 54 Ky. L.J. 643, 667 (1966). Are such features present in the student-athlete/university relationship? See Richard Salgado, *A Fiduciary Duty to Teach Those Who Don't Want to Learn: The Potentially Dangerous Oxymoron of "College Sports,"* 17 Seton Hall J. Sports & Ent. L. 135 (2007) (arguing that under certain limited circumstances a fiduciary relationship exists between student-athletes and their institutions).

Hendricks v. Clemson University, 578 S.E.2d 711 (S.C. 2003), arose out of an academic advisor's erroneous advice regarding course selection that contributed to a student-athlete's ineligibility to play baseball. Hendricks sued Clemson University alleging, *inter alia*, breach of fiduciary duty; the South Carolina Tort Claims Act shielded Clemson, a public university, from negligence liability. Noting that historically the imposition of fiduciary duties has been reserved for legal or business settings in which one entrusts money to another, the South Carolina Supreme Court refused to recognize the relationship between a student and a university academic advisor as fiduciary in nature. See also *Knelman v. Middlebury Coll.*, 898 F.Supp.2d 697 (D. Vt. 2012) (concluding that it is highly unlikely the Vermont Supreme Court would recognize a fiduciary relationship between a student-athlete and university).

b. *Respondeat Superior.* Courts have also addressed the question of whether student-athletes' relationships with their institution can give rise to, on the basis of respondeat superior, institutional liability for acts committed by student-athletes. In *Hanson v. Kynast*, 494 N.E.2d 1091 (Ohio 1986), a lacrosse player for Ohio State University sustained serious injuries after he was thrown to the ground by Kynast, a player on Ashland University's lacrosse team. In a lawsuit against Kynast and Ashland, Hanson turned to respondeat superior as a basis for holding Ashland responsible for Kynast's conduct. In rejecting this theory, the court articulated the rule that a master and servant or a principal and agent relationship exists only where one party exercises control of the other whose actions are directed toward attaining an objective sought by the master or principal. It found that a student is a buyer of educational services that he or she retains for his or her own benefit and is therefore not an agent of the institution. On the question of control, the court concluded:

> [A] student who attends a university of his choice, receives no scholarship or compensation, voluntarily becomes a member of the university lacrosse team that engages in intercollegiate contests with other universities for which games no attendance fee is charged, who purchases his own equipment and who receives instructions from a coach while preparing for and playing such games, but is not otherwise controlled by the coach, and who participates in the games as a part of his total educational experience while attending school, is not an agent of the university at the time he is playing the game of lacrosse.

Id. at 1096. Does this rationale apply to student-athletes who have an athletic scholarship?

c. *Special Relationship.* In addition to tort claims asserting educational malpractice, student-athletes have argued that their "special relationship" with colleges justifies the imposition of a legal duty to protect them from foreseeable, unreasonable risks of physical harm on the playing field, an issue discussed more fully in Chapter 11. See *McFadyen v. Duke University*, 786 F. Supp. 2d 887 (M.D. N.C. 2011) (in a suit by three lacrosse players accused and later exonerated of charges of sexual assault and rape, the players alleged actions taken by Duke University violated the relationship of trust and confidence the university had with them; the court held that the university owed no fiduciary duty to the players, and even though a special relationship existed between the university and the players as student-athletes, the duty of care owed to the players was limited to the context of athletics and did not extend to all facets of student life).

2.   *NCAA Academic Reform Legislation*

a.   Academic Reform—Generally

How likely is it that a Kevin Ross-type scenario would occur today? NCAA rules seek, in part, to reduce the likelihood that a student-athlete will leave college after three or four years with the learning deficiencies of a Kevin Ross. These rules include "initial eligibility standards" and "satisfactory progress rules." With respect to the latter, NCAA rules require that, as a condition to eligibility for participation, student-athletes take a curriculum that allows them to make progress toward obtaining a degree. In 2002, the NCAA heightened these requirements. The changes in "satisfactory progress rules" were a part of Division I academic reforms enacted by the NCAA between 2002 and 2004. Another component of the NCAA's reform efforts were the significant revisions made to its initial eligibility rules; NCAA-revised eligibility rules deemphasize standardized test scores (i.e., the SAT and ACT), place greater emphasis on high school grades, and increase the number of core course requirements. (Initial eligibility requirements are also discussed in Chapter 9, *infra.*) The NCAA adopted another component of its academic reform legislation with its 2004 approval of the Academic Progress Rate (APR), which is an "incentive/disincentive program" and is discussed *infra.*

Some academics and college administrators lauded the revisions as likely to achieve their goal of improving graduation rates. Others, however, warned that the revised rules may have a negative impact on academic achievement. Some are concerned that more athletes will be steered toward "jock majors"—fields of study that allow student-athletes to "maneuver through the maze of academic requirements and remain eligible to compete." Welch Suggs, *Jock Majors,* Chron. Higher Educ. A33 (Jan. 17, 2003). As expressed by one commentator, "[T]he march toward tougher standards and, the NCAA hopes, higher graduation rates begs a crucial question, however: What do numbers matter if players are being sent into academic programs that won't give them a meaningful education or marketable skills?" *Id.* at A34. The clustering of players in particular majors is not a new phenomenon. Whether the revised standards will contribute to this practice is uncertain at this time. For a recent examination of majors by football players see Stripling, *Inside Auburn's Secret Effort to Advance an Athlete-Friendly Curriculum,* Chron. Higher Educ., Feb 16, 2018; David Biderman, *Why Football Players Don't Speak Spanish,* http://online.wsj.com/article/SB100014240527487 03743504575493773613076844.html.

In 2012, the NCAA again adopted heightened Division I initial eligibility standards that became effective August 1, 2016. Substantial changes were made to the core course requirements such as when core courses must be completed at the required GPA in those courses. The modifications also articulate the academic requirements for academic redshirts. For a detailed discussion of these requirements see NCAA, 2018-19 NCAA Division I Manual Article 14 (2018); NCAA, *2016 NCAA Division I Initial-Eligibility Academic Requirements*, http://www .ncaa.org/sites/default/files/High_School_IE_Standards.pdf (2016).

b.   Academic Reform — Academic Progress Rate

As noted above, in 2004, the NCAA adopted legislation that instituted a metric known as the Academic Progress Rate (APR). It was designed to give a real-time "snapshot" into the academic progress of individual teams at member institutions. In commenting on this reform, then-NCAA president Myles Brand, stated, "For the first time, the NCAA will have the ability to hold institutions and teams accountable for the academic progress of their student athletes." Welch Suggs, *NCAA Weighs New Penalties for Academic Laggards*, Chron. Higher Educ., April 23, 2004, A42 (discussing NCAA's incentives/disincentives program).

To calculate an institution's APR, the NCAA examines each scholarship-receiving student-athlete on an intercollegiate team at a member institution and determines whether the player has remained academically eligible to participate in intercollegiate athletics and whether the student has chosen to remain enrolled at the school. Teams are awarded one point for meeting each of these standards during a given semester, resulting in each athlete earning the school a possible maximum of two points per semester and four points per year if the institution uses a two-semester calendar; alternatively, schools that use a quarter system can be awarded a maximum of eight total points per athlete. After determining each athlete's individual score, each team gets a final APR score; 1,000 is the maximum APR a team can earn. The NCAA initially established 925 as the minimum score an institution should achieve to avoid being immediately (or contemporaneously) penalized. Initially, the failure of a team to reach a 925 benchmark exposed colleges to the assessment of penalties including scholarship and recruiting restrictions and a team's loss of eligibility for postseason competition. For additional discussion of how the Academic Progress Rate works, see Michelle B. Hosick, *Academic Success Stories Transcend Improved APRs*, NCAA News, June 9, 2010; Michelle B. Hosick, *Division I Beginning Major APR Assessment*, NCAA News, June 9, 2010.

In 2011, the NCAA Board of Directors enacted enhanced academic performance measures. One change, which took effect in 2012-2013, increased the APR benchmark to 930 (which corresponds to a 50 percent graduation rate). The potential impact of the changes to the APR penalty structure were realized in dramatic fashion when the NCAA declared that because of a low four-year APR, the University of Connecticut men's basketball team, which in 2011 was the NCAA national champion, would be ineligible to participate in postseason play during the 2012-2013 season. Connecticut appealed the NCAA's penalty arguing that its men's basketball team's APR for 2010-2011 and the first semester of 2011 were perfect. Its appeal was rejected.

Overall APR numbers released over the past several years indicate positive trends. NCAA officials attribute improved student-athlete academic performance, as measured by the APR, to several policy adjustments, including: (1) more stringent progress-toward-degree requirements; (2) a rule allowing student-athletes who fit a certain academic profile to transfer; (3) increased core course requirements for incoming student-athletes; and (4) a requirement that transfer student-athletes earn an eligibility point in order to receive financial aid at the school to which they are transferring.

Apart from the improved academic performance of student-athletes, the success of the APR program can be measured by the way in which it and other academic measures are becoming part of the fabric of Division I institutions. For example, the NCAA created a head coach APR portfolio, a database that was first made public in 2010 and provided details of the APRs earned by teams associated with a head coach. Some institutions are also incorporating APR clauses into coaching contracts, which give monetary incentives and disincentives for coaches who achieve or fail to achieve APR benchmarks.

Since their inception, APRs have generally been on an upward trajectory. The overall four-year APR for the 2017-18 academic year (which measures the metric for students enrolled in school between the 2014-15 and 2017-18 academic years) was 983. This represents the highest ever recorded APR and compares to a 979 APR reported for the 2014-15 academic year. For 2017-18, the four-year rates for football and men's basketball were 964 and 967, respectively. At 982, women's basketball maintained its previous high APR. Other notable APRs include those for limited resource schools, which realized an overall increase from 945 for 2010-11 to 969 for 2017-18. Historically black colleges and universities (HBCUs) realized a 960 APR in 2017-18, which compares to a 918 APR reported by HBCUs for the 2010-11 academic year. In 2019-20, eight schools will be ineligible for postseason competition as a result of their low APRs, which is a decrease from seventeen teams ineligible in 2017-18. Michelle B. Hosick, *Low Academic Rates Cause Lost Postseason, Penalties* (May 8, 2019), https://www.ncaa.org/about/resources/media-center/news/low-academic-rates-cause-lost-postseason-penalties. During 2019, the NCAA's Committee on Academics conducted a holistic review of the APR metric that examined which student-athletes to include in the rate and how best to account for transfers and assign penalties. Michelle B. Hosick, *Division I College Athletes Match Record-High Academic Performance*, May 8, 2019, https://www.ncaa.org/about/resources/media-center/news/division-i-college-athletes-match-record-high-academic-performance.

Student-athlete progress-toward-degree requirements from the 2018-2019 NCAA Division I Manual are as follows.

NCAA BYLAW, ARTICLE 14

Eligibility: Academic and General Requirements
  14.4 Progress-Toward-Degree Requirements
    14.4.1 Progress-Toward-Degree Requirements. To be eligible to represent an institution in intercollegiate athletics competition, a student-athlete shall maintain progress toward a baccalaureate or equivalent degree at that institution as determined by the regulations of that institution subject to controlling legislation of the conference(s) or similar association of which the institution is a member and applicable NCAA legislation.
    14.4.2 Eligibility for Financial Aid and Practice. Eligibility for institutional financial aid and practice during each academic year after a student-athlete's initial year in residence or after the student-athlete has used one season of eligibility in a sport shall be based upon the rules of the institution and the conference(s), if any, of which the institution is a member.

14.4.3 Eligibility for Competition

14.4.3.1 Fulfillment of Credit-Hour Requirements. Eligibility for competition shall be determined based upon satisfactory completion of at least:

(a) Twenty-four semester or 36 quarter hours of academic credit prior to start of the student-athlete's second year of collegiate enrollment (third semester, fourth quarter);

(b) Eighteen semester or 27 quarter hours of academic credit since the beginning of the previous fall term or since the beginning of the certifying institution's preceding regular two semesters or three quarters (hours earned during the summer may not be used to fulfill this requirement) (See Bylaw 14.4.3.1.4); and

(c) Six semester or six quarter hours of academic credit during the preceding regular academic term (e.g., fall semester, winter quarter) in which the student-athlete has been enrolled full time at any collegiate institution. . . .

14.4.3.2 Fulfillment of Percentage of Degree Requirements. A student-athlete who is entering his or her third year of collegiate enrollment shall have completed successfully at least 40 percent of the course requirements in the student's specific degree program. A student-athlete who is entering his or her fourth year of collegiate enrollment shall have completed successfully at least 60 percent of the course requirements in the student's specific degree program. A student-athlete who is entering his or her fifth year of collegiate enrollment shall have completed successfully at least 80 percent of the course requirements in the student's specific degree program. The course requirements must be in the student's specific degree program (as opposed to the student's major).

PROBLEM 3-3

Skip Baxter, the starting center for his high school basketball team and consensus All-American, was recruited by more than 100 colleges and universities. Over the course of his senior year, Baxter received numerous letters from University of Denton (UD) personnel touting UD's: (1) elite basketball program and its penchant for developing National Basketball Association (NBA) quality players; (2) academic requirements for scholarship athletes; (3) fitness and training facilities; and (4) academic and vocational resources. Baxter visited UD to meet the staff and see the school. Shortly thereafter, he made a verbal commitment to attend UD, which the UD basketball staff acknowledged by letter and e-mail.

Prior to making the verbal commitment, Baxter received visits at his home in North Carolina. On one occasion, Baxter was visited by the head coach, assistant coach, and athletic trainer. During the group visit, head coach David Lyons told Baxter that if he made a verbal commitment to attend UD, Lyons would discontinue efforts to recruit another center in Baxter's class. Lyons, who had a reputation for developing college basketball players, particularly centers who left college to play in the NBA, also told Baxter that he and his coaching staff would do everything possible to develop Baxter's basketball skills. Lyons stated: "You will start as center during your freshman year. We will build the team around you. We will also provide you with the resources to enable you to remain academically eligible and earn a degree in four or five years." Lyons also told Baxter, "Under no circumstances will I accept a head coaching position at any other institution during the four years that you play for UD. If a player makes a commitment to me, I make one to the player. I love it here and plan to remain for years to come."

Baxter and his mother signed a National Letter of Intent for him to attend UD and UD's Statement of Financial Assistance. Two weeks later, Coach Lyons signed an agreement with a highly regarded NBA team. Shortly thereafter, UD appointed a new basketball coach, Richard Douglas, who contacted Baxter and assured him that the commitments, goals, and play system used by the Lyons regime would not be changed. Around the same time, however, Baxter learned via the Internet and other media that another highly regarded center, John Williams, had signed a Letter of Intent with UD. Lyons had recruited Williams.

During fall practice, Baxter competed with Williams for the starting center position. In contrast to Williams, virtually no attention was directed toward developing Baxter's basketball skills during fall practice (or thereafter). Nevertheless, Baxter outperformed Williams during fall practice and the first two games of the season (the only games in which Baxter played; he started in neither game). Notwithstanding Baxter's performance, Douglas decided that Williams would be his center because he possessed a better attitude than Baxter. When questioned by the local media about what some viewed as an irrational decision, Coach Douglas stated that he and Baxter had a few personality clashes and that Williams possessed a better attitude. When questioned by one reporter at a press conference, Douglas said, "I didn't recruit Baxter, I don't like his entitlement attitude, and I don't have to play him. I'm the coach of this team, not Baxter. He'll be lucky if I offer him a scholarship next year."

To make matters worse, Baxter did not perform well academically. Coach Douglas and his basketball staff limited the time Baxter could meet with academic tutors to two hours per week. This is substantially less time than is afforded other players on the team.

Baxter and his mother are extremely unhappy with developments at UD and have come to you for advice as to what options, including litigation, are available to Baxter. What would you advise? In responding, identify any additional facts that would assist you in your analysis of Baxter's options.

3.   *Federal Constitutional Rights Issues*

This section considers the federal constitutional rights of an intercollegiate athlete that must be respected and not infringed by a public university, which constitutes a "state actor." The Fourteenth Amendment of the United States Constitution requires that a public university must not deprive a student-athlete of life, liberty, or property without providing procedural (i.e., adequate notice of conduct that is prohibited and requires a fair hearing) and substantive (i.e., privacy rights, liberty interest in not being subjected to arbitrary or capricious procedures) due process. The following materials consider whether student-athletes at public universities have a property right or liberty interest in playing intercollegiate athletics. It considers their First Amendment rights of free speech and religious liberty. Athletes' equal protection rights also are briefly considered.

PROBLEM 3-4

You serve as legal counsel to a state legislative committee whose chairperson wants you to draft legislation recognizing a property right in participation in intercollegiate athletics at the state's public universities. The legislator is irate because her daughter was not permitted to try out for the football team at the public university she attends. Her daughter believes that she could earn an athletic scholarship if given the opportunity to demonstrate her ability as a kicker and would increase her future job opportunities by playing college football. When the legislator and her daughter asked the football coach why she was not permitted to try out, the coach simply said he thought it was best that she not be permitted without providing any specific reasons. When the legislator discussed the matter with a well-known sports lawyer, she said it was unlikely that a court would require the university to justify why her daughter was not permitted to try out for the football team because she does not have a property right that would trigger federal due process protection. Considering the following case, was the lawyer's advice correct? What advice would you give to the legislator regarding the pros and cons of a state law expressly creating a property right to participate in intercollegiate athletics at the state's public universities?

PROBLEM 3-5

You are general counsel at a Division I university. Your faculty athletics representative (FAR), who also serves as chairman of your institution's faculty athletics committee (FAC), which is given authority to hear scholarship termination cases, has asked you for advice regarding the creation of guidelines or standards for that process. At present, the FAC has broad discretion to hear such cases, and there are no institutional rules or guidelines governing the process. In responding to the FAR's request, consider the benefits and difficulties associated with discretion and with written guidelines. You should also consider whether the FAC should maintain written records of their deliberations and decisions.

HYSAW v. WASHBURN UNIVERSITY OF TOPEKA

690 F. Supp. 940 (D. Kan. 1987)

SAFFELS, Judge.

This civil rights and breach of contract case arises out of a dispute early in Washburn University's 1986 football season. Several black football players complained that they were being treated in a racially-discriminatory manner by the coaching staff and administration. The dispute culminated in those players boycotting team practices and the administration removing those players from the team. The players now claim defendants infringed upon their free speech, liberty and property rights in violation of 42 U.S.C. § 1983, violated 42 U.S.C. § 1981, and breached their contracts with Washburn University. Defendants ask for summary judgment on all of plaintiffs' claims.

The court has reviewed the uncontroverted facts submitted by defendants, plaintiffs' responses to them, and supporting documents and deposition

testimony, and has determined that for purposes of this motion, the uncontroverted facts are as follows:

1. Plaintiffs are all black Americans recruited to play football for Washburn
   University.
2. Defendant John L. Green is the president of defendant Washburn University.
3. Defendant Jerry Robertson is the Athletic Director at defendant
   Washburn University.
4. Defendant Larry Elliott is the head football coach at defendant
   Washburn University.
5. Each of the plaintiffs were awarded football scholarships for the 1986-
   87 school year. Plaintiffs Neil Chapman ("Chapman"), Vernon Hysaw
   ("Hysaw"), and Eugene Battle ("Battle") were told they would receive
   scholarships to cover tuition, fees, books, room and board. Plaintiff
   Randy Craven received a scholarship to cover tuition, fees and books; a
   federally-funded Pell Grant was to cover the cost of his room and board.
   Plaintiff Tony McDonald also was to receive a scholarship sufficient to
   cover tuition, fees and books, with a Pell Grant to pay for his room
   and board.
6. Before receiving their scholarships, each of the plaintiffs executed an
   agreement indicating that they accepted the financial aid awards. The
   written agreements did not promise that the plaintiffs would be allowed
   to play football for Washburn.
7. Early in the 1986 football season, several black football players on the
   Washburn team began expressing discontent with their scholarships.
   They complained that promises of full scholarships had not been carried
   out; many also felt that white players on the team were being favored by
   the coaching staff and that lesser white players had been awarded better
   scholarships than some of the black players.
8. On August 26, 1986, several of the black players, along with the president of the Washburn Black Student Alliance (B.S.A.), met with defendants Green and Robertson about their concerns. The following day,
   the players met with defendant Elliott and with financial aid officials.
9. After those meetings, the B.S.A. president composed a letter to defendant Green outlining the concerns of the black players.
10. The players again met with the B.S.A. president after football practice
    on August 27, 1986. At that meeting, they decided that they were not
    satisfied with the administration's response to their complaints. To pro-
    test the administration's response, the players agreed to boycott team
    practice.
11. The players prepared a letter containing a list of those players who would
    be boycotting; the letter indicated that the boycott was due to their dis-
    satisfaction with the administration's response to their complaints.
12. On August 28, 1986, the players did not attend team practice.
13. On August 29, 1986, defendant Robertson responded to the players'
    boycott; he outlined the administration's position on their complaints.
    He also indicated that "missing practice without an excuse from the
    coaching staff is a violation of disciplinary rules affecting all players
    and will be treated in the same manner as any player's unexcused
    absence."
14. The players voted on August 29, 1986, to continue their boycott of prac-
    tice and positional meetings.

15. Several additional meetings were held between the players and the administration. Some players were subsequently allowed to rejoin the team by meeting certain conditions set out by the administration.

16. On September 1, 1986, defendant Robertson met with the plaintiffs. Robertson told them that they would be allowed to retain their scholarships if they met the following conditions: 1) issue an apology through the news media to Washburn and its administration, 2) apologize to the football team at a team meeting, 3) participate in five early morning practices, 4) agree to be kept out of the first game that season, and 5) "exhibit total commitment and support to the Washburn University football program."

17. Plaintiffs refused to comply with the administration's requests.

18. Defendants then refused to allow plaintiffs to return to the team.

19. Defendants claim that the reasons plaintiffs were not allowed to return to the team were that they had missed practice and positional meetings and had failed to show leadership. Plaintiffs claim they were not allowed to return because they boycotted in protest of the alleged racial mistreatment of black football players at Washburn.

20. All plaintiffs received the financial aid allocations promised them for the 1986-87 school year.

I. VIOLATIONS OF 42 U.S.C. § 1981

Defendants argue summary judgment is in order on plaintiffs' section 1981 claims because plaintiffs had no contractual interest in playing football for Washburn University. The facts do establish that defendants complied with their obligations under the written contracts. Therefore, there can be no violation of section 1981 with regard to any claims plaintiffs have that they were denied scholarship monies awarded under the 1986-87 agreements or prevented from playing football as allegedly promised by their contracts. However, a review of the Pre-trial Order in this case indicates that plaintiffs' section 1981 claims go far beyond the issue of whether defendants breached the 1986-87 written scholarship agreements. They claim that throughout their playing careers at Washburn, white players with equal or less ability were given greater opportunities to make more beneficial scholarship contracts and were allowed greater opportunities to participate in the Washburn football program. If proven, these actions might constitute violations of 42 U.S.C. § 1981. While the court does not express any opinion concerning the merits of this claim, it is unable to grant summary judgment at the present time because defendants have not addressed plaintiffs' claim in full. . . .

II. VIOLATIONS OF 42 U.S.C. § 1983

Plaintiffs claim defendants infringed on their property, liberty, and free speech rights in violation of 42 U.S.C. § 1983. The court will grant partial summary judgment in favor of defendants.

A. PROPERTY RIGHTS

Plaintiffs first argue that defendants violated their property rights without affording them due process. They argue they held a property interest in contractual rights to play football for Washburn, and argue that by breaching their scholarship contracts the defendants have deprived them of a property right without due process.

Our analysis begins with *Board of Regents v. Roth*, 408 U.S. 564, 33 L. Ed. 2d 548, 92 S. Ct. 2701 (1972). In *Roth*, the United States Supreme Court set out the standard for determining whether an alleged deprivation of a property right violated due process. We must determine whether plaintiffs possessed a property right protected under the Constitution. Property rights "are created and their dimensions are defined by existing rules or understandings that stem from an independent source such as state law." *Roth*, 408 U.S. at 577. Only after a protectable property interest has been established do we then determine whether due process was afforded.

Plaintiffs claim defendants deprived them of their contractual rights under the scholarship agreements to play football for Washburn University. However, plaintiffs have only established a property right in the scholarship funds. No deprivation of those funds took place. Plaintiffs had no other protectable property interest. "To have a property interest in a benefit, a person clearly must have more than an abstract need or desire for it. He must have more than a unilateral expectation of it. He must, instead, have a legitimate claim of entitlement to it." *Roth*, 408 U.S. at 577. Plaintiffs concede that the only source for their alleged property interest is their scholarship agreements. The court has determined that the only interests created by those agreements are interests in receiving scholarship funds. Any other terms plaintiffs attempt to read into those agreements are, without supporting evidence, no more than "unilateral expectations." The court will therefore grant defendants' summary judgment motion on this claim.

B.   LIBERTY INTERESTS

Plaintiffs Battle and Chapman next argue that defendants infringed upon their liberty interests in pursuing a college football career. This claim arises out of those plaintiffs' efforts to be recruited by the nearby Emporia State University football team after they were dismissed from the Washburn team. The additional uncontroverted facts for purposes of this portion of the motion are as follows. . . .

4. After they were dismissed from the Washburn team, plaintiffs Battle and Chapman sought recruitment by the Emporia State University football team.
5. The head coach at Emporia spoke with defendant Elliott about the two plaintiffs.
6. Defendant Elliott commented to the Emporia coach about the plaintiffs' failure to attend practice and positional meetings. He allegedly told the coach the plaintiffs were lazy and were troublemakers.
7. Based on this information, the Emporia coach did not recruit Battle and Chapman.

Again, the court must start its analysis with *Board of Regents v. Roth*. A due process claim is made out only if the liberty interest allegedly violated is protectable under the Constitution. Again we look to an independent source of law to determine whether plaintiffs held a legitimate interest in the right to pursue a college football career. Only if this right is a protected liberty right under state law have plaintiffs made out a Section 1983 violation.

The plaintiffs concede that no right to pursue a college football career exists under well-established Tenth Circuit law. *See, e.g., Colorado Seminary (Univ. of Denver) v. NCAA*, 570 F.2d 320, 321 (10th Cir. 1978) (interest of student athlete in participating in intercollegiate sports did not rise to level of constitutionally protected right invoking due process); *see also Justice v. NCAA*, 577 F. Supp. 356, 366 (D. Ariz. 1983) (participation in intercollegiate athletics is not a constitutionally protected interest). Furthermore, the court rejects plaintiffs' contention that the rule of *Paul v. Davis*, 424 U.S. 693, 47 L.Ed.2d 405, 96 S. Ct. 1155 (1976), commands a denial of summary judgment here. The Court in *Paul* held that damage to an individual's reputation by a state official is not enough to establish a due process violation. Something more must be shown; a tangible interest must be established. *Paul*, 424 U.S. at 709-10.

The court finds no tangible interest here. *Roth* held that defamatory comments made by a government employer which cast a cloud over an employee's future employment prospects could constitute a deprivation of liberty. Plaintiffs now ask this court to extend the holding in *Roth* to the present situation; in effect, they are asking the court to equate government employment with a football scholarship. The court is unwilling to take such a giant leap. While no constitutional right to a government job exists, the Supreme Court has noted that qualification for a government job is a "privileg[e] of first-class citizenship." *Anti-Fascist Committee v. McGrath*, 341 U.S. 123, 183, 95 L. Ed. 817, 71 S. Ct. 624 (1950) (J. Douglas, concurring). Plaintiffs have offered no reason why a right to pursue a collegiate athletic career should be afforded the same status, and the court likewise sees no reason to do so.

If plaintiffs have made out any claim here, it is one for defamation under Kansas law. The rule in *Paul* dictates that every violation of state tort law does not rise to a violation of section 1983 when committed by a state official. Even claims of defamation are not enough, standing alone, to invoke the protections of section 1983. Plaintiffs have shown nothing in addition to their defamation charges which would justify invoking section 1983, and defendants' motion on this issue will be granted. . . .

C.   FREE SPEECH INTERESTS

Plaintiffs next claim that defendants violated their first amendment right to free speech by removing them from the team after they protested racial mistreatment. Defendants first argue summary judgment is appropriate because the players were removed from the team simply for missing practices and a positional meeting. They allege the discharge had nothing to do with the players' protest, and they point to the team policy that unexcused absences from team practices or positional meetings may result in disciplinary action, including dismissal from the team.

However, plaintiffs point out that in defendant Elliott's deposition, he admitted that if a player were to miss practice in protest of racial mistreatment, the absence would be excused. If this were the case, then plaintiffs' absences may have been excused, and defendants' reasons for dismissing the players would be inadequate. If the facts were to establish that the plaintiffs were disciplined for protesting racial mistreatment, defendants may have infringed upon plaintiffs' first amendment rights. Summary judgment would therefore be inappropriate. . . .

III.   BREACH OF CONTRACT

Plaintiffs finally claim that defendants breached their scholarship contracts. Defendants argue that summary judgment is in order, because the only promise made in those contracts was to pay plaintiffs their scholarship money, and this was done. No other promises were made.

The law in Kansas is well-established that when a written contract exists and its language is clear and unambiguous, the language controls. . . . Plaintiffs argue they were promised that they would be allowed to play football during the 1986-87 season. Yet the written scholarship contracts they signed make no indication of such promises. In fact, the only promises in those written contracts were that the players would receive money. Plaintiffs provide no other evidence, other than "understandings" and "expectations," that they were promised a position on the 1986 team.

We then turn to the written language of the scholarship agreement to ascertain whether defendants breached those terms. The court finds that defendants met all obligations under the contracts. They promised to pay Chapman, Hysaw and Battle "full" scholarships for the 1986-87 school year, and Craven and McDonald were to receive "partial" scholarships. Plaintiffs concede that they received all disbursements on time. Defendants, therefore, met all their obligations under the contracts.

The court rejects the assertion that defendants' threats on September 1, 1986, constituted a breach of their scholarship agreements. They argue that any disbursements made after September 3, 1986, when suit was filed, only constitute mitigation of damages. However, the evidence does not indicate that the administration announced on September 1, 1986, "We hereby revoke your scholarships." Plaintiff has only shown the court that on September 1, defendants threatened to pull the scholarships. The evidence also indicates that the administration chose not to follow through with that threat, and instead paid all amounts promised. Whether the administration chose to comply with the agreement because of the suit the players had filed or for any other reason, their motivation is not controlling. The facts plainly indicate that all terms of the scholarship contracts were met, and plaintiffs concede this point. No breach of contract occurred, and summary judgment will be granted. . . .

IT IS BY THE COURT THEREFORE ORDERED that defendants' motion for summary judgment is granted in part and denied in part. Summary judgment is granted in favor of the defendants on plaintiffs' claims of property and liberty deprivation under 42 U.S.C. 1983 and on plaintiffs' claims of breach of contract. Summary judgment is denied on plaintiffs' claims under 42 U.S.C. § 1981 and for first amendment violations under 42 U.S.C. § 1983.

NOTES AND QUESTIONS

1. *Due Process Analysis.* In *Hysaw,* what property rights and liberty interests regarding intercollegiate athletics were asserted by the plaintiffs? Which ones did the court recognize, and which ones were rejected? What parallels, if any, exist in the claims raised by the plaintiffs in *Hysaw* and *Ross v. Creighton University*? Did the court in *Hysaw* take a literal approach in analyzing the student-athlete/ university contract or one based on the parties' reasonable expectations?

In *Richard v. Perkins*, 373 F. Supp. 2d 1211, 1219 (D. Kan. 2005), the same federal district court that decided *Hysaw* re-affirmed the general rule that there is no property right in intercollegiate athletics participation, while recognizing that a student-athlete has a liberty interest in not being treated in an arbitrary and capricious manner regarding removal from an intercollegiate sports team, which is sufficient to trigger judicial review for purposes of ensuring his substantive due process rights were not violated. See *Brands v. Sheldon Community School, supra* in Chapter 2, which considered this issue in the context of interscholastic athletics.

In *Conard v. University of Washington*, 834 P.2d 17 (Wash. 1992), two student-athletes alleged that the University of Washington (UW)'s refusal to renew their football scholarships violated their federal due process rights by claiming there was a "common understanding" that the duration of these scholarships would be four to five years. UW did not renew their scholarships because of their alleged violation of football team rules. The Washington Supreme Court began its analysis by stating: "Unless a legitimate claim of entitlement to the renewal of plaintiffs' scholarships was created by the terms of the contract, by a mutually explicit understanding, or by substantive procedural restrictions on the part of the decision maker, plaintiffs have no constitutional due process protections." *Id.* at 22. The court concluded that the duration of the athletic scholarship was for only one year and that none of its terms established any entitlement to renewal. As to plaintiffs' assertion of a mutual understanding of renewal, it stated, "the fact that scholarships are, in fact, normally renewed does not create a 'common law' of renewal, absent other consistent and supportive UW policies or rules." *Id.* at 22. The court found plaintiffs failed to present evidence of such rules or policies and that their misconduct precluded them from satisfying the conditions for renewal of their scholarships. Recognizing that procedural guarantees limiting a decision maker's discretion may create a protected property interest, the court concluded: "[E]ven though the DIA manual speaks to due process, such a procedural guaranty cannot create a protected property interest in a vacuum. There must be some substantive standard and explicitly mandatory language to give the hearing substance." *Id.* at 26.

Hysaw recognizes that a student-athlete has a property right in the financial value of an existing athletic scholarship, which may be revoked by a public university for misconduct if appropriate procedural due process (i.e., fair notice and a hearing) is provided. *Austin v. Univ. of Oregon*, 925 F.3d 1133 (9th Cir. 2019) (sexual assault); *Mattison v. E. Stroudsburg Univ.*, 2013 WL 1563656 (M.D. Pa. Apr. 12, 2013) (marijuana use); *Marsh v. Del. State Univ.*, 2006 WL 141680 (D. Del.) (violation of the university's drug and weapons policies). See also *Doe v. Allee*, 242 Cal. Rptr.3d 109, 130-131 (Cal. Ct. App. 2019) (stating "[f]or practical purposes, common law requirements for a fair disciplinary hearing at a private university mirror the due process protections at public universities," and holding that a student-athlete removed from the football team and expelled for alleged sexual misconduct was denied a fair hearing).

2.   *Theoretical Perspectives.* According to one commentator, student-athletes historically advanced four theories in asserting their constitutionally protected property right in college sports eligibility and participation:

The economic rationale views intercollegiate athletics as a training ground for professional sports and argues that the property right is derived from the collegians' economic interests in uninterrupted preparation for lucrative careers as professional athletes. . . .

The educational rationale views participation in college athletics as an integral facet of the student athlete's educational experience. . . . This reasoning is premised upon the longstanding recognition that the opportunity to pursue an education is a sufficiently important interest that it cannot be impaired without due process. . . .

The scholarship per se rationale claims that the loss of an athletic scholarship per se is a denial of a property interest in athletic eligibility. The athletes who suffer such losses are likely to incur financial hardships, which may cut off the opportunity to continue attending college and to earn a degree. The deprivation of the scholarships, then, is also a deprivation of benefits to which the athletes were entitled according to the terms of their awards; the continued receipt of those benefits is a property interest which cannot be denied without due process. . . .

The contractual rationale maintains that the contractual provisions of the athletic scholarship create a property right to athletic eligibility. The scholarships are contracts that have conferred upon the athletes certain benefits, including the right to participate in intercollegiate athletics, which cannot be denied without due process.

Brian L. Porto, Note, *Balancing Due Process and Academic Integrity in Intercollegiate Athletics: The Scholarship Athlete's Limited Property Interest in Eligibility*, 62 Ind. L.J. 1151, 1158-1159 (1987).

Professor Porto notes that most courts have rejected the economic rationale "[b]ecause so few former college athletes ever sign a professional contract, college athletes' economic interests in professional sports opportunities are speculative and not of constitutional dimensions." *Id.* at 1158. For example, in *Colorado Seminary v. NCAA*, 417 F. Supp. 885 (D. Colo. 1976), *affirmed*, 570 F.2d 320 (10th Cir. 1978), the court stated:

[W]hile plaintiffs' characterization of the distinctive importance of collegiate athletics as a forum may be a sadly accurate reflection of the true significance of today's amateur athletic competition, the interest in future professional careers must . . . be considered speculative and not of constitutional dimensions. . . . Nor do the interests in postseason competition or appearances on television seem to be of a constitutionally greater magnitude. . . .

Id. at 24-25. See also *Equity in Athletics, Inc. v. Dep't of Educ.*, 675 F. Supp. 2d 660, 681 (W.D. Va. 2009) (adopting the majority rule that college athletes possess no property interest in athletic participation); *Hart v. NCAA*, 550 S.E.2d 79, 86 (W. Va. 2001) ("[A] student's ability to participate in athletic contests is not a right recognized by the law of this State. "[P]articipation in interscholastic athletics . . . does not rise to the level of a constitutionally protected 'property' or 'liberty' interest. . . .").

State courts have reached the same conclusion in contexts other than federal constitutional law litigation. *NCAA v. Yeo*, 171 S.W.3d 863, 869 (Tex. 2005) (rejecting a student-athlete's claim that she possessed a property or liberty interest under the Texas constitution because of her unique "reputation as a world-class athlete in her home country of Singapore, which was separate and apart from her intercollegiate swimming career"); *McAdoo v. Univ. of N.C. at Chapel Hill*, 736 S.E.2d 811, 823-24 (N.C. Ct. App 2013), *rev. denied*, (alleged loss of future income as an NFL player caused by a university's determination that a student-athlete was ineligible to play football his senior year is too speculative to afford the player standing to assert a contract-based claim).

Scholars have advocated that a contract rationale justifies judicial recognition that student-athletes have a property right in college sports participation. See, e.g., Timothy Davis, *Student-Athlete Perspective Economic Interests: Contractual Dimensions*, 19 T. Marshall L. Rev. 585 (1994); John P. Sahl, *College Athletes and Due Process*, 21 Ariz. St. L.J. 621 (1989); Brian L. Porto, Note, *Balancing Due Process and Academic Integrity in Intercollegiate Athletics: The Scholarship Athlete's Limited Property Interest in Eligibility*, 62 Ind. L.J. 1150 (1987).

In support of the contractual rationale, one commentator explains:

> Even if a court did not agree that an athletic scholarship is an explicit contract which confers a property interest upon an awardee, that court could agree that where an athlete is recruited by a university and both parties anticipate the athlete's participation in athletics, an implied contract has been formed, creating a property interest in continued eligibility. . . .
>
> Implied contracts exist where the school and the student athlete anticipate the latter's participation in the athletic program. . . . In college athletics, intense recruiting battles among schools for the services of highly skilled athletes are commonplace. These battles indicate that the combatant universities anticipate that the scholarship athletes who enroll at each institution will represent that institution in athletics competition. The scholarship agreement is the sort of "mutually explicit understanding," . . . which supports a claim of entitlement to participate in intercollegiate athletics.

Id. at 1168-1169.

Despite scholarly support, courts generally have rejected the contract rationale as the basis for establishing a property interest in intercollegiate athletics participation. See, e.g., *Lesser v. Neosho Cty. Cmty. Coll.*, 741 F. Supp. 854, 865 (D. Kan. 1990) (relying on *Hysaw*, court rules that contractually enforceable scholarship terms promised only financial aid, not a position on university's baseball team).

If you were a judge, would you be willing to adopt any of the foregoing rationales as the basis for finding a property interest in intercollegiate athletics participation?

3. Hysaw *First Amendment Free Speech Analysis.* What was the underlying factual basis of the plaintiffs' denial of free speech claims? Why did the court refuse to grant the university's summary judgment motion? As adults, are the plaintiffs' free speech rights entitled to more or less protection than high school students, whose rights were discussed by *Wildman v. Marshalltown Sch. Dist., supra,* in Chapter 2? See generally *Pinard v. Clatskanine Scho. Dis. 6J*, 446 F.3d 964, 978 (9th Cir. 2006) ("[I]f the plaintiffs can show that their protected speech was a 'substantial or motivating factor' in the defendant's decision to suspend them from the team permanently, and the defendants fail to show that they 'would have taken the same action even in the absence' of that speech, then the defendants violated plaintiffs' First Amendment rights.").

In *Ridpath v. Board of Governors Marshall University*, 447 F.3d 292 (4th Cir. 2006), a compliance officer at Marshall University became aware of a number of violations of NCAA rules, including the school's practice of providing student-athletes with jobs at "above-market" wages. After bringing this information to the attention of university officials, the compliance officer alleged he was prevented from assisting in the investigation, blamed for the violations, and subjected to "corrective action" resulting in a transfer to another position on campus that significantly diminished his ability to obtain future employment in his chosen occupation of athletic compliance. The Sixth Circuit ruled that a public university employer "contravenes a public employee's First Amendment rights when it discharges or refuses to rehire the employee or when it makes decisions relating to the promotion, transfer, recall and hiring in the exercise of that employee's free speech rights." *Id.* at 316. The court held that the plaintiff had sufficiently alleged that he was speaking as a private citizen and not as a public employee, and that his interest in exercising his First Amendment rights was not outweighed by the university's interest in his speech because the school was unable to show how the plaintiff's remarks had interfered with its legitimate operations. He also produced testimony supporting his claim that "but for" his speaking out against the school's conduct, he would not have been terminated from his position as a compliance officer. Because the evidence suggested that university administrators attempted to use their positions to intimidate the plaintiff so that he would remain silent regarding the investigation, the court found that he had properly alleged First Amendment claims for retaliation and chilling of his free speech rights. See Chris Hanna et al., *College Athletics Whistle-Blower Protection,* 27 J. Legal Aspect Sport 209 (2017) (advocating for enhanced protection for athletic personnel who report possible NCAA violations).

4. Hysaw *Equal Protection Analysis.* Discrimination based on race, ethnicity, or national origin triggers strict judicial scrutiny and requires a compelling justification and that the differing treatment be no broader than necessary to achieve such an objective. In *Priester v. Lowndes County,* 354 F.3d 414, 424 (5th Cir. 2004), the Fifth Circuit explained: "To state a claim of racial discrimination under the Equal Protection Clause and section 1983, the plaintiff 'must allege and prove' that he received treatment different from that received by similarly situated individuals and that the unequal treatment stemmed from a discriminatory intent." What facts would the *Hysaw* plaintiffs have to prove to establish their race discrimination claims?

    Claims alleging that a student-athlete has been discriminated against based on gender or sex are addressed in *Davenport v. Randolph County Bd. of Education, supra,* in Chapter 2 as well as generally in Chapter 10.

5. *First Amendment Freedom of Religion Issues.* As noted in Chapter 2, religious liberty issues often arise in the interscholastic athletics context, and similar issues arise at the intercollegiate level. Some of the areas in which religious liberties issues have arisen in the intercollegiate athletic context include the following: (1) recognition of religious activity on the part of student-athletes, coaches, and athletic personnel (see, e.g., Gil Fried & Lisa Bradley, *Applying the First Amendment to Prayer in a Public University Locker Room: An Athlete's and Coach's Perspective,* 4 Marq. Sports L.J. 301 (1994)); (2) accommodation of the religious interests of competitors (e.g., coaches and conferences have been known to be sensitive to the religious interests of student-athletes and have rescheduled events and relieved student-athletes of practice and other obligations so that they could exercise their religious conscience); and (3) accommodation of religious educational institutions

(e.g., Brigham Young University refuses to participate in athletic events on Sunday, the Sabbath for members of the Church of Jesus Christ of Latter-day Saints, which has resulted in its being placed in brackets in the NCAA men's basketball tournament that will permit adherence to its Sabbath).

Even though it is not subject to the constraints of the federal constitution because it is not a state actor (see *NCAA v. Tarkanian, infra*), the NCAA has exempted brief religious observances by student-athletes from its general rule that prohibits players from celebrating or drawing attention to themselves on the football field. This includes pausing to pray or express religious gratitude in the end zone after scoring a touchdown. Do you agree with this exemption? Does it favor religion over other significant interests of student-athletes?

Student-athletes at the intercollegiate level are generally older and more mature than high school student-athletes. As such, prayers in a public high school locker room, particularly if they are led or sponsored by the coach, are arguably more offensive to impressionable high school athletes than they might be to intercollegiate student-athletes who play for a public university. Does this distinction in levels of maturity provide a legitimate basis for permitting more religion or religious exercise on the part of intercollegiate student-athletes?

It also should be noted that federal statutes and state constitutional provisions might provide intercollegiate athletes with greater protection of their freedom of religion than does the First Amendment.

PROBLEM 3-6

You are general counsel at a major university, and a Muslim student-athlete has asked to meet with you to discuss a dispute he has with his coach. The coach insists that student-athletes maintain a rigorous diet, which includes eating certain meals each day. The Muslim student desires to follow his religious conscience and fast on certain days and avoid eating some of the meals prescribed by the coach. He also eats a more vegetarian diet than the high-protein fare established by the coach. Before the meeting, you call the coach, and he says that although he respects the student-athlete for his religious conviction, it is imperative that he eat with the team for health purposes and to maintain team morale. He is fearful that yielding to this student-athlete's religious beliefs would open a Pandora's box, permitting student-athletes to contrive all kinds of reasons for getting out of his strict dietary regimen. The coach also indicates that the diet was devised after consultation with the team's athletic trainer in order to maximize student-athletes' athletic performance. What do you say to the student-athlete? Is it likely that he has a cognizable legal action on First Amendment grounds against the coach and university? Would your legal analysis change based upon whether the sport in which the student-athlete participates is football or golf? In considering these issues, review the legal discussion in Chapter 2 B (2) (b) (ii).

4. *Are Student-Athletes University Employees?*

As you read the following cases and materials, consider the legal implications of characterizing student-athletes as university employees as well as the public policy reasons for not doing so.

a. Eligibility to Receive Workers' Compensation Benefits

As illustrated by *Waldrep*, although historically courts were divided over the question of whether scholarship student-athletes are covered by workers' compensation statutes, the modern trend is not to judicially characterize student-athletes as employees.

WALDREP v. TEXAS EMPLOYERS INSURANCE ASSN.

21 S.W.3d 692 (Tex. Ct. App. 2000)

YEAKEL, Judge.

Appellant Alvis Kent Waldrep, Jr. was awarded workers' compensation benefits by the Texas Workers' Compensation Commission (the "Commission") for an injury he sustained while playing football for Texas Christian University ("TCU"). Appellee Texas Employers Insurance Association ("TEIA"), in receivership, Texas Property and Casualty Insurance Guaranty Association appealed the award to the district court. Following a trial *de novo*, a jury found that Waldrep had failed to prove that he was an employee of TCU at the time of his injury. The district court rendered judgment that Waldrep take nothing against TEIA. Waldrep appeals the judgment, claiming that (1) he was an employee as a matter of law. . . . We will affirm the district court's judgment.

BACKGROUND

Waldrep graduated from high school in Alvin, Texas in 1972. During his junior and senior years, TCU was among many schools interested in recruiting Waldrep, a young man known for his athletic ability as well as his good academic record. Tommy Runnels, a TCU assistant football coach, visited Waldrep frequently at his home and school, attempting to interest Waldrep in TCU's football and academic programs. During one home visit, Waldrep's mother asked Runnels what would happen if Waldrep were injured during his football career at TCU. Runnels assured Waldrep and his family that TCU would "take care of them" and emphasized that Waldrep would keep his scholarship even if he were injured and could not play football.

Waldrep was very impressed with the facilities at TCU and believed that his abilities would fit in well with TCU's football program. He was also aware that recruitment and his future involvement in athletics at TCU were governed by the rules of the Southwest Athletic Conference ("Southwest Conference")[3] and the National Collegiate Athletic Association ("NCAA"). To affirm his intent to attend school at TCU and participate in TCU's football program, Waldrep signed two documents. First, Waldrep signed a pre-enrollment form ("Letter of Intent") . . ., which demonstrated his formal desire to play football for TCU and penalized him if he decided to enter a different school within the Southwest Conference. . . . Waldrep later signed a financial aid agreement ("Financial Aid Agreement") . . ., ensuring that Waldrep's room, board, and tuition would

---

3. At the time, TCU was a member of the Southwest Conference. That athletic conference no longer exists.

be paid while attending TCU and that Waldrep would receive ten dollars per month for incidentals. This cash payment was generally referred to as "laundry money." Both documents were contingent on Waldrep's meeting TCU's admission and scholastic requirements for athletic awards.

In August 1972, Waldrep enrolled at TCU. In October 1974, while playing football for TCU against the University of Alabama, Waldrep was critically injured. He sustained a severe injury to his spinal cord and was paralyzed below the neck. Today, Waldrep has no sensation below his upper chest. In 1991, Waldrep filed a workers' compensation claim for his injury.

DISCUSSION

STATUS AS AN EMPLOYEE FOR WORKERS' COMPENSATION PURPOSES

The question presented to this Court is whether there is some evidence (more than a mere scintilla) supporting the jury's failure to find that Waldrep was an employee of TCU at the time of his injury. Stated another way, could any reasonable and fair-minded person conclude that Waldrep was not employed by TCU when injured? We answer this question affirmatively.

We are confronted with a situation novel to Texas jurisprudence: whether, for workers' compensation law purposes, a recipient of a scholarship or financial aid from a university becomes that university's employee by agreeing in return to participate in a university-sponsored program. Cases decided under the various workers' compensation statutes in effect from time to time have almost uniformly determined the existence of an employer-employee relationship by an analysis of whether the claimant of workers' compensation benefits was an *employee* as distinguished from an *independent contractor*. . . . These authorities do not conveniently overlay the facts presented here, as there is no allegation that Waldrep was an independent contractor. Yet they are instructive in one significant aspect: one may receive a benefit from another in return for services and not become an employee.

The jury charge defined "employee" as "a person in the service of another under a contract of hire, express or implied, oral or written, whereby the employer has the right to direct the means or details of the work and not merely the result to be accomplished. . . ." (Footnote omitted.) Thus, in failing to find that Waldrep was TCU's employee, the jury may have believed that there was no contract of hire between Waldrep and TCU or, if there was, it did not give TCU the right to direct the means or details of Waldrep's "work." We will examine both possibilities. . . .

EXISTENCE OF CONTRACT OF HIRE

For the purpose of workers' compensation law, the employer-employee relationship may be created *only* by a contract. . . . Waldrep strongly urges that the Letter of Intent and Financial Aid Agreement are express contracts of hire that set forth the terms of Waldrep's "employment." However, we do not find these documents to be so clear. At best, they only partially set forth the relationship between Waldrep and TCU. By their terms, they generally bound Waldrep to TCU to the exclusion of other Southwest Conference schools, if he intended to participate in athletics, and extended him financial aid so long as he complied with the admission and scholastic requirements of TCU and the rules and regulations of both TCU and the Southwest Conference. These requirements, rules, and regulations are not specifically described in either of the agreements. Nor does the record in this case set them forth in any detail. The Letter of Intent and Financial Aid Agreement are also silent with regard to whether any rules or regulations of the NCAA would apply to Waldrep or affect his relationship with TCU. Yet it is undisputed that before Waldrep signed the Letter of Intent and Financial Aid Agreement, both he and TCU understood that his recruitment and future football career at TCU would be governed by and subject to the rules of the NCAA.

TEIA, on the other hand, posits that Waldrep clearly and simply did not have a contract of hire. . . .

Mindful of the district court's definition of employee, the jury was left to determine if there was a "contract of hire" between Waldrep and TCU. We observe that "the most basic policy of contract law . . . is the protection of the justified expectations of the parties." *DeSantis v. Wackenhut Corp.*, 793 S.W.2d 670, 677 (Tex. 1990). Was it the expectation of Waldrep and TCU that Waldrep would become TCU's employee? To form a contract, the parties must mutually assent to its terms. Whether there is such assent is determined "based on objective standards of what the parties said and did and not on their alleged subjective states of mind." *American Nat'l Ins. Co. v. Paul*, 927 S.W.2d 239, 244 (Tex. App.—Austin 1996, writ denied) (quoting *Adams v. Petrade Int'l, Inc.*, 754 S.W.2d 696, 717 (Tex. App.—Houston [1st Dist.] 1988, writ denied)). Because the Letter of Intent and Financial Aid Agreement do not evidence the entire agreement between Waldrep and TCU, we consider them against "the background of circumstances surrounding [their] execution." *Brown*, 395 S.W.2d at 702 (citing *Allison v. Campbell*, 117 Tex. 277, 298 S.W. 523 (Tex. Comm. App. 1927, opinion adopted)). We may also look to the parties' conduct after execution of the documents, and such conduct "may be a strong factor in determining just what the real agreement contemplated." *Maryland Cas. Co. v. Brown*, 131 Tex. 404, 115 S.W.2d 394, 396 (Tex. 1938).

On the facts of this record, any contract of hire must have been a contract whereby TCU hired Waldrep to attend the university, remain in good standing academically, and play football. However, if Waldrep played football for pay, he would have been a professional, not an amateur. The evidence reflects that the actions of both Waldrep and TCU were consistent with a joint intention that Waldrep be considered an amateur and not a professional. It is undisputed that before Waldrep signed the Letter of Intent and Financial Aid Agreement, both he and TCU understood that his recruitment and future football career at TCU would be governed by and subject to the rules of the NCAA. The record indicates that the NCAA's policies and rules in effect at that time exhibited a concerted effort to ensure that each school governed by these rules made certain that student-athletes were not employees. Indeed, the rules declared that the fundamental policy of the NCAA was "to maintain intercollegiate athletics as an integral part of the educational program and the athlete as an integral part of the student body, and, by so doing, retain a clear line of demarcation between college athletics and professional sports." (citation omitted). Following its policy, the evidence reflects that the NCAA rules made the principle of amateurism foremost and established several requirements to ensure that the student-athlete would not be considered a professional. . . . For example, the NCAA had strict rules against student-athletes taking pay for participation in sports, and student-athletes were ineligible to participate if they were receiving or had received a salary from a professional sports organization.

Additionally, the record reflects that Waldrep and TCU did not treat the financial aid Waldrep received as "pay" or "income." First, as previously noted, the NCAA rules provided that student-athletes would be ineligible if they used their skill for pay in any form; however, that same rule goes on to state that "a student-athlete may accept scholarships or educational grants-in-aid from his institution" as these benefits do not conflict with the NCAA rules. (Citation omitted.) As the NCAA rules were based upon a principle of amateurism and strictly prohibited payment for play, these two provisions together indicate that the NCAA and its participating institutions did not consider the acceptance of financial aid from the institution to be "taking pay." Moreover, the rules provided that any financial aid that exceeded tuition and fees, room and board, required course-related supplies and books, and incidental expenses of fifteen dollars per month would be considered "pay" for participation in intercollegiate athletics. . . . TCU gave Waldrep financial aid for these items but nothing more, indicating that TCU did not intend to pay Waldrep for his participation. Of equal significance, TCU never placed Waldrep on its payroll, never paid him a salary, and never told him that he would be paid a salary. There is no evidence that Waldrep expected a salary. No social security or income tax was withheld from Waldrep's grant-in-aid. *See Continental Ins. Co. v. Wolford*, 526 S.W.2d 539, 540 (Tex. 1975) (withholding taxes is *indicia* of employee status). Waldrep never filed a tax return reporting his financial aid.

The evidence further reflects that Waldrep and TCU intended that Waldrep participate at TCU as a *student*, not as an *employee*. During the recruitment process, TCU never told Waldrep that he would be an employee, and Waldrep never told TCU that he considered himself to be employed. Moreover, a basic purpose of the NCAA, which governed Waldrep's intercollegiate football career, was to make the student-athlete an integral part of the student body. *See NCAA Manual* at 5. According to the NCAA rules, "an amateur student-athlete is one who engages in athletics for the education, physical, mental and social benefits he derives therefrom, and to whom athletics is an avocation." *NCAA Manual* at 6. Of importance is the evidence that Waldrep was aware when he signed the Letter of Intent and Financial Aid Agreement that he would still receive financial aid even if hurt or unable to play football, as long as he complied with the rules of the Southwest Conference. Thus, TCU could not "fire" Waldrep as it could an employee. . . . In addition, when Waldrep signed the agreements, he still had to meet the scholastic requirements for athletic awards and qualify for admission to TCU in order to enroll and participate in the football program. Waldrep testified that he knew when he signed the agreements that in order to play football at TCU he would have to maintain certain academic requirements as a student. Thus, his academic responsibilities dictated whether he could continue to play football.

Financial-aid awards are given to many college and university students based on their abilities in various areas, including music, academics, art, and athletics. Sometimes these students are required to participate in certain programs or activities in return for this aid. But, as the Supreme Court of Indiana observed, "scholarship recipients are considered to be students seeking advanced educational opportunities and are not considered to be professional athletes, musicians or artists employed by the university for their skill in their respective areas." *Rensing v. Indiana State Univ. Bd. of Trustees*, 444 N.E.2d 1170, 1174 (Ind. 1983).

Although the record in this case contains facts from which the jury could have found that Waldrep and TCU were parties to a contract of hire, there is also probative evidence to the contrary. Viewing the evidence in the light most favorable to the jury's verdict, we hold that the record before us reflects more than a mere scintilla of evidence that Waldrep was not in the service of TCU under a contract of hire.

RIGHT TO DIRECT THE MEANS OR DETAILS OF WALDREP'S WORK

If, however, we assume the jury found that a contract existed between Waldrep and TCU, we must determine whether there is some evidence concerning TCU's right to direct the means or details of Waldrep's "work." The definition of "employee" submitted to the jury correctly states the recognized test to determine whether an employer-employee relationship exists: the *right* of the employer to direct or control the means or details of the employee's work. *See Mayo,* 688 S.W.2d at 243 (ultimate test in deciding employment question is right of alleged employer to control specifics of worker's performance) (citing *Hartsfield,* 390 S.W.2d at 471). To determine whether there is a right of control, "we first must look to the terms of the employment contract." *Allstate Ins. Co. v. Scott,* 511 S.W.2d 412, 414 (Tex. Civ. App.—El Paso 1974, writ ref'd n.r.e.). Where there is no express contract or where the terms of the contract are indefinite, the *exercise* of control "may be the best evidence available to show the actual terms of the contract." *Newspapers, Inc. v. Love,* 380 S.W.2d 582, 590 (Tex. 1964); *see Scott,* 511 S.W.2d at 414. However, "'the *right* to control' remains the supreme test and the 'exercise of control' necessarily presupposes a right to control which must be related to some agreement expressed or implied." *Love,* 380 S.W.2d at 590 (emphasis added); *see Scott,* 511 S.W.2d at 414 ("the exercise of control, while evidentiary only and not the true test, is the best evidence available in determining the right of control").

The record reflects that TCU *exercised* direction and control over all of the athletes in its football program, including non-scholarship players, while they were participating in the *football program.* Waldrep admitted that his high school coaches exercised the same type of control over his participation in sports as the coaches at TCU. Waldrep further testified that he did everything that the coaches told him to do because he wanted to, because he loved the game, and because he wanted to be the best, not because he had to. The evidence is clear that TCU did not have the right to direct or control all of Waldrep's activities during his tenure at the school. The NCAA rules protected Waldrep's financial-aid award even if his physical condition prevented him from playing football for any reason. *See NCAA Manual* at 8. Moreover, TCU could not simply cancel Waldrep's grant-in-aid based on his "athletic ability or his contribution to [the] team's success," or even, in certain circumstances, if he quit. *Id.*

The fact that the athletic department at TCU established practice and meeting times to be observed by those playing football does not establish that TCU had the *right* to direct and control all aspects of the players' activities while enrolled in the university. Waldrep's acceptance of financial aid from TCU did not subject him to any extraordinary degree of control over his academic activities.

Waldrep clearly presented evidence that TCU *exercised* direction or control over some of his activities while a student at the university. Perhaps the jury might have found this sufficient to prove that TCU had the *right* to direct the means or details of Waldrep's activities, but the jury declined to do so. Viewing the evidence in the light most favorable to the jury's verdict, we hold that the record before us reflects more than a mere scintilla of evidence disputing TCU's right of control.

The district court properly left the jury to determine the issue of employ-ment. The circumstances presented in the record before us do not establish an employer-employee relationship as a matter of law. We hold that there is some evidence to support the jury's verdict declining to find that Waldrep was an employee of TCU at the time of his injury.

CONCLUSION

In conclusion, we note that we are aware college athletics has changed dramat-ically over the years since Waldrep's injury. Our decision today is based on facts and circumstances as they existed almost twenty-six years ago. We express no opinion as to whether our decision would be the same in an analogous situation arising today; therefore, our opinion should not be read too broadly. Having disposed of all of the issues before us, we affirm the district court's judgment.

Affirmed.

NOTES AND QUESTIONS

1. *Employment Status.* What test was adopted in *Waldrep* to determine if the plaintiff was an employee for workers' compensation benefits? What are the elements of the standard adopted? The court affirmed the jury's find-ing that Waldrep was not a university employee when he suffered a per-manently disabling injury during a game. Although Waldrep received an athletic scholarship for participating in university-sponsored athletics, the court found that it was not the expectation of the parties that he thereby became a paid university employee. According to the court, what was the parties' expectation regarding the nature of Waldrep's relationship with TCU? On what sources did the court rely in arriving at its characterization of the parties' expectations regarding their relationship?

2. *Requisite Degree of Control for Employee Status.* The *Waldrep* court concludes that even though the university "*exercised* direction and control over all of the athletes in its football program" (emphasis in original), TCU did not have the "right to direct or control all of Waldrep's activities during his tenure at the school."

   Moreover, Waldrep's participation in football "did not subject him to any extraordinary degree of control over his academic activities." What is the relevance of the right of control? Is the court's analysis of the degree of control exercised by athletic departments over student-athletes accurate? Which factor seems most influential in the court's assessment that the req-uisite right to control for workers' compensation purposes is absent?

   In *University of Colorado v. Derdeyn*, 863 P.2d 929 (Colo. 1993), the uni-versity argued that its drug-testing program did not violate the federal or Colorado constitutions, in part because of student-athletes' lessened expec-tation of privacy. In support of its defense, the university emphasized the extent of control that universities exercise over student-athletes. Consider the following comments of the Colorado Supreme Court:

   > CU argues that student athletes' expectations of privacy with regard to uri-nalysis are diminished because they submit to extensive regulation of their

on- and off-campus behavior, including maintenance of required levels of academic performance, monitoring of course selection, training rules, mandatory practice sessions, diet restrictions, attendance at study halls, curfews, and prohibitions on alcohol and drug use. . . .

CU's athletic director testified in relevant part that the NCAA sets limits on financial aid awards, playing seasons, squad size, and years of eligibility; that the NCAA requires that CU maintain records of each athlete's academic performance; that the "athletes that eat at training tables are football and men's basketball and the other athletes eat in the dorms or at their off-campus residences"; that some coaches within their discretion impose curfews; that athletes are required to show up for practice; that athletes are "advised . . . on what they should take for classes"; that "we have a required study hall in the morning and in the evening"; and that it is "fair to say that the athletes are fairly well regulated." A student athlete testified in relevant part that "Yes . . . if you are an NCAA athlete, you have to keep a certain grade average," and "Yes . . . if your grades drop below that average, then you are not eligible for competition."

Although it is obviously not amenable to precise calculation, it is at least doubtful that the testimony relied upon by CU fully supports CU's assertion that its student athletes are "extensively regulated in their on and off-campus behavior," especially with regard to all of the particulars that CU asserts.

Id. at 940-41.

3. *Statutory Exclusion.* Some early cases held that an injured intercollegiate athlete could recover workers' compensation benefits if he held a university job unrelated to athletics. See, e.g., *Van Horn v. Indus. Accident Comm'n*, 33 Cal. Rptr. 169 (Cal. Ct. App. 1963); *Univ. of Denver v. Nemeth*, 257 P.2d 423 (Colo. 1953). After *Van Horn*, the California legislature amended its workers' compensation statute to expressly exclude student-athletes from its coverage. See Cal. Lab. Code §3352(a)(7) (Deering Supp. 2013). For examples of similar legislation, see Haw. Rev. Stat. Ann. §386-1 (Michie Supp. 2017); N.Y. Workers' Comp. §2(4) (McKinney 2018); Or. Rev. Stat. §656.027(13) (2008); and 21 Vt. Stat. Ann. §601(14(b)) (LexisNexis 2018). In contrast, Nebraska has established an administrative system for providing medical and disability benefits to injured university athletes without characterizing them as university employees. See, e.g., Neb. Rev. Stat. §85-106.05 (2019).

4. *Judicial Characterizations.* Most states do not expressly include or exclude scholarship athletes from coverage under their respective workers' compensation statutes or provide a system of compensation for injured university athletes. Thus, courts must determine whether or not scholarship athletes are covered "employees."

Despite some early contrary authority, as illustrated by *Van Horn* and *Nemeth*, courts now generally hold that athletes who suffer injuries while participating in intercollegiate athletics are not entitled to workers' compensation benefits. Relying on policy considerations, these courts refuse to find that a student's receipt of an athletic scholarship establishes an employment relationship with a university, a prerequisite for workers' compensation coverage. See e.g., *Rensing v. Ind. State Univ. Bd. of Trustees*, 444 N.E.2d 1170 (Ind. 1983) (the court found that no employer/employee relationship existed because the university and injured student did not intend to create a contract of employment); *Coleman v. W. Mich. Univ.*, 336 N.W.2d 224 (Mich. Ct. App. 1983) (applying "economic reality" to find that although the plaintiff's athletic scholarship constituted "wages," and the university had a limited right to control the plaintiff's activities and discipline him, conducting a football program was not an integral part of the university's business, which was to provide an academic education). *Id.* at 226-227. See also *Berger v. NCAA*, 2016 WL 614365 (S.D. Ind.) (holding that women's track and field athletes were not employees for purposes of the Fair Labor Standards Act), *aff'd* 845 F.3d. 104 (7th Cir. 2016); *Kavanagh v. Trs. of Boston Univ.*, 795 N.E.2d 1170 (Mass. 2003) (the provision of scholarships or other financial aid to student-athletes did not create an employment relationship for purposes of respondeat superior); *Shephard v. Loyola Marymount Univ.*, 102 Cal. App. 4th 837 (Cal. Ct. App. 2 Dist. 2002) (holding that a student-athlete was not an employee for the purpose of bringing a lawsuit pursuant to the California Fair Employment and Housing Act (FEHA).

5. *Scholarly Views.* Several legal commentators have criticized courts' refusals to include injured scholarship athletes within the coverage of workers' compensation statutes. Frank P. Tiscione, *College Athletics and Workers' Compensation: Why the Courts Get It Wrong in Denying Student-Athletes Workers' Compensation Benefits When They Get Injured*, 14 Sports Law. J. 137 (2007). Scholars have also debated whether student-athletes should be considered employees of their schools. See Richard T. Karcher, *Big-Time College Athletes' Status as Employees*, 33 ABA J. Lab. & Emp. L. 31 (2017); Robert A. McCormick & Amy Christian McCormick, *Myth of the Student-Athlete: The College Athlete as Employee*, 81 Wash. L. Rev. 71 (2006); Nathan McCoy & Kerry Knox, Comment, *Flexing Union Muscle—Is It the Right Game Plan for Revenue Generating Student-Athletes in Their Contest for Benefits Reform with the NCAA?*, 69 Tenn. L. Rev. 1051 (2002).

Professor Timothy Davis posits that two models of intercollegiate athletics emerge from judicial decisions and scholarly discourse. Under the amateur/education model, the student-athlete is viewed as an amateur, and college athletics is considered an integral part of the educational purpose of universities. The competing model, the commercial/education model, assumes that college sport is a commercial enterprise subject to the same economic considerations as any other industry. Despite the considerable impact of economic factors on college sports, education remains a component of the conceptualization of college sports. In the following excerpt, Professor Davis comments on the influence of judicial conceptualizations of college sports pursuant to one of these models on the resolution of cases involving student-athlete entitlement to workers' compensation.

> [L]egal doctrine and philosophical visions of college athletics combine to shape the judicial response to a student-athlete's status as an employee for worker's compensation purposes. Courts declining to define student-athletes as employees adopt the views of intercollegiate athletics embodied in the amateur/education model of college sports. The judiciary in these cases perceives college sports as serving an academic function where intercollegiate athletics are simply an avocation of the student.
>
> Juxtaposed with these decisions are cases in which the judiciary recognizes the impact of commercialism on college sports and on the student-athlete's relationship with his university. Here, the duality of the student-athlete's role—a student on the one hand and an employee on the other—provides the framework from which the relevant issues are analyzed. Employment status stems from the quid pro quo that earmarks the contractual obligations between a student-athlete and his institution. Nevertheless, these cases

recognize that the student-athlete is still a student, hence creating an educational component to college sports.

The student-athlete worker's compensation decisions also illustrate the significant extent to which a court's reliance on a particular conceptual model influences the ultimate disposition of the case. Recognizing these judicial tendencies, parties to disputes arising within intercollegiate athletics construct their policy and legal arguments upon these two competing conceptual schemes.

Timothy Davis, *Intercollegiate Athletics: Competing Models and Conflicting Realities*, 25 Rutgers L.J. 269 (1994). Other discussions regarding the current as well as proposed models for intercollegiate athletics may be found in Matthew Mitten & Stephen F. Ross, *A Regulatory Solution to Better Promote the Educational Values and Economic Sustainability of Intercollegiate Athletics*, 92 Or. L. Rev. 837 (2014); William W. Berry III, *Educating Athletes Re-Envisioning the Student-Athlete Model*, 81 Tenn. L. Rev. 795 (2014).

6. *Institutional Payment of Medical Expenses.* If an injury prevents a student-athlete from participating in intercollegiate athletics, NCAA bylaws permit a university to continue his or her scholarship so that the athlete can complete his or her education. Absent a valid contract, however, a university has no obligation to pay for an injured athlete's medical expenses. See *Searles v. Trs. of St. Joseph's Coll.*, 695 A.2d 1206, 1211-12 (Me. 1997); *Reed v. Univ. of N.D.*, 543 N.W.2d 106, 110 (Minn. Ct. App. 1996); *Reed v. Univ. of N.D.*, 589 N.W.2d 880, 884 (N.D. 1999). Moreover, an athlete's past service to a university as an intercollegiate athlete is not valid consideration for the university's agreement to pay for medical expenses arising out of an athletic injury. See *Cardamone v. Univ. of Pittsburgh*, 384 A.2d 1228 (Pa. Super. Ct. 1978). On the other hand, NCAA schools are required to certify that student-athletes have health insurance. The NCAA permits schools to require student-athletes to have their own insurance or to be covered by their parents' policy, but many universities provide medical care or health insurance for their student-athletes.

If a TCU athletic official had orally promised Waldrep that the university would provide him with all necessary medical treatment for future sustained injuries as an inducement to play a sport, would this promise be enforceable? See *Eberhart v. Morris Brown Coll.*, 352 S.E.2d 832, 834 (Ga. Ct. App. 1987) (limiting recovery to only those medical expenses incurred in connection with an athletic injury).

7. *NCAA Insurance Programs.* Since August 1, 1992, the NCAA has provided catastrophic athletic injury insurance covering the more than 400,000 student-athletes who suffer serious injuries while participating in intercollegiate athletics at member institutions. This plan, which provides for a maximum lifetime benefit of $20 million, compensates for educational benefits and lost earnings, as well as lifetime rehabilitation, medical costs, and dental expenses. Catastrophic injuries that fall within a covered loss are defined as:

i. The inability of the Insured Person, as the result of a Covered Accident, to engage in substantially the same activities as the Insured Person had engaged in immediately prior to the Covered Accident; and

ii. The irrevocable loss suffered by the Insured Person, as a result of the Covered Accident, of: a) speech; or b) hearing of both ears; or c) sight in both eyes; or d) use of both arms; or e) use of both legs; or f) use of one arm and one leg; or g) severely diminished mental capacity due to brain stem or other neurological injury such that the Insured Person is unable to perform normal daily functions.

NCAA, *NCAA Catastrophic Injury Insurance Program Benefit Summary for 8/1/17 through 7/31/20* at p. 7, https://ncaaorg.s3.amazonaws.com/ncaa/insurance/2017-20INS_NCAACatastrophicBenefitSummary.pdf.

The NCAA also has established a program that enables qualified "exceptional" student-athletes to obtain a preapproved loan to purchase disability insurance. This policy is designed to protect talented student-athletes against the loss of expected future earnings should they suffer a disabling injury or illness while in college. NCAA, *Exceptional Student-Athlete Disability Insurance Program,* http://www.ncaa.org/about/resources/insurance/student-athlete-insurance-programs.

8. *California "Student Athlete Bill of Rights."* In September 2012, California enacted a law (effective with the 2013-2014 academic year) that requires any California four-year university whose athletic program receives $10 million or more in media revenues (currently Stanford University; the University of California, Berkeley; the University of California, Los Angeles; and the University of Southern California) to provide an academic scholarship for up to five academic years, or until graduation, to a student-athlete who suffers a career-ending injury causing the loss of an athletic scholarship.

b.   Student-Athlete Unionization and Related Issues

On August 17, 2015, the National Labor Relations Board declined to exercise jurisdiction in a much-heralded case raising the issue of whether Northwestern University's football players, who receive grant-in-aid scholarships, are employees within the meaning of Section 2(3) of the National Labor Relations Act. The players also sought to have the NLRB "direct an election in a unit of these grant-in-aid players." As you read this case, ask yourself the following questions: 1) whether the NLRB's ruling was correct (and wise); 2) if you were a member of Congress, would you support legislation recognizing NCAA student-athletes as university employees; 3) what would be the likely implications of doing so; 4) and has the NCAA responded appropriately to address the concerns that led to this unionization effort, and if not, what more should be done and how should it be funded?

NORTHWESTERN UNIVERSITY
AND
COLLEGE ATHLETES PLAYERS ASSOCIATION (CAPA), PETITIONER

Case 13-RC-121359
August 17, 2015

BY CHAIRMAN PEARCE AND MEMBERS MISCIMARRA, HIROZAWA, JOHNSON, AND MCFERRAN

SUMMARY OF FACTS

Northwestern is a university with its main campus in Evanston, Illinois. During the 2013-2014 academic year, about 112 athletes were on the football team, of whom 85 received a grant-in-aid scholarship. The scholarship is worth about $61,000 per year (or more, if the recipient enrolls in summer classes). The scholarship amount is calculated based on tuition, fees, room, board, and books, and the scholarship funds are directly applied to those expenses. [N]one of the money is directly disbursed to the players, except that upperclassmen living off-campus receive a monthly stipend earmarked for their room and board (and disbursed to them in the form of a personal check).

The football team — along with Northwestern's 18 other varsity sports — is part of the Department of Athletics and Recreation. Head Coach Pat Fitzgerald oversees a staff of 13 assistant coaches; in addition, the team is supported by various other personnel, including strength and conditioning coaches, athletic trainers, video office personnel, and football operations staff. Fitzgerald reports to Athletic Director James J. Phillips, who in turn reports to Northwestern's president, Morton Schapiro.

Northwestern is a member of both the National Collegiate Athletic Association (the NCAA) and The Big Ten Conference (Big Ten). Its athletes compete under the auspices of these organizations, and the school's athletics program operates within certain constraints by which members of these associations agree to be bound. For example, the NCAA dictates the maximum number of grant-in-aid scholarships a school can award, caps the number of players who can participate in preseason football practices, sets the minimum academic requirements that football players must meet to remain eligible to play (including the requirements that players be enrolled as students, carry a full class load, and maintain a certain minimum grade point average (GPA)), controls the terms and content of the scholarship, defines amateur status that players must maintain (including prohibiting players from retaining agents or profiting from their names and likenesses), and regulates the number of mandatory practice hours that can be imposed on the players. . . . Northwestern's football team competes in the NCAA Division I Football Bowl Subdivision (FBS), college football's highest level of play. At present, about 125 schools compete at that level. Only 17 of those schools–including Northwestern–are private colleges or universities, and Northwestern is the only private school in the 14-member Big Ten.

Scholarship players are required to devote substantial hours to football activities, but they are also full-time students. They receive no academic credit for their football endeavors. Although some players testified that they learned valuable skills and life lessons from playing football and consider Coach Fitzgerald to be a "teacher," playing football does not fulfill any sort of degree requirement, and no coaches teach courses or are part of the academic faculty.

Northwestern's football program generated some $30 million in revenue during the 2012-2013 academic year, although the program also incurred close to $22 million in expenses. Over a 10-year period ending in 2012-2013, the football program generated about $235 million in revenue and incurred roughly $159 million in expenses. . . . According to Department of Athletics Chief Financial Officer Steve Green, although the football program generates net revenue, the Department of Athletics' overall annual expenses exceed revenues, and Northwestern must subsidize the department to balance its budget.

ANALYSIS

The parties . . . have largely focused on whether the scholarship players in the petitioned-for unit are statutory employees. If the players are not statutory employees, then the Board lacks authority to direct an election or certify a representative. . . . [A]s the Supreme Court has stated . . . even when the Board has the statutory authority to act (which it would in this case, were we to find that the scholarship players were statutory employees), "the Board sometimes properly declines to do so, stating that the policies of the Act would not be effectuated by its assertion of jurisdiction . . ." [citation omitted]. [W]e address this case without explicit congressional direction, but "[t]he absence of explicit congressional direction . . . does not preclude the Board from reaching any particular type of employment."

After careful consideration of the record and arguments of the parties and amici, we have determined that, even if the scholarship players were statutory employees (which, again, is an issue we do not decide), it would not effectuate the policies of the Act to assert jurisdiction. Our decision is primarily premised on a finding that, because of the nature of sports leagues (namely the control exercised by the leagues over the individual teams) and the composition and structure of FBS football (in which the overwhelming majority of competitors are public colleges and universities over which the Board cannot assert jurisdiction), it would not promote stability in labor relations to assert jurisdiction in this case.

[T]his case involves novel and unique circumstances. The Board has never before been asked to assert jurisdiction in a case involving college football players, or college athletes of any kind. . . . And the scholarship players do not fit into any analytical framework that the Board has used in cases involving other types of students or athletes. [T]he scholarship players bear little resemblance to the graduate student assistants or student janitors and cafeteria workers whose employee status the Board has considered in other cases. The fact that the scholarship players are students who are also athletes receiving a scholarship to participate in what has traditionally been regarded as an extracurricular activity (albeit a nationally prominent and extraordinarily lucrative one for many universities, conferences, and the NCAA) materially sets them apart from the Board's student precedent. Yet at the same time, the scholarship players are unlike athletes in undisputedly professional leagues, given that the scholarship players are required, inter alia, to be enrolled full time as students and meet various academic requirements, and they are prohibited by NCAA regulations from engaging in many of the types of activities that professional athletes are free to engage in, such as profiting from the use of their names or likenesses. [E]ven if scholarship players were regarded as analogous to players for professional sports teams who are considered employees for purposes of collective bargaining, such bargaining has never involved a bargaining unit consisting of a single team's players, where the players for competing teams were unrepresented or entirely outside the Board's jurisdiction. [N]othing in our precedent requires us to assert jurisdiction in this case. Given the absence of any controlling precedent, we find it appropriate to consider whether the Board should exercise its discretion to decline to assert jurisdiction in this case, even assuming the Board is otherwise authorized to act.

Notwithstanding the dissimilarities, discussed above, FBS football does resemble a professional sport in a number of relevant ways. [I]nstitutions that have FBS teams are engaged in the business of staging football contests from which they receive substantial revenues (via gate receipts, concessions and merchandise sales, and broadcasting contracts). [Citation omitted.] As in professional sports, the activity of staging athletic contests must be carried out jointly by the teams in the league or association involved. [Citations omitted.]

For this reason, as in other sports leagues, academic institutions that sponsor intercollegiate athletics have banded together and formed the NCAA to, among other things, set common rules and standards governing their competitions, including those applicable to FBS football. The NCAA's members have also given the NCAA the authority to police and enforce the rules and regulations that govern eligibility, practice, and competition. The record demonstrates that the NCAA now exercises a substantial degree of control over the operations of individual member teams, including many of the terms and conditions under which the scholarship players (as well as walk-on players) practice and play the game. As in professional sports, such an arrangement is necessary because uniform rules of competition and compliance with them ensure the uniformity and integrity of individual games, and thus league competition as a whole. There is thus a symbiotic relationship among the various teams, the conferences, and the NCAA. As a result, labor issues directly involving only an individual team and its players would also affect the NCAA, the Big Ten, and the other member institutions. Many terms applied to one team therefore would likely have ramifications for other teams. . . . [S]uch an arrangement is seemingly unprecedented; all previous Board cases concerning professional sports involve league-wide bargaining units. [Citations omitted.]

Just as the nature of league sports and the NCAA's oversight renders individual team bargaining problematic, the way that FBS football itself is structured and the nature of the colleges and universities involved strongly suggest that asserting jurisdiction in this case would not promote stability in labor relations. Despite the similarities between FBS football and professional sports leagues, FBS is also a markedly different type of enterprise. In particular, of the roughly 125 colleges and universities that participate in FBS football, all but 17 are state-run institutions. As a result, the Board cannot assert jurisdiction over the vast majority of FBS teams because they are not operated by "employers" within the meaning of Section 2(2) of the Act. [Citation omitted.] More starkly, Northwestern is the only private school that is a member of the Big Ten, and thus the Board cannot assert jurisdiction over any of Northwestern's primary competitors. This too is a situation without precedent because in all of our past cases involving professional sports, the Board was able to regulate all, or at least most, of the teams in the relevant league or association.

[A]sserting jurisdiction in this case would not promote stability in labor relations. Because most FBS teams are created by state institutions, they may be subject to state labor laws governing public employees. Some states, of course, permit collective bargaining by public employees, but others limit or prohibit such bargaining. At least two states–which, between them, operate three universities that are members of the Big Ten–specify by statute that scholarship athletes at state schools are not employees. [A]sserting jurisdiction would not [promote stability] because the Board cannot regulate most FBS teams. . . .

[W]e [also] observe that the terms and conditions of Northwestern's players have changed markedly in recent years and that there have been calls for the NCAA to undertake further reforms that may result in additional changes to the circumstances of scholarship players. For example, the NCAA's decision to allow FBS teams to award guaranteed 4-year scholarships, as opposed to 1-year renewable scholarships, has reduced the likelihood that scholarship players who become unable to play will lose their educational funding, and possibly their educational opportunity. [O]ur decision to decline jurisdiction in this case is based on the facts in the record before us, and that subsequent changes in the treatment of scholarship players could outweigh the considerations that motivate our decision today.

For these reasons, we conclude, without deciding whether the scholarship players are employees under Section 2(3), that it would not effectuate the policies of the Act to assert jurisdiction in this case.

We emphasize that our decision today does not concern other individuals associated with FBS football, but is limited to Northwestern's scholarship football players. In this regard, we observe that the Board has exercised jurisdiction in other contexts involving college athletics. The Board has, for example, adjudicated cases involving athletic coaches, college physical plant employees who performed functions in support of athletic events, and referees. Our decision today should not be understood to extend to university personnel associated with athletic programs.

Further, we are declining jurisdiction only in this case involving the football players at Northwestern University; we therefore do not address what the Board's approach might be to a petition for all FBS scholarship football players (or at least those at private colleges and universities). . . . [T]he Board's decision not to assert jurisdiction does not preclude a reconsideration of this issue in the future. For example, if the circumstances of Northwestern's players or FBS football change such that the underpinnings of our conclusions regarding jurisdiction warrant reassessment, the Board may revisit its policy [citations omitted].

CONCLUSION

The Board has never asserted jurisdiction, or even been asked to assert jurisdiction, in a case involving scholarship football players or similarly situated individuals, and for the reasons stated above, we decline to do so in this case. Processing a petition for the scholarship players at this single institution under the circumstances presented here would not promote stability in labor relations. Moreover, recent changes, as well as calls for additional reforms, suggest that the situation of scholarship players may well change in the near future. For these reasons and the others set forth above, even if the scholarship players were statutory employees (which the Board does not here decide), we have concluded that it will not effectuate the policies of the Act to assert jurisdiction in this case.

NOTES AND QUESTIONS

1. *Analysis of* Northwestern University. Do you agree with the NLRB's determination that even if Northwestern scholarship football players are statutory employees, "it would not effectuate the policies of the [National Labor Relations Act] to assert jurisdiction" and permit them to decide whether to unionize? Is the NLRB's decision sound public policy consistent with the objectives of federal labor law? If intercollegiate athletes cannot unionize, what other laws require them to receive fair benefits and compensation for their playing services?

2. *Should Public University Student-Athletes Be Permitted to Unionize?* As noted in the NLRB's decision, some states such as Michigan and Ohio passed legislation prohibiting intercollegiate athletes at public universities, who do

not have the right to unionize under federal labor law, from unionizing under state labor laws applicable to public employees. If you were advising a state legislative committee, would you recommend that they permit inter-collegiate athletes at public universities within the state to unionize? What would the implications of such a decision be for the universities, internally and within the NCAA and their respective conferences? For discussions of student-athletes and their efforts to unionize see Marc Edelman, *The Future of College Athlete Players Unions: Lesson Learned from Northwestern University and Potential Next Steps in the College Athletes' Rights Movement*, 38 Cardozo L. Rev. 1627 (2017); Karcher, *supra*; William B. Gould, Glenn M. Wong & Eric Weitz, *Full Court Press: Northwestern University, A New Challenge to the NCAA*, 35 Loy. L.A. Ent. L. Rev. 1 (2014).

3. *Minimum Wage for Student-Athletes?* In *Berger v NCAA*, 162 F.Supp.3d 845 (S.D. Ind. 2016), the court ruled that three University of Pennsylvania wom-en's track & field athletes had standing to assert a Fair Labor Standards Act (FLSA) claim solely against their alleged employer (Penn), effectively denying their request to certify a plaintiff class of all current and former NCAA Division I women's and men's student-athletes on rosters from aca-demic year 2012-13 to the present against the NCAA and 123 Division I uni-versities. It also held that the student-athletes are not "employees" under the FLSA because "the revered tradition of amateurism in college sports" constitutes "an essential part of the 'economic reality' of the relationship between Plaintiffs and Penn." It concluded "students at Penn who choose to participate in sports—whether NCAA sports, club sports, or intramural sports—as part of their educational experience do so because they view it as beneficial to them." In affirming the district court's decision, the Seventh Circuit ruled that former student-athletes' relationships to the NCAA were too tenuous for the athletes to be considered NCAA employees. Addressing whether student-athletes were employees of their universities, the court adopts the district court's reasoning in concluding that "student-athletes are not employees and are not entitled to a minimum wage under the FLSA." *Berger v. NCAA*, 843 F.3d 285, 293 (2016).

In *Dawson v. NCAA*, 250 F.Supp.3d 401 (N.D. Cal. 2017), the court, rely-ing on *Berger*, dismissed ex-USC linebacker Lamar Dawson's complaint that the NCAA and Pac-12 violated the FLSA and the California Labor Code by not paying college football players minimum wage or overtime pay. It held that "the premise that revenue generation is determinative of employ-ment status is not supported by the case law." The Ninth Circuit affirmed the lower court decision. *Dawson v. NCAA*, 932 F.3d 905 (9th Cir. 2019). Examining three factors to be considered in determining employee status under an economic reality test, the court concluded: (1) Dawson's schol-arship from USC engendered no expectation of compensation from the NCAA or the PAC-12 because neither defendant provided him with a schol-arship; (2) the NCAA's and PAC-12's regulatory roles did not convey upon either entity the power to fire or hire Dawson—neither entity selected who would play on the football team nor had any actual supervisory power over players; and (3) NCAA rules were not promulgated or implemented in an effort to evade the law. The court also held that "under California law, student-athletes are generally deemed not to be employees of their schools." *Id.* at *7. But see *Livers v. NCAA*, 2018 WL 3609839 (E.D. Pa.

Jul. 26, 2018) (applying economic realities test, the court concludes plaintiff student-athlete allege facts sufficient, at this stage, to establish he was an FSLA employee of Villanova University). See Christine Colwell, *Playing for Pay or Playing to Play: Student-Athletes as Employees Under the Fair Labor Standards Act,* 79 La. L. Rev. 899 (2019) (surveying cases involving student-athletes as employees under the FSLA).

D.   NCAA RULES ENFORCEMENT PROCESSES AND LEGAL LIMITS THEREON

Pursuant to section 1.3.1 ("Basic Purpose") of its constitution, the NCAA has established an amateur/education model of intercollegiate athletics:

> The competitive athletics programs of member institutions are designed to be a vital part of the educational system. A basic purpose of the NCAA is to maintain intercollegiate athletics as an integral part of the education program and the athlete as an integral part of the student body and, by doing so, retain a clear line of demarcation between intercollegiate athletics and professional sports.

See NCAA, 2019-20 *NCAA Division I Manual,* http://www.ncaapublications.com/productdownloads/D119.pdf.

From its inception in December 1905 to the present, the NCAA members retained control over their own programs, a fundamental principle known today as Institutional Autonomy. NCAA members propose and adopt rules for the association, and each institution is responsible for acting in compliance with those regulations. See *2019-20 NCAA Division I Manual,* Bylaw 2.1.1. Rules compliance has always been a concern of the NCAA membership, and at the 1948 annual convention, the NCAA made its first attempt at becoming a regulatory body by instituting the Sanity Code. This attempt was short lived, as the only penalty for violators was expulsion, and the membership failed to vote out seven institutions that were found to have committed violations. It was not until the 1950s, when Walter Byers was hired as the first full-time executive director and the national association office was established, that the NCAA became a regulatory enforcement body. See Ronald A. Smith, *Pay for play: A history of big-time college athletic reform,* 2011 for a complete history of the NCAA governance and enforcement.

NCAA CONSTITUTION AND DIVISION I BYLAWS, 2019-20 NCAA DIVISION I MANUAL

2.1   THE PRINCIPLE OF INSTITUTIONAL CONTROL AND RESPONSIBILITY

2.1.1   Responsibility for Control. It is the responsibility of each member institution to control its intercollegiate athletics program in compliance with the rules and regulations of the Association. The institution's president or chancellor is responsible for the administration of all aspects of the athletics program, including approval of the budget and audit of all expenditures. . . .

2.1.2 Scope of Responsibility. The institution's responsibility for the conduct of its intercollegiate athletics program includes responsibility for the actions of its staff members and for the actions of any other individual or organization engaged in activities promoting the athletics interests of the institution.

6.01 GENERAL PRINCIPLE

6.01.1 Institutional Control. The control and responsibility for the conduct of intercollegiate athletics shall be exercised by the institution itself and by the conference(s), if any, of which it is a member. Administrative control or faculty control, or a combination of the two, shall constitute institutional control.

Over time, the NCAA's member institutions have promulgated detailed, extensive rules to maintain academic integrity, amateurism, and competitive balance in intercollegiate athletics. The Association's rules enforcement and disciplinary system includes a large enforcement staff that investigates and prosecutes rules violations. The Committee on Infractions functions like a trial court and imposes sanctions, while the Infractions Appeals Committee acts like an appellate court. The NCAA has contractual authority to sanction only its member institutions, but because the member institutions must comply, it also has the effective ability to indirectly sanction coaches and other institutional personnel, student-athletes, and other representatives of a university's athletics interests for their rules' violations.

The NCAA has separate internal processes for resolving student-athlete eligibility issues and rules violations. For example, there are NCAA committees that consider university requests on behalf of student-athletes for waivers of eligibility requirements or reinstatement of eligibility for violations of amateurism rules. The NCAA Committee on Competitive Safeguards and Medical Aspects of Sport hears appeals of student-athlete drug testing violations and determines appropriate disciplinary sanctions.

The following materials provide an overview of the NCAA's internal rules enforcement processes, including some examples of significant infractions cases, as well as the federal laws that must be complied with in exercising this governing authority. The NCAA's rules enforcement processes are not subject to the constraints of the U.S. Constitution (e.g., due process requirements) because the NCAA is not a state actor (*see NCAA v. Tarkanian, infra*), although it exercises nationwide plenary governing authority and many of its member institutions are public universities that comply with the requirements of the federal constitution. Courts also have held that the U.S. Constitution precludes state laws from regulating the NCAA's rules enforcement processes (*NCAA v. Miller, infra*) to avoid the risk of potentially burdensome and conflicting requirements. The NCAA is a private association of member colleges and universities, and it must comply with its own rules, which are the product of a contract between its members, and the law of private associations (*Bloom v. NCAA, infra*). Courts have expressed a reluctance to permit federal civil rights laws (*NCAA v. Smith, infra*) or state constitutional provisions (*Brennan v. Bd. of Trustees for University of Louisiana Systems, infra*) to be used to invalidate NCAA student-athlete eligibility determinations or sanctions for rules violations.

1. Application of Federal Constitutional Law to NCAA Rules Enforcement Processes

The U.S. Constitution imposes constraints on public universities and colleges, whose conduct constitutes state action. However, the U.S. Supreme Court has ruled that the NCAA is not a state actor; therefore, its rules and enforcement processes are not subject to the same limits as those of its public member institutions in its governance of intercollegiate athletics.

NCAA v. TARKANIAN

488 U.S. 179 (1988)

Justice STEVENS delivered the opinion of the Court.

When he became head basketball coach at University of Nevada, Las Vegas (UNLV) in 1973, Jerry Tarkanian inherited a team with a mediocre 14-14 record. Four years later the team won 29 out of 32 games and placed third in the championship tournament sponsored by the National Collegiate Athletic Association (NCAA), to which UNLV belongs.

Yet in September 1977 UNLV informed Tarkanian that it was going to suspend him. No dissatisfaction with Tarkanian, once described as "the 'winningest' active basketball coach," motivated his suspension. Rather, the impetus was a report by the NCAA detailing 38 violations of NCAA rules by UNLV personnel, including 10 involving Tarkanian. The NCAA had placed the University's basketball team on probation for two years and ordered UNLV to show cause why the NCAA should not impose further penalties unless UNLV severed all ties during the probation between its intercollegiate athletic program and Tarkanian.

Facing demotion and a drastic cut in pay, Tarkanian brought suit in Nevada state court, alleging that he had been deprived of his Fourteenth Amendment due process rights in violation of 42 U.S.C. § 1983. Ultimately Tarkanian obtained injunctive relief and an award of attorney's fees against both UNLV and the NCAA. . . . NCAA's liability may be upheld only if its participation in the events that led to Tarkanian's suspension constituted "state action" prohibited by the Fourteenth Amendment and were performed "under color of state law within the meaning of § 1983. . . ."

I

THE NCAA INVESTIGATION OF UNLV

On November 28, 1972, the Committee on Infractions notified UNLV's president that it was initiating a preliminary inquiry into alleged violations of NCAA requirements by UNLV. As a result of that preliminary inquiry, some three years later the Committee decided that an "Official Inquiry" was warranted and so advised the UNLV president on February 25, 1976. That advice included a series of detailed allegations concerning the recruitment of student athletes during the period between 1971 and 1975. Many of the allegations implicated Tarkanian. It requested UNLV to investigate and provide detailed information concerning each alleged incident.

With the assistance of the Attorney General of Nevada and private counsel, UNLV conducted a thorough investigation of the charges. On October 27,

1976, it filed a comprehensive response containing voluminous exhibits and sworn affidavits. The response denied all of the allegations and specifically concluded that Tarkanian was completely innocent of wrongdoing. Thereafter, the Committee conducted four days of hearings at which counsel for UNLV and Tarkanian presented their views of the facts and challenged the credibility of the NCAA investigators and their informants. Ultimately the Committee decided that many of the charges could not be supported, but it did find 38 violations of NCAA rules, including 10 committed by Tarkanian. Most serious was the finding that Tarkanian had violated the University's obligation to provide full cooperation with the NCAA investigation. . . .

The Committee proposed a series of sanctions against UNLV. The Committee also requested UNLV to show cause why additional penalties should not be imposed against UNLV if it failed to discipline Tarkanian by removing him completely from the University's intercollegiate athletic program during the probation period. UNLV appealed most of the Committee's findings and proposed sanctions to the NCAA Council. After hearing arguments from attorneys representing UNLV and Tarkanian, the Council on August 25, 1977 unanimously approved the Committee's investigation and hearing process and adopted all its recommendations.

UNLV'S DISCIPLINE OF TARKANIAN

Promptly after receiving the NCAA report, the president of UNLV directed the University's vice president to schedule a hearing to determine whether the Committee's recommended sanctions should be applied. Tarkanian and UNLV were represented at that hearing, the NCAA was not. Although the vice president expressed doubt concerning the sufficiency of the evidence supporting the Committee's findings, he concluded that "given the terms of our adherence to the NCAA we cannot substitute—biased as we must be—our own judgment on the credibility of witnesses for that of the infractions committee and the Council." . . . [H]e advised the president that he had three options:

1. Reject the sanction requiring us to disassociate Coach Tarkanian from the athletic program and take the risk of still heavier sanctions, e.g., possible extra years of probation.
2. Recognize the University's delegation to the NCAA of the power to act as ultimate arbiter of these matters, thus reassigning Mr. Tarkanian from his present position—though tenured and without adequate notice—even while believing that the NCAA was wrong.
3. Pull out of the NCAA completely on the grounds that you will not execute what you hold to be their unjust judgments. . . .

[T]he president accepted the second option and notified Tarkanian that he was to be completely severed of any and all relations, formal or informal, with the University's Intercollegiate athletic program during the period of the University's NCAA probation.

TARKANIAN'S LAWSUIT AGAINST UNLV

The day before his suspension was to become effective, Tarkanian filed an action in Nevada state court for declaratory and injunctive relief against UNLV and a number of its officers. He alleged that these defendants had, in violation of 42 U.S.C. § 1983, deprived him of property and liberty without the due process of law guaranteed by the Fourteenth Amendment to the United States Constitution. Based on a stipulation of facts and the testimony offered by Tarkanian, the trial court enjoined UNLV from suspending Tarkanian on the ground that he had been denied procedural and substantive due process of law. UNLV appealed.

The NCAA, which had not been joined as a party, filed an amicus curiae brief arguing that there was no actual controversy between Tarkanian and UNLV; thus, the suit should be dismissed. Alternatively, the NCAA contended that the trial court had exceeded its jurisdiction by effectively invalidating the enforcement proceedings of the NCAA, even though the Association was not a party to the suit. Should a controversy exist, the NCAA argued, it was a necessary party to litigate the scope of any relief. Finally, it contested the trial court's conclusion that Tarkanian had been denied due process. The Nevada Supreme Court concluded that there was an actual controversy but agreed that the NCAA was a necessary party and therefore reversed and remanded to permit joinder of the NCAA. *University of Nevada v. Tarkanian*, 95 Nev. 389, 594 P.2d 1159 (1979).

THE LAWSUIT AGAINST NCAA

Tarkanian consequently filed a second amended complaint adding the NCAA. . . . [T]he trial judge conducted a two-week bench trial and resolved the issues in Tarkanian's favor. The court concluded that NCAA's conduct constituted state action for jurisdictional and constitutional purposes, and that its decision was arbitrary and capricious. It reaffirmed its earlier injunction barring UNLV from disciplining Tarkanian or otherwise enforcing the Confidential Report. Additionally, it enjoined the NCAA from conducting "any further proceedings against the University," from enforcing its show-cause order, and from taking any other action against the University that had been recommended in the Confidential Report. . . .

. . . The Nevada Supreme Court agreed that Tarkanian had been deprived of both property and liberty protected by the Constitution and that he was not afforded due process before suspension. It thus affirmed the trial court's injunction insofar as it pertained to Tarkanian, but narrowed its scope "only to prohibit enforcement of the penalties imposed upon Tarkanian in Confidential Report No. 123(47) and UNLV's adoption of those penalties. . . ."

As a predicate for its disposition, the State Supreme Court held that the NCAA had engaged in state action. Several strands of arguments supported this holding. First, the court assumed that it was reviewing "UNLV's and the NCAA'[s] imposition of penalties against Tarkanian," . . . [and not] the NCAA's proposed sanctions against UNLV if it failed to discipline Tarkanian appropriately. Second, it regarded the NCAA's regulatory activities as state action because "many NCAA member institutions were either public or government supported. . . ." Third, it stated that the right to discipline a public employee "is traditionally the exclusive prerogative of the state" and that UNLV could not escape its responsibility for such disciplinary action by delegating that duty to a private entity. . . . Summing up its holding that the NCAA's activities constituted state action, the Nevada Supreme Court stated:

> The first prong [of *Lugar v. Edmondson Oil Co.*, 457 U.S. 922 (1982)] is met because no third party could impose disciplinary sanctions upon a state university employee unless the third party received the right or privilege from the university. Thus, the

deprivation which Tarkanian alleges is caused by the exercise of a right or privilege created by the state. Also, in the instant case, both UNLV and the NCAA must be considered state actors. By delegating authority to the NCAA over athletic personnel decisions and by imposing the NCAA sanctions against Tarkanian, UNLV acted jointly with the NCAA.

II

Embedded in our Fourteenth Amendment jurisprudence is a dichotomy between state action, which is subject to scrutiny under the Amendment's Due Process Clause, and private conduct, against which the Amendment affords no shield, no matter how unfair that conduct may be. . . .

In this case, Tarkanian argues that the NCAA was a state actor because it misused power that it possessed by virtue of state law. He claims specifically that UNLV delegated its own functions to the NCAA, clothing the Association with authority both to adopt rules governing UNLV's athletic programs and to enforce those rules on behalf of UNLV. Similarly, the Nevada Supreme Court held that UNLV had delegated its authority over personnel decisions to the NCAA. Therefore, the court reasoned, the two entities acted jointly to deprive Tarkanian of liberty and property interests, making the NCAA as well as UNLV a state actor.

These contentions fundamentally misconstrue the facts of this case. In the typical case raising a state action issue, a private party has taken the decisive conduct as state action. This may occur if the State creates the legal framework governing the conduct . . . if it delegates its authority to the private actor, . . . or sometimes if it knowingly accepts the benefits derived from unconstitutional behavior. . . . [I]n the usual case we ask whether the State provided a mantle of authority that enhanced the power of the harm-causing individual actor.

This case uniquely mirrors the traditional state action case. Here the final act challenged by Tarkanian—his suspension—was committed by UNLV. When it decides to impose a serious disciplinary sanction upon one of its tenured employees, it must comply with the terms of the Due Process Clause of the Fourteenth Amendment to the Federal Constitution. . . .

The mirror image presented in this case requires us to step through an analytical looking glass to resolve it. Clearly UNLV's conduct was influenced by the rules and recommendations of the NCAA, the private party. But it was UNLV, the state entity, that actually suspended Tarkanian. Thus the question is not whether UNLV participated to a critical extent in the NCAA's activities, but whether UNLV's actions in compliance with the NCAA rules and recommendations turned the NCAA's conduct into state action.

We examine first the relationship between UNLV and the NCAA regarding the NCAA's rule-making. UNLV is among the NCAA's members and participated in promulgating the Association's rules; it must be assumed, therefore, that Nevada had some impact on the NCAA's policy determinations. Yet the NCAA's several hundred other public and private member institutions each similarly affected those policies. Those institutions, the vast majority of which were located in states other than Nevada, did not act under color of Nevada law. It necessarily follows that the source of the legislation adopted by the NCAA is not Nevada but the collective membership, speaking through an organization that is independent of any particular State. . . .

State action nonetheless might lie if UNLV, by embracing the NCAA's rules, transformed them into state rules and the NCAA into a state actor. . . . UNLV engaged in state action when it adopted the NCAA's rules to govern its own behavior, but that would be true even if UNLV had taken no part in the promulgation of those rules. UNLV retained the authority to withdraw from the NCAA and establish its own standards. The University alternatively could have stayed in the Association and worked through the Association's legislative process to amend rules or standards it deemed harsh, unfair, or unwieldy. Neither UNLV's decision to adopt the NCAA's standards nor its minor role in their formulation is a sufficient reason for concluding that the NCAA was acting under color of Nevada law when it promulgated standards governing athlete recruitment, eligibility, and academic performance.

Tarkanian further asserts that the NCAA's investigation, enforcement proceedings, and consequent recommendations constituted state action because they resulted from a delegation of power by UNLV. UNLV, as an NCAA member, subscribed to the statement in the Association's bylaws that NCAA "enforcement procedures are an essential part of the intercollegiate athletic program of each member institution. . . ." [A s]tate may delegate authority to a private party and thereby make that party a state actor. . . . But UNLV delegated no power to the NCAA to take specific action against any University employee. The commitment by UNLV to adhere to NCAA enforcement procedures was enforceable only by sanctions that the NCAA might impose on UNLV itself.

Indeed, the notion that UNLV's promise to cooperate in the NCAA enforcement proceedings was tantamount to a partnership agreement or the transfer of certain University powers to the NCAA is belied by the history of this case. It is quite obvious that UNLV used its best efforts to retain its winning coach — a goal diametrically opposed to the NCAA's interest in ascertaining the truth of its investigators' reports. During the several years that the NCAA investigated the alleged violations, the NCAA and UNLV acted much more like adversaries than like partners engaged in a dispassionate search for the truth. The NCAA cannot be regarded as an agent of UNLV for purposes of that proceeding. It is more correctly characterized as an agent of its remaining members which, as competitors of UNLV, had an interest in the effective and evenhanded enforcement of NCAA's recruitment standards. . . .

The NCAA enjoyed no governmental powers to facilitate its investigation. It had no power to subpoena witnesses, to impose contempt sanctions, or to assert sovereign authority over any individual. Its greatest authority was to threaten sanctions against UNLV, with the ultimate sanction being expulsion of the University from membership. Contrary to the premise of the Nevada Supreme Court's opinion, the NCAA did not — indeed, could not — directly discipline Tarkanian or any other state university employee. The express terms of the Confidential Report did not demand the suspension unconditionally; rather, it requested "the university . . . to show cause" why the NCAA should not impose additional penalties if UNLV declines to suspend Tarkanian. . . . Even the university's vice president acknowledged that the Report gave the university options other than suspension: UNLV could have retained Tarkanian and risked additional sanctions, perhaps even expulsion from the NCAA, or it could have withdrawn voluntarily from the Association.

Finally, Tarkanian argues that the power of the NCAA is so great that UNLV had no practical alternative to compliance with its demands. We are not at all sure this is true . . ., but even if we assume that a private monopolist can impose its will on a state agency by a threatened refusal to deal with it, it does not follow that such a private party is therefore acting under color of state law. . . .

It would be ironic indeed to conclude that the NCAA's imposition of sanctions against UNLV—sanctions that UNLV and its counsel, including the Attorney General of Nevada, steadfastly opposed during protracted adversary proceedings—is fairly attributable to the State of Nevada. It would be more appropriate to conclude that UNLV has conducted its athletic program under color of the policies adopted by the NCAA, rather than that those policies were developed and enforced under color of Nevada law.

The judgment of the Nevada Supreme Court is reversed and the case is remanded to that court for further proceedings not inconsistent with this opinion.

It is so ordered.

Justice WHITE, with whom Justice BRENNAN, Justice MARSHALL, and Justice O'CONNOR join, dissenting.

. . . I agree with the majority that this case is different on its facts from many of our prior state action cases. As the majority notes, in our "typical case raising a state action issue, a private party has taken the decisive step that caused the harm to the plaintiff." . . . In this case, however, the final act that caused the harm to Tarkanian was committed, not by a private party, but by a party conceded to be a state actor.

But the situation presented by this case is not unknown to us and certainly is not unique. In both *Adickes v. S.H. Kress & Co.*, 398 U.S. 144 (1970), and *Dennis v. Sparks*, 449 U.S. 24 (1980), we faced the question of whether private parties could be held to be state actors in cases in which the final or decisive act was carried out by a state official. In both cases we held that the private parties could be found to be state actors, if they were "jointly engaged with state officials in the challenged action. . . ."

On the facts of the present case, the NCAA acted jointly with UNLV in suspending Tarkanian. First, Tarkanian was suspended for violations of NCAA rules, which UNLV embraced in its agreement with the NCAA. . . .

Second, the NCAA and UNLV also agreed that the NCAA would conduct the hearings concerning violations of its rules. Although UNLV conducted its own investigation into the recruiting violations alleged by the NCAA, the NCAA procedures provide that it is the NCAA Committee on Infractions that "determine[s] facts related to alleged violations," subject to an appeal to the NCAA Council. . . .

Third, the NCAA and UNLV agreed that the findings of fact made by the NCAA at the hearings it conducted would be binding on UNLV. By becoming a member of the NCAA, UNLV did more than merely "promise to cooperate in the NCAA enforcement proceedings." . . . [T]he NCAA's findings were final and not subject to further review by any other body . . ., and it was for that reason that UNLV suspended Tarkanian, despite concluding that many of those findings were wrong. . . .

In short, it was the NCAA's findings that Tarkanian had violated NCAA rules, made at NCAA-conducted hearings, all of which were agreed to by UNLV in its membership agreement with the NCAA, that resulted in Tarkanian's suspension by UNLV. [T]he majority relies on the fact that the NCAA did not have any power to take action directly against Tarkanian as indicating that the NCAA was not a state actor. . . . But the same was true in [our decision in *Dennis*]: the private parties did not have any power to issue an injunction against the plaintiff.

Only the trial judge, using his authority granted under state law, could impose the injunction.

Next, the majority points out that UNLV was free to withdraw from the NCAA at any time. . . . But of course the trial judge in *Dennis* could have withdrawn from his agreement at any time as well. That he had that option is simply irrelevant to finding that he had entered into agreement. What mattered was not that he could have withdrawn, but rather that he did not do so.

Finally, the majority relies extensively on the fact that the NCAA and UNLV were adversaries throughout the proceedings before the NCAA. . . . But this opportunity for opposition, provided for by the terms of the membership agreement between UNLV and the NCAA, does not undercut the agreement itself. Surely our decision in *Dennis* would not have been different had the private parties permitted the trial judge to seek to persuade them that he should not grant the injunction before finally holding the judge to his agreement with them to do so. The key there, as with any conspiracy, is that ultimately the parties agreed to take the action.

The majority states in conclusion that "[I]t would be ironic indeed to conclude that the NCAA's imposition of sanctions against UNLV—sanctions that UNLV and its counsel, including the Attorney General of Nevada, steadfastly opposed during protracted adversary proceedings—is fairly attributable to the State of Nevada." . . . Had UNLV refused to suspend Tarkanian, and the NCAA responded by imposing sanctions against UNLV, it would be hard indeed to find any state action that harmed Tarkanian. But that is not this case. Here, UNLV did suspend Tarkanian, and it did so because it embraced the NCAA rules governing conduct of its athletic program and adopted the results of the hearings conducted by the NCAA concerning Tarkanian, as it had agreed that it would. Under these facts, I would find that the NCAA acted jointly with UNLV and therefore is a state actor.

I respectfully dissent.

NOTES AND QUESTIONS

1. *Analysis of* Tarkanian. Comparing the reasoning of the majority and the dissent, which appears to be the stronger argument? What would be the effects of a Supreme Court ruling that the NCAA is a state actor on the NCAA's rules enforcement processes?

2. *Dormant Commerce Clause Limit on State Regulatory Authority.* In response to *Tarkanian*, the Nevada legislature enacted a statute requiring "any national collegiate athletic association to provide a Nevada institution, employee, student-athlete, or booster who is accused of a rules infraction with certain procedural due process protections during an enforcement proceeding in which sanctions may be imposed." *NCAA v. Miller*, 10 F.3d 633, 637 (9th Cir. 1993). The federal district court upheld the statute, but the Ninth Circuit reversed:

> The Statute would force the NCAA to regulate the integrity of its product in every state according to Nevada's procedural rules. Thus, if a university in state X ("U of X") engaged in illicit practices while recruiting a high school quarterback from state Y, the NCAA would have to conduct its enforcement proceeding according to Nevada law in order to maintain uniformity in its

rules. Nevada procedures do not allow the Committee on Infractions to consider some types of evidence, like hearsay and unsworn affidavits, that it is permitted consider under the NCAA Bylaws. As a result, if its case against the U of X were based on unsworn affidavits from unavailable witnesses, the NCAA might not have enough admissible evidence to prove that there was a violation of the recruiting rules. The NCAA could be forced to allow the U of X to use an illegally recruited quarterback from state Y because it could not prove a rules violation under the strictures of Nevada law. In this way, the Statute could control the regulation of the integrity of a product in interstate commerce that occurs wholly outside Nevada's borders. The Commerce Clause forbids that sort of extraterritorial effect.

The Statute's extraterritorial reach also violates the Commerce Clause because of its potential interaction or conflict with similar statutes in other jurisdictions. "Generally speaking, the Commerce Clause protects against inconsistent legislation arising from the projection of one state regulatory regime into the jurisdiction of another State." [Citation omitted.]

Nevada is not the only state that has enacted or could enact legislation that establishes procedural rules for NCAA enforcement proceedings. Florida, Illinois, and Nebraska have also adopted due process statutes and similar legislation has been introduced in five other states. Those statutes could easily subject the NCAA to conflicting requirements. For example, suppose that state X required proof of an infraction beyond a reasonable doubt, while state Y only required clear and convincing evidence, and state Z required infractions to be proven by a preponderance of the evidence. Given that the NCAA must have uniform enforcement procedures in order to accomplish its fundamental goals, its operation would be disrupted because it could not possibly comply with all three statutes. Nor would it do to say that it need only comply with the most stringent burden of persuasion (beyond a reasonable doubt), for a state with a less stringent standard might well consider its standard a maximum as well as a minimum. The serious risk of inconsistent obligations wrought by the extra-territorial effect of the Statute demonstrates why it constitutes a per se violation of the Commerce Clause.

Id. at 639-640. Because the NCAA is engaged in interstate commerce, Congress has authority pursuant to the Commerce Clause to enact federal legislation that would directly regulate the NCAA. What would be the advantages and disadvantages of federal regulation?

3. In *Cohane v. NCAA*, 2005 WL 2373472 (W.D.N.Y. 2005), the district court held that an NCAA investigation of a men's basketball coach did not constitute state action despite cooperation in the investigation on the part of his employer, a public university. On appeal, however, the Second Circuit concluded that the district court erred in concluding that the coach could not prove a set of facts showing that the NCAA was a state actor by engaging in joint activity with a public university. The complaint alleged that the university forced the coach's resignation immediately upon learning of the charges in an attempt to placate the NCAA, actively participated in the case against the coach, and intimidated witnesses into giving false statements to NCAA investigators. These allegations, combined with others, if proven, could show joint activity between the university and the NCAA to deprive the coach of a property right in his university contract without due process. The court further stated that the coach may be able to show that the public university's assistance and the exercise of its authority over student-athlete witnesses enabled the NCAA to

issue the alleged defamatory report and impose sanctions on him, which gave rise to his federal constitutional law claim that the NCAA violated his due process rights. *Cohane v. NCAA*, 215 Fed. Appx. 13, 2007 WL 247710 (2d Cir. 2007), *cert. denied*, 128 S. Ct. 641 (2007). Does *Cohane* provide a means of judicially characterizing the NCAA as a state actor because of its joint conduct with its public member institutions that is consistent with *Tarkanian*?

2. *The NCAA Infractions Process, Institutional and Personnel Rules Violations, and Sanctions*

In 1954, to ensure fairness and a level playing field in intercollegiate athletics, the NCAA formed the Committee on Infractions (COI) to interpret NCAA rules and impose penalties on member institutions for rules violations. Concerns were frequently raised regarding the way the COI enforced the rules against member institutions. Although *Tarkanian* held the NCAA did not have to afford constitutionally mandated procedural due process in its investigative processes or to those appearing before the COI, its member institutions voluntarily revised their rules enforcement procedures to address these concerns. A Special Committee to Review the National Collegiate Athletic Association Enforcement and Infractions Process (Review Committee) was formed to evaluate the enforcement process of the NCAA to ensure timeliness, fairness, and consistency. The Review Committee issued a report in 1991 that included a series of recommended reforms designed to bring greater fairness to the NCAA's rules enforcement and infractions processes. The establishment of an appellate body, the Infractions Appeals Committee (IAC), was based on one of these recommendations. In 2012, the Division I board of directors adopted major reforms, including re-characterizing rules infractions and their severity along with adding more members to the COI to expedite the hearing process. These changes were designed to establish and strengthen a culture of shared responsibility among head coaches, the compliance community, institutional leadership, and conferences for upholding the values of intercollegiate athletics. The NCAA defines the Infractions Program in Bylaw 19.

NCAA CONSTITUTION AND DIVISION I
BYLAWS, 2019-20 NCAA DIVISION I MANUAL

19.01 [INFRACTIONS PROGRAM] GENERAL PRINCIPLES.
  19.01.1 Mission of the infractions Program. It is the mission of the NCAA infractions program to uphold integrity and fair play among the NCAA membership, and to prescribe appropriate and fair penalties if violations occur. One of the fundamental principles of the infractions program is to ensure that those institutions and student-athletes abiding by the NCAA constitution and bylaws are not disadvantaged by their commitment to compliance. The program is committed to the fairness of procedures and the timely resolution of infractions cases. The ability

to investigate allegations and penalize infractions is critical to the common interests of the Association's membership and the preservation of its enduring values.

19.01.2 Accountability. The infractions program shall hold institutions, coaches, administrators and student-athletes who violate the NCAA constitution and bylaws accountable for their conduct, both at the individual and institutional levels.

19.01.4 Penalty structure. The infractions program shall address the varying levels of infractions and, for the most serious infractions, include guidelines for a range of penalties, which the Committee on Infractions, subject to review by the Infractions Appeals Committee, or the Independent Resolution Panel may prescribe. Penalties shall depend on the relative severity of the infraction(s), the presence of aggravating or mitigating factors and, in some cases, the existence of extenuating circumstances.

19.01.5 Exemplary Conduct. Individuals employed by or associated with member institutions for the administration, the conduct or the coaching of intercollegiate athletics are, in the final analysis, teachers of young people. Their responsibility is an affirmative one, and they must do more than avoid improper conduct or questionable acts. Their own moral values must be so certain and positive that those younger and more pliable will be influenced by a fine example. Much more is expected of them than of the less critically placed citizen.

The Division I enforcement and infractions process is described in Bylaw 19.5 Enforcement Staff Review and Investigation of Alleged Violations. The process begins when the enforcement staff learns of information regarding a potential compliance violation. The enforcement staff determines whether there is sufficient evidence indicating the need for a full investigation or if the issue can be resolved without a formal investigation. If an investigation is warranted, the enforcement staff represents the membership in gathering all relevant information. Information may be shared with the institution if it could assist in stopping an ongoing violation. *2019-20 NCAA Division I Manual,* Bylaw 19.5.1.

A Notice of Inquiry is provided to the president or chancellor of the member institution before the enforcement staff visits the institution to conduct an inquiry. Institutions are obligated to cooperate with the investigation (Bylaw 19.2.3) and may not make public disclosures about the case until a final decision has been announced (Bylaw 19.01.3; Bylaw 19.5.8). Individuals who may have information to assist with the investigation will be interviewed by the enforcement staff; those individuals are obligated to provide truthful information (Bylaw 19.5.5.2) and may be represented by personal legal counsel (Bylaw 19.5.4). An institutional representative may be present during these interviews (Bylaw 19.5.6.1). If information gathered does not appear to require a Notice of Allegations for Level I and Level II violations, or involve Level III allegations, the investigation will be terminated (Bylaw 19.5.10). Otherwise, the institution may pursue a negotiated resolution with the enforcement staff, subject to the approval of a hearing panel of the COI (Bylaw 19.5.12) or proceed to summary disposition or an infractions hearing.

If the institution, involved individuals, and the enforcement staff agree, a jointly produced written report containing findings of fact, identification of rules violations, and proposed penalties may be submitted to the COI to invoke the summary disposition process (Bylaw 19.6). If the written report is accepted, the hearing panel for the COI will prepare a report of its decision, forward the report to the parties, and publicly announce the resolution of the case (Bylaw 19.6.4.3). If the hearing panel accepts the findings of fact, but proposes additional penalties, the institution and/or involved parties may either accept the penalties or request an expedited hearing before the panel. After the hearing, the panel will provide a written report and announce its decision; appeals will be made to the IAC (Bylaw 16.4.5). If the panel rejects the proposed findings of fact, the case will proceed with a Formal Notice of Allegations (Bylaw 19.7).

The Notice of Allegations is quite similar to a legal complaint identifying all involved parties and stating with specificity all alleged violations of NCAA rules, the level of each violation, the processing level of the case, all factual information, aggravating and/or mitigating factors, and the available hearing procedures (Bylaw 19.7.1). Similar to an answer to a complaint, the institution and involved individuals have 90 days to respond (Bylaw 19.7.2), and the enforcement staff have an additional 60 days to provide a written reply to the institutional response (Bylaw 19.7.3). The assigned hearing panel of the COI will hear the case according to the procedures applicable to the most serious allegations (Bylaw 19.7.7).

The COI is composed of 24 individuals including current or former college or university presidents, senior institutional administrators, athletics directors, former coaches, conference officers, institutional faculty or staff, athletics personnel with compliance experience, and public representatives with formal legal training not associated with a member institution or conference (Bylaw 19.3.1). Members serve three-year terms and are limited to a total of nine years of service. Cases involving Level I or Level II violations are typically heard by panels of five to seven members of the full COI (Bylaw 19.3.3). The panel will determine findings of fact, whether there are violations of the NCAA constitution and bylaws, and what penalties are appropriate given the circumstances (Bylaw 19.3.6). Bylaw 19.7.8.3.1, adopted in August 2018, allows the COI to consider facts established by courts, agencies, accrediting bodies, or commission reports in addition to evidence gathered by the enforcement staff. The panel may sanction parties who disrupt proceedings or fail to behave in a professional and civil manner. The COI hearing panel prepares and approves the final written infractions decision and releases it to the parties. A redacted report is released to the public shortly thereafter (Bylaw 19.8.1). The COI is also responsible for monitoring compliance with penalties (Bylaw 19.3.6).

Division I implemented a four-tier characterization of violations and sanctions on August 1, 2013, replacing the former two-tier system of major and secondary violations, which is still utilized by Divisions II and III. Level I (severe breach of conduct) describes "[v]iolations that seriously undermine or threaten the integrity of the NCAA collegiate model as set forth in the Constitution and bylaws, including any violation that provides or is intended to provide a substantial or extensive recruiting, competitive or other advantage, or a substantial or extensive impermissible benefit." Level II (significant breach of conduct) consists of "[v]iolations that provide or are intended to provide more than a minimal but less than a substantial or extensive recruiting, competitive or other advantage . . . or . . . conduct that may compromise the integrity of the NCAA collegiate model as set forth in the Constitution and bylaws." Level III (breach of conduct) consists of "[v]iolations that are isolated or limited in nature; provide no more than a minimal recruiting, competitive or other advantage; and do not include more than a minimal impermissible benefit. Multiple Level IV violations may collectively be considered a breach of conduct." Level IV (incidental issues) consists of "[m]inor infractions that are inadvertent and isolated, technical in nature and result in a negligible, if any, competitive advantage. Level IV infractions generally will not affect a student-athlete's eligibility for intercollegiate athletics." *2019-20 NCAA Division I Manual,* Bylaw 19.1.

There are a range of potential sanctions for each level of violations based on their respective severity. Core penalties for Level I and Level II violations include limiting postseason competition, financial penalties such as fines or reduction or elimination of revenue sharing in postseason competition, scholarship reductions, show-cause orders related to disciplinary or corrective actions for individuals in violation of NCAA rules, head coach restrictions including suspension, recruiting restrictions, and institutional probation (Bylaw 19.9.5). Additional Level I or Level II penalties are enumerated in Bylaw 19.9.7 and may include suspension or termination of institutional membership, public reprimand or censure, vacation of records, prohibition against television appearances, and/or disassociation of an individual from interaction with the athletics department. Level III penalties may include declaring a student-athlete ineligible, forfeiting contests, restrictions on off campus recruiting, fines, reduction of scholarships, suspension of coaches and/or staff members, show-cause orders, public reprimand, and/or institutional recertification (Bylaw 19.9.8). As of August 1, 2019, those individuals impacted by show-cause penalties are provided an opportunity to appeal (Bylaw 19.9.9).

In addition to prescribed penalties, the COI panel has discretion to increase or decrease penalties:

19.9.2 Factors Affecting Penalties. The hearing panel shall determine whether any factors that may affect penalties are present for a case. The panel shall weigh any factors and determine whether a party should be subject to standard penalties or should be classified with aggravation or mitigation and, therefore, subject to a higher or lower range of penalties. . . .

19.9.2.1 Aggravation. An aggravated case is one in which aggravating factors for a party outweigh mitigating factors for that party. A case should not be classified as aggravated solely because the number of aggravating factors is larger than the number of mitigating factors. An egregious aggravating factor may outweigh multiple mitigating factors.

19.9.2.2 Standard. A standard case is one in which no mitigating or aggravating factors are present for a party or in which aggravating and mitigating factors for that party are generally of equal weight.

19.9.2.3 Mitigation. A mitigated case is one in which mitigating factors for a party outweigh aggravating factors for that party. A case should not be classified as mitigated solely because the number of mitigating factors is larger than the number of aggravating factors.

Institutions and/or involved individuals may appeal the findings, conclusions, penalties, corrective actions, and/or requirements of the COI by submitting a notice of intent to appeal within 15 days after the release of the public infractions decision (Bylaw 19.10.2). The IAC is a five-member panel appointed by the Division I Board of Directors consisting of current or former institutional or conference members and at least one person from the general public not affiliated with any institution, conference, coach, or student-athlete. The IAC will consider information contained in the COI proceedings, the written materials submitted in support of the appeal as well as the enforcement staff rebuttals, and oral arguments presented during the appeals hearing (Bylaw 19.10.4). New information will be remanded to the COI for further proceedings, which may result in an amended COI decision (Bylaw 19.02.2). If a party requests an appeal oral argument, they may be represented by legal counsel. The IAC may question representatives, the COI panel, enforcement staff and others to determine the issues related to the appeal (Bylaw 19.10.5). Upon conclusion of the appeal, the IAC will deliberate privately and prepare a written decision. The IAC will not set aside COI findings of fact and conclusions unless the appealing party is able to show the factual finding is "clearly contrary to the information presented to the panel; the facts found by the panel do not constitute a violation of the NCAA constitution and bylaws; or there was a procedural error and but for the error, the panel would not have made the finding or conclusion" (Bylaw 19.10.1.2). The IAC written decision is first distributed to the appealing parties, the COI, and other NCAA staff, and then a redacted version is released to the public (Bylaw 19.10.6). Decisions of the IAC are final and binding (Bylaw 19.10.7). COI and IAC cases are published on the NCAA website. Those cases collectively constitute a growing body of private law that internally governs intercollegiate athletics.

Another newly instituted infractions process, effective August 1, 2019, is Independent Accountability Resolution. This process allows the NCAA to resolve select infractions cases before a hearing panel comprised completely of members external to the Association if this will best serve the interests of the Association (Bylaw, 19.11). Four new bodies will be created:

1. The Independent Accountability Oversight Committee will be responsible for the new Independent Accountability Resolution structure, consulting with the Board of Directors and appointing individuals to serve on the various committees.
2. The Infractions Referral Committee will determine which cases will be heard through the independent accountability resolution structure. (See Bylaw 19.11.3.1 for the standard for referral.)
3. The Independent Resolution Panel will hear and decide cases.
4. The Complex Case Unit will determine whether supplemental investigation is needed, investigate, and process violations substantiated through final resolution by the Independent Resolution Panel (Bylaw 19.11.2).

What are the advantages and/or unexpected consequences of using individuals from outside a voluntary membership organization to enforce compliance and adjudicate penalties?

For scholarly review of the NCAA's enforcement process, see, e.g., Timothy Davis and Christopher Hairston, *Majoring in Infractions: The Evolution of the National Collegiate Athletic Association Enforcement Structure*, 92 Ore. L. Rev. 979 (2014); Jerry R. Parkinson, *Scoundrels: An Inside Look at the NCAA Infractions and Enforcement Processes*, 12 Wyo. L. Rev. 215 (2012); Josephine (Jo) R. Potuto and Jerry R. Parkinson, *If It Ain't Broke, Don't Fix It: An Examination of the NCAA Division I Infractions Committee's Composition and Decision-Making Process*, 89 Neb. L. Rev. 437 (2011).

a.   Institutions and the Infractions Process

The following excerpts from reported decisions of the IAC, COI, and NCAA are illustrative of procedural and substantive issues that often arise in the NCAA rules enforcement process. As you read the following cases, think about the level of violation (review the definitions of Level I-IV violations, *supra*) that would likely be found now by the COI or IAC based on the facts in each case. Note that the Division I four-tier structure is intended to impose severe consequences (postseason bans, scholarship reductions, recruiting limits, head coach suspensions, show-cause orders and financial penalties) for serious NCAA rules violations, but seeks to align sanctions more predictably commensurate with the severity of the violations while considering aggravating and mitigating circumstances in each case.

In the following case involving serious violations of the NCAA's amateurism rules, the University of Southern California, a repeat offender, appealed a series of substantial penalties imposed by the COI on the grounds that they are inconsistent with past precedent and are unfair.

THE UNIVERSITY OF SOUTHERN CALIFORNIA
PUBLIC INFRACTIONS APPEALS COMMITTEE REPORT

May 26, 2011

[EDS. Beginning in October 2004 and continuing until November 2005, the former football student-athlete, his stepfather, and his mother agreed to form a partnership with two individuals to form a sports agency. Shortly after the agreement was reached the former football student-athlete and his family began asking for financial and other assistance from the partners. During the course of this relationship, the agency partners gave the former football student-athlete and his family impermissible benefits including several thousand dollars, an automobile, housing, a washer and dryer, air travel, hotel lodging, and transportation, among others. Because of the receipt of these benefits, the former football student-athlete competed while ineligible.

On January 8, 2006, one of the agency partners called the assistant football coach asking for assistance in convincing the former student-athlete to adhere to the agency agreement or reimburse the partners for money and benefits they provided. The assistant football coach failed to alert the university compliance staff of this information and later provided false and misleading information to the enforcement staff regarding his knowledge of the violations. Based on these actions, the Committee on Infractions (COI) found that the assistant football coach violated NCAA ethical conduct rules and violated NCAA legislation by failing to report knowledge of possible violations.

The former football student-athlete and his family also received benefits from another sports marketing agency during his time at the university. On a number of occasions from November 2005 to January 2006, an individual who triggered NCAA agent rules provided impermissible benefits to the former football student-athlete, as well as his friends and family. These benefits included air travel, transportation, lodging, and repairs to the automobile that was purchased by the previous agency partners.

Although the former football student-athlete participated in an interview with enforcement staff, he refused to cooperate fully with the investigation. He failed to provide the requested information that, if it existed, could have substantiated his claim that he was not involved in NCAA rules violations.

The case also includes multiple impermissible inducements and extra benefits for a former men's basketball student-athlete, his brother, his girlfriend, and his girlfriend's mother. From August 2006 through May 2008, a representative affiliated with a professional sports agency and his associate provided cash, lodging, transportation, meals, air travel, professional personal trainers, a cell phone, wireless service, a television, watches, shoes, and clothing, among other benefits.

The former head men's basketball coach, assistant men's basketball coach, institutional compliance staff, faculty athletics representative, and athletics director all knew this representative had previously committed two separate NCAA violations. One of these violations involved the former men's basketball student-athlete, and in the other violation the representative was found to have provided benefits to a student-athlete. These university officials also knew that the representative was acting as the point person in the recruitment of the former men's basketball student-athlete, yet it failed to take steps to monitor the recruitment.

The COI also found the football program violated coaching staff limit rules. In August 2008, the former head football coach hired a consultant for the entire 2008 regular playing season. The consultant attended practice sessions, analyzed video footage of contests, and discussed with the former head football coach his observations and analyses of the university's special teams. These activities led the university to exceed the maximum number of countable coaches.

Further, from November 2006 to March 2009, a former women's tennis student-athlete used an athletics department long-distance access code to make 123 unauthorized international telephone calls to family members. The total value of the calls is more than $7,000.

The COI acknowledged the difficulty of the investigation. Investigations of amateurism cases are often laborious given the significant effort by those involved to avoid leaving a paper trail or other evidence. It also noted that a number of key individuals, including the former football and basketball student-athletes, refused to cooperate fully with the investigation.

In determining the penalties, the committee considered the university's self-imposed penalties, corrective actions, and cooperation. The committee seriously contemplated imposing a television ban penalty in this case. However, after careful consideration, it ultimately decided that the penalties imposed adequately responded to the nature of violations and the level of institutional responsibility.

The penalties include four-year probation; a two-year football postseason ban; a one-year basketball postseason ban; vacation of regular and postseason wins for all three involved sports; scholarship reductions for football and basketball; and recruiting restrictions for men's basketball. They also include a $5,000 financial penalty; forfeiture of revenue from the 2008 NCAA Division I Men's Basketball Championship Tournament; and limitations for access granted to boosters and non-university personnel to team charters, sidelines, practices, locker rooms, and camps for men's basketball and football. The university must also disassociate itself from three boosters, including the former football and

men's basketball student-athletes involved in the case. As part of the disassociation, the university will not be able to accept financial contributions or other
assistance for the athletics department from these individuals or provide them
with any benefit or privileges. In addition, the assistant football coach received a
one-year show-cause penalty, which prohibits him from engaging in any recruiting activity with prospective student-athletes.

Issues on appeal include the following: (1) the penalties imposed on the
University of Southern California (USC) should be reduced because they "are
not supported by the facts and are excessive," and (2) the COI's findings of certain violations should be set aside as contrary to the evidence.

The IAC also rejected the university's assertion that the COI had "erred in
concluding that sports marketer A, sports marketer B, and agency were representatives of USC's athletic interests" on the ground that the IAC was persuaded
that there was sufficient evidence for the COI's conclusions regarding these
issues.

The IAC rejected the university's argument that the COI's finding of lack of
institutional control "should be set aside because some of the facts found by the
[COI] did not constitute a violation of NCAA rules, and the [COI] failed to consider a number of mitigating factors." One of the institution's principal arguments regarding this point was that the COI had imposed a heightened duty to
monitor elite student-athletes and that "NCAA bylaws do not establish a 'heightened duty' standard, nor do they differentiate between 'elite' athletes and other
student-athletes." The IAC did find that the COI's statements inappropriately
established a new or different standard not permitted by the applicable bylaws.

Despite these and related arguments, the IAC found no basis on which to
reverse the COI's finding of lack of institutional control. More particularly, the
IAC determined that there was evidence sufficient to permit the COI to hold
that the institution had devoted inadequate resources to its compliance program, especially when the institution learned that problems with the compliance program were developing.]

The institution argues that the penalties imposed by the COI were excessive.
More specifically, the institution argues that (a) the COI "has imposed significantly lesser sanctions in major infractions cases based on similar violations";
(b) "abused its discretion in imposing a two-year post-season ban and drastic
scholarship reductions in football for the violations in this case"; and (c) "the
scholarship reductions are excessive, particularly when considering the unintended actual impact."

The committee states in the Alabama case as follows:

> An abuse of discretion in the imposition of a penalty occurs if the penalty: (1) was
> not based on a correct legal standard or was based on a misapprehension of the
> underlying substantive legal principles; (2) was based on a clearly erroneous fac-
> tual finding; (3) failed to consider and weigh material factors; (4) was based on a
> clear error of judgment, such that the imposition was arbitrary, capricious, or irra-
> tional; or (5) was based in significant part on one or more irrelevant or improper
> factors. . . .

Guided by that standard, we find no error or abuse of discretion in the imposition of either the two-year postseason ban or the grants-in-aid reduction.

We note in particular the [COI's] recognition that this was the institution's
sixth major infraction case involving football, and that the institution had last
been before the [COI] in June 2001, fewer than four years before the violations

which occurred in this case. Thus, the institution was a "repeat violator" under Bylaw 19.5.2.3 and therefore at risk for enhanced penalties set forth in Bylaw 19.5.2.3.2. As the [COI] stated in its response to the institution's appeal:

> Although the COI ultimately chose not to impose any of the enhanced penalties, it noted that "stiff sanctions are warranted in light of the serious violations found by the committee and the fact that the institution is a 'repeat violator.'" Those stiff penalties are particularly warranted because the school failed to take to heart the lessons it should have learned in 2001.

Thus, we believe that the penalties imposed make clear to other institutions the message which the [COI] intended to convey:

> Similar strong penalties will be meted out to institutions that do [not] take the problems of sports agents and their runners seriously. It is not enough for institutions simply to educate student athletes about the dangers of unscrupulous agents. Schools must have appropriate staff and procedures in place to combat this significant problem. An institution that does not foster a climate of compliance on its campus should expect serious consequences.

In reaching this decision, this committee [IAC] closely considered both the institution and the [COI's] substantial arguments regarding the application to this case of prior decisions of both the [COI] and this committee [citations omitted]. Indeed, we have recognized since the University of Mississippi (May 1, 1995) case that a "factor of particular significance in considering an appeal of penalties is the review and analysis of the penalty or penalties imposed when compared with the penalty or penalties imposed in other cases with similar characteristics." [Citation omitted.] Given this latitude afforded the [COI], there is no basis on which to conclude that the [COI] departed from prior decisions, much less to any impermissible extent.[2]

The institution placed particular reliance on the [COI's] decision in the 1996 Florida State case, arguing that the case "illustrates how the [COI] historically has penalized universities for amateurism violations." [Citation omitted.] While the institution's observation regarding that case may be correct, we also must make clear the principle of guidance from prior decisions is not an unyielding directive. It is instead a matter of considered judgment to be applied along with all other factors which this committee has recognized should guide the [COI] and this committee. And, one very important factor in the application of that principle, and in determining the extent to which a prior decision should guide a present decision, is change in the matters to which the decision of the [COI] and this committee are directed. The [COI] should not be strictly bound to a decision made fifteen years earlier, when the circumstances of intercollegiate athletics were qualitatively different than those which presently obtain. This, of course, does not mean that prior decisions provide no restraint on or guidance to the [COI] and this committee, or that insignificant changes in the environment in which NCAA member institutions operate can justify ignoring those prior decisions. It means only that the guidance provided by prior decisions is,

---

2. We note in particular the [COI's] extensive discussion of the Alabama, Michigan, and Florida State cases [citation omitted]. While we do not necessarily agree with all of the [COI's] points made there, the discussion makes clear that none of the facts of, or penalties imposed in, those cases demonstrate an abuse of discretion in this case.

and always has been, a matter of judgment. In this case, we cannot say that the [COI] improperly exercised that judgment.

NOTES AND QUESTIONS

1. *Post-USC Litigation.* In late October 2010, O.J. Mayo, the basketball player involved in the USC case, and Rodney Guillory, a man Mayo considered a mentor but whom the NCAA characterized in less charitable terms, filed a $25 million defamation, false light invasions of privacy, and negligent misrepresentation lawsuit against the NCAA. The NCAA Infractions Report accused Guillory of giving Mayo automobile transportation, skills instruction, free dinners and clothing, and other recruiting inducements. Guillory contends that the report fails to take into consideration the fact that the ride was in Guillory's car, the meals were home-cooked, the skills instruction was not prearranged or paid for by anyone, and the clothing was left over from a variety of basketball camps. The NCAA moved to strike Guillory's complaint, because (1) the report was a protected matter of public interest, and (2) Guillory was unlikely to prevail at trial. (Code Civ. Proc. §425.16.) The trial court granted the NCAA's motion, and the appellate court affirmed. *Guillory v. National Collegiate Athletic Assn.*, 2012 WL 2831806 (Cal. Ct. App.). In its decision, the COI did not address these facts. Should the COI and IAC have addressed these seemingly mitigating factors? Should the COI and IAC make it clear that they considered all relevant facts, including ones that have a potential to mitigate?

   Todd McNair, the former assistant football coach at the University of Southern California also filed a lawsuit against the NCAA arising from the Reggie Bush scandal and the NCAA infractions report findings. In the COI report, the NCAA imposed sanctions on McNair for unethical conduct and prohibited him from engaging in recruiting activities or interacting with prospective student-athletes. It also required McNair's employer during the penalty period to monitor McNair's compliance and report to the COI to affirm compliance. McNair's contract was not renewed by USC, and he was unable to find other coaching employment since that time. He filed a lawsuit against the NCAA claiming defamation — libel by publishing falsehoods in the COI and Appeals Committee reports and slander by oral statements made by NCAA officials. Additional causes of action included interference with prospective economic advantage, interference with contractual relations, breach of contract, and negligence.

   The NCAA filed a motion to dismiss under the anti-SLAAP statute, claiming McNair only filed his complaint to censor, intimidate, or silence the NCAA by burdening them with the cost of a legal defense or a settlement. The trial court denied the special motion to strike, finding that McNair had shown a probability of prevailing on the merits for his defamation claim based on admissible evidence that the COI report was inaccurate. The court found that McNair had presented admissible evidence showing the COI report contained false statements. The NCAA's timely appeal ensued.

   In an unpublished opinion, *McNair v. National Collegiate Athletic Assn.*, 234 Cal. App. 4th 25, 183 Cal. Rptr. 3d 490, 2015 Cal. App. LEXIS 112 (Cal. App. 2d Dist., Feb. 6, 2015), the California Court of Appeals drew its own conclusions as to the veracity of the statements contained in the COI report and upheld the trial court decision that McNair demonstrated a probability of prevailing on the merits of his defamation claim. However, the court dismissed the interference with contractual relations and interference with prospective economic advantage claims for failure to demonstrate a likelihood of success on the merits. The negligence, contract, and declaratory relief claims were not deemed protected activity under the anti-SLAAP statute.

The case was finally heard before a jury in Los Angeles County Superior Court in May 2018. After deliberating for three days, the jury found 9-3 in favor of the NCAA. McNair was deemed a limited purpose public figure, and the jury was not sufficiently convinced that the NCAA's findings were false. They also struggled with whether the NCAA acted with "actual malice" in issuing the COI report. Only the defamation claim was litigated as all other claims were dropped before the trial; however, it has been suggested that a negligence claim may have been a better option. *See* Michael McCann, *Ex-USC Coach Todd McNair Losing Trial to NCAA Shows Why Defamation Lawsuits Are Tricky to Win*, https://www.si.com/college-football/2018/05/21/todd-mcnair-usc-loses-ncaa-defamation-lawsuit. Can a limited purpose public figure ever win a defamation case against the NCAA? Why would a plaintiff have better success with a negligence claim if a COI report contains false information?

2. *Repeat Major Offenders and the "Death Penalty."* Should USC's football program have been suspended (given the so-called "death penalty"), as was the case with Southern Methodist University in 1987? In cases involving highly successful and competitive teams, like the one at USC, what sanctions are most effective in maintaining academic values and student welfare? Under the current Division I four-tier rules enforcement structure, what penalties could have been imposed?

3. *IAC Precedent and the Rule of Law.* In the USC case, the IAC makes it clear that past precedent is not binding but is merely a "matter of judgment." NCAA Bylaw 19.9.6 gives the hearing panel the ability to adjust penalties due to "extenuating circumstances." What are the advantages and disadvantages of this policy?

4. *High-Profile Student-Athletes.* While the IAC indicates that it is not adopting a new standard for institutional duty to monitor higher profile student-athletes, it appears that institutions with higher profile student-athletes are being held to a standard that requires closer scrutiny of their activities and relationships. If so, what steps should USC and other institutions with higher profile student-athletes take to ensure compliance with NCAA rules?

On July 8, 2011, after the decision in the *USC* infractions case and in the midst of serious problems in its own football program, officials at the Ohio State University altered its oversight of its student-athletes, many of whom are higher profile athletes who are likely to play professionally. See Encarnacion Pyle and Bill Rabinowitz, *Ohio State Alters Oversight of Athletes*, Columbus Dispatch, July 8, 2011. Gene Smith, OSU's athletic director states "We want to go further than where we've been." The article describes a series of steps that OSU is taking to oversee the purchases and relationships of its student-athletes, including receiving in-depth information regarding automobile purchases and usage, checking of game passes to ascertain whether there might be any improper relationships that might jeopardize a student-athlete's amateur status, and even examining the bank accounts of student-athletes. Is this extensive degree of monitoring appropriate and fair to student-athletes?

5. *The Ohio State University Case.* On December 20, 2011, in *The Ohio State Public Infractions Report,* the Ohio State University was cited for failure to monitor, preferential treatment, and extra benefit violations in its football program, according to findings by the COI. Eight football student-athletes received more than $14,000 in cash payments or preferential treatment from the owner of a Columbus, Ohio, tattoo parlor. In addition to free or discounted tattoos and cash for memorabilia received by these student-athletes, one football student-athlete received a loan and discount on a car in violation of NCAA rules. The COI also found that former head coach Jim Tressel concealed these NCAA violations after he was notified of the situation. In its report, the COI expressed "great concern" over the "fact that the former head coach became aware of these violations and decided not to report the violations to institutional officials, the Big Ten Conference or the NCAA." The COI found that Tressel engaged in unethical conduct for not report- ing these NCAA rule violations; as a sanction, he received a five-year show- cause order that limits his athletically related duties and applies to any NCAA member school that may consider employing him. The penalties imposed on Ohio State, some of which were self-imposed by the university and adopted by the COI, included a one-year postseason ban for the 2012 football season, scholarship reductions, disassociation of both an involved booster and a former student-athlete, forfeiture of almost $340,000, and forfeiture of all of the team's wins during the 2010 season.

6. *The University of Miami Case.* On October 22, 2013, the NCAA Committee of Infractions (COI) decided an infractions case involving the University of Miami. The case garnered significant public attention, particularly because the NCAA enforcement staff had improperly obtained information for its case. NCAA staff had encouraged a lawyer in a judicial proceeding to ask questions of a potential witness who had refused to provide testimony to the NCAA, which lacks subpoena power. NCAA President Mark Emmert acknowledged that the manner in which evidence from that witness in the Miami case was obtained was "shocking." In evaluating the facts and impos- ing sanctions, the NCAA noted that:

> [T]he [Committee on Infractions] only considered information obtained appropriately during the investigative process and presented at the hear- ing. . . . [The case involved serious violations of NCAA rules] including 18 general allegations of misconduct with 79 issues within those allegations. These were identified through an investigation that included 118 interviews of 81 individuals. Additionally, the committee had the responsibility of deter- mining the credibility of individuals who submitted inconsistent statements and information provided by a booster who is now in federal prison. In reaching its conclusions, the committee found, in most instances, corrobo- ration through supporting documentation and the statements of [multiple] individuals.

See NCAA, *University of Miami lacked institutional control resulting in a decade of violations,* http://www.ncaa.org/about/resources/media-center/press- releases/university-miami-lacked-institutional-control-resulting-decade- violations.

In sanctioning Miami, the COI acknowledged that the University had cooperated in the investigation and had self-imposed major sanctions, including bowl and league championship bans. After concluding that the University "lacked institutional control" for over a decade regarding many of its athletic teams by failing to monitor a major booster, coaches, and student-athletes, the COI censured and then sanctioned the University with three years of probation, a loss of twelve scholarships (nine in football and three in basketball), and numerous other lesser sanctions for men's football, basketball, baseball, and track and field as well as women's swimming and diving, basketball, soccer, track and field, rowing, and tennis. Two former assistant football coaches and one assistant basketball coach received two-year orders to show cause, effectively prohibiting them from coaching for two years. The former associate athletics director for compliance received a letter of admonishment. Miami did not appeal the COI decision.

7. *Post-Season Bans.* In *The University of California, Berkeley Public Infractions Appeals Committee Report* (11/18/2002), a case discussing sanctions for institutional rules violations under Division I's former two-tier system of NCAA rules infractions, the IAC acknowledged that a ban on post-season competition affects student-athletes who had nothing to do with the violations. They suggested a fairer penalty might be to allow the institution to compete in postseason, but to prohibit the institution from reaping any financial awards associated with the contest: "Such a penalty would minimize the adverse impact on student-athletes, who individually have done nothing wrong, and instead would penalize the institution, which has failed in its responsibilities." The new penalty structure still allows post-season competition bans, but it also includes financial penalties, negating revenues received by the institution during the years the violations occurred, and reduction or elimination of NCAA revenue distributions. What objectives are furthered by imposing a ban on postseason competition for repeated and/or serious violations of NCAA rules? Are financial penalties a better option? What unintended consequences might this sanction have?

MATERIALS REGARDING THE BINDING CONSENT DECREE IMPOSED BY THE NATIONAL COLLEGIATE ATHLETIC ASSOCIATION AND ACCEPTED BY THE PENNSYLVANIA STATE UNIVERSITY

(Consent Decree 2012)

In 2012, the NCAA and The Penn State University entered into a binding consent decree regarding allegations of sexual abuse of young boys occurring in Penn State athletics facilities. NCAA, *Binding Consent Decree Imposed by the National Collegiate Athletic Association and Accepted by the Pennsylvania State University,* https://www.ncaa.org/sites/default/files/Binding%20Consent%20Decree.pdf. Understanding this unprecedented binding consent decree requires an understanding of the developments leading up to the decree. On November 17, 2011, NCAA President Emmert wrote a letter to Penn State President Rodney Erickson in which he stated, in pertinent part:

As we have discussed, on November 5, 2011, the NCAA first learned about allegations of sexual abuse of young boys occurring in the athletic facilities of Pennsylvania State University, perpetrated by a former assistant head football coach. Further, at the same time the NCAA learned that these alleged acts occurred over two decades and that individuals with present or former coaching responsibilities may have been aware of this behavior. The recount of these tragic events in the Grand Jury Report is deeply troubling, and if true, individuals who were in a position to monitor and act upon learning of potential abuses appear to have been acting starkly contrary to the values of higher education, as well as the NCAA. I am writing to notify you that the NCAA will examine Penn State's exercise of institutional control over its intercollegiate athletics program, as well as the actions, and inactions, of relevant responsible personnel.

Letter from Mark A. Emmert, President, NCAA to Rodney Erickson, President, Pennsylvania State University (Nov. 17, 2011), available at http://www.psu.edu/ur/2011/NCAA.pdf.

President Emmert then stated the NCAA constitutional and bylaw provisions requiring institutional control, monitoring, and ethical conduct, and added:

[T]o prepare for potential inquiry, the university should provide relevant information and data in response to the following questions:

1. How has Penn State and/or its employees complied with the Articles of the [NCAA] Constitution and bylaws [implicated in this case?]
2. How has Penn State exercised institutional control over the issues identified in and related to the Grand Jury Report? Were there procedures in place that were or were not followed? What are the institution's expectations and policies to address conduct that has been alleged in this matter upon discovery by any party?
3. Have each of the alleged persons to have been involved or have notice of the issues identified in and related [to this matter] behaved consistent with principles and requirements governing ethical conduct and honesty? If so, how? If not, how?
4. What policies and procedures does Penn State have in place to monitor, prevent and detect the issues identified in [this case] or to take disciplinary or corrective action if such behaviors are found?

Penn State responded quickly, hiring the law firm of Judge Louis Freeh, former FBI director, to investigate the matter. In compiling their report, Freeh's law firm and those working with it interviewed 430 university and other individuals and reviewed over 3.5 million e-mails and documents. The Freeh report concluded, "Our most saddening finding is the total disregard [by Penn State officials] for the safety and welfare of [the abuse] victims." See Genaro C. Armas, *PSU formally requests more time from NCAA*, http://timesbulletin.com/PrintArticle.aspx?aid=170495&uid=1b7cad03-2773-4f17-9eba-8c3eeafacb3a.

Rather than engaging in further investigation or hearings, President Emmert and the Executive Committee of the NCAA responded quickly by proposing a Binding Consent Decree. In a press release regarding the Decree, the NCAA noted:

By perpetuating a "football first" culture that ultimately enabled serial child sexual abuse to occur, The Pennsylvania State University leadership failed to value and uphold institutional integrity, resulting in a breach of the NCAA constitution and rules. The NCAA Division I Board of Directors and NCAA Executive Committee directed Association President Mark Emmert to examine the circumstances and determine appropriate action in consultation with these presidential bodies.

"As we evaluated the situation, the victims affected by Jerry Sandusky and the efforts by many to conceal his crimes informed our actions," said Emmert. "At our core, we are educators. Penn State leadership lost sight of that."

According to the NCAA conclusions and sanctions, the Freeh Report "presents an unprecedented failure of institutional integrity leading to a culture in which a football program was held in higher esteem than the values of the institution, the values of the NCAA, the values of higher education, and most disturbingly the values of human decency."

NCAA, Penn State Failures Draw Unprecedented NCAA Sanctions, http://www.ncaa .org/about/resources/media-center/news/penn-state-failures-draw-unprecedented-ncaa-sanctions.

[EDS. The sanctions imposed in the Penn State Consent Decree included a $60 million fine; a four-year postseason ban on participation in postseason play in the sport of football, beginning with the 2012-2013 academic year and expiring at the conclusion of the 2015-2016 academic year; a four-year reduction in football scholarships; five years of probation, including the appointment of an on-campus, independent Integrity Monitor and periodic reporting; vacation of all wins of the Penn State football team from 1998 to 2011 (which will be reflected in the career record of Coach Joe Paterno. See NCAA, *Binding Consent Decree Imposed by the National Collegiate Athletic Association and Accepted by The Pennsylvania State University,* https://www.ncaa.org/sites/default/files/ Binding%20Consent%20Decree.pdf.]

NOTES AND QUESTIONS

1. *NCAA Authority to Sanction Penn State.* The NCAA was subjected to significant criticism for presenting Penn State University with a consent decree to avoid the potential imposition of the "death penalty" on its football program rather than adjudicating this case through its Division I COI and IAC processes. Critics argued that the NCAA did not have authority to intervene in a case involving sexual abuse of young men by a former coach; which is a criminal and tort law matter that should have been left to the judicial system. See, e.g., Matthew J. Mitten, *The Penn State 'Consent Decree': The NCAA's Coercive Means Don't Justify Its Laudable Ends, but is There a Legal Remedy?,* 41 Pepp. L. Rev. 321 (2014). Was it appropriate for the NCAA to discipline Penn State for a crime committed by a former employee? The NCAA was under significant public pressure to act promptly in the matter. What counsel would you offer the NCAA in responding to the extreme public pressure that was being exerted on it to act and demonstrate its commitment to the victims of the abuse? Mitten, *supra,* at 347 (The NCAA "should adopt proactive reforms requiring greater individual and institutional responsibility to take affirmative steps to protect the health, safety, and welfare of all persons exposed to known or foreseeable risks of harm by the operation of its athletics program, reforms that provide clear notice of specific action or inaction that violates NCAA rules and potential sanctions").

2. *Sanctions.* There have also been objections that the sanctions imposed on Penn State were unprecedented in their severity. Do you think the sanctions were excessive? Subsequent to the consent decree, the NCAA gradually reduced or eliminated the sanctions, including the football post season ban

and scholarship limits, based on the NCAA's assessment that Penn State had taken significant steps to build a culture of compliance, in which the athletics department is subjected to meaningful oversight. In January 2015, to settle a lawsuit by a Pennsylvania state senator challenging the legality of the consent decree, the NCAA vacated all of the sanctions with the exception of the $60 million fine to be used to prevent child abuse that it permitted to be spent in Pennsylvania. Does reduction of these sanctions evidence that they were excessive? It has been reported that the NCAA leadership seriously considered the suspension of the football program (the "death penalty"), but they refrained from doing so, in part, because they believed that they had tailored the penalties in a manner that was designed to penalize Penn State and help the university avoid such actions in the future. The willingness to not suspend the football program also was an inducement to Penn State to enter into the Consent Decree. Should the NCAA have invoked the "death penalty"?

3. *Costs of Monitoring Compliance.* In a 2011 infractions case involving Boise State University, the COI found numerous major violations involving more than 75 prospects and student-athletes in five sports over the course of five years, including football, men's and women's cross country and track and field, and men's and women's tennis. One of the lessons learned from the Boise State case is that failure to monitor one sport, even a minor sport, may adversely impact others, including those which produce revenue.

> In an October 2012 compliance report filed with the NCAA, Ohio State reported that it was devoting significantly more financial and personnel resources to ensure compliance with NCAA rules. For example, it increased the size of its compliance department to 12 full-time employees, including one that focuses exclusively on its football program and another whose primary responsibility is to counsel and oversee elite student-athletes likely to play professional sports after their intercollegiate careers end. Should other Power Five conference universities increase resources allocated to the compliance and monitoring processes?
>
> The USC and Ohio State infractions cases were decided prior to the October 30, 2012, NCAA announcement regarding the use of four levels of infractions, but it may be argued the high level of monitoring expected in those cases essentially held the institutions and their personnel to a presumption of responsibility, which is an underlying basis of the new enforcement structure. Is it feasible for smaller and less commercially successful athletic programs to provide such monitoring, given the vast majority of NCAA university athletic programs do not generate net revenues? Is lack of funding a justification for lack of self-enforcement?

Failure to monitor is a Level II violation, which most institutions try to avoid by implementing rules education programs for all employees, student-athletes, and alumni and boosters and establishing policies and procedures to identify potential problems. However, the athletics department cannot possibly monitor every affiliated person every minute of every day. A tweet of song lyrics from a University of North Carolina at Chapel Hill football student-athlete was the catalyst for an NCAA impermissible benefits investigation that discovered so much more. As you read the materials, consider the interaction of the athletics department and the academic departments within the university and the obligation to monitor.

MATERIALS RELATED TO THE UNIVERSITY OF NORTH CAROLINA INFRACTIONS CASES AND ACADEMIC SCANDAL

In the summer of 2010 the NCAA notified the University of North Carolina, Chapel Hill athletics compliance office it had received information leading them to believe football student-athletes may be receiving impermissible benefits from an agent. The UNC compliance staff began investigating immediately, and the ensuing investigation discovered seven football student-athletes had received benefits including transportation, jewelry, accommodations, meals, and cash from agents, a jeweler, various financial advisors, and five former UNC football student-athletes; the impermissible benefits were worth over $27,000. The investigation also uncovered a close personal relationship between an agent and an assistant football coach at the university as well as evidence the assistant coach had received payments from the agent. All seven student-athletes were declared ineligible; three were declared permanently ineligible by the NCAA Student-Athlete Reinstatement staff.

Academic improprieties by a former undergraduate student who was employed by the athletics department in the academic support program from 2008 to 2009 were also discovered during the investigation. The tutor provided impermissible assistance to three football student-athletes: she wrote conclusory paragraphs for five papers, provided an outline and thesis statement for another paper, revised a draft document adding four sentences and making grammatical corrections, and provided citations and works cited pages for two papers. The tutor graduated in 2009, but continued to work part-time for the academic support program that summer until the athletics department discovered she was socializing with student-athletes and then chose not to renew her contract. The former student continued to provide academic assistance for 11 football student-athletes for the 2009-2010 academic year; she also assisted one with a $150 airline fee to change his ticket and paid outstanding campus parking tickets worth $1,789 for another.

The Committee on Infractions found UNC in violation of the following:

- Bylaw 10.1 Unethical conduct by the tutor and assistant coach
- Bylaw 14.11.1 Impermissible participation by ineligible football student-athletes in the 2008, 2009 and 2010 seasons
- Bylaw 16.11.2 Impermissible benefits
- Bylaw 19.01.3 Failure to cooperate by the assistant coach and tutor
- Bylaws 12.1.2.1.6 and 12.3.1.2 Preferential treatment and benefits from prospective agents
- Bylaw 11.2.2 Failure to report outside income by the assistant coach
- Constitution 2.8.1 Failure to monitor

The Committee on Infractions acknowledged the University "self-discovered the academic fraud and took decisive action when the former assistant coach's violations came to light. It cooperated fully, was not a repeat violator and, although there is a finding of failure to monitor, the institution exhibited appropriate control over the athletics program." University of North Carolina, Chapel Hill Public Infractions Report, March 12, 2012, p. 28, https://apsa.unc .edu/files/2019/06/NCAA-Public-Infractions-Report-Appendix-2-March-2012 .pdf. Penalties levied on the university included a public reprimand, one-year postseason ban, reduction of 15 football scholarships, vacation of records, dissociation letters, a $50,00 fine, and three years' probation, many of which were self-imposed.

Per Bylaw 19.5.11, NCAA investigations are limited to four years prior to the date of the self-reported violations or notice of inquiry. A UNC working group, in cooperation with the NCAA enforcement staff, had discovered "serious anomalies related to the course offerings and methods of instruction within the Department of African and Afro-American Studies." The Hartlyn-Andrews Report investigated all courses offered by the African and Afro-American Studies department from 2007 to 2011 and identified 54 courses with academic anomalies. These anomalies included: courses that operated as independent studies but were registered as lecture courses; courses where student work was not supervised or graded by the instructor of record; and unauthorized grade changes. There was no evidence of students receiving grades who had not submitted written work, nor any evidence that student-athletes received more favorable treatment than students who were not athletes. See https://carolinacommitment.unc.edu/files/2012/05/HartlynAndrews-report.pdf.

While the University was deeply embarrassed by the academic improprieties, the media accused the institution of covering up an athletics scandal by limiting the scope of the investigation. In response, then UNC Chancellor Holden Thorp invited former North Carolina Governor James G. Martin to lead an independent review to address questions of further academic anomalies. The Martin Report examined all course sections in all departments from Fall 1994 through Summer 2012 and conducted interviews with 84 faculty, staff, students, and others. Academic improprieties were discovered as early as 1997 and persisted through 2007 and were limited to the AFAM department. The majority of students associated with these courses were not student-athletes, and the percentage of student-athletes in these classes was consistent with enrollment numbers for regular classes within the department. Martin concluded this was an embarrassing academic scandal isolated to two individuals within a single department within the university. See James G. Martin, *The University of North Carolina at Chapel Hill Academic Anomalies Report Findings*, December 19, 2012. https://carolinacommitment.unc.edu/files/2013/01/UNC-Governor-Martin-Final-Report-and-Addendum-1.pdf.

UNC proceeded to institute over 70 policy changes on campus to assure the integrity of its academic programs. See *Actions and Initiatives: Moving Forward Together* at https://carolinacommitment.unc.edu/actions-and-initiatives/. On June 4, 2015, the NCAA issued a notice of allegations to the University of North Carolina, stating:

> It is important to remember the following information about the NCAA members' rules on academic misconduct:
>
> • An NCAA member school is responsible for determining if violations of its academic standards occurred.
> • Schools are responsible for the quality of the degree programs offered for all students, including student-athletes. Generally, academic issues are managed first and foremost by the faculty member in the classroom, second by that faculty member's department head, next by their dean, then the provost and finally the president or chancellor. NCAA rules do not address course curriculum, rigor or content.

- Ultimately, member schools must determine if the courses for which they are giving credit and the degrees they are awarding meet the academic standards of the school and its overall mission.
- While schools are in the best position to determine compliance with academic standards on campus, the enforcement staff will consider if other infractions occurred.
- These might include violations of progress toward degree requirements, extra benefit rules or ethical conduct obligations. Any alleged violation of NCAA rules would be investigated and decided through the formal infractions process.

See NCAA, *NCAA sends Notice of Allegations to University of North Carolina,* http://www.ncaa.org/about/resources/media-center/news/ncaa-sends-notice-allegations-university-north-carolina.

In April of 2016, the NCAA issued an amended notice of allegations (NOA) involving the University of North Carolina. On August 3, 2016, the University of North Carolina responded with a 73-page response to the NCAA's amended or revised notice of allegations. In their response, UNC argued:

> The Amended Notice of Allegations refer to core academic issues of course structure, content, and administrative oversight that are beyond the scope of authority granted to the NCAA by its members. Such matters concern fundamental issues of institutional and academic integrity, not athletics compliance, and the University has addressed them with its accreditor. They are not the proper subject of an NCAA enforcement option.

Julian Council, *UNC responds strongly to the NCAA's revised Notice of Allegations,* http://www.tarheelblog.com/2016/8/3/12361714/unc-ncaa-allegations-notice-of-allegations-response.

The Committee on Infractions issued its decision on October 12, 2017, essentially agreeing with the university that this was an academic scandal outside the purview of the NCAA and finding only a failure to cooperate by the former AFAM chair and department administrator, and issued a show-cause order for the department chair who had resigned in 2011. See *University of North Carolina at Chapel Hill Public Infractions Decision,* October 13, 2017, https://www.ncaa .org/sites/default/files/Oct2017_University-of-North-Carolina-at-Chapel-Hill_ InfractionsDecision_20171013.pdf.

NOTES AND QUESTIONS

1. Does the NCAA's position—that it lacks a legal obligation to exercise oversight as to how classes are taught by member institutions—indicate a reluctance on the part of the NCAA to get involved in academic matters? If so, might this provide a means by which schools can contrive academic programs that provide their students-athletes with an athletic competitive advantage (e.g., by creating weak classes that are designed to optimize eligibility on the part of student-athletes)? Would such a plan deprive participating student-athletes of an education, which is the benefit of the academic bargain between the university and the athlete? Should such a plan constitute an infraction or merely a potential cause of action against the school? See *Ross v. Creighton, infra.*
2. Bylaw 14.02.1, adopted April 28, 2016, states: "All institutional staff members and student-athletes are expected to act with integrity and honesty in

all academic matters. Post-enrollment academic misconduct includes any violation or breach of an institutional policy regarding academic honesty or integrity (e.g., academic offense, academic honor code violation, plagiarism, academic fraud)." Does this bylaw strike the right balance between academic independence at the institutional level and maintaining academic integrity in intercollegiate athletics, as well as a level playing field, on a national level? Does an athletics department have the ability to monitor institutional academic honesty or integrity?

b.   Coaches, Other Institutional Personnel, and the Infractions Process

As illustrated by *NCAA v. Tarkanian, supra,* the NCAA has indirect authority to sanction coaches and other university employees for violations of its rules. Over time, the NCAA has moved from a subjective standard (whether the head coach actually knew of the offense by an assistant coach) to an objective standard (whether the head coach should have known), and, finally, to a rebuttable presumption standard (the head coach is presumed to know of such violations unless the head coach can rebut by proving that he or she took reasonable steps to oversee activities by assistant coaches). The rule published in the *NCAA Division I Manual 2019-20* is as follows:

> **11.1.1.1   Responsibility of Head Coach.** An institution's head coach is presumed to be responsible for the actions of all institutional staff members who report, directly or indirectly, to the head coach. An institution's head coach shall promote an atmosphere of compliance within his or her program and shall monitor the activities of all institutional staff members involved with the program who report, directly or indirectly, to the coach.

The following COI decision involves the former head basketball coach at the University of Southern Mississippi, Donnie Tyndall, who was sanctioned with a ten-year order to show cause for a series of level I and level II violations. The coach had gone on to another university, but he was summarily fired when this decision was rendered. This case may well have terminated his college coaching career. Other members of his coaching staff were removed from their positions as part of a series of corrective actions taken by the University of Southern Mississippi in the case.

UNIVERSITY OF SOUTHERN
MISSISSIPPI PUBLIC INFRACTIONS DECISION
April 8, 2016

[EDS. This is a lengthy decision. We begin with Section IV, Analysis.]

ANALYSIS

The violations in this case all occurred in the men's basketball program. Within weeks of beginning their employment at USM, the former head coach and his staff formulated and commenced a plan to arrange fraudulent academic credit for prospective student-athletes. The former head coach also facilitated the payment of impermissible benefits to two nonqualifier student-athletes. The actions of the basketball staff constituted unethical conduct, and some members of the staff failed to cooperate in the investigation. The violations fall into five areas: (1) the former head coach and members of his staff implementing a plan of academic fraud; (2) student-athlete 3's high school coach and student-athlete 4's prep school coach providing impermissible benefits to student-athletes 3 and 4 during their year-in-residence; (3) unethical conduct, failure to cooperate and violation of head coach responsibility legislation by the former head coach; (4) failure to cooperate by student-athlete 4's prep school coach; and (5) unethical conduct and failure to cooperate by graduate assistant B and the former associate head coach.

A. ACADEMIC FRAUD, IMPERMISSIBLE INDUCEMENTS AND BENEFITS, AND INELIGIBLE PARTICIPATION

From June 2012 through May 2014, the former head coach, former associate head coach and graduate assistants A and B were knowingly involved in arranging fraudulent academic credit for seven prospective student-athletes. The institution, enforcement staff and graduate assistant A substantially agreed to the facts and that Level I violations occurred. The former head coach agreed that academic fraud occurred, but did not agree that he knew of the activities, orchestrated them or was involved in any way. The former associate head coach and graduate assistant B did not respond to the notice of allegations. The panel concludes that Level I violations occurred and that the former head coach, the former associate head coach and graduates assistants A and B were involved in the violations. . . .

Within weeks of their arrival at the institution, the former head coach, former associate head coach, former assistant coach A and the two graduate assistants formulated and began executing a plan to complete online academic coursework for prospective student-athletes. Former assistant coach A and graduate assistant A both admitted that they completed online coursework for multiple prospects. Computer metadata confirmed that graduate assistant A, along with graduate assistant B, were involved in the fraud. The scheme continued for the two years the staff served at the institution, during which time the staff members arranged for fraudulent academic credit for seven prospects. Their actions violated NCAA Bylaws 10.01.1, 10.1 and 10.1-(b). When student-athlete 8's advisor told the former head coach that someone would have to pay for student-athlete 8's online courses, the former head coach purchased prepaid credit cards to cover the costs. He passed the cards to former assistant coach A, who in turn gave them to the graduate assistants. The graduate assistants used the cards to cover the fees for student-athlete 8's online courses. When the former head coach purchased the cards and caused them to be used for student-athlete 8's course registrations, he provided an impermissible benefit in violation of NCAA Bylaws 10.01.1, 10.1, 10.1-(c) and 13.2.1. Due to the actions of the men's basketball staff members, the institution allowed student-athletes 1, 2, 6, 7 and 9 to compete and receive competition-related expenses while ineligible, in violation of NCAA Bylaws 12.11.1, 14.01.1, 14.10.1, 14.11.1 and 16.8.1.1.

B. IMPERMISSIBLE FINANCIAL AID, IMPERMISSIBLE BENEFITS AND INELIGIBLE PARTICIPATION . . .

During the 2012-13 and 2013-14 academic years, the institution allowed student-athlete 3's high school coach and student-athlete 4's prep school coach to provide funds to pay toward their tuition, room and board during their years in residence. The institution violated NCAA eligibility and extra benefit legislation when it subsequently allowed student-athlete 3 to compete while ineligible. The institution substantially agreed to the facts and that Level II violations occurred. The enforcement staff asserted that the former head coach provided the funds and that Level I violations occurred. The panel concludes that Level II violations occurred. . . .

C. THE FORMER HEAD COACH'S UNETHICAL CONDUCT, FAILURE TO COOPERATE AND FAILURE TO PROMOTE AN ATMOSPHERE OF COMPLIANCE

The former head coach engaged in a number of actions designed to thwart the investigation. Specifically, he acted in an unethical manner, failed to cooperate with the investigation and/or failed to promote an atmosphere of compliance when he: (1) deleted emails pertinent to the enforcement staff's inquiry; (2) provided false or misleading information during his three interviews with the enforcement staff and institution; (3) contacted other interviewees and individuals with knowledge of the investigation; and (4) directed the involvement of members of his coaching staff in a pattern of academic fraud. The enforcement staff and institution substantially agreed on the facts and that Level I violations occurred. The former head coach agreed that he deleted emails and contacted other individuals, but he did not agree that he did so in an effort to hinder the investigation. He also agreed that he was responsible for the actions of his staff members under NCAA head coach responsibility legislation, but did not agree that he directed a plan of academic fraud, was aware of it or provided false information regarding the fraud. The former head coach's conduct violated NCAA Bylaws 10 and 11. The panel concludes that the Level I violations occurred. . . .

[T]he former head coach did not set a tone for rules compliance in his program or otherwise meet his responsibilities as a head coach. Head coaches violate NCAA head coach responsibility legislation when they do not make rules adherence the foundation of their programs. Indiana University (2008) (head coach failed to promote an atmosphere of compliance when he did not monitor his staff's rules compliance); University of Connecticut (2011) (head coach who did not take steps to stop or report known rules violations violated his responsibilities); University of Tennessee (2011) (head coach failed to promote an atmosphere of compliance when he asked prospects and a prospect's father to withhold information); and University of Central Florida (2012) (head coach failed to discourage, stop or report impermissible activities by boosters). The former head coach sent a message that strict adherence to rules compliance was not a high priority in his program when he: (1) planned and implemented a scheme to involve members of his coaching staff in academic fraud; (2) deleted emails pertinent to the investigation; (3) contacted interviewees during the investigation; and (4) instructed former assistant coach A to contact student-athlete 8 and tell him to lie. Further, although he monitored the actions taken by the staff members as they engaged in academic fraud, the duty to monitor includes a responsibility to set the proper tone for rules compliance. The former head coach acknowledged that he was responsible for the actions of his staff under NCAA Bylaw 11.1.1.1. His actions further demonstrate that he failed to promote an atmosphere of compliance and failed to monitor his staff, as also required by the bylaw.

PENALTIES

Head Coach Restrictions: The former head coach engaged in unethical conduct when he planned and orchestrated a scheme of academic fraud involving seven prospective student-athletes over two years. He involved members of his staff in the scheme and directed their activities. Further, he failed to fully disclose information relevant to the investigation and took affirmative steps to obstruct the investigation. Finally, he failed in his duty to promote an atmosphere of compliance and to monitor the activities of the staff who reported directly and indirectly to him. Specifically, the former head coach deleted relevant emails; provided false or misleading information regarding his knowledge of, and role in, the academic fraud; had the [Director of Basketball Operations] fabricate a fraudulent compliance document; and contacted interviewees and others involved in the investigation in an attempt to influence the investigation and learn what others were saying to the enforcement staff. Therefore, the former head coach will be informed in writing by the NCAA that the panel prescribes a 10-year show-cause order pursuant to NCAA Bylaw 19.9.5.5. The show-cause period shall run from April 8, 2016, through April 7, 2026.

The terms of the show-cause are as follows: a. Any member institution employing the former head coach during the period of the show cause shall suspend him from all coaching duties; and b. Pursuant to NCAA Bylaw 19.9.5.5, as a result of the former head coach's NCAA Bylaw 11.1.1.1 violation, and following the period of the show-cause, any member institution employing the former head coach shall suspend him for the first 50 percent of the first season he is employed. . . .

NOTES AND QUESTIONS

1. *Orders to Show Cause.* Orders to show cause are used as a means of disciplining coaches (and other personnel associated with an institution's athletics program) for NCAA rules violations by preventing employment as a coach at another NCAA member university during a prescribed period of time. While a coach is given the opportunity to show cause why the sanctions should not apply in a certain future context, it is highly unlikely that the effective suspension from coaching will be lifted until the sanction has been fulfilled. The NCAA exercises broad discretion in issuing orders to show cause and otherwise penalizing coaches who violate ethical conduct and other NCAA rules by providing false information in an investigation. See, e.g., *Southeastern Louisiana University Public Infractions Report,* Apr. 9, 2015 (2-year Order to Show Cause for the volleyball coach at Southeastern Louisiana University); and Emily James, *Syracuse did not control athletics; basketball coach failed to monitor,* http://www.ncaa.org/about/resources/media-center/news/syracuse-did-not-control-athletics-basketball-coach-failed-monitor.

2. *Practical Lawyering Issues.* As legal counsel for Coach Tyndall, would you advise him to appeal to the IAC? If so, on what grounds? How would you advise a coach that you represent to prevent an unethical conduct violation and to avoid termination of employment and/or being subject to an order to show cause that may prevent employment at another NCAA institution?

3. *Notoriety and Power of Coaches.* In the Penn State and other cases, the NCAA has expressed concern regarding the power of nationally prominent coaches

and the potential adverse effects of that power on the broader university community. As university legal counsel, is there anything that you might suggest to help the president and athletic director (neither whom may be as well known nationally or locally) in their efforts to restrain a prominent coach inclined to violate NCAA rules?

4. *Presumptive Knowledge Standard for Head Coaches.* Coaches are now subject to a presumptive knowledge standard rather than focusing on a coach's subjective or objective knowledge: if an NCAA rules violation occurs, the head coach is presumed responsible. Head coaches are also expected to provide training and monitoring materials to instruct their assistant coaches. If they do so, such instruction may mitigate the head coach's presumed responsibility in the case of a "rogue" assistant coach. If such training and monitoring do not occur, the head coach will be held accountable for the acts of a "rogue" assistant coach, even if the head coach was unaware of the assistant coach's violation of the rules. In short, coaches are being held to a very strict level of responsibility under the new structure. Is this rebuttable presumption standard appropriate and reasonable?

5. *Significant Sanctions Imposed on Coaches.* Not surprisingly, institutions are now self-imposing penalties on coaches that include termination and permanent dissociation from the program and the university. For example, in May of 2011, Ohio State University forced head football coach Jim Tressel to "retire" for failing to disclose that two players received impermissible extra benefits (e.g., discounted tattoos and cash for selling sports memorabilia) and permitting them to play in games during the 2010 season.

> Even if the subject conduct does not violate NCAA rules, institutions also terminate coaches in order to avoid harm to the university's brand or reputation. A recent example is Baylor University's May 2016 firing of its successful football coach, Art Briles, in response to an independent report finding that he had not adequately dealt with or reported allegations that his players had been engaged in sexual violence and assault. The Athletics Director Ian McCaw and Chancellor Ken Starr, who served as special prosecutor in an investigation involving President Bill Clinton, also were pressured to resign. For a summary of the Baylor investigative reports, see Nicole Auerbach, *Summary of outside report: Baylor failed sexual assault victims,* http://www.usatoday.com/story/sports/ncaaf/big12/2016/05/26/baylor-investigation-pepper-hamilton-report-sexual-assault/84979090/. How should a coach or university leader deal with allegations of a sexual assault or some other act by a team's players, which, if true, would reflect poorly on the university or might constitute a violation of NCAA rules? How can they balance the right to privacy, the right of innocence until proven guilty, and related interests of student-athletes, coaches, and other personnel with the immediate and long-term interests of the University and the athletic team?

PROBLEM 3-7

You are vice president and legal counsel for a large public Division I FBS institution. The president of the university has given you responsibility for acting as her liaison with the athletics program regarding possible infractions of NCAA rules. Your men's football and basketball teams have regularly been ranked in the top 25 in the nation. Your coaches are well known in the local community and nationally, are quite popular, and are well liked by legislators throughout the state. Indeed, they are better known and more popular than the president in whose administration you serve. Not surprisingly, the coaches have been given wide budgetary latitude. They have raised and allocated funds for the hiring of additional academic advisors and tutors to work with their student-athletes in an effort to increase their graduation rates.

It is December, and your football and basketball teams have each enjoyed substantial success. Your football team is scheduled to play in an FBS Bowl, and your basketball team is 10-1 and ranked fifth in the country. The university community is thrilled by the successes of your most visible programs. However, your institution's faculty athletics representative (FAR) has asked to meet with you and the athletic director as soon as possible to convey some important concerns that have been raised by some faculty and staff members on campus. When contacted, the athletic director also indicated that he has heard some rumors that he thinks he should share with you, although with the upcoming bowl game he is very busy and would like to put off the meeting until after the first of the year.

When you suggest the possibility of delaying the meeting until after the first of the year to your FAR, she responds by indicating that the problems she wants you to consider are significant and may implicate the eligibility of players on the men's basketball and football teams. This certainly was not what you wanted to hear, but it makes it clear that you need to hold the meeting as soon as possible. You communicate this to the athletic director, who reluctantly agrees.

At the meeting, the FAR states that staff members associated with the university's academic support program have indicated that they have strong reason to believe that the academic advisors and tutors working directly with the basketball and football teams may have helped student-athletes research and write papers during the recently concluded finals period. Additionally, the FAR noted that she was contacted immediately after finals by a professor who is concerned about possible cheating by a number of student-athletes in his class. The professor teaches a large psychology class, and he gave a multiple-choice exam that could be taken at the testing center on campus at any time. After discovering that a number of students in the class, almost all of whom were prominent student-athletes, did so well on the exam that they raised their grades in the class from the D range to the B range, the faculty member examined the grade sheets and discovered that the student-athletes missed only five to seven questions on a 100-question exam. Of even greater concern to the professor was the fact that the student-athletes overwhelmingly missed the same questions. The student-athletes suspected of cheating include an All-American linebacker on the football team and the star center on the basketball team, as well as three other starters on the football team and one other starter on the basketball team.

The athletic director, who joins you in being stunned by the professor's allegations of possible cheating among student-athletes, then shares his concerns. He has learned that a major donor at the university, who owns three major car dealerships, may have loaned cars to a couple of student-athletes. The athletic director confesses that he received a call from a reporter with the local newspaper who said he saw the quarterback on the football team driving a new Ford Explorer, which caused him to spend a day observing student-athletes arriving and departing from the athletics facilities on campus. When he did so, the reporter noted that at least four other student-athletes arrived in new cars that could be traced, based on their plates, to the dealerships owned by the major donor. Upon inquiring of the student-athletes and the donor, the athletic director was told by the student-athletes that they were permitted to use the cars because their older cars were in the shop. The donor, in turn, confirmed the student-athlete's statements and added, when asked whether this was common practice, "Sure, we commonly do this for our best customers." The athletic director was hesitant to inquire further at the time, but he was unsettled about the donor's response.

You are obviously quite concerned about these statements. After the meeting, you call the president and relate what has happened. She instructs you to call the coaches and see what they have to say about the matter and set up meetings for you to discuss your concerns with the student-athletes suspected of cheating. She then wants you to get back to her so that she can determine whether a full investigation is in order. When told about the cars, she muses, "I wondered about that. Last week, I went to a banquet at the athletic department and noticed that a number of the athletes were driving what appeared to be new, high-priced automobiles." She said that she will personally contact the donor, because she is involved in delicate discussions with him regarding a multimillion-dollar gift from his family to the university, which would be used to build an addition to the business building that would be named after the donor.

When you call the coaches regarding possible cheating, each of them responds by requesting the identity of the faculty member and the names of the student-athletes. When you are reluctant to give the names at this stage, each coach responds indicating his belief it was Professor Norse in the psychology department, who has long been an opponent of athletics at the university. They add that they are not surprised that the athletes missed the same questions because they generally study together. Both coaches are reluctant to help set up meetings with the student-athletes until school starts after the first of the year, arguing that it would be very disruptive to their practice and playing schedules and that the students were going home for the holidays on the few days that they have off during December. When told of allegations that the basketball and football academic advisors and tutors may have helped write papers, the coaches scoff, again noting that there is bad blood between the university's academic support staff and the basketball and football advisors and tutors, because the university personnel think the athletic academic advisors get preferential treatment and perks, including necessary traveling with the teams to provide academic and tutoring support on the road. They agree to talk with the advisors and the student-athletes and get back to you to set up a meeting after the first of the year.

After these conversations with the coaches, which you found to be disheartening and unhelpful, you call the president to ask whether she can help get the coaches to set up meetings with the student-athletes, the academic advisors and tutors, and the donor as soon as possible. She responds that she will do her best and get back to you. You do not hear from her for a week, despite two follow-up e-mails you sent to her during the week. When you finally reach her, she apologizes for not getting back to you sooner and indicates that, after speaking with the coaches, she thinks it would be best to wait to set up the meetings until after the first of the year, when the student-athletes are back on campus on a full-time basis and athletics personnel are not busy preparing for the football bowl game and the prestigious holiday tournament that the basketball team is participating in during December.

In analyzing the preceding factual scenario, consider the following questions:

a. Who is your client? Do you see any potential conflicts of interest (consider which individuals may have violated NCAA rules), and if so, what steps should you take to comply with your ethical duties as an attorney?

b. Are you satisfied with the responses you received from the president and the coaches? What should you do? Are there possible implications for you personally if you fail to take appropriate action until after the first of the year?

c. Whom do you want to interview, and what facts would you try to discover to determine whether any of the allegations are true? What NCAA rules may have been violated and how are they likely to be characterized within the Division I Levels I-IV rules violation structure?

d. If you find that the allegations are true, what action would you recommend the university take to fulfill its self-reporting obligation? What other voluntary self-corrective actions would you advise? What if the university president refuses to follow your advice?

e. Going forward, what is your advice to prevent similar problems from arising in the future (i.e., what reporting, follow-up, or other investigative procedures designed to deal with possible infractions should be implemented)?

PROBLEM 3-8

Midwestern State University was highly interested in seeing Joe Fastball, a junior college baseball star, don a Midwestern State baseball uniform and compete for the team in the upcoming season. In an effort to recruit Fastball, Midwestern State's assistant baseball coach promised the junior college star that his wife would be able to travel with the baseball team to each away game. Furthermore, the assistant coach assured Fastball that he would help his wife secure full-time employment.

Fastball accepted the assistant coach's "offer" and enrolled in Midwestern State. Fastball was happy to see that the assistant coach was true to his word in that he immediately arranged for Fastball's wife to work part-time before switching to a full-time job in the mailroom of the apartment complex where the assistant baseball coach both lives and works part-time as a manager. In an additional gesture of gratitude toward Fastball, the assistant coach loaned his automobile to Fastball and his wife on several occasions so the two of them could run local errands.

Joe was not the only member of the Fastball family who, in the eyes of the assistant coach, had an aptitude for the game of baseball. On several occasions, the assistant coach called on Joe's father, Scout Fastball, to watch a prospective student-athlete compete in a high school baseball game and share his opinion of the prospective student-athlete's performance with the assistant coach. As the relationship between Scout and the assistant coach continued to grow, the assistant coach gave more and more recruitment-related responsibilities to Scout. On one occasion, Scout was asked to hand-deliver a National Letter of Intent to a prospective student-athlete. On another occasion, Scout introduced a different prospective student-athlete and his family to Midwestern State's head baseball coach.

Although Scout was in regular contact with the assistant baseball coach, he was never compensated by Midwestern State for his efforts. According to the NCAA, Scout was not actually a certified recruiter; he was merely a representative of Midwestern State's athletic interests.

Fastball was not the only student-athlete for whom the assistant baseball coach performed favors. While in Oklahoma for winter break, the assistant coach offered to provide Sam Slugger, a Midwestern State baseball player, with transportation from Oklahoma to Midwestern State's campus (a distance of 1,350 miles) so Slugger could enroll in the institution for the spring semester. Slugger accepted this offer. Upon returning to Midwestern State's campus, the assistant baseball coach allowed Slugger to borrow his automobile for personal errands on approximately two occasions.

When baseball season arrived, Midwestern State certified both Fastball and Slugger as initial enrollees with four years of eligibility. Both were allowed to practice, travel with the team, compete, and receive financial aid. Fastball and Slugger, however, had both previously attended and competed for other institutions: Fastball for a junior college and Slugger for both a junior college and a four-year institution. The assistant baseball coach knew that both individuals had competed as student-athletes for other institutions and thus could not be eligible under NCAA rules governing transfers from two- and four-year institutions.

During the following summer, three Midwestern State student-athletes, one of whom was Fastball, were awarded academic credit for classes in which they did not perform any work or take any exams and which they did not even attend. In fact, none of the three student-athletes was aware that they were enrolled in the class in question. When two of the student-athletes, after finding they had received a grade of "A," approached the assistant coach, he told them not to be concerned about the situation. After being informed that the credits may have been fraudulent, the assistant coach took no action to report or investigate the matter. Although the academic credits were indeed fraudulent, Fastball was certified as eligible to compete for Midwestern State the following season.

Identify the NCAA rules violations raised by the foregoing facts and determine each violation's likely characterization in the Division I Levels I-IV rules structure. What action, if any, would you advise Midwestern State to take regarding Joe Fastball?

3. Student-Athlete Eligibility Issues

a. Amateurism, Academic, and Ethics Rules

When a student-athlete violates a rule of the NCAA, both the student-athlete and member institution may be subject to the resultant penalties. Rules violations can be minor, sometimes requiring little more than a waiver of the rule as it applies to the student-athlete in a given instance. They can also be more serious, requiring the imposition of stronger penalties. Unlike institutions and personnel, however, student-athletes are largely subjected to sanctions at the institutional or conference level under NCAA Rules. The NCAA, however, oversees this process to ensure that its member institutions are acting consistently and in a manner that maintains a level playing field for intercollegiate athletics. For example, during the fall of 2015, the University of Georgia suspended its star running back Todd Gurley for four games for accepting more than $3,000 in cash from multiple individuals for autographed memorabilia and other items over a two-year period of time.

Student-athletes who have been penalized for violating an NCAA or conference rule (e.g., Todd Gurley) will have to seek reinstatement. The Student-Athlete Reinstatement Committee (SARC) oversees the reinstatement process. Professor Jo Potuto, a former member and chair of the NCAA's Committee on Infractions (COI), summarizes the NCAA's student-athlete reinstatement process as follows:

> The consequences to a student-athlete for committing an NCAA bylaw violation are determined by the [Student-Athlete Reinstatement Committee] (SARC) and its staff. In academic year 2010-11, the last year for which data are reported, approximately 1,850 student-athlete violations were sufficiently serious to trigger the formal involvement of the NCAA student-athlete reinstatement process. Student-athletes are ineligible to compete from the point at which they commit a violation until their eligibility status is resolved.
>
> Even for the most serious student-athlete violations, the NCAA enforcement staff conducts no investigation, makes no allegation of violations, and compiles no evidence to support allegations. Instead, the university at which a student-athlete is enrolled investigates, determines the relevant facts, decides whether a violation was committed, reports any findings of violations to the NCAA enforcement staff, and typically reports those findings to the SARC staff and requests reinstatement to eligibility of the culpable student-athlete. There is no fact-finding by any NCAA committee, no adversarial hearing before an adjudicatory body analogous to the COI, and no appeal of a SARC decision to an internal NCAA appellate body equivalent to the IAC. The exclusive role of the SARC and its staff is to ensure that a university provides a fully developed factual record to support its conclusion as to the seriousness of the violation reported, to assess the degree of student-athlete culpability based on the facts that an institution reports, and to decide whether and under what conditions a student-athlete may be reinstated to competition eligibility.
>
> [Generally matters are disposed of by the staff and member institution]. [T]he SARC hears university appeals from staff decisions. To limit the scope of the reinstatement staff's discretion and enhance the likelihood that cases with similar facts are treated similarly across all NCAA member institutions, the SARC has adopted guidelines that prescribe reinstatement conditions (sanctions) for particular violations. For minor violations, there is no withholding of a student-athlete from competition. Serious violations can result in withholding for a substantial number of competitions (including permanent ineligibility), a decrease in the total number of years (five) a student-athlete has to compete, and sometimes both consequences.

See Josephine (Jo) R. Potuto and Matthew J. Mitten, *Comparing NCAA and Olympic Athlete Eligibility Dispute Resolution Systems in Light of Procedural Fairness and Substantive Justice*, 7 Harv. J. Sports & Ent. L. 1 at 17-20 (2016).

Professor Potuto argues that there are strong policy and practical reasons that support such a process for dealing with most student-athlete issues at the institutional and staff level, leaving only the most egregious and challenging issues to be dealt with by SARC:

> By staffing the SARC with faculty and staff from member universities, the NCAA student-athlete reinstatement process incorporates expertise in both the areas of NCAA bylaws and also campus protocols. An approach by which student-athletes are ineligible from the time they commit a violation until their eligibility is

restored incentivizes a university with information about his or her possible violation of an NCAA rule to work expeditiously to investigate and report it. It is consistent with the NCAA's guiding principle of institutional control, including an institution's obligation to educate student-athletes regarding eligibility requirements; to monitor for potential violations; to cooperate with the NCAA to ensure bylaw compliance; and to report violations when uncovered. Putting the onus for rules compliance squarely on member institution facilitates enforcement of NCAA rules by precluding student-athletes from competing pending determination of their eligibility to do so, thereby avoiding the problem of attempting to offset any institutional competitive advantage gained if they competed but ultimately were determined to have been ineligible.

Id. at 19-21. She adds, however, that there are two possible flaws in the system:

> The first flaw is the likelihood of uneven rules enforcement that impact competitive equity among NCAA member institutions that are not equally adept at uncovering violations or willing to undertake the same thorough and probing job of deciding whether violations were committed . . . Another significant flaw is the current widespread perception of inconsistent decisions across cases considered by the SARC. In its own right, a perception of internal inconsistency and unfairness ill serves the NCAA, which also may contribute to a reluctance by trial judges and juries to defer to NCAA decisions that result in a student-athlete's ineligibility.

Id. at 21.

Institutions may also submit requests for waivers of NCAA student-athlete eligibility rules in other areas. For example, an incoming student-athlete, through his or her institution, may seek a waiver of NCAA or conference academic eligibility requirements. See NCAA, *2016-17 Initial-Eligibility Waiver Directive NCAA Divisions I and II,* http://www.ncaa.org/sites/default/files/IEW_Directive_20160616.pdf. In determining whether to grant an institution's request for a waiver from the NCAA's academic eligibility rules on behalf of a student-athlete, the directive instructs staff to weigh the following factors:

> [T]he staff will weigh the student-athlete's deficiency against the overall academic record and the mitigating circumstances asserted for the student-athlete's failure to satisfy minimum legislated initial-eligibility requirements. The larger the deficiency, the more significant and compelling the mitigation must be to provide relief. Further, all mitigating circumstances are analyzed to determine whether they directly impacted the student-athlete's ability to satisfy initial-eligibility requirements and whether they were within the student-athlete's control. Grade-point average deficiencies are analyzed stringently, as they generally reflect the entire academic record.

Institutions may seek a waiver from any rule on behalf of a student-athlete, but such waivers have to be justified. Justifying a waiver—providing reasons why an NCAA or conference rule should not apply in a particular instance—is part of the challenging work done by compliance personnel at a member institution. Some member institutions also have more stringent rules than those required by the NCAA or the member's conference. For example, a school may require a higher academic standard than that required by the NCAA, and a student-athlete who fails to meet that standard will have to seek a waiver from a faculty committee or other academic officer within the university.

Under private contract and association law, courts generally are quite deferential to the NCAA regarding its interpretation and enforcement of its own rules and regulations, particularly its student-athlete eligibility rules.

BLOOM v. NCAA

93 P.3d 621 (Colo. App. 2004)

DAILEY, J.

I.   BACKGROUND

[Jeremy] Bloom, a high school football and track star, was recruited to play football at CU. Before enrolling there, however, he competed in Olympic and professional World Cup skiing events, becoming the World Cup champion in freestyle moguls. During the Olympics, Bloom appeared on MTV, and thereafter was offered various paid entertainment opportunities, including a chance to host a show on Nickelodeon. Bloom also agreed to endorse commercially certain ski equipment, and he contracted to model clothing for Tommy Hilfiger.

Bloom became concerned that his endorsements and entertainment activities might interfere with his eligibility to compete in intercollegiate football. On Bloom's behalf, CU first requested waivers of NCAA rules restricting student-athlete endorsement and media activities and, then, a favorable interpretation of the NCAA rule restricting media activities.

The NCAA denied CU's requests, and Bloom discontinued his endorsement, modeling, and media activities to play football for CU during the 2002 fall season. However, Bloom instituted this action against the NCAA for declaratory and injunctive relief, asserting that his endorsement, modeling, and media activities were necessary to support his professional skiing career, something which the NCAA rules permitted.

In his complaint, Bloom alleged: (1) as a third-party beneficiary of the contract between the NCAA and its members, he was entitled to enforce NCAA bylaws permitting him to engage in and receive remuneration from a professional sport different from his amateur sport; (2) as applied to the facts of this case, the NCAA's restrictions on endorsements and media appearances were arbitrary and capricious; and (3) those restrictions constituted improper and unconscionable restraints of trade.

For these reasons, Bloom requested that the NCAA restrictions be declared inapplicable, and that the NCAA and CU be enjoined from applying them, to activities originating prior to his enrollment at CU or wholly unrelated to his prowess as a football player. . . .

IV.   STANDING

We reject the NCAA's assertion that Bloom lacked standing to pursue claims for breach of contract or arbitrary and capricious action on the part of the NCAA.

A party has standing to seek relief when he or she has suffered actual injury to a legally protected interest. . . .

A person not a party to an express contract may bring an action on the contract if the parties to the agreement intended to benefit the nonparty, provided that the benefit claimed is a direct and not merely incidental benefit of the contract. While the intent to benefit the nonparty need not be expressly recited in the contract, the intent must be apparent from the terms of the agreement, the surrounding circumstances, or both. . . .

Here, the trial court found, and we agree, that the NCAA's constitution, bylaws, and regulations evidence a clear intent to benefit student-athletes. And because each student-athlete's eligibility to compete is determined by the NCAA, we conclude that Bloom had standing in a preliminary injunction hearing to contest the meaning or applicability of NCAA eligibility restrictions. *See Hall v. NCAA*, 985 F. Supp. 782, 796-97 (N.D. Ill. 1997) (given importance of NCAA's function to benefit student-athletes, and NCAA's role in determining eligibility of student-athletes, court assumed student-athlete was likely to succeed in proving third-party beneficiary standing vis-a-vis the contract between the NCAA and its members); *see also NCAA v. Brinkworth*, 680 So. 2d 1081, 1083 (Fla. Dist. Ct. App. 1996).

With respect to a claim of arbitrary and capricious action, the Kentucky Supreme Court observed that "relief from our judicial system should be available if voluntary athletic associations act arbitrarily and capriciously toward student-athletes." *NCAA v. Lasege*, 53 S.W.3d 77, 83 (Ky. 2001). . . .

Courts are reluctant to intervene, except on the most limited grounds, in the internal affairs of voluntary associations. . . . Even then, it would appear that a plaintiff must ordinarily allege an invasion of some type of civil or property right to have standing. *See Van Valkenburg v. Liberty Lodge No. 300, supra*, 619 N.W.2d at 609; *see also Levant v. Whitley*, 755 A.2d 1036, 1043-44 n. 11 (D.C. 2000) (surveying circumstances in which courts intervene in disputes involving voluntary membership associations).

Here, Bloom is not a member of the NCAA, and he does not have a constitutional right to engage in amateur intercollegiate athletics at CU. *See, e.g., Graham v. NCAA*, 804 F.2d 953, 955 (6th Cir. 1986); *Colo. Seminary (Univ. of Denver) v. NCAA*, 570 F.2d 320, 321 (10th Cir. 1978); *Hart v. NCAA*, 209 W. Va. 543, 550 S.E.2d 79, 86 (2001). Nor does he assert any property interest in playing football for CU.

However, to the extent Bloom's claim of arbitrary and capricious action asserts a violation of the duty of good faith and fair dealing that is implied in the contractual relationship between the NCAA and its members, his position as a third-party beneficiary of that contractual relationship affords him standing to pursue this claim. *See O'Reilly v. Physicians Mut. Ins. Co.*, 992 P.2d 644, 646 (Colo. App. 1999) (implied duty of good faith and fair dealing requires "parties to the agreement to perform their contractual obligations in good faith and in a reasonable manner"); *see also Hall v. NCAA, supra*, 985 F. Supp. at 784 (implied duty of good faith and fair dealing "requires that a party vested with contractual discretion exercise that discretion reasonably, not arbitrarily or capriciously"); *Dayan v. McDonald's Corp.*, 125 Ill. App. 3d 972, 991, 81 Ill. Dec. 156, 466 N.E.2d 958, 972 (1984) (implied duty to deal fairly and in good faith requires party vested with discretion to act reasonably and not "arbitrarily, capriciously, or in a manner inconsistent with the reasonable expectations of the parties").

In sum, we conclude that Bloom has third-party beneficiary standing to pursue what in essence are two claims for violation of his contractual rights.

V. PROBABILITY OF SUCCESS

Bloom contends that the trial court erred in assessing the probability of success on his contract claims. We disagree.

Initially, we note that, as a third-party beneficiary, Bloom has rights no greater than those of the parties to the contract itself, here, the NCAA and its member institutions. . . .

A. INTERPRETATION OF NCAA BYLAWS

In interpreting a contract, we seek to give effect to the intent and the reasonable expectations of the parties. . . . To determine the intent and expectations of the parties, we view the contract in its entirety, not in isolated portions, . . . and we give words and phrases their plain meaning according to common usage.

If its meaning is clear and unambiguous, the contract is enforced as written. . . . If, however, the contract is susceptible of more than one reasonable interpretation, it is ambiguous, and its meaning must be determined as an issue of fact. . . . In resolving an ambiguity, a court will follow the construction placed upon it by the parties themselves before the controversy arose. . . .

The interpretation of a contract and the determination whether it is ambiguous are questions of law subject to de novo review by this court. . . .

Bloom relies on NCAA Bylaw 12.1.2, which states that "[a] professional athlete in one sport may represent a member institution in a different sport." He asserts that, because a professional is one who "gets paid" for a sport, a student-athlete is entitled to earn whatever income is customary for his or her professional sport, which, in the case of professional skiers, primarily comes from endorsements and paid media opportunities.

We recognize that, like many others involved in individual professional sports such as golf, tennis, and boxing, professional skiers obtain much of their income from sponsors. We note, however, that none of the NCAA's bylaws mentions, much less explicitly establishes, a right to receive "customary income" for a sport.

To the contrary, the NCAA bylaws prohibit every student-athlete from receiving money for advertisements and endorsements. In this regard, NCAA Bylaw 12.5.2.1 states:

> Subsequent to becoming a student-athlete, an individual shall not be eligible for participation in intercollegiate athletics if the individual: (a) Accepts any remuneration for or permits the use of his or her name or picture to advertise, recommend or promote directly the sale or use of a commercial product or service of any kind, or (b) Receives remuneration for endorsing a commercial product or service through the individual's use of such product or service.

Additionally, while NCAA Bylaw 12.5.1.3 permits a student-athlete to continue to receive remuneration for activity initiated prior to enrollment in which his or her name or picture is used, this remuneration is only allowed, if, as pertinent here, "the individual became involved in such activities for reasons independent of athletics ability; . . . no reference is made in these activities to the individual's name or involvement in intercollegiate athletics; [and] . . . the individual does not endorse the commercial product."

Further, NCAA Bylaw 12.4.1.1 prohibits a student-athlete from receiving "any remuneration for value or utility that the student-athlete may have for the employer because of the publicity, reputation, fame or personal following that he or she has obtained because of athletics ability."

Unlike other NCAA bylaws, the endorsements and media appearance bylaws do not contain any sport-specific qualifiers. *See, e.g.*, NCAA Bylaw 12.3.1 (ineligibility of student-athlete to compete in intercollegiate sport based on agreement with agent to market athlete's athletic ability or reputation "in that sport").

In our view, when read together, the NCAA bylaws express a clear and unambiguous intent to prohibit student-athletes from engaging in endorsements and paid media appearances, without regard to: (1) when the opportunity for such activities originated; (2) whether the opportunity arose or exists for reasons unrelated to participation in an amateur sport; and (3) whether income derived from the opportunity is customary for any particular professional sport.

The clear import of the bylaws is that, although student-athletes have the right to be professional athletes, they do not have the right to simultaneously engage in endorsement or paid media activity and maintain their eligibility to participate in amateur competition. And we may not disregard the clear meaning of the bylaws simply because they may disproportionately affect those who participate in individual professional sports.

Further, the record contains ample evidence supporting the trial court' conclusion that this interpretation is consistent with both the NCAA's and its member institutions' construction of the bylaws. An NCAA official testified that both the endorsement and media appearance provisions have been consistently applied and interpreted in a nonsport-specific manner. Indeed, another NCAA official related that association members had resisted efforts to change the endorsement rule to be sport-specific. Although the evidence is conflicting, the record supports the trial court's conclusion that, from the beginning, CU understood that the endorsement and media activity rules were nonsport-specific in scope.

Thus, even if the bylaws were viewed as ambiguous, the record supports the trial court's conclusion that the bylaws would ultimately be interpreted in accordance with the NCAA's and its member institutions' construction of those bylaws.

B. APPLICATION OF BYLAWS TO BLOOM

The United States Supreme Court has recognized the NCAA as "the guardian of an important American tradition," namely, amateurism in intercollegiate athletics. *See NCAA v. Bd. of Regents*, 468 U.S. 85, 101, 104 S.Ct. 2948, 2960, 82 L. Ed. 2d 70 (1984).

Under that tradition, "college sports provided an important opportunity for teaching people about character, motivation, endurance, loyalty, and the attainment of one's personal best—all qualities of great value in citizens. In this sense, competitive athletics were viewed as an extracurricular activity, justified by the university as part of its ideal objective of educating the whole person." James J. Duderstadt, Intercollegiate Athletics and the American University 70 (Univ. Mich. Press 2003).

The NCAA's "Principle of Amateurism" states:

> Student-athletes shall be amateurs in an intercollegiate sport, and their participation should be motivated primarily by education and by the physical, mental and social benefits to be derived. Student participation in intercollegiate athletics is an

avocation, and student-athletes should be protected from exploitation by professional and commercial enterprises.

NCAA Const. art. 2.9.

The NCAA's purpose, in this regard, is not only "to maintain intercollegiate athletics as an integral part of the educational program," but also to "retain a clear line of demarcation between intercollegiate athletics and professional sports." NCAA Const. art. 1, § 1.3.1.

Here, the trial court found that application of the endorsement and media appearance rules in Bloom's case was rationally related to the legitimate purpose of retaining the "clear line of demarcation between intercollegiate athletics and professional sports."

The trial court noted that salaries and bonuses are an acceptable means for attaining income from professional sports, but endorsement income is not acceptable if a student-athlete wishes to preserve amateur eligibility. According to NCAA officials: (1) endorsements invoke concerns about "the commercial exploitation of student-athletes and the promotion of commercial products"; and (2) it is not possible to distinguish the precise capacity in which endorsements are made. A CU official related that generally, the endorsement rule prevents students from becoming billboards for commercialism, and in Bloom's case, there would "be no way to tell whether he is receiving pay commensurate with his . . . football ability or skiing ability."

In this respect, the trial court observed:

> In an honest world where there is no attempt to avoid an ideal, there wouldn't be an impact on amateurism if Mr. Bloom was allowed to be compensated as is customary for professional skiers; however, it's naive to think that we live in such a world. There are those who would be less than honest and seek profit for profit's sake. . . .
>
> If Mr. Bloom was allowed to receive the [endorsement] income that is customary for professional skiers, it is not difficult for me to imagine that some in other professional sports would decide that in addition to direct monetary compensation . . . endorsements or promotion of goods would become customary.

Similar concerns underlie the NCAA's prohibition on paid entertainment activity. Paid entertainment activity may impinge upon the amateur ideal if the opportunity were obtained or advanced because of the student's athletic ability or prestige, even though that activity may further the education of student-athletes such as Bloom, a communications major. As the trial court noted, there are "various shades of gray within which such events could fall." And, as should be evident, the NCAA does not prohibit *unpaid* internships, externships, or other educational opportunities in the entertainment field.

In this case, Bloom presented evidence that some of his acting opportunities arose not as a result of his athletic ability but because of his good looks and on-camera presence. However, the record contains evidence that Bloom's agent and the Tommy Hilfiger company marketed Bloom as a talented multi-sport athlete, and a representative from a talent agency intimated that Bloom's reputation as an athlete would be advantageous in obtaining auditions for various entertainment opportunities. Further, the NCAA indicated, when asked to interpret its rules, that it was unable, due to insufficient information, to determine which of Bloom's requested media activities were, in fact, unrelated to his athletic ability or prestige.

Under these circumstances, we perceive no abuse of the trial court's discretion in failing to fault the NCAA for refusing to waive its rules, as requested by CU, to permit Bloom "to pursue any television and film opportunities while he is a student-athlete at CU." *See Cole v. NCAA*, 120 F. Supp. 2d 1060, 1071-72 (N.D. Ga. 2000) (NCAA decisions regarding "challenges of student-athletes are entitled to considerable deference," and courts are reluctant to replace the NCAA as the "decision-maker on private waiver applications"); *see also NCAA v. Lasege, supra*, 53 S.W.3d at 83 (voluntary athletic associations "should be allowed to 'paddle their own canoe' without unwarranted interference from the courts").

Bloom also asserts that the NCAA is arbitrary in its application of the endorsement and media bylaws. He notes that, while the NCAA would bar him from accepting commercial endorsements, it will allow colleges to commercially endorse athletic equipment by having students wear the equipment, with identifying logos and insignias, while engaged in intercollegiate competition. But the trial court determined, and we agree, that this application of the bylaws has a rational basis in economic necessity: financial benefits inure not to any single student-athlete but to member schools and thus to all student-athletes, including those who participate in programs that generate no revenue.

Bloom further argues that the NCAA is arbitrary in the way it applies its bylaws among individual students. Bloom presented evidence that, in one instance, a student-athlete was permitted to make an unpaid, minor appearance in a single film. But the NCAA could rationally conclude that this situation was different: Bloom did not seek permission to make an unpaid appearance in one specific instance; he wanted to take advantage of any number of television and film opportunities, and he wanted to be paid. Bloom also presented evidence that a second student-athlete was permitted to appear on television while he participated in his professional sport. But Bloom did not show that the NCAA would prohibit him from appearing on television while participating in his professional sport. . . .

Bloom has thus failed to demonstrate any inconsistency in application which would lead us to conclude that the NCAA was arbitrarily applying its rules.

Finally, we are not convinced that the NCAA treated Bloom unfairly in the manner in which it denied the requests to waive or interpret its rules.

Although Bloom is correct that he was not permitted to personally petition the NCAA, he effectively submitted three petitions to the NCAA with the full assistance and support of CU. The trial court's finding that Bloom had "an ability to fully present his . . . position through the membership institution" is amply supported by the record.

Further, the court found, with record support, that the NCAA requested additional information on CU's petition (evidencing that the NCAA was not acting arbitrarily or capriciously), and that there was no evidence that the NCAA gave CU's petition any less consideration than its other "hundreds of administrative and waiver requests."

The record thus supports the trial court's findings that the NCAA's administrative review process is reasonable in general and that it was reasonably applied in this case. As such, these findings, as well as those with respect to the NCAA's application of its bylaws, are not manifestly arbitrary, unreasonable, or unfair. . . .

For these reasons, we agree with the trial court that Bloom failed to demonstrate a reasonable probability of success on the merits.

VI. OTHER ISSUES

. . . In light of this conclusion, we need not address whether, as the trial court found, Bloom also failed to show that a preliminary injunction would not disserve the public interest and was justified by the balance of equities in the case. Consequently, we do not address the parties' remaining arguments, including the validity of the NCAA's restitution rule, NCAA Bylaw 19.8, or the effect, if any, of the federal Commerce Clause on the trial court's ability to fashion a remedy for Bloom in this case.

Accordingly, the trial court's order is affirmed.

NOTES AND QUESTIONS

1. *Judicial Deference to Private Associations.* *Bloom* illustrates that, as is true for other private sports governing bodies, courts afford considerable deference to the NCAA in enforcing its rules and regulations even vis-à-vis non-members such as intercollegiate athletes. See also *NCAA v. Brinkworth*, 680 So. 2d 1081, 1085 (Fla. Ct. App. 1996) (in upholding NCAA procedures for considering a student-athlete's request for a waiver of a rule requiring completion of four years of intercollegiate competition within five years, the court concluded that because the "procedures were adequate and fair, there was no basis on which to intervene in the internal affairs of the NCAA"); *Hispanic College Fund, Inc. v. NCAA*, 826 N.E.2d 652, 657 (Ind. App. 2005) (upholding an NCAA decision to add a twelfth Division 1-A regular season game because no allegation that "NCAA's actions were fraudulent, otherwise illegal, or that they abused civil or property rights having their origin elsewhere"). Notwithstanding the general policy of judicial abstention from interference, courts will intervene and grant appropriate relief when the NCAA or an athletic conference has acted in violation of its own rules, regulations, and policies. See, e.g., *Gulf South Conference v. Boyd*, 369 So. 2d 553, 557 (Ala. 1979) (holding that "the general non-interference doctrine concerning voluntary associations does not apply in cases involving disputes between college athletes themselves and college athletic associations" because "the athlete is not even a member of the athletic association" and "has no voice or bargaining power concerning [its] rules and regulations"; finding the student eligible to play football because the athletic conference incorrectly declared him ineligible in violation of its own rules); *California State Univ., Hayward v. NCAA*, 121 Cal. Rptr. 85, 88-89 (Cal. App. 1975) ("It is true that courts will not interfere with the disciplining or expelling of members of such associations where the action is taken in good faith and in accordance with its adopted laws and rules. But if the decision of the tribunal is contrary to its laws and rules, it is not authorized by the bylaws of the association, a court may review the ruling of the board and direct the reinstatement of the member").

2. *Contractual Relationships.* What was the significance of third-party beneficiary contract law in *Bloom*? Why did the *Bloom* court hold that the NCAA's application of its endorsement and media bylaws was not arbitrary or capricious? For law review commentary regarding *Bloom*, see, for example, Michael A. Corgan, *Permitting Student-Athletes to Accept Endorsement Deals: A Solution to the Financial Corruption of College Athletics Created by Unethical Sports*

Agents and the NCAA's Revenue-Generating Scheme, 19 Vill. Sports & Ent. L.J. 371 (2012); Bill Cross, *The NCAA as Publicity Enemy Number One*, 58 U. Kan. L. Rev. 1221 (2010); Joel Eckert, *Student-Athlete Contract Rights in the Aftermath of* Bloom v. NCAA, 59 Vand. L. Rev. 905 (2006). In contrast to *Bloom*, in *Knelman v. Middlebury College*, 2012 WL 4481470 (D. Vt. 2012), the court refused to grant third-party beneficiary status to a student-athlete. It concluded that the student-athlete failed to demonstrate that Middlebury College and the NCAA intended to confer on the athlete the benefit of provisions in the NCAA manual articulating the responsibility of institutions to ensure that coaches exhibit fairness and honesty in their relationships with student-athletes.

In *Oliver v. National Collegiate Athletic Assn.*, 920 N.E.2d 203 (Ohio Ct. Common Pleas, 2009), a college baseball player sued the NCAA, alleging breach of contract and tortious interference with contractual relations and seeking declaratory and injunctive relief to prevent it from rendering him ineligible for violating its rules. After a bench trial, an Ohio Court of Common Pleas held that (1) the NCAA bylaw prohibiting an attorney representing a student-athlete from being present during contract negotiations between the athlete and a professional sports organization violated the NCAA's contractual obligation of good faith and fair dealing to its member universities' student-athletes; (2) the NCAA bylaw allowing the NCAA to impose penalties on student-athletes and institutions (i.e., "restitution rule") violated its contractual obligation of good faith and fair dealing; and (3) an injunction was necessary to prevent the plaintiff from suffering irreparable harm. The court's decision subsequently was vacated pursuant to a settlement between the parties. For scholarly discussion of the *Oliver* case, see Brandon D. Morgan, Oliver v. NCAA: *NCAA's No Agent Rule Called Out, But Remains Safe*, 17 Sports Law. J. 303 (2010); T. Matthew Lockhart, Oliver v. NCAA: *Throwing a Contractual Curveball at the NCAA's "Veil of Amateurism,"* 35 U. Dayton L. Rev. 175 (2010); James Halt, *Andy Oliver Strikes Out the NCAA's "No-Agent" Rule for College Baseball*, 19 J. Legal Aspects Sport 185 (2009). What kinds of problems does the *Oliver* decision portend for the NCAA?

In 2016, the NCAA liberalized rules previously limiting Division I men's basketball and baseball student-athletes' ability to interact with professional teams. NCAA president Mark Emmert stated that this will allow student-athletes the ability to "develop an objective reality of what their prospects" are without potentially losing their eligibility. The rule change will allow athletes to enter their respective draft multiple times and provides a later date for when an athlete must remove their name from the NBA draft to preserve their eligibility. Prior to the rule change, student-athletes gauging their professional basketball interests could not participate in the NBA draft combine. Now, student-athletes can participate in the NBA draft combine and one tryout per NBA team to determine their pro potential without losing their eligibility. In regards to baseball, the rule changes allow for high school baseball players to hire an agent and still preserve collegiate eligibility. Under the previous rule, high school athletes would lose eligibility if they hired an agent.

3. NCAA v. Lasege. Consistent with *Bloom*, in *NCAA v. Lasege*, 53 S.W.3d 77 (Ky. 2001), the Supreme Court of Kentucky ruled in favor of the NCAA, which had prohibited a University of Louisville basketball player from participating in intercollegiate sports. Prior to his matriculation at Louisville, Lasege

played basketball in Russia under a professional contract and engaged in other conduct that the NCAA found violated its amateurism rules. Consequently, the NCAA deemed him ineligible to participate in intercollegiate competition. Louisville declared Lasege ineligible but subsequently requested that the NCAA reinstate his eligibility. The NCAA rejected the request, concluding that Lasege had compromised his amateur status by accepting "preferential treatment, benefits, or services" for his participation in the Russian basketball league. *Id.* at 2.

After Louisville exhausted its appeals within the NCAA regulatory process, Lasege filed an action against the NCAA in which he sought a temporary injunction to reverse the NCAA's decision and reinstate his eligibility. The trial court granted Lasege's request. It found that a substantial question existed as to whether the NCAA acted arbitrarily and capriciously. The trial court stated that the NCAA ignored overwhelming mitigating circumstances (e.g., economic and cultural disadvantage, ignorance of NCAA rules, and coercion associated with execution of the profession contract) and engaged in disparate treatment with respect to Lasege. Accordingly, it issued the injunction, and Lasege played during the 2000-2001 basketball season.

The Kentucky Supreme Court reversed the trial court's decision in favor of the plaintiff and the court of appeals' affirmance thereof. It characterized the trial court's order as clearly erroneous. Moreover, it identified the NCAA as the party in the best position to determine a player's eligibility.

> We have held that a ruling is arbitrary and capricious only where it is "clearly erroneous, and by 'clearly erroneous' we mean unsupported by substantial evidence." Here, the NCAA's ruling has strong evidentiary support — Lasege unquestionably signed contracts to play professional basketball and unquestionably accepted benefits. Contrary to the trial court's allegations of disparate treatment, the NCAA submits that no individual has ever had his or her eligibility reinstated after committing a combination of rules violations akin to those compiled by Lasege. The NCAA's eligibility determinations are entitled to a presumption of correctness — particularly when they stem from conceded violations of NCAA regulations. Although we recognize that Lasege's mitigation evidence is relevant to review of the NCAA's determination, we believe the trial court simply disagreed with the NCAA as to the weight which should be assigned to this evidence. Accordingly, we believe the trial court abused its discretion when it found that Lasege had a high probability of success on the merits of his claim.

Id. at 85.

4. *Proposed Heightened Judicial Review.* Consider the following view:

> To ensure that student-athletes are not denied the lifetime educational benefits of athletic participation opportunities without adequate justification, courts should apply a higher level of judicial scrutiny than the traditional common law rational basis or arbitrary and capricious standards. We do not advocate *de novo* or strict judicial review, but the significant educational and potential economic benefits of athletic participation (e.g., a scholarship or professional sports career) warrant more than courts merely asking the very deferential and frequently outcome determinative question of whether an eligibility rule or its application is merely rational or arbitrary and capricious. We propose a uniform heightened level of judicial scrutiny that allows a student-athlete to prove, by clear and

convincing evidence, that his or her exclusion from athletic participation does not substantially further an important and legitimate interest of an interscholastic or intercollegiate sports governing body or educational institution.

This standard would better balance the parties' respective interests in an athletic eligibility dispute, but it poses the risk of unwarranted judicial micromanagement of high school and college athletics and potentially more litigation. On the other hand, because a student-athlete has a significant burden of persuasion to satisfy, an adverse eligibility determination will be judicially vacated in relatively few cases.

Matthew J. Mitten and Timothy Davis, *Athlete Eligibility Requirements and Legal Protection of Sports Participation Opportunities*, 8 Va. Sports & Ent. L.J. 71 (2008). Do you agree?

5. *Legality of Restitution Rule.* The *Lasege* court also validated NCAA Bylaw 19.8, which permits the organization to seek restitution from its member institutions as a result of rules violations such as those that Louisville committed when it allowed Lasege to play:

> By becoming a member of the NCAA, a voluntary athletic association, U of L agreed to abide by its rules and regulations. NCAA Bylaw 19.8 is one of those regulations, and it specifically provides that the NCAA can attempt to restore competitive equity by redistributing wins and losses and imposing sanctions upon a member institution which allows an ineligible player to participate under a subsequently-vacated court order, even if that order requires the institution to allow the player to participate.

Id. at 87.

Quoting from an Indiana Supreme Court decision involving the Indiana High School Athletic Association (IHSAA), the court explained:

Undeniably, the Restitution Rule imposes hardship on a school that, in compliance with an order of a court which is later vacated, fields an ineligible player. On the other hand, use of an ineligible player imposes a hardship on other teams that must compete against the teams fielding ineligible players. While schools will contend that is unfair when they have to forfeit victories earned with an ineligible player on the field because they complied with a court order, competing schools will reply that it is unfair when they have to compete against a team with an ineligible student athlete because a local trial judge prohibited the school or the IHSAA from following the eligibility rules. The Restitution Rule represents the agreement of IHSAA members on how to balance those two competing interests. The Restitution Rule may not be the best method to deal with such situations. However, it is the method which the member schools have adopted. And in any event, its enforcement by the IHSAA does not impinge upon the judiciary's function. [Citation omitted.]

Id. at 87-88.

What are the advantages and disadvantages of the restitution rule? See also Richard G. Johnson, *Submarining Due Process: How the NCAA Uses Its Restitution Rule to Deprive College Athletes of Their Right of Access to the Courts . . . Until* Oliver v. NCAA, 11 Fla. Coastal L. Rev. 459 (2010).

6. *Use of Federal Civil Rights Laws to Challenge NCAA Eligibility Rules.* In *NCAA v. Smith,* 525 U.S. 459 (1999), Renee Smith sued the NCAA after she was denied a waiver of the Post-baccalaureate Bylaw, which allowed a student-athlete to continue competing as a graduate student, but only at the same

institution at which the student-athlete earned his or her undergraduate degree. Smith sought to utilize her remaining athletics eligibility as a graduate student at another institution. When the NCAA denied the graduate institution's application for a waiver, Smith filed a lawsuit claiming the NCAA violated Title IX because the Association granted more waivers for male student-athletes than for female student-athletes. In an opinion written by Justice Ginsburg, the Supreme Court held the NCAA is not a recipient of federal funds and therefore not required to comply with Title IX. What would have been the likely outcome of this case if Smith, like *Bloom*, had attacked the validity of the bylaw on its face?

Like *Tarkanian*, *Smith* holds that certain laws applicable to the NCAA's member institutions do not apply to the NCAA. Is this good policy? Note that educational institutions acting collectively through the NCAA may legally accomplish as a group what they could not individually. In *Cureton v. NCAA*, 198 F.3d 107 (3d Cir. 1999), the Third Circuit considered the two issues not decided by *Smith*. The *Cureton* plaintiffs alleged that the NCAA's Proposition 16 minimum standardized test score requirement for freshman student-athlete eligibility has a racially discriminatory impact in violation of Title VI of the Civil Rights Act of 1964, 42 U.S.C. §§2000d et seq., which applies to any program or activity receiving federal financial assistance. The court rejected plaintiffs' contention that the NCAA is subject to Title VI based on federal funds received by the National Youth Sports program or the degree of its control over its member institutions. It found no evidence that the National Youth Sports program's practices affected the NCAA's broader practices, including adoption and enforcement of Proposition 16. Relying on *Tarkanian*, the court held that the NCAA does not in fact "control" its members:

> Similarly, the ultimate decision as to which freshmen an institution will permit to participate in varsity intercollegiate athletics and which applicants will be awarded athletic scholarships belongs to the member schools. The fact that the institutions make these decisions cognizant of NCAA sanctions does not mean that the NCAA controls them, because they have the option, albeit unpalatable, of risking sanctions or voluntarily withdrawing from the NCAA.

Id. at 117.

However, in some instances, courts have held that federal antidiscrimination laws such as Title VI, the Americans with Disabilities Act of 1990, and the Rehabilitation Act of 1972 apply to the NCAA. See Chapters 9 and 11.

b. NCAA Drug Testing Program

The NCAA's drug testing program, applicable to all student-athletes, was initiated in 1986. It was created (1) so that no one participant could gain an artificially induced advantage, (2) so that no one participant might be pressured to use chemical substances in order to remain competitive, and (3) to safeguard the health and safety of student-athletes. See NCAA, *NCAA Drug Testing Program 2019-20*, https://ncaaorg.s3.amazonaws.com/ssi/substance/2019-20SSI_DrugTestingProgramBooklet.pdf. As a condition to participating in intercollegiate athletics, student-athletes are required to provide written consent to random drug testing for substances prohibited by the NCAA during NCAA championship competition and out-of-season testing programs. The NCAA's list of banned substances includes performance-enhancing drugs such as anabolic steroids, stimulants (e.g., cocaine and amphetamines), and certain illegal recreational drugs such as marijuana and heroin. As illustrated by the following case, courts also provide significant deference to the NCAA in its efforts to prevent student-athletes from using banned substances and its imposition of disciplinary sanctions for doing so. See generally Josephine (Jo) R. Potuto and Matthew J. Mitten, *Comparing NCAA and Olympic Athlete Eligibility Dispute Resolution Systems in Light of Procedural Fairness and Substantive Justice,* 7 Harv. J. Sports & Ent. L. 1 at 23-26 (2016).

BRENNAN v. BOARD OF TRUSTEES FOR UNIVERSITY OF LOUISIANA SYSTEMS

691 So. 2d 324 (La. App. 1997)

LOTTINGER, Chief Judge.

Plaintiff, John Patout Brennan (Brennan), a student-athlete at the University of Southwestern Louisiana (USL), tested positive for [use of the banned anabolic steroid testosterone in the second of three random drug tests administered by the NCAA]. Brennan requested and received two administrative appeals in which he contended that the positive test results were "false" due to a combination of factors, including heavy drinking and sexual activity the night before the test, and his use of nutritional supplements. Following the unsuccessful appeals, USL complied with the NCAA regulations and suspended Brennan from intercollegiate athletic competition for one year. Brennan brought this action against USL's governing body, the Board of Trustees for University of Louisiana Systems (Board of Trustees), seeking to enjoin enforcement by USL of the suspension.

In his petition, Brennan alleged that, by requiring him to submit to the NCAA's drug testing program, USL violated his right of privacy and deprived him of a liberty and property interest without due process in contravention of Article I, Sections 2 and 5 of the Louisiana Constitution. The NCAA moved to intervene on the grounds that the drug testing policies and procedures that Brennan placed at issue were developed, administered, conducted and enforced by the NCAA. The intervention was granted. . . .

VALIDITY OF THE DRUG TEST

. . . After reviewing the record in this case in its entirety, we conclude that the trial judge committed manifest error in finding that the drug test results were flawed. . . .[2]

Upon close review, we find that the record does not contain a reasonable factual basis for the trial judge's conclusion that the test results were flawed.

---

2. Brennan tested positive for the anabolic steroid testosterone. Testosterone that is introduced into the body from external sources (exogenous testosterone) appears in the urine. To identify the presence of exogenous testosterone, the urine is tested to measure the ratio of testosterone to another hormone called epitestosterone (the T/E ratio). The NCAA has adopted a 6 to 1 ratio as a standard for a positive test result for the presence of exogenous testosterone.

According to the experts, sex and alcohol alone could not have caused the drastic increase in Brennan's T/E ratio. Brennan admitted to taking nutritional supplements which likely contained testosterone. Experts testified that Brennan's elevated T/E ratio was consistent with having consumed nutritional supplements which likely contained testosterone. The pattern established by Brennan's three drug tests indicated that he had been exposed to testosterone. Considering the evidence contained in the record, we conclude that the trial judge was clearly wrong in finding that the test results were flawed. . . .

A. BRENNAN'S CONSTITUTIONAL CLAIMS

Brennan claims that his constitutional rights to privacy and due process were violated. The Louisiana Constitution's protection of privacy provisions contained in Article 1, § 5 does not extend so far as to protect private citizens against the actions of private parties. *Carr v. City of New Orleans*, 622 So. 2d 819, 822 n. 3 (La. App. 4th Cir.), *writ denied*, 629 So. 2d 404 (La. 1993). Nor do the due process provisions of Article 1, § 2 provide a cause of action against private actors. *Delta Bank & Trust Company v. Lassiter*, 383 So. 2d 330, 334 (La. 1980). Thus, in order to prevail on the merits of either constitutional claim, Brennan must first show that USL was a state actor when it enforced the NCAA's rules and recommendations. . . .

In the present case, Brennan asserts that USL, not the NCAA, violated his constitutional rights to privacy and due process. Without question, USL is a state actor even when acting in compliance with NCAA rules and recommendations. While we conclude that there is state action in this case, the preliminary injunction could only be issued on the constitutional claims if Brennan made a prima facie showing that he had a privacy interest which was invaded or that he had a property or liberty interest which was entitled to due process protection.

2. *Brennan's Privacy Interest*

In determining whether USL violated Brennan's right of privacy, we are guided by the California Supreme Court's recent decision in *Hill v. National Collegiate Athletic Association*, 7 Cal. 4th 1, 26 Cal. Rptr. 2d 834, 865 P.2d 633 (Cal. 1994). Therein several student-athletes filed suit against the NCAA challenging its drug testing program as an invasion of the right of privacy. While the court recognized that the drug testing program impacts privacy interests, it reasoned that there was no constitutional violation when the student-athletes' lower expectations of privacy were balanced against the NCAA's countervailing interests.

After discussing aspects of communal undress, the necessity of physical examinations, as well as the fact that student-athletes share personal information with their coaches and trainers on a routine basis, the court concluded that student-athletes have a diminished expectation of privacy. The court further noted that:

> Drug testing has become a highly visible, pervasive, and well accepted part of athletic competition, particularly on intercollegiate and professional levels. It is a reasonably expected part of the life of an athlete, especially one engaged in advanced levels of competition, where the stakes and corresponding temptations are high.
>
> The student athlete's reasonable expectation of privacy is further diminished by two elements of the NCAA's drug testing program—advance notice and the opportunity to consent to testing.

Id. at 860, 865 P.2d at 658-59. Balanced against the diminished privacy interests of the student-athletes, the *Hill* court found that the drug testing program was reasonably calculated to further the NCAA's interests of safeguarding the integrity of intercollegiate athletic competition and in protecting the health and safety of student-athletes.

Although Brennan filed suit against USL, the state actor, rather than the NCAA, we conclude, as did the court in *Hill*, that there was no violation of a privacy interest. Brennan, like the student-athletes in *Hill*, has a diminished expectation of privacy. Additionally, we note that USL shares the NCAA's interests in ensuring fair competition in intercollegiate sports as well as in protecting the health and safety of student-athletes. While a urine test may be an invasion of privacy, in this case, it is reasonable considering the diminished expectation of privacy in the context of intercollegiate sports and there being a significant interest by USL and the NCAA that outweighs the relatively small compromise of privacy under the circumstances.

Because Brennan could not make a prima facie showing that he had a privacy interest which was unjustly violated, he could not prevail on the merits of the right of privacy claim.

3.   *Brennan's Property or Liberty Interest*

To prevail on the due process claim, Brennan must show the existence of some property or liberty interest which has been adversely affected by state action. *Delta Bank & Trust Company v. Lassiter*, 383 So. 2d at 334. However, it is clear that participation in intercollegiate athletics is not a property right, but is a privilege not protected by Constitutional due process safeguards. *See Marino v. Waters*, 220 So. 2d 802, 806 (La. App. 1st Cir. 1969); *La. State Bd. of Educ. v. NCAA*, 273 So. 2d 912, 916 (La. App. 3d Cir. 1973). Because a student-athlete has no liberty or property interest in participating in intercollegiate athletics, Brennan could not make a prima facie showing that he would prevail on the merits of his due process claim.

In sum, Brennan could not make a prima facie showing that he would prevail on the merits of either constitutional claim; therefore, these claims could not be the basis for the issuance of the preliminary injunction. . . .

For the foregoing reasons, the judgment of the trial court issuing the preliminary injunction is reversed.

NOTE AND QUESTIONS

The *Brennan* court rejected the plaintiff's indirect challenge to the NCAA's drug testing program. What factors were considered in the court's conclusion that the NCAA's justifications for drug testing outweigh the student-athlete's privacy interests? If the drug test was positive for recreational drugs instead of performance-enhancing substances, does that change the analysis?

NCAA rules impose an affirmative duty on an institution to notify and educate its student-athletes regarding the NCAA's banned substances list and drug protocol. Regarding plaintiff's contention that USL negligently failed to provide this information, the *Brennan* court held:

> While Brennan claimed not to have received adequate information or warnings,
> the overwhelming evidence supports a conclusion to the contrary. According to

the documentary evidence, Brennan was aware of and given the opportunity to review the NCAA drug testing program, he was provided a summary of NCAA rules, given an opportunity to ask questions about the rules and to review the NCAA manual. Brennan was told to inquire of the USL athletic department before taking anything at all, prescription or non-prescription. Thus, the only possible basis for a tort claim was USL's failure to specifically warn against taking nutritional supplements. However, in light of the warnings which were given by USL and the information which was received by Brennan, we cannot say that the relevant jurisprudence supports a finding that USL was negligent in failing to specifically warn against consuming nutritional supplements.

691 So. 2d at 331.

The sanction generally imposed on a student-athlete who tests positive for a banned substance is ineligibility to participate in any intercollegiate sports for one calendar year and loss of one season of eligibility. (Athletes ineligible to participate in Olympic or international sports competitions for violating the World Anti-Doping Code also are ineligible to participate in NCAA intercollegiate sports during the period of their suspension.) The student-athlete, in conjunction with his or her institution, has the right to appeal the finding of a positive drug test to the NCAA's Committee on Competitive Safeguards and Medical Aspects of Sports. Effective August 1, 2005, the NCAA's drug-testing protocol was modified to make it more consistent with the World Anti-Doping Code (discussed in Chapter 4) by now allowing consideration of a reduced penalty based on the student-athlete's relative degree of fault for a doping violation. After a hearing, the committee may reduce the length of the student-athlete's suspension to one-half season of competition in their particular sport or determine that no suspension is appropriate based on extenuating circumstances.

E. ANTITRUST LAW

The following cases illustrate that federal antitrust law provides an important limit on the NCAA's internal governance of intercollegiate athletics and protects the economic rights of its member institutions, coaches, student-athletes, and others. As you read these materials, consider how well judicial precedent applying antitrust law to NCAA rules and decisions has furthered the interests of college sports fans.

1. Introduction

The purpose of antitrust law is to preserve a competitive marketplace and protect consumer welfare. Economic competition is harmed when anticompetitive conduct inhibits or prevents the market's ability to achieve lower prices, better products, and more efficient methods of production, all of which benefit consumers. *Sullivan v. NFL*, 34 F.3d 1091, 1097 (1st Cir. 1994), *cert. denied*, 513 U.S. 1190 (1995) ("injury to competition" is "measured by a reduction in output and an increase in prices in the relevant market").

Section One of the Sherman Act, 15 U.S.C. §1, provides that "[e]very contract, combination . . . or conspiracy in restraint of trade or commerce" is illegal.

Section Two of the Sherman Act, 15 U.S.C. §2, prohibits monopolization or attempts to monopolize trade or commerce. Both statutory provisions apply only to anticompetitive restraints affecting interstate trade or commerce. Courts have consistently held that the NCAA's general business activities and governance of intercollegiate athletics have a national scope and satisfy this requirement. *NCAA v. Miller*, 10 F.3d 633 (9th Cir. 1993); *Hennessey v. NCAA*, 564 F.2d 1136 (5th Cir. 1977); *Justice v. NCAA*, 577 F. Supp. 356 (D. Ariz. 1983). For example, the NCAA conducts national championships in numerous men's and women's intercollegiate sports and sells the national broadcasting rights to these events, promulgates a wide variety of rules applicable to its member schools located throughout the country, and engages in a nationwide system of policing and rules enforcement activities.

The NCAA has no blanket exemption from the federal antitrust laws merely because it is a nonprofit organization whose members are predominantly colleges and universities with educational objectives. In *Hennessey v. NCAA*, 564 F.2d 1136 (5th Cir. 1977), the Fifth Circuit observed that "[w]hile the participating athletics [*sic*] may be amateurs, intercollegiate athletics in its management is clearly business, and big business at that." *Id.* at 1150. The court concluded, "[w]hile organized as a non-profit organization, the NCAA and its member institutions are, when presenting amateur athletics to a ticket-paying, television-buying public, engaged in a business venture of far greater magnitude than the vast majority of 'profit-making' enterprises." *Id.* at 1149, n.14.

The collective adoption and enforcement of NCAA rules by its member universities as well as other agreements concerning the production, marketing, and governance of intercollegiate athletics constitute concerted action for purposes of §1 of the Sherman Act, which is the focus of this section.[1] *NCAA v. Bd. of Regents*, 707 F.2d 1147, 1153 (10th Cir. 1983) ("The NCAA is essentially an integration of the rulemaking and rule-enforcing activities of its member institutions"). As a result, virtually all NCAA rules and agreements among NCAA members are potentially subject to antitrust challenge. For the reasons discussed in *NCAA v. Board of Regents, infra*, §1's broad statutory language has been judicially interpreted to prohibit only unreasonable restraints of trade that have anticompetitive economic effects. For purposes of antitrust law, the validity of a challenged NCAA rule is determined by whether it has a predominantly anticompetitive commercial effect that harms college sports fans (i.e., it is an unreasonable restraint of trade) or whether it is appropriate and necessary regulation that benefits fans more than unbridled market competition among universities producing intercollegiate athletics (i.e., it is a reasonable restraint of trade).

Despite the more than 100-year history of the NCAA's national governance of college sports, there was little federal antitrust litigation challenging its rules, enforcement activities, or other collective action of its members before the early 1970s, when the financial rewards for fielding winning big-time football and basketball programs escalated as public demand for intercollegiate sports viewing and television revenues skyrocketed. Since then, the increasing commercialization of intercollegiate athletics, which is now a multibillion-dollar industry,

---

1. There has been relatively little litigation asserting §2 claims against the NCAA, which historically have been unsuccessful. See, e.g., *Association for Intercollegiate Athletics for Women v. NCAA*, 735 F.2d 577 (D.C. Cir. 1984) (rejecting an allegation that the NCAA unlawfully used its monopoly regulatory power over men's intercollegiate sports to facilitate its entry into the regulation of women's intercollegiate sports, and to force the Association of Intercollegiate Athletics for Women, a competing national governing body, out of existence).

has spawned several antitrust suits against the NCAA and its member universities and/or their respective athletic conferences asserting that their rules
or collective agreements unreasonably restrain trade and harm the plaintiffs'
economic interests. Membership in the NCAA is unquestionably an economic
necessity if a school desires to participate in "big-time" intercollegiate athletics.
Nonmember universities cannot compete in NCAA championship events, do
not have the prestige and visibility to consistently attract a large number of the
best student-athletes to their programs, and do not generate the substantial
economic revenues that NCAA schools do. Perhaps because there currently is
no viable existing alternative to NCAA membership, some universities whose
individual economic interests have been harmed by its regulations or rules
enforcement actions have brought antitrust litigation against the NCAA. In
addition to its member universities, NCAA rules indirectly govern and affect
the economic interests of student-athletes, coaches, athletic departments,
other university personnel, and alumni even though they lack an effective
voice and/or vote in the NCAA's rule-making and enforcement process; each
of these groups have been plaintiffs in antitrust litigation against the NCAA.
See Peter C. Carstensen and Paul Olszowski, *Antitrust Law, Student-Athletes, and
the NCAA: Limiting the Scope and Conduct of Private Economic Regulation,* 1995
Wis. L. Rev. 545, 549-552.

Private plaintiffs must suffer economic loss and be directly affected by the
alleged antitrust violation to have *standing* to bring an antitrust suit and to recover
damages (which are automatically trebled) and/or injunctive relief. *McCormack
v. NCAA,* 845 F.2d 1338 (5th Cir. 1988) (Southern Methodist University (SMU)
alumni did not have standing to challenge severe NCAA sanctions imposed on
SMU for its amateurism rules violations because their alleged economic injury,
devaluation of their college degrees, was too indirect). Because the antitrust
laws are intended to protect competition and consumers rather than individual
marketplace competitors, an antitrust plaintiff also must prove that the anticompetitive effects of the challenged restraint (i.e., "*antitrust injury*") caused
the plaintiff's economic loss. See, e.g., *Marucci v. NCAA,* 751 F.3d 368 (5th Cir.
2014) (dismissing an aluminum bat manufacturer's antitrust claim because it
failed to prove the NCAA's standards for bats injures competition in the market
for non-wood baseball bats); *Warrior Sports, Inc. v. NCAA,* 623 F.3d 281 (6th Cir.
2010) (dismissing a lacrosse stick manufacturer's antitrust claims because NCAA
regulation of lacrosse equipment increases rather than reduces economic competition and permits plaintiff to "compete in the market on the same footing as
all other participants"); *Association for Intercollegiate Athletics for Women v. NCAA,*
735 F.2d 577 (D.C. Cir. 1984) (dismissing a women's intercollegiate athletics
governing body claim that NCAA sponsorship of women's intercollegiate sports
championships violates antitrust laws; universities chose to participate in NCAA
women's championships because they are a "superior product," demonstrating
legal competition on the merits).

2. Antitrust Law Limits on NCAA Governance and Rules

At the outset, keep in mind that NCAA intercollegiate athletics is based on a
philosophical *amateur/education model,* although Division 1 FBS football and
men's basketball have evolved into a *commercial/education* model. As with efforts
to apply federal labor and state worker's compensation laws to college sports,

the plaintiffs in the following antitrust cases effectively are seeking to establish a *commercial/professional model* for NCAA sports that generate net revenues
because of their widespread popularity. While you study how courts have applied
Sherman Act §1 to intercollegiate athletics, consider whether you believe this
to be an appropriate objective. In addition, consider the following questions:

1. Is the challenged rule or conduct a commercial restraint reducing economic competition among NCAA member schools, or is it non-economic
   internal regulation making college sports a more attractive product to college sports fans?
2. If it is a commercial restraint, which NCAA justifications are procompetitive economic justifications (e.g., amateurism, academics, competitive balance, health and safety, others)?
3. How much deference should courts and juries give the NCAA regarding
   its chosen means of achieving procompetitive economic objectives (i.e.,
   substantially less restrictive alternative analysis)?
4. Finally, if the plaintiff(s) are persons or business entities other than sports fans,
   is consumer harm presumed or is it required to be proven as part of a §1 claim?

a. Output Market Restraints

This landmark Supreme Court case addresses how antitrust law limits the
NCAA's regulatory authority in the output market in which goods or services
are produced for public consumption, in particular, televised college football
games. It establishes the analytical framework for determining whether an
NCAA rule or decision unreasonably restrains trade.

NCAA v. BOARD OF REGENTS
OF THE UNIVERSITY OF OKLAHOMA

468 U.S. 85 (1984)

Justice STEVENS delivered the opinion of the Court.
    The University of Oklahoma and the University of Georgia contend that the
National Collegiate Athletic Association has unreasonably restrained trade [in
violation of §1 of the Sherman Act] in the televising of college football games....
    ... With the exception of football, the NCAA has not undertaken any regula-
tion of the televising of athletic events....
    [EDS. In separate agreements, the NCAA granted the American Broadcasting
Company (ABC) and the Columbia Broadcasting System (CBS) the right to
each telecast 14 regular season football games in accordance with certain
"ground rules." Each network agreed to pay a specified "minimum aggregate
compensation to the participating NCAA member institutions" during the four-
year period in an amount that totalled $131,750,000.
    The ground rules provided that the carrying networks make alternate selec-
tions of those games they wished to televise, and thereby obtain the exclusive
right to submit a bid at an essentially fixed price to the institutions involved. The
plan also contained "appearance requirements" and "appearance limitations"
which pertained to each of the two-year periods that the plan was in effect.
The basic requirement imposed on each of the two networks was that it must

schedule appearances for at least 82 different member institutions during each two-year period. Under the appearance limitations no member institution was eligible to appear on television more than a total of six times and more than four times nationally, with the appearances to be divided equally between the two carrying networks. The number of exposures specified in the contracts also set an absolute maximum on the number of games that could be broadcast.

Thus, although the current plan was more elaborate than any of its predecessors, it retained the essential features of each of them. It limited the total amount of televised intercollegiate football and the number of games that any one team could televise. No NCAA member university was permitted to make any sale of television rights except in accordance with the basic plan.

Some years ago, five major conferences together with major football-playing independent institutions organized the College Football Association (CFA). The original purpose of the CFA was to promote the interests of major football-playing schools within the NCAA structure. The Universities of Oklahoma and Georgia, respondents in this Court, were members of the CFA.

Beginning in 1979, CFA members began to advocate that colleges with major football programs should have a greater voice in the formulation of football television policy than they had in the NCAA. They developed an independent television plan and entered into a 1981 contract with the National Broadcasting Co. (NBC) that would have permitted a greater number of its members games to be televised, and would have increased the overall football television revenues realized by CFA members. In response the NCAA publicly announced that it would take disciplinary action against any CFA member that complied with the CFA-NBC contract, which would apply to other sports as well as football. Although respondents obtained a preliminary injunction against the NCAA's threatened disciplinary action, most CFA members were reluctant to enter into the proposed contract with NBC and the agreement was never consummated.]

II

There can be no doubt that the challenged practices of the NCAA constitute a "restraint of trade" in the sense that they limit members' freedom to negotiate and enter into their own television contracts. In that sense, however, every contract is a restraint of trade, and as we have repeatedly recognized, the Sherman Act was intended to prohibit only unreasonable restraints of trade.

It is also undeniable that these practices share characteristics of restraints we have previously held unreasonable. The NCAA is an association of schools which compete against each other to attract television revenues, not to mention fans and athletes. As the District Court found, the policies of the NCAA with respect to television rights are ultimately controlled by the vote of member institutions. By participating in an association which prevents member institutions from competing against each other on the basis of price or kind of television rights that can be offered to broadcasters, the NCAA member institutions have created a horizontal restraint—an agreement among competitors on the way in which they will compete with one another. A restraint of this type has often been held to be unreasonable as a matter of law. Because it places a ceiling on the number of games member institutions may televise, the horizontal agreement places an artificial limit on the quantity of televised football that is available to broadcasters and consumers. By restraining the quantity of television rights available for sale, the challenged practices create a limitation on output; our cases have held that such limitations are unreasonable restraints of trade. Moreover, the District Court found that the minimum aggregate price in fact operates to preclude any price negotiation between broadcasters and institutions, thereby constituting horizontal price fixing, perhaps the paradigm of an unreasonable restraint of trade.

Horizontal price fixing and output limitation are ordinarily condemned as a matter of law under an "illegal per se" approach because the probability that these practices are anticompetitive is so high; a per se rule is applied when "the practice facially appears to be one that would always or almost always tend to restrict competition and decrease output." *Broadcast Music, Inc. v. Columbia Broadcasting System, Inc.*, 441 U.S. 1, 19-20, 99 S. Ct. 1551, 1562, 60 L. Ed. 2d 1 (1979). In such circumstances a restraint is presumed unreasonable without inquiry into the particular market context in which it is found. Nevertheless, we have decided that it would be inappropriate to apply a per se rule to this case. This decision is not based on a lack of judicial experience with this type of arrangement, on the fact that the NCAA is organized as a nonprofit entity, or on our respect for the NCAA's historic role in the preservation and encouragement of intercollegiate amateur athletics. Rather, what is critical is that this case involves an industry in which horizontal restraints on competition are essential if the product is to be available at all.

As Judge Bork has noted: "[S]ome activities can only be carried out jointly. Perhaps the leading example is league sports. When a league of professional lacrosse teams is formed, it would be pointless to declare their cooperation illegal on the ground that there are no other professional lacrosse teams." R. Bork, *The Antitrust Paradox* 278 (1978). What the NCAA and its member institutions market in this case is competition itself—contests between competing institutions. Of course, this would be completely ineffective if there were no rules on which the competitors agreed to create and define the competition to be marketed. A myriad of rules affecting such matters as the size of the field, the number of players on a team, and the extent to which physical violence is to be encouraged or proscribed, all must be agreed upon, and all restrain the manner in which institutions compete. Moreover, the NCAA seeks to market a particular brand of football—college football. The identification of this "product" with an academic tradition differentiates college football from and makes it more popular than professional sports to which it might otherwise be comparable, such as, for example, minor league baseball. In order to preserve the character and quality of the "product," athletes must not be paid, must be required to attend class, and the like. And the integrity of the "product" cannot be preserved except by mutual agreement; if an institution adopted such restrictions unilaterally, its effectiveness as a competitor on the playing field might soon be destroyed. Thus, the NCAA plays a vital role in enabling college football to preserve its character, and as a result enables a product to be marketed which might otherwise be unavailable. In performing this role, its actions widen consumer choice—not only the choices available to sports fans but also those available to athletes—and hence can be viewed as procompetitive.

Respondents concede that the great majority of the NCAA's regulations enhance competition among member institutions. Thus, despite the fact that this case involves restraints on the ability of member institutions to compete in terms of price and output, a fair evaluation of their competitive character requires consideration of the NCAA's justifications for the restraints.

Our analysis of this case under the Rule of Reason, of course, does not change the ultimate focus of our inquiry. Both per se rules and the Rule of Reason are employed "to form a judgment about the competitive significance of the restraint." . . .

III

Because it restrains price and output, the NCAA's television plan has a significant potential for anticompetitive effects.[28] The findings of the District Court indicate that this potential has been realized. The District Court found that if member institutions were free to sell television rights, many more games would be shown on television, and that the NCAA's output restriction has the effect of raising the price the networks pay for television rights. Moreover, the court found that by fixing a price for television rights to all games, the NCAA creates a price structure that is unresponsive to viewer demand and unrelated to the prices that would prevail in a competitive market. And, of course, since as a practical matter all member institutions need NCAA approval, members have no real choice but to adhere to the NCAA's television controls.

The anticompetitive consequences of this arrangement are apparent. Individual competitors lose their freedom to compete. Price is higher and output lower than they would otherwise be, and both are unresponsive to consumer preference. This latter point is perhaps the most significant, since "Congress designed the Sherman Act as a 'consumer welfare prescription.'" *Reiter v. Sonotone Corp.*, 442 U.S. 330, 343, 99 S. Ct. 2326, 2333, 60 L. Ed. 2d 931 (1979). A restraint that has the effect of reducing the importance of consumer preference in setting price and output is not consistent with this fundamental goal of antitrust law. Restrictions on price and output are the paradigmatic examples of restraints of trade that the Sherman Act was intended to prohibit. At the same time, the television plan eliminates competitors from the market, since only those broadcasters able to bid on television rights covering the entire NCAA can compete. Thus, as the District Court found, many telecasts that would occur in a competitive market are foreclosed by the NCAA's plan.

Petitioner argues, however, that its television plan can have no significant anticompetitive effect since the record indicates that it has no market power — no ability to alter the interaction of supply and demand in the market.[38] We must reject this argument for two reasons, one legal, one factual.

As a matter of law, the absence of proof of market power does not justify a naked restriction on price or output. To the contrary, when there is an agreement not to compete in terms of price or output, "no elaborate industry analysis is required to demonstrate the anticompetitive character of such an agreement." *Professional Engineers*, 435 U.S., at 692, 98 S. Ct., at 1365. Petitioner does not quarrel with the District Court's finding that price and output are not responsive to demand. Thus

---

28. In this connection, it is not without significance that Congress felt the need to grant professional sports an exemption from the antitrust laws for joint marketing of television rights. See 15 U.S.C. §§ 1291-1295. The legislative history of this exemption demonstrates Congress' recognition that agreements among league members to sell television rights in a cooperative fashion could run afoul of the Sherman Act.

38. Market power is the ability to raise prices above those that would be charged in a competitive market.

the plan is inconsistent with the Sherman Act's command that price and supply be responsive to consumer preference. We have never required proof of market power in such a case. This naked restraint on price and output requires some competitive justification even in the absence of a detailed market analysis.

As a factual matter, it is evident that petitioner does possess market power. The District Court employed the correct test for determining whether college football broadcasts constitute a separate market—whether there are other products that are reasonably substitutable for televised NCAA football games. Petitioner's argument that it cannot obtain supracompetitive prices from broadcasters since advertisers, and hence broadcasters, can switch from college football to other types of programming simply ignores the findings of the District Court. It found that intercollegiate football telecasts generate an audience uniquely attractive to advertisers and that competitors are unable to offer programming that can attract a similar audience. These findings amply support its conclusion that the NCAA possesses market power. . . .

Thus, the NCAA television plan on its face constitutes a restraint upon the operation of a free market, and the findings of the District Court establish that it has operated to raise prices and reduce output. Under the Rule of Reason, these hallmarks of anticompetitive behavior place upon petitioner a heavy burden of establishing an affirmative defense which competitively justifies this apparent deviation from the operations of a free market. We turn now to the NCAA's proffered justifications. . . .

V

Throughout the history of its regulation of intercollegiate football telecasts, the NCAA has indicated its concern with protecting live attendance. This concern, it should be noted, is not with protecting live attendance at games which are shown on television; that type of interest is not at issue in this case. Rather, the concern is that fan interest in a televised game may adversely affect ticket sales for games that will not appear on television. Although the NORC studies in the 1950's provided some support for the thesis that live attendance would suffer if unlimited television were permitted, the District Court found that there was no evidence to support that theory in today's market. Moreover, as the District Court found, the television plan has evolved in a manner inconsistent with its original design to protect gate attendance. Under the current plan, games are shown on television during all hours that college football games are played. The plan simply does not protect live attendance by ensuring that games will not be shown on television at the same time as live events.

There is, however, a more fundamental reason for rejecting this defense. The NCAA's argument that its television plan is necessary to protect live attendance is not based on a desire to maintain the integrity of college football as a distinct and attractive product, but rather on a fear that the product will not prove sufficiently attractive to draw live attendance when faced with competition from televised games. At bottom the NCAA's position is that ticket sales for most college games are unable to compete in a free market. The television plan protects ticket sales by limiting output—just as any monopolist increases revenues by reducing output. By seeking to insulate live ticket sales from the full spectrum of competition because of its assumption that the product itself is insufficiently attractive to consumers, petitioner forwards a justification that is inconsistent with the basic policy of the Sherman Act. "[T]he Rule of Reason does not support a defense based on the assumption that competition itself is unreasonable."

VI

Petitioner argues that the interest in maintaining a competitive balance among amateur athletic teams is legitimate and important and that it justifies the regulations challenged in this case. We agree with the first part of the argument but not the second.

Our decision not to apply a per se rule to this case rests in large part on our recognition that a certain degree of cooperation is necessary if the type of competition that petitioner and its member institutions seek to market is to be preserved. It is reasonable to assume that most of the regulatory controls of the NCAA are justifiable means of fostering competition among amateur athletic teams and therefore procompetitive because they enhance public interest in intercollegiate athletics. The specific restraints on football telecasts that are challenged in this case do not, however, fit into the same mold as do rules defining the conditions of the contest, the eligibility of participants, or the manner in which members of a joint enterprise shall share the responsibilities and the benefits of the total venture.

The NCAA does not claim that its television plan has equalized or is intended to equalize competition within any one league. The plan is nationwide in scope and there is no single league or tournament in which all college football teams compete. There is no evidence of any intent to equalize the strength of teams in Division I-A with those in Division II or Division III, and not even a colorable basis for giving colleges that have no football program at all a voice in the management of the revenues generated by the football programs at other schools.

The interest in maintaining a competitive balance that is asserted by the NCAA as a justification for regulating all television of intercollegiate football is not related to any neutral standard or to any readily identifiable group of competitors.

The television plan is not even arguably tailored to serve such an interest. It does not regulate the amount of money that any college may spend on its football program, nor the way in which the colleges may use the revenues that are generated by their football programs, whether derived from the sale of television rights, the sale of tickets, or the sale of concessions or program advertising. The plan simply imposes a restriction on one source of revenue that is more important to some colleges than to others. There is no evidence that this restriction produces any greater measure of equality throughout the NCAA than would a restriction on alumni donations, tuition rates, or any other revenue-producing activity. At the same time, as the District Court found, the NCAA imposes a variety of other restrictions designed to preserve amateurism which are much better tailored to the goal of competitive balance than is the television plan, and which are "clearly sufficient" to preserve competitive balance to the extent it is within the NCAA's power to do so. And much more than speculation supported the District Court's findings on this score. No other NCAA sport employs a similar plan, and in particular the court found that in the most closely analogous sport, college basketball, competitive balance has been maintained without resort to a restrictive television plan.

Perhaps the most important reason for rejecting the argument that the interest in competitive balance is served by the television plan is the District Court's

unambiguous and well-supported finding that many more games would be televised in a free market than under the NCAA plan. The hypothesis that legiti-
mates the maintenance of competitive balance as a procompetitive justification
under the Rule of Reason is that equal competition will maximize consumer
demand for the product. The finding that consumption will materially increase
if the controls are removed is a compelling demonstration that they do not in
fact serve any such legitimate purpose.

VII

The NCAA plays a critical role in the maintenance of a revered tradition of amateurism in college sports. There can be no question but that it needs ample latitude to play that role, or that the preservation of the student-athlete in higher
education adds richness and diversity to intercollegiate athletics and is entirely
consistent with the goals of the Sherman Act. But consistent with the Sherman
Act, the role of the NCAA must be to preserve a tradition that might otherwise
die; rules that restrict output are hardly consistent with this role. Today we hold
only that the record supports the District Court's conclusion that by curtailing
output and blunting the ability of member institutions to respond to consumer
preference, the NCAA has restricted rather than enhanced the place of intercollegiate athletics in the Nation's life. Accordingly, the judgment of the Court
of Appeals is
  Affirmed.

Justice WHITE, with whom Justice REHNQUIST joins, dissenting.
  Although some of the NCAA's activities, viewed in isolation, bear a resemblance to those undertaken by professional sports leagues and associations, the Court errs in treating intercollegiate athletics under the NCAA's
control as a purely commercial venture in which colleges and universities
participate solely, or even primarily, in the pursuit of profits. Accordingly,
I dissent. . . .
  The NCAA, in short, "exist[s] primarily to enhance the contribution made
by amateur athletic competition to the process of higher education as distinguished from realizing maximum return on it as an entertainment commod-
ity." *Association for Intercollegiate Athletics for Women v. NCAA*, 558 F. Supp. 487,
494 (DC 1983), *aff'd*, 236 U.S. App. D.C. 311, 735 F.2d 577 (1984). In pursuing
this goal, the organization and its members seek to provide a public good—a
viable system of amateur athletics—that most likely could not be provided
in a perfectly competitive market. *See Hennessey v. NCAA*, 564 F.2d 1136, 1153
(CA5 1977). "Without regulation, the desire of member institutions to remain
athletically competitive would lead them to engage in activities that deny
amateurism to the public. No single institution could confidently enforce
its own standards since it could not trust its competitors to do the same."
Note, *Antitrust and Nonprofit Entities*, 94 Harv. L. Rev. 802, 817-818 (1981). The
history of intercollegiate athletics prior to the advent of the NCAA provides
ample support for this conclusion. By mitigating what appears to be a clear
failure of the free market to serve the ends and goals of higher education, the
NCAA ensures the continued availability of a unique and valuable product,
the very existence of which might well be threatened by unbridled competition in the economic sphere.

In pursuit of its fundamental goal and others related to it, the NCAA imposes numerous controls on intercollegiate athletic competition among its members, many of which "are similar to those which are summarily condemned when undertaken in a more traditional business setting." [Citation omitted.] Thus, the NCAA has promulgated and enforced rules limiting both the compensation of student-athletes and the number of coaches a school may hire for its football and basketball programs; it also has prohibited athletes who formerly have been compensated for playing from participating in intercollegiate competition, restricted the number of athletic scholarships its members may award, and established minimum academic standards for recipients of those scholarships; and it has pervasively regulated the recruitment process, student eligibility, practice schedules, squad size, the number of games played, and many other aspects of intercollegiate athletics. One clear effect of most, if not all, of these regulations is to prevent institutions with competitively and economically successful programs from taking advantage of their success by expanding their programs, improving the quality of the product they offer, and increasing their sports revenues. Yet each of these regulations represents a desirable and legitimate attempt "to keep university athletics from becoming professionalized to the extent that profit making objectives would overshadow educational objectives." *Kupec v. Atlantic Coast Conference*, 399 F. Supp. 1377, 1380 (MDNC 1975). Significantly, neither the Court of Appeals nor this Court questions the validity of these regulations under the Rule of Reason.

Notwithstanding the contrary conclusion of the District Court and the majority, . . . I do not believe that the restraint under consideration in this case—the NCAA's television plan—differs fundamentally for antitrust purposes from the other seemingly anti-competitive aspects of the organization's broader program of self-regulation. The television plan, like many of the NCAA's actions, furthers several complementary ends. Specifically, the plan is designed "to reduce, insofar as possible, the adverse effects of live television . . . upon football game attendance and, in turn, upon the athletic and related educational programs dependent upon the proceeds therefrom; to spread football television participation among as many colleges as practicable; to reflect properly the image of universities as educational institutions; to promote college football through the use of television; to advance the overall interests of intercollegiate athletics; and to provide college football television to the public to the extent compatible with these other objectives." More generally, in my view, the television plan reflects the NCAA's fundamental policy of preserving amateurism and integrating athletics and education. . . .

IV

Finally, I return to the point with which I began—the essentially noneconomic nature of the NCAA's program of self-regulation. Like Judge Barrett, who dissented in the Court of Appeals, I believe that the lower courts "erred by subjugating the NCAA's educational goals (and, incidentally, those which Oklahoma and Georgia insist must be maintained in any event) to the purely competitive commercialism of [an] 'every school for itself' approach to television contract bargaining." . . .

For all of these reasons, I would reverse the judgment of the Court of Appeals.

NOTES AND QUESTIONS

1. *Commercial or Noncommercial Regulation?* The Supreme Court's majority characterizes the NCAA's restrictions on televised college football games as commercial activity subject to judicial scrutiny under the Sherman Act. They conclude that NCAA members "compete against each other to attract television revenues, not to mention fans and athletes," and therefore are economic competitors in some instances. By contrast, the dissenting justices, in an opinion written by Justice White (who played college football at the University of Colorado and finished second in the 1937 Heisman Trophy balloting) emphasizes the "essentially non-economic nature of the NCAA's program of self-regulation" and asserts that the majority erroneously treats intercollegiate athletics "as a purely commercial venture in which . . . universities participate solely, or even primarily, in the pursuit of profits." They suggest that, unlike the conduct of professional sports leagues, the antitrust laws should not be applied to NCAA regulation of intercollegiate athletics. Do the differences between professional sports and intercollegiate athletics justify not subjecting its governance by the NCAA to federal antitrust law?

   Tom McMillen, a former Congressman and All-American college basketball player at the University of Maryland, argues that *Board of Regents* was wrongly decided because "the NCAA's loss of monopoly broadcast power [has led] to an escalating competition for money among schools." McMillen supports Justice White's dissent, arguing that "the NCAA monopoly 'fosters the goal of amateurism by spreading revenues among various schools and reducing the financial incentives towards professionalism.'" Tom McMillen, Opinion, *"Whizzer" White Had It Right When It Came to TV Money*, NCAA News, May 27, 2002. Given the twenty-first-century realities of commercialized college basketball and football, do you agree or disagree with his view?

2. *Per Se Illegality Versus Rule of Reason Scrutiny.* To determine whether an agreement unreasonably restrains trade, courts historically have applied either per se or rule-of-reason analysis. The objective of either standard is "to form a judgment about the competitive significance of the restraint," although the respective application of these tests is quite different. Restraints found to be predominantly anticompetitive are unreasonable and thus illegal under Sherman Act §1. Under the per se rule, certain restraints are conclusively presumed to be illegal as a matter of law because of their significant adverse effects on competition and lack of redeeming procompetitive virtues. Under the rule of reason, the anticompetitive effects of the challenged restraint are balanced against its procompetitive effects on a case-by-case basis, considering the specific facts introduced into evidence by the parties. Although the Supreme Court notes that horizontal agreements among competitors in the same industry to fix prices and limit output generally are illegal per se, why does it analyze the legality of the NCAA's college football television plan (which was found to be an output restriction raising the price networks paid for television rights) under the rule of reason?

3. *Application of the Rule of Reason.* The plaintiff has the burden of pleading and proving that the challenged restraint has actual or potential significant

anticompetitive effects. How did the plaintiffs do this in the *Board of Regents* case? Why didn't they have to prove that the NCAA possessed "market power" (i.e., "the ability to raise prices above those that would be charged in a competitive market")?

After plaintiffs proved the requisite anticompetitive effects of the television plan, the NCAA has "a heavy burden of establishing an affirmative defense" to justify this agreement. Which procompetitive justifications offered by the NCAA in defense of its television plan were recognized by the Court as valid? Did the NCAA's television plan further any of these valid justifications as a matter of fact? Even if it did, are there viable alternative means of accomplishing these objectives that do not impose significant anticompetitive effects?

On the other hand, do you agree with the dissent's view that "the television plan reflects the NCAA's fundamental policy of preserving amateurism and integrating athletics and education"? Should these "primarily noneconomic values pursued by educational institutions" justify restraints that would be illegal in other industries, including professional sports?

4. *Board of Regents'* Effect on Consumer Welfare. The Supreme Court observes that "Congress designed the Sherman Act as a 'consumer welfare prescription.'" In other words, the federal antitrust laws are intended to ensure that consumers receive the benefits of a competitive marketplace. How have college football fans benefited from judicial invalidation of the NCAA's television plan?

5. *Post-*Board of Regents *College Sports Television Contracts.* Although *Board of Regents* determined that the NCAA (i.e., its collective 1,100-plus member colleges and universities) cannot agree among themselves to limit the total number of televised college football games or to fix the price of broadcasting rights, it did not prohibit smaller groups of NCAA universities from jointly selling television or other media rights to college football games or other athletic events. Today, college sports television contracts generally are negotiated and entered into by athletic conferences on behalf of their member universities with network television (e.g., ABC, CBS, NBC, or Fox) or cable television broadcasters (e.g., ESPN). In *Association of Independent Television Stations, Inc. v. College Football Association,* 637 F. Supp. 1289 (W.D. Okla. 1984), the court rejected a television broadcaster's contention that a series of contracts conveying exclusive rights to televise Big Eight Conference football games to other broadcasters is per se illegal because it limited the number of available games that the plaintiff could televise. The court noted that these contracts have potential procompetitive efficiencies: "In the marketing of television rights, just as in the management of the live contest itself, some cooperation is necessary if the product, live college football television, is to be available at all." *Id.* At 1297. The court found that the conference television package creates a new product—namely, a "national series of games"—that creates more effective competition in the live college football television market. In addition, the marketing of exclusive television rights may provide incentives to broadcasters to promote and develop programs fully (which they might not otherwise do), thereby increasing the number of available television broadcasts to consumers, a collective business practice that generally does not violate antitrust law.

b.   Input Market Restraints

Board of Regents held that NCAA rules that unreasonably restrain the intercollegiate athletics output market (e.g., a limit on the total number of televised
college football games), which have clear adverse effects on consumer welfare,
violate antitrust law. Next, we consider the validity of NCAA rules limiting competition among universities in the input market for the resources necessary
to produce intercollegiate sports such as the services of coaches and student-
athletes, whose effects on consumer welfare are more difficult to determine.

i.   *Coaches' Salaries*

LAW v. NCAA

134 F.3d 1010 (10th Cir. 1998)

EBEL, Circuit Judge.

Defendant-Appellant the National Collegiate Athletic Association ("NCAA")
promulgated a rule limiting annual compensation of certain Division I entry-
level coaches to $16,000. Basketball coaches affected by the rule filed a class
action challenging the restriction under Section 1 of the Sherman Antitrust
Act. . . .

I.   BACKGROUND

. . . During the 1980s, the NCAA became concerned over the steadily rising costs
of maintaining competitive athletic programs, especially in light of the requirements imposed by Title IX of the 1972 Education Amendments Act to increase
support for women's athletic programs. . . . At the same time, many institutions
felt pressure to "keep up with the Joneses" by increasing spending on recruiting
talented players and coaches and on other aspects of their sports programs in
order to remain competitive with rival schools. In addition, a report commis-
sioned by the NCAA known as the "Raiborn Report" found that in 1985, 42%
of NCAA Division I schools reported deficits in their overall athletic program
budgets, with the deficit averaging $824,000 per school . . . [and] that 51% of
Division I schools responding to NCAA inquiries on the subject suffered a net
loss in their basketball programs alone that averaged $145,000 per school.

Part of the problem identified by the NCAA involved the costs associated
with part-time assistant coaches. The NCAA allowed Division I basketball
teams to employ three full-time coaches, including one head coach and two
assistant coaches, and two part-time coaches. The part-time positions could
be filled by part-time assistants, graduate assistants, or volunteer coaches.
The NCAA imposed salary restrictions on all of the part-time positions. . . .
The NCAA limited compensation to part-time assistants to the value of
full grant-in-aid compensation based on the value of out of-state graduate
studies.

Despite the salary caps, many of these part-time coaches earned $60,000 or
$70,000 per year. Athletic departments circumvented the compensation limits
by employing these part-time coaches in lucrative summer jobs at profitable

sports camps run by the school or by hiring them for part-time jobs in the physical education department in addition to the coaching position. Further, many of these positions were filled with seasoned and experienced coaches, not the type of student assistant envisioned by the rule.

In January of 1989, the NCAA established a Cost Reduction Committee (the "Committee") to consider means and strategies for reducing the costs of intercollegiate athletics "without disturbing the competitive balance" among NCAA member institutions. . . . It became the consensus of the Committee that reducing the total number of coaching positions would reduce the cost of intercollegiate athletic programs.

The Committee proposed an array of recommendations to amend the NCAA's bylaws, including proposed Bylaw 11.6.4 that would limit Division I basketball coaching staffs to four members—one head coach, two assistant coaches, and one entry-level coach called a "restricted-earnings coach." The restricted-earnings coach category was created to replace the positions of part-time assistant, graduate assistant, and volunteer coach. . . .

A second proposed rule, Bylaw 11.02.3, restricted compensation of restricted-earnings coaches in all Division I sports other than football to a total of $12,000 for the academic year and $4,000 for the summer months (the "REC Rule" for restricted-earnings coaches). The Committee determined that the $16,000 per year total figure approximated the cost of out-of-state tuition for graduate schools at public institutions and the average graduate school tuition at private institutions, and was thus roughly equivalent to the salaries previously paid to part-time graduate assistant coaches. . . . The REC Rule did not prevent member institutions from using savings gained by reducing the number and salary of basketball coaches to increase expenditures on other aspects of their athletic programs. . . .

The NCAA adopted the proposed rules, including the REC Rule, by majority vote in January of 1991, and the rules became effective on August 1, 1992.[5] The rules bind all Division I members of the NCAA that employ basketball coaches. The schools normally compete with each other in the labor market for coaching services. . . .

III.   RULE OF REASON ANALYSIS

. . . The NCAA does not dispute that the REC Rule resulted from an agreement among its members. However, the NCAA does contest the district court's finding that on the record before it, there was no genuine dispute of fact that the REC Rule is an unreasonable restraint of trade.

---

5. Other cost-saving measures were adopted that, *inter alia*, limited:

- the number of coaches who could recruit off campus.
- off-campus contacts with prospective student-athletes.
- visits by prospective student-athletes.
- printed recruiting materials.
- the number of practices before the first scheduled game.
- the number of games and duration of seasons.
- team travel and training table meals.
- financial aid grants to student-athletes.

Two analytical approaches are used to determine whether a defendant's conduct unreasonably restrains trade: the *per se* rule and the rule of reason. The *per se* rule condemns practices that "are entirely void of redeeming competitive rationales." Once a practice is identified as illegal *per se*, a court need not examine the practice's impact on the market or the procompetitive justifications for the practice advanced by a defendant before finding a violation of antitrust law. Rule of reason analysis, on the other hand, requires an analysis of the restraint's effect on competition. A rule of reason analysis first requires a determination of whether the challenged restraint has a substantially adverse effect on competition. The inquiry then shifts to an evaluation of whether the procompetitive virtues of the alleged wrongful conduct justifies the otherwise anticompetitive impacts. The district court applied the rule of reason standard to its analysis of the REC Rule.

Horizontal price-fixing is normally a practice condemned as illegal *per se*. . . . By agreeing to limit the price which NCAA members may pay for the services of restricted-earnings coaches, the REC Rule fixes the cost of one of the component items used by NCAA members to produce the product of Division I basketball. As a result, the REC Rule constitutes the type of naked horizontal agreement among competitive purchasers to fix prices usually found to be illegal *per se*. . . . [T]he Supreme Court in *NCAA v. Board of Regents* departed from the general treatment given to horizontal price-fixing agreements by refusing to apply a *per se* rule and instead adopting a rule of reason approach in reviewing an NCAA plan for televising college football that involved both limits on output and price-fixing. . . .

. . . *Board of Regents* does not turn on whether the agreement in question is based on input components or output products. Rather, *Board of Regents* more generally concluded that because horizontal agreements are necessary for sports competition, all horizontal agreements among NCAA members, even those as egregious as price- fixing, should be subject to a rule of reason analysis. . . .

. . . Under this approach, the plaintiff bears the initial burden of showing that an agreement had a substantially adverse effect on competition. If the plaintiff meets this burden, the burden shifts to the defendant to come forward with evidence of the procompetitive virtues of the alleged wrongful conduct. If the defendant is able to demonstrate procompetitive effects, the plaintiff then must prove that the challenged conduct is not reasonably necessary to achieve the legitimate objectives or that those objectives can be achieved in a substantially less restrictive manner. Ultimately, if these steps are met, the harms and benefits must be weighed against each other in order to judge whether the challenged behavior is, on balance, reasonable.

A. ANTICOMPETITIVE EFFECT

We first review whether the coaches in this case demonstrated anticompetitive effect so conclusively that summary judgment on the issue was appropriate. A plaintiff may establish anticompetitive effect indirectly by proving that the defendant possessed the requisite market power within a defined market or directly by showing actual anticompetitive effects, such as control over output or price. A naked, effective restraint on market price or volume can establish anticompetitive effect under a truncated rule of reason analysis. . . .

. . . Thus, where a practice has obvious anticompetitive effects—as does price-fixing—there is no need to prove that the defendant possesses market power.

Rather, the court is justified in proceeding directly to the question of whether the procompetitive justifications advanced for the restraint outweigh the anti-competitive effects under a "quick look" rule of reason.

We find it appropriate to adopt such a quick look rule of reason in this case. Under a quick look rule of reason analysis, anticompetitive effect is established, even without a determination of the relevant market, where the plaintiff shows that a horizontal agreement to fix prices exists, that the agreement is effective, and that the price set by such an agreement is more favorable to the defendant than otherwise would have resulted from the operation of market forces. Under this standard, the undisputed evidence supports a finding of anticompetitive effect. The NCAA adopted the REC Rule to reduce the high cost of part-time coaches' salaries, over $60,000 annually in some cases, by limiting compensation to entry-level coaches to $16,000 per year. The NCAA does not dispute that the cost-reduction has effectively reduced restricted-earnings coaches' salaries. Because the REC Rule was successful in artificially lowering the price of coaching services, no further evidence or analysis is required to find market power to set prices. Thus, in the case at bar, the district court did not need to resolve issues of fact pertaining to the definition of the relevant market in order to support its decision on summary judgment that the REC Rule is a naked price restraint. . . .

B.   PROCOMPETITIVE RATIONALES

Under a rule of reason analysis, an agreement to restrain trade may still survive scrutiny under section 1 if the procompetitive benefits of the restraint justify the anticompetitive effects. Justifications offered under the rule of reason may be considered only to the extent that they tend to show that, on balance, "the challenged restraint enhances competition." *Board of Regents*, 468 U.S. at 104, 104 S. Ct. at 2961.

In *Board of Regents* the Supreme Court recognized that certain horizontal restraints, such as the conditions of the contest and the eligibility of participants, are justifiable under the antitrust laws because they are necessary to create the product of competitive college sports. Thus, the only legitimate rationales that we will recognize in support of the REC Rule are those necessary to produce competitive intercollegiate sports. The NCAA advanced three justifications for the salary limits: retaining entry-level coaching positions; reducing costs; and maintaining competitive equity. We address each of them in turn.

1.   *Retention of Entry-Level Positions*

The NCAA argues that the plan serves the procompetitive goal of retaining an entry-level coaching position. The NCAA asserts that the plan will allow younger, less experienced coaches entry into Division I coaching positions. While opening up coaching positions for younger people may have social value apart from its affect [*sic*] on competition, we may not consider such values unless they impact upon competition. . . .[14]

---

14. Similarly, the NCAA cannot be heard to argue that the REC Rule fosters the amateurism that serves as the hallmark of NCAA competition. While courts should afford the NCAA plenty of room under the antitrust laws to preserve the amateur character of intercollegiate athletics, courts have only legitimized rules designed to ensure the amateur status of student athletes, not coaches.

The NCAA also contends that limiting one of the four available coaching positions on a Division I basketball team to an entry-level position will create more balanced competition by barring some teams from hiring four experienced coaches instead of three. However, the REC Rule contained no restrictions other than salary designed to insure that the position would be filled by entry-level applicants; it could be filled with experienced applicants. . . . In fact, the evidence in the record tends to demonstrate that at least some schools designated persons with many years of experience as the restricted-earnings coach. . . . . Thus, the NCAA failed to present a triable issue of fact as to whether preserving entry-level positions served a legitimate procompetitive end of balancing competition.

2. *Cost Reduction*

The NCAA next advances the justification that the plan will cut costs. However, cost-cutting by itself is not a valid procompetitive justification. If it were, any group of competing buyers could agree on maximum prices. Lower prices cannot justify a cartel's control of prices charged by suppliers, because the cartel ultimately robs the suppliers of the normal fruits of their enterprises. Further, setting maximum prices reduces the incentive among suppliers to improve their products. Likewise, in our case, coaches have less incentive to improve their performance if their salaries are capped. . . .

The NCAA adopted the REC Rule because without it competition would lead to higher prices. The REC Rule was proposed as a way to prevent Division I schools from engaging in behavior the association termed "keeping up with the Joneses," *i.e.*, competing. However, the NCAA cannot argue that competition for coaches is an evil because the Sherman Act "precludes inquiry into the question whether competition is good or bad."

While increasing output, creating operating efficiencies, making a new product available, enhancing product or service quality, and widening consumer choice have been accepted by courts as justifications for otherwise anticompetitive agreements, mere profitability or cost savings have not qualified as a defense under the antitrust laws. . . . The NCAA's cost containment justification is illegitimate because . . . [r]educing costs for member institutions, without more, does not justify the anticompetitive effects of the REC Rule.

The NCAA argues that reducing costs can be considered a procompetitive justification because doing so is necessary to maintain the existence of competitive intercollegiate sports. . . .

We are dubious that the goal of cost reductions can serve as a legally sufficient justification for a buyers' agreement to fix prices even if such cost reductions are necessary to save inefficient or unsuccessful competitors from failure. Nevertheless, we need not consider whether cost reductions may have been required to "save" intercollegiate athletics and whether such an objective served as a legitimate procompetitive end because the NCAA presents no evidence that limits on restricted-earning coaches' salaries would be successful in reducing deficits, let alone that such reductions were necessary to save college basketball. Moreover, the REC Rule does not equalize the overall amount of money Division I schools are permitted to spend on their basketball programs. There is no reason to think that the money saved by a school on the salary of a restricted-earnings coach will not be put into another aspect of the school's basketball program, such as equipment or even another coach's salary, thereby increasing inequity in that area. . . .

3. Maintaining Competitiveness

We note that the NCAA must be able to ensure some competitive equity between member institutions in order to produce a marketable product: a "team must try to establish itself as a winner, but it must not win so often and so convincingly that the outcome will never be in doubt, or else there will be no marketable 'competition.'" Michael Jay Kaplan, Annotation, *Application of Federal Antitrust Laws to Professional Sports*, 18 A.L.R. FED. 489 § 2(a) (1974). The NCAA asserts that the REC Rule will help to maintain competitive equity by preventing wealthier schools from placing a more experienced, higher-priced coach in the position of restricted-earnings coach. . . .

While the REC Rule will equalize the salaries paid to entry-level coaches in Division I schools, it is not clear that the REC Rule will equalize the experience level of such coaches.[15] Nowhere does the NCAA prove that the salary restrictions enhance competition, level an uneven playing field, or reduce coaching inequities. Rather, the NCAA only presented evidence that the cost reductions would be achieved in such a way so as to maintain without "significantly altering," "adversely affecting," or "disturbing" the existing competitive balance. The undisputed record reveals that the REC Rule is nothing more than a cost-cutting measure and shows that the only consideration the NCAA gave to competitive balance was simply to structure the rule so as not to exacerbate competitive imbalance. Thus, on its face, the REC Rule is not directed towards competitive balance nor is the nexus between the rule and a compelling need to maintain competitive balance sufficiently clear on this record to withstand a motion for summary judgment.[16]

Affirmed.

NOTES AND QUESTIONS

1. *Standard for Analyzing Input Market Restraints.* The *Law* court recognized that coaching services are a necessary input to produce intercollegiate athletic competition, and the court analyzed the legality of fixed maximum salaries for restricted-earnings basketball coaches (the "REC Rule") under the same antitrust standard used by *Board of Regents* to invalidate restraints on the sale of output (e.g., television rights) by NCAA members. Do NCAA restrictions affecting the output market or input market present the most significant antitrust concerns from the perspective of consumers?

2. *Application of "Quick Look" Rule of Reason.* In *Law*, the Tenth Circuit affirmed the trial court's grant of summary judgment in favor of the plaintiff basketball coaches. Applying the "quick look" rule of reason (why does the court do so?), it concluded that capping the salaries of restricted-earnings coaches is illegal as a matter of law. Why wasn't it necessary to have the jury balance the anticompetitive effects of fixing these coaches' salaries with the NCAA's claimed procompetitive justifications, which occurs when the full

---

15. For example, some more-experienced coaches may take restricted-earnings coach positions with programs such as those at Duke or North Carolina, despite the lower salary, because of the national prominence of those programs. In fact, absent the REC Rule, the market might produce greater equity in coaching talent, because a school with a less-prominent basketball program might be able to entice a more-experienced coach away from a prominent program by offering a higher salary.

16. Because we hold that the NCAA did not establish evidence of sufficient procompetitive benefits, we need not address question of whether the plaintiffs were able to show that comparable procompetitive benefits could be achieved through viable, less anticompetitive means.

rule of reason is applied? To answer these questions, carefully review part III of *Law*, particularly the Tenth Circuit's explanation of the parties' respective burdens of proof under the rule of reason. Note that an antitrust claim can be resolved by the court as a matter of law at any stage of the rule of reason analysis if a party fails to satisfy its required burden of proof.

3. *NCAA's Procompetitive Justifications.* Why does the court reject the NCAA's argument that the REC Rule is a procompetitive means of preventing a "keep up with the Joneses" type of spending in its members' athletic programs? Is the rule necessary to ensure competitive balance among NCAA members, to preserve the amateur nature of NCAA sports, or to achieve any other legitimate procompetitive justification?

4. *REC Rule Damages Award and Settlement.* Coaches whose economic interests were adversely affected by the NCAA's REC Rule (including those coaching sports other than basketball) ultimately won a jury verdict of $22.3 million, which, with mandatory trebling, resulted in a total award of $66.9 million from the NCAA. The NCAA ultimately agreed to pay $54.5 million as part of a settlement to resolve all damage claims, and the court awarded approximately $20 million in attorney fees and costs to the plaintiffs' attorneys. See *Law v. NCAA*, 108 F. Supp. 2d 1193 (D. Kan. 2000) (approving the revised settlement plan as fair, reasonable, and adequate).

5. *Permissible NCAA Cost Containment?* Before *Board of Regents*, courts held that NCAA limits on the size of coaching staffs, which were found to be a legitimate cost-cutting measure that promoted competitive balance by preventing more successful and economically powerful universities from expanding their football programs, do not violate the antitrust laws. *Hennessey v. NCAA*, 564 F.2d 1136 (5th Cir. 1977); *Board of Regents of the Univ. of Oklahoma v. NCAA*, 561 P.2d 499 (Okla. 1977). Is an NCAA-mandated reduction of coaches in a particular sport an antitrust violation under *Board of Regents*? Review the other NCAA cost-saving measures described in footnote 5 of *Law* that were not challenged by the plaintiffs and consider which ones would survive antitrust scrutiny under the rule of reason. Would NCAA-mandated cost-cutting or caps on total expenditures in some men's sports (e.g., football) in an effort to comply with Title IX gender equity requirements violate antitrust law? *See* John C. Weistart, *Can Gender Equity Find a Place in Commercialized College Sports?*, 3 Duke J. Gender L. & Pol'y 191 (1995).

6. *NCAA Limits on Revenue Streams.* If NCAA limits on costs (e.g., part-time coaches' salaries) violate antitrust law, are NCAA limits on its members' potential sources of revenue (e.g., advertising rights) an antitrust violation?

Adidas America, Inc., a leading sporting goods manufacturer, alleged that an NCAA bylaw limiting the size of trademarks on player uniforms and equipment illegally restrains the sale of advertising and promotional rights by NCAA universities. In denying Adidas's requested injunctive relief against NCAA enforcement of the bylaw, the federal district court found this to be noncommercial regulation not subject to antitrust law. It concluded that *Law* did not require the challenged advertising restrictions to be characterized as commercial activity within the scope of the Sherman Act. Finding the bylaw's purpose to be protecting student-athletes from commercial exploitation and avoiding excessive advertising that could potentially interfere with the basic function of player uniforms, the court explained that the bylaw "is an incidental by-product of the NCAA's legitimate attempt to maintain the amateurism and integrity of college sports,

and it does not economically benefit the NCAA or its member institutions." *Adidas America, Inc. v. NCAA*, 40 F. Supp. 2d 1275 (D. Kan. 1999).
When reading the materials below, note how the law subsequently has
evolved and consider the probability that courts would reach a different
conclusion today.

ii.   Student-Athlete Eligibility Rules and Scholarship Restrictions

PROBLEM 3-9

In *Bloom v. NCAA, supra,* Jeremy Bloom alleged that NCAA bylaws prohibiting
student-athletes from being paid for advertisements and endorsements restrain
trade and violate antitrust law. As you read the following materials, consider
how a court is likely to resolve the merits of his claim.

In *Board of Regents, supra,* the Supreme Court recognized that NCAA schools
compete against each other to attract student-athletes to their intercollegiate
athletic programs. Although uniform eligibility rules both define and limit the
permissible nature and scope of economic competition among NCAA members
for student-athletes' services, lower courts historically characterized all NCAA
student-athlete eligibility rules as noncommercial activity not subject to antitrust
scrutiny. For example, in *Smith v. NCAA*, 139 F.3d 180, 185-86 (3d Cir. 1998), the
Third Circuit upheld the dismissal of a student-athlete's claim that an NCAA
bylaw (which subsequently was repealed) prohibiting her from participating
in intercollegiate athletics while enrolled in a graduate program at a university
other than her undergraduate institution violated §1:

> The Supreme Court addressed the applicability of the Sherman Act to the NCAA
> in [*Board of Regents*], holding that the NCAA's plan to restrict television coverage
> of intercollegiate football games violated section 1. The Court discussed the pro-
> competitive nature of the NCAA's activities such as establishing eligibility require-
> ments as opposed to the anticompetitive nature of the television plan. Yet, while
> the Court distinguished the NCAA's television plan from its rule making, it did not
> comment directly on whether the Sherman Act would apply to the latter.
>
> Although insofar as we are aware no court of appeals expressly has addressed
> the issue of whether antitrust laws apply to the NCAA's promulgation of eligibility
> rules, *cf. McCormack v. National Collegiate Athletic Assn*, 845 F.2d 1338, 1343 (5th Cir.
> 1988) (assuming without deciding that the NCAA's eligibility rules were subject
> to antitrust scrutiny and holding that the "no-draft" and "no-agent" rules do not
> have an anticompetitive effect), many district courts have held that the Sherman
> Act does not apply to the NCAA's promulgation and enforcement of eligibility
> requirements. *See Gaines v. National Collegiate Athletic Assn*, 746 F. Supp. 738, 744-
> 46 (M.D. Tenn. 1990) (holding that antitrust law cannot be used to invalidate
> NCAA eligibility rules, but noting in dicta that the "no-agent" and "no-draft" rules
> have primarily procompetitive effects); *Jones v. National Collegiate Athletic Assn*, 392
> F. Supp. 295, 303 (D. Mass. 1975) (holding that antitrust law does not apply to
> NCAA eligibility rules); *College Athletic Placement Service, Inc. v. National Collegiate
> Athletic Assn*, 1975-1 Trade Cas. (CCH) T 60,117, available in 1974 WL 998, *2, *3
> (D.N.J. 1974) (holding that the NCAA's adoption of a rule furthering its noncom-
> mercial objectives, such as preserving the educational standards of its members, is
> not within the purview of antitrust law), *aff'd*, 506 F.2d 1050 (3d Cir. 1974) (table).
>
> We agree with these courts that the eligibility rules are not related to the NCAA's
> commercial or business activities. Rather than intending to provide the NCAA with

a commercial advantage, the eligibility rules primarily seek to ensure fair competition in intercollegiate athletics. Based upon the Supreme Court's recognition that the Sherman Act primarily was intended to prevent unreasonable restraints in "business and commercial transactions," and therefore has only limited applicability to organizations which have principally noncommercial objectives, we find that the Sherman Act does not apply to the NCAA's promulgation of eligibility requirements.

After and consistent with *Smith*, courts generally upheld, as a matter of law, the validity of NCAA and athletic conference student-athlete eligibility rules and dismissed antitrust challenges to them. *Tanaka v. University of S. Cal.*, 252 F.3d 1059 (9th Cir. 2001); *Bleid Sports v. NCAA*, 976 F. Supp. 2d 911, 916 (E.D. Ky. 2013) (E.D. Ky.). *But see White v. NCAA*, 2006 WL 8066802 (C.D. Cal.) (refusing to dismiss a §1 antitrust challenge to an NCAA rule limiting the value of an athletic scholarship to university tuition, room and board, and books because it limits economic competition among universities for prospective student-athletes). Without any detailed legal or factual analysis, eligibility rules were presumed necessary to preserve amateurism, academic values, and/or competitive balance in intercollegiate athletics, notwithstanding scholarly commentary that these rules should be characterized as commercial activity with their respective net competitive effects individually analyzed under the rule of reason. See, e.g., Daniel E. Lazaroff, *The NCAA in Its Second Century: Defender of Amateurism or Antitrust Recidivist?*, 83 Or. L. Rev. 329 (2007); Matthew J. Mitten, *University Price Competition for Elite Students and Athletes: Illusions and Realities*, 36 S. Tex. L. Rev. 59 (1995).

Courts also have ruled that NCAA or athletic conference sanctions against member institutions for rules violations do not violate antitrust law. In *Commonwealth of Pennsylvania v NCAA*, 948 F. Supp. 2d 416 (M.D. Pa. 2013), the court dismissed an antitrust suit filed by the Commonwealth of Pennsylvania, which alleged that unprecedented NCAA disciplinary sanctions imposed on Penn State University arising out of serial child molestation by a former football coach will cripple the ability of its football program to compete on the playing field and reduce its ability to generate revenues for the university in violation of §1 of the Sherman Act. Initially, the court observed that "Penn State is not a party to this action and takes no position in this litigation" and that "the complaint limits [judicial] review to the question of whether [Governor Corbett] has articulated a violation of federal antitrust law." *Id.* at 420, 422. It explained that the complaint "must point to harm directed at commercial activity of the type the Sherman Act is designed to address" for §1 to apply to the NCAA's challenged conduct, and concluded this requirement is not met because "the complaint is devoid of allegations that [the NCAA] sought to regulate commercial activity or obtain any commercial advantage for itself by imposing sanctions on Penn State." *Id.* at 422, 427. *See also Bassett v. NCAA*, 528 F.3d 426, 430 (6th Cir. 2008) (dismissing an antitrust challenge to sanctions imposed on a coach for violation of NCAA rules governing recruiting, improper benefits to athletes, and academic fraud because it was "not within the purview of antitrust law as it is not related to NCAA's commercial or business activities"); *Hairston v. Pacific-10 Conference*, 101 F.3d 1315, 1320 (9th Cir. 1995) (dismissing an antitrust challenge to penalties imposed on the university because the penalties were not shown to be an unreasonable restraint on trade); *McCormack v. NCAA*, 845 F.2d 1338, 1343, 1345 (5th Cir. 1988) ("hold[ing] that the NCAA's eligibility rules are reasonable" and "do not violate antitrust laws"). Do you agree that even arbitrary, capricious, and/or unreasonable NCAA sanctions should not be subject to antitrust challenge?

In *Agnew v. NCAA*, 683 F.3d 328, 339 (7th Cir. 2012), the Seventh Circuit considered "whether and when the Sherman Act applies to the NCAA and its member schools in relation to their interaction with student-athletes." Based on *Board of Regents*, the court stated that certain forms of NCAA regulation such as student-athlete eligibility rules are "presumptively procompetitive" and should be judicially characterized as reasonable restraints "'in the twinkling of an eye' . . . at the motion-to-dismiss stage" of a §1 claim. *Id.* at 341. However, the Seventh Circuit distinguished eligibility rules from NCAA maximum limits on the number of scholarships a university may award for a particular sport and their one-year duration, which it found have adverse commercial effects on student-athletes that must be justified under the rule-of-reason scrutiny. The court explained:

> Most—if not all—eligibility rules . . . fall comfortably within the presumption of procompetitiveness afforded to certain NCAA regulations, as both parties agree. Beyond the obvious fact that the Supreme Court explicitly mentioned eligibility rules as a type that "fit[s] into the same mold" as other procompetitive rules, they are clearly necessary to preserve amateurism and the student-athlete in college football. Indeed, they define what it means to be an amateur or a student-athlete, and are therefore essential to the very existence of the product of college football. . . . There may not be such a thing as a student-athlete, for instance, if it was not for the NCAA rules requiring class attendance, and thus no "detailed analysis," *Am. Needle, 130 S. Ct. at 2216-17, would be necessary to deem such rules procompetitive. Cf. Bd. of Regents, 468 U.S. at 102, 104 S. Ct. 2948. The same goes for bylaws eliminating the eligibility of players who receive cash payments beyond the costs attendant to receiving an education—a rule that clearly protects amateurism.*
>
> The Bylaws at issue in this case, however, are not eligibility rules, nor do we conclude that they "fit into the same mold" as eligibility rules. (citation omitted). These Bylaws—a one-year limit to scholarships and a limit on scholarships per team—are not inherently or obviously necessary for the preservation of amateurism, the student-athlete, or the general product of college football. The Bylaws at issue, especially the prohibition against multi-year scholarships, seem to be aimed at containing university costs, not preserving the product of college football, though evidence presented at a later stage could prove that the Bylaws are, in fact, key to the survival of the student-athlete and amateurism. . . .
>
> The NCAA's limitation on athlete compensation *beyond* educational expenses . . . directly advances the goal of maintaining a "clear line of demarcation between intercollegiate athletics and professional sports," and thus is best categorized as an eligibility rule aimed at preserving the existence of amateurism and the student-athlete. The Bylaws at issue in this case, on the other hand, are not directly related to the separation of amateur athletics from pay-for-play athletics, as explained in the preceding paragraphs. Nor do they help preserve the existence of the student-athlete (as a facial matter, anyway), since they actually limit the number of athletes awarded financial aid and the amount of financial aid that an athlete can be awarded. Thus, financial aid rules do not always assist in the preservation of amateurism or the existence of student-athletes, so the regulations at issue cannot be presumptively procompetitive simply because they relate to financial aid.

Id. at 343-345. While *Agnew* was pending, but before it was decided by the Seventh Circuit, the NCAA amended its bylaws to permit Division I universities to award multiyear athletic scholarships. See Michelle Brutlag Hosick, *Multiyear*

Scholarships to Be Allowed, http ://www.ncaa.com/news/ncaa/article/2012-02-17/multiyear-scholarships-be-allowed.

Applying *Agnew*, in *Rock v NCAA*, 2013 WL 4479815 (S.D. Ind.), a case involving a former FCS football player who sought damages for non-renewal of his athletic scholarship, the court ruled that an antitrust challenge to NCAA limits on the maximum number of Division I football scholarships its member universities could award (85 for FBS teams, and 63 for FCS teams) and former prohibitions against multi-year scholarships constitutes commercial activity subject to §1.

In *Deppe v. NCAA*, 893 F.3d 498 (7th Cir. 2018), the Seventh Circuit affirmed the dismissal of a Division I FBS football player's antitrust challenge to the NCAA's "year in residence" bylaw, which requires Division I athletes to fulfill a full academic year residency requirement at the university to which he or she transfers before being eligible to play intercollegiate sports. It held that this bylaw "is an eligibility rule clearly meant to preserve the amateur character of college athletics and is therefore presumptively procompetitive under [*Board of Regents* and *Agnew*]." *Id.* at 499. In support of its conclusion, the court observed: "Deppe argues that at bottom, the year-in-residence rule serves economic interests because it 'preserves the hegemony of the top 'Power 5' conferences—the most powerful group of schools in the NCAA. He asserts that these schools recruit the most talented high-school athletes and that the year-in-residence rule prevents those student-athletes from transferring to less powerful schools. But the rule impedes transfers in both directions. Without it, the 'Power 5' schools could poach rising stars from smaller schools, which would risk eroding the amateur character of the college game." *Id.* at 503.

The following case sharply diverges from *Smith, Agnew,* and other cases by holding that NCAA eligibility rules, which prohibit student-athletes from being paid any economic compensation for or related to playing intercollegiate athletics other than an athletic scholarship, are commercial restraints subject to rule of reason analysis, but it upholds the NCAA's authority to maintain the amateur nature of intercollegiate athletics.

O'BANNON v. NATIONAL COLLEGIATE ATHLETIC ASSOCIATION

802 F.3d 1049 (9th Cir. 2015), *cert. denied*, 137 S. Ct. 277 (2016)

BYBEE, Circuit Judge:

. . . For more than a century, the National Collegiate Athletic Association (NCAA) has prescribed rules governing the eligibility of athletes at its more than 1,000 member colleges and universities. Those rules prohibit student-athletes from being paid for the use of their names, images, and likenesses (NILs). The question presented in this momentous case is whether the NCAA's rules are subject to the antitrust laws and, if so, whether they are an unlawful restraint of trade.

After a bench trial and in a thorough opinion, the district court concluded that the NCAA's compensation rules were an unlawful restraint of trade. It then enjoined the NCAA from prohibiting its member schools from giving student-athletes scholarships up to the full cost of attendance at their respective schools and up to $5,000 per year in deferred compensation, to be held in trust for student-athletes until after they leave college. As far as we are aware, the district court's decision is the first by any federal court to hold that any aspect of the

NCAA's amateurism rules violate the antitrust laws, let alone to mandate by injunction that the NCAA change its practices.

We conclude that the district court's decision was largely correct. Although we agree with the Supreme Court and our sister circuits that many of the NCAA's amateurism rules are likely to be procompetitive, we hold that those rules are not exempt from antitrust scrutiny; rather, they must be analyzed under the Rule of Reason. Applying the Rule of Reason, we conclude that the district court correctly identified one proper alternative to the current NCAA compensation rules — *i.e.,* allowing NCAA members to give scholarships up to the full cost of attendance — but that the district court's other remedy, allowing students to be paid cash compensation of up to $5,000 per year, was erroneous. We therefore affirm in part and reverse in part. . . .

III

A. *BOARD OF REGENTS* DID NOT DECLARE THE NCAA'S AMATEURISM RULES "VALID AS A MATTER OF LAW"

We consider, first, the NCAA's claim that, under *Board of Regents,* all NCAA amateurism rules are "valid as a matter of law." . . .

[T]he NCAA contends that any Section 1 challenge to its amateurism rules must fail as a matter of law because the *Board of Regents* Court held that those rules are presumptively valid. We disagree.

The *Board of Regents* Court certainly discussed the NCAA's amateurism rules at great length, but it did not do so in order to pass upon the rules' merits, given that they were not before the Court. Rather, the Court discussed the amateurism rules for a different and particular purpose: to explain why NCAA rules should be analyzed under the Rule of Reason, rather than held to be illegal per se. . . .

What is more, even if the language in *Board of Regents* addressing amateurism were *not* dicta, it would not support the tremendous weight that the NCAA seeks to place upon it. The Court's opinion supports the proposition that the preservation of amateurism is a legitimate procompetitive purpose for the NCAA to pursue, but the NCAA is not asking us to find merely that its amateurism rules are procompetitive; rather, it asks us to hold that those rules are essentially exempt from antitrust scrutiny. Nothing in *Board of Regents* supports such an exemption. To say that the NCAA's amateurism rules are procompetitive, as *Board of Regents* did, is not to say that they are automatically lawful; a restraint that serves a procompetitive purpose can still be invalid under the Rule of Reason if a substantially less restrictive rule would further the same objectives equally well. *See Bd. of Regents,* 468 U.S. at 101 n. 23 ("While as the guardian of an important American tradition, the NCAA's motives must be accorded a respectful presumption of validity, it is nevertheless well settled that good motives will not validate an otherwise anticompetitive practice."). . . .

In sum, we accept *Board of Regents'* guidance as informative with respect to the procompetitive purposes served by the NCAA's amateurism rules, but we will go no further than that. The amateurism rules' validity must be proved, not presumed.

B. THE COMPENSATION RULES REGULATE "COMMERCIAL ACTIVITY"

The NCAA next argues that we cannot reach the merits of the plaintiffs' Sherman Act claim because the compensation rules are not subject to the Sherman Act at all. The NCAA points out that Section 1 of the Sherman Act applies only to "restraint[s] of trade or commerce," 15 U.S.C. § 1, and claims that its compensation rules are mere "eligibility rules" that do not regulate any "commercial activity."

This argument is not credible. Although restraints that have no effect on commerce are indeed exempt from Section 1, the modern legal understanding of "commerce" is broad, "including almost every activity from which the actor anticipates economic gain." Phillip Areeda & Herbert Hovenkamp, *Antitrust Law: An Analysis of Antitrust Principles and Their Application,* ¶ 260b (4th ed. 2013). That definition surely encompasses the transaction in which an athletic recruit exchanges his labor and NIL rights for a scholarship at a Division I school because it is undeniable that both parties to that exchange anticipate economic gain from it. . . .

[T]he NCAA's Postbaccalaureate Bylaw challenged in [*Smith v. NCAA*] was a true "eligibility" rule, akin to the rules limiting the number of years that student-athletes may play collegiate sports or requiring student-athletes to complete a certain number of credit hours each semester. As the *Smith* court expressly noted, the Postbaccalaureate Bylaw was "not related to the NCAA's commercial or business activities." By contrast, the rules here—which regulate what compensation NCAA schools may give student-athletes, and how much—*do* relate to the NCAA's business activities: the labor of student-athletes is an integral and essential component of the NCAA's "product," and a rule setting the price of that labor goes to the heart of the NCAA's business. Thus, the rules at issue here are more like rules affecting the NCAA's dealings with its coaches or with corporate business partners—which courts have held to be commercial—than they are like the Bylaw challenged in *Smith.* . . .

We therefore conclude that the NCAA's compensation rules are within the ambit of the Sherman Act. . . .

IV

Like the district court, we follow the three-step framework of the Rule of Reason: "[1] The plaintiff bears the initial burden of showing that the restraint produces significant anticompetitive effects within a relevant market. [2] If the plaintiff meets this burden, the defendant must come forward with evidence of the restraint's procompetitive effects. [3] The plaintiff must then show that any legitimate objectives can be achieved in a substantially less restrictive manner." *Tanaka v. Univ. of S. Cal.,* 252 F.3d 1059, 1063 (9th Cir. 2001).

A. SIGNIFICANT ANTICOMPETITIVE EFFECTS WITHIN A RELEVANT MARKET

[T]he district court made the following factual findings: (1) that a cognizable "college education market" exists, wherein colleges compete for the services of athletic recruits by offering them scholarships and various amenities, such as coaching and facilities; (2) that if the NCAA's compensation rules did not exist, member schools would compete to offer recruits compensation for their NILs; and (3) that the compensation rules therefore have a significant anti-competitive effect on the college education market, in that they fix an aspect of the "price" that recruits pay to attend college (or, alternatively, an aspect of the price that schools pay to secure recruits' services). These findings have substantial support in the record. . . .

The "combination[s] condemned by the [Sherman] Act" also include "price-fixing . . . by purchasers" even though "the persons specially injured . . . are sellers, not customers or consumers." *Mandeville Island Farms, Inc. v. Am. Crystal Sugar Co. ., 334 U.S. 219, 235, 68 S. Ct. 996, 92 L. Ed. 1328 (1948). At trial, the plaintiffs demonstrated that the NCAA's compensation rules have just this kind of anti-competitive effect: they fix the price of one component of the exchange between school and recruit, thereby precluding competition among schools with respect to that component. The district court found that although consumers of NCAA football and basketball may not be harmed directly by this price-fixing, the "student-athletes themselves are harmed by the price-fixing agreement among FBS football and Division I basketball schools." The athletes accept grants-in-aid, and no more, in exchange for their athletic performance, because the NCAA schools have agreed to value the athletes' NILs at zero, "an anticompetitive effect." This anticompetitive effect satisfied the plaintiffs' initial burden under the Rule of Reason. . . .*

B.   PROCOMPETITIVE EFFECTS

[T]he NCAA offered the district court four procompetitive justifications for the compensation rules: (1) promoting amateurism, (2) promoting competitive balance among NCAA schools, (3) integrating student-athletes with their schools' academic community, and (4) increasing output in the college education market. The district court accepted the first and third and rejected the other two.

[T]he NCAA focuses its arguments to this court entirely on the first proffered justification—the promotion of amateurism. We therefore accept the district court's factual findings that the compensation rules do not promote competitive balance, that they do not increase output in the college education market, and that they play a limited role in integrating student-athletes with their schools' academic communities, since we have been offered no meaningful argument that those findings were clearly erroneous.

[The] district court found, and the record supports that there is a concrete procompetitive effect in the NCAA's commitment to amateurism: namely, that the amateur nature of collegiate sports increases their appeal to consumers. We therefore conclude that the NCAA's compensation rules serve the two procompetitive purposes identified by the district court: integrating academics with athletics, and "preserving the popularity of the NCAA's product by promoting its current understanding of amateurism." . . .

We note that the district court's findings are largely consistent with the Supreme Court's own description of the college football market as "a particular brand of football" that draws from "an academic tradition [that] differentiates [it] from and makes it more popular than professional sports to which it might otherwise be comparable, such as, for example, minor league baseball." *Bd. of Regents, 468 U.S. at 101-02.* "*Thus, the NCAA plays a vital role in enabling college football to preserve its character, and as a result enables a product to be marketed which might otherwise be unavailable.*" *Id.* at 102. But, as *Board of Regents* demonstrates, not every rule adopted by the NCAA that restricts the market is necessary to preserving the "character" of college sports. We thus turn to the final inquiry—whether there are reasonable alternatives to the NCAA's current compensation restrictions.

C.   SUBSTANTIALLY LESS RESTRICTIVE ALTERNATIVES

The third step in the Rule of Reason analysis is whether there are substantially less restrictive alternatives to the NCAA's current rules. We bear in mind that—to be viable under the Rule of Reason—an alternative must be "virtu-ally as effective" in serving the procompetitive purposes of the NCAA's current rules, and "without significantly increased cost." . . .

Not only do plaintiffs bear the burden at this step, but the Supreme Court has admonished that we must generally afford the NCAA "ample latitude" to superintend college athletics. *Bd. of Regents,* 468 U.S. at 120 . . .

The district court identified two substantially less restrictive alternatives: (1) allowing NCAA member schools to give student-athletes grants-in-aid that cover the full cost of attendance; and (2) allowing member schools to pay student-athletes small amounts of deferred cash compensation for use of their NILs. We hold that the district court did not clearly err in finding that raising the grant-in-aid cap would be a substantially less restrictive alternative, but that it clearly erred when it found that allowing students to be paid compensation for their NILs is virtually as effective as the NCAA's current amateur-status rule.

1.   Capping the permissible amount of scholarships at the cost of attendance

. . . All of the evidence before the district court indicated that raising the grant-in-aid cap to the cost of attendance would have virtually no impact on amateurism: Dr. Mark Emmert, the president of the NCAA, testified at trial that giving student-athletes scholarships up to their full costs of attendance would not violate the NCAA's principles of amateurism because all the money given to students would be going to cover their "legitimate costs" to attend school. Other NCAA witnesses agreed with that assessment. Nothing in the record, moreover, suggested that consumers of college sports would become less interested in those sports if athletes' scholarships covered their full cost of attendance, or that an increase in the grant-in-aid cap would impede the integration of stu-dent-athletes into their academic communities. . . .

A compensation cap set at student-athletes' full cost of attendance is a sub-stantially less restrictive alternative means of accomplishing the NCAA's legit-imate procompetitive purposes. And there is no evidence that this cap will significantly increase costs; indeed, the NCAA already permits schools to fund student-athletes' full cost of attendance. The district court's determination that the existing compensation rules violate Section 1 of the Sherman Act was cor-rect and its injunction requiring the NCAA to permit schools to provide com-pensation up to the full cost of attendance was proper.

2.   Allowing students to receive cash compensation for their NILs

In our judgment, however, the district court clearly erred in finding it a viable alterative to allow students to receive NIL cash payments untethered to their education expenses. . . .

We cannot agree that a rule permitting schools to pay students pure cash com-pensation and a rule forbidding them from paying NIL compensation are both *equally* effective in promoting amateurism and preserving consumer demand. Both we and the district court agree that the NCAA's amateurism rule has pro-competitive benefits. But in finding that paying students cash compensation would promote amateurism as effectively as not paying them, the district court ignored that not paying student-athletes is *precisely what makes them amateurs.* . . .

The difference between offering student-athletes education-related compen-sation and offering them cash sums untethered to educational expenses is not minor; it is a quantum leap. Once that line is crossed, we see no basis for return-ing to a rule of amateurism and no defined stopping point; we have little doubt that plaintiffs will continue to challenge the arbitrary limit imposed by the district court until they have captured the full value of their NIL. At that point the NCAA will have surrendered its amateurism principles entirely and transitioned from its "particular brand of football" to minor league status. In light of that, the meager evidence in the record, and the Supreme Court's admonition that we must afford the NCAA "ample latitude" to superintend college athletics, *Bd. of Regents,* 468 U.S. at 120, we think it is clear the district court erred in concluding that small payments in deferred compensation are a substantially less restrictive alternative restraint. . . .

V

. . . In this case, the NCAA's rules have been more restrictive than necessary to maintain its tradition of amateurism in support of the college sports market. The Rule of Reason requires that the NCAA permit its schools to provide up to the cost of attendance to their student athletes. It does not require more.

We vacate the district court's judgment and permanent injunction insofar as they require the NCAA to allow its member schools to pay student-athletes up to $5,000 per year in deferred compensation. We otherwise affirm. . . .

THOMAS, Chief Judge, concurring in part and dissenting in part:

I largely agree with all but one of the majority's conclusions. I respectfully disagree with the majority's conclusion that the district court clearly erred in ordering the NCAA to permit up to $5,000 in deferred compensation above student-athletes' full cost of attendance.

I

. . . There was sufficient evidence in the record to support the award. The district court's conclusion that the proposed alternative restraint satisfied the Rule of Reason was based on testimony from at least four experts—including three experts presented by the NCAA—that providing student-athletes with small amounts of compensation above their cost of attendance most likely would not have a significant impact on consumer interest in college sports. It was also based on the fact that FBS football players are currently permitted to accept Pell grants in excess of their cost of attendance, and the fact that Division I tennis recruits are permitted to earn up to $10,000 per year in prize money from athletic events before they enroll in college. The majority characterizes the weight of this evidence as "threadbare." I respectfully disagree.

The NCAA's own expert witness, Neal Pilson, testified that the level of deferred compensation would have an effect on consumer demand for college athletics, but that paying student-athletes $5,000 per year in trust most likely would not have a significant impact on such demand. He also testified that any negative impact that paying student-athletes might have on consumer demand could be partially mitigated by placing the compensation in a trust fund to be paid out after graduation. . . .

The majority also dismisses the testimony given by expert witness Dr. Daniel Rascher demonstrating that consumer interest in major league baseball and the Olympics increased after baseball players' salaries rose and professional athletes were allowed to compete in the Olympics. The majority reasons that major league baseball and the Olympics are "not fit analogues to college sports," speculating that college sports would be more significantly transformed by professionalism than have the Olympics. However, the majority does not offer any evidentiary support for the distinction, nor explain how or why the district court clearly erred in crediting this testimony. . . .

The district court accepted the testimony of multiple experts that small amounts of compensation would not affect consumer demand, and then used the lowest amount suggested by one of the NCAA's experts. The district court was within its right to do so.

II

The disagreement between my view and the majority view largely boils down to a difference in opinion as to the procompetitive interests at stake. The majority characterizes our task at step three of the Rule of Reason as determining "whether the alternative of allowing students to be paid NIL compensation unrelated to their education expenses is 'virtually as effective' in preserving *amateurism* as not allowing compensation." This conclusion misstates our inquiry. Rather, we must determine whether allowing student-athletes to be compensated for their NILs is 'virtually as effective' in preserving *popular demand for college sports* as not allowing compensation. In terms of antitrust analysis, the concept of amateurism is relevant only insofar as it relates to consumer interest. . . .

The district court determined that "the evidence presented at trial suggests that consumer demand for FBS football and Division I basketball-related products is not driven by the restrictions on student-athlete compensation but instead by other factors, such as school loyalty and geography." . . .

. . . The NCAA insists that consumers will flee if student-athletes are paid even a small sum of money for colleges' use of their NILs. This assertion is contradicted by the district court record and by the NCAA's own rules regarding amateurism. . . . Division I schools have spent $5 billion on athletic facilities over the past 15 years. The NCAA sold the television rights to broadcast the NCAA men's basketball championship tournament for 12 years to CBS for $10.8 billion dollars. The NCAA insists that this multi-billion dollar industry would be lost if the teenagers and young adults who play for these college teams earn one dollar above their cost of school attendance. That is a difficult argument to swallow. Given the trial evidence, the district court was well within its rights to reject it. . . .

NOTES AND QUESTIONS

1. *Commercial v. Noncommercial Student-Athlete Eligibility Rules.* Is there a principled distinction between student-athlete eligibility rules, characterized as commercial restraints by *O'Bannon* (e.g., NCAA NIL rules), that are subject to antitrust scrutiny and those considered to be noncommercial (e.g., academic requirements such as the NCAA's former postbaccalaureate rule in *Smith*) that are not? Should the objectives or effects of the particular eligibility rule be the determining factor for purposes of antitrust law?

In *Marshall v. ESPN, Inc.*, 111 F. Supp. 3d 815 (M.D. Tenn. 2015), a group of current and former NCAA Division I basketball and football players sued television broadcasters, college athletics conferences, and licensing entities (but not the NCAA), alleging they were forced to sign unconscionable waivers of their otherwise existing right to compensation for use of their publicity rights in the advertising and promotion of college basketball and football game broadcasts in violation of §1. Contrary to *O'Bannon*, the court dismissed plaintiffs' claims based on *Board of Regents, Smith,* and *Agnew* and concluded: "Right or wrong, under NCAA rules, other than the requirement that an athlete be a student, there can be no more basic eligibility rule for amateurism than that the athlete not be paid for playing his or her sport." *Id.* at 834. *Marshall* follows the majority judicial view holding that NCAA student-athlete eligibility rules to preserve amateurism are not commercial restraints subject to antitrust challenge even if they effectively reduce the cost of an essential input necessary to produce intercollegiate athletics (i.e., student-athletes' economic benefits for their playing services). If cost reduction is not a valid justification for fixing the price of coaches' salaries (*Law v. NCAA, supra*), should it be a judicially accepted implicit justification for limiting the compensation for student-athletes' services below the full cost of attendance?

2. *Analysis of* O'Bannon. Why did the Ninth Circuit affirm the district court's finding that NCAA rules barring student-athletes from receiving any share of the revenues the NCAA and its member schools earn from products using student-athletes' names, images, and likenesses violate §1? The Ninth Circuit three-judge panel agrees that not permitting student-athletes to receive a full cost of attendance scholarship is an antitrust violation, but the majority and dissent sharply disagree regarding the district court's determination that an additional $5,000 annual stipend will not preclude the NCAA's legitimate procompetitive purposes from being achieved. Do you agree with the Ninth Circuit majority's conclusion that the district court "clearly erred when it found that allowing students to be paid compensation for their NILs is virtually as effective as the NCAA's current amateur-status rule," or the dissent's view that "[i]n terms of antitrust analysis, the concept of amateurism is relevant only insofar as it relates to consumer interest" in intercollegiate athletics? See generally Matthew J. Mitten, *Why and How the Supreme Court Should Have Decided O'Bannon v NCAA*, 62 Antitrust Bull. 62 (2017) (asserting that the Supreme Court should have granted a writ of certiorari in *O'Bannon* and suggesting how it should have decided this case).

From the perspective of the fans, what distinguishes college sports (e.g., Division I FBS football and basketball) from their corresponding professional sports (e.g., NFL football and NBA basketball)? Is preserving "amateurism" as defined by NCAA student-athlete eligibility rules necessary for Division I FBS football and basketball to maintain their enormous popularity that generates multi-billion revenues annually? Note that NCAA rules permit student-athletes to play professionally in one sport without losing their eligibility to participate in another intercollegiate sport; for example, Seattle Seahawks quarterback Russell Wilson played minor league baseball while also playing college football at North Carolina State University and the University of Wisconsin. Subject to certain conditions and requirements, former professional athletes in a sport are eligible to participate in NCAA Division II and Division III athletics in the same sport. Division

II Bylaws 12.1.3, 15.2.5.4 and 15.2.5.5; Division III Bylaw 12.1.2. In April 2002, the Division I Management Council rejected proposals that would have permitted student-athletes to enter professional drafts and compete as professionals and retain limited eligibility to compete in Division I intercollegiate athletics. Does (should) Division II and Division III deregulation of amateurism undercut the validity of the NCAA's argument that its Division I amateurism rules are necessary to preserve the distinction between intercollegiate and professional sports?

After the *O'Bannon* district court decision, the NCAA redefined and increased the value of an athletic scholarship to permit student-athletes to receive an economic benefit equal to the full cost of attendance at his or her university, which is consistent with the Ninth Circuit majority's ruling. See discussion of this NCAA legislation in Section C of this chapter, *supra.*

On February 3, 2017, the NCAA agreed to pay $208.7 million to settle the damages portion of the lawsuit filed by former student-athletes who claimed that capping the economic value of their scholarships at the costs of tuition, room, board, books, and fees violated federal antitrust law (*Alston v. NCAA,* 3:14-cv-01011 (N.D. Cal.)). Judge Claudia Wilken approved the settlement on December 6, 2017. More than 43,000 Division I men's and women's basketball players and Football Bowl Subdivision football players who played during the period from March 2010 through the 2016–17 seasons will receive a payment based on the difference between this amount and the full cost of attendance at their respective schools, which averages approximately $6,763. In July 2018, the Ninth Circuit affirmed the district court's award of $40.8 million in attorneys' fees and $1.5 million in administrative costs to the *O'Bannon* plaintiffs because "the award of injunctive relief against the NCAA in an antitrust action brought by private parties is an 'excellent result.'" *O'Bannon v. NCAA,* 739 Fed. Appx. 890, 894 (9th Cir. 2018).

3. *Preserving Competitive Balance. Board of Regents* held that maintaining on-field competitive balance among NCAA universities that regularly compete against each other in intercollegiate athletics is a legitimate procompetitive justification for NCAA rules that restrict economic competition among them. "Competitive balance" has the dual meaning of "parity" (i.e., the extent to which all teams playing at the same level are able to play close and exciting games during a season of competition) and "potential to change" (i.e., teams' ability to improve their relative performance in terms of on-field success vis-à-vis other teams over time). Gary R. Roberts, *The NCAA, Antitrust, and Consumer Welfare,* 79 Tul. L. Rev. 2631, 2664-2665. (1996). Does preservation of competitive balance require uniform limits on student-athlete compensation within each level of intercollegiate athletics competition (e.g., Division I FBS and FCS, II, and III football)? Or is price competition for student-athletes' playing services among athletic conferences within each NCAA division a substantially less restrictive alternative means of maintaining competitive balance?

4. *Increasing Output of Intercollegiate Athletics.* The *O'Bannon* district court rejected the NCAA's defense that its amateurism rules enable its member schools to offer and fund women's sports and less popular men's sports because it "is not a legitimate procompetitive justification." *In re NCAA Student-Athlete Name & Likeness Licensing Litigation,* 37 F. Supp. 3d 1126, 1151 (N.D. Cal. 2014). It ruled: "The NCAA cannot restrain competition in the 'college education' market for Division I football and basketball recruits

or in the 'group licensing' market for Division I football and basketball teams' publicity rights in order to promote competition in those markets for women's sports or less prominent men's sports." *Id.* It further noted that the defense fails because financial support for these sports could be provided through less restrictive alternatives such as mandating "Division I schools and conferences redirect a greater portion of the licensing revenue generated by football and basketball to these other sports." *Id.* On the other hand, the court held that increasing "the total 'output' of Division I football and basketball, as measured by the total number of teams, players, scholarships, and games . . . is potentially procompetitive because it increases output in the relevant market." *Id.* at 1152. See generally Nathan Boninger, *Antitrust and the NCAA: Sexual Equality in Collegiate Athletics as a Procompetitive Justification for NCAA Compensation Restrictions*, 65 UCLA L. Rev. 754, 758-759 (2018) (advocating that maintaining equality of intercollegiate athletic opportunities for both sexes is a legitimate procompetitive justification under the Rule of Reason, which justifies NCAA cap on student-athlete financial aid at the full cost of attendance).

5.   In re NCAA Athletic Grant-In-Aid Cap Antitrust Litigation. In March 2019, a California federal district court (Judge Wilken) held that NCAA student-athlete amateurism eligibility rules (1) limiting the value of an athletics scholarship to the full cost of attendance; (2) prohibiting compensation and benefits unrelated to education over its value; and (3) limiting compensation and benefits related to education over its value for the services of Division I men's and women's and FBS football players "constitute horizontal price-fixing agreements enacted and enforced with monopsony power." *In re NCAA Athletic Grant-In-Aid Cap Antitrust Litigation*, 375 F.Supp.3d 1058, 1109 (N.D. Cal. 2019). It determined that none of these rules furthered the procompetitive objective of integrating these student-athletes into their respective academic communities and/or improved the academic outcomes or benefits they receive from a college education. The court concluded that the first two rules furthered the procompetitive objective of "help[ing] maintain consumer demand for college sports as a distinct product by preventing unlimited cash payments unrelated to education" and that there are "no less restrictive alternatives for achieving this objective." *Id.* at 1101. It permitted the NCAA to continue limiting the value of athletics scholarships to not less than the full cost of attendance and prohibiting additional compensation and benefits unrelated to education, thereby rejecting plaintiffs' request for an injunction against enforcement of any NCAA rules limiting compensation for their services (which would have created a competitive market subject to regulation by its member conferences).

Regarding the third rule, the court found no "procompetitive justification for caps on education-related benefits . . . inherently limited by their actual cost and that can be provided in kind, not in cash" (*Id.* at 1104), enjoining the NCAA's attempts to prohibit universities from providing tangible items related to the pursuit of academic studies (e.g., computers, musical instruments, science equipment), expenses for study abroad, and post-eligibility paid internships and scholarships to complete degrees at other institutions. Because such restrictions might maintain consumer demand for college sports, it permitted the NCAA "to limit academic and graduation awards and incentives . . . provided in cash or a cash-equivalent to a level that the record shows is not demand-reducing or inconsistent with NCAA amateurism." *Id.* at 1106. Because the NCAA currently permits student-athletes to receive cash-equivalent Visa cards valued at $5,600 for high levels of team performance in Division I basketball and FBS football (which expert testimony established had not reduced consumer demand for these sports), the court permanently enjoined the NCAA from limiting the annual value of university-provided academic and graduation awards and incentives to less than this amount. In summary, the court explained:

> Restricting non-cash education-related benefits and academic awards that can be provided on top of a grant-in-aid has not been proven to be necessary to preserving consumer demand for Division I basketball and FBS football as a product distinct from professional sports. Allowing each conference and its member schools to provide additional education-related benefits without NCAA caps and prohibitions, as well as academic awards, will help ameliorate their anticompetitive effects and may provide some of the compensation student-athletes would have received absent Defendants' agreement to restrain trade.

Id. at 1110.

Both sides have filed appeals, which are pending before the Ninth Circuit. Is the district court's ruling consistent with *Board of Regents*, specifically its dicta that the NCAA "needs ample room" to maintain "a revered tradition of amateurism in college sports"? Does its injunctive relief conflict with *O'Bannon*, which the NCAA contends held that NCAA rules limiting student-athletes' economic benefits to the value of the full cost of attendance at their respective universities are valid as a matter of law?

6. *Is Conditional Antitrust Immunity the Solution?* As a member of Congress, would you support adoption of a federal statute immunizing the NCAA and its member institutions from Sherman Act §1 antitrust liability conditioned on certain requirements they must satisfy to ensure that commercialized intercollegiate athletics are primarily an educational endeavour and that student-athletes receive valuable educational benefits in exchange for their playing services? See, e.g., Matthew J. Mitten & Stephen F. Ross, *A Regulatory Solution to Better Promote the Educational Values and Economic Sustainability of Intercollegiate Athletics*, 92 Ore. L. Rev. 837, 844 (2014) (advocating "establishment of an independent federal regulatory commission, which would provide an inclusive and transparent rule-making process readily accessible to all intercollegiate athletics stakeholders and the public. To ensure that its rules have a reasonable basis, we propose independent review through arbitration. Although the commission's rules would not be legal mandates, their voluntary adoption by the NCAA and its member institutions would immunize anticompetitive restraints in connection with big-time college sports from judicial scrutiny under federal and state antitrust laws."); Daniel E. Lazaroff, *Antitrust Exemption for the NCAA: Sound Policy or Letting the Fox Loose in the Henhouse?*, 41 Pepperdine Law Review 229, 248 (2014) (arguing that an antitrust exemption should not be given to the NCAA "[u]ntil and unless a sufficient regulatory scheme is devised to ensure that any commercial restraints on coaches' salaries and player 'compensation' would serve sound policy goals and expand overall athletic opportunities . . .").

PROBLEM 3-10

After a successful tryout, Talented Freshman (TF) was selected to be a "walk-on" member of the Big University football team. TF was not a heavily recruited high school football player, and he was not offered a scholarship to play football at any NCAA Football Bowl Subdivision (formerly Division I-A) university. TF was offered a partial athletic scholarship to play football by two NCAA Division II universities. NCAA Division III colleges and universities do not offer any athletic scholarships. Big University's head football coach wants to offer TF a full scholarship to play football during his freshman year. However, he cannot do so because Big University already has awarded 85 football scholarships, which is the maximum number that NCAA rules permit Division I FBS universities to award each year. TF feels he has earned a football scholarship and is very upset that Big University cannot give him one. He files an antitrust suit alleging that the NCAA's scholarship limit is an illegal output restriction designed to reduce the costs of producing Division I FBS football, which violates §1 of the Sherman Act. Does TF have a valid antitrust claim?

CHAPTER

4

Regulating Olympic and
International Athletics

A. INTRODUCTION

The Olympic Games and other international sports competitions such as the Fédération Internationale de Football Association (FIFA) World Cup demonstrate that sport is a universal cultural phenomenon, which is a tremendously popular and significant part of the world's twenty-first-century global economy, giving rise to numerous important national and international legal issues.

Because of the increasing globalization of sports and the historical European domination of the governance of Olympic and international sports competition, it is important to have a basic understanding of the European model of sport. Traditionally, European sport has been based on a sociocultural model, with the objective of promoting athletic participation opportunities for all through club sports. In Europe, a hierarchical or pyramid system of governance applies for both "amateur" and "professional" competition in a sport, with a worldwide regulatory authority at its apex. For example, within each country, regional federations govern soccer in their respective local areas; these regional federations are members of a national federation, which in turn is part of the Union of European Football Associations (UEFA), a confederation of 53 national federations recognized by soccer's international governing body, FIFA. Pursuant to a vertical solidarity system, the grassroots amateur clubs traditionally have received some financial support from the country's national federation and top-tier professional clubs, as well as some government subsidies. European sports leagues are "open" and have a promotion and relegation system; each year, the best two to four teams in a league are promoted to the next higher league and the corresponding worst teams are relegated to the next lower league. See generally Richard Parish and Samuli Miettinen, The Sporting Exception in European Union Law 17-22 (2008); James A. R. Nafziger, *European and North American Models of Sports Organization*, in Research Handbook on International Sports Law 88-111 (James A.R. Nafziger and Stephen F. Ross, eds.) (Edward Elgar Publishing 2011).

This chapter initially provides an overview of the Olympic Games and describes how Olympic sports are structured and governed pursuant to an international hierarchy based on the European model of sport. It then discusses how Olympic sports are internally governed within the United States and regulated by one of the few U.S. sports-specific statutes, the Ted Stevens Olympic and Amateur Sports Act. After considering the general reluctance of U.S. courts and other national courts to use their respective domestic laws to regulate Olympic and international sports competitions, this chapter describes the jurisdiction and role of the Court of Arbitration for Sport in resolving Olympic and international sports disputes (e.g., athlete disciplinary sanctions for misconduct, challenged competition results, and doping violations and sanctions).

1. Origin, History, and Objectives of the Olympic Games

The Olympic Games have been held during two distinct historical time periods. The Ancient Olympics began in 776 B.C. in Elis, Greece, in the valley of Olympia, to honor the mythical Greek god Zeus. The Olympics likely were not the first athletic competitions in Greece, but they represented the dawn of organized athletic activity for the Western world.

The first Olympic Games consisted of one event—a 200-meter footrace—and were subsequently expanded to include boxing, wrestling, chariot racing, and the pentathlon. Competitors included local residents in addition to those who lived outside the Greek city-states. Because of the highly competitive nature of the ancient Greeks, a victory at the Games was considered one of the greatest athletic accomplishments. The prize for winning was a simple olive tree branch, which the Greeks believed would transfer its sacred vitality to the recipient. This simple prize demonstrated the magnitude of the honor of an Olympic victory and emphasized the importance of athletics and competition in Greek life. As the Ancient Olympics grew in importance, athletes evolved from amateurs to professionals and began to train for their sports year-round, and to receive substantial gifts and money from their home cities and others.

The purpose of the Ancient Olympics, which is the same as for the modern Olympic Games (if not as easily recognizable today), was to promote goodwill and unity among different nations through athletic competition. To facilitate this objective, a peace agreement, called "ekecheiria," or "sacred truce," was established that provided for a three-month truce on fighting surrounding the time of the Olympic Games, which were held every four years. From their inception, the Ancient Games continued for almost 1,200 years without interruption. They were even held in 480 B.C. during the Persian War, and took place despite the Romans taking control of Greece in 146 B.C. The Games embodied the Greek ideal of transforming violent urges into playful athletic competition; they also provided a forum for Greeks from all city-states to gather in attempted unification through athletic competition and religious ceremonies. In A.D. 393, the Ancient Olympics were abolished by the Christian Byzantine emperor Theodosius I because they were perceived to be a pagan festival. See generally Nostos Hellenic Information Society (UK), *Brief History of the Olympic Games*, available at http://www.nostos.com/olympics.

In 1892, Baron Pierre de Courbetin, a French nobleman, initiated an effort to re-establish the Olympic Games. At the Congress of Paris in 1894, representatives of 13 nations, including the United States, met to create the modern Olympic

Games. The International Olympic Committee (IOC) was created, and the Olympic Games (initially consisting of only traditional summer Olympic events) were scheduled to be held every fourth year. Returning to their country of origin, in 1896 the first modern Olympic Games were held in Athens, Greece, in which 300 athletes from 13 countries participated in various events in ten sports.

Courbetin chose the Latin words "Citius, altius, fortius" as the motto of the modern Olympic Movement. It connotes not only athletic achievement, but also moral and educational development—"Citius: fast not only in the race, but with a quick and vibrant mind as well. Altius: higher, not only toward a coveted goal, but also toward the uplifting of an individual. Fortius: not only more courageous in the struggles on the field of play, but in life, also." Pierre de Courbetin, *Olympism—Selected Writings* at 585 (International Olympic Committee 2000). He emphasized that "[t]he most important thing in the Olympic Games is not winning but taking part; the essential thing in life is not conquering but fighting well." *Id.*

In 1914 Courbetin designed the now widely recognized Olympic rings, consisting of five interlocking rings of blue, yellow, black, green, and red with a white background. He explained that they "represent the five parts of the world now won over to Olympism, ready to accept its fruitful rivalries. In addition, the six colors combined in this way to reproduce the colors of every country without exception." *Id.* at 594.

The Olympic Winter Games began in 1924 in Chamonix, France, and were held in the same years as the Summer Games until 1986, when the IOC began scheduling Summer and Winter Olympic competitions in four-year cycles alternating two years apart. The Olympic Games were canceled in 1916, 1940, and 1944 because of World Wars I and II. In modern times, the Ancient Games' Olympic truce has been renewed by the IOC with the "view to protecting, as far as possible, the interests of the athletes and sport in general, and to encourage searching for peaceful and diplomatic solutions to the conflicts around the world." International Olympic Committee, *Olympic Truce*, available at https://www.olympic.org/olympic-truce. The Paralympic Games, first held in Rome, Italy, in 1960, with 400 participating athletes from 23 countries, arose out of the Stoke Mandeville Games, a 1948 competition in Great Britain for wheelchair athletes, in which 16 injured World War II servicemen and women participated in archery. International Paralympic Committee, *Paralympics—History of the Movement,* https://www.paralympic.org/the-ipc/history-of-the-movement.

2.   *Organization, Governance, and Structure of the Olympic Movement*

The modern Olympic Movement "is the concerted, organised, universal and permanent action, carried out under the supreme authority of the IOC, of all individuals and entities who are inspired by the values of Olympism." International Olympic Committee, *Olympic Charter*, Fundamental Principles of Olympism (in force as from 9 October 2018). "Olympism is a philosophy of life, exalting and combining in a balanced whole the qualities of body, will and mind. Blending sport with culture and education, Olympism seeks to create a way of life based on the joy of effort, the educational value of good example, social responsibility and respect for universal fundamental ethical principles." *Id.* Numerous organizations and persons are part of the Olympic Movement, including the International Olympic Committee (IOC); international sports federations (IFs), the international governing bodies for each Olympic sport; National Olympic Committees (NOCs); national governing bodies (NGBs) or national federations (NFs) (the term generally used in European countries) for each Olympic sport in each country; the World Anti-Doping Agency (WADA); Court of Arbitration for Sport (CAS); and the Olympic Museum, as well as thousands of individual athletes, judges, and coaches.

The Olympic Charter governs the Olympic Movement, which codifies the fundamental principles, rules, and bylaws adopted by the IOC, and establishes rules for the production and operation of the Olympic Games. It states that the IOC is the "supreme authority" of the Olympic Movement, and all members are bound by its provisions and the IOC's decisions regarding its application or interpretation. *Id.*, Chap. 1, Rule 1 (1 and 4). The IOC is an "international non-governmental not-for-profit organization" domiciled in Lausanne, Switzerland. *Id.*, Chap. 2, Rule 15 (1). It is the "authority of last resort on any question concerning the Olympic Games" (*Id.*, Chap. 5, Rule 58), although those adversely affected by an IOC decision may submit the dispute to final and binding arbitration before the Court of Arbitration for Sport. *Id.*, Chap. 6, Rule 61. Despite its plenary worldwide governing authority, the IOC must rely on the agreement of the IFs and NOCs—and the willingness of national governments—to enforce its decisions and those of the CAS.

The IOC is governed by its individual members and an executive board comprised of the IOC president, four vice-presidents, and ten other members, all of whom are elected by secret ballot for an eight-year term. IOC members are elected individuals who serve as its representatives in their respective home countries (105 persons as of June 2019), but they are not representatives of their respective countries of residence or their country's official delegates. The current IOC president, Thomas Bach of Germany, who began his term in September 2013, frequently states: "[S]port is one of the few things with the power to unite all people in an increasingly fragile world. Sport is an anchor of stability for so many people, regardless of background, nationality or belief." Thomas Bach, *Sport: An Anchor of Society in a Fragile World,* available at https://www.olympic .org/news/sport-an-anchor-of-stability-in-a-fragile-world (30 December 2016).

Like the IOC, the IFs are private nongovernmental organizations. Each IF is recognized by the IOC as the worldwide governing body for a particular sport (or group of sports); its members are the NGBs or NFs that serve as its affiliates for the subject sport(s) in each country. An IF's statutes, practices, and activities must conform to the Olympic Charter and be approved by the IOC Executive Board. The IFs establish and enforce the rules for their respective sports; establish eligibility criteria for Olympic sports competition (subject to IOC approval); select referees, judges, or umpires for competitions; establish and provide an internal dispute resolution process; and are responsible for the technical control and direction of their sports during the Olympic Games. There are approximately 70 summer, winter, and IOC-recognized IFs, which have formed the following associations to discuss their common issues and to establish their events calendars: Association of Summer Olympic International Federations (ASOIF), the Association of International Olympic Winter Sports Federations (AIOWF), the Association of the IOC Recognised International Sports Federations (ARISF), and the General Association of International Sports Federations (GAISF).

There are more than 200 NOCs, which develop and protect the Olympic Movement within their respective countries. Most represent a single nation, although the IOC does recognize independent territories, commonwealths, protectorates, and geographical areas as national governing bodies for Olympic sports. The NOCs are responsible for encouraging the development of high-performance sport and sports opportunities for all their citizens; recognizing NGBs or NFs for Olympic sports; preventing discrimination and violence in sport; and adopting and implementing the World Anti-Doping Code. Each NOC has exclusive authority regarding the representation of its country at the Olympic Games, and selects its Olympic teams and athletes based on the recommendations of the NGB for the particular sport. The NOCs also have the authority to designate which cities may apply to host the Olympics within their respective countries.

In carrying out their responsibilities, NOCs frequently cooperate with government agencies and other nongovernmental bodies to promote sports. Each NOC must preserve its "autonomy and resist all pressures of any kind, including but not limited to political, legal, religious or economic pressures which may prevent them from complying with the Olympic Charter." Olympic Charter, *supra*, Chap. 4, Rule 27 (6). The NOCs are subject to the laws of their respective nations as well as the provisions of the Olympic Charter and the governing authority of the IOC. For example, the United States Olympic and Paralympic Committee (USOPC) must comply with the Ted Stevens Olympic and Amateur Sports Act, 36 USC §§220501 et seq., and other applicable federal and state laws.

An NGB or NF is the national governing authority for a particular sport that is affiliated with the corresponding IF and is recognized by the country's NOC. It must comply with the Olympic Charter and IF rules as well as "exercise a specific, real and on-going sports activity." Olympic Charter, *supra*, Chap. 4, Rule 29. It serves a function at the national level similar to that of the corresponding IF at the international level of athletic competition. Each NGB recognized by the USOPC (e.g., USA Track & Field) serves as the United States' member representative in the IF for its particular sport (e.g., IAAF). Like NOCs, NGBs and NFs also are subject to applicable domestic laws within their respective countries.

In summary, the following diagram illustrates that a series of hierarchical contractual relationships defines the Olympic Movement's governing structure:

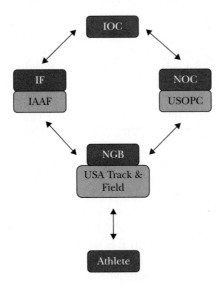

The IOC is responsible for ensuring the regular celebration of the Olympic Games and Winter Olympic Games and exclusively owns all related rights. It selects a host city entrusted with responsibility for organizing the Olympic Games or Winter Olympic Games along with the country's NOC, which forms an Organizing Committee for the Olympic Games (OCOG) to fulfill all responsibilities connected with the organization and hosting of the Olympic Games. An OCOG must treat every sport equally; abide by the IFs' rules of competition; ensure that no political demonstrations disrupt the Games; construct the necessary venues, stadiums, and other facilities; provide food and lodging for all athletes and officials; provide medical services; and accommodate the media. In addition, in light of recent world events, OCOGs now face the daunting task of ensuring the security of those competing in and attending the Games. All profits realized by the host city, OCOG, or NOC from the Games must be "applied to the development of the Olympic Movement and of sport." Olympic Charter, *supra*, Chap. 5, Rule 32 (5).

The Olympic Charter states that "[t]he Olympic Games are competitions between athletes in individual or team events, and not between countries." Olympic Charter, *supra*, Chap. 1, Rule 6 (1). (In reality, is this an accurate characterization given the athletic rivalries that have developed among various countries, including the United States and Russia)? Is this objective furthered when the sports media list medal counts by country and promote a strong spirit of nationalism?) To participate in the Olympic Games, a competing athlete must satisfy several conditions, including being a national of the country of the IOC-recognized NOC that is entering him or her as well as compliance with the Olympic Charter, applicable IF rules for the subject sport, and the World Anti-Doping Code. Olympic Charter, *supra*, Chap. 5, Rules 40-43. The Olympic Charter prohibits any "kind of demonstration or political, religious or racial propaganda" in any Olympic venues by athletes and others. Olympic Charter, *supra*, Chap. 5, Rule 50.

B. REGULATION OF OLYMPIC SPORTS WITHIN THE UNITED STATES

Participation in the Olympics, the Paralympic Games, and other international athletic competitions is an important part of U.S. culture. Since the modern Olympic Games began in 1896, the United States has hosted the Olympic Games in 1904 (St. Louis), 1932 (Los Angeles), 1984 (Los Angeles), and 1996 (Atlanta); and the Winter Olympic Games in 1932 (Lake Placid), 1960 (Squaw Valley), 1980 (Lake Placid), and 2002 (Salt Lake City). Los Angeles will host the 2028 Olympic Games. The United States has entered teams each year that the Olympic Games have been held with the exception of 1980, when it boycotted the Moscow Games to protest the Soviet Union's military invasion of Afghanistan. Since 1896 through the 2018 Olympic Winter Games, U.S. athletes and teams have won 2,515 medals in the Summer Games (1,023 gold, 788 silver, and 704 bronze) and 305 medals in the Winter Games (105 gold, 110 silver, and 90 bronze). The United States team has won the most combined total medals (2,367) in the Paralympic Summer Games and Paralympic Winter Games (847 gold, 778 silver, and 742 bronze medals).

1.   Basis of Governing Body Authority and Legal Limits Thereon

DeFRANTZ v. U.S. OLYMPIC COMMITTEE

492 F. Supp. 1181 (D.D.C. 1980)

Pratt, District Judge.

Plaintiffs, 25 athletes and one member of the Executive Board of defendant United States Olympic Committee (USOC), have moved for an injunction barring defendant USOC from carrying out a resolution, adopted by the USOC House of Delegates on April 12, 1980, not to send an American team to participate in the Games of the XXIInd Olympiad to be held in Moscow in the summer of 1980. Plaintiffs allege that in preventing American athletes from competing in the Summer Olympics, defendant has exceeded its statutory powers and has abridged plaintiffs' constitutional rights.

For the reasons discussed below, we find that plaintiffs have failed to state a claim upon which relief can be granted. Accordingly, we deny plaintiffs' claim for injunctive and declaratory relief and dismiss the action.

THE FACTS

In essence, the action before us involves a dispute between athletes who wish to compete in the Olympic Games to be held in Moscow this summer and the United States Olympic Committee, which has denied them that opportunity in the wake of the invasion and continued occupation of Afghanistan by Soviet military forces. Because this dispute confronts us with questions concerning the statutory authority of the USOC, its place and appropriate role in the international Olympic movement, and its relationship to the United States Government and with certain United States officials, we begin with a brief discussion of the organizational structure of the Olympic Games and the facts which have brought this action before us. These facts are not in dispute.

According to its Rules and By-laws, the International Olympic Committee (IOC) governs the Olympic movement and owns the rights of the Olympic games. IOC Rules provide that National Olympic Committees (NOC) may be established "as the sole authorities responsible for the representation of the respective countries at the Olympic Games," so long as the NOC's rules and regulations are approved by the IOC. The USOC is one such National Olympic Committee.

The USOC is a corporation created and granted a federal charter by Congress in 1950. Pub L. No. 81-805, 64 Stat. 899. This charter was revised by the Amateur Sports Act of 1978 Pub. L. No. 95-606, 92 Stat. 3045, 36 U.S.C. §§ 371 et seq. Under this statute, defendant USOC has "exclusive jurisdiction" and authority over participation and representation of the United States in the Olympic Games.

The routine procedure initiating the participation of a national team in Olympic competition is the acceptance by the NOC of an invitation from the Olympic Organizing Committee for the particular games. In accordance with this routine procedure under IOC Rules, the Moscow Olympic Organizing Committee extended an invitation to the USOC to participate in the summer games. Recent international and domestic events, however, have made acceptance of this invitation, which must come on or before May 24, 1980, anything but routine.

On December 27, 1979, the Soviet Union launched an invasion of its neighbor, Afghanistan. That country's ruler was deposed and killed and a new government was installed. . . .

President Carter termed the invasion a threat to the security of the Persian Gulf area as well as a threat to world peace and stability and he moved to take direct sanctions against the Soviet Union. . . .

As the affidavit of then Acting Secretary of State Warren Christopher makes clear, the Administration was concerned that "[t]he presence of American competitors would be taken by the Soviets as evidence that their invasion had faded from memory or was not a matter of great consequence or concern to this nation." The Administration's concern was sharpened because "[t]he Soviet Union has made clear that it intends the Games to serve important national political ends. For the U.S.S.R., international sports competition is an instrument of government policy and a means to advance foreign policy goals."

With these concerns in mind, the Administration strenuously urged a boycott of the Moscow games. On January 20, 1980, President Carter wrote the President of the United States Olympic Committee to urge that the USOC propose to the IOC that the 1980 summer games be transferred from Moscow, postponed, or cancelled if the Soviet forces were not withdrawn within a month. On January 23, 1980, the President delivered his State of the Union Message, in which he said that he would not support sending American athletes to Moscow while Soviet military forces remained in Afghanistan.

Following these statements, the United States House of Representatives passed, by a vote of 386 to 12, a Concurrent Resolution opposing participation by United States athletes in the Moscow Games unless Soviet troops were withdrawn from Afghanistan by February 20th. The Senate passed a similar resolution by a vote of 88 to 4. . . .

After what USOC President Kane describes in his affidavit as "full, open, complete and orderly debate by advocates of each motion," the House of Delegates, on a secret ballot, passed by a vote of 1,604 to 798, a resolution [not to enter a U.S. team in the Moscow Olympics]. . . .

Plaintiffs describe these attempts by the Administration to persuade the USOC to vote not to send an American team to Moscow as "a campaign to coerce defendant USOC into compliance with the President's demand for a boycott of the Olympic Games." In addition, plaintiffs' complaint alleges that the President and other Executive Branch officials threatened to terminate federal funding of the USOC and that they raised the possibility of revoking the federal income tax exemption of the USOC if the USOC did not support the President's decision to boycott the 1980 Games. The complaint also alleges that these officials state that the Federal government would provide increased funding to the USOC if the USOC supported a boycott. . . .

Plaintiffs allege that unredressed, these violations will result in great and irreparable injury to the athletes. "Many would lose a once-in-a-lifetime opportunity to participate in the Olympic Games, and the honor and prestige that such participation affords. Most of the class members are at or near their physical peaks at the present time and will not physically be capable of reaching the same or higher levels at a later period of their lives."

In summary, plaintiffs ask this court to declare the April 12, 1980 resolution of the USOC House of Delegates null and void because it violated statutory authority and constitutional provisions and to permanently enjoin the USOC from carrying out that resolution. . . .

ANALYSIS

1. THE AMATEUR SPORTS ACT OF 1978

Plaintiffs allege in their complaint that by its decision not to send an American team to compete in the summer Olympic Games in Moscow, defendant USOC has violated the Amateur Sports Act of 1978. . . . Reduced to their essentials, these allegations are that the Act does not give, and that Congress intended to deny, the USOC the authority to decide not to enter an American team in the Olympics, except perhaps for sports-related reasons, and that the Act guarantees to certain athletes a right to compete in the Olympic Games which defendant denied them. . . .

(a) *The USOC's Authority Not to Send a Team to Moscow*

The United States Olympic Committee was first incorporated and granted a federal charter in 1950. However, predecessors to the now federally-chartered USOC have existed since 1896, and since that time, they have exercised the authority granted by the International Olympic Committee to represent the United States as its National Olympic Committee in matters pertaining to participation in Olympic games. It is unquestioned by plaintiffs that under the International Olympic Committees Rules and By-laws, the National Olympic Committees have the right to determine their nation's participation in the Olympics. IOC Rule 24B provides that "NOCs shall be the sole authorities responsible for the representation of the respective countries at the Olympic Games . . ." and Chapter 5, paragraph 7 of the By-laws to Rule 24 provides that [r]*epresentation* covers the decision to participate. . . ." (emphasis supplied). Nothing in the IOC Charter, Rules or By-laws requires a NOC, such as the USOC, to accept an invitation to participate in any particular Olympic contest and the President of the IOC has said that participation in the Olympic games is entirely voluntary. As defendant has argued, an invitation to participate is just that, an invitation which may be accepted or declined.

Because defendant USOC clearly has the power under IOC Rules to decide not to enter an American team in Olympic competition, the question then becomes whether the Amateur Sports Act of 1978, which rewrote the USOC's charter, denies the USOC that power. . . .

Plaintiffs' argument is simple and straightforward: The Act by its terms does not expressly confer on the USOC the power to decline to participate in the Olympic Games, and if any such power can be inferred from the statute, the power must be exercised for sports-related reasons. Defendant and the Government respond that the Act gives the USOC broad powers, including the authority to decide not to accept an invitation to send an American team to the Olympics.

The principal substantive powers of the USOC are found in § 375(a) of the Act. In determining whether the USOC's authority under the Act encompasses the right to decide not to participate in an Olympic contest, we must read these provisions in the context in which they were written. In writing this legislation, Congress did not create a new relationship between the USOC and the IOC. Rather, it recognized an already long-existing relationship between the two and statutorily legitimized that relationship with a federal charter and federal incorporation. The legislative history demonstrates Congressional awareness that the USOC and its predecessors, as the National Olympic Committee for the United States, have had a continuing relationship with the IOC since 1896. Congress was necessarily aware that a National Olympic Committee is a creation and a creature of the International Olympic Committee, to whose rules and regulations it must conform. The NOC gets its power and its authority from the IOC, the sole proprietor and owner of the Olympic Games.

In view of Congress' obvious awareness of these facts, we would expect that if Congress intended to limit or deny to the USOC powers it already enjoyed as a National Olympic Committee, such limitation or denial would be clear and explicit. No such language appears in the statute. . . . [W]e find a compatibility and not a conflict between the Act and the IOC Rules on the issue of the authority of the USOC to decide whether or not to accept an invitation to field an American team at the Olympics. The language of the statute is broad enough to confer this authority, and we find that Congress must have intended that the USOC exercise that authority in this area, which it already enjoyed because of its long-standing relationship with the IOC. We accordingly conclude that the USOC has the authority to decide not to send an American team to the Olympics.

Plaintiffs next argue that if the USOC does have the authority to decide not to accept an invitation to send an American team to the Moscow Olympics, that decision must be based on "sports-related considerations." . . .

The provision on which plaintiffs place reliance by analogy is specifically concerned with eliminating the feuding between various amateur athletic organizations and national governing bodies which for so long characterized amateur athletics. As all parties recognize, this friction, such as the well-publicized power struggles between the NCAA and the AAU, was a major reason for passage of the Act, and the provisions plaintiffs cite, among others, are aimed at eliminating this senseless strife, which the Senate and House Committee reports indicate had dramatically harmed the ability of the United States to compete effectively in international competition. In order to eliminate this internecine squabbling, the Act elevated the USOC to a supervisory role over the various amateur athletic organizations, and provided that the USOC establish procedures for the swift and equitable settlement of these disputes. As indicated above, it also directed that the national governing bodies of the various sports could only withhold their approvals of international competition for sports-related reasons. Previously, many of these bodies had withheld their sanction of certain athletic competitions in order to further their own interests at the expense of other groups and to the detriment of athletes wishing to participate.

In brief, this sports-related limitation is intimately tied to the specific purpose of curbing the arbitrary and unrestrained power of various athletic organizations subordinate to the USOC not to allow athletes to compete in international competition below the level of the Olympic Games and the Pan American Games. This purpose has nothing to do with a decision by the USOC to exercise authority granted by the IOC to decide not to participate in an Olympic competition. . . .

We therefore conclude that the USOC not only had the authority to decide not to send an American team to the summer Olympics, but also that it could do so for reasons not directly related to sports considerations.

(b)   Athletes' Statutory Right to Compete in the Olympics

Plaintiffs argue that the Act provides, "in express terms" an "Athlete's Bill of Rights," pointing to the following provisions in the Act's "objects and purposes" section, which directs that the USOC shall:

provide for the swift resolution of conflicts and disputes involving amateur athletes, national governing bodies, and amateur sports organizations, and protect
the opportunity of any amateur athlete, coach, trainer, manager, administrator, or
official to participate in amateur athletic competition. (emphasis supplied).

36 U.S.C. § 374(8). . . .

The Senate Report makes clear that the language relied on by plaintiffs is
not designed to provide any substantive guarantees, let alone a Bill of Rights.
Further, to the extent that any guarantees of a right to compete are included in
the USOC Constitution as a result of this provision, they do not include a right
that amateur athletes may compete in the Olympic Games despite a decision by
the USOC House of Delegates not to accept an invitation to enter an American
team in the competition. This provision simply was not designed to extend so
far. Rather, it was designed to remedy the jurisdictional disputes among amateur
athletic bodies, not disputes between athletes and the USOC itself over the exercise of the USOC's discretion not to participate in the Olympics.

(c)   Statutory Cause of Action

Plaintiffs argue that they have a private cause of action under the Amateur
Sports Act of 1978 to maintain an action to enforce their rights under that Act.
This argument assumes (1) the existence of a right and (2) the capability of
enforcing that right by a private cause of action. As the foregoing discussion
establishes, we have found that the statute does not guarantee plaintiffs a right
to compete in the Olympics if the USOC decides not to send an American team
to the Olympic Games and we have found that defendant has violated no provision of the Act. Thus, the "right" the plaintiffs seek to enforce under the Act
simply does not exist. (Plaintiffs have pointed to no express private right of
action in the statute, and none exists). Under these circumstances, we cannot
find that plaintiffs have an implied private right of action under the Amateur
Sports Act to enforce a right which does not exist. . . .

[W]e find that plaintiffs have no implied private right of action under the
Amateur Sports Act of 1978 to maintain this suit.

2.   CONSTITUTIONAL CLAIMS

Plaintiffs have alleged that the decision of the USOC not to enter an American
team in the summer Olympics has violated certain rights guaranteed to
plaintiffs under the First, Fifth and Ninth Amendments to the United States
Constitution. This presents us with two questions: (1) whether the USOC's
decision was "governmental action" (state action), and, assuming state action
is found, (2) whether the USOC's decision abridged any constitutionally protected rights.

(a)   State Action

Although federally chartered, defendant is a private organization. Because
the Due Process Clause of the Fifth Amendment, on which plaintiffs place great
reliance, applies only to actions by the federal government, plaintiffs must show
that the USOC vote is a "governmental act," i.e., state action. . . .

Plaintiffs clearly recognize this, but they argue that by the actions of certain
federal officials, the federal government initiated, encouraged, and approved
of the result reached (i.e., the vote of the USOC not to send an American team
to the summer Olympics). Plaintiffs advance a novel theory. Essentially, their

argument is that the campaign of governmental persuasion, personally led by President Carter, crossed the line from "governmental recommendation," which plaintiffs find acceptable and presumably necessary to the operation of our form of government, into the area of "affirmative pressure that effectively places the government's prestige behind the challenged action," and thus, results in state action. We cannot agree. . . .

Here there is no such control. The USOC is an independent body, and nothing in its chartering statute gives the federal government the right to control that body or its officers. Furthermore, the facts here do not indicate that the federal government was able to exercise any type of "de facto" control over the USOC. The USOC decided by a secret ballot of its House of Delegates. The federal government may have had the power to prevent the athletes from participating in the Olympics even if the USOC had voted to allow them to participate, but it did not have the power to make them vote in a certain way. All it had was the power of persuasion. We cannot equate this with control. To do so in cases of this type would be to open the door and usher the courts into what we believe is a largely nonjusticiable realm, where they would find themselves in the untenable position of determining whether a certain level, intensity, or type of "Presidential" or "Administration" or "political" pressure amounts to sufficient control over a private entity so as to invoke federal jurisdiction.

We accordingly find that the decision of the USOC not to send an American team to the summer Olympics was not state action, and therefore, does not give rise to an actionable claim for the infringements of the constitutional rights alleged.

(b)   Constitutionally Protected Rights

Assuming arguendo that the vote of the USOC constituted state action, we turn briefly to plaintiffs' contention that by this action they have been deprived of their constitutional rights to liberty, to self-expression, to travel, and to pursue their chosen occupation of athletic endeavor. Were we to find state action in this case, we would conclude that defendant USOC has violated no constitutionally protected right of plaintiffs. . . .

Plaintiffs have been unable to draw our attention to any court decision which finds that the rights allegedly violated here enjoy constitutional protection, and we can find none. Plaintiffs would expand the constitutionally-protected scope of liberty and self-expression to include the denial of an amateur athlete's right to compete in an Olympic contest when that denial was the result of a decision by a supervisory athletic organization acting well within the limits of its authority. Defendant has not denied plaintiffs the right to engage in every amateur athletic competition. Defendant has not denied plaintiffs the right to engage in their chosen occupation. Defendant has not even denied plaintiffs the right to travel, only the right to travel for one specific purpose. We can find no justification and no authority for the expansive reading of the Constitution which plaintiffs urge. To find as plaintiffs recommend would be to open the floodgates to a torrent of lawsuits. The courts have correctly recognized that many of life's disappointments, even major ones, do not enjoy constitutional protection. This is one such instance.

At this point, we find it appropriate to note that we have respect and admiration for the discipline, sacrifice, and perseverance which earns young men and women the opportunity to compete in the Olympic Games. Ordinarily, talent alone has determined whether an American would have the privilege of participating in the Olympics. This year, unexpectedly, things are different. We express no view on the merits of the decision made. We do express our understanding of the deep disappointment and frustrations felt by thousands of American athletes. In doing so, we also recognize that the responsibilities of citizenship often fall more heavily on some than on others. Some are called to military duty. Others never serve. Some return from military service unscathed. Others never return. These are the simple, although harsh, facts of life, and they are immutable.

NOTES AND QUESTIONS

1. *USOPC's Contractual and Legal Obligations.* In June 2019, the USOC changed its name to the United States Olympic and Paralympic Committee (USOPC) to be more inclusive by putting "sports for those with physical and intellectual impairments on the same level as those with exceptional abilities." As the *DeFrantz* court observed, the USOPC is authorized by the IOC to represent the United States in all matters relating to participation in the Olympic Games. It is bound by contract to follow the IOC's Charter, rules and regulations, and executive board decisions. Did it comply with its obligation to resist political pressure not to do anything contrary to the Olympic Charter? If it violated the Olympic Charter, would the *DeFrantz* plaintiffs have a valid legal basis for obtaining effective relief from a U.S. court? For background information and an in-depth analysis of the U.S. boycott of the 1980 Olympic Games, see James A. R. Nafziger, International Sports Law (2d ed.) at 260-264 (Transnational Publishers, Inc. 2004). In addition to the United States, more than 60 other countries, including Japan, West Germany, China, the Philippines, Argentina, and Canada, were part of this boycott. In response, 14 Eastern Bloc countries including the Soviet Union, Cuba, and East Germany (but not Romania) boycotted the 1984 Olympic Games in Los Angeles.

   The USOPC also must comply with the provisions of the Amateur Sports Act (ASA), which was amended in 1998 by the Ted Stevens Olympic and Amateur Sports Act, 36 U.S.C. §220501 et seq. It has a federal statutory obligation to ensure "the most competent representation possible" for the U.S. in each event of the Olympic, Paralympic, and Pan-American Games. 36 U.S.C. §220503(4). Its mission is "[t]o support U.S. Olympic and Paralympic athletes in achieving sustained competitive excellence while demonstrating the values of the Olympic Movement, thereby inspiring all Americans." United States Olympic Committee, *Bylaws of the United States Olympic Committee*, §2.1 (effective March 7, 2019), available at http://www.teamusa.org/Footer/Legal/Governance-Documents.

   What if the USOPC has conflicting obligations under IOC rules and federal law? For example, the IOC requires that a majority of the members of an NOC's governing body must be affiliated with the Olympic Movement, but Congress enacted legislation requiring that a majority of the USOC's board of directors be independent. During June 2003 congressional hearings regarding this legislation, Senator John McCain asked why "a corporation chartered by the U.S. Congress has to comply with the IOC." Vicki Michaelis, *McCain Seeks Swift USOC Fix*, USA Today, June 25, 2003, at 8C. See *Michels v. USOC*, 741 F.2d 155, 159 (7th Cir. 1984) (J. Posner, concurring) (observing that an international sports governing body "can thumb its collective nose at the U.S. Olympic Committee" for disregarding its rules and that the IOC could disqualify an American team); *Akiyama v. U.S. Judo Inc.*, 181 F. Supp. 2d 1179, 1188 (W.D. Wash. 2002) (noting that a U.S. court's invalidation of an NGB's rule because it violates federal law prohibiting religious discrimination "would have no force over international organizations who are not parties to this litigation or in international competitions such as the Olympics and World Championships").

2. *USOPC's Governing Authority.* As the coordinating body within the U.S. for Olympic and international athletic competition, the USOPC selects one sports organization as the NGB for each Olympic sport. With some exceptions, the USOPC effectively acts as the NGB for Paralympics sports in the U.S. The ASA requires that arbitration be used to finally resolve disputes regarding which organization is entitled to be the NGB for a particular sport, and the USOPC is bound to accept a judicially confirmed arbitration award. *United States Wrestling Federation v. Wrestling Division of the AAU, Inc.*, 545 F. Supp. 1053 (N.D. Ohio 1982).

3. *USOPC and NGBs Not State Actors.* The U.S. Supreme Court has confirmed that the USOPC is a private entity, not a state actor, whose conduct is not subject to the constraints of the federal constitution. In *San Francisco Arts & Athletics, Inc. v. United States Olympic Committee*, 483 U.S. 522, 543-44 (1987), the Court explained:

> The fact that Congress granted it a corporate charter does not render the USOC a [g]overnment agent. All corporations act under charters granted by a government, usually by a State. They do not thereby lose their essentially private character. . . . Moreover, the intent on the part of Congress to help the USOC obtain funding does not change the analysis. The Government may subsidize private entities without assuming constitutional responsibility for their actions.

Although the USOC's activities serve a national interest, the Court concluded that the coordination of amateur sports is not a traditional governmental function and found no evidence that the federal government coerced or significantly encouraged the USOC's exercise of its exclusive control over the Olympic marks.

For similar reasons, lower courts have held that the U.S. NGBs also are not "state actors"; therefore, their rules and conduct are not subject to the constraints of the federal constitution. *Behagen v. Amateur Basketball Assn. of the United States*, 884 F.2d 524 (10th Cir. 1989); *Harding v. United States Figure Skating Assn.*, 851 F. Supp. 1476 (D. Ore. 1994), *vacated on other grounds*, 879 F. Supp. 1053 (1995).

4. *No Private Right of Action Under ASA.* The ASA does not create any substantive athletic participation rights that athletes can enforce in litigation against the USOPC or an NGB. Consistent with *DeFrantz*, courts have ruled that athletes have no implied private right of action under the ASA. See, e.g., *Slaney v. International Amateur Athletic Federation*, 244 F.3d 580 (7th Cir. 2001); *Martinez v. USOC*, 802 F.2d 1275 (10th Cir. 1986); *Oldfield v. Athletic Congress*, 779 F.2d 505 (9th Cir. 1985). On September 27, 2006, Congress amended the ASA to expressly state that it creates no private right of action for athletes to sue the [USOPC] or an NGB. 36 U.S.C. § 220505(b)(9).

5. *ASA Preemption of State Law Claims.* In *Slaney v. Int'l Amateur Athletic Federation*, 244 F.3d 580 (7th Cir.), *cert. denied,* 534 U.S. 828 (2001), the Seventh Circuit ruled that middle-distance runner Mary Decker Slaney's state contract and tort claims against the USOPC, which arose out of her suspension from track and field competition for a doping offense, are preempted by the ASA:

> Beginning with the often quoted language from the concurrence in *Michels v. United States Olympic Committee*, the district court reiterated that "there can be few less suitable bodies than the federal courts for determining the eligibility, or procedures for determining the eligibility, of athletes to participate in the Olympic Games." 741 F.2d 155, 159 (7th Cir. 1984) (Posner, J., concurring). From there, the court cited numerous cases which have adopted the principle that eligibility decisions fall within the USOC's exclusive jurisdiction over all matters pertaining to United States participation in the Olympic Games. For example, in *Dolan v. United States Equestrian Team, Inc.*, 257 N.J. Super. 314, 608 A.2d 434, 437 (App. Div. 1992), the court focused on the need for uniformity in determining questions of eligibility, and held "that it would be inappropriate to attribute different or unique meanings to [the Amateur Sports Act's] provisions in New Jersey and thus create a jurisdictional sanctuary from the Congressional determination that these types of disputes should be resolved outside the judicial processes." Similarly, in *Walton-Floyd v. United States Olympic Committee*, 965 S.W.2d 35, 40 (Tex. Ct. App. 1998), the court noted that "[t]he interest of maintaining consistent interpretations among jurisdictions requires the Act to preempt claims asserted under state tort law. To hold a common law duty exists outside the scope of the Act, thereby enabling an individual athlete to bring suit, threatens to override legislative intent and opens the door to inconsistent interpretations of the Act." We agree with the district court and the courts in *Dolan* and *Walton-Floyd* that strict questions of athletes' eligibility are preempted by the Amateur Sports Act's grant of exclusive jurisdiction to the USOC over all matters pertaining to United States participation in the Olympic Games.

Id. at 594-595.

In *Lee v. United States Taekwondo Union*, 331 F. Supp. 2d 1252 (D. Haw. 2004), the plaintiff alleged that he was removed as coach of the 2004 U.S. Olympic taekwondo team because of his Korean ancestry. Consistent with *Slaney*, the court held that his state-law claims challenging the national governing body's eligibility requirements, and his seeking reinstatement as coach of the team, were preempted by the ASA. It ruled that the ASA does not supersede or nullify federal antidiscrimination laws and permitted him to assert his federal race discrimination claim under 42 U.S.C. §1981. Although he could recover money damages for successfully proving his claim at trial, the court refused to grant preliminary injunctive relief ordering his reinstatement, because doing so would interfere with the USOC's exclusive authority to establish a process for resolving Olympic sport participation disputes pursuant to the ASA, which is discussed *infra*.

6. *Implied Antitrust Immunity.* Because the ASA provides the USOPC with "exclusive jurisdiction . . . over all matters pertaining to United States participation in the Olympic Games, the Paralympic Games, and the Pan-American Games, including representation of the United States in the games" (36 U.S.C. § 220503(3)), courts have held that the USOPC and NGBs have implied immunity from antitrust claims arising out of an athlete's ineligibility to participate in an Olympic sport. *Behagen v. Amateur Basketball Assn.*

of the United States, 884 F.2d 524, 529 (10th Cir. 1989) (antitrust immunity for NGB's enforcement of IF's athlete eligibility rules). See also *Gold Medal LLC v. USA Track & Field,* 899 F.3d 712 (9th Cir. 2018) (regulations restricting commercial advertising on athlete apparel during Olympic Trials are immune from antitrust challenge because they enable USOPC and its NGBs to generate sponsorship revenues to support U.S. teams' participation in the Olympic Games); *JES Properties v. USA Equestrian,* 458 F.3d 1224 (11th Cir. 2006) (an NGB rule that minimizes event scheduling conflicts and furthers congressional intent regarding governance of amateur athletics is immune from antitrust scrutiny); but see *Championsworld LLC v. United States Soccer Federation, Inc.,* 726 F. Supp. 2d 961, 970 (N.D. Ill. 2010) (because the U.S. NGB for soccer "has no clear mandate from Congress to govern the whole of professional soccer in the U.S.," it "is not entitled to an exemption from the antitrust laws regarding professional soccer, except to the extent necessary for [it] to oversee Olympic and related events"); *TYR Sport Inc. v. Warnaco Swimwear Inc.,* 679 F. Supp. 2d 1120 (C.D. Cal. 2009) (USA Swimming has no implied antitrust immunity from the claim that it conspired with Speedo, a corporate sponsor, to exclusively promote, to disparage a competing manufacturer's high-end competitive swimwear, and to persuade Olympic-caliber swimmers to switch to Speedo's "LZR Racer" suit).

2. Legal Framework for Resolving Domestic Athlete Participation Disputes

The USOPC generally grants the recognized NGB for each sport the authority to select U.S. athletes to participate in the Olympic, Paralympic, and Pan-American Games as well as other international athletic competitions. An NGB must provide all athletes with an equal opportunity to participate "without discrimination on the basis of race, color, religion, sex, age, or national origin." 36 U.S.C. §220522(a)(8). Each NGB has an affirmative duty to encourage and support athletic participation opportunities for women and those with disabilities. 36 U.S.C. §220524(6)-(7). An NGB's eligibility and participation criteria for U.S. athletes to participate in the Olympic, Paralympic, and Pan-American Games must be consistent with those of the IF for its sport. 36 U.S.C. §220522(a)(14). An NGB has plenary domestic authority to regulate Olympic and other international athletic competition in a sport, but it has no authority to regulate high school or college athletic competition (36 U.S.C. §220526(a)) or professional sports in the United States. Notably, almost 80% of U.S. team athletes who participated in the 2016 Rio Olympic Games had ties to United States intercollegiate athletic programs, and 41 United States athletes who competed at the 2016 Rio Paralympic Games participated in U.S. intercollegiate varsity sports as an athlete with a disability. Nancy Gillen, *USOPC to launch Olympic and Paralympic campaigns to promote collegiate sport opportunities,* available at https://www.insidethegames.biz/articles/1082488/uspoc-launch-collegiate-sport-campaign (July 23, 2019).

The NGBs have wide latitude to select athletes for their teams and to discipline athletes for misconduct, but they must follow and apply their respective rules consistently and provide athletes with appropriate notice of prohibited and required conduct as well as a fair opportunity to be heard if disputes arise. As previously discussed in *Slaney,* the ASA preempts litigation of state law claims by athletes arising out of eligibility disputes except for a breach of contract action to require the USOPC or an NGB to follow its own internal dispute resolution procedures. *Pliuskaitis v. USA Swimming, Inc.*, 243 F.Supp.3d 1217 (D. Utah 2017), *aff'd*, 720 Fed. Appx. 481 (10th Cir. 2018).

In *Harding v. U.S. Figure Skating*, 851 F. Supp. 1476 (D. Or. 1994), *vacated on other grounds*, 879 F. Supp. 1053 (D. Or. 1995), the court preliminarily enjoined the United States Figure Skating Association (USFSA) from conducting a disciplinary proceeding against Tonya Harding until she had sufficient time to prepare a defense to its charges against her. Outside a Detroit ice rink Harding's associates clubbed figure skater Nancy Kerrigan's knee, which forced her to withdraw from the USFSA Championship, which was won by Harding and earned her a performance-based spot on the U.S. Olympic team. Thereafter, USFSA instituted a disciplinary proceeding against Harding for alleged unethical conduct. This incident also led to a criminal investigation regarding Harding's knowledge of, or involvement in, the attack on Kerrigan.

The court found that USFSA violated its bylaws, which required a disciplinary proceeding to be held on a date "reasonably convenient for all parties." Observing that "[w]hen one party to a contract is given discretion in the performance of some aspect of the contract, that discretion must be exercised in good faith," it concluded that the date unilaterally set by USFSA "was arbitrary and manifestly unreasonable, and would severely prejudice plaintiff's chances of obtaining a fair hearing." *Id.* at 1479. It cautioned that "courts should rightly hesitate before intervening in disciplinary hearings held by private associations. . . . Intervention is appropriate only in the most extraordinary circumstances, where the association has clearly breached its own rules, that breach will imminently result in *serious* and irreparable harm to the plaintiff, and the plaintiff has exhausted all internal remedies." *Id.* at 1478. Rejecting Harding's request that the disciplinary hearing be postponed until after resolution of the criminal charges against her, the court "merely ordered defendant to comply with the requirement in its own bylaws that the hearing be set at a time reasonably convenient for all parties" and refused to "take any position upon the merits of the disciplinary proceeding." *Id.* at 1480. See also *USA Track & Field, Inc. v. Leach*, 2016 WL 6584699 (S.D. Ind., Nov. 7, 2016) (court refuses to intervene in parties' dispute and grant injunctive relief before pending NGB administrative proceeding has "run its course to a final decision").

The USOPC and all NGBs must comply with the ASA's legal framework for protecting the participation opportunities of Olympic sport athletes. The ASA mandates that the USOC establish a procedure for "swift and equitable resolution" of disputes "relating to the opportunity of an amateur athlete . . . to participate" in the Olympics, Paralympics, Pan-American Games, and world championship competitions." 36 U.S.C. §220509(a). Such disputes often arise out of an athlete's dissatisfaction with an NGB's resolution of a team selection issue, or alternatively, its imposition of a disciplinary sanction on an athlete. The USOPC is required to hire an athlete ombudsman to provide independent advice to athletes (free of charge) regarding eligibility disputes.

Section 9 of the USOPC's Bylaws creates both procedural and limited substantive rights for an "amateur athlete," defined as "any athlete who meets the eligibility standards established by the [NGB] or Paralympic Sports Organization for the sport in which the athlete competes," which generally includes professional athletes. USOC Bylaws, Section 1.3(c). Section 9.1 prohibits an NGB from "deny[ing] or threaten[ing] to deny . . . the opportunity to participate" in a protected competition to an athlete otherwise qualified to do so, who has the right to file a complaint with the USOC against an NGB that allegedly did so. An athlete dissatisfied with the USOC's resolution of the complaint may submit the dispute with the NGB to final and binding Section 9 arbitration conducted in accordance with the Commercial Rules of the AAA.

The AAA arbitration proceeding generally is held in person or telephonically before a single arbitrator selected by the parties from a closed pool maintained by the AAA. The athlete and the NBG generally are represented by legal counsel. The arbitrator must render a timely written and reasoned award resolving the parties' dispute, which is final and binding. The arbitration award usually is published on the USOPC's website at https://www.teamusa.org/Footer/Legal/Arbitration-and-Hearing-Panel-Cases/Section-9.

For example, *Hyatt v. United States Judo, Inc.*, AAA Case Number: 01-14-0000-7635 (2014) involved a dispute arising out of United States Judo (USJ)'s rules and process for selecting athletes to compete in the 2014 International Judo Federation (IJF) Junior World Championships, a protected competition. Claimant Alex Hyatt, who placed second in the girls' Junior 48 kg. weight division at USJ's 2014 Scholastic Nationals, contended that the winner of this event, Gabriela Prado, should not have been permitted to compete because she did not make weight by the time established by USJ's written rules for this competition. Therefore, as the second-place finisher, she was entitled to represent the U.S. in the girls' 48 kg. weight division at the IJF Junior World Championships pursuant to USJ's rules. The Arbitrator initially observed that:

> Section 9 jurisprudence requires [Ms. Hyatt] to prove [USJ] breached its approved and published Athlete Selection Procedures for the [2014 IJF Junior World Championships], applied them inconsistently to athletes similarly situated, acted in bad faith towards or with bias against [her], and/or violated applicable federal or state laws (e.g., Ted Stevens Olympic and Amateur Sports Act) [by a preponderance of evidence].

Id. at 10. Applying *de novo* review, the Arbitrator determined that USJ breached its published athlete selection rules (and Ms. Prado's substantive contract rights) for the 2014 U.S. Junior World Team by granting Ms. Prado a 30-minute extension of time to make weight and ordered it to name Ms. Hyatt as the U.S. entrant in the girls' 48 kg. weight division for the 2014 IJF Junior World Championships Team.

In February 2018, Congress created the United States Center for Safe Sport ("Center") to exercise exclusive jurisdiction over the USOPC and NGBs with the objective of protecting Olympic sport athletes from "abuse, including emotional, physical, and sexual abuse, in sports." 36 U.S.C. §220541(a) (2). The Center is responsible for developing training, oversight practices, policies, and procedures to prevent such abuse. 36 U.S.C. §220541(a) (3). It has established an arbitration procedure "to resolve allegations of sexual abuse . . . to determine the opportunity of [any Olympic sport] athlete, coach, trainer, manager, administrator, or official, who is the subject of such an allegation, to participate in [Olympic sport athletic competitions]" (36 U.S.C. §220541(b)(1)) by JAMS arbitrators in accordance with the Commercial Rules of the AAA. To protect the safety of other athletes, the Center's rules permit an NGB to impose an interim suspension on an athlete accused of sexual abuse pending final resolution of the allegations by the Center or JAMS arbitration. If an NGB's suspension denies an athlete the opportunity to participate in a protected competition, the athlete has the right to bring a AAA Section 9 arbitration proceeding to challenge the suspension, which may be nullified by the arbitrator if it is unauthorized or is not an appropriate and proportionate interim measure necessary to protect athletes from an imminent threat of harm to their safety or well-being. See, e.g., *Lopez and USA Taekwondo Inc.*, AAA Case No. 01-19-0000-5335 (2019).

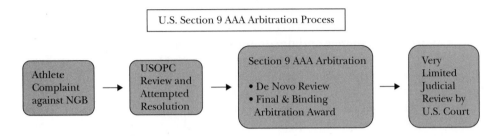

Arbitral resolution of a Section 9 athlete eligibility dispute bars the merits of the arbitrator's decision from being relitigated in a subsequent judicial proceeding. *Pliuskaitis v. USA Swimming, Inc.*, 243 F.Supp.3d 1217 (D. Utah 2017), *aff'd*, 720 Fed.Appx. 481 (10th Cir. 2018). The following case provides an example of the very limited scope of judicial review of a AAA arbitration award affecting an athlete's eligibility to participate in an Olympic sport. It also illustrates the need for all affected parties to have the opportunity to be heard and raises questions regarding which substantive issues should be within the arbitrators' authority to decide on the merits.

LINDLAND v. U.S. WRESTLING ASSOCIATION, INC.

227 F.3d 1000 (7th Cir. 2000)

EASTERBROOK, Circuit Judge.

Readers of our prior opinions (or the sports pages) know that Keith Sieracki and Matt Lindland both believe that they are entitled to be the U.S. entrant in the 76 kilogram weight class of Greco-Roman wrestling at the 2000 Olympic Games. They have met twice in championship bouts where the Olympic spot was the victor's reward: Sieracki won the first by a score of 2-1; Lindland won the second by a score of 8-0. Each claims that his victory entitles him to the slot in Sydney. Lindland protested the result of the first match through the hierarchy of USA Wrestling, the national governing body for amateur wrestling. After USA Wrestling rejected his protests, Lindland commenced arbitration, which was his right under the Ted Stevens Olympic and Amateur Sports Act. See 36 U.S.C. § 220529(a). Arbitrator Burns ordered the rematch, which Lindland won. USA Wrestling was unwilling to accept this outcome; instead of sending Lindland's name to the United States Olympic Committee (USOC) as its nominee for the Games, it told the USOC to send Sieracki and listed Lindland only as a person eligible to compete in the event of injury. Lindland then sought confirmation of the Burns Award under § 9 of the Federal Arbitration Act, 9 U.S.C. § 9, and in an opinion issued on August 24 we held that Lindland is entitled to that relief—which, we pointedly added, means that he is entitled to be USA Wrestling's nominee to the USOC.

Later that day, USA Wrestling informed the USOC that Sieracki remained its nominee. Its explanation for this defiance was that a second arbitrator, in a proceeding initiated by Sieracki, had disagreed with Arbitrator Burns and directed USA Wrestling to make Sieracki its nominee on the basis of his victory in the first match. USA Wrestling had no excuse for following Arbitrator Campbell's unreviewed award rather than a decision of a federal court confirming Arbitrator Burns's award, and on August 25 we issued a writ of mandamus requiring the district court to ensure that USA Wrestling implemented the Burns Award "immediately and unconditionally." On August 26 USA Wrestling finally complied, but the USOC then refused to accept Lindland as a member of the team, asserting that USA Wrestling's nomination of Lindland was untimely because Sieracki's name already had been sent to the International Olympic Committee (IOC) in Lausanne, Switzerland.

Lindland then returned to the district court, asking it to compel the USOC to send his name to the IOC. Sieracki fought back by asking a different district court (in Denver, Colorado) to confirm the Campbell Award. The district judge in Denver sensibly transferred that request to the Northern District of Illinois under 28 U.S.C. § 1404, consolidating all proceedings arising out of the dispute. The Northern District ordered the USOC to request the IOC to substitute Lindland for Sieracki. The USOC has done so, and the IOC has made the substitution. The Northern District also denied Sieracki's petition to confirm the Campbell Award. . . .

Lindland had argued to Arbitrator Burns that USA Wrestling's grievance proceedings were flawed. Arbitrator Burns agreed and ordered the rematch as a remedy in lieu of directing USA Wrestling to reconsider Lindland's protest to the judging of his match with Sieracki. Arbitrator Campbell went over the same ground, disagreed with Arbitrator Burns about the adequacy of USA Wrestling's processes and added that in his view the result of the first match (which everyone calls "Bout #244") had not been affected by any errors in applying the scoring rules for Greco-Roman Wrestling. It is not a surprising view for Arbitrator Campbell to have taken, because the proceedings began amicably. Sieracki initiated the arbitration to defend his initial victory, and USA Wrestling, the respondent, likewise defended both the scoring of the match and the conduct of its internal appeals. (Lindland intervened to defend the Burns Award, but, having already won the rematch, was more interested in preserving that victory than in litigating from scratch.) What *is* surprising was that Arbitrator Campbell not only approved the result of the original Bout #244 and the adequacy of USA Wrestling's grievance procedures but also directed it to ignore the result of the rematch—that is, Arbitrator Campbell directed USA Wrestling not to implement the Burns Award.

Sieracki argues that the Campbell Award is no less confirmable under the standards of the Federal Arbitration Act than was the Burns Award, see 9 U.S.C. § 10, and if he is entitled to confirmation of the Campbell Award then we should set aside the confirmation of the Burns Award (because relief from the BurnsAward is *part* of the Campbell Award). Certainly there is no evidence that the Campbell Award is the result of "corruption," "fraud," "evident partiality," or any similar bar to confirmation. The district court refused to enforce the Campbell Award because the Burns Award had been enforced already, and it read *Consolidation Coal Co. v. United Mine Workers*, 213 F.3d 404 (7th Cir. 2000), as precluding enforcement of incompatible awards. Only one of these athletes can be on the Olympic Team, and the district judge thought that federal courts should not order the USOC to send both. . . .

Definitive resolution of the right way to handle conflicting awards, after one has been confirmed, may await another day. The Campbell Award could not be confirmed even if it were the sole award. It is doubly flawed: first, the entire proceeding appears to have been *ultra vires*; second, the award violates the Commercial Rules of the American Arbitration Association, under which the proceeding was conducted. 36 U.S.C. § 220529(b)(2). Because Arbitrator Campbell exceeded his powers, his award cannot be confirmed. 9 U.S.C. § 10(a)(4).

Sieracki initiated an arbitration not to contest a final decision by USA Wrestling but to protest the Burns Award. Sieracki filed his demand for arbitration on August 11, two days after the Burns Award and three days before his rematch with Lindland (and thus before any issues associated with that bout could have arisen). The Stevens Act does not authorize arbitration about the propriety of another arbitrator's decision. . . .

What is arbitrable is "a determination of . . . the USOC, though some of its powers have been delegated to national governing bodies such as USA Wrestling. . . . Lindland exhausted his remedies within USA Wrestling and obtained "a determination of the corporation [i.e., USOC] under section 220527 . . . of this title," and thus was entitled to arbitrate his grievance. Sieracki, by contrast, did not initiate any proceedings within the scope of § 220527. . . . No other provision of which we are aware supports arbitration whose *sole* subject is the decision of a prior arbitrator. The Stevens Act would be self-destructive if it authorized such proceedings, which would lead to enduring turmoil (as happened here) and defeat the statute's function of facilitating final resolution of disputes, see § 220529(d).

Even if the second arbitration had been authorized, however, the outcome would have been forbidden by the rules under which it was conducted. Rule 48 of the AAA's Commercial Rules provides that an "arbitrator is not empowered to redetermine the merits of any claim already decided." . . . Arbitrators are not ombudsmen; they are authorized to resolve disputes under contracts and rules, not to declare how the world should work in the large. Arbitrator Campbell did not misinterpret Rule 48; he decided to ignore it utterly. The whole point of the Campbell proceeding was to redecide the issues that had been before Arbitrator Burns, and the Campbell Award directs USA Wrestling to disregard the Burns Award. Campbell observed, correctly, that Sieracki was not a party to the Burns proceedings, but the other participants in the proceedings before Arbitrator Campbell *were* parties to the Burns proceedings. By the time Campbell acted, the Burns Award had "already decided" that the nomination to the Olympic team would depend on a rematch between Sieracki and Lindland. Whatever powers Campbell possessed *vis-a-vis* Sieracki, he lacked the power to order USA Wrestling to nominate anyone other than the winner of the rematch. The Campbell Award therefore is not entitled to confirmation. . . .

For completeness, we add that none of the parties' arguments persuades us that the order confirming the Burns Award should be reconsidered. Sieracki, USA Wrestling, and the USOC continue to assert that the Burns proceedings were flawed because Sieracki was not a party to them. These submissions ignore the language of the Stevens Act, which provides for arbitration between an aggrieved athlete and the national governing body, not for arbitration among athletes. In arbitration the national governing body, by defending its decision (as USA Wrestling vigorously did), also defends the interests of the winning athlete. Doubtless the constitution or bylaws of the USOC or USA Wrestling could designate as additional parties those athletes potentially affected by the proceedings, but they do not do so. Arbitrator Campbell himself remarked that "customarily in a USOC Article IX arbitration . . . the competing athlete who does not initiate the arbitration . . . is not a participant and is not considered a necessary party by the USOC." If the USOC now favors a different approach, it should change its own rules rather than ask a federal court to disregard an award that was reached following normal procedures. . . .

. . . One of [the USOC's] rules specifies that the winner of Bout #244 would be USA Wrestling's nominee in the 76 kilogram classification. Lindland is the winner of Bout #244 and the recipient of USA Wrestling's (belated) nomination. Under the USOC's own rules, therefore, Lindland is entitled to the position on the Olympic Team. . . .

Affirmed.

NOTES AND QUESTIONS

1. *Analysis of* Lindland. If you were Keith Sieracki's counsel, what would have been your advice when Matt Lindland instituted an AAA arbitration proceeding seeking a rematch? The Federal Arbitration Act, 9 U.S.C. §§1 et seq., enables an athlete (such as Lindland, who won a silver medal at the 2000 Sydney Olympics) to seek judicial confirmation and enforcement of an arbitration award if an NGB or the USOPC refuses to comply with it. Why did the Seventh Circuit confirm and enforce the Burns arbitration award, but not the Campbell award?

   A court's review of an arbitration award is very limited, focusing primarily on jurisdictional and procedural issues. In *Gault v. United States Bobsled and Skeleton Federation*, 578 N.Y.S.2d 683, 685 (N.Y. App. Div. 1992), a New York appellate court explained: "Although we also may disagree with the arbitrator's award and find most unfortunate the increasing frequency with which sporting events are resolved in the courtroom, we have no authority to upset it when the arbitrator did not exceed his authority." A court will vacate or refuse to confirm an arbitration award that is "the result of 'corruption,' 'fraud,' 'evident partiality,' or any similar bar to confirmation." *Lindland*, 227 F.3d at 1003. See also *Westerbeke Corp. v. Daihatsu Motor Co., Ltd*, 304 F.2d 200, 208 (2d Cir. 2002) ("an arbitral decision may be vacated when an arbitrator has exhibited a 'manifest disregard of law,'" but standard of review is "severely limited" and requires "something beyond and different from a mere error in the law or failure on the part of the arbitrators to understand or apply the law").

   The Amateur Sports Act provides:

   > In any lawsuit relating to the resolution of a dispute involving the opportunity of an amateur athlete to participate in the Olympic Games, the Paralympic Games, or the Pan-American Games, a court shall not grant injunctive relief against [the USOPC] within 21 days before the beginning of such games if [the USOPC], after consultation with the chair of the Athletes' Advisory

> Council, has provided a sworn statement in writing . . . to such court that its constitution and bylaws cannot provide for the resolution of such dispute prior to the beginning of such games.

36 U.S.C. §220509(a). The *Lindland* court observed that this statutory provision "is designed to prevent a court from usurping the [USOPC's] powers when time is too short for its own dispute-resolution machinery to do its work." 227 F.3d at 1007. However, the Seventh Circuit held this provision did not preclude judicial authority to order the USOPC to comply with the Burns arbitration award because it was both issued and confirmed outside the ASA's 21-day window.

2. Lindland *Aftermath.* The multi-stage litigation arising out of two conflicting AAA arbitration awards illustrates the need for Section 9 athlete participation disputes to be resolved by a single arbitration proceeding, in which all affected athletes have a fair and full opportunity to be heard that results in a final and binding award. After *Lindland*, the USOPC amended its bylaws to provide that an athlete instituting Section 9 arbitration and the NGB must identify all individuals (usually athletes) either believes "may be adversely affected by the arbitration." The AAA is responsible for providing notice to those individuals, who may choose to participate in the arbitration as a party. An individual who receives notice is bound by the arbitration award even if he or she chooses not to participate in the arbitration. USOPC Bylaw 9.8.

Regarding disputed competition results, USOPC Bylaw 9.13 was amended as follows:

> The final decision of a referee during a competition regarding a field of play decision (a matter set forth in the rules of the competition to be within the discretion of the referee) shall not be reviewable through or the subject of these complaint procedures unless the decision is (i) outside the authority of the referee to make or (ii) the product of fraud, corruption, partiality or other misconduct of the referee. For purposes of this Section, the term 'referee' shall include any individual with discretion to make field of play decisions.

PROBLEM 4-1

After failing to qualify as a member of the 2002 U.S. Olympic 1,000-meter speedskating team, Tommy O'Hare alleged that Apolo Ohno and Rusty Smith conspired to enable Shani Davis to win the final qualifying race for this event and earn a spot on the team. The U.S. Speedskating Code of Conduct requires fair play and responsible conduct by all athletes competing in events. In an arbitration proceeding, Ohno, who had already qualified for a spot on the U.S. Olympic team for this event, testified that he held back during the race to prevent injury. Three other U.S. speed skaters initially claimed to have heard Ohno and Smith discussing a plan to ensure that Davis won the qualifying event, which they ultimately retracted. The race referee and official timer stated their belief that Ohno had not skated to the best of his ability, but he did not violate any racing rule. Three assistant race referees testified that it was a clean race. As an arbitrator, how would you resolve this dispute? If you found that the race had been "fixed" or "manipulated," what relief would you order?

C. LIMITS ON USE OF NATIONAL LAW TO REGULATE OLYMPIC AND INTERNATIONAL ATHLETIC COMPETITION

A U.S. court generally has no personal jurisdiction (i.e., valid authority to render a legally binding judgment against the defendant) over a nonresident international athletics governing body, such as an IF or the IOC, unless an athlete's claims arise out of its activities within both the United States and forum state. For example, in *Reynolds v. Int'l Amateur Athletic Federation,* 23 F.3d 1110 (6th Cir. 1994), the Sixth Circuit held that an Ohio court had no jurisdiction to hear American world-class sprinter Butch Reynolds' state law claims against the IAAF (then based in London, England), which alleged that his positive drug test was erroneous (his urine sample was collected at an event in Monaco and tested in Paris, France). The merits of Reynolds's legal claims had been resolved adversely to him in an IAAF arbitration proceeding held in London. Consider whether an IF should be subject to a U.S. court's jurisdiction based on its U.S. member NGB's domestic activities, such as enforcing its athlete eligibility determinations. In other words, does personal jurisdiction exist if the NGB functions as the IF's agent in the United States? See *Behagen v. Amateur Basketball Assn. of United States of America,* 744 F.2d 731, 732-734 (10th Cir. 1984) (record evidence establishes that an IF "is its members" and governs the sport through its member organizations in each country, which raises a question of fact whether a German-based IF is subject to a U.S. court's jurisdiction).

Like *Reynolds,* other courts have dismissed claims against FIFA and the IOC on lack of personal jurisdiction grounds. *Mehr v. FIFA,* 115 F. Supp. 3d 1035, 1051 (N.D. Cal. 2015) ("allegation that FIFA requires its members, such as U.S. Soccer, to 'follow FIFA's rules and the Laws of the Game' and also requires the members of its members (*i.e.,* U.S. Soccer's members) to follow those rules and laws, even if true" is insufficient to make it subject to a U.S. court's jurisdiction; "[t]o find otherwise would be to suggest that FIFA is subject to personal jurisdiction everywhere in the United States where soccer is played"); *Shepherd v. USOC,* 94 F. Supp. 2d 1136 (D. Col. 2000) (a U.S. court has no personal jurisdiction over the IOC merely because it requires the USOPC, which is not an IOC member, to act in accordance with the Olympic Charter).

Even if personal jurisdiction over an international sports governing body exists, U.S. courts are very reluctant to apply U.S. federal or state law to IOC or IF rules, which are the product of a private international agreement intended to provide for uniform, worldwide governance of sport. In *Martin v. IOC,* 740 F.2d 670 (9th Cir. 1984), the Ninth Circuit affirmed the denial of a preliminary injunction to require the organizers of the 1984 Los Angeles Summer Olympic Games to include 5,000- and 10,000-meter track events for women as existed for men. The court rejected plaintiffs' claims that the IOC's failure to include these events constituted illegal gender discrimination, even though "the women runners made a strong showing that the early history of the modern Olympic Games was marred by blatant discrimination against women." *Id.* at 673. The majority explained:

> [W]e find persuasive the argument that a court should be wary of applying a state statute to alter the content of the Olympic Games. The Olympic Games are organized and conducted under the terms of an international agreement—the

Olympic Charter. We are extremely hesitant to undertake the application of one state's statute to alter an event that is staged with competitors from the entire world under the terms of that agreement.

Id. at 677.

The *Martin* dissenting judge argued:

The IOC made concessions to the widespread popularity of women's track and field by adding two distance races this year. The IOC refused, however, to grant women athletes equal status by including all events in which women compete internationally. In so doing, the IOC postpones indefinitely the equality of athletic opportunity that it could easily achieve this year in Los Angeles. When the Olympics move to other countries, some without America's commitment to human rights, the opportunity to tip the scales of justice in favor of equality may slip away. Meanwhile, the Olympic flame—which should be a symbol of harmony, equality, and justice—will burn less brightly over the Los Angeles Olympic Games.

Id. at 683.

A Colorado federal district court denied a pro se plaintiff's request for a temporary restraining order against the enforcement of the Switzerland-based United World Wrestling's eligibility rule prohibiting athletes 60 years of age and older from participating in the Veterans World Championships. Even assuming personal jurisdiction over the defendant, it ruled that plaintiff failed to establish a likelihood of success on his federal antitrust and denial of equal protection claims or state breach of fiduciary duty claim. The court also held that "ineligibility for participation in athletic competitions alone does not constitute irreparable harm." *Wirs v. United World Wrestling*, 2017 WL 8943750 (D. Colo.), *vacated as moot*, 2018 WL 672081 (D. Colo.).

U.S. courts also have rejected state discrimination law claims by foreign athletes seeking to march under flags of countries not recognized by the IOC in opening ceremonies in the Olympic Games or Olympic Winter Games held in the United States. *Spindulys v. Los Angeles Olympic Organizing Comm.*, 175 Cal. App. 3d 206, 220 Cal. Rptr. 565 (Cal. App. 1985); *Ren-Guey v. Lake Placid 1980 Olympic Games*, 72 A.D.2d 439, 424 N.Y.S.2d 533, *aff'd*, 49 N.Y.2d 771, 429 N.Y.S.2d 473 (1980).

Is it appropriate for courts to refuse to apply laws prohibiting discrimination to Olympic and other international sports events held in the United States?

Canadian and British courts also have declined to use their respective national laws to regulate international sports governing bodies or to invalidate their rules. *Sagen v. Vancouver Organizing Committee for the 2010 Olympic & Paralympic Games*, 98 B.C.L.R. 4th 141 (Can. B.C.) (the British Columbia Court of Appeals rejected a gender discrimination claim and ruled that the IOC's decision not to include women's ski jumping as an event in the Vancouver Olympic Games, while including men's ski jumping events, did not violate the Canadian Charter of Rights and Freedoms); *Gasser v. Stinson* (Queens Bench Division 1988) (although English restraint of trade laws applied to the London-based IAAF, the court refused to interfere with "honest decisions of bodies exercising jurisdiction over sporting and other activities which those bodies exercising jurisdiction are far better fitted to judge than courts" and upheld an athlete's doping sanction); *Cowley v. Heatley* (Chancery Div., July 24, 1986) (unreported case) ("The concepts of natural justice and the duty to be fair must not be allowed to discredit themselves by making unreasonable requirements and imposing undue burdens" on a sports organization's internal governance decisions).

On the other hand, European Union law has been used to invalidate international sports governing body rules such as FIFA's athlete transfer and nationality rules. See, e.g., *UEFA v. Bosman* (ECJ 1995), discussed in Chapter 7 E. In December 2017, the European Commission ruled that an International Skating Union (ISU) rule imposing severe penalties (including a threatened lifetime ban from participating in the Winter Olympic Games) on athletes participating in unauthorized speed skating competitions violates European Union competition laws. European Commissioner Margrethe Vestager, who is responsible for ruling on competition policy, stated: "International sports federations play an important role in athletes' careers — they protect their health and safety and the integrity of competitions. However, the severe penalties the ISU imposes on skaters also serve to protect its own commercial interests and prevent others from setting up their own events. The ISU now has to comply with our decision, modify its rules, and open up new opportunities for athletes and competing organisers, to the benefit of all ice skating fans."

As previously discussed, a U.S. athlete's dispute with the USOC or an NGB is resolved by AAA arbitration. By comparison, a U.S. athlete's dispute with the IOC or an IF generally will be resolved before a foreign arbitration panel (e.g., the Court of Arbitration for Sport, *infra*). An international treaty, the United Nations Convention on the Recognition and Enforcement of Foreign Arbitral Awards ("New York Convention"), 9 U.S.C. §201, to which the United States is a party, provides a mechanism for national courts to review foreign arbitration awards. The following case illustrates that in accordance with the Convention, U.S. courts generally will recognize and confirm foreign sports arbitration awards affecting U.S. athletes, which precludes re-litigating their merits under national or state laws.

SLANEY v. INTERNATIONAL AMATEUR ATHLETIC FEDERATION

244 F.3d 580 (7th Cir.), *cert. denied*, 534 U.S. 828 (2001)

FLAUM, Chief Judge.

Former Olympic runner Mary Decker Slaney ("Slaney") brought suit against the International Amateur Athletic Federation ("IAAF") and the United States Olympic Committee ("USOC") shortly after an IAAF arbitration panel determined that Slaney had committed a doping offense. Slaney's complaint raised a litany of state-law claims [arising out of her positive test for the banned substance testosterone based on an elevated T/E ratio and suspension by the IAAF, the international governing federation for track and field]. . . .

I.   BACKGROUND

In the course of her storied career, middle-distance runner Mary Decker Slaney has captured a multitude of United States and world records. She is considered by many to be one of the most celebrated female athletes of the past century, as well as one of the greatest runners of all-time. . . .

. . . In June of 1996, she competed in the 5000- and 1500-meter races in the national trials for the Atlanta Olympics. Following her 5000-meter race, Slaney provided the USOC with a urine sample, which was tested for prohibited substances including exogenous testosterone.

Because current technology cannot detect the presence of prohibited testosterone in the body, testing programs measure the ratio of testosterone to epitestosterone ("T/E") in the body. This test, referred to as the T/E test, assumes that an ordinary T/E ratio in humans is one to one, and thus any ratio of above six to one is consistent with "blood doping." The ratio was established at six to one in order to account for non-doping factors that might cause elevated ratios in female athletes. Factors which may influence the T/E ratio include an individual changing birth control pills, age, menstrual cycle, bacterial contamination of the urine sample, and alcohol use.

Slaney's test . . . revealed that Slaney's T/E ratio [9.5:1 and 11.6:1] was elevated significantly beyond the permitted six to one ratio. . . . The IAAF's investigating doctor analyzed Slaney's samples, her past test results, and two additional samples. Slaney claimed that her elevated level was the result of (1) her menstrual cycle, and (2) her changing of birth control pills. Furthermore, Slaney posited that there was no scientific validity to the hypothesis that a T/E ratio above six to one was not normal for female athletes. Nonetheless, on February 5, 1997, the IAAF adopted the investigating doctor's recommendation and found Slaney's specimen positive for the prohibited substance testosterone.

As a result of the IAAF's decision, IAAF and USOC rules required the [United States Track & Field Association ("USATF")] to hold a hearing to determine whether Slaney had committed a doping offense. . . .

Slaney received her hearing before the USATF Doping Hearing Board on September 14, 1997. The Hearing Board, unpersuaded by the testimony of the IAAF's investigating doctor, unanimously determined that no doping violation had occurred. . . .

The IAAF was unsatisfied with the USATF Hearing Board's findings, and invoked arbitration of the USATF's decision. Slaney and the USATF opposed arbitration, but both were represented before the IAAF Arbitral Panel ("the Tribunal"). In late January 1999, the Tribunal issued an interlocutory decision upholding the IAAF's interpretation of how to adjudicate a testosterone doping offense, and found that the rules were neither vague nor inconsistent. Thus, once the IAAF showed that Slaney had a T/E ratio greater than six to one, Slaney had to come forth and show by clear and convincing evidence that the elevated ratio was attributable to a pathological or physiological condition. Believing that it was scientifically impossible to prove by clear and convincing evidence that her high T/E ratio was due to pathological or physiological factors, Slaney withdrew from the arbitration, followed by the USATF. Ultimately, the Tribunal ruled that Slaney had committed a doping offense. . . .

. . . [T]he district court held that the United Nations Convention on the Recognition and Enforcement of Foreign Arbitral Awards, 9 U.S.C. § 201 ("New York Convention"), barred Slaney's claims against the IAAF, as those claims had been the subject of a valid arbitration decision. . . .

A.   STATE-LAW CLAIMS AGAINST THE IAAF

. . . Slaney challenges the district court's decision dismissing her IAAF claims, arguing that (1) Slaney is not subject to the New York Convention, in that she has never agreed—in writing or by actions—to arbitrate all disputes with the

IAAF; (2) the claims raised in Slaney's complaint are separate and distinct from the matter decided by the IAAF; and (3) she has defenses under the New York Convention that preclude enforcement of the IAAF arbitration award against her.

. . . According to 9 U.S.C. § 201, the Convention on the Recognition and Enforcement of Foreign Arbitral Awards (New York Convention) shall be enforced in the United States courts. Article II of the Convention speaks to the requirements of states that have signed on to the Convention. Specifically, the section states that "[e]ach Contracting State shall recognize an agreement in writing under which the parties undertake to submit to arbitration all or any differences which have arisen or which may arise between them in respect of a defined legal relationship, whether contractual or not, concerning a subject matter capable of settlement by arbitration."

. . . If an award has been rendered, that award must be enforced unless the party against whom enforcement is sought presents evidence that one of the limited defenses enumerated under Article V of the Convention is applicable. For purposes of this appeal, we note that both the United States and Monaco are signatories to the Convention, such that the United States is bound to enforce arbitral awards validly rendered in that country.

In analyzing the merits of Slaney's appeal, we proceed in a systematic fashion. First, we must examine the decision rendered by the IAAF arbitration panel and determine the specific findings made by that Tribunal. Second, we shall examine the state-law causes of action that Slaney now brings against the IAAF in her complaint to the district court, and determine whether in fact those claims seek relitigation of an issue determined by the arbitration. If we determine that adjudication of Slaney's present claims would necessitate a reexamination of matters decided by the arbitration decision, we must resolve whether the arbitration decision, which took place on foreign soil, should be recognized by the courts, and thus deprive us of subject-matter jurisdiction over the present claims. Finally, assuming that we are theoretically obligated to recognize the decision of the Tribunal, we must inquire whether any defense to enforcement is applicable.

1. *Decision of the Tribunal*

. . . [T]he Tribunal notes that the initial burden of proof rests with the IAAF to show that an athlete has a T/E ratio greater than the 6:1 established limit. If the IAAF can do so, according to the Tribunal, the Federation has provided sufficient evidence for the sample to be deemed positive. At that point, the burden is shifted to the athlete, who must prove by clear and convincing evidence that the elevated T/E ratio was due to pathological or physiological conditions. In making this analysis, the Tribunal drew from the IAAF rules on testing for testosterone.

With the evidentiary procedure established, the Tribunal continued to consider whether Slaney had committed a doping offense. The Tribunal noted that the IAAF had established that both of Slaney's specimens had been analyzed as having T/E ratios significantly higher than 6:1. The tribunal also observed that Slaney's longitudinal study revealed a previous T/E ratio high of 3:1; meaning that her present ratio, by the most modest of calculations, was more than three times greater than she had ever previously tested. Thus the burden was shifted to Slaney to produce a valid explanation for the findings. The Tribunal noted that Slaney had produced no evidence, let alone that of a clear and convincing nature, to prove that her elevated ratio was the result of pathological or physiological factors. Since Slaney had withdrawn from the proceedings, and refused to tender her medical records to the Tribunal, the panel was forced to conclude under the burden-shifting procedure it had outlined that Slaney was guilty of a doping offense on June 17, 1996.

2. Slaney's Present Complaint and Its Relationship to the Tribunal's Decision

Keeping in mind the orbit of the Tribunal's decision, we now turn to examine Slaney's present state-law causes of action against the IAAF. Slaney raises six such claims: breach of contract, negligence, breach of fiduciary duty of good faith and fair dealing, fraud, constructive fraud, and negligent misrepresentation. . . . [W]e note that her complaints center around the claim that the IAAF violated its obligations to Slaney by "using the T/E ratio as a proxy for doping in women." Thus, she alleges that the Federation failed to properly investigate her urine sample. Though Slaney does not specify how she was damaged by the implementation of the T/E test . . . the answer is apparent. The implementation by the IAAF of a burden-shifting approach to proving ingestion of testosterone damaged Slaney in that, as a result, she was unable to disprove that she had committed the offense—resulting in her suspension.[1]

We conclude that Slaney's present complaint seeks to address issues decided by the Tribunal. During the course of the IAAF arbitration, Slaney presented two positions: (1) that the IAAF's T/E ratio test for determining ingestion of exogenous testosterone was invalid, and (2) that it could not be proven that Slaney had committed a doping violation. . . . As our inquiry above made transparent, Slaney's state-law claims against the IAAF seek deliberation on the identical issues. For example, in order to adjudicate whether Slaney's Fifth Count (negligence against the IAAF) is a valid claim, the court would be required to delve into whether the cause of action makes the *prima facie* case. That probing would require that the court assess whether the IAAF in fact breached its obligations to Slaney. Slaney claims that the IAAF had a duty to properly test her for drug use. Since Slaney asserts that the IAAF breached this duty by employing the T/E test, the court would *de facto* be required to determine whether the implementation of that test constituted a breach of the duty to properly test athletes. Of course, the court could not reach that decision without addressing the validity of the test itself. Likewise, any examination of damages would require an assessment of whether Slaney was properly found guilty of a doping offense. Thus, we accept the district court's finding that allowing Slaney's current action would undermine or nullify the Tribunal's decision.

3. Application of the New York Convention

[W]e now turn to the critical issue of whether we are required to acknowledge the foreign arbitration decision. If we are, then unless Slaney can present a defense to enforcement, we cannot exercise subject-matter jurisdiction over her present claims, as that would require prohibited relitigation of previously decided issues.

---

1. We note that Slaney walks a tightrope throughout this portion of her appellate argument. On the one hand, in order to raise many of the causes of action she alleges, Slaney must establish that there is a contractual relationship between her and the IAAF. However, in order to maintain the action as a whole against the IAAF, Slaney must avoid any suggestion that she has a contractual relationship with the IAAF whereby she has agreed to abide by their rules, including those which compel arbitration of all disputes.

Slaney's primary contention in this regard is that the arbitration between herself and the IAAF need not be enforced by federal courts in that it did not satisfy the requirements of the New York Convention. First, Slaney points out that there is no agreement in writing between her and the IAAF in which she agreed to submit her claims to arbitration. . . . The IAAF counters that Slaney, by becoming a member of the USATF, agreed to abide by all IAAF rules. Included within those rules is the requirement that she arbitrate all disputes with the IAAF. . . . Additionally, because the IAAF suggests that Slaney participated in the IAAF arbitration, she cannot now raise the procedural defense of lack of an arbitration agreement.

Whether Slaney's written agreement to follow the rules of the USATF would satisfy the requirement of an agreement in writing for purposes of enforcing an arbitration agreement with the IAAF is a question we need not resolve. Instead, we direct our inquiry to whether Slaney was a party to the IAAF arbitration, and what results flow from that fact. An examination of Slaney's actions following the IAAF's submission of the matter to the Tribunal leads to only one conclusion: Slaney was a participant in the arbitration. During the arbitration, Slaney's counsel appeared before and presented arguments to the Tribunal. Her counsel called an expert witness to testify on Slaney's behalf, filed a motion to dismiss, and a motion for summary judgment. Furthermore, Slaney's counsel moved for an interlocutory ruling regarding the burden of proof the Tribunal would apply. Given this level of participation, the district court was correct to reject Slaney's contention that she was merely an interested athlete in the proceedings. . . .

We see no reason why, even in the absence of a writing, ordinary rules of contract law should not apply. . . . Non-signatories to an arbitration agreement may nevertheless be bound according to ordinary principles of contract and agency, including estoppel. Our judicial system is not meant to provide a second bite at the apple for those who have sought adjudication of their disputes in other forums and are not content with the resolution they have received. Slaney had the opportunity to show that she had never agreed to arbitrate the dispute when she was notified of the arbitration, but she let that opportunity pass. Slaney could not "sit back and allow the arbitration to go forward, and only after it was all done . . . say: oh by the way, we never agreed to the arbitration clause. That is a tactic that the law of arbitration, with its commitment to speed, will not tolerate."

. . . Thus, we find that the Tribunal's decision must be recognized by this court, and unless a defense is present, must bar her present claims.

4. New York Convention Defenses

Slaney alternatively suggests that even if we are to determine that she is bound by the arbitration panel's decision, the New York Convention provides exceptions in which a court need not enforce a foreign arbitral decision, and that those defenses to enforcement are applicable to the Tribunal's decision.

The first such defense raised by Slaney is that the Tribunal's decision should not be enforced because she was denied the opportunity to present her case. Slaney contends that under the IAAF rules, the IAAF has the burden of proving beyond a reasonable doubt that a doping offense has occurred. Her defense, she puts forth, was that the IAAF could not scientifically prove beyond a reasonable doubt that any prohibited substance was in her urine. Thus, when the Tribunal concluded it was bound by the IAAF's position—that upon a showing that an athlete had a T/E ratio greater than 6:1 the burden shifted to the athlete to show by clear and convincing evidence that the elevated ratio was due to a pathological or physiological condition—the Tribunal in effect denied Slaney a meaningful opportunity to present her case.

Article V(1)(b) of the New York Convention states that recognition and enforcement of an award may be refused if the party against whom it is invoked furnishes proof that it "was not given proper notice of the appointment of the arbitrator or of the arbitration proceedings or *was otherwise unable to present his case*." (Emphasis added.) . . . As we have noted, in order to comport with the requirement that a party to a foreign arbitration be able to present her case, we require that the arbitrator provide a fundamentally fair hearing. A fundamentally fair hearing is one that "meets the minimal requirements of fairness—adequate notice, a hearing on the evidence, and an impartial decision by the arbitrator." Nevertheless, parties that have chosen to remedy their disputes through arbitration rather than litigation should not expect the same procedures they would find in the judicial arena. . . .

. . . Our examination of these cases leads us to conclude that Slaney's allegation has no merit. This defense to enforcement of a foreign arbitration need not apply when a panel employs a burden-shifting test in a fair manner. Slaney was not denied an opportunity to present her evidence. Rather, the arbitrator's decision merely maintained the same standard of proof the IAAF had always been guided by. As such, Slaney's complaint does not truly attack the procedure implemented by the arbitration panel, but rather an underlying evidentiary decision of the panel. . . .

Slaney's final submission on this issue is that "presuming she had committed a doping offense based on a test that is scientifically invalid and discriminatory towards female athletes violated the 'most basic notions of morality and justice.'" Slaney further postulates that "eliminating the presumption of [her] innocence based upon her elevated T/E ratio also violates . . . explicit public policy that is well defined and dominant and is ascertained by reference to the laws and legal precedents and not from general considerations of supposed public interests."

According to Article V(2)(b) of the New York Convention, "Recognition and enforcement of an arbitral award may also be refused if the competent authority in the country where recognition and enforcement is sought finds that: . . . [t]he recognition or enforcement of the award would be contrary to the public policy of that country." . . . In *Fotochrome, Inc. v. Copal Co.*, 517 F.2d 512, 516 (2d Cir. 1975), the Second Circuit noted that the public policy defense is exceedingly narrow. While Slaney states that the Tribunal's decision meets the stringent requirements of that case and others, in that the Tribunal's decision violated the "most basic notions of morality and justice," and that enforcement would entail a violation of a paramount legal principle that is "ascertained by reference to the laws and legal precedents and from general considerations of supposed public interests," *Industrial Risk Insurers v. M.A.N. Gutehoffnungshutte GmbH*, 141 F.3d 1434, 1445 (11th Cir. 1998), she provides little support for her contention.

Reduced to its essence, Slaney contends that the burden-shifting approach adopted by the IAAF violates United States public policy. We disagree. According to the parties, proving the presence of exogenous testosterone in the body by scientific tests is not possible at the present time. Therefore, the IAAF has adopted the rebuttable presumption of ingestion from a high T/E ratio in an athlete's urine, as detailed throughout this opinion. Were the IAAF not to make use of the rebuttable presumption, it would be nearly impossible, absent eyewitness proof, to ever find that an athlete had ingested testosterone. . . . We hope that at some juncture, science will develop a means for detecting exogenous testosterone in athletes, such that an athlete's T/E ratio of 11.6:1 can be discounted if it is based on innocent factors. However, until that point in time, we are confident that requiring an athlete to prove by clear and convincing evidence that her elevated ratio was due to pathological or physiological factors does not invoke a violation of United States public policy as federal case law has required in order for a court to refuse to enforce a foreign arbitral award.

Thus, having found that (1) Slaney participated in the IAAF arbitration, (2) her present state-law complaint seeks to relitigate issues decided by the IAAF Tribunal, (3) the New York Convention mandates enforcement of the arbitrator's decision, and (4) there is no defense that should bar enforcement of the arbitration decision, we find that the district court did not err in dismissing Slaney's state-law claims against the IAAF. . . .

NOTES AND QUESTIONS

1. *Analysis of* Slaney. The New York Convention treaty requires national courts of signatory countries to enforce valid arbitration awards if the parties agreed in writing to arbitrate their dispute. What defenses to judicial enforcement of foreign arbitration awards are established by the New York Convention? Do you agree that requiring Slaney "to prove by clear and convincing evidence that her elevated T/E ratio was due to pathological or physiological factors" does not violate United States public policy? If the Seventh Circuit had refused to recognize and enforce the IAAF arbitration award, would this provide Slaney with an effective legal remedy for her alleged harm as a practical matter?

2. *Valid Foreign Arbitration Award Precludes Re-litigation of Its Merits.* The *Lindland* case, *supra*, illustrates the offensive use of a domestic arbitral award to obtain judicial enforcement of the prevailing party's rights. On the other hand, *Slaney* illustrates the defensive use of a foreign arbitral award by the prevailing party in arbitration (i.e., IAAF) to preclude re-litigation of the same claims by the losing party (i.e., Mary Decker Slaney) in a judicial forum (i.e., Indiana federal court). This dual approach is consistent with the prevailing judicial preference that Olympic and international sports-related disputes be resolved by arbitration. See generally James A.R. Nafziger, *Arbitration of Rights and Obligations in the International Sports Arena*, 35 Val. U. L. Rev. 357 (2001).

PROBLEM 4-2

Andy is a junior at Aquatic State University and the NCAA champion in the 100-meter butterfly swimming event. In the recently completed Olympic Trials conducted under the auspices of United States Swimming, Inc. (USS), he finished fourth in this event, only 0.01 second behind the third-place finisher. He failed to make the United States Olympic team because only the top three finishers qualify for this event. Andy believes that the winner of this event used an "illegal kick" during the race and should have been disqualified. He timely filed a complaint with the USS race officials overseeing this event, which was rejected on its merits within one hour after the race ended. The next day, USS's executive committee denied his appeal. Andy wants to sue USS, the USOPC, and the International Olympic Committee and obtain a court order enabling him to participate as a member of Team USA in the Olympic 100-meter butterfly swimming event, which will be held in the United States in 20 days. What advice would you give him?

D.   COURT OF ARBITRATION FOR SPORT

1.   *Overview*

The materials in the previous section illustrate the inherent problems of adjudication of Olympic and international sports disputes by national courts. There are potential jurisdictional and conflicts-of-law problems as well as inherent difficulties in attempting to apply a specific country's laws to the rules and decisions of international sports organizations such as the IOC and IFs whose governing authority is exercised worldwide. The increasing commercialization of Olympic and international sports competitions and the corresponding rising tide of legal disputes generated the need for an independent international tribunal with final and binding authority, whose decisions would be respected and enforced, if necessary, by national courts.

In 1983, the IOC established the Court of Arbitration for Sport (CAS), which is based in Lausanne, Switzerland, to resolve legal disputes in sports fairly, effectively, and efficiently. Its creation recognizes the need for international sport's legal regulation to be uniform and protective of the integrity of athletics competitions, while also safeguarding all athletes' legitimate rights and adhering to fundamental principles of natural justice. Tricia Kavanagh, *The Doping Cases and the Need for the International Court of Arbitration for Sport (CAS)*, 22 Univ. New S. Wales L.J. 721 (1999). The CAS "provides a forum for the world's athletes and sports federations to resolve their disputes through a single, independent and accomplished sports adjudication body that is capable of consistently applying the rules of different sports organizations." Richard H. McLaren, *The Court of Arbitration for Sport: An Independent Arena for the World's Sports Disputes*, 35 Val. U. L. Rev. 379, 381 (2001). It is "a unifying institution that can help deliver sport back to its origins . . . [and] ensures fairness and integrity in sport through sound legal control and the administration of diverse laws and philosophies." *Id.*

Despite its designation as a "court," the CAS is an arbitral tribunal whose jurisdiction is based on the parties' written agreement to submit their dispute to the CAS for final adjudication. The IOC and all Olympic IFs have agreed to CAS jurisdiction. By rule, the IFs require their respective member NGBs and athletes to submit all disputes with the IF to CAS arbitration. Interested third parties, such as athletes whose interests may be affected, may intervene in CAS proceedings, which avoids the problem of conflicting arbitration awards raised by the *Lindland* case, *supra*. All parties in a CAS proceeding have the right to be represented by counsel. CAS arbitrators have legal training and recognized competence in the fields of sport and/or international arbitration. They must be fluent in French or English, which are the working languages of the CAS.

Since 1994, the International Council of Arbitration for Sport (ICAS), a group of 20 distinguished jurists and lawyers with a sports and/or arbitration background (some of whom are Olympians) also based in Lausanne, has overseen the CAS and appointed its group of approximately 400 arbitrators, managed its budget, and promulgated the Code of Sports-Related Arbitration (Code), which governs CAS arbitration proceedings.

The CAS *ordinary arbitration procedure* is used to resolve sports-related commercial disputes, such as issues regarding sponsorship contracts, media rights to sports events, and contracts between athletes and their agents. Pursuant to Article R45 of the Code, the dispute is resolved according to the law chosen by the parties, or Swiss law if none has been chosen. The proceedings usually are confidential and do not result in the publication of an award by the CAS.

The CAS *appeals arbitration procedure* is used to resolve appeals from final decisions of sports federations (requiring the exhaustion of all available internal administrative remedies) involving a variety of disputes, including discipline for misconduct, athlete eligibility issues, competition results, and doping. These proceedings usually are before a three-person panel. Each party selects one arbitrator, and the president of the CAS appeals arbitration procedure (who is an ICAS member) appoints the third arbitrator who serves as the president of the panel. The applicable substantive law generally is the particular sport governing body's rules (e.g., IOC or IF rules) and the law of the country in which it is domiciled (the IOC and most IFs are based in Switzerland), although the CAS panel has rarely exercised authority to resolve the dispute according to the "rules of law" it deems appropriate (and must give its reasons for doing so). Article R58 of the Code. As a CAS panel explained: "First, CAS is an adjudicative, not legislative body. It is not for CAS to write the rules of the FEI. As long as those rules are not incompatible with some relevant aspect of ordre public, be it competition law, the law of human rights, or Swiss statute, we have to apply them as they stand." *Hansen v. FEI*, CAS 2009/A/1768. The Code generally provides for the case to be decided and a written operative part of the award (i.e., ultimate adjudication of the material issues) to be provided to the parties within three months after the case file is transferred to the CAS panel, with a written final reasoned award.

The CAS *ad hoc Division* operates at the site of each Olympic Games (as well as some other major international sports competitions) to provide for expedited resolution of all disputes arising during the Games or during a period of ten days preceding the Games Opening Ceremony (e.g., team selection disputes, nationality requirement issues, or doping violations). Pursuant to Article 61 (2) of the Olympic Charter and a clause contained in the Olympic Athlete Entry Form, all members of the Olympic Movement are subject to CAS jurisdiction for any dispute in connection with the Olympic Games. According to Article 17 of the Arbitration Rules for the Olympic Games, the applicable substantive laws are the Olympic Charter and the general principles and rules of law that the arbitration panel deems appropriate. All disputes are resolved by a panel of three arbitrators from a pool of CAS arbitrators specifically chosen by the ICAS for the Olympic Games. Their decision, which must be written and provide reasons, generally must be rendered within 24 hours of the filing of a request for CAS adjudication. See generally Richard H. McLaren, *Introducing the Court of Arbitration for Sport: The Ad Hoc Division at the Olympic Games*, 12 Marq. Sports L. Rev. 517 (2001).

For the first time in Olympic history, at the 2016 Rio Olympic Games, the IOC transferred its power to resolve doping-related issues arising during the Olympic Games as a first-instance authority to an on-site CAS *Anti-Doping Division* (ADD), which resolved several cases in accordance with the IOC Anti-Doping Rules applicable to the Olympic Games. The CAS ADD also operated during the 2018 Pyeongchang Olympic Winter Games and will continue to do so at future Olympic Games and Olympic Winter Games. CAS ADD awards rendered during the Olympic Games and Olympic Winter Games may be appealed to the CAS ad hoc Division or Appeals Division. In 2019, the CAS ADD's jurisdiction was expanded to act as a first-instance authority on behalf of any sports entity (e.g., an IF) that delegates its anti-doping rules adjudication and sanctioning powers to it. A three-arbitrator CAS ADD award is final and binding on the parties, and a sole arbitrator CAS ADD may be appealed to the CAS Appeals Division for final and binding adjudication.

Article R27 provides that the Code's procedural rules apply when the "parties have agreed to refer a sports-related dispute to CAS." See generally Despina Mavromati & Matthieu Reeb, *The Code of the Court of Arbitration for Sport—Commentary, Cases, and Materials* (Wolters Kluwer Int'l 2015) ("Mavromati & Reeb") (a comprehensive treatise analyzing Code provisions and explaining CAS arbitration procedures). Regardless of its geographical location, the "seat" of any CAS arbitration is always considered to be Lausanne, Switzerland, and Swiss law governs the procedural aspects of all CAS arbitrations. This ensures uniform procedural rules for all CAS arbitrations, which provides a stable legal framework and facilitates efficient dispute resolution in locations convenient for the parties.

In both Appeals Division and ad hoc Division proceedings, the CAS panel provides *de novo* review of the sport's governing body (or CAS ADD) decision rather than the very deferential, error-based "arbitrary and capricious" or "rational basis" standards that national courts generally apply when reviewing sport governing body rules and decisions. Article R57 provides that a CAS panel has "full power to review the facts and the law" and "may issue a new decision which replaces the decision challenged or annul the decision and refer the case back to the previous instance." In *D'Arcy v. Australian Olympic Committee*, CAS 2008/A11574 at 3, the CAS panel observed that "each party has a right to advance a completely fresh case on the facts" and "it is the duty of the [appeal panel] to make its independent determination of whether the Appellant's contentions are correct, not to limit itself to assessing the correctness of the 'award or decision' from which the appeal was brought." By providing the parties with a full and fair opportunity to be heard during the CAS arbitration, any due process deficiencies in the sport's governing body internal adjudication proceedings are effectively remedied. (Does CAS *de novo* review effectively counterbalance the monolithic authority of Olympic and international sports governing bodies?)

A CAS arbitration award resolves the subject dispute, orders appropriate relief (including damages and allocation of costs), is binding on the parties, and generally is a final adjudication (in some instances CAS ADD awards may be appealed). Although CAS arbitration awards do not constitute binding precedent or have a stare decisis effect, CAS panels have frequently cited to and relied on prior Appeals Division and ad hoc Division awards in subsequent similar cases. This effectively "accord[s] to previous CAS awards a substantial precedential value and it is up to the party advocating a jurisprudential change to submit persuasive arguments and evidence to that effect." *Anderson, et al. v. IOC*, CAS

2008/A/1545. Pursuant to Article R59, the CAS Secretary General reviews all Appeals Division awards for form (e.g., errors in grammar, spelling, or calculation of numbers are corrected) and "may also draw the attention of the Panel to fundamental issues of principle." This review includes pointing out any departure from well-established CAS jurisprudence without adequate reasons and suggesting revisions in an effort to "ensure that there is no unjustified change in the CAS established case law under the same or similar conditions." Mavromati & Reeb at 367. Non-confidential CAS Appeals Division, ad hoc Division, and ADD awards, which are indexed and published on the CAS website at tas-cas.org., are collectively creating a rich body of Olympic and international sports law, a so-called *lex sportiva*. See generally James A.R. Nafziger, International Sports Law (2d ed.) at 48-61 (Transnational Publishers, Inc. 2004) (observing that CAS awards "provide guidance in later cases, strongly influence later awards, and often function as precedent," which reinforce and help elaborate "established rules and principles of international sports law").

Because the "seat" of all CAS arbitrations is Lausanne, Switzerland (regardless of where the arbitration occurs), CAS arbitration awards are subject to judicial review by the Swiss Federal Tribunal (SFT), Switzerland's highest court. The SFT has ruled that "the CAS is a true arbitral tribunal independent of the parties," which "offers the guarantees of independence upon which Swiss law makes conditional the valid exclusion of ordinary judicial recourse." *G. v. Federation Equestre Internationale* (Swiss Federal Tribunal 1993) in Digest of CAS Awards 1986-1998 at 561, 568-569 (Reeb, ed. 1998). In a 2003 case, the SFT rejected the plaintiffs' contention that the CAS is not impartial when it decides a dispute between an athlete and the IOC. It ruled that the CAS, whose operations have been overseen by the ICAS since 1994, is sufficiently independent from the IOC for its arbitration decisions "to be considered true awards, equivalent to the judgments of State courts." *A. and B. v. IOC and FIS (Lazutina), A. and B. v. IOC and FIS,* in Digest of CAS Awards III 2001-2003 (Matthieu Reeb ed., 2004) at 674, 689.

In *Canas v. ATP Tour,* 4P.172/2006 (1st Civ. Law Ct., March 22, 2007), the SFT refused to enforce a contractual waiver of an athlete's right to appeal a CAS award, which was a condition of participating in any events organized or sponsored by the Association of Tennis Professionals Tour. The athlete's agreement to arbitrate a doping dispute before the CAS is enforceable because it "promotes the swift settlement of [sports] disputes . . . by specialized arbitral tribunals that offer sufficient guarantees of independence and impartiality." On the other hand, the SFT recognized the importance of ensuring that "the parties, especially professional athletes, do not give up lightly their right to appeal awards issued by a last instance arbitral body before the supreme judicial authority of the state in which the arbitral tribunal is domiciled." It explained this apparent contradiction by stating "this logic is based on the continuing possibility of an appeal acting as a counterbalance to the 'benevolence' with which it is necessary to examine the consensual nature of recourse to arbitration where sporting matters are concerned."

Article 190(2) of the Swiss Federal Code on Private International Law of December 18, 1987 ("PILA") specifies only very limited procedural or substantive grounds for challenging a CAS award before the SFT; for example, if the CAS panel was not independent and impartial, if the award is outside the CAS panel's jurisdiction, if the parties' rights to be heard and treated equally were violated, or if the award is incompatible with Swiss public policy. *Raducan v. International Olympic Committee,* 5P.427/2000 (2d Civil Court, Dec. 4, 2000) (Swiss public policy requires international sports governing bodies to act in good faith and treat all athletes equally). The SFT has vacated very few CAS awards on any of these grounds. See, e.g., *Canas v. ATP Tour*, 4P.172/2006 (1st Civ. Law Ct., March 22, 2007) (award vacated because it violated the athlete's right to a fair hearing by not providing reasons for rejecting arguments that his doping sanction violated Delaware, U.S., and European Union law); *Matuzalem v. FIFA*, 4A_558/2011(1st Civil Court, March 27, 2012) at 6 (vacating a CAS award on public policy grounds because it disregarded "fundamental legal principles and consequently becomes completely inconsistent with the important, generally recognized values, which according to dominant opinions in Switzerland should be the basis of any legal order").

In a landmark April 30, 2019 award, a CAS panel determined that South American middle- distance runner Caster Semenya (winner of two gold medals in the women's 800-meters race) and Athletics South Africa (ASA) did not establish that the IAAF's Eligibility Regulations for the Female Classification (Athletes with Differences of Sex Development) (DSD Regulations) are "invalid." The Panel found that the DSD Regulations are discriminatory but that on the basis of the evidence submitted by the parties, such discrimination is a necessary, reasonable, and proportionate means of achieving the legitimate objective of ensuring fair competition in female athletics in certain events and protecting the "protected class" of female athletes in those events.

The DSD Regulations establish requirements governing the eligibility of women with certain differences of sex development (DSD) to participate in the female classification in eight events (Restricted Events) at international athletics competitions, including the 400-meter, 800-meter, and 1,500-meter races in which Semenya regularly participates. The applicability of the regulations is limited to "46 XY DSD" (i.e., when the affected individual has XY chromosomes); no individuals with XX chromosomes are subjected to any restricted eligibility conditions. Athletes with 46 XY DSD have testosterone levels well into the male range. Female athletes with 46 XY DSD who have a natural testosterone level of above 5 nmol/L and experience a "material androgenizing effect" from that enhanced testosterone level must reduce their natural testosterone level to within the normal female range (i.e., below 5 nmol/L) and maintain that reduced level for a continuous period of at least six months to be eligible to compete in a Restricted Event. There is no required surgical intervention to achieve this level. Despite its finding that the submitted evidence did not negate the prima facie proportionality of the DSD Regulations, the CAS panel noted that this conclusion may change without careful attention to the fairness of their implementation and application in individual cases.

Semenya and ASA have filed an appeal with the SFT on the ground that the CAS award upholding the IAAF regulations "violate essential and widely recognised public policy values, including the prohibition against discrimination, the right to physical integrity, the right to economic freedom and respect for human dignity." The SFT initially suspended implementation of the DSD Regulations (which allowed Semenya to compete in some IAAF-sanctioned 800-meters races pending its resolution of their appeal), but soon thereafter reversed its decision, which prevents her from continuing to compete in this event and indicates the appeal is unlikely to be successful.

A CAS award is a foreign arbitration award in all countries except Switzerland and is subject to judicial review by national courts of countries that are parties to the New York Convention (e.g., the United States, as discussed in *Slaney, supra*).

A national court may refuse to recognize and enforce it on substantially the same grounds as those in the PILA, including that doing so "would be contrary to the public policy of that country." Similar to the SFT, U.S. courts have construed this defense very narrowly, while generally confirming and enforcing CAS awards. *Championsworld LLC v. United States Soccer Federation, Inc.*, 890 F. Supp. 2d 912, 930 (N.D. Ill. 2012) (confirming a CAS ordinary arbitration procedure award resolving a commercial dispute, concluding that "enforcing the award would not violate the public policy of the United States"); *Gatlin v. USADA*, 2008 WL 2567657 at *1 (N.D. Fla. 2008) (confirming CAS Appeals Division doping award and rejecting U.S. athlete's claim that it is contrary to public policy and should not be judicially enforced because it violates the Americans with Disabilities Act). See generally Matthew J. Mitten, *Judicial Review of Olympic and International Sports Arbitration Awards: Trends and Observations,* 10 Pepperdine Dispute Resolution J. 51 (2009).

The following graphic illustrates the CAS Appeals Division and ad hoc Division arbitration processes as well as the two methods of judicial review by national courts:

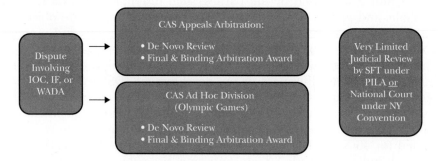

The following cases are illustrative examples of CAS ad hoc Division and Appeals Division jurisprudence regarding governing body disciplinary action against athletes for misconduct or corruption, disputed competition results, and athletes' doping violations and sanctions.

2.   *Governing Body Disciplinary Action*

SAMOA NOC AND SPORTS FEDERATION, INC. v. INTERNATIONAL WEIGHTLIFTING FEDERATION (IWF)

**Arbitration CAS ad hoc Division (O.G. Sydney 2000) 042
Award of September 12, 2000**

PANEL: The Hon. Michael Beloff (England), President; The Hon. Justice Tricia Kavanagh (Australia); Prof. Richard McLaren (Canada)

This is an appeal by the Claimant, the Samoan NOC ("NOC"), against a decision of the Respondent ("IWF") to support the suspension of Ofisa Junior Ofisa ("Ofisa"), ordered by the Samoan Weightlifting Federation ("SWF"), preventing him from participating in the Olympic Games in the 85.0-kg class. At issue, then, is the ability of Ofisa to participate in such competition. . . .

In May 2000, Ofisa competed in Oceania-Commonwealth and South Pacific Weightlifting Championships in Nauru. He won three gold medals and was selected to represent Samoa by the Samoan NOC as appears from a form for confirmation of participation signed by the NOC dated 18 May 2000.

Thereafter allegations were made that Ofisa had sex with a female minor in Nauru. There has been no charge, no arrest, no extradition proceedings . . . and Ofisa has denied the allegations in affidavit form.

By letter dated 23rd May 2000, the Samoan Weightlifting Federation informed IWF that Ofisa was suspended as a member of SWF until 7th June 2001 "due to serious misconduct at the recent Oceania Weightlifting Championships." We do not have a copy of the relevant constitution or rules of the SWF, but it is accepted that the SWF enjoyed powers to suspend a weightlifter for misconduct at the material time.

On 1st September 2000, Dr. Ajan, Secretary General of the IWF, circulated a document to, *inter alia*, NOC that IWF had, in accordance with its constitution, adopted SWF's decision of Ofisa's suspension and [endorsed] it to the Sydney Olympics. . . .

By a further letter dated 6th September 2000, IWF repeated the substance of its letter of 1st September 2000.

On 7th September 2000, Ofisa instituted injunction proceedings in Samoa against JJW Wallwork (the President of SWF) and SWF, both of whom were subject to its jurisdiction, seeking an order in effect lifting the suspension on grounds of misconstruction of the SWF constitution, taking into account irrelevant matters (the suggestion being that Ofisa was penalized because he did not support Wallwork in elections to the NOC), breach of both the main rules of natural justice, malice and disproportionate penalty. . . .

On 8th September 2000, the Samoan Supreme Court [enjoined Wallwork and SWF from continuing to suspend Ofisa and attempting to enforce the suspension to prevent him from competing in international weight lifting competitions and the Sydney Olympic Games] ("the interim order"). . . .

On 8th September 2000, NOC appealed to CAS stating that: "Since Court order has lifted the suspension of [Ofisa], the only cause of action that IWF [can take] is likewise to lift its endorsement of said suspension of Ofisa." . . .

The IWF adheres to its earlier decision.

In Law . . .

The IWF decision expressly assumed the validity of the SWF decision to suspend: the letters of 1st September and 6th September both refer to the adoption of the SWF decision.

On the evidence before us there were and are arguable grounds to challenge the validity of the SWF decision. A failure to accord Ofisa any kind of hearing as well as apparent bias on the part of the effective decision maker, if established, makes it fatally flawed.

It is, however, unnecessary for us to form a concluded view about either the way in which the SWF decision was reached or the legal consequence thereof. The Supreme Court of Samoa has set the suspension aside until further order. There is no reason for us not to accept the interim order at face value. It was for that reason that we rejected an application on behalf of the IWF to adduce evidence said to be relevant to the allegations against Ofisa. To have entertained such evidence would necessarily have involved going behind the order of the Samoan Court (in this instance the Chief Justice). It is the Samoan Court to which such evidence should have been (or should be) addressed.

Although the Samoan Court order does not bind the IWF directly, it indirectly affects it, since if the SWF decision is set aside, the foundations of the IWF decision are removed. The IWF decision required the SWF decision to be valid: the Samoan Court has held that it is not to be treated as valid. That decision which the IWF purported to adopt (and to continue to adopt) no longer has any weight in law.

The IWF decision is not supported on any other ground. Therefore we find that the decision of the IWF must be set aside. The IWF have made no independent examination of the allegations against Ofisa or come to any conclusion about them independently of the SWF.

For the avoidance of doubt, our decision is not to be taken as any precedent should an athlete be validly suspended by an IF: nor should it be read as confirming that an athlete may participate in the Olympic Games where he/she is guilty of serious sexual or other offences. However Ofisa is entitled, until trial, to the presumption of innocence. Other Tribunals than CAS may have to decide in accordance with the appropriate rules and principles which govern their jurisdiction, whether the allegations against him have substance or not.

The CAS ad hoc Division rules: The decision of the IWF that Ofisa Jr. Ofisa cannot participate in the Sydney Olympic Games is no longer effective and is therefore set aside.

NOTES AND QUESTIONS

1. *Analysis of* Samoa NOC. Why was it necessary for the athlete to seek relief from the CAS *ad hoc Division* to participate in the Sydney Olympic Games? *Samoa NOC* illustrates that, in accordance with Article R58 of the Code and Article 17 of the Arbitration Rules for the Olympic Games, the CAS must consider applicable transnational, national, and local laws (including judicial decisions) when deciding the merits of cases.

2. *Legality and Predictability Requirements for Athlete Disciplinary Sanctions.* In *Vanakorn v. FIS*, CAS 2014/A/3832 & 3833, a CAS panel provided the following summary:

> [E]very sanction requires an express and valid rule providing that someone could be sanctioned for a specific offense. . . . Pursuant to CAS jurisprudence, the different elements of the rules of a federation shall be clear and precise, in the event they are legally binding for the athletes. Inconsistencies/ambiguities in the rules must be construed against the legislator (here: FIS) . . . [W]hen interpreting the rules of a federation, it is necessary to consider whether the spirit of the rule (in as much as it may differ from the strict letter) has been violated. It follows that an athlete or official, when reading the rules, must be able to clearly make the distinction between what is prohibited and what is not. In line with many CAS awards, . . . *"the principle of legality and predictability of sanctions which requires a clear connection between the incriminated behaviour and the sanction and calls for narrow interpretation of the respective provision."*

3. *Disciplinary Sanctions for On-Field Misconduct.* In *Suárez, FC Barcelona & Uruguayan Football Ass'n v. FIFA*, CAS 2014/A/3665, 3666 & 3667, the CAS panel upheld the FIFA Appeal Committee's finding that Luis Suárez, a Uruguayan professional football player, committed an assault on Italian player Giorgio Chiellini by biting him during a 2014 World Cup match between Italy and Uruguay, in violation of FIFA regulations. Noting that Suárez' assault on Chiellini was intentional and unprovoked, and rejecting his contention that the scope and duration of these sanctions were not predictable consequences of his misconduct, the CAS panel upheld the imposition of suspensions of nine consecutive games from participation in any Uruguayan national team matches and four consecutive months from playing in any official football matches at any level, as well as a significant fine. It concluded that the principles of legality and predictability were satisfied because "the disciplinary rules have been properly adopted, describe the infringement and provide, directly or by reference, for the relevant sanction." However, it vacated a four-month ban on his participation in any football-related activity and entry into any football stadium because they were not authorized or proportionate sanctions for his offense. It agreed with the Appeal Committee's conclusion that in determining the appropriate sanction for Suárez' assault "the remorse of an offender can hardly be given any weight when the same offender had in precedent occasions committed the same infringement and in those occasions had already expressed its remorse and pledged not to repeat that infringement."

4. *Match Fixing and Corruption Sanctions.* Illegal betting and match fixing pose an increasing threat to the integrity of Olympic and international sports competitions, and recent high-profile scandals have occurred in cricket and soccer. In July 2011, IOC president Jacques Rogge stated:

> I can't open my newspapers without finding an article on the prevalence of cheating and match fixing. . . . It is a world problem and it is a very pernicious problem. With the introduction of broadband, you can bet worldwide. The danger is that from illegal betting comes match fixing and you see more and more attempts to manipulate matches. It is as dangerous as doping for the credibility of sport. It's only the beginning of a huge battle.

Owen Gibson, *London's Olympic Preparations Best of Any Games, Says IOC President*, Guardian, July 25, 2011, http://www.guardian.co.uk/sport/2011/jul/25/london-olympics-preparations-ioc-president.

In *Kollerer v. Association of Tennis Professionals, Women's Tennis Assn., International Tennis Federation & Grand Slam Committee*, CAS 2011/A/2490, the CAS panel upheld a lifetime ban imposed on Daniel Kollerer, an Austrian professional tennis player, for attempting to fix matches three times during 2009 and 2010. This disciplinary action was based on the findings of the Tennis Integrity Unit, an initiative formed by four international tennis governing bodies to investigate breaches of the Uniform Tennis Anti-Corruption Program (UTACP) and to impose appropriate penalties. The CAS ruled that the UTACP's standard of proof requiring that a corruption offense be proved by a preponderance of evidence was contractually agreed to by Kollerer and does not violate Florida law (which governs the UTACP).

Rejecting Kollerer's contention that a higher standard for proof of corruption (i.e., clear and convincing evidence) is required, the panel concluded that there "is no universal (minimum) standard of proof for match-fixing offences" and that applying the UTACP's standard would not "violate any rules of national and/or international public policy." Acknowledging that consistency among different sport governing bodies may be desirable, in the absence of any agreed uniform requirement, each body can decide for itself which standard of proof to apply subject to national and/or international public policy." Because the ATP's Player Council did not object to it, the CAS panel determined that the preponderance of evidence standard was not void on the ground of unconscionability even though Kollerer was required to agree to it as a condition of participating in ATP tennis tournaments. Given the seriousness of match-fixing allegations and potential adverse effects on an accused athlete's career and reputation, do you believe the preponderance of evidence standard provide an adequate level of due process?

3. Disputed Competition Results

During the 2004 Athens Olympics, American Paul Hamm came from twelfth place to win the gold medal in men's all-around gymnastics when he earned scores of 9.837 in both the parallel bars and the high bar, the competition's final two events. However, judges incorrectly deducted one-tenth of a point from the start value of South Korean gymnast Yang Tae-Young's parallel bars routine. Because of this error, Yang received a lower score for his routine. Yang's final overall score was 0.049 points behind Hamm, which resulted in his winning the bronze medal rather than the gold medal.

The Korean Olympic Committee (KOC) protested the start value attributed to Yang's parallel bars routine because it was lower than he had previously received for the same routine in the gymnastics team and qualifying competitions. Acknowledging this error, the International Gymnastics Federation (FIG) suspended the three judges responsible for incorrectly determining the start value of Yang's routine.

The IOC refused to issue duplicate gold medals to both Hamm and Yang as proposed by the KOC and the USOC. However, IOC president Jacques Rogge stated that the IOC would respect a request by the FIG to correct the error in Yang's score and to reallocate the medals for the men's all-around gymnastics competition. The FIG, however, refused to change the competition results or award a duplicate gold medal to Yang because a timely protest on his behalf had not been made to the appropriate official in charge of the competition's judging.

The FIG subsequently attempted to send a letter to Hamm stating that Yang was the "true winner" of this event because of the judges' scoring error. The FIG's letter suggested that Hamm's voluntary decision to return his gold medal would be regarded "as the ultimate demonstration of fair play by the whole world." The USOPC rejected the FIG's proposal and refused to forward the letter to Hamm.

Yang and the KOC petitioned the CAS to correct the judging error and to rule that Yang was entitled to receive the gold medal in the men's all-around gymnastics competition.

YANG TAE YOUNG v. INTERNATIONAL GYMNASTICS FEDERATION

Arbitration CAS 2004/A/704
Award of October 21, 2004

PANEL: The Hon. Michael Beloff (England); Mr. Dirk-Reiner Martens (Germany); Mr. Sharad Rao (Kenya).

[EDS. In gymnastics, an individual competitor's score is awarded by a combination of start values based on the degree of difficulty in a particular routine and on execution as determined by the FIG's Code of Points. The primary purpose of this Code is to provide an objective means of evaluating gymnastics exercises, and each gymnast "has the right [t]o have his performance judged correctly, fairly, and in accordance with the stipulations of the Code of Points."

Unlike sports such as diving, an evaluation of the start value of a gymnastics routine is not made before its performance because gymnasts will frequently modify a planned routine in response to competitive circumstances, or will fail to execute a planned element. The judges' assessment of start values is in part subjective and in part objective. Elements that make up start values such as a Belle or a Morisue are objectively identified. Whether any element has been fully performed is a matter of subjective judgment. In this case, the three judges responsible for determining the start value of Yang's parallel bars routine erroneously characterized a Belle as a Morisue, giving him a start value of 9.9 rather than 10. Video analysis confirmed that his start value should have been 10.]

. . . [A]s was conceded on behalf of Yang and KOC, the protest even *if* made *before* the Medal Ceremony was certainly made *after* the competition had ended with the conclusion of the sixth rotation [for the high bar]. . . .

It is, however, notable that all the provisions we have recited refer to the role of the persons/bodies *vis a vis a competition*. . . . We consider that this sufficiently identifies that any appeal must be dealt with during, not after a competition. After a competition, the person/body is effectively functus officio. This interpretation conforms with the natural expectation of both participants, spectators and the public at large that at the close of a competition in any sport, gymnastics included, the identity of the winner should be known, and not subject to alteration thereafter save where exceptionally, for example, the purported winner is proved to have failed a drug test and so been disqualified. . . .

The extent to which, if at all, a Court including CAS can interfere with an official's decision is not wholly clear. An absolute refusal to recognize such a decision as justiciable and to designate the field of play as "*a domain into which the King's writ does not seek to run*" in Lord Atkin's famous phrase would have a defensible purpose and philosophy. It would recognize that there are areas of human activity which elude the grasp of the law, and where the solution to disputes is better found, if at all, by agreement. It would contribute to finality. It would uphold, critically, the authority of the umpire, judge or referee, whose power to control competition, already eroded by the growing use of technology such as video replays, would be fatally undermined if every decision taken could be judicially reviewed. And, to the extent that the matter is capable of analysis in conventional legal terms, it could rest on the premise that any contract that the player has made in entering into a competition is that he or she should have the benefit of honest "field of play" decisions, not necessarily correct ones.

Sports law does not, however, have a policy of complete abstention. In *Mendy v. AIBA* where the challenge was to a referee's decision to disqualify a boxer for a low blow (CAS OG 96/06), the CAS ad hoc Panel accepted jurisdiction, even over a game rule, but considered it inappropriate to exercise it. It said . . .

> [T]he referee's decision, is a purely technical one pertaining to the rules which are the responsibility of the federation concerned. It is not for the ad hoc Panel to review the application of these rules. This restraint is all the more necessary since, far from where the action took place, the ad hoc Panel is less well-placed to decide than the referee in the ring or the ring judges. The above-mentioned restraint must be limited to technical decisions or standards; it does not apply when such decisions are taken in violation of the law, social rules, or general principles of law, which is not the case in this particular instance. . . .

In short courts may interfere only if an official's field of play decision is tainted by fraud or arbitrariness or corruption; otherwise although a Court may have jurisdiction it will abstain as a matter of policy from exercising it. . . .

[EDS. The CAS rejected Yang's claim that the judges' scoring decision was arbitrary because one judge's head was lowered at the start of his routine, causing him to not observe a second of Yang's initial sequence. Quoting *KOC v. ISU*, *infra*, the arbitrators explained that "arbitrary" or "bad faith" means "more than that the decision is wrong or one that no sensible person could have reached. If it were otherwise, every field of play decision would be open to review on the merits. . . . [E]ach of those phrases means there must be some evidence of preference for, or prejudice against, a particular team or individual."]

While in this instance we are being asked, not to second guess an official but rather to consider the consequences of an admitted error by an official so that the "field of play" jurisprudence is not directly engaged, we consider that we should nonetheless abstain from correcting the results by reliance of an admitted error. An error identified with the benefit of hindsight, whether admitted or not, cannot be a ground for reversing a result of a competition. We can all recall occasions where a video replay of a football match, studied at leisure, can show that a goal was given, when it should have been disallowed (the Germans may still hold that view about England's critical third goal in the World Cup Final in 1966), or vice versa, or where in a tennis match a critical line call was mistaken. However, quite apart from the consideration, which we develop below, that no one can be certain how the competition in question would have turned out had the official's decision been different, for a Court to change the result would on this basis still involve interfering with a field of play decision. Each sport may have within it a mechanism for utilising modern technology to ensure a correct decision is made in the first place (e.g., cricket with run-outs) or for immediately subjecting a controversial decision to a process of review (e.g., gymnastics) but the solution for error, either way, lies within the framework of the sport's own rules; it does not licence judicial or arbitral interference thereafter. If this represents an extension of the field of play doctrine, we tolerate it with equanimity. Finality is in this area all important: rough justice may be all that sport can tolerate. As the CAS Panel said in *KOC v. IOC*:

> There is a more fundamental reason for not permitting trial, by television or otherwise, of technical, judgmental decisions by referees. Every participant in a sport in which referees have to make decisions about events on the field of play must

accept that the referee sees an incident from a particular position, and makes his decision on the basis of what he or she sees. Sometimes mistakes are made by referees, as they are players. That is an inevitable fact of life and one that all participants in sporting events must accept. But not every mistake can be reviewed. It is for that reason that CAS jurisprudence makes it clear that it is not open to a player to complain about a "field of play" decision simply because he or she disagrees with that decision.

There is another and powerful consideration, well-articulated on behalf of Hamm. Had the competition been on one apparatus only, i.e., the parallel bars, then the conclusion that the judging error led to a disarray in the medal positions would follow as night follows day. (We put on one side the contention . . . that Yang had the benefit of the error—a failure by AB Judges to deduct points for a gymnastic fault exceeding the stipulated number of pauses during his exercise. . . .) But the event was not a single apparatus event, but an all around one.

After the parallel bars there was one more apparatus on which the competitors had to perform, i.e., the high bar. We have no means of knowing how Yang would have reacted had he concluded the competition in this apparatus as the points leader rather than in third position. He might have risen to the occasion; he might have frozen (his marks on the high bar were in fact below expectation and speculation is inappropriate.) So it needs to be clearly stated that while the error *may* have cost Yang a gold medal, it did not necessarily do so. . . .

There are two victims of this unusual sequence of events, Hamm and Yang. Hamm because, as he eloquently explained, a shadow of doubt has been cast over his achievement in winning the sport's most prestigious prize. Yang because he may have been deprived of an opportunity of winning it. Both Hamm and Yang are superb athletes at the pinnacle of their sport: neither was in any way responsible for the Judge's error: each has comported himself with dignity which this controversy has subsisted. Nonetheless the Court of Arbitration is not Solomon: nor can it mediate a solution acceptable to both gymnasts or their respective NOCs. CAS must give a verdict based on its findings of fact viewed in the context of the relevant law.

For the reasons set out above, we dismiss this appeal.

NOTES AND QUESTIONS

1. *Scope of CAS Jurisdiction to Resolve Disputes Regarding Competition Results.* Even if rules provide that an athletics governing body's final determination of competition results is not appealable, "CAS will always have jurisdiction to overrule the Rules of any sport federation if its decision making bodies conduct themselves with a lack of good faith or not in accordance with due process." *Hellenic Olympic Committee and Kaklamanakis v. International Sailing Federation,* CAS ad hoc Division (O.G. Athens 2004) 009.

    In *Neykova v. FISA & IOC,* CAS ad hoc Division (O.G. Sydney 2000) 012, in Digest of CAS Awards II 1998-2000, at 674, the applicant claimed that television video called into question the accuracy of the official finish of the 2002 Olympics women's single sculls event and indicated the possibility of mechanical error in the photo finish depicted by the official race camera. Because of the 0.0012-second difference between the first- and second-place finishers and the videotape evidence, applicant asked the CAS to declare the race a dead heat and award two gold medals. Rejecting this claim, the CAS panel stated:

> The issue presented here, however, is somewhat different to that of a typical official's field of play decision, in that it is the accuracy of the technical equipment used that is being challenged and not the judgment of any official. Be this as it may, it is not necessary for this panel to determine to what extent a challenge of a field of play decision based on faulty equipment may be reopened by CAS. Indeed, the Applicant, who has the burden of proof, has not proved that the technical equipment was deficient. Therefore, even if *arguendo* the decision could be reopened, the Application would have to be dismissed for lack of proof.

If the applicant had proven that the official race equipment was defective, how should the CAS panel have resolved this case?

2. *Other Notable Controversies Regarding Olympic Sports Competition Results.* During the 2002 Olympics, by a 5-4 judges' decision, a Russian pairs figure-skating team won the gold medal despite making a few technical errors, while the silver medalist Canadian team skated flawlessly. Shortly thereafter, the French competition judge claimed the French skating federation president had pressured her to vote for the Russians. (Although the French judge later recanted her accusation, the ISU suspended her and the French federation president for three years plus the 2006 Olympics.) Based on a recommendation from the ISU, the IOC's executive board voted to also award gold medals to the Canadian team. Because there was no evidence of any Russian involvement in the matter, the Russian team was permitted to keep its gold medals. This scandal led the ISU to change significantly its methods of judging skaters' performances. If the IOC had allowed the initial competition results to stand, would the Canadian team have prevailed in an appeal to the CAS?

During the 2014 Sochi Winter Olympic Games, the Canadian and Slovenian national Olympic committees (whose skiers finished fourth and sixth, respectively) asserted that the three French skiers who won gold, silver, and bronze medals in the men's ski cross event shaped the lower legs of their ski suits, which created an aerodynamic effect that provided them with a competitive advantage in violation of FIS rules. They sought disqualification of the French skiers and invalidation of their race results, which would have resulted in their respective skiers winning the gold and bronze medals. The CAS ad hoc Division panel ruled it could not resolve the merits of their contention because their protests were not filed within 15 minutes after the competition ended as clearly required by FIS rules:

> The Panel concludes that the Applicants' delay of more than six hours in filing a written Protest is not justified in the circumstances of this case: the Applicants, in fact, became aware of the possibility that the three French competitors may have violated Articles 4511.4 and 222.1 ICR at the time the Big Final of the Competition was run. . . . Holding the contrary would contravene the natural expectation of athletes, sports governing bodies, spectators, and the public that competition results are final unless promptly and properly protested within a reasonable amount of time after the competition ends. In addition, it is not for this Panel, but for the competent FIS bodies, to change the rules governing protests.

Alpine Canada Alpin, Canadian Olympic Committee & Olympic Committee of Slovenia v. FIS & IOC, CAS ad hoc Division (O.G. Sochi 2014) 04-05.

PROBLEM 4-3

During the Olympic Games, with only seconds left in a game in which the Ruritanian team led 3-2, a Ruritanian soccer player elbowed a Slobovian soccer player in the head. This injury ultimately caused him to lose the sight in his right eye. At the time of this incident, the Slobovian player was ten feet directly in front of the Ruritanian goal (within the Ruritanian penalty area) and was preparing to kick the ball toward the net. The force of the blow caused him to lose control of the ball. Although he clearly observed this incident, the Coste Pobrian referee did not call this a foul or award a penalty kick to the Slobovian team. If the Slobovian team had made the penalty kick, it would have tied the game and advanced to the medal round of the competition rather than the Coste Pobre soccer team.

FIFA's "laws of the game" for soccer provide as follows: The referee will send a player off the field and show him the red card for being guilty of "serious foul play" or "violent conduct." The opposing team will be awarded a penalty kick if, inside his own penalty area, a player "strikes or attempts to strike an opponent in a manner considered by the referee to be too careless, reckless or using excessive force." These rules also provide that "[t]he decisions of a referee regarding facts connected with a play are final."

After the soccer match ended, FIFA's Match Protest Committee reviewed a videotape of the incident, but it rejected the Slobovian team's challenge to the referee's refusal to call a foul and its request for a penalty kick. As a result, the Ruritanian team was declared the winner of the match. This decision was upheld by FIFA's Executive Board later the same day.

Discuss how the CAS should resolve the Slobovian soccer team's appeal of FIFA's decision.

4.   *Doping Violations and Sanctions*

a.   Strict Liability Standard, Clear Notice Requirement, and Proportionate and Authorized Sanctions

As a policy matter, CAS jurisprudence has upheld a sport's governing body's adoption and use of a strict liability standard (i.e., liability without any personal fault) for doping offenses. In *USA Shooting and Q. v. Int'l Shooting Union* (*Quigley*), CAS 94/129, in Matthieu Reeb, Digest of CAS Awards 1986-1998 (1998) at 187, a CAS panel stated:

> It is true that a strict liability test is likely in some sense to be unfair in an individual case, such as that of Q., where the athlete may have taken medication as the result of mislabelling or faulty advice for which he or she is not responsible—particularly in the circumstances of sudden illness in a foreign country. But it is also in some sense "unfair" for an athlete to get food poisoning on the eve of an important competition. Yet in neither case will the rules of the competition be altered to undo the unfairness. Just as the competition will not be postponed to await the

athlete's recovery, so the prohibition of banned substances will not be lifted in recognition of its accidental absorption. The vicissitudes of competition, like those of life generally, may create many types of unfairness, whether by accident or the negligence of unaccountable persons, which the law cannot repair.

Furthermore, it appears to be a laudable policy objective not to repair an accidental unfairness to an individual by creating an intentional unfairness to the whole body of other competitors. This is what would happen if banned performance-enhancing substances were tolerated when absorbed inadvertently. Moreover, it is likely that even intentional abuse would in many cases escape sanction for lack of proof of guilty intent. And it is certain that a requirement of intent would invite costly litigation that may well cripple federations—particularly those run on modest budgets—in their fight against doping.

In *Quigley*, the CAS panel stated that doping rules must provide clear notice to protect athletes' legitimate expectations. It explained that if a strict liability test is adopted, "it becomes even more important that the rules for the testing procedure are crystal clear, that they are designed for reliability, and that it may be shown that they have been followed." Moreover, "as a general matter, if breaches of specific requirements laid down by a federation for the testing procedure are sufficiently material as to call into question the validity and correctness of the positive result, any athlete would be entitled to have that federation's decision overturned." The CAS panel ruled that the athlete, who tested positive for a banned stimulant in medication prescribed by a physician for bronchitis while competing in a skeet shooting competition in Egypt, did not commit a doping violation because the IF rule defined doping as the use of a banned substance "with the aim of attaining an increase in performance." The (ironic) language of this rule did not clearly articulate a strict liability standard for doping offenses.

Applying these principles, the CAS Ad Hoc Division for the 1998 Nagano Winter Olympics overturned the IOC's decision to strip the winner of the giant slalom event of his gold medal for a positive marijuana test. The CAS panel ruled that the IOC's sanction lacked a valid basis because neither its rules nor those of the international skiing federation clearly banned the usage of marijuana. Olympic athletes were tested for marijuana solely to compile a database for determining whether its usage is a sports-related problem justifying its ban. *R. v. IOC*, CAS ad hoc Division (O.G. Nagano 1998) 002, in Digest of CAS Awards 1986-1998 at 419 (Reeb, ed. 1998).

NOTES AND QUESTIONS

1. *Strict Liability Standard.* Why did the CAS panel uphold strict liability for a doping violation? Does this standard appropriately balance all parties' interests?

   Consistent with *Quigley*, the CAS Ad Hoc Division for the Sydney Summer Olympics upheld clearly defined IOC strict liability doping rules requiring Romanian gymnast Andreea Raducan to forfeit her gold medal in the women's individual all-around competition in artistic gymnastics. She tested positive for pseudoephedrine, a banned substance, after taking a cold and flu tablet prescribed by the Romanian gymnastics team doctor on the same day she competed in this event. The CAS panel ruled that this doping violation justified the stripping of her gold medal "as a matter of fairness to all other athletes." Raducan did not challenge the identity or integrity of her urine sample or the validity of its analysis, but pointed out a discrepancy between the recorded total volume of her collected urine sample (62 mL) and that which arrived at the laboratory (80 mL in the A sample, and 20 mL in the B sample). The CAS panel ruled that "the minor irregularity revealed in the record showing the volume of urine taken cannot reasonably be considered to have affected the results of what is a valid test." It also rejected her claimed defenses: (1) pseudoephedrine impaired (rather than enhanced) her athletic performance; (2) heavier athletes would not produce positive test results if taking the same dosage of the drug as she did; and (3) she is a 16-year-old minor who should not be found guilty of doping under these circumstances. *Raducan v. IOC,* CAS ad hoc Division (O.S. Sydney 2000) 011, in CAS Awards-Sydney: The Decisions Delivered by the ad hoc Division of the Court of Arbitration for Sport During the 2000 Olympic Games in Sydney (2000) at 111.

Do you agree with the CAS panel's decision? (Note that Olympic athletes had the ability to seek prior approval to take a particular medication from the IOC's medical staff, a process not utilized by Raducan.)

Raducan unsuccessfully appealed the CAS panel's decision to the Swiss Federal Tribunal. (Why didn't she appeal to an Australian court in Sydney?) Recognizing there should be "a very special rigor in the scrupulous application of the testing procedures issued by [a] sporting body," the Swiss court found that the recorded sample volume discrepancy did not impact the positive results of the sample analysis. Because Raducan admitted taking cold medication containing a prohibited substance, it upheld the CAS's finding of a doping violation because the relevant IOC rule defined it to include "evidence of the use thereof." *Raducan v. International Olympic Committee,* 5P.427/2000 (2d Civil Court, Dec. 4, 2000).

2.   *Proportionate and Authorized Sanctions.* In *Chagnaud v. FINA,* CAS 95/141, the CAS panel concluded:

> [T]he system of strict liability of the athlete must prevail when sporting fairness is at stake. This means that, once a banned substance is discovered in the urine or blood of an athlete, he must automatically be disqualified from the competition in question, without any possibility for him to rebut this presumption of guilt (irrebuttable presumption). It would indeed be shocking to include in a ranking an athlete who had not competed using the same means as his opponents, for whatever reasons.

However, it ruled that sports governing bodies "should make allowance for an appreciation of the subjective elements in each case" in order to determine "a just and equitable sanction." Rather than a fixed minimum sanction for all doping offenses (e.g., a two-year suspension), the CAS panel expressed its preference for "a sliding scale of suspension periods depending on the degree of fault of the athlete." Applying this principle of proportionality, it reduced a swimmer's suspension from the two-year period provided by FINA's rules to approximately 13½ months because her coach mistakenly gave her a tablet that she did not know contained a banned substance shortly before an event.

b.   World Anti-Doping Code

On November 10, 1999, the World Anti-Doping Agency (WADA), an international collaborative effort between governments and sports organizations to combat doping in sport, was established in Lausanne, Switzerland. Its purpose is to promote harmonization and standardization for athlete drug testing as well as to establish effective minimum standards for doping controls, especially for out-of-competition tests, and uniform, fair, and proportionate sanctions for antidoping rule violations (ADRVs).

On March 5, 2003, at the World Conference on Doping in Sport held in Copenhagen, Denmark, almost 80 national governments and all of the major international sports federations approved the first World Anti-Doping Code (WADC). The WADC seeks to harmonize regulations regarding anti-doping across all sports and all countries of the world. The WADC subsequently has been revised twice, and its current version became effective on January 1, 2015. World Anti-Doping Agency, *World Anti-Doping Code* 2015 (WADC), available at https://www.wada-ama.org/sites/default/files/resources/files/wada-2015-world-anti-doping-code.pdf. Pursuant to Article 23.1 of the WADC, the IOC, International Paralympic Committee, NOCs, and virtually all IFs as well as WADA and all national anti-doping organizations are signatories thereto and have adopted the WADC, which applies to their respective NGBs and athletes.

In July 2008, the U.S. Senate ratified the International Convention Against Doping in Sport adopted by the United Nations Educational, Scientific, and Cultural Organization on October 19, 2005, which is based on the WADC. On August 4, 2008, shortly before the Beijing Olympics began, President Bush signed the treaty's instrument of ratification. The National Collegiate Athletic Association and U.S. professional sports leagues and their respective athletes, which are not members of an international sports federation or currently directly regulated by the federal government, are not automatically subject to the WADC merely because the United States is a party to this treaty. The NCAA's drug testing program is discussed in Chapter 3. In accordance with federal labor law, doping regimens for unionized professional sports leagues are established by collective bargaining. See Chapter 7. It is important to note that all U.S. intercollegiate and professional athletes must agree to comply with the WADC as a condition of competing in the Olympic Games and other international sports competitions.

The WADC seeks to protect all athletes' "fundamental right to participate in doping-free sport and thus promote health, fairness and equality." Purpose, Scope and Organization of the World Anti-doping Program and the *Code*, WADC at 11. The WADC states: "Anti-doping rules, like *competition* rules, are sport rules governing the conditions under which sport is played. *Athletes* or other *Persons* accept these rules as a condition of participation and shall be bound by these rules.". Introduction, WADC at 16. It provides that "[t]hese sport-specific rules and procedures . . . are not intended to be subject to or limited by any national requirements and legal standards applicable to such proceedings, although they are intended to be applied in a manner which respects the principles of proportionality and human rights." *Id.* at 17. "When reviewing the facts and law in a given case, all courts, arbitral hearing panels and other adjudicating bodies should be aware of and respect the distinct nature of the anti-doping rules in the *Code* and the fact that those rules represent the consensus of a broad spectrum of stakeholders around the world with an interest in fair sport." *Id.*

Article 4.2.1 of the WADC states that the prohibited list shall identify the substances and methods whose usage are prohibited both in-competition and out-of-competition because of their potential to enhance performance in future competitions or their masking potential, as well as those substances and methods that are prohibited only in-competition. Article 4.3 states that WADA will consider putting a substance or method on its prohibited list if it meets any two of three criteria: (1) "medical or scientific evidence or pharmacological effect or experience demonstrates that it, alone or in combination, has the potential to enhance or enhances sport performance"; (2) medical or scientific evidence or pharmacological effect or experience demonstrates that its usage represents "an actual or potential health risk" to an athlete; or (3) WADA has determined that its usage "violates the spirit of sport."

Pursuant to Article 2.1, the presence of a prohibited substance (or its metabolites or markers) in an athlete's urine or blood sample (e.g., by positive laboratory analysis of both A and B samples) is an ADRV, and "it is not necessary that intent, [f]ault, negligence or knowing [u]se [by the athlete] be demonstrated." An athlete's use or attempted use of a prohibited substance or method (Article 2.2); evading, refusing, or failing to submit to sample collection (Article 2.3); and "whereabouts failures" (i.e., "three missed tests and/or filing failures" within a 12-month period) also constitute ADRVs. (Article 2.4)

Article 3.1 provides that an "anti-doping organization shall have the burden of establishing that an [ADRV] has occurred . . . to the comfortable satisfaction [i.e., "greater than a mere balance of probability but less than proof beyond a reasonable doubt"] of the hearing panel, bearing in mind the seriousness of the allegation which is made."

Section 3.2 permits an ADRV to be "established by any reliable means, including admissions." In *USADA v. Montgomery*, CAS 2004/O/645, the CAS panel found a violation of the IAAF's anti-doping rules based on sprinter Tim Montgomery's admitted usage of prohibited substances in a conversation with fellow sprinter Kelli White (who had previously admitted to doping and accepted a two-year suspension from competition) and refusal to testify in his defense. According to White, she and Montgomery had "a small discussion about whether or not the Clear made our calves tight?" He asked her, "Does it make your calves tight?" After she responded in the affirmative, Montgomery placed a phone call in her presence to someone (believed to be BALCO president Victor Conte) and stated "she said that it makes her calves tight too." It concluded: "[B]ecause he has not offered any evidence of his own concerning his admission to Ms. White of his use of the Clear [THG], the Panel can only rely on the testimony of Ms. White. That testimony is more than merely adverse to Mr. Montgomery; it is fatal to his case." For scholarly commentary analyzing CAS jurisprudence regarding proof of doping violations by evidence other than positive laboratory test results, see Richard H. McLaren, *An Overview of Non-Analytical Positive & Circumstantial Evidence Cases in Sports*, 16 Marq. Sports L. Rev. 193 (2006); Michael Straubel, *Enhancing the Performance of the Doping Court: How the Court of Arbitration for Sport Can Do Its Job Better*, 36 Loy. U. Chi. L.J. 1203, 1266-1270 (2005).

As another example, in *Pechstein and Deutsche Eisschnelllauf Gemeinschaft e. V. v. ISU*, CAS 2009/A/1912 & 1913, the CAS panel held that the International Skating Union (ISU) could use a blood-profiling program that measured hemoglobin and hematocrit levels and the percentage of reticulocytes ("% retics") in an athlete's blood to prove she committed a doping violation. Claudia Pechstein, an elite German speed skater who participated in five Olympic Games from 1992 to 2006 and won five gold and two bronze medals, provided numerous blood and urine samples as part of the ISU's anti-doping program from February 2, 2000, to April 30, 2009. None of them tested positive for a banned substance. During this same period the ISU collected more than 90 blood samples from her as part of its blood-profiling program. The ISU charged Pechstein with a doping offense based on high retics values percentages in her blood of 3.49 on February 6, 2009, and 3.54 and 3.38 on February 7, 2009, along with a February 18, 2009, value of 1.37. Normal retics values percentages fall within a range of 0.4 to 2.4.

The CAS panel determined that the ISU satisfied its burden of proving: (i) the blood samples used to acquire the athlete's hematological values and portray her profile were properly taken, (ii) there was a reliable chain of custody of the blood samples from the place of collection to the laboratory, (iii) the machine used to analyze the blood samples . . . was a reliable equipment to record accurate hematological values, (iv) the transmission of those values to, and storage in, the ISU data base was reliable, and (v) the hematological values of Ms Pechstein are reliable evidence of her use of a prohibited method in violation of Article 2.2 of the ISU ADR.

After considering complex scientific evidence and expert testimony, it concluded that Pechstein committed an ADRV:

> [T]he ISU has discharged its burden of proving to the comfortable satisfaction of the Panel that the abnormal values of % retics recorded by Ms Pechstein in Hamar on 6 and 7 February 2009, and the subsequent sharp drop recorded on 18 February 2009, cannot be reasonably explained by any congenital or subsequently developed abnormality. The Panel finds that they must, therefore, derive from the Athlete's illicit manipulation of her own blood, which remains the only reasonable alternative source of such abnormal values.

Article 9 provides that an in-competition ADRV (e.g., positive test for a prohibited substance) requires disqualification of an individual's competition results along with forfeiture of any medals, points, and prizes. For a discussion of the retroactive disqualification of an individual athlete's competitive results after an ADRV until an athlete is suspended from competing, see generally Markus Manninen & Brent J. Nowicki, *"Unless Fairness Requires Otherwise": A Review of Exceptions to Retroactive Disqualification of Competitive Results for Doping Offenses,* CAS Bulletin 2/2017.

Article 10 establishes standard sanctions for ADRVs (i.e., two years or four years of ineligibility to participate in athletic competitions under the auspices of sport governing bodies adopting the WADC for a particular time period). For purposes of determining individual sanctions pursuant to Article 10, Article 4.2.2 states that all prohibited substances are "specified substances" except "anabolic agents [e.g., steroids] and hormones and those stimulants and hormone antagonists and modulators so identified on the prohibited list."

As illustrated by the following case, the standard sanction for an ADRV may be reduced in "exceptional circumstances" if the athlete bears "no fault or negligence" or "no significant fault or negligence." As you read it, consider the WADC's definition of "fault":

> Fault is any breach of duty or any lack of care appropriate to a particular situation. Factors to be taken into consideration in assessing an Athlete or other Person's degree of Fault include, for example, the Athlete's or other Person's experience,

whether the Athlete or other Person is a Minor, special considerations such as impairment, the degree of risk that should have been perceived by the Athlete and the level of care and investigation exercised by the Athlete in relation to what should have been the perceived level of risk. In assessing the Athlete's or other Person's degree of Fault, the circumstances considered must be specific and relevant to explain the Athlete's or other Person's departure from the expected standard of behavior. Thus, for example, the fact that an Athlete would lose the opportunity to earn large sums of money during a period of Ineligibility, or the fact that the Athlete only has a short time left in his or her career, or the timing of the sporting calendar, would not be relevant factors to be considered in reducing the period of Ineligibility under Article 10.5.1 or 10.5.2.

Appendix One Definitions, WADC at 134.

NADO ITALIA v. ERRANI AND ITF

Arbitration CAS 2017/A/5302
Award of 8 June 2018

PANEL: Dr Christoph Vedder (Germany); Mr Ken Lalo (Israel); Mr Jacopo Tognon (Italy)

[EDS. Sara Errani, a 30-year-old international-level professional tennis player of Italian nationality, admittedly tested positive for letrozole, a specified substance, during a February 16, 2017 drug test conducted by the International Tennis Federation (ITF), the IF for the sport of tennis. Errani denies ingesting letrozole intentionally and contends it inadvertently entered her system through a pill of her mother's anti-cancer medication "Femara," which fell into a meal her mother prepared and her family ate on February 14 or 15, 2017. After a hearing and considering her "unblemished record," "evidence which we accept," and "having otherwise been meticulous in taking precautions to ensure compliance with" the ITF's anti-doping rules based on the 2015 WADC, the ITF's Independent Tribunal (IT) characterized her level of fault as "at the lowest end of the scale" and imposed a sanction of two months of ineligibility. Acknowledging the lack of any evidence that she took letrozole intentionally, Nado Italia, the Italian national anti-doping organization, challenged her "food contamination hypothesis" and contended there is no basis for reducing her sanction below the generally applicable two-year period of ineligibility for the presence of a specified substance in her system.]

IX. MERITS

[A]ccording to Article R57 of the Code, the [CAS] Panel has the power to review the facts and the law *de novo.* . . .

THE PERIOD OF INELIGIBILITY, ARTICLES 10.2 AND 10.4 THROUGH 10.6
[TENNIS ANTI-DOPING PROTOCOL]

The regular sanction, Article 10.2

For an Anti-Doping Rule Violation (ADRV) in the form of the presence of a prohibited substance according to Article 2.1, Article 10.2.1 (b) provides, if the substance is a specified substance, for a period of ineligibility of four years if the ADRV was intentional. Pursuant to Article 3.4.1, letrozole is a specified substance.

Neither before the IT nor in the present proceedings did the ITF . . . establish or even claim that the Athlete administered letrozole intentionally.

Therefore, according to Article 10.2.2 . . . the regular sanction to be applied would be a period of two years of ineligibility, subject to a potential elimination or reduction in accordance with Articles 10.4, 10.5, and 10.6.

Elimination of the sanction for no fault or negligence, Article 10.4

Although the Athlete had claimed before the IT that she did not bear any fault or negligence, which was rejected by the IT, such argument was not submitted in support of her appeal before the Panel nor raised by any other Party.

Reduction of the sanction for no significant fault or negligence, Art. 10.5

Pursuant to Article 10.5.1, where an ADRV involves a specified substance and an athlete can establish that he or she bore no significant fault or negligence, the period of ineligibility shall be between no period, at a minimum, and two years of ineligibility, at a maximum.

According to Article 8.6.2, the applicable standard of proof for the Athlete to establish no significant fault or negligence is "*by a balance of probability.*"

SOURCE OF THE PROHIBITED SUBSTANCE

As set forth in the *Definitions*, the first condition to be met for establishing no significant fault or negligence is "*that the Athlete must ... establish how the Prohibited Substance entered his or her system.*"

Therefore, . . . the Athlete had to establish by a balance of probability that she ingested letrozole, which was contained in the Femara medication of her mother, through the meal prepared by her mother. As to the understanding of what exactly means "*by a balance of probability*", the Panel adheres to the general approach established by CAS panels in consistent case law [which is] the occurrence of the scenario suggested by the Athlete must be more likely than its non-occurrence and not the most likely among competing scenarios. . . .

Based on the written and oral evidence and expert-evidence provided before it the Panel accepts, but just slightly, as the IT did, that the occurrence of the food contamination scenario is more likely than its non-occurrence.

Against the background that on, at least, one previous occasion a Femara pill fell out of the box and of the day-to-day routine of her mother taking her medication, the storage of the Femara box in the immediate proximity to the place where the meals were prepared and relying particularly on the testimony of [her mother], which the Panel found most credible, it is deemed more likely than not that a pill of Femara found its way into the broth or the tortellini filling and that the Athlete ingested an amount of letrozole sufficient to cause the AAF.

The concentration of letrozole found in the Athlete's samples is not non-compatible with the single intake of the amount of letrozole corresponding to one or less than one pill of Femara. The expert[s] concur that, due to the large variation in individual excretion time of letrozole and the lack of reliable scientific studies, the explanation of a single pill of Femara mixed in the food and the inadvertent ingestion of an amount of letrozole equal to one or less than a pill cannot be ruled out but is an acceptable explanation.

Degree of fault, Article 10.5.1 (a)

In order to be entitled to a reduction or elimination of the sanction for no significant fault or negligence, the Athlete must establish that her "*Fault or negligence, when viewed in the totality of the circumstances and taking into account the criteria for No Fault or Negligence, was not significant in relationship*" to the ADRV.

No Fault or Negligence is defined as a situation where an athlete "*did not know or suspect, and could not reasonably have known or suspected even with the exercise of utmost caution,*" that he/she committed an ADRV.

The Cilic principles accommodated

Those elements are to be understood and applied in accordance with the established CAS case law as determined, in particular (CAS 2013/A/3327 *Cilic v. ITF*, CAS 2013/A/3335 *ITF v Cilic*) [which applied the 2009 WADC]. As determined in *Cilic*, an "*objective*" and a "*subjective level of fault*" must be taken into consideration. The objective level of fault or negligence points to "*what standard of care could have been expected from a reasonable person in the athlete's situation*" and the subjective level consists in "*what could have been expected from that particular athlete, in the light of his particular capacities.*"

[The] level of care to be expected from athletes is their high responsibility to take care that no prohibited substance enters their system as it is set forth in Article 2.2.2: "*It is each Player's personal duty to ensure that no Prohibited Substance enters his/her body. A Player is responsible for any Prohibited Substance or any Metabolites or Markers found to be present in his/her Sample.*" . . .

In order to find into which category of fault a particular case might fall, [*Cilic*] suggested as "*helpful to consider both the objective and subjective level of fault*" and that the objective element should be "*foremost in determining*" in determining the category of fault. . . .

Under the 2015 WADA Code, the sanctions regime has been changed considerably:

- the regular sanction for an ADRV in the form of the presence of a prohibited substance, according to Article 10.2.1 2015 WADA Code, amounts to 4 years if a specified substance is involved and the ADO has established that the ADRV was intended;
- if the ADRV was not intentional, pursuant to Article 10.2.2 WADA Code 2015 the regular sanction for the presence of a specified substance shall be two years, as in the present case;
- at that stage, concerning the regular sanction, the legal situations under both the 2009 and the 2015 edition of the WADA Code coincide;
- the sanctions regime, however, differs in respect to the potential reduction of the sanction: whereas, under Article 10.4 [of the] 2009 WADA Code, in the event of a specified substance, in the absence of intent, a reduction was possible for any kind of fault including significant fault or negligence, now, under the 2015 WADA Code, with respect to a specified substance, according to Article 10.5.1.1, a reduction can only be considered if an athlete can establish that he or she bore no significant fault or negligence;
- as a consequence, a reduction can no longer be granted for the category of significant fault but only for a normal or light degree of fault or negligence.

Therefore, the *Cilic* principles are to be accommodated accordingly. The time span of 24 months which is still available now covers only two instead of three categories of fault:

- normal degree of fault: over 12 months and up to 24 months with a standard normal degree leading to an 18-month period of ineligibility; and
- light degree of fault: 0–12 months with a standard light degree leading to a 6-month period of ineligibility.

The other guiding principles identified in *Cilic* in order to determine the degree of fault in an individual case continue to be applicable. The objective elements of the level of fault identified in *Cilic* (par. 75) which, according to that panel, have "*foremost*" relevance, however, relate to the intake of an unknown product by the athlete in question, exclusively and have no meaning for the case before the Panel.

The subjective elements of the level of fault identified in *Cilic* (par. 76) are of supportive weight:

- the athlete's youth and/or experience
- language or environmental problems encountered by the athlete
- the extent of anti-doping education received by the athlete
- other "*personal impairments*" such as having taken a product over a long period of time without incident, previously having checked the product's ingredients
- suffering from a high degree of stress
- the awareness of the athlete being reduced by a careless but understandable mistake and may be partly applicable to the Athlete involved in the present proceedings.

The application of the re-defined Cilic principles

For establishing that an athlete bore no significant fault or negligence, "*the totality of the circumstances*" must be considered "*taking into account the criteria for no fault or negligence.*" For no fault, an athlete must exercise "*utmost caution,*" i.e., he or she must take every conceivable effort that no prohibited substance enters his/her body. In order to determine the degree of fault or negligence displayed by the Athlete, the Panel, having accepted and based on the Athlete's explanation that she inadvertently ingested letrozole through the meal cooked by her mother, examined how significant her departure from that level of care was.

The Athlete's responsibility includes that she is responsible for the behaviour of her entourage, be it her coaches, medical staff etc. or, in the present case, the members of her family living in the same house and, in particular, her mother who was preparing the food which was consumed by the whole family, including the Athlete, on 13 and/or 14 February 2017.

The degree of fault exercised by the Athlete's mother is to be imputed to the Athlete herself because she entrusted her mother to prepare the meal she ate. The Femara box was stored in the kitchen close to the space where meals were prepared; that situation was changed by her after she concluded that the Femara medication most likely was the source of the AAF. The Athlete's mother was a pharmacist and knew or must have known that Femara contained letrozole. She was aware or must have been aware of the doping warning on the back of the Femara box. She knew that her daughter was a high-profile tennis player and, therefore, was under a strict obligation to avoid ingesting any prohibited substance. Previously, at least once, when she took her daily medication, a Femara pill had fallen out of the blister package. Femara pills do not quickly, if at all, dissolve in the broth or the tortellini filling and could have been removed.

Also personally the Athlete bore a degree of fault or negligence. According to the Athlete's statement made before the Panel, which corresponds with her oral statement before the IT, she did not know that her mother was suffering from cancer and took Femara. Nevertheless, although she had a separate apartment in the house, she could and should have known that the Femara box was stored in the kitchen close to the spot where her mother was cooking because the kitchen and dining room, in a family house, are places common to the family. The pictures presented as evidence show that the Femara box was in plain sight. The Athlete, after having lived for years abroad had moved to her parents' house without establishing or suggesting even basic controls to ensure a safe and clean environment for a professional athlete. Similarly to suggesting what the Athlete needed or wanted to eat to ensure her condition, weight etc. she had to suggest basic actions to avoid contamination even if she did not know about the existence of the Femara box.

OBJECTIVE ELEMENTS OF FAULT

In order to determine the degree of fault, i.e. that extent to which the Athlete did deviate from the responsibility to exercise utmost caution, the objective elements of the level of fault, "*the standard of care that would have been expected from a reasonable person in the Athlete's situation*" are to be identified. The Athlete was under the obligation to control her environment. In the same way the Athlete had to control her daily training program, her diet, the supplements she takes, and her environment away from home, she was also obliged to control the environment at home. Athletes must exercise the same level of care at home in a family environment as at outside places like restaurants. The Athlete was expected to tell her mother to ensure to buy clean food at reliable places, to guard the food from contamination. She should have seen the kitchen with all the boxes of pills lying on the working surface. At home, it was much easier to control her environment than in public places such as restaurants.

The Athlete, in order to comply with her personal responsibility as an experienced athlete in anti-doping matters, should have checked the kitchen and the cooking facilities. Had she done so, she would have checked the Femara box and seen the doping warning on its back. Similar to a food contamination situation, the Athlete could not just confer the responsibility of preparing the meals to her mother. She herself had to ensure that the meals were not contaminated. Even considering that the Athlete lived in a separate room or apartment in her parent's house, the Panel does not accept as an excuse that she did not even see the kitchen because that was her mother's place.

Under the objective elements of fault, the Athlete did not meet the required level of care and displayed a normal degree of fault or negligence.

SUBJECTIVE ELEMENTS OF FAULT

[I]n addition to the objective elements of fault which are of foremost relevance, the Panel also considered the subjective elements identified in the *Cilic* decision (see para. 187 above) and finds that most of those elements do not apply to the Athlete. She was experienced, had enjoyed an anti-doping education and took care about her food when travelling. At home, she encountered no language or other cultural barriers. She was not under a high degree of stress. However, the Panel accepts that her awareness was reduced "*by a careless but understandable mistake.*"

The Panel takes into consideration the particular situation of the family dinner on 13 and/or 14 February 2017. After the entire family returned from the Fed Cup where the Athlete had competed, her mother prepared her favourite dish which she has liked since her childhood. The Athlete was not aware that her mother suffered from cancer and took Femara. But she knew that her mother was a pharmacist and the latter was aware that her daughter was a high-ranking tennis player under a strict anti-doping obligation. In this situation, the Athlete could be sure that her mother would do everything to protect her daughter against prohibited substances and food contamination. She was relaxed and did not expect that she may be confronted with contaminated food. The Panel acknowledges that the Athlete was in a position to feel safe and accepts that the subjective element of "*a careless but understandable mistake*" on the occasion of the family dinner on 13 and/or 14 February 2017 lowers the degree of fault or negligence exercised by the Athlete.

Having thoroughly considered the partly new and modified evidence, the Panel comes to the conclusion that the Athlete's personal departure from the objective and subjective standards of care, expected to be exercised by her, together with her mother's fault which is imputed to her, amounts to a light degree of fault, however in its upper range.

In application of the re-adjusted *Cilic* principles the Panel determines that a period of ineligibility of 10 months is to be imposed upon the Athlete. . . .

NOTES AND QUESTIONS

1. *Analysis of* Errani. Are you convinced that Ms. Errani proved how the prohibited substance entered her system "by a balance of probability"? Do you agree with the CAS panel's determination that she "bore a degree of fault or negligence" (which was not "significant") for her ADRV, and that it was "normal" based of objective factors but "light" considering subjective factors? Do you agree with its determination that a 10-month suspension is appropriate under the circumstances considering her objective and subjective fault?

2. *"Exceptional Circumstances" Justifying a Reduced Sanction.* The existence of "exceptional circumstances" under the WADC establishing "no fault or negligence" or "no significant fault or negligence" for a doping violation is necessarily a fact-specific inquiry to determine the reasonableness of an athlete's action (or inaction) to ensure that he or she does not ingest or use a banned substance.

    (a) *Article 10.4 ("No fault or negligence").* The Comment to Article 10.4 provides:

    > This Article . . . will only apply in exceptional circumstances, for example, where an Athlete could prove that, despite all due care, he or she was sabotaged by a Competitor. Conversely, No Fault or Negligence would not apply in the following circumstances: (a) a positive test resulting from a mislabeled or contaminated vitamin or nutritional supplement [Athletes are responsible for what they ingest (Article 2.1.1) and have been warned against the possibility of supplement contamination]; (b) the Administration of a Prohibited

Substance by the Athlete's personal physician or trainer without disclosure to the Athlete [Athletes are responsible for their choice of medical personnel and for advising medical personnel that they cannot be given and Prohibited Substance]; and (c) sabotage of the Athlete's food or drink by a spouse, coach or other Person within the Athlete's circle of associates [Athletes are responsible for what they ingest and for the conduct of these Persons to whom they entrust access to their food and drink]. However, depending on the unique facts of a particular case, any of the referenced illustrations could result in a reduced sanction under Article 10.5 based on No Significant Fault or Negligence.

In *Pobyedonostev v. IIHF*, CAS 2005/A/990, the CAS panel found that an ice hockey player's positive test for norandrosterone was caused by emergency hospital treatment in Europe following his on-ice injury. Unknown to him, while unconscious in the hospital, he was treated for a heart condition with a steroid called retabolil that contained norandrosterone. He left the hospital 24 hours after receiving treatment, resumed training soon afterward, and did not discover he had been treated with retabolil for his heart condition until long after his positive test. The panel determined he was without any fault or negligence because, under the circumstances, he had no reason to suspect he had been treated with any medication for a heart condition.

By comparison, in *Medvedev v. Russian Anti-Doping Agency*, CAS 2017/A/5317, a CAS sole arbitrator rejected a cyclist's assertion that he bore "no fault or negligence" for a positive test for furosemide (a specified substance) in medication given to him two days before his sample collection by an emergency room physician who treated him for head, shoulder, and hip injuries suffered during a training ride. Factually distinguishing *Pobyedonostev*, the CAS arbitrator determined that the cyclist did not use "utmost caution" to avoid his ADRV, which is required to establish "no fault or negligence." Finding it likely he was aware that the physician had prescribed furosemide but did not take it "once he was responsible for his own care again," the arbitrator concluded "at the very least, [he] should have made further inquiries and sought disclosure as to the ramifications of his treatment." The arbitrator explained: "it was his duty as a professional athlete . . . to ensure that he did his best to avoid *and mitigate* any violation, including the continuing presence in his body of a prohibited substance."

In *ITF and WADA v. Gasquet*, Arbitration CAS 2009/A/1926 & 1930, the CAS panel determined that a professional tennis player's positive urine test for a small amount of cocaine more likely than not resulted from kissing a previously unknown woman in a nightclub multiple times. The panel concluded:

> [U]nder the given circumstances, even if the Player exercised the utmost caution, he could not have been aware of the consequences of kissing a girl who he had met in a totally unsuspicious environment. It was simply impossible for the Player, even when exercising the utmost caution, to know that in kissing Pamela, he could be contaminated with cocaine. The Player therefore acted without fault or negligence.

The CAS panel determined that "the [ITF Anti-doping] Programme cannot impose an obligation on an athlete never to go out to any restaurant or nightclub where he might meet an attractive stranger whom he might later be tempted to kiss. This would be an unrealistic and impractical expectation that should not be imposed on athletes by sanctioning bodies in their endeavors to defeat doping." See also *WADA v Gil Roberts*, CAS 2017/A/ 5296 (determining that athlete had no fault or negligence for out of competition positive test for probenecid from kissing his girlfriend, who had taken capsules of Moxylong containing this substance purchased in India for a sinus infection, because he had no way of knowing he was exposing himself to a doping violation).

(b) *Article 10.5 ("No significant fault or negligence").*

In *Sharapova v. ITF*, CAS 2016/A/4643, the CAS panel ruled that professional tennis player Maria Sharapova's fault or negligence for the presence of meldonium (a prohibited, non-specified substance) in her system was "not significant" and reduced the 24-month suspension imposed on her by the ITF IT to 15 months. Her January 26, 2016 sample collection tested positive for this substance, which was added to WADA's Prohibited List for 2016, published on its website on September 29, 2015. For approximately ten years, she had been legally taking Mildronate (a heart medication containing meldonium), most of the time on the basis of her doctor's prescription, without violating any anti-doping rules. No specific warning had been issued by WADA, the ITF, or the Women's Tennis Association regarding meldonium's changed listing as a prohibited substance, and no case of an Olympic sport athlete testing positive for meldonium or any prior case involving a tennis player had been significantly publicized. The panel found that Sharapova continued taking meldonium "with the good faith belief that it was appropriate and compliant with the relevant rules and her anti-doping obligations, as it was over a long period of her career, and that she was not clearly informed by the relevant anti-doping authorities of the change in the rules."

The CAS panel observed:

> a period of ineligibility can be reduced based on [no significant fault] NSF only in cases where the circumstances justifying a deviation from the duty of exercising the "utmost caution" are truly exceptional, and not in the vast majority of cases. However, in the Panel's opinion, the "bar" should not be set too high for a finding of NSF. In other words, a claim of NSF is (by definition) consistent with the existence of some degree of fault and cannot be excluded simply because the athlete left some "stones unturned." As a result, a deviation from the duty of exercising the "utmost caution" does not imply per se that the athlete's negligence was "significant" . . . . [A]n athlete can always read the label of the product used or make Internet searches to ascertain its ingredients, cross-check the ingredients so identified against the Prohibited List or consult with the relevant sporting or anti-doping organizations, consult appropriate experts in anti-doping matters and, eventually, not take the product. However, an athlete cannot reasonably be expected to follow all such steps in each and every circumstance. To find otherwise would render the NSF provision in the WADC meaningless.

On the other hand, the panel determined that Sharapova bore some fault for her positive drug test, which precluded more than a nine-month reduction from the standard two-years ineligibility for the unintentional presence of a prohibited non-specified substance in her system. Although "athletes are permitted to delegate elements of their anti-doping obligations," an athlete who does so "is at fault if he/she chooses an unqualified person as her delegate, if he/she fails to instruct him properly or set out clear procedures he/she must follow in carrying out his task, and/or if he/she fails to exercise supervision and control over him/her in the carrying out of the task." It determined that Sharapova's selection of her agent and his company to ensure compliance with her anti-doping obligations was reasonable but that she negligently failed to provide instructions regarding how to perform this task or to supervise such actions. In addition, she did not disclose her usage of Mildronate on any anti-doping control forms, which would have been a factor mitigating her degree of fault.

In *FIS v. Johaug and NIF*, CAS 2017/A/5015 & CAS 2017/A/5110, a cross-country skier unknowingly ingested Trofodermin (which contained clostebol, a prohibited non-specified substance) provided by a physician to heal her lip sores. The tube of this medication (which was in her possession for approximately 12 days before providing the urine sample giving rise to her positive test result for a very small amount of clostebol) clearly listed "Clostebol acetate" as an ingredient, and the box containing it had a conspicuous doping-related warning label. Although she did not provide "even a cursory check of the label" or make any effort to verify by Internet research whether any of the medication's listed ingredients were on the WADA Prohibited List, the CAS panel determined she had no significant fault or negligence for her ADRV because "she had acted upon the advice of Dr. Bendiksen, her skiing team doctor and a highly-respected expert in anti-doping, and that the Trofodermin had been provided by him." It observed: "Considering Ms Johaug's extremely high level of experience and success as an international athlete, her failure to conduct a basic check is very surprising. Throughout her ten-year career as a professional cross-country skier she has been subject to approximately 140 doping control tests. As such, she should have been very familiar with the rigorous standards expected of an athlete such as herself. Therefore, in light of her personal capacities, Ms Johaug would certainly have been expected to at very least check the label and conduct a basic internet search." Based on the totality of the circumstances, including her negligence, a majority of the panel determined that an 18-month suspension is appropriate.

In *Lea v. USADA*, CAS 2016/A/4371, a CAS panel determined that a professional cyclist did not have significant fault or negligence for an in-competition positive drug test for oxycodone (a specified substance) caused by taking one tablet of Percocet as a sleep aid late at night approximately 12 to 12 and a half hours before a morning race the next day. A long-time trusted sports medicine physician had prescribed the Percocet, a permissible out-of-competition medication he knew contained oxycodone, which was foreseeably used by cyclists for pain relief on non-riding days during multi-day cycling competitions and/or as a sleep aid, without providing any warnings regarding the risk of a positive in-competition drug test even if taken "out-of-competition" (defined by the WADC as 12 hours before the beginning of a competition in which the athlete will participate). The cyclist was generally aware that metabolites of ingredients of Percocet medication, including oxycodone, may remain in his system beyond its period of therapeutic effectiveness, which is approximately four hours. USADA's Science Director, testified that oxycodone metabolites can remain in one's system 24 to 72 hours after ingestion, but there was no record evidence that the IF for cycling, USADA, or WADA websites or the GlobalDRO.com (the primary Internet resources athletes should check to obtain information about products or substances before taking them) contained this information. Also no record showed evidence that any of these resources warned that oxycodone or its metabolites could remain in an athlete's system longer than 12 hours after ingesting it and result in a positive in-competition test even if medication containing it was taken out-of-competition. After reviewing prior CAS cases with similar facts, the CAS panel imposed a six-month suspension based on the athlete's relatively low level of fault for taking a Percocet tablet the day before a cycling event without trying to determine how long it could remain in his system.

In *Medvedev, supra*, the CAS sole arbitrator determined that this WADC provision "clearly requires that the Athlete remain under a duty to deal appropriately with the presence of a prohibited substance in his or her body *after* ingestion," which "involves consultation and might lead to withdrawal from competition for example, as well as a retroactive TUE [therapeutic use] application (albeit that there was no specific separate obligation for him to apply for the same)." However, he concluded that the cyclist's fault was not "significant" and justified a reduction in the standard two-year period of ineligibility:

> The starting point in a case of this nature of the ADRV is the ingestion of a single pill of furosemide by the Athlete at the direction of an emergency room doctor while the Athlete was in an uncontroverted, mentally incapacitated state. Under these circumstances, and not taking away from the Athlete's duty to mitigate such inadvertent ingestion . . ., a 6-month period of ineligibility is appropriate.

Regarding determination of the athlete's level of fault or negligence, are the foregoing CAS awards reasonably consistent based on their respective facts, or are different CAS panels and arbitrators applying the same standard inconsistently?

3. *Exclusivity of WADA Code Sanctions.* A CAS panel determined that sports governing bodies that are signatories to the WADC are prohibited by contract from imposing sanctions for doping violations other than those prescribed by the code. *USOC v. IOC*, CAS 2011/A/2422 (invalidating an IOC rule precluding any person sanctioned with a suspension of more than six months for a doping violation on or after July 1, 2008, from participating in the next Olympic Games after expiration of the suspension); *British Olympic Association (BOA) v. WADA*, CAS 2011/A/2658 (invalidating a BOA bylaw declaring any British athlete previously found guilty of a doping offense to be permanently ineligible to represent Great Britain in the Olympic Games).

4. *Team or National Responsibility for Doping Violations.* In *USOC v. IOC & IAAF*, CAS 2004/A/725, the CAS panel reversed the IAAF's decision to disqualify the United States 1,600-meter relay team (which won the gold medal in the 2000 Sydney Games) because of Jerome Young's 1999 positive drug test. In June 2004, the panel found that Young, who competed in a preliminary round as a member of the American 1,600-meter Olympic relay team, had committed a 1999 doping offense and should have been ineligible to participate in the 2000 Sydney Games (resulting in the loss of his gold medal).

In July 2004, the IAAF determined that the U.S. team's first-place finish in the 1,600-meter relay should be annulled because of Young's ineligibility to compete in the 2000 Olympics. The CAS panel found that the IAAF's rules in effect in 2000 concerned only the disqualification, ineligibility, and annulment of an individual athlete's performance results:

> To take a rule that plainly concerns individual ineligibility and the annulment of individual results, and then to stretch and complement and construe it in order that it may be said to govern the results achieved by teams, is the sort of legal abracadabra that lawyers and partisans in the fight against doping in sport can love, but in which athletes should not be required to engage in order to understand the meaning of the rules to which they are subject. . . .

See also *Tzagaev v. Int'l Weightlifting Federation*, Arbitration CAS ad hoc Division (O.G. Sydney 2000) 010 (annulling IWF's decision to prohibit all Bulgarian weightlifters from further participation in the Sydney Olympics after three of them tested positive for banned substances because "suspension of an entire federation from participation in the Olympic Games, including innocent athletes who have not committed a doping offence or any other violation of the applicable rules, at least requires an explicit, and unambiguous legal basis").

Article 11.2 of the WADC permits the sport's governing body to impose "an appropriate sanction on a team" (e.g., loss of points, disqualification) if two or more of its athletes commit an ADRV during a competition or event. Article 11.3 allows it to establish competition or event rules with stricter consequences; for example, the IOC could disqualify a team from the Olympic Games "based on a lesser number of anti-doping rule violations during the period of the Games." Comment to Article 11.3.

A CAS panel upheld membership suspensions of the All-Russia Athletic Federation (ARAF) and Russian Paralympic Committee (RPC) imposed by the IAAF and International Paralympic Committee (IPC), respectively, based on evidence of a state-sponsored doping scheme, which prohibited the entry of Russian teams in the 2016 Olympic and Paralympic Games, 2018 Paralympic Games, and other international competitions under the auspices of the IAAF and IPC. *ROC and 68 Athletes v IAAF* & IOC, CAS 2016/O/4684 (upholding IAAF Competition Rules rendering athletes whose national federation is suspended by the IAAF ineligible for competitions held under the IAAF Rules, including track and field events in the Olympic Games, unless individual athletes satisfy specific criteria); *RPC v. IPC*, CAS 2016/A/4745 ("the RPC is the responsible entity having the obligation to the IPC as well as [its] members to ensure that no violations of the anti-doping system occur within Russia . . . and that the RPC breached its obligations and conditions of membership of the IPC"), which award was confirmed by the SFT. The CAS ad hoc Division upheld an IOC Executive Board Decision precluding Russian athletes in any of the 28 Olympic summer sports from participating in the 2016 Olympic Games unless he or she individually satisfied strict anti-doping requirements (except the rule prohibiting the participation of any athlete ever previously sanctioned for an ADRV even if the period of ineligibility had ended). *Anastasia Karabelshlkova & Ivan Podshivalov v. World Rowing Federation (FISA) & IOC* (O.G. Rio de Janeiro 2016) 013.

5. *Litigation Challenging CAS Doping Awards.* As previously discussed, the SFT and other national courts that are parties to the New York Convention have jurisdiction to review and either confirm or vacate CAS arbitration awards. Article 22.4 of the 2015 WADC provides: "Each government will respect arbitration as the preferred means of resolving doping related-disputes, subject to human and fundamental rights and applicable national law."

In reviewing CAS doping awards, national courts of countries other than Switzerland generally have been as deferential as the SFT. In *Pechstein v. International Skating Union*, KZR 6/15 (June 7, 2016), the German Federal Court of Justice in Civil Matters confirmed the validity of a CAS award upholding a two-year ban on speed skater Claudia Pechstein for blood doping, which foreclosed her subsequent suit in a German court against the ISU seeking $5.18 million in damages for lost income during her allegedly wrongful suspension from competition. It rejected her contention that the CAS award is not enforceable under the New York Convention because it violated German public policy on two grounds: 1) there was no valid CAS arbitration agreement between Pechstein and the ISU, because she was required to enter into it as a condition of participating in the ISU's World Speed Skating Championship, during which she was found to have engaged in blood doping; and 2) the CAS process for choosing an arbitration panel is unfair because it is skewed in favor of international sports governing bodies such as the IOC, IFs, and NOCs, based on a closed list of arbitrators from which parties are required to select arbitrators, and because of the procedure by which the CAS panel president is appointed.

The court ruled that the CAS arbitration provision is valid because she was not required to agree to it "by any unlawful threat or misrepresentation or by physical coercion." Observing that "the fight against doping is of paramount importance worldwide," it explained "[A] uniform system of arbitration is intended to implement the anti-doping rules of the WADC in an effective manner and in accordance with uniform case law. If this task were left to the courts in the individual states, the goal of international sporting arbitration would be jeopardised." Finding that the CAS "is independent of the sports federations and Olympic Committees that support it," the court concluded: "[t]he procedure of drawing up the list of arbitrators of the CAS indicates no structural imbalance impairing the independence and neutrality of the CAS to such an extent that its position as a 'true' court of arbitration could be called into question." See also *Gatlin v. U.S. Anti-Doping Agency, Inc.*, 2008 WL 2567657, at *1 (N.D. Fla. 2008) ("Pursuant to the [New York Convention], claims that have been properly submitted to arbitration and ruled upon by entities such as CAS are barred from relitigation in this forum").

In *Adrian Mutu & Claudia Pechstein v. Switzerland*, Nos. 40575/10 and 67474/10 (ECHR Oct. 2018), the European Court of Human Rights (ECHR) ruled that the CAS is a genuine independent arbitrational tribunal and that its procedures generally comply with due process rights required by the European Convention on Human Rights (Convention). The ECHR determined that the CAS should have allowed German speed skater Claudia Pechstein to have a public arbitration hearing to comply with the Convention's requirement that hearings be public. (Thereafter, the CAS Code was amended to permit public hearings in disciplinary and/or ethics matters at the request of an athlete.) See also *National Federation of Sportspersons' Associations and Unions v. France*, Nos. 48151/11 and 77769/

13 (ECHR Jan. 18, 2018) (rejecting claim that WADA's "whereabouts system" for out-of-competition drug testing violates Article 8 of the European Convention of Human Rights concerning "respect for private and family life" because its invalidation would increase the dangers of doping to the health of athletes and would contravene the European and international consensus regarding the need for unannounced testing as part of effective doping control).

On the other hand, in *Meca-Medina and Majcen v. Comm'n of European Communities*, [2006] 5 C.M.L.R. 18 (ECJ 3d Chamber 2006), the European Court of Justice (ECJ) ruled that two professional swimmers could challenge their doping sanctions in litigation under European Union law, specifically the Treaty of Rome's competition and freedom to provide services provisions, after unsuccessful CAS arbitration. After the swimmers tested positive for nandrolone, FINA, the Swiss-based international federation for swimming, suspended them from competition for four years. Although the CAS reduced the length of their suspension to two years, the athletes filed suit claiming their doping sanctions violated the Treaty, rather than appealing to the Swiss Federal Tribunal. The ECJ ruled the Treaty provisions applied because the challenged doping rules, although "purely sporting in nature," have the requisite effect on economic activity by banning applicants from professional swimming. Acknowledging that doping rules have legitimate objectives (including ensuring healthy rivalry among athletes), the ECJ ruled that "the restrictions thus imposed by those rules must be limited to what is necessary to ensure the proper conduct of competitive sport." Although the European Union is not a signatory of the New York Convention, all of its member countries are signatories.Should CAS awards be judicially reviewed on legal grounds other than those set forth in the Swiss Federal Code on Private International Law or the New York Convention, and is doing so consistent with the objectives of the WADC? See generally Matthew J. Mitten, *The Court of Arbitration for Sport's Jurisprudence: International Legal Pluralism in a World Without Boundaries*, 30 Ohio St. J. on Disp. Res. 1, 41 (2014) ("On balance, a consistent body of CAS jurisprudence that is uniformly applied to all the world's Olympic athletes with limited disruption by national courts probably is better than the risk of a potentially conflicting body of international sports law unduly influenced by nationalistic interests through broader judicial review").

Comment: United States ADRV Dispute Resolution Process

The U.S. Anti-Doping Agency (USADA) was formed in 2000 and is an independent anti-doping agency for Olympic sports in the U.S. Its operations are funded primarily by the federal government and USOPC. USADA provides drug education, conducts drug testing of U.S. athletes and foreign nationals residing in the U.S. or participating in Olympic sport athletic events in the U.S., investigates ADRVs (e.g., positive test results and evidence of non-analytical positive anti-doping rule violations), and prosecutes anti-doping rule violations. Its website is usada.org. See generally Travis T. Tygart, *Winners Never Dope and Finally, Dopers Never Win: USADA Takes Over Drug Testing of United States Olympic Athletes*, 1 DePaul J. Sports L. & Contemp. Probs. 124 (2003).

Applying the applicable IF anti-doping rules (which are based on the WADC) (e.g., the IAAF's anti-doping rules if a U.S. sprinter tests positive for a banned substance), a USADA review board considers written submissions to deter-mine whether there is sufficient evidence of doping to warrant a hearing. If so, USADA proposes doping charges and sanctions that are consistent with the IF's rules for the athlete. WADA or an IF may challenge USADA's disposition of a doping matter by appealing to the CAS. See *WADA v. USADA, USBSF, and Zachery Lund,* CAS ad hoc Division (O.G. Turin 2006) 001 (upholding WADA's contention that USADA erroneously concluded that Zachery Lund, a member of the American skeleton race team who failed to check the IF website, which clearly listed the banned substance for which he tested positive, had "no fault or negligence" for his doping violation).

If the athlete or other alleged violator does not accept USADA's proposed doping charges and sanctions, he or she may request a hearing before an American Arbitration Association (AAA) panel (a right provided by the ASA if the sanction would preclude participation in a "protected competition"), whose members are also U.S. CAS arbitrators. Special AAA Supplementary Procedures apply to USADA doping arbitrations, including rules that provide the panel with broad discretion to "determine the admissibility, relevance, and material-ity of evidence offered (Rule R-28(c)) and that permit the panel to "consider the evidence of witnesses by declaration or affidavit, but shall give it only such weight as [it] deems it entitled to after consideration of any objection made to its admission" (Rule R-29(a)). See *Jacobs v. USA Track & Field,* 374 F.3d 85 (2d Cir. 2004) (rejecting an athlete's petition to compel arbitration pursuant to AAA Commercial Rules). In the AAA arbitration proceeding, USADA and the athlete are adverse parties. The IF or WADA may observe the AAA arbitration proceeding or participate as a party. Rule R-4.

Externalizing this process through USADA and using AAA arbitration to resolve doping disputes (in contrast to the former system of internal adjudica-tion by the U.S. NGB for the subject sport) has enhanced the credibility of the U.S. anti-doping efforts within the international community and has resulted in the disposition of doping cases in a manner more acceptable to all concerned parties. See generally Anne Benedetti and Jim Bunting, *There's a New Sheriff in Town: A Review of the United States Anti-Doping Agency,* [2003] I.S.L.R. 19 (conclud-ing that "USADA has laid a strong foundation to combat doping at the national level" and "is achieving international and national respect for its commitment to eradicate doping among U.S. athletes").

Any of the parties in the AAA arbitration proceeding (e.g., athlete or USADA) as well as the IF or WADA may appeal the award to the CAS appeals division, whose decision is final and binding. (This is a unique procedure that applies only to AAA doping awards because an arbitration award generally cannot be appealed to and reconsidered *de novo* by another panel of different arbitrators.) For example, in a widely publicized case, a majority of the three-person AAA panel upheld a USADA doping charge against Floyd Landis, the winner of the 2006 Tour de France bicycle race, based on a French laboratory's finding of exogenous testosterone in his urine. Although Landis proved that the French lab deviated from the international standards for laboratory analysis, USADA proved to the comfortable satisfaction of the panel that its departure from the standards did not cause Landis's positive test results. *USADA v. Landis,* AAA 30 190 00847 06 (Sept. 20, 2007). In its *de novo* review of the AAA award based on Landis's appeal, a CAS panel unanimously agreed with the majority's ruling. It awarded USADA $100,000 in costs, to be paid by Landis, because, *inter alia,* all he proved were "some minor procedural imperfections" by the French lab, and all his multiple defenses were "unfounded" and "barely arguable." *Landis v. USADA*, CAS 2007/A/1394.

The following graphic illustrates the three potential stages of the adjudicative process for resolving doping violation proceedings prosecuted by USADA:

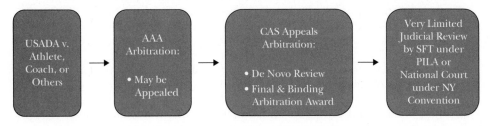

USADA has adopted an aggressive stance in its efforts to combat doping by U.S. athletes, as evidenced by its proceedings against athletes for doping offenses based on circumstantial evidence of usage of banned substances (i.e., non-analytical positives). *Armstrong v. Tygart*, 2012 WL 3569682 (W.D. Tex.), arose out of USADA's July 2012 charges that Lance Armstrong, although he had never tested positive for a banned substance, had committed several anti-doping rule violations, including use or attempted use of EPO, blood transfusions, testosterone, corticosteroids, and masking agents. USADA also alleged that Armstrong possessed banned substances, engaged in their trafficking, and had been involved in a doping conspiracy with five others beginning in January 1998 and continuing until he retired from cycling in 2009. It sought to invalidate all of his competition results from August 1, 1998 (including his seven Tour de France cycling titles) to the present and to impose a lifetime period of ineligibility for future competitions sanctioned by sports governing bodies that are signatories to the WADA Code.

Armstrong alleged that the arbitration procedures in USADA doping prosecutions violated his federal constitutional due process rights:

> Specifically, he complains of the following alleged procedural deficiencies: (1) he was not provided an adequate charging document; (2) he has no guarantee of a hearing by the appellate arbitral panel; (3) he has no right to cross-examine or confront witnesses against him; (4) he has no right to an impartial arbitration panel; (5) he has no right to disclosure of exculpatory evidence; (6) he has no right to disclosure of cooperation agreements or inducements provided by USADA; (7) he has no right to obtain investigative witness statements; (8) he has no right to obtain full disclosure of laboratory analyses or an impartial assessment of their accuracy; and (9) he has no right to judicial review of the arbitrators' decision by a United States court.

Id. at *6.

Acknowledging that "it is very possible" that USADA is not a state actor, the court concluded that "the USADA arbitration rules, which largely follow those of the American Arbitration Association (AAA), are sufficiently robust to satisfy the requirements of due process." It also stated:

> The Supreme Court has already rejected challenges to arbitration based on speculation of bias by arbitration panels (challenge 4, above), the relatively narrow discovery available in arbitration as compared to judicial proceedings (challenges 5, 6, 7, and 8), and limited judicial review options (challenge 9). See *Gilmer*

v. Interstate/Johnson Lane Corp., 500 U.S. 20, 30-32 & n.4 (1991). This Court does likewise, and also rejects Armstrong's other challenges.

Like the Supreme Court, this Court declines to assume either the pool of potential arbitrators, or the ultimate arbitral panel itself, will be unwilling or unable to render a conscientious decision based on the evidence before it. Further, Armstrong has ample appellate avenues open to him, first to the Court of Arbitration for Sport (CAS), where he is entitled to de novo review, and then to the courts of Switzerland, as permitted by Swiss law, if he so elects. Further, the record shows CAS routinely grants hearings in cases such as Armstrong's, and this Court declines to presume it will break with tradition in this particular instance. Thus, the Court rejects challenges (2), (4), and (9). With respect to challenges (5), (6), and (7), as Armstrong admits, such disclosures are only applicable to criminal matters, and there is no reason to believe they would be required under UCI's rules (which Armstrong argues are applicable and, presumably, valid), much less the Federal Rules of Civil Procedure. Challenge (8) again asks this Court to predict what may occur at arbitration, and to assume the arbitration panel will give undue weight to adverse laboratory findings, both of which the Court declines to do. Though USADA's woefully inadequate charging letter makes it difficult to say with certainty, it appears USADA's evidence will revolve more around eyewitness testimony than lab results. In any case, Armstrong's lawyers will have the opportunity to question the reliability of any adverse test results at arbitration, and the Court must presume the arbitration panel will discount the weight of those results to the extent it finds them unreliable or unpersuasive. Similarly, Armstrong will be able to call into question the reliability of any witness testimony, by affidavit or otherwise, that was not subject to cross-examination, and the panel may discount the weight of that evidence accordingly. The Court thus rejects challenges (3) and (8).

Id. at *8.

Observing that "Armstrong is asking a court of the United States to decide matters which are designed to be resolved by, and with direct input from, members of the international community," the court ruled that it lacked subject matter jurisdiction over Armstrong's state common law due process and tortious interference with contract claims:

> The Court agrees with the reasoning of *Slaney* and *Harding,* that federal courts should not interfere with an amateur sports organization's disciplinary procedures unless the organization shows wanton disregard for its rules, to the immediate and irreparable harm of a plaintiff, where the plaintiff has no other available remedy. To hold otherwise would be to turn federal judges into referees for a game in which they have no place, and about which they know little.

Id. at *10. See also *Graham v. USADA*, 2011 WL 1261321 (E.D. N.C.) (the court lacks jurisdiction over coach's claims against USADA challenging his lifetime suspension from coaching Olympic athletes in amateur sports).

Thereafter, Armstrong refused to participate in the USADA arbitration process. Was this what you would have advised him to do? On October 10, 2012, USADA published its 200-page "reasoned decision" with numerous exhibits, including testimony from 11 of Armstrong's former U.S. Postal Service cycling teammates, detailing its evidence that Armstrong was the central figure in the "most sophisticated, professionalized and successful doping program that sport has ever seen" and imposed the foregoing sanctions. After reviewing USADA's report, the Union Cycliste Internationale (UCI), the international governing body for cycling, recognized these sanctions rather than appealing to the CAS. The UCI's president Pat McQuaid stated, "I was sickened by what I read in the USADA report," and "Lance Armstrong deserves to be forgotten in cycling."

PROBLEM 4-4

Popeye, a U.S. weightlifter, won the gold medal during the most recent International Weightlifting Federation (IWF) championships with a world record lift for the super-heavyweight class. The same day he tested positive for nandrolone, a performance-enhancing anabolic steroid metabolite, which is not a "specified substance." The IWF invalidated his competition results (requiring him to return the gold medal) and suspended him from participating in any future weightlifting competitions for four years. Popeye filed a timely appeal with the CAS. At the hearing, a Canadian weightlifting coach testified that he saw a Bulgarian weightlifter (who ultimately won the silver medal) spike Popeye's Gatorade with an unidentified liquid on the day before the competition. Popeye did not see this happen because he left his bottle of Gatorade unattended in the gym while he went to the bathroom. The U.S. weightlifting team physician testified that nandrolone is a clear liquid that is tasteless and odorless and readily mixes with other liquids. In his opinion, ingesting nandrolone one day before a competition would not enhance a weightlifter's performance. Both the A and B samples of Popeye's urine were tested by a WADA-accredited lab and were found to contain small amounts of nandrolone. Based on the applicable 2015 WADC provisions, comments, and definitions, as well as the foregoing CAS precedent, consider how a CAS panel is likely to resolve Popeye's appeal of the action taken by the IWF.

CHAPTER

5

Coaches' Contracts and
Related Issues

A. INTRODUCTION

It was once common for coaches to negotiate contracts with professional teams or educational institutions without the assistance of lawyers or agents. In fact, many coaching contracts were sealed with a handshake. Contracts between coaches and their institutions, however, are now the norm, and the changing landscape of sports has transformed the manner in which coaching contracts are consummated. The past several years have been marked by escalating salaries paid to football and men's basketball coaches. Increased compensation has been accompanied, however, by expanded duties and increased pressure on these coaches to win. The end result is a profession notable for high visibility and job stress but low job security. Consequently, the terms that regulate the rights and duties of parties to coaching contracts take on more significance than perhaps in the past. Notes one author, coaching contracts are "sophisticated endeavors — no standard forms, no two that look the same, no union protecting their interests, and no data bank that correctly reports the intricacies of their packages." Martin J. Greenberg, *College Coaching Contracts Revisited: A Practical Perspective*, 12 Marq. Sports L. Rev. 127, 127 (2001). Given these and other dynamics, coaches require the assistance of agents or lawyers in drafting and negotiating contracts that adequately protect the interests of both parties.

Those who represent coaches in contract negotiations must be prepared to address a myriad of issues, including the scope of a coach's responsibilities, the duration of a contract, reassignment to noncoaching positions, termination of the relationship for cause and without cause, entitlement to perquisites and fringe benefits, and buyout provisions. The materials that follow are intended to provide a glimpse at clauses that increasingly find their way into coaching contracts and provide the source of disputes. The following discussion also briefly examines other issues that confront those who enter into the coaching profession. (Issues involving coaches are also discussed in other chapters, including Chapters 9 and 10, which examine racial and gender equity.)

B. IS THERE A PROPERTY INTEREST IN A COACHING POSITION?

KISH v. IOWA CENTRAL COMMUNITY COLLEGE

142 F. Supp. 2d 1084 (N.D. Iowa 2001)

BENNETT, Chief Judge.

I. INTRODUCTION

A. FACTUAL BACKGROUND

Plaintiff Charles R. (Chad) Kish entered into a written "Extracurricular Contract With Coach" with defendant Iowa Central Community College (Iowa Central) on September 14, 1999. Iowa Central is a community college in Fort Dodge, Iowa, which is organized pursuant to Iowa Code Ch. 260C. Under the Extracurricular Contract With Coach, Kish was to perform the duties of Women's Basketball Coach from September 7, 1999, for a period of nine months and eighteen days, and such other time as might be assigned to coach post-season or other related duties. The contract provided, among other things, as follows: "This contract is not continuing in nature and may be terminated at the pleasure of the Board [of Iowa Central]." . . . On September 14, 1999, Vice President of Financial Affairs Charles D. Peterson . . . advised Kish in writing that his employment as Retention Coordinator for the remainder of the 1999-2000 college year had been authorized, presumably by Iowa Central's Board of Trustees. . . . The particulars of this position, as stated in Vice President Peterson's letter, included the following:

> The period of your employment shall begin on September 7, 1999, and continue through June 30, 2000. Your employment, however, may be terminated at any time if there is a need to reduce staff because of the uncertainties of funding, reduction in enrollment, discontinuance of programs or services, or for other just cause.

Id. Kish accepted this position as well as the head coaching job. Kish's combined salary for both positions was approximately $31,000. Kish worked approximately thirty hours per week at the Retention Coordinator job and that position provided almost two-thirds of his salary and benefits.

Kish's coaching career at Iowa Central apparently did not begin smoothly. Dr. Paxton, the President of Iowa Central, first raised concerns with Kish's coaching during a meeting with Kish on September 23, 1999. Complaints and comments critical of the women's basketball program, Kish's coaching, and practice schedules continued during the fall of 1999. . . . Eventually, on Thursday, November 4, 1999, Kish contends that he was terminated from *all duties* at Iowa Central during a meeting with [Tom Beneke, the Vice President of Iowa Central] and Dennis Pilcher, the Athletic Director for Iowa Central. . . (emphasis added).

II. LEGAL ANALYSIS

[EDS. The court concluded that Kish failed to "meet his burden to generate a genuine issue of material fact on the essential element that Iowa Central breached a term of either of his contracts of employment." It therefore granted defendant summary judgment on Kish's breach of contract and wrongful discharge claims.]

B.   DUE PROCESS

1.   Arguments of the Parties

Iowa Central . . . contends that Kish has no property right in his employment as a coach, where his coaching contract stated that it was not "continuing" in nature and that he served "at the pleasure" of the Board. Furthermore, Iowa Central contends that Kish has not been deprived of any such property right, if it existed, where he was suspended *with pay* from the coaching job and told to continue in his job as Retention Coordinator. Finally, Iowa Central contends that Kish never requested a post-deprivation hearing and did not take advantage of opportunities he was given by Iowa Central to review his suspension as head women's basketball coach.

Kish . . . contends that both of his contracts were sufficient to create cognizable property rights entitled to due process protection. He contends further that he was not suspended, but terminated, as women's basketball coach, which impinged upon that property right. He also contends that he requested due process review via the letter from his counsel to the Equity Coordinator of Iowa Central, but that his request was ignored.

2.   Due Process and Property Interests

Kish's due process claim . . . fails as a matter of law. Due process claims are generally subjected to a two-part analysis: (1) is the asserted interest protected by the due process clause; and if so, (2) what process is due? [Citations omitted.] As this court has previously explained,

> When a public employee asserts a protected property interest in his or her employment, the public employee must show that the protected property interest is derived from a source such as state law, which requires a showing that the employee could have been fired only for good cause. . . . While a public employee with a protected property interest in continued employment is entitled to due process before termination, [Citations omitted], where the claimant can show only that he or she was an at-will employee, the claimant lacks the necessary property interest in his or her employment. . . .

Randall v. Buena Vista County Hosp., 75 F. Supp. 2d 946, 953-54 (N.D. Iowa 1999). Similarly, the Eighth Circuit Court of Appeals recently explained,

> To succeed on a procedural due process claim, [a public employee] must establish that he had a constitutionally protected property interest, that is, a "legitimate claim of entitlement" to continued employment by the [public entity]. [Citation omitted]. If a public employee may not be terminated except for good cause, that is a property interest entitled to due process protection. [Citation omitted]. On the other hand, an at-will probationary employee does not have a protected property interest in continued public employment. [Citation omitted].

Somers v. City of Minneapolis, 245 F.3d 782, 785 (8th Cir. 2001). Recognizing these same standards, the Eighth Circuit Court of Appeals has concluded that language providing that a public employee serves "at the pleasure" of an administrative board or executive is "inconsistent with the . . . conclusion that [the employee] could only be removed for cause," and thus the employee had no protected property interest. [Citation omitted].

3.   Analysis of the Record

Under these standards, as a matter of law, Kish had no cognizable property interest in his coaching contract. The contract expressly states, "This contract is not continuing in nature and may be terminated at the pleasure of the Board [of Iowa Central]. . . ." Nor are the authorities cited by Kish to the contrary. . . .

In *Winegar* [*v. Des Moines Independent Community School District*, 20 F.3d 895 (8th Cir.), *cert. denied*, 513 U.S. 964 . . . (1994)], the court explained the circumstances under which such a property interest arises, as follows:

> Typically, this interest arises from contractual or statutory limitations on the employer's ability to terminate an employee. [Citation omitted.] A property interest in employment can also be created by implied contract, arising out of customs, practices, and de facto policies. [Citation omitted.]

Winegar, 20 F.3d at 899. Whatever the parties may have agreed about the teacher's property interest in his employment in *Winegar*, it is clear that Kish has not demonstrated any contractual or statutory limitations on Iowa Central's ability to terminate his coaching contract, nor has he demonstrated that a protectible [sic] property interest arose from any implied contract arising out of customs, practices, or de facto policies. . . . Instead, Kish's coaching contract expressly provided to the contrary, by stating, "This contract is not continuing in nature and may be terminated at the pleasure of the Board [of Iowa Central]."

Because Kish has failed to generate a genuine issue of material fact on the essential element of his due process claim that he had a protectible [sic] property interest in his employment as Women's Basketball Coach at Iowa Central . . . Iowa Central is entitled to summary judgment on Kish's due process claim as to that position. Iowa Central apparently concedes that Kish had a property interest in his retention coordinator position, and the court notes that, unlike Kish's coaching contract, the retention coordinator position could not be terminated, except under specified conditions, including a "just cause" requirement. . . . However, Kish cannot maintain his claim of a due process violation as to this position, because he was reinstated to it, with full pay and benefits, agreed to the reinstatement, and worked for two days after reinstatement, then abandoned the position. In other words, Kish received all the process he was due with regard to his termination from his retention coordinator position, because he was promptly reinstated with full pay and benefits. A due process hearing could not have provided him with more. Therefore, Iowa Central is entitled to summary judgment on Kish's due process claim in its entirety. . . .

Therefore, Iowa Central's motion for summary judgment is granted. Judgment in favor of Iowa Central shall enter on all claims.

IT IS SO ORDERED.

NOTES AND QUESTIONS

1. *Analysis of* Kish. In *Kish*, the district court rejected the plaintiff's argument that a property interest requiring due process arose from his contract.

In reaching this conclusion, the court found that Kish possessed no claim of entitlement to his position as coach. How did the court characterize Kish's contract with Iowa Central? Was this characterization a predicate to finding that Kish possessed no property interest in his coaching position?

2. *Due Process. Kish* aligns with cases in which courts have addressed whether a coach should be afforded due process prior to being terminated. See e.g., *Jones v. Wash. Interscholastic Athletic Ass'n.*, 2008 WL 351013 (W.D. Wash. Feb. 6, 2008) (there is no fundamental right to coach an interscholastic or high school football team). In *Price v. University of Alabama*, 318 F. Supp. 2d 1084 (N.D. Ala. 2003), the University of Alabama terminated its head football coach, Mike Price, for indiscretions relating to his attendance at a charity golf tournament. Subsequent to his firing, Price filed suit alleging, *inter alia*, that his termination violated his Fifth and Fourteenth Amendment rights because the university failed to give him notice of the charges and refused to allow him to present evidence at a hearing before his termination. At the time Price was fired, he had not signed a contract with the university. The court concluded that Price possessed no property interest in his coaching position at the university because of his failure to accept the terms of the employment contract offered by the university and because any agreement he had with the university was not in writing.

A terminated coach may, under limited circumstances, be entitled to due process protections even though he or she is employed under a contract of indefinite duration. The contours of a plaintiff's right to due process were explored in *Kingsford v. Salt Lake City Sch. Dist.*, 247 F.3d 1123 (10th Cir. 2001). There the court held that because the coach did not sign an employment contract for a definite term, his employment was presumed to be at will, and he possessed no property interest in his position. The court further stated, however, that "[a]n implied-in-fact promise to terminate only for cause can be demonstrated by 'conduct of the parties, announced personnel policies, practices of that particular trade or industry, or other circumstances which show the existence of such a promise.'" *Id.* See *Jacobeit v. Rich Twp. High Sch. Dist. 227*, 673 F. Supp. 2d 653 (N.D. Ill. 2009) (even though coach and school had not entered into an express written contract, property interest gave rise to due process right where a form of de facto tenure existed, since the school district's established practice was to retain coaches unless certain specified acts occurred); *Ridpath v. Bd. of Governors Marshall Univ.*, 447 F.3d 292 (4th Cir. 2006) (university's labeling as "corrective action" its reassignment of athletic director to a position outside the athletic department created a charge of a serious character defect, which in turn gave rise to a liberty interest and entitled plaintiff to Fourteenth Amendment due process protections); but see *Kennedy v. Bremerton Sch. Dist.*, 869 F.3d 813 (9th Cir. 2017) (a high school football coach who was placed on paid administrative leave for refusing to discontinue kneeling and praying at the 50-yard line following football games, failed to plead a cognizable First Amendment retaliation claim); *Williams v. Bd. of Regents of the Univ. of Minn.*, 763 N.W.2d 646 (Minn. App. 2009) (coach's failure to comply with university's grievance procedures precluded his due process property interest claim premised on an alleged contract between him and the university).

Statements that defame a coach's reputation potentially may infringe on his or her liberty interest. See *Campanelli v. Bockrath*, 100 F.3d 1476 (9th Cir. 1996) (statements by public officials charging that coach abused players verbally and psychologically presented question of fact as to whether such statements placed a stigma on coach's "good name, reputation, honor and integrity" so as to foreclose his freedom to take advantage of employment opportunities as a college basketball coach and thereby infringed on his liberty interest); *McNair v. NCAA*, 2015 WL 8053286 (Cal.App. 2d Dist., Dec. 7, 2015) (ruling former assistant coach's defamation allegations related to statements in NCAA Committee on Infractions and Infractions Appeals Committee reports were sufficient to go to a jury; a jury ultimately ruled against plaintiff); but see *Sanchez v. Dubois*, 291 Fed. Appx. 187 (10th Cir. 2008) (cross country coach whose contract was terminated following a history of poor performance, including a failure to follow NCAA practice reporting guidelines, failed to establish violation of liberty interest where institution's reporting of secondary violation to the NCAA was confidential and therefore was never published).

PROBLEM 5-1

William Barr was the head coach of the Richmond football team for ten years. His contract term was August 11, 2019, to August 10, 2022. During a football game, a local sports reporter informed Mr. Reynolds, Richmond's principal, that Barr had shouted a racial epithet at a player on the opposing team. At some point after this game, the principal met with the school district's superintendent and discussed the renewal of Barr's coaching contract. In January 2020, at the conclusion of the football season, Reynolds informed Barr that he would be fully compensated for the entire term of his coaching contract, but that all of Barr's duties as coach would cease immediately. (Barr received the total amount due under his coaching contract.) Reynolds provided no reasons for terminating Barr and did not afford Barr a hearing to contest his termination. The school denied Barr's request that he be permitted to present evidence at a hearing as to why his contract should be renewed. Mr. Reynolds announced to the local newspaper that "Coach Barr's contract will not be renewed." Reynolds made no comments as to the reasons why the contract would not be renewed. Following his termination, Barr sent out applications for several head football coaching positions but received no job offers.

Barr has filed suit alleging breach of contract and depravation of his fundamental rights to continued employment and to the protection of his reputation. Consider the preceding materials in determining whether Barr is likely to prevail on his claims. Also see *Puchalski v. Sch. Dist. of Springfield*, 161 F. Supp. 2d 395 (E.D. Penn. 2001).

C. COMPENSATION ISSUES

In the event that a coach is justifiably terminated pursuant to one of the circumstances set forth in his or her contract, the institution is not liable to the coach for any damages other than those that may be specified in the contract between the parties. Coaches, however, often are terminated prior to the lapse of the contract term because of the poor performance of the team or other matters such as conflicts between a coach and a team owner or university administrators. Assuming the termination is unjustified (i.e., without cause), the coach is entitled to compensation for the duration of the contract term of employment. Therefore, if a coach with a three-year contract is unjustifiably terminated after the second year of his or her contract with a team, the coach generally would be entitled to compensation for the third year of the three-year contract term. In these circumstances, it is not unusual for the coach and institution to disagree over what compensation the coach is owed. These issues are addressed in the following case.

1. *What Constitutes Compensation?*

RODGERS v. GEORGIA TECH ATHLETIC ASS'N.

303 S.E.2d 467 (Ga. Ct. App. 1983)

POPE, Judge.

Franklin C. "Pepper" Rodgers brought this breach of contract action against the Georgia Tech Athletic Association to recover the value of certain perquisites which had been made available to him as the head coach of football at the Georgia Institute of Technology. Both parties moved for summary judgment, Rodgers' motion encompassing only the issue of liability under his contract of employment with the Association. The trial court granted the Association's motion and denied Rodgers' motion. The issue presented for resolution by this appeal is whether Rodgers is entitled to recover the value of certain perquisites or "fringe benefits" of his position as head coach of football under the terms of his contract of employment with the Association.

Rodgers was removed from his coaching position by vote of the Association's Board of Trustees on December 18, 1979, notwithstanding a written contract of employment through December 31, 1981. In addition to an annual salary, the contract provided that Rodgers, as an employee of the Association, would be entitled "to various insurance and pension benefits and perquisites" as he became eligible therefore. Rodgers makes no claim for base salary, health insurance and pension plan benefits, all of which were provided voluntarily by the Association through December 31, 1981, the expiration date of the contract. Rather, his claim is solely for the value of the aforesaid "perquisites," to which he claims entitlement under this employment contract.

Rodgers lists some 29 separate items as such perquisites. In support of his motion for summary judgment, Rodgers categorized these items into two groups: A. Items provided directly to him by the Association but discontinued when Rodgers was relieved of his duties, and B. Items provided by sources other than the Association by virtue of his position as head coach of football. These items are listed in the Appendix to this opinion.

The subject contract was in the form of a letter from the Association dated April 20, 1977 offering Rodgers the position of head coach of football for three years at an annual salary plus certain benefits and perquisites. This contract provided that Rodgers could be terminated for illness or other incapacity continuing for three months, death, or "any conduct or activity involving moral turpitude or which in the opinion of [the Board of Trustees] would constitute an embarrassment to the school." Rodgers accepted this contract on April 25, 1977. This contract was extended until January 1, 1982 by a subsequent letter agreement between the parties. At its December 18, 1979 meeting, the Association's Board of Trustees determined that a change should be made in the position of head coach of football. The following statement was approved and released to the press: "The Board of Trustees of the Georgia Tech Athletic Association met at its regular December meeting this morning. After full discussion, the Board determined that in the best interest of Georgia Tech, with full respect for Coach Pepper Rodgers, a change should be made in the position of Head Coach of Football. The Board stated that it would, of course, honor the financial contractual obligation to Coach Rodgers and that Doug Weaver, the Athletic Director, had been directed to immediately pursue the obtaining of a new head coach."

Rodgers contends that he was terminated or fired from his employment by the Association. However, the evidence of record supports the Association's view that Rodgers was merely relieved of his duties as the head coach of football yet remained an employee of the Association, albeit without any function or duties, for the duration of his contract. In either event, this disassociation of Rodgers from his position and duties was not "for cause" pursuant to the terms of the contract. Therefore, the Association was obligated to pay Rodgers that part of the amount set forth in the contract "which he himself was entitled to receive as compensation for his services." *Southern Cotton Oil Co. v. Yarborough*, 26 Ga. App. 766, 770, 107 S.E. 366 (1921).

In addition to a salary, health insurance and pension benefits, the contract provided that Rodgers, as an employee of the Association, was entitled to "perquisites" as he became eligible therefor. The term "perquisites" is defined as "[e]moluments or incidental profits attaching to an office or official position, beyond the salary or regular fees." Black's Law Dictionary 1299 (4th ed. 1968). The term is also defined as "a privilege, gain, or profit incidental to an employment in addition to regular salary or wages; *esp*: one expected or promised [e.g.,] the [perquisites] of the college president include a home and car. . . ." Webster's Third New International Dictionary 1685 (1981). Thus, Rodgers was entitled to the perquisites (or their value) for which he was eligible during the duration of his contract. The problem presented here for resolution is to determine whether any of the items listed in the Appendix were indeed perquisites to which Rodgers was entitled pursuant to his contract.

First, we must determine the intention of the parties as to the scope of the perquisites to which Rodgers was entitled under the contract. See Code Ann. § 20-702 (now OCGA § 13-2-3). The pertinent language of the contract provides: "You, as Head Coach of Football, will devote your time, attention, skill, and efforts to the performance of your duties as Head Coach under the policies established by the Athletic Board and the Athletic Director, and you will receive compensation at [an] annual rate of $35,175.00 payable in equal monthly installments. In addition, as an employee of the Association, you will be entitled to various . . . perquisites as you become eligible therefore." The Association contends that the language "as an employee of the Association" limited Rodgers' eligibility for perquisites to those items common to all Association employees. Rodgers argues that he was not only entitled to those perquisites common to all Association employees, but that he was also entitled to additional perquisites for which he became eligible as the head coach of football. Since the contract is susceptible to either construction, it is ambiguous. This ambiguity may be resolved by applying the appropriate rules of construction.

"If a contract is so framed as to be susceptible of two constructions, that interpretation which is least favorable to the author . . . should generally be accepted. [Cits.] 'When it is possible to do so without contravening any rule of law, the courts will construe a contract as binding on both the parties, where, from the language of the contract, the conduct of the parties, and all the attendant circumstances, it appears that the intention of the parties was that both should be bound [thereby], and substantial justice requires that the contract be given effect. [Cits.]'" *Bridges v. Home Guano Co.*, 33 Ga. App. 305, 309, 125 S.E. 872 (1924). . . . The subject contract was drafted by the Association. Moreover, the record discloses that Rodgers, during his tenure as head coach of football, did receive perquisites in addition to those received by other Association employees. Accordingly, we conclude that the parties intended that Rodgers would receive perquisites, as he became eligible therefore, based upon his position as head coach of football and not merely as an employee of the Association.

We must next determine the nature of the items for which Rodgers seeks damages, i.e., whether the items listed in the Appendix are perquisites vel non. We will first address ourselves to those items listed in Section A of the Appendix and address separately those items listed in Section B. (a) The Association asserts that Rodgers was not entitled to any of the items listed in Section A because they were expense account items—"tools" to enable him to more effectively execute his duties as head coach of football. Rodgers counters that those items were an integral part of the total compensation package that he received as head coach of football and constituted consideration for his contract of employment. We certainly agree with the Association that Rodgers would be entitled to recover only "compensatory damages that he suffered by reason of the breach of his contract; in other words, that the proper measure of damages arising from the breach of the contract of employment was actual loss sustained by the breach, and not the gross amount of [his] wages and expenses [under the contract]." *Southern Cotton Oil Co. v. Yarborough, supra,* 26 Ga. App. at 770, 107 S.E. 366. . . . However, the evidence offered as to the nature of the items in Section A was in considerable dispute. The fact that these items were not reported as taxable income by Rodgers is not conclusive as to their nature . . . nor is the fact that Rodgers reimbursed the Association for occasional "personal" expenses which it had paid. Thus, with three exceptions, we cannot say as a matter of law either that Rodgers was entitled to the items listed in Section A as perquisites of his employment, or that he was not.

The three exceptions to this finding are the services of a secretary, the services of an administrative assistant, and the cost of trips to football conventions, clinics, etc. The undisputed purpose of the services of the secretary and administrative assistant was to assist Rodgers in fulfilling his duties under the contract. Since Rodgers had been relieved of his duties as head coach of football, and, thus, had no responsibilities under the contract, he had no need for these support services. This is true even though the secretary and administrative assistant may have occasionally provided personal services to Rodgers beyond their duties to him as head coach of football since, as Rodgers admits, their primary functions were to provide services to the head coach of football. Also, since Rodgers had been relieved of his coaching duties, the Association was not obligated to pay his expenses for trips to various football-related activities, these costs clearly being business-related and not in the nature of compensation. . . .

(b) We turn our attention finally to those items in Section B of the Appendix—items which Rodgers asserts were perquisites he received from sources other than the Association by virtue of his position as head coach of football at Georgia Tech. . . . [W]e must now determine whether Rodgers may recover the items in Section B under his breach of contract theory.

"[T]he consideration of a contract need not flow directly from the promis[or] [here, the Association], but may be the promise or undertaking of one or more third persons." *Bing v. Bank of Kingston*, 5 Ga. App. 578, 580, 63 S.E. 652 (1908). "Damages growing out of a breach of contract, in order to form the basis of a recovery, must be such as can be traced solely to the breach, must be capable of exact computation, must have arisen naturally and according to the usual course of things from such breach, and must be such as the parties contemplated as a probable result of the breach." *Sanford-Brown Co. v. Patent Scaffolding Co.*, 199 Ga. 41, 33 S.E.2d 422 (1945). "As a general rule, a party is entitled to recover profits that would have resulted from a breach of a contract into which he has entered, where the breach is the result of the other party's fault. And while a breach of the original contract will not ordinarily entitle a plaintiff to recover as damages the profits of collateral enterprises or subcontracts, yet where the knowledge of the subcontract [or collateral enterprise] is within the contemplation of the parties when the original contract is made, and is known to have been made with reference thereto, anticipated profits shown to be certain, fixed in amount, and the direct fruit of the contract, are recoverable. Profits are excluded only when there are no criteria, definite and certain, upon which an adjudication can be based. They then become speculative and imaginary." *Carolina Portland Cement Co. v. Columbia Improvement Co.*, 3 Ga. App. 483(2), 60 S.E. 279 (1908).

We will apply the foregoing legal principles to the facts of record. Can Rodgers' loss of the items in Section B be traced solely to the Association's breach of the contract? Rodgers testified that he received these perquisites as a result of his being head coach of football at Georgia Tech. The record discloses, however, that the items relating to housing and the cost of premiums on a life insurance policy were discontinued several years prior to the Association's breach of contract and were, in fact, not related to the breach. Thus, these items were properly excluded by the trial court. The remaining items were discontinued as the direct result of Rodgers being relieved of his duties as head coach of football.

Are the remaining items in Section B capable of exact computation? A "gift" is defined as "[a] voluntary transfer of personal property without consideration." Black's Law Dictionary 817 (4th ed. 1968). A gift, then, being a *voluntary* transaction and *without consideration,* can not form an enforceable part of the consideration of a contract. Although Rodgers may have received gifts of money and personalty [sic] during his tenure as head coach of football, such voluntary contributions to his financial well-being are totally incapable of exact computation, for a gift made in one year is no assurance of a similar gift in the next. In fact, Rodgers concedes that he did not receive these gifts each year. Thus, the item which listed various financial gifts was properly excluded from recovery. The items now remaining are sufficiently capable of computation. *See generally Hoffman v. Louis L. Battey Post etc. Am. Legion*, 74 Ga. App. 403, 410-11, 39 S.E.2d 889 (1946).

Did these remaining items arise naturally and according to the usual course of things, and were they such as the parties contemplated as a probable result of a breach? There is no evidence of record showing that the Association had any knowledge of Rodgers' free lodging at certain Holiday Inns or of his membership in Terminus International Tennis Club. Thus, the loss of these items could not be such as was contemplated as a probable result of a breach of the contract. The evidence was in dispute as to the remaining items—profits from his television and radio shows and from his summer football camp plus the loss of use of a new automobile and tickets to professional sporting events—i.e., whether such items were contemplated by the parties at the time the contract was executed as perquisites or fringe benefits to which Rodgers would be entitled as the result of his position as head coach of football at Georgia Tech. These items are of the type commonly provided to head coaches at major colleges and universities. There was some evidence that the Association knew that Rodgers would receive (and, in fact, did receive) these benefits as the result of his head coaching position and that his removal from that position would result in the loss of these benefits. In fact, some members of the Association assisted Rodgers in obtaining many of these items. Also, there was at least some evidence by which the amount of these items could be fixed. Therefore, summary judgment in favor of the Association as to these items was inappropriate. . . . For these same reasons, summary judgment in favor of Rodgers was properly denied.

In summary, a question of fact remains as to whether Rodgers is entitled to recover those items listed in Section A of the Appendix not excluded in this opinion and also those items in Section B not heretofore excluded, any recovery being subject to proof of the amount of his damages as set forth in this opinion. All items which have been excluded are denoted by asterisks in the Appendix.

Judgment affirmed in part; reversed in part.

DEEN, P.J., and SOGNIER, J., concur.

APPENDIX

A. Benefits and Perquisites Received by Rodgers Directly from the Georgia Tech Athletic Association.
   (1) gas, oil, maintenance, repairs, other automobile expenses;
   (2) automobile liability and collision insurance;
   (3) general expense money;
   (4) meals available at the Georgia Tech training table;
   (5) eight season tickets to Georgia Tech home football games during fall of 1980 and 1981;
   (6) two reserved booths, consisting of approximately 40 seats at Georgia Tech home football games during fall of 1980 and 1981;
   (7) six season tickets to Georgia Tech home basketball games for 1980 and 1981;
   (8) four season tickets to Atlanta Falcon home football games for 1980 and 1981;
   (9) four game tickets to each out-of-town Georgia Tech football game during fall of 1980 and 1981;
   (10) pocket money at each home football game during fall of 1980 and 1981;
   (11) pocket money at each out-of-town Georgia Tech football game during fall of 1980 and 1981;
   (12) parking privileges at all Georgia Tech home sporting events;
   *(13) the services of a secretary;
   *(14) the services of an administrative assistant;
   (15) the cost of admission to Georgia Tech home baseball games during spring of 1980 and 1981;

*(16)   the cost of trips to football coaches' conventions, clinics, and meetings and to observe football practice sessions of professional and college football teams;

(17)   initiation fee, dues, monthly bills, and cost of membership at the Capital City Club;

(18)   initiation fee, dues, monthly bills, and cost of membership at the Cherokee Country Club;

(19)   initiation fee and dues at the East Lake Country Club.

B.   Benefits and Perquisites Received by Rodgers from Sources Other Than the Georgia Tech Athletic Association by Virtue of Being Head Coach of Football.

(1)   profits from Rodgers' television football show, "The Pepper Rodgers Show," on Station WSB-TV in Atlanta for the fall of 1980 and 1981;

(2)   profits from Rodgers' radio football show on Station WGST in Atlanta for the fall of 1980 and 1981;

(3)   use of a new Cadillac automobile during 1980 and 1981;

(4)   profits from Rodgers' summer football camp, known as the "Pepper Rodgers Football School," for June, 1980 and June, 1981;

*(5)   financial gifts from alumni and supporters of Georgia Tech for 1980 and 1981;

*(6)   lodging at any of the Holiday Inns owned by Topeka Inn Management, Inc. of Topeka, Kansas, for the time period from December 18, 1979 through December 31, 1981;

*(7)   the cost of membership in Terminus International Tennis Club in Atlanta for 1980 and 1981;

(8)   individual game tickets to Hawk basketball and Braves baseball games during 1980 and 1981 seasons;

*(9)   housing for Rodgers and his family in Atlanta for the period from December 18, 1979 through December 31, 1981;

*(10)   the cost of premiums of a $400,000.00 policy on the life of Rodgers for the time period from December 18, 1979 through December 31, 1981.

NOTES AND QUESTIONS

1.   *Compensation of College Coaches.* A major component of what has been characterized as the athletics arms race in big-time intercollegiate athletics is escalating salaries paid to coaches. As of January 2004, 23 college football coaches earned at least $1 million. Mary Jo Sylvester & Tom Witosky, *Athletic Spending Grows as Academic Funds Dry Up,* USA Today, Feb. 18, 2004, at 1A. In 2011, the average compensation for major-college football coaches was $1.4 million, a 55 percent increase over the average pay in 2006. Erik Brady, Jodi Upton & Steve Berkowitz, *Salaries for College Football Coaches Back on Rise,* USA Today, Nov. 11, 2011, http://www.usatoday.com/sports/college/football/story/2011-11-17/cover-college-football-coaches-salaries-rise/51242232/1. The escalation continued in 2012 when 66 major-college football coaches had annual salaries in excess of $1 million, 42 had compensation in excess of $2 million, 13 had compensation in excess of $3 million, 4 had compensation in excess of $4 million, and 2 had compensation in excess of $5 million. Erik Brady,

Steve Berkowitz & Jodi Upton, *College Football Coaches Continue to See Salary Explosion*, USA Today, Nov. 20, 2012, http://www.usatoday.com/story/sports/ncaaf/2012/11/19/college-football-coaches-contracts-analysis-pay-increase/1715435/. In 2015, the average salary for a Football Bowl Subdivision coach exceeded $2 million. Steve Berkowitz & Christopher Schnaars, *Find Out What College Football Coaches Make — If You Like Your Blood to Boil*, USA Today (Oct. 20, 2015). For the 2018 football season, the average salary for a FBS head coach had increased to $2.6 million. Steve Berkowitz, *Analysis: After Dabo Swinney's deal, how high can college football salaries go? Keep Watching*, USA Today (Apr. 26, 2019).

Factors fueling the dramatic rise in the salaries of college football coaches include the proliferation of money from football bowl games and television contracts. Another factor has been the substantial rise since the mid-1990s in agents representing coaches in their contract negotiations. Increased competition for coaches fueled by the willingness of NFL teams to hire college coaches and colleges to hire NFL coaches has also contributed to rising salaries. Other variables include promotion by coaches and their agents and the illegality of efforts to cap coaches' salaries. For an insightful article discussing the economics of college coaching contracts see Richard T. Karcher, *The Coaching Carousel in Big-Time Intercollegiate Athletics: Economic Implications and Legal Considerations*, 20 Fordham Intell. Prop. Media & Ent. L.J. 1 (2009). Acknowledging the foregoing factors, Professor Karcher identifies several additional factors that have contributed to the dramatic increase in coaches' salaries, including: "the desire to win and the prospects of generating more revenue, the granting of contract extensions to keep winning coaches from being poached . . . , the payment of huge buyouts when coaches do not win, and the tremendous leverage that coaches have over schools in the hiring and contract negotiation process." *Id.* at 4. He also attributes the increase to the refusal of colleges to pay student-athletes a portion of the income generated in football and men's basketball. *Id.* at 44-45. See Richard Johnson, *A history of skyrocketing college football coach salaries from Walter Camp to Nick Saban*, SBNation (Oct. 4, 2019) (providing a historical overview of the increase in football coach salaries); Jasmine Harris, *How Bonuses for Winning Coaches Became a Tradition in College Football*, HigherEdJobs (Dec. 24, 2018) (discussing the historical emergence of bonus provisions in football coaching contracts).

Examples of the approximate annual compensation (which includes university- and nonuniversity-based compensation, excluding bonuses) earned by FBS head football coaches in 2018 include:

- Nick Saban (University of Alabama): $8.3 million
- Urban Meyer (The Ohio State University): $7.6 million
- Jim Harbaugh (University of Michigan): $7.5 million
- Jimbo Fisher (Texas A & M): $7.5 million

2018 NCAA Salaries: NCAAF Coaches, USA Today (Oct. 3, 2018), https://sports.usatoday.com/ncaa/salaries/football/coach.

Examples of the approximate annual compensation for head basketball coaches in 2019 include:

- John Calipari (University of Kentucky): $9.27 million
- Mike Krzyzewski (Duke University): $7.05 million

- Tom Izzo (Michigan State University): $4.16 million
- Tony Bennet (University of Virginia): $4.15 million

2019 NCAA Salaries: NCAAB Coaches, USA Today (Mar. 11, 2019), https://sports.usatoday.com/ncaa/salaries/mens-basketball/coach.

2. *Bonuses and Perquisites.* Perquisites and various performance incentives continue to represent significant components of college coaches' salaries. In 2013, 57% of the income of Division I FBS head coaches was derived from "radio, television, Internet, speeches, alumni club appearances, and similar engagements," summer camps, and endorsements. Randall Thomas & Lawrence Van Horn, *College Football Coaches' Pay and Contracts: Are They Overpaid and Unfairly Treated?,* 91 Indiana L. J. 189, 217-18 (2016).

   Is the compensation paid to Division I-A coaches justified? See Thomas & Van Horn, *supra* at 203 (arguing that college football coaches "create value for their universities far in excess of the value they capture").

3. *Compensation and Athlete Academic Performance.* Should the contracts of college coaches include financial incentives and disincentives related to the academic performance and off-campus conduct of student-athletes? Professor Linda Greene's analysis of the contracts of head football coaches revealed the following:

   > [T]his review of head football coach contracts revealed a trend toward explicit head football coach responsibility for student-athlete academic performance as either a term of the contract or a factor in bonus determination. . . . In contrast, fewer contracts impose a duty of responsibility for athlete misbehavior or penalize or reward the coach for improper or unlawful conduct of their student-athletes. . . . The . . . trend of contracts without explicit coach responsibility for athlete misconduct seems counterintuitive. . . .

   Linda S. Greene, *Football Coach Contracts: What Does the Student-Athlete Have to Do with It?,* 76 UMKC L. Rev. 665, 688-89 (2008).

4. *Required Public Disclosure.* Should documents relating to coaches' third-party income be disclosed to the public? What is the public's interest in such disclosure? In *University Sys. of Maryland v. Baltimore Sun Co.,* 847 A.2d 427 (Md. 2004), a newspaper sought disclosure, under Maryland's Public Information Act (MPIA), of income and compensation information concerning two University of Maryland head coaches, football coach Ralph Friedgen and basketball coach Gary Williams. The Maryland Court of Appeals held that the "employment contracts and any amendments thereto, side letters or documents reflecting the total compensation of monies paid directly by the University" to the coaches must be disclosed. *Id.* at 441. It reasoned that disclosure was essential to the public obtaining an understanding of the salaries paid to coaches. With respect to outside income, the case was remanded for a determination of whether this "income is intimately connected to [Williams's] activities as coach. . . ." *Id.* at 443.

5. *Memorandum of Understanding.* Increasingly, colleges and coaches will enter into a memorandum of understanding ("MOU") before executing a formal contract. The MOU will typically outline the elements of the terms that will eventually appear in the formal contract. These terms include salary, contract duration, perquisites, "incentive pay, guaranteed pay from television, radio and shoe contracts, termination benefits" and buyout clauses. Thomas & Van Horn, *supra* at 207; James K. Gentry, *In Coaching Contracts,*

Deals Within the Deal, N.Y. Times, Jan. 1, 2012; see also Randal S. Thomas & R. Lawrence Van Horn, *Are College Presidents Like Football Coaches? Evidence from Their Employment Contracts,* 58 Ariz. L. Rev. 901 (2016) (discussing MOUs in coaching contracts); Chris Low, *Greg Schiano's agreement with Tennessee wasn't signed by chancellor,* ESPN (Nov. 17, 2017), https://www.espn.com/college-football/story/_/id/21590353/university-tennessee-chancellor-did-not-sign-memorandum-understanding-greg-schiano (discussing the dispute involving the University of Tennessee and a coach, Greg Schiano, who signed a memorandum of understanding to become the university's head football coach before the university backed out of the deal).

The MOU can often play a key role in disputes between colleges and coaches. On October 13, 2009, the University of Kentucky agreed to pay $3 million to settle a $6 million breach of contract action filed by its former head men's basketball coach, Billy Gillispie. Gillispie, who was hired in 2007, never signed a formal contract and coached under a memorandum of understanding. The university argued in defense that it owed Gillispie nothing because the memorandum was not an enforceable contract.

2. Termination and Breach

As the following materials reveal, whether an institution or a club has grounds for justifiably terminating a coach turns principally on the terms of the parties' contract. As *Leach* demonstrates, however, other legal principles influence the legal relationship between the parties.

LEACH v. TEXAS TECH UNIVERSITY

335 S.W.3d 386 (Tex. App. 2011)
(review denied, Feb. 17, 2012)

BRIAN QUINN, Chief Justice.

[EDS. On December 30, 2009, Texas Tech University fired its highly successful head football coach, Mike Leach, who compiled a 10-season record of 84-43. The for-cause termination was based on allegations that the coach had improperly treated a player who had suffered a concussion. On January 10, 2010, Leach, who had signed a five-year contract extension on January 1, 2009, filed a lawsuit against Texas Tech alleging wrongful termination and defamation. Leach alleged the university fired him to avoid making an $800,000 bonus payment due to Leach on December 31, 2009. In 2010, a judge rejected Texas Tech's sovereign immunity defense and allowed Leach's breach of contract claim to move forward. The university appealed the ruling. The appellate court ruling demonstrates the significance of contract law in disputes between coaches and their teams. It also shows, however, that other factors may ultimately determine an institution's liability to a terminated coach.]

We have been asked to determine whether the common law doctrine of sovereign immunity barred the suit of Mike Leach against Texas Tech University (the University), its Chancellor Kent Hance, its regents Jerry Turner and Larry Anders, its president Guy Bailey, its athletic director Gerald Myers, and its employee/attorney Charlotte Bingham. Applying the doctrine via a plea to the court's jurisdiction, the trial court dismissed all but one cause of action averred by Leach. The one remaining encompassed the allegation of breached contract. The trial court refused to dismiss it because the University "by and through its conduct . . . waived [its] immunity from suit. . . ." We affirm in part, reverse in part, and render in part the trial court's order. . . .

THE LAW OF SOVEREIGN IMMUNITY

It is clear that sovereign immunity is alive and well in Texas. As it now exists, it provides a double shield to the entities it protects. They are insulated from both liability and suit. *Tex. A & M University–Kingsville v. Lawson*, 87 S.W.3d at 520-21; *Federal Sign v. Texas S. Univ.*, 951 S.W.2d 401, 405 (Tex. 1997). That is, one can neither sue for payment nor compel payment from the State without legislative consent. *Federal Sign v. Texas S. Univ.*, 951 S.W.2d at 405. Given this double shield, defeating one still meant the other stood. Take, for instance, the subject of contracts. In Texas, when the State executes such an obligation it loses its immunity from liability. *Id.* at 405-06. Yet, it remains protected from being forced into litigation via suit. *Id.* So, while it must perform and, like any other party to a contract, is responsible for its failure to do so, it cannot be sued for damages without its permission if it opts to forego performance. In other situations, the converse is also true; the State may grant someone permission to sue it but retain its insulation from being forced to pay. *Id.*; *Ben Bolt-Palito Blanco Consol. Indep. Sch. Dist. v. Tex. Political Subdivisions Prop./Cas. Joint Self-Insurance Fund*, 212 S.W.3d 320, 323-24 (Tex. 2006) (explaining the nature of the immunity). The logic behind that circumstance is not ours to debate for that is the law as declared by our Supreme Court.

That sovereign immunity extends to state universities is similarly clear. *Ben Bolt-Palito Blanco Consol. Indep. Sch. Dist. v. Tex. Political Subdivisions Prop./Cas. Ins. Joint Self-Insurance Fund*, 212 S.W.3d at 324. Of less clarity, however, is the manner by which a university or the State, for that matter, waives immunity.

Admittedly, our Supreme Court has declared that it has "consistently deferred to the Legislature" to effectuate waiver. *Id.* at 326, quoting *Tex. Natural Res. Comm'n v. IT-Davy*, 74 S.W.3d 849, 854 (Tex. 2002). That is, we have been told that only the legislature can remove the insulation. *Id.* . . .

If one invokes a statute as basis for defeating immunity, that statute must clearly and unambiguously abrogate the shield. Tex. Gov't Code Ann. § 311.034 (Vernon Supp. 2010). On the other hand, if the purported waiver is founded upon non-statutory grounds, then we must search precedent to determine whether the factual situation has already been addressed by the Supreme Court. *E.g.*, *Federal Sign v. Texas S. Univ.*, *supra* (wherein the court clearly held that executing a contract waives immunity from liability). If that court has not, then we defer to the legislature's general authority to act on the matter, except when the circumstances compel the judiciary to intervene, if ever. With that said, we turn to the issues posed to us by the parties.

APPLICATION OF SOVEREIGN IMMUNITY — LEACH ISSUES

A.   WAIVER BY OPERATING PROCEDURE

We first address Leach's argument that the University's immunity was waived by statute. The statute in question is § 109.001(c) of the Texas Education Code. Through it, the legislature wrote:

The governance, control, jurisdiction, organization, and management of the Texas Tech University System is hereby vested in the present board of regents of Texas Tech University, which will hereinafter be known and designated as the board of regents of the Texas Tech University System. The board by rule may delegate a power or duty of the board to an officer, employee, or other agent of the board.

Tex. Educ. Code Ann. § 109.001(c) (Vernon 2002). Per that grant, the University enacted specific "operating policy and procedures" allowing an employee to "elect to remove such issues of grievance or complaint from further consideration through . . ." the school's administrative process if the employee "files substantially the same issues . . . with any external agency or court. . . ." Leach reads this as consent from the University to sue it in state court. We disagree for several reasons.

First, and assuming arguendo that any state-supported university has the power to waive its immunity, such a waiver is not explicit in the "operating policy and procedures" at issue. Recognizing that an employee may end an internal grievance proceeding if the same complaint is encompassed within a later suit speaks to whether the person must exhaust internal administrative remedies before suing. It does not speak to the matter of waiving immunity. Indeed, nothing in the procedure even mentions immunity, much less its waiver. . . .

Finally, and to the extent Leach argues that the University's operating procedures are comparable to state statutes, we abide by the legislature's unambiguous directive regarding the waiver of immunity. Again, per that directive, a statute "shall not be construed" as waiving immunity unless the "waiver is effected by clear and unambiguous language." Tex. Gov't Code Ann. § 311.034 (Vernon Supp. 2010). Those words plainly mean that any waiver one attempts to derive from a statute must be clear and unambiguous. And, the statute underlying Leach's claim of waiver is § 109.001(c). According to him, it purports to vest the University's regents with the power to do most anything they want, including the power to waive immunity. Yet, nothing in it expressly addresses immunity or its waiver.

B. WHISTLEBLOWER CLAIM

Next, Leach argues that the trial court erred in dismissing his whistleblower claim. We again disagree and overrule the issue.

[EDS. The court noted that claims asserted pursuant to the Texas Whistleblower's Act are not barred by sovereign immunity. It concluded, however, that Leach failed to allege facts to establish a cognizable claim under the Act.]

C. CONSTITUTIONAL CLAIMS

We next address the argument that the trial court erred in dismissing Leach's [state] constitutional claims. The claims in question involve the purported taking without compensation of Leach's property and his termination without due process. We overrule the issues in part.

1. Takings Claim

[EDS. The court held that a claim alleging a breach of contract, non-payment of salary, does not amount to a taking.] [W]hen the State withholds property under color of a contractual right, such as when it believes the contract was not properly performed, it is not acting as a sovereign invoking powers of eminent domain, but rather as a private party to a contract invoking rights expressed or implicit in the contract. *Id.* at 599. Thus, the takings clause appearing under Texas Constitution art. I, § 17 does not apply to contractual disputes. . . .

2. *Denial of Due Course of Law*

As for the dispute regarding due process, Leach argues that he was denied constitutionally protected interests without due course of law. The property rights at issue were to 1) continue employment for a term of years (except when terminated for cause) and 2) specific compensation accruing while so employed. And because he tendered sufficient evidence establishing the constitutional claim, it allegedly was error for the trial court to use the doctrine of sovereign immunity to dismiss it. We sustain the issue for several reasons.

Sovereign immunity bars a trial court from adjudicating lawsuits through which a complainant seeks money damages from the State. *Tex. Natural Res. & Conservation Comm'n v. IT-Davy*, 74 S.W.3d 849, 853 (Tex. 2002). It does not pretermit legal actions against a governmental entity seeking equitable relief to redress violations of the Texas Constitution. *City of Elsa v. M.A.L.*, 226 S.W.3d 390, 392 (Tex. 2007). . . . One means of determining whether constitutional violations have occurred that survive the invocation of sovereign immunity is through prosecuting a declaratory action. . . . Leach requested such declaratory relief here when seeking a declaration of whether he was denied a constitutionally protected interest by the University without due course of the law. See Tex. Const. art. I, § 19 (stating that "[n]o citizen of this State shall be deprived of life, liberty, property, privileges or immunities, or in any manner disfranchised, except by the due course of the law of the land"). Admittedly, he cannot avoid the shield of sovereign immunity by simply morphing a demand for monetary relief into one for declaratory relief, *City of El Paso v. Heinrich*, 284 S.W.3d at 370-71, and that is what the University contended he did here. That is, it argued through its plea to the court's jurisdiction that his pleadings regarding the due course of law violations were "a disguised attempt to obtain money damages under the 2009 Contract recast as a declaratory judgment claim." Yet, whether Leach had a constitutionally protected interest (property or liberty) that was denied him without due process is quite distinct from whether the University breached the employment contract. It is possible for there to be a due process violation without a breach of contract or a breach of contract without a due process violation. So, simply because both types of claims may be included in the same petition does not ipso facto mean that the constitutional allegation is a mere "disguised attempt to obtain money damages" for a breach of contract. Examining the nature of the relief sought is determinative for one may invoke the jurisdiction of Texas courts via a declaratory action to redress, through equitable remedies, unconstitutional acts. *City of Elsa v. M.A.L., supra.* So, the trial court had jurisdiction to declare whether Leach was denied due course of law even though it cannot adjudicate the attempt to recover damages for breach of contract. The same may be true for other choses-in-action that he may assert and which are independent of his breach of contract claim; they must be assessed on an individual basis. . . .

[EDS. The court's discussion of the trial court's dismissal of Leach's complaint against university officials is omitted.]

THE UNIVERSITY'S APPELLATE ISSUES

A. BREACH OF CONTRACT

Through its sole issue, the University argues that the trial court erred in refusing to dismiss Leach's breach of contract allegation. Again, the trial court refused to do so because it reasoned that the University "waived its immunity from suit . . . by and through its conduct." We sustain the issue.

As previously mentioned, the Supreme Court left open, in *Federal Sign*, the question of whether the state entity may waive its immunity through its conduct. Yet, whether the idea of waiving immunity through conduct extends to choses-in-action sounding in breach of contract is not an open question. In *General Servs. Comm'n. v. Little-Tex Insulation Co.*, Little-Tex sued Texas A&M for breach of contract and argued that the school waived its immunity by accepting the benefits of the contract. The proposition was rejected by the Supreme Court after acknowledging that it had left open "the question of whether the State's conduct may waive its immunity from suit." *General Servs. Comm'n v. Little-Tex Insulation Co.*, 39 S.W.3d at 595. The Court rather clearly stated that "there is but one route to the courthouse for breach-of-contract claims against the State, and that route is through the Legislature." *Id.* at 597. . . .

Admittedly, the factual circumstances in *Little-Tex* differ from those before us. And, because of that Leach argues that the holding does not control the outcome here. Though the circumstances may differ between the two suits, the Supreme Court in *Little-Tex* actually focused not upon the facts underlying the cause of action but rather upon the cause of action itself, that is, the claim of breached contract. Nor did it simply say that a governmental entity retains its immunity even though it accepted contractual benefits. Rather, it told us that there was only one way the State could be sued for breach of contract and that involved first garnering the legislature's approval via chapter 107 of the Texas Civil Practice and Remedies Code. . . .

In sum, we reverse those portions of the trial court's order 1) dismissing, for want of jurisdiction, Leach's due course of law claim and request for non-monetary declaratory and equitable relief founded upon it and 2) concluding that Texas Tech University waived its sovereign immunity from the breach of contract claim due to its conduct. We next dismiss, for want of jurisdiction, the appellate issue involving whether Bailey, Myers, and Bingham were properly dismissed by the trial court, render judgment dismissing Leach's claim of breached contract against the University, and affirm the remainder of the order granting the pleas to the trial court's jurisdiction.

NOTES AND QUESTIONS

1. *Termination for "Cause" Defined.* A wide array of events may give an institution or team a right to terminate a coach for cause. At the collegiate level, contracts typically contain provisions allowing an institution the right to terminate a coach if the coach has committed serious violations of NCAA rules and regulations. Similarly, a contract may include a provision that grants the institution the discretion to terminate a head coach if a member of his or her coaching staff commits an NCAA rules violation, if such violation was under the control or direction of the head coach. Among the more common provisions in coaching contracts at both the collegiate and professional levels are those that permit termination for cause if a coach: (1) refuses or is unable (e.g., because of death or incapacity) to perform duties either stipulated in the contract or reasonably associated with the position of coach; (2) is convicted of a serious criminal offense; (3) engages in fraud or dishonesty in the performance of his or her duties;

and (4) participates or encourages participation in gambling or betting involving sports. Finally, coaching contracts typically give colleges or professional clubs the right to terminate a coach if he or she engages in conduct that is detrimental to the best interests of the institution or club. For a detailed discussion of termination provisions, see Adam Epstein, *An Explanation of Interesting Clauses in Sports*, 21 J. Legal Aspects of Sport 5, 17-22 (2011) (discussing the evolution of termination provisions in sports); Karcher, *supra* (discussing termination provisions in coaching contracts); Martin J. Greenberg, *Termination of College Coaching Contracts: When Does Adequate Cause to Terminate Exist and Who Determines Its Existence?*, 17 Marq. Sports L. Rev. 197 (2006) (discussing what constitutes just cause); Robert H. Lattinville & Robert A. Boland, *Coaching in the National Football League: A Market Survey and Legal Review*, 17 Marq. Sports L. Rev. 109 (2006) (discussing termination provisions included in NFL coaching contracts); see also Patricia Sánchez Abril & Nicholas Greene, *Contracting Correctness: A Rubric for Analyzing Morality Clauses*, 74 Wash. & Lee L. Rev. 3, 69-70 (2017) (discussing the enforceability of a morals clause in a college coach's contract).

In *Cole v. Valley Ice Garden, L.L.C.*, 113 P.3d 275 (Mont. 2005), a five-year employment contract between a coach and a professional hockey team provided the coach could be terminated for cause. The agreement failed to define cause. After the team terminated the coach because of his team's poor performance, the coach filed a wrongful termination suit against the team. The coach argued that because the contract failed to expressly require that he maintain a specific win/loss ratio, the court could not imply such a term into the agreement. Relying on definitions from other contexts to lend meaning to the term "cause," the court ruled for the team, finding that "discharging the coach of a professional sports team which is performing poorly, despite management's good faith efforts, is a discretionary decision related to the legitimate needs of the business and constitutes 'cause.'" *Id.* at 280. See *Chang v. Univ. of R.I.*, 606 F. Supp. 1161, 1256 (D. R.I. 1985) (identifying a win-loss record as an objective measure for evaluating a coach).

2. *Termination for Rules Violations and Non-Sports-Related Indiscretions.* Institutions and teams have terminated coaches for exercises of poor judgment that range from abusive conduct toward players, to violating NCAA rules, to off-the-field indiscretions. Indeed, in 2003, the number and severity of incidents involving alleged and established improper conduct by coaches in intercollegiate basketball reached such a level that, in a move characterized as unprecedented, the National Association of Basketball Coaches convened a mandatory ethics summit for all NCAA Division I men's head coaches. One of the most notorious incidents, which provided a major catalyst for the coaching summit, involved Dave Bliss, former head men's basketball coach at Baylor University. Bliss was forced to resign following an investigation revealed that: Bliss lied to school officials who were investigating the death of Baylor basketball player Patrick Dennehy; Bliss instructed coaches and players to lie to those investigators and to portray Dennehy as a drug dealer; and Bliss improperly paid the tuition for players on the basketball team. See Jeff Caplan, *Baylor's Situation Catalyst for Summit*, Star-Telegram (Sept. 5, 2003). Other 2003 incidents involving poor judgment and indiscretions by coaches included the following (in many of these cases,

the coaches in question soon received subsequent coaching opportunities, as noted parenthetically):

- Mike Price's termination as the University of Alabama's head coach for conduct that included a visit to a topless bar and reports that a young woman charged $1,000 for room service at a hotel at which Price stayed. (Price subsequently became head football coach at the University of Texas at El Paso from 2004 until his retirement in 2012.)
- University of Washington's firing of head football coach Rick Neuheisel after he admitted that he bet more than $6,000 on the NCAA Division I men's basketball tournament (in December 2007, Neuheisel was named head football coach of the UCLA Bruins until November 2011 when the university fired him. In 2019, Neuheisel was briefly employed as head coach of the Arizona franchise of the Alliance of American Football before the league's abrupt collapse.)
- Larry Eustachy's resignation as Iowa State University's head men's basketball coach after the release of a photograph showing him surrounded by and kissing younger women and drinking a beer at a college party following a basketball game. (In 2004, Eustachy became head basketball coach at the University of Southern Mississippi and later assumed the same position in 2012 at Colorado State University ("CSU"). In early 2018, CSU paid Eustachy $750,000 after he agreed to resign in the wake of allegations that he emotionally and verbally abused players.)

Craig Bennett et al., *One Year Later: A Look Back at College Scandals, the People Involved and Where They Stand*, USA Today, June 15, 2004, at C3; Welch Suggs, *A Hard Year in College Sports*, Chron. Higher Educ., Dec. 19, 2003, at A37; John L. Pulley & Welch Suggs, *Coaches Will Be Coaches?*, Chron. Higher Educ., May 16, 2003, at A40.

Notwithstanding the negative attention such indiscretions attract, coaches in high profile collegiate athletics continue to find themselves embroiled in scandal and suffering employment-related consequences. In a highly publicized 2012 incident, Bobby Petrino, the successful former head football coach at the University of Arkansas, was terminated following revelations of an affair with a female staff employee and misleading statements he made to university officials. See Tom Weir, *Petrino Dumped by Arkansas*, USA Today (April 11, 2012). In December 2012, Petrino was appointed head football coach at Western Kentucky University. In October 2015, the University of Southern California ("USC") fired its head football coach Steve Sarkisian. The termination occurred in the aftermath of incidents in which Sarkisian slurred his words during a speech and showed signs of intoxication during a game and a team meeting. Sarkisian entered an alcohol treatment program after he was fired. He later sued USC seeking $30 million in damages alleging that he was wrongfully terminated instead of being able to seek treatment. In July 2018, an arbitrator ruled in favor of USC. Although Sarkisian lost the suit, he soon reestablished his career, signing a contract in January 2019 to be the offensive coordinator for the University of Alabama Crimson Tide.

The terminations or forced resignations of coaches for conduct such as that noted above raises several questions. Are coaches held to standards that are too high, particularly if the indiscretion does not involve rules violations or matters related to the athletics program? What signal does a school send when it hires a coach so quickly after the coach was terminated for such behavior elsewhere? Do schools signal that such behavior is irrelevant to being an effective coach and that terminations for such behavior have more to do with saving face in the media and among some supporters than with running a successful athletic program? What interest does a university have in regulating the personal behavior of coaches? Which clause or clauses within a coach's contract is an institution likely to contend justify its termination of a coach for cause for nonathletic-related behavior? See generally Greenberg, *Termination of College Coaching Contracts, supra.*

Two cases illustrate the issues involved when a court determines whether NCAA rules violations constitute grounds for a good-cause termination. In *O'Brien v. Ohio State University.*, 2007 WL 2729077 (Ohio Ct. App. Sept. 20, 2007), the former head coach of Ohio State's men's basketball team was terminated for violating NCAA rules prohibiting institutional representatives from providing extra benefits to players (giving a loan to a student-athlete). Plaintiff filed a breach of contract action alleging wrongful termination. The dispositive issue was whether O'Brien's violations of NCAA rules constituted a material breach of contract so as to discharge the university's obligations and allow it to terminate him without pay. In concluding that O'Brien's failure to comply with NCAA rules did not constitute a material breach, the court found that compliance with NCAA rules represented only one of the coach's duties stipulated in the contract. The court also identified contract language providing that the contracting party's failure to perform in each instance would not necessarily justify termination for cause. Since O'Brien's violation of NCAA rules and his failure to promptly report his violations were not so fundamental that they defeated "the essential purpose of the contract" and "thus rendered performance by defendant impossible," the court held that O'Brien's breach was not material and defendant did not have cause to terminate his employment. The court upheld the trial court's damages award of approximately $2.49 million.

In *Harrick v. NCAA*, 454 F. Supp. 2d 1255 (N.D. Ga. 2006), the head coach resigned and an assistant coach's contract was not renewed as the result of an NCAA investigation concerning rules violations while the two coached at the University of Georgia. Plaintiffs Jim Harrick, Sr., and Jim Harrick, Jr., asserted that the NCAA had tortiously interfered with their contracts with the university. In analyzing this claim, the court found that plaintiffs failed to establish an essential element—"the defendant is a 'third party' i.e., a 'stranger' to the contract with which the defendant allegedly interfered." *Id.* at 1260. The court found NCAA member schools require their employees to sign documents in which they agree to abide by NCAA legislation. According to the court, both plaintiffs signed their employment contracts and certified that they understood they were subject to NCAA guidelines. "The NCAA was 'an essential entity' in the employment relationships at issue. . . . Therefore, the NCAA is not a stranger to the contracts, and thus, cannot be liable for tortious interference with those contracts." *Id.* See also *Bassett v. NCAA*, 528 F.3d 426 (6th Cir. 2008) (coach who resigned his position as assistant football coach at the University of Kentucky, amid allegations of NCAA rules infractions, failed to establish a cognizable fraud claim. It would have been unreasonable for him to rely on the alleged misrepresentation of the athletic director that the coach's infractions would not be investigated. In addition, any alleged agreement between the coach and athletic director that they would ignore their respective obligations to report infractions was unenforceable as against public policy); see also Joshua Lens, *NCAA Head Coach Responsibilities Legislation,* 14 DePaul J. Sports L. 33 (2018) (discussing NCAA legislation imposing increased accountability on head coaches for any NCAA violation within their programs).

The termination of a coach for cause will not necessarily result in a denial of compensation. In 2017-18, several terminated coaches received sizable payments following their terminations. For example, Baylor University paid its former head football coach $15 million after it terminated him as a consequence of sexual assault allegations brought by women students against Baylor football players. In January 2018, USA Today reported that buyouts for head and assistant football coaches and athletic directors at the close of the 2017-18 season would likely cost major college athletic departments at public universities at least $110 million. Steve Berkowitz, *Analysis: Coaching Buyouts to Cost at Least $110M,* USA Today (Jan. 9, 2018).

3. *College Basketball Scandal.* In September 2017, federal prosecutors issued a criminal complaint against four assistant men's basketball coaches: Chuck Person (Auburn University), Tony Bland (University of Southern California), Emanuel "Book" Richardson (University of Arizona), and Lamont Evans (University of Oklahoma). The complaint alleged solicitation of bribes and wire services fraud arising from coaches funneling money from Adidas to the families of high school basketball recruits to influence the recruits to attend and play basketball at certain universities. Michael McCann, *Unpacking Louisville's Countersuit Against Rick Pitino,* SI.com. (Dec. 14, 2017); see also Sealed Complaint, United States v. Person (S.D.N.Y. Sept. 25, 2017), https://www.justice.gov/usao-sdny/press-release/file/999001/download. The complaint followed a two-year FBI investigation of college basketball coaches, Adidas executives, and agents. Mitch Sherman, *Everything You Need to Know About the College Basketball Scandal,* ESPN.com (Feb. 23, 2018); Aaron Moody, *Here's a Master Guide to College Basketball Corruption Scandal and FBI Investigation,* The News & Observer (Oct. 4, 2018).

Each coach pled guilty to bribery and conspiracy and was sentenced as follows:

- Bland: One hundred hours of community service and two years of probation; *Ex-USC Assistant Bland Avoids Sentence After Plea,* ESPN (June 5, 2019).
- Richardson: Three months in jail; *Ex-Arizona Assistant Gets 3 Month Sentence,* ESPN (June 6, 2019).
- Evans: Three months in jail; *Ex-Oklahoma State Coach Lamont Evans Sentenced to Three Months in Prison,* Sports Illustrated (June 7, 2019).
- Persons: Two years' of probation and 200 hours of community service; Kyle Boone, *College Basketball Corruption Trial: Ex-Auburn Assistant Person Avoids Prison Time,* CBS Sports (July 17, 2019), https://www.cbssports.com/college-basketball/news/college-basketball-corruption-trial-ex-auburn-assistant-chuck-person-avoids-prison-time/.

Shortly after the investigation was made public, the University Louisville terminated its head men's basketball coach Rick Pitino. Because Louisville terminated Pitino for cause, Louisville asserted it was not obligated to pay Pitino compensation based on a liquidated damages provision in the parties' contract. In November 2017, Pitino sued Louisville for breach of contract seeking "payments of $4,307,000 per year, through 2026," which is allegedly consistent with the liquidated damages provision of the parties' contract.

In December 2017, Louisville asserted a counterclaim against Pitino asserting:

> Pitino is liable for breach of contract, negligence and unlawful interference with business relationships between the university and the NCAA, Atlantic Coast Conference, media companies, TV networks and sponsors. Louisville also demands that Pitino indemnify the school for any penalties it must pay to the NCAA for wrongdoing connected to his acts.

McCann, *supra.* In August 2018, Pitino's lawsuit was dismissed pursuant to a clause in the parties' contract requiring arbitration.

4. *College Admission Scandal.* In March, 2019, prosecutors revealed a wide-ranging illicit college admission scheme tied to NCAA athletics. The mastermind, Rick Singer, "admitted to funneling portions of $25 million in bribes from rich parents to coaches, test-cheaters and others to get their children into some of the nation's top universities." Joey Garrison, *Felicity Huffman is Just the Beginning: Who's Guilty in the College Admissions Scandal— and Who's Still Fighting,* USA Today (June 4, 2019). One aspect of the scheme, dubbed "Varsity Blues," allegedly involved coaches helping "undeserving students" gain admissions to elite universities by portraying the students as top athletes when they were not. *College Admissions Scandal: Your Questions Answered,* NY Times (Mar. 14, 2019).

Among the coaches facing federal charges are: Jovan Vavic (USC Men's Water Polo Coach), Gordon Ernst (Georgetown Women's Tennis Coach), William Ferguson (Wake Forest Women's Volleyball Coach), Jorge Salcedo (UCLA Men's Soccer Coach), Ali Krosroshahin (USC Women's Soccer Coach), Laura Janke (USC Assistant Women's Soccer Coach), Rudy Meredith (Yale Women's Soccer Coach), John Vandemoer (Stanford Sailing Coach), and Michael Center (Texas Men's Tennis Coach). Andrew Das, Marc Tracy & Naila-Jean Meyers, *The Coaches Connected to the College Admission Fraud Case,* NY Times (Mar. 12, 2019). The actions taken by universities against the coaches range from termination to administrative leave. *Id.* To date, Meredith, Center, Janke, and Khosroshahin have agreed to plead guilty, and Vandemoer has already pled guilty and been sentenced to one day in prison (already served), six-months home confinement, and two years of probation. Varsity Blues and its NCAA enforcement implications are discussed in Chapter 3(E)(2)(b).

5. *Termination for Abusive Conduct.* When a coach crosses the thin line that separates appropriate tough discipline from abuse, institutions are justified in terminating a coach for cause. Throughout his coaching career, former Texas Tech and Indiana University men's basketball coach Bobby Knight fended off criticism that he verbally and physically abused his players. In 2002, Knight sued Indiana University for breach of contract and defamation following his termination for violating a "zero tolerance" behavior policy when he grabbed a student by the arm. He alleged the termination

caused him to lose more than $2 million in media and clothing contracts, endorsements, and camp fees. In October 2003, a judge dismissed Knight's lawsuit. The state judge noted that Knight's contract contained a provision that allowed IU to terminate him at will and that IU was not required to give Knight another chance.

In *Campanelli v. Bockrath*, 100 F.3d 1476 (9th Cir. 1996), Louis Campanelli was fired as head coach of the men's basketball team at the University of California at Berkeley. Newspaper accounts attributed Campanelli's firing to his conduct toward players. A *Washington Post* article described Campanelli as "an abusive bully" who "perpetuate[d] a cycle of abuse" and psychologically attacked his players. Tony Kornheiser, *When the Boot Fits*, Wash. Post, Feb. 17, 1993, at C1. In another matter, Winston Bennett pled guilty to fourth-degree assault. Bennett was suspended and later fired from his position as head men's basketball coach at Kentucky State University after he struck a player in the face. The player later filed assault charges that ended in the plea bargain. Bennett was ordered to complete 200 hours of community service and to obtain anger management counseling or serve 90 days in jail. *Finish Line*, Rocky Mountain News, Feb. 27, 2004, at 22C.

The Iowa Supreme Court has ruled that evidence showing that a coach engaged in threatening and intimidating treatment of student-athletes is sufficient to support a good-cause termination. *Bd. of Dirs. of Ames Cmty. Sch. Dist. v. Cullinan*, 745 N.W. 2d 487 (Iowa 2008); see *Dortch v. N.Y. City Dept. of Educ.*, 2016 WL 2621076 (E.D.N.Y. Mar. 3, 2016) (coach's verbal abuse of players provided a legitimate non-retaliatory reason for termination); see also Adam Epstein & Barbara Osborne, *Teaching Ethics with Sports: Recent Developments*, 28 Marq. Sports L. Rev. 301 (2018) (discussing abusive, criminal, and other improper conduct by high school and college coaches and the ethical dimensions of coaching).

Another incident involved Jim Leavitt. The University of South Florida terminated Leavitt for cause following allegations that Leavitt had mistreated a walk-on running back. The coach disputed allegations that he had grabbed a player by his throat and struck him during halftime of a game and filed a wrongful termination suit against the university. On January 11, 2011, the University of South Florida and Leavitt reached a settlement that paid Leavitt $2.75 million. Specifically, the settlement included $2 million for "salary and benefits" and $750,000 for Leavitt's contributions to building USF's "nationally respected" football program. *Jim Leavitt Gets $2.75M in Settlement*, ESPN (Jan. 11, 2011), http://sports.espn.go.com/ncf/news/story?id=6013605.

In April of 2013, video footage emerged of former Rutgers University head men's basketball coach, Mike Rice, physically assaulting his players. Brittany Brady, *Rutgers coach fired after abusive video broadcast*, CNN.com (Apr. 4, 2013), http://www.cnn.com/2013/04/03/sport/rutgers-video-attack/. The video showed Rice throwing basketballs at his players and forcefully pushing them while verbally insulting them. *Id.* Although such coaching tactics are certainly not novel and are viewed by some as appropriate hard-nose coaching, others find them appalling. Rutgers initially punished Rice with a three-game suspension and a $75,000 fine, but the University terminated him after it was pressured by state officials. *Id.* Still, Rice received $475,000 in severance pay. Angela Delli Santi, *Rutgers, Mike Rice Settlement: Fired Basketball Coach to Receive $475,000 Under Agreement*, Huffington Post (Apr. 18, 2013), http://www.huffingtonpost.com/2013/04/18/rutgers-mike-rice-settlement-coach-paid_n_3113310.html.

Allegations of coaches mistreating athletes have led to the termination of women coaches as well. Georgia Tech fired its head women's basketball coach, MaChelle Joseph, for her alleged emotional and mental mistreatment of her players. Longtime UNC head women's basketball coach, Sylvia Hatchell, resigned after a university-commissioned report allegedly concluded Hatchell had made racially insensitive comments to players and had exerted pressure on medical staff to clear injured players to return to play. Hatchell denied the allegations. Madeline Holcombe, *UNC's women's basketball coach resigns after review finds she made 'racially insensitive' comments*, CNN (Apr. 19, 2019), https://www.cnn.com/2019/04/19/us/unc-womens-basketball-sylvia-hatchell-resigns/index.html.

6. *Illegal Discrimination Claims.* In contesting their terminations, coaches are asserting with increased frequency that the terminations violated federal and state constitutional and statutory prohibitions against age, gender, or racial discrimination. See, e.g., *Miller v. Bd. of Regents of Univ. of Minn.*, 2018 WL 659851 (D. Minn. Feb. 2, 2018) (three female coaches asserting federal and state claims alleging gender and sexual orientation discrimination); *Ghioroaie-Panait v. Rolle*, 2018 WL 1722395 (M.D. Ala. Feb. 2, 2018) (refusing to dismiss a white assistant coach's claims that his contract was not renewed as a result of racial and national origin discrimination); *Ranieri v. Highlands Falls-Fort Montgomery Sch. Dist.*, 198 F. Supp. 2d 542 (S.D.N.Y. 2002) (football coach established prima facie case of age discrimination under the Age Discrimination in Employment Act, but failed to show that employer's nondiscriminatory reason for declining to rehire him was pretextual); *Maddox v. Univ. of Tenn.*, 62 F.3d 843 (6th Cir. 1995) (university not liable under Americans with Disabilities Act and Rehabilitation Act of 1973 because its discharge of coach was not based solely on his disability—alcoholism).

7. *Negligent Misrepresentation. Williams v. Smith*, 820 N.W.2d 807 (Minn. 2012), demonstrates the need for coaches to exercise caution in representations made to prospective employees. James Williams, an assistant basketball coach at Oklahoma State University, was contacted by Tubby Smith, head men's basketball coach at the University of Minnesota, about an assistant basketball coach position at Minnesota. Following several communications during which salary and other terms were discussed, Smith orally offered Williams the position, which Williams orally accepted. Thereafter, athletic administrators expressed concerns to Smith regarding the commission of NCAA rules infractions by Williams. Following further communications between Smith and Williams, and after Williams had submitted his resignation to OSU, Williams was officially informed that Minnesota would not hire him because of his previous major NCAA rules infractions.

A jury awarded over $1 million in damages based on Williams's negligent misrepresentation claim. In affirming the jury verdict, the court of appeals found that Smith owed a duty of care to Williams during the hiring negotiations, and there was evidence sufficient to support the jury's finding that Williams reasonably relied on Smith's representations regarding his authority to hire Williams. *Id.* at 4. The Minnesota Supreme Court reversed, explaining:

> We conclude that the legal relationship between Williams and Smith is not the type of relationship entitled to legal protection, and therefore no duty of care against negligent misrepresentation is owed. . . . First, their relationship in negotiating potential employment was not a professional, fiduciary, or special relationship in which one party had superior knowledge or expertise. . . . Second, the nature of the relationship between Williams and Smith does not support a duty of care in this case. The relationship between Williams and Smith in their discussions of Williams' prospective employment as an assistant basketball coach was that of two sophisticated business people, both watching out for their individual interests while negotiating at arm's length.

Id. at 10-11.

3. *Liquidated Damages*

It is not uncommon for coaches to attempt to move up to a more prestigious college or university. For this reason, institutions increasingly seek some form of compensation when a coach leaves an institution prior to the expiration of the term of his or her contract. When the coach quits before his or her contract has expired, that coach has committed a breach of contract. The options theoretically available to an institution are to seek negative injunctive relief (affirmative injunctive relief is unavailable), to sue for damages, or simply to cancel the contract and allow the coach to leave. Institutions will most likely resort to an increasingly popular additional option: seek compensation under a buyout or liquidated-damages provision. The amounts due to institutions under such provisions are often paid by the breaching coaches' new institutions. The *DiNardo* case discusses the validity of liquidated damages provisions in coaching contracts.

PROBLEM 5-2

James Williams signed a five-year contract to serve as head basketball coach for Big-Time University. His annual compensation was $2,500,000. At the time the parties contracted, they were both represented by attorneys. The parties' contract included the following language:

> 4. James Williams recognizes that his promise to work for Big-Time University for the entire term of this five (5) year Contract is of the essence of his Contract with the University. Williams also recognizes that the University is making a highly valuable investment in his continued employment by entering into this Contract and its investment would be lost were he to resign or otherwise terminate his employment with the University prior to the expiration of this Contract. Accordingly, in the event of such resignation or termination, Williams will pay to the University as liquidated damages an amount equal to his base and supplemental salary, multiplied by the number of years (or portion(s) thereof) remaining on the Contract.

Nine months into his contract with Big-Time, Williams called Big-Time's athletic director and requested permission to speak to other schools regarding employment. The athletic director granted his request. Shortly thereafter, Williams terminated his relationship with Big-Time and agreed to become the head basketball coach at Rival University at a higher salary.

Big-Time filed suit alleging breach of contract and seeking to recover as damages the amount stipulated in paragraph 4. Williams argued that, among other things, Big-Time waived its claims and/or damages asserted against him, paragraph 4 was unconscionable and otherwise unenforceable as a penalty, and Big-Time failed to allege actual damages. Is Big-Time likely to succeed in its breach of contract action and recover the prayed-for relief? In responding, consult the materials that follow.

VANDERBILT UNIVERSITY v. DiNARDO
174 F.3d 751 (6th Cir. 1999)

GIBSON, Circuit Judge.

Gerry DiNardo resigned as Vanderbilt's head football coach to become the head football coach for Louisiana State University. As a result, Vanderbilt University brought this breach of contract action. The district court entered summary judgment for Vanderbilt, awarding $281,886.43 pursuant to a damage provision in DiNardo's employment contract with Vanderbilt. DiNardo appeals, arguing that the district court erred in concluding: (1) that the contract provision was an enforceable liquidated damage provision and not an unlawful penalty under Tennessee law; (2) that Vanderbilt did not waive its right to liquidated damages. . . . We affirm the district court's ruling that the employment contract contained an enforceable liquidated damage provision and the award of liquidated damages under the original contract. . . .

On December 3, 1990, Vanderbilt and DiNardo executed an employment contract hiring DiNardo to be Vanderbilt's head football coach. Section one of the contract provided:

> The University hereby agrees to hire Mr. DiNardo for a period of five (5) years from the date hereof with Mr. DiNardo's assurance that he will serve the entire term of this Contract, a long-term commitment by Mr. DiNardo being important to the University's desire for a stable intercollegiate football program. . . .

The contract also contained reciprocal liquidated damage provisions. Vanderbilt agreed to pay DiNardo his remaining salary should Vanderbilt replace him as football coach, and DiNardo agreed to reimburse Vanderbilt should he leave before his contract expired. Section eight of the contract stated:

> Mr. DiNardo recognizes that his promise to work for the University for the entire term of this 5-year Contract is of the essence of this Contract to the University. Mr. DiNardo also recognizes that the University is making a highly valuable investment in his continued employment by entering into this Contract and its investment would be lost were he to resign or otherwise terminate his employment as Head Football Coach with the University prior to the expiration of this Contract. Accordingly, Mr. DiNardo agrees that in the event he resigns or otherwise terminates his employment as Head Football Coach (as opposed to his resignation or termination from another position at the University to which he may have been reassigned), prior to the expiration of this Contract, and is employed or performing services for a person or institution other than the University, he will pay to the University as liquidated damages an amount equal to his Base Salary, less amounts that would otherwise be deducted or withheld from his Base Salary for income

and social security tax purposes, multiplied by the number of years (or portion(s) thereof) remaining on the Contract.

During contract negotiations, section eight was modified at DiNardo's request so that damages would be calculated based on net, rather than gross, salary.

Vanderbilt initially set DiNardo's salary at $100,000 per year. DiNardo received salary increases in 1992, 1993, and 1994. . . .

[EDS. The facts relating to an Addendum under which DiNardo allegedly agreed to extend the term of his contract with Vanderbilt for an additional two years are omitted.]

In November 1994, Louisiana State University contacted Vanderbilt in hopes of speaking with DiNardo about becoming the head football coach for L.S.U. [Paul] Hoolahan [Vanderbilt's athletic director] gave DiNardo permission to speak to L.S.U. about the position. On December 12, 1994, DiNardo announced that he was accepting the L.S.U. position.

Vanderbilt sent a demand letter to DiNardo seeking payment of liquidated damages under section eight of the contract. Vanderbilt believed that DiNardo was liable for three years of his net salary: one year under the original contract and two years under the Addendum. DiNardo did not respond to Vanderbilt's demand for payment.

Vanderbilt brought this action against DiNardo for breach of contract. . . .

I

DiNardo first claims that section eight of the contract is an unenforceable penalty under Tennessee law. DiNardo argues that the provision is not a liquidated damage provision but a "thinly disguised, overly broad non-compete provision," unenforceable under Tennessee law. . . .

Contracting parties may agree to the payment of liquidated damages in the event of a breach. . . . The term "liquidated damages" refers to an amount determined by the parties to be just compensation for damages should a breach occur. . . . Courts will not enforce such a provision, however, if the stipulated amount constitutes a penalty. . . . A penalty is designed to coerce performance by punishing default. . . . In Tennessee, a provision will be considered one for liquidated damages, rather than a penalty, if it is reasonable in relation to the anticipated damages for breach, measured prospectively at the time the contract was entered into, and not grossly disproportionate to the actual damages. . . . When these conditions are met, particularly the first, the parties probably intended the provision to be for liquidated damages. However, any doubt as to the character of the contract provision will be resolved in favor of finding it a penalty. . . .

The district court held that the use of a formula based on DiNardo's salary to calculate liquidated damages was reasonable "given the nature of the unquantifiable damages in the case." The court held that parties to a contract may include consequential damages and even damages not usually awarded by law in a liquidated damage provision provided that they were contemplated by the parties. . . . The court explained:

> The potential damage to [Vanderbilt] extends far beyond the cost of merely hiring a new head football coach. It is this uncertain potentiality that the parties sought to address by providing for a sum certain to apply towards anticipated expenses

and losses. It is impossible to estimate how the loss of a head football coach will affect alumni relations, public support, football ticket sales, contributions, etc. . . . As such, to require a precise formula for calculating damages resulting from the breach of contract by a college head football coach would be tantamount to barring the parties from stipulating to liquidated damages evidence in advance.

Id. at 642.

DiNardo contends that there is no evidence that the parties contemplated that the potential damage from DiNardo's resignation would go beyond the cost of hiring a replacement coach. He argues that his salary has no relationship to Vanderbilt's damages and that the liquidated damage amount is unreasonable and shows that the parties did not intend the provision to be for liquidated damages.

DiNardo's theory of the parties' intent, however, does not square with the record. The contract language establishes that Vanderbilt wanted the five-year contract because "a long-term commitment" by DiNardo was "important to the University's desire for a stable intercollegiate football program," and that this commitment was of "essence" to the contract. Vanderbilt offered the two-year contract extension to DiNardo well over a year before his original contract expired. Both parties understood that the extension was to provide stability to the program, which helped in recruiting players and retaining assistant coaches. Thus, undisputed evidence, and reasonable inferences therefrom, establish that both parties understood and agreed that DiNardo's resignation would result in Vanderbilt suffering damage beyond the cost of hiring a replacement coach.

This evidence also refutes DiNardo's argument that the district court erred in presuming that DiNardo's resignation would necessarily cause damage to the University. That the University may actually benefit from a coaching change (as DiNardo suggests) matters little, as we measure the reasonableness of the liquidated damage provision at the time the parties entered the contract, not when the breach occurred, *Kimbrough & Co.*, 939 S.W.2d at 108, and we hardly think the parties entered the contract anticipating that DiNardo's resignation would benefit Vanderbilt.

The stipulated damage amount is reasonable in relation to the amount of damages that could be expected to result from the breach. As we stated, the parties understood that Vanderbilt would suffer damage should DiNardo prematurely terminate his contract, and that these actual damages would be difficult to measure. *See Kimbrough & Co.*, 939 S.W.2d at 108. . . .

Vanderbilt hired DiNardo for a unique and specialized position, and the parties understood that the amount of damages could not be easily ascertained should a breach occur. Contrary to DiNardo's suggestion, Vanderbilt did not need to undertake an analysis to determine actual damages, and using the number of years left on the contract multiplied by the salary per year was a reasonable way to calculate damages considering the difficulty of ascertaining damages with certainty. *See Kimbrough & Co.*, 939 S.W.2d at 108. The fact that liquidated damages declined each year DiNardo remained under contract, is directly tied to the parties' express understanding of the importance of a long-term commitment from DiNardo. Furthermore, the liquidated damages provision was reciprocal and the result of negotiations between two parties, each of whom was represented by counsel.

We also reject DiNardo's argument that a question of fact remains as to whether the parties intended section eight to be a "reasonable estimate" of damages. The liquidated damages are in line with Vanderbilt's estimate of its actual damages. . . . Vanderbilt presented evidence that it incurred expenses associated with recruiting a new head coach of $27,000.00; moving expenses for the new coaching staff of $86,840; and a compensation difference between the coaching staffs of $184,311. The stipulated damages clause is reasonable under the circumstances, and we affirm the district court's conclusion that the liquidated damages clause is enforceable under Tennessee law.

[EDS. The court's discussion of whether Vanderbilt waived its right to liquidated damages when it granted DiNardo permission to discuss a coaching position with L.S.U., the enforceability of an addendum to the parties' contract, and the duration of DiNardo's contract if the addendum was deemed to be enforceable is omitted.]

Accordingly, we affirm the district court's judgment that the contract contained an enforceable liquidated damage provision, and we affirm the portion of the judgment reflecting damages calculated under the original five-year contract. We reverse the district court's judgment concluding that the Addendum was enforceable as a matter of law. We remand for a resolution of the factual issues as to whether Larry DiNardo's approval was a condition precedent to the enforceability of the Addendum and, if so, whether the condition was satisfied by Larry DiNardo's failure to object.

DAVID A. NELSON, Circuit Judge, concurring in part and dissenting in part.

If section eight of the contract was designed primarily to quantify, in an objectively reasonable way, damages that the university could be expected to suffer in the event of a breach, such damages being difficult to measure in the absence of an agreed formula, the provision is enforceable as a legitimate liquidated damages clause. If section eight was designed primarily to punish Coach DiNardo for taking a job elsewhere, however, the provision is a penalty unenforceable under Tennessee law. My colleagues on the panel and I are in agreement, I believe, on both of these propositions. We disagree, however, as to section eight's primary function.

It seems to me that [section 8 of the contract] was designed to function as a penalty, not as a liquidation of the university's damages. Insofar as the court holds otherwise, I am constrained to dissent. In all other respects, I concur in Judge Gibson's opinion and in the judgment entered pursuant to it.

My principal reasons for viewing section eight as a penalty are these: (1) although the damages flowing from a premature resignation would normally be the same whether or not Coach DiNardo took a job elsewhere, section eight does not purport to impose liability for liquidated damages unless the coach accepts another job; (2) the section eight formula incorporates other variables that bear little or no relation to any reasonable approximation of anticipated damages; and (3) there is no evidence that the parties were attempting, in section eight, to come up with a reasonable estimate of the university's probable loss if the coach left. I shall offer a few words of explanation on each of these points.

Section eight does not make Coach DiNardo liable for any liquidated damages at all, interestingly enough, unless, during the unexpired term of his contract, he "is employed or performing services for a person or institution other than the University. . . ." But how the coach spends his post-resignation time could not reasonably be expected to affect the university's damages; should the coach choose to quit in order to lie on a beach somewhere, the university would presumably suffer the same damages that it would suffer if he quit to coach for another school. The logical inference, therefore, would seem to be that section eight was intended to penalize the coach for taking another job, and was not intended to make the university whole by liquidating any damages suffered as a result of being left in the lurch.

This inference is strengthened, as I see it, by a couple of other anomalies in the stipulated damages formula. First, I am aware of no reason to believe that damages arising from the need to replace a prematurely departing coach could reasonably be expected to vary in direct proportion to the number of years left on the coach's contract. Section eight, however, provides that for every additional year remaining on the contract, the stipulated damages will go up by the full amount of the annual take-home pay contemplated under the contract. Like the "other employment" proviso, this makes the formula look more like a penalty than anything else.

Second, the use of a "take-home pay" measuring stick suggests that the function of the stick was to rap the coach's knuckles and not to measure the university's loss. Such factors as the number of tax exemptions claimed by the coach, or the percentage of his pay that he might elect to shelter in a 401(k) plan, would obviously bear no relation at all to the university's anticipated damages.

Finally, the record before us contains no evidence that the contracting parties gave any serious thought to attempting to measure the actual effect that a premature departure could be expected to have on the university's bottom line. On the contrary, the record affirmatively shows that the university did not attempt to determine whether the section eight formula would yield a result reasonably approximating anticipated damages. The record shows that the university could not explain how its anticipated damages might be affected by the coach's obtaining employment elsewhere, this being a subject that the draftsman of the contract testified he had never thought about. And the record shows that the question of why the number of years remaining on the contract would have any bearing on the amount of the university's damages was never analyzed either.

In truth and in fact, in my opinion, any correspondence between the result produced by the section eight formula and a reasonable approximation of anticipated damages would be purely coincidental. What section eight prescribes is a penalty, pure and simple, and a penalty may not be enforced under Tennessee law. . . .

NOTES AND QUESTIONS

1. *Analysis of* DiNardo. What is the likely practical effect of buyout clauses such as that in *DiNardo?* Are liquidated damages clauses such as in *DiNardo* intended primarily to deter a coach from leaving an institution or to compensate an institution for the damages attributable to the loss of a coach's services? Do you agree or disagree with the concurring/dissenting judge's argument that Section 8 constituted an unenforceable penalty? In the absence of a liquidated-damages provision, how might an institution calculate the damages caused by the departure of a successful football or basketball coach? Are damages resulting from a coach's breach too uncertain to quantify? See Richard T. Karcher, *Redress for a No-Win Situation: Using Liquidated Damages in Comparable Coaches' Contracts to Assess a School's Economic Damages from the Loss of a Successful Coach,* 64 S.C. L. Rev. 429 (2012) (discussing the reasons that support validating liquidated-damages provisions in coaching contracts).

Shortly after the trial began, DiNardo settled the dispute by agreeing to pay Vanderbilt an undisclosed sum. As an attorney representing DiNardo, what would be your strategy during settlement negotiations? What would be your strategy as counsel representing Vanderbilt?

A state appellate court cited to *DiNardo* in upholding a $1.2 million damages award to a university based on a liquidated damages provision in a head men's basketball coach's contract. *Kent State Univ. v. Ford*, 26 N.E.3d 868 (Ohio Ct. App. 2015). In a related action, an appellate court found that issues of material fact precluded summary judgment on claims that Bradley University wrongly interfered with Ford's contract with Kent State and that Kent State was entitled to recover attorneys' fees. *Kent State Univ. v. Bradley Univ.*, 2019 WL 2269154 (Ohio. Ct. App. May 28, 2019).

2. University of West Virginia v. Rodriguez. The validity of a $4 million liquidated-damages provision was at issue in a lawsuit filed by the University of West Virginia against its former head football coach Rich Rodriguez, who left the school in 2007 to assume the same position at the University of Michigan. The disputed provision was included in the Rodriguez/West Virginia contract after the coach had received an offer from another school. Rodriguez argued: he was induced by fraud and improper pressure to sign the agreement; the disputed clause was an unenforceable penalty provision; and West Virginia breached the contract by failing to abide by an oral commitment to reduce the agreed-on damage amount in the event that he resigned before the end of his contract term. The university argued the clause was valid and entered into in good faith. In July 2008, Rodriguez agreed to a $4 million settlement pursuant to which Rodriguez and Michigan paid $1.5 million and $2.5 million, respectively, to West Virginia. Michigan also paid his attorney fees incurred in the litigation. Rodriguez's new contract with Michigan included a $4 million liquidated-damages provision. Vicki Smith, *Rodriguez, Michigan to Pay WVU $4 Million*, Pittsburgh Trib. (Jul. 10, 2008). Three years later, Rodriquez was fired by Michigan and the university agreed to pay him $2.5 million of the $4 million buyout provided for in the parties' contract. Nick Bunkley, *Looking to Start Over, Michigan Fires Rodriquez*, NY Times (Jan. 5, 2011). In November 2011, Rodriguez was hired as the head coach at the University of Arizona.

3. *Exclusivity of Liquidated Damages and Availability of Injunctive Relief.* The question before a state superior court judge in Massachusetts was whether a liquidated-damages provision constituted the sole remedy available to the university in *Northeastern Univ. v. Brown*, 17 Mass. L.Rptr. 443 (Mass. Super. 2004). In July 2003, Northeastern University entered into a contract to have Donald Brown serve as its head football coach through the end of the 2007-2008 football season. The contract provided in part as follows:

> Coach [Brown] agrees to devote full time and effort to the University and agrees not to seek, discuss, negotiate for, or accept other employment during the term of this Agreement without first obtaining the written consent of the President of the University. Such consent shall not be unreasonably withheld.

Id. at *1. The contract also provided that in the event that Brown left Northeastern prior to the end of the contract term, he would pay the university $25,000. Six months after he signed the contract, Brown accepted an offer to coach the University of Massachusetts football team. Northeastern thereupon sought an injunction to prevent Brown from coaching at the University of Massachusetts.

In determining whether the liquidated damages provision was Northeastern's exclusive remedy, the judge concluded that, when specific performance is sought, a liquidated-damages provision is not the exclusive remedy. In doing so, the judge emphasized the general applicability of rules of contract law to the sports context. Citing section 361 of the Restatement (Second) of Contracts, the court stated, "Specific performance or an injunction may be granted to enforce a duty even though there is a provision for liquidated damages for breach of that duty." *Id.* at *3.

Within a month of granting an interim injunction, the judge reversed himself, lifted the injunction, and instructed the parties to settle. Eventually, the parties worked out a settlement under which the University of Massachusetts agreed to pay Northeastern $150,000 and to suspend Brown from coaching the first three games of the 2004-05 season. Mark Blaudschun, *Settlement Is Reached on Brown UMass, NU End Coach Saga*, Boston Globe, May 13, 2004, at E1.

Applying general rules of contract law, did the judge reach the right decision in lifting the injunction?

PROBLEM 5-3

Coach entered into a five-year contract with University at an annual base salary of $250,000, not including perquisites, which contained the following provision:

NOTICE OF APPOINTMENT AND CONTRACT: During the term of Coach's contract, Coach shall hold the appointment, title, and duties of Head Coach in the University's men's basketball program, except that at any time during the Appointment Term with 30 days' notice, the appointment, title, and duties of Head Coach may be terminated and another title and duty assigned. The University's termination of Coach's appointment, title, and duties as Head Coach of the men's basketball program, and its reassignment of Coach to other appointment, title, and duties within the University, shall be within the discretion of the University and may be exercised with or without cause.

During the first two years of his contract, the basketball team had a losing record of 8 wins and 45 losses. University, which previously had a highly regarded men's basketball program, lost money on its men's basketball program, and attendance was down during these two years. In a letter to Coach dated March 15, University's athletic director stated:

University hereby notifies you that your appointment as Head Coach of University's men's basketball team, and all duties associated with your title as Head Coach, will terminate as of April 16. University hereby offers to reassign you to the position of compliance coordinator for NCAA rules and regulations. A change in leadership of the basketball team is required, and this reassignment is for the good of the athletic department. If you accept University's offer of reassignment, it will take effect April 16. You will continue to receive your annual base salary of $250,000 for each of the remaining three years of your contract, except you will not be entitled to receive perquisites that are normally associated with the position of head basketball coach.

Coach is very upset and believes University's reassignment of him constitutes an effort to get him to resign. He is also concerned that accepting a noncoaching position will detrimentally affect his ability to secure a future coaching position. Coach would like nothing better than to sue University and comes to you for advice. What advice would you offer to Coach? What are the legal and professional consequences of Coach accepting the reassignment or of Coach rejecting the reassignment? What type of compromise might Coach consider? In advising Coach, consider the following materials: *Monson v. State*, 901 P.2d 904 (Or. Ct. App. 1995); *Dennison v. Murray State Univ.*, 465 F. Supp. 2d 733 (W.D. Ky. 2006) (even though the athletic director's contract stated that the university could only reassign him to a job with responsibilities consistent with the duties of an athletic director, the university acted properly in reassigning plaintiff to the position of Director of Corporate and Foundation Giving, since the contract also included a provision providing it was subject to all university policies, which included its transfer/reassignment policy); Martin J. Greenberg & Brandon Leibsohn, *The Disappearance of a Dinosaur: Reassignment Clauses Are Losing Their Footing in College Coaches' Contracts*, 25 Marq. Sports L. Rev. 39 (2014).

4. Sexual Harassment of Student-Athletes by Coaches

This comment examines the sexual harassment of female student-athletes by male coaches and responsibilities imposed on coaches to address alleged sexual misconduct committed by student-athletes.

With regard to sexual harassment by coaches, one of the more prominent cases involved allegations made by two female soccer players against the male coach of the University of North Carolina women's soccer team. The players alleged, among other things, that the coach made inappropriate sexual comments to them and uninvited sexual advances toward them. One of the two soccer players settled with the university for $70,000 and an agreement that the coach would undergo sensitivity training. *UNC Will Pay Settlement in Dorrance Case*, Charlotte Observer, March 24, 2004, at 6C.

In subsequently dismissing the remaining player's action, a federal district court noted that the plaintiff's complaint revolved around sexually related comments and statements made by her soccer coach that allegedly amounted to "hostile environment" sexual harassment in violation of Title IX. *Jennings v. Univ. of N.C. at Chapel Hill*, 340 F. Supp. 2d 679 (M.D.N.C. 2004). The court adopted the following standard as controlling whether such a claim is actionable under Title IX: "[T]he sexual harassment must be 'so severe, pervasive, and objectively offensive that it can be said to deprive the victims of access to the educational opportunities or benefits provided by the school.'" *Id.* at *5 (quoting *Davis v. Monroe Cnty. Sch. Bd. of Educ.*, 526 U.S. 629, 650 (1999)). Applying this standard, the court dismissed the plaintiff's Title IX claim:

> While inappropriate in some respects and quite possibly offensive to her, the conduct that she alleges occurred was not "severe, pervasive and objectively offensive" to the point of depriving her of educational opportunities. The comments Ms. Jennings claims to have found offensive occurred less than weekly. When comments were made, they were not severe, especially when the social context is considered. . . . The players were teasing and joking amongst themselves on these

occasions. Mr. Dorrance [the women's soccer coach] did not initiate these discussions or steer the players' conversation in the direction of sex. The comments were only "mere utterances," and were not physically threatening. There is no evidence, beyond Ms. Jennings' own vague assertion, that the atmosphere at practice interfered with her performance on the field or in the classroom. . . .

As for the inquiries Mr. Dorrance allegedly made directly to Ms. Jennings, one of these occurred in a group setting and was only mildly related to any sort of sexual topic. In the setting of an athletic practice where players are discussing their social activities, a coach inquiring about a player's weekend, or about whether a certain person is her boyfriend, is not harassment. . . .

Id.

A three-judge panel of the Fourth Circuit affirmed the district court ruling. *Jennings v. Univ. of N.C. at Chapel Hill*, 444 F.3d 255 (4th Cir. 2006). It stated a cognizable hostile environment claim arises under Title IX if a plaintiff establishes: "(1) that she belongs to a protected group (e.g., a student at an institution covered by Title IX); (2) that she was subjected to harassment based on her sex; (3) that the harassment was sufficiently severe or pervasive to create an abusive educational environment; and (4) a cognizable basis for imputing institutional liability under Title IX." *Id.* at 267-68. The court concluded that no reasonable jury could find that Coach Dorrance's "remarks during Jennings' two-year tenure on the team were sufficiently severe or pervasive to create a sexually hostile educational environment." *Id.* at 275. After considering the case *en banc*, however, the court ruled that the plaintiff alleged sufficient facts for a jury to find that Dorrance subjected Jennings to sexual harassment. *Jennings v. Univ. of N.C.*, 482 F.3d 686 (4th Cir. 2007). It found that a jury could reasonably find that Dorrance's persistent harassment was sufficiently degrading to young women to create a hostile or abusive environment.

In *Simpson v. University of Colorado Boulder*, 500 F.3d 1170 (10th Cir. 2007), the plaintiffs alleged they were sexually assaulted at a party by football players and recruits. According to the plaintiffs, the university had an official policy that paired recruits with "female ambassadors" to ensure that the recruits would be shown a good time. In determining the viability of the plaintiffs' Title IX claim, the court framed the central issue as whether a risk existed that a sexual assault might occur during a recruiting visit. The court found evidence sufficient to establish such a risk, including: the head football coach's general knowledge of the serious risk of sexual assault during recruiting visits; the coach's specific knowledge that assaults had occurred during recruiting visits at CU; the coach's maintenance of an unsupervised player-host program notwithstanding this knowledge; the inadequacy of steps taken by CU to reduce the risk of sexual assaults during recruiting visits; and conduct by the head coach in resisting recruiting reforms.

In settlement of the plaintiffs' claims, CU agreed to pay them a total of $2.5 million. The settlement terms also required CU to hire an external Title IX monitor to focus on the university's sexual harassment and gender discrimination issues and to add staff to its victims' assistance center. Allison Sherry, *$2.85 Million CU Settles Case Stemming from Recruit Scandal*, Denver Post, Dec. 6, 2007, at A01.

For examples of other cases in which male coaches have been accused of sexually harassing female athletes, see *Bostic v. Smyrna Sch. Dist.*, 418 F.3d 355 (2d Cir. 2005) (although acknowledging that a teacher's harassment of a student falls within the ambit of Title IX, the court refused to hold the school liable because there was no proof that the school had actual knowledge of a sexual relationship between a 15-year-old student and her track coach); *Doe v. Rains Cty. Indep. Sch. Dist.*, 76 F.3d 666 (5th Cir. 1996); *Mandy v. Indep. Sch. Dist. No. 1 of Del. Cty. Okla.*, 2017 WL 2783990 (N.D. Okla. June 27, 2017) (although girls' basketball coach had an inappropriate relationship with a minor, a player on the basketball team, the court granted summary judgment in favor of the defendant because the school possessed no knowledge that the coach posed a threat to any of the girls on the team and once the school became aware of the coach's inappropriate relationship, the coach was immediately fired); *Remphrey v. Cherry Hill Twp. Bd. of Ed.*, 2017 WL 25391 (D.N.J. Jan. 20, 2017) (denying defendants' motion for summary judgment where school officials took no action after it was brought to their attention that a high school coach had inappropriately flirted with and touched female students); *Ericson v. Syracuse Univ.*, 35 F. Supp. 2d 326 (S.D.N.Y. 1999) (plaintiffs alleged cognizable claim that coach harassed female student-athletes and that university officials had actual notice of the harassment). See generally Deborah L. Brake, *Going Outside of Title IX to Keep Coach-Athlete Relationships in Bounds*, 22 Marq. Sports L. Rev. 395 (2012); Caitlin M. Cullitan, *"I'm His Coach, Not His Father": A Title IX Analysis of Sexual Harassment in College Sports*, 12 Tex. Rev. Ent. & Sports L. 53 (2010); Diane Heckman, *Title IX and Sexual Harassment Claims Involving Educational Athletic Department Employees and Student-Athletes in the Twenty-First Century*, 8 Va. Sports & Ent. L.J. 223 (2009).

What factors may contribute to cases of sexual harassment by male coaches against female student-athletes? Are there unique aspects of college sports that warrant a careful balancing of preventing potential sexual harassment claims against those unique features? Two commentators have identified the following three factors as creating special opportunities for sexual harassment: (1) the coach/student-athlete relationship, which is marked by the immense authority and power coaches exercise over student-athletes, and the one-on-one contact coaches have with student-athletes; (2) the physical nature of sports, in which coaches often apply a hands-on approach to instructing athletes, and frequent physical contact between coaches and athletes in the form of a congratulatory pat on the back; and (3) focus on the athlete's body, around which daily discussions between coach and student-athlete revolve. See Maureen A. Weston, *Tackling Abuse in Sport Through Dispute System Design*, 13 U. St. Thomas L. J. 434 (2017) (discussing the increased risk of sexual or physical abuse in the athlete-coach relationship and proposing a dispute system designed to address such matters); Nancy Hogshead-Makar & Sheldon E. Steinbach, *Intercollegiate Athletics' Unique Environment for Sexual Harassment Claims: Balancing the Realities of Athletics with Preventing Potential Claims*, 13 Marq. Sports L. Rev. 173 (2003).

In February 2018, Larry Nassar, a former doctor for USA Gymnastics and Michigan State University, was sentenced to 40 to 175 years in prison after pleading guilty to three counts of criminal sexual assault. Eric Levenson, *Larry Nassar Apologizes, gets 40 to 125 Years for Decades of Sexual Abuse*, CNN https://www.cnn .com/2018/02/05/us/larry-nassar-sentence-eaton/index.html (last updated Feb. 5, 2018). Nearly 200 women accused Nassar of sexually assaulting them over a period spanning two decades. Caroline Kitchener & Alia Wong, *The Moral Catastrophe at Michigan State*, The Atlantic (Sept. 12, 2018). On top of the sentence related to sexual assault, Nassar will first serve a 60-year sentence in federal prison for possession of child pornography. *Id.* In addition to USA Gymnastics, these other national governing bodies have been publicly accused of mishandling complaints of abuse: USA Taekwondo, USA Swimming, USA Figure Skating, USA Speed Skating, and USA Volleyball. Katherine Hampel, *Whose Fault Is It Anyway? How Sexual Abuse Has Plagued the United States Olympic Movement and Its Athletes,* 29 Marq. Sports L. Rev. 547 (2019).

In the aftermath of these incidents, the U.S. Center for SafeSport was created in March 2017 to handle all investigations of sexual abuse in U.S. Olympic and Paralympic organizations. SafeSport's website states: "The Center provides services to sport entities on abuse prevention techniques, policies and programs and provides a safe professional and confidential place for individuals to report sexual abuse within the U.S. Olympic and Paralympic Movements." U.S. Center for SafeSport, *Who We Are,* https://safesport.org/who-we-are. SafeSport has exclusive authority to investigate and manage hearings of actual or suspected sexual misconduct and to impose sanctions ranging from written warnings to permanent ineligibility. *Id.* at *Safesport Practices and Procedures for the U.S. Olympic and Paralympic Movement.* SafeSport maintains and provides access to a centralized searchable database containing all SafeSport disciplinary measures along with all known disciplinary records received from NGBs. *Id.* at *Centralized Disciplinary Database.*

In February 2018, Congress passed the Protecting Young Victims from Sexual Abuse and Safe Sport Authorization Act of 2017, or the SafeSport Act, which requires any adult within an Olympic National Governing Body to immediately report any allegation or reasonable suspicion of abuse to SafeSport. 36 U.S.C. § 220542. As of the end of 2018, the Center had received more than 1,800 reports of sexual misconduct or abuse. Nancy Armour & Rachel Axon, *SafeSport CEO Shellie Pfohl Will Step Down at Year's End,* USA Today (last updated Feb. 21, 2019).

Attention has also focused on the reporting and other responsibilities of athletic administrators, including head coaches and athletic directors at the collegiate level. Ten female students at Baylor University asserted Title IX violations based in part on the alleged failure of athletic administrators to appropriately address male student-athletes' sexual assault of female students. A report filed by Pepper Hamilton, the law firm retained by Baylor to investigate the allegations, found widespread shortcomings by the university. The resulting scandal led the NCAA to send a notice of allegations to the university and to the termination of the head football coach, the disciplining of the athletic director and his resignation, and the demotion and eventual resignation of the university's president.

Increasingly, coaches' contracts include provisions expressly requiring them to report credible allegations of sexual assault and other conduct that could violate Title IX. Coaching contracts may include provisions expressly incorporating a university's rules and policies, including an institution's Title IX policy. Although it did not involve sexual assault, former Ohio State University head football coach, Urban Meyer, and the university's athletic director, Gene Smith, were both suspended for three games in 2018 for their failure to act on knowledge they allegedly possessed of domestic abuse accusations by the wife of a former assistant football coach. Doha Madani, *Ohio State Suspends Meyer for 3 Games for his Silence on Domestic Abuse,* Huffington Post (Aug. 22, 2018).

D.   CONTRACT NEGOTIATION EXERCISE

You are an attorney representing Coach Reynolds, who is widely regarded as an up-and-coming head college football coach. He began his head football coaching career at Midwest U, a poorly regarded Division I university. Prior to his arrival at Midwest U, the school's football team had suffered through eight consecutive losing seasons. After Reynolds assumed the head coaching position, he immediately turned around Midwest U's football program. From the second through the fifth year of his five-year contract at Midwest U, the team qualified for postseason play. Moreover, his student-athletes graduated at a rate far above the average nationwide graduation rate for college football players. He runs what is considered a very clean program.

Reynolds has been approached by his alma mater, Southeastern U, to become its head coach because of the resignation of its long-time successful coach. After extensive negotiations, Reynolds tentatively agrees to become the head coach of Southeastern U, subject to finalizing the details of the contract. Southeastern U has a strong program in a moderately strong conference, but not one of the elite conferences. The general counsel for Southeastern U is concerned that Reynolds will use the institution as a steppingstone to a school in an elite conference. Reynolds, on the other hand, wants to retain the flexibility to leave Southeastern U before his contract term ends if such an offer becomes available. Reynolds is also interested in making certain that he obtains the types of incentives and bonuses that he believes he deserves given his past success. In addition, Coach Reynolds, who is 45, wants to secure the future of his family. Reynolds is married and has four children, ages 8, 10, 13, and 17. The 17-year-old will enter college a year from now.

At the end of this chapter is a sample contract. Analyze the sample contract from the perspectives of the general counsel for Southeastern U and the agent representing Coach Reynolds. Discuss terms that should be modified, deleted, or added. In addition to the sample contract, the following resources may assist you in developing your negotiation points.

1.   Summaries of Coaches' Contracts

The following summaries provide select compensation information that may assist you in developing a negotiation strategy.

CLEMSON UNIVERSITY

Coach: Dabo Swinney[1]
Term: Ten years—Jan. 1, 2019, through Dec. 31, 2028
Estimated total annual compensation: $9.3 million
Base salary: $245,000
TV/radio/personal services: $8,755,000 annual average split between supplemental and licensing income

---

1. Salary information for Coach Swinney was obtained from the following source: Manie Robinson & Mollie R. Simon, *Clemson gives Dabo Swinney Largest Contract in Football History,* The Greenville News (Apr. 26, 2019).

Supplemental:

$5,505,000: 2019
$5,505,000: 2020
$5,755,000: 2021
$5,755,000: 2022
$6,005,000: 2023
$6,255,000: 2024
$6,505,000: 2025
$6,755,000: 2026
$7,255,000: 2027
$7,255,000: 2028

Licensing: $2,500,000 per year

Perks and other terms: $1,000,000 Split Dollar Life Insurance Premium executed by September 1, 2019. In 2022, parties are required to negotiate a new contract in good faith within 120 days after the team appears in the College Football Playoff Semi-Final Game (or current existing equivalent). If the parties fail to reach an agreement and the university does not offer terms to make Swinney at least the third-highest-paid active head coach in college football, Swinney's liquidated damages are waived for the remainder of the contract. This review is not required if a new contract is negotiated in the prior year. The buyout for Swinney increases if Swinney leaves for the head coach position at the University of Alabama.

Termination/liquidated damages: There are separate provisions if Swinney or the University seek a buyout.

Swinney (amount in parenthesis is the higher buyout if Swinney leaves for the head coach position at the University of Alabama):

January 1, 2019, through December 31, 2020: $4,000,000 ($6,000,000)
January 1, 2021, through December 31, 2022: $3,000,000 ($4,500,000)
January 1, 2023, through December 31, 2025: $2,000,000 ($3,000,000)
January 1, 2026, through December 31, 2027: $1,000,000 ($1,500,000)
January 1, 2027, through December 31, 2028: $0

University

January 1, 2019, through December 31, 2020: $50,000,000
January 1, 2021, through December 31, 2022: $47,500,000
January 1, 2023, through December 31, 2023: $45,000,000
January 1, 2024, through December 31, 2028: 100% remaining total compensation (Base + Supplement + Licensing)

Retention Bonus:

$1,000,000 if coach is employed Spring 2021
$1,000,000 if coach is employed Spring 2023

PERFORMANCE BONUSES

ACC Championship Appearance: $50,000 + $150,000 for Win

Non-CFP Bowl Game Appearance (with 8+ Regular Season Wins): $50,000
Or
CFP NY6 Bowl Game Appearance: $100,000
Or
CFP Semifinal Appearance: $200,000
CFP National Championship Appearance: $200,000
CFP National Champion: $250,000
AP National Coach of the Year: $50,000

THE OHIO STATE UNIVERSITY

Coach: Ryan Day[2]
Term: Five years—Jan. 2, 2019, through Jan. 31, 2024
Estimated total annual compensation: $4.5 million
Base salary: $850,000
TV/radio/personal services: $2,600,000 in Year 1, $2,100,000 in Years 2-5
Perks and other terms: $250,000 annual payments on December 31 of each year into a RCP II pension plan. If Coach is not employed by the University on December 31 of a contract year, a payment shall be made to the pension plan equal to $250,000 multiplied by the percentage of the year Coach worked for the University. $10,000 for one annual appearance on behalf of Coca-Cola. A $1,400,000 marketing deal with Nike. Additional stipend of $1,200 per month. For each home football game: 12 tickets; 5 press booth credential tickets; use of suite by spouse, family, and guests; 10 complementary suite tickets with ability to purchase 8 additional; ability to purchase 20 additional non-suite tickets at face value. 3 season parking passes. 2 tickets to each home men's basketball game. Ability to earn supplemental compensation by participating in Ohio State youth football camp. 100 hours of private aircraft use: 50 hours for recruiting and 50 for private use. Membership and monthly dues at local golf course.
Retention Bonus:

> $250,000 if coach is employed as of January 31, 2022
> $250,000 if coach is employed as of January 31, 2024

Termination/liquidated damages: If Coach is fired other than for cause, Coach is to receive continued payment of base salary, media payments, beverage sponsor payment, and equipment payments for the next 12 months or until January 31, 2024, whichever occurs first. Contract may be terminated by the University if Coach or his staff fails to report known or suspected NCAA violations. Contract may be terminated if Coach violates any law of the United States or the State of Ohio.

If Coach terminates the agreement early, he owes Ohio State damages equivalent to the remaining salaries of all assistant coaches for the remainder of the contract period and owes compensation depending on when the contract was terminated:

---

2. Salary information for Coach Day was obtained from the following source: *Ohio State Trustees Approve Ryan Day Contract, Gene Smith Extension,* The Ohio State University (June 3, 2019), https://news.osu.edu/ohio-state-trustees-approve-ryan-day-contract-gene-smith-extension/.

Between January 2, 2019, and January 31, 2020: $3,000,000
Between February 1, 2020, and January 31, 2021: $2,000,000
Between February 1, 2021, and January 31, 2022: $1,500,000
Between February 1, 2022, and January 31, 2023: $1,000,000
Between February 1, 2022, and January 31, 2024: $500,000

PERFORMANCE BONUSES

Big Ten East Division Champion: $50,000
Winner of Big Ten East Championship Game: $100,000
CFP Bowl Game Appearance: $200,000
CFP Semi-Final Appearance: $250,000
CFP Final Appearance: $350,000
Big Ten Coach of the Year: $50,000
National Coach of the Year: $100,000

Annual Cumulative Team Grade Point Averages

   3.0: $50,000
   3.3: $100,000
   3.5: $150,000

MIAMI (OHIO) UNIVERSITY

Coach: Chuck Martin[3]
Term: Three years— Feb. 1, 2018, through January 31, 2021
Total annual compensation: $522,300
Base salary: $472,300
TV/radio/personal services: $50,000
Perks and other terms: 25 tickets to each home football game, 4 tickets to each home men's basketball game, 4 tickets to each home ice hockey game, and 4 tickets to each home women's basketball game, one automobile, insurance, and reimbursement for moving expenses.
Termination/liquidated damages: "If Coach's employment . . . is terminated by Miami *other than for cause* . . . at any time prior to February 1, 2017, Miami shall pay to Coach, as liquidated damages and not as compensation, an amount equal to the Coach's then Guaranteed Annual Payment (one year's Base Salary and Media Services Compensation) prorated over the remainder of the term of this Agreement. . . ."
"Upon Coach's obtaining new employment, Miami's obligation to pay Coach as set forth in this [section] shall be reduced by Coach's total compensation received from any new employment or any other payments for services rendered by him."
"If Coach[] obtains a position as an NCAA Division I football coach with another institution of higher education or a professional football team prior to the

---

3. Salary information for Coach Martin was obtained from the following source: *Chuck Martin New Multi-Year Contract,* Miami University, Ohio (Feb. 2018), http://miamioh.edu/_files/documents/athletics/public-records/ica-2018/chuck-martin-new-multi-year-contract.pdf.

expiration of this Agreement then Coach shall pay to Miami in equal monthly installments within one (1) year of the date of obtaining such position a sum equal to an amount equal to the Coach's then current Guaranteed Annual Payment."

PERFORMANCE BONUSES

MAC Championship: $8.333% of Guaranteed Annual Payment
Participation in Post-Season Bowl Game: 8.333% of Guaranteed Annual Payment
Or
Appearance in BCS Championship semi-finals or finals, Orange, Sugar, Rose, Fiesta, Peach or Cotton Bowl Game: 16.666% of Guaranteed Annual Payment
Game Incentive: 9 Regular Season Wins—$10,000; 10 Regular Season Wins—$15,000; 11 Regular Season Wins—$25,000
Undefeated Regular Season: 8.333% of Guaranteed Annual Payment
MAC Coach of the Year: 4.167% of Guaranteed Annual Payment
National Coach of the Year: 8.333% of Guaranteed Annual Payment
Top 25 BCS Ranking at the End of Regular Season: 8.333% of Guaranteed Annual Payment
Winning National Championship: 40% of Guaranteed Annual Payment
Yearly Graduation Rate: If 80% or better: 4.167% of Guaranteed Annual Payment
Multi-Year Academic Progress Rate (APR) of 970 or Above: 4.167% of Guaranteed Annual Payment
Or
Highest Multi-Year Academic Progress Rate (APR) in the MAC: 8.333% of Guaranteed Annual Payment

2.   *Helpful Resource Materials*

In addition to materials previously cited in this chapter, students may wish to refer to the following materials in developing a negotiating strategy:

- Michael L. Buckner, *Structuring College Coaches' Employment Agreements: Important Clauses and Issues in Agreements*—*Part One*, 3 Holland & Knight LLP Newsletter, no. 2 (Second Quarter 2000), at 1, http://www.mondaq.com/unitedstates/x/14556/Structuring+College+Coaches+Employment+Agreements+Important+Clauses+And+Issues+In+Agreements+Part+One.
- Canadian Professional Coaches Association, *A Guide to Employment Contracts for Coaches*, Section 3: The Coaching Contract: Basic Elements (2000), http://www.swimontario.com/userfiles/file/Club%20Services/AGM/2009/Presentations/Corbett/employmentcontractsforcoaches.pdf.
- Martin J. Greenberg, *A Study of Division I Assistant Football and Men's Basketball Coaches' Contracts*, 18 Marq. Sports L. Rev. 25 (2007).
- Greenberg, *Termination of College Coaching Contracts, supra.*
- Martin J. Greenberg, *College Coaching Contracts Revisited: A Practical Perspective*, 12 Marq. Sports L. Rev. 127 (2001).
- Martin J. Greenberg, *College Coaching Contracts: A Practical Perspective*, 1 Marq. Sports L.J. 207 (1991).

- Harvey M. Shrage & Curt Hamakawa, *The Impact of Teacher Collective Bargaining Agreements on High School Coaches*, 27 Marq. Sports L. Rev. 373 (2017).
- Edward Stoner, II, and Arlie Nogay, *The Model University Coaching Contract ("MCC"): A Better Starting Point for Your Next Negotiation*, 16 J.C. & U.L. 43 (1989).

3.   *Sample Contract*

HEAD FOOTBALL COACH'S EMPLOYMENT CONTRACT

This contract, dated January 6, 2016, is between Texas State University (Texas State) and Everett Withers (Coach).

1. EMPLOYMENT

1.01.   <u>Employment.</u> Subject to the terms of this contract, Texas State employs the Coach as its Head Football Coach and the Coach accepts this employment. As Head Coach, the Coach shall report directly to Texas State's Director of Athletics. This employment does not grant the Coach a claim to tenure.

1.02.   <u>Duties.</u> As Head Football Coach, the Coach agrees to perform the following duties:

   a.   To perform faithfully and conscientiously the duties assigned by the Director of Athletics as specified in this contract.

   b.   To devote full time attention and energy to the duties of Head Football Coach; to promote Texas State's athletic program; and to avoid business or professional activities that prevent or distract the Coach from performing his duties.

   c.   To comply with the laws, policies, and rules that govern Texas State and its students and employees. These laws, policies, and rules include: (1) the Rules and Regulations of the Board of Regents, The Texas State University System; (2) the rules of the National Collegiate Athletic Association (NCAA); and (3) the applicable conference rules.

   d.   To use his best efforts to assure that all assistant coaches, employees, and others for whom the Coach is responsible perform their duties and comply with these laws, policies, and rules and to assume full responsibility for violations that jeopardize the University's standing with the NCAA or the applicable conference.

1.03   <u>Support Staff.</u> The Coach may select, retain, or reassign assistant coaches in consultation with the Director of Athletics, subject to NCAA and applicable conference rules.

1.04.   <u>Evaluation.</u> The Director of Athletics will evaluate the Coach's performance periodically, but not less often than annually. The standards for evaluation include:

   a.   The usual and customary coaching activities, including positive instruction of and interaction with the student-athletes on field performance, cooperating with academic departments, and making best efforts to assure satisfactory academic progress.

   b.   The football team's competitiveness and performance on the field;

   c.   Recruiting;

d.   Assisting Texas State's Alumni Association, Bobcat Club and other development activities;

e.   Cooperating with news media as provided in subsection f below;

f.   Representing Texas State, The Texas State University System (TSUS) and the University's athletic programs positively in private and public forums. This representation includes a strict requirement not to make statements to the press or in public that disparage or reflect negatively on the Board of Regents, TSUS, Texas State, its Department of Athletics, its football program, or any of the above's regents, administrators or employees; and

g.   Performing duties assigned in writing by the Director of Athletics.

2. COMPENSATION

2.01.   Salary. In consideration for the Coach's satisfactory services under this contract, Texas State agrees to pay the Coach an annual salary and other compensation shown on Attachment A, which is made a part of this contract for all purposes. The base salary and the media and outside appearance compensation are payable in monthly installments on the first working day of each month of this contract. Texas State may, in its discretion, increase this salary to reflect increases, bonuses, and merit given its other staff employees or otherwise to compensate for increases in his duties or responsibilities.

2.02.   Deductions. The compensation that Texas State pays is subject to the same payroll deductions that apply to Texas State's other staff employees. These deductions include, for example, income tax and FICA withholding, health care deductions, and contributions to retirement plans.

2.03.   Benefits. The Coach is eligible to participate in health and life insurance, retirement programs, benefits, and other voluntary payroll deduction programs on the same basis, and with the same employer contributions, that apply to Texas State's other staff employees.

3. TERM AND TERMINATION

3.01.   Term and Extensions. This contract will begin on January 6, 2016, and will terminate on January 5, 2021. At the end of each year of this contract, if it is satisfied with the Coach's performance, Texas State will present and recommend an extension of this contract to the President and the Chancellor of The Texas State University System. The parties will negotiate and agree on the length of each such extension, with the understanding that any extension plus the years remaining on the contract will not exceed five years. Texas State will use its best efforts to secure approval for each extension.

3.02.   Replacing Prior Contracts. This contract supersedes and replaces all prior contracts and agreements between the parties respecting the Coach's employment.

3.03.   <u>Buyout.</u> If Texas State terminates this Contract without cause, Texas State will pay Coach as liquidated damages an amount equal to 50% of the remaining outstanding Guaranteed Salary as set forth in Attachment A, scheduled to be paid to Coach through the end of the Term (i.e., January 5, 2021). Said amount will be paid to Coach during the remainder of the scheduled Term in equal installments in accordance with Texas State's normal payroll policy, or may be paid in a lump sum at the option of Texas State University. Coach will have no duty to mitigate Texas State's liquidated damages hereunder, and there will be no set off should Coach secure another job prior to January 5, 2021.

3.04.   <u>Coach's Resignation.</u> Coach shall have the right to terminate this Contract at any time during the Term. If Coach terminates this Contract for any reason other than death, disability, or significant health issue, then Coach agrees to pay Texas State as liquidated damages an amount equal to 50% of the remaining outstanding Guaranteed Salary as set forth in Attachment A, scheduled to be paid to Coach through the end of the Term (i.e., January 5, 2021). Said amount will be paid to Texas State within a one year period from the date of Coach's resignation, in 3 equal installments, with the first installment to be paid within 6 months of date of Coach's resignation.

3.05.   <u>Requirement to Follow Rules and Laws.</u> The Coach is required to follow all of Texas State's rules and policies, including those of The Texas State University System. The Coach is also required to follow local ordinances and state and federal laws.

   a.   Major violations of rules, policies, or laws subject the Coach to immediate termination of employment without further compensation.

   b.   As provided in the Rules and Regulations of the Board of Regents, The Texas State University System (Chapter V, Section 1.13), Texas State may terminate this contract for cause without penalty and the Coach is not entitled to prior notice or reasons for non-renewal. "Cause" includes failure to perform the duties in Sections 1.04, with the exception of 1.04 (b), and 3.06 of this contract or otherwise for conduct constituting lewdness, moral turpitude, or any violation of the ethical policies in Chapter VIII of the System Rules and Regulations.

   c.   Under these circumstances the Coach may grieve the termination using the grievance procedures available to Texas State's staff employees in UPPS No. 04.04.41 or in the System Rules and Regulations, which govern in the event of a conflict.

3.06.   <u>Requirement to Follow NCAA and Conference Rules.</u> The Coach is required to follow all applicable rules of the NCAA and the applicable conference, including the NCAA requirement to maintain an atmosphere of compliance with staff members and assistant coaches. If the Coach is found to be knowingly involved in significant or repetitive violations of these rules the Coach is subject to disciplinary action as set forth in NCAA and/or conference enforcement regulations. These disciplinary actions include suspension without pay or termination of employment.

    a.   Further, if the NCAA or the conference imposes restrictions on the Coach's recruiting off campus, Texas State may suspend the Coach without pay or terminate his employment without further liability.

    b.   Disciplinary sanctions up to and including termination relating to these provisions are within the discretion of the NCAA or the conference and apply notwithstanding any other provisions in this contract.

4. OUTSIDE EMPLOYMENT AND ATHLETICALLY RELATED INCOME

4.01.   Approval Required. Before seeking, negotiating for, or accepting other full-time or part-time employment during the term of this contract, the Coach will inform the Director of Athletics of his intention to do so and will receive the Director of Athletics's approval. Outside employment must conform to state of Texas, NCAA, applicable conference, Texas State and TSUS laws and policies. Approval will not be unreasonably withheld.

4.02.   Athletically Related Income. Annually the Coach is required to receive approval from the Director of Athletics for athletically related income and benefits received from sources other than Texas State. The Coach's request must precede the receipt of such income and must be in writing and must provide the amount and the source of the income. These sources include income from: (1) annuities; (2) sports camps; (3) housing benefits, including preferential housing arrangements; (4) country club memberships; (5) complimentary ticket sales; (6) radio and television programs; (7) endorsement or consultation contracts with athletic shoe, apparel, or equipment manufacturers; and (8) bonuses other than those included in this contract.

5. PERSONAL SERVICES

5.01.   Other Coaching Employment. During the term of this contract, the Coach agrees not to accept employment as a coach at any institution that is a member of the same conference that Texas State is a member of, without first notifying the Director of Athletics and receiving his written approval. Permission will not be unreasonably withheld.

5.02.   Enforcement. If Texas State is compelled to bring legal action to enforce its rights under this section 5, it will be entitled to its costs and attorney fees if it prevails, in whole or in part, in the cause of legal action.

6. GENERAL PROVISIONS

6.01.   Governing Law. The laws of the State of Texas will govern this contract. The parties will perform their obligations in Hays County, Texas. Neither Texas State nor TSUS waive their constitutional, statutory, or common law immunities or defenses as agencies of the State.

6.02.   <u>Entire Contract.</u> This contract constitutes the entire agreement of the parties
respecting this subject and it supersedes any prior written or oral understandings
of the parties. This contract may not be amended except in writing, signed by the
parties or their representatives.

Texas State University:

By: _Denise M. Trauth_   _(signature)_
Denise M. Trauth   Head Football Coach
President

By: _Larry Teis_
Larry Teis
Director of Athletics

By: _(signature)_
Brian McCall, Ph.D.
Chancellor, The Texas State University System

Approved as to legal form: _(signature)_
Fernando Gomez, Vice Chancellor and General Counsel
The Texas State University System

ATTACHMENT A

COMPENSATION PACKAGE

Guaranteed Salary:

Year 1 - $650,000
Year 2 - $675,000
Year 3 - $700,000
Year 4 - $725,000
Year 5 - $750,000

Guaranteed salary includes compensation for radio, television, and outside appearances. These appearances include radio and TV shows during each football season and additional radio shows for bowl games or a special season wrap-up show, plus departmental appearances at support organization lunches and special fundraising events.

Monthly Car Allowance:	$550
Monthly Cell Phone Allowance:	$50

ATHLETIC PERFORMANCE INCENTIVE:

Bowl game:	one month's salary

ACADEMIC PERFORMANCE INCENTIVES (NOT CUMMULATIVE):

Greater than 960	$7,500
Greater than 970	$10,000
Greater than 980	$12,500

OTHER FINANCIAL CONSIDERATIONS:

Moving expenses - reimbursed according to university policy and state law

CHAPTER
6

Professional Sports League Governance and Legal Regulation

A. INTRODUCTION

This chapter begins our exploration of the regulation of legal and business relationships within professional sports in the United States. The greatest emphasis is on North American major league team sports, particularly the National Football League (NFL), the National Basketball Association (NBA), Major League Baseball (MLB), and the National Hockey League (NHL), as well as Major League Soccer (MLS). The internal governance and legal regulation of individual-performer sports such as auto racing, golf, mixed martial arts, and tennis also are briefly considered. Professional sports enterprises are for-profit entertainment businesses that are overwhelmingly driven by economics, which significantly influences most of the league or governing body's decision-making and creates most of the legal issues. Like other for-profit industries, where money is to be made, legal issues surge in the wake.

This chapter initially describes the development of the North American professional sports industries (particularly team sports) as well as their unique features and primary components. We then examine the structure, operation, and internal governance of professional sports leagues, which generally consist of independently owned and operated clubs with a commissioner vested with broad "best interests" of the game authority. Finally, we explore the role of state contract, fiduciary duty, and private association laws, and of then federal antitrust law in regulating the relationships among the league, clubs, and its commissioner as well as rival sports leagues and associations.

North American professional sports league or association labor relations issues are covered in Chapter 7. When U.S. professional athletes compete in Olympic and other international sports events, the associated governance and legal issues in general are significantly different and usually require the application of foreign laws or international law, which are addressed in Chapter 4. Recent unionization efforts as well as antitrust and employment law litigation seeking to professionalize intercollegiate athletics are discussed in Chapter 3.

B.   ORIGIN AND EVOLUTION OF MODERN PROFESSIONAL SPORTS INDUSTRIES

The origins of today's most popular American individual and team professional sports are at least somewhat shrouded in mystery. The great American pastime of baseball may not be American in origin at all. Although legend long held—and a century-old MLB investigation claimed to confirm—that Abner Doubleday invented baseball in Cooperstown, New York, in 1839, the more accurate view is that baseball was first played on the Elysian Fields in New Jersey in 1845, perhaps as a derivative of the English game of rounders.

Football, the American version, has equally obscure beginnings. Most would attribute its modern origin to soccer-like games at Harvard in 1871, when the rules were altered to allow players to scoop up the round ball and run with it. At that point, football began to be played with more than feet. In the early 1900s, it had reached sufficient levels of mayhem (causing the deaths of several college football players) to be condemned by the old Rough Rider himself, Theodore Roosevelt.

The origin of the word *hockey* is uncertain. Some of the theories are certainly amusing. It may have come from the French word *hoquet,* meaning "shepherd's crook." A more fanciful theory is that French explorers in North America observed Iroquois Indians playing a version of the game, striking a hard ball with sticks, and yelling "Hogee!" or "It hurts!" What is known is that something resembling the modern version was played in Canada as early as the 1830s.

The one sport whose origins seem uncontroversial is basketball. Dr. James Naismith did nail a peach basket to a wall in the gymnasium in Springfield, Massachusetts, YMCA during the winter of 1891 to provide the youth with an indoor sport to play when snow and wind prevented outdoor activity. Dr. Naismith first instructed his charges to play soccer (undisputedly of British origin) in the gym, but their lack of ball control resulted in broken windows, leading him to develop a game in which players used their hands rather than their feet to control the ball.

As popular as these sports are today, none can rival the origin of golf and its journey to the modern day. It was so popular that in 1457 the king of Scotland had his parliament ban it, lest it detract from more serious pursuits such as archery. But this ban was largely ignored and was completely overturned when King James IV of Scotland took up the game in the early sixteenth century. His granddaughter Mary, Queen of Scots, was a great devotee of the sport and took the game with her to France. She attracted the attention of a host of young male admirers, known as *cadets,* who followed her over the meadows. They eventually were called *caddies.* Most caddies today probably are unaware of their noble lineage.

This brief history highlights the unique appeal that sports have always had throughout the history of the United States, and these are but summary examinations of only a few of the current professional sports that might be explored. It is not surprising that sports have evolved into one of the twenty-first century's most popular forms of entertainment, and that they generate billions of dollars in revenue from a variety of sources, including gate receipts, media contracts, trademark licensing, and sponsorships.

1.   *Evolution of Sports into a Business and Profession*

Sports as activities, diversions, and cohesive unifiers have been a significant part of American society for centuries, but sports as professions, businesses, and industries are of more recent vintage. Contemporaneously with the industrial revolution in the 1800s, a sports revolution occurred as well. This was no coincidence. Recreational activity became a business, and business evolved into industry. For sports, the roots were perhaps not as obvious as the invention of steam locomotion or electricity harnessed into light, but sports took advantage of emerging industrial technologies just as surely as the wings of birds inspired the flight of man.

Each new step in the advancement of technology led to increased opportunities for sports exposure and thus expansion. Transportation was the first crucial ingredient. Communications was the second. The two have been powerful concomitants—necessary elements to allow sports to transcend the confines of the ballpark or arena and to enter the homes of millions of sports fans, initially through radio, then via television, and more recently the Internet and mobile devices. Although the movers and shakers in early professional sports ventures could not have recognized fully the enormous commercial potential within their grasp, such is not true today. The preeminent sports business entrepreneurs are those with the greatest vision and ability to exploit this vast revenue-generating potential. Sports as commercial successes owe much to technological advances and to deepened understanding of business and marketing techniques. There is still the game itself, with on-field winners and losers, but there is a driving force—off-field economic success—that is equally influential in just how, when, and where a game is played and who ultimately plays it.

In the United States, the sport of baseball was the pioneer for professional players, teams, and leagues. The Cincinnati Red Stockings are generally acknowledged as the first truly professional team, touring the country in 1869 and taking on all challengers. The National League, which still exists today, was founded in 1876. Although it bears perhaps small resemblance to its current structure within Major League Baseball, and some might take issue with it being designated as the first professional sports league, it was certainly a bellwether on the road to professionalization.

Decades later than baseball, other professional sports leagues began to form. The NFL began in 1919, 1920, or 1921. In 1919, it called itself the American Professional Football Conference, short thereafter changing its name to the American Professional Football Association. The league's struggles led to its near demise in 1920 and its restart in 1921, so when it actually began can be debated. By whatever definition, however, the NFL's ultimate astounding success and popularity are beyond dispute.

The NHL actually predated the NFL, starting in 1918 in the aftermath of a one-year wonder, the National Hockey Association. The "national" designation, however, signified Canada, not the United States. The first U.S. team, the Boston Bruins, did not join the league until 1924. Today the number of American clubs significantly exceeds that of Canadian clubs. Four of the original six clubs were located in the United States, with this trend continuing as the NHL expanded. Still, for most of the twentieth century, NHL players were almost exclusively Canadian. This changed, however, as grassroots amateur hockey leagues developed in the United States and as Eastern European players flooded into the league following the break-up of the Soviet Union and the end of the Cold War.

The history of professional basketball has been circuitous. Players used to be *cagers*, which referred to the wire netting originally surrounding the court to keep the players from hurtling into the stands near the sidelines. This makeshift, precarious nature of the court was a fitting description for the business of basketball as well. Through the 1920s and 1930s, the sport gained popularity but headed in directions both unknown and uncharted. The end of World War II provided the American public with more leisure time to seek new diversions, which generally resulted in the increased popularity of professional sports, including basketball. The National Basketball Association (NBA)'s genesis was the Basketball Association of America (BAA) in 1946.

Soccer, known to the rest of the world as "football," is truly global in its nature and fan appeal, more so than any other American team sport. Its World Cup is the premier worldwide team sports event (with apologies to the NFL's Super Bowl). Although Major League Soccer lags behind the other American sports leagues economically, its fan base is large and growing.

Tennis and golf are very popular individual performer sports both in the United States and globally. Professional tennis tournaments began in the 1920s, but amateur tournaments were more popular. The professional players were reduced to barnstorming, with the prevailing champion taking on the latest challenger from the amateur ranks. The big tournaments were closed to professionals. Only with the arrival of the open tennis era in 1968 did professional tennis truly emerge. Golf also had its share of early professional tournaments, with the U.S. Open dating from 1895 and, in 1921, Walter Hagen's win in the first Professional Golfers' Association Championship. However, it was not until after World War II that professional players began dominating the sport of golf. Tennis and golf are more global than virtually all team sports except soccer because the top players in both sports come from all parts of the world. Despite loyal and avid fans, the overall level of fan support for these sports pales in comparison to team sports, at least in the United States.

Auto racing is one of the country's most popular professional spectator sports, although some might be reluctant to characterize it as a sport. The first Indianapolis 500 Mile Race was held in 1911. The National Association for Stock Car Auto Racing (NASCAR) has been in existence since 1951. NASCAR and IndyCar each sponsor an annual series of auto races at tracks throughout the United States.

The Ultimate Fighting Championship (UFC), a promoter of professional mixed martial arts (MMA) competitions involving martial arts, wrestling, and other combat sports created in 1993, has developed a huge following worldwide. As MMA's popularity has grown, other MMA promotors, such as Bellator MMA, have begun to challenge UFC for market dominance. MMA competition has a long history, which can be traced to the Ancient Olympic Games in Athens. Vale Tudo, a Brazilian form of MMA that means "anything goes," reinvigorated public interest in MMA about 80 years ago. The New York legislature's March 2016 vote to legalize MMA competitions in the state (which are now legal nationwide) is viewed by many as removing the final obstacle to its acceptance as a legitimate mainstream sport.

2.   Unique Features of Professional Team Sports

Professional team sports have several unique features that significantly influence how they are operated, structured, and internally governed, which give rise to complex legal issues. It is important to keep these features in mind in analyzing and developing an understanding of how general areas of law, particularly contract, fiduciary duty, private association, and antitrust law, have been judicially applied to regulate professional team sports.

A professional sports team must have other teams to play against on a regular basis for individual game and seasonal championship competition to exist, which is why multiple teams join together to form national or continental sports leagues such as MLB, MLS, NBA, NFL, or NHL. To sustain fans' interest and to generate the very substantial revenues necessary for a North American major professional sports league to produce a financially viable entertainment product, on-field competition among league teams cannot be too one-sided in favor of any single team from year to year. Team owners, players, and ultimately consumers tire of being perennial losers (although a few teams in each league have an unfortunate knack for annually doing so).

Without any agreed-on limitations, there is nothing to prevent teams from being off-field economic competitors. Although on-field competition in the form of close, exciting games economically benefits the league and its member clubs by increasing fan support and total revenues, too much off-field economic competition among teams can be harmful, not only to individual teams but also the league as a whole. Thus, a sports league's financial viability and the economic health of all teams necessitate some limits on economic competition among member clubs, so that a league and its clubs can collectively compete against other professional leagues and other forms of entertainment.

Economic competition for fan patronage (which may be national, regional, and/or local) exists among the various North American sports leagues, either those that offer games in the same sport (e.g., MLB Cubs and White Sox teams in Chicago) or those that offer different sports (e.g., in addition to the two MLB clubs, MLS Fire, NBA Bulls, NFL Bears, and NHL Blackhawks in Chicago). Each team needs a large local fan base and must appeal to consumers with limited discretionary income and recreational time who may transfer their allegiance as the on-field success of the various local teams ebbs and flows. For example, NBA and NHL clubs in the same city, whose playing seasons largely overlap, often experience the whims of fair-weather fans.

There are no analogous business models in other industries comparable to the unique features of a professional sports league. The strong desire to compete successfully on the playing field with the simultaneous need to limit economic competition among league clubs to some degree presents significant challenges to businesspeople accustomed to ruthless competition in other industries. To work both competitively and cooperatively as part of a professional sports league can be very difficult and frequently leads to business and legal disputes.

When players (along with their unions and agents) are added to this mix, business and legal issues multiply in their complexity. Highly skilled players are essential to the game's attractiveness to consumers and economic success. Sports leagues, as commercial enterprises, thrive on the special talents of players, their celebrity status, and their resulting marketability. Major league professional athletes have unique talents and playing abilities, but their necessarily symbiotic relationship with the league and teams for their respective sports often gives rise to contentious economic and legal issues, which are analyzed in Chapter 7.

The following section explores in greater depth how the respective roles of teams, leagues, players, and other important components of sports industries interact and often conflict. This interplay illustrates the need for legal regulation of this complex web of relationships.

3.   The Principal "Players" in the Professional Sports Industries

The old cliché "you can't tell the players without a scorecard" aptly describes why we cannot appreciate the broad dimensions of professional sports business and legal problems unless we identify the various parties' differing interests and how they both intersect and conflict. The following discussion concerning the principal professional sports industry players (i.e., components) uses the team-sports model, which has some common elements with the individual-performer sports industry.

In general, the league, its commissioner, and its teams are aligned on one side; the players, their labor union, and player-agents are on the other side. However, there are a host of related entities that play integral roles in a professional sports league's operations. Television and Internet media, advertisers and corporate sponsors, and financial institutions are just a few of the heavyweights that influence the professional team sports and individual-performer sports industries. Each of these components adds a layer of complexity and raises corresponding legal issues.

a.   Leagues

North American professional sports leagues, which generally are "closed" (i.e., new clubs are added only by supramajority vote of existing clubs) in contrast to "open" European professional leagues (i.e., a national promotion and relegation system discussed *infra*) and have an "independent" commissioner, have existed since baseball's National League was founded in 1876. In essence, a sports league is a group of team owners that join together in a formal association defined by a series of contracts to produce, market, and sell its product: organized athletic competition among its member teams. The formation of a league raises complex questions as to its legal relationship with and between its member clubs. Consider the multitude of important issues that must be considered and resolved: for example, number, ownership, and location of league clubs; league internal governance; business relationships with others, such as league clubs' host cities, broadcasters, and sponsors, etc.

b.   Clubs or Teams

The terms clubs and teams are used interchangeably in the professional sports context. Each major professional league (e.g., MLB, NBA, NFL, NHL, and MLS) has several member clubs located throughout the United States or Canada, which are expanded (or contracted) from time to time. Indeed, the growth in the popularity of a particular sport is generally measured by the historical expansion of a league's number of teams. By the same token, a decline in interest is often marked by a reduction in teams and perhaps the demise of an entire league, which often occurs when a new league seeks to compete with the established league in the same sport.

With few exceptions (e.g., Green Bay Packers), league clubs generally are separately owned and operated by private parties (usually very wealthy individuals) that have an exclusive geographical territory (shared in the largest markets such as New York, Los Angeles, Chicago, and others), which share revenues but not profits or losses. Within a particular league, all clubs are not on equal footing. Their on-field competitive success, business approach, and profitability frequently vary substantially. A club's geographical location is a significant factor that determines its potential consumer (fan) and economic base. Another important factor is the club's ownership, which in turn determines who operates and manages the club, thereby undoubtedly influencing who plays for the team and its performance level as well as its generally corresponding economic performance.

The legal nature and character of the interrelationships between a league and its member clubs, as well as among them, are very important, particularly for the purposes of federal antitrust law, which constrains a league's internal governance autonomy.

c.   Commissioners

The concept of a league commissioner with broad governing authority came to fruition when major league baseball club owners appointed their first commissioner, Judge Kenesaw Mountain Landis, to his throne in 1920. This bold step was taken to ensure that baseball would not experience another scandal such as befell the Chicago White Sox in 1919 when several of its players allegedly accepted money to purposefully lose the World Series. Commissioner Landis was given sweeping power to act "in the best interests of baseball," which he and his successors have used when necessary. The other North American major professional sports leagues have followed baseball's example by adopting a league commissioner model of governance. The existence of a commissioner with broad powers invites legal conflict; there have been several disputes regarding a league commissioner's exercise of "best interests" authority in a wide variety of situations, as wil be explored later in this chapter.

d.   Players

For a professional athlete, sports are his or her livelihood, with many professional athletes earning multi-million-dollar salaries. Most professional athletes have relatively short playing careers (especially at the major league level), however, and they must be cognizant of the cold realities of this frequently harsh business, which may implicate their legal rights. The multitude of legal issues involving players and the league or their respective clubs (primarily contract, labor, and antitrust law matters) are explored in Chapter 7.

e.   Players Associations/Unions

A players association exists for each major league team sport for the purpose of advancing the players' interests. It generally is a labor union chosen by the players that represents them in labor and employment matters with the league and clubs. Professional sports give rise to unique labor relations issues not typically found in other industries, which are considered in Chapter 7.

f.   Agents

Player agents (sometimes referred to as sports agents) generally are lawyers and trained professionals who represent team sport athletes in contract negotiations with their respective clubs. They also represent individual performer sport athletes. Player agents frequently handle, or participate in, the management of most aspects of their players' business affairs. As discussed in Chapter 8, agents who represent professional athletes are subject to both federal and state laws, and they are regulated by the major league sport's players union if they represent any of its member players.

g.   Other Industries Integral to Modern Professional Sports

Several industries have both contributed to and benefited from the operation of professional sports leagues and associations. A prime example is the media, which extensively broadcasts, comments on, and reports about professional sports. Society today is pervasively connected to North American professional sports, which can be accessed domestically and throughout many parts of the world through television, radio, print media, the Internet, and mobile devices. Pervasive media coverage of sports has stimulated enormous consumer interest in professional sports as well as in collateral products such as trademarked merchandise and activities such as fantasy sports and gambling. Media broadcasting rights fees have injected billions of dollars into the professional sports industries. Corporations selling a variety of goods and services provide huge sums to professional sports leagues, associations, and athletes for advertising and sponsorships. This produces a complex set of often conflicting economic interests and objectives with corresponding intellectual property legal issues, which are discussed in Chapter 12.

C.   INTERNAL LEAGUE GOVERNANCE AND COMMISSIONER AUTHORITY

A professional sports league or association generally has a constitution and bylaws that establish its internal system of governance pursuant to a contract among its member clubs. One particular individual, usually designated as the commissioner, often is given substantial authority to oversee the league's general operations and business affairs. As discussed in Chapter 7, if professional team sport athletes (or league employees such as umpires and referees) form a labor union that negotiates a collective bargaining agreement with club owners, it takes precedence over the league's constitution and bylaws regarding most labor relations issues and matters. Standardized player contract terms, which generally are collectively bargained, also take precedence over the league constitution and bylaws. However, other negotiated terms of individual player contracts do not. The following material primarily focuses on relations and disputes between leagues and their member clubs. To a limited extent, it also considers the nature and scope of the regulatory authority of associations formed to govern individual-performer sports. Because the athletes in these sports are independent contractors (rather than team employees who can unionize and collectively bargain under federal labor law), state contract, fiduciary duty, and private association laws generally are used to resolve internal governance actions that affect them.

1. Scope of Judicial Review of Internal League Governance

United States professional sports leagues and associations are private entities that are not subject to the constraints of the United States Constitution because their conduct, decisions, and rules do not constitute "state action." *Long v. National Football League*, 870 F. Supp. 101 (W.D. Pa. 1994), *aff'd*, 66 F.3d 311 (3d Cir. 1994). The league or association constitution, bylaws, and rules create binding contractual rights and responsibilities if they are reasonable, do not infringe on other parties' rights, and do not violate applicable laws. Thus, the legal relationships among professional sports league clubs or sports association members are primarily governed by contract law and the law of private associations. Federal antitrust law also plays a significant role in regulating the internal governance of professional leagues and associations.

A sport's governing body has a legal obligation to follow its own rules and bylaws; its failure to do so may give rise to a breach of contract claim by an aggrieved member whose interests are harmed. In general, courts will intervene and provide appropriate relief only "(1) where the rules, regulations or judgments of the association are in contravention to the laws of the land or in disregard of the charter or bylaws of the association and (2) where the association has failed to follow the basic rudiments of due process of law." *Charles O. Finley & Co. v. Kuhn*, 569 F.2d 527, 544 (7th Cir. 1978). In addition, courts will do so if an association's decision-making process is arbitrary or capricious or is tainted by malice or bad faith.

Courts recognize that professional sports leagues and associations must be given considerable latitude in rule making and enforcement in order to accomplish their legitimate objectives. See, e.g., *Mayfield v. NASCAR*, 674 F.3d 369 (4th Cir. 2012) (enforcing the disciplinary suspension imposed on a professional race car driver for breaching contractual obligation to comply with NASCAR's Substance Abuse Policy as well as a release of liability and covenant not to sue NASCAR for any claims arising out of the implementation of its policy). They generally are permitted to freely establish their respective systems of self-governance, and courts are reluctant to interfere with or second-guess their internal decision making. Their members generally are bound by the terms of the sports league or association's constitution, bylaws, and other governing documents, which collectively create contractual obligations and rights, unless there is a breach of fiduciary duty, a conflict of interest, bad faith, or violation of applicable laws, such as, for example, federal antitrust law. But otherwise there is broad discretion accorded to a sports league or association to interpret its own rules without judicial intervention, as illustrated by the following cases.

In *Koszela v. NASCAR*, 646 F.2d 749 (2d Cir. 1981), the Second Circuit rejected the claims of a stock car owner and driver that NASCAR misapplied its rules in determining that another car and driver were the winners of two races. The court found that the plaintiffs' membership contract with NASCAR did not provide for an administrative appeal or judicial review of NASCAR official decisions regarding race procedures or determination of car positions. The court concluded that the plaintiffs had been given an opportunity to be heard by NASCAR officials and had exhausted all available rights. The court affirmed the dismissal of the plaintiffs' claims and held that NASCAR was not in violation of any contractual duties owed to the plaintiffs.

A similar result was reached in *Crouch v. National Association for Stock Car Auto Racing, Inc.*, 845 F.2d 397 (2d Cir. 1988), in which the court reviewed whether

NASCAR violated its own procedures in determining the winner of a stock car race. The court initially drew a distinction between reviewing the merits of decisions made by private organizations and reviewing the procedures used in reaching those decisions. The court recognized the appropriateness of intervening if there were inadequate procedures to safeguard a member's rights, but the plaintiffs did not make any such assertions. Nor were there any allegations that NASCAR violated its own rules or that NASCAR officials acted in bad faith in reviewing the plaintiffs' challenge to their determination of the official race results. The Second Circuit held that the lower court erred in delving into NASCAR's rulebook and conducting what was essentially an inquiry *de novo*. Instead, the proper approach was to defer to an association's interpretation of its own rules absent a showing of bad faith or violation of any state or federal laws.

Despite a general judicial reluctance to oversee a professional sports organization's affairs, courts will nevertheless provide a forum for resolution of internal governance disputes. At least at the major league level, a professional sports league is often without direct competition from another league. Because of the for-profit and monopolistic nature of major professional sports leagues and associations, there is a judicially recognized need for some limited oversight to prevent exploitation and blatant unfairness toward any of the organization's members or participants. As the *Koszela* court observed, when a sports organization has such a "strangle-hold" that all teams or individuals desiring to participate in a sport must join it, "rigid adherence to a 'hands off' policy is inappropriate." 646 F.2d at 754.

Gilder v. PGA Tour, Inc., 727 F. Supp. 1333 (D. Ariz. 1989), *aff'd*, 936 F.2d 417 (9th Cir. 1991), illustrates that courts will intervene when individuals with vested interests breach their fiduciary duty when governing a professional sports association's affairs. The Ninth Circuit held that touring professional golfers serving on the PGA's board of directors (who had endorsement deals with manufacturers of V-shaped grooved irons) owe a fiduciary duty to act in the best interests of the association and are prohibited from using their position for potential personal gain. Their vote to amend the PGA bylaws' voting procedures, which resulted in U-shaped grooved irons being banned, breached this fiduciary duty. See also *Blalock v. Ladies Professional Golf Assn.*, 359 F. Supp. 1260 (N.D. Ga. 1973) (the suspension of a professional golfer for alleged rule violations by a governing board that included competing tour players infringed her right to a fair disciplinary hearing; her competitors, sitting in judgment of her, unlawfully had authority to exercise unfettered, subjective discretion to discipline her for their own potential financial benefit).

In summary, the foregoing cases illustrate that courts generally are reluctant to interfere with the internal affairs of a professional sports league or association absent specific breaches of contract, failure to provide procedural due process, bad faith conduct, or a violation of state (e.g., fiduciary duty) or federal (e.g., antitrust) law.

2.   *League Commissioner "Best Interests" Power*

The major professional sports leagues in the United States have all adopted a model of organization and governance that places an independent commissioner, selected by and answerable to the league club owners, in control of internal affairs. The commissioner generally is more powerful than a chairperson of the board of a corporation and probably wields more power than a typical president of a company. As noted above, the first commissioner in any sport was Judge Kenesaw Mountain Landis, who assumed that position in baseball in 1920 to ensure that the infamous Black Sox scandal arising out of the 1919 World Series would not recur. Reportedly, at his insistence, Judge Landis was accorded the authority to do whatever was necessary to protect the "best interests" of baseball. This same sweeping power—to act in the best interests of the sport—describes the decision-making, disciplinary, and dispute resolution powers and duties vested in all commissioners of the North American major professional sports leagues.

Regarding Major League Baseball, former commissioner Bud Selig described this role as follows:

> Along with inherent administrative authority to further baseball's best interests (analogous to the United States president's executive order authority), the MLB commissioner historically and currently has enjoyed broad investigative, remedial, preventative, and disciplinary power to ensure that baseball players, coaches, and other personnel engage in honest athletic competition and to refrain from activities that harm the sport's integrity such as gambling on or improperly influencing the results of baseball games. In addition, the commissioner's "best interests" power encompasses plenary authority to take appropriate steps to preserve league-wide competitive balance as well as fair play (both on-field and off-field) among MLB league clubs. This authority enables the MLB commissioner to maintain the integrity of and public confidence in the game of baseball.

Allan H. "Bud" Selig and Matthew J. Mitten, *Baseball Jurisprudence: Its Effects on America's Pastime and Other Professional Sports Leagues*, 50 Ariz. St. L. J. 1171, 1174 (2018).

A league's commissioner is an integral part of the league's governance structure whose role may consist of the following functions:

1. To create a fair and impartial internal authority to resolve disputes within the league and to enforce independently a disciplinary process—these being essential to maintain the game's integrity and provide rudimentary due process protections necessary to avoid judicial oversight of league affairs.
2. To take action when needed to restrain the unwarranted exercise of power by the league's owners to the detriment of fans and others, again to avoid judicial intervention.
3. To serve as a centralized administrative authority to facilitate efficient decision making and league governance.
4. To be a skillful mediator when owners cannot agree.
5. To be the lead negotiator for league-wide contracts, such as the all-important television deals.
6. At times, to become involved in labor disputes between the owners and the players—in fact, in some leagues, the commissioner is the lead negotiator on behalf of the owners. (Such is the case today in the NBA and the NHL.)

For a general overview of a league's organizational structure, its commissioner's governing authority, and its objectives, see Gregor Lentze, *The Legal Concept of Professional Sports Leagues: The Commissioner and an Alternative Approach from a Corporate Perspective*, 6 Marq. Sports L.J. 65 (1995).

Despite having the above powers, it must be emphasized that a league commissioner does not have unfettered independence or authority. At times, he or she must walk a tightrope to avoid undermining or losing his or her authority. The commissioner, for example, has contractually defined disciplinary authority over the league's club owners, but his or her job security is subject to the will of these owners. For instance, MLB commissioner Fay Vincent resigned in August 1992 under pressure from MLB club owners after making a series of controversial decisions.

A sports league commissioner's authority is contractual in nature and derived from the league's constitution and bylaws. The most sweeping power that a league commissioner is typically granted is the ability to take action deemed necessary to further the best interests of the sport. As illustrated by the following case, although interpretation of the nature and scope of the commissioner's contractual authority ultimately is a question for judicial resolution, courts usually provide substantial deference to the commissioner's judgment.

CHARLES O. FINLEY & CO., INC. v. KUHN

569 F.2d 527 (7th Cir.), *cert. denied*, 439 U.S. 876 (1978)

SPRECHER, Circuit Judge.

The two important questions raised by this appeal are whether the Commissioner of baseball is contractually authorized to disapprove player assignments which he finds to be "not in the best interests of baseball" where neither moral turpitude nor violation of a Major League Rule is involved, and whether the provision in the Major League Agreement whereby the parties agree to waive recourse to the courts is valid and enforceable.

The defendant Bowie K. Kuhn is the Commissioner of baseball (Commissioner), having held that position since 1969. On June 18, 1976, the Commissioner disapproved the assignments of the contracts of [Joe] Rudi, [Rollie] Fingers and [Vida] Blue to the Red Sox and Yankees "as inconsistent with the best interests of baseball, the integrity of the game and the maintenance of public confidence in it." The Commissioner expressed his concern for (1) the debilitation of the Oakland club, (2) the lessening of the competitive balance of professional baseball through the buying of success by the more affluent clubs, and (3) "the present unsettled circumstances of baseball's reserve system." . . .

II

Basic to the underlying suit brought by Oakland and to this appeal is whether the Commissioner of baseball is vested by contract with the authority to disapprove player assignments which he finds to be "not in the best interests of baseball." In assessing the measure and extent of the Commissioner's power and authority, consideration must be given to the circumstances attending the creation of the office of Commissioner, the language employed by the parties in drafting their contractual understanding, changes and amendments adopted from time to time, and the interpretation given by the parties to their contractual language throughout the period of its existence. . . .

In November, 1920, the major league club owners unanimously elected federal Judge Kenesaw Mountain Landis as the sole Commissioner of baseball and appointed a committee of owners to draft a charter setting forth the Commissioner's authority. In one of the drafting sessions an attempt was made to place limitations on the Commissioner's authority. Judge Landis responded by refusing to accept the office of Commissioner.

On January 12, 1921, Landis told a meeting of club owners that he had agreed to accept the position upon the clear understanding that the owners had sought "an authority . . . outside of your own business, and that a part of that authority would be a control over whatever and whoever had to do with baseball." Thereupon, the owners voted unanimously to reject the proposed limitation upon the Commissioner's authority, they all signed what they called the Major League Agreement, and Judge Landis assumed the position of Commissioner. Oakland has been a signatory to the Major League Agreement continuously since 1960. The agreement, a contract between the constituent clubs of the National and American Leagues, is the basic charter under which major league baseball operates.

The Major League Agreement provides that "[t]he functions of the Commissioner shall be . . . to investigate . . . any act, transaction or practice . . . not in the best interests of the national game of Baseball" and "to determine . . . what preventive, remedial or punitive action is appropriate in the premises, and to take such action. . . ." Art. I, Sec. 2(a) and (b).

The Major League Rules, which govern many aspects of the game of baseball, are promulgated by vote of major league club owners. Major League Rule 12(a) provides that "no . . . (assignment of players) shall be recognized as valid unless . . . approved by the Commissioner."

The Major Leagues and their constituent clubs severally agreed to be bound by the decisions of the Commissioner and by the discipline imposed by him. They further agreed to "waive such right of recourse to the courts as would otherwise have existed in their favor." Major League Agreement, Art. VII, Sec. 2.

Upon Judge Landis' death in 1944, the Major League Agreement was amended in two respects to limit the Commissioner's authority. First, the parties deleted the provision by which they had agreed to waive their right of recourse to the courts to challenge actions of the Commissioner. Second, the parties added the following language to Article I, Section 3:

> No Major League Rule or other joint action of the two Major Leagues, and no action or procedure taken in compliance with any such Major League Rule or joint action of the two Major Leagues shall be considered or construed to be detrimental to Baseball.

The district court found that this addition had the effect of precluding the Commissioner from finding an act that complied with the Major League Rules to be detrimental to the best interests of baseball.

The two 1944 amendments to the Major League Agreement remained in effect during the terms of the next two Commissioners, A. B. "Happy" Chandler and Ford Frick. Upon Frick's retirement in 1964 and in accordance with his recommendation, the parties adopted three amendments to the Major League Agreement: (1) the language added in 1944 preventing the Commissioner from finding any act or practice "taken in compliance" with a Major League Rule to be "detrimental to baseball" was removed; (2) the provision deleted in 1944 waiving any rights of recourse to the courts to challenge a Commissioner's decision was restored; and (3) in places where the language "detrimental to the best interests of the national game of baseball" or "detrimental to baseball" appeared those words were changed to "not in the best interests of the national game of Baseball" or "not in the best interests of Baseball."

The nature of the power lodged in the Commissioner by the Major League Agreement is further exemplified "(i)n the case of conduct by organizations not parties to this Agreement, or by individuals not connected with any of the parties hereto, which is deemed by the Commissioner not to be in the best interests of Baseball" whereupon "the Commissioner may pursue appropriate legal remedies, advocate remedial legislation and take such other steps as he may deem necessary and proper in the interests of the morale of the players and the honor of the game." Art. I, Sec. 4.

The Commissioner has been given broad power in unambiguous language to investigate any act, transaction or practice not in the best interests of baseball, to determine what preventive, remedial or punitive action is appropriate in the premises, and to take that action. He has also been given the express power to approve or disapprove the assignments of players. In regard to nonparties to the agreement, he may take such other steps as he deems necessary and proper in the interests of the morale of the players and the honor of the game. Further, indicative of the nature of the Commissioner's authority is the provision whereby the parties agree to be bound by his decisions and discipline imposed and to waive recourse to the courts. . . .

III

Despite the Commissioner's broad authority to prevent any act, transaction or practice not in the best interests of baseball, Oakland has attacked the Commissioner's disapproval of the Rudi-Fingers-Blue transactions on a variety of theories which seem to express a similar thrust in differing language.

The complaint alleged that the "action of Kuhn was arbitrary, capricious, unreasonable, discriminatory, directly contrary to historical precedent, baseball tradition, and prior rulings and actions of the Commissioner." In pre-trial answers to interrogatories, Oakland acknowledged that the Commissioner could set aside a proposed assignment of a player's contract "in an appropriate case of violation of (Major League) Rules or immoral or unethical conduct." . . .

The plaintiff has argued that it is a fundamental rule of law that the decisions of the head of a private association must be procedurally fair. Plaintiff then argued that it was "procedurally unfair" for the Commissioner to fail to warn the plaintiff that he would "disapprove large cash assignments of star players even if they complied with the Major League Rules."

In the first place it must be recalled that prior to the assignments involved here drastic changes had commenced to occur in the reserve system and in the creation of free agents. In his opinion disapproving the Rudi, Fingers and Blue assignments, the Commissioner said that "while I am of course aware that there have been cash sales of player contracts in the past, there has been no instance in my judgment which had the potential for harm to our game as do these assignments, particularly in the present unsettled circumstances of baseball's reserve system and in the highly competitive circumstances we find in today's sports and entertainment world."

Absent the radical changes in the reserve system, the Commissioner's action would have postponed Oakland's realization of value for these players. Given those changes, the relative fortunes of all major league clubs became subject to a host of intangible speculations. No one could predict then or now with certainty that Oakland would fare better or worse relative to other clubs through the vagaries of the revised reserve system occurring entirely apart from any action by the Commissioner.

In the second place, baseball cannot be analogized to any other business or even to any other sport or entertainment. Baseball's relation to the federal antitrust laws has been characterized by the Supreme Court as an "exception," an "anomaly" and an "aberration." Baseball's management through a commissioner is equally an exception, anomaly and aberration, as outlined in Part II hereof. In no other sport or business is there quite the same system, created for quite the same reasons and with quite the same underlying policies. Standards such as the best interests of baseball, the interests of the morale of the players and the honor of the game, or "sportsmanship which accepts the umpire's decision without complaint," are not necessarily familiar to courts and obviously require some expertise in their application. While it is true that professional baseball selected as its first Commissioner a federal judge, it intended only him and not the judiciary as a whole to be its umpire and governor.

. . . [T]he Commissioner was vested with broad authority and that authority was not to be limited in its exercise to situations where Major League Rules or moral turpitude was involved. When professional baseball intended to place limitations upon the Commissioner's powers, it knew how to do so. In fact, it did so during the 20-year period from 1944 to 1964.

The district court found and concluded that the Rudi-Fingers-Blue transactions were not, as Oakland had alleged in its complaint, "directly contrary to historical precedent, baseball tradition, and prior rulings." During his almost 25 years as Commissioner, Judge Landis found many acts, transactions and practices to be detrimental to the best interests of baseball in situations where neither moral turpitude nor a Major League Rule violation was involved, and he disapproved several player assignments.

On numerous occasions since he became Commissioner of baseball in February 1969, Kuhn has exercised broad authority under the best interests clause of the Major League Agreement. Many of the actions taken by him have been in response to acts, transactions or practices that involved neither the violation of a Major League Rule nor any gambling, game-throwing or other conduct associated with moral turpitude. Moreover, on several occasions Commissioner Kuhn has taken broad preventive or remedial action with respect to assignments of player contracts. . . .

We conclude that the evidence fully supports, and we agree with, the district court's finding that "(t)he history of the adoption of the Major League Agreement in 1921 and the operation of baseball for more than 50 years under it, including: the circumstances preceding and precipitating the adoption of the Agreement; the numerous exercises of broad authority under the best interests clause by Judge Landis and . . . Commissioner Kuhn; the amendments to the Agreement in 1964 restoring and broadening the authority of the Commissioner; . . . and most important the express language of the Agreement itself are all to the effect that the Commissioner has the authority to determine whether any act, transaction or practice is 'not in the best interests of baseball,' and upon such determination, to take whatever preventive or remedial action he deems appropriate, whether or not the act, transaction or practice complies with the Major League Rules or involves moral turpitude." Any other conclusion would involve the courts in not only interpreting often complex rules of baseball to determine if they were violated but also, as noted in the Landis case, the "intent of the (baseball) code," an even more complicated and subjective task.

We conclude that the evidence fully supports, and we agree with, the district court's finding and conclusion that the Commissioner "acted in good faith, after investigation, consultation and deliberation, in a manner which he determined to be in the best interests of baseball" and that "(w)hether he was right or wrong is beyond the competence and the jurisdiction of this court to decide." . . .

V

Following the bench trial, the district court reached its decision in favor of the Commissioner without considering the impact of Article VII, Section 2 of the Major League Agreement, wherein the major league baseball clubs agreed to be bound by the Commissioner's decisions and discipline and to waive recourse to the courts. . . .

Even in the absence of a waiver of recourse provision in an association charter, "[i]t is generally held that courts . . . will not intervene in questions involving the enforcement of bylaws and matters of discipline in voluntary associations." . . .

. . . This clause can be upheld as coinciding with the common law standard disallowing court interference. We view its inclusion in the Major League Agreement merely as a manifestation of the intent of the contracting parties to insulate from review decisions made by the Commissioner concerning the subject matter of actions taken in accordance with his grant of powers. . . .

Even if the waiver of recourse clause is divorced from its setting in the charter of a private, voluntary association . . . we think that it is valid under the circumstances here involved. Oakland claims that such clauses are invalid as against public policy. This is true, however, only under circumstances where the waiver of rights is not voluntary, knowing or intelligent, or was not freely negotiated by parties occupying equal bargaining positions. The trend of cases in many states and in the federal courts supports the conclusion of the district court under the circumstances presented here that "informed parties, freely contracting, may waive their recourse to the court." . . .

Although the waiver of recourse clause is generally valid . . . we do not believe that it forecloses access to the courts under all circumstances. Thus, the general rule of nonreviewability which governs the actions of private associations is subject to exceptions (1) where the rules, regulations or judgments of the association are in contravention to the laws of the land or in disregard of the charter or bylaws of the association and (2) where the association has failed to follow the basic rudiments of due process of law. . . . We therefore hold that, absent the applicability of one of these narrow exceptions, the waiver of recourse clause contained in the Major League Agreement is valid and binding on the parties and the courts.

We affirm the district court's judgments. . . .

NOTES AND QUESTIONS

1. In the wake of the Messersmith-McNally arbitration, discussed in Chapter 7, MLB clubs in 1976 entered a new era in which the free agency of players became a reality. How clubs would deal with this was uncertain. In anticipation of potential problems, Commissioner Bowie Kuhn issued warnings to

clubs that violations of rules to prevent tampering with another club's players would be punished by various sanctions. In particular, a club was prohibited from having direct or indirect dealings with a potential free agent prior to the end of the season.

The general manager of the Atlanta Braves, John Alevizos, and later the owner, Ted Turner, were charged with improper contacts and public remarks concerning Gary Matthews, who at the time played for the San Francisco Giants. In the first instance, after a hearing, Commissioner Kuhn held that Alevizos had violated the anti-tampering rules on two occasions and fined the Braves club $5,000 for each violation. In addition, the club lost its first-round selection in the next amateur player draft. This disciplinary action was accepted by the Braves. Subsequently, at a cocktail party, owner Ted Turner informed the Giants co-owner, Robert Lurie, that the Braves would do anything necessary to sign Matthews after the season officially ended. These comments were overheard by several witnesses and reported in San Francisco newspapers. Lurie and the Giants filed a complaint with the commissioner. After a second hearing, the commissioner ruled that Turner's statements violated the anti-tampering rules by contravening the new collective bargaining agreement's re-entry draft procedures.

The commissioner declined to nullify Matthews's new contract with the Braves because Matthews had not engaged in any misconduct. The punishment levied was to suspend Turner from baseball for one year and to order a forfeiture of the Braves' first-round selection in the amateur draft, which was to follow the one in which Atlanta had already forfeited its first-round choice.

The Braves and Turner brought suit to overturn these rulings. See *Atlanta National League Baseball Club v. Kuhn*, 432 F. Supp. 1213 (N.D. Ga. 1977). The questions before the court revolved around the explicit powers accorded the commissioner in these situations. The commissioner argued that he had broad powers to act in the best interest of baseball and impose appropriate discipline at his sole discretion, whereas the Braves asserted he was given explicit powers to deal with the current situation and could act only as specifically authorized. The court concluded that the commissioner had proper discretionary authority to suspend Turner for one year, but not to strip the Braves club of a draft choice because this sanction "is simply not among the penalties authorized for this offense."

2. Both *Finley* and *Atlanta National League Baseball Club* upheld the MLB commissioner's exercise of his "best interests" of the game authority. Read together, what judicial precedent is established by these two cases? Do these decisions collectively establish and further sound public policy regarding the scope of judicial review of league commissioner decisions? Should courts provide similar deference to a league commissioner's decisions that adversely affect third parties, such as the communities in which league franchises are located, or fans in general?

3. Although a court will not second-guess a league commissioner's exercise of discretionary judgment, as *Atlanta National League Baseball Club* illustrates, it will require that the commissioner have valid authority to take any challenged action.

In an unpublished opinion, a federal district court held that the MLB commissioner could not order involuntary realignment of the teams in the National League pursuant to his "best interests" of the game authority. In *Chicago National League Ball Club, Inc. v. Vincent*, 1992 WL 179208 (N.D. Ill.

1992), the Chicago Cubs successfully challenged Commissioner Vincent's authority to transfer the club to the Western Division of the National League. In 1992, ten National League clubs voted to realign their two divisions so that the Cubs and St. Louis Cardinals would move to the Western Division, and the Atlanta Braves and Cincinnati Reds would move to the Eastern Division. The Cubs and New York Mets voted against the proposed realignment. The National League Constitution required approval by three-fourths of the league's clubs for divisional realignment but provided that no club could be transferred to a different division without its consent. Nevertheless, acting on the request of several National League clubs to intervene, Commissioner Vincent ordered the proposed realignment in accordance with his "best interests" power.

The court preliminarily enjoined the commissioner's order from taking effect based on its finding that he exceeded his authority and impaired the Cubs' contract rights under the National League Constitution. Although the Major League Agreement empowered the commissioner to resolve disputes among member clubs and conferred broad "best interests" power, this authority did not extend to disputes whose resolution is otherwise expressly provided for in the constitution of either Major League. Relying on the statutory construction principle that the specific governs the general, the court held that the commissioner could not use his general "best interests" authority to unilaterally abrogate the Cubs' express right under the National League Constitution not to be moved to another division without its consent.

4.   When exercising disciplinary authority, courts require that a league commissioner provide due process to the party subject to sanctions pursuant to the exercise of his "best interests" power. *Finley*, 569 F.2d at 544 and n.65 ("the procedure must not be a sham designed merely to give colorable propriety to an inadequate process"). A party is entitled to notice of the alleged misconduct and a fair opportunity to be heard. *Professional Sports, Ltd. v. Va. Squires Basketball Club Ltd. Partnership*, 373 F. Supp. 946, 951 (W.D. Tex. 1974); *American League Baseball Club of New York v. Johnson*, 179 N.Y. Supp. 498, 506 (N.Y. Sup. Ct. 1919), *aff'd*, 179 N.Y.S. 898 (1920). The league's constitution generally establishes procedural safeguards or enables the commissioner to formulate rules necessary to satisfy the minimum requirements of due process in connection with a disciplinary proceeding. *Rose v. Giamatti*, 721 F. Supp. 906, 916 (S.D. Ohio 1989) (observing that under Major League Agreement, "Commissioner is given virtually unlimited authority to formulate his own rules of procedure for conducting ['not in the best interests' of baseball] investigations, the only limitations being that whatever rules he adopts must recognize the right of any party in interest to appear before him and be heard").

A league commissioner must act in an impartial and fair manner without prejudging a disciplinary matter. In *Rose v. Giamatti*, No. A8905178, 1989 WL 111447 (Ct. Com. Pl. Ohio, Hamilton Co. June 26, 1989), a state trial judge temporarily enjoined MLB commissioner Bart Giamatti from holding a disciplinary hearing to determine whether Pete Rose, the manager of the Cincinnati Reds, placed bets on MLB games. The court relied on affidavit testimony alleging that Rose was being denied his right to a fair hearing before the commissioner. After reviewing a report prepared by his special investigator and upon which he intended to rely, the commissioner wrote a letter to a federal judge regarding Ron Peters, a convicted drug dealer who was awaiting sentencing. The letter stated that Peters had provided sworn testimony concerning allegations that Rose had bet on MLB games, and that the commissioner was satisfied that Peters had told the truth to his special investigator. Commissioner Giamatti and Rose ultimately entered into a settlement agreement pursuant to which Rose accepted a lifetime suspension from baseball. See generally Matthew B. Pachman, Note, *Limits on the Discretionary Powers of Professional Sports Commissioners: A Historical and Legal Analysis of Issues Raised by the Pete Rose Controversy,* 76 Va. L. Rev. 1409 (1990).

5. *Commissioner's Exercise of "Best Interests" Authority Creates a Conflict of Interest.* In 2010, the NBA purchased the floundering New Orleans Hornets, giving Commissioner David Stern supervisory authority over a league club. A year later, Hornets general manager Dell Demps engineered a three-way trade with the Houston Rockets and Los Angeles Lakers, which involved sending the Hornets' All-Star point guard Chris Paul to the Lakers. Before the trade was finalized, however, Stern vetoed it, raising questions as to whether he was doing so in the best interests of the Hornets, in the best interests of the NBA, or for other reasons. Stern publicly justified his decision as being in the "best interests" of the Hornets. Many in the NBA community, however, viewed the proposed trade (which reportedly would have given the Hornets several players and a 2012 first round draft pick) as advantageous to the Hornets and believed that, in reality, Stern was pressured to quash the deal by a group of owners of other teams who were leery that it would too greatly benefit the Lakers. Demps was angered by Stern's decision and considered quitting, and Paul — before later being dealt to the Los Angeles Clippers — contemplated suit under an anti-collusion clause in the NBA Collective Bargaining Agreement that prevents the league from conspiring with teams regarding player transactions. See Sam Amick, *Lakers, Hornets, Rockets, Resubmit Paul Trade for League Approval,* Sports Illustrated, Dec. 10, 2011, http://sports illustrated.cnn.com/2011/writers/sam_amick/12/10/chris.paul/index.html; Mitch Lawrence, *Paul Eyes Court Assist,* N.Y. Daily News, Dec. 13, 2011, at 68.

Stern's refusal to permit the trade raises a host of questions. Is it possible to act both in the "best interests" of a particular team and in the "best interests" of a league in this situation? If not, in the event that a league owns a team in the league, should the league appoint an independent party to have ultimate supervisory authority over that team? Assuming that other NBA team owners influenced Stern's decision, can it nevertheless be justified by his "best interests" authority? Does your answer depend on whether the owners opposed to his decision constitute a minority or a majority of the league's owners?

OAKLAND RAIDERS v. NATIONAL FOOTBALL LEAGUE

131 Cal. App. 4th 621, 32 Cal. Rptr. 3d 266 (Cal. App. 2005)

PREMO, J.

The Oakland Raiders (Raiders), a member club of an unincorporated association known as the National Football League (NFL or League), sued the NFL and its commissioner, Paul Tagliabue. The Raiders alleged that the NFL and Tagliabue (collectively, defendants) took various actions that were discriminatory towards the Raiders and placed it at a competitive disadvantage vis-à-vis other member clubs. One legal theory that the Raiders advanced was breach of fiduciary duty. . . .

Broadly speaking, the complaint alleged that the Raiders was discriminated against and treated unfavorably as compared with the other member clubs. The alleged breaches of fiduciary duty included: "singling the Raiders out" from other clubs and "treating the Raiders disparately and adversely"; permitting other member clubs to violate NFL rules, thereby giving them a competitive advantage over the Raiders; requiring that the Raiders (over its objection) participate with other member clubs in the European football league known as the "World League of American Football"; concealing information from the Raiders and excluding its participation in a lawsuit involving the former owner of the New England Patriots, William H. Sullivan, Jr.; and denying Al Davis (former Raiders' managing general partner) and his family permission to buy the Oakland Athletics baseball team, notwithstanding that defendants permitted violations of the League's "Cross-ownership Rule" by other club owners. In addition, the Raiders alleged that Tagliabue committed further breaches of fiduciary duty: by removing Davis from the Management Council Executive Committee in September 1995; by removing Raiders' representatives from NFL committees, and by excluding the Raiders from participating in significant NFL committees, thereby placing the Raiders at a competitive disadvantage; and by concealing from the Raiders certain rules violations by other member clubs. . . .

[Granting defendants' motion for summary judgment, the trial court held] that (1) defendants owed no fiduciary duties to the Raiders, and (2) even were the breach of fiduciary duty claim legally viable, the court was required to abstain from deciding it. . . .

III.   WHETHER DEFENDANTS OWED FIDUCIARY DUTIES TO THE RAIDERS

We first examine whether there was a fiduciary relationship between defendants and the Raiders as a matter of law. . . .

As the Ninth Circuit Court of Appeals has previously recognized, "[t]he NFL is [a] unique business organization." (*Los Angeles Memorial Coliseum Com'n v. N.F.L.* (9th Cir. 1984) 726 F.2d 1381, 1401.) It is perhaps for this reason that there is no authority cited by the parties — or known by this court to exist — that is definitive on the question of whether the NFL or its commissioner owes fiduciary duties to one of the NFL's member clubs (in this case, the Raiders). . . .

The Raiders relies extensively on *Jones v. H.F. Ahmanson & Co.*, 1 Cal. 3d 93, 81 Cal. Rptr. 592, 460 P.2d 464 (Cal. 1969), in support of its assertion that defendants owed the Raiders fiduciary duties. For a number of reasons, *Jones* is inapposite. In *Jones*, the Supreme Court held definitively that majority shareholders owe fiduciary duties to the corporation and its minority shareholders "to use their ability to control the corporation in a fair, just, and equitable manner." Thus, under the circumstances presented in that case, the court concluded that "when, as here, no market [for the corporation's stock] exists, the controlling shareholders may not use their power to control the corporation for the purpose of promoting a marketing scheme that benefits themselves alone to the detriment of the minority."

Most notably, the discussion of fiduciary duties in *Jones* was premised on the existence of a *corporation, controlling shareholders, and minority shareholders*. No such organizational structure is presented in the instant appeal. To the contrary, it is without dispute that the NFL is *an unincorporated not-for-profit association* of 31 (now 32) member clubs. Indeed, we acknowledged this organizational status in a prior appeal by the Raiders. (See *Oakland Raiders, supra*, 93 Cal. App. 4th 572, 578, 113 Cal. Rptr. 2d 255.) As such, neither the NFL nor its member clubs fit the *Jones* model of fiduciary duties owed by majority shareholders to their corporation and to minority shareholders. . . .

The Raiders has cited no cases—and we are aware of none—in which it has been held as a blanket proposition that a voluntary unincorporated association and/or its leadership owes fiduciary duties to its members. A voluntary association, although it has some attributes of a legal entity, is not the equivalent of a corporation. . . .

Finally, we reject the Raiders' intimation that a fiduciary relationship exists between it and the defendants because of an alleged joint venture. A joint venture, of necessity, "requires an agreement under which the parties have (1) a joint interest in a common business, (2) an understanding that profits and losses will be shared, and (3) a right to joint control. [Citations.]" Here, there is no sharing of profits and losses by member clubs indicative of a joint venture. As one federal district court concluded, specifically with respect to the NFL: "Strictly speaking, the NFL teams are not engaged in a joint venture. 'A joint venture is a joint business undertaking of two or more parties who share the risks as well as the profits of the business.' [Citation.] Though the NFL teams share revenues, they do not share profits or losses." (*Los Angeles Memorial Coliseum v. N.F.L.* (S.D. Cal. 1979) 468 F. Supp. 154, 162, fn. 9; see also *Los Angeles Memorial Coliseum Com'n v. N.F.L., supra*, 726 F.2d 1381, 1390 [NFL clubs do not share "profits and losses . . . a feature common to partnerships"].) There is thus no merit to the Raiders' claim for breach of fiduciary duty arising out of a joint venture.

We conclude therefore that the relationship between the Raiders, on the one hand, and the NFL and Tagliabue, on the other hand, is not one under which a fiduciary relationship exists as a matter of law. . . .

IV. APPLICABILITY OF ABSTENTION DOCTRINE . . .

The Raiders contends that the trial court also erred by concluding that it was required to abstain from this intra-association dispute . . .

. . . [T]he abstention doctrine . . . applies broadly to intra-association disputes, irrespective of whether the particular dispute concerns a claimed breach of association bylaws.

This conclusion is consistent with other cases . . . (See *Berke v. TRI Realtors* (1989) 208 Cal. App. 3d 463, 469, 257 Cal. Rptr. 738 [abstention doctrine means that "[c]ourts must guard against unduly interfering with an organization's autonomy by substituting judicial judgment" for the organization's]; *California Trial Lawyers Assn. v. Superior Court* (1986) 187 Cal.App. 3d 575, 580, 231 Cal. Rptr. 725 (*California Trial Lawyers*).) In *California Trial Lawyers*, the court found that the . . . "policy of judicial restraint control[led]" to preclude judicial intervention in interpreting the bylaws of a voluntary association of attorneys that impacted the election of the association's president. In so holding, the court explained that "[t]his reluctance to intervene in internecine controversies, the resolution of which requires that an association's constitution, bylaws, or rules be construed, is premised on the principle that the judiciary should generally accede to any interpretation by an independent voluntary organization of its own rules which is not unreasonable or arbitrary."

In this instance, the trial court properly held that it was barred by the abstention doctrine from resolving the dispute between the Raiders and defendants. Ignoring for the moment that the Raiders' breach of fiduciary duty claim is not viable as a matter of law, the underlying basis for the claim is not one for an asserted breach of the NFL constitution. The court correctly concluded—after a discussion in its order of each alleged act that the Raiders claimed constituted breaches of fiduciary duty—that the Raiders had not shown any evidence of a violation of a clear and unambiguous provision of the NFL constitution. . . .

In short, the court correctly construed and applied the abstention doctrine . . . We observe that the rationale of abstention from intra-association disputes applies with particular force in this instance. Given the unique and specialized nature of this association's business—the operation of a professional football league—there is significant danger that judicial intervention in such disputes will have the undesired and unintended effect of interfering with the League's autonomy in matters where the NFL and its commissioner have much greater competence and understanding than the courts. . . .

[The court affirmed the granting of summary judgment for defendants.]

NOTES AND QUESTIONS

1. *Analysis of* Oakland Raiders. If the court had ruled that the NFL commissioner owed the Raiders club a fiduciary duty, what would this mean? Would it facilitate or inhibit effective league governance? Is the court's ruling that the California state law abstention doctrine applies consistent with *Finley*'s view of when judicial intervention in league internal governance is appropriate?

2. *Legal Duties of League Clubs in Exercising Governing Authority.* Courts have imposed an implied covenant of good faith and fair dealing in contracts governing the internal affairs of professional sports leagues. For example, in a case arising out of the Oakland Raiders' proposed relocation to Los Angeles in the early 1980s, the Ninth Circuit applied California law and ruled that league teams owed each other a reciprocal duty "to refrain from doing anything to injure the right of the other to receive the benefits of the agreement . . . [and] the duty to do everything that the contract presupposes that he will do to accomplish the purpose." *Los Angeles Memorial Coliseum Commission v. National Football League (Raiders II)*, 791 F.2d 1356, 1361 (9th Cir. 1986). Concerning franchise relocation, the court held that each league club must exercise its contractual discretionary right of approval or disapproval in good faith (i.e., reasonably). Is this duty satisfied if a club votes in a manner consistent with the league's best interests? Is it breached if a club votes solely in furtherance of its own economic interests?

Depending on how a sports league is legally structured, its member clubs may have a fiduciary duty to act and vote on matters of internal governance consistent with the league's best interests, which imposes a more stringent obligation than the implied covenant of good faith and fair dealing. In *Professional Hockey Corp. v. World Hockey Assn.*, 191 Cal. Rptr. 773, 777 (Cal. Ct. App. 1983), the court ruled that each club's representative on the board of directors of a professional sports league structured as a corporation "owes the league as a whole the traditional fiduciary duties in this commonly shared corporate purpose." It explained: "The law requires, irrespective of the competitive personal feelings the various owners of teams may have towards each other, when they or their representatives sit on the board of directors of [the league] to the extent they have common corporate goals, they have a duty to make decisions for the benefit of the corporation, the hockey league as a whole." In dicta, *Oakland Raiders* suggests that the member clubs of a league structured as an unincorporated association (e.g., the NFL) rather than a corporation do not owe a fiduciary duty to the league because they do not share profits and losses like a partnership. If not, each club has no legal duty to place the league's interests ahead of its individual interests when making internal governance decisions, which would be constrained by its contractual obligations and the implied covenant of good faith and fair dealing's reasonableness requirement. See generally Nadelle Grossman, *What is the NBA?*, 25 Marq. Sports L. Rev. 101, 104 (2014) ("[I]t is essential to determine what the NBA's structure is for purposes of state organization law because of the consequences that might flow from that structure. . . . Importantly, the cooperative nature of NBA team-owners' profit-seeking and the absence of any other explicit organizational form suggest that the NBA is a partnership. As a partnership, team-owners would owe the NBA and the other members fiduciary duties.").

PROBLEM 6-1

Soon after an audio recording became public in which Los Angeles Clippers owner Donald Sterling made racist comments indicating that he did not welcome African Americans at Clippers games, NBA Commissioner Adam Silver fined him $2.5 million and indefinitely banned him from having any involvement in the management or operation of the club. Sterling's comments promptly attracted substantial outrage: Clippers team members protested by tossing their warm-up jackets on the floor at midcourt and wearing their team jerseys inside out before a game, several companies terminated their sponsorship agreements with the Clippers, and a number of NBA players publicly condemned his remarks and suggested the possibility of boycotting Clippers games. Consider whether this disciplinary action against Sterling was a valid exercise of Commissioner Silver's "best interests" authority, and whether a court would uphold it if challenged by Sterling. Assuming that the other 29 NBA club owners had voted unanimously to require Sterling to sell the Clippers, would their decision be legally valid and enforceable?

PROBLEM 6-2

Assume that the NFL constitution requires an affirmative vote of 75% of the 32 NFL clubs (at least 24 votes) for a team to relocate outside of its "home territory" (the area within a 75-mile radius of its current stadium). Twenty-eight NFL clubs vote in favor of allowing the St. Louis Rams to relocate to Los Angeles, but only 23 NFL clubs (including the Chargers) vote to approve the San Diego Chargers' request to move to LA, which would require the club to share a new stadium with the Rams. The Rams owner not only votes against permitting the

Chargers to move to LA, but he also aggressively lobbies and convinces eight other club owners to cast negative votes. Evaluate the likely success of the Chargers' claim that the Rams owner's vote and lobbying against the Chargers' move to LA breached the Rams club's fiduciary duty and covenant of good faith and fair dealing.

D.   ANTITRUST LAW LIMITS ON LEAGUE GOVERNANCE AND RULES

Federal antitrust law is one of the primary bodies of public law used to regulate professional sports outside the context of labor relations. In the following materials we consider the objectives of antitrust law and the unique economic aspects of professional sports vis-à-vis other for-profit industries; MLB's common law antitrust immunity and other sports-specific antitrust exemptions; and the judicial application of antitrust law to professional sports league rules, internal governance, and business decisions that affect member clubs, consumers, and others.

1.   Nature and Purposes of Antitrust Law

The federal antitrust laws prohibit agreements and collective action that unreasonably restrain trade under §1 of the Sherman Act (15 U.S.C. §1) as well as monopolization and attempted monopolization under §2 (15 U.S.C. §2). The purpose of the antitrust laws is to preserve a competitive marketplace and protect consumer welfare. Competition is hurt when conduct harms the market's ability to achieve lower prices, better products, and more efficient methods of production—all of which benefit consumers. *Sullivan v. NFL*, 34 F.3d 1091, 1097 (1st Cir. 1994), *cert. denied*, 513 U.S. 1190 (1995).

Professional sports leagues and organizations are commercial enterprises that compete against other available entertainment options for consumer interest and economic support. Because of the unique nature of professional sports (particularly team sports), it is very difficult for courts and juries to apply antitrust law in a principled and consistent fashion to challenged league or association rules and collective decisions. Traditional antitrust law jurisprudence does not provide a simple means of accurately measuring whether a particular practice enhances or harms consumer welfare (i.e., sports fans).

Like any other business enterprise, the member clubs of a professional sports league collectively seek to maximize their profits. However, unlike members of other industries that sell the same product and compete among themselves for consumer support (for example, McDonald's, Wendy's, and Burger King franchised fast food systems), a professional sports league's member clubs do not have an economic self-interest in driving each other out of business. To the contrary, league clubs have an inherent economic interdependence. As one court explained:

> Professional teams in a league . . . must not compete too well with each other, in a business way. On the playing field, of course, they must compete as hard as they can all the time. But it is not necessary and indeed it is unwise for all the teams

to compete as hard as they can against each other in a business way. . . . [If this happened,] not only would the weaker teams fail, but eventually the whole league, both the weaker and the stronger teams, would fail, because without a league no team can operate profitably.

United States v. NFL, 116 F. Supp. 319, 323 (E.D. Pa. 1953).

To further league clubs' collective economic interests, it is essential that on-field competitive balance among teams exists within the league and that the outcome of games be relatively uncertain to maintain fan interest in the league's product:

> For maximum customer receptivity and profit it is in the best interest of any club that its opponents not generally be viewed by the public as totally incompetent and utterly unable to compete effectively. For if the latter occurs, thousands of customers will not spend their dollars for tickets to view hundreds of games when the contest seems to present no more of a challenge than an ant confronting an elephant.

Philadelphia World Hockey Club, Inc. v. Philadelphia Hockey Club, Inc., 351 F. Supp. 462, 504 (E.D. Pa. 1972).

League clubs do not share profits like the members of a typical business joint venture or partnership, and they do not subsidize an individual team's economic losses. However, to maintain the financial integrity of all member clubs, to protect economically weaker teams from stronger ones, and to further all clubs' collective interest in producing competitive games, professional sports leagues share certain revenues (e.g., broadcasting, trademark licensing, sponsorship rights, etc.) as well as limit the permissible degree of economic competition among their teams. Substantial economic disparities may have the undesirable effect of adversely impacting competition among league clubs on the playing field.

As one court observed:

> Teams with impressive records tend to show bigger revenues than teams in the cellar. On the very most basic level, going to the playoffs means more games, and therefore more gate receipts, and more fan following and therefore higher rights fees from local broadcasting (which belong 100% to the teams) — in other words, more money. . . .
>
>   In addition, and to complete the circle, more money means a better chance at making the playoffs again. The richest teams enjoy competitive advantages on the court over the poorest teams — in the ability to bid for free agents or to pay to keep their own players who opt for free agency, and so field a strong team; in the ability to charter flights for away games, and so field an alert team; in the ability to hire top notch staffs, and so field a well-coached team, and more.

Chicago Prof. Sports Ltd. Partnership v. NBA, 754 F. Supp. 1336, 1341-1342 (N.D. Ill. 1991).

Ironically, league limits on off-field economic competition among clubs may be necessary to preserve and enhance the on-field competition between clubs that is attractive to the sport's fans. On the other hand, in North America, historically and currently there has been only one financially viable major professional league for football, men's and women's basketball, hockey, soccer, and baseball (with the American League and National League effectively operating as a single baseball league under the auspices of Major League Baseball). As is discussed later in this chapter, a sports league may have either monopoly power or a significant degree of market power that may enable it and/or its member clubs to engage in conduct with predominantly anticompetitive effects that harm existing or prospective clubs and their owners, local communities, other sports leagues and franchises, and ultimately, sports fans.

2.   *MLB's Antitrust Law Immunity and Other Exemptions*

In 1890, Congress enacted the Sherman Act pursuant to its authority to regulate interstate commerce. To be subject to scrutiny under the federal antitrust laws, a defendant's business activities or its allegedly anticompetitive conduct must have the requisite nexus to interstate trade or commerce. *Summit Health, Ltd. v. Pinhas*, 500 U.S. 322 (1991).

In 1922, the Supreme Court decided its first antitrust case involving professional sports, deciding specifically the issue of whether organized professional baseball is subject to the Sherman Act. Pursuant to a December 1915 "peace agreement" with the American League and National League (which had been in operation since 1876 and 1901, respectively), the recently formed Federal League was dissolved. However, the Baltimore club refused to be part of this settlement and brought an antitrust lawsuit with broad allegations that the American League and National League had conspired to monopolize professional baseball in violation of the Sherman Act. It alleged that the two leagues had induced some Federal League club owners to "betray and desert the other clubs" by entering into the settlement in order "to wreck entirely the Federal League"; and by collectively enforcing the "reserve clause" (providing their respective league clubs with perpetual rights to a player even after his contract expired, which prevented the Federal League from competing for those players).

In *Federal Baseball Club of Baltimore, Inc. v. National League of Professional Baseball Clubs*, 259 U.S. 200 208-09 (1922), the Supreme Court ruled that professional baseball is a business (i.e., it constitutes "trade or commerce") but that it is not interstate commerce as required to be regulated by the Sherman Act:

> The business is giving exhibitions of baseball, which are purely state affairs. It is true that, in order to attain for these exhibitions the great popularity that they have achieved, competitions must be arranged between clubs from different cities and States. But the fact that in order to give the exhibitions the Leagues must induce free persons to cross state lines and must arrange and pay for their doing so is not enough to change the character of the business. According to the distinction insisted upon in *Hooper v. California*, 155 U.S. 648, 655 . . . the transport is a mere incident, not the essential thing. That to which it is incident, the exhibition, although made for money would not be called trade or commerce in the commonly accepted use of those words. As it is put by the defendants, personal effort, not related to production, is not a subject of commerce. That which in its consummation is not commerce does not become commerce among the States because the transportation . . . takes place. To repeat the illustrations given by the Court below, a firm of lawyers sending out a member to argue a case . . . does not engage in such commerce because the lawyer . . . goes to another State.

In a 1953 case, *Toolson v. New York Yankees*, 346 U.S. 356 (1953), the Supreme Court reaffirmed *Federal Baseball Club*. In a per curiam opinion, the Court reasoned that baseball had been allowed to develop for more than 30 years without being subject to the antitrust laws. The Court also observed that Congress did not eliminate baseball's antitrust exemption, thereby evidencing its intention that organized baseball not be covered by the antitrust laws. In dissent, Justices Burton and Reed vigorously argued that professional baseball is interstate in nature and that Congress has not expressly exempted baseball from the Sherman Act.

On the other hand, after *Toolson*, the Supreme Court held that other professional sports such as football (*Radovich v. National Football League*, 352 U.S. 445 (1957)); basketball (*Haywood v. NBA*, 401 U.S. 1204 (1971)); and boxing (*United States v. International Boxing Club of N.Y., Inc.*, 348 U.S. 236 (1955)) are subject to antitrust law because their respective business activities occur in interstate commerce. Regarding baseball, lower court decisions continued to follow *Toolson* and held that professional baseball retained its immunity from federal antitrust law. See, e.g., *Salerno v. American League of Prof'l Baseball Clubs*, 429 F.2d 1003 (2d Cir. 1970); *Portland Baseball Club, Inc. v. Baltimore Baseball Club, Inc.*, 282 F.2d 680 (9th Cir. 1960).

This background set the stage for the Supreme Court's 1972 reconsideration of whether professional baseball is subject to federal antitrust law.

FLOOD v. KUHN
407 U.S. 258 (1972)

Mr. Justice BLACKMUN delivered the opinion of the Court.

For the third time in 50 years the Court is asked specifically to rule that professional baseball's reserve system is within the reach of the federal antitrust laws. . . .

[EDS. Curt Flood rose to fame as a center fielder with the Cardinals during the years 1958-1969 and distinguished himself as a star player. But at the age of 31, in October 1969, Flood was traded to the Philadelphia Phillies of the National League in a multiplayer transaction. He was not consulted about the trade. He was informed by telephone and received formal notice only after the deal had been consummated. That December he complained to the commissioner of baseball and asked that he be made a free agent and be placed at liberty to strike his own bargain with any other major league team. His request was denied. Thereafter, he filed an antitrust challenge to baseball's reserve system, which effectively precluded him from contracting with the major league baseball club of his choice. Flood declined to play for Philadelphia in 1970, despite a $100,000 salary offer, and he sat out the year. After the season was concluded, Philadelphia sold its rights to Flood to the Washington Senators. Washington and the petitioner were able to come to terms for 1971 at a salary of $110,000. Flood started the season, but apparently because he was dissatisfied with his performance, he left the Washington club on April 27. At the time of his suit, he had not played baseball since then. Relying on *Federal Baseball Club* and *Toolson*, the Second Circuit affirmed the district court's dismissal of Flood's suit.]

. . . It seems appropriate now to say that:

1. Professional baseball is a business and it is engaged in interstate commerce.
2. With its reserve system enjoying exemption from the federal antitrust laws, baseball is, in a very distinct sense, an exception and an anomaly. *Federal Baseball* and *Toolson* have become an aberration confined to baseball.

Baseball is in interstate commerce but still exempt — stare decisis

3. Even though others might regard this as "unrealistic, inconsistent, or illogical," the aberration is an established one, and one that has been recognized not only in Federal Baseball and *Toolson*, but in *Shubert, International Boxing*, and *Radovich*, as well, a total of five consecutive cases in this Court. . . . It is an aberration that has been with us now for half a century, one heretofore deemed fully entitled to the benefit of stare decisis, and one that has survived the Court's expanding concept of interstate commerce. It rests on a recognition and an acceptance of baseball's unique characteristics and needs.

4. Other professional sports operating interstate—football, boxing, basketball, and, presumably, hockey and golf—are not so exempt.

5. The advent of radio and television, with their consequent increased coverage and additional revenues, has not occasioned an overruling of *Federal Baseball* and *Toolson*.

Congress not silent

6. The Court has emphasized that since 1922 baseball, with full and continuing congressional awareness, has been allowed to develop and to expand unhindered by federal legislative action. Remedial legislation has been introduced repeatedly in Congress but none has ever been enacted. The Court, accordingly, has concluded that Congress as yet has had no intention to subject baseball's reserve system to the reach of the antitrust statutes. This, obviously, has been deemed to be something other than mere congressional silence and passivity.

7. The Court has expressed concern about the confusion and the retroactivity problems that inevitably would result with a judicial overturning of *Federal Baseball*. It has voiced a preference that if any change is to be made, it come by legislative action that, by its nature, is only prospective in operation.

8. The Court noted in *Radovich*, 352 U.S., at 452, 77 S. Ct., at 394, that the slate with respect to baseball is not clean. Indeed, it has not been clean for half a century.

This emphasis and this concern are still with us. We continue to be loath, 50 years after *Federal Baseball* and almost two decades after *Toolson*, to overturn those cases judicially when Congress, by its positive inaction, has allowed those decisions to stand for so long and, far beyond mere inference and implication, has clearly evinced a desire not to disapprove them legislatively.

Accordingly, we adhere once again to *Federal Baseball* and *Toolson* and to their application to professional baseball. We adhere also to *International Boxing* and *Radovich* and to their respective applications to professional boxing and professional football. If there is any inconsistency or illogic in all this, it is an inconsistency and illogic of long standing that is to be remedied by the Congress and not by this Court. If we were to act otherwise, we would be withdrawing from the conclusion as to congressional intent made in *Toolson* and from the concerns as to retrospectivity therein expressed. Under these circumstances, there is merit in consistency even though some might claim that beneath that consistency is a layer of inconsistency. . . .

The judgment of the Court of Appeals is affirmed. . . .

Mr. Justice MARSHALL, with whom Mr. Justice BRENNAN joins, dissenting.

. . . The importance of the antitrust laws to every citizen must not be minimized. They are as important to baseball players as they are to football players, lawyers, doctors, or members of any other class of workers. Baseball players cannot be denied the benefits of competition merely because club owners view other economic interests as being more important, unless Congress says so.

Has Congress acquiesced in our decisions in *Federal Baseball Club* and *Toolson?* I think not. Had the Court been consistent and treated all sports in the same way baseball was treated, Congress might have become concerned enough to take action. But, the Court was inconsistent, and baseball was isolated and distinguished from all other sports. In *Toolson* the Court refused to act because Congress had been silent. But the Court may have read too much into this legislative inaction.

Americans love baseball as they love all sports. Perhaps we become so enamored of athletics that we assume that they are foremost in the minds of legislators as well as fans. We must not forget, however, that there are only some 600 major league baseball players. Whatever muscle they might have been able to muster by combining forces with other athletes has been greatly impaired by the manner in which this Court has isolated them. It is this Court that has made them impotent, and this Court should correct its error.

We do not lightly overrule our prior constructions of federal statutes, but when our errors deny substantial federal rights, like the right to compete freely and effectively to the best of one's ability as guaranteed by the antitrust laws, we must admit our error and correct it. We have done so before and we should do so again here.

To the extent that there is concern over any reliance interests that club owners may assert, they can be satisfied by making our decision prospective only. Baseball should be covered by the antitrust laws beginning with this case and henceforth, unless Congress decides otherwise.

NOTES AND QUESTIONS

1. *Analysis of* Flood. If all other professional sports leagues, organizations, and governing bodies are subject to the federal antitrust laws, why should baseball retain its common law antitrust immunity? What are "baseball's unique characteristics and needs" that the Supreme Court relies on to justify its antitrust exemption? If you were a member of Congress, would you vote to take away baseball's antitrust exemption?

   In *Flood,* the Supreme Court majority waxed nostalgic:

   > Then there are the many names, celebrated for one reason or another, that have sparked the diamond and its environs and that have provided tinder for recaptured thrills, for reminiscence and comparisons, and for conversation and anticipation in-season and off-season: Ty Cobb, Babe Ruth, Tris Speaker, Walter Johnson, Henry Chadwick, Eddie Collins, Lou Gehrig, Grover Cleveland Alexander, Rogers Hornsby, Harry Hooper, Goose Goslin, Jackie Robinson, Honus Wagner, Joe McCarthy, John McGraw, Deacon Phillippe, Rube Marquard, Christy Mathewson, Tommy Leach, Big Ed Delahanty, Davy Jones, Germany Schaefer, King Kelly, Big Dan Brouthers, Wahoo Sam Crawford, Wee Willie Keeler, Big Ed Walsh, Jimmy Austin, Fred Snodgrass, Satchel Paige, Hugh Jennings, Fred Merkle, Iron Man McGinnity, Three-Finger Brown, Harry and Stan Coveleski, Connie Mack, Al Bridwell, Red Ruffing, Amos Rusie, Cy Young, Smokey Joe Wood, Chief Meyers, Chief Bender, Bill Klem, Hans Lobert, Johnny Evers, Joe Tinker, Roy Campanella, Miller Huggins, Rube Bressler, Dazzy Vance, Edd Roush, Bill Wambsganss, Clark Griffith, Branch Rickey, Frank Chance, Cap Anson, Nap Lajoie, Sad Sam Jones, Bob O'Farrell, Lefty O'Doul, Bobby Veach, Willie Kamm, Heinie Groh,

Lloyd and Paul Waner, Stuffy McInnis, Charles Comiskey, Roger Bresnahan, Bill Dickey, Zack Wheat, George Sisler, Charlie Gehringer, Eppa Rixey, Harry Heilmann, Fred Clarke, Dizzy Dean, Hank Greenberg, Pie Traynor, Rube Waddell, Bill Terry, Carl Hubbell, Old Hoss Radbourne, Moe Berg, Rabbit Maranville, Jimmie Foxx, Lefty Grove.

407 U.S. at 263. One scholar asserts that "[Justice] Blackmun's list is worthy of attention. The list lies at the heart of his curious and quite exceptional celebration of [baseball] in what was a critical sports law decision." Roger I. Abrams, *Blackmun's List*, 6 Va. Sports & Ent. L.J. 181, 189 (2007). He notes that "[a]lthough Blackmun took considerable time in his opinion to celebrate the national game, he could not have considered how the reserve system, which the Court's opinion upheld, affected the lives of the men he memorialized." *Id.* at 192.

Flood has generated significant scholarly commentary, with most of it criticizing the Supreme Court's decision as an unprincipled judicial aberration. See, e.g., Edmund P. Edmonds, *Over Forty Years in the On-Deck Circle: Congress and the Baseball Antitrust Exemption*, 19 T. Marshall L. Rev. 627 (1994); Connie Mack and Richard M. Blau, *The Need for Fair Play: Repealing the Federal Baseball Antitrust Exemption*, 45 Fla. L. Rev. 201 (1993); Robert G. Berger, *After the Strikes: A Reexamination of Professional Baseball's Exemption from the Antitrust Laws*, 45 U. Pitt. L. Rev. 209 (1983). Nevertheless, some scholars argue that its congressional or judicial repeal almost one hundred years later would potentially do more harm than good. Nathaniel Grow, *In Defense of Baseball's Antitrust Exemption*, 49 Am. Bus. L.J. 211, 215 (2012) ("Congress has obtained considerable leverage over baseball throughout the years by threatening to revoke the sport's antitrust exemption. Congress has used this power to help extract various procompetitive concessions from MLB, benefits that would not have been directly obtained via antitrust litigation alone"); Gary Roberts, *On the Scope and Effect of Baseball's Antitrust Exclusion*, 4 Seton Hall J. Sport L. 321, 323 (1994) ("while it is in theory unjustified to treat baseball differently from other sports and, while problems exist in baseball which concern both the public and Congress, trying to abolish the exclusion would be politically futile and unlikely to further the public interest").

2. *Lower Courts' Interpretation of* Flood. Most courts have broadly construed *Flood* to exempt all aspects of the "business of baseball" from the federal antitrust laws, not only player-management labor relations. See, e.g., *City of San Jose v MLB*, 766 F.3d 686 (9th Cir.), *cert. denied*, 136 S. Ct. 36 (2015) ("*Flood*'s congressional acquiescence rationale applies with special force to franchise relocation. In 1998, Congress passed the Curt Flood Act, which withdrew baseball's antitrust exemption with respect to the reserve clause and other labor issues, but explicitly maintained it for franchise relocation"). In addition, courts have ruled that baseball's antitrust immunity encompasses the exercise of the MLB Commissioner's "best interests of baseball authority" (*Charles O. Finley & Co., Inc. v. Kuhn*, 569 F.2d 527 (7th Cir. 1978)), and a state attorney general's investigation of a proposed sale and relocation of a baseball franchise (*Major League Baseball v. Crist*, 331 F.3d 1177 (11th Cir. 2003); *Minnesota Twins Partnership v. Hatch*, 592 N.W.2d 847 (Minn. 1999)).

Federal appellate courts continue to construe baseball's antitrust exception broadly and the Supreme Court has declined to review their decisions. In *Right Field Rooftops, LLC v. Chicago Cubs Baseball Club LLC*, 870 F.3d 682 (7th

Cir. 2017), the Seventh Circuit affirmed the dismissal of attempted monopolization claims by owners of buildings with rooftops overlooking Wrigley Field alleging that Chicago Cubs team representatives threatened to block rooftop views as leverage to force a sale of the rooftops at below-market prices to the Ricketts family, which owns the club, and demanded that they set minimum ticket prices to avoid having their views blocked. The court explained: "By attempting to set a minimum ticket price, purchasing rooftops, threatening to block rooftops with signage that did not sell to the Cubs, and beginning construction at Wrigley Field, the Cubs' conduct is part and parcel of the 'business of providing public baseball games for profit' that *Federal Baseball* and its progeny exempted from antitrust law." *Id.* at 689. See also *Miranda v Selig*, 860 F.3d 1237, 1242 (9th Cir.), *cert denied*, 138 S. Ct. 507 (2017) (holding that baseball's antitrust exception extends to MLB's labor relationship with minor league baseball players, which its member clubs employ and pay; although the Curt Flood Act of 1998 subjects MLB's labor relations with major league players to federal antitrust law, "it explicitly maintained the baseball exemption for anything related to the employment of minor league baseball players — including the use of reserve clauses"); *Wyckoff v. Office of the Commissioner of Baseball*, 2017 WL 3856454 (2d Cir. 2017), *cert. denied*, 138 S. Ct. 2621 (2018) (affirming dismissal of an antitrust suit brought by MLB scouts on the grounds that the relationship between scouts and MLB teams are "central to the business of baseball" and is protected by baseball's antitrust exemption).

Other courts have distinguished *Flood* and narrowly limited the scope of its antitrust immunity to the reserve clause and matters integral to baseball's structure. See, e.g., *Laumann v. NHL*, 56 F. Supp. 3d 280, 297 (S.D.N.Y. 2014) (declining "to apply the exemption to a subject that is not central to the business of baseball . . . namely baseball's contracts for television broadcast rights," which Congress did not intend to exempt in enacting the *Curt Flood Act of 1998); Postema v. National League of Professional Baseball Clubs*, 799 F. Supp. 1475 (S.D.N.Y. 1992) (no antitrust immunity for a common law restraint of trade claim concerning baseball's employment relations with its umpires because *Flood* limits exemption to baseball's "unique characteristics and needs"). One federal district court, in *Piazza v. Major League Baseball*, 831 F. Supp. 420 (E.D. Pa. 1993), and Florida state courts have ruled that baseball's antitrust exemption does not extend to decisions involving the sale and location of baseball franchises. *Butterworth v. National League of Professional Baseball Clubs*, 644 So. 2d 1021 (Fla. 1994); *Morsani v. Major League Baseball*, 663 So. 2d 653 (Fla. Dist. App. Ct. 1995). See generally Allan H. "Bud" Selig, Thomas J. Ostertag, and Matthew J. Mitten, *Baseball's Antitrust Exemption for Franchise Decisions: Its Justifications and Antitrust Law Implications for Other Professional Leagues*, 2019 Wisconsin L. Rev. 421, 427-432 (reviewing evolution and judicial scope of baseball's antitrust exemption).

What are the policy reasons in favor of construing baseball's antitrust exemption broadly? Narrowly?

3. Former MLB Commissioner Bud Selig has explained the importance of baseball's antitrust immunity:

> Baseball's antitrust exemption provides the MLB commissioner and league clubs with substantial internal governing autonomy regarding their economically interdependent business affairs. It enables MLB to prevent unilateral relocation by a club into another club's home territory, or to reject the geographical movement of a club that would be inconsistent with MLB's

league-wide interests, either of which generally also implicates consumer welfare considerations (i.e., the interests of baseball fans in the team's current location). It also protects their collective right to approve or disapprove the purchase and sale of clubs without fear of potential antitrust liability.

In addition, this antitrust exemption has enabled development of baseball's national minor league system, which provides a popular, relatively inexpensive form of entertainment in small and medium communities throughout the U.S. and has facilitated a very successful system of player development that creates thousands of employment opportunities for aspiring MLB players. Development of future MLB players through the minor league system is a proven means of building a competitive MLB team as illustrated by the recent postseason success of clubs such as the Kansas City Royals (2015 World Series champions and 2014 World Series American League representative), the Chicago Cubs (2016 World Series champions, its first championship since 1908), and the Houston Astros (2017 World Series champions, the first championship in its history).

Allan H. "Bud" Selig and Matthew J. Mitten, *Baseball Jurisprudence: Its Effects on America's Pastime and Other Professional Sports Leagues*, 50 Ariz. St. L. J. 1171, 1187-1188 (2018).

4. *Curt Flood Act of 1998.* In 1998, Congress modified the Sherman Act to provide MLB players with the same antitrust remedies as other professional athletes such as football and basketball players. 15 U.S.C. §26b. This legislation is the product of a joint lobbying effort by the MLB players union and major league club owners pursuant to a provision in their 1994 CBA to do so. This law gives MLB players the same right to sue under antitrust laws concerning MLB employment terms as other professional athletes have in their sports. 15 U.S.C. §26b(c). It is important to understand that this legislation is not intended to affect judicial construction and application of the nonstatutory labor exemption (which is discussed in Chapter 7) to baseball players' antitrust claims brought against professional baseball organizations. 15 U.S.C. §26b(d)(4). In other words, MLB players do not have any antitrust remedies for certain terms and conditions of their employment arising out of an ongoing collective bargaining process. *Brown v. Pro Football, Inc.*, 518 U. S. 231 (1996).

 The act expressly permits antitrust challenges only to conduct or agreements by those persons "in the business of organized professional major league baseball directly relating to or affecting employment of major league baseball players to play baseball at the major league level." 15 U.S.C. §26b(a). It does not provide a basis for challenging conduct or agreements relating to employment as a minor league baseball player, the amateur or first-year player draft, or any reserve clause applied to minor league players. 15 U.S.C. §26b(b)(1). *Miranda v Selig*, 860 F.3d 1237, 1242 (9th Cir.), *cert denied*, 138 S. Ct. 507 (2017).

The act is not intended to affect the applicability or inapplicability of the antitrust laws to any areas other than MLB labor relations issues. It has no prospective or retroactive effect on judicial construction of the scope of baseball's antitrust exemption on any other matters. Rejecting an argument that the act is a congressional endorsement of baseball's antitrust exemption, one court explained: "I take Congress at its word and resolve this case without reliance on the Curt Flood Act as affecting the outcome one way or the other. I conclude that the business of baseball *is* exempt; the exemption was well established long prior to adoption of the Curt Flood Act and certainly was not *repealed* by that Act." *Major League Baseball v. Butterworth*, 181 F. Supp. 2d 1316, 1331 n.16 (N.D. Fla. 2001), *aff'd on other grounds, Major League Baseball v. Crist*, 331 F.3d 1177 (11th Cir. 2003).

5. *Sports Broadcasting Act (SBA) of 1961.* This federal law, codified at 15 U.S.C. §1291, *et seq.,* expressly permits professional sports league clubs to pool and sell or transfer "all or any part of the rights of such league's member clubs in the sponsored telecasting of the games." Legislative history indicates that the SBA is intended to "enable the member clubs . . . to pool their separate rights in the sponsored broadcasting of their games and to permit the league to sell the resulting package of pooled rights to a purchaser, such as a television network, without violating the antitrust laws." S. Rep. No. 1087, 87th Cong. at 1 (1961), reprinted in 1961 U.S.C.C.A.N. 3042, 3042. It was enacted in response to *U.S. v. NFL*, 116 F. Supp. 319 (E.D. Pa. 1953), the only sports industry antitrust suit ever filed by the federal government, which held that the NFL's territorial broadcast restrictions on its member clubs' licensing of television rights to their home games violated Sherman Act §1.

As one court observed, "The purpose of the SBA . . . was to establish the legality of a practice which tends to restrain competition, package sales to the networks." *Chicago Prof'l Sports Limited Partnership v. NBA (Bulls I)*, 754 F. Supp. 1336, 1352 (N.D. Ill. 1991), *aff'd*, 961 F.2d 667 (7th Cir. 1992). Congress provided professional sports leagues with this limited antitrust exemption to protect their home game ticket sales, especially those of the economically weaker clubs, and to facilitate the sharing of television broadcast revenues among clubs, thereby preserving the league's competitive balance, product integrity, and existence.

The SBA does not define "sponsored telecasting," although its legislative history evidences Congress's intent to exclude league-pooled television rights packages with games shown on closed circuit and subscription television from antitrust immunity. Telecasting of Professional Sports Contests: Hearing Before the Antitrust Committee of the House Committee on the Judiciary on H.R. 8757, 87th Cong. 1st Sess. at 5 (1961). This has given rise to litigation concerning the types of broadcasts encompassed within the meaning of "sponsored telecasting," which courts have narrowly construed. See, e.g., *Shaw v. Dallas Cowboys Football Club, Inc.*, 172 F.3d 299, 300 (3d Cir. 1999) (the package sale of television broadcast rights to a satellite distributor is not "sponsored telecasting" immune from antitrust scrutiny); *Chicago Prof'l Sports Ltd. Partnership v. NBA (Bulls III)*, 808 F. Supp. 646, 650 (N.D. Ill. 1992) ("sponsored telecasting" encompasses only "free television," such as "national network and local over-the-air broadcasting provided at no direct cost to viewers," not the league's pooled television rights contract with a cable television programming service).

The SBA does not confer an antitrust exemption for any joint agreement that prohibits a purchaser of a league's pooled television rights from telecasting the games in a particular area "except within the home territory of a member club of the league on a day when such club is playing a game at home." 15 U.S.C. §1292. Thus, prohibiting telecasts of other league games into a club's home territory when it has a home game does not violate antitrust laws; whereas, any other collective limits on the territorial scope of broadcasts of league games may be an antitrust violation.

6. *State Antitrust Law.* In *Flood*, the Supreme Court held that the Supremacy and dormant Commerce Clauses of the United States Constitution bar state antitrust law regulation of organized baseball because of its exemption from federal antitrust law. The Court observed that national uniformity is necessary in connection with baseball's reserve system and that state antitrust regulation would conflict with national antitrust policy.

Regarding sports other than baseball that are subject to federal antitrust regulation, courts generally hold that applying state antitrust laws to a professional sports league's interstate activities (e.g., labor disputes) violates the Dormant Commerce Clause. In *Partee v. San Diego Chargers Football Co.*, 668 P.2d 674, 678 (Cal. 1983), the California Supreme Court explained:

> Professional football is a nationwide business. . . . The necessity of a nationwide league structure for the benefit of both teams and players for effective competition is evident as is the need for a nationally uniform set of rules governing the league structure. Fragmentation of the league structure on the basis of state lines would adversely affect the success of the competitive business enterprise, and differing state antitrust decisions if applied to the enterprise would likely compel all member teams to comply with the laws of the strictest state.

In light of these concerns, is any state regulation of professional sports other than the recognition and enforcement of valid contracts appropriate? Considering that many businesses are national in their operations, does the rationale of the court overly protect professional sports leagues vis-à-vis other industries from state antitrust law regulation?

3. Application of Sherman Act §1

If there are no applicable antitrust law exemptions or immunities, it is necessary to consider the merits of a claim alleging that a particular league rule or agreement among its member clubs violates Sherman Act §1. As you study how courts have applied §1 to professional sports leagues, keep in mind antitrust law's underlying principle that an unrestrained competitive market is the best means of promoting consumer welfare (i.e., sports fans' interests). But is it important to recognize that professional team sports are a unique entertainment market product (i.e., a particular brand of athletic competition such as NFL football), which are collectively produced by economically interdependent league clubs. Consider the nature and scope of the agreements and cooperation among league clubs that are necessary to produce sports competition in a form attractive to fans. For example, there must be agreement regarding the rules of game and scheduling of games. What else is necessary? Also consider that league clubs' internal governance rules and decisions often have adverse economic effects on themselves, those desiring to join the league, manufacturers of collateral products such as trademarked merchandise, broadcasters, and sports fans: when do they violate §1?

a. Concerted Action Requirement

The express language of Sherman Act §1 broadly prohibits "[e]very contract, combination in the form of trust or otherwise, or conspiracy" that restrains trade, which literally encompasses virtually all professional sports league rules (which are the product of an agreement among league clubs) and decisions. Nevertheless, as a defense to Sherman Act §1 claims, professional sports leagues (particularly the NFL) historically argued that the league and its member clubs jointly produce a single product (e.g., NFL football) that no individual club is capable of producing. Therefore, a professional sports league's rules and member clubs' collective governance should not be subject to §1 because they are not economic competitors who produce separate products. At the outset it is necessary to resolve an important threshold issue: is a professional sports league a single economic entity whose agreements and rules are not subject to §1 scrutiny, or is it a joint venture of separate economic entities (i.e., its clubs) whose collective conduct is subject to §1?

Singleentity issue [handwritten margin note]

In 1974, the so-called "single entity defense" was first judicially addressed in *San Francisco Seals, Ltd. v. National Hockey League*, 379 F. Supp. 966 (C.D. Cal. 1974), in which a federal district court held that the member clubs of the NHL are not legally capable of conspiring to restrain trade in the alleged relevant market. The owner of the San Francisco Seals club asserted that league members' refusal to permit the team to relocate to Vancouver, British Columbia, violated §1. The court found the relevant market to be "the production of professional hockey games before live audiences . . . [in] the United States and Canada." *Id.* at 969. Finding that "the plaintiff and defendants are acting together as one single business enterprise, competing against other similarly organized professional leagues," the court concluded "they are not competitors in the economic sense in this relevant market." *Id.* at 969-970. Because the parties cooperated in producing hockey games, the court held that the league's refusal to permit the plaintiff's relocation was not a conspiracy to restrain trade as a matter of law.

Most federal appellate courts subsequently refused to accept the single economic entity defense. For example, in *Los Angeles Memorial Coliseum Comm'n v. NFL (Raiders I)*, 726 F.2d 1381 (9th Cir.), *cert. denied*, 469 U.S. 990 (1984), the Ninth Circuit rejected the NFL's claim that the league is in essence a single economic entity, like a partnership that shares profits and losses, precluding application of §1, which prohibits only agreements among business entities with economically separate interests that restrain trade:

> Our inquiry discloses an association of teams sufficiently independent and competitive with one another to warrant rule of reason scrutiny under § 1 of the Sherman Act. The NFL clubs are, in the words of the district court, "separate business entities whose products have an independent value." The member clubs are all independently owned. Most are corporations, some are partnerships, and apparently a few are sole proprietorships. Although a large portion of League revenue, approximately 90%, is divided equally among the teams, profits and losses are not shared, a feature common to partnerships or other "single entities." In fact, profits vary widely despite the sharing of revenue. The disparity in profits can be attributed to independent management policies regarding coaches, players, management personnel, ticket prices, concessions, luxury box seats, as well as franchise location, all of which contribute to fan support and other income sources.
>
> In addition to being independent business entities, the NFL clubs do compete with one another off the field as well as on to acquire players, coaches, and management personnel. In certain areas of the country where two teams operate in close proximity, there is also competition for fan support, local television and local radio revenues, and media space.

Id. at 1389-1390. See also *North American Soccer League v. National Football League*, 670 F.2d 1249, 1252 (2d Cir. 1981), *cert. denied*, 459 U.S. 1074 (1982) (NFL teams are "separate economic entities engaged in a joint venture" whose joint conduct is subject to scrutiny under §1).

After *Raiders I*, in *Copperweld Corp. v. Independence Tube Corp.*, 467 U.S. 752 (1984), the Supreme Court held that legally separate business entities with a "complete unity of interest," such as a parent corporation and its wholly owned subsidiary, are not subject to §1 of the Sherman Act. It reasoned that this business arrangement is "like a multiple team of horses drawing a vehicle under the control of a single driver"; therefore, there is no sudden joining of previously diverse economic forces raising the prospect of collusive anticompetitive conduct. The court observed that internal coordination within a single business enterprise is often necessary for effective competition and that a business entity's internal organizational structure is irrelevant to the resulting anticompetitive consequences. The Court explained that the Sherman Act contains a "basic distinction between concerted and independent action," with the result that anticompetitive independent conduct by a single entity does not violate §1.

Although there is no complete unity of interest between professional sports league teams like there is between a corporate parent and a wholly owned subsidiary or among the members of a partnership, some of *Copperweld*'s reasoning suggests a professional sports league and its member clubs should be treated as a single economic entity for antitrust purposes. Thereafter, in *Brown v. Pro Football, Inc.*, 518 U.S. 231, 248 (1996), the Supreme Court observed "that the clubs that make up a professional sports league are not completely independent economic competitors, as they depend upon a degree of cooperation for economic survival." The Court did not specifically consider whether league clubs are separate economic entities whose collective action is subject to §1, or whether a sports league and its members are an economically integrated single business enterprise whose conduct is not covered by §1.

Thereafter, most lower courts refused to construe *Copperweld* and *Brown* as requiring the conclusion that a professional sports league and its member clubs are a single entity as a matter of law whose joint conduct is not subject to §1. See *Sullivan v. National Football League*, 34 F.3d 1091 (1st Cir. 1994); *Shaw v. Dallas Cowboys Football Club, Ltd.*, 1998 WL 419765 (E.D. Pa. 1998), *aff'd on other grounds*, 172 F.3d 299 (3d Cir. 1999). Some courts reasoned that league clubs do not satisfy *Copperweld*'s "complete unity of interest" standard because they often act in furtherance of their own individual economic interests rather than the league's collective economic interests. *Sullivan v. NFL*, 34 F.2d 1091, 1099 (1st Cir. 1994), *cert. denied*, 513 U.S. 1190 (1995).

By contrast, in *Chicago Professional Sports Limited Partnership v. National Basketball Association*, 95 F.3d 593 (7th Cir. 1996), the Seventh Circuit suggested the single entity defense should not be rejected based simply on how professional sports leagues are structured and governed. The court proposed that a functional approach, which analyzes whether league clubs are economic competitors in the alleged relevant market that is restrained (as *San Francisco Seals* did), be used to determine the appropriateness of applying §1 on a case-by-case basis. In other words, whether the particular challenged conduct has the requisite degree of economic integration to be considered that of a single economic entity requires a facet-by-facet analysis of each league's operations.

Judge Easterbrook observed that the NBA is closer to a single firm than a group of independent firms when acting in the broadcast market:

> Whether the NBA itself is more like a single firm, which would be analyzed only under § 2 of the Sherman Act [which prohibits monopolization or attempted

monopolization], or like a joint venture, which would be subject to the Rule of Reason under § 1, is a tough question under *Copperweld*. It has characteristics of both. Unlike the colleges and universities that belong to the National Collegiate Athletic Association . . . the NBA has no existence independent of sports. It makes professional basketball; only it can make "NBA Basketball" games. . . . From the perspective of fans and advertisers (who use sports telecasts to reach fans), "NBA Basketball" is one product from a single source even though the Chicago Bulls and Seattle Supersonics [two of the NBA's clubs] are highly distinguishable.

Id. at 599.

Relying on *Chicago Professional Sports*, in *American Needle, Inc. v. New Orleans La. Saints*, 496 F. Supp. 2d 941 (N.D. Ill. 2007), the NFL argued that its member clubs function as a single economic entity in jointly producing NFL football and collectively licensing their intellectual property (e.g., trademarked merchandise), which does not constitute the requisite concerted action under §1. The district court agreed and held that "with regard to the facet of their operations respecting exploitation of intellectual property rights, the NFL and its 32 teams are, in the jargon of antitrust law, acting as a single entity." *Id.* at 943. The Seventh Circuit affirmed, concluding that "the record amply establishes that since 1963, the NFL teams have acted as one source of economic power—under the auspices of NFL Properties—to license their intellectual property collectively and to promote NFL football." *American Needle, Inc. v. National Football League*, 538 F.3d 736, 744 (7th Cir. 2008).

Because the Seventh Circuit's ruling conflicted with the precedent from other circuits, American Needle petitioned the Supreme Court for a writ of certiorari. Although it had prevailed in the lower courts, the NFL also petitioned the Supreme Court for review, hoping it would accept the single entity defense and effectively provide professional sports leagues with immunity from Sherman Act §1.

AMERICAN NEEDLE, INC. v. NATIONAL FOOTBALL LEAGUE
560 U.S. 183 (2010)

STEVENS, Justice.

. . . Originally organized in 1920, the NFL is an unincorporated association that now includes 32 separately owned professional football teams. Each team has its own name, colors, and logo, and owns related intellectual property. Like each of the other teams in the league, the New Orleans Saints and the Indianapolis Colts, for example, have their own distinctive names, colors, and marks that are well known to millions of sports fans.

Prior to 1963, the teams made their own arrangements for licensing their intellectual property and marketing trademarked items such as caps and jerseys. In 1963, the teams formed National Football League Properties (NFLP) to develop, license, and market their intellectual property. Most, but not all, of the substantial revenues generated by NFLP have either been given to charity or shared equally among the teams. However, the teams are able to and have at times sought to withdraw from this arrangement.

Between 1963 and 2000, NFLP granted nonexclusive licenses to a number of vendors, permitting them to manufacture and sell apparel bearing team insignias. Petitioner, American Needle, Inc., was one of those licensees. In December 2000, the teams voted to authorize NFLP to grant exclusive licenses, and NFLP granted Reebok International Ltd. an exclusive 10-year license to manufacture and sell trademarked headwear for all 32 teams. It thereafter declined to renew American Needle's nonexclusive license.

American Needle filed this action in the Northern District of Illinois, alleging that the agreements between the NFL, its teams, NFLP, and Reebok violated §§ 1 and 2 of the Sherman Act. In their answer to the complaint, the defendants averred that the teams, NFL, and NFLP were incapable of conspiring within the meaning of § 1 "because they are a single economic enterprise, at least with respect to the conduct challenged." . . .

As the case comes to us, we have only a narrow issue to decide: whether the NFL respondents are capable of engaging in a "contract, combination . . . , or conspiracy" as defined by § 1 of the Sherman Act, 15 U.S.C. § 1, or, as we have sometimes phrased it, whether the alleged activity by the NFL respondents "must be viewed as that of a single enterprise for purposes of § 1." *Copperweld Corp. v. Independence Tube Corp.*, 467 U.S. 752, 771, 104 S. Ct. 2731, 81 L. Ed. 2d 628 (1984). . . .

The meaning of the term "contract, combination . . . or conspiracy" is informed by the "'basic distinction'" in the Sherman Act "'between concerted and independent action'" that distinguishes § 1 of the Sherman Act from § 2. *Copperweld*, 467 U.S., at 767. Section 1 applies only to concerted action that restrains trade. Section 2, by contrast, covers both concerted and independent action, but only if that action "monopolize[s]," 15 U.S.C. § 2, or "threatens actual monopolization," *Copperweld*, 467 U.S. at 767, a category that is narrower than restraint of trade. Monopoly power may be equally harmful whether it is the product of joint action or individual action.

Congress used this distinction between concerted and independent action to deter anticompetitive conduct and compensate its victims, without chilling vigorous competition through ordinary business operations. The distinction also avoids judicial scrutiny of routine, internal business decisions. . . .

As *Copperweld* exemplifies, "substance, not form, should determine whether a[n] . . . entity is capable of conspiring under § 1." 467 U.S., at 773, n. 21. This inquiry is sometimes described as asking whether the alleged conspirators are a single entity. That is perhaps a misdescription, however, because the question is not whether the defendant is a legally single entity or has a single name; nor is the question whether the parties involved "seem" like one firm or multiple firms in any metaphysical sense. The key is whether the alleged "contract, combination . . . , or conspiracy" is concerted action-that is, whether it joins together separate decisionmakers. The relevant inquiry, therefore, is whether there is a "contract, combination . . . or conspiracy" amongst "separate economic actors pursuing separate economic interests," *id.*, at 769, such that the agreement "deprives the marketplace of independent centers of decisionmaking," *ibid.*, and therefore of "diversity of entrepreneurial interests," *Fraser v. Major League Soccer, L.L. C.*, 284 F.3d 47, 57 (C.A.1 2002) (Boudin, C. J.), and thus of actual or potential competition. . . .

The NFL teams do not possess either the unitary decisionmaking quality or the single aggregation of economic power characteristic of independent action. Each of the teams is a substantial, independently owned, and independently managed business. . . . The teams compete with one another, not only on the playing field, but to attract fans, for gate receipts and for contracts with managerial and playing personnel.

Directly relevant to this case, the teams compete in the market for intellectual property. To a firm making hats, the Saints and the Colts are two potentially competing suppliers of valuable trademarks. When each NFL team licenses its intellectual property, it is not pursuing the "common interests of the whole" league but is instead pursuing interests of each "corporation itself," *Copperweld*, 467 U.S., at 770, teams are acting as "separate economic actors pursuing separate economic interests," and each team therefore is a potential "independent cente[r] of decisionmaking," *id.*, at 769. Decisions by NFL teams to license their separately owned trademarks collectively and to only one vendor are decisions that "depriv[e] the marketplace of independent centers of decisionmaking," *ibid.*, and therefore of actual or potential competition. See *NCAA*, 468 U.S., at 109, n. 39.

In defense, respondents argue that by forming NFLP, they have formed a single entity, akin to a merger, and market their NFL brands through a single outlet. But it is not dispositive that the teams have organized and own a legally separate entity that centralizes the management of their intellectual property. An ongoing § 1 violation cannot evade § 1 scrutiny simply by giving the ongoing violation a name and label. . . .

The NFL respondents may be similar in some sense to a single enterprise that owns several pieces of intellectual property and licenses them jointly, but they are not similar in the relevant functional sense. Although NFL teams have common interests such as promoting the NFL brand, they are still separate, profit-maximizing entities, and their interests in licensing team trademarks are not necessarily aligned. Common interests in the NFL brand "*partially* unit[e] the economic interests of the parent firms," Brodley, Joint Ventures and Antitrust Policy, 95 Harv. L. Rev. 1521, 1526 (1982) (emphasis added), but the teams still have distinct, potentially competing interests.

It may be, as respondents argue, that NFLP "has served as the 'single driver'" of the teams' "promotional vehicle," "'pursu[ing] the common interests of the whole.'" But illegal restraints often are in the common interests of the parties to the restraint, at the expense of those who are not parties. It is true, as respondents describe, that they have for some time marketed their trademarks jointly. But a history of concerted activity does not immunize conduct from § 1 scrutiny. . . .

Respondents argue that nonetheless, as the Court of Appeals held, they constitute a single entity because without their cooperation, there would be no NFL football. It is true that "the clubs that make up a professional sports league are not completely independent economic competitors, as they depend upon a degree of cooperation for economic survival." *Brown*, 518 U.S., at 248. But the Court of Appeals' reasoning is unpersuasive.

The justification for cooperation is not relevant to whether that cooperation is concerted or independent action. A "contract, combination . . . or conspiracy," § 1, that is necessary or useful to a joint venture is still a "contract, combination . . . or conspiracy" if it "deprives the marketplace of independent centers of decisionmaking," *Copperweld*, 467 U.S., at 769. See *NCAA*, 468 U.S., at 113 ("[J]oint ventures have no immunity from antitrust laws"). Any joint venture involves multiple sources of economic power cooperating to produce a product. And for many such ventures, the participation of others is necessary. But that does not mean that necessity of cooperation transforms concerted action into independent action; a nut and a bolt can only operate together, but an agreement between nut and bolt manufacturers is still subject to § 1 analysis. Nor does it mean that once a group of firms agree to produce a joint product, cooperation amongst those firms must be treated as independent conduct. The mere fact that the teams operate jointly in some sense does not mean that they are immune.

The question whether NFLP decisions can constitute concerted activity covered by § 1 is closer than whether decisions made directly by the 32 teams are covered by § 1. This is so both because NFLP is a separate corporation with its own management and because the record indicates that most of the revenues generated by NFLP are shared by the teams on an equal basis. Nevertheless we think it clear that for the same reasons the 32 teams' conduct is covered by § 1, NFLP's actions also are subject to § 1, at least with regards to its marketing of property owned by the separate teams. NFLP's licensing decisions are made by the 32 potential competitors, and each of them actually owns its share of the jointly managed assets. Apart from their agreement to cooperate in exploiting those assets, including their decisions as the NFLP, there would be nothing to prevent each of the teams from making its own market decisions relating to purchases of apparel and headwear, to the sale of such items, and to the granting of licenses to use its trademarks.

We generally treat agreements within a single firm as independent action on the presumption that the components of the firm will act to maximize the firm's profits. But in rare cases, that presumption does not hold. Agreements made within a firm can constitute concerted action covered by § 1 when the parties to the agreement act on interests separate from those of the firm itself, and the intrafirm agreements may simply be a formalistic shell for ongoing concerted action.

For that reason, decisions by the NFLP regarding the teams' separately owned intellectual property constitute concerted action. Thirty-two teams operating independently through the vehicle of the NFLP are not like the components of a single firm that act to maximize the firm's profits. The teams remain separately controlled, potential competitors with economic interests that are distinct from NFLP's financial well-being. Unlike typical decisions by corporate shareholders, NFLP licensing decisions effectively require the assent of more than a mere majority of shareholders. And each team's decision reflects not only an interest in NFLP's profits but also an interest in the team's individual profits. The 32 teams capture individual economic benefits separate and apart from NFLP profits as a result of the decisions they make for the NFLP. NFLP's decisions thus affect each team's profits from licensing its own intellectual property. "Although the business interests of" the teams "will *often* coincide with those of the" NFLP "as an entity in itself, that commonality of interest exists in every cartel." *Los Angeles Memorial Coliseum Comm'n v. NFL,* 726 F.2d 1381, 1389 (C.A.9 1984) (emphasis added). In making the relevant licensing decisions, NFLP is therefore "an instrumentality" of the teams. . . .

Football teams that need to cooperate are not trapped by antitrust law. "[T]he special characteristics of this industry may provide a justification" for many kinds of agreements. *Brown,* 518 U.S., at 252, 116 S. Ct. 2116 (Stevens, J., dissenting). The fact that NFL teams share an interest in making the entire league successful and profitable, and that they must cooperate in the production and scheduling of games, provides a perfectly sensible justification for making a host of collective decisions. But the conduct at issue in this case is still concerted activity under the Sherman Act that is subject to § 1 analysis.

When "restraints on competition are essential if the product is to be available at all," *per se* rules of illegality are inapplicable, and instead the restraint must be judged according to the flexible Rule of Reason. *NCAA,* 468 U.S., at 101;

see *id.*, at 117 ("Our decision not to apply a *per se* rule to this case rests in large part on our recognition that a certain degree of cooperation is necessary if the type of competition that petitioner and its member institutions seek to market is to be preserved"); see also *Dagher*, 547 U.S., at 6. In such instances, the agreement is likely to survive the Rule of Reason. See *Broadcast Music, Inc. v. Columbia Broadcasting System, Inc.*, 441 U.S. 1, 23, 99 S. Ct. 1551, 60 L. Ed. 2d 1 (1979) ("Joint ventures and other cooperative arrangements are also not usually unlawful . . . where the agreement . . . is necessary to market the product at all"). And depending upon the concerted activity in question, the Rule of Reason may not require a detailed analysis; it "can sometimes be applied in the twinkling of an eye." *NCAA*, 468 U.S., at 109, n. 39.

Other features of the NFL may also save agreements amongst the teams. We have recognized, for example, "that the interest in maintaining a competitive balance" among "athletic teams is legitimate and important," *NCAA*, 468 U.S., at 117. While that same interest applies to the teams in the NFL, it does not justify treating them as a single entity for § 1 purposes when it comes to the marketing of the teams' individually owned intellectual property. It is, however, unquestionably an interest that may well justify a variety of collective decisions made by the teams. What role it properly plays in applying the Rule of Reason to the allegations in this case is a matter to be considered on remand.

Accordingly, the judgment of the Court of Appeals is reversed, and the case is remanded for further proceedings consistent with this opinion.

NOTES AND QUESTIONS

1. Do you agree with the Supreme Court's rejection of the single entity defense and its reasoning? Should all league rules and agreements among league clubs (e.g., rules of the game, scheduling of games, the number of teams qualifying for the playoffs, selection of a commissioner) be subject to judicial scrutiny under §1? Does *American Needle* inhibit the ability of a league and its member clubs to adopt rules and to make joint decisions that enhance the league's likelihood of more effectively competing with other producers in the U.S. entertainment market?

2. *Post-*American Needle *Cases and Scholarly Debate.* In *Deutscher Tennis Bund v. ATP Tour, Inc.*, 610 F.3d 820, 835-837 (3d Cir. 2010), the Third Circuit construed *American Needle* soon after it was decided by the Supreme Court, suggesting that an agreement among the Association of Tennis Professionals' member tournaments regarding the stratification of ATP tennis tournaments is not immune from §1 scrutiny:

> At trial, ATP contended it constitutes a single enterprise, and under *Copperweld*, its internal decisions cannot violate § 1 of the Sherman Act. It asserted each of its tournament members is dependent on the others to produce a common product-a marketable annual professional tennis tour that competes with other forms of entertainment, within and without the sports arena. ATP maintained its members do not compete but instead cooperate to produce the Tour, and its adoption of the Brave New World plan was the core activity of producing this product. For their part, the Federations contended ATP operates in the market for top tier men's professional tennis players, and individual tournaments compete to attract top players. They asserted the Brave New World plan was an agreement unreasonably restraining trade in this alleged market. . . .

[T]he agreement among the ATP's tournament members in the Brave New World Plan might have deprived the marketplace of potential competition. Professional sports teams or tournaments always have an interest in obtaining the best players possible. *Brown v. Pro Football, Inc.*, 518 U.S. 231, 116 S. Ct. 2116, 135 L. Ed. 2d 521 (1996). The record in this case indicates that the individual tennis tournaments traditionally compete for player talent. An agreement restricting this competition should not necessarily be immune from § 1 scrutiny merely because the tournaments cooperate in various aspects of producing the ATP Tour. "The justification for cooperation is not relevant to whether that cooperation is concerted or independent action." *Am. Needle*, 130 S. Ct. 2201, 2214 (2010). The necessity of cooperation does not "transform[ ] concerted action into independent action. The mere fact that the teams operate jointly in some sense does not mean that they are immune." *Id.*

In *In re National Football League Sunday Ticket Antitrust Litigation*, 2019 WL 3788253 (9th Cir.) at *10, the Ninth Circuit rejected the NFL's argument that because "each NFL game broadcast is a copyrighted work jointly authored by the NFL, the two competing teams, and the broadcast network, and the agreement of all participants is necessary in order to create the telecasts at all," the plaintiffs' §1 challenge to its "Sunday Ticket" package of NFL game broadcasts should be dismissed as a matter of law. The court ruled:

> In the absence of a legal requirement that the NFL teams, NFL, and broadcasters coordinate in filming and broadcasting live games, the Los Angeles Rams (for instance) could contract for their own telecast of Rams games and then register the telecasts for those games with the Rams (and perhaps the team against whom they are playing). Only the agreements that are the subject of plaintiffs' antitrust action prevent such independent actions. Thus, we reject the defendants' argument that *American Needle* is inapposite; here, like in *American Needle*, the agreements not to compete concern separately owned intellectual property, and impose an unlawful restraint on independent competition.

Id. at *11. See also *Laumann v. NHL*, 907 F. Supp. 2d 465 (S.D.N.Y. 2012) (alleged agreements among MLB and NHL clubs to create exclusive local television territories and broadcasting rights for each club, and to grant their respective leagues the exclusive right to sell television and internet broadcasting rights to those games outside these local territories, are subject to §1 scrutiny because they are actual or potential competitors for the sale of these rights).

By contrast, in *Washington v. National Football League*, 880 F. Supp.3d 1004, 1006 (D. Minn. 2012), another federal district court rejected a group of former NFL players' allegations that the NFL's refusal to pay them royalties for the use of their images in game films for promotional purposes violated §1 because "Here, unlike in *American Needle*, the intellectual property involved is historical football game footage, something that the individual teams do not separately own, and never have separately owned. Rather, the NFL owns the game footage, either alone or in conjunction with the teams involved in the game being filmed." See also *Spinelli v. NFL*, 96 F. Supp.3d 81, 114 (S.D.N.Y. 2015) (NFL teams' agreement to exclusively license photos does not violate the Sherman Act because "many if not most of the photographs at issue contain intellectual property owned by the NFL and at least one NFL Club").

Which of the foregoing developing lines of judicial precedent is most consistent with *American Needle*?

Scholarly commentary regarding the post-*American Needle* application of the single entity defense to the joint conduct of U.S professional sports league clubs, outside the context of intellectual property licensing and other restrictions, is divided. One commentator has stated that "because differences do exist between the various leagues' structures, *American Needle* should not be read to automatically foreclose the possibility that another league could assert a colorable case for single entity status." Nathaniel Grow, American Needle *and the Future of the Single Entity Defense Under Section One of the Sherman Act*, 48 Am. Bus. L.J. 449, 497 (2011). A different commentator has observed, "*American Needle* is unclear . . . whether a court should treat a league pooling all of the teams' revenues and costs as a single economic entity or as a cartel. By stressing the potential for competition, *American Needle* suggests treatment as a cartel, but by focusing on incentives to maximize league profits, the decision suggests single-entity treatment." Gregory J. Werden, American Needle *and the Application of the Sherman Act to Professional Sports Leagues*, 18 Vill. Sports & Ent. L.J. 395, 404-406 (2011). Another has suggested *American Needle* leaves open the possibility that any "core activity" of a professional sports league (e.g., the rules of the game; equipment, club ownership, club relocation, and broadcast restrictions; player restraints) may be effectively immune from §1 scrutiny. James A. Keyte, American Needle: *A New Quick Look for Joint Ventures*, 25 Antitrust 48, 51-52 (2010). Others, however, assert that *American Needle* "put[s] an end to the argument that a sports league [as currently structured] is a single entity immune from antitrust scrutiny" and "reinforces the need to view skeptically any argument purporting to define a zone of conduct as automatically lawful without regard to its competitive effects." Meir Feder, *Is There Life After Death for Sports League Immunity?* American Needle *and Beyond*, 18 Vill. Sports & Ent. L.J. 407, 428 (2011). See also Allan H. "Bud" Selig, Thomas J. Ostertag, and Matthew J. Mitten, *Baseball's Antitrust Exemption for Franchise Decisions: Its Justifications and Antitrust Law Implications for Other Professional Leagues*, 2019 Wisconsin L. Rev. 421, 444-445 ("The justifications for MLB's antitrust exemption . . . support judicial application of the single entity defense to bar Sherman Act § 1 challenges to other leagues' rules and decisions regarding the number and ownership of their clubs and whether to permit a club to relocate to an area in which there would be no economic competition with another league team. League rules and decisions regarding these specific matters are the product of collective action among existing league clubs, but these aspects of internal governance do not reduce any actual or potential economic competition among those clubs.").

3. Consider how an existing professional sports league could be restructured (or a new league could be structured or governed) to have the requisite complete unity of economic interest under *American Needle* and *Copperweld* to justify its characterization as a single economic entity. It could be governed by a separate economic entity that wholly owns and controls all of its member clubs. *Fraser v. Major League Soccer, LLC*, 284 F.3d 47, 56 (1st Cir. 2002), *cert. denied*, 537 U.S. 885 (2002) ("If ordinary investors decided to set up a company that would own and manage all of the teams in a league, it is hard to see why this arrangement would fall outside *Copperweld*'s safe harbor"). See also Gregory J. Werden, American Needle *and the Application of the Sherman Act to Professional Sports Leagues*, 18 Vill. Sports & Ent. L.J. 395, 403 (2011) ("A professional

sports league entirely owned and operated by a single person undoubtedly would be treated as a single economic entity, even though the teams compete on the field of play, and even though the teams have separate identities and fan loyalties"). Alternatively, the league could be an independent company with separate ownership and control from its clubs similar to NASCAR's business model. See generally Stefan Szymanski and Stephen F. Ross, Fans of the World, Unite! A (Capitalist) Manifesto for Sports Consumers 70-107 (2008).

b.   Unreasonable Restraint of Trade

If §1 applies, it is necessary to then consider whether the challenged league rule or agreement among its clubs unreasonably restrains trade. The production of professional sports athletic competition requires many aspects of cooperation, and professional leagues and their member clubs are economically interdependent. One team cannot survive without other league teams as on-field competitors. To offer an attractive product desirable to consumers (e.g., close and exciting games), a professional sports league must maintain on-field competitive balance among its member teams and preserve the long-term financial viability of each club. In an effort to achieve these objectives, league rules may either prohibit certain conduct by an individual club owner or require its approval by a majority of other member clubs to avoid harming the league's collective economic interests. League rules or its member clubs' collective decisions may limit an individual club owner's ability to sell or relocate the club, contract with third parties in an effort to maximize the team's revenues, or take other desired action. Thus, league rules and internal agreements precluding or limiting economic competition among league clubs are not irrefutably presumed to be anticompetitive and per se illegal.

It is well settled law that the Rule of Reason, which involves a complicated case-by-case analysis, is the applicable standard for evaluating the competitive effects of collective action by professional sports league members or organizations under §1 of the Sherman Act. *American Needle, Inc. v. NFL*, 560 U.S. 183 (2010); *National Collegiate Athletic Assn. v. Board of Regents of the Univ. of Oklahoma*, 468 U.S. 85 (1984). Virtually all professional sports industry rules or agreements that allegedly violate §1 require detailed consideration of both their anticompetitive effects and procompetitive benefits to determine their net competitive consequences and effect on consumer welfare. If the restraint has predominately anticompetitive effects, it is unreasonable and illegal. Conversely, if it has predominately procompetitive effects, it is reasonable and legal. Regarding judicial application of the Rule of Reason to restraints in the professional team sports industry, focus on these questions as you read the following principal cases:

1.   Does the particular restraint reduce intrabrand (among league clubs) and/or interbrand (with other forms of entertainment) economic competition?
2.   If the restraint does so, is it a procompetitive means that promotes and is reasonably necessary to produce the league's brand of athletic competition?
3.   Even if so, is there a substantially less restrictive alternative means of achieving the league's procompetitive objectives?
4.   Because antitrust law's primary objective is to benefit consumers, also consider the restraint's net or overall effects on sports fans: that is, does it benefit or harm their interests?

The following materials analyze §1 claims by a prospective club owner denied entry into a league and by an existing club owner whose individual revenue-generating capacity has allegedly been harmed by league rules as well as antitrust claims asserted by third parties, including consumers. The range of circumstances giving rise to antitrust claims are considerable and include acquisition, ownership, and sale of franchises; franchise relocations; and league restrictions on an individual club's sale or licensing of intellectual property rights to third parties.[1]

i. Acquisition, Ownership, and Sale of a Franchise

LEVIN v. NBA

385 F. Supp. 149 (S.D.N.Y. 1974)

OWEN, District Judge.

The plaintiffs, two businessmen, in 1972 had an agreement to buy the Boston Celtics basketball team, one of the 17-member National Basketball Association.

The N.B.A., as its constitution recites, is a joint venture "organized to operate a league consisting of professional basketball teams each of which shall be operated by a member of the Association." It has been in existence since 1946. Each of its joint venturers holds a franchise to operate a team. While the teams compete vigorously on the basketball court, the joint venturers are dependent upon one another as partners in the league format to make it possible. N.B.A. operates through its Board of Governors which consists of one governor designated by each member. Action by the Board on a transfer of membership requires the affirmative vote of three-quarters of the members of the Board. [EDs. When the plaintiffs applied to become owners of the Celtics franchise, only two votes were cast favorable to their application, thirteen were opposed, and one club owner was not present.]

Plaintiffs immediately demanded and were granted a personal hearing before the Board. Following the presentation of their case a second vote was taken. It was, however, to identical effect.

There is a sharp dispute on the reason for the rejection. Plaintiffs contend that they were rejected because of their friendship and business associations with one Sam Schulman, owner of the Seattle SuperSonics, who was an anathema to the other members of the league. . . .

On the other hand, the reason given by the N.B.A. for the rejection was that the business association between the plaintiffs and Schulman violated the "conflict of interest" provision of the N.B.A. constitution. That provision reads: A member shall not exercise control, directly or indirectly, over any other member of the Association. . . . This provision is necessary, N.B.A. claims, in order that the league may enjoy public support because there is in fact, and the public

---

1. The internal governance of individual-performer sports also has given rise to §1 antitrust claims. For example, restrictions on the use of playing equipment (*Gunter Harz Sports v. United States Tennis Assn.*, 511 F. Supp. 1103 (D. Neb. 1981)) and race car tires (*Race Tires America, Inc. v. Hoosier Racing Tire Corp.*, 614 F.3d 57 (3d Cir. 2010)), player eligibility (*Toscano v. PGA Tour, Inc.*, 201 F. Supp. 2d 1106 (E.D. Cal. 2002)), and player discipline (*Blalock v. LPGA*, 359 F. Supp. 1260 (N.D. Ga. 1973)) as well as a requirement that caddies wear bibs with advertising (*Hicks v. PGA Tour Inc.*, 897 F.3d 1109 (9th Cir. 2018)) have been challenged on antitrust grounds.

believes there is, intense competition in the league framework between the teams operated by the N.B.A. members.

In any event plaintiffs, rejected, sold their rights in the Celtics elsewhere and commenced this action.

In order to survive defendants' motion for summary judgment, plaintiffs must demonstrate that the conduct complained of is a violation of the antitrust laws. While it is true that the antitrust laws apply to a professional athletic league, and that joint action by members of a league can have antitrust implications, this is not such a case. Here the plaintiffs wanted to join with those unwilling to accept them, not to compete with them, but to be partners in the operation of a sports league for plaintiffs' profit. Further, no matter which reason one credits for the rejection, it was not an anti-competitive reason. Finally, regardless of the financial impact of this rejection upon the plaintiffs, if any, the exclusion of the plaintiffs from membership in the league did not have an anticompetitive effect nor an effect upon the public interest. The Celtics continue as an operating club, and indeed are this year's champion. . . .

Since there was no exclusion of plaintiffs from competition with the alleged excluders, nor anti-competitive acts by them and no public injury occasioned thereby, the defendants' acts did not constitute a violation of the antitrust laws and defendants' motion for summary judgment is granted.

MID-SOUTH GRIZZLIES v. NFL
720 F.2d 772 (3d Cir. 1983)

GIBBONS, Circuit Judge.

. . . The suit concerns the defendants' refusal to grant the plaintiffs a football franchise. . . .

I.   BACKGROUND

In 1974 and 1975 the Grizzlies participated in the World Football League from a home team location in Memphis, Tennessee. The members of that league could be found to have been competitors of the members of the NFL in the national market for network television revenue. The World Football League disbanded, however, halfway through the 1975 football season. The NFL had no franchise at Memphis, and a home team designation for that location would not infringe upon the home territory of any NFL member. Upon the demise of the World Football League the Grizzlies applied to the NFL for admission to the league with a designated home territory at Memphis.

At meetings with the NFL Expansion Committee, and with the full NFL membership, the Grizzlies urged that it had in place at Memphis an established, functioning professional football enterprise. The application was rejected. . . .

II.   THE COMPLAINT

The Grizzlies' complaint . . . does not charge that the provisions of the NFL's Constitution and By-Laws reserving to its members franchise exclusivity for designated home territories violates the antitrust laws. Indeed, the Grizzlies sought such an exclusive franchise for themselves. Thus this case does not present any issue of possible antitrust violation from the exclusion of potential competitors in the designated exclusive home territories. . . .

. . . The complaint alleges that Memphis is a highly desirable submarket for major league professional football, that the refusal to consider it as a home territory for a franchise was made pursuant to an agreement or understanding or conspiracy among NFL members, the NFL and the Commissioner, that no valid basis for rejection of the Grizzlies was articulated or formulated by the defendants, and that the rejection amounted to an unreasonable restraint of trade, or a group boycott. One motive for that conspiracy is alleged to have been a desire to punish, intimidate and restrain plaintiffs from participation in major league professional football because they had entered into competition with NFL members by participating in the World Football League. The exclusion, so motivated, and having the effects alleged, is said to be a violation of Section 1 of the Sherman Act. . . .

IV. THE MERITS

A. SHERMAN ACT SECTION 1

. . . In this case there is no dispute about the requisite concert of action among the defendants. The defendants do deny injury to competition in any relevant market from their rejection of the Grizzlies' application. They urge that any limitations on actual or potential competition in any relevant market were insulated from antitrust scrutiny by the 1961 and 1966 statutes referred to, or, are reasonable as a matter of law. They also urge that as a matter of law there was no competition among league members or between league members and nonmembers in other markets to which the Grizzlies point.

The Grizzlies identify as the relevant product market major-league professional football, and as the relevant geographic market the United States. The trial court found these markets to be relevant. The court observed as well that "[t]here is no doubt that the NFL currently has a monopoly in the United States in major league football." The Grizzlies pose as the question on this appeal "whether it can be said as a matter of law that defendants neither acquired nor maintained monopoly power over any relevant market in an unlawful manner."

As to the acquisition of dominant position and monopoly power, the facts are undisputed. Long before the Grizzlies and the World Football League came into existence, Congress authorized the merger of the two major football leagues extant in 1966, and granted to the merged league the power to pool television revenues. That congressional decision conferred on the NFL the market power which it holds in the market for professional football. Congress could not have been unaware that necessary effect of the television revenue sharing scheme which it approved for the NFL would be that all members of that league would be strengthened in their ability to bid for the best available playing and coaching personnel, to the potential disadvantage of new entrants. . . .

But, the Grizzlies urge, the 1966 statute did not confer the authority to abuse the market power, even though it may have authorized its acquisition. Rather, the merger was approved only "if such agreement increases rather than decreases the number of professional clubs so operating." 15 U.S.C. § 1291. Paraphrasing their argument, it is the Grizzlies' contention that the statute which authorized NFL acquisition of monopoly power in the professional football market required not only that the league members refrain from abusing that power against potential competitors, but that it take affirmative steps to share its market power with others.

. . . The only basis on which the Grizzlies seek recovery . . . is that they were denied admission to the monopoly, and thus were deprived of a share of the NFL's monopoly power. No claim is made that abuse of NFL market power led to the demise of the World Football League, and no issue is before us concerning activities of the NFL, since that demise, which may have inhibited the development of competition by another football league. The NFL structure as a barrier to entry to the market by another football league is relevant in this case only to the extent that it bears on the obligation to permit entry to the NFL.

There are two possible sources of any NFL obligation to permit entry to its shared market power; the 1966 statute, and the Sherman Act. Each will be considered separately.

The provision in the 1966 statute that "such agreement increases rather than decreases the number of professional football clubs so operating" cannot reasonably be construed as addressing competition, the preservation of which is the object of the Sherman Act. The basic thrust of the 1966 statute is to authorize an arrangement which eliminated competition among the only two viable competitors then in the professional football market. The reference to an increase in the number of professional football teams "so operating" is a reference to professional teams operating under the antitrust exemption for television revenue sharing provided in the 1961 statute. Thus what the 1966 statute suggests is that more home team territories would be added, not to increase competition in professional football, but to permit geographic enlargement of the NFL's market power. . . .

Since the 1966 statute is not directed at preservation of competition in the market for professional football, and cannot be construed as conferring any economic benefit on the class to which the Grizzlies belong, we conclude that it does not oblige the NFL to permit entry by any particular applicant to the NFL shared market power.

We turn, therefore, to the Sherman Act. As noted above, Sherman Act liability requires an injury to competition. In this case the competition inquiry is a narrow one, because the Grizzlies are not seeking recovery as potential competitors *outside* the NFL. They identify as the antitrust violation the league's negative vote on their application for membership. . . .

The NFL's stated reasons for rejecting the Grizzlies' application included scheduling difficulties created by the presence of an odd number of teams, a long-running collective bargaining dispute with league players, several pending antitrust lawsuits, and league concern over legislation prohibiting television blackouts in home team territories, all of which allegedly made consideration of expansion unpropitious. The Grizzlies contend that there are material issues of disputed fact as to the accuracy of these reasons. They contend that at trial they could prove that the motivation for their rejection was to punish them for having attempted in the past to compete with the NFL in the World Football League, or to reserve the Memphis location for friends of present league team owners.

Assuming, without deciding, that the summary judgment record presents disputed fact issues with respect to the actual motivation of the NFL members, those disputed facts are not material, under Section 1 of the Sherman Act, if the action complained of produced no injury to competition.

As to competition with NFL members in the professional football market, including the market for sale of television rights, the exclusion was patently pro-competitive, since it left the Memphis area, with a large stadium and a significant metropolitan area population, available as a site for another league's franchise, and it left the Grizzlies' organization as a potential competitor in such a league. If there was any injury to competition, actual or potential, therefore, it must have been to intra-league competition. . . .

. . . The Grizzlies do not challenge the legality of the NFL's revenue sharing arrangements, and seek to participate in them. The Grizzlies emphasize that there nevertheless remains a not insignificant amount of intra-league non-athletic competition. We need not, in order to affirm the summary judgment, accept entirely the NFL's position that there is no intra-league competition. Conceivably within certain geographic submarkets two league members compete with one another for ticket buyers, for local broadcast revenue, and for sale of the concession items like food and beverages and team paraphernalia. Thus rejection of a franchise application in the New York metropolitan area, for example, might require a different antitrust analysis than is suggested by this record. But the Grizzlies were obliged, when faced with the NFL denial of the existence of competition among NFL members and a potential franchisee at Memphis, to show some more than minimal level of potential competition, in the product markets in which league members might compete. They made no such showing. The record establishes that the NFL franchise nearest to Memphis is at St. Louis, Mo., over 280 miles away. There is no record evidence that professional football teams located in Memphis and in St. Louis would compete for the same ticket purchasers, for the same local broadcast outlets, in the sale of team paraphernalia, or in any other manner. . . .

Since on the record before us the Grizzlies have shown no actual or potential injury to competition resulting from the rejection of their application for an NFL franchise, they cannot succeed on their section 1 Sherman Act claim. . . .

NOTES AND QUESTIONS

1. *Antitrust Analysis of League Restrictions on Purchase and Sale of Clubs.* The *Levin* court held that a league's rejection of a proposed sale of an existing team does not harm *intrabrand* economic competition among league clubs. See also *Fishman v. Estate of Wirtz*, 807 F.2d 520, 542-544 (7th Cir. 1986) (a league's mere selection of one prospective franchise owner over another does not have anticompetitive effects for purposes of antitrust law). Why not?

   Other courts have held that a league's denial of a prospective owner's bid to purchase a club may have an anticompetitive effect on the market for the purchase and sale of its clubs. In *Piazza v. Major League Baseball*, 831 F. Supp. 420 (E.D. Pa. 1993), the court refused to dismiss the plaintiffs' §1 claim alleging that MLB club owners conspired to prevent them from buying the San Francisco Giants. The plaintiffs' complaint alleged injury to competition in the market for ownership of major league professional baseball teams, particularly the market for ownership of the Giants club. They averred that they were competing with other potential bidders to acquire ownership of the Giants franchise and that defendants directly and substantially interfered with competition in this market. Distinguishing *Levin* on the ground that it did not involve an alleged reduction of competition among bidders for an existing franchise, the court ruled that the plaintiffs sufficiently alleged an injury to competition in a relevant product market.

One court has suggested that a league rule banning a club owner's sale of a minority interest in a franchise to the public may violate the antitrust laws. In *Sullivan v. National Football League*, 34 F.3d 1091 (1st Cir. 1994), the First Circuit held that an NFL policy prohibiting the sale of an ownership interest in a league club through a public stock offering raises a fact question regarding whether it is anticompetitive. The former owner of the New England Patriots franchise claimed he was precluded from selling 49 percent of his team to the public and thereby forced to sell the club at a depressed price to private buyers. He asserted that, absent the NFL's policy, he would have been able to retain a majority interest in the Patriots and earn future profits from continued ownership of the club.

Sullivan observed that the league's public ownership policy "compromises the entire process by which competition for club ownership occurs," rather than merely preventing transfers of club ownership, which do not adversely affect competition. *Id.* at 1099. The jury found the relevant market to be the "nationwide market for the sale and purchase of ownership interests in the National Football League member clubs, in general, and in the New England Patriots, in particular." *Id.* at 1097. The court rejected the NFL's contention that, as a matter of law, its clubs do not compete against each other for the sale of their ownership interests and ruled that whether NFL teams are economic competitors in this market is a fact question. The court found sufficient evidence to support the jury's determination that the NFL's policy against public ownership of franchises is anticompetitive because it interferes with consumer demand for ownership interests in NFL teams and prevents ownership by a class of persons that may be more efficient operators of teams than private owners.

On the other hand, the First Circuit recognized that the NFL's public ownership policy has a legitimate procompetitive objective. It contributes to the league's ability to effectively function by preventing a potential detrimental conflict of interest between team shareholders' short-term dividend interests and the league's long-term interest in maintaining each club's financial integrity and competitiveness. The court observed, however, that modifying the NFL's policy to permit a club's sale of minority, nonvoting shares of team stock to the public with limits on the size of an individual's holdings might accomplish this objective in a substantially less restrictive manner. It ultimately reversed the jury's verdict in the plaintiff's favor, because erroneous jury instructions had been given, and remanded the case for a new trial. The retrial of the case resulted in a hung jury, and the parties settled before it was tried for the third time.If the rejection of a prospective club owner is based on adequate evidence of its lack of the minimally necessary financial capital, character and fitness, or business skills to successfully operate a league franchise, it is a procompetitive means of furthering the league's ability to compete against other forms of entertainment. *National Basketball Assn. v. Minnesota Professional Basketball Limited Partnership*, 56 F.3d 866 (8th Cir. 1995) (affirming a preliminary injunction against the sale of an NBA club without league approval and a denial of the prospective owner based on inadequate financial resources).Is antitrust law the best means of resolving disputes regarding the purchase and sale of professional sports franchises? Is consumer welfare furthered by doing so?

2. *Antitrust Analysis of Restrictions on League Entry.* Why did the Third Circuit reject the Grizzlies' claim that the denial of its application for an NFL expansion club reduced *intrabrand* economic competition among NFL clubs? Given the fact that the NFL's Tennessee Titans currently play in Nashville, would the NFL's refusal to place a team in Memphis today be an antitrust violation? See generally *City of Oakland v. Oakland Raiders*, 2019 WL 3344624 (N.D. Cal.) at *10 (observing that "neither Oakland's complaint nor its opposition brief address what sort of structure Oakland believes would be permissible if the current limitation on the number of teams is not—do the antitrust laws require the NFL to admit any team interested in joining? If not, what number would be an allowable limit, and would Oakland have fared differently if the limit had been set at that number?"); Stephen F. Ross, *Antitrust Options to Redress Anticompetitive Restraints and Monopolistic Practices by Professional Sports Leagues*, 52 Case W. Res. L. Rev. 133, 150-151 (2001) (noting "considerable conceptual and remedial problems with any finding that a sports league's refusal to expand to permit a *particular* franchise to enter its joint venture constitutes an unreasonable restraint of trade").

The Memphis Grizzlies did not allege the NFL's conduct caused the demise of the WFL or inhibited the development of a rival professional football league, which would give rise to potential §2 monopolization and/or attempted monopolization claims that are discussed *infra*. Thus, the NFL's denial of the Grizzlies' application for an expansion franchise did not reduce competition in the *interbrand* market (i.e., among competing professional football leagues or other forms of consumer entertainment), which the Third Circuit characterized as "patently procompetitive" rather than anticompetitive. What was the court's rationale for this conclusion, and does it further the welfare of NFL fans? See Thomas A. Piraino, Jr., *The Antitrust Rationale for the Expansion of Professional Sports Leagues*, 57 Ohio St. L.J. 1677, 1677-1678 (1996) (arguing that "owners refusal to expand their leagues to meet demand for additional franchises . . . has the effect of reducing the importance of consumer preference in setting price and output [and] is not consistent with this fundamental goal of antitrust law").

3. *League Contraction Issues.* After the conclusion of the 2001 season and expiration of the collective bargaining agreement with the MLB Players Association, MLB announced its intention to contract two teams prior to the 2002 season. However, after entering into a new collective bargaining agreement, MLB ultimately agreed not to contract any teams at least through the 2006 season. Based on *Memphis Grizzlies,* under what circumstances (if any) would a professional sports league's decision to contract one or more of its clubs potentially violate the antitrust laws?

In *Metropolitan Sports Facilities Comm'n v. Minnesota Twins Partnership*, 638 N.W.2d 214, 224 (Minn. Ct. App. 2002), the Minnesota court of appeals affirmed the trial court's injunction requiring the Minnesota Twins to play its 2002 home games in the Metrodome, and prohibiting MLB from interfering with this contractual obligation by eliminating the Twins club. It concluded that money damages are inadequate to compensate a public stadium authority for the breach of a playing facility lease with an MLB club:

> [L]egal commentators have recognized that money damages are not sufficient to compensate for the harm suffered by a community for the loss of a professional sports team." *Id.* See, e.g., Matthew J. Mitten and Bruce

> W. Burton, *Professional Sports Franchise Relocations From Private Law Public Law Perspectives: Balancing Marketplace Competition, League Autonomy, and the Need for Level Playing Field,* 56 Md. L. Rev. 57, 70-71 (1997). According to these commentators, "Merely allowing a city to recover contract damages for the premature loss of a team does not provide adequate compensation for the city's lost benefit of the bargain in providing the public, financial inducements necessary to attract or retain a sports franchise. . . . The city's real benefits of the bargain are the highly valued, intangible benefits. . . . The value of such benefits is virtually impossible to quantify and, therefore, is not recoverable for a team owner's breach of contract.

The court concluded that "the use agreement at issue here is not a typical commercial lease" because "[T]he benefit of the bargain that the commission received was the Twins promise to play their home games at the Metrodome for the duration of their lease. Indeed, the stated purpose for building and operating the stadium was to attract major league sport franchises to play at the stadium for the enjoyment of fans." *Id.* at 222-223.

4. *Closed v. Open Professional Sports Leagues.* North American major professional leagues are closed, which means the requisite majority of its existing clubs (usually three-fourths) must agree to the entry of new clubs, thereby providing each league with a monopoly over its particular sport at the major league level of play. Courts have not been receptive to claims that a closed league structure violates antitrust law. *Warnock v. NFL,* 356 F. Supp. 2d 535 (W.D. Pa. 2005), *aff'd,* 154 Fed. Appx. 291 (3d Cir. 2005), *cert. denied,* 547 U.S. 1021 (2006) (a Pittsburgh municipal taxpayer lacks standing to sue the NFL and its member clubs for allegedly violating antitrust law by acting in concert to force the league's cities, including Pittsburgh, to build new football stadiums). *Hamilton County Bd. of County Comm'rs v. NFL,* 491 F.3d 310 (6th Cir. 2007) (dismissing a county's antitrust claim against the NFL after it agreed to highly favorable lease terms to prevent the Bengals club from relocating because its officials knew or should have known the NFL was a monopoly during lease negotiations); *State v. Milwaukee Braves, Inc.,* 144 N.W.2d 1 (Wis. 1966) (based on MLB's antitrust immunity, the Wisconsin Supreme Court reversed a trial court ruling that the National League and its member clubs violated state antitrust law by allowing the Milwaukee Braves to move to Atlanta and by refusing to provide a replacement team in Milwaukee).

By comparison, professional sports leagues in other parts of the world, particularly Europe, generally are open: "membership in the league is contingent on success. Professional sports leagues in soccer, rugby, basketball, and cricket are organized in ascending tiers (generally called divisions), and every year the teams with the worst record are relegated to a lower division and replaced by the most successful teams from that lower division." Stephen F. Ross and Stephan Szymanski, *Open Competition in League Sports,* 2002 Wis. L. Rev. 625, 626. Consider the pros and cons of their following proposal:

> A system of promotion and relegation places a significant limit on the monopoly power of sports leagues. The system preserves the integrity of the league itself and indeed allows leagues to legitimately expand or contract to most effectively market the product. . . . Promotion and relegation is in fact an ideal structure for surgical intervention to promote entry, since it involves replacing the least efficient incumbent (in terms of wins) with the most efficient entrant.

> Moreover, entry is only conditional on continuing success, so that a relegated incumbent has an opportunity to recapture its position the following season.

Id. at 629.

5. *Classification of Professional Sports Leagues.* In *North American Soccer League LLC v. United States Soccer Federation, Inc.*, 883 F.3d 32 (2d Cir. 2018), the Second Circuit upheld the authority of the United States Soccer Federation (USSF), the governing body for soccer in the United States and Canada, to promulgate and apply its Professional League Standards (Standards), which establish requirements for professional soccer leagues seeking Division I, II, or III designation (which occurs annually). Major League Soccer (MLS) has been designated as the only Division I men's soccer league since its 1995 inception, the North American Soccer League (NASL) was the only Division II league from 2011 to 2017, and the United Soccer Leagues, LLC (USL) historically has been the only Division III league. NASL asserted that USSF promulgated and applied its Standards pursuant to a conspiracy with its membership and others (including MLS) to preclude NASL and other leagues from competing with MLS in the Division I men's soccer market. Because the NASL failed to prove "a clear likelihood of its success on the merits" of its antitrust claim, the Second Circuit affirmed the lower court's denial of its requested preliminary injunction prohibiting USSF from separating professional soccer leagues into three divisions and ordering the NASL's designation as a Division II men's professional soccer for the 2018 season. It held that USSF did not conspire to restrain competition among U.S. and Canadian men's professional soccer leagues and that its Standards and their application to NASL does not violate the full rule of reason. Although USSF has market power to prevent competition among soccer leagues through the application of its Standards, the Second Circuit determined that "in the context of a soccer industry historically prone to collapse," the Standards' requirements (e.g., minimum-team count, time zones, market size, stadium capacity, and financial viability) have the countervailing procompetitive effects of generating fan interest and promoting league quality and stability without any "viable less restrictive alternatives."

ii.   *Franchise Relocation*

Pursuant to its franchise agreement with the league, a club owner generally has the exclusive right to operate its team in a particular city, although large markets such as New York City, Los Angeles, and Chicago may have two league clubs. For economic reasons, a club may want to relocate the team to another city to increase its local revenues and/or to play in a new facility. See Steve Rushin, *Moving Violations: Relocation Saga Is a Tale of More Than Two Cities*, Sports Illustrated, available at http://www.si.com/nfl/2016/01/21/relocation-nfl-los-angeles-rams-raiders-chargers (providing a history of North American major league club relocations). For example, in 2016, the St. Louis Rams relocated back to the Los Angeles metropolitan area (specifically, Inglewood), where its club owner will build a $1.86 billion stadium, which Forbes estimates will triple the club's value to $3 billion. The Chargers, which moved from San Diego, will share the stadium. Although only 2 of the 18 NFL clubs in existence during the league's 1922 formation are in same city (the Chicago Bears and the Green

Bay Packers), other sports' clubs such as the Cincinnati Reds (the oldest major league professional sports franchise in the U.S.) and the NHL's Original 6 clubs (the Boston Bruins, Chicago Black Hawks, Detroit Red Wings, Montreal Canadians, New York Rangers, and Toronto Maple Leafs) are in their original host cities.

In recent years, local communities, including mid-major cities such as Nashville, Memphis, Charlotte, and Oklahoma City as well as Seattle have provided multimillion-dollar public subsidies for playing facilities to attract major league professional sports franchises. Many other communities have made similar investments of public funds to keep their local sports franchises and prevent them from relocating elsewhere. Courts generally rule that these arrangements are a legitimate use of state and local tax dollars to promote the public good, although these significant public expenditures combined with favorable lease terms provide substantial economic benefits to privately owned professional sports clubs. See, e.g., *Libertarian Party of Wis. v. State*, 546 N.W.2d 424, 438 (Wis. 1996) (bonds issued by a local professional baseball park district are "obligations of . . . a revenue-producing enterprise that serves a public purpose"); *Lifteau v. Metropolitan Sports Facilities Comm'n*, 270 N.W.2d 749 (Minn. 1978) (construction of a publicly owned sports facility for use by professional sports teams has a public purpose for which public funds may be expended).

Depending on the specific circumstances, a sports league's refusal to permit one of its clubs to relocate to another city may violate antitrust law. Former Oakland Raiders owner Al Davis' antitrust litigation against the NFL provides an example of a rare successful case arising out of the league's initial rejection of his 1980 request to move the Raiders from Oakland to Los Angeles.

LOS ANGELES MEMORIAL COLISEUM COMMISSION v. NFL (RAIDERS I)

726 F.2d 1381 (9th Cir.), *cert. denied*, 469 U.S. 990 (1984)

ANDERSON, Circuit Judge:

These appeals involve the hotly contested move by the Oakland Raiders, Ltd. professional football team from Oakland, California, to Los Angeles, California. . . .

I. FACTS

In 1978, the owner of the Los Angeles Rams, the late Carroll Rosenbloom, decided to locate his team in a new stadium, the "Big A," in Anaheim, California. That left the Los Angeles Coliseum without a major tenant. Officials of the Coliseum then began the search for a new National Football League occupant. They inquired of the League Commissioner, Pete Rozelle, whether an expansion franchise might be located there but were told that at the time it was not possible. They also negotiated with existing teams in the hope that one might leave its home and move to Los Angeles. . . .

[EDS. The L.A. Coliseum ran into a major obstacle in its attempts to convince a team to move because it was located in the home territory of the Rams franchise. The obstacle was Rule 4.3 of Article IV of the NFL Constitution, which as amended, stated, "The League shall have exclusive control of the exhibition of football games by member clubs within the home territory of each member. No member club shall have the right to transfer its franchise or playing site to a different city, either within or outside its home territory, without prior approval by the affirmative vote of three-fourths of the existing member clubs of the League."

After the Oakland Raiders' lease with the Oakland Coliseum expired in 1978, Al Davis, the club's managing general partner, and L.A. Coliseum officials signed a March 1, 1980, "memorandum of agreement" outlining the terms of the Raiders' proposed relocation to Los Angeles. At an NFL meeting on March 3, 1980, Davis announced his intentions. Over Davis's objection that Rule 4.3 was illegal under the antitrust laws, the NFL teams voted 22-0 against the move on March 10, 1980, with five teams abstaining. That vote did not meet Rule 4.3's requirement of three-quarters approval.

An antitrust action against the NFL and its member clubs brought by the Raiders in Los Angeles federal court resulted in a verdict in favor of the Raiders, and the jury awarded the Raiders $11.55 million in damages, which was automatically trebled as a prevailing party in an antitrust suit.]

B. RULE OF REASON

. . . In a quite general sense, the case presents the competing considerations of whether a group of businessmen can enforce an agreement with one of their co-contractors to the detriment of that co-contractor's right to do business where he pleases. More specifically, this lawsuit requires us to engage in the difficult task of analyzing the negative and positive effects of a business practice in an industry which does not readily fit into the antitrust context. Section 1 of the Sherman Act was designed to prevent agreements among competitors which eliminate or reduce competition and thereby harm consumers. Yet, as we discussed in the context of the single entity issue, the NFL teams are not true competitors, nor can they be.

The NFL's structure has both horizontal and vertical attributes. On the one hand, it can be viewed simply as an organization of 28 competitors, an example of a simple horizontal arrangement. On the other, and to the extent the NFL can be considered an entity separate from the team owners, a vertical relationship is disclosed. In this sense the owners are distributors of the NFL product, each with its own territorial division. In this context it is clear that the owners have a legitimate interest in protecting the integrity of the League itself. Collective action in areas such as League divisions, scheduling and rules must be allowed, as should other activity that aids in producing the most marketable product attainable. Nevertheless, legitimate collective action should not be construed to allow the owners to extract excess profits. In such a situation the owners would be acting as a classic cartel. Agreements among competitors, i.e., cartels, to fix prices or divide market territories are presumed illegal under § 1 because they give competitors the ability to charge unreasonable and arbitrary prices instead of setting prices by virtue of free market forces.

On its face, Rule 4.3 divides markets among the 28 teams, a practice presumed illegal, but, as we have noted, the unique structure of the NFL precludes application of the per se rule. Instead, we must examine Rule 4.3 to determine whether it reasonably serves the legitimate collective concerns of the owners or instead permits them to reap excess profits at the expense of the consuming public.

1. Relevant Market

The NFL contends it is entitled to judgment because plaintiffs failed to prove an adverse impact on competition in a relevant market. . . .

In the antitrust context, the relevant market has two components: the product market and the geographic market. Product market definition involves the process of describing those groups of producers which, because of the similarity of their products, have the ability—actual or potential—to take significant amounts of business away from each other. A market definition must look at all relevant sources of supply, either actual rivals or eager potential entrants to the market. . . .

. . . The Raiders attempted to prove the relevant market consists of NFL football (the product market) in the Southern California area (the geographic market). The NFL argues it competes with all forms of entertainment within the United States, not just Southern California. . . .

That NFL football has limited substitutes from a consumer standpoint is seen from evidence that the Oakland Coliseum sold out for 10 consecutive years despite having some of the highest ticket prices in the League. A similar conclusion can be drawn from the extraordinary number of television viewers—over 100 million people—that watched the 1982 Super Bowl, the ultimate NFL product. NFL football's importance to the television networks is evidenced by the approximately $2 billion they agreed to pay the League for the right to televise the games from 1982-1986. . . .

To some extent, the NFL itself narrowly defined the relevant market by emphasizing that NFL football is a unique product which can be produced only through the joint efforts of the 28 teams. Don Shula, coach of the Miami Dolphins, underscored this point when he stated that NFL football has a different set of fans than college football.

The evidence from which the jury could have found a narrow pro football product market was balanced, however, with other evidence which tended to show the NFL competes in the first instance with other professional sports, especially those with seasons that overlap with the NFL's. On a broader level, witnesses such as Pete Rozelle and Georgia Frontierre (owner of the L.A. Rams) testified that NFL football competes with other television offerings for network business, as well as other local entertainment for attendance at the games.

In terms of the relevant geographic market, witnesses testified, in particular Al Davis, that NFL teams compete with one another off the field for fan support in those areas where teams operate in close proximity such as New York City-New Jersey, Washington, D.C.-Baltimore, and formerly San Francisco-Oakland. Davis, of course, had firsthand knowledge of this when his team was located in Oakland. Also, the San Francisco Forty-Niners and the New York Giants were paid $18 million because of the potential for harm from competing with the Oakland Raiders and the New York Jets, respectively, once those teams joined the NFL as a result of the merger with the American Football League. Al Davis also testified at length regarding the potential for competition for fan support between the Raiders and the Los Angeles Rams once his team relocated in Los Angeles. . . .

. . . We find that this evidence taken as a whole provided the jury with an adequate basis on which to judge the reasonableness of Rule 4.3 both as it affected competition among NFL teams and among stadia. . . .

D. Antitrust Law Limits on League Governance and Rules

2.   *The History and Purpose of Rule 4.3*

The NFL has awarded franchises exclusive territories since the 1930s. In the early days of professional football, numerous franchises failed and many changed location in the hope of achieving economic success. League members saw exclusive territories as a means to aid stability, ensuring the owner who was attempting to establish an NFL team in a particular city that another would not move into the same area, potentially ruining them both.

Rule 4.3 is the result of that concern. Prior to its amendment in 1978, it required unanimous League approval for a move into another team's home territory. That, of course, gave each owner an exclusive territory and he could vote against a move into his territory solely because he was afraid the competition might reduce his revenue. Notably, however, the League constitution required only three-quarters approval for all other moves. The 1978 amendment removed the double-standard, and currently three-quarters approval is required for all moves.

That the purpose of Rule 4.3 was to restrain competition among the 28 teams may seem obvious and it is not surprising the NFL admitted as much at trial. It instead argues that Rule 4.3 serves a variety of legitimate League needs, including ensuring franchise stability. We must keep in mind, however, that the Supreme Court has long rejected the notion that "ruinous competition" can be a defense to a restraint of trade. . . .

3.   *Ancillary Restraints and the Reasonableness of Rule 4.3*

. . . We assume, with no reason to doubt, that the agreement creating the NFL is valid and the territorial divisions therein are ancillary to its main purpose of producing NFL football. The ancillary restraint must then be tested under the rule of reason, *id.*, the relevance of ancillarity being it "increases the probability that the restraint will be found reasonable." As we have already noted, the rule of reason inquiry requires us to consider the harms and benefits to competition caused by the restraint and whether the putative benefits can be achieved by less restrictive means.

The competitive harms of Rule 4.3 are plain. Exclusive territories insulate each team from competition within the NFL market, in essence allowing them to set monopoly prices to the detriment of the consuming public. . . . The harm from Rule 4.3 is especially acute in this case because it prevents a move by a team into another existing team's market. If the transfer is upheld, direct competition between the Rams and Raiders would presumably ensue to the benefit of all who consume the NFL product in the Los Angeles area.

The NFL argues, however, that territorial allocations are *inherent* in an agreement among joint venturers to produce a product. This inherent nature, the NFL asserts, flows from the need to protect each joint venturer in the "legitimate fruits of the contract, or to protect him from the dangers of an unjust use of those fruits by the other party." We agree that the nature of NFL football requires some territorial restrictions in order both to encourage participation in the venture and to secure each venturer the legitimate fruits of that participation.

Rule 4.3 aids the League, the NFL claims, in determining its overall geographical scope, regional balance and coverage of major and minor markets. Exclusive territories aid new franchises in achieving financial stability, which protects the large initial investment an owner must make to start up a football team. Stability arguably helps ensure no one team has an undue advantage on the field. Territories foster fan loyalty which in turn promotes traditional rivalries between teams, each contributing to attendance at games and television viewing.

Joint marketing decisions are surely legitimate because of the importance of television. [15 U.S.C. §1291] grants the NFL an exemption from antitrust liability, if any, that might arise out of its collective negotiation of television rights with the networks. To effectuate this right, the League must be allowed to have some control over the placement of teams to ensure NFL football is popular in a diverse group of markets.

Last, there is some legitimacy to the NFL's argument that it has an interest in preventing transfers from areas before local governments, which have made a substantial investment in stadia and other facilities, can recover their expenditures. In such a situation, local confidence in the NFL is eroded, possibly resulting in a decline in interest. All these factors considered, we nevertheless are not persuaded the jury should have concluded that Rule 4.3 is a reasonable restraint of trade. The same goals can be achieved in a variety of ways which are less harmful to competition.

As noted by Justice Rehnquist, a factor in determining the reasonableness of an ancillary restraint is the "possibility of less restrictive alternatives" which could serve the same purpose. Here, the district court correctly instructed the jury to take into account the existence of less restrictive alternatives when determining the reasonableness of Rule 4.3's territorial restraint. . . .

The NFL argues that the requirement of Rule 4.3 that three-quarters of the owners approve a franchise move is reasonable because it deters unwise team transfers. While the rule does indeed protect an owner's investment in a football franchise, no standards or durational limits are incorporated into the voting requirement to make sure that concern is satisfied. Nor are factors such as fan loyalty and team rivalries necessarily considered.

The NFL claims that its marketing and other objectives are indirectly accounted for in the voting process because the team owners vote to maximize their profits. Since the owners are guided by the desire to increase profits, they will necessarily make reasonable decisions, the NFL asserts, on such issues of whether the new location can support two teams, whether marketing needs will be adversely affected, etc. Under the present Rule 4.3, however, an owner need muster only seven friendly votes to prevent three-quarters approval for the sole reason of preventing another team from entering its market, regardless of whether the market could sustain two franchises. A basic premise of the Sherman Act is that regulation of private profit is best left to the marketplace rather than private agreement. The present case is in fact a good example of how the market itself will deter unwise moves, since a team will not lightly give up an established base of support to confront another team in its home market.

The NFL's professed interest in ensuring that cities and other local governments secure a return on their investment in stadia is undercut in two ways. First, the local governments ought to be able to protect their investment through the leases they negotiate with the teams for the use of their stadia. Second, the NFL's interest on this point may not be as important as it would have us believe because the League has in the past allowed teams to threaten a transfer to another location in order to give the team leverage in lease negotiations.

Finally, the NFL made no showing that the transfer of the Raiders to Los Angeles would have any harmful effect on the League. Los Angeles is a market large enough for the successful operation of two teams, there would be no scheduling difficulties, facilities at the L.A. Coliseum are more than adequate, and no loss of future television revenue was foreseen. Also, the NFL offered no evidence that its interest in maintaining regional balance would be adversely affected by a move of a northern California team to southern California.

It is true, as the NFL claims, that the antitrust laws are primarily concerned with the promotion of *interbrand* competition. . . . To the extent the NFL is a product which competes with other forms of entertainment, including other sports, its rules governing territorial division can be said to promote interbrand competition. Under this analysis, the territorial allocations most directly suppress intrabrand, that is, NFL team versus NFL team, competition. A more direct impact on intrabrand competition does not mean, however, the restraint is reasonable. The finder of fact must still balance the gain to interbrand competition against the loss of intrabrand competition. Here, the jury could have found that the rules restricting team movement do not sufficiently promote interbrand competition to justify the negative impact on intrabrand competition.

To withstand antitrust scrutiny, restrictions on team movement should be more closely tailored to serve the needs inherent in producing the NFL "product" and competing with other forms of entertainment. An express recognition and consideration of those objective factors espoused by the NFL as important, such as population, economic projections, facilities, regional balance, etc., would be well advised. *See* L. Kurlantzick, *Thoughts on Professional Sports and the Antitrust Laws*, 15 Conn. L.R. 183, 206 (1983). Fan loyalty and location continuity could also be considered. *Id.* at 206-207. Al Davis in fact testified that in 1978 he proposed that the League adopt a set of objective guidelines to govern team relocation rather than continuing to utilize a subjective voting procedure.

Some sort of procedural mechanism to ensure consideration of all the above factors may also be necessary, including an opportunity for the team proposing the move to present its case. . . . In the present case, for example, testimony indicated that some owners, as well as Commissioner Rozelle, dislike Al Davis and consider him a maverick. Their vote against the Raiders' move could have been motivated by animosity rather than business judgment.

Substantial evidence existed for the jury to find the restraint imposed by Rule 4.3 was not reasonably necessary to the production and sale of the NFL product. Therefore, the NFL is not entitled to judgment notwithstanding the verdict. . . .

V. CONCLUSION

The NFL is an unique business organization to which it is difficult to apply antitrust rules which were developed in the context of arrangements between actual competitors. . . .

We believe antitrust principles are sufficiently flexible to account for the NFL's structure. To the extent the NFL finds the law inadequate, it must look to Congress for relief.

The judgment finding the NFL liable to . . . the Raiders, and enjoining the NFL from preventing the Raiders from relocating in Los Angeles is Affirmed.

NOTES AND QUESTIONS

1. *Determination of Anticompetitive Effect.* Why was the NFL's refusal to allow the Raiders to move to Los Angeles anticompetitive? Note that the Raiders' proposed 1980 relocation to Los Angeles would result in a shared market with

the Rams, while leaving the San Francisco Forty-Niners as the only NFL club in the Bay area. How do you accurately measure the net effect on *intrabrand competition* as a result of an increased number of NFL teams in Los Angeles with a corresponding reduction of NFL clubs in the Bay area?

2. *League Procompetitive Justifications for Territorial Restrictions.* The NFL argued that its rules concerning franchise relocation are necessary to promote *interbrand* competition with other forms of entertainment, which was based on Supreme Court precedent holding that preserving interbrand competition among sellers of different brands of competing products is the primary objective of antitrust law. See *Continental TV, Inc. v. GTE Sylvania, Inc.,* 433 U.S. 36 (1977) (a non-sports case holding that vertical territorial restrictions are to be analyzed under the rule of reason because of their economic potential for facilitating interbrand competition). Which specific justifications did *Raiders I* recognize as procompetitive?

3. *Less Restrictive Alternative Analysis. Raiders I* held that "restrictions on team movement should be more closely tailored to serve the needs inherent in producing the NFL 'product' and competing with other forms of entertainment." What would you advise the NFL to do in response to the court's admonition? Does judicial and jury consideration of post-hoc less restrictive alternatives to achieve a league's procompetitive objectives unduly interfere with the league's internal governance?

4. *Calculation of Damages and Offset.* In *Los Angeles Memorial Coliseum Comm'n v. National Football League (Raiders II),* 791 F.2d 1356 (9th Cir. 1986), the Ninth Circuit affirmed the jury's finding that the Raiders' gross lost profits from the two-year delay in moving to Los Angeles as a result of the NFL's vote against this move amounted to $11,554,382. Because the NFL's relocation rule is not a per se illegal rule and was invalid only as applied to the Raiders' proposed move to Los Angeles, the club could recover only those damages caused by the NFL's antitrust violation. The court initially observed that, prior to 1980, when the Raiders sought to relocate to Los Angeles, the NFL as a whole owned the right to expand into the Los Angeles area and the corresponding value of this expansion opportunity. When the Raiders subsequently moved into this market without league approval, the club appropriated this expansion value for itself, which increased its value by approximately $25 million. Its move out of Oakland created a potential expansion opportunity for the NFL, but the Los Angeles market was a significantly more lucrative venue. Therefore, "the accumulated value of that business opportunity is not something to which the Raiders became entitled as a result of the liability verdict," and this "excess value should have been offset against the Raiders' lost profits from the two years they were precluded from moving to Los Angeles . . . less the value of the 'Oakland opportunity' that was returned to the NFL." *Id.* at 1372-1373. "As a result, the injunction permitting the Raiders to play NFL football in Los Angeles provided them with a windfall benefit beyond the scope of the antitrust verdict." *Id.* at 1372. Is *Raiders II* consistent with *Raiders I*?

5. *Post-*Raiders *Antitrust Litigation by League Clubs.* In *National Basketball Assn. v. SDC Basketball Club, Inc.,* 815 F.2d 562, 567 (9th Cir. 1987), the Ninth Circuit held that league rules regarding franchise relocation, including requiring a club to seek league approval before moving, are not per se illegal; rather "rule of reason analysis governed a professional sports league's efforts to restrict franchise movement." The court explained that "objective

factors and procedures . . . are 'well advised,' and might be sufficient to demonstrate procompetitive purposes that would save the restriction from the rule of reason, [t]hey are not, however, necessary conditions to the legality of franchise relocation rules." *Id.* at 568. See also *In re Dewey Ranch Hockey, LLC*, 414 B.R. 577 (D. Ariz. 2009) (a bankruptcy court rejects the attempt by a prospective purchaser of the Phoenix Coyotes NHL club to use the federal bankruptcy laws to avoid required NHL approval to purchase and relocate the club to Hamilton, Ontario). What advice would you give to a league commissioner and its clubs regarding the antitrust validity of franchise relocation rules under current law?

6. *What Laws Protect the Community's Interest in Its Local Sports Teams?* The relocation of professional sports franchises causes great upset among the local populace and has spawned litigation against club owners by their respective host cities, states, or local governing bodies. Such litigation is motivated by the potential loss of economic benefits to a city and its local businesses, outstanding bond indebtedness to finance the departing club's playing facility, and wounded community pride resulting from the loss of a major league professional sports franchise. These lawsuits generally have sought to prevent the loss of the local team, or to at least prevent it from moving before its stadium lease expires. See generally Matthew J. Mitten and Bruce W. Burton, *Professional Sports Franchise Relocations from Private Law and Public Law Perspectives: Balancing Marketplace Competition, League Autonomy, and the Need for a Level Playing Field*, 56 Md. L. Rev. 57 (1997).

To protect a host community's legitimate interests in local sports teams, should antitrust law impose a fairness requirement on a professional sports league when making franchise relocation decisions? Would doing so further antitrust law's primary objective of enhancing consumer welfare by prohibiting anticompetitive conduct? See *City of Oakland v. Oakland Raiders*, 2019 WL 3344624 (N.D. Cal.) at *5 (dismissing antitrust claims against NFL and its member clubs for permitting Raiders club to relocate to Las Vegas based on their arguments that "Oakland has not alleged antitrust injury, because allowing the Raiders to move to a city willing to provide more funding promotes, rather than impairs, competition, and because [NFL] restrictions on relocation tended to benefit rather than harm Oakland in its efforts to keep the team from leaving").

In an unsuccessful effort to prevent the Raiders from moving to Los Angeles, the City of Oakland attempted to "take" the NFL club's franchise pursuant to its eminent domain authority. In *City of Oakland v. Oakland Raiders*, 183 Cal. Rptr. 673 (Cal. 1982), the California Supreme Court held that state law permitted the taking of intangible property such as a professional sports franchise, and that doing so could be proven to constitute a valid public purpose. However, a California intermediate appellate court subsequently ruled that the use of eminent domain to prevent the Raiders from relocating to Los Angeles would violate the Dormant Commerce Clause, even though this was an intrastate move the NFL clubs had unanimously voted against. *City of Oakland v. Oakland Raiders*, 220 Cal. Rptr. 153 (Cal. Ct. App. 1985). Observing that eminent domain could be used to "bar indefinitely defendant's business from relocating out of Oakland," the court concluded, "[t]his is the precise brand of parochial meddling with the national economy that the commerce clause was designed to prohibit." *Id.* at 157.

A well-drafted stadium lease is the most effective means of protecting a host community's public investment in the playing facility that houses a local team and ensuring that the local populace receives the full benefit of its contractual bargain. See generally Bruce W. Burton and Matthew J. Mitten, *New Remedies for Breach of Sports Facility Use Agreements: Time for Marketplace Realism*, 88 Iowa L. Rev. 811 (2003). For example, requiring a club to pay agreed liquidated damages of several million dollars for breach of a playing facility lease may be an effective means of protecting a host community's interests. Finding that damages are not an adequate remedy for breach of a playing facility lease and that the premature relocation of a team causes irreparable harm to a city and its fans, some courts have enjoined a club from breaching its facility lease by scheduling and playing home games outside its host city prior to the lease's expiration. See, e.g., *City of New York v. New York Yankees*, 458 N.Y.S.2d 486 (N.Y. Sup. Ct. 1983); *City of New York v. New York Jets Football Club, Inc.*, 394 N.Y.S.2d 799 (N.Y. Sup. Ct. 1977).

PROBLEM 6-3

In 1994, the Oakland Raiders left Los Angeles (LA) to move back to Oakland, which is approximately 370 miles north of LA. The Los Angeles Rams moved from Anaheim, a city within the LA metropolitan area, to St. Louis in 1995 to take advantage of a very favorable stadium lease. Since its creation, the Chargers club has played its home games in a stadium in downtown San Diego, which is located approximately 120 miles south of downtown LA.

Assume that the stadium leases of the Oakland Raiders, San Diego Chargers, and St. Louis Rams expired after the 2015 NFL season. The owners of these three clubs filed applications to relocate their respective teams to Los Angeles (LA), the second largest city in the United States, which has not had an NFL team for more than two decades. Since 1995, 25% of the Chargers' ticket sales have been from fans in Orange, Riverside, and LA counties (the southernmost counties in the LA metropolitan area), who attended the team's games in San Diego. The NFL constitution requires the affirmative vote of 75% of the 32 NFL clubs (at least 24 votes) for a team to relocate outside of its "home territory" (the area within a 75-mile radius of its current stadium). Twenty-eight NFL clubs vote in favor of allowing the Rams to relocate to LA, but only 23 clubs vote in favor of the Chargers' proposed move to LA, which would require the club to share a new stadium with the Rams. Thirty NFL clubs (all except the San Francisco 49ers and the Oakland Raiders) vote against allowing the Raiders to relocate to LA.

A. Evaluate the likely success of the Chargers' claim that the NFL club owners' vote not to allow the club to move to LA violates §1 of the Sherman Act.
B. Assuming all other elements of §1 are satisfied, evaluate the likely success of the Raiders' claim that the NFL club owners' vote not to allow the team to move to LA is an unreasonable restraint of trade.

iii.   Restrictions on Intellectual Property Rights Licensing and Sales

The four major North American professional sports leagues (NFL, MLB, NBA, and NHL) are geographically dispersed throughout the United States and

Canada. Their respective clubs are located in cities with vastly different populations and economic bases; for example, large-market metropolitan areas such as New York City, Los Angeles, and Chicago, as well as much smaller markets like Kansas City, Milwaukee, and Pittsburgh. Thus, league clubs' respective revenue-generating potential from ticket sales (including personal seat licenses), concessions, parking fees, sponsorships, merchandising rights, and game broadcasts within differing local markets varies considerably.

As a means of preventing significant disparities in local revenue streams from inhibiting or destroying on-field competitive balance and fan interest in league games, the NFL, MLB, NBA, and NHL have implemented varying degrees of revenue sharing among their member clubs. In each league, national television and broadcasting rights revenues are shared equally among league clubs. Individual clubs' trademarks and logos are collectively licensed by a central league authority, with revenues distributed to league clubs on a pro rata basis. A recent trend is for leagues to require their clubs' Internet rights to be consolidated and centrally licensed (rather than, or with limits on, an individual club's exploitation) with revenues shared among league clubs. Gate receipts from individual ticket sales frequently are also shared between the home and visiting teams in an agreed percentage.

The NFL currently has the most significant degree of revenue sharing among its member clubs, which provides the Green Bay Packers, located in a metropolitan area of approximately 100,000 people, with the financial resources to compete effectively on the field with large market clubs such as the Chicago Bears. Except for designated local advertising and facility-related revenues, NFL clubs share virtually all other revenues in an effort to jointly produce exciting games between closely matched teams that attract fan interest.

In testimony before Congress, former NFL commissioner Pete Rozelle stated that "revenue sharing is the key to maintaining geographic and competitive balance in professional football . . . and ensure[s] that each club, irrespective of the size of its community, stadium, or television market, has a comparable opportunity to field a championship team." See William J. Hoffman, Comment, *Dallas' Head Cowboy Emerges Victorious in a Licensing Showdown with the NFL*: National Football League Properties v. Dallas Cowboys Football Club, 7 Seton Hall J. Sport L. 255, 262 (1997).

The exclusive licensing or sale of pooled intellectual property rights by a central league marketing arm, along with corresponding restrictions on individual clubs, is designed to (and often does) maximize their aggregate economic value and the total revenue generated by the league. However, the pro rata revenue shares received by the most popular individual league clubs or those in the largest markets may be significantly less than the percentage of league revenues generated by the intellectual property associated with those clubs. Such conduct may force the league to bring breach of contract and trademark infringement litigation to protect its clubs' collective economic interests and exclusive sponsorship agreements from being harmed. See, e.g., *NFL Properties, Inc. v. Dallas Cowboys Football Club, Ltd.*, 922 F. Supp. 849 (S.D.N.Y. 1996) (alleging that the Dallas Cowboys used NFL and club marks without authorization to solicit sponsorship agreements with Dr. Pepper, Pepsi, and Nike, which were competitors of official NFL sponsors, in violation of the federal Lanham Act, which prohibits unauthorized use of another's trademark that creates a likelihood of confusion, as well as state contract, misappropriation, and tortious interference with contract laws).

In response, league-imposed restrictions on a club's sale of sponsorship and merchandising rights have been challenged on antitrust grounds. See, e.g., *Dallas Cowboys Football Club, Ltd. v. NFL Trust*, 1996 WL 601705 (S.D.N.Y. 1996) (alleging that NFL Trust and Licensing Agreements create a price-fixing cartel that precludes free competition in pro football sponsorship and merchandising markets); Complaint, *New York Yankees Partnership v. Major League Baseball Enterprises, Inc*, 97-1153-CIV-T-2513 (M.D. Fla. filed May 19, 1997) (asserting that MLB Properties is a "cartel organized at the behest of a large group of the less successful Major League Clubs" that illegally restrains trade). Both cases settled before being judicially resolved on the merits, but the following case squarely addressed similar antitrust claims by a trademark licensee against Major League Baseball.

MAJOR LEAGUE BASEBALL PROPERTIES, INC. v. SALVINO, INC.

542 F.3d 290 (2d Cir. 2008)

KEARSE, Circuit Judge.

   [EDS. Defendant Salvino, Inc., which was sued for trademark infringement because of its unauthorized use of Major League Baseball clubs' trademarks, alleged that the collective trademark licensing arrangement of Major League Baseball Properties, Inc. (MLBP) violates §1 of the Sherman Act. MLBP is the worldwide exclusive licensing agent for all 30 MLB clubs' trademarks on retail products and acts as their agent for quality control and trademark protection. It charged "a standard royalty percentage" license for products bearing or incorporating an MLB club's trademarks "irrespective of variations in the Clubs' popularity as reflected by their respective fan bases." The dollar amount of royalties that each licensee pays to MLBP varies with its sales rather than being uniform. Each club receives a pro rata share of the profits from licensing royalties regardless of the amount of revenues generated by the licensing of its trademarks. A prospective licensee can request and obtain from MLBP a license to use the trademarks of one, some, or all MLB clubs. MLBP did not limit the number of products it would license or the number of companies to which it granted licenses for any particular products. The defendant was licensed by MLBP to use MLB clubs' trademarks on several products, but it did not have a license to use those marks in connection with a line of plush, bean-filled bears that it called "Bammers."]

II. DISCUSSION

On appeal, Salvino contends that the district court erred in ruling that the centralization in MLBP of the licensing of MLB Intellectual Property for use on retail products is to be analyzed under the rule of reason. Salvino principally adheres to the contention on which it relied in the district court, *i.e.*, that MLBP's operations should be evaluated only under a stricter standard-either the *per se* standard or the "quick-look" standard-and that under those stricter standards, summary judgment was inappropriate. In support of this contention, it characterizes the Clubs' agreement to make MLBP their exclusive licensor as "naked horizontal price and output restrictions [that] traditionally fall within the per se proscriptions." . . .

B. MODES OF ANALYSIS UNDER THE SHERMAN ACT

. . . "To justify a *per se* prohibition a restraint must have manifestly anticompetitive effects, . . . and lack . . . any redeeming virtue. . . ." [Citation omitted.] Accordingly, the Supreme Court has repeatedly " 'expressed reluctance to adopt *per se* rules . . . "where the economic impact of certain practices is not immediately obvious." ' " [citations omitted]. . . .

In a few cases, the Supreme Court has ruled that the challenged practice should neither be held a *per se* violation of the Sherman Act nor be subjected to full-blown rule-of-reason analysis, but rather should be held illegal on the basis of an "abbreviated or 'quick-look' [rule-of-reason] analysis" because "the great likelihood of anticompetitive effects can easily be ascertained." *California Dental Ass'n v. FTC,* 526 U.S. 756, 770, 119 S. Ct. 1604, 143 L. Ed. 2d 935 (1999) . . .

The Court has applied quick-look analysis only "to business activities that are so plainly anticompetitive that courts need undertake only a cursory examination before imposing antitrust liability." . . .

C. THE RECORD IN THE PRESENT CASE

Salvino contends that . . . "[t]he conduct at issue here [constitutes] naked horizontal price and output restrictions [that] traditionally fall [ ] within the per se proscriptions." . . .

. . . [T]he record in this case does not show any reduction in the licensing of the Clubs' intellectual property; rather MLBP presented evidence that there were sizeable increases. According to this evidence, when MLBP became the Clubs' exclusive licensor in 1987, there were approximately 100 licensees; in the first year thereafter, the number of licensees more than doubled. And in the years since, the number has continued to grow, with MLBP having, at the time of its summary judgment motion in this case, more than 300 licenses outstanding for some 4,000 products in the United States, along with licenses to some 170 licensees for sales of products outside of the United States. . . .

In sum, Salvino has pointed to no evidence in the record to support its contention that there has been a horizontal agreement to limit "output," and the only evidence of record—which Salvino has not genuinely disputed—is that output has greatly increased. We turn now to Salvino's contention that there has been a horizontal agreement on "price." . . .

While Salvino contends that its challenge concerns "naked . . . price restrictions," it is important to focus on precisely what conduct Salvino characterizes as "price" restrictions. Although price usually refers to the amount of money a seller charges a buyer for the product, Salvino has made no assertions that there is an agreement as to the fees that the licensees of the MLB Intellectual Property are required to pay MLBP. Instead, throughout this litigation, the conduct that Salvino has contended is *per se* illegal price fixing is the Clubs' agreement to share equally in the profits from MLBP's licensing of the Clubs' intellectual property. . . .

With the recognition that what Salvino calls a "price" restriction is in actuality an agreement for profit sharing, and bearing in mind that, as discussed in the preceding section, there is no genuine dispute that "output" since MLBP became the Clubs' exclusive licensing agent with respect to all retail products bearing Club intellectual property has increased rather than decreased. . . .

. . . Salvino has presented no evidence to suggest that the licensing of MLB Intellectual Property is not entirely responsive to demand. MLBP does not issue licenses that are not requested; there is no evidence that an entity that wishes to obtain a license for particular intellectual property is required to accept or pay for a license that encompasses other intellectual property as well.

Moreover, it may be presumed that a prospective licensee, acting in its own economic self-interest, requests licenses only with respect to products that it believes will be purchased. Thus, MLBP grants licenses that are responsive to the licensees' anticipation of consumer demand.

Further, a licensee's actual sales of products bearing MLB Intellectual Property are, by definition, responsive to consumer demand. Assuming that the licensees assess consumer demand correctly, they will sell more products bearing logos of a Club that is more popular-more popular either because of its success on the playing field or because of a dedicated fan base-than products bearing logos of a less popular Club. Accordingly, because the license requires the licensee to pay a percentage of its sales prices, the licensee will pay MLBP higher dollar amounts with respect to the intellectual property of the more popular Clubs. Thus, the dollar amounts of the license fees received by MLBP with respect to the intellectual property of the various Clubs are not uniform from Club to Club, but instead are plainly responsive both to the relative quality of the various Major League Baseball teams and to the preferences of the buyers. Indeed, the fact that MLBP receives proportionately higher revenues with respect to some Clubs than others is the cornerstone of what Salvino complains of as "price" restrictions, *i.e.,* the Clubs' agreement to share the profits equally.

Finally, MLBP-licensed products that are not desired by the consumer are not purchased. And because the licenses granted by MLBP require payments of percentages of the licensee's sales, products left behind by the consumer do not result in payments to MLBP or to the Clubs. . . .

In the present case, the district court observed that antitrust challenges to the operations of sports leagues have generally been analyzed by the courts under the rule of reason, rather than being held illegal *per se,* because competition among the teams in their fields of play is to an extent dependent upon the teams' cooperation with each other in various other respects. . . .

[T]he MLB Entertainment Product comprises some 2,400 interrelated regular-season Major League Baseball games played each year, followed by play-off games for the American and National League championships, and culminating in the World Series. The production of this entertainment requires the joint efforts of the 30 Clubs; it cannot be produced by any one Club individually or even by a few Clubs. In creating the MLB Entertainment Product, the Clubs plainly do not operate separately or independently but rather are interdependent entities in an organization that is highly integrated.

It is undisputed that the production and value of the MLB Entertainment Product affect the value of MLB Intellectual Property. For example, when the Major League Baseball players were on strike in 1994 and 1995, sales of products bearing MLB Intellectual Property decreased; when the strike ended, sales of those products increased. Further, the value of the intellectual property of a particular Club is dependent in part on that Club's membership in MLB . . . (and in part on the Club's popularity. Although every Club no doubt has a core of die-hard fans, a Club's popularity is affected principally by its success on the baseball field and by how the play of each game relates to the season as a whole.

Moreover, it cannot be disputed that the performance aspect of a Club's popularity is related to the Clubs' interdependence. Obviously, a team cannot win games or championships unless it has opponents. Thus, even Clubs that fail to achieve winning records, and that have only small steadfast fan bases, contribute to the popularity of the more successful Clubs. . . . Direct licensing by the Clubs . . . would result in the more popular Clubs granting more licenses and receiving more income for their intellectual property than the less popular Clubs would grant and receive. This inequality in licensing income, however, would "over-compensat[e] the popular team for the joint efforts of all Clubs." (Fisher Report ¶ 81.)

Further, the disproportionate distribution of licensing income would foster a competitive imbalance among the Clubs. The concept of "competitive balance" reflects the expected equality of opportunity to compete and prevail on the field. Competitive balance also relates to the fans' expectations that each team is a potential champion-i.e. that each Club has a reasonable opportunity to win each game and also to compete for a championship. . . .

There is no genuine dispute here that maintaining the value of the MLB Entertainment Product requires competitive balance among the Clubs. Fisher calls "competitive balance . . . critical to the success of MLB." And Salvino acknowledges that *MLB teams,* like all teams in sports leagues, *need to cooperate in terms of* scheduling, rulemaking, league format, *competitive balance* and both the live performance and televising of games, in order to create and market the product, which is baseball games. Accordingly, Fisher opined that "*all* the Clubs must be rewarded in order to ensure continued league-wide efforts as well as to foster competitive balance." . . .

D. RULE OF REASON

Finally, given the present record, we see no error in the district court's analysis of Salvino's claim under the rule of reason. The court noted that Salvino had proffered no evidence that the centralization of licensing in MLBP caused any actual injury to competition or any evidence that MLBP possessed power in the relevant market.

CONCLUSION

. . . The judgment of the district court is affirmed.

NOTES AND QUESTIONS

1. *Analysis of* Salvino. Why does the Second Circuit hold that the full rule of reason applies to a §1 claim challenging centralized league licensing of its clubs' trademarks? How is this anticompetitive? What are its potential pro-competitive benefits and its effects on consumers?
2. American Needle v. NFL. In contrast to *Salvino*, the challenged conduct in *American Needle, supra,* was the validity of a league trademark licensor's granting of product category exclusivity to a single licensee for a fixed, up-front licensing fee. Plaintiff alleged that NFLP's grant of an exclusive license to manufacture apparel and headwear bearing the trademarks of the NFL and its individual clubs resulted in termination of its nonexclusive license to design, manufacture, and sell headwear bearing NFL clubs' trademarks, which had been in effect for more than 20 years when it expired and was not renewed. It alleged that this agreement violated §1 by reducing competition in the wholesale market for the distribution and sale of apparel

and headwear products bearing the trademarks of NFL clubs. See generally Marc Edelman, *Upon Further Review: Will the NFL's Trademark Licensing Practices Survive Full Antitrust Scrutiny? The Remand of* American Needle v. Nat'l Football League, 16 Stan. J.L. Bus. & Fin. 183, 219 (2011) ("[W]hile the MLB arrangement maintains some level of competition among licensees to sell MLB licensed items, the NFL arrangement does not allow multiple licensees to compete against each other to sell NFL teams' apparel and headwear").

It is arguable that exclusive product licensing has direct anticompetitive effects not reasonably necessary to achieve the procompetitive benefits of collective trademark licensing by league clubs (e.g., lower transaction and trademark rights enforcement costs, enhanced competitive balance among league clubs); therefore, it should be invalidated under the quick-look rule of reason:

> The procompetitive justifications for collective exclusive trademark licensing clearly could be achieved in a substantially less restrictive manner other than by granting one licensee the exclusive rights to use league clubs' trademarks in connection with particular products. For example, offering licenses with the same terms (including appropriate quality control provisions) to two or more competing companies to produce and sell merchandise bearing or incorporating league clubs' trademarks.

Matthew J. Mitten, *From* Dallas Cap *to* American Needle *and Beyond: Antitrust Law's Limited Capacity to Stitch Consumer Harm from Professional Sports Club Trademark Monopolies*, 86 Tul. L. Rev. 901, at 931-932 (2012).

Nevertheless, on remand, the district court refused to apply the "quick look" Rule of Reason. *American Needle, Inc. v. New Orleans Louisiana Saints*, 2014 WL 1364022 (N.D. Ill.). The parties subsequently reached a settlement pursuant to which the NFL paid an undisclosed sum to American Needle, and NFLP's exclusive product licensing regime remained intact. See also *Dang v. San Francisco Forty Niners*, 964 F. Supp. 2d 1097, 1102 (N.D. Cal. 2013) (allegation by a consumer that he paid an "anticompetitive overcharge for his purchase" of an item of apparel bearing an NFL team's logo because of the NFL's current exclusive license with Reebok; case subsequently settled).

3. Consistent with *Salvino*, in *Madison Square Garden, L.P. v. NHL*, 270 Fed. Appx. 56, 2008 WL 746524 (2d Cir.), the Second Circuit ruled that requiring the New York Rangers NHL club to migrate its website to a common technology platform managed by the NHL, rather than allowing its independent operation, is not clearly anticompetitive conduct that violates §1 under the "quick look" Rule of Reason. It affirmed the lower court's finding that the NHL's challenged conduct has several plausible procompetitive effects, including a standardized website layout to attract national sponsors and advertisers interested in uniform exposure across the NHL.com network, which is a key element of the NHL's strategy to enhance its national brand to better compete against other sports and entertainment products.

Courts have expressed a similar reluctance to invalidate league restrictions on member clubs' individual sale of intellectual property rights such as television broadcasting rights under the "quick look" Rule of Reason. In *Chicago Professional Sports Ltd. Partnership v. NBA*, 95 F.3d 593 (7th Cir. 1996), the Seventh Circuit held that the NBA's limit on the number of games a club may televise on a superstation (e.g., WGN) and a league-imposed tax on televised games must be evaluated under a full Rule of Reason analysis, which would require proof that the NBA has market power from the perspective of television viewers or advertisers.

The following case is an example of a consumer class action lawsuit (which have been relatively rare) claiming that a professional sports league's television and Internet broadcasting restrictions violate antitrust law by eliminating intrabrand economic competition among its clubs for the sale of these rights.

LAUMANN v. NATIONAL HOCKEY LEAGUE

56 F. Supp. 3d 280 (S.D.N.Y. 2014)

SCHEINDLIN, District Judge.

I. INTRODUCTION

Plaintiffs bring these putative class actions against the National Hockey League ("NHL") and various individual clubs in the league (the "NHL Defendants"); Major League Baseball ("MLB") and various individual clubs in the league (the "MLB Defendants") (together the "League Defendants"); multiple regional sports networks ("RSNs") that produce and distribute professional baseball and hockey programming; two multichannel video programming distributors ("MVPDs" or "distributors"), Comcast and DIRECTV (together with the RSNs, the "Television Defendants" or "broadcasters"); Madison Square Garden Company and the New York Rangers Hockey Club (the "MSG Defendants"); and New York Yankees Partnership and Yankees Entertainment & Sports Network, LLC ("YES") (together the "Yankee Defendants"). Plaintiffs allege violations under Sections 1 and 2 of the Sherman Antitrust Act (the "Sherman Act"). [The NHL and MLB Defendants moved for summary judgment.]

II. BACKGROUND

NHL is an unincorporated association of thirty major league professional ice hockey clubs, nine of which are named as defendants in *Laumann*. MLB is an unincorporated association of thirty professional baseball clubs, nine of which are named as defendants in *Garber*. The clubs within each League are competitors—both on the field and in the contest to broaden their fan bases. However, the clubs must also coordinate in various ways in order to produce live sporting events, including agreeing upon the game rules and setting a schedule of games for the season. Both leagues divide their member teams into geographic territories and assign each team a home television territory ("HTT") for broadcasting purposes. Neither the Comcast Defendants nor the DIRECTV Defendants played a role in the initial creation of the Leagues' HTTs.

The structure of the territorial broadcasting system is largely uncontested. By League agreement, each club agrees to license its games for telecast only within its designated HTT. The clubs then contract with RSNs through Rights Agreements. The Rights Agreements generally provide each RSN the exclusive right to produce a club's games and telecast them in the HTT. The Agreements do not permit the RSNs to license telecasts for broadcast outside the HTTs. The Rights Agreements also require the RSNs to provide their telecasts to the Leagues without charge for use in the out-of-market packages ("OOM packages"). The clubs keep the revenue from their respective Rights Agreements. There are significant differences in the economic value of the various HTTs.

In order to produce the telecasts of live games, the RSNs invest in equipment, production facilities, and a large staff. They also produce "shoulder" programming such as pre-game and post-game shows. The RSNs then sell their programming to MVPDs like Comcast and DIRECTV through Affiliation Agreements, and the MVPDs televise the programming through standard packages sold to consumers within the HTT. Even when an MVPD agrees to carry a RSN, it does not always distribute that RSN throughout its entire territory. The MVPDs acquire the rights to broadcast the games subject to the territorial restrictions in the RSNs' agreements with the Leagues. The MVPDs black out games in unauthorized territories in accordance with those restrictions.

Fans can watch out-of-market games in one of two ways. *First,* some games are televised nationally through contracts between the Leagues and national broadcasters like ESPN and Fox. The clubs have agreed to allow the Leagues to negotiate national contracts on their behalf. The Leagues' agreements with national broadcasters contain provisions requiring the Leagues to preserve the HTTs. The revenues from national broadcasts are shared equally among the clubs.

Second, the Leagues produce OOM packages in both television and Internet format. The television packages—NHL Center Ice and MLB Extra Innings—are available for purchase through MVPDs, including Comcast and DIRECTV. The Internet packages—NHL GameCenter Live and MLB.tv—are available for purchase directly from the Leagues. The OOM packages are comprised of local RSN programming from each of the clubs. As with the national broadcasts, revenues from the OOM packages are shared equally among the clubs.

Each of the OOM packages requires the purchase of the full slate of out-of-market games, even if a consumer is only interested in viewing the games of one team. The OOMs exclude in-market games to "avoid diverting viewers from local RSNs that produce the live game feeds that form the OOM packages."

In sum, each RSN is the sole producer of its club's games and the sole distributor of those games within the HTT aside from limited nationally broadcasted games. The OOM packages do not show in-market games to avoid competition with the local RSN. Additionally, the territorial broadcast restrictions allow each RSN to largely avoid competing with out-of-market games produced by other RSNs.

Internet streaming rights are owned by the Leagues and/or the clubs. The RSNs have no right to license their programming for Internet streaming directly. The Internet OOM packages are the primary way for fans to view games on the Internet. Additionally, some MVPDs have negotiated with the Leagues to provide Internet streaming of out-of-market games to subscribers of the OOM television packages. Internet streaming of in-market games remains largely unavailable to consumers. . . .

B.   THE LEAGUE DEFENDANTS ARE NOT ENTITLED TO SUMMARY JUDGMENT

While territorial divisions of a market are normally per se violations, the Supreme Court has held that a per se approach is inappropriate in the context of sports broadcasting restrictions due to the necessary interdependence of the teams within a League. On the other hand, the procompetitive benefit of the challenged scheme here is not so obvious that the case can be resolved in favor of defendants in the " 'twinkling of an eye.' " Therefore the rule of reason is the appropriate standard in this case.

Plaintiffs have carried their initial burden of showing an actual impact on competition. The clubs in each League have entered an express agreement to limit competition between the clubs—and their broadcaster affiliates—based on geographic territories. There is also evidence of a negative impact on the output, price, and perhaps even quality of sports programming. Plaintiffs' expert, Dr. Roger G. Noll, attests that consumers pay higher prices for live game telecasts, and have less choice among the telecasts available to them, than they would in the absence of the territorial restrictions. Similarly, Dr. Noll estimates that the price of OOM packages would decrease by about fifty percent in a world without the restrictions. Finally, defendants have not argued in these motions that the Leagues lack market power.

Defendants respond by identifying various procompetitive effects of the territorial broadcast restrictions. They claim that the rules: 1) prevent free riding, 2) preclude competition with joint venture products, 3) incentivize investment in higher quality telecasts, 4) maintain competitive balance, 5) preserve a balance between local loyalty and interest in the sport as a whole, and 6) increase the overall number of games that are telecast. Plaintiffs deny that the territorial rules serve the above interests and also challenge the validity of the interests in light of the territorial rules' overall economic impact on competition.

First, defendants argue that the territorial rules prevent free riding. Although avoiding free riding can be a legitimate procompetitive goal in certain contexts, it is not clear how free riding would pose a threat in this case. Defendants argue that the clubs would "free ride" on the popularity and publicity of the Leagues if they were permitted to license their games nationally. However, the same argument could be made for any revenue-producing activity that an individual team undertakes, including local ticket sales. Defendants also claim that the clubs would "free ride" off the OOM packages by nationally licensing individual club broadcasts, but it is the clubs and RSNs who create the programming in the first place. If anything, the OOM packages benefit from the labor and investment of the clubs and RSNs, not the other way around. Defendants' theory of free riding is unclear and unpersuasive.

Second, defendants argue that the Leagues have an unassailable right to prevent the clubs from competing with the "joint venture." However, no case cited by defendants stands for the proposition that a joint venture may always prevent its members from competing with the venture product regardless of anticompetitive consequences. Rather, in each case, the court concluded based on the facts presented that the restraint in question caused no actual harm to competition. "If the fact that potential competitors shared in profits or losses from a venture meant that the venture was immune from §1, then any cartel could evade the antitrust law simply by creating a joint venture to serve as the exclusive seller of their competing products."

Third, defendants argue that territorial exclusivity encourages the RSNs to invest in higher-quality telecasts, including high-definition cameras, announcers, audio-visual effects, and related pre-game and post-game programming. However, the incentive for added investment is inflated profit stemming from limited competition. "[T]he Rule of Reason does not support a defense based on the assumption that competition itself is unreasonable." To the extent that the Leagues defend *content* exclusivity rather than territorial exclusivity, Dr. Noll predicts that increased competition would overall improve output and consumer satisfaction, an argument that applies with equal force to the quality of telecasts.

Fourth, defendants argue that the territorial restrictions foster competitive balance between the teams and prevent excessive disparities in team quality. Maintaining competitive balance is a legitimate and important goal for professional sports leagues. However, it is unclear whether the territorial restrictions at issue here really serve that purpose. On the one hand, the restrictions protect less popular clubs from competition with more popular teams in their own HTTs. On the other hand, the system requires small market teams to refrain from broadcasting in larger, more populous markets, while big market teams forego only smaller, less populous markets. It is not immediately clear whether the restrictions help or harm competitive balance overall.

Defendants also claim that the revenue sharing aspects of the OOM packages and national broadcasts foster competitive balance. However, there is support in the economic community for the theory that revenue sharing in fact exacerbates competitive imbalance. Even accepting the premise that revenue sharing is beneficial, defendants have not explained why broadcasting contracts are a better mechanism than more direct, limited forms of revenue sharing.

Fifth, defendants claim that they have a legitimate pro-competitive interest in maintaining "a balance between the promotion of [hockey and baseball] as [ ] national game[s] and the need to incentivize Clubs to build their local fan bases." Aside from the fact that these two goals appear to conflict, defendants have not explained what the ideal balance would be, or how they might quantify it. There is no objective measure the Leagues could aspire to attain. Therefore defendants cannot establish that this particular balance between local and national interests is better for consumers, or for demand, than the balance that would prevail in a free market. Moreover, the Leagues purport to bolster regional interest and team loyalty by consciously depriving consumers of out-of-market games they would prefer, which is generally not a permissible aim under the antitrust laws.

Finally, defendants argue that the number of telecasts created and broadcast is greater under the territorial restrictions than it would be in the plaintiffs' "but-for" world. According to defendants, while almost every game is currently available to consumers in one format or another (national broadcast, local RSN, or OOM package), a system dependent on consumer demand could not guarantee that every game would be available everywhere because less popular teams would struggle to get their games produced or televised on their own. Destroying the HTTs would also destroy content exclusivity because OOMs and both competing teams would be able to sell the same game in the same areas. As a result, RSNs would be loathe to give their telecasts to the Leagues to create OOM packages, depriving consumers of the ability to access any and all out-of-market games as they do now. Similarly, national broadcasters would refuse to enter into national contracts without the assurance of exclusivity. Because plaintiffs do not challenge the legality of the OOM packages or national broadcasts, defendants argue, the territorial system is also immune from challenge as a matter of law.

These arguments are far from compelling. Just because plaintiffs do not directly challenge the legality of the OOM packages and national broadcasts does not mean that preserving them is sufficient justification for the territorial rules. Even the complete disappearance of OOM packages would not necessarily cause consumer harm if the same content could be distributed in another form (such as by RSNs nationwide). The OOMs are simply one form of delivering the content to consumers—a form made necessary by the territorial rules themselves. Moreover, it is certainly conceivable that the OOMs would continue to exist absent the territorial restrictions, given the low added cost of creating the packages and the convenience of bundling to many consumers.

Defendants' assumption that market demand would be insufficient to ensure access to the same number of games is questionable. Indeed, the Television Defendants insist that the sports rights are so valuable that they would compete for those rights vigorously even in the absence of the territorial rules. Moreover, "[a] restraint that has the effect of reducing the importance of consumer preference in setting price and output is not consistent with th[e] fundamental goal of antitrust law." While defendants have identified some conceivable procompetitive effects from the territorial rules, plaintiffs have produced equally plausible (if not more plausible) arguments in opposition. It certainly cannot be said that defendants have established procompetitive benefits to the economy as a matter of law.

Defendants [assert] that plaintiffs must identify a less restrictive alternative for any procompetitive effect defendants can identify, even if the overall effect on the economy is overwhelmingly anticompetitive. Such an interpretation, however, is inconsistent with the Supreme Court's mandate that "the essential inquiry [under the rule of reason] . . . [is] whether or not the challenged restraint enhances competition." Indeed, in *United States v. Visa U.S.A., Inc.*, the Second Circuit balanced the alleged procompetitive and anticompetitive effects of the exclusivity rules before requiring the Government to propose any less restrictive alternatives.

Most of defendants' claimed pro-competitive effects are disputable, and the overall effect on the economy is even less conclusive, especially in light of Dr. Noll's testimony that abolishing the territorial restrictions would decrease the cost of sports programming without diminishing output. Far from being implausible, plaintiffs' "but-for" world is at least as likely as defendants' prognostications. Plaintiffs have raised a genuine issue of material fact regarding the overall competitive impact of the territorial rules, foreclosing the possibility of summary judgment for the Leagues under the rule of reason.

NOTE AND QUESTIONS

1. From the perspective of consumers, what are the anticompetitive effects of the league Internet and television broadcasting restrictions? Are there any legitimate procompetitive justifications for these restrictions? If so, why does the *Laumann* court refuse to grant summary judgment for the NHL and MLB? Subsequently, the court ruled that the legality of the challenged NHL and MLB territorial restraints should be adjudicated on a class-wide basis, observing, "Every class member has suffered an injury, because every class member, as a consumer in the market for baseball or hockey broadcasting, has been deprived of an option—a la carte channels—that would have been available absent the territorial restraints." *Laumann v. NHL*, 2015 WL 2330107 (S.D.N.Y.) at *11. Thereafter, the NHL and MLB both settled these cases by agreeing to offer a full-season Internet subscription for all league teams for a lower price than previously offered as well as a full-season

Internet subscription for a single team. Is this a good settlement agreement from the perspective of NHL and MLB fans if it does not also permit individual clubs to sell subscriptions for televised games to consumers outside their respective home territories?

2. In *In re National Football League Sunday Ticket Antitrust Litigation*, 2019 WL 3788253 (9th Cir.), a group of individuals and commercial establishments alleged that an exclusive agreement between the NFL and DirecTV, pursuant to which DirecTV created its "Sunday Ticket" satellite television package of NFL game broadcasts and received the exclusive rights to broadcast all NFL games not shown on over-the-air local television within any given geographical area, is anticompetitive and violates federal antitrust law. Pursuant to the "Teams-NFL Agreement," the 32 NFL clubs pool their game telecasting rights and give the NFL exclusive authority to exercise those rights, which precludes a club from individually entering into telecasting rights agreements with networks, satellite TV providers, or internet streaming services. Under the "NFL-Network Agreement," CBS and Fox coordinate to create a single telecast for every Sunday-afternoon NFL game, which is shown in some but not all television markets in the U.S. Under the "NFL-DirecTV Agreement," the NFL allows DirecTV to obtain all live game telecasts produced by CBS and Fox, package those telecasts, and deliver the bundled telecasts to NFL Sunday Ticket subscribers, which enables them to view local and all out-of-market NFL games. Fans are required to buy the entire "Sunday Ticket" package of NFL games (which requires purchase of a basic television package from DirecTV) and cannot purchase out-of-market NFL games individually or a particular team's games.

Reversing the district court's dismissal of plaintiffs' claims, the Ninth Circuit ruled:

> Because we assume that the NFL's interlocking agreements are not protected by the SBA, [*NCAA v. Bd. of Regents*] controls our analysis. In that case, the Supreme Court held that an agreement among college football teams and the NCAA violated Section 1 of the Sherman Act because the agreement eliminated competition in the market for college football telecasts. Here, the interlocking agreements impose similar restrictions. First, the Supreme Court noted in *NCAA* that the agreement at issue "limits the total amount of televised intercollegiate football and the number of games that any one team may televise." The complaint here alleges that the interlocking agreements in this case impose analogous limitations: plaintiffs assert that the Teams-NFL and NFL-DirecTV Agreements limit the "amount of televised [professional] football" that one team may televise because they restrict the number of telecasts made to a single telecast for each game.
>
> . . .
>
> Because the complaint alleges that the interlocking agreements in this case involve the same sorts of restrictions that *NCAA* concluded constituted an injury to competition, we likewise conclude that the complaint plausibly alleges an injury to competition. Further, because the alleged restrictions on the production and sale of telecasts constitute "a naked restriction" on the number of telecasts available for broadcasters and consumers, the plaintiffs were not required to establish a relevant market.

Id. at *8-9. What advice would you give to the NFL after this ruling?

4.   *Sherman Act §2 Limits on Dominant Sports League Responses to the Formation of Rival Leagues*

This section considers antitrust issues arising out of the formation of a new league that challenges an established league's dominance of a major professional league sport. Our focus here is on challenged restraints affecting interbrand competition between professional sports leagues or clubs that sell competing products within the U.S. sports industry. Similar issues have arisen in connection with competition between promoters of individual performer sports such as tennis, auto racing, rodeo competitions, and mixed martial arts. See, e.g., *Deutscher Tennis Bund v. ATP Tour, Inc.*, 610 F.3d 820 (3d Cir. 2010); *Kentucky Speedway, LLC v. National Assn. for Stock Car Auto Racing, Inc.*, 588 F.3d 908 (6th Cir. 2009); *Volvo N. Am. Corp. v. Men's Int'l Prof'l Tennis Council*, 857 F.2d 55 (2d Cir. 1988); *Elite Rodeo Ass'n v. Prof'l Rodeo Cowboys Ass'n*, 2016 WL 429886 (N.D. Tex.); *Le v. Zuffa*, 216 F.Supp.3d 1154 (D. Nev. 2016). Interbrand competition exists among sellers of different brands of products that are reasonable substitutes from the perspective of consumers. For example, this encompasses competition between professional leagues in the same sports (e.g., NFL and XFL football) or other sports with overlapping seasons (e.g., basketball and hockey), as well as competition between clubs in a different sport within the same geographical area (e.g., the Chicago Bulls NBA team and the Chicago Blackhawks NHL team).

Most antitrust challenges to restraints on interbrand competition have been brought under §2 of the Sherman Act, which prohibits monopolization or attempted monopolization. Unlike §1, which governs only concerted action, §2 applies to unilateral conduct. Monopolization requires proof that (1) the defendant possesses monopoly power in the relevant market; and (2) the defendant has willfully acquired or maintained that power rather than having grown or developed power as a consequence of a superior product, business acumen, or historical accident. *United States v. Grinnell Corp.*, 384 U.S. 563, 570-571 (1966). Attempted monopolization requires proof "(1) that the defendant has engaged in predatory or anticompetitive conduct with (2) a specific intent to monopolize and (3) a dangerous probability of achieving monopoly power." *Spectrum Sports, Inc. v. McQuillan*, 506 U.S. 447, 456 (1993). Although the elements of monopolization and attempted monopolization are different, both require analysis of the defendant's degree of control or power in the relevant market and a determination of whether its conduct is legal and fair competition on the merits or is illegal exclusionary conduct with anticompetitive market effects.

Determining whether a professional sports league has monopoly power for Sherman Act §2 purposes requires a definition of both the relevant product and the geographical markets and a calculation of the defendant's market share in order to evaluate the actual or potential anticompetitive effects of the challenged league rules or conduct. Although courts generally require at least a 70 percent market share to justify a finding of monopoly power, no rigid mathematical approach is used in §2 sports antitrust cases. Rather, the dispositive issue is whether the league has the ability to exclude rivals and prevent economic competition, which is the essence of monopoly power.

For example, in *American Football League v. National Football League*, 323 F.2d 124, 130–31 (4th Cir. 1963), the Fourth Circuit ruled that the NFL did not have sufficient control of the market to prevent a newly formed rival from competing with it:

> The relevant market is nationwide, though the fact that there are a limited number of desirable sites for team locations bears upon the question of [the NFL]'s power to monopolize the national market.
>
> The District Court's finding that [the NFL] did not have the power to monopolize the relevant market appears plainly correct. In 1959, it occupied eleven of the thirty-one apparently desirable sites for team locations, but its occupancy of some of them as New York and San Francisco-Oakland was not exclusive, for those metropolitan areas were capable of supporting more than one team. Twenty of the thirty-one potentially desirable sites were entirely open to American. Indeed, the fact that the American League was successfully launched, could stage a full schedule of games in 1960, has competed very successfully for outstanding players, and has obtained advantageous contracts for national television coverage strongly supports the District Court's finding that [the NFL] did not have the power to prevent, or impede, the formation of the new league. Indeed, at the close of the 1960 season, representatives of the American League declared that the League's success was unprecedented.

There has been a historical tendency toward single U.S. major professional leagues for the most popular North American team sports of baseball, football, basketball, and hockey, as well as soccer. Competition among rival leagues in the same sport has never continued for any significant period of time. See generally Paul Weiler, Leveling the Playing Field: How the Law Can Make Sports Better for Fans, 324-328 (2001) (analyzing historical and economic reasons for this phenomenon). The professional women's basketball landscape in the late 1990s provides a prime example. Two competing leagues, the American Basketball League (ABL) and the Women's National Basketball Association (WNBA), began play at roughly the same time. The ABL, despite having some of the best women's basketball players in the country on its clubs' rosters, ceased operations after only a few years of existence because of its inability to market its product and finance its operations as well as the WNBA, many of whose clubs are owned and operated by the NBA teams in their respective locations. The WNBA remains America's only professional women's basketball league, and it was not been challenged since.

There may be certain inherent conditions in the professional sports industries that predispose each sport to dominance by one league at the major league level; the mere fact there is only a single major league for a particular sport does not violate §2 of the Sherman Act. One potential reason for this phenomenon is that fans may prefer a single champion for the highest level of competition within the sport. If so, over time, fans will prefer the product of one league over that of another, thereby leading to the demise of the disfavored league. There is no §2 violation if a league's market dominance results from winning the off-field competitive economic struggle by providing a superior entertainment product that is most desirable to sports fans. In *American Football League, supra,* the court held that the NFL could expand its business operations in response to increasing consumer demand for its product and compete with the AFL for the best available remaining geographical areas in which to place a professional football franchise, which is legal, fair competition on the merits.

On the other hand, this phenomenon may be the result of an established league's efforts to unfairly exclude a rival league, which reduces interbrand competition and harms consumers by reducing available entertainment options and increasing their cost. See generally Stephen F. Ross, *Antitrust Options to Redress Anticompetitive Restraints and Monopolistic Practices by Professional Sports Leagues,* 52 Case W. L. Rev. 133, 158-165 (2001) (providing historical description of dominant leagues' successful exclusionary practices to achieve and maintain monopoly power).

To be economically viable, a major professional sports league needs several resources, including (1) club owners with the financing and business acumen to successfully operate its member clubs, (2) teams in several large cities throughout the country with the population and economic base to support them, (3) access to adequate playing facilities, (4) major league-quality players, and (5) a national television broadcasting contract. Even if a new league is able to satisfy these minimum requirements, its long-term survival as a profitable independent entity is not ensured. Upstart leagues often fold after a relatively short period of existence because of financial problems or improper management and strategic business decisions. Or fans may choose to support an established league rather than a new league.

The following cases provide illustrative examples of Sherman Act §2 litigation against an established league for allegedly restricting access to essential inputs that a rival league needed to engage in competition.

PHILADELPHIA WORLD HOCKEY CLUB, INC. v. PHILADELPHIA HOCKEY CLUB, INC.

351 F. Supp. 462 (E.D. Pa. 1972)

HIGGINBOTHAM, District Judge.

I. INTRODUCTION

. . . [F]rom what in 1917 was a relatively minor sports attraction, the National Hockey League has skated into the 1970's to a position of substantial wealth, power, broad spectator interest, international recognition and many superstars, all crescendoing into huge profits for both its owners and players. . . .

Since 1971, the World Hockey Association (hereinafter referred to as WHA) has attempted to enter major league professional hockey to become a real competitor in this field where the National Hockey League (hereinafter referred to as NHL) has for so long held a total monopolistic position as the sole supplier of major league hockey competition. The basic issue is whether through their reserve clause, affiliation agreements, and market power dominance, the National Hockey League has violated the federal antitrust laws and if such a violation is found, whether the WHA is entitled to relief at this preliminary injunction stage. . . .

II. FINDINGS OF FACT

[EDS. The presence of qualified players of major league professional caliber is essential to the successful conduct of major league professional ice hockey competition. Unlike professional football and basketball, which can draw on an ample supply of talented players developed in competition at the college level in the United States at no cost to the member clubs of the professional leagues, the NHL has never had such a ready-made source of talent. It has invested millions of dollars to help support a system of amateur league and minor league hockey in Canada and the United States that gives youngsters an opportunity to play hockey and to develop their skills, and also provides a source of potential players of major league caliber.

There are more than 50,000 amateur hockey players in Canada and the United States, but very few have sufficiently developed skills to play immediately in the NHL. In 1972, approximately 7,000 Canadian players attained the age of 20 and were eligible for the NHL draft; only 152 were drafted by NHL clubs. Any and all of these 50,000 amateur players, including those subject to the NHL draft or actually drafted by an NHL club, but not successfully signed, are available to play in the WHA or any other hockey league.

Prior to the formation of the WHA in 1971, the NHL was the only major league professional hockey association in North America. In addition to the NHL, there are three other professional hockey leagues in North America. These are the American Hockey League (AHL), the Western Hockey League (WHL), and the Central Hockey League, formerly the Central Professional Hockey League (CHL), with a total of 24 teams. The best players are found in the NHL, the next best in the American and Western Hockey Leagues, and the lowest level of professional players is in the Central Hockey League. The International and Eastern Hockey Leagues are amateur or at best semiprofessional leagues; their players are generally less talented than those in the minor professional leagues.

NHL clubs have invested large sums for the development and support of professional minor league hockey clubs in Canada and the United States, many of which could not continue to operate without the subsidies provided by the NHL clubs. The NHL requires that each of its member teams must have an affiliation with a "player development team." Thus, at least 16 of the 24 professional minor league teams are owned or operated by or affiliated with NHL teams. All of the teams in the CHL are owned by NHL teams. In addition to the teams owned by NHL members, "there are almost an unlimited number of affiliations and loaning arrangements of various kinds."

The willingness of the NHL clubs to invest so heavily in the development of hockey players in the amateur and minor leagues is based in large part on their belief that if a player developed through this system signs a standard contract with an NHL club, that club will, because of the "reserve" clause, have the perpetual right to his services as a professional hockey player. NHL club owners have been insistent on the continuation of the reserve clause basically in its present form, and after unionizing, the NHL players have been consistently against this type of reserve clause.

In 1971, a special and highly confidential NHL Presidential Study Committee, which had representatives from six NHL clubs, was established to make recommendations with regard to several problems faced by the NHL in light of the formation of the WHA. In May 1972, the NHL Board of Governors established a Legal Committee to develop and implement a policy with regard to players who had signed contracts with the WHA. It promptly employed a law firm to aid in this task. NHL president Campbell subsequently suggested that NHL clubs send a form letter to all players, particularly those who had signed with the WHA, reminding them of the club's contract rights and threatening litigation to enforce the reserve clause. NHL clubs sent such letters to particular players and instituted legal actions against 11 NHL players who had signed contracts with WHA teams to seek enforcement of the league's reserve clause. The targets of the suits included several well-known players, such as Bobby Hull, Derek Sanderson, and Gerry Cheevers.

More than 200 of the 345 of the players signed by WHA teams for the 1972-1973 playing season were subject to reserve clauses in their 1971-1972 contracts with the NHL, AHL, CHL, and WHL. Approximately 58 to 60 of them played for an NHL team during the past season. The remainder (more than 140 players) played with a minor league team last year. Of the 345 players who signed WHA contracts, four or five were enjoined from playing with their WHA teams as a result of the enforcement of the NHL's reserve clause.]

III. THE LABOR EXEMPTIONS OF THE SHERMAN ACT

[EDS. The court held that the nonstatutory labor exemption, which is considered in Chapter 7, does not immunize the NHL's reserve clause from antitrust scrutiny.]

IV. THE RELEVANT MARKET

A. RELEVANT PRODUCT MARKET

. . . In the leading case discussing relevant product market, *United States v. E.I. DuPont De Nemours & Co.*, 351 U.S. 377, 76 S. Ct. 994, 100 L. Ed. 1264 (1956), the Supreme Court stated:

> The varying circumstances of each case determine the result. In considering what is the relevant market for determining the control of price and competition, no more definite rule can be declared than that commodities reasonably interchangeable by consumers for the same purposes make up that "part of the trade or commerce," monopolization of which may be illegal.

351 U.S. at 395, 76 S. Ct. at 1007.

. . . The NHL argues that the relevant market for anti-trust purposes should include at a minimum both major league professional hockey and minor league professional hockey. Further, the NHL urges that from a realistic view of hockey the relevant market should be expanded beyond the professional and semi-professional leagues to include also the amateur leagues. In contrast, the WHA asserts that the relevant market is only major league professional hockey, namely the hockey played today in the National Hockey League. I find that the relevant market is major league professional hockey.

The rationale of *International Boxing Club v. United States*, 358 U.S. 242, 249-250, 79 S. Ct. 245, 250, 3 L. Ed. 2d 270 (1959), is decisive here. From the vastness of innumerable boxing contests, the Court isolated as a relevant market championship boxing contests. They noted the common denominators of all boxing contests, whether championship or not, were: one ring, two boxers, and a fight under a similar set of rules, before a greater or lesser number of spectators. But, in spite of the apparent "physical identity of the product," the determinative difference in championship bouts was money: more revenue from (1) more spectators, (2) television rights, (3) movie rights, and (4) higher ticket prices.

Similarly, any hockey match whether in the NHL, the minor professional hockey leagues, or in the amateur leagues always includes one hockey rink, 12 hockey players, two referees, and a similar set of rules, before a greater or lesser number of spectators. That major league professional hockey is the relevant product here is substantiated by . . . higher ticket prices, increased television revenues, and greater players' skill and salaries.

Of course, the consumer is no longer king in sports; he has lost the unilateral power to demand and always get high quality competition. Yet, though his voice is weak, he is not totally impotent. He can withdraw his support when the level of performance becomes so outrageously low that he feels the admission price does not justify the quality of performance observed. There is a point where even avid fans will not support minor league performances for major league prices. This residuum of discretion in the sports fan to refrain from paying high prices for low performance is an additional factor in separating the minor leagues from the major professional league market.

A review of the record convinces me that above all else, the NHL owners are probably more shrewd as businessmen than they are as enthusiasts of sports. It is inconceivable that they would pay much larger salaries to major league players for any reason other than the fact that these players are more skillful, generally have more professional hockey experience, and as a group at least in the profits returned to the owners are worth the salaries paid. This profit pattern of payment to the players conclusively establishes that major and minor league hockey players are not interchangeable products. . . . I find the relevant product market to be major league professional hockey as it is currently played in the NHL.

B. RELEVANT GEOGRAPHIC MARKET

In *Brown Shoe Co. v. United States*, 370 U.S. 294, 336-337, 82 S. Ct. 1502, 1530, 8 L. Ed. 2d 510 (1962), the Supreme Court articulated the requirements for selecting the appropriate and relevant geographic market. The Court noted as follows:

> . . . The geographic market selected must, therefore, both "correspond to the commercial realities" (footnote omitted) of the industry and be economically significant. Thus, although the geographic market in some instances may encompass the entire Nation, under other circumstances it may be as small as a single metropolitan area. . . .

The record establishes that almost all of the hockey players currently playing in the NHL, began their skating careers in either Canadian or United States amateur hockey. The typical players' journey to the "big league" carried them through at least one of the five semi-professional leagues which play throughout the United States and Canada. Further, the NHL and WHA have teams at the present solely in the United States and Canada. Against this factual background presented by the plaintiffs, the defendants urge that the plaintiffs have available a potentially large source of supply of European players. However, in order to be guilty of monopolization under § 2 of the Sherman Act, 15 U.S.C. § 2, the WHA need not prove that the NHL has an international monopoly in the hockey players' market. The language of the Sherman Act itself does not require a monopolization of *all* the trade or commerce, but rather *any part* of the trade or commerce among the several states or with foreign nations.

. . . I find that the relevant geographic market here is the United States and Canada. . . .

VI.   THE SHERMAN ACT § 2

. . . The WHA charges that the NHL has through a series of agreements and other concerted actions monopolized, conspired to monopolize, and attempted to monopolize major league professional hockey by (1) controlling the pool of players capable and available to play major league professional hockey, and (2) expanding the NHL so as to exclude the WHA from participation in major league professional hockey. . . .

. . . I hold that in the circumstances of this case, the three year restraint following the expiration of a current contract (considering this factor along with the other numerous interlocking agreements NHL has fashioned and shaped over the years to monopolize a hockey player's professional career) is unreasonable, and in violation of Section 2 of the Sherman Act. . . .

B.   MONOPOLY POWER

. . . Here, through the use, *inter alia*, of (1) Standard Players' Contracts, including the "reserve clause" in paragraph 17 of that contract, (2) the agreements between the NHL and three of the major semi-professional leagues, and (3) the agreements between the professional and semi-professional leagues and the amateur leagues, it is clear that the NHL overwhelmingly controls the supply of players who are capable and available for play in a new league where the level of internal competitions fairly approaches the levels currently existing in the NHL. In an attempt to minimize the NHL's extraordinary degree of control over the players, the NHL asserts that there are many other available players who will shortly be able to play major league professional hockey. However, the relevant market place is the market place of *today*, not the market place of 1980 or even the market place of 1975. A monopolist may not today excuse his present predatory practices because someday in the future his total domination of the market place may be lessened.

The NHL's monopoly power is their power to control overwhelmingly the supply of hockey players who are today available for play in any major professional league. It is that total control by the NHL which I hold is proscribed by § 2 of the Sherman Act. One who builds the most modern steel mill cannot operate without an adequate supply of iron ore. The 50,000 amateur hockey players allegedly available to the WHA are not the "iron ore" from which viable competition can be built. If the WHA is to compete effectively for attendance and television rights with commensurate payments, the WHA must have a "show" which is equal or nearly equal to that of the NHL today. Since the WHA is a newcomer, the quality of play need not instantly equal that of the NHL, but there must be a prospect that the product will be nearly equal in a relatively short period of time.

. . . I find that the NHL possesses monopoly power in the relevant market. . . .

The mere possession of monopoly power in the relevant market does not alone constitute a violation of section 2 of the Sherman Act. There must also be "(2) the willful acquisition or maintenance of that power as distinguished from growth or development as a consequence of a superior product, business acumen, or historic accident." *United States v. Grinnell*, 384 U.S. 563, 86 S. Ct. 1698, 1704, 16 L. Ed. 2d 778 (1966). The activities of the NHL go beyond mere possession of monopoly power in the relevant market to breach these aforementioned prohibitions articulated in *United States v. Grinnell, supra.*

The NHL has willfully acquired and maintained its monopoly power through the use of the many agreements. . . . Its continuing and overriding goal is to maintain a monopoly over the supply of major league professional hockey players.

The NHL employs devices such as reserve clauses, Standard Player Contracts, an NHL semi-professional league Joint-Affiliation Agreement, and control over the amateurs through the Pro-Am Agreement in which the amateurs agreed to recognize the NHL as the "sole and exclusive governing body of professional hockey." If the NHL reserve clause were valid for those players whose contracts terminated in September, 1972, then the NHL would have the power, directly or indirectly, to prevent any player under "contract" to the NHL or one of its affiliated minor professional leagues from playing with any other team or league outside the NHL System.

Upon reading the self-serving tributes for its expenditure of millions of dollars to develop amateur and minor league hockey, one might infer that the millions were spent solely for the honor and glory of amateur and minor league hockey. The NHL's motives were not quite so noble; these expenditures to develop the amateur and minor professional leagues were essential to maintain the NHL's monopolistic position. . . .

Keeping in mind both the many agreements employed by National Hockey League and its continuing expansion, it is apparent that the National Hockey League's intent is and was the willful acquisition and maintenance of a position as the only major professional hockey league in the United States and Canada. . . .

VII.   PRELIMINARY INJUNCTIVE RELIEF

. . . Here, the injunction restraining the NHL from enforcing or attempting to enforce its reserve clause is not a contest involving just one superstar. Rather, it is a dispute of a substantially larger magnitude. The superstars in issue are many, Bobby Hull, Derek Sanderson, Gerry Cheevers, John McKenzie, to name just a few of the players whose former NHL clubs will be precluded from enjoying their services as a result of this injunction. However, the players directly affected include more than 200 players who but for the formation of the WHA and the issuance of this preliminary injunctive relief would still be obligated to play with the NHL if the reserve clause is valid. . . .

The NHL is no shaky institution which will collapse if it loses a few superstars or even many average players during the pendency of this preliminary injunction. The NHL is merely sustaining the fate which monopolists must face when they can no longer continue their prior total dominance of the market. For the reality of today is that the federal antitrust laws preclude the continued implementation of NHL President Campbell's fondest dream that it remains "the *only* major professional hockey league operating from coast-to-coast in the United States [and] Canada." (Emphasis added.) . . .

The WHA and its member teams have demonstrated that they will be immediately irreparably injured by the enforcement of the reserve clause in that they will be deprived of the services of professional caliber players vital to the existence of a major professional league. . . .

For the foregoing reasons, the Preliminary Injunction should be granted. . . .

NOTES AND QUESTIONS

1. *Relevant Market for Players.* Why did the court find that "major and minor league hockey players are not interchangeable products"? Under what circumstances, if any, would it be appropriate to include college and minor league players in the same product market as major league players? Note that the current relevant geographical market for players (i.e., source of supply) in sports such as baseball, basketball, soccer, and hockey extends beyond the United States or North America, given the large number of foreign-born players playing in North American sports leagues. *Fraser v. Major League Soccer, L.L.C.,* 284 F.3d 47 (1st Cir. 2002) (upholding jury's finding of a worldwide labor market for elite soccer players).

2. *Fair Competition for Players Versus Illegal Exclusionary Conduct.* Although *Philadelphia World Hockey Club* recognized the need for "some type of intraleague reserve system," why did the court find that the NHL's player restraints violated §2? What relief did the court order to remedy this antitrust violation?

   A dominant league's clubs are free to compete fairly with a rival league's clubs for the services of the best available players, *American Football League v. National Football League,* 205 F. Supp. 60, 77 (D. Md. 1962), *aff'd,* 323 F.2d 124 (4th Cir. 1963), and to enforce valid, existing player contracts, thereby preventing their players from switching leagues before their respective contracts expire. See, e.g., *Winnipeg Rugby Football Club, Ltd. v. Freeman,* 140 F. Supp. 365 (N.D. Ohio 1955); *Philadelphia Ball Club v. Lajoie,* 51 A. 973 (Pa. 1902). As one court explained, "Nobody has ever thought, so far as we can find, that in the absence of some monopolistic purpose everyone had not the right to offer better terms to another's employee so long as the latter is free to leave." *Washington Capitols Basketball Club, Inc. v. Barry,* 419 F.2d 472, 478 (9th Cir. 1969).

UNITED STATES FOOTBALL LEAGUE v. NFL
842 F.2d 1335 (2d Cir. 1988)

Winter, Circuit Judge.

This appeal follows a highly publicized trial and jury verdict of $1.00. The plaintiff is a now-defunct professional football league that began play in this decade; the defendant is a football league founded nearly seventy years ago. The older of the two leagues, the National Football League, is a highly successful entertainment product. . . . After three seasons and losses in the neighborhood of $200 million, the USFL played its last game in July 1985. Meanwhile, in

October, 1984, blaming its older competitor for its difficulties, the USFL instituted this litigation. Plans to play in the fall of 1986 were abandoned after the jury's verdict that is the principal subject of this appeal. . . .

. . . The jury's finding of illegal monopolization of a market of major-league professional football was based upon evidence of NFL attempts to co-opt USFL owners, an NFL Supplemental Draft of USFL players, an NFL roster increase, and NFL conduct directed at particular USFL franchises. These activities, however, were hardly of sufficient impact to support a large damages verdict or to justify sweeping injunctive relief. For that reason, the USFL candidly admits that "at the heart of this case" are its claims that the NFL, by contracting with the three major networks and by acting coercively toward them, prevented the USFL from acquiring a network television contract indispensable to its survival. The jury expressly rejected the television claims. . . .

In 1970, the NFL entered into a contract with ABC to televise a game nationally on Monday nights. Since then, all three major television networks have broadcast NFL games, and the NFL's annual revenues from television have increased by more than 800 percent. . . .

The ABC, CBS and NBC contracts from 1970 onward have given each network rights of first negotiation and first refusal to decide whether to continue its NFL contract for subsequent years. The NFL's 1982-86 contracts were non-exclusive and did not forbid a network from televising another football league's games at any time when it was not broadcasting NFL games. NBC was thus legally free to televise to a particular city another league's games on Sunday afternoons directly opposite NFL games on CBS when there was no NFL game scheduled for NBC to be televised to that city. CBS had a similar option. ABC was legally free to televise another league's games all afternoon each Sunday. All three networks were legally free to telecast another league's games in prime time. Because the NFL was forbidden by its network contracts to televise games on cable, cable television contracts were open to a competing league, although such contracts are less lucrative than network contracts. When the NFL's network contracts expired in 1981 and 1986, the networks were free to contract with a competing league's games for all time slots.

The NFL's three-network "tie-up" was a central issue at trial. The USFL claimed that the NFL intentionally set out to tie up the three networks as a means of excluding competitors. In support of its theory, the USFL introduced a memorandum from NFL general counsel Jay Moyer written during the NFL's 1973 network contract negotiations stating that "an open network may well be an open invitation to formation of a new league." Commissioner Rozelle testified, however, that in 1970, before contacting ABC and signing the Monday night football contract with it, he unsuccessfully approached CBS and NBC, both of which already televised NFL games, about their interest in prime-time football. . . .

The USFL also sought to show that the NFL had placed unlawful pressure on the networks to prevent the broadcast of USFL games. Much of this evidence consisted of statements by USFL representatives and hearsay and speculation by third parties. Officials from the three networks and one cable network testified that the NFL had not exerted any pressure on them regarding the broadcast of USFL games. Several network officials did testify, however, that they feared that televising the USFL in the fall might jeopardize their NFL relationships. . . . Executives from all three major networks also testified that by 1986, after the USFL had left several large television markets and was encountering financial and other difficulties, the USFL was not an attractive entertainment product. . . .

6.   MANAGEMENT OF THE USFL

The USFL was conceived and organized in 1981 to play in the spring rather than the fall. Its founders believed that public demand for football was not satisfied by the NFL's and the colleges' fall seasons; that cable television, which could not televise NFL games under the existing NFL-network contracts, would offer unique opportunities for television revenues and exposure; that a spring football league would face limited competition; that there was a sufficient supply of football players for two leagues; and that a spring league could draft college players and put them on the field even before the NFL draft.

The USFL's founders placed a high priority on the fans' perception of the quality of play. They intended to use major stadiums and to hire well-known coaches. At the same time, they wanted the league to control costs. For its first season, therefore, the USFL established budget guidelines for player salaries of between $1.3 and $1.5 million per team.

The USFL's founders did not seek to obtain a television contract for fall play. Before fielding a team, however, the USFL received bids for a spring television contract from ABC and NBC and from two cable networks, ESPN and the Turner Broadcasting System. The league entered a four-year contract with ABC, and a two-year contract with ESPN. . . . The USFL began with eight of its twelve teams in the nation's top ten television markets. The ABC contract required the USFL to field teams in the three largest television markets (New York, Los Angeles, and Chicago) and in at least four of the five other top-ten television markets in which teams were originally located (Philadelphia, Boston, Detroit, San Francisco/Oakland and Washington).

The USFL's first year of play, 1983, was a mixed success. The league received extensive media exposure when it signed Heisman Trophy winner Herschel Walker to a three-year, $3,250,000 contract. The Nielsen television rating for the first week of games was 14.2, a figure comparable to NFL ratings. As the season went on, however, the USFL's television ratings declined. . . . Average attendance for the year was approximately 25,000. Nevertheless, these figures were consistent with the league's and networks' preseason projections.

On the financial side, the picture was not as bright. The USFL lost a total of almost $40 million, or an average of $3.3 million per team. The league had projected losses of only about $2 million per year for each team over the first three years. The unanticipated financial losses were chiefly the result of the failure to stay within the original salary guidelines. . . .

The USFL's second year was marked by change. Four teams shifted locations. For example, the owner of the Chicago franchise exchanged that franchise for the Phoenix franchise, taking his winning Chicago coach and players while the original Phoenix team moved to Chicago under a new owner. The league, over the objection of some owners, expanded from twelve teams to eighteen. Five of the original owners left the league. Some of the new owners, notably Donald Trump of the New Jersey Generals, believed that the USFL ought to play in the fall. Thereafter, the issue of when to play became divisive, and several owners came to believe that Trump was trying to bring about a merger with the NFL that would include only some USFL teams.

The NFL introduced extensive evidence designed to prove that the USFL followed Trump's merger strategy, and that this strategy ultimately caused the USFL's downfall. The merger strategy, the NFL argued, involved escalating financial competition for players as a means of putting pressure on NFL expenses, playing in the fall to impair NFL television revenues, shifting USFL franchises out of cities where NFL teams played into cities thought to be logical expansion (through merger) cities for the NFL, and, finally, bringing the antitrust litigation now before us.

Throughout the second half of 1983 and early 1984, several USFL owners escalated spending on player salaries. . . . The USFL's spending on players greatly outpaced its revenues. The owner of the Los Angeles team, for example, committed the team to $13.1 million in salaries and bonuses for just one season. He even entered into a multiyear, $40 million contract with just one player, Steve Young of Brigham Young University.

By the end of the 1984 season, USFL franchises in two of the top three television markets, Chicago and Los Angeles, had failed, and only four of the original owners remained in the league. The league was not a failure as entertainment, however. Despite a decline in the USFL's television ratings . . . ABC exercised its option to carry the USFL in the spring of 1985 at $14 million and offered a new contract worth $175 million for four years in the spring beginning in 1986. ESPN offered a contract worth $70 million over three years.

Nevertheless, during an August 1984 owners' meeting, the USFL decided to move to the fall in 1986. This decision was made despite: (i) ABC's warning that such a move would breach its contract for the spring of 1985 and 1986; (ii) the contrary recommendations of a management consulting firm, McKinsey & Company, which the USFL had retained for $600,000 to consider the advisability of a fall season; and (iii) the contrary recommendations of the USFL's directors of operations and marketing.

Moreover, Eddie Einhorn, a USFL owner who was to represent the USFL in negotiations to secure a network contract for the fall, warned that moving from large television markets to "merger" cities too quickly might preclude the securing of a network contract. Nevertheless, in the ensuing months, the USFL withdrew from Chicago, Detroit, Philadelphia, Pittsburgh and Washington, D.C. — each a large television market with an NFL team — and moved into Baltimore (which had lost its NFL team in 1984) and Orlando (which had no NFL team). Through mergers, the USFL bolstered franchises in Oakland (which had lost the NFL Raiders to Los Angeles) and Phoenix (which had been discussed as a possible NFL expansion city). The decision to move to the fall damaged the USFL's relations with ABC and ESPN. The former withheld a significant portion of the USFL's rights fees for the 1985 season, while the latter demanded a renegotiation of its proposed 1985-87 USFL contract. . . .

. . . The USFL's 1985 "lame-duck" spring season appears to have been affected adversely by the now publicly announced move to the fall. The league's television ratings declined to 4.1 on ABC and 2.0 on ESPN. By the end of the season, several owners had withdrawn financial support for their teams, and a number of clubs were no longer meeting their payrolls and other bills. The USFL scheduled eight teams for its fall 1986 season, which was ultimately cancelled after the verdict in this case. Only one team (New Jersey), was in a top-ten television market. One other team (Tampa Bay), was in a top-twenty market. Three teams were located in Florida (Jacksonville, Orlando and Tampa Bay) but only one was west of the Mississippi River (Phoenix). In three years, USFL teams had left fourteen of the twenty-two cities in which they had played. . . .

DISCUSSION

On appeal, the USFL raises a host of claims with respect to the NFL's liability, the district court's evidentiary rulings, damages charge, and denial of injunctive relief.

1.   LIABILITY

a.   The Sports Broadcasting Act

The USFL contends that the Sports Broadcasting Act of 1961 limits the antitrust exemption for pooled-rights contracts to a single contract with one network. . . .

In any event, the passage of the 1966 NFL-AFL merger statute provides conclusive evidence that Congress did not intend the 1961 Act to prohibit NFL contracts with more than one network. When considering this legislation, Congress was explicitly informed that the merged league would continue to broadcast its games on "at least 2 networks," and no concern whatsoever was expressed in Congress that such conduct was either undesirable or would go beyond the scope of the 1961 Act's exemption. . . . The lack of a "one network" limitation in the 1966 merger bill thus dooms the USFL's claims. Accordingly, we hold that the mere existence of the NFL contracts with the three networks does not violate the antitrust laws. . . .

h.   Essential-Facilities Charge

Finally, the USFL contends that it was held to an improperly high standard of proof on its "essential-facilities" claim. We set out the pertinent charge:

> Plaintiffs allege that defendants violated Sections [1] and [2] of the Sherman Act by conspiring to and in fact denying plaintiffs access to a satisfactory national broadcast television contract for future seasons, with any one of the three networks. The legal basis for this particular claim by plaintiffs is that a network contract is an essential facility which the USFL or any other professional football league needs in order to compete in major league professional football. . . .

In order to prove their essential "facilities" claim, plaintiffs must prove all of the following elements by a preponderance of the evidence:

> First: That a national broadcast television contract with at least one of the three networks, CBS, NBC or ABC is essential to the ability of a professional football league to compete successfully in the United States;
>
> Second: that potential competitors of the NFL cannot as a practical matter, duplicate the benefits of a network contract;
>
> Third: That the defendants control access to each of the three networks, that is, the defendants themselves have the ability by their actions to deny actual or potential competitors, such as the USFL, access to national broadcast television — access to a national broadcast television contract;
>
> Fourth: That the defendants through their actions have exercised their ability to deny actual or potential competitors access to a national broadcast television contract by denying the USFL such access;

Fifth: That a national broadcast television contract between one or more of the networks and a professional football league other than the NFL would not interfere with any of the defendants' lawful dealings with those networks.

The USFL argues first that this charge erred in failing to distinguish between a network television contract in the spring and one in the fall. The charge did, however, address the USFL's denial of "access to a *satisfactory* national broadcast contract for future seasons" (emphasis added). The jury was well aware of the USFL's claim that a spring contract was unsatisfactory as an "inferior facility" or "minor league." It thus either rejected that characterization of spring football or rejected the USFL's claim that the NFL could deny the USFL access to a network in the fall. . . .

3.   THE DISTRICT COURT'S DAMAGES INSTRUCTIONS

. . . The jury was given the following nominal damages instruction:

Just because you have found the fact of some damage resulting from a given unlawful act, that does not mean that you are required to award a dollar amount of damages resulting from that act. You may find, for example, that you are unable to compute the monetary damages resulting from the wrongful act, except by engaging in speculation or guessing, or you find that you cannot separate out the amount of the losses caused by the wrongful act from the amount caused by other factors, including perfectly lawful competitive acts and including business decisions made by the plaintiffs or the plaintiffs' own mismanagement. Or you may find that plaintiffs failed to prove an amount of damages.

You may decline to award damages under such circumstances, or you may award a nominal amount, say $1.

The jury's $1.00 award was consistent with this instruction. The NFL offered much evidence of self-destructive USFL decisions, and the jury's nominal award suggests that it credited this proof, as it was free to do. . . .

4.   THE DISTRICT COURT'S DENIAL OF INJUNCTIVE RELIEF

Finally, the USFL claims that the district court should have granted sweeping injunctive relief under Section 16 of the Clayton Act, 15 U.S.C. § 26 (1982). In particular, the USFL requested membership in the NFL, separation of the NFL into two leagues, each league being limited to one network, or a prohibition on the NFL from broadcasting its games in more than one afternoon time slot on Sunday. Judge Leisure held that the requested relief was unrelated to the monopolization of the market for major-league professional football verdict and not justified by the record as a whole.

The USFL contends that the jury's monopolization verdict compelled the district court to "pry open to competition [the] market that has been closed by defendants' illegal restraints." However, this argument simply glosses over the critical fact that the jury did not find the NFL liable on any of the USFL's television-related claims. With regard to the findings implied by the monopolization verdict that the NFL engaged in predatory conduct through attempts to co-opt USFL owners, creation of a Supplemental Draft, or expansion in roster size, Judge Leisure denied relief on the ground that the USFL provided no evidence that such conduct was likely to continue or recur. The USFL has not asked us to overturn that denial of relief.

Instead, the USFL seeks sweeping injunctive relief on the ground that the NFL's single-league structure, in conjunction with television contracts with the three networks, creates an impenetrable barrier to entry by a competing league into the market of professional football. No matter what the jury found, however, such relief would not have been appropriate. First, Congress has authorized the NFL's single-league structure and its joint economic operations. Second, at the time the district court denied the relief, the NFL's contracts with the networks had expired. . . . There was only free competition between the NFL's product and the USFL's product. Of course, the district court also properly rejected this claim in view of the jury's outright rejection of all of the USFL's television-related claims.

What the USFL seeks is essentially a judicial restructuring of major-league professional football to allow it to enter. Because of the explicit congressional authorization in 1966 for the NFL-AFL merger and single-league operation, the USFL does not attack the league structure directly. Instead, the USFL asks us to prevent networks from broadcasting, and fans from watching, NFL games in the hope that they will turn to the USFL. Absent a showing of an unlawful barrier to entry, however, new sports leagues must be prepared to make the investment of time, effort and money that develops interest and fan loyalty and results in an attractive product for the media. The jury in the present case obviously found that patient development of a loyal following among fans and an adherence to an original plan that offered long-run gains were lacking in the USFL. Instead, the USFL quickly changed to a strategy of competition with the NFL in the fall, hoping thereby to force a merger of a few USFL teams into the NFL. That led to a movement of USFL teams out of large television markets and a resultant reduction in value of USFL games to television. As USFL owner and negotiator Einhorn predicted, abandoning major television markets precluded the possibility of obtaining a network contract. The USFL hoped, however, that if a merger did not occur, a jury verdict in the instant litigation followed by a decree effectively forcing a network to televise its product would save the day. Instead, the jury found that the failure of the USFL was not the result of the NFL's television contracts but of its own decision to seek entry into the NFL on the cheap.

CONCLUSION

For the foregoing reasons, we affirm the jury's verdict and the judgments entered thereon. . . .

NOTES AND QUESTIONS

1. *USFL Relief for NFL's §2 Violations.* Why did the jury award the USFL only $1 in damages (which is automatically trebled under the antitrust laws)? Note that the USFL, by proving the NFL was guilty of monopolization, was awarded approximately $5.5 million in attorney fees as a prevailing party.

   The Second Circuit refused to grant the USFL's proposed "sweeping injunctive relief," which it characterized as "essentially a judicial restructuring of major league professional football." What did the USFL ask the court to do, and why were these proposals rejected? Alternatively, what future NFL conduct (if any) should be enjoined to remedy the NFL's §2 violations and establish a competitive market for professional football in the United States?

2. *Policy Considerations.* What form of judicial relief for a §2 violation is in the best interests of sports fans—simply enjoining specific exclusionary practices, or requiring a league to restructure its business operations and/or to divest certain aspects?

   Some commentators argue that the historical pattern of anticompetitive practices by the dominant major professional sports leagues justify breaking the existing monopoly leagues into two or more independent competing leagues. James Quirk and Rodney Fort, Hard Ball—The Abuse of Power in Pro Team Sports, 171-186 (1999); Stephen Ross, *Monopoly Sports Leagues*, 73 Minn. L. Rev. 643 (1989). Professors Quirk and Fort explain:

   > We don't want the courts or regulatory bodies to be micromanaging the sports industry—instead, we want owners and general managers of teams to make the same kinds of decisions they make today, but in a competitive market environment, not in the present monopoly setup. If there is one thing about which economists are in agreement, it is that decentralized decision making in a competitive market environment leads to outcomes that are in the best interests of consumers, and that is all we are proposing here. . . .
   >
   > Our proposal does not involve the creation of a regulatory authority nor the intervention of courts into the day-to-day decision making in pro team sports. Instead, under our solution, the role of the government and the courts in pro team sports would be what it is in every other industry, as a corrective to monopolistic abuses if they arise again in the future.

   Quirk and Fort at 177-178, 182.

   However, others question whether doing so ultimately would be an effective remedy: "A once-and-for-all intervention to break up each current league monopoly into three or four competing leagues would provide the ideal solution . . . [but] there remains the crucial practical question of whether competition among major leagues can endure over the longer run." Paul Weiler, Leveling the Playing Field: How the Law Can Make Sports Better for Fans 333 (2000).

3. *Complementary Upstart Leagues.* Perhaps recognizing the difficulty of successfully competing with the dominant major leagues in the market and of obtaining effective relief through antitrust law for illegal exclusionary practices, some recent upstart leagues have purposefully assumed a nonthreatening posture. For example, the Big 3 league is a popular 3-on-3 half-court basketball league founded in 2017 with rosters composed largely of former NBA players for whom "the NBA is no longer an option." Ben Ladner, *An NBA Offseason Role Realized, the BIG3 Now Has Grander Ambitions*, SI.com, Aug. 9, 2018, https://www.si.com/nba/2018/08/09/big-3-ice-cube-kobe-bryant-nba-offseason-metta-world-peace-nate-robinson. Because the Big 3 league's brand of basketball differs substantially from NBA basketball, and because the Big 3 does not compete for current NBA players, it has positioned itself as a potential NBA partner rather than a competitor. The Alliance of American Football (AAF), a spring football league that began play in 2019, did not deviate from football's traditional rules as the Big 3 diverged from basketball's traditional rules. But, like the Big 3, the AAF sought to cooperate rather than compete with the dominant league in the market. Rather than challenge the NFL, the AAF sought to serve as an informal NFL minor league system through borrowing and developing fringe NFL players. Megan Armstrong, *NFL Discussing Loaning QBs, Other Players to AAF,*

Bill Polian Says, Bleacher Report, March 6, 2019, https://bleacherreport.com/articles/2823898-nfl-discussing-loaning-qbs-other-players-to-aaf-bill-polian-says. The Big 3 league is thriving, but the AAF folded during its first season due to financial mismanagement. By offering a variation that capitalizes on a preexisting major sport's popularity without infringing any of the dominant league's rights, these upstart leagues provide a new product to sports fans that is entirely consistent with the free market objectives of antitrust law.

PROBLEM 6-4

Since the American Basketball League (ABL) ceased operations, the WNBA has been the only women's professional basketball league in the United States. It has 12 teams, primarily in cities in which NBA teams play. It is a summer league that plays its regular season and playoff games from May through October to avoid any significant overlap with the NBA season. Each WNBA team has a roster of 12 players and plays 34 regular season games. CBS nationally televises 40 of the league's games per year.

Because of the increasing popularity of women's professional basketball, a group of wealthy investors is seeking to resurrect the ABL as an eight-team league with franchises in different American cities than the WNBA's clubs. They plan to play a 24-game regular season, with each club having a roster of ten players. The ABL's season will run from November through January.

The WNBA's commissioner is considering whether the league should increase its regular season to 36 games and allow all 12 teams (rather than the current eight teams with the best regular season records) to participate in the WNBA playoffs. This would extend the WNBA's season into November. She also is pondering whether to recommend that the WNBA proceed with its recent plan to expand into Boston and Denver, two cities in which ABL franchises will be located. She also is concerned about the enforceability of a provision in the WNBA standard player contract that prohibits a player from playing professional basketball for anyone other than her current team while the contract is in effect.

Advise the WNBA commissioner regarding whether the league's proposed actions or its standard player contract provision either individually or in combination violate §2, and how she can minimize any potential antitrust liability.

CHAPTER
7

Labor Relations in Professional Sports

A. INTRODUCTION

Contract, labor, and antitrust law historically have been the most important areas of law regulating labor relations between professional athletes and professional sports clubs and leagues, or the organizers of individual performer sports events. The chronology of professional sports leagues reveals a corresponding chronology regarding the prevailing legal principles that have helped shape the development of the professional sports industries during particular periods of time. Contract law was the first guiding light. Antitrust law concerns did not play a major role until the 1950s. Labor relations and labor law weighed in heavily, at least as to team sports, in the late 1960s. From the 1970s to the present day, the combination of contracts, antitrust, and labor law has significantly influenced the development of professional sports leagues in the United States. Together, these three areas of law are of great importance in understanding how and why professional sports leagues and associations have developed into their present forms and methods of business operation as well as how they will evolve in the future.

This chapter begins by exploring the basic application of contract law in professional sports and then turns to labor law with an analysis of five important, interrelated labor law areas that have substantially affected professional sports. These five areas are (1) the collective bargaining process, collective bargaining agreements, and uniform player contracts; (2) professional team sports drug testing regimes; (3) the activities of either a league and its clubs or the players union that constitute unfair labor practices under the National Labor Relations Act (NLRA); (4) the duty of a players union to represent all of its constituents fairly; and (5) the labor arbitration process established to resolve disputes between players and the league or their clubs, including discipline for on-field or off-field player conduct. This chapter then explores the complex intersection between labor and antitrust law, including the statutory and nonstatutory labor exemptions and the application of antitrust law to professional sports industry labor market restraints. Finally, because there is a global labor market for many professional sports (e.g., soccer, basketball, hockey, and baseball), this chapter briefly explores some European and other international labor relations issues.

B.   CONTRACT LAW

Owners of the first professional sports teams encountered player contract problems almost from the outset of their business operations. When an outstanding player was contractually bound to play for a particular club, but another club desired his services, legal problems ensued.

1.   *The Early Cases*

One of the first player contract disputes involved Samuel Washington Wise, who in 1882 refused to honor his contract with the Cincinnati club of the then-newly formed, but ultimately short-lived, American Association baseball league. In 1884, Tony Mullane, one of the better-known pitchers in that era, was sued by the also short-lived Union Association baseball league as a result of a contract dispute. Little is known about the results of these cases.

More is known about contract disputes that emerged in the Players League, another ill-fated baseball league that existed briefly in the late 1890s. The question raised in two early cases was whether star players Buck Ewing and John Montgomery Ward could escape being bound by their contracts with the National League's New York club or, to the contrary, be enjoined from jumping to the nascent Players League. In both cases the players prevailed. See *Metropolitan Exhibition Co. v. Ewing*, 42 F. 198 (C.C.S.D.N.Y. 1890); *Metropolitan Exhibition Co. v. Ward*, 9 N.Y.S. 779 (N.Y. Sup. Ct. 1890).

The *Ewing* court recognized the availability of a negative injunction in appropriate circumstances. If granted, a player in breach of an existing contract would be prohibited from playing for another club. The court, however, held that the subject player contract was not sufficiently definite to warrant a negative injunction. The club's right to retain rights to the player at the end of the contract was not adequately defined, and there was insufficient evidence of general custom and usage in the trade to define the contract's terms.

The *Ward* court also recognized the appropriateness of granting injunctive relief in some cases, focusing on the requirement that there be a likelihood that the club would succeed at trial on the merits on its breach of contract claim against the player. The court expressed concern about the player contract's indefinite terms and its lack of mutuality. As to the latter point, which was at issue in many of these early cases, the court emphasized that the club could terminate the contract almost at will, while the player was potentially bound to play for the club as long as it wanted him. The court concluded that this situation evidenced a lack of required mutuality of contractual obligations sufficient to deny injunctive relief.

The leading early sports contract case emanated from conflicts associated with the formation of the American League in 1900, which motivated National League star Napoleon Lajoie's efforts to leave the league's Philadelphia club and join its crosstown rival in the new American League.

PHILADELPHIA BALL CLUB, LTD. v. LAJOIE

51 A. 973 (Pa. 1902)

POTTER, J.

The defendant in this case contracted to serve the plaintiff as a baseball player for a stipulated time. During that period he was not to play for any other club. He violated his agreement, however, during the term of his engagement, and, in disregard of his contract, arranged to play for another and a rival organization. The plaintiff, by means of this bill, sought to restrain him during the period covered by the contract. The court below refused an injunction, holding that to warrant the interference prayed for "the defendant's services must be unique, extraordinary, and of such a character as to render it impossible to replace him; so that his breach of contract would result in irreparable loss to the plaintiff." In the view of the court, the defendant's qualifications did not measure up to this high standard. The trial court was also of opinion that the contract was lacking in mutuality, for the reason that it gave plaintiff an option to discharge defendant on 10 days' notice, without a reciprocal right on the part of defendant.

. . . We think, however, that in refusing relief unless the defendant's services were shown to be of such a character as to render it impossible to replace him he has taken extreme ground. It seems to us that a more just and equitable rule is . . . "[w]here one person agrees to render personal services to another, which require and presuppose a special knowledge, skill, and ability in the employée, so that in case of a default the same service could not easily be obtained from others, although the affirmative specific performance of the contract is beyond the power of the court, its performance will be negatively enforced by enjoining its breach. . . . The damages for breach of such contract cannot be estimated with any certainty, and the employer cannot, by means of any damages, purchase the same service in the labor market." We have not found any case going to the length of requiring, as a condition of relief, proof of the impossibility of obtaining equivalent service. It is true that the injury must be irreparable; but, as observed by Mr. Justice Lowrie in *Com. v. Pittsburgh & C.R. Co.*, 24 Pa. 160, 62 Am. Dec. 372: "The argument that there is no 'irreparable damage' would not be so often used by wrongdoers if they would take the trouble to discover that the word 'irreparable' is a very unhappily chosen one, used in expressing the rule that an injunction may issue to prevent wrongs of a repeated and continuing character, or which occasion damages which are estimated only by conjecture, and not by any accurate standard." We are therefore within the term whenever it is shown that no certain pecuniary standard exists for the measurement of the damages. . . .

The court below finds from the testimony that "the defendant is an expert baseball player in any position; that he has a great reputation as a second baseman; that his place would be hard to fill with as good a player; that his withdrawal from the team would weaken it, as would the withdrawal of any good player, and would probably make a difference in the size of the audiences attending the game." We think that, in thus stating it, he puts it very mildly, and that the evidence would warrant a stronger finding as to the ability of the defendant as an expert ball player. He has been for several years in the service of the plaintiff club, and has been re-engaged from season to season at a constantly increasing salary. He has become thoroughly familiar with the action and methods of the other players in the club, and his own work is peculiarly meritorious as an integral part of the team work which is so essential. In addition to these

Well known bts + very skilled

features which render his services of peculiar and special value to the plaintiff, and not easily replaced, Lajoie is well known, and has great reputation among the patrons of the sport, for ability in the position which he filled, and was thus a most attractive drawing card for the public. He may not be the sun in the baseball firmament, but he is certainly a bright particular star. We feel, therefore, that the evidence in this case justifies the conclusion that the services of the defendant are of such a unique character, and display such a special knowledge, skill, and ability, as renders them of peculiar value to the plaintiff, and so difficult of substitution that their loss will produce "irreparable injury," in the legal significance of that term, to the plaintiff. . . .

But the court below was also of the opinion that the contract was lacking in mutuality of remedy, and considered that as a controlling reason for the refusal of an injunction. The opinion quotes the nineteenth paragraph of the contract, which gives to the plaintiff a right of renewal for the period of six months, beginning April 15, 1901, and for a similar period in two successive years thereafter. The seventeenth paragraph also provides for the termination of the contract upon 10 days' notice by the plaintiff. But the eighteenth paragraph is also of importance, and should not be overlooked. It provides as follows: "(18) In consideration of the faithful performance of the conditions, covenants, undertakings, and promises herein by the said party of the second part, inclusive of the concession of the options of release and renewal prescribed in the seventeenth and nineteenth paragraphs, the said party of the first part, for itself and its assigns, hereby agrees to pay to him for his services for said term the sum of twenty-four hundred dollars, payable as follows," etc. And, turning to the fifth paragraph, we find that it provides expressly for proceedings, either in law or equity, "to enforce the specific performance by the said party of the second part, or to enjoin said party of the second part from performing services for any other person or organization during the period of service herein contracted for; and nothing herein contained shall be construed to prevent such remedy in the courts, in case of any breach of this agreement by said party of the second part, as said party of the first part, or its assigns, may elect to invoke."

We have, then, at the outset, the fact that the paragraphs now criticised and relied upon in defense were deliberately accepted by the defendant, and that such acceptance was made part of the inducement for the plaintiff to enter into the contract. We have the further fact that the contract has been partially executed by services rendered, and payment made therefor, so that the situation is not now the same as when the contract was wholly executory. The relation between the parties has been so far changed as to give to the plaintiff an equity, arising out of the part performance, to insist upon the completion of the agreement according to its terms by the defendant. This equity may be distinguished from the original right under the contract itself, and it might well be questioned whether the court would not be justified in giving effect to it by injunction, without regard to the mutuality or nonmutuality in the original contract. The plaintiff has so far performed its part of the contract in entire good faith, in every detail, and it would therefore be inequitable to permit the defendant to withdraw from the agreement at this late day. . . .

. . . In the contract now before us the defendant agreed to furnish his skilled professional services to the plaintiff for a period which might be extended over three years by proper notice given before the close of each current year. Upon the other hand, the plaintiff retained the right to terminate the contract upon 10 days' notice and the payment of salary for that time and the expenses of defendant in getting to his home. But the fact of this concession to the plaintiff is distinctly pointed out as part of the consideration for the large salary paid to the defendant, and is emphasized as such; and owing to the peculiar nature of the services demanded by the business, and the high degree of efficiency which must be maintained, the stipulation is not unreasonable. Particularly is this true when it is remembered that the plaintiff has played for years under substantially the same regulations.

We are not persuaded that the terms of this contract manifest any lack of mutuality in remedy. Each party has the possibility of enforcing all the rights stipulated for in the agreement. It is true that the terms make it possible for the plaintiff to put an end to the contract in a space of time much less than the period during which the defendant has agreed to supply his personal services; but mere difference in the rights stipulated for does not destroy mutuality of remedy. Freedom of contract covers a wide range of obligation and duty as between the parties, and it may not be impaired, so long as the bounds of reasonableness and fairness are not transgressed. . . .

. . . The defendant sold to the plaintiff, for a valuable consideration, the exclusive right to his professional services for a stipulated period, unless sooner surrendered by the plaintiff, which could only be after due and reasonable notice and payment of salary and expenses until the expiration. Why should not a court of equity protect such an agreement until it is terminated? The court cannot compel the defendant to play for the plaintiff, but it can restrain him from playing for another club in violation of his agreement. No reason is given why this should not be done, except that presented by the argument, that the right given to the plaintiff to terminate the contract upon 10 days' notice destroys the mutuality of the remedy. But to this it may be answered that, as already stated, the defendant has the possibility of enforcing all the rights for which he stipulated in the agreement, which is all that he can reasonably ask. Furthermore, owing to the peculiar nature and circumstances of the business, the reservation upon the part of the plaintiff to terminate upon short notice does not make the whole contract inequitable.

In this connection another observation may be made, which is that the plaintiff, by the act of bringing this suit, has disavowed any intention of exercising the right to terminate the contract on its own part. This is a necessary inference from its action in asking the court to exercise its equity power to enforce the agreement made by the defendant not to give his services to any other club. Besides, the remedy by injunction is elastic and adaptable, and is wholly within the control of the court. If granted now, it can be easily dissolved whenever a change in the circumstances or in the attitude of the plaintiff should seem to require it. The granting or refusal of an injunction or its continuance is never a matter of strict right, but is always a question of discretion, to be determined by the court in view of the particular circumstances.

Upon a careful consideration of the whole case, we are of opinion that the provisions of the contract are reasonable, and that the consideration is fully adequate. The evidence shows no indications of any attempt at overreaching or unfairness. Substantial justice between the parties requires that the court should restrain the defendant from playing for any other club during the term of his contract with the plaintiff. . . .

The specifications of error are sustained, and the decree of the court below is reversed, and the bill is reinstated; and it is ordered that the record be remitted to the court below for further proceedings in accordance with this opinion.

NOTES AND QUESTIONS

1. *Negative Injunction.* Although the relevant contractual language was essentially the same, the *Lajoie* court (unlike the *Ewing* and *Ward* courts) held that the subject contract was sufficiently definite and mutual to be enforceable. Which of these differing judicial views is most persuasive? Why? For the past century, *Lajoie* has represented the prevailing judicial view regarding the availability of equitable relief to remedy a professional athlete's breach of contract. Pursuant to the so-called negative injunction, a player is not ordered to perform for his former club but is instead ordered not to perform for his new club or elsewhere. A negative injunction may be granted if the court concludes that damages alone (which may be uncertain and difficult to ascertain) are not an adequate legal remedy for loss of a player's services. How would a club's damages for a player's nonperformance because of his breach of contract be calculated? (Hint: The standard measure of damages for breach of contract is to award the nonbreaching party the "benefit of the bargain," otherwise termed the expectation interest.) What is the appropriate nature and scope of injunctive relief?

2. *Affirmative Injunction.* Because of the Thirteenth Amendment prohibition of involuntary servitude and judicial reluctance to police compliance with the terms of an employment contract, courts generally do not order a player to honor his or her contract. Is it ever appropriate for a court to order a player under contract to play for his or her current club? See Geoff Rapp, *Affirmative Injunctions in Athletic Employment Contracts: Rethinking the Place of the Lumley Rule in American Sports Law,* 16 Marq. Sports L. Rev. 261 (2006) (arguing in favor of specific performance enforceable by affirmative injunction as a remedy for a player's holdout in breach of his employment contract).

3. The legal victory by the Philadelphia National League club was largely illusory. After the Pennsylvania court's decision, Lajoie was traded by the Philadelphia American League club to its American League counterpart in Cleveland. The National League attempted to enforce its Pennsylvania decree in Ohio but was rebuffed. See *Philadelphia Baseball Club v. Lajoie,* 13 Ohio Dec. 504 (1902). Thus, Lajoie never returned to the National League. The only practical effect of the Pennsylvania decision was that Lajoie did not risk contempt of court by playing in that state until the National and American Leagues reached an agreement in 1903 that allowed players such as Lajoie to remain with their chosen ball clubs.

4. Lajoie, known as the "Big Frenchman," achieved several notable milestones in his long baseball career. His .422 batting average in 1901 is still the American League single-season high mark, topped in the post-1900 era only by Rogers Hornsby's .424 record in 1924 for the St. Louis Cardinals. Lajoie's playing career spanned 21 seasons. He had 9,589 official at bats, 3,251 hits, and compiled a career batting average of .339. He was elected to baseball's Hall of Fame in the second year of its existence. The only players selected ahead of him were Babe Ruth, Walter Johnson, Ty Cobb, Christy Mathewson, and Honus Wagner.

2. *Modern Judicial View*

By and large, cases such as *Lajoie* have arisen when a rival league is formed and players are enticed to abandon their present teams, lured by more lucrative contracts offered by new clubs. Such was the situation not only in *Lajoie* but also in the *Ward* and *Ewing* cases. During the twentieth century, several new professional leagues were created, particularly after World War II. The increasing popularity of sport, aided in great part by the developing technologies of radio and television, inspired an entrepreneurial spirit in the industry. As an established league's revenues increased, so did the economic incentives for new rival leagues to form.

Baseball's National League, after being challenged by the upstart American League at the beginning of the twentieth century, joined with the American League in 1903 to create Major League Baseball. But the combined leagues then had to fight off the Federal League (founded in 1914) and later the Mexican League (founded in 1946). In 1949 the National Basketball Association (formed in 1946 as the Basketball Association of America) renamed itself after absorbing teams from the original National Basketball League, then faced challenges from the American Basketball League (1961) and the American Basketball Association (1967). The World Hockey Association (founded in 1972) lasted a few tenuous years in competition with the National Hockey League, with the WHA finally succumbing as four of its clubs were absorbed by the more established league. The National Football League, as it became increasingly popular, dealt with a myriad of rivals, notably the All-America Football Conference (1946), the American Football League (AFL) (1960), the World Football League (1973), and the United States Football League (1983). The XFL (2001), which lasted only one season originally, has planned a relaunch 2020, but its low salaries and spring schedule signal that it hopes to merely coexist with, rather than challenge, the NFL.

Some rival leagues lasted only a year, while others persevered longer. Some new leagues were sufficient nuisances that a few of their teams were permitted to join the established league. The most successful rival league that developed in the twentieth century, in addition to baseball's American League, was the AFL, which was allowed to merge in its entirety with the NFL through an act of Congress (which is discussed in *Mid-South Grizzlies v. NFL, supra* in Chapter 6).

The formation of rival leagues led to much litigation. Clubs in established leagues brought breach of contract suits and sought negative injunctions against players seeking to jump to clubs in new leagues. (As discussed in Chapter 6D, the upstart league frequently responded by asserting antitrust law claims against the established league and its clubs.)

Two issues typically raised in breach of contract suits require close scrutiny: (1) whether a negative injunction is necessary to prevent imminent and irreparable harm to the breaching player's former club; and (2) whether the requested injunction is reasonable in its duration and scope. Although other issues such as mutuality of obligation frequently were raised in the early cases, these two issues historically have been more important.

a. Imminent and Irreparable Harm

The *Lajoie* court concluded that a professional player of Lajoie's status was sufficiently special to merit injunctive relief to prevent his breach of contract. The court focused on the irreparable harm to Lajoie's club if it lost a player of his ability prior to the expiration of his contract, observing that "[h]e may not be the sun in the baseball firmament, but he is certainly a bright particular star." 51 A. at 974.

More recently, courts have not required that a player be irreplaceable, only that it be shown that the player has unique skills not *easily* replaced, and in evaluating whether a professional athlete has "unique" skills, courts have reached different conclusions using varying measures. In *Winnipeg Rugby Football Club v. Freeman*, 140 F. Supp. 365 (N.D. Ohio 1955), a federal court opined that even if the player was not unique by simply being a "good" NFL player, he might be unique in the Canadian Football League, where the quality of play might be lower. Thus, the player, who was in breach, was enjoined from playing for an NFL club. In *Dallas Cowboys Football Club, Inc. v. Harris*, 348 S.W.2d 37 (Tex. Civ. App. 1961), the court ruled that a player who played for only one year with minimal success could be found to be not "unique," though the subject player had not yet proved his "nonunique" status. Based on these cases and others, even if a court considers evidence that a player is not unique, the player has a substantial burden to prove this factually. Today, it is probably a safe assumption that those who make the major leagues in any sport are almost certain to be characterized as "unique."

The standard player contracts in all major leagues have a provision stating that the player acknowledges he is unique and that a negative injunction can be obtained against him if he refuses to perform. Although this is not necessarily conclusive and a court or arbitrator might refuse to enforce this provision, this is highly unlikely. Thus, the odds are increased that a major league professional athlete will be found to have unique skills.

b. Duration and Scope of the Injunction

The greatest hurdle to obtaining a negative injunction relates to its scope and duration. If a court finds the requested injunction will create an unreasonable hardship to the party sought to be restrained, the injunction will be denied or its scope may be limited. What constitutes unreasonableness, or undue harshness, varies with the particular circumstances. Factors considered by a court may include the length of the requested injunction, its geographical reach, the types of employment or activities prohibited under the injunction, and its potential effects in preventing employment or other opportunities for the restrained party. However, these factors are balanced against the resulting damage to the plaintiff if an injunction is not granted.

In the absence of an express agreement, an injunction normally will not be imposed beyond the time period specified in the contract. For example, when basketball star Rick Barry decided to abandon the NBA for the ABA, he had an option year remaining on his NBA contract. Faced with an injunction barring his immediate move to the ABA, Barry simply sat out his option year and did not play for anyone. After that year, when he did join the ABA, his old NBA club sought a further injunction preventing him from playing in the ABA until he fulfilled his option year obligation. However, the court ruled that the duration of his contract had lapsed and that an injunction would not be granted for any additional length of time. See *Lemat Corp. v. Barry*, 275 Cal. App. 2d 671 (1969).

The granting of an injunction becomes more complicated when it is international in scope. In *Winnipeg Football Club v. Freeman, supra*, a U.S. court upheld a Canadian contract and enforced a negative injunction that enjoined the breaching player from playing in the NFL while his CFL contract was in effect. Today, contracts may be entered into and performed on a global basis.

Traditionally, courts have hesitated to order an injunction with extraterritorial effect that requires enforcement abroad. However, *Boston Celtics v. Shaw*, discussed at length later in this chapter, illustrates that U.S. courts may no longer be reluctant to do so. A U.S. court confirmed an arbitration award ordering Brian Shaw to honor a valid contract with the Boston Celtics and not to continue playing basketball with an Italian basketball team. The duration and scope of an injunction may present complex issues when the activity contemplated in the contract is a single event, such as a tennis or golf tournament or exhibition, or a boxing match. The following case raises several important issues related to the appropriateness of a negative injunction in such circumstances. A critical analysis of the court's reasoning should produce arguments both for and against the court's final disposition of the matter.

LEWIS v. RAHMAN

147 F. Supp. 2d 225 (S.D.N.Y. 2001)

CEDARBAUM, District Judge.

[EDS. In one of two related contract disputes, Lennox Lewis, the then-former heavyweight champion of the world, claimed a contractual right to fight a rematch against Hasim Rahman, the then-current heavyweight champion of the world, within 150 days of an April 21, 2001 bout in which Rahman defeated Lewis. A Provision of Services Agreement (PSA) obligated the boxers to a boxing match on April 21, 2001. The agreement included a provision entitling Lewis to a rematch bout within 150 days after the April 21, 2001 match in the event that Rahman won the bout. A subsequent amendment to the PSA (hereinafter "Addendum") stated as follows:

> [I]f Fighter [Rahman] is declared the winner of the bout by the applicable boxing commission, he agrees to participate in a rematch within 150 days of the date of the bout upon the terms and conditions that may be negotiated by promoter.

Although Lewis was the favorite, he was defeated in the bout by Rahman, who thereby became the World Boxing Council, International Boxing Federation, International Boxing Organization, and linear heavyweight champion (linear is a "term used in the industry to describe the boxer whose championship can be traced back in a straight line to a single, undisputed champion"). Thereafter, the representatives of Lewis and Rahman negotiated a deal for a rematch that would have granted HBO exclusive rights, but the deal fell through when HBO failed to present a check for a $3 million signing bonus to Rahman as had been negotiated.]

On the evening of May 9, 2001, Rahman and Hoffman [Rahman's manager] met with [boxing promoter Don] King in King's hotel room in New York. King offered Rahman an Exclusive Promotional Agreement (the "King agreement"). The King agreement promised a signing bonus to Rahman of $5 million. It also provided that Rahman's first bout would be against Brian Nielsen on August 4, 2001, and that his second bout would be a "unification bout" against the [World Boxing Association] WBA champion. The winner of that bout would hold the heavyweight title of all four sanctioning organizations. Rahman signed the King agreement, and King gave him $200,000 in cash and a check for $4.8 million. After Rahman signed the King agreement, his opponent in the August 4, 2001 bout was changed from Nielsen to David Izon. Rahman has not yet signed a Bout Agreement to fight Izon.

Lennox Lewis was an extremely credible witness. He testified that he has been a boxer since the age of 12. He fought in over 300 amateur fights before turning professional at age 23. He represented Canada in the 1984 and 1988 Olympic Games. In 1998, he won the Olympic gold medal for boxing. He has fought 36 professional bouts. Prior to the loss to Rahman, Lewis had lost only one professional fight. Lewis described the rigorous training program he undertakes to prepare for each fight, as well as the physical risks he assumes when he boxes. He testified that it was a material condition of his bout with Rahman that Rahman agree to a prompt rematch if he won the bout. Lewis wants an immediate rematch both because of his age and because he fears that other boxers will try to freeze him out of title contention. He will be 36 years old this fall.

Emmanuel Steward, Lewis' manager and trainer, was also a very credible witness. He testified that Lewis is reaching the age at which a boxer's skills begin to diminish. Steward testified that Lewis has fought longer and more often than most heavyweight boxers, especially champions, and has suffered even more wear and tear than other boxers his age. He further testified that Lewis needs to fight three or four times a year to maintain his weight and keep his skills sharp. Because of his age and the relatively large number of fights he has fought in his amateur and professional careers, Lewis plans to retire in two years.

I find that Lewis would suffer irreparable harm were he denied the opportunity to regain his championship title. It is undisputed that the heavyweight championship is the most prestigious title in professional boxing. The opportunity to fight for the heavyweight championship, and especially the opportunity to regain the championship, cannot be measured in money. Because of his age, Lewis has only a limited time to regain his title and restore his reputation. Rahman, in contrast, is only 28 years old. Even if he chose not to box for 18 months, he would still have several productive years left in his career. Rahman concedes that he has a contractual obligation to fight Lewis in a rematch eventually, although he prefers to fight an interim bout. When asked if he wished to fight Lewis immediately, he said, "I don't have a problem with it." . . .

DISCUSSION

Lewis has a right to a rematch on August 18, 2001. . . . By signing the Addendum, Rahman expressly agreed to fight Lewis in a rematch within 150 days. . . . Defendants' fraudulent inducement defense fails. A contract may be voided if it is induced by fraud, as where "one party possesses superior knowledge, not readily available to the other, and knows the other is acting on the basis of mistaken knowledge." *Brass v. American Film Tech., Inc.*, 987 F.2d 142, 150 (2d Cir. 1993). There is no evidence that the terms of the rematch provision were not readily available to Hoffman and Rahman. It is clear on the face of the Addendum that Rahman was agreeing to 1) a rematch within 150 days, 2) the terms of the PSA and 3) the grant of certain future rights to Lion [Lewis' promotion company]. Rahman's and Hoffman's failure to ask Kushner [Rahman's former promoter] questions about paragraphs 5 and 7 of the Addendum, even if believed, does not show fraud on the part of CKP [Kushner's promotion company] or Lion [Lewis promotion company].

Defendants' other argument . . .—that the WBC rule against immediate rematches . . .—[is] equally without merit. Violation of the WBC's rule may cause the WBC to refuse to sanction the Lewis-Rahman rematch. WBC sanction, however, is not required by the PSA . . . or the Addendum. Moreover, only Lewis, and not Rahman, can be harmed by the withholding of the WBC sanction. Whether or not the bout is sanctioned, if Rahman should win the rematch, he would keep all the titles; if he should lose, he would lose all the titles. . . .

Neither the Addendum nor the PSA contains an express negative covenant pursuant to which Rahman agreed not to fight anyone else before he fights the rematch. But, under New York law, a negative covenant will be implied where the party from whom performance is sought is a unique and extraordinary talent. *Harry Rogers Theatrical Enterprises, Inc. v. Comstock*, 225 A.D. 34, 232 N.Y.S. 1, 4 (1st Dep't 1928). Rahman holds the heavyweight championship title. He is therefore both unique and extraordinary.

INJUNCTIVE RELIEF

Several courts have granted equitable relief to enforce negative covenants where, as here, the party to be enjoined is a unique and extraordinary boxing talent. *Madison Square Garden Corp. v. Carnera*, 52 F.2d 47 (2d Cir. 1931); *Madison Square Garden Boxing, Inc. v. Shavers*, 434 F. Supp. 449 (S.D.N.Y. 1977); *Arias v. Solis*, 754 F. Supp. 290 (E.D.N.Y. 1991); but see *Machen v. Johansson*, 174 F. Supp. 522 (S.D.N.Y. 1959).

"The basic requirements to obtain injunctive relief have always been a showing of irreparable injury and the inadequacy of legal remedies." *Ticor Title Insurance Co. v. Cohen*, 173 F.3d 63, 68 (2d Cir. 1999). Lewis would be irreparably harmed if he were denied the opportunity to regain the championship. The value of the opportunity to regain the heavyweight championship while he still has the ability to do so cannot be measured or compensated for in money damages.

In contrast, an injunction will not impose a significant burden on Rahman. Rahman concedes that he has an obligation to fight a rematch with Lewis eventually, and he testified that he does not have a problem fighting the rematch first. Moreover, the evidence at trial demonstrates that Rahman will earn several million dollars in a rematch bout. The potential harm to Lewis should injunctive relief be denied greatly outweighs the relatively minor burden the injunction imposes on Rahman.

Defendants, in their post-trial submissions, now argue that lack of mutuality precludes injunctive relief. See *Lawrence v. Dixey*, 119 A.D. 295, 104 N.Y.S. 516 (1st Dep't 1907). This argument is unavailing. Lion has exercised its option under the rematch provision, binding itself and Lewis to fight the rematch on the terms described in the PSA and to negotiate in good faith for a purse that exceeds the stipulated minimum. The Lawrence doctrine is, therefore, inapplicable.

A preponderance of the credible evidence shows that Lewis will not be able to fight for more than the next two years. Even during the next two years, his boxing abilities may diminish. An injunction for 18 months provides an effective remedy for Lewis' irreparable harm and does not unfairly impede Rahman. Cf. *Machen*, 174 F. Supp. at 529-531 (denying injunctive relief based on the finding that a limited injunction would be ineffective and an indefinite injunction would unduly burden the defendant).[6] If I were to limit the injunction to 150 days, as Rahman urges, I would be permitting Rahman to escape his obligation by letting a short period of time elapse. As soon as Rahman complies with his obligation, he will be free to fight other bouts. The power to end the restriction is in his hands.

CONCLUSION

The foregoing Opinion constitutes my findings of fact and conclusions of law pursuant to Fed. R. Civ. P. 52(a). Defendant Hasim Rahman is hereby enjoined from engaging in any heavyweight bout for the next 18 months unless and until he complies with his contractual obligation to fight a rematch with Lennox Lewis under the terms and conditions of the Provision of Services Agreement. . . .

PROBLEM 7-1

Driver Johnny Joe Milton has compiled an enviable record on the NASCAR circuit since joining the Il Penseroso racing team two years ago. In fact, he has been so successful that he has attracted the attention of other race team owners, including Claude Forsooth. Despite the fact that Johnny has a year remaining on his three-year contract with Il Penseroso, not to mention two one-year options exercisable by Il Penseroso, Johnny agrees to leave that group and join Forsooth and his Formula One racing team. Though Johnny regrets leaving the NASCAR circuit, he looks forward to the new challenges of Formula One. He will race mainly in Europe in Grand Prix events but will also be in the United States for such races as the Indy 500 and two or three similar events.

Il Penseroso's owner, Alfonse Allegro, is not about to allow Johnny to leave his team that easily. He points to wording in his written contract with Johnny whereby Johnny promises to render "his race driving services *exclusively*" to Il Penseroso for the term of the contract. Allegro files suit against Johnny for breach of contract and seeks a worldwide injunction to restrain him from racing for Forsooth for the three-year remaining duration of his contract.

Considering the arguments likely to be raised by the parties, how should the court rule?

C. LABOR LAW

1. *Historical Overview*

Our nation's labor laws have become predominant influences in the structure and operations of professional sports leagues in the United States. If sports

---

6. *Machen* did not involve a right to fight to regain the heavyweight championship. Accordingly, Eddie Machen's interest in fighting a rematch with the defendant, and the harm resulting from the loss of that opportunity, were not comparable to Lewis's injury.

leagues engage in interstate commerce, which almost all do, they come under the aegis of our national labor laws. Players are employees of teams; when players organize into groups to voice and advance their interests collectively, they become labor unions. The federal labor laws have had a profound impact on the development of professional sports leagues, particularly those at the major league level, for more than 50 years. To understand these effects more fully, we first need to consider the general role of the National Labor Relations Act (NLRA), and then analyze its application to professional sports industries.

The NLRA, 29 U.S.C. §§151 et seq., was enacted by Congress in 1935. The NLRA, which is known as the Wagner Act, and its numerous amendments (in particular the Taft-Hartley Act of 1947 and the Landrum-Griffin Act of 1959) provide the basic legal structure governing management-worker relations in the United States. Section 7 of the NLRA provides three basic rights for workers: (1) the right to form, join, and assist labor organizations; (2) the right to bargain collectively through representatives chosen by the workers; and (3) the right to engage in "concerted activities" such as picketing and strikes to advance and protect their interests. 29 U.S.C. §157.

Section 8(a) of the NLRA details prohibited employer conduct, including interference with employees' rights to organize and bargain collectively, domination or interference with the formation or administration of a labor union, discrimination against employees to discourage union membership, retaliation against employees for exercising their rights, and refusing to bargain in good faith. 29 U.S.C. §158(a). All of these prohibited employer actions may constitute unfair labor practices. The NLRA also prohibits unfair labor practices by a labor union; for example, a refusal to bargain collectively in good faith. 29 U.S.C. §158(b).

The oversight and enforcement of these rights comes under the jurisdiction of the National Labor Relations Board (NLRB) and the federal courts. The NLRB enforces the federal labor laws by adjudicating claims of "unfair labor practices" allegedly committed by either management or labor. The NLRB also administers the machinery that determines appropriate units or groups of employees qualified to vote in a union representation election, and that conducts such elections to determine which, if any, union will represent all employees who are part of that unit.

The NLRB also determines which issues are subject to negotiation under labor law, delving into questions concerning the required scope of bargaining. Under the NLRA, *scope of bargaining* includes all issues relating to wages, hours, and terms and conditions of employment. 29 U.S.C. §158(d). Wages include pay, fringe benefits, and bonus payments; hours encompass time spent on the job; and working conditions cover factors influencing the work environment, such as work rules, seniority, and safety. Most important, these three areas—wages, hours, and working conditions—are considered *mandatory* subjects of bargaining. If either labor or management requests bargaining on issues that are mandatory under labor law, the other side must bargain over these in good faith. A failure to do so is an unfair labor practice that violates §8 of the NLRA. However, what actually constitutes an issue of wages, hours, or conditions of employment is not always crystal clear. In particular, it is not uncommon for labor and management to disagree regarding what is a condition of employment. Such disputes must be resolved by the NLRB.

If an issue is not a *mandatory* subject of bargaining, it is either a *permissive* or *illegal* subject. See *NLRB v. Wooster Div. of Borg-Warner Corp.*, 356 U.S. 342 (1958).

Mandatory
v. Permissive
v. Illegal

It is *permissive* if it is a nonmandatory lawful subject of bargaining. It is an *illegal* subject of bargaining if one or more laws prohibit it from being implemented (e.g., discriminatory treatment of certain employees based on their race), even if it were successfully negotiated. If a subject is permissive, management may negotiate with a union on that issue, but is not required to do so. If the subject is illegal, neither side has either the duty or freedom to bargain over such issues.

For purposes of the NLRA, there are two additional important factors to consider. First, a union that is duly certified by the NLRB pursuant to the prescribed procedures becomes the exclusive bargaining agent for all employees within the unit. As a practical matter, all active players in a U.S. professional sports league come under the aegis of the union that has been chosen to represent them. A player is not required to become a member of the union that the NLRB recognizes for his or her league. The player is bound, however, by the union's actions and the terms of any collective bargaining agreements that the union negotiates with the league and its member clubs.

The second factor is equally important. Those who are not currently active players in the league (as defined by the bargaining unit) are *not* members of the union and, as such, have no vote and little voice in union affairs. Even so, to a large extent, the actions of the union may affect their rights. For example, college players who want to play professionally usually find that their eligibility to do so is determined by the collective bargaining agreement between the league and the players union. The same may be true for foreign players and others such as high school graduates seeking the opportunity to play in an American professional league that is unionized. The extent to which management and labor, by their agreement, can effectively control prospective players outside the bargaining unit has been the subject of extensive litigation and is explored later in this chapter.

Until 1969, the NLRB expressed reluctance to assert jurisdiction over labor relations in the context of professional sports. For example, it had declined to do so for the thoroughbred horse-racing industry, which was deemed to be merely a local activity. See *Walter A. Kelley*, 139 N.L.R.B. 744 (1962); *Los Angeles Turf Club, Inc.*, 90 N.L.R.B. 20 (1950). However, in its landmark ruling in *American League of Professional Baseball Clubs and Association of National Baseball League Umpires*, 180 N.L.R.B. 190 (1969), the NLRB recognized the interstate nature of professional sports and the appropriateness of having federal labor law govern the relationships between league clubs and their players.

THE AMERICAN LEAGUE OF PROFESSIONAL BASEBALL CLUBS AND ASSN. OF NATIONAL BASEBALL LEAGUE UMPIRES

180 N.L.R.B. 190 (1969)

Upon the entire record in this case, including the briefs, the National Labor Relations Board finds:

1. The Petitioner seeks an election in a unit of umpires employed by the American League of Professional Baseball Clubs (hereinafter called the Employer or the League). The Employer, while conceding the Board's constitutional and statutory power to exercise jurisdiction herein, nevertheless urges

the Board, as a matter of policy, not to assert jurisdiction pursuant to Section 14(c) of the Act.

The Employer is a nonprofit membership association consisting of 12 member clubs located in 10 states and the District of Columbia. Operating pursuant to a constitution adopted and executed by the 12 member clubs, the Employer is engaged in the business of staging baseball exhibitions and, with its counterpart the National League of Professional Baseball Clubs, constitutes what is commonly known as "major league baseball." The Employer currently employs, among other persons, the 24 umpires requested herein, and one umpire-in-chief. . . .

The Board's jurisdiction under the Act is based upon the commerce clause of the Constitution, and is coextensive with the reach of that clause. In 1922 the Supreme Court in *Federal Baseball Club of Baltimore v. National League of Professional Baseball Clubs*, 259 U.S. 200, although characterizing baseball as a "business," ruled that it was not interstate in nature, and therefore was beyond the reach of the nation's antitrust laws. However, subsequent Supreme Court decisions appear to proceed on the assumption that baseball, like the other major professional sports, is now an industry in or affecting interstate commerce, and that baseball's current antitrust exemption has been preserved merely as a matter of judicial *stare decisis*. Thus, in both the *Toolson* and *Radovich* decisions the Supreme Court specifically stated that baseball's antitrust status was a matter for Congress to resolve, implying thereby that Congress has the power under the commerce clause to regulate the baseball industry. Since professional football and boxing have been held to be in interstate commerce and thus subject to the antitrust laws, it can no longer be seriously contended that the Court still considers baseball alone to be outside of interstate commerce. Congressional deliberations regarding the relationship of baseball and other professional team sports to the antitrust laws likewise reflect a Congressional assumption that such sports are subject to regulation under the commerce clause. It is, incidentally, noteworthy that these deliberations reveal Congressional concern for the rights of employees such as players to bargain collectively and engage in concerted activities. Additionally, legal scholars have agreed, and neither the parties nor those participating as *amici* dispute, that professional sports are in or affect interstate commerce, and as such are subject to the Board's jurisdiction. Therefore, on the basis of the above, we find that professional baseball is an industry in or affecting commerce, and as such is subject to Board jurisdiction under the Act.

Section 14(c)(1) of the National Labor Relations Act, as amended, permits the Board to decline jurisdiction over labor disputes involving any "class or category of employers, where, in the opinion of the Board, the effect of such labor dispute on commerce is not sufficiently substantial to warrant the exercise of its jurisdiction. . . ." The Employer and other employers contend that because of baseball's internal self-regulation, a labor dispute involving The American League of Professional Baseball Clubs is not likely to have any substantial effect on interstate commerce; and that application of the National Labor Relations Act to this Employer is contrary to national labor policy because Congress has sanctioned baseball's internal self-regulation. The Employer also contends that effective and uniform regulations of baseball's labor relations problems is not possible through Board processes because of the sport's international aspects.

The Petitioner and other employee representatives contend, on the other hand, that Section 14(c) precludes the Board from declining jurisdiction, as any labor dispute arising in this industry will potentially affect millions of dollars of interstate commerce and have nationwide impact. They assert that baseball's self-regulation is controlled entirely by employers, and therefore has not and will not prevent labor disputes from occurring in this industry. Additionally, it is submitted that Congressional intent does not preclude, and national labor policy requires, Board jurisdiction—for without a national forum for uniform resolution of disputes, the industry might be subject to many different labor laws depending upon the State in which any particular dispute arises.

We have carefully considered the positions of the parties, and the *amicus* briefs, and we find that it will best effectuate the mandates of the Act, as well as national labor policy, to assert jurisdiction over this Employer. We reach this decision for the following reasons:

Baseball's system for internal self-regulation of disputes involving umpires is made up of the Uniform Umpires Contract, the Major League Agreement, and the Major League Rules, which provide, among other things, for final resolution of disputes through arbitration by the Commissioner. The system appears to have been designed almost entirely by employers and owners, and the final arbiter of internal disputes does not appear to be a neutral third party freely chosen by both sides, but rather an individual appointed solely by the member club owners themselves. We do not believe that such a system is likely either to prevent labor disputes from arising in the future, or, having once arisen, to resolve them in a manner susceptible or conductive to voluntary compliance by all parties involved. Moreover, it is patently contrary to the letter and spirit of the Act for the Board to defer its undoubted jurisdiction to decide unfair labor practices to a disputes settlement system established unilaterally by an employer or group of employers. Finally, although the instant case involves only umpires employed by the League, professional baseball clubs employ, in addition to players, clubhouse attendants, bat boys, watchmen, scouts, ticket sellers, ushers, gatemen, trainers, janitors, office clericals, batting practice pitchers, stilemen, publicity, and advertising men, grounds keepers and maintenance men. . . . As to these other categories, there is no "self-regulation" at all. This consideration is of all the more consequence for those employees in professional baseball whose interests are likely to call the Board's processes into play, the great majority are in the latter-named classifications.

We can find, neither in the statute nor in its legislative history, any expression of a Congressional intent that disputes between employers and employees in this industry should be removed from the scheme of the National Labor Relations Act. . . .

There is persuasive reason to believe that future labor disputes—should they arise in this industry—will be national in scope, radiating their impact far beyond individual State boundaries. As stated above, the Employer and its members are located and conduct business in 10 States and the District of Columbia. The stipulated commerce data establishes that millions of dollars of interstate commerce are involved in its normal business operations. The nature of the industry is such that great reliance is placed upon interstate travel. Necessarily, then, we are not here confronted with the sort of small, primarily intrastate employer over which the Board declines jurisdiction because of failure to meet its prevailing monetary standards. Moreover, it is apparent that the Employer, whose operations are so clearly national in scope, ought not have its labor relations problems subject to diverse state labor laws.

The Employer's final contention, that Board processes are unsuited to regulate effectively baseball's international aspects, clearly lacks merit, as many if not most of the industries subject to the Act have similar international features.

Accordingly, we find that the effect on interstate commerce of a labor dispute involving professional baseball is not so insubstantial as to require withholding assertion of the Board's jurisdiction, under Section 14(c) of the Act, over Employers in that industry, as a class. As the annual gross revenues of this Employer are in excess of all of our prevailing monetary standards, we find that the Employer is engaged in an industry affecting commerce, and that it will effectuate the policies of the Act to assert jurisdiction herein. . . .

Accordingly, we find that the umpires are not supervisors, and thus the Employer's motion to dismiss on this ground is hereby denied. We further find that the following employees of the Employer constitute a unit appropriate for the purposes of collective bargaining within the meaning of Section 9(b) of the Act: All persons employed as umpires in the American League of Professional Baseball Clubs, but excluding all other employees, office clerical employees, guards, professional employees and supervisors as defined in the Act. . . .

NOTES

1. Shortly after *American League of Professional Baseball Clubs* was decided, the first collective bargaining agreements were entered in the major professional sports leagues. Labor and management reached rudimentary (by today's standards) but significant agreements. Within months of each other, the National Basketball Association (NBA), the National Football League (NFL), and Major League Baseball (MLB) all reached formal agreements with the players unions in their respective leagues. The National Hockey League (NHL) also reached a series of less formal agreements with the National Hockey League Players Association. Professional sports league labor relations have been significantly more complex and governed primarily by federal labor law since then.

2. The benefits to athletes of unionization and collective bargaining are perhaps most clearly seen when examining baseball's minor leagues. Nothing in the law prevents minor league players from unionizing, but they have not done so, perhaps due to the challenges involved in organizing a diverse group of young players with relatively short careers who play in several regional leagues throughout the nation. Since MLB players formed the MLBPA, MLB minimum salaries have increased by roughly 5,000%. Over the same time period, minor league salaries have increased by less than 100%, and some minor league players make a mere $1,200 per month. Because there is no collective bargaining relationship with their respective league clubs, a group of minor league players in 2014 turned to the courts, alleging, in *Senne v. Kansas City Royals Baseball*, 105 F. Supp. 3d 981 (N.D. Cal. 2015), that their compensation violates the Fair Labor Standards Act (FLSA). Plaintiffs brought the class action against Major League Baseball and each of its thirty franchises in the United States District Court for the Northern District of California. Although plaintiffs cleared a major hurdle in March 2017 by securing class certification, the United States Congress derailed the case a year later when it passed the Save America's Pastime Act (SAPA), amending FLSA to generally exclude professional baseball players from

the statute's protections. Christopher R. Deubert, *What Might the Supreme Court's Decision in Epic Systems Mean for Sports?*, Sports Law Blog, June 13, 2018, http://sports-law.blogspot.com/2018/05/the-save-americas-pastime-act.html. The legislation, which followed years of MLB lobbying and which was quietly inserted on page 1,967 of a 2,232-page, $1.3 billion omnibus spending bill, has been widely criticized as an MLB power play to quash the *Senne* case and any future such litigation attempts. Mike Axisa, *Congress' 'Save America's Pastime Act' would allow teams to pay minor-leaguers less than minimum wage*, CBSSports.com, March 22, 2018, https://www.cbssports.com/mlb/news/congress-save-americas-pastime-act-would-allow-teams-to-pay-minor-leaguers-less-than-minimum-wage/; Whitney McIntosh, *How Congress screwed over Minor League Baseball players, explained*, SBNation.com, March 23, 2018, https://www.sbnation.com/mlb/2018/3/23/17152778/spending-bill-minor-league-baseball-explained-save-americas-pastime. Indiana University Kelley School of Business Professor Nathaniel Grow, however, argues that the legislation may not be a death knell for minor league baseball players' future FLSA claims. Specifically, he argues sloppy drafting permits the interpretation that the statute bars FLSA claims related to work during the playing season, but does not bear on such claims related to off-season work. Nathaniel Grow, *The Save America's Pastime Act and Its Implications for the Future of Minor-League Baseball*, Kelley School of Business Research Paper No. 18-45, April 27, 2018, https://ssrn.com/abstract=3169957.

Several NFL cheerleaders, who like minor league baseball players are not unionized and are concerned that their compensation violates the FLSA, have filed similar suits. See Alexandra Sifferlin, *NFL Cheerleaders File Suit Saying They Make as Little as $2.85 per Hour*, Time.com, Feb. 14, 2014, http://time.com/44069/cheerleaders-rebel-over-low-wages/. The suits allege unlawfully low pay and bad working conditions. In September 2014, the Oakland Raiders reached a $1.25 million settlement with its former cheerleaders, Eric Morath, *Cheerleaders vs. NFL Teams: A Fair-Wage Fight*, WSJ.com, Sept. 5, 2014, http://www.wsj.com/articles/cheerleaders-vs-nfl-teams-a-fair-wage-fight-1409939356, and in March 2015, the Tampa Bay Buccaneers settled with its cheerleaders for $825,000. Marissa Payne, *Tampa Bay Buccaneers cheerleaders get $825,000 in wage lawsuit settlement*, WashPost.com, March 7, 2015, http://www.washingtonpost.com/blogs/early-lead/wp/2015/03/07/tampa-bay-buccaneers-cheerleaders-ger-825000-in-wage-lawsuit-settlement/. San Francisco 49ers cheerleaders did not fare as well with their challenge, which a federal court dismissed in July 2017. *Kelsey K. v. NFL Enterprises LLC, et al.*, 2017 WL 3115169 (N.D. Ca. July 21, 2017). A similar suit against the Milwaukee Bucks, which expanded the FLSA battle to the NBA, was settled in 2017. *Milwaukee Bucks settle lawsuit over cheerleader pay*, USAToday.com, April 26, 2017, *Milwaukee Bucks settle lawsuit over cheerleader pay*, USAToday.com, Apr. 26, 2017, https://www.usatoday.com/story/sports/nba/2017/04/26/milwaukee-bucks-settle-lawsuit-over-cheerleader-pay/100953804/.

A former New Orleans Saints cheerleader brought a different sort of challenge in March 2018, filing an Equal Employment Opportunity Commission charge against the NFL. Bailey Davis, who was fired because of a photo she posted on social media, argued that the Saints maintain different sets of rules for players and cheerleaders regarding social media use and interaction between the two groups. For instance, the club has rules that prohibit Saints cheerleaders from having contact with Saints players, whether in person or on social media, but the club places no such restrictions on players. Davis asserts this inequity violates the NFL Personal Conduct Policy's prohibition on gender-based employment discrimination. Davis offered to drop her action in exchange for one dollar in nominal damages and a meeting NFL Commissioner Roger Goodell to establish a "binding set of rules" for all NFL clubs with respect to their treatment of cheerleaders. *Report: Former Saints cheerleader, others seek $1 settlement, meeting, other terms,* New Orleans Advocate, April 24, 2018, https://www.theadvocate.com/new_orleans/news/article_2bfd0510-47f4-11e8-8b9b-7740a09228ed.html https://www.theadvocate.com/new_orleans/news/article_2bfd0510-47f4-11e8-8b9b-7740a09228ed.html. No such meeting or settlement occurred, and the case has gone to arbitration. Chelsea Brasted, *Girls can't run the world if we don't stick together,* Nola.com, Apr. 9, 2019, https://www.nola.com/opinions/article_ae75cc75-54ef-5051-a4b4-fef06da93d7f.html.

2. Collective Bargaining in the Professional Sports Industries

The primary basis for determining legal relationships between owners and players in professional sports is the collective bargaining agreement (CBA) reached between the players association and the owners' multiemployer bargaining unit. The collective bargaining agreement under our nation's labor laws is the predominant legal source and prevails over a league's enunciated rules or the individual agreements reached between a player and a league. This also applies to other employee unions, such as umpires and referees.

The primary focus of bargaining between players and owners has shifted over the past decades since the first agreements in the late 1960s. Those first agreements largely concentrated on job security for the players and focused on pension plans, minimum salaries, and fringe benefits such as health and life insurance. These are still important considerations, but as the economics of sports have changed, so has much of the emphasis of collective bargaining. Two general areas, driven by economics, have dictated a shift in focus on collective bargaining.

The first of these areas are concerns of the players around so-called player mobility issues—those relating to the initial allocation of players through a draft and the later restraints on player movement through free agency. The second arises from a league's concern that free agency has strained the player market by greatly increasing player salaries and other benefits. Thus, the response has been to seek restrictions on spending by team owners. Because owners have seemingly been unable to control themselves, probably fearing that other owners would not be similarly inclined, owners through their leagues have sought such constraints as salary caps, luxury or competitive balance taxes, and other devices aimed to discourage excessive spending.

These two areas have a direct impact on players' wages and conditions of employment and thus are mandatory subjects of bargaining, so much so that they have often been central issues of contention. More than one strike or lockout has been triggered in the various leagues over issues relating to player mobility and salary caps.

a. Salary Caps and Competitive Balance Taxes

The NBA was the first league to institute anything approaching a comprehensive cap on salaries. This occurred in 1983, at a time when the NBA was clearly struggling financially. In an unprecedented move, the league opened its books for inspection. The picture was bleak. The players association (NBPA) reluctantly acquiesced to a cap on player salaries, although it was months after the "agreement" was reached before the full details were formulated and the new collective bargaining agreement was signed. Even then, the cap was fraught with vagueness. No one had contemplated the many ways in which its provisions could be circumvented. But restraints came into existence under what later became known as a "soft cap." The "soft" was a reference to the many ways by which a team could exceed the cap and still be within its provisions.

The chief exception, often used, was to pay salaries to a team's veteran players that sent the overall team salary far beyond the official league team limit. This became known as the "Larry Bird Exception," because the famous Celtics Hall of Famer was completing the final year of his first contract when the new collective bargaining agreement was to take effect. When the league and the union fashioned a method by which veterans were not penalized by the cap if their original team was willing to pay their asking price on the market, Bird was the prime example of the largesse accorded to the league's superstars. It is also true that representatives of Bird had worked behind the scenes to ensure that he was not injured by the new cap. In one fashion or another, an exception was carved that has provided millions for the many top players in the NBA since 1983. Also of note is that, since its first inception, the NBA cap has gone through several revisions, including more explicit limits on both veteran and rookie salaries, but it still remains, in most respects, a "soft" cap approach. (For the most recent specifics of the NBA salary cap, see 2017 NBA CBA, Article VII. For the WNBA, see 2014 WNBA CBA, Article VII.)

Ten years later, the NFL instituted its salary cap. The notable difference from the NBA efforts was that the NFL got its players to agree to a "hard cap." Under this, a team maximum salary is determined each year based on prior and projected team revenues. Every team has to fit its total salaries into that maximum figure, with no give at the top. This sounds fairly simple, but it is not. The agreement has led to multiple schemes to restructure player contracts to free up room under the salary cap in a particular year. By this device, players enter into a new contract wherein their immediate salary is low, but a signing bonus gives them most of the monies that would have been received under their previous contracts. The signing bonus, however, is then allocated equally over the years of the new contract, thus reducing the club's immediate cap obligation. Another device to change a club's cap obligation is to have the player sacrifice the immediate income provided in their previous contract for even greater future rewards in a new agreement struck between the parties.

However, the cap has also led to clubs being hesitant about guaranteed income, leaving players vulnerable to later release, causing their big salaries to suddenly evaporate. In other words, the large salaries reported in the newspapers are often highly illusory. Even so, despite the cap's obvious difficulties, the NFL has used it to maintain its position as the most prosperous organization in professional sports. Overall, player salaries continue to rise on average each year, team revenues increase annually, and the owners benefit by sharp increases in the values of their franchises. (For the latest formulations of the NFL cap, see 2011 NFL CBA, Article XIV.)

The economics of Major League Baseball breed local revenue disparities among large and small market clubs. In an effort to remedy this disparity, national broadcast, trademark licensing, and Internet (i.e., Major League Baseball Advanced Media (MLBAM)) revenues are equally shared among MLB clubs, and Commissioner Rob Manfred has broad authority to redistribute MLB central fund revenues created by each club's payment of a fixed percentage of its locally generated revenues. In addition, because MLB has never had a salary cap, it has collectively bargained attempts to curtail some clubs' profligate spending on player salaries by requiring them to pay some type of tax if their annual aggregate spending exceeds a certain amount. The first attempt was a so-called "luxury tax," which expired under the terms of the collective bargaining agreement provision that created it. The 2002 CBA created a "competitive balance tax," which is similar to the earlier tax and requires teams above a certain aggregate player salary level to pay a tax into MLB coffers for distribution to lower-income clubs. The "competitive balance tax" is also used to help finance an Industry Growth Fund, established in 1997, to "promote the growth of baseball in the United States and Canada, as well as throughout the world." With some negotiated modifications, this tax has continued to be a key feature of subsequent MLB CBAs. (In general, see 2012 MLB CBA, Articles XXIII and XXIV, and 2017 MLB CBA, Articles XXIII and XXIV.)

The NHL had no salary cap or competitive balance tax through 2004, and the players had long staunchly opposed the imposition of any such salary controls. When the NHL CBA expired at the end of the 2004 season, however, the owners refused to enter a new CBA without a salary cap, which triggered a collective bargaining stalemate and led to the cancellation of the 2004-2005 season. Only after a ten-month lockout did the NHL and NHLPA agree to a salary cap. The cap remains in place in the current NHL CBA, which continues through the 2021-2022 season. The basic contours of the cap are discussed in section C.2.c.iv, *infra*.

For various perspectives on efforts by leagues to impose constraints and limits on player salaries, see Scott Bukstein, *Preparing for Another Round of Collective Bargaining in the National Basketball* Assocation, 22 Jeffrey S. Moorad Sports L.J. 373 (2015); Matthew J. Parlow, *Lessons from the NBA Lockout: Union Democracy, Public Support, and the Folly of the National Basketball Players* Association, 67 Okla. L. Rev. 1 (2014); Justin Hunt, *To Share or Not to Share: Revenue Sharing Structures in Professional Sports*, 13 Tex. Rev. Ent. & Sports L. 139 (2012); Zachary Golden, Note, *Is This Heaven? No, It's I.O.U.: Why Major League Baseball Must Modify Its Current Revenue-Sharing and Luxury-Tax Procedures*, 45 Suffolk U. L. Rev. 125 (2011); Justin Hunt, *Why Single Is Better: The Implications of a Multi-Entity Ruling on Revenue Sharing and the NFL Salary Cap*, 10 Va. Sports & Ent. L.J. 17 (2010); William B. Gould, *Labor Issues in Professional Sports: Reflections on Baseball, Labor and Antitrust Law*, 15 Stan. L. & Pol'y Rev. 61 (2004).

b. Collective Bargaining Provisions on Player Mobility

Beginning in the 1890s with the National League, major professional leagues and their clubs unilaterally established rules tying players to a particular team through a draft of players initially entering the league, a "reserve clause" that purportedly gave a club perpetual rights to a player even after his contract expired, and other restrictions on player movement to other teams. Only a trade of the player allowed him to move to a new team—at least within the league in which he currently played. In some instances, as discussed *infra*, NFL, NBA, and NHL players successfully challenged free agency restrictions on antitrust grounds, a means of legal recourse not available to MLB players because of baseball's broad common law antitrust immunity. However, MLB players gained free agency through a 1976 landmark labor arbitration decision, *National & American League Professional Baseball Clubs v. Major League Baseball Players Association*, discussed *infra*. In modern times, the nature and scope of restrictions on player mobility usually are a contentious part of collective bargaining negotiations in all of the major professional leagues that are unionized.

The main existing restraints are summarized as follows:

The Draft. All major American sports leagues hold one or more drafts per year to divide rights to new players among their member clubs. Although a player draft (depending on its number of rounds and other factors) may violate antitrust law, the players associations in each of these leagues, for diverse reasons, have agreed to some form of a draft. In most instances, the number of rounds in the draft has been reduced, most notably in the NBA and NFL. But the bottom line is that the best players are drafted and have little initial choice where they will play. Player eligibility for the draft has also changed over the years. MLB continues to allow players right out of high school to be drafted, as well as those who go to college and become eligible again at a later date. The NFL has relaxed its eligibility rules somewhat, but most players are not eligible to be drafted to play in the league until they are three years out of high school. The NBA generally requires that players be a year out of high school to be eligible, but Commissioner Adam Silver has signaled a desire to eliminate that requirement in the near future. The NHL allows 18- and 19-year-olds to be drafted in certain early rounds of its draft, but not in the later rounds. A veritable montage of differing league rules provides (or does not provide) for the drafting of foreign players.

If all of this sounds confusing, do not be alarmed. It is. The end result is that along with issues of free agency, trade, and related topics, discussed below, those who represent athletes or teams need to have thorough knowledge of the collective bargaining provisions, as well as league rules, that have a significant effect on how one does business in the sports industry.

Uniform Player Contract. By whatever name it is called, "uniform" or "standard" or something else, it is a contract signed by every player in a league, as well as those seeking to enter the league and join a team's preseason training camp. In all major sports leagues, at least in the United States, the uniform player contract is an important part of the collective bargaining agreement, with its terms and legal effects governed by U.S. labor laws. It is referenced here because many of its terms incorporate several of the restraints on player mobility. As an illustration of its overriding importance, we consider one example (the NBA Uniform Player Contract) later in this chapter.

Free Agency. Over the years, free agency has been a major battleground. For decades, the players lost the battles. As noted previously, this changed with the legal victories via antitrust lawsuits and arbitration in the 1970s. Even so, a player is not entirely free to play for the club of his choice, because the players associations for each league have agreed to some type of restrictions on free agency. Arguably the most stringent are in MLB, where a player must have six full major league seasons to be eligible for free agency, which is earned by credited time on a major league roster. Each day is counted, so that a player who is shuttled back and forth between the major and minor leagues by his club may need more than six seasons to earn six years of credited service. Only an MLB player's right to salary arbitration after three full years of credited service softens the impact. (See the discussion of salary arbitration, *infra*.)

The NBA's approach to free agency concentrates on the top players entering the league (i.e., those taken in the first round of the draft). Contracts between a club and a first-round pick last for a guaranteed two seasons, with the club holding an option for a third and fourth season.

In the NFL, the player's rights may be retained by his initial club (or one to which he is traded) for four years (or, in the case of first round draft picks, for five years).

The NHL uses a complicated set of criteria to determine if a player is a restricted or unrestricted free agent, which depends on either the player's length of service or age.

In all four major sports leagues, the player's current contract must expire before he may become a free agent. For example, even if an MLB player fulfills the six years of credited service, he is not a free agent if he is contractually bound to his current club (e.g., if he signed a three-year contract at the end of his fifth year).

In summary, though free agency is much easier for a player to achieve now than it was a few years ago, there are still strings attached through the draft, free agency eligibility requirements and conditions, the current club's rights of first refusal, free agent compensation systems, and other mechanisms pursuant to the league CBA and uniform player contracts. (General references to the above include 2011 NBA CBA, Article X *Draft* and Article XI *Free Agency*; 2011 NFL CBA, Article VI *College Draft* and Articles VIII, IX, and X, various types of free agency; 2012 MLB CBA, Article XX *Reserve System*; and 2005 NHL CBA, Article 8 *Entry Draft* and Article 10 *Free Agency*.)

c.   Key Provisions of the NBA, NFL, MLB, and NHL CBAs as of August 2016

i.   *NBA Collective Bargaining Agreement, 2017-2024*

In December 2016, the NBA and NBPA both declined to trigger an opt-out provision in their previous CBA that would have potentially led to a work stoppage. Instead, they agreed to a new CBA in place until the end of the 2023-2024 season.

Central features of the agreement are:

- The 50-50 split of basketball-related revenue remains unchanged.
- Minimum salaries rise by 45%.
- Teams are now each able to develop two players in the NBA Developmental League, known as the D League, on two-way contracts, which will substantially increase those players' salaries.
- The rule that permits players one year out of high school to play in the NBA, known as the "one-and-done" rule, remains in place, but both sides agree that the rule may need revision.

- The season will start a week earlier than it has in recent years, and there will be no more than six preseason games.
- Teams will less frequently play on successive days, and no team will play four games in five days more than once during a season.
- No team may offer a player over 38 years of age a five-year maximum contract (the threshold was previously 36 years of age).

ii. NFL Collective Bargaining Agreement, 2011-2020

After months of negotiation and a lockout by the owners that began in March 2011 and extended through much of the summer, the NFL and NFLPA came together to forge a new collective bargaining agreement with only one preseason game lost.[1]

Central features of the agreement are as follows:

- The ten-year agreement will be in existence through the 2020 season. There will be no opt-out provision allowing either side to terminate the agreement before that date. This differs from the 2006 CBA that allowed the owners to end the agreement two years before its scheduled date, which led to early and extended labor strife. Although the NFL had sought to expand the regular schedule to 18 games per team, the season will remain at 16 games pending further discussions.
- The new CBA includes new provisions to protect player health and safety, including reduced mandatory off-season workouts and fewer contact practices during the season, along with enhanced injury protection benefits. Retired NFL players will receive $1 billion collectively in additional health insurance and disability benefits.
- A good number of contentious issues dealt with the division of money and the salary cap. Both sides received something in the compromise that ensued. The players' share of league-wide revenue is reduced from 50 percent to 47 percent, but revenue is defined to be more inclusive as to the sources of income that are included.
- The salary cap and bonus cap for 2012 was set at $125 million per team.[2] Importantly, in addition to a revised and expanded definition of "revenue," each team had to spend at least 89 percent of the salary cap, but the league as a whole had to spend 99 percent of the cap during the following two years, a significant advance for the players.
- There is a rookie wage scale, and all players taken in the regular draft must sign four-year contracts, with first-round picks also giving their club an option to extend their contracts for a fifth year.

1. Fifteen months after the NFL locked out its players, it locked out its game day officials. Like the NFL's dispute with the NFLPA, its dispute with the National Football League Referees Association (NFLRA) revolved around financial issues, with the NFLRA demanding increased salaries and enhanced pension benefits for officials. Throughout the 2012 NFL preseason and for the first three weeks of the regular season, replacement officials officiated games, but following weeks of criticism regarding missed calls and poor game management—highlighted by an outcry over an officiating error that gave the Seattle Seahawks a last-second win over the Green Bay Packers during the season's third week—a new eight-year CBA was reached on September 27, 2012.

2. The salary cap has increased steadily thereafter, and the projected NFL salary cap for the 2019 season is $188.2 million.

- Veteran players whose contracts have expired become unrestricted free agents if they have four years of league experience.
- Disputes concerning the terms of the CBA will be resolved by arbitration, rather than judicial oversight by a federal court, as had been provided by Judge David Doty since 1993.
- The *Brady v. NFL* lawsuit, see *infra*, was settled as part of the agreement. Also settled was another pending suit in Minnesota federal district court before Judge Doty in which the NFL was found to have breached its duty to obtain the maximum value for its television contracts by accepting a lower amount in exchange for guaranteed payments even if no football was played during the 2012 season.[3]

In the CBA's aftermath, many commentators concluded that the NFL got the better of the NFLPA at the bargaining table, particularly with respect to the agreed percentage of revenue sharing between the NFL clubs and players. In 2017, evidently dissatisfied the revenue split as well as other aspects of the CBA, Smith declared that a work stoppage at the CBA's conclusion was "almost a virtual certainty." Although the NFL and NFLPA in April 2019 announced that they had begun informal discussions toward a new CBA, in May 2019, Smith doubled down, warning all NFL player agents to prepare for "work stoppage of at least a year of length." Michael Shapiro, *NFLPA Director DeMaurice Smith Tells Agents to Plan for Work Stoppage After 2020*, SI.com, May 28, 2019, https://www.si.com/nfl/2019/05/28/demaurice-smith-nflpa-work-stoppage-collective-bargaining-agreement.

iii.   MLB Collective Bargaining Agreement, 2017-2021

In December 2016, MLB clubs and players reached agreement on a new CBA, which will last through the 2021 season. Unlike the contentious labor relations that have plagued other major American sports leagues and their players' union in the recent past, MLB clubs and players have resolved their labor issues with relatively little contention since 1995. MLB remains the only major U.S. professional sports league with no salary cap. The new CBA is similar to the previous one, although it does feature some new provisions.

Central features of the current MLB CBA are as follows:

- The regular season has been extended to give players four extra off-days.
- World Series home field advantage is now assigned to the team with the best record rather than the team in the league that wins the All-Star game.

---

3. The most contentious issue arising from the new CBA has been the discretion afforded the Commissioner in handing down disciplinary measures. Partly in response to the ongoing investigation and appeal of Tom Brady's 2015 suspension for allegedly conspiring to deflate footballs below authorized air pressure levels (see discussion later in this chapter of *National Football League Management Council v. National Football League Players Ass'n*, 820 F.3d 527 (2d Cir. 2016)), the NFLPA has pressed the NFL for a new disciplinary appeals process that would remove the Commissioner as arbiter and appoint an appeals officer in his place. *NFL, NFLPA working on a deal to strip Roger Goodell of disciplinary power*, SportsIllustrated.com, March 15, 2016, http://www.si.com/nfl/2016/03/15/nflpa-deal-strip-commissioner-roger-goodell-disciplinary-power. For a thorough exploration of the NFL CBA and the process that produced it, see Chris Deubert, *All Four Quarters: A Retrospective and Analysis of the 2011 Collective Bargaining Process and Agreement in the National Football League*, 19 UCLA Ent. L. Rev. 1 (2012).

- A player now has ten days to accept a qualifying offer from a club rather than seven days.
- The number of MLB games played outside of the continental United States and Canada will increase over the next five years, with games taking place in Mexico, Puerto Rico, the Dominican Republic, Asia, and the United Kingdom.
- The Major League minimum salary will increase (from the 2017 level of $535,000) to $545,000 in 2018 and to $555,000 in 2019, and it will be subject to a cost-of-living adjustment in 2020 and 2021.
- The number of in-season random drug tests has been increased from 3,200 to 4,800, with all players on 40-man rosters subject to random tests during the offseason.
- A smokeless tobacco ban has been implemented throughout MLB, but all smokeless tobacco users who saw MLB action in 2016 or earlier are grandfathered in.
- New anti-hazing and anti-bullying policies have been implemented.

In early 2019, MLB and MLBPA negotiated a number of substantial rules changes that became effective for the 2019 season: shorter inning breaks; restricted mound visits; adjustments to All-Star bonus payments; and the creation of a joint committee to consider further changes. For the 2020 season, changes include an increase of MLB's active player roster limit from 25 to 26; elimination of the 40-player active player roster limit in September; and a requirement that relief pitchers must (absent illness or injury) pitch to "either a minimum of three batters or the end of a half-inning." *MLB, MLPBPA announce on-field agreement*, MLB, Mar. 14, 2019, https://www.mlb.com/press-release/mlb-mlbpa-announce-rule-changes.

iv.   NHL Collective Bargaining Agreement, 2013-2022

In 2012, the NHL experienced its second work stoppage in eight years. As noted in section C.2.a above, the first work stoppage caused the cancellation of an entire season and created a widespread sense that the league might not survive. The NHL and the NHLPA, however, eventually reached a collective bargaining agreement that included, among other provisions, a salary cap tied to revenues (something the NHLPA initially vowed it would never accept) and an immediate rollback of 24 percent on all existing contracts (e.g., a contract that paid a player $1 million in 2005-2006 was reduced to $760,000), and as a result, the league not only survived; it thrived. Revenues increased, and as they did, so too did the salary cap. Indeed, the salary cap for the 2012-2013 season was $70.2 million, $31.2 million higher than when the cap was initially instituted in 2005.

When the 2005 CBA neared expiration in September 2012, renewal discussions began, but as in 2004 the NHL and NHLPA negotiated to a stalemate, and a month before the 2012-2013 season was scheduled to begin, the 2005 CBA expired with no new agreement, sparking another lockout. Negotiations dragged on through the fall of 2012 and resulted in the cancellation of hundreds of games before the parties signed a Memorandum of Understanding reflecting the terms of a new, ten-year CBA on Saturday, January 12, 2013. This new CBA has an opt-out clause for both the NHL and the NHLPA. The owners have the first option to terminate on September 1, 2019.

Central features of the agreement are as follows:

- The salary cap for the first full season under the agreement was $64 million. For all subsequent seasons the salary cap will be determined by a complex formula that considers hockey-related revenues from the previous season, the cost of preliminary benefits (e.g., pension funding, group insurance programs, and individual bonuses), and the number of teams playing in the league.[4]
- The new agreement provides a 50-50 split of hockey related revenues between owners and players. This provision represents a substantial concession for players, who under the previous CBA received a 57 percent share of such revenues.
- Individual player contracts are limited to seven years, with an exception (permitting eight-year contracts) for players who re-sign with their current clubs.
- The minimum player salary for the 2012-2013 season was $525,000. By the start of the 2021-2022 season, that figure will have risen to $750,000.
- A player's on-ice infractions can result in fines in an amount up to 50 percent of the player's salary and non-performance-based bonuses divided by the number of days in the regular season. Fines, however, cannot exceed $10,000 for the first infraction and $15,000 for each subsequent infraction. More egregious offenses may result in suspension.
- Random drug testing of players will occur during the preseason, the regular season, the play-offs, and the off-season. Notably, the agreement modifies the Prohibited Substances List to include amphetamines and other stimulants. The agreement also considers the creation of a committee to study the issue of human growth hormone (HGH) testing and to make recommendations on whether an HGH testing program should be established in the NHL.
- Each NHL club will be required—upon the NHL's request—to participate in at least one international trip during the term of the CBA, and the NHL and NHLPA will work together to develop and pursue other international opportunities involving NHL players.
- Any NHL club not generating regular-season gate revenues equaling 75 percent or more of the league-wide gate revenue average will be subject to oversight from the league's Revenue Sharing Oversight Committee and may be eligible for financial assistance from the league's new Industry Growth Fund. Clubs seeking such assistance must submit business plans explaining the steps they will take to improve business performance.
- The newly created Owner-Player Relations Committee will meet twice a year to discuss matters of mutual interest and will ensure that there exists consistent communication between players and owners as to how to best grow the game for their mutual benefit and that of the fans.

In January 2019, the NHL and NHLPA announced that they had entered preliminary discussions regarding renewal of their CBA, an effort to engender good will and avoid the high tensions surrounding previous negotiations. Kevin

---

4. In June 2019, the NHL set the league's salary cap at $81.5 million per club for the 2019-20 season.

Allen, *Opinion: NHL, NHLPA have started CBA talks on a positive note, and that's different*, USA Today (Jan. 25, 2019), https://www.usatoday.com/story/sports/nhl/columnist/allen/2019/01/25/nhl-nhlpa-cba-labor-talks-different-vibe/2682988002/.

d. Uniform Player Contracts

The *uniform* or *standard* player contract (UPC), which is the product of collective bargaining between the players' union and league clubs' bargaining representative, is a staple in the world of professional team sports. The UPC reproduced *infra* is an edited version of the one used by the NBA, which is incorporated as Exhibit A to the league's current collective bargaining agreement. Although the terms of each league's UPC may vary slightly, most provisions are remarkably similar. The UPC, which is subject to the provisions of the league CBA, has a hierarchical contract status that places it above a league's constitution and bylaws, followed by the individually negotiated terms of the contract between a player and his or her club. Often, it mentions, and thus incorporates, other collective bargaining provisions.

e. Individual Player Contracts

In general, depending on the status of the particular player, several of the following terms are considered negotiable:

1. Basic salary and length of contract
2. Bonuses—signing, roster, performance (individual and team)
3. Guaranteed income (with details when this is applicable)
4. Trade provisions (assignment of contract) and possible limitations
5. Special benefits
6. Added injury protection
7. Personal conduct provisions

Not all of these provisions are negotiated in every individual player contract. Some amendments or modifications of the terms of the UPC may be prohibited by a league's CBA, which was an issue considered in *Boston Celtics v. Shaw, infra.* Other terms may be unobtainable because of a particular club's unwillingness to negotiate and the player's lack of bargaining leverage (which usually depends on his level of talent).

PROBLEM 7-2

Prior to examining the NBA Uniform Player Contract, review the following questions that will assist in directing your attention to particular provisions and inform you of the many variables that parties must consider during contract negotiation.

a. The NBA collective bargaining agreement prescribes three-year contracts for first-round rookie draftees, with restricted free agent status thereafter. In general, if the team and player are not restricted as to the term of years (other than the five-year veteran maximum), what considerations go into the determination of the length of the contract?

b. Provision 7 provides that if a player is not in good physical condition, he may be suspended by the team. What if an NBA player is suspended for this reason and then signs with a European club? Can his NBA team enjoin him from playing in Europe? Consider the cases on negative injunctions in section B, as well *Boston Celtics v. Shaw* in section C.6, *infra*.

c. Provision 9 states that the player recognizes he possesses unique skills and thus can be enjoined if he is in breach of contract. What is the legal effect of this language? Can a judge or arbitrator decide that, despite this declaration, the player in fact does not have unique skills? On this point, is this to be decided exclusively by arbitration? Or does the team (or player) have the right to have this decided by a court? See Provision 17.

d. Provision 10 addresses the assignment of a player's contract. After the assignment (or trade), suppose the team that acquires the player fails to pay the player all that is owed under the contract. Does the player have recourse against his old club, as well as his current employer? Does Provision 10 provide a definitive answer to this question? Is the general law on assignments of contracts relevant?

e. The termination provisions in Provision 16 must be studied with great care, particularly section (a)(iii) as to a player's failure to exhibit sufficient skill. This provision embodies what was traditionally termed the right of a club to "cut" a player. That term, for good reason, has largely been discarded. Essentially, however, this provision allows a team to terminate the contract of a player if the club, for whatever reason, feels the player does not have sufficient skills to make the team. If there are no other safeguards in the contract, the player is paid to the date of termination, he or she is released under the procedures applicable in the league (generally through the so-called waiver system), and the contract is terminated with no further obligations owed by player or club. The question is, can there ever be any bases for a player to contest the club's use of this provision? (Hint: What if a player claims he was injured when he was released? What if he claims he cursed at the coach and incurred the personal enmity of the coach? In section C.6, on labor arbitrations, *infra*, examine the cases for other possible examples.)

f. Provision 17 stipulates that arbitration is the proper method for resolution of disputes arising from the player-team contract. It excludes Provision 9 from the purview of interpretation by an arbitrator. What does this mean?

g. What provisions often found in individual contracts between a player and a team are not included in the Uniform Player Contract? How does one introduce these into the player-team negotiations? Where does one go to find out whether any such limitations exist?

NBA UNIFORM PLAYER CONTRACT

THIS AGREEMENT made this ___ day of _____, is by and between _____ (hereinafter called the "Team"), a member of the National Basketball Association (hereinafter called the "NBA" or "League") and an individual whose address is shown below (hereinafter called the "Player"). In consideration of the mutual promises hereinafter contained, the parties hereto promise and agree as follows:

1. TERM.

The Team hereby employs the Player as a skilled basketball player for a term of _____ year(s) from the 1st day of September.

2. SERVICES.

The services to be rendered by the Player pursuant to this Contract shall include: (a) training camp, (b) practices, meetings, workouts, and skill or conditioning sessions conducted by the Team during the Season, (c) games scheduled for the Team during any Regular Season, (d) Exhibition games scheduled by the Team or the League during and prior to any Regular Season, (e) if the Player is invited to participate, the NBA's All-Star Game (including the Rookie-Sophomore Game) and every event conducted in association with such All-Star Game, but only in accordance with Article XXI of the Collective Bargaining Agreement currently in effect between the NBA and the National Basketball Players Association (hereinafter the "CBA"), (f) Playoff games scheduled by the League subsequent to any Regular Season, (g) promotional and commercial activities of the Team and the League as set forth in this Contract and the CBA, (h) any NBADL Work Assignment in accordance with Article XLI of the CBA, and (i) any service in the NBADL pursuant to a Two-Way Contract.

3. COMPENSATION.

(a) Subject to paragraph 3(b) below, the Team agrees to pay the Player for rendering the services and performing the obligations described herein the Compensation described in Exhibit 1, Exhibit 1A, Exhibit 1B, or Exhibit 10 hereto, as applicable (less all amounts required to be withheld by any governmental authority, and exclusive of any amount(s) which the Player shall be entitled to receive from the Player Playoff Pool). For Standard NBA Contracts, unless otherwise provided in Exhibit 1 or Exhibit 1A, such Compensation shall be paid in twenty-four (24) equal semi-monthly payments beginning with the first of said payments on November 15th of each year covered by this Contract ("contract year") and continuing with such payments on the first and fifteenth of each month until said Compensation is paid in full. For Two-Way Contracts, Compensation shall be paid as follows: (i) the Player's Two-Way NBADL Salary shall be paid in twenty-four (24) equal semi-monthly payments beginning with the first of said payments on November 15th of each contract year and continuing with such payments on the first and fifteenth of each month until said Compensation is paid in full (each such payment date, a "Semi-Monthly Payment Date"); (ii) for each NBA Day of Service that the Player accrues prior to the first Semi-Monthly Payment Date and between each subsequent Semi-Monthly Payment Date (each such period, an "NBA Day of Service Payment Period"), the Player shall be paid a payment equal to (x) the Two-Way NBA Salary daily rate, less (y) the Two-Way NBADL Salary daily rate, multiplied by (z) the number of NBA Days of Service that the Player accrues during such NBA Day of Service Payment Period, with such payment, if applicable, made on the Semi-Monthly Payment Date two weeks after the completion of the NBA Day of Service Payment Period.

(b) The Team agrees to pay the Player $2,000 per week, pro rata, less all amounts required to be withheld by any governmental authority, for each week (up to a maximum of four (4) weeks for Veterans and up to a maximum of five (5) weeks for Rookies) prior to the Team's first Regular Season game that the Player is in attendance at NBA training camp or Exhibition games; provided, however, that no such payments shall be made if, prior to the date on which he is required to attend training camp, the Player has been paid $10,000 or more in Compensation with respect to the NBA Season scheduled to commence immediately following such training camp. Any Compensation paid by the Team pursuant to this A-3 subparagraph shall be considered an advance against any Compensation owed to the Player pursuant to paragraph 3(a) above, and the first scheduled payment of such Compensation (or such subsequent payments, if the first scheduled payment is not sufficient) shall be reduced by the amount of such advance; except that in the case of Two-Way Players, any Compensation paid by the Team pursuant to this subparagraph shall be considered an advance against such player's Two-Way NBA Salary only, and the first scheduled payment of such Two-Way NBA Salary (or such subsequent payments, if the first scheduled payment is not sufficient) shall be reduced by the amount of such advance.

(c) The Team will not pay and the Player will not accept any bonus or anything of value on account of the Team's winning any particular NBA game or series of games or attaining a certain position in the standings of the League as of a certain date, other than the final standing of the Team.

4. EXPENSES.

The Team agrees to pay all proper and necessary expenses of the Player, including the reasonable lodging expenses of the Player while playing for the Team "on the road" and during the NBA training camp period (defined for this paragraph only to mean the period from the first day of training camp through the day of the Team's first Exhibition game) for as long as the Player is not then living at home. . . .

5. CONDUCT.

(a) The Player agrees to observe and comply with all Team rules, as maintained or promulgated in accordance with the CBA, at all times whether on or off the playing floor. Subject to the provisions of the CBA, such rules shall be part of this Contract as fully as if herein written and shall be binding upon the Player.

(b) The Player agrees: (i) to give his best services, as well as his loyalty, to the Team, and to play basketball only for the Team and its assignees; (ii) to be neatly and fully attired in public; (iii) to conduct himself on and off the court according to the highest standards of honesty, citizenship, and sportsmanship; and (iv) not to do anything that is materially detrimental or materially prejudicial to the best interests of the Team or the League.

(c) For any violation of Team rules, any breach of any provision of this Contract, or for any conduct impairing the faithful and thorough discharge of the duties incumbent upon the Player, the Team may reasonably impose fines and/or suspensions on the Player in accordance with the terms of the CBA.

(d) The Player agrees to be bound by Article 35 of the NBA Constitution, a copy of which, as in effect on the date of this Contract, is attached hereto.

The Player acknowledges that the Commissioner is empowered to impose fines upon and/or suspend the Player for causes and in the manner provided in such Article, provided that such fines and/or suspensions are consistent with the terms of the CBA.

(e) The Player agrees that if the Commissioner, in his sole judgment, shall find that the Player has bet, or has offered or attempted to bet, money or anything of value on the outcome of any game participated in by any Team or NBADL team, the Commissioner shall have the power in his sole discretion to suspend the Player indefinitely or to expel him as a player for any Team, and the Commissioner's finding and decision shall be final, binding, conclusive, and unappealable.

(f) The Player agrees that he will not, during the term of this Contract, directly or indirectly, entice, induce, or persuade, or attempt to entice, induce, or persuade, any player or coach who is under contract to any NBA Team to enter into negotiations for or relating to his services as a basketball player or coach, nor shall he negotiate for or contract for such services, except with the prior written consent of such Team. Breach of this subparagraph, in addition to the remedies available to the Team, shall be punishable by fine and/or suspension to be imposed by the Commissioner.

(g) When the Player is fined and/or suspended by the Team or the NBA, he shall be given notice in writing (with a copy to the Players Association), stating the amount of the fine or the duration of the suspension and the reasons therefor.

6. WITHHOLDING.

(a) In the event the Player is fined and/or suspended by the Team or the NBA (or, as applicable, the NBADL or an NBADL team), the Team shall withhold the amount of the fine or, in the case of a suspension, the amount provided in Article VI of the CBA (or, as applicable, Article XLI) from any Current Base Compensation due or to become due to the Player with respect to the contract year in which the conduct resulting in the fine and/or the suspension occurred (or a subsequent contract year if the Player has received all Current Base Compensation due to him for the then current contract year). If, at the time the Player is fined and/or suspended, the Current Base Compensation remaining to be paid to the Player under this Contract is not sufficient to cover such fine and/or suspension, then the Player agrees promptly to pay the amount directly to the Team. In no case shall the Player permit any such fine and/or suspension to be paid on his behalf by anyone other than himself. . . .

7. PHYSICAL CONDITION.

(a) The Player agrees to report at the time and place fixed by the Team in good physical condition and to keep himself throughout each NBA Season in good physical condition.

(b) If the Player, in the judgment of the Team's physician, is not in good physical condition at the date of his first scheduled game for the Team, or if, at the beginning of or during any Season, he fails to remain in good physical condition (unless such condition results directly from an injury sustained by the Player as a direct result of participating in any basketball practice or game played for the Team during such Season), so as to render the Player, in the judgment of the Team's physician, unfit to play skilled basketball, the Team shall have the right to suspend such Player until such time as, in the judgment of the Team's physician, the Player is in sufficiently good physical condition to play skilled basketball. In the event of such suspension, the Base Compensation payable to the Player for any Season during such suspension shall be reduced in the same proportion as the length of the period during which, in the judgment of the Team's physician, the Player is unfit to play skilled basketball, bears to the length of such Season. Nothing in this subparagraph shall authorize the Team to suspend the Player solely because the Player is injured or ill.

(c) If, during the term of this Contract, the Player is injured as a direct result of participating in any basketball practice or game played for the Team, the Team will pay the Player's reasonable hospitalization and medical expenses (including doctor's bills), provided that the hospital and doctor are selected by the Team, that the Team shall be obligated to pay only those expenses incurred as a direct result of medical treatment caused solely by and relating directly to the injury sustained by the Player. . . .

(d) The Player agrees to provide to the Team's coach, trainer, or physician prompt notice of any injury, illness, or medical condition suffered by him that is likely to affect adversely the Player's ability to render the services required under this Contract, including the time, place, cause, and nature of such injury, illness, or condition.

(e) Should the Player suffer an injury, illness, or medical condition, he will submit himself to a medical examination, appropriate medical treatment by a physician designated by the Team, and such rehabilitation activities as such physician may specify. Such examination when made at the request of the Team shall be at its expense, unless made necessary by some act or conduct of the Player contrary to the terms of this Contract. . . .

8. PROHIBITED SUBSTANCES/DOMESTIC VIOLENCE.

The Player acknowledges that this Contract may be terminated in accordance with the express provisions of (i) Article XXXIII (Anti-Drug Program) of the CBA or (ii) the Joint NBA/NBPA Policy on Domestic Violence, Sexual Assault, and Child Abuse, and that any such termination will result in the Player's immediate dismissal and disqualification from any employment by the NBA and any of its Teams. Notwithstanding any terms or provisions of this Contract (including any amendments hereto), in the event of such termination, all obligations of the Team, including obligations to pay Compensation, shall cease, except the obligation of the Team to pay the Player's earned Compensation (whether Current or Deferred) to the date of termination.

9. UNIQUE SKILLS.

The Player represents and agrees that he has extraordinary and unique skill and ability as a basketball player, that the services to be rendered by him hereunder cannot be replaced or the loss thereof adequately compensated for in money damages, and that any breach by the Player of this Contract will cause irreparable injury to the Team, and to its assignees. Therefore, it is agreed that in the event it is alleged by the Team that the Player is playing, attempting or threatening to play, or negotiating for the purpose of playing, during the term of this Contract, for any other person, firm, entity, or organization, the Team and its assignees (in addition to any other remedies that may be available to them judicially or by way of arbitration) shall have the right to obtain from any court or arbitrator having jurisdiction such equitable relief as may be appropriate, including a decree enjoining the Player from any further such breach of this Contract, and enjoining the Player from playing basketball for any other person, firm, entity, or organization during the term of this Contract. The Player agrees that this right may be enforced by the Team or the NBA. In any suit, action, or arbitration proceeding brought to obtain such equitable relief, the Player does hereby waive his right, if any, to trial by jury, and does hereby waive his right, if any, to interpose any counterclaim or set-off for any cause whatever.

10. ASSIGNMENT.

(a) The Team shall have the right to assign this Contract to any other NBA Team, and the Player agrees to accept such assignment and to faithfully perform and carry out this Contract with the same force and effect as if it had been entered into by the Player with the assignee Team instead of with the Team.

(b) In the event that this Contract is assigned to any other NBA Team, all reasonable expenses incurred by the Player in moving himself and his family to the home territory of the Team to which such assignment is made, as a result thereof, shall be paid by the assignee Team. . . .

(d) If the Player, without a reasonable excuse, does not report to the Team to which this Contract has been assigned within the time provided in subsection (c) above, then (i) upon consummation of the assignment, the Player may be disciplined by the assignee Team or, if the assignment is not consummated or is voided as a result of the Player's failure to so report, by the assignor Team, and (ii) such conduct shall constitute conduct prejudicial to the NBA under Article 35(d) of the NBA Constitution, and shall therefore subject the Player to discipline from the NBA in accordance with such Article.

11. VALIDITY AND FILING.

(a) This Contract shall be valid and binding upon the Team and the Player immediately upon its execution.

(b) The Team agrees to file a copy of this Contract, and/or any amendment(s) thereto, with and as directed by the Commissioner of the NBA as soon as practicable by email, but in no event may such filing be made more than forty-eight (48) hours after the execution of this Contract and/or amendment(s).

(c) If pursuant to the NBA Constitution and By-Laws or the CBA, the Commissioner disapproves this Contract (or any amendment(s) thereto) within ten (10) days from the first business day following the day on which this Contract (or amendment) is first received, as directed, in his office, this Contract (or amendment) shall thereupon terminate and be of no further force or effect and the Team and the Player shall thereupon be relieved of their respective rights and liabilities thereunder, provided that such ten (10) day period shall be fifteen (15) days for any Contract (or amendment) so received during the period each year from July 1 through the date that is fourteen (14) days following the last day of the Moratorium Period. If the Commissioner's disapproval is subsequently overturned in any proceeding brought under the arbitration provisions of the CBA (including any appeals), the Contract shall again be valid and binding upon the Team and the Player, and the Commissioner shall be afforded another ten-day period to disapprove the Contract (based on the Team's Room at the time the Commissioner's disapproval is overturned) as set forth in the foregoing sentence. The NBA will inform the Players Association if the Commissioner disapproves this Contract (or any amendment(s) thereto) no later than one (1) day following the date of such disapproval.

12. PROHIBITED ACTIVITIES.

The Player and the Team acknowledge and agree that the Player's participation in certain other activities may impair or destroy his ability and skill as a basketball player, and the Player's participation in any game or exhibition of basketball other than at the request of the Team may result in injury to him. Accordingly, the Player agrees that he will not, without the written consent of the Team, engage in any activity that a reasonable person would recognize as involving or exposing the participant to a substantial risk of bodily injury including, but not limited to: (i) sky-diving, hang gliding, snow skiing, rock or mountain climbing (as distinguished from hiking), water or jet skiing, white-water rafting, rappelling, bungee jumping, trampoline jumping, and mountain biking; (ii) any fighting, boxing, or wrestling; (iii) using fireworks or participating in any activity involving firearms or other weapons; (iv) riding on electric scooters or hoverboards; (v) driving or riding on a motorcycle or moped or fourwheeling/off-roading of any kind; (vi) riding in or on any motorized vehicle in any kind of race or racing contest; (vii) operating an aircraft of any kind; (viii) engaging in any other activity excluded or prohibited by or under any insurance policy which the Team procures against the injury, illness or disability to or of the Player, or death of the Player, for which the Player has received written notice from the Team prior to the execution of this Contract; or (ix) participating in any game or exhibition of basketball, football, baseball, hockey, lacrosse, or other team sport or competition. If the Player violates this Paragraph 12, he shall be subject to discipline imposed by the Team and/or the Commissioner of the NBA. Nothing contained herein shall be intended to require the Player to obtain the written consent of the Team in order to enable the Player to participate in, as an amateur, the sports of golf, tennis, handball, swimming, hiking, softball, volleyball, and other similar sports that a reasonable person would not recognize as involving or exposing the participant to a substantial risk of bodily injury.

13. PROMOTIONAL ACTIVITIES.

(a) The Player agrees to allow the Team, the NBA, or any League related entity to take pictures of the Player, alone or together with others, for still photographs, motion pictures, television, or other Media (as such term is defined in Article XXVIII of the CBA), at such reasonable times as the Team, the NBA or the League-related entity may designate. No matter by whom taken, such images may be used in any manner desired by either the Team, the NBA, or the League-related entity for publicity or promotional purposes for Teams or the NBA. The rights in any such images taken by the Team, the NBA, or the League-related entity shall belong to the Team, the NBA, or the League-related entity, as their interests may appear.

(b) The Player agrees that, during any year of this Contract, he will not make public appearances, participate in radio or television programs, permit his picture to be taken, write or sponsor newspaper or magazine articles, or sponsor commercial products without the written consent of the Team, which shall not be withheld except in the reasonable interests of the Team or the NBA. The foregoing shall be interpreted in accordance with the decision in Portland Trail Blazers v. Darnell Valentine and Jim Paxson, Decision 86-2 (August 13, 1986).

(c) Upon request, the Player shall consent to and make himself available for interviews by representatives of the media conducted at reasonable times.

(d) In addition to the foregoing, and subject to the conditions and limitations set forth in Article II, Section 8 of the CBA, the Player agrees to participate, upon request, in all other reasonable promotional activities of the Team, the NBA, and any League-related entity. For each such promotional appearance made on behalf of a commercial sponsor of the Team, the Team agrees to pay the Player $3,500 subject to Article II, Section 8 of the CBA, or, if the Team agrees, such higher amount that is consistent with the Team's past practice and not otherwise unreasonable.

14. LEAGUE PROMOTION.

(a) The NBA, all League-related entities, and the Teams may use, and may authorize others to use, in League Promotions, the Player's name, nickname, picture, portrait, likeness, signature, voice, caricature, biographical information, or other identifiable feature (collectively, "Player Attributes"). The NBA, all League-related entities, and the Teams shall be entitled to use the Player's Player Attributes individually pursuant to the preceding sentence and may, but shall not be required to, use the Player's Player Attributes in a group or as one of multiple players. As used herein, "League Promotion" shall mean any and all uses intended to publicize, promote or market (including in any and all Media) (i) the NBA, any League-related entity that generates BRI (as defined in Article VII of the CBA), any Team, or any Player, (ii) any game in which a Team participates (including a Pre- Season, Exhibition, Regular Season, and Playoff game), including the sale of tickets to any such game, (iii) any telecast or other exhibition or distribution of (x) any such game or (y) any NBA-related or Team-related program or content, (iv) any NBA or Team facility, platform, or event, including the sale of tickets to any such event, or public service activity conducted by the NBA, a League-related entity that generates BRI, or a Team, or (v) the sport of basketball. For purposes of clarity, the foregoing rights of the NBA, League-related entities, and the Teams include the right and authority to use, and to authorize others to use, after the term of this Contract, any Player Attributes fixed in a tangible medium (e.g., filmed, photographed, recorded or otherwise captured) during the term of this Contract solely for the purposes described herein. . . .

15. TEAM DEFAULT.

In the event of an alleged default by the Team in the payments to the Player provided for by this Contract, or in the event of an alleged failure by the Team to perform any other material obligation that it has agreed to perform hereunder, the Player shall notify both the Team and the League in writing of the facts constituting such alleged default or alleged failure. If neither the Team nor the League shall cause such alleged default or alleged failure to be remedied within five (5) days after receipt of such written notice, the Players Association shall, on behalf of the Player, have the right to request that the dispute concerning such alleged default or alleged failure be referred immediately to the Grievance Arbitrator in accordance with the provisions of the CBA. If, as a result of such arbitration, an award issues in favor of the Player, and if neither the Team nor the League complies with such award within ten (10) days after the service thereof, the Player shall have the right, by a further written notice to the Team and the League, to terminate this Contract.

16. TERMINATION.

(a) The Team may terminate this Contract upon written notice to the Player if the Player shall:

> (i) at any time, fail, refuse, or neglect to conform his personal conduct to standards of good citizenship, good moral character (defined here to mean not engaging in acts of moral turpitude, whether or not such acts would constitute a crime), and good sportsmanship, to keep himself in first class physical condition, or to obey the Team's training rules;

(ii) at any time commit a significant and inexcusable physical attack against any official or employee of the Team or the NBA (other than another player), or any person in attendance at any NBA game or event, considering the totality of the circumstances, including (but not limited to) the degree of provocation (if any) that may have led to the attack, the nature and scope of the attack, the Player's state of mind at the time of the attack, and the extent of any injury resulting from the attack;

(iii) at any time, fail, in the sole opinion of the Team's management, to exhibit sufficient skill or competitive ability to qualify to continue as a member of the Team; provided, however, (A) that if this Contract is terminated by the Team, in accordance with the provisions of this sub-paragraph, prior to January 10 (or, in the case of a Two-Way Contract, prior to January 20) of any Season, and the Player, at the time of such termination, is unfit to play skilled basketball as the result of an injury resulting directly from his playing for the Team, the Player shall (sub-ject to the provisions set forth in Exhibit 3) continue to receive his full Base Compensation, or, in the case of a Two-Way Contract, his full Two-Way NBADL Salary plus any Two-Way NBA Salary that has been earned by the Player), less all workers' compensation benefits (which, to the extent permitted by law, and if not deducted from the Player's Compensation by the Team, the Player hereby assigns to the Team) and any insurance provided for by the Team paid or payable to the Player by reason of said injury, until such time as the Player is fit to play skilled basketball, but not beyond the Season during which such termination occurred; and provided, further, (B) that if this Contract is terminated by the Team, in accordance with the provisions of this subparagraph, during the period from the January 10 (or, in the case of a Two-Way Contract, from the January 20) of any Season through the end of such Season, the Player shall be entitled to receive his full Base Compensation for said Season (or, in the case of a Two-Way Contract, his Two-Way Annual NBADL Salary for such NBADL Regular Season (prorated as necessary if the Two-Way Contract was entered into after the start of the NBADL Regular Season) plus (i) any Two-Way NBA Salary earned by such Two-Way Player during such NBA Regular Season prior to the date of termination, less (ii) such Two-Way Player's Two-Way NBADL Salary covering the number of NBA Days of Service accrued by such Two-Way Player during such NBA Regular Season prior to the date of termination); or

(iv) at any time, fail, refuse, or neglect to render his services hereunder or in any other manner materially breach this Contract.

(b) If this Contract is terminated by the Team by reason of the Player's failure to render his services hereunder due to disability caused by an injury to the Player resulting directly from his playing for the Team and rendering him unfit to play skilled basketball, and notice of such injury is given by the Player as provided herein, the Player shall (subject to the provisions set forth in Exhibit 3) be entitled to receive his full Base Compensation for the Season in which the injury was sustained (or, in the case of a Two-Way Contract, his Two-Way Annual NBADL Salary for such NBADL Regular Season (pro-rated as necessary if the Two-Way Contract was entered into after the start of the NBADL Regular Season) plus (i) any Two-Way NBA Salary earned by such Two-Way Player during such NBA Regular Season prior to the date of termination, less (ii) such Two-Way Player's Two-Way NBADL Salary covering the number of NBA Days of Service accrued by such Two-Way Player during such NBA Regular Season prior to the date of termination), less all workers' compensation benefits (which, to the extent permitted by law, and if not deducted from the Player's Compensation by the Team, the Player hereby assigns to the Team) and any insurance provided for by the Team paid or payable to the Player by reason of said injury.

(c) Notwithstanding the provisions of paragraph 16(b) above, if this Contract is terminated by the Team prior to the first game of a Regular Season by reason of the Player's failure to render his services hereunder due to an injury or condition sustained or suffered during a preceding Season, or after such Season but prior to the Player's participation in any basketball practice or game played for the Team, payment by the Team of any Compensation earned through the date of termination under paragraph 3(b) above, payment of the Player's board, lodging, and expense allowance during the training camp period, payment of the reasonable traveling expenses of the Player to his home city, and the expert training and coaching provided by the Team to the Player during the training season shall be full payment to the Player.

(d) If this Contract is terminated by the Team during the period designated by the Team for attendance at NBA training camp, payment by the Team of any Compensation earned through the date of termination under paragraph 3(b) above, payment of the Player's board, lodging, and expense allowance during such period to the date of termination, payment of the reasonable traveling expenses of the Player to his home city, and the expert training and coaching provided by the Team to the Player during the training season shall be full payment to the Player.

(e) If this Contract is terminated by the Team after the first game of a Regular Season, except in the case provided for in subparagraphs (a)(iii) and (b) of this paragraph 16, (A) with respect to a Standard NBA Contract, the Player shall be entitled to receive as full payment hereunder a sum of money which, when added to the salary which he has already received during such Season, will represent the same proportionate amount of the annual sum set forth in Exhibit 1 or Exhibit 1A hereto as the number of days of such Regular Season then past bears to the total number of days of such Regular Season, plus the reasonable traveling expenses of the Player to his home, and (B) with respect to a Two-Way Contract, the Player shall be entitled to receive as full payment hereunder a sum of money which, when added to the salary which he has already received during such Season, shall equal the sum of the Player's Two-Way NBA Salary (reflecting the number of NBA Days of Service the Player has accrued up until the date of termination) and the Player's Two-Way NBADL Salary (reflecting the number of NBADL Days of Service the Player has accrued up until the date of termination), plus the reasonable traveling expenses of the Player to his home.

(f) If the Team proposes to terminate this Contract in accordance with subparagraph (a) of this paragraph 16, it must first comply with the following waiver procedure:

(i) The Team shall request the NBA Commissioner to request waivers from all other clubs. Such waiver request may not be withdrawn.

(ii) Upon receipt of the waiver request, any other NBA Team may claim assignment of this Contract at such waiver price as may be fixed by the League, the priority of claims to be determined in accordance with the NBA Constitution and By-Laws.

(iii) If this Contract is so claimed, the Team agrees that it shall, upon the assignment of this Contract to the claiming Team, notify the Player of such assignment as provided in paragraph 10(c) hereof, and the Player agrees he shall report to the assignee Team as provided in said paragraph 10(c).

(iv) If the Contract is not claimed prior to the expiration of the waiver period, it shall terminate, and the Team shall promptly deliver written notice of termination to the Player.

(v) The NBA shall promptly notify the Players Association of the disposition of any waiver request.

(vi) To the extent not inconsistent with the foregoing provisions of this subparagraph (f), the waiver procedures set forth in the NBA Constitution and By-Laws, a copy of which, as in effect on the date of this Contract, is attached hereto, shall govern.

(g) Upon any termination of this Contract by the Player, all obligations of the Team to pay Compensation shall cease on the date of termination, except the obligation of the Team to pay the Player's Compensation to said date.

17. DISPUTES.

In the event of any dispute arising between the Player and the Team relating to any matter arising under this Contract, or concerning the performance or interpretation thereof (except for a dispute arising under paragraph 9 hereof or as provided in paragraph 14 above), such dispute shall be resolved in accordance with the Grievance and Arbitration Procedure set forth in . . . the CBA.

18. PLAYER NOT A MEMBER.

Nothing contained in this Contract or in any provision of the NBA Constitution and By-Laws shall be construed to constitute the Player a member of the NBA or to confer upon him any of the rights or privileges of a member thereof.

19. RELEASE.

The Player hereby releases and waives any and all claims he may have, or that may arise during the term of this Contract, against (a) the NBA and its related entities, the NBADL and its related entities, and every member of the NBA or the NBADL, and every director, officer, owner, stockholder, trustee, partner, and employee of the NBA, NBADL and their respective related entities and/or any member of the NBA or NBADL and their related entities (excluding persons employed as players by any such member), and (b) any person retained by the NBA and/or the Players Association in connection with the NBA/NBPA Anti-Drug Program, the Grievance Arbitrator, the System Arbitrator, and any other arbitrator or expert retained by the NBA and/or the Players Association under the terms of the CBA, in both cases (a) and (b) above, arising out of, or in connection with, and whether or not by negligence, (i) any injury that is subject to the provisions of paragraph 7 hereof, (ii) any fighting or other form of violent and/or unsportsmanlike conduct occurring during the course of any practice, any NBADL game, and/or any NBA Exhibition, Regular Season, and/or Playoff game (in all cases on or adjacent to the playing floor or in or adjacent to any facility used for such practices or games), (iii) the testing procedures or the imposition of any penalties set forth in paragraph 8 hereof and in the NBA/NBPA Anti-Drug Program, or (iv) any injury suffered in the course of his employment as to which he has or would have a claim for workers' compensation benefits. The foregoing shall not apply to any claim of medical malpractice against a Team-affiliated physician or other medical personnel.

20. ENTIRE AGREEMENT.

This Contract (including any Exhibits hereto) contains the entire agreement between the parties and, except as provided in the CBA, sets forth all components of the Player's Compensation from the Team or any Team Affiliate, and there are no other agreements or transactions of any kind (whether disclosed or undisclosed to the NBA), express or implied, oral or written, or promises, undertakings, representations, commitments, inducements, assurances of intent, or understandings of any kind (whether disclosed or undisclosed to the NBA) (a) concerning any future Renegotiation, Extension, or other amendment of this Contract or the entry into any new Player Contract, or (b) involving compensation or consideration of any kind (including, without limitation, an investment or business opportunity) to be paid, furnished, or made available to the Player, or any person or entity controlled by, related to, or acting with authority on behalf of the Player, by the Team or any Team Affiliate.

EXAMINE THIS CONTRACT CAREFULLY
BEFORE SIGNING IT.

THIS CONTRACT INCLUDES EXHIBITS _____, WHICH ARE ATTACHED HERETO AND MADE A PART HEREOF.

EXCERPT FROM NBA CONSTITUTION
MISCONDUCT

35. The provisions of this Article 35 shall govern all Players in the Association, hereinafter referred to as "Players."

(a) Each Member shall provide and require in every contract with any of its Players that they shall be bound and governed by the provisions of this Article. Each Member, at the direction of the Board of Governors or the Commissioner, as the case may be, shall take such action as the Board or the Commissioner may direct in order to effectuate the purposes of this Article.

(b) The Commissioner shall direct the dismissal and perpetual disqualification from any further association with the Association or any of its Members, of any Player found by the Commissioner after a hearing to have been guilty of offering, agreeing, conspiring, aiding or attempting to cause any game of basketball to result otherwise than on its merits.

(c) If in the opinion of the Commissioner any act or conduct of a Player at or during an Exhibition, Regular Season, or Playoff game has been prejudicial to or against the best interests of the Association or the game of basketball, the Commissioner shall impose upon such Player a fine not exceeding $50,000, or may order for a time the suspension of any such Player from any connection or duties with Exhibition, Regular Season, or Playoff games, or he may order both such fine and suspension.

(d) The Commissioner shall have the power to suspend for a definite or indefinite period, or to impose a fine not exceeding $50,000, or inflict both such suspension and fine upon any Player who, in his opinion, (i) shall have made or caused to be made any statement having, or that was designed to have, an effect prejudicial or detrimental to the best interests of basketball or of the Association or of a Member, or (ii) shall have been guilty of conduct that does not conform to standards of morality or fair play, that does not comply at all times with all federal, state, and local laws, or that is prejudicial or detrimental to the Association.

(e) Any Player who, directly or indirectly, entices, induces, persuades or attempts to entice, induce, or persuade any Player, Coach, Trainer, General Manager or any other person who is under contract to any other Member of the Association to enter into negotiations for or relating to his services or negotiates or contracts for such services shall, on being charged with such tampering, be given an opportunity to answer such charges after due notice and the Commissioner shall have the power to decide whether or not the charges have been sustained; in the event his decision is that the charges have been sustained, then the Commissioner shall have the power to suspend such Player for a definite or indefinite period, or to impose a fine not exceeding $50,000, or inflict both such suspension and fine upon any such Player.

(f) Any Player who, directly or indirectly, wagers money or anything of value on the outcome of any game played by a Team in the league operated by the Association shall, on being charged with such wagering, be given an opportunity to answer such charges after due notice, and the decision of the Commissioner shall be final, binding and conclusive and unappealable. The penalty for such offense shall be within the absolute and sole discretion of the Commissioner and may include a fine, suspension, expulsion and/or perpetual disqualification from further association with the Association or any of its Members.

(g) Except for a penalty imposed under Paragraph (f) of this Article 35: (i) any challenge by a Team to the decisions and acts of the Commissioner pursuant to Article 35 shall be appealable to the Board of Governors, who shall determine such appeals in accordance with such rules and regulations as may be adopted by the Board in its absolute and sole discretion, and (ii) any challenge by a Player to the decisions or acts of the Commissioner pursuant to Article 35 shall be governed by the provisions of the NBA/NBPA Collective Bargaining Agreement then in effect.

NOTE

Provision 7, "Physical Condition," is discussed in Problem 7-2, *supra.* Examinations assessing physical condition are a standard part of pre-draft evaluations. They serve to protect clubs contemplating large roster expenditures from signing players with physical limitations or ailments that might compromise the players' ability and, therefore, limit their monetary value. In some cases, they also alert players to life-threatening conditions potentially exacerbated by playing. For instance, in 2014, Isaiah Austin, who starred at Baylor University and was projected to be a first-round NBA draft pick, was diagnosed with Marfan Syndrome after a routine physical examination at the NBA Combine. The condition increases a person's risk of a cardiac incident when exercising vigorously. While the diagnosis certainly would have impacted clubs' perspectives on drafting him, Austin withdrew from the draft altogether and ended his basketball career out of concern for his health.

In some instances, however, a player refuses to take a test that might impact his market value even if it might reveal important information about his health. An example of such a problem is illustrated by the dispute between the NBA's Chicago Bulls and its center, Eddy Curry. Before the start of the 2005-2006 season, the Bulls requested that Curry submit to DNA testing to determine if he had a genetic predisposition for a condition that might lead to a fatal heart attack. Curry had experienced an irregular heartbeat toward the end of the prior season that caused him to miss the Bulls' final 17 games. Deaths by other players, including the Celtics' Reggie Lewis, from this condition led the Bulls to insist on this examination. Curry refused, the union backed him, and the dispute seemed headed to arbitration. Curry was traded to the Knicks, which did not require this testing before signing him to a multiyear, multimillion-dollar guaranteed contract. The issue thus became moot. Even so, the underlying question as to how far clubs may go to protect their interests through medical tests is an important one that likely will be considered in future CBA negotiations.

PROBLEM 7-3

The following problem provides an opportunity to consider the nature and scope of a league commissioner's authority to discipline a player for on-field conduct as well as limitations on this authority established by the league CBA and UPC.

Stars Candy Company has contracted with Stan Tallace of the Portland Flyers to advertise its candy by prominently displaying a tattoo of its company logo on his upper arm during the World Basketball League (WBL) playoffs. WBL rules do not prohibit players from having visible tattoos. Stars hopes that fans watching Flyers games in person and on national television will see its logo on Tallace's arm, and that this advertising will significantly increase its candy sales. Stars has offered to pay Tallace a substantial undisclosed amount of money (depending on how far the Flyers advance in the playoffs) for displaying the Stars tattoo, which is temporary and will wash off in a few months.

After learning about Stars's proposed advertising deal with Tallace, WBL commissioner Don Bern announced that no player would be permitted to display a tattoo of any company's logo on his body during a WBL game. He stated that any WBL player doing so would be suspended indefinitely and fined $250,000. Bern is concerned that Stars' proposal will disrupt the league's business relationship with Westle, which has paid the WBL a $15 million sponsorship fee to be advertised as the "WBL's Official Candy" during nationally televised WBL regular season and playoff games for the next three years.

The WBL Uniform Player Contract (UPC) does not prohibit players from having tattoos, but it does prohibit players from "sponsoring commercial products without the consent of the WBL and his club, which shall not be withheld except to protect the reasonable interests of the WBL and player's club." The UPC also provides, "Player agrees that the Commissioner has the right to fine Player a reasonable amount and/or suspend Player as deemed appropriate for conduct judged by Commissioner to be detrimental to the WBL or professional basketball."

Neither Stars nor Westle has a sponsorship agreement with the Flyers, but the club sells both Stars and Westle candy at concession stands in its playing facility in Portland. The Flyers' sale of Stars candy to their fans does not violate any WBL rules or regulations. The Flyers have no objections to Stars's proposed advertising deal with Tallace.

Tallace believes he has a First Amendment right to display expressive material, including the Stars logo, on his skin in the form of a tattoo. He points out that Bern took no action against Philadelphia 99ers' player Andy McPherson for producing music with lyrics offensive to gay people and women, although McPherson is earning a lot of money from sales and streams of the music.

Does Bern have the authority to prohibit Tallace from displaying a Stars logo tattoo during WBL playoff games and to impose the threatened discipline if he does so?

3.   *Professional Team Sports Drug Testing Programs*

Two types of drug problems have plagued professional sports in recent years. One is performance-enhancing drugs such as anabolic steroids, which are taken to help the athlete perform better despite their associated health risks. The use of these banned drugs constitutes a form of cheating that provides an unfair competitive advantage over clean athletes not using these substances. The other is the widespread use of "recreational" drugs such as marijuana and cocaine. Various questions are posed by the regulation of either type of drug by a professional sports league. One is whether sports club owners and leagues have any legitimate reason to interfere with the private decisions made by individual athletes, at least in instances when their on-field athletic performances are not impaired and no threat is posed to the safety of others. Second, because the usage and possession of these drugs for other than legitimate medical reasons are illegal in most United States jurisdictions (although many states are increasingly legalizing marijuana), does the damage done to the image of sports outweigh an individual's freedom to choose?

Three major issues differentiate the legal framework governing drug testing in professional sports as contrasted with interscholastic, intercollegiate, and Olympic sports, which is discussed in other chapters. First, professional sports leagues are private in nature. There are no public professional sports leagues, in contrast to the thousands of public universities and public high school systems. Thus, the U.S. Constitution rarely supports any legal challenge to drug testing programs in the professional ranks because no governmental or "state" action, which is required to assert federal constitutional law claims, is involved. Thus, players such as Terry Long of the Pittsburgh Steelers, who tested positive for anabolic steroids, have been unable to show a sufficient nexus between a professional sports league's drug policies and the actions of government officials or state actors to assert any federal constitutional claims. *Long v. National Football League*, 66 F.3d 311 (3d Cir. 1995).

Second, despite the lack of federal constitutional law oversight, professional sports leagues are in many respects more constrained in their ability to implement drug testing programs than are universities or other educational institutions. Professional team sport athletes are usually employees either of a club, the league, or both. When athletes agree to have a union represent them, they gain the protections of the National Labor Relations Act, pursuant to which drug testing programs are mandatory subjects of collective bargaining. Consequently, in most major league professional team sports, leagues and teams cannot unilaterally institute drug programs that must be implemented through collective bargaining with the agreement of the players union. Although one would expect a players' union to consent to a drug testing program because drug usage has adverse health effects on players, its nature and scope as well as sanctions for violations often are the subject of considerable debate and negotiation. Individual athlete privacy concerns, the validity of testing measures for specific substances, and the consequences of proven drug usage have caused player unions to have significant trepidation about wide-ranging testing procedures and the penalties for impermissible drug use. As new drugs enter the scene, and new pressures arise, problems multiply.

Third, a strong reason for union hesitancy to agree to stringent drug testing programs is pressure from athletes and their agents. A great deal is at stake for professional athletes, arguably more so than for amateur athletes at the interscholastic and intercollegiate levels, or even Olympic athletes. Professional careers may end prematurely through noncompliance with league drug testing and treatment programs. Salaries, bonuses, and endorsement opportunities may be lost, often costing a professional athlete thousands, even millions, of dollars. Economically, the stakes are high. Consequently, both the players union and the clubs' multi-employer bargaining unit must scramble to reach reasonable solutions, with common ground and compromise frequently difficult to achieve.

In general, two overriding concerns need to be addressed and resolved in collective bargaining agreements if adequate drug testing programs are to be implemented. One is protection of privacy of the individual players, to the maximum extent possible. Second, there must be a clear and definite articulation of the program's purposes, procedures, and sanctions. See generally E. Tim Walker, Comment, *Missing the Target: How Performance-Enhancing Drugs Go Unnoticed and Endanger the Lives of Athletes*, 10 Vill. Sports & Ent. L.J. 181 (2003) (comparing drug testing policies of various sports leagues and organizations); Mark M. Rabuano, *An Examination of Drug-Testing as a Mandatory Subject of Collective Bargaining in Major League Baseball*, 4 U. Pa. J. Lab. & Emp. L. 439 (2002).

Current collectively bargained suspensions for a first drug testing violation are 80 games for MLB players, 4 games for NFL players, 25 games for NBA players, and 20 games for NHL players, numbers that increase significantly for subsequent offenses. For example, MLB players face a 162-game suspension for a second positive test and a lifetime ban (which can later be lifted after two years by the MLB commissioner) for a third positive drug test.

A brief history and summary of the major professional sports leagues' respective drug testing policies follows.

a.   NBA Drug Policy

The 2005 CBA was the NBA's first attempt to effectively address drug use among players. The NBA subsequently has addressed player drug use several times, most recently in Article XXXIII of the 2017 CBA. The most notable provisions are as follows:

- Prohibited drugs include benzodiazepines, cocaine, GHB, ketamine, LSD, methamphetamine, opiates (such as heroin, codeine, morphine, and oxycodone), PCP, and marijuana.
- Sanctions vary depending on the drug detected in the tests. Steroids and marijuana are separated from the others. Marijuana use triggers the lightest penalties, starting with a mandatory marijuana treatment program for the first violation and progressing to a 5-game suspension. Use of Steroids and Performance-Enhancing Drugs (SPED) results in a 25-game suspension and

a mandatory SPED program for the first offense and can lead to immediate dismissal.

- Testing procedures provide safeguards through a two-sample testing protocol.
- All players are subject to four random drug tests per season and two tests during the off-season.
- Players may be tested on game day by way of either blood tests after the game or urine tests before the game-day shoot-around.
- Human growth hormone (HGH) testing may occur up to three times per year and the sanctions for a positive result are the same as for a SPED positive result.

b. WNBA Drug Policy

The Women's National Basketball Association (WNBA) also has a drug testing, treatment, and sanctions program in its CBA. The WNBA's program is very similar to the NBA's; however, the use of steroids is subject to, among other things, a $1,000-per-day fine if a player enters the WNBA Steroid Program and fails to comply with its dictates. The first violation triggers an 8-game suspension and the second violation triggers a 20-game suspension. A third violation results in disqualification for a period of not less than two years, and the player's contract shall be voided. Reinstatement after the mandatory two-year suspension is discretionary and requires approval of both the WNBA and the WNBA Players Association (WNBPA). (See 2014 WNBA CBA, Article XXI and Exhibit 2, "Anti-Drug Program.")

c. NFL Drug Policy

The NFL's drug policies have steadily evolved since 1982, with the 1994 CBA presenting the first truly comprehensive approaches to drug testing, sanctions, and treatment. The major aspects of the NFL's drug testing program under that CBA and as augmented since can be summarized as follows:

1. Steroids are dealt with severely. A first offense results in a four-game suspension, and a second offense results in a ten-game suspension. A subsequent violation triggers a suspension of at least two seasons. Recreational drugs (such as marijuana, opiates, PCP, and amphetamines) are dealt with somewhat more leniently, with a series of fines — and then ultimately suspension — for repeated violations.
2. There are also sanctions for alcohol abuse and for drug offenses discovered through criminal prosecutions that result in either a guilty or no-contest verdict or plea by a player. The penalties for drug use discovered by criminal violations are more severe than those discovered through testing.
3. The commissioner has reserved the right to impose more stringent sanctions when drug trafficking is involved. The player effectively agrees to be subject to enhanced discipline by signing the standard NFL Player Contract, which stipulates that the commissioner has the right to suspend a player or terminate his contract for using or distributing to other players performance enhancing drugs or stimulants.

The current NFL CBA, which was entered into in 2011, continues the earlier testing procedures. (See 2011 NFL CBA, Article 39 Section 7, "Substance Abuse.") In September 2014, the NFL and NFLPA agreed on additional drug testing and substance abuse policies, which represented a major advance in the league and union working together to address the issues. Among other things, the new policies permit Human Growth Hormone (HGH) testing on non-game days and require that an independent arbitrator hears appeals for positive test violations. Ryan Wilson, *NFL players vote to adopt new drug-testing policies*, CBSSports.com, Sept. 12, 2014, http://www.cbssports.com/nfl/eye-on-football/24706854/nfl-players-vote-to-adopt-new-drug-testing-policies.

d. MLB Drug Policy

The MLBPA first agreed to allow random drug testing for steroids in 2003. Subsequently, in part because of pressures applied by Congress, increased testing was implemented and much harsher suspensions were collectively bargained and incorporated into MLB CBAs. Beginning with the off-season following the 2012 season, all Major League baseball players have been subject to random, unannounced testing.

A monumental development in the MLB drug saga was the December 2007 Mitchell Report, a 409-page tome that traces the use of steroids and human growth hormone by present and former MLB players. In this report, 85 individuals were named as having used at least one type of drug. Probably most notable among the names was Roger Clemens, because he had not previously been identified as a likely steroids user and, until this report, was clearly headed for the Baseball Hall of Fame. As with Barry Bonds, also named in the report, that honor is now in serious doubt. Former Senator George Mitchell spent almost two years and an estimated $20 million investigating allegations from various sources. Mitchell and his investigative team interviewed numerous individuals, but without any subpoena power, he had to rely on persons appearing voluntarily.

The report itself did not result in any punishments being levied against current players. It did, however, raise consciousness as to the degree of performance-enhancing drug use in the sport of baseball. In addition, the report contained three significant recommendations. First, MLB should create a department solely to investigate drug use allegations with the authority to investigate circumstantial evidence of drug usage, such as drug shipment records. Second, it should expand education efforts to increase players' awareness of the dangers of taking performance-enhancing steroids. Third, MLB should establish an independent drug testing program, under which neither teams nor players would have any advance notice of testing.

In 2013, another MLB performance-enhancing drug scandal erupted, raising (and, for some, confirming) fears that doping was prevalent in the MLB. After a lengthy investigation, MLB persuaded Anthony Bosch, the founder of the Biogenesis "anti-aging" clinic in Coral Gables, Florida, to "turn over a cache of material, including emails, ledgers and phone records that allegedly confirmed ballplayers were doping." Julie K. Brown, *A-Rod, 12 others suspended in Biogenesis scandal*, Miami Herald, Aug. 6, 2013, http://www.miamiherald.com/2013/08/06/3543980/a-rod-12-others-suspended-in-biogenesis.html. Over a dozen players, including New York Yankees superstar Alex Rodriguez, were given lengthy suspensions. With the help of the MLBPA, he immediately challenged the 211-day suspension. In an arbitration proceeding chaired by Frederic

Horowitz, he argued that Bosch's testimony was not credible; MLB engaged in egregious misconduct during the investigation; and MLB could not prove by clear and convincing evidence that he had used performance-enhancing drugs. The arbitration panel determined that Rodriguez had violated MLB's drug testing program, but it reduced his suspension's length to one full season (162 games) and any post-season games for which his team qualified. See *MLBPA v. Office of the Commissioner of Baseball*, MLB Arbitration Panel Decision No. 131., 32-34 (Jan. 13, 2014) (Horowitz, Manfred, and Prouty).

In 2011, MLB's drug testing program was expanded to include testing for HGH. In 2014, MLB and the MLBPA agreed to increase the number of in-season and out-of-season random drug tests, expanded the list of banned substances, and increased the penalties for positive tests. As noted above, first time offenders are suspended for 80 games for testing positive for the use of banned performance-enhancing substances, which increases to a season-long 162-game suspension for a second positive test and a lifetime ban for a third. An arbitrator may reduce a suspension for a first or second violation by up to fifty percent if a player proves by clear and convincing evidence that a positive test was not caused by his "significant fault." Paul Hagen, *MLB, MLBPA agree to improve joint drug program*, MLB.com, March 28, 2014, http://mlb.mlb.com/news/article/mlb/mlb-mlbpa-agree-to-improve-joint-drug-program?ymd=20140328&content_id=70316506&vkey=news_mlb.

In 2016, Jennry Meija became the first MLB player to receive a lifetime suspension for a third positive test, but he was reinstated by MLB Commissioner Rob Manfred in 2017. Citing Meija's contrition and his "commitment to comply with the program in the future," Commissioner Manfred utilized his broad discretion to reinstate Meija, who became eligible to return to MLB in 2019. Andy Torres, *Mejia conditionally allowed to return from drug ban in 2019*, Associated Press, July 6, 2018, https://www.usatoday.com/story/sports/mlb/2018/07/06/mejia-conditionally-allowed-to-return-from-drug-ban-in-2019/36683649/.

e.   NHL Drug Policy

In 1986, reports of widespread cocaine use by NHL players caused then-NHL president John Ziegler and Alan Eagleson, head of the NHLPA, to announce a mandatory drug testing program. But it was subsequently rejected by the players and was never instituted. In 1996, the NHLPA and players agreed to a four-step drug testing program with in-patient treatment for a first offense and escalating sanctions for each subsequent offense, culminating with a fourth stage that imposed a minimum one-year suspension with no guarantee of reinstatement. Little information regarding the details of the NHL's early drug testing program, which were not included in the NHL's CBA, was made publicly available in order to protect the privacy of NHL players.

This approach was substantially altered by the 2005 CBA, and the alterations were reaffirmed in the 2012 CBA, which remains in effect. For a first positive test, a player is suspended for 20 games without pay. For a second positive test, the suspension is 60 games without pay. There is also a mandatory referral to the NHL substance abuse program for both a first and second offense. For a third positive test, there is a "permanent" suspension without pay, although the player can apply for reinstatement after a minimum period of two years. The player's reinstatement is a discretionary decision to be made by a special committee.

NOTES AND QUESTIONS

1. Professional athletes' use of performance-enhancing drugs have given rise
    to criminal prosecutions. In 2011, MLB superstar Barry Bonds was tried for
    perjury and obstruction of justice in relation to a governmental investigation
    of steroid use in MLB. Several years earlier, federal authorities had seized
    drug testing information for approximately 100 MLB players who tested pos-
    itive for performance-enhancing drugs in 2003, reportedly including Bonds,
    David Ortiz, Manny Ramirez, Alex Rodriguez, and Sammy Sosa. The Ninth
    Circuit held that the seizure violated the players' federal constitutional rights,
    see *U.S. v. Comprehensive Drug Testing, Inc.*, 621 F.3d 1162 (9th Cir. 2010), and as
    a result, federal authorities were ordered to return the seized information to
    the MLBPA for destruction. The government was permitted to retain Bonds's
    positive test results and used them in securing his criminal conviction, but the
    conviction was ultimately overturned on appeal.[5] Roger Clemens was feder-
    ally prosecuted twice for perjury and obstruction of justice with respect to a
    steroid investigation, but unsuccessfully both times.

    The outcomes of the Bonds and Clemens trials convinced some observ-
    ers that high-profile MLB players accused of performance-enhancing drug
    usage are—whether because of technicalities or expensive lawyers—more
    likely than not to "get off," and that criminal prosecutions are a waste of
    scarce government resources. See, e.g., Jerome Solomon, *Bonds Able to Coax
    His Biggest Walk*, Hous. Chron., April 14, 2011, at 1 (addressing Bonds's
    and Clemens's prosecutions). Other observers argue that performance-
    enhancing drug development tends to outpace performance-enhancing
    drug detection technology, resulting in the continuous creation of unde-
    tectable performance-enhancing drugs. Although the decade-long inquiry
    that prompted the United States Anti-Doping Agency's August 2012 life-
    time ban of renowned cyclist Lance Armstrong was widely hailed as a victory
    for the fight against doping, it starkly revealed (1) the myriad means by
    which athletes can manipulate drug testing procedures (Armstrong passed
    over 500 drug tests during his career, never failed one, and was ultimately
    sanctioned only on the strength of circumstantial evidence and extensive
    testimony from fellow cyclists before finally admitting his doping history
    in a televised interview with Oprah Winfrey), and (2) the exorbitant costs
    involved in such investigations. See Alexander Wolff and David Epstein, *A
    Massive Fraud Now More Fully Exposed*, Sports Illustrated, Oct. 22, 2012, at 40.

    If performance-enhancing drug detection is challenging and in some
    cases virtually impossible, and if users will rarely be held accountable (and
    in those cases only if exorbitant investigatory resources are expended), does
    it make sense to permit performance-enhancing drug use by adult profes-
    sional athletes? Consider the following opinion column excerpt:

---

5. Bonds later brought a claim against MLB arguing that collusion among MLB clubs prevented
him from getting a job after the allegations of his steroid use surfaced. He presented evidence
that all other MLB free agents with statistics similar to his were able to get jobs following the 2007
season and argued that his failure get a job indicated collusion. Arbitrator Frederic Horowitz, in
ruling for MLB, acknowledged that Bonds' numbers were good but found that nothing directly
evidenced collusion among clubs. See John Heyman, *MLB prevails over Barry Bonds in collusion case
over his career ending*, CBSSports.com, August 27, 2015, http://www.cbssports.com/mlb/news/mlb-
prevails-over-barry-bonds-in-collusion-case-over-his-career-ending/.

Athletes should be permitted to use performance enhancers, so long as the users are monitored for safety. . . . [T]he sporting world must ultimately accept that the distinctions between doping and nutritional supplements, illegal enhancements and scientific training, no longer exist. Elite sports are already thoroughly enmeshed in a laboratory world of pharmaceuticals, medicine, and high tech nutrition. Any athlete who wants a banned drug can get it. And as we've seen repeatedly, designer drugs co-evolve with tests, staying one step ahead of authorities and allowing savvy athletes to juice unnoticed.

Imagine a world where performance enhancement was open and regulated. Instead of forcing athletes to sneak through back alleys to stay competitive, sports authorities should admit that drugs are essential—then help athletes cope with the side effects. Once legalized, drug use would still have limits, but they would be established by physicians and athletes—based on their ability to handle performance enhancers. Bad outcomes would be far less frequent if players were not forced to rely on quacks. . . . Innovation in performance enhancers would accelerate in the light of day.

Drea Knufken, *Could Doping Be Effectively Legalized, Regulated?*, Bus. Pundit, May 20, 2010, http://www.businesspundit.com/?s=Could+Doping+Be+Effectively+Legalized. Do you agree that "the distinctions between doping and nutritional supplements, illegal enhancements and scientific training, no longer exist"? Whether or not you agree with this statement, do you agree with the author's ultimate point? What negative consequences might flow (in the sporting world and in society generally) from the author's proposed regimen?

2. Several states and the District of Columbia have legalized the recreational use of marijuana, complicating sports leagues' prohibition of its use. Although NFL drug use rules contain a therapeutic medicinal marijuana use exemption, at the time of this writing no player has obtained an exemption permitting his use of marijuana for medical reasons. Former Detroit Lions running back Mike James, having overcome an addiction to pain-relieving opioids, was the first player in league history to file for the exemption, but his petition was denied. Rick Maese, *An NFL Running Back Says He Needs One Thing To Continue His Football Career: Weed*, May 1, 2018, https://www.washingtonpost.com/news/sports/wp/2018/05/01/an-nfl-running-back-says-he-needs-one-thing-to-continue-his-football-career-weed/?utm_term=.c3c69e413fbf.

Some professional sports organizations, while continuing to ban marijuana, are beginning to permit athletes to use cannabidiol (CBD), an anti-inflammatory compound extracted from cannabis. For instance, the World Anti-Doping Agency (WADA) has removed CBD from its banned substance list. Justin Pentelute, *Guest Opinion: FIFA Athletes Can Use CBD. It's Time for US Sports to Follow Suit*, Leafly.com, July 5, 2018, https://www.leafly.com/news/politics/guest-opinion-fifa-athletes-can-use-cbd-its-time-for-us-sports-to-follow-suit. In June of 2018, BIG3, the up-and-coming professional three-on-three basketball league featuring former NBA players, became the first U.S. pro sports league to permit CBD use for pain management. Josh Peter, *BIG3 Becomes First U.S. Pro Sports League to Permit Use of Marijuana Ingredient*, USAToday.com, June 27, 2018, https://www.usatoday.com/story/sports/basketball/2018/06/27/big-3-becomes-first-pro-league-permit-use-marijuana-ingredient/738878002/.

3. As illustrated by the following problem, a professional athlete who tests positive for drugs or violates drug laws may be subject to consequences in addition to suspension from playing the particular sport and/or potential criminal prosecution.

PROBLEM 7-4

a. *Loss of Signing Bonus.* Traditionally, the typical signing bonus provision in a team sport player's contract contained language such as:

> It is expressly understood that no part of the bonus herein provided is part of any salary in the contract specified above . . . and that such obligations of Club are not terminable if such contract is terminated pursuant to the League's waiver system.
>
> In the event Player, in any of the years specified above, fails or refuses to report to Club, fails or refuses to practice or play with Club, or leaves Club without its consent, then, upon demand by Club, Player will return to Club the proportionate amount of the total bonus not having been earned at the time of Player's default.

Assume an NFL Player received a $4 million signing bonus when he entered into a four-year contract with Club. After playing for one year, he tested positive for a prohibited substance in training camp before the start of the second year of his contract. He received a four-game suspension for this offense pursuant to the applicable collective bargaining agreement. Club now requests that Player return a proportionate amount of his bonus money (i.e., one-sixteenth of the $4 million bonus he received).

Player argues he has not failed or refused to report to practice or to play, and thus he is not in breach of his contract. He argues that his bonus was earned when he received it. What would be the result (i.e., does the Player have to repay any of his bonus)?

Is the preceding contract language adequate to address situations such as the Player's foregoing conduct? What alternative contract language do you suggest to clarify the responsibilities and rights of both Club and Player in a similar future situation?

b. *Endorsement Contracts.* Suppose Player, a professional tennis star, entered an endorsement contract with Nibok Shoes. Pursuant to guarantees and bonuses based on Player's performance on the professional tennis circuit, Player had the potential to earn sums in excess of $2 million over the term of the contract. The endorsement agreement, has the following provision:

> 14. Termination by Company
>
> Company shall have the right to terminate this Agreement on fifteen days prior written notice to Player or his legal representative in the event of the occurrence of any of the following contingencies:
>
> . . . (c) If Player has engaged in illegal or immoral conduct resulting in a felony conviction, or if he has otherwise conducted himself in a manner which is not reasonably in keeping with the standards of professional athletics.

Player was stopped for speeding, and the arresting officer observed a small amount of marijuana in a transparent bag in his car. Player was charged with speeding and the illegal possession of a "prohibited substance." Both charges are misdemeanors. Company, for multiple reasons, immediately announced it was terminating Player's endorsement contract, stating its product endorsers are expected to maintain the highest standards of personal conduct.

In the meantime, Player has pled guilty to the speeding charge and not guilty to the illegal drug possession charge. Company is adamant regarding its decision to terminate the contract.

Considering the likely respective legal positions of Company and Player, how would you resolve their dispute as either a judge or arbitrator? What better contractual language might have been drafted from the perspective of Player? From the perspective of Company?

4.   Unfair Labor Practices

Section 8(d) of the National Labor Relations Act (NLRA) imposes a mutual obligation on representatives of both management and labor "to meet at reasonable times and confer in good faith with respect to wages, hours, and other terms and conditions of employment," so-called mandatory subjects of collective bargaining. 29 U.S.C. §158(d). Either side's failure to do so constitutes an unfair labor practice. However, this obligation "does not compel either party to agree to a proposal or require the making of a concession." *Id.* Labor disputes are to be resolved by collective bargaining or resort to economic coercion in the form of a strike by players or a lockout by league clubs.

The NLRB enforces the requirements of the NLRA and polices the unionization and collective bargaining processes. After an administrative hearing, the NLRB is empowered to order either labor or management to cease and desist from engaging in any unfair labor practice. 29 U.S.C. §160(a). The NLRB may petition the appropriate federal circuit court for judicial enforcement of its orders. 29 U.S.C. §160(e). Upon issuance of an administrative complaint alleging that a party has committed an unfair labor practice, the NLRB may petition a federal district court for appropriate interlocutory relief as warranted by the alleged illegal conduct. 29 U.S.C. §160(j). Failure to comply with an injunction may result in contempt sanctions.

In the context of professional sports, allegations of unfair labor practices have arisen in a variety of circumstances. A refusal by the league's multiemployer bargaining unit to bargain over a mandatory subject of collective bargaining is a relatively common allegation, which is explored more fully later. Other illustrative examples of alleged unfair labor practices arising in the professional sports industry are discussed in the following sections.

a.   League Interference with Players' Rights to Unionize

Section 8(a) prohibits an employer from attempting to interfere with the rights of employees to choose freely which union represents them and from discriminating against any employee to encourage or discourage union membership. 29 U.S.C. §158(a)(1) and (2).

The Arena Football League (AFL) club owners' actions in 2000 offer an interesting example of activity that potentially runs afoul of Section 8(a). In February of that year, the owners threatened to cancel the 2000 season after several players filed an antitrust suit alleging that the owners had agreed to restrict competition among themselves for players' services. The players had formed the Arena Football League Players Association (AFLPA), but they had not yet unionized. Subsequently, AFL club owners recognized the Arena Football League Players Organizing Committee (AFLPOC) as the players' collective bargaining representative, negotiated an interim labor agreement with AFLPOC, and reinstated the league's 2000 season.

In September 2000, the NLRB filed unfair labor practice charges against the AFL alleging that its club owners both threatened players and illegally promised them benefits to coerce them to accept AFLPOC as their union. The complaint asserted that the AFLPOC was unduly sympathetic to league management and had been formed primarily at the club owners' behest to immunize them from antitrust liability (the statutory and nonstatutory labor exemptions that protect a professional sports league and its member clubs from antitrust liability if the players have unionized are discussed *infra*).

After the NLRB's complaint was filed, the AFL reached a settlement that resolved both the unfair labor practice claims and the pending antitrust litigation. The net effect of the settlement was that players received $5 million in damages, the AFL withdrew its recognition of AFLPOC as the players' collective bargaining representative, players regained the right to choose which union was to represent them, and players gained free agency concessions.

b. League Refusal to Recognize Players Union as Exclusive Bargaining Representative

Player associations in professional sports date as far back as the 1880s, but effective associations were not formed until the 1950s and 1960s. It was several years before these associations, functioning as unions, were able to obtain the first collective bargaining agreements with the various major professional sports leagues. A difficult threshold task was to obtain full recognition as the players' exclusive bargaining representative, especially by a newly formed league. This was particularly true in the case of the now-defunct North American Soccer League (NASL). Two cases underscore the difficulties that a newly formed union faced in its initial efforts to collectively bargain with NASL club owners. The legal principles developed in these cases have general application to labor relations involving professional team sports.

In *North American Soccer League v. National Labor Relations Board*, 613 F.2d 1379 (5th Cir. 1980), the NASL disputed the NLRB's certification of "all NASL players of clubs based in the United States" as the appropriate collective bargaining unit, which was requested by the players union. The Fifth Circuit upheld the NLRB's determination that there is a "joint employer relationship" among the NASL and its member clubs:

> The League exercises a significant degree of control over essential aspects of the clubs' labor relations, including but not limited to the selection, retention, and termination of the players, the terms of individual player contracts, dispute resolution and player discipline. Furthermore, each club granted the NASL authority over not only its own labor relations but also, on its behalf, authority over the labor relations of the other member clubs.

Id. at 1382.

The court then concluded that a "leaguewide unit of players" for purposes of collective bargaining is appropriate:

> Notwithstanding the substantial financial autonomy of the clubs, the Board found they form, through the League, an integrated group with common labor problems and a high degree of centralized control over labor relations. In these circumstances the Board's designation of a leaguewide bargaining unit as appropriate is reasonable, not arbitrary or capricious.

Id. at 1383. This effectively required the NASL's member clubs to function as a multiemployer collective bargaining unit in labor relations issues with the players. See also *Brown v. Pro Football, Inc.*, 518 U.S. 231 (1996) (recognizing the need for multiemployer collective bargaining in professional team sports).

Once certified, the union is the exclusive bargaining representative of the league's players. 29 U.S.C. §159(a). In *Morio v. North American Soccer League*, 501 F. Supp. 633 (S.D.N.Y. 1980), the court enjoined the NASL from refusing to collectively bargain with the players union and continuing to negotiate contracts with individual players. To avoid undermining the union's authority, the league's "duty to bargain with the exclusive representative carries with it the negative duty not to bargain with individual employees." *Id.* at 639. The court required the NASL to maintain the present terms of player contracts, except for its illegal unilaterally imposed changes, until an agreement or impasse was reached pursuant to good faith bargaining with the players union.

A decision by the British Columbia Labour Relations Board demonstrates that issues pertaining to the determination of the appropriate bargaining unit in the sports labor context are still being contested. During the prolonged NHL lockout of 2004-2005, Vancouver Canucks players sought certification as a separate union under British Columbia Labour Law. (Labor law in Canada is controlled by the laws of each province rather than on a national basis.) The National Hockey League and the owners of the Canucks, the Orca Bay Hockey Limited Partnership, resisted this effort. The initial decision by a British Columbia labor panel favored the establishment of a separate bargaining unit of Canucks players, which was overturned by the British Columbia Labour Relations Board. See *Orca Bay Hockey Limited Partnership (Orca Bay) and National Hockey League (NHL) and British Columbia Chapter of the National Hockey League Players Association (BC-NHLPA)*, Case number 55143, July 31, 2007.

The Board noted that despite the earlier decision favoring the Canucks players' application, the NHLPA continued bargaining on a league-wide basis with the NHL on behalf of all NHL players, including Canucks players. Even after a new collective bargaining agreement was entered into between the NHLPA and NHL, the BC-NHLPA, acting on behalf of the Canucks players, pursued its application for British Columbia certification as a separate bargaining unit.

In a lengthy decision, the Board concluded:

> Orca Bay is the employer, but Orca Bay itself is an integral part of the NHL, just as the BC-NHLPA is an integral part of the NHLPA, and the Canucks players, as a team, are an integral part of the hockey league within which they play. All three elements . . . are well served by their current league-wide bargaining structure. This is a crucial factor in our finding that the applied for bargaining unit is

inappropriate. If this circumstance were to change, . . . it may be we would have to revisit our decision. However, in light of the present circumstances, we find that the bargaining unit applied for is inappropriate.

Similarly, in a publicly available legal opinion provided in connection with the 2012 NHL lockout, Professor William Gould, a former chair of the National Labor Relations Board, stated:

> It is my opinion that collective bargaining for North American sports leagues has to be conducted on a league-wide basis to meet the interests of the parties, labor and management, as well as the public. Public policy and labor law have promoted leaguewide bargaining under the laws of the United States. This is the way that it has been treated under the laws of the United States, and it is my view that it would be contrary to U.S. labor law and the requirements of sound collective bargaining between the parties for the existing league-wide bargaining unit involving the parties, the National Hockey League and the National Hockey League Players' Association, to be fragmented by the creation of separate bargaining units for the Canadian teams, as well as separate rules governing the right to engage in strikes and lockouts which would balkanize the bargaining unit and disrupt the orderly collective bargaining process. . . .
>
>   The law relating to NLRB assertion of jurisdiction over conduct engaged in outside the United States has particular significance for professional sports. This is because so many sports, like baseball and basketball, as well as hockey, possess both American and Canadian franchises and thus give rise to litigation involving relationships between organized labor and multi-employer entities in so-called "mixed territory" cases. The fact that professional sports are *sui generis* and involve player movement, scheduling, roster arrangements, and the like, between different employers in the multi-employer association requires the involvement of the administrative process in the territory which possesses the majority of franchises. In professional sports, including hockey, the overwhelming majority are to be found in the United States, where the National Labor Relations Board possesses exclusive jurisdiction, which is why in my opinion the NLRB has the jurisdiction to intervene in the "mixed territory" relationship between the NHL and the NHLPA.

Letter from William B. Gould, IV, to Heenan Blaikie, LLP, re *Colby Armstrong, et al. and The National Hockey League Players Association v. Club de Hockey Canadien Inc. and the National Hockey League,* November 30, 2012.

c. Retaliation Against Union Activists

Section 8(a)(3) prohibits an employer from discriminating against any employee to encourage or discourage union membership. 29 U.S.C. §158(a)(3). The release of a player because of his union activities, if proved, is an unfair labor practice.

In *Nordstrom d/b/a Seattle Seahawks,* 292 NLRB 899 (1989), Sam McCullum asserted that the Seattle Seahawks NFL club cut him from the team's final roster in violation of §8(a)(3). McCullum started as a wide receiver for the Seahawks during the 1976-1981 seasons. In 1981 his teammates selected him to be their union player representative. McCullum's union activities incurred head coach Jack Patera's ire, particularly for his orchestration of a "solidarity handshake" between his teammates and players on the opposing team prior to the first 1982 preseason game. Despite starting all of the Seahawks 1982 preseason games,

McCullum was cut shortly after the club acquired Roger Carr, another wide receiver.

McCullum and the NFL Players Association claimed that his union activities were a "motivating factor" in the termination of his employment with the Seahawks. The club asserted that he would have been cut even without his participation in union activities based on his relative skills in comparison to the team's other wide receivers. The Seahawks claimed a stronger team need for Carr's services and the inability to keep McCullum as a fifth wide receiver without harming the need for players at other positions.

In a divided opinion, the NLRB affirmed the administrative law judge's ruling that McCullum's termination was illegal discrimination based on his role "as a fairly aggressive union spokesman." Patera's attempted heavy fines for team players' participation in the solidarity handshake evidenced his animus toward union activity for which McCullum was the focal point. Patera also had the final authority regarding player cuts, and there was some evidence that Carr was acquired to enable McCullum's release because of his union activities. A dissenting NLRB member concluded that McCullum's release was a valid exercise of team management's business judgment regarding its personnel needs, which decision would have been made absent any antiunion motivation.

The effectiveness of available administrative remedies can be questioned, however, because it may be a lengthy period of time before an NLRB proceeding and appeals are concluded. See *Nordstrom v. NLRB*, 984 F.2d 479 (D.C. Cir. 1993) (affirming $301,000 award of back pay to McCullum for the period he would have been employed by the Seahawks but for his unlawful termination, 11 years after his 1982 release).

This case illustrates the difficulty of determining why a player active in union activities was cut by a team. Does federal labor law potentially interfere with a club's efforts to field its best possible team? As a player agent, what is your advice to a marginal veteran player who is interested in serving as the team's union representative? As the club's general counsel, what is your advice to team management regarding cutting a player serving as the team's union representative?

Section 8(a)(3) retaliation claims are, predictably, even more complex when athletes' right to unionize is unclear. Unlike NFL players, Ultimate Fighting Championship (UFC) fighters are not unionized. In February 2018, UFC fighter Leslie Smith launched an effort, dubbed Project Spearhead, to organize fighters into a union. Two months later, when Smith's contract with UFC expired, UFC declined to renew it. Smith attributes UFC's declination to its distaste for her organizing efforts, and in May 2018 she filed an NLRB retaliation charge against UFC. Jaclyn Diaz, *UFC, Fighter Spar Over Union Activity*, Bloomberg Law, May 2, 2018, https://news.bloomberglaw.com/daily-labor-report/ufc-fighter-spar-over-union-activity. In addition to the challenge that the Seattle Seahawks' Sam McCullum faced of establishing the adverse action at issue related to his union activities, Smith had to establish the threshold requirement that UFC fighters are "employees" eligible under the NLRA to unionize and that the statute's anti-retaliation provisions protect her.

UFC classifies its fighters as independent contractors (who are not capable of unionizing under the NLRA) rather than employees (who are), but Smith alleged this is a misclassification. She argued that UFC exerts substantial control over the fighters (e.g., they must wear a required uniform, are restricted in how they may display their sponsors' names and logos, and may not participate in bouts organized by other combat organizations), and, therefore, the fighters should be considered employees. Keith J. Brodie, *UFC Enters NLRB Independent Contractor Cage Match*, National Law Review, May 3, 2018, https://www .natlawreview.com/article/ufc-enters-nlrb-independent-contractor-cage-match.

In September 2018, the NLRB dismissed the matter but did not reach the issue of UFC's classification of its fighters. The Board found that, although Smith provided sufficient evidence to establish she tried to organize MMA fighters, she provided insufficient evidence to establish the UFC's nonrenewal of her contract was based on her union organizing efforts. Finding as such, the NLRB determined it was "unnecessary to decide whether Smith is a statutory employee."[6] Smith's appeal of its ruling to a federal appellate court is pending.

d.   Discrimination Against Striking Workers

Players have a statutory right to strike, which is an important aspect of our national labor laws designed to facilitate peaceful and productive collective bargaining relations. If the players strike, league clubs may hire replacement players for the duration of their strike as the NFL did during the 1987 three-week strike by its players. In the alternative, a professional sports league may choose to cease operations and lock out its players as the NHL did in 2004 and 2012, and as the NFL and NBA did in 2011. In each of the major professional sports leagues, who has the greater economic leverage to exercise in a labor dispute, club owners or players? Whatever the case, as illustrated below, a league and its member clubs are prohibited from retaliating against striking players.

NFL MANAGEMENT COUNCIL AND NFLPA

309 N.L.R.B. 78 (1992)

By Chairman STEPHENS and Members DEVANEY and OVIATT.

The parties began negotiations for a successor to the 1982-1987 agreement early in 1987. These negotiations were unsuccessful and, on September 21, 1987, after the second week of regular season play, the players went out on strike. The Respondents immediately began hiring temporary replacements for the striking players. Because certain Clubs were unable to assemble complete teams in time for the games scheduled for September 27-28, 1987, the Respondents canceled those games.

The Respondents also substantially modified the NFL's complex personnel rules governing the hiring of players and their eligibility to play in a game. . . .

Only players on a Club's Active list were eligible to play in a game. The Respondents' rules usually provide that, for games played on a Saturday or Sunday, each Club must establish its Active list for the game by 2 p.m. New York time the day prior to that game. For Monday night games, the deadline is 2 p.m. New York time the day of the game.

In response to the strike, the Respondents substantially modified these rules. On September 29, 1987, the NFL Management Council Executive Committee

---

6. *ZUFFA, LLC, d/b/a Ultimate Fighting Championship ("UFC") Case 04-CA-219498*, https://usatm-majunkie.files.wordpress.com/2018/10/leslie-smith-ufc-labor-complaint-dismissal-letter.pdf   (last visited May 14, 2019).

(CEC) eliminated roster limits until 4 p.m. New York time on October 3, 1987. Clubs were permitted an unlimited number of players on their Inactive lists with a 45-player Active list limit for participating in the games on October 4-5. The deadline for establishing the Active lists was set at 4 p.m. New York time on October 3, and a deadline of 12 p.m. noon local time on Friday (October 2) was established for signing nonroster players. The CEC also established a deadline of 12 p.m. noon local time on October 2 for strikers to report in order to be eligible to play in the Sunday or Monday games.

On October 1, the above rules were modified to establish a 3 p.m. Friday New York time deadline for strikers to report in order to be eligible for that weekend's games or for Clubs to sign nonroster players.

On October 5, the CEC further modified its eligibility rules for returning strikers. The deadline for signing nonroster players was moved back to 4 p.m. New York time Saturday for teams playing on Sunday, and to 4 p.m. New York time on Monday for teams playing that night. For strikers, however, the reporting deadline was set at 1 p.m. New York time on Wednesdays. Strikers reporting after that time were not eligible to play in the following weekend's game, could not be paid for that game, and were exempt from counting against the Club's Active or Inactive list until 4 p.m. New York time on the day following that game. This rule was in effect on Thursday October 15, when the Union advised the Respondents that the strike was over; on the basis of this rule all strikers who had not reported prior to the deadline were declared ineligible to play in the games scheduled for October 18-19 and were not paid for that game. . . .

The judge found, and we agree, that the Union unconditionally offered to return to work on Thursday October 15. For the reasons that follow, we find that the Respondents unlawfully discriminated against the strikers by maintaining and enforcing the Wednesday eligibility deadline to preclude their participation in or payment for the games played on October 18-19.

The Supreme Court has recognized that "there are some practices which are inherently so prejudicial to union interests and so devoid of significant economic justification . . . that the employer's conduct carries with it an inference of unlawful intent so compelling that it is justifiable to disbelieve the employer's protestations of innocent purpose." *American Ship Building Co. v. NLRB*, 380 U.S. 300 (1965). If an employer's conduct falls within this category, "the Board can find an unfair labor practice even if the employer introduces evidence that the conduct was motivated by business considerations." *NLRB v. Great Dane Trailers*, 388 U.S. 26, 34 (1967).

On the other hand, if the impact on employee rights of the discriminatory conduct is comparatively slight, an antiunion motivation must be proved to sustain the charge if the employer has come forward with evidence of legitimate and substantial business justifications for the conduct. Thus, in either situation, once it has been proved that the employer engaged in discriminatory conduct which could have adversely affected employee rights to some extent, the burden is upon the employer to establish that it was motivated by legitimate objectives since proof of motivation is most accessible to him.

Applying these principles to this case, we find as an initial matter that the Wednesday deadline rule clearly constitutes discriminatory conduct which adversely affects employee rights. On its face, the rule discriminates against strikers by applying different, and more stringent, standards for eligibility to participate in NFL games (and to be paid for such participation). Moreover, the rule also adversely affects one of the most significant rights protected by the

Act—the right to strike. The Board and the courts, applying the principles of *Great Dane*, have long recognized that the right to strike includes the right to full and complete reinstatement upon unconditional application to return. . . .

As in *Laidlaw*, the Respondents—in reliance on their Wednesday reporting deadline—offered the striking employees who reported for work on October 15 "less than the rights accorded by full reinstatement" (i.e., the right to participate in the games scheduled for October 18-19 and to be paid for those games). . . . Thus, the Wednesday deadline adversely affected the striking employees in the exercise of their right to strike or to cease participating in the strike, by prohibiting the full and complete reinstatement, for the October 18-19 games, of those employees who chose to return to work after the Respondents' deadline had passed.

We need not decide whether, as the General Counsel contends, the Respondents' conduct was inherently destructive of employee rights. Even assuming that the impact on employee rights of the Wednesday deadline rule for strikers was "comparatively slight," the burden still rests with the Respondents to establish "legitimate and substantial business justifications" for the rule. For the reasons that follow, we find that the Respondents have not made the required showing.

The Respondents assert that the Wednesday deadline was justified by the Clubs' need for sufficient time to prepare returning players for game conditions. In this regard, the Respondents presented evidence that the strikers' physical condition would be expected to deteriorate as the strike progressed. In addition, NFL Management Council official Eddie LeBaron testified that players could not maintain their "football condition" without participating in practices involving physical contact. The Respondents also assert that they particularly did not wish to risk injuries to so-called franchise players.

The Respondents also assert that the rule is justified by their goal of ensuring that each Club operates from the same competitive position. Thus, the Wednesday deadline would give each Club the same amount of preparation time with returning players, prevent situations in which a replacement squad was "mismatched" against a squad composed of veterans who had reported late in the week, and ensure that Clubs could prepare for specific players during the Wednesday and Thursday practices when game plans were typically practiced.

Finally, the Respondents assert that the Wednesday deadline was justified in light of substantial administrative difficulties allegedly posed if strikers returned at a late date in the week. These alleged difficulties included the question of how to merge replacement squads and strikers, as well as the logistics of practicing and evaluating two squads of players at the same time and arranging transportation to away games for late-reporting players.

In evaluating the Respondents' justifications, we initially note the unprecedented nature of the Wednesday deadline and the absence of any evidence that the Respondents have imposed a deadline of this type on employees outside of a strike setting. In particular, the record shows that players who withheld their services in pursuit of individual goals (i.e., players holding out for a more lucrative contract) are not subject to comparable restraints on their status on their return. Rather, such players are eligible to play immediately so long as they are included in the Club's active roster. . . .

It is undisputed that the Wednesday deadline was only applicable to striking players. The Respondents could and did sign nonstrikers to contracts subsequent to the date the strikers were declared ineligible. . . .

Under these circumstances, we find that the Respondents have not established legitimate and substantial justifications for the deadline rule. While it may be true that some striking employees' physical conditioning declined during the strike, the same considerations were present in the case of holdouts and of replacement players. . . .

We also find that the Respondents' asserted competitiveness concerns are unpersuasive. Although the Respondents were entitled to ensure that all clubs operated under the same rules, adopting a deadline which discriminated against strikers was unnecessary to the achievement of this goal. The Respondents' argument that Clubs needed the practice time provided by the Wednesday deadline to prepare the strikers to play (and, for the purpose of those practices, needed to know who would be playing for its opponent) is contradicted by their willingness to allow nonstrikers with substantially less preparation time to play in those games. . . .

The Respondents also provide no explanation for the fact that the initial deadline for returning strikers, 12 noon on Friday (later modified to 3 p.m. New York time), would have provided the Clubs with less time to accomplish the reinstatement of returning strikers than they actually had when the strikers reported on October 15. . . .

In sum, the Respondents' Wednesday deadline prohibited employees who returned from the strike on October 15 from playing in the following weekend's games and prohibited their Club from paying them for that game on the basis of their absence from the Club during the strike. The only players subject to such restrictions were those who chose to participate in the strike, a concerted activity protected by the Act. Players absent from their Club for other reasons were not subject to any similar restriction on their eligibility to participate in games; players ineligible to play for other reasons were nevertheless still entitled to be paid. Accordingly, for the reasons stated above, we find that the Respondents' maintenance and enforcement of its Wednesday deadline rule violated Section 8(a)(1) and (3) of the Act. . . .

To remedy the unfair labor practices which we have found, we shall order the Respondents to cease and desist, and to take certain affirmative action necessary to effectuate the purposes of the Act. Specifically, we shall order the Respondents to make whole all employees who were denied wages and declared ineligible for the games played on October 18 and 19, 1987, on the basis of the Respondents' Wednesday eligibility rule for strikers, with interest computed in the manner set forth in the judge's decision. The Respondents shall also make whole those injured players denied compensation on account of their participation in the strike in the manner set forth in the judge's decision. . . .

e.   Breach of Duty to Bargain in Good Faith and to Provide Relevant Information Concerning Mandatory Subjects of Collective Bargaining

As noted previously, both the league's labor representatives and the players union have a duty to collectively bargain over wages, hours, and other terms and conditions of employment. The players union generally wants to bargain over a wide range of issues, but league clubs may be reluctant to do so. The following cases consider what constitutes mandatory subjects of collective bargaining in the context of professional sports labor relations as well as the parties' mutual obligation to provide relevant information concerning these subjects to the other side.

SILVERMAN v. MAJOR LEAGUE BASEBALL PLAYER RELATIONS COMMITTEE, INC. (SILVERMAN I)
516 F. Supp 588 (S.D.N.Y. 1981)

WERKER, District Judge.

. . . Since 1966 the Major League baseball players have been represented by the Players Association. During this time the respondent [Major League Baseball Player Relations Committee, Inc. (PRC)] has been the exclusive collective bargaining agent of twenty-six Major League clubs. The Board of Directors of the PRC is empowered to formulate labor policy for the clubs and direct all negotiations with the Players Association. C. Raymond Grebey, Director of Player Relations of PRC, has been designated by the PRC Board as the official spokesman for the PRC in all collective bargaining matters. . . .

The Players Association and the PRC bargain to establish an agreement on pensions, allowances, and a variety of rules governing players' employment. Except as to a base salary, under the various agreements negotiated by the parties, the Players Association has waived its right to bargain with the PRC about individual player salaries. Thus, above a minimum salary, the subject has been left to each individual player to negotiate with his club.

Prior to 1975, when a Major League baseball player's employment contract expired, he was precluded from negotiating for employment with any other team except his own. In December 1975, as the result of grievances filed by the Players Association on behalf of John Messersmith and David McNally, an arbitrator found that Major League clubs could not reserve a player for more than one year ("option year") past the expiration of his contract. A player who completes the option year without signing a renewal contract with his team becomes a "free agent" who is able to negotiate with other clubs.

In 1976 the Players Association and the PRC entered into a collective bargaining agreement, effective January 1, 1976 through December 31, 1979, which provided, *inter alia*, for "free agency" as established by the Messersmith-McNally decision. Pursuant to this agreement, however, a player was required to serve six years in the Major Leagues before becoming a "free agent." The agreement also provided for "compensation" in the form of an amateur player draft choice to each club which lost a "free agent" player selected by more than two clubs for negotiation rights. After four years of experimenting with this new system, the Players Association and the PRC commenced negotiations for a new collective bargaining agreement on November 11, 1979.

On January 16, 1980, the PRC presented a proposal which recognized the difference in quality, as measured by skill and ability, among the various players choosing to become "free agents." Under this proposal, as finally offered on May 12, 1980, a team losing a "free agent" selected by less than four clubs will not be afforded replacement player "compensation." If a player is selected for negotiation rights by four to seven clubs, the club signing a contract with the player must compensate the player's former club with an amateur draft choice, as before. However, if a player is selected by eight or more clubs, and meets certain minimum performance standards, the signing club must compensate the former club with not only an amateur draft choice, but also a professional player of the former club's choice from a list of unprotected players under contract with the signing club. In this third category, the player is referred to as a "ranking free agent" or "premium" player. Each club may retain 40 players under the contract. Depending upon the performance level of the "free agent" signed, the signing team may protect from 15 to 18 of its 40 players.

The Players Association adamantly opposed this proposal as having a negative impact on player salaries. Since the proposal requires a club signing a "ranking free agent" to give up a professional player as well as an amateur draft choice, the Association predicts that the number of clubs willing to bid for a "premium" player and the salaries they would offer would be limited by the knowledge that they would be required to forfeit a player of perhaps comparable quality. Correspondingly, the player's present club could then offer him less to insure his remaining with the team.

As negotiations progressed, various matters were being resolved, but it became apparent that the issue of additional replacement player "compensation" was a significant impediment to settlement. . . . On December 8, 1980, Bowie Kuhn, Commissioner of Baseball, delivered a speech at the Annual Convention of Professional Baseball. Commenting on the financial difficulties facing the industry, Commissioner Kuhn expressed concern about escalating player salaries brought about by "free agency." He cited the companion problem of "compensation" as a threat to competitive balance in baseball and thus expressed a concern about adequate replacement talent for the loss of a "free agent." Sounding a clarion call to owners and players alike to recognize the need to correct the system of "free agency" which has given rise to these problems, he predicted further financial loss without cooperation between the two groups. . . .

By letter of February 27, 1981, the Players Association requested the PRC to provide certain financial information for all member clubs. The Players Association premised the appropriateness of its request on Commissioner Kuhn's December 1980 speech which the Association interpreted as an affirmation of its belief that the "compensation" proposal was motivated by financial concerns.

Mr. Miller explained that the requested financial data was "necessary for the Players Association to properly discharge its duties and responsibilities . . . as the exclusive collective bargaining representative of all major league players, for purposes of preparation for and conduct of the ongoing negotiations."

On March 13, 1981, the PRC, through Mr. Grebey, refused to comply with the Association's request, repeating the PRC's position that its bargaining stance regarding "compensation" was not based on "economic incapacity or inability." . . .

. . . Grebey [subsequently] stated that the PRC had "never advanced the position nor taken refuge in argumentation which either directly or indirectly claims an inability to pay as a defense for (its) position in collective bargaining." Rather, the objective of the PRC in proposing the plan for "compensation," explained Mr. Grebey, "is to enhance player balance between clubs losing a quality free agent over the long term by providing replacement personnel that will: (1) compensate for the loss of a player; (2) compensate for the general inability of clubs to overcome this added turn-over on a club roster through additions from the Minor Leagues; and (3) provide equity balance in compensation, reflecting the different levels of skill and ability of players who chose to become free agents as evidenced by our experience of the past four years."

Meanwhile, during this second round of negotiations, various statements by club owners appeared in the media. These statements all reflect an expression of concern about the financial well-being of the baseball industry and/or the level of player salaries. . . .

Believing that the PRC's bargaining position on the issue of player "compensation" was based at least in part on the financial difficulties of certain member clubs, on May 7, 1981, the Players Association filed an unfair labor practice charge with the Board alleging respondents' failure to bargain in good faith by refusing to comply with the Players Association's request for financial disclosure in violation of Sections 8(a)(1) and (5) of the Act, 29 U.S.C. §§ 158(a)(1) and (5).

Following investigation and pursuant to Section 10(b) of the Act, 29 U.S.C. § 160(b), the Board filed a complaint charging respondents with violating Sections 8(a)(1) and (5) of the Act. A hearing on this complaint before an administrative law judge of the Board is scheduled to commence on June 15, 1981.

The temporary injunctive relief sought by petitioner requires respondents to rescind their February 19, 1981, action by which they exercised their right under the 1980 basic agreement and unilaterally implemented their bargaining proposal regarding "compensation." This relief, if granted, would thus preclude the Players Association, under the terms of the basic agreement, from commencing a strike. Petitioner argues that if its request for relief is not granted, the Players Association and the baseball player-employees it represents will be forced to strike within forty-eight hours after this Court rules, or be bound through the end of 1983 by the PRC's proposal. Petitioner emphasizes that obvious irreparable harm to the players, owners and fans would flow from a decision by the Players Association to strike.

The Association contends that if petitioner should prevail in the proceedings presently before the administrative law judge, the Board would be unable to adequately remedy the PRC's alleged unfair labor practice by ordering the clubs to disclose the financial information which the Association seeks, since the Board cannot undo the effects of a strike which would ensue as a result of the denial of petitioner's instant request for relief.

Respondents vigorously oppose petitioner's application as a tactic by the Players Association to avoid the consequences of a contract freely bargained for and entered into by it. . . .

The Board alleges in its petition that the public statements by club owners regarding claims of financial difficulties created a reasonable belief on the part of the Players Association that respondents' bargaining position during this second round of negotiations was based, "at least in part, on the present or prospective financial difficulties of certain of Respondents' member clubs." Although Marvin Miller has expressed some doubt as to club owners' inability to pay rising player salaries, he nevertheless takes the position that the Players Association must have the financial information it requests if it is to fulfill its duty of fair representation. If deprived of that information, the Association claims that it must blindly decide whether to press its demands and risk the loss of jobs for its members if the clubs cannot survive under the "compensation" terms proposed by the Association, or to recede from it position and accept the

PRC's proposal without verifying owners' claims of financial distress caused by "free agency." Thus, the Association brought an unfair labor practice charge against the PRC for its failure to disclose the requested financial data after the clubs allegedly put into issue their inability to pay.

In *N.L.R.B. v. Truitt Manufacturing Co.*, 351 U.S. 149, 76 S. Ct. 753, 100 L.Ed. 1027 (1956), the Supreme Court laid to rest the question of whether an employer, bound by the National Labor Relations Act to bargain in good faith, could claim that it was financially unable to pay higher wages and then refuse a union's request to produce financial data to substantiate the claim. Holding that such conduct supported a finding of failure to bargain in good faith, in violation of Section 8(a)(5) of the Act, 29 U.S.C. § 158(a)(5), the Court explained:

> Good-faith bargaining necessarily requires that claims made by either bargainer should be honest claims. This is true about an asserted inability to pay an increase in wages. If such an argument is important enough to present in the give and take of bargaining, it is important enough to require some sort of proof of its accuracy.

However, *Truitt's* progeny have held that an employer is required to disclose its financial condition only when the employer claims an inability to pay, however phrased, during the course of bargaining. . . .

Petitioner admits that at no time during bargaining sessions have respondents made a claim of inability to pay. Nevertheless, petitioner urges the Court to find that public statements made by several club owners as well as the Commissioner of Baseball about the financial condition of the industry are sufficient to support a finding of reasonable cause to believe that respondents have injected the inability to pay into the negotiations.

The cases cited by petitioner in support of its position are simply inapposite. In each case, inability to pay was put in issue at the bargaining table. . . .

Thus, Petitioner concedes, as it must, that the Board and courts have never found that an employer has injected financial condition into negotiations, absent statements or conduct by the employer at the bargaining table. Nevertheless, it urges this Court to find, on the basis of statements by Commissioner Kuhn and various owners, that the financial issue has become relevant to the negotiations regarding "compensation" because of the unique nature of collective bargaining in baseball. Mindful that this Court must be "hospitable" to the views of the Regional Director, however novel, . . . I am nevertheless convinced that the Board's position is wrong, and thus will not "defer to the statutory construction urged by (it)."

It is the PRC Board of Directors which is charged with the exclusive authority to formulate the collective bargaining position of the clubs and to negotiate agreements with the Players Association. Indeed, Grebey, the official spokesman for the PRC in collective bargaining matters, has consistently denied that the clubs' financial status is at issue in the current negotiations.

Commissioner Kuhn's remarks in December 1980 at the convention cannot be imputed to the PRC as a statement of its bargaining position. First, petitioner's attempt to establish an agency relationship between the Commissioner and the PRC is unavailing. As Commissioner of Baseball, Kuhn presides at the regular joint meetings of the Major Leagues, but does not request nor preside at special meetings called by the PRC. Moreover, while Kuhn is responsible for disciplining players who may then file grievances against him in his capacity as Commissioner, he has likewise ordered the clubs to cease certain action when the interests of baseball warranted his intercession, as when he directed the clubs to open their training camps in the spring of 1976. . . .

In a multi-employer bargaining unit as large and publicly visible as the Major League Baseball Clubs, it is inevitable that extraneous statements will be made by individuals affiliated in some way with the group which are inconsistent with the official position of the unit. This only underscores the necessity, recognized by the PRC, for centralized bargaining responsibility and authority. Clearly, individual expressions of opinion cannot serve to bind the entire bargaining unit in the absence of authority to speak for the group. . . .

The Act has provided for collective bargaining between the parties through their authorized representatives. If this Court were to find that the several public statements by club officials and the Commissioner were sufficient to support a finding that the PRC and its negotiating team view the respondents' "compensation" proposal as related to the financial condition of the clubs, it would do violence to the intent and purpose of the Act which limits the jurisdiction of this Court. . . .

To accept petitioner's argument would permit disgruntled employers in a multi-employer unit who disagreed with the negotiation policies of their representatives to force negotiation issues into the courts, thereby "conducting labor management relations by way of an injunction," a result clearly contrary to the purpose of the Act. . . .

Thus, I cannot find that the comments by several club officials and the Commissioner, relied upon by petitioner, are statements of policy on behalf of the PRC which would support a claim of inability to pay.

Moreover, the issue of salary, above a minimum rate, is not a subject of collective bargaining between the Players Association and the PRC. Rather, individual players negotiate independently with the clubs as to their salary. Indeed, it is the high player salaries which have resulted from the negotiation of individual contracts by players and clubs which Commissioner Kuhn addressed in his 1980 speech. Noting that player salaries are increasing at a more rapid rate than revenues, he opined that bargaining of individual contracts has led to this problem. . . .

The court is mindful that a strike may result from its denial of petitioner's request for a 10(j) injunction. Indeed, the industry has suffered a strike in the past. Nevertheless, in struggling with a temptation and even compulsion to prevent a strike in the public interest, I am bound by the law. The possibility of a strike, although a fact of life in labor relations, offers no occasion for this Court to distort the principles of law and equity. The resolution of the "compensation" issue is left to the parties through the negotiation process.

PLAY BALL!!!

SO ORDERED.

NOTES AND QUESTIONS

1. Unfortunately for MLB and its fans, the judge's "order" to "play ball" was a wish, not a command enforceable by contempt sanctions. On June 10, 1981, he declined to grant the NLRB's request to enjoin the PRC from unilaterally implementing its bargaining proposal regarding "compensation" for lost free agents. The players went on strike two days later. The strike lasted 50 days, eliminating much of the season and resulting in a "split season"

that left all parties dissatisfied. It is hard to determine what would have happened if the judge had granted the injunction. In all likelihood, the strike would have been postponed at least until after the 1981 season. In the interim, perhaps the PRC and MLBPA would have found compromise and reached a new collective bargaining agreement, possibly averting a strike altogether.

The *Silverman I* judge was following well-established legal precedent in denying the injunction based on the circumstances. It generally takes more than a few outsider comments, even by owners, about potential economic hardship to require the clubs to open their books. In general, league clubs prefer not to disclose information about their finances. However, there have been some instances in which disclosure of league financial information has occurred. In 1982, the NFLPA filed a successful unfair labor practices claim, pursuant to which the NFL was required to divulge the terms of its television contracts to allow the players association to evaluate its fair share of such proceeds. In 1982-1983, the National Basketball Association voluntarily opened its books to demonstrate to players the tenuous state of its finances, thus leading to the first professional sports collective bargaining agreement with an aggregate player salary cap.

2. One tactic used by MLB club owners in 1981 foreshadowed what has become a common practice. The club owners built a "war chest" in anticipation of the strike, primarily strike insurance costing the insurers millions of dollars. Since then, insurance companies have been reluctant to assume such risks even for the payment of hefty premiums. Instead, both sides regularly accumulate funds received from their respective constituents (i.e., club owners or players) or third-party sources (e.g., media contracts or intellectual property licensing royalties) for economic protection against a protracted strike.

In 2008, anticipating that the 2011 NFL CBA expiration would trigger a work stoppage, NFL owners appeared to begin building a "war chest" of their own. Rather than relying on insurance, however, they negotiated television contract extensions that would produce revenue during the 2011 season even if no games were played. These extensions created a $4 billion fund for the NFL, and recognizing the economic leverage that this money created for the NFL owners, the NFLPA sued to prevent them from accessing it. See *White v. National Football League*, 766 F. Supp. 2d 941, 948 (D. Minn. 2011). In the suit, the NFLPA alleged that the NFL brokered a relatively weak deal for pre-work stoppage revenues, which were shared with players, in exchange for the robust $4 billion deal, which would not be shared with players if a work stoppage were to occur. The court decided in the NFLPA's favor, finding that "the NFL renegotiated the broadcast contracts to benefit its exclusive interest at the expense of, and contrary to, the joint interests of the NFL and the Players[,] which constitutes 'a design . . . to seek an unconscionable advantage' and is inconsistent with good faith." *White*, 766 F. Supp. 2d at 951 (internal citations omitted).

3. Players unions, for their part, tend to systematically prepare for potential labor stoppages as well. For instance, as it became increasingly clear that a 2011 NFL work stoppage was likely, the NFLPA tried to brace players economically through raising their financial awareness and encouraging them to save funds equal to at least three game checks in case of a work stoppage. In addition, the NFLPA took out a secret insurance policy sufficient to pay each player $200,000 in the event the lockout extended into the season. In

fact, the insurance fund may have helped turn the tide in the CBA negotiations: when the players revealed its existence during what had devolved
into a stalemate, it "got the [owners'] attention," signaling that the players
might not break solidarity for fear of financial hardship as quickly as was
previously assumed. Jim Trotter, *Players' Secret Lockout Insurance Could Have
Sparked Talks*, Sports Illustrated, July 15, 2011, http://sportsillustrated.cnn
.com/2011/writers/jim_trotter/07/15/secret-lockout-fund/index.html.

Similarly, about 200 NBA players bought lockout insurance prior to
the 2011 NBA lockout to ensure income flow despite the work stoppage.
Moreover, some NBA players chose to ensure income flow by playing basketball in foreign leagues during the lockout under contracts that allowed
them to return to the NBA mid-season in the event labor peace was achieved.

Both sides must negotiate in good faith over wages, hours, and other terms
and conditions of player employment. The league cannot unilaterally implement new terms relating to mandatory subjects of collective bargaining until the
parties have reached an impasse in collective bargaining negotiations. It is an
unfair labor practice to violate either of these requirements.

Soon after the NFL's first collective bargaining agreement was reached, NFL
club owners, at the league commissioner's behest, unilaterally adopted a rule
imposing an automatic $200 fine on all players leaving the bench and going
onto the field of play during altercations transpiring in the heat of battle. The
NFLPA alleged that this unilateral conduct constituted a refusal to bargain with
the union in violation of §8(a)(5). The owners contended that the commissioner promulgated this rule pursuant to his authority under the collective bargaining agreement to fine a player for conduct detrimental to the NFL. The
Eighth Circuit affirmed the NLRB's determination that the rule was promulgated by the NFL club owners rather than the commissioner. Because the rule
establishes a term or condition of employment, it is a mandatory subject of
bargaining and its unilateral implementation is an unfair labor practice. See
National Football League Players Assn. v. National Labor Relations Bd., 503 F.2d 12
(8th Cir. 1974).

The following case, which arose out of the 1994 MLB players strike, considers
the important distinction between mandatory and permissive subjects of collective bargaining.

SILVERMAN v. MAJOR LEAGUE BASEBALL PLAYER
RELATIONS COMMITTEE, INC. (SILVERMAN II)

880 F. Supp. 246 (S.D.N.Y. 1995)

SOTOMAYOR, District Judge.

. . . On March 15, 1995, on the basis of charges filed by [the Major League
Baseball Players Association (the "Players")], the [NLRB] issued a Complaint
and Notice of Hearing alleging, *inter alia*, that [the Major League Baseball
Player Relations Committee, Inc. (the PRC)] had violated Sections 8(a)(1) and
(5) of the Act by unilaterally eliminating, before an impasse had been reached,
salary arbitration for certain reserve players, competitive bargaining for certain free agents, and the anti-collusion provision of their collective bargaining
agreement, Article XX(F). After the Board concluded that there was reasonable

cause to believe that a violation of the Act had occurred and that injunctive relief was just and proper, it filed this Petition on March 27, 1995. . . .

The most recent Basic Agreement between the parties extended from January 1990 through December 1993. The Agreement covered a multitude of employment terms and conditions. The pertinent provisions of the Agreement to the issues before me involve the Agreement's reserve and free agency systems. Essentially, the free agency system permits players who have completed six major-league playing seasons to set their wages with individual owner clubs. . . . The anti-collusion provision of the Basic Agreement, Subsection F of Article XX, provides, in relevant part, that the wage process between the free agent individual player and club owner is an individual matter to be determined solely by each Player and each Club for his or its own benefit. Players shall not act in concert with other Players and the Clubs shall not act in concert with other Clubs. . . .

In the matter before me, the NLRB has charged the Owners with violating §§ 8(a)(1) & (5) of the Act, that is, of violating the duty to bargain collectively in good faith with the Players. . . .

The potential subject matter of parties engaged in collective bargaining has been divided by the Supreme Court into two categories: mandatory and permissive subjects of bargaining. . . . Mandatory subjects are those encompassed in Section 8(d) in the phrase "wages, hours, and other terms and conditions of employment," while permissive subjects are all other matters. The distinction between mandatory and permissive subjects of bargaining is crucial in labor disputes, because it determines to what extent one party may compel the other to bargain over a given proposal: mandatory subjects require the parties to bargain in good faith, whereas no such requirement adheres to permissive subjects. It is not always obvious whether or not a provision relates to "wages, hours, and other terms and conditions of employment," and the mandatory/permissive distinction is the subject of much case law.

The distinction between mandatory and permissive subjects of bargaining is also important upon expiration of a collective bargaining agreement, in the period before the parties have instituted a successor agreement. During the interim between agreements, the Supreme Court has held, the parties must honor the terms and conditions of the expired contract that involve mandatory subjects of bargaining, at least until the parties reach a good faith impasse. . . . A unilateral change of an expired provision on a mandatory topic, such as one involving wages, is an unfair labor practice, as it violates the duty to bargain collectively in good faith. The provision of the expired agreement survives only until the parties reach a new agreement or until the parties bargain in good faith to impasse. The policy behind the rule retaining the mandatory terms of the expired agreement is that it will be more effective in promoting peaceful negotiations than a rule allowing a change in the status quo during the critical bargaining period. . . .

In the matter before me, the Owners do not deny that they changed provisions in the expired contract; specifically, that they revoked the salary arbitration clause and eliminated section XX(F), the free agency anti-collusive provision. The Owners assert, however, that their changes were allowed because the provisions concerned a statutorily permissive topic, i.e., who would collectively bargain for them over free agent and reserve player salaries. The NLRB maintains that the Owners' changes involved mandatory subjects, and the Owners thereby committed an unfair labor practice by undermining the collective bargaining process. . . .

Collective bargaining in the context of professional sports presents issues different from most other contexts. On the one hand, the talent of an individual athlete can provide him with extraordinary bargaining power, but on the other hand, a player may sell his talent only to a circumscribed group of owners, who have something akin to monopoly power in the sport at issue. These circumstances in professional sports have given rise to the development of the reserve/free agency system, which, perhaps not surprisingly, is quite different from other models of collective bargaining in less specialized and unique industries.

To look for guidance, then, in deciding whether the Board had reasonable cause for making its determination that the provisions changed by the Owners were mandatory, I find most helpful precedent that involves professional sports. *Accord, Wood v. Nat'l Basketball Ass'n*, 809 F.2d 954, 961 (2d Cir. 1987) (collective bargaining between athletes and their leagues "raise[s] numerous problems with little or no precedent in standard industrial relations"). And in the sports context, courts have overwhelmingly held that the constituent parts of reserve/free agency systems are mandatory, not permissive, subjects of bargaining.

For example, this Circuit held in *Wood* that the agreement between professional basketball players and team owners "is a unique bundle of compromises," and matters such as salary caps, minimum individual salaries, fringe benefits, minimum aggregate team salaries, guaranteed revenue sharing, and first refusal provisions are all mandatory subjects of bargaining, as "[e]ach of them is intimately related to 'wages, hours, and other terms and conditions of employment.' " . . . Likewise, in *Mackey v. Nat'l Football League*, 543 F.2d 606, 615 (8th Cir. 1976), *cert. dismissed*, 434 U.S. 801, 98 S. Ct. 28, 54 L. Ed. 2d 59 (1977), the Eighth Circuit held that the Rozelle Rule, even though it does not on its face deal with wages, hours, and other terms and conditions of employment, is a mandatory subject of bargaining because it "operates to restrict a player's ability to move from one team to another and depresses player salaries." *See also, Powell v. Nat'l Football League*, 930 F.2d 1293, 1298-99 (8th Cir. 1989) (agreements establishing first refusal and compensation system are mandatory subjects).

I recognize that these precedents, which address the question of whether wage topics trump the antitrust laws, do not deal with the issue before me, i.e., the continuation of reserve and free agency systems in which individual owners competitively bid for players after the expiration of a collective bargaining agreement and pending the completion by Player and Owner representatives of negotiations over a successor agreement. The owners argue that the right to bid competitively or collectively must be a permissive topic of bargaining, because if it were a mandatory topic, the Owners would be forced to give up their statutory right to bargain collectively.

Courts in addressing the antitrust area of law have easily recognized, however, that the essence of collective bargaining in professional sports is the establishment and maintenance of reserve and free agency systems in which owners agree to bid competitively for some players and collectively for others. The Owners' argument has a superficial appeal in its attempt to harken back to the unionizing cry of employees when they banded together to create this nation's labor laws. What the Owners have missed here, and the NLRB has not, is that the statutory right to join collective bargaining units belongs to employees, not to employers. The NLRA gives only employees the section 7 right to bargain collectively through an elected representative. The only reciprocal statutory right the Act imposes on employers and employees is that they bargain with the other in good faith. In other words, the term "employer union" for collective bargaining purposes is not meaningful.

The extent of statutory protection for an employer is that it may select a representative for the purpose of bargaining free of coercion from a labor union. . . . This right is not a statutory right for a group of employers to bargain collectively through one representative. In fact, while many multi-employer bargaining units, like the PRC, have been formed, the NLRB and the union must consent to the such formation. *See, e.g., NLRB v. Johnson Sheet Metal, Inc.*, 442 F.2d 1056, 1060 (10th Cir. 1971) ("[t]he basic test of the appropriateness of a multi-employer bargaining unit is whether it was created with the approval, express or implied, of the parties"). . . .

Maintaining the reserve/free agency systems in the interim between collective bargaining agreements does not alter the rights of Owners to have the PRC represent them for purposes of negotiating a successor agreement or to continue to oppose the inclusion of the systems in any successor agreement. The Owners can, if they successfully bargain, end the free agency and salary arbitration systems, exclude the anti-collusion provision, and create an entirely new system. What they cannot do is alter particular individual's wages until the system is changed by agreement or until the parties negotiate to impasse. That is the nub of all wage negotiations which are inherently mandatory subjects of bargaining. It must be remembered that many employers are forced to continue sometimes onerous and debilitating wage obligations until the collective bargaining process runs its course, just as many employees may earn less than they would in a system that more closely duplicates the free market. Having freely entered into the free agency and reserve systems in their Basic Agreement, the Owners are bound to that system until they bargain in good faith to an impasse.

In view of the abundant case law in the professional sports context that has found that constituent parts of the reserve/free agency system are mandatory subjects of collective bargaining, I find that the Board had substantial reasonable cause to conclude, and a substantial likelihood of success ultimately in establishing, that the unilateral changes made by the Owners to the free agency system before impasse violated the rule against changes to mandatory subjects of bargaining. In summary, the Board has clearly met its injunctive remedy standard in demonstrating that the Owners committed an unfair labor practice by their unilateral abrogation of Article XX(F) and the free agency system.

For substantially similar reasons, I find that salary arbitration for reserve players is also a mandatory part of the collective bargaining process between the Players and the Owners. . . .

I find injunctive relief here warranted for several reasons. An important public interest in the process of collective bargaining will be irreparably harmed if an injunction does not issue. This strike has captivated the public's attention, given the popularity of the sport as well as the protracted nature and well-documented bitterness of the strike. Thus, this strike is about more than just whether the Players and Owners will resolve their differences. It is also about how the principles embodied by federal labor law operate. In a very real and immediate way, this strike has placed the entire concept of collective bargaining on trial. It is critical, therefore, that the Board ensure that the spirit and letter of federal labor law be scrupulously followed. If the Board is unable to enforce the NLRA, public confidence in the collective bargaining process will be permanently and severely undermined. . . . Issuing the injunction before Opening Day is important to ensure that the symbolic value of that day is not tainted by an unfair labor practice and the NLRB's inability to take effective steps against its perpetuation.

Although this public interest alone justifies the issuance of an injunction, I also find that returning the parties to the status quo will permit them to salvage some of the important bargaining equality that existed before the February 6 unfair labor practices were committed. Before February 6, the Players had the right to attempt to salvage the upcoming season and avoid the continuing damage to their short professional careers by offering to return to work under the terms of the Basic Agreement before replacement players were used in the regular season. . . .

Finally, the Owners argue that even if there is reasonable cause to believe that they committed unfair labor practices, the resulting injury to the Players is merely lost wages which can be compensated through damages. The Owners' argument is flawed because there is more than money involved in the systems at issue here and because there is no adequate way to reconstruct the systems to fully recompense the losses of free agents or reserve players.

Salary is just one factor a free agent considers when seeking and accepting offers. A free agent may wish to join a team because of personal reasons such as family considerations, or because of promises of more playing time. Likewise, a free agent may select a team that pays less money but whose coaching staff and team roster make it a World Series contender. . . .

The protections of the NLRA extend to non-monetary bargaining topics that are "terms and conditions of employment." . . . In professional baseball, whether to leave a team, where to go and why are of "deep concern" to the affected players and the loss of those choices in the terms and conditions of employment cannot be adequately recompensed by money. The only adequate remedy to protect these important personal rights, rights which the NLRB is empowered to protect, is to issue an injunction and thereby restore the status quo. . . .

Similarly, to the extent the salary arbitration system is intimately intertwined with the choice for both owners and players between free agency or arbitration, it is nearly impossible to reconstruct retrospectively the factors that would have influenced each side's decision at the time of election. Hence, even though it is easier later to reconstruct the actual process of salary arbitration and more precisely determine a lost wage from that process, monetary damages are insufficient to recompense for the harm caused in eliminating the salary arbitration process as a choice in the integrated reserve/free agency systems.

Free agency, salary arbitration, and the reserve systems are three aspects of the professional baseball wage structure which are inexorably linked. . . .

Thus, a poisoning of the free agency bargaining process will also affect the wage negotiations of reserve and salary arbitration players. Conversely, the loss of salary arbitration in the reserve system skews the choice of free agency rights. The unusual wage structure in this monopoly industry makes it extraordinarily difficult if not nearly impossible to reconstruct past market conditions for purposes of retroactive damage calculations. Where "monetary damages are difficult to ascertain or are inadequate," an injunction is appropriate. In short, in balancing the equities, I find that the harm to the public, the players, and the NLRB compels the issuance of a Section 10(j) injunction in this case.

. . . This injunction is to remain in effect until either (1) the Players and Owners enter into a new collective bargaining agreement that replaces the expired Basic Agreement, or (2) the final disposition of the matters pending before the National Labor Relations Board . . . or (3) a finding of this court, upon petition of the Players or Respondents . . . demonstrating that an impasse in good faith bargaining has occurred despite a reasonable passage of time negotiating in good faith the full mandatory bargaining terms of the expired Basic Agreement. . . .

NOTES AND QUESTIONS

1. William Gould was Chairman of the NLRB when the foregoing matter came before the Board. In his book, Labored Relations: Law, Politics and the NLRB—A Memoir (2000), Professor Gould discusses his experiences in being confirmed by the U.S. Senate after his nomination by President Clinton and his tenure on the NLRB. He devotes a chapter to an analysis of the MLB labor conflict and strike in 1994-1995 and the Board's role in those matters.

In 1995, he also discussed these matters in the Cambridge Lectures at Queen's College, University of Cambridge, England. In unpublished remarks, he stated:

> Labor law has become a dominant element in the resolution of professional sports disputes. . . . The National Labor Relations Act of 1935, as amended, provides for a secret ballot method of resolving disputes about union recognition and representation, as well as a balanced system of unfair labor practice prohibitions applicable to both management and labor. But it does not provide a mechanism for resolving contract negotiations issues except for requiring the parties to bargain in good faith.
>
> The baseball dispute has involved the unfair labor practices portions of the Board's jurisdiction. On March 26 of this year, the Board determined to seek injunctive relief against unilateral changes in free agency and salary arbitration procedures which had been instituted by the owners prior to that time. The relevant portions of the duty to bargain obligation require that both sides bargain in "good faith"—that is, with a good faith intent to consummate a collective bargaining agreement (entering into an agreement is not required under the statute) until the point of impasse or deadlock on all mandatory subjects of bargaining. . . .
>
> Notwithstanding the *Curt Flood* decision's adherence to the doctrine of *stare decisis*, the fact of the matter is that labor law, whatever its deficiencies, has played a significant role in the world of baseball and in other professional sports. The statutory support for collective bargaining has been facilitated by virtue of the Board's assertion of jurisdiction. Arbitration awards creating free agency were enforced in the federal courts under the standards of deference accorded arbitration awards by the United States Supreme Court for the past 35 years. And, perhaps most important of all, the 1995 baseball season has been played because of the Board's March 26 decision to intervene in federal district court to obtain an injunction. This injunction prompted the players to agree to go back to work. The owners then agreed to accept them without a lockout. . . .
>
> The Board has no authority to oblige the parties to continue the 1995 season—or to fashion an agreement for them. Under our system of voluntary collective bargaining, that process is for the parties themselves. The Board's only role is to insure adherence to the proper procedures, to rid the process of unlawful impediments, and to provide for an appropriate framework for future collective bargaining.

2. Shortly after *Silverman II* was decided, MLB players ended their strike and began playing the 1995 season, even though its start date was delayed. Why did the owners not declare a lockout at this point to exert economic pressure on the players in an effort to obtain their agreement to the disputed terms of employment? Why doesn't the NLRB and why don't courts review the reasonableness of the parties' respective collective bargaining positions on the merits?

3. The foregoing cases and Professor Gould's observations return to a continuing inquiry—what are (and what are not) mandatory subjects of bargaining in the professional sports industries? By the express terms of §8(d), this means "wages, hours, and other terms and conditions of employment." But what does this terminology mean as applied to both the business surrounding a sport and to the sport itself? Consider which of the following examples are mandatory subjects of bargaining:

    a. Whether players can be fined for leaving the bench and going onto the field when there is an altercation among other players.
    b. The placement (distance from the basket) of the three-point line in basketball.
    c. The height of the pitcher's mound. (It was lowered in the late 1960s to reduce the perceived advantage given to pitchers.)
    d. The dimensions of the hockey rink or a baseball field.
    e. The addition (in the National League) or elimination (in the American League) of baseball's designated hitter rule.
    f. The expansion or contraction of the number of teams in a league.
    g. The movement of a franchise (in any sport) from one city to another.
    h. The determination of whether foreign players are eligible for a league's draft.

5. *Union's Duty of Fair Representation*

Labor unions representing professional athletes face unique challenges. They must represent the diverse interests of several hundred extremely talented athletes who have overcome difficult odds to rise to the top of a very elite profession. The small number of athletes who ever get the chance to play their sport at a major league level for even a brief period are far outnumbered by those who would seek to invade their ranks. Even within their membership ranks are telling divisions within a spectrum including a relatively few superstars, several very good players, numerous marginal players, and some perennial benchwarmers.

The career of a major league professional athlete is, on average, very short in relation to most other careers; for example, the average NFL player's career is approximately 3.25 years. Thus, the substantial economic rewards that may be gained in the brief time allotted to a professional athlete must be grasped eagerly. That is why professional athletes have turned to agents, attorneys, accountants, marketing specialists, and others in an effort to maximize their earning potential. It is also why the task of the labor union representing them is a difficult one.

The NLRA grants to a union exclusive negotiating and other rights to act on behalf of all members of the collective bargaining unit. As a result, the union sometimes has the ability to sacrifice particular individuals' rights to further the collective good. In 1944, the Supreme Court held that the NLRA implicitly required a union to fairly represent all members of the collective bargaining unit. *Steele v. Louisville & N.R. Co.*, 323 U.S. 192 (1944). Under the "hiring hall" concept, this duty has been extended to include incoming rookie players (e.g., *Wood v. NBA*, discussed *infra*) and even those at the time ineligible to play in the league (e.g., *Clarett v NFL*, discussed *infra*). It is well established that a union's breach of its duty of fair representation is an unfair labor practice, see *Miranda Fuel Co.*, 140 N.L.R.B. 181 (1962), and that an employee harmed by such a breach may seek both compensatory and punitive damages. 15 Am. Jur. 2d *Proof of Facts* § 5.1 (2019).

Because the nonstatutory labor exemption (which is discussed *infra*) precludes any antitrust challenge to the terms of the collective bargaining agreement, the union's duty to fairly represent all current and prospective players' interests becomes particularly significant. The following case illustrates the difficulty proving that a union has breached its duty of fair representation.

PETERSON v. KENNEDY

771 F.2d 1244 (9th Cir. 1985)

REINHARDT, Circuit Judge.

[EDS. James Peterson brought suit against the National Football League Players Association and two of its attorneys. He claimed that the union, through its attorneys, had furnished him with inaccurate advice on which he detrimentally relied in pursuing a grievance against his former ball club, the Tampa Bay Buccaneers. The district court granted a judgment notwithstanding the verdict (JNOV) for defendants after the jury had decided in Peterson's favor. Peterson appealed the JNOV as well as summary judgment and directed verdict rulings in favor of the union attorneys. The following excerpts relate to the granting of the JNOV.]

Peterson's breach of duty claim is based principally on allegations that the union, through its representatives, erroneously advised him to file an injury grievance and that the union failed to rectify its error while there still was time to do so. We assume *arguendo* that the advice was in fact erroneous, although it is not entirely clear that such was the case. Viewed in a light most favorable to Peterson, the evidence presented at trial established, *inter alia*, that: Kennedy, after being informed that Peterson's 1977 contract contained an "injury protection" clause, advised Peterson's agent to file an injury grievance against Tampa Bay; based on Kennedy's advice, Peterson designated his claim as an injury grievance; the union failed to recognize its error within the 60 day period in which a non-injury grievance could have timely been filed; union representatives assured Peterson on many occasions during this 60 day period that the union was handling his grievance for him; as a result of the union's assurances, Peterson failed to file a non-injury grievance within the 60 day period.

The district court concluded that the evidence presented was legally insufficient to sustain the jury's verdict that the union breached its duty of fair representation. We agree. After reviewing all of the evidence in the light most favorable to Peterson, we conclude that the union did not breach its duty of fair representation; the record is devoid of evidence that the union acted in an arbitrary, discriminatory, or bad faith manner.

The duty of fair representation is a judicially established rule imposed on labor organizations because of their status as the exclusive bargaining representative for all of the employees in a given bargaining unit. The Supreme Court recently explained the basis and scope of the duty:

> The duty of fair representation exists because it is the policy of the National Labor Relations Act to allow a single labor organization to represent collectively the interests of all employees within a unit, thereby depriving individuals in the unit of the ability to bargain individually or to select a minority union as their representative. In such a system, if individual employees are not to be deprived of all effective means of protecting their own interests, it must be the duty of the representative organization to "serve the interests of all members without hostility or discrimination toward any, to exercise its discretion with complete good faith and honesty, and to avoid arbitrary conduct." . . .

A union breaches its duty of fair representation only when its conduct toward a member of the collective bargaining unit is "arbitrary, discriminatory, or in bad faith." *Vaca v. Sipes*, 386 U.S. at 190, 87 S. Ct. at 916. The duty is designed to ensure that unions represent fairly the interests of all of their members without exercising hostility or bad faith toward any. It stands "as a bulwark to prevent arbitrary union conduct against individuals stripped of traditional forms of redress by the provisions of federal labor law." . . .

The Supreme Court has long recognized that unions must retain wide discretion to act in what they perceive to be their members' best interests. . . . To that end, we have "stressed the importance of preserving union discretion by narrowly construing the unfair representation doctrine." . . . We have emphasized that, because a union balances many collective and individual interests in deciding whether and to what extent it will pursue a particular grievance, courts should "accord substantial deference" to a union's decisions regarding such matters.

A union's representation of its members "need not be error free." . . . We have concluded repeatedly that mere negligent conduct on the part of a union does not constitute a breach of the union's duty of fair representation. . . .

Peterson recognizes and does not challenge the established principle that a union's negligence cannot give rise to a suit for breach of the duty of fair representation. Furthermore, he does not contend that the NFLPA or any of its representatives acted toward him or his grievance in a discriminatory or bad faith manner. Rather, Peterson claims that the union breached its duty to represent him fairly because its mishandling of his grievance was so egregious as to constitute "arbitrary" conduct.

Whether in a particular case a union's conduct is "negligent," and therefore non-actionable, or so egregious as to be "arbitrary," and hence sufficient to give rise to a breach of duty claim, is a question that is not always easily answered. A union acts "arbitrarily" when it simply ignores a meritorious grievance or handles it in a perfunctory manner, . . . for example, by failing to conduct a "minimal investigation" of a grievance that is brought to its attention. . . . We have said that a union's conduct is "arbitrary" if it is "without rational basis," . . . or is "egregious, unfair and unrelated to legitimate union interests." . . . In *Robesky v. Qantas Empire Airways Ltd.*, 573 F.2d 1082, 1089-90 (9th Cir. 1978), we held that a union's unintentional mistake is "arbitrary" if it reflects a "reckless disregard" for the rights of the individual employee, but not if it represents only "simple negligence violating the tort standard of due care." In *Dutrisac v. Caterpillar*

Tractor Co., 749 F.2d 1270, 1274 (9th Cir. 1983), we concluded that unintentional union conduct may constitute a breach of the duty of fair representation in situations where "the individual interest at stake is strong and the union's failure to perform a ministerial act completely extinguishes the employee's right to pursue his claim."

There are some significant general principles that emerge from our previous decisions. In all cases in which we found a breach of the duty of fair representation based on a union's arbitrary conduct, it is clear that the union failed to perform a procedural or ministerial act, that the act in question did not require the exercise of judgment and that there was no rational and proper basis for the union's conduct. For example, we found a union acted arbitrarily where it failed to: (1) disclose to an employee its decision not to submit her grievance to arbitration when the employee was attempting to determine whether to accept or reject a settlement offer from her employer, . . . (2) file a timely grievance *after* it had decided that the grievance was meritorious and should be filed, . . . (3) consider individually the grievances of particular employees where the factual and legal differences among them were significant, . . . or (4) permit employees to explain the events which led to their discharge before deciding not to submit their grievances to arbitration. . . .

We have never held that a union has acted in an arbitrary manner where the challenged conduct involved the union's judgment as to how best to handle a grievance. To the contrary, we have held consistently that unions are not liable for good faith, non-discriminatory errors of judgment made in the processing of grievances. . . . We have said that a union's conduct may not be deemed arbitrary simply because of an error in evaluating the merits of a grievance, in interpreting particular provisions of a collective bargaining agreement, or in presenting the grievance at an arbitration hearing. . . . In short, we do not attempt to second-guess a union's judgment when a good faith, non-discriminatory judgment has in fact been made. It is for the union, not the courts, to decide whether and in what manner a particular grievance should be pursued. We reaffirm that principle here.

Sound policy reasons militate against imposing liability on unions for errors of judgment made while representing their members in the collective bargaining process. In *Dutrisac*, we recognized that holding unions liable for such errors would serve ultimately to "defeat the employees' collective bargaining interest in having a strong and effective union." . . . If unions were subject to liability for "judgment calls," it would necessarily undermine their discretion to act on behalf of their members and ultimately weaken their effectiveness. In the long run, the cost of recognizing such liability would be borne not by the unions but by their memberships. Not only would the direct costs of adverse judgments be passed on to the members in the form of increased dues, but, more importantly, unions would become increasingly reluctant to provide guidance to their members in collective bargaining disputes. Such a result would be inconsistent with our oft-repeated commitment to construe narrowly the scope of the duty of fair representation in order to preserve the unions' discretion to decide how best to balance the collective and individual interests that they represent.

Freeing a union from liability for ordinary acts of negligence in the performance of its representational responsibilities requiring judgment on its part, reflects a balance of the union's organizational interest against the individual interests of its members. Our cases, and those of the Supreme Court, tip the balance in favor of the union, and accept the consequence of uncompensated loss sustained by an individual union member. Whether liability for a loss occasioned by ordinary negligence of the union might be spread more equitably among the membership as a whole, rather than be borne by the individual member who is harmed, is no longer an open question.

In applying the foregoing principles to the case at hand, we conclude, as a matter of law, that Peterson failed to establish that the NFLPA breached its duty of fair representation. As mentioned, Peterson does not contend that the union acted in a discriminatory or bad faith manner toward either him or his grievance. He relies exclusively on his claim that the union's error was so egregious as to be "arbitrary." We disagree. The alleged error was one of judgment. Viewing the evidence in the light most favorable to Peterson, the most that can be said is that the union provided him with incorrect advice and did not alter its judgment until it was too late to rectify the error. In this case, deciding whether to file an injury or a non-injury grievance was not a purely mechanical function; the union attorneys were required to construe the scope and meaning of the injury and non-injury grievance provisions of the collective bargaining agreement and to determine which of the two grievance procedures was more appropriate. As we have indicated earlier, the answer was not as simple as a literal reading of the two contract sections might indicate.

Peterson also contends that the union failed adequately to investigate the facts and circumstances of his claim before advising him to file an injury grievance. Peterson does not specify exactly what the union neglected to do; however, his only possible claim appears to be that the union failed to examine copies of his contracts with Tampa Bay before rendering its advice. We find this contention insufficient as a matter of law. Both Peterson and his agent testified that they informed Kennedy of the inclusion of the "injury protection" clause in Peterson's 1977 contract and described its substance to him. We do not believe that a further examination of that provision, or of any other provision in Peterson's contracts, would have better enabled Kennedy to advise Peterson as to which form of grievance to file. It was the grievance and arbitration provisions of the standard collective bargaining agreement, rather than the "injury protection" clause of Peterson's contract, that the union was required to construe in order to determine which grievance procedure was applicable to Peterson's claim. Examining the text of the injury protection clause would not have materially influenced the union's judgment in that regard.

Although the union's representatives may have erred in initially advising Peterson to file an injury grievance and in failing to recognize its mistake in time to file a non-injury grievance in its stead, we are unwilling to subject unions to liability for such errors in judgment. Accordingly, we affirm the district court's conclusion that the evidence presented was insufficient, as a matter of law, to support the jury's verdict against the union. . . .

NOTES AND QUESTIONS

1. The *Peterson* case clarifies the nature of the duty of fair representation that the union owes to its members. What is the standard adopted by the court and its underlying policy justification?

   It bears noting that this case involves a unique, narrow set of circumstances. As previously discussed, other player union actions affect, perhaps adversely and unfairly, not only its members but also others brought within the overall sway of professional sports labor relations. Regarding the NFL's current draft eligibility rules, could Maurice Clarett (who did not meet the age eligibility threshold when he attempted to enter the draft) have successfully asserted that the NFLPA did not fairly represent him and others in negotiations with the NFL regarding initial player eligibility requirements? See generally Matthew J. Mitten and Timothy Davis, *Athlete Eligibility Requirements and Legal Protection of Sports Participation Opportunities*, 8 Va. Sports & Ent. L.J. 71, 107 (2009) ("Under existing law a minimum age eligibility rule (or a *de facto* equivalent) for professional athletes is not a form of prohibited discrimination that breaches a players union's duty of fair representation").

2. As is more fully considered in section C.6 of this chapter, arbitration generally is the predominant method of resolving disputes in the professional sports industries. Thus, it is important to note the impact of *Vaca v. Sipes*, 386 U.S. 171 (1967), in which the Supreme Court held that a union has the authority to control whether an employee's grievance proceeds to arbitration. In other words, an aggrieved player has no "absolute right" to arbitration if the player's claim is subject to the union's control, although a player can establish that the union failed to represent his or her interests fairly by proving that its actions were arbitrary, discriminatory, or in bad faith. As *Peterson* illustrates, this is a high standard to meet.

3. *Eller v. NFLPA*, 872 F. Supp. 2d 823 (D. Minn. 2012), *aff'd*, 731 F.3d 752 (8th Cir. 2013), which grew out of the 2011 NFL lockout, explores the scope of a union's duty to represent retired players in collective bargaining negotiations. When the NFL and NFLPA agreed to a new ten-year CBA that ended the lockout, a group of retired players who alleged their interests were not represented in the negotiations that produced the CBA sued the NFLPA and several player leaders involved with the union for breach of fiduciary duty and intentional interference with prospective economic advantage. The defendants moved for 12(b)(6) dismissal, which the court granted based on its finding that the NFLPA had done nothing to "assume any legally enforceable fiduciary duty towards the retired players" and that any harm to the retired players resulting from the NFLPA's good faith negotiations with the NFL could not be attributed to improper interference. *Id.* at 833. The court also seemed to doubt whether they suffered any harm, noting that "a better package of benefits was in fact obtained for the retired players in the 2011 CBA as compared to those in the former CBA." *Id.* at 834.

    Eller distinguished *Parrish v. NFLPA*, 2009 WL 88484 (N.D. Cal. Jan. 19, 2009), a class action suit regarding the licensing of retired players' images, in which that court found the NFLPA had assumed a fiduciary duty to this group of players. In *Parrish*, retired players who had signed a "Retired Player Group License Agreement" with the NFLPA alleged that the union breached its duty to market their names and likenesses. The court found that the NFLPA not only failed to market the retired players, but also actively worked against their interests by devoting a grossly disproportionate measure of its marketing efforts to promoting active, and therefore more profitable, NFL players. In awarding $7.1 million in compensatory damages and $21 million in exemplary damages to the class of plaintiffs, the court stressed that the NFLPA held itself out to the retired players as a "marketing agent," which assumed an affirmative duty to promote the retired players' names and licenses. *Id.* at *2.

While the district court's judgment in *Parrish* was pending appeal, the retired players and the NFLPA settled the matter, resulting in a $26.25 million payment to the retired players.

4. In January 2017, Philadelphia Eagles' offensive lineman Lane Johnson sued both the NFLPA and NFL in response to a ten-game suspension the NFL imposed upon him for violating the league's performance-enhancing drug policy. In the suit, Johnson argued that the defendants conspired to "insulate their collectively bargained drug policy from lawful scrutiny" and to withhold information from him. His claims against the NFLPA alleged, among other things, that the NFLPA breached its duty of fair representation to him. Specifically, he asserted that due to his public statements impugning the quality of the NFLPA's representation, the NFLPA retaliated against him "by abdicating its representative duties and abandoning [him] to the caprice of the [NFL]." Michael McCann, *Lane Johnson's bold move to sue his own union is rare, but not unprecedented,* Sports Illustrated, Jan. 11, 2017, https://www.si.com/nfl/2017/01/11/lane-johnson-suspension-lawsuit-nfl-nflpa-peds. After years of motions practice, the court dismissed the last of Johnson's claims in August 2019, concluding that his case was built on "speculation" and "conjecture." Mike Curley, *NFL Gets Quick Win In Eagles Player's Suit Over Drug Ban,* Law360, Aug. 2, 2019, https://www.law360.com/employment/articles/1184816/nfl-gets-quick-win-in-eagles-player-s-suit-over-drug-ban.

6.   *Labor Arbitration*

Labor arbitration's impact on the professional sports industry has been substantial and long lasting. When the first professional sports industry CBAs were successfully negotiated in the late 1960s, basic provisions for arbitration of many types of grievances were included in these agreements. Often it was designated that the commissioner of the league would be the arbitrator. This was later deemed unsatisfactory by the players because they understandably believed that the commissioner was in reality representing the interests of the league and the owners, who had chosen and pay him or her. Consequently, the players union and league generally agreed that most grievances would be decided by an independent and impartial arbitrator or panel of arbitrators or by a panel consisting of a representative of each side that was chaired by an impartial arbitrator who was usually the deciding vote. To a certain degree, all these models continue in various configurations today.

Except for certain player disciplinary matters that are resolved exclusively by the league commissioner, most disputes between a player and the league or club are resolved by some form of independent arbitration. There are three general types of disputes that are resolved by arbitration; examples of each are provided and analyzed in the following materials.

The first are matters deemed by management or the players association to be very significant far beyond the bounds of that particular arbitration; for example, the following 1975 landmark arbitration involving baseball players Dave McNally and Andy Messersmith. Although this arbitration technically involved only those two individuals, the decision by arbitrator Peter Seitz effectively laid the groundwork for a free agency system benefiting all MLB players. Consequently, the decision should be studied for its long-term effects as well as its immediate resolution. It effectively forced the MLB club owners to collectively bargain with the players over significant modifications to the "reserve system" that had existed in baseball almost from the inception of the National League in 1876. This arbitration proceeding was also significant because the players had recently failed in their antitrust law challenge to the reserve system, because the Supreme Court affirmed the continuing validity of baseball's common law antitrust immunity in its 1972 *Flood v. Kuhn* decision. Thus, the result the MLB players could not accomplish in court through antitrust law was obtained under the auspices of labor law by an arbitrator who gave them a favorable interpretation regarding the meaning and duration of baseball's "reserve clause." This arbitration decision is joined by others that have far-reaching implications. Baseball's collusion arbitrations in the 1980s show that an arbitrator, by enforcing collective bargaining provisions, can effectively require the owners to adhere to the system of free agency established by the CBA. In a series of three arbitrations MLB players were awarded in excess of $280 million for the collusive actions of the club owners that violated the CBA.

A second type of arbitration has been instituted through collective bargaining to establish a league-wide system for dealing with specific disputes that a team and a player are unable to resolve through individual negotiations, such as player salary arbitration in MLB and the NHL. For various reasons, both leagues have recognized that several factors may coalesce to thwart successful bargaining that determines an individual player's salary. Therefore, in carefully defined circumstances, a player's salary for the ensuing season may be determined in an arbitration proceeding.

The third category of matters that generally are submitted to arbitration are grievances arising out of a contract dispute between a player and his club. These are numerous, with multiple grievances filed in every league on a yearly basis. It is harder to see the broader effects of these arbitration decisions, which, strictly speaking, do not create binding precedent with the same legal effect as court decisions. However, it is evident that arbitrators pay close attention to earlier arbitration decisions resolving similar disputes, particularly those involving parties in the same league as the current dispute.

a.   Wide-Impact Arbitration

The *McNally-Messersmith* arbitration is a leading example of arbitration in the professional sports industries that has significantly altered the way a league conducts its business with players.

NATIONAL & AMERICAN LEAGUE PROFESSIONAL BASEBALL CLUBS v. MAJOR LEAGUE BASEBALL PLAYERS ASSN.

66 Labor Arbitration 101 (1975)

SEITZ, Arbitrator.

. . . The Chairman understands the dispute in arbitration to be as follows: The Association claims that the terms of the Uniform Player Contracts of [Andy] Messersmith and [Dave] McNally, respectively, having expired, the two players are at liberty to negotiate contract relationships with any of the other clubs in the leagues and that they are not to be regarded as having been "reserved" by the Los Angeles and Montreal clubs, respectively, in such manner as to inhibit clubs from dealing with them.

The leagues and the clubs assert that the terms of the contracts of these players have not expired; that they are still under contract; and that, in any event, the grievants have been duly "reserved" by their respective clubs; and, accordingly, they are not free to deal with other clubs for the performance of services for the 1976 season; nor are such other clubs free to deal with them for that season excepting under circumstances and conditions not here obtaining. . . .

[EDS. Arbitrator Seitz then proceeded to explain there were two general issues before him. The first was a jurisdictional question — that is, whether these matters were properly the subject of arbitration. The second was the issues on the merits, which of course would be reached only if the arbitrator ruled that he had jurisdiction to hear the dispute.

On the first issue, Seitz held that the case was properly before him. He did so despite language in Article XV of the MLB collective bargaining agreement that specified "*this Agreement does not deal with the reserve system.*" Despite this language, Seitz found that time and again questions arose in other aspects of the Agreement that necessitated interpretations of the reserve system in order to clarify these other provisions. Consequently, he found that he did have jurisdiction to hear the dispute and thus proceeded to the merits. A fuller discussion of the jurisdiction issue is in *Kansas City Royals v. Major League Baseball Players Association*, 532 F.2d 615 (8th Cir. 1976), *infra.*]

. . . I have reached the conclusion that, as a matter of contract construction, the position of the Players Association in the dispute has merit and deserves to be sustained. . . .

No one challenges the rights of a Club to renew a Player's contract with or without his consent under § 10(a) [of the MLB Uniform Player Contract], "for the period of one [renewal] year." I read the record, however, as containing a contention by the leagues that when a Club renews a Player's contract for the renewal year, the contract in force during that year contains the "right of renewal" clause as one of its terms, entitling the Club to renew the contract in successive years, to perpetuity, perhaps, so long as the Player is alive and the Club has duly discharged all conditions required of it. This is challenged by the Players Association whose position it is that the contractual relationship between the Club and the Player terminates at the end of the first renewal year. Thus, it claims that there was no longer any contractual bond between Messersmith and the Los Angeles Club [after the renewal year.]

The league's argument is based on the language in § 10(a) of the Player's Contract that the Club "may renew this contract for the period of one year *on the same terms*" (emphasis supplied); and that among those "terms" is the right to further contract renewal.

In the law of contract construction, as I know it, there is nothing to prevent parties from agreeing to successive renewals of the terms of their bargain (even to what has been described as "perpetuity"), provided the contract expresses that intention with explicit clarity and the right of subsequent renewals does not have to be implied. . . .

There is nothing in Section 10(a) which, explicitly, expresses agreement that the Players Contract can be renewed for any period beyond the first renewal year. The point the leagues present must be based upon the implication or assumption, that if the renewed contract is "on the same terms" as the contract for the preceding year (with the exception of the amount of compensation) the right to additional renewals must have been an integral part of the renewed contract. I find great difficulties, in so implying or assuming, in respect of a contract providing for the rendition of personal services in which one would expect a more explicit expression of intention. . . .

We now turn to the Major League Rules, as to which it has already been stated that, by virtue of § 9(a) of the Uniform Players Contract and Article XIII of the Basic Agreement, they are a part of the agreements of the parties if not inconsistent with the provisions of the Basic Agreement and the Players Contract.

The parties are in sharp conflict on this. The leagues claim that there is exclusive reservation of a player's services under Rule 4-A(a) regardless of the continued existence of any contractual relationship between the Club and the Player. Thus, Counsel for the National League asserted that:

> The club may continue the pattern of career-long control over the player and that this pattern of career-long control is not essentially dependent upon the renewal clause (Section 10-A) at all.

The Players Association, on the other hand, asserts that in the absence of a nexus or linkage of contract between the Player and the Club, there can be no exclusive reservation of the right to his future services. . . .

These provisions and others in the very Rules which, allegedly, establish the kind of reservation of services for which the leagues contend, all subsume the existence of a *contractual relation*. The leagues would have it that it is only when there is a release or assignment that a contract must have been in existence; but even if there were no contract in existence (the players' contract having expired) a Club, by placing the name of a player on a list, can reserve exclusive rights to his services from year to year for an unstated and indefinite period in the future. I find this unpersuasive. It is like the claims of some nations that persons once its citizens, wherever they live and regardless of the passage of time, the swearing of other allegiances and other circumstances, are still its own nationals and subject to the obligations that citizenship in the nation imposes. This "status" theory is incompatible with the doctrine or policy of freedom of contract in the economic and political society in which we live and of which the professional sport of baseball ("the national game") is a part. . . .

Finally, on this point, it is evident that traditionally, the leagues have regarded the existence of a contract as a basis for the reservation of players. In Club's Exhibit No. 15 there is set forth the Cincinnati Peace Compact of the National and American Leagues, signed January 10, 1903 — probably the most important step in the evolution and development of the present Reserve System. In that document it provided:

> Second — A *reserve rule* shall be recognized, by which each and every club may reserve *players under contract*, and that a uniform contract for the use of each league shall be adopted. (Emphasis supplied.)

This emphasis on the existence of a contract for reservation of a player to be effective was perpetuated in the Major League Rules to some of which I have referred. It is even found in Rule 3(g) in which, however, it is referred to disjunctively along with acceptance of terms "or by which he was reserved." However, *even in Rule 3(g),* reading it analytically and construing it syntactically, one may reasonably reach the conclusion — *no contract, no reservation.* The provision says there shall be no dealings between a player and a club other than the one "with which he is under *contract*, or acceptance of terms, *or by which he is reserved.*" (Emphasis supplied.) . . .

Thus, I reach the conclusion that, absent a contractual connection between Messersmith and the Los Angeles Club after September 28, 1975, the Club's action in reserving his services for the ensuing year by placing him on its reserve list was unavailing and ineffectual in prohibiting him from dealing with other clubs in the league and to prohibit such clubs from dealing with him.

In the case of McNally whom the Montreal Club had placed on its disqualified list, a similar conclusion has been reached. . . .

I am not unmindful of the testimony of the Commissioner of Baseball and the Presidents of the National and American League given at the hearings as to the importance of maintaining the integrity of the Reserve System. It was represented to me that any decision of the Arbitration Panel sustaining the Messersmith and McNally grievances would have dire results, wreak great harm to the Reserve System and do serious damage to the sport of baseball.

Thus, for example, it was stated that a decision favoring these grievants would encourage many other players to elect to become free agents at the end of the renewal years; that this would encourage clubs with the largest monetary resources to engage free agents, thus unsettling the competitive balance between clubs, so essential to the sport; that it would increase enormously the already high costs of training and seasoning young players to achieve the level of skills required in professional baseball and such investments would be sacrificed if they became free agents at the end of a renewal year; that driven by the compulsion to win, owners of franchises would over-extend themselves financially and improvident bidding for players in an economic climate in which, today, some clubs are strained, financially; that investors will be discouraged from putting money in franchises in which several of the star players on the club team will become free agents at the end of a renewal year and no continuing control over the players' services can be exercised; and that even the integrity of the sport may be placed in hazard under certain circumstances.

I do not purport to appraise these apprehensions. They are all based on speculations as to what may ensue. Some of the fears may be imaginary or exaggerated; but some may be reasonable, realistic and sound. After all, they were voiced by distinguished baseball officials with long experience in the sport and a background for judgment in such matters much superior to my own. However, as stated above, at length, it is not for the Panel (and especially the writer) to determine what, if anything, is good or bad about the reserve system. The Panel's sole duty is to interpret and apply the agreements and undertakings of the parties. If any of the expressed apprehensions and fears are soundly based, I am confident that the dislocations and damage to the reserve system can be avoided or minimized through good faith collective bargaining between the parties. There are numerous expedients available and arrangements that can be made that will soften the blow—if this decision, indeed, should be regarded as a blow. This decision is not the end of the line by any means. The parties, jointly, are free to agree to disregard it and compose their differences as to the reserve system in any way they see fit. . . .

However strong my conviction that the basic dispute should be determined by the parties, in collective bargaining rather than by an Arbitration Panel, that Panel could not justify any further delay, and the accompanying Award, accordingly, is being rendered. The parties are still in negotiation, however, and continue to have an opportunity to reach agreement on measures that will give assurance of a reserve system that will meet the needs of the clubs and protect them from the damage they fear this decision will cause, and, at the same time, meet the needs of the players. . . .

Grievance upheld.

NOTES AND QUESTIONS

1. Do you agree with Arbitrator Seitz's conclusion that the parties' dispute was an arbitrable matter? Was Arbitrator Seitz remiss in his failure to address business custom and usage in his opinion? Or does he indirectly address past business practices?

2. The MLB club owners were given advance notice of the probable success of the Messersmith and McNally grievances. Rather than attempting to reach an agreement with MLBPA regarding new free agency provisions, the owners appealed the arbitrator's decision in federal court, which usually is an unsuccessful endeavor. In *Kansas City Royals v. Major League Baseball Players Assn.*, 532 F.2d 615 (8th Cir. 1976), the Eighth Circuit affirmed the district court's confirmation of the *Messersmith-McNally* arbitration decision, which effectively enabled these two players to become free agents and to sign new contracts with the respective clubs of their choosing. Holding that when an "arbitrator ha[s] jurisdiction, judicial review of his award is limited to the question of whether it draws its essence from the collective bargaining agreement," the Eighth Circuit held that the merits of the award satisfied this requirement. *Id.* at 621. A detailed examination of the *Messersmith-McNally* decision and its subsequent appeal to the courts is found in Charles P. Korr, The End of Baseball As We Knew It: The Players Union, 1960-81, 149-67 (2002); Robert C. Berry and William B. Gould IV, *A Long Deep Drive to Collective Bargaining: Of Players, Owners, Brawls and Strikes*, 31 Case Western L. Rev. 685, 749-53 (1981).

3. After going through a period of readjustment, in which every MLB player was given one opportunity to be a free agent, the club owners and players union entered into a new CBA providing that a player can earn free agent status after six years of credited major league service. This basic threshold is still the standard today, as was explored in the foregoing MLB provisions on free agency detailed in section C.2.b, *supra*. Why would the players agree to a six-year standard? Are there good reasons why MLB players generally have a longer wait before free agency than other professional team sport players?

b.   Defining the Scope of Judicial Review

In the following case, the Supreme Court describes the very limited scope of judicial review of labor arbitration decisions and provides an example of the rare vacatur of an arbitration award. As you read this case, consider the breadth of judicial deference afforded arbitrators, the reasons for it, and whether it is appropriate.

MAJOR LEAGUE BASEBALL PLAYERS ASSN. v. GARVEY

532 U.S. 504 (2001)

PER CURIAM.

The Court of Appeals for the Ninth Circuit here rejected an arbitrator's factual findings and then resolved the merits of the parties' dispute instead of remanding the case for further arbitration proceedings. . . .

In the late 1980's, petitioner Major League Baseball Players Association (Association) filed grievances against the Major League Baseball Clubs (Clubs), claiming the Clubs had colluded in the market for free-agent services after the 1985, 1986 and 1987 baseball seasons, in violation of the industry's collective-bargaining agreement. A free agent is a player who may contract with any Club, rather than one whose right to contract is restricted to a particular Club. In a series of decisions, arbitrators found collusion by the Clubs and damage to the players. The Association and Clubs subsequently entered into a Global Settlement Agreement (Agreement), pursuant to which the Clubs established a $280 million fund to be distributed to injured players. The Association also designed a "Framework" to evaluate the individual player's claims, and, applying that Framework, recommended distribution plans for claims relating to a particular season or seasons.

The Framework provided that players could seek an arbitrator's review of the distribution plan. The arbitrator would determine "only whether the approved Framework and the criteria set forth therein have been properly applied in the proposed Distribution Plan." (*Garvey I*). The Framework set forth factors to be considered in evaluating players' claims, as well as specific requirements for lost contract-extension claims. Such claims were cognizable "'only in those cases where evidence exists that a specific offer of an extension was made by a club prior to collusion only to thereafter be withdrawn when the collusion scheme was initiated.'"

Respondent Steve Garvey, a retired, highly regarded first baseman, submitted a claim for damages of approximately $3 million. He alleged that his contract with the San Diego Padres was not extended to the 1988 and 1989 seasons due to collusion. The Association rejected Garvey's claim in February 1996, because he presented no evidence that the Padres actually offered to extend his contract. Garvey objected, and an arbitration hearing was held. He testified that the Padres offered to extend his contract for the 1988 and 1989 seasons and then withdrew the offer after they began colluding with other teams. He presented a June 1996 letter from Ballard Smith, Padres' President and CEO from 1979 to 1987, stating that, before the end of the 1985 season, Smith offered to extend Garvey's contract through the 1989 season, but that the Padres refused to negotiate with Garvey thereafter due to collusion.'"

The arbitrator denied Garvey's claim, after seeking additional documentation from the parties. In his award, he explained that "'there exists . . . substantial doubt as to the credibility of the statements in the Smith letter.'" He noted the "stark contradictions" between the 1996 letter and Smith's testimony in the earlier arbitration proceedings regarding collusion, where Smith, like other owners, denied collusion and stated that the Padres simply were not interested in extending Garvey's contract. The arbitrator determined that, due to these contradictions, he "'must reject [Smith's] more recent assertion that Garvey did not receive [a contract] extension'" due to collusion, and found that Garvey had not shown a specific offer of extension. He concluded that:

> The shadow cast over the credibility of the Smith testimony coupled with the absence of any other corroboration of the claim submitted by Garvey compels a finding that the Padres declined to extend his contract not because of the constraints of the collusion effort of the clubs but rather as a baseball judgment founded upon [Garvey's] age and recent injury history.

Garvey moved in Federal District Court to vacate the arbitrator's award, alleging that the arbitrator violated the Framework by denying his claim. The District Court denied the motion. The Court of Appeals for the Ninth Circuit reversed by a divided vote. The court acknowledged that judicial review of an arbitrator's decision in a labor dispute is extremely limited. But it held that review of the merits of the arbitrator's award was warranted in this case, because the arbitrator " 'dispensed his own brand of industrial justice.' " The court recognized that Smith's prior testimony with respect to collusion conflicted with the statements in his 1996 letter. But in the court's view, the arbitrator's refusal to credit Smith's letter was "inexplicable" and "bordered on the irrational," because a panel of arbitrators, chaired by the arbitrator involved here, had previously concluded that the owners' prior testimony was false. The court rejected the arbitrator's reliance on the absence of other corroborating evidence, attributing that fact to Smith and Garvey's direct negotiations. The court also found that the record provided "strong support" for the truthfulness of Smith's 1996 letter. The Court of Appeals reversed and remanded with directions to vacate the award.

The District Court then remanded the case to the arbitration panel for further hearings, and Garvey appealed. The Court of Appeals, again by a divided vote, explained that *Garvey I* established that "the conclusion that Smith made Garvey an offer and subsequently withdrew it because of the collusion scheme was the only conclusion that the arbitrator could draw from the record in the proceedings." (*Garvey II*). Noting that its prior instructions might have been unclear, the Court clarified that *Garvey I* "left only one possible result—the result our holding contemplated—an award in Garvey's favor." The Court of Appeals reversed the District Court and directed that it remand the case to the arbitration panel with instructions to enter an award for Garvey in the amount he claimed.

The parties do not dispute that this case arises under § 301 of the Labor Management Relations Act, 1947, as the controversy involves an assertion of rights under an agreement between an employer and a labor organization. Although Garvey's specific allegation is that the arbitrator violated the Framework for resolving players' claims for damages, that Framework was designed to facilitate payments to remedy the Clubs' breach of the collective-bargaining agreement. Garvey's right to be made whole is founded on that agreement.

Judicial review of a labor-arbitration decision pursuant to such an agreement is very limited. Courts are not authorized to review the arbitrator's decision on the merits despite allegations that the decision rests on factual errors or misinterprets the parties' agreement. We recently reiterated that if an " 'arbitrator is even arguably construing or applying the contract and acting within the scope of his authority,' the fact that 'a court is convinced he committed serious error does not suffice to overturn his decision.' " It is only when the arbitrator strays from interpretation and application of the agreement and effectively "dispenses his own brand of industrial justice" that his decision may be unenforceable. When an arbitrator resolves disputes regarding the application of a contract, and no dishonesty is alleged, the arbitrator's "improvident, even silly, fact-finding" does not provide a basis for a reviewing court to refuse to enforce the award.

In discussing the courts' limited role in reviewing the merits of arbitration awards, we have stated that "'courts . . . have no business weighing the merits of the grievance [or] considering whether there is equity in a particular claim.'" When the judiciary does so, "it usurps a function which . . . is entrusted to the arbitration tribunal." Consistent with this limited role, we said in *Misco* that "even in the very rare instances when an arbitrator's procedural aberrations rise to the level of affirmative misconduct, as a rule the court must not foreclose further proceedings by settling the merits according to its own judgment of the appropriate result." That step, we explained, "would improperly substitute a judicial determination for the arbitrator's decision that the parties bargained for" in their agreement. Instead, the court should "simply vacate the award, thus leaving open the possibility of further proceedings if they are permitted under the terms of the agreement."

To be sure, the Court of Appeals here recited these principles, but its application of them is nothing short of baffling. The substance of the Court's discussion reveals that it overturned the arbitrator's decision because it disagreed with the arbitrator's factual findings, particularly those with respect to credibility. The Court of Appeals, it appears, would have credited Smith's 1996 letter, and found the arbitrator's refusal to do so at worst "irrational" and at best "bizarre." But even "serious error" on the arbitrator's part does not justify overturning his decision, where, as here, he is construing a contract and acting within the scope of his authority.

In *Garvey II*, the court clarified that *Garvey I* both rejected the arbitrator's findings and went further, resolving the merits of the parties' dispute based on the court's assessment of the record before the arbitrator. For that reason, the court found further arbitration proceedings inappropriate. But again, established law ordinarily precludes a court from resolving the merits of the parties' dispute on the basis of its own factual determinations, no matter how erroneous the arbitrator's decision. Even when the arbitrator's award may properly be vacated, the appropriate remedy is to remand the case for further arbitration proceedings. The dissent suggests that the remedy described in *Misco* is limited to cases where the arbitrator's errors are procedural. *Misco* did involve procedural issues, but our discussion regarding the appropriate remedy was not so limited. If a remand is appropriate *even* when the arbitrator's award has been set aside for "procedural aberrations" that constitute "affirmative misconduct," it follows that a remand ordinarily will be appropriate when the arbitrator simply made factual findings that the reviewing court perceives as "irrational." The Court of Appeals usurped the arbitrator's role by resolving the dispute and barring further proceedings, a result at odds with this governing law.

For the foregoing reasons, the Court of Appeals erred in reversing the order of the District Court denying the motion to vacate the arbitrator's award, and it erred further in directing that judgment be entered in Garvey's favor. The judgment of the Court of Appeals is reversed, and the case is remanded for further proceedings consistent with this opinion.

Justice STEVENS, dissenting.

It is well settled that an arbitrator "does not sit to dispense his own brand of industrial justice." We have also said fairly definitively, albeit in dicta, that a court should remedy an arbitrator's "procedural aberrations" by vacating the award and remanding for further proceedings. Our cases, however, do not provide significant guidance as to what standards a federal court should use in assessing whether an arbitrator's behavior is so untethered to either the agreement of the parties or the factual record so as to constitute an attempt to "dispense his own brand of industrial justice." Nor, more importantly, do they tell us how, having made such a finding, courts should deal with "the extraordinary circumstance in which the arbitrator's own rulings make clear that, more than being simply erroneous, his finding is completely inexplicable and borders on the irrational." *Garvey v. Roberts*, 203 F.3d 580 (9th Cir. 2000). Because our case law is not sufficiently clear to allow me to conclude that the case below was wrongly decided—let alone to conclude that the decision was so wrong as to require the extraordinary remedy of a summary reversal—I dissent from the Court's disposition of this petition.

Without the benefit of briefing or argument, today the Court resolves two difficult questions. First, it decides that even if the Court of Appeals' appraisal of the merits is correct—that is to say, even if the arbitrator did dispense his own brand of justice untethered to the agreement of the parties, and even if the correct disposition of the matter is perfectly clear—the only course open to a reviewing court is to remand the matter for another arbitration. That conclusion is not compelled by any of our cases, nor by any analysis offered by the Court. As the issue is subject to serious arguments on both sides, the Court should have set this case for argument if it wanted to answer this remedial question.

Second, without reviewing the record or soliciting briefing, the Court concludes that, in any event, "no serious error on the arbitrator's part is apparent in this case." At this stage in the proceedings, I simply cannot endorse that conclusion. After examining the record, obtaining briefing, and hearing oral argument, the Court of Appeals offered a reasoned explanation of its conclusion. Whether or not I would ultimately agree with the Ninth Circuit's analysis, I find the Court's willingness to reverse a fact bound determination of the Court of Appeals without engaging that court's reasoning troubling.

NOTES AND QUESTIONS

1. What standard does *Garvey* adopt for determining when an arbitrator's award will be judicially vacated? Does this provide sufficient guidance to lower courts regarding the appropriate level of deference to be afforded an arbitrator's decision? What concern is expressed by the dissent in *Garvey*? See generally Jaime D. Byrnes and Alison B. Prout, Major League Baseball Players Association v. Garvey: *Revisiting the Standard for Arbitral Review*, 7 Harv. Negot. L. Rev. 389 (2004); Emily Huitsing, *Retaining Bargained-For Finality and Judicial Review in Labor Arbitration Decisions: Dual Interests Preserved in Major League Baseball*, 2002 J. Disp. Resol. 453.

2. *Scope of Judicial Review.* For further discussions of the limited scope of judicial review of arbitration awards, see *Major League Umpires Ass'n v. American League of Professional Baseball Clubs*, 357 F.3d 272, 280 (3d Cir. 2004) (explaining that an arbitration award may be vacated if the arbitrator demonstrates manifest disregard for the CBA, which occurs when the arbitrator's award

is totally unsupported by principles of contract construction); *National Football League Players Assn. v. Pro-Football, Inc.*, 857 F. Supp. 71, 75-76 (D.D.C. 1994) (although arbitration decisions should be afforded deference even if the arbitrator makes errors of fact and law, an award will not be upheld if it compels violation of law or conduct contrary to well-established public policy); *Morris v. New York Football Giants, Inc.*, 150 Misc. 2d 271, 575 N.Y.S.2d 1013, 1017 (Sup. Ct. 1991) (refusing to compel arbitration where circumstances made it clear that arbitrator was deprived of the requisite neutrality); *Dryer v. Los Angeles Rams*, 709 P.2d 826, 830 (Cal. 1985) ("Normally a claim that the grievance procedures are unfair or inadequate cannot be asserted until the aggrieved party has attempted to implement the procedures and found them to be unfair.").

c. Salary Arbitration

Both MLB and the NHL use arbitration to resolve salary disputes between teams and individual players; arbitration is available only in limited situations but has far-reaching effects on player salaries within the league. MLB CBA salary arbitration provisions apply to players who have between three (or in some cases slightly less) and six years of credited major league service. One of the most notable aspects of baseball salary arbitration is that it utilizes "final offer arbitration." This means that, without knowing what the other side will submit as a salary figure, the team and the player each submit an amount for a one-year contract. This requires substantial thought by both parties, because the arbitration panel must select one figure or the other. There can be no compromise. Thus, if the matter is decided by arbitration, the end result will be a one-year contract (with no bonuses) at a salary submitted by the club or the player. The club may release its rights to the player at any time consistent with the terms of the applicable CBA.

What are the advantages and disadvantages of MLB's system of final offer arbitration? Does it result in greater leverage for clubs, players, or neither? Commentators have noted that despite owners' expressed dislike for final offer arbitration, they have an historical track record of success. In a study of 417 baseball salary arbitrations between 1974 and 1999, clubs prevailed in 236 cases and players prevailed in 181 cases. Roger I. Abrams, *Inside Baseball's Salary Arbitration Process*, 6 U. Chi. L. Sch. Roundtable 55, 64 (1999) (also providing historical and practical overviews of the final offer arbitration process).

The authors of another empirical study of baseball's final offer arbitration concluded:

> Aggressive offers by players trigger arbitration and that more aggressive offers are associated with inferior financial outcomes in arbitration. Overall, clubs appear to outperform players in arbitration. Unexpectedly high or low offers are less common for players who have previously been through arbitration, which suggests that learning occurs. Our results are inconsistent with simple one-sided asymmetric-information models of arbitration. The results are more consistent with an optimism model or a model in which players are risk-loving.

Amy Farmer, Paul Pecorino and Victor Stango, *The Causes of Bargaining Failure: Evidence from Major League Baseball*, 47 J.L. & Econ. 543, 543 (2004).

For other scholarly discussions of baseball salary arbitration, see Jeff Monhait, *Baseball Arbitration: An ADR Success*, 4 Harv. J. Sports & Ent. L. 105, 144 (2013); William B. Gould, *Labor Issues in Professional Sports: Reflections on Baseball, Labor and Antitrust Law*, 15 Stan. L. & Pol'y Rev. 61 (2004); Stuart J. Riemer, *Albert Pujols: Major League Baseball Salary Arbitration from a Unique Perspective*, 22 Cardozo Arts & Ent. L.J. 219 (2004); Brien M. Wassner, *Major League Baseball's Answer to Salary Disputes and the Strike Final Offer Arbitration: A Negotiation Tool Facilitating Adversary Agreement*, 6 Vand. J. Ent. L. & Prac. 5 (2003); Jonathan M. Conti, *The Effect of Salary Arbitration on Major League Baseball*, 5 Sports Law. J. 221 (1998); David J. Faurot and Stephen McAllister, *Salary Arbitrations and Pre-Arbitration Negotiation in Major League Baseball*, 45 Indus. & Lab. Rel. Rev. 697 (1992).

Unlike MLB's final offer arbitration, the NHL's salary arbitration system is premised on a conventional arbitration model. Like MLB's system, the NHL's salary arbitration system contains eligibility requirements that must be met in order for players to seek salary arbitration; procedures are in place for selecting arbitrators, and limitations are imposed on the factors the arbitrator can consider in determining a player's compensation. Because it is based on a conventional arbitration model, the salary determined by the arbitrator can "be either one of the two offers made by the parties or an amount ranging anywhere between the two." Melanie Aubut, *When Negotiations Fail: An Analysis of Salary Arbitration and Salary Cap Systems*, 10 Sports Law. J. 189, 205 (2003). Another notable difference is the binding effect of the arbitrator's award. Generally, the arbitrator's decision is final and binding on the player and club. As a result of a compromise agreed to by the NHL and NHLPA in 1995 during a period of considerable player/management conflict, NHL club owners have a limited right to reject a salary arbitration award (a walk-away right). "Each club can exercise the right up to three times in two continuous years and not more than twice in the same year." *Id.* at 206. When this right is exercised, the player becomes a free agent. "If the player is unable to obtain a better offer from another team, he can then return to his previous team and accept the offer that was last on the table prior to his becoming a free agent." *Id.* See also Stephen J. Bartlett, *Contract Negotiations and Salary Arbitration in the NHL: An Agent's View*, 4 Marq. Sports L.J. 1 (1993). The current provisions are set forth in 2012 NHL CBA, Article 12.

d.   Contract Dispute Arbitration

The third major category of arbitration relates to disputes arising out of team-player contracts. The nature of the disputes that have developed over the years runs the gamut. They include disputes as to whether a contract was properly formed, what consequences flow from a material breach of a contract, what rights a club (or league) has to discipline a player, guaranteed salaries, bonus provisions, and side deals to the standard player contract. The following materials provide some examples of the myriad issues that have been raised through arbitration in professional sports.

One general question can be posed at this point: If more attention had been paid to the drafting of language in the CBA, UPC, or particular individual player's contracts, would the problems leading to the arbitration have been avoided or alleviated? Often the answer will be "yes." If so, consider alternative provisions to gain a fuller appreciation of the rewards of good "preventive" contract drafting.

i.   Failure to Honor Contract and Remedies for Enforcement

The negative injunction cases considered earlier in this chapter illustrate some of the legal problems that have confronted sports leagues when rival leagues were formed. However, modern times have given new meaning to what is meant by rival leagues, which may be in foreign countries. Do the old rules developed more than a century ago when U.S. professional sports leagues were primarily regional still apply? To further complicate matters, CBAs sometimes require that these issues go to arbitration.

The following case is one of the more important cases involving a player/team conflict; it has continuing relevance, despite being decided almost 30 years ago, because in the twenty-first century a global labor market exists for most major professional team sports. The case relies on basic legal principles enunciated over 100 years ago in landmark cases such as *Ward, Ewing,* and *Lajoie* (discussed in section B, *supra*) and provides an opportunity to reexamine them. As you read this case, consider whether domestic arbitration provides an effective means of resolving disputes with international implications.

BOSTON CELTICS LIMITED PARTNERSHIP v. BRIAN SHAW
908 F.2d 1041 (lst Cir. 1990)

BREYER, Chief Judge.

I.   BACKGROUND

A.   FACTS

The basic facts, which are not in dispute, include the following:

(a)   In 1988, soon after Shaw graduated from college, he signed a one-year contract to play for the Celtics.

(b)   In 1989, Shaw signed a two-year contract to play with the Italian team Il Messaggero Roma ("Il Messaggero"). The team agreed to pay him $800,000 for the first year and $900,000 for the second year. The contract contains a clause permitting Shaw to cancel the second year (1990-91). It says that Shaw has the right to rescind the second year of this Agreement . . . [if he] returns to the United States to play with the NBA . . . by delivering a registered letter to [Il Messaggero] . . . between June 20, 1990 and July 20, 1990.

(c)   At the end of January 1990 Shaw signed a five-year "Uniform Player Contract" with the Celtics. The contract contains standard clauses negotiated by the National Basketball Association ("NBA") franchise owners and the National Basketball Players Association (the "Players Association"). It adopts by cross-reference arbitration provisions contained in the NBA-Players Association Collective Bargaining Agreement. In the contract, the Celtics promise Shaw a $450,000 signing bonus and more than $1 million per year in compensation. In return, Shaw promises the Celtics, among other things, that he will cancel his second year with Il Messaggero. The contract says that the "Player [*i.e.*, Shaw] and Club [*i.e.*, the Celtics] acknowledge that Player is currently under contract with Il Messaggero Roma (the 'Messaggero Contract') for the 1989-90 & 1990-91 playing seasons. The Player represents that in accordance with the terms of the Messaggero Contract, the Player has the right to rescind that contract prior to the 1990-91 season *and the player hereby agrees to exercise such right of rescission* in the manner and at the time called for by the Messaggero Contract." (Emphasis added.)

(d)   On June 6, 1990, Shaw told the Celtics that he had decided to play for Il Messaggero during the 1990-91 season and that he would not exercise his right of rescission.

B.   PROCEDURAL HISTORY

On June 11, 1990, the Celtics invoked their right under the Collective Bargaining Agreement (cross-referenced in the Contract) to an "expedited" arbitration proceeding. The arbitrator held a two-day hearing on June 13 and 14. He found that Shaw's refusal to rescind the Il Messaggero contract violated Shaw's contract with the Celtics. He ordered Shaw to rescind the Il Messaggero contract (on June 20) and not to play for any team other than the Celtics during the term of his Celtics contract. On June 15, Shaw said he still did not intend to rescind the Il Messaggero contract.

The Celtics responded immediately by asking the federal district court to use its authority under § 301 of the Labor Management Relations Act, 29 U.S.C. § 185, to enforce the award. . . . The Celtics asked the court for "expedited enforcement" of the award and for a preliminary injunction. After receiving Shaw's response (in the form of an opposition, a motion to dismiss, a brief, and supporting affidavits), and after holding an oral hearing, on June 26, the court granted the Celtics' motion to expedite, ordered Shaw to cancel the Il Messaggero agreement "forthwith," and "enforced" the award. Shaw now appeals this district court decision, attacking both the preliminary injunction and the order enforcing the arbitration award.

II.   THE LEGAL MERITS

Shaw makes two basic categories of argument in his effort to show that the district court lacked the legal power to enter its order. First, he says that the arbitration award was itself unlawful. Second, he says that regardless of the lawfulness of the award, the district court followed improper procedures. We shall address these arguments in turn and explain why we find each not persuasive.

A.   THE ARBITRATOR'S DECISION

Shaw says that the district court should not have enforced the arbitrator's award because that award was itself unlawful, for any of five separate reasons.

1.   The termination promise. Shaw argues that the arbitrator could not reasonably find that he broke a contractual promise to the Celtics because, he says, the Celtics had previously agreed with the Players Association that contracts with individual players such as Shaw would not contain promises of the sort here at issue, namely, a promise to cancel a contract to play with a different team. Shaw says that this previous agreement between the Celtics and the Players Association renders his promise to terminate Il Messaggero "null and void." To support this argument, he points to Article I, § 2 of the Collective Bargaining Agreement, which Shaw and the Celtics, through

cross-reference, made part of their individual agreement. Section 2 says, "Any amendment to a Uniform Player Contract [of the type Shaw and the Celtics used], other than those permitted by this [Collective Bargaining] Agreement, shall be null and void." The Agreement permits amendments (a) "in . . . respect to the compensation . . . to be paid the player," (b) "in respect to specialized compensation arrangements," (c) in respect to a "compensation payment schedule," and (d) in respect to "protect[ion]" of compensation in the event of contract termination. Shaw says that his promise to cancel the Il Messaggero agreement was an amendment to the Uniform Players Contract that does not concern compensation, specialized compensation, compensation schedules, or compensation protection; therefore, it is "null and void." . . .

Shaw's argument, while logical, fails to show that the arbitrator's contrary finding is unlawful. The reasons it fails are fairly straightforward. First, the argument concerns the proper interpretation of a contract negotiated pursuant to a collective bargaining agreement. Second, federal labor law gives arbitrators, not judges, the power to interpret such contracts. The Supreme Court, noting the strong federal policy favoring the voluntary settlement of labor disputes, has written that a labor arbitration award is valid so long as it "draws its essence" from the labor contract. . . .

Third, one can find "plausible arguments" favoring the arbitrator's construction. Shaw's "rescission" promise defines the beginning of the compensation relationship. It also plausibly determines, at the very least, whether Shaw's compensation will begin at $1.1 million (and continue for three years) or whether it will begin at $1.2 million (and continue for only two years). . . . More importantly, and also quite plausibly, Shaw's overall compensation might have been much different had he declined to promise to play for the Celtics in 1990-91, thereby forcing the Celtics, perhaps, to obtain the services of a replacement for that year. The NBA Commissioner, who reviews all player contracts, found that the term was related to "compensation," as did the arbitrator. We cannot say that their findings lack any "plausible" basis . . .

In sum, we find the arbitration award lawful. . . .

B. THE DISTRICT COURT PROCEEDINGS

The district court, as we have pointed out, issued a preliminary injunction requiring Shaw to rescind "forthwith" his contract with Il Messaggero and forbidding him to play basketball for any team other than the Celtics during the term of his Celtics contract. The court also "enforced" an arbitration award containing essentially the same terms. Shaw argues that both the preliminary injunction and the enforcement order are unlawful. Since the district court correctly upheld the award's validity, Shaw's only remaining arguments are that the district court lacked discretion to award preliminary injunctive relief and that it mismanaged the proceedings below. We discuss both points briefly.

1. *The preliminary injunction.* . . .

The only legal question before us, therefore, is whether the district court acted outside its broad equitable powers when it issued the preliminary injunction. That is to say, did the court improperly answer the four questions judges in this Circuit must ask when deciding whether to issue a preliminary injunction. They are: (1) have the Celtics shown a likelihood of success on the merits?

(2) have they shown that failure to issue the injunction would cause the Celtics "irreparable harm?" (3) does the "balance of harms" favor Shaw or the Celtics? and (4) will granting the injunction harm the "public interest?" Our examination of the record has convinced us that the court acted well within the scope of its lawful powers. . . .

To begin with, the Celtics have shown a clear likelihood of success on the merits. As we pointed out in section "A," the arbitration award is lawful, and courts have authority to enforce lawful arbitration awards. The Celtics also have demonstrated irreparable harm. Without speedy relief, they will likely lose the services of a star athlete next year, . . . and, unless they know fairly soon whether Shaw will, or will not play for them, they will find it difficult to plan intelligently for next season. Indeed, in his contract Shaw expressly represents and agrees that he has extraordinary and unique skill and ability as a basketball player, . . . and that any breach by the Player of this contract will cause irreparable injury to the Club.

Further, the court could reasonably find that the "balance of harms" favors the Celtics. Of course, a preliminary injunction, if ultimately shown wrong on the merits, could cause Shaw harm. He might lose the chance to play in the country, and for the team, that he prefers. On the other hand, this harm is somewhat offset by the fact that ultimate success on the merits—*i.e.*, a finding that Shaw was not obligated to terminate Il Messaggero after all—would likely result in the following scenario: Shaw might still be able to sign with Il Messaggero and, if not, he would always have the Celtics contract of over $5 million to fall back upon. At the same time, the court's failure to issue the injunction, if the merits ultimately favored the Celtics, could cause them serious harm of the sort just mentioned (*i.e.*, significantly increased difficulty in planning their team for next season). Given the very small likelihood that Shaw would ultimately prevail on the merits, and the "comparative" harms at stake, the district court could properly decide that the overall "balance" favored the Celtics, not Shaw.

Finally, the court could properly find that issuing a preliminary injunction would not harm the public interest. Indeed, as we have pointed out, the public interest favors court action that "effectuate[s]" the parties' intent to resolve their disputes informally through arbitration. . . . Where the dispute involves a professional basketball player's obligation to play for a particular team, one could reasonably consider expeditious, informal and effective dispute-resolution methods to be essential, and, if so, the public interest favoring court action to "effectuate" those methods of dispute-resolution would seem at least as strong as it is in respect to work-related disputes typically arising under collective bargaining agreements. . . .

Shaw makes an additional argument. He notes that courts will not provide equitable relief such as an injunction to a party with "unclean hands," and he argues that the Celtics' hands are not clean. To support this argument, he has submitted an affidavit saying, in effect, that he signed the contract in a weak moment. His trip to Italy had made him "homesick"; he was "depressed" by what he viewed as undeserved and "negative criticism" in the Italian press; he was not represented by an agent; the Celtics had been urging him to sign up; he read the contract only for about 20 minutes while he was driving around Rome with a Celtics official; and no one ever explained to him that if he did not sign and played with Il Messaggero for another year, he would become a "free agent," able to bargain thereafter with any American team, perhaps for an even greater salary than the Celtics were willing to pay him.

Other evidence in the record, however, which Shaw does not deny, shows that he is a college graduate; that he has played under contract with the Celtics before; that the contract is a standard form contract except for a few, fairly simple, rather clear, additions, . . . that he had bargained with the Celtics for an offer that increased from $3.4 million (in December) to $5.4 million (less than one month later); that he looked over the contract before signing it; that he told the American consul in Rome (as he signed it) that he had read and understood it; and that he did not complain about the contract until he told the Celtics in June that he would not honor it.

Given this state of the record, the district court could easily, and properly, conclude that the Celtics' hands were not "unclean." . . .

In sum, issuance of the preliminary injunction was legally proper. For these reasons, the order of the district court is *Affirmed.*

NOTES AND QUESTIONS

1. Although it could not require Shaw to play for the Celtics (why not?), what did the *Shaw* district court do to enforce the arbitrator's award? Shaw thus faced a dilemma—stay abroad indefinitely or comply with the court's negative injunction by returning to the Celtics. He ultimately chose the latter option.

2. The NBA collective bargaining agreement is more explicit than most in detailing the negotiable items that are allowed either to change language in the UPC or to add new provisions. In this instance, the Celtics persuaded Shaw to agree to send a letter to his Italian club, Il Messaggero, stating that Shaw was exercising his option to terminate the second year of his contract. Did the arbitrator properly rule that this agreement did not contravene the NBA CBA provisions on allowable amendments? What is the appropriate role of the First Circuit in reviewing the arbitrator's decision?

3. *Shaw* illustrates the deference U.S. courts provide to valid arbitration decisions (with the grounds for successful judicial appeal being very limited). In considering whether an Italian court would enforce a U.S. arbitration award enjoining Shaw from playing for Il Messaggero, national courts generally enforce foreign arbitration awards if the parties that it binds had a valid written arbitration agreement, there were no procedural defects in the arbitration process, and the award does not violate the country's public policy pursuant to the Convention on the Recognition and Enforcement of Foreign Arbitral Awards (New York Convention), a 1958 treaty entered into by the United States. Because all of these requirements were not satisfied, in *Dynamo v. Ovechkin*, 412 F. Supp. 2d 24 (D.D.C. 2006), a federal district court refused to enforce the decision of a Russian arbitrator that Alexander Ovechkin, who was playing for the NHL's Washington Capitals, had a contractual obligation to play during the 2005-2006 season for a Russian hockey team, Dynamo Moscow. Because neither the Capitals nor Ovechkin were parties to the Russian arbitration proceeding, the court held that they were not bound by the arbitration award and it was not enforceable in the United States under the New York Convention. *Dynamo* and *Shaw* illustrate the

growing complexity of sports labor issues as a global market for the services of professional players continues to develop.

ii.   Club and League Power to Discipline

We now shift our focus to the authority of clubs and leagues to discipline players. Player disciplinary matters are a major source of arbitration disputes in professional sports. As you examine the following materials, consider who serves as arbitrator, what standard the arbitrator uses in determining whether the club or league had a legitimate basis for disciplining a player, and how different courts view the appropriate scope of arbitral and commissioner authority.

NATIONAL FOOTBALL LEAGUE MANAGEMENT COUNCIL v. NATIONAL FOOTBALL LEAGUE PLAYERS ASS'N

820 F.3d 527 (2d Cir. 2016)

PARKER, Circuit Judge. . . .

[EDS. On January 18, 2015, during the National Football League's American Football Conference Championship Game between the New England Patriots and the Indianapolis Colts, the Colts suspected that the Patriots were using game balls that were inflated below the permissible range of 12.5 to 13.5 pounds per square inch (psi). At halftime, League officials tested all of the game balls—half of which the Patriots supplied and half of which the Colts supplied. All of the Colts balls were determined to be properly inflated, but all of the Patriots' balls were determined to be underinflated. Within a week, the League retained Theodore V. Wells, Jr., Esq., and his law firm of Paul, Weiss, Rifkind, Wharton & Garrison to conduct an independent investigation into whether the balls had been tampered with before or during the game. The investigation concluded that it was "more probable than not" that two Patriots equipment officials—Jim McNally and John Jastremski—had deliberately deflated the balls and that quarterback Tom Brady had been "at least generally aware" of McNally and Jastremski's actions. In concluding as such, the investigators noted that Brady had previously publicly asserted his preference for throwing softer game balls and that text messages between McNally and Jastremski about ball deflation frequently referenced Brady and his preference. They also noted that, after not communicating by text or phone with Jastremski for over six months, Brady texted Jastermski several times and spoke with him by phone for 25 minutes when the investigation was announced. Additionally, they reported that Brady had impaired the investigation by refusing "to make available any documents or electronic information (including text messages and emails)." On May 11, 2015, NFL Commissioner Roger Goodell suspended Brady for four games pursuant to Article 46 of the NFL-NFLPA Collective Bargaining Agreement between the NFL and the NFL Players Association for engaging in "conduct detrimental to the integrity of and public confidence in the game of professional football." Brady, through the Association, appealed the suspension, and Commissioner Goodell exercised his discretion under the CBA to serve as the hearing officer. While the appeal was pending, it was revealed that on the day Wells was to interview Brady during the investigation, Brady ordered his assistant to destroy his cell phone. On July 28, 2015, the Commissioner issued a final decision affirming the four-game suspension. Shortly thereafter, the League brought an action in federal district court to confirm the award, and the Association brought an action to vacate the award. The two actions were consolidated before the United States District Court for the Southern District of New York, which granted the Association's motion to vacate the award and denied the League's motion to confirm it on the grounds that Brady lacked notice that he could be suspended rather than simply fined for the conduct and that the Commissioner was evidently partial and should have recused himself at least in some regards. *Nat'l Football League Mgmt. Council v. Nat'l Football League Players Ass'n,* 125 F. Supp. 3d 449 (S.D.N.Y. 2015). The League appealed the decision.]

The basic principle driving both our analysis and our conclusion is well established: a federal court's review of labor arbitration awards is narrowly circumscribed and highly deferential—indeed, among the most deferential in the law. Our role is not to determine for ourselves whether Brady participated in a scheme to deflate footballs or whether the suspension imposed by the Commissioner should have been for three games or five games or none at all. . . . Our obligation is limited to determining whether the arbitration proceedings and award met the minimum legal standards established by the Labor Management Relations Act, 29 U.S.C. § 141 *et seq.* (the "LMRA"). . . . These standards do not require perfection in arbitration awards. Rather, they dictate that even if an arbitrator makes mistakes of fact or law, we may not disturb an award so long as he acted within the bounds of his bargained-for authority.

Here, that authority was especially broad. The Commissioner was authorized to impose discipline for . . . "conduct detrimental to the integrity of, or public confidence, in the game of professional football." In their collective bargaining agreement, the players and the League mutually decided many years ago that the Commissioner should investigate possible rule violations, should impose appropriate sanctions, and may preside at arbitrations challenging his discipline. Although this tripartite regime may appear somewhat unorthodox, it is the regime bargained for and agreed upon by the parties, which we can only presume they determined was mutually satisfactory.

Given this substantial deference, we conclude that this case is not an exceptional one that warrants vacatur. Our review of the record yields the firm conclusion that the Commissioner properly exercised his broad discretion to resolve an intramural controversy between the League and a player. Accordingly, we REVERSE the judgment of the district court and REMAND with instructions to confirm the award. . . .

DISCUSSION

Article 46 of the CBA empowers the Commissioner to take disciplinary action against a player whom he "reasonably judge[s]" to have engaged in "conduct detrimental to the integrity of, or public confidence in, the game of professional football." A disciplined player is entitled to appeal to the Commissioner and seek an arbitration hearing, and the Commissioner may appoint either himself or someone else to serve as arbitrator.

On this appeal, the Association does not contest the factual findings of the Commissioner. Nor does the Association dispute that the Commissioner was entitled, under Article 46, to determine that Brady's "participat[ion] in a scheme to tamper with game balls" was "conduct detrimental" worthy of a four-game suspension. The parties disagree, however, as to whether other aspects of the CBA and the relevant case law require vacatur of the award. . . .

LACK OF ADEQUATE NOTICE

The Association's chief ground for vacatur, relied upon by the district court, is that the Commissioner improperly suspended Brady pursuant to the "conduct detrimental" clause of Article 46 because Brady was only on notice that his conduct could lead to a fine under the more specific "Discipline for Game–Related Misconduct" section of the League Policies for Players (the "Player Policies").

The Association argues that the Commissioner was not permitted to impose a four-game suspension under Article 46 because the Player Policies mandated only a fine for equipment infractions. The Association further contends that the award is additionally defective because the Commissioner failed to make findings as to the applicability or interpretation of the Player Policies. *See Clinchfield Coal Co. v. Dist. 28, United Mine Workers,* 720 F.2d 1365, 1369 (4th Cir. 1983) ("Where . . . the arbitrator fails to discuss critical contract terminology, which terminology might reasonably require an opposite result, the award cannot be considered to draw its essence from the contract"). . . . We conclude that the equipment provision does not apply and, in any event, the punishments listed for equipment violations are minimum ones that do not foreclose suspensions.

The Association . . . argues that equipment violations include "ball or equipment tampering" and "equipment tampering such as ball deflation." But [the Other Uniform/Equipment Violations section of the Player Policies] says nothing about tampering with, or the preparation of, footballs and, indeed, does not mention the words "tampering," "ball," or "deflation" at all. Moreover, there is no other provision of the Player Policies that refers to ball or equipment tampering, despite an extensive list of uniform and equipment violations ranging from the length of a player's stockings to the color of his wristbands. On the other hand, Article 46 gives the Commissioner broad authority to deal with conduct he believes might undermine the integrity of the game. The Commissioner properly understood that a series of rules relating to uniforms and equipment does not repeal his authority vested in him by the Association to protect professional football from detrimental conduct. . . . [T]he Commissioner's decision to discipline Brady pursuant to Article 46 was "plausibly grounded in the parties' agreement," which is all the law requires. *See Wackenhut,* 126 F.3d at 32.

Even were the district court and the Association correct, and they are not, that Brady could be punished only pursuant to the Player Policies and its "Other Uniform/Equipment Violations" provision, it would not follow that the only available punishment would have been a fine. While the Player Policies do specify that, with regard to "Other Uniform/Equipment Violations," "[f]irst offenses will result in fines," the 2014 Schedule of Fines . . . makes clear that the "[f]ines listed below are minimums." The Schedule of Fines goes on to specify that "[o]ther forms of discipline, including higher fines and suspension may also be imposed, based on the circumstances of the particular violation." . . . . [T]hese provisions make clear that even first offenders are not exempt from punishment, and serious violations may result in suspension. But even if other readings were plausible, the Commissioner's interpretation of this provision as allowing for a suspension would easily withstand judicial scrutiny because his interpretation would be at least "barely colorable," which, again, is all that the law requires. *See In re Andros Compania Maritima, S.A.*, 579 F.2d 691, 704 (2d Cir. 1978).

* * *

The district court also concluded that the award was invalid because "[n]o NFL policy or precedent provided notice that a player could be subject to discipline for general awareness of another person's alleged misconduct." *Nat'l Football League*, 125 F. Supp. 3d at 466. This conclusion misapprehends the record. The award is clear that it confirmed Brady's discipline not because of a general awareness of misconduct on the part of others, but because Brady both "participated in a scheme to tamper with game balls" and "willfully obstructed the investigation by . . . arranging for destruction of his cellphone."

The Association takes a somewhat different tack and argues that the Commissioner was bound to the Wells Report's limited conclusion that Brady was at least "generally aware" of the inappropriate activities of Patriots equipment staff. But the Association offers no persuasive support for its contention that the universe of facts the Commissioner could properly consider was limited by the Wells Report. Nothing in Article 46 limits the authority of the arbitrator to examine or reassess the factual basis for a suspension. In fact, in providing for a hearing, Article 46 strongly suggests otherwise. Because the point of a hearing in any proceeding is to establish a complete factual record, it would be incoherent to both authorize a hearing and at the same time insist that no new findings or conclusions could be based on a record expanded as a consequence of a hearing. . . .

The issue before the Commissioner was whether the discipline imposed on Brady was warranted under Article 46, and that was the issue he decided. The Commissioner did not develop a new basis for the suspension, nor did he deprive Brady of an opportunity to confront the case against him. We see nothing in the CBA that suggests that the Commissioner was barred from concluding, based on information generated during the hearing, that Brady's conduct was more serious than was initially believed.

Moreover, the Wells Report did not limit itself to a finding of "general awareness." It also found that "it is unlikely that [McNally and Jastremski] would deflate game balls without Brady's knowledge and approval" or that they "would personally and unilaterally engage in such conduct in the absence of Brady's awareness and consent." The Commissioner's shift from "knowledge and approval" to "participation" was not, as the *542 Association argues, a "quantum leap," but was instead a reasonable reassessment of the facts that gave rise to Brady's initial discipline, supplemented by information developed at the hearing.

We therefore find that the Commissioner was within his discretion to conclude that Brady had "participated in a scheme to tamper with game balls." Because the parties agree that such conduct is "conduct detrimental," the district court erred in concluding that the Commissioner's deviation from the Wells Report's finding of general awareness was a ground for vacatur. . . .

The district court held and the Association contends that Brady's suspension cannot be sustained on the grounds that he obstructed the Commissioner's investigation. The court reasoned that "[n]o player suspension in NFL history has been sustained for an alleged failure to cooperate with — or even allegedly obstructing — an NFL investigation." *Nat'l Football League*, 125 F. Supp. 3d at 465 (internal quotation marks omitted). The League, on the other hand, argues that not only is the deliberate obstruction of a league investigation "conduct detrimental" within the meaning of Article 46, but also the destruction of the cell phone permitted the Commissioner to draw an adverse inference against Brady that supported the finding that he participated in the deflation scheme.

. . . [T]he Association insists that because the award is invalid in light of the Commissioner's failure to discipline Brady under the Player Policies, the award cannot be salvaged on the alternative theory that Brady could have been suspended for his obstruction of the investigation [including the destruction of his cell phone]. Specifically, the Association contends that "once it becomes clear that Brady's non-cooperation led to the adverse inference about ball tampering, it's back to square one: The only penalty of which Brady had notice was the collectively bargained *fine* for equipment violations." This argument fails for the simple reason that, as we have explained, the Player Policies are inapplicable and, in any event, suspensions may be imposed for violations of the League's equipment policies. . . .

At oral argument, the Association contended, for the first time, that Brady had no notice that the destruction of the cell phone would even be at issue in the arbitration proceeding. . . . For a number of reasons, the Association's assertion that Brady lacked notice that the destruction of the cell phone would be an issue in the arbitration has no support in the record. The League's letter to Brady notifying him of his suspension pointed to Brady's "failure to cooperate fully and candidly with the investigation, including by refusing to produce any relevant electronic evidence (emails, texts, etc.)." Having been given clear notice that his cooperation with the investigation was a subject of significant interest, we have difficulty believing that either Brady or the Association would have been surprised that the destruction of the cell phone was of importance to the Commissioner.

At oral argument, the Association further contended that the Commissioner was improperly punishing Brady for destroying his cell phone because he was required to institute a new disciplinary action (so that Brady could then appeal any determination that he had destroyed his cell phone). This argument fails because, as set forth in the original disciplinary letter, Brady was punished for failing to cooperate, and it is clear from the Commissioner's decision that Brady's cell phone destruction was part and parcel of the broader claim that he had failed to cooperate.

Further, as we stated with regard to general awareness, nothing in Article 46 limits the arbitrator's authority to reexamine the factual basis for a suspension by conducting a hearing. Additionally, the Commissioner did not increase the punishment as a consequence of the destruction of the cell phone—the four-game suspension was not increased. Rather, the cell phone destruction merely provided further support for the Commissioner's determination that Brady had failed to cooperate, and served as the basis for an adverse inference as to his participation in the scheme to deflate footballs.

Finally, any reasonable litigant would understand that the destruction of evidence, revealed just days before the start of arbitration proceedings, would be an important issue. It is well established that the law permits a trier of fact to infer that a party who deliberately destroys relevant evidence the party had an obligation to produce did so in order to conceal damaging information from the adjudicator. *See, e.g., Residential Funding Corp. v. DeGeorge Fin. Corp.*, 306 F.3d 99, 106-07 (2d Cir. 2002); *Byrnie v. Town of Cromwell*, 243 F.3d 93, 107-12 (2d Cir. 2001); *Kronisch v. United States*, 150 F.3d 112, 126 (2d Cir. 1998). These principles are sufficiently settled that there is no need for any specific mention of them in a collective agreement, and we are confident that their application came as no surprise to Brady or the Association. . . .

EVIDENT PARTIALITY

The Association's final contention is that the Commissioner was evidently partial . . . and should have recused himself . . . because it was improper for him to adjudicate the propriety of his own conduct. This argument has no merit. . . . We may vacate an arbitration award "where there was evident partiality . . . in the arbitrator[]." 9 U.S.C. § 10(a)(2). "Evident partiality may be found only 'where a reasonable person would have to conclude that an arbitrator was partial to one party to the arbitration.'" *Scandinavian Reins. Co. v. Saint Paul Fire & Marine Ins. Co.*, 668 F.3d 60, 64 (2d Cir. 2012) (quoting *Applied Indus. Materials Corp. v. Ovalar Makine Ticaret Ve Sanayi, A.S.*, 492 F.3d 132, 137 (2d Cir. 2007)). The party seeking vacatur must prove evident partiality by "clear and convincing evidence." *Kolel Beth Yechiel Mechil of Tartikov, Inc. v. YLL Irrevocable Tr.*, 729 F.3d 99, 106 (2d Cir. 2013). However, arbitration is a matter of contract, and consequently, the parties to an arbitration can ask for no more impartiality than inheres in the method they have chosen. *Williams v. Nat'l Football League*, 582 F.3d 863, 885 (8th Cir. 2009); *Winfrey v. Simmons Foods, Inc.*, 495 F.3d 549, 551 (8th Cir. 2007). . . . Here, the parties contracted in the CBA to specifically allow the Commissioner to sit as the arbitrator . . . knowing full well that the Commissioner had the sole power of determining what constitutes "conduct detrimental," and thus knowing that the Commissioner would have a stake both in the underlying discipline and in [the] arbitration. . . . Had the parties wished to restrict the Commissioner's authority, they could have fashioned a different agreement.

CONCLUSION

For the foregoing reasons, we REVERSE the judgment of the district court and REMAND with instructions for the district court to confirm the arbitration award.

NOTES AND QUESTIONS

1. *"Deflate-gate" in Context.* The Second Circuit's decision in *National Football League Management Council v. National Football League Players Ass'n*, better known as the "deflate-gate" case, was a huge win for Commissioner Goodell, who had been derided as "a dictator" and called "judge, jury, and executioner" by league players, while being a stern disciplinarian throughout his tenure as commissioner.

    Consider the "deflate-gate" outcome in the context of the sharp blow Commissioner Goodell's authority had suffered three years earlier in connection with the New Orleans Saints' "bounty-gate" scandal. In that matter, having concluded that the Saints had instituted a system of financial incentives for injuring opposing players, Commissioner Goodell stripped the Saints of two future second round draft picks, fined the club $500,000, and suspended the Saints general manager Mickey Loomis, Head Coach Sean Payton, and Assistant Head Coach Joe Vitt as well as several Saints players for various lengths of time. Loomis, Payton, and Vitt appealed their suspensions (which were not subject to the constraints of the NFL CBA), but Commissioner Goodell heard and denied their appeals.

Goodell's suspensions of Saints players Scott Fujita, Will Smith, Anthony Hargrove, and Jonathan Vilma spawned what stood, until deflate-gate, as perhaps the most intense and complex dispute over league commissioner disciplinary authority in American sports history. The central issue in "bounty-gate," as in "deflate-gate," was the appropriate scope of Goodell's disciplinary power over NFL players and the manner in which he exercised it. Also as in "deflate-gate," Goodell used his power under the CBA to both issue suspensions and to serve as the "arbitrator" in hearing the suspension appeals by the Saints players.

The NFLPA also sought to have the dispute involving the players resolved along an alternative adjudicatory track by initiating a separate proceeding before an Independent System Arbitrator, pursuant to Article 15 of the NFL CBA, arguing that the System Arbitrator rather than the Commissioner had jurisdiction over the bounty system allegations because they constituted an allegedly impermissible "undisclosed agreement" (over which the System Arbitrator would have jurisdiction) rather than alleged "conduct detrimental to the league" (over which Commissioner Goodell would have jurisdiction). See *Complaint*, ¶51, *NFLPA v. NFL Mgmt. Council*, No. 2:12-cv-01744 (E.D. La. 2012).

The System Arbitrator, in a decision issued in June 2012, deferred jurisdiction to Commissioner Goodell, asserting that the allegations, if proved, would not constitute an impermissible "undisclosed agreement" and that they would, therefore, be more appropriately analyzed as alleged "conduct detrimental to the league." *Id.* ¶53. The NFLPA promptly appealed the System Arbitration Award to an Appeals Panel provided for in the CBA. *Id.* ¶55.

While the NFLPA's appeal from the System Arbitrator's decision was pending, Commissioner Goodell rejected the NFLPA's original appeal to him, and the NFLPA responded by suing the NFL on behalf of Fujita, Smith, and Hargrove, claiming he acted with evident partiality in hearing the appeal and, in any event, lacked jurisdiction to dispense punishment in, or arbitrate, the matter in the first place. See *NFLPA v. NFL Mgmt. Council*, No. 2:12-cv-01744 (E.D. La. 2013). The fourth suspended player, Jonathan Vilma, sued Commissioner Goodell separately, alleging that Commissioner Goodell made defamatory statements about him that caused permanent harm to his reputation. See *Vilma v. Goodell*, 917 F. Supp. 2d 591 (E.D. La. 2012). The NFL then countered with a grievance against the NFLPA alleging that Vilma's defamation suit violated the CBA.

Vilma's defamation suit was ultimately dismissed, but he filed another lawsuit, this time against the NFL, arguing that Commissioner Goodell failed to serve as a neutral arbiter and that he failed to issue a timely decision on the appeal in accordance with the CBA. See *Vilma v. NFL*, No. 2:12-cv-01718 (E.D. La. 2012). In this suit, Vilma sought injunctive relief to vacate the suspension and allow him to participate in team activities.

As the parties awaited decisions in these cases, the Appeals Panel considering the appeal from the System Arbitration Award issued a summary of its decision on September 7, 2012, in which it found that the "alleged bounty program was both an undisclosed agreement to provide compensation to players and an agreement to cause or attempt to cause injury to players (conduct detrimental to the league)," and thus, both the System Arbitrator and the Commissioner would have jurisdiction to impose punishments under their respective powers. *CBA Appeals Panel Summary Decision* at 3. But because the record did not reveal whether Commissioner Goodell issued the punishments under the "conduct detrimental" to the NFL clause (for which he would have authority) or the "undisclosed agreement" clause (for which he would not have authority), the Appeals Panel vacated the System Arbitration Award and remanded the matter to Commissioner Goodell for redetermination. *Id.* at 4.

Roughly a month later, on October 9, 2012, after meetings with the players and their attorneys, Commissioner Goodell reissued his decision to punish the players, explaining that the "players confirmed many of the key facts disclosed in [the] investigation" and clearly stated that the punishments were for *conduct detrimental* to the league. NFL Communications, *Discipline Reaffirmed for Four Players Suspended for Participation in Saints' Bounty Program,* press release, Oct. 9, 2012. However, he reduced the lengths of the suspensions for two of the players: Scott Fujita and Anthony Hargrove (the punishments for Smith and Vilma remained the same). *Id.*

Three days following Goodell's reissued decision, all four players appealed and requested that this time Goodell recuse himself and therefore not handle the appeal of his own decision. Goodell agreed to recusal and appointed former NFL Commissioner Paul Tagliabue to hear the appeals.

On December 11, 2012, over seven months after Goodell initially issued the players' suspensions, Tagliabue vacated them. In doing so, he did not dispute the essence of what Goodell's investigation uncovered. Indeed, he generally affirmed Goodell's factual findings. He insisted, though, that "[u]nlike [the] Saints' broad organizational misconduct, player appeals involve sharply focused issues of alleged individual player misconduct in several different aspects, [and in this instance] this entire case had been contaminated by the coaches and others in the Saints' organization." Jesse Reed, *Reviewing the Entire Timeline of Saints, Bountygate Scandal,* Bleacher Report, Dec. 11, 2012, http://bleacherreport.com/articles/1441646-reviewing-the-complete-timeline-of-nfl-saints-bountygate-scandal. Therefore, Tagliabue did not find the suspensions appropriate, and in vacating them he dealt both Goodell and the concept of broad league commissioner player disciplinary authority a resounding defeat.

Do you agree with the outcome in the deflate-gate case? In bounty-gate? Why would the NFLPA assent in a CBA to such a disciplinary structure? Is it appropriate (even if permitted under a CBA) for a league commissioner to both make disciplinary decisions and serve as the arbitrator of appeals from those decisions? Might this structure ultimately call in to question the legitimacy of the commissioner's office? Note that the Missouri Supreme Court refused to enforce an employment contract provision requiring an NFL club's former equipment manager to arbitrate his age discrimination claim before Commissioner Goodell. Although the court compelled arbitration, it held that requiring an NFL club employee to agree that the NFL Commissioner be the sole arbitrator of disputes with the club is unconscionable outside the context of a collective bargaining agreement. *State ex rel. v. Kerr,* 461 S.W.3d 798 (Mo. 2015).

2. Latrell Sprewell v. Golden State Warriors. While friction between a coach and one of his or her players is not unusual, it rarely raises to the level that it

did between Golden State Warriors coach P.J. Carlesimo and his star player Latrell Sprewell during practice on December 1, 1997. After Carlesimo repeatedly criticized Sprewell for his lack of effort, Sprewell responded with, "What the f*** do you want me to do?," at which point Carlesimo told Sprewell, "Get the f*** out of here." Sprewell then grabbed Carlesimo by the neck, choked him, and threatened to kill him. After being ushered to the locker room and showering, Sprewell returned to the gym and again advanced towards Carlesimo before being restrained. Upon leaving the gym for the second time, Sprewell again threatened to kill Carlesimo. After fully reviewing the incident, the Warriors terminated Sprewell's contract, and the NBA Commissioner, David Stern, decided to suspend Sprewell for a year. The Grievance Arbitrator, John Feerick, upheld the suspension but reduced its length to the remainder of the 1997-1998 season (68 games).

Believing that no suspension for his actions was appropriate, Sprewell sought to vacate the arbitrator's award upholding it. Affirming the district court's refusal to vacate it, the Ninth Circuit explained that "judicial scrutiny of an arbitrator's decision in a labor dispute 'is extremely limited'" and that vacatur is only warranted: "(1) when the award does not draw its essence from the collective bargaining agreement; (2) when the arbitrator exceeds the scope of the issues submitted; (3) when the award runs counter to public policy; and (4) when the award is procured by fraud." *Sprewell v. Golden State Warriors*, 266 F.3d 979, 986 (9th Cir. 2001). Applying this standard, the Ninth Circuit concluded that the arbitrator's award should stand.

3. *Malice at the Palace.* A 2004 incident ranking among the NBA's ugliest moments produced another important arbitration award and judicial case considering a league commissioner's player disciplinary authority. On November 19, 2004, Commissioner Stern suspended Indiana Pacers forward Ron Artest for the remainder of the season, guard Stephen Jackson for 30 games, forward Jermaine O'Neal for 25 games, and guard Anthony Johnson for 5 games in response to their involvement in a fight during a game against the Detroit Pistons that spilled into the stands and involved fans. Following the suspensions, the NBPA filed an appeal to the grievance arbitrator, stating that the suspensions were inconsistent with the terms of the NBA CBA. The grievance arbitrator reduced Jermaine O'Neal's suspension from 25 games to 15 games but did not alter the others players' suspensions. The NBA then filed suit in *National Basketball Assn. v. National Basketball Players Assn.*, 2005 WL 22869 (S.D.N.Y., 2005), arguing that the grievance arbitrator wrongly concluded he had authority to reduce O'Neal's suspension. The court, however, disagreed, finding that the parties clearly and unmistakably agreed in the CBA, the NBA constitution, and other supporting documents to arbitrate disciplinary disputes, and that the grievance arbitrator did not exceed his authority. As such, the reduction stood, giving the NBPA a victory in its effort to check the Commissioner's disciplinary authority. *National Basketball Assn. v. National Basketball Players Assn.*, 2005 WL 22869 (S.D.N.Y., 2005).

4. *Club and League Power to Discipline Players for Off-Field Conduct.* The NFL confronted this issue in 2014 when two star players, Ray Rice and Adrian Peterson, engaged in highly publicized episodes of domestic abuse. Rice struck his then-fiancé (and now wife) in an Atlantic City casino's elevator, knocking her unconscious, and Peterson beat his four-year-old son with a switch, causing welts on his bottom, thighs, and scrotum.

NFL Commissioner Roger Goodell initially suspended Rice for two games and was widely assailed for it. He was accused of indifference to domestic abuse and NFL players' involvement in it, and he was called upon to resign by commentators and anti-domestic violence advocates. Shortly after the punishment was announced, a video emerged that was taken from a different camera angle than those previously released, and it clearly showed Rice unleashing a brutal punch that struck his fiancé in the face. After the second video's release, Commissioner Goodell suspended Rice indefinitely, asserting that Rice misled him during the initial investigation. Goodell was roundly criticized on many grounds. Some commentators argued that the brutality of the attack was implicit in the originally released video and that the punishment should have been indefinite suspension from the beginning. Others alleged that league officials had access to the second video for months and had suppressed it. Still others viewed the second suspension as arbitrary and as unjust and refuted Goodell's assertion that Rice misled him. Ultimately Rice appealed the suspension, and on December 1, 2014, he was immediately reinstated. The arbitrator, former U.S. District Court Judge Barbara Jones, found that the second penalty imposed on Rice was arbitrary and that Goodell had no power to issue the second suspension. *Ray Rice wins appeal, eligible to sign,* ESPN.com, Dec. 1, 2014, http://espn.go.com/nfl/story/_/ id/11949855/ray-rice-baltimore-ravens-wins-appeal-eligible-reinstatement.

On September 12, 2014, while the NFL was addressing the Rice domestic abuse scandal, Peterson was indicted for child abuse. Two days later, the Minnesota Vikings deactivated him, and in early November, Peterson pled no contest to the charges and was placed on probation, fined $4,000 and ordered to complete 80 hours of community service. Once the criminal case was resolved, the NFL suspended Peterson for the remainder of the season for violating the personal conduct policy, which he appealed. On December 12, 2014, the arbitrator, former NFL executive Harold Henderson, upheld the Commissioner's discipline and denied the appeal. *Adrian Peterson's appeal denied,* ESPN.com, Dec. 14, 2014, http://espn.go.com/nfl/story/_ /id/12020801/adrian-peterson-appeal-suspension-denied. Peterson and the NFLPA then filed a federal suit seeking to vacate the arbitration award because Henderson exceeded his authority. Josh Katzowiz, *NFLPA files lawsuit vs. NFL in Adrian Peterson suspension case,* CBSSports.com, Dec. 15, 2014, http://www.cbssports.com/nfl/eye-on-football/24890919/report-nflpa-files-lawsuit-vs-nfl-in-adrian-peterson-case. The Eighth Circuit reversed the district court's vacatur, concluding that "the parties bargained to be bound by the decision of the arbitrator, and the arbitrator acted within his authority." Matt Bonesteel, *Federal appeals court sides with NFL in Adrian Peterson case,* WashPost. com, Aug. 4, 2016, https://www.washingtonpost.com/news/early-lead/wp/ 2016/08/04/federal-appeals-court-sides-with-nfl-in-adrian-peterson-case/.

The Rice and Peterson matters raise a host of important questions about a league's power to discipline a player. Should a league's disciplinary power apply to off-the-field conduct in the same way it applies to on-the-field conduct? Should the fact that prosecutors choose to indict a player for off-the-field conduct (as they did with respect to Peterson but not with respect to Rice) impact a league's disciplinary authority or decisions? To avoid impropriety or the appearance of impropriety in any given case (e.g., a former league executive ruling for the league in a dispute with a player), should all appeals from league disciplinary decisions be heard by the same non-league affiliated independent arbitrator or arbitration body?

In December 2014, the NFL's 32 owners unanimously passed a new Personal Conduct Policy to address concerns regarding players' on-the-field as well as off-the-field conduct. With respect to off-the-field conduct, the policy "provides for clinical evaluations and follow-up education, counseling or treatment programs for anyone arrested or charged with conduct that would violate the policy; states clubs are obligated to promptly report any possible violations that come to their attention; and forms a conduct committee of NFL owners who will review the policy annually and recommend appropriate changes." In addition, the policy reassigns initial disciplinary authority in personal conduct matters from Commissioner Goodell to a "member of the league office staff who will be a highly-qualified individual with a criminal justice background." Tom Pelissero, *NFL owners pass new personal conduct policy*, USA Today, Dec. 10. 2014, http://www.usatoday.com/story/sports/nfl/2014/12/10/roger-goodell-nfl-owners-personal-conduct-policy/20199033/.

Notwithstanding passage of the Personal Conduct Policy (PCP) and the NFL's "No More" anti-domestic violence campaign, which was launched in early 2015, domestic violence committed by players, and the league's response to it, has continued to cause great concern as well as litigation. In August of 2016, the NFL suspended New York Giants kicker Josh Brown for one-game as punishment for assaulting his wife in the summer of 2015. The suspension sparked widespread outrage as insufficient under the PCP and as trivializing domestic violence. In August of 2017, after having investigated domestic violence allegations against Dallas Cowboys running back Ezekiel Elliott related to incidents that occurred a year earlier, the NFL imposed a much harsher penalty against Elliott than it initially had against Brown: a six-game suspension. The following month, the NFL added six games to Brown's suspension. Brown, by then out of the league, did not appeal his suspension. Elliott, however, appealed his suspension.

As in the Adrian Peterson case, Commissioner Goodell used his power under the NFL CBA to appoint an arbitrator of his choice to hear the appeal and again appointed Harold Henderson, who again sided with Goodell, upholding Elliott's suspension and denying his appeal. The NFLPA then sued the NFL in federal court, claiming, as it had in the Peterson and "deflate-gate" cases, that the disciplinary process was fundamentally unfair. In a flurry of federal district and appellate court decisions, the principle one being *National Football League Management Council v. National Football League Players Ass'n*, 296 F. Supp. 3d (S.D.N.Y. 2017), the suspension was put on hold and reinstated three times before Elliott and the NFLPA finally dropped the lawsuit in November of 2017 and Elliott began serving the suspension. Jenna Thomas, *The Ezekiel Elliott suspension explained in a 2-minute read*, SBNation.com, Dec. 17, 2017, https://www.sbnation.com/2017/11/19/16666714/ezekiel-elliott-nfl-suspension-cowboys-ex. The Elliott case further cemented Goodell's disciplinary authority as granted to him by the CBA and again showed that courts generally defer to the parties' chosen dispute resolution process.

Some legal scholars find fault with the NFLPA's litigation strategy, which they say "routinely frames the motion to vacate in federal court under the very narrow standard appropriate to judicial review of an independent labor arbitrator." Steven Ross and Roy Eisenhardt, *Clear Statement Rules and the Integrity of Labor Arbitration*, 10 Arbitration L. Rev. 1, 3 (2018). They believe this is the wrong standard for reviewing Article 46 Commissioner discipline: "The appropriate standard is the common law baseline that would have existed were the employees not protected by a collective bargaining agreement." *Id.* at 34.

The NFL is not the only sports league for which domestic violence has been a problem. It impacts all sports leagues, just as it impacts all of society. Indeed, in August of 2015, in the wake of the Rice and Peterson matters as well as other incidents of professional athletes committing domestic violence, MLB and the MLBPA announced a Joint Domestic Violence, Sexual Assault & Child Abuse Policy. Under the policy, the league can "suspend players with pay when legal charges are pending in 'exceptional cases'" and can discipline players "for 'just cause'" even when there has been no criminal conviction. See *New MLB domestic violence policy has no maximum, minimum penalties*, ESPN.com, Aug. 21, 2015, http://espn.go.com/mlb/story/_/id/13485353/mlb-players-union-announce-domestic-violence-policy. Yankees' relief pitcher Aroldis Chapman, who had allegedly choked his girlfriend but was not charged with a crime, was the first player suspended under this policy. His suspension lasted 30 games during the 2016 season. A player may challenge the discipline imposed under the policy before a neutral arbitrator or arbitration panel, but Chapman opted not to do so. See *Aroldis Chapman banned 30 games under MLB domestic violence policy*, ESPN.com, Mar. 1, 2016, http://espn.go.com/mlb/story/_/id/14878838/aroldis-chapman-new-york-yankees-suspended-30-games.

For differing perspectives on disciplining players in professional sports, see Joshua S. E. Lee, *Sports Scandals from the Top-Down: Comparative Analysis of Management, Owner, and Athletic Discipline in the NFL & NBA*, 23 Jeffery S. Moorad Sports L. J. 69 (2014); Michael R. Wilson, *Why So Stern?: The Growing Power of the NBA Commissioner*, 7 DePaul J. Sports L. Contemp. Probs. 45 (2010); Janine Young Kim and Matthew J. Parlow, *Off-Court Misbehavior: Sports Leagues and Private Punishment*, 99 J. Crim. L. & Criminology 573 (2009); Colin J. Daniels and Aaron Brooks, *From the Black Sox to the Sky Box: The Evolution and Mechanics of Commissioner Authority*, 10 Tex. Rev. Ent. & Sports L. 23 (2008).

5. *Preemption of State Claims.* This is an important threshold issue that has arisen in post-disciplinary litigation by unionized professional athletes against their respective leagues and clubs as well as more frequently in other litigation in which breach of contract or tort claims are asserted. In *Sprewell, supra* Note 2, the Ninth Circuit observed:

> The Supreme Court has held that federal law exclusively governs suits for breach of a CBA, while concomitantly preempting state law claims predicated on such agreements. *See Allis-Chalmers Corp. v. Lueck*, 471 U.S. 202, 210, 105 S. Ct. 1904, 85 L. Ed. 2d 206 (1985). The Court has expanded the preemptive reach of section 301 [of the Labor Management Relations Act] beyond contract claims, holding that section 301 "also preempts tort claims which, 'as applied, would frustrate the federal labor-contract scheme established in § 301.'" . . . A state law claim is preempted by section 301 when it is "substantially dependent" on analysis of a CBA. . . . Stated alternatively, "[i]f the plaintiff's claim cannot be resolved without interpreting the applicable CBA . . . it is preempted." . . . "[T]he bare fact that a collective bargaining agreement will be consulted in the course of state-law litigation," however, does not require that the state-claim be extinguished. . . . Nor is a state-law claim preempted merely because the defendant has raised a defense based on the terms of a CBA.

266 F.3d at 990.

The court ruled that Sprewell's state law unfair business practices claim based on the Warriors' termination of his player contract and NBA disciplinary action imposed on him resulting from his altercation with his former coach was preempted by Section 301 of the Labor Relations Act because it "requires an interpretation of the disciplinary provisions of the CBA." *Id.* at 992.

On the other hand, the court held that Sprewell's state claims alleging that his team and the league interfered with his contracts with third parties by issuing defamatory media reports were not preempted. The Ninth Circuit ruled these claims arose under California law independent of the terms of the collective bargaining agreement.

Following *Sprewell,* courts have continued to struggle with preemption issues. For instance, in *Atwater v. NFLPA,* 2009 WL 3254925 (N.D. Ga. March 27, 2009), six former NFL players and their spouses sued the NFL and the NFLPA alleging that the NFLPA breached its duty to them by negligently performing background checks on certain financial advisors who participated in the NFLPA's Financial Advisors Program. The NFLPA filed a motion for summary judgment asserting that Section 301 preempted all of plaintiffs' state claims. In addressing the issue, the federal district court—using a slightly different formulation than that used in *Sprewell,* but one also endorsed by the Supreme Court—stated that a tort action is governed by federal law if it is "inextricably intertwined" with a collective bargaining agreement. *Id.* at *6. Finding that the plaintiffs' state claims fell within the parameters of this standard and that resolution of those claims would therefore require an interpretation of the CBA, the court granted defendants' motion for summary judgment regarding preemption of plaintiffs' state claims.

In *Duerson v. National Football League,* 2012 WL 1658353 (N.D. Ill. May 11, 2012), a case in which the family of deceased former Chicago Bears safety Dave Duerson sued the NFL for wrongful death under the theory that Duerson's suicide resulted from brain damage he suffered while playing in the league, the court commented on the factually intensive nature of Section 301 preemption questions: "As one would expect in case-by-case analysis, in some situations preemption is found and in others it is not." *Id.* at *5. The court ruled that the Duersons' claims were preempted because they were "substantially dependent on the interpretation of CBA provisions." *Id.* at *5-6. In *Dent v. Nat'l Football League,* 2014 WL 7205048 (N.D. Cal.), a group of eight former NFL players brought suit against the NFL, asserting that to keep players in games, NFL teams routinely, and sometimes illegally, supplied players with large amounts of powerful pain-killing drugs without regard for the adverse medical effects such dosages could have on players' health. Citing Section 301 of the Labor Management Relations Act, which governs "[s]uits for violation of contracts between an employer and a labor organization," the NFL moved to dismiss the suit, arguing that even if the plaintiffs' claims were true, the NFL CBA provided the exclusive bargained-for remedies and pointed out that in some cases the plaintiffs had previously sought those remedies. The district court granted the NFL's motion to dismiss because "preemption does not require that the preempted state law claim be replaced by an analogue claim in the collective-bargaining agreement . . . . Nevertheless, the types of claims asserted in the operative complaint are grievable in important respects under the various CBAs." *Id.* at *2, 11. The Ninth Circuit disagreed, rejecting the NFL's argument that the players should be bound by the CBA's grievance procedures. *Dent v. Nat'l Football League*, 902 F.3d 1109 (9th Cir. 2018). On remand, the district court found for the NFL on the merits, determining that the players failed to establish that the NFL breached its duty of care in distributing controlled substances. *Dent v. Nat'l Football League*, 2019 WL 1745118, at *1 (N.D. Cal.).

iii.   Side Deals and Undisclosed Agreements

It is generally required that all agreements between a club and player be filed with the league, and leagues generally do not recognize undisclosed side deals. This does not necessarily mean side deals are unenforceable in a court of law, but they may be prohibited by league rules or a collective bargaining agreement. With the prevalence of league salary caps and other restrictive devices that limit player salaries, the temptation to enter side deals in an effort to provide additional player compensation has increased. The response by leagues has been to impose sanctions on the involved parties, so both clubs and players (as well as their agents) must hesitate before exploring prohibited or undisclosed means of compensation.

For example, in *Arbitration Between National Football League Players Association (Elvin Bethea) and NFL Management Council (Houston Oilers)* (April 17, 1978), Elvin Bethea, a defensive lineman for the Houston Oilers, agreed to a lower salary after he was encouraged by the Oilers owner, head coach, and general manager to participate in a cattle-feeding partnership from which he expected to receive 10 percent of the profits. The operation was a failure, and the partnership was dissolved. Bethea demanded that the Oilers pay him the yearly profit he expected to receive from the cattle-feeding venture over the term of his three-year contract, but the club refused. In protest, Bethea skipped training camp for six to eight days and was fined. Bethea initiated a noninjury grievance, claiming that the club was liable to him for $20,000, $40,000, and $60,000 for 1977, 1978, and 1979. He also sought immediate payment of all salary monies previously deferred. Arbitrator Searce concluded that:

> The partnership was established over a month before his player contracts and not as a package deal. The agreement did not set forth as a condition that Bethea would have to sign his player contracts. Also, neither the agreement nor the parties' conversations contained an express guarantee of returns from the partnership.

Thus, Searce found that the partnership agreement was not part of the NFL Player Contract and the club was not in breach of contract or in violation of Article XIX.

As a more recent example, *In the Matter of National Basketball Association Minnesota Timberwolves, Joe Smith and Eric Fleisher* (Nov. 9, 2000), an arbitrator found that Joe Smith, a Minnesota Timberwolves player, and the club entered into an undisclosed letter agreement dated January 22, 1999. Apparently, the letter agreement provided for a series of contracts that would be signed in the future requiring that the Timberwolves pay Smith a total of $84 million. The NBA argued that "the undisclosed agreement kept other teams from enticing Smith away because Smith had figuratively in his pocket the promise of many millions in the future, a promise that other teams could not make consistently with the CBA." The letter agreement constituted a violation of Article XIII, §2, which prohibits undisclosed agreements.

It was clear that the NBA commissioner possessed the power to void Smith's contract for the upcoming season. The narrow issue before the arbitrator was the commissioner's authority to void any player contract Smith and the Timberwolves might enter into in the future. After reviewing the CBA, arbitrator Kenneth M. Dam wrote, "I conclude that the Commissioner does have the authority to void contracts not yet entered into at the time of the violation. . . . If the Commissioner, having voided the existing contract, simply voids the same contract when resubmitted (with new signatures and a new signature date), he is still voiding 'upon a violation of Section 2.'" The arbitrator also noted that the matter before him extended beyond the imposition of a penalty on Smith, but also involved the need to maintain competitive balance and the integrity of the league's salary cap, which are primary objectives that the rule against undisclosed agreements is designed to further. See Jeffrey A. Mishkin, *Dispute Resolution in the NBA: The Allocation of Decision Making Among the Commissioner, Impartial Arbitrator, System Arbitrator, and the Courts*, 35 Val. U. L. Rev. 449, 456-57 (2001) (discussing the Smith matter).

D.   THE INTERSECTION OF ANTITRUST AND LABOR LAW

One of the more perplexing aspects of labor relations in professional sports is the intersection of antitrust law and labor law. It is important to understand the inherent tension between these two bodies of federal law. Labor law permits employees and employers to engage in joint conduct among themselves, and with each other, that otherwise may violate antitrust law.

The objective of federal antitrust law is to promote competition among buyers and sellers of goods and services (including labor). Section 1 of the Sherman Act prohibits agreements that unreasonably restrain interstate trade or commerce. 15 U.S.C. §1. Applied literally, §1 prohibits both employees and employers from engaging in joint activity or making agreements that unreasonably restrain the labor market. Section 1 requires employers in an industry (e.g., league clubs) to compete independently for employee (e.g., player) services. Similarly, employees such as professional athletes must individually compete for employment with teams. Theoretically, consumers will benefit because the operation of free market forces in the labor market will result in the most efficient allocation of human resources.

On the other hand, federal labor law permits employees of private employers, including professional athletes, to unionize and collectively bargain, which is an allowable form of anticompetitive behavior. Multiemployer bargaining within an industry, which is similarly anticompetitive, is legal under labor law. Such concerted action among otherwise competing groups of employees (e.g., players) and employers (e.g., league clubs) squarely conflicts with §1 of the Sherman Act.

In the early 1900s, employers outside the professional sports industries successfully used §1 of the Sherman Act (enacted in 1890) to thwart employees' efforts to unionize and collectively bargain their terms of employment. See *Loewe v. Lawlor*, 208 U.S. 274 (1908) (union subject to §1 liability for boycotting hat manufacturers in an effort to obtain higher wages and working conditions). In 1914, Congress responded by enacting §6 of the Clayton Act, which provides in relevant part:

> The labor of a human being is not a commodity or article of commerce. Nothing contained in the antitrust laws shall be construed to forbid the existence and operation of labor . . . organizations, instituted for the purposes of mutual help . . . or to forbid or restrain individual members of such organizations from lawfully carrying out the legitimate objects thereof; nor shall such organizations, or the members thereof, be held or construed to be illegal combinations or conspiracies in restraint of trade, under the antitrust laws.

15 U.S.C. §17.

In 1934, Congress enacted the Norris-LaGuardia Act, 29 U.S.C. §§101-115, because courts were narrowly construing the scope of union activities immunized from antitrust liability under §6 of the Clayton Act. The combined effect of these laws is to create a *statutory labor exemption*, which provides a labor union with immunity from antitrust liability for its unilateral efforts to further its members' economic interests. Thus, in general, union collective bargaining activities over issues of wages, hours, and conditions of employment as well as strikes, picketing, and boycotts of employers do not violate antitrust law. *United States v. Hutcheson*, 312 U.S. 219 (1941). To facilitate the collective bargaining process, courts have held that the activities of multiemployer bargaining units to further their members' common interests, such as collective strike insurance and lockouts, also are protected by the statutory exemption. *Kennedy v. Long Island Rail Road Co.*, 319 F.2d 366 (2d Cir. 1963), *cert. denied*, 375 U.S. 830 (1963).

In the 1970s, in addition to labor law, players sought to use antitrust law to advance their economic interests by challenging league-imposed labor market restraints such as player drafts and free agency restrictions. In defense, professional leagues and clubs asserted that the statutory labor exemption bars these antitrust claims (an ironic assertion given that the exemption primarily is intended to shield union activity from antitrust immunity). Courts have uniformly rejected this argument. *Smith v. Pro Football, Inc.*, 593 F.2d 1173, 1175 n.2 (D.C. Cir. 1978) ("athletes have standing to challenge player restrictions in professional sports since the restraints operate directly on, and to the detriment of, the employee"); *Mackey v. National Football League*, 543 F.2d 606, 618 (8th Cir. 1976) ("restraints on competition within the market for players' services fall within the ambit of the Sherman Act"); *McNeil v. National Football League*, 790 F. Supp. 871, 881 (D. Minn. 1992) (rejecting league's contention that "restraints that operate solely in a labor market are outside the scope of the antitrust laws").

In *Brown v. Pro Football, Inc.*, 1992 WL 88039 at *4 (D.D.C Mar. 10, 1992), *rev'd on other grounds*, 50 F.3d 1041 (D.C. Cir. 1995), the court explained:

> Contrary to defendants' assertion, wage-fixing restraints which affect the labor market are considered price-fixing restraints subject to the antitrust laws. Section 6 of the Clayton Act does not exempt such restraints from antitrust liability: "It is readily apparent that Congress, in enacting § 6, was concerned with the right of labor and similar organizations to continue engaging in [activities which otherwise would be considered antitrust violations], including the right to strike, not with the right of employers to band together for joint action in fixing the wages to be paid by each employer."

Throughout the 1970s, NFL players successfully challenged the then-existing 16-round draft and certain free agency restrictions on antitrust grounds. See, e.g., *Smith v. Pro Football, Inc.*, 593 F.2d 1173 (D.C. Cir. 1978); *Kapp v. National Football League*, 586 F.2d 644 (9th Cir. 1978); *Mackey v. National Football League*, 543 F.2d 606 (8th Cir. 1976). Antitrust litigation challenging similar restraints unilaterally implemented by the NBA and NHL also was successful. *Robertson v. National Basketball Assn.*, 389 F. Supp. 867 (S.D.N.Y. 1975); *Philadelphia World Hockey Club, Inc. v. Philadelphia Hockey Club, Inc.*, 351 F. Supp. 462 (E.D. Pa. 1972). From the players' perspective, the antitrust laws became powerful weapons for effectuating changes in how sports leagues conduct business vis-à-vis the players. However, MLB's unique common law antitrust exemption barred professional baseball players' antitrust claims. *Flood v. Kuhn*, 407 U.S. 258 (1972).

Although federal antitrust law may be used by players to invalidate league rules that effectively limit their salaries or ability to play for the club of their choosing as well as other restraints on their employment, it is only prohibitory rather than remedial in nature. In other words, although antitrust law prohibits league clubs from unreasonably restraining the market for player services, it does not require them to agree to or implement any particular terms and conditions of employment. Courts that struck down various restraints observed that the collective bargaining process governed by labor law, rather than antitrust litigation, should resolve labor disputes between players and clubs. *Smith v. Pro Football, Inc.*, 593 F.2d 1173, 1188 (D.C. Cir. 1978) ("We are not required in this case to design a draft that would pass muster under the antitrust laws"); *Mackey v. National Football League*, 543 F.2d 606, 623 (8th Cir. 1976) ("The parties are far better situated to agreeably resolve what rules governing player transfers are best suited for their mutual interests than the courts"). See also *Philadelphia World Hockey Club, Inc. v. Philadelphia Hockey Club, Inc.*, 351 F. Supp. 462 (E.D. Pa. 1972); *Flood v. Kuhn*, 316 F. Supp. 271 (S.D.N.Y. 1970). As a result, leagues and their member clubs attempted to reinstate player restraints such as the draft, free agent restrictions, and a salary cap (usually in modified form) through collective bargaining with player unions. However, the statutory labor exemption, which applies only to unilateral union conduct, does not immunize the terms of collective bargaining agreements with employers from antitrust challenge. *Connell Construction Co. v. Plumbers, Local 100*, 421 U.S. 616 (1975); *Mackey v. National Football League*, 543 F.2d 606, 611 (8th Cir. 1976) (this exemption "does not extend to concerted action or agreements between unions and non-labor groups").

Connell Construction recognized the need for a *nonstatutory labor exemption* to further "the strong labor policy favoring the association of employees to eliminate competition over wages and working conditions" through collective bargaining. 421 U.S. at 622. The following materials explore the contours of the nonstatutory labor exemption in the context of collective bargaining between league clubs and players unions as well as whether nonimmunized player restraints violate antitrust law. While reading and analyzing these cases, consider the following questions: (1) Does the nonstatutory labor exemption immunize the terms of an existing collective bargaining agreement from antitrust challenge? If so, why and under what conditions? (2) If the collective bargaining agreement has expired, are its provisions still protected by this exemption, and if so, for how long? (3) After a collective bargaining agreement expires, can league clubs unilaterally implement new terms and practices that are permissible under labor law without incurring antitrust liability? (4) If the nonstatutory labor exemption is not applicable, when do player restraints (e.g., player drafts, limits on player salaries, veteran free agency restrictions) violate antitrust law? As a matter of policy, also consider whether courts are appropriately balancing the competing objectives of antitrust law and labor law regarding labor relations in professional sports.

1. *Judicial Application of the Nonstatutory Labor Exemption to Terms of an Existing Collective Bargaining Agreement*

Mackey v. NFL, 543 F.2d 606 (8th Cir. 1976), is an early case considering the intersection of antitrust and labor law, which was decided a few years after the first collective bargaining agreements were reached in professional team sports. Today *Mackey* is important primarily for historical reasons because it established the elements of the nonstatutory labor exemption and provided an initial judicial view regarding the underlying rationale for this antitrust immunity. Subsequent cases, particularly *Powell v. NFL* and *Brown v. Pro Football, Inc.*, supra, have expanded significantly the scope of the nonstatutory labor exemption, thereby limiting *Mackey's* current importance.

Mackey considered the validity of the NFL's Rozelle Rule, so named because it was unilaterally fashioned and applied by then-commissioner Pete Rozelle from 1963 until it was successfully challenged on antitrust grounds by a group of NFL players. This rule had two components, which adversely affected free agent players' mobility and salaries. First, if a club signed a free agent who had previously played for another club, the signing club owed the other club "compensation." Second, if the two clubs could not agree what the "compensation" should be, Commissioner Rozelle made that determination. This compensation, either agreed to by the clubs or ordered by the commissioner, could be in the form of draft choices, players, cash, or a combination thereof.

MACKEY v. NFL
543 F.2d 606 (8th Cir. 1976)

LAY, Circuit Judge.

This is an appeal by the National Football League (NFL), twenty-six of its member clubs, and its Commissioner, Alvin Ray "Pete" Rozelle, from a district court judgment holding the "Rozelle Rule" to be violative of § 1 of the Sherman Act, and enjoining its enforcement. This action was initiated by a group of present and former NFL players . . . alleg[ing] that the defendants' enforcement of the Rozelle Rule constituted an illegal combination and conspiracy in restraint of trade denying professional football players the right to freely contract for their services. Plaintiffs sought injunctive relief and treble damages. . . .

The district court held that the defendants' enforcement of the Rozelle Rule constituted a concerted refusal to deal and a group boycott, and was therefore a per se violation of the Sherman Act. Alternatively, finding that the evidence offered in support of the clubs' contention that the Rozelle Rule is necessary to the successful operation of the NFL insufficient to justify the restrictive effects of the Rule, the court concluded that the Rozelle Rule was invalid under the Rule of Reason standard. Finally, the court rejected the clubs' argument that the Rozelle Rule was immune from attack under the Sherman Act because it had been the subject of a collective bargaining agreement between the club owners and the National Football League Players Association (NFLPA). . .

HISTORY

. . . For a number of years, the NFL has operated under a reserve system whereby every player who signs a contract with an NFL club is bound to play for that club, and no other, for the term of the contract plus one additional year at the option of the club. . . . Once a player signs a Standard Player Contract, he is bound to his team for at least two years. He may, however, become a free agent at the end of the option year by playing that season under a renewed contract rather than signing a new one. A player "playing out his option" is subject to a 10% salary cut during the option year.

Prior to 1963, a team which signed a free agent who had previously been under contract to another club was not obligated to compensate the player's former club. In 1963, after R.C. Owens played out his option with the San Francisco 49ers and signed a contract with the Baltimore Colts, the member clubs of the NFL unilaterally adopted the following provision, now known as the Rozelle Rule, as an amendment to the League's Constitution and Bylaws:

> Whenever a player, becoming a free agent in such manner, thereafter signed a contract with a different club in the League, then, unless mutually satisfactory arrangements have been concluded between the two League clubs, the Commissioner may name and then award to the former club one or more players, from the Active, Reserve, or Selection List (including future selection choices) of the acquiring club as the Commissioner in his sole discretion deems fair and equitable; any such decision by the Commissioner shall be final and conclusive.

. . . During the period from 1963 through 1974, 176 players played out their options. Of that number, 34 signed with other teams. In three of those cases, the former club waived compensation. In 27 cases, the clubs involved mutually agreed upon compensation. Commissioner Rozelle awarded compensation in the four remaining cases. . . .

THE LABOR EXEMPTION ISSUE

. . . To determine the applicability of the nonstatutory exemption we must first decide whether there has been any agreement between the parties concerning the Rozelle Rule. . . .

GOVERNING PRINCIPLES

Under the general principles surrounding the labor exemption, the availability of the nonstatutory exemption for a particular agreement turns upon whether the relevant federal labor policy is deserving of pre-eminence over federal antitrust policy under the circumstances of the particular case. . . .

We find the proper accommodation to be: First, the labor policy favoring collective bargaining may potentially be given pre-eminence over the antitrust laws where the restraint on trade primarily affects only the parties to the collective bargaining relationship. . . . Second, federal labor policy is implicated sufficiently to prevail only where the agreement sought to be exempted concerns a mandatory subject of collective bargaining. . . . Finally, the policy favoring collective bargaining is furthered to the degree necessary to override the antitrust laws only where the agreement sought to be exempted is the product of bona fide arm's-length bargaining. . . .

APPLICATION

Applying these principles to the facts presented here, we think it clear that the alleged restraint on trade effected by the Rozelle Rule affects only the parties to the agreements sought to be exempted. Accordingly, we must inquire as to the other two principles: whether the Rozelle Rule is a mandatory subject of collective bargaining, and whether the agreements thereon were the product of bona fide arm's-length negotiation. . . .

MANDATORY SUBJECT OF BARGAINING

Under § 8(d) of the National Labor Relations Act, 29 U.S.C. § 158(d), mandatory subjects of bargaining pertain to "wages, hours, and other terms and conditions of employment. . . ." See *NLRB v. Borg-Warner Corp.*, 356 U.S. 342, 78 S. Ct. 718, 2 L. Ed. 2d 823 (1958). Whether an agreement concerns a mandatory subject depends not on its form but on its practical effect. . . .

On its face, the Rozelle Rule does not deal with "wages, hours and other terms or conditions of employment" but with inter-team compensation when a player's contractual obligation to one team expires and he is signed by another. Viewed as such, it would not constitute a mandatory subject of collective bargaining. The district court found, however, that the Rule operates to restrict a player's ability to move from one team to another and depresses player salaries. There is substantial evidence in the record to support these findings. Accordingly, we hold that the Rozelle Rule constitutes a mandatory bargaining subject within the meaning of the National Labor Relations Act.

BONA FIDE BARGAINING

The district court found that the parties' collective bargaining history reflected nothing which could be legitimately characterized as bargaining over the Rozelle Rule; that, in part due to its recent formation and inadequate finances, the NFLPA, at least prior to 1974, stood in a relatively weak bargaining position vis-a-vis the clubs; and that "the Rozelle Rule was unilaterally imposed by the NFL and member club defendants upon the players in 1963 and has been imposed on the players from 1963 through the present date."

On the basis of our independent review of the record, including the parties' bargaining history as set forth above, we find substantial evidence to support the finding that there was no bona fide arm's-length bargaining over the Rozelle Rule preceding the execution of the 1968 and 1970 agreements. The

Rule imposes significant restrictions on players, and its form has remained unchanged since it was unilaterally promulgated by the clubs in 1963. The provisions of the collective bargaining agreements which operated to continue the Rozelle Rule do not in and of themselves inure to the benefit of the players or their union. . . .

In view of the foregoing, we hold that the agreements between the clubs and the players embodying the Rozelle Rule do not qualify for the labor exemption. . . .

NOTES AND QUESTIONS

1. In the context of player restraints, the *Mackey* case recognized that the nonstatutory labor exemption may immunize a professional league and its member clubs from antitrust liability. According to *Mackey*, what are the elements of the nonstatutory labor exemption? Why was it found to be inapplicable in this case?

2. In a related case, the Eighth Circuit strongly suggested that none of the terms of the current collective bargaining agreement are subject to antitrust scrutiny, regardless of whether the challenged specific provision(s) were the product of bona fide arm's-length (i.e., quid pro quo) negotiation as apparently required by *Mackey*. In that case, *Reynolds v. National Football League*, 584 F.2d 280 (8th Cir. 1978), the precise question before the court was the fairness of the settlement in the *Mackey* antitrust litigation. This settlement resulted in a new collective bargaining agreement between the NFL Management Council for the owners and the National Football League Players Association. Several NFL players objected to the settlement terms and corresponding provisions in the new collective bargaining agreement. The court held that the overall settlement was fair and denied the players' protests.

   After *Mackey*, other federal appellate courts broadly held that the terms of existing collective bargaining agreements are not subject to antitrust attack. In *McCourt v. California Sports, Inc.*, 600 F.2d 1193 (6th Cir. 1979), the Sixth Circuit rejected an antitrust challenge to the NHL's "equalization payment" compensation system. At issue was the compensation that a club signing a free agent must pay to his former club. An NHL bylaw establishing the procedure for determining this compensation was incorporated into the league's collective bargaining agreement. Pursuant to this procedure, an arbitrator ordered that Dale McCourt be transferred from the Detroit Red Wings to the Los Angeles Kings as compensation for the former club's free agency acquisition of Rogatien Vachon. McCourt asserted that the bylaw violated antitrust law. The court found that the nonstatutory labor exemption barred McCourt's antitrust claims because all three elements of the *Mackey* test were satisfied. The court concluded "that the inclusion of the reserve system in the collective bargaining agreement was the product of good faith, arm's length bargaining." *Id.* at 1203.

   In *Wood v. National Basketball Assn.*, 809 F.2d 954 (2d Cir. 1987), the Second Circuit held that even players such as draft-eligible rookies who are not yet playing in the league are barred from challenging the terms of an existing collective bargaining agreement on antitrust grounds. Despite being the Philadelphia 76ers' first-round draft choice, the club offered Leon Wood only a one-year, $75,000 contract. Because the 76ers' player payroll exceeded the amount permitted by the NBA's salary cap, this was the maximum amount that the club could offer Wood pursuant to the league's collective bargaining agreement. Wood claimed that the NBA salary cap and college draft violated antitrust law by reducing competition among league clubs for the services of college basketball players.

The Second Circuit initially observed that antitrust law should not be used "to subvert fundamental principles of our federal labor policy," which encourages collective bargaining by workers. *Id.* at 959. Refusing to address the merits of Wood's antitrust claims, the court explained:

> Freedom of contract is an important cornerstone of national labor policy for two reasons. First, it allows an employer and a union to agree upon those arrangements that best suit their particular interests. . . . Courts cannot hope to fashion contract terms more efficient than those arrived at by the parties who are to be governed by them. Second, freedom of contract furthers the goal of labor peace. To the extent that courts prohibit particular solutions for particular problems, they reduce the number and quality of compromises available to unions and employers for resolving their differences.
>
> Freedom of contract is particularly important in the context of collective bargaining between professional athletes and their leagues. Such bargaining relationships raise numerous problems with little or no precedent in standard industrial relations. As a result, leagues and player unions may reach seemingly unfamiliar or strange agreements. If courts were to intrude and to outlaw such solutions, leagues and their player unions would have to arrange their affairs in a less efficient way. It would also increase the chances of strikes by reducing the number and quality of possible compromises.

Id. at 960.

Relying on labor law policy that "allows employees to seek the best deal for the greatest number" through union collective bargaining on their behalf, the court held that "Wood's [antitrust] claim is beyond peradventure one that implicates the labor market and subverts federal labor policy." *Id.* at 959 and 963. Thus, Wood's only potentially viable claim for harm to his individual economic interests was against the NBA players union for breaching its duty of fair representation.

In contrast to *Wood*, which involved an NBA first-round draft choice who was eligible to join the players union as soon as he signed a contract with the club that drafted him, the following case involves an athlete's claim that a professional sports league's eligibility rules, which have the imprimatur of the players union, exclude him from league employment in violation of antitrust law. *Clarett* raises the concept of the "hiring hall" in labor relations, pursuant to which a union can enter into agreements that affect prospective future employees outside the bargaining unit.

CLARETT v. NFL
369 F.3d 124 (2d Cir. 2004), *cert. denied*, 544 U.S. 961 (2005)

SOTOMAYOR, Circuit Judge.

[EDS. Maurice Clarett wanted to play in the National Football League despite his inability to comply with a league rule limiting eligibility to players three seasons removed from their high school graduation. Clarett was a star freshman football player while attending Ohio State University (OSU) and was in his sophomore year at the time he filed this lawsuit. He claimed he was ready, willing, and able to play in the NFL and that his exclusion violated antitrust law.

In his short collegiate career, Clarett's credentials as a football player were impressive. In the 2002-2003 collegiate season, Clarett—the first freshman starter at running back for OSU since 1943—led his team to an undefeated (14-0) season that was capped by a 31-24 double-overtime victory over University of Miami in the Fiesta Bowl, OSU's first national championship in 34 years. As a result of his resounding freshman-year success, Clarett was named the Big Ten Freshman of the Year and voted the best running back in college football by *The Sporting News*.

Ohio State suspended Clarett for the entire 2003 college football season because of concerns that he violated NCAA amateurism rules. When this suit was filed there was some question whether the NCAA would permit him to play during the 2004 season, and the NFL may have been his only real option for playing football the next year.

The current CBA took effect on May 6, 1993, and was to expire in 2007. That CBA, along with the League's Constitution and Bylaws, comprehensively outlines the relationship between the players and the League, covering the operation of the League, player salary and the player draft, including detailed rules by which the teams select new players. Two provisions of that CBA are at issue here. Article III, section 1, provides:

> This Agreement represents the complete understanding of the parties on all subjects covered herein, and there will be no change in the terms and conditions of this Agreement without mutual consent. . . . [T]he NFLPA and the Management Council *waive all rights to bargain with one another concerning any subject covered or not covered in this Agreement* for the duration of this Agreement, *including the provisions of the NFL Constitution and Bylaws. . . .*

Article IV, section 2, entitled "No Suit," provides:

> [N]either the NFLPA nor any of its members, agents acting on its behalf, nor any members of its bargaining unit will sue, or support financially or administratively any suit against, the NFL or any Club relating to the presently existing provisions of the Constitution and Bylaws of the NFL as they are currently operative and administered. . . .

Clarett and the NFL disagree on whether these two provisions establish that the NFL and the players union actually bargained over the terms of the Constitution and Bylaws (which contained the eligibility rule at issue), or merely bargained away the NFLPA's ability to bargain over or challenge the Bylaws' provisions.

With respect to the 2004 draft, the Commissioner issued a release that included the following iteration of the Rule:

> **SPECIAL ELIGIBILITY.** . . . Any applications for special eligibility must be in the Commissioner's office no later than Thursday, January 15, 2004, if the player is to be considered for inclusion in the League's principal draft scheduled for April 24-25, 2004. Applications will be accepted only for college players for whom at least three full *college seasons* have elapsed since their high school graduation. . . .]

. . . Clarett argues that the NFL clubs are horizontal competitors for the labor of professional football players and thus may not agree that a player will be hired only after three full football seasons have elapsed following that player's high school graduation. That characterization, however, neglects that the labor market for NFL players is organized around a collective bargaining relationship that is provided for and promoted by federal labor law, and that the NFL clubs, as a multi-employer bargaining unit, can act jointly in setting the terms and conditions of players' employment and the rules of the sport without risking antitrust liability. For those reasons, the NFL argues that federal labor law favoring and governing the collective bargaining process precludes the application of the antitrust laws to its eligibility rules. . . .

Relying on *Mackey*, the district court below held that the nonstatutory exemption provides no protection to the NFL's draft eligibility rules, because the eligibility rules fail to satisfy any of the three *Mackey* factors. . . .

We, however, have never regarded the Eighth Circuit's test in *Mackey* as defining the appropriate limits of the nonstatutory exemption. . . .

Clarett does not contend that the NFL's draft eligibility rules work to the disadvantage of the NFL's competitors in the market for professional football or in some manner protect the NFL's dominance in that market. *Compare N. Am. Soccer League v. Nat'l Football League*, 670 F.2d 1249 (2d Cir. 1982). He challenges the eligibility rules only on the ground that they are an unreasonable restraint upon the market for players' services. . . . Thus, we need not decide here whether the *Mackey* factors aptly characterize the limits of the exemption in cases in which employers use agreements with their unions to disadvantage their competitors in the product or business market, because our cases have counseled a decidedly different approach where, as here, the plaintiff complains of a restraint upon a unionized labor market characterized by a collective bargaining relationship with a multi-employer bargaining unit. . . .

Our decisions in *Caldwell, Williams*, and *Wood* all involved players' claims that the concerted action of a professional sports league imposed a restraint upon the labor market for players' services and thus violated the antitrust laws. In each case, however, we held that the nonstatutory labor exemption defeated the players' claims. Our analysis in each case was rooted in the observation that the relationships among the defendant sports leagues and their players were governed by collective bargaining agreements and thus were subject to the carefully structured regime established by federal labor laws. We reasoned that to permit antitrust suits against sports leagues on the ground that their concerted action imposed a restraint upon the labor market would seriously undermine many of the policies embodied by these labor laws, including the congressional policy favoring collective bargaining, the bargaining parties' freedom of contract, and the widespread use of multi-employer bargaining units. . . .

Clarett argues that he is physically qualified to play professional football and that the antitrust laws preclude the NFL teams from agreeing amongst themselves that they will refuse to deal with him simply because he is less than three full football seasons out of high school. Such an arbitrary condition, he argues, imposes an unreasonable restraint upon the competitive market for professional football players' services, and, because it excludes him from entering that market altogether, constitutes a *per se* antitrust violation. The issue we must decide is whether subjecting the NFL's eligibility rules to antitrust scrutiny would "subvert fundamental principles of our federal labor policy." . . . For the reasons that follow, we hold that it would and that the nonstatutory exemption therefore applies.

Although the NFL has maintained draft eligibility rules in one form or another for much of its history, the "inception of a collective bargaining relationship" between the NFL and its players union some thirty years ago "irrevocably alter[ed] the governing legal regime." . . . Our prior cases highlight a number of consequences resulting from the advent of this collective bargaining relationship that are relevant to Clarett's litigation. For one, prospective players no longer have the right to negotiate directly with the NFL teams over the terms and conditions of their employment. That responsibility is instead committed to the NFL and the players union to accomplish through the collective bargaining process, and throughout that process the NFL and the players union are to have the freedom to craft creative solutions to their differences in light of the economic imperatives of their industry. Furthermore, the NFL teams are permitted to engage in joint conduct with respect to the terms and conditions of players' employment as a multi-employer bargaining unit without risking antitrust liability. The arguments Clarett advances in support of his antitrust claim, however, run counter to each of these basic principles of federal labor law.

Because the NFL players have unionized and have selected the NFLPA as its exclusive bargaining representative, labor law prohibits Clarett from negotiating directly the terms and conditions of his employment with any NFL club, . . . and an NFL club would commit an unfair labor practice were it to bargain with Clarett individually without the union's consent. . . . The terms and conditions of Clarett's employment are instead committed to the collective bargaining table and are reserved to the NFL and the players union's selected representative to negotiate. . . .

The players union's representative possesses "powers comparable to those possessed by a legislative body both to create and restrict the rights of those whom it represents." . . . In seeking the best deal for NFL players overall, the representative has the ability to advantage certain categories of players over others, subject of course to the representative's duty of fair representation. (Citation omitted.) The union representative may, for example, favor veteran players over rookies . . . and can seek to preserve jobs for current players to the detriment of new employees and the exclusion of outsiders. (Citations omitted.) This authority and exclusive responsibility is vested in the players' representative "once a mandatory collective bargaining relationship is established and continues throughout the relationship." (Citation omitted.) For the duration of that relationship, federal labor law then establishes a " 'soup-to-nuts array' of rules, tribunals and remedies to govern [the collective bargaining] process." . . .

Clarett's argument that antitrust law should permit him to circumvent this scheme established by federal labor law starts with the contention that the eligibility rules do not constitute a mandatory subject of collective bargaining and thus cannot fall within the protection of the non-statutory exemption. Contrary to the district court, however, we find that the eligibility rules are mandatory bargaining subjects. Though tailored to the unique circumstance of a professional sports league, the eligibility rules for the draft represent a quite literal condition for initial employment and for that reason alone might constitute a mandatory bargaining subject.

. . . Similarly, the complex scheme by which individual salaries in the NFL are set, which involves, *inter alia*, the NFL draft, league-wide salary pools for rookies, team salary caps, and free agency, was built around the longstanding restraint on the market for entering players imposed by the eligibility rules and the related expectations about the average career length of NFL players. The eligibility rules in other words cannot be viewed in isolation, because their elimination might well alter certain assumptions underlying the collective bargaining agreement between the NFL and its players union. . . .

Clarett, however, argues that the eligibility rules are an impermissible bargaining subject because they affect players outside of the union. But simply because the eligibility rules work a hardship on prospective rather than current employees does not render them impermissible. (Citation omitted.) The eligibility rules in this respect are not dissimilar to union demands for hiring hall arrangements that have long been recognized as mandatory subjects of bargaining. (citation omitted.) In such hiring hall arrangements, the criteria for employment are set by the rules of the hiring hall rather than the employer alone. . . . Nevertheless, such an arrangement constitutes a permissible, mandatory subject of bargaining despite the fact that it concerns prospective rather than current employees. . . .

As a permissible, mandatory subject of bargaining, the conditions under which a prospective player, like Clarett, will be considered for employment as an NFL player are for the union representative and the NFL to determine. Clarett, however, stresses that the eligibility rules are arbitrary and that requiring him to wait another football season has nothing to do with whether he is in fact qualified for professional play. But Clarett is in this respect no different from the typical worker who is confident that he or she has the skills to fill a job vacancy but does not possess the qualifications or meet the requisite criteria that have been set. In the context of this collective bargaining relationship, the NFL and its players' union can agree that an employee will not be hired or considered for employment for nearly any reason whatsoever so long as they do not violate federal laws such as those prohibiting unfair labor practices, 29 U.S.C. § 201 *et seq.*, or discrimination. . . .

Even accepting that an individual club could refuse to consider him for employment because he is less than three full seasons out of high school, Clarett contends that the NFL clubs invited antitrust liability when they agreed amongst themselves to impose that same criteria on every prospective player. As a consequence of the NFL's unique position in the professional football market, of course, such joint action deprives Clarett of the opportunity to pursue, at least for the time being, the kind of high-paying, high-profile career he desires. In the context of collective bargaining, however, federal labor policy permits the NFL teams to act collectively as a multi-employer bargaining unit in structuring the rules of play and setting the criteria for player employment. Such concerted action is encouraged as a matter of labor policy and tolerated as a matter of antitrust law. . . .

The threat to the operation of federal labor law posed by Clarett's antitrust claims is in no way diminished by Clarett's contention that the rules were not bargained over during the negotiations that preceded the current collective bargaining agreement. The eligibility rules, along with the host of other NFL rules and policies affecting the terms and conditions of NFL players included in the NFL's Constitution and Bylaws, were well known to the union, and a copy of the Constitution and Bylaws was presented to the union during negotiations. Given that the eligibility rules are a mandatory bargaining subject for the reasons set out above, the union or the NFL could have forced the other to the bargaining table if either felt that a change was warranted. . . .

. . . [T]he collective bargaining agreement itself makes clear that the union and the NFL reached an agreement with respect to how the eligibility rules would be handled. In the collective bargaining agreement, the union agreed to waive any challenge to the Constitution and Bylaws and thereby acquiesced in the continuing operation of the eligibility rules contained therein—at least for the duration of the agreement. . . . The value of such a clause to the NFL is obvious, as control over any changes to the eligibility rules is left in the hands of management at least until the expiration of the collective bargaining agreement. Although it is entirely possible that the players union might not have agreed entirely with the eligibility rules, the union representative might not have regarded any difference of opinion with respect to the eligibility rules as sufficient to warrant the expenditure of precious time at the bargaining table in light of other important issues.

Clarett would have us hold that by reaching this arrangement rather than fixing the eligibility rules in the text of the collective bargaining agreement or in failing to wrangle over the eligibility rules at the bargaining table, the NFL left itself open to antitrust liability. Such a holding, however, would completely contradict prior decisions recognizing that the labor law policies that warrant withholding antitrust scrutiny are not limited to protecting only terms contained in collective bargaining agreements. . . . The reach of those policies, rather, extends as far as is necessary to ensure the successful operation of the collective bargaining *process* and to safeguard the "unique bundle of compromises" reached by the NFL and the players' union as a means of settling their differences. It would disregard those policies completely to hold that some "particular *quid pro quo* must be proven to avoid antitrust liability" . . . or to allow Clarett to undo what we assume the NFL and its players' union regarded as the most appropriate or expedient means of settling their differences. . . .

[EDS. The Second Circuit reversed the district court's ruling regarding the applicability of the nonstatutory labor exemption and vacated its order that Clarett be made eligible for the 2004 NFL draft.]

NOTES AND QUESTIONS

1. *Clarett* characterizes professional sports league player eligibility rules as "a permissible, mandatory subject of collective bargaining." Consistent with *Clarett*, in *National Hockey League Players' Assn. v. Plymouth Whalers*, 419 F.3d 462, 474 (6th Cir. 2005), the Sixth Circuit upheld a rule prohibiting 20 year-old U.S. college hockey players from playing in the Ontario Hockey League (which has three U.S. clubs), determining that "any anti-competitive effect of a properly bargained collective bargaining agreement is excluded from antitrust scrutiny by [the] non-statutory antitrust exemption." Do these cases appropriately preclude an excluded player's antitrust claims against a league whose member clubs have agreed not to employ him even if he has the requisite skills and talent? Although Maurice Clarett could not use antitrust law to challenge his exclusion from the NFL draft, did he have an effective labor law remedy?

2. *Maurice Clarett Postscript.* After losing his suit and his chance to play in the NFL, Clarett's life took a sharp downward spiral. In February 2006, Clarett was indicted and charged with two counts of aggravated robbery and four lesser robbery charges for taking property from two people at gunpoint

in an alley behind a bar in Columbus, Ohio. Several months later, while charges were still pending in that matter, Clarett was arrested after he refused to pull over after a traffic violation, was pursued by police, and was eventually found to have three handguns and an AK-47 assault rifle in the vehicle. In September 2006, Clarett pled guilty to aggravated robbery and carrying a concealed weapon and was sentenced to seven and a half years in prison (with release possible after three and a half years) as well as five years of probation. He was released from prison in April 2010 for good behavior and, after his release, reenrolled in classes at Ohio State, played professional football with the Omaha Nighthawks of the United Football League, and began playing rugby. He now speaks frequently to groups of collegiate and professional athletes, offering his story as a cautionary tale.

3. The NFL is not the only American professional sports league with an age eligibility rule. With narrow exceptions, the NBA limits eligibility to players who are 19 years old and one year removed from their high school graduation (notably, Commissioner Silver has pushed to reduce the eligibility age to 18). The WNBA has a similar rule, although the thresholds are 22 years old and four years removed from high school graduation. MLB and the NHL have lower age eligibility thresholds than the NFL, NBA, or WNBA, while MLS, the PGA, the LPGA, and the USTA have no age eligibility requirements at all. What accounts for the differences in age eligibility criteria among the various leagues and associations? In *Clarett v. National Football League*, 306 F. Supp. 2d 379, 408 (S.D.N.Y. 2004), *judgment rev'd in part, vacated in part*, 369 F.3d 124 (2d Cir. 2004), the NFL argued that its age eligibility rules are necessary to protect "younger and/or less experienced players—that is, players who are less mature physically and psychologically—from heightened risks of injury in NFL games," but if this is so, wouldn't a similar age eligibility rule be prudent in hockey, which, like football, is a physically punishing game? If you believe that different sports' particular physical demands adequately explain the variety of age eligibility requirements, consider the basketball context: although the rules governing play in the NBA and WNBA are no different with regard to physical contact, a player must be roughly three years older to play in the WNBA than in the NBA. This means women basketball players face a three-year delay in earning salaries and endorsements as compared with their male counterparts. Because the WNBA is a partially-owned subsidiary of the NBA, in that some WNBA clubs are owned and operated by NBA clubs, might the different age eligibility thresholds make the NBA vulnerable to a sex discrimination claim? It bears noting that the NBA and WNBA age eligibility rules discussed in this paragraph do not apply to international players. What justifies having international basketball players face less stringent age eligibility criteria than American basketball players?

2. *Judicial Extension of the Scope of the Nonstatutory Labor Exemption Beyond the Terms of an Existing Collective Bargaining Agreement and Limitation of Antitrust Remedies*

The 1980s saw unprecedented labor strife in the NFL, which forced courts to consider the appropriate duration and scope of the nonstatutory labor exemption as well as its underlying policy justifications. Although the NFL has been a party to most litigation concerning the applicability of this exemption, the legal principles developed in these cases apply throughout the professional sports industry.

In 1982, with the expiration of the existing CBA (negotiated in 1977) and with league revenues steadily increasing, the NFL and the NFLPA entered into negotiations over a new CBA. The NFLPA sought a much more beneficial deal including a guarantee that players be paid 55 percent of league-wide revenues, but the owners balked. The players then voted to go on strike, and the owners responded by barring all players from team facilities. After a two-month standoff that shortened and nearly doomed the 1982 season, the two sides entered into a new five-year CBA incorporating among other things a first refusal/compensation system, which existed in the 1977 CBA and allowed a team to keep its free agent players if it exercised a right of first refusal and matched any other team's offer for the player.

When the 1982 CBA neared its expiration in 1987, the two sides began negotiations to renew the CBA, but talks broke down and the players again voted to strike. This time, team owners, after canceling one week of games, hired replacement players—pejoratively called "scabs"—and continued the season. After three games featuring primarily replacement players, the striking players voted to end the strike and return to their teams. That same day, Marvin Powell, along with eight other NFL players and the NFLPA, sued the NFL for violating antitrust law. They argued that when the two sides reached an "impasse" in negotiating a new CBA, the nostatutory labor exemption that protected the terms of the expired CBA (including the first refusal/compensation system) from antitrust scrutiny ceased to exist. In *Charles D. Bonanno Linen Service, Inc. v. NLRB*, 454 U.S. 404, 412 (1982), the Supreme Court defined "impasse" as "a temporary deadlock or hiatus in negotiations 'which in almost all cases is eventually broken, through either a change of mind or the application of economic force'" and observed that an impasse may be "brought about intentionally by one or both parties as a device to further, rather than destroy, the bargaining process."

The district court held that "once the parties reach impasse concerning player restraint provisions those provisions will lose their immunity and further imposition of those conditions may result in antitrust liability." See *Powell v. National Football League*, 678 F. Supp. 777, 788-789 (D. Minn. 1988), *rev'd*, 930 F.2d 1293 (8th Cir. 1989). The NFL promptly appealed to the Eighth Circuit, arguing that the "district court's standard [provides the NFLPA] with undue motivation to generate impasse in order to pursue an antitrust suit for treble damages." *Powell v. National Football League*, 930 F.2d 1293, 1299 (8th Cir. 1989).

In a 2-1 decision, the Eighth Circuit reversed the district court and ruled that "the nonstatutory labor exemption protects agreements conceived in an ongoing collective bargaining relationship from challenges under the antitrust laws . . . and extends beyond impasse." *Id.* at 1303. The majority explained:

> Both relevant case law and the more persuasive commentators establish that labor law provides a comprehensive array of remedies to management and [the] union, even after impasse. After a collective bargaining agreement has expired, an employer is under an obligation to bargain with the union before it may permissibly make any unilateral change in terms and conditions of employment which constitute mandatory subjects of collective bargaining. After impasse, an employer may make unilateral changes that are reasonably comprehended within

its pre-impasse proposals. We are influenced by those commentators who suggest that, given the array of remedies available to management and unions after impasse, a dispute such as the one before us "ought to be resolved free of intervention by the courts" where "the union has had a sufficient impact in shaping the content of the employer's offers" and where the challenged restraint is "clothed with union approval."

Id. at 1302.

The dissent observed: "The majority purports to reject the owners' argument that the labor exemption in this case continues indefinitely. The practical effect of the majority's opinion, however, is just that—because the labor exemption will continue until the bargaining relationship is terminated either by a NLRB decertification proceeding or by abandonment of bargaining rights by the union." *Id.* at 1305.

The NFLPA interpreted the *Powell* decision to mean that as long as the union remained intact, players would have no recourse under antitrust law. To preserve their antitrust rights, the NFLPA disclaimed its authority to represent the players as a labor union, and player representatives from the league's 24 clubs unanimously voted to end the NFLPA's status as the players' collective bargaining representative and to restructure the organization as a voluntary professional association. The NFLPA filed a labor organization termination notice with the U.S. Department of Labor and discontinued collective bargaining on behalf of NFL players. Thereafter, Freeman McNeil and other NFL players filed an antitrust suit challenging the league's Plan B free agency restrictions, which allowed clubs to retain limited rights to 37 players each season, thereby substantially limiting their ability to sign with other clubs.

A threshold issue in the antitrust case was whether the NFLPA was continuing to function as the players union and whether its disclaimer of authority to do so was a sham, as the NFL asserted. The trial court held that the NFLPA's disclaimer was sufficient to terminate the nonstatutory labor exemption, which enabled the *McNeil* plaintiffs to assert their antitrust claims. The court explicitly rejected the NFL's contention that the NFLPA must decertify as a labor union, which would require a determination by the National Labor Relations Board that its certification as a union was no longer operative. *Powell v. NFL,* 764 F. Supp. 1351 (D. Minn. 1991). See also *McNeil v. National Football League,* 790 F. Supp. 871, 885 (D. Minn. 1992).

The *McNeil* plaintiffs ultimately prevailed on the merits of their antitrust claims. The jury found that certain aspects of the NFL's Plan B first refusal/compensation system for veteran players violated §1 of the Sherman Act. *McNeil,* 790 F. Supp. at 896-897. Four of the plaintiffs were awarded substantial damages. *Id.* at 897.

After the *McNeil* verdict, another group of NFL players filed a class action suit seeking damages caused by the Plan B free agency restrictions invalidated on antitrust grounds in that case. The NFL ultimately settled all antitrust litigation challenging the validity of the player restraints and paid a $115 million settlement. *White v. NFL,* 41 F.3d 402 (8th Cir. 1994). The NFLPA then resumed functioning as a union and negotiated a new CBA with the NFL, which was incorporated into the settlement agreement.

Powell, which immunized the terms of an expired CBA from antitrust challenge as long as there is an ongoing collective bargaining process, illustrates that labor law rather than antitrust law generally regulates labor relations in the professional sports industry. This principle was reaffirmed and expanded by the Supreme Court in the following case.

BROWN v. PRO FOOTBALL, INC.

518 U.S. 231 (1996)

Breyer, Justice.

The question in this case arises at the intersection of the Nation's labor and antitrust laws. A group of professional football players brought this antitrust suit against football club owners. The club owners had bargained with the players' union over a wage issue until they reached impasse. The owners then had agreed among themselves (but not with the union) to implement the terms of their own last best bargaining offer. The question before us is whether federal labor laws shield such an agreement from antitrust attack. . . .

I

We can state the relevant facts briefly. In 1987, a collective-bargaining agreement between the National Football League (NFL or League), a group of football clubs, and the NFL Players Association, a labor union, expired. The NFL and the Players Association began to negotiate a new contract. In March 1989, during the negotiations, the NFL adopted Resolution G-2, a plan that would permit each club to establish a "developmental squad" of up to six rookie or "first-year" players who, as free agents, had failed to secure a position on a regular player roster. . . . Squad members would play in practice games and sometimes in regular games as substitutes for injured players. Resolution G-2 provided that the club owners would pay all squad members the same weekly salary.

The next month, April, the NFL presented the developmental squad plan to the Players Association. The NFL proposed a squad player salary of $1,000 per week. The Players Association disagreed. It insisted that the club owners give developmental squad players benefits and protections similar to those provided regular players, and that they leave individual squad members free to negotiate their own salaries.

Two months later, in June, negotiations on the issue of developmental squad salaries reached an impasse. The NFL then unilaterally implemented the developmental squad program by distributing to the clubs a uniform contract that embodied the terms of Resolution G-2 and the $1,000 proposed weekly salary. The League advised club owners that paying developmental squad players more or less than $1,000 per week would result in disciplinary action, including the loss of draft choices.

In May 1990, 235 developmental squad players brought this antitrust suit against the League and its member clubs. The players claimed that their employers' agreement to pay them a $1,000 weekly salary violated the Sherman Act. See 15 U.S.C. § 1 (forbidding agreements in restraint of trade). The Federal District Court denied the employers' claim of exemption from the antitrust laws; it permitted the case to reach the jury; and it subsequently entered judgment on a jury treble-damages award that exceeded $30 million. . . .

The Court of Appeals (by a split 2-to-1 vote) reversed. The majority interpreted the labor laws as "waiv[ing] antitrust liability for restraints on competition imposed through the collective-bargaining process, so long as such restraints operate primarily in a labor market characterized by collective bargaining." (citation omitted.) The court held, consequently, that the club owners were immune from antitrust liability. . . . Although we do not interpret the exemption as broadly as did the Appeals Court, we nonetheless find the exemption applicable, and we affirm that court's immunity conclusion.

The immunity before us rests upon what this Court has called the "nonstatutory" labor exemption from the antitrust laws. *Connell Constr. Co. v. Plumbers,* 421 U.S. 616, 622, 95 S. Ct. 1830, 1835, 44 L. Ed. 2d 418 (1975). . . . The Court has implied this exemption from federal labor statutes, which set forth a national labor policy favoring free and private collective bargaining. . . .

As a matter of logic, it would be difficult, if not impossible, to require groups of employers and employees to bargain together, but at the same time to forbid them to make among themselves or with each other *any* of the competition-restricting agreements potentially necessary to make the process work or its results mutually acceptable. Thus, the implicit exemption recognizes that, to give effect to federal labor laws and policies and to allow meaningful collective bargaining to take place, some restraints on competition imposed through the bargaining process must be shielded from antitrust sanctions. . . .

The petitioners and their supporters concede, as they must, the legal existence of the exemption we have described. They also concede that, where its application is necessary to make the statutorily authorized collective-bargaining process work as Congress intended, the exemption must apply both to employers and to employees. . . . Consequently, the question before us is one of determining the exemption's scope: Does it apply to an agreement among several employers bargaining together to implement after impasse the terms of their last best good-faith wage offer? We assume that such conduct, as practiced in this case, is unobjectionable as a matter of labor law and policy. On that assumption, we conclude that the exemption applies.

Labor law itself regulates directly, and considerably, the kind of behavior here at issue — the postimpasse imposition of a proposed employment term concerning a mandatory subject of bargaining. Both the Board and the courts have held that, after impasse, labor law permits employers unilaterally to implement changes in pre-existing conditions, but only insofar as the new terms meet carefully circumscribed conditions. For example, the new terms must be "reasonably comprehended" within the employer's preimpasse proposals (typically the last rejected proposals), lest by imposing more or less favorable terms, the employer unfairly undermined the union's status. . . . The collective-bargaining proceeding itself must be free of any unfair labor practice, such as an employer's failure to have bargained in good faith. . . .

Although the case law we have cited focuses upon bargaining by a single employer, no one here has argued that labor law does, or should, treat multiemployer bargaining differently in this respect. Indeed, Board and court decisions suggest that the joint implementation of proposed terms after impasse is a familiar practice in the context of multiemployer bargaining. . . . We proceed on that assumption. . . .

In these circumstances, to subject the practice to antitrust law is to require antitrust courts to answer a host of important practical questions about how collective bargaining over wages, hours, and working conditions is to proceed — the very result that the implicit labor exemption seeks to avoid. And it is to place in jeopardy some of the potentially beneficial labor-related effects that multi-employer bargaining can achieve. That is because unlike labor law, which some-times welcomes anticompetitive agreements conducive to industrial harmony, antitrust law forbids all agreements among competitors (such as competing employers) that unreasonably lessen competition among or between them in virtually any respect whatsoever. . . .

If the antitrust laws apply, what are employers to do once impasse is reached? If all impose terms similar to their last joint offer, they invite an antitrust action premised upon identical behavior (along with prior or accompanying conversa-tions) as tending to show a common understanding or agreement. If any, or all, of them individually impose terms that differ significantly from that offer, they invite an unfair labor practice charge. Indeed, how can employers safely discuss their offers together even before a bargaining impasse occurs? A preimpasse discussion about, say, the practical advantages or disadvantages of a particular proposal invites a later antitrust claim that they agreed to limit the kinds of action each would later take should an impasse occur. The same is true of post-impasse discussions aimed at renewed negotiations with the union. Nor would adherence to the terms of an expired collective-bargaining agreement elimi-nate a potentially plausible antitrust claim charging that they had "conspired" or tacitly "agreed" to do so, particularly if maintaining the status quo were not in the immediate economic self-interest of some. (Citation omitted.) All this is to say that to permit antitrust liability here threatens to introduce instability and uncertainty into the collective-bargaining process, for antitrust law often forbids or discourages the kinds of joint discussions and behavior that the collective bargaining process invites or requires.

We do not see any obvious answer to this problem. We recognize, as the Government suggests, that, in principle, antitrust courts might themselves try to evaluate particular kinds of employer understandings, finding them "reason-able" (hence lawful) where justified by collective-bargaining necessity. But any such evaluation means a web of detailed rules spun by many different nonex-pert antitrust judges and juries, not a set of labor rules enforced by a single expert administrative body, namely the Board. The labor laws give the Board, not antitrust courts, primary responsibility for policing the collective-bargaining process. And one of their objectives was to take from antitrust courts the author-ity to determine, through application of the antitrust laws, what is socially or economically desirable collective-bargaining policy. . . .

III

A

Petitioners claim that the implicit exemption applies only to labor-management *agreements*—a limitation that they deduce from case-law language. . . . The lan-guage, however, reflects only the fact that the cases previously before the Court involved collective-bargaining agreements. . . . The language does not reflect the exemption's rationale. . . .

Nor do we see how an exemption limited by petitioners' principle of labor-management consent could work. One cannot mean the principle lit-erally—that the exemption applies only to understandings embodied in a collective-bargaining agreement—for the collective-bargaining process may take place before the making of any agreement or after an agreement has expired. Yet a multiemployer bargaining process itself necessarily involves many procedural and substantive understandings among participating employers as well as with the union. Petitioners cannot rescue their principle by claiming that the exemption applies only insofar as *both* labor and management consent to those understandings. Often labor will not (and should not) consent to certain common bargaining positions that employers intend to maintain. . . .

B

The Solicitor General argues that the exemption should terminate at the point of impasse. After impasse, it says, "employers no longer have a duty under the labor laws to maintain the status quo," and "are free as a matter of labor law to negotiate individual arrangements on an interim basis with the union."

Employers, however, are not completely free at impasse to act independently. The multiemployer bargaining unit ordinarily remains intact; individual employers cannot withdraw. . . . The duty to bargain survives; employers must stand ready to resume collective bargaining. . . . And individual employers can negotiate individual interim agreements with the union only insofar as those agreements are consistent with "the duty to abide by the results of group bargaining." . . .

The problem is aggravated by the fact that "impasse" is often temporary . . . and it may occur several times during the course of a single labor dispute, since the bargaining process is not over when the first impasse is reached. . . . Employers who erroneously concluded that impasse had *not* been reached would risk antitrust liability were they collectively to maintain the status quo, while employers who erroneously concluded that impasse *had* occurred would risk unfair labor practice charges for prematurely suspending multiemployer negotiations.

The Solicitor General responds with suggestions for softening an "impasse" rule by extending the exemption after impasse "for such time as would be reasonable in the circumstances" for employers to consult with counsel, confirm that impasse has occurred, and adjust their business operations. . . . But even as so modified, the impasse-related rule creates an exemption that can evaporate in the middle of the bargaining process, leaving later antitrust courts free to second-guess the parties' bargaining decisions and consequently forcing them to choose their collective-bargaining responses in light of what they predict or fear that antitrust courts, not labor law administrators, will eventually decide. . . .

C

Petitioners and their supporters argue in the alternative for a rule that would exempt postimpasse agreement about bargaining "tactics," but not postimpasse agreement about substantive "terms," from the reach of antitrust. . . . They recognize, however, that both the Board and the courts have said that employers can, and often do, employ the imposition of "terms" as a bargaining "tactic." . . . This concession as to joint "tactical" implementation would turn the presence of an antitrust exemption upon a determination of the employers' primary purpose or motive. . . . But to ask antitrust courts, insulated from the bargaining process, to investigate an employer group's subjective motive is to ask them to conduct an inquiry often more amorphous than those we have previously discussed. And, in our view, a labor/antitrust line drawn on such a basis would too often raise the same related (previously discussed) problems. . . .

D

. . . Petitioners also say that irrespective of how the labor exemption applies elsewhere to multiemployer collective bargaining, professional sports is "special." We can understand how professional sports may be special in terms of, say, interest, excitement, or concern. But we do not understand how they are special in respect to labor law's antitrust exemption. We concede that the clubs that make up a professional sports league are not completely independent economic competitors, as they depend upon a degree of cooperation for economic survival. . . . In the present context, however, that circumstance makes the league more like a single bargaining employer, which analogy seems irrelevant to the legal issue before us.

We also concede that football players often have special individual talents, and, unlike many unionized workers, they often negotiate their pay individually with their employers. . . . But this characteristic seems simply a feature, like so many others, that might give employees (or employers) more (or less) bargaining power, that might lead some (or all) of them to favor a particular kind of bargaining, or that might lead to certain demands at the bargaining table. We do not see how it could make a critical legal difference in determining the underlying framework in which bargaining is to take place. . . . Indeed, it would be odd to fashion an antitrust exemption that gave additional advantages to professional football players (by virtue of their superior bargaining power) that transport workers, coal miners, or meat packers would not enjoy. . . .

For these reasons, we hold that the implicit ("nonstatutory") antitrust exemption applies to the employer conduct at issue here. That conduct took place during and immediately after a collective-bargaining negotiation. It grew out of, and was directly related to, the lawful operation of the bargaining process. It involved a matter that the parties were required to negotiate collectively. And it concerned only the parties to the collective-bargaining relationship.

Our holding is not intended to insulate from antitrust review every joint imposition of terms by employers, for an agreement among employers could be sufficiently distant in time and in circumstances from the collective-bargaining process that a rule permitting antitrust intervention would not significantly interfere with that process. *See, e.g.,* 50 F.3d at 1057 (suggesting that exemption lasts until collapse of the collective-bargaining relationship, as evidenced by decertification of the union); *El Cerrito Mill & Lumber Co.,* 316 N.L.R.B., at 1006-1007 (suggesting that "extremely long" impasse, accompanied by "instability" or "defunctness" of multiemployer unit, might justify union withdrawal from group bargaining). We need not decide in this case whether, or where, within these extreme outer boundaries to draw that line. Nor would it be appropriate for us to do so without the detailed views of the Board, to whose "specialized judgment" Congress "intended to leave" many of the "inevitable questions concerning multi-employer bargaining bound to arise in the future." . . .

The judgment of the Court of Appeals is affirmed.

Justice STEVENS, dissenting.

. . . The statutory labor exemption protects the right of workers to act collectively to seek better wages, but does not "exempt concerted action or agreements between unions and nonlabor parties." *Connell Constr. Co. v. Plumbers,* 421 U.S. 616, 621-22, 95 S. Ct. 1830, 1834-1835, 44 L. Ed. 2d 418 (1975). It is the judicially crafted, nonstatutory labor exemption that serves to accommodate the conflicting policies of the antitrust and labor statutes in the context of action between employers and unions. . . .

Consistent with basic labor law policies, I agree with the Court that the judicially crafted labor exemption must also cover some collective action that employers take in response to a collective-bargaining agent's demands for higher wages. Immunizing such action from antitrust scrutiny may facilitate collective bargaining over labor demands. . . .

In my view, however, neither the policies underlying the two separate statutory schemes, nor the narrower focus on the purpose of the nonstatutory exemption, provides a justification for exempting from antitrust scrutiny collective action initiated by employers to depress wages below the level that would be produced in a free market. Nor do those policies support a rule that would allow employers to suppress wages by implementing noncompetitive agreements among themselves on matters that have not previously been the subject of either an agreement with labor or even a demand by labor for inclusion in the bargaining process. That, however, is what is at stake in this litigation.

II

In light of the accommodation that has been struck between antitrust and labor law policy, it would be most ironic to extend an exemption crafted to protect collective action by employees to protect employers acting jointly to deny employees the opportunity to negotiate their salaries individually in a competitive market. Perhaps aware of the irony, the Court chooses to analyze this case as though it represented a typical impasse in an unexceptional multiemployer bargaining process. In so doing, it glosses over three unique features of the case that are critical to the inquiry into whether the policies of the labor laws require extension of the nonstatutory labor exemption to this atypical case.

First, in this market, unlike any other area of labor law implicated in the cases cited by the Court, player salaries are individually negotiated. The practice of individually negotiating player salaries prevailed even prior to collective bargaining. The players did not challenge the prevailing practice because, unlike employees in most industries, they want their compensation to be determined by the forces of the free market rather than by the process of collective bargaining. Thus, although the majority professes an inability to understand anything special about professional sports that should affect the framework of labor negotiations . . . in this business it is the employers, not the employees, who seek to impose a noncompetitive uniform wage on a segment of the market and to put an end to competitive wage negotiations.

Second, respondents concede that the employers imposed the wage restraint to force owners to comply with league-wide rules that limit the number of players that may serve on a team, not to facilitate a stalled bargaining process, or to revisit any issue previously subjected to bargaining. The employers could have confronted the culprits directly by stepping up enforcement of roster limits. They instead chose to address the problem by unilaterally preventing players from individually competing in the labor market.

Third, although the majority asserts that the "club owners had bargained with the players' union over a wage issue until they reached impasse," . . . that hardly constitutes a complete description of what transpired. When the employers' representative advised the union that they proposed to pay the players a uniform wage determined by the owners, the union promptly and unequivocally responded that their proposal was inconsistent with the "principle" of individual salary negotiation that had been accepted in the past and that predated collective bargaining. The so-called "bargaining" that followed amounted to nothing more than the employers' notice to the union that they had decided to implement a decision to replace individual salary negotiations with a uniform wage level for a specific group of players.

Given these features of the case, I do not see why the employers should be entitled to a judicially crafted exemption from antitrust liability. We have explained that "[t]he nonstatutory exemption has its source in the strong labor policy favoring the association of employees to eliminate competition over wages and working conditions." (Citation omitted.) I know of no similarly strong labor policy that favors the association of employers to eliminate a competitive method of negotiating wages that predates collective bargaining and that labor would prefer to preserve.

Even if some collective action by employers may justify an exemption because it is necessary to maintain the "integrity of the multiemployer bargaining unit," . . . no such justification exists here. The employers imposed a fixed wage even though there was no dispute over the pre-existing principle that player salaries should be individually negotiated. They sought only to prevent certain owners from evading roster limits and thereby gaining an unfair advantage. . . .

The point of identifying the unique features of this case is not, as the Court suggests, to make the case that professional football players, alone among workers, should be entitled to enforce the antitrust laws against anticompetitive collective employer action. . . . Other employees, no less than well-paid athletes, are entitled to the protections of the antitrust laws when their employers unite to undertake anticompetitive action that causes them direct harm and alters the state of employer-employee relations that existed prior to unionization. Here that alteration occurred because the wage terms that the employers unilaterally imposed directly conflict with a pre-existing principle of agreement between the bargaining parties. In other contexts, the alteration may take other similarly anticompetitive and unjustifiable forms. . . .

IV

Congress is free to act to exempt the anticompetitive employer conduct that we review today. In the absence of such action, I do not believe it is for us to stretch the limited exemption that we have fashioned to facilitate the express statutory exemption created for labor's benefit so that unions must strike in order to restore a prior practice of individually negotiating salaries. I therefore agree with the position that the District Court adopted below.

"Because the developmental squad salary provisions were a new concept and not a change in terms of the expired collective bargaining agreement, the policy behind continuing the nonstatutory labor exemption for the terms of a collective bargaining agreement after expiration (to foster an atmosphere conducive to the negotiation of a new collective bargaining agreement) does not apply. To hold that the nonstatutory labor exemption extends to shield the NFL from antitrust liability for imposing restraints never before agreed to by the union would not only infringe on the union's freedom to contract . . . but would also contradict the very purpose of the antitrust exemption by not promoting execution of a collective bargaining agreement with terms mutually acceptable to employer and labor union alike. Labor unions would be unlikely to sign collective bargaining agreements with employers if they believed that they would be forced to accept terms to which they never agreed." [Citation omitted.]

Accordingly, I respectfully dissent.

NOTES AND QUESTIONS

1. Is judicial extension of the nonstatutory labor exemption to enable league clubs to unilaterally implement new player restraints that the union has *never* agreed to justified? The *Brown* majority's broad construction of the nonstatutory labor exemption expands the parameters of allowable actions by the clubs after the collective bargaining agreement has expired without fear of antitrust liability. For example, league clubs can propose new player restraints, bargain to impasse, and then unilaterally implement these terms and lock the players out until the union agrees to the terms' inclusion in a new collective bargaining agreement. Does this foster or impede the settlement of labor disputes between league clubs and their players? Given that neither side has an antitrust remedy as long as there is an ongoing collective bargaining process, are the parties' respective economic weapons and available labor law remedies sufficient to enable the fair and efficient resolution of disputes concerning mandatory subjects of collective bargaining?

    The *Brown* majority focuses on what is necessary to make the collective bargaining process work and concludes that a multiemployer bargaining unit should not be liable for conduct that is lawful under labor law. By contrast, the dissenting justice concludes that allowing a union to use antitrust law furthers the labor law policy goal of achieving higher wages for workers. Do you favor the majority's process-oriented approach or the dissent's results-oriented view?

    Congress enacted the federal labor laws, which permit unionization and collective bargaining, because of concern that the disparity of bargaining power between individual workers and large employers would result in employee wage levels that are too low for the good of our national economy. Although players in the NFL, NBA, MLB, and NHL have unionized, they generally want free market competition for their services among league clubs to determine their individual salaries. Unlike employees in other industries, major league professional athletes have unique talents and skills that generally are not fungible or readily interchangeable. Each player's individual market value varies based on the nature of his or her respective talents and skills relative to those of other league players. Do these distinctions justify a special legal rule regarding the nature and scope of the nonstatutory labor exemption's application to professional sports?

2. According to *Brown*, when does the nonstatutory labor exemption end? If the multiemployer bargaining unit for a league's clubs commits an unfair labor practice, does the players union also have an antitrust remedy?

    In an effort to circumvent *Brown*'s broad construction of the nonstatutory labor exemption, professional soccer players chose not to unionize and engage in collective bargaining with Major League Soccer when the league was initially formed. Instead, they unsuccessfully claimed that the league and the operator/investors of its member clubs violated antitrust law by conspiring to eliminate competition for their services. *Fraser v. Major League*

Soccer, 284 F.3d 47 (1st Cir. 2002). Thereafter, the MLS players unionized. Although this issue was not raised in the *Fraser* litigation, does *Brown* allow players to deprive a league of the antitrust immunity conferred by the non-statutory labor exemption through not unionizing?

3. Because professional baseball has a broad common law antitrust exemption, MLB players historically have not been able to use antitrust law to challenge league rules restricting their ability to become free agents. *Flood v. Kuhn*, 407 U.S. 258 (1972). In 1998, Congress modified the Sherman Act to provide MLB players with the same right to sue under antitrust law concerning their employment terms as other professional athletes have in their sports. 15 U.S.C. §27b(c). See detailed discussion in Chapter 6, D-2. What is the practical effect of this statutory provision regarding the ability of MLB players to assert antitrust claims arising out of labor disputes?

From 1993, when the NFLPA and the NFL negotiated a new CBA, through 2011, the two parties enjoyed relative labor peace, continually renewing the CBA with some modifications. In the spring of 2011, the then-existing CBA expired before the NFL and the NFLPA were able to agree to new terms and an extension. This led to the NFL's lockout of the players, which set the stage for the following precedent-setting case, which precludes injunctive relief in a labor dispute.

BRADY v. NATIONAL FOOTBALL LEAGUE
644 F.3d 661 (8th Cir. 2011)

COLLOTON, Circuit Judge.

This appeal arises from an action filed by nine professional football players and one prospective football player ("the Players") against the National Football League and its thirty-two separately-owned clubs, more commonly known as football teams (collectively, "the NFL" or "the League"). On March 11, 2011, a collective bargaining agreement between the League and a union representing professional football players expired. The League had made known that if a new agreement was not reached before the expiration date, then it would implement a lockout of players, during which the athletes would not be paid or permitted to use club facilities. The League viewed a lockout as a legitimate tactic under the labor laws to bring economic pressure to bear on the players as part of the bargaining process. *See Am. Ship Bldg. Co. v. NLRB*, 380 U.S. 300, 301-02, 318 (1965).

The players, aware of the League's strategy, opted to terminate the union's status as their collective bargaining agent as of 4:00 p.m. on March 11, just before the agreement expired. Later that day, the Players filed an action in the district court alleging that the lockout planned by the League would constitute a group boycott and price-fixing agreement that would violate § 1 of the Sherman Antitrust Act. The complaint explained that "the players in the NFL have determined that it is not in their interest to remain unionized if the existence of such a union would serve to allow the NFL to impose anticompetitive restrictions with impunity." The plaintiffs also alleged other violations of the antitrust laws and state common law.

The League proceeded with its planned lockout on March 12, 2011. The Players moved for a preliminary injunction in the district court, urging the court to enjoin the lockout as an unlawful group boycott that was causing irreparable harm to the Players. The district court granted a preliminary injunction, and the League appealed. We conclude that the injunction did not conform to the provisions of the Norris-LaGuardia Act, 29 U.S.C. § 101 *et seq.*, and we therefore vacate the district court's order. . . .

B.

Since 1993, the players and the League have operated under [the *White v. NFL* Stipulation and Settlement Agreement (SSA), which resolved the *McNeil v. NFL* antitrust litigation and led to a new collective bargaining agreement (CBA) between the NFL and the National Football League Players Assocation (NFLPA) shortly thereafter], and the district court has continued to oversee the settlement by resolving numerous disputes over the terms of the SSA and CBA. *White v. NFL*, 585 F.3d 1129, 1133 (8th Cir. 2009). Whenever the NFL and the NFLPA have agreed to change a provision in the CBA, a conforming change has also been made to the SSA. *Id.* at 1134. The SSA has been amended several times over the past eighteen years, most recently in 2006, when the NFL and the NFLPA reached an agreement on a new CBA that would last through the 2012-2013 football season. The 2006 SSA and CBA gave both sides the right to opt out of the final two years of each agreement upon written notice.

In May 2008, the NFL opted out of the final two years of the SSA and CBA, citing concerns about operating costs and other elements of the agreements. As a result, the SSA and CBA were scheduled to expire in early March 2011. Although the NFL and the NFLPA engaged in more than two years of negotiations toward a new CBA, the League and the players were unable to reach an agreement. The League filed an unfair labor practice charge with the NLRB in February 2011, asserting that the union failed to confer in good faith. The Players say that the charge is meritless.

As the deadline approached, a substantial majority of NFL players voted to end the NFLPA's status as their collective bargaining representative. On March 11, 2011—the expiration date of the SSA and CBA—the NFLPA notified the NFL that it disclaimed interest in continuing to serve as the players' collective bargaining representative, effective at 4:00 p.m. The NFLPA also amended its bylaws to prohibit collective bargaining with the League or its agents, filed a labor organization termination notice with the Department of Labor, asked the Internal Revenue Service to reclassify the NFLPA as a professional association rather than a labor organization, and notified the NFL that it would no longer represent players bringing grievances against the League.

The League filed an amended unfair labor practice charge on March 11, alleging that the NFLPA's disclaimer was a "sham" and that the combination of a disclaimer by the union and subsequent antitrust litigation was "a ploy and an unlawful subversion of the collective bargaining process." The Players dispute the charge, citing an advice memorandum of an associate general counsel of the NLRB in *Pittsburgh Steelers, Inc.*, No. 6-CA-23143, 1991 WL 144468 (NLRB G.C. June 26, 1991). The memorandum concluded that the NLFPA's 1989 disclaimer was valid, and that it was "irrelevant" whether the disclaimer was motivated by "litigation strategy," so long as the disclaimer was "otherwise unequivocal and adhered to." *Id.* at *2 & n. 8.

The Players, funded by the NFLPA, commenced this action on the same day as the disclaimer, March 11, 2011. Four of the plaintiffs are under contract with an NFL club; five are free agents, and one is a prospective player who had entered the 2011 NFL draft and was ultimately selected in that draft. The Players brought this action on behalf of themselves and a putative class consisting of players who are under contract with any NFL club, free agents seeking employment with any NFL club, and college or other players who have not previously been under contract with any NFL club and who are eligible to play as a rookies for any club. As the case comes to us, no class has been certified.

The Players explained in their complaint that "[t]he players . . . have ended the role of the NFLPA as their collective bargaining representative and no longer have a collective bargaining relationship with the NFL defendants." They asserted, based on the Supreme Court's language in [*Brown v. Pro Football*], that the nonstatutory labor exemption therefore no longer protects the League from antitrust liability. The complaint alleged that the NFL's planned lockout was an illegal group boycott and price-fixing arrangement that violated § 1 of the Shevrman Act. . . .

The complaint further alleged that the League planned to institute or to continue several anticompetitive practices that would violate § 1 of the Sherman Act, including a limitation on the amount of compensation that can be paid to recently drafted first-year "rookie" players, a cap on salaries for current players, and "franchise player" and "transition player" designations that restrict the ability of free agents to join a team other than their former team. The Players requested damages and declaratory and injunctive relief regarding these practices, including an injunction prohibiting the League from implementing or continuing the lockout. . . .

On April 25, 2011, the district court granted the Players' motion to enjoin the lockout, rejecting the League's assertions that the court lacked jurisdiction to enter the injunction, that the court should defer to the primary jurisdiction of the NLRB, and that the League is in any event immune from antitrust liability under the nonstatutory labor exemption. *See Brady v. NFL*, No. 11-639, 2011 WL 1535240, at *37 (D. Minn. Apr. 25, 2011) [hereinafter *Brady I*]. . . .

The League appealed, challenging the district court's application of the Norris-LaGuardia Act, the doctrine of primary jurisdiction, and the nonstatutory labor exemption. This court granted the NFL's motion to expedite the appeal and its motion for a stay of the district court's order pending appeal. We now consider the merits of the appeal.

II.

We consider first the League's contention that the Norris-LaGuardia Act deprived the district court of jurisdiction to enter the injunction. The NLGA, enacted in 1932, curtails the authority of a district court to issue injunctions in a labor dispute. "Congress was intent upon taking the federal courts out of the labor injunction business except in the very limited circumstances left open for federal jurisdiction under the Norris-LaGuardia Act." *Marine Cooks & Stewards v. Pan. S.S. Co.*, 362 U.S. 365, 369 (1960). . . .

To determine whether the NLGA forbids or places conditions on the issuance of an injunction here, we begin with the text of the statute. Section 1 provides that "[n]o court of the United States . . . shall have jurisdiction to issue any . . .

temporary or permanent injunction in a case involving or growing out of a labor dispute, except in strict conformity with the provisions of this chapter." 29 U.S.C. § 101. As noted, the district court concluded that the Act is inapplicable to this action, because the case is not one "involving or growing out of a labor dispute."

Section 13(c) of the Act states that "[t]he term 'labor dispute' includes *any controversy concerning terms or conditions of employment,* or concerning the association or representation of persons in negotiating, fixing, maintaining, changing, or seeking to arrange terms or conditions of employment, regardless of whether or not the disputants stand in the proximate relation of employer and employee." 29 U.S.C. § 113(c) (emphasis added). This lawsuit is a controversy concerning terms or conditions of employment. The Players seek broad relief that would affect the terms or conditions of employment for the entire industry of professional football. In particular, they urge the court to declare unlawful and to enjoin several features of the relationship between the League and the players, including the limit on compensation that can be paid to rookies, the salary cap, the "franchise player" designation, and the "transition player" designation, all of which the Players assert are anticompetitive restrictions that violate § 1 of the Sherman Act. . . .

The Act also states expressly that "[a] case shall be held to involve or grow out of a labor dispute when the case involves persons who are engaged in the same industry, trade, craft, or occupation." 29 U.S.C. § 113(a). This case, of course, involves persons engaged in the "same industry," namely, professional football. The statute continues that such a case "shall be held to involve or grow out of a labor dispute" when "such dispute is . . . between one or more employers or associations of employers and one or more employees or associations of employees." *Id.* This dispute is between one or more employers or associations of employers (the League and the NFL teams) and one or more employees (the Players under contract). By the plain terms of the Act, this case "shall be held to involve or grow out of a labor dispute."

The district court reached a contrary conclusion by departing from the text of § 13(a). The court thought the phrase "one or more employees or associations of employees" did not encompass the Players in this dispute, because "one or more employees" means "individual *unionized* employee or employees." *Brady I,* 2011 WL 1535240, at 24 n. 43 (emphasis added). We see no warrant for adding a requirement of unionization to the text.

A similar argument did not persuade the Supreme Court in *New Negro Alliance v. Sanitary Grocery Co.,* 303 U.S. 552 (1938). There, a company sought an injunction against the New Negro Alliance, which the Supreme Court described as "a corporation composed of colored persons, organized for the mutual improvement of its members and the promotion of civic, educational, benevolent, and charitable enterprises." *Id.* at 555. The Alliance allegedly had conspired to picket and boycott one of the company's grocery stores to pressure the store to employ African-American clerks. *Id.* at 555-56. The company claimed, among other things, that the Alliance's acts were "unlawful, [and] constitute[d] a conspiracy in restraint of trade." . . .

. . . Although no labor organization was involved in the dispute, and the company argued that "a recognized labor union or unions or individual members thereof were involved" in all but one of the "labor dispute" precedents cited by the Alliance, Brief for Respondent at 24, *New Negro Alliance,* 303 U.S. 552 (No. 511), the Court ruled that the definitions in the Act "plainly embrace the controversy which gave rise to the instant suit and classify it as one arising out of a dispute defined as a labor dispute." *New Negro Alliance*, 303 U.S. at 560. The Court observed that § 13(a) provides that a case shall be held to involve or grow out of a labor dispute "when the case involves any conflicting or competing interests in a 'labor dispute' . . . of 'persons participating or interested' therein," and ruled that the Alliance and its individual members were "persons interested in the dispute." *Id.* (internal quotation omitted). If § 13(a) were limited to controversies involving unions or unionized employees, then the Court could not have reached this conclusion. . . .

The text of the Norris-LaGuardia Act and the cases interpreting the term "labor dispute" do not require the present existence of a union to establish a labor dispute. Whatever the precise limits of the phrase "involving or growing out of a labor dispute," this case does not press the outer boundary. The League and the players' union were parties to a collective bargaining agreement for almost eighteen years prior to March 2011. They were engaged in collective bargaining over terms and conditions of employment for approximately two years through March 11, 2011. At that point, the parties were involved in a classic "labor dispute" by the Players' own definition. Then, on a single day, just hours before the CBA's expiration, the union discontinued collective bargaining and disclaimed its status, and the Players filed this action seeking relief concerning industry-wide terms and conditions of employment. Whatever the effect of the union's disclaimer on the League's immunity from antitrust liability, the labor dispute did not suddenly disappear just because the Players elected to pursue the dispute through antitrust litigation rather than collective bargaining.

III.

The Players argue alternatively that even if this case does involve or grow out of a labor dispute, the district court's injunction conforms to the provisions of the NLGA, and should be affirmed on this alternative ground. The League counters that § 4 of the Act includes a flat prohibition on injunctions against a lockout, and, alternatively, that even if the court has authority to enjoin a lockout under certain circumstances, the district court did not comply with the procedural requirements set forth in § 7 of the Act.

A.

Section 4 of the NLGA, 29 U.S.C. § 104, is entitled, "Enumeration of specific acts not subject to restraining orders or injunctions." It provides:

> No court of the United States shall have jurisdiction to issue any restraining order or temporary or permanent injunction in any case involving or growing out of any labor dispute to prohibit any person or persons participating or interested in such dispute . . . from doing, whether singly or in concert, any of the following acts:
> (a) Ceasing or refusing to perform any work or to remain in any relation of employment. . . .

The League relies on § 4(a). It argues that this subsection forbids an injunction to prohibit a lockout. There is no uniform definition of the term "lockout," but one "practical definition" used by this court is "a refusal by [an employer] to furnish available work to its regular employees." *Laclede Gas Co. v. NLRB*, 421 F.2d 610, 615 & n. 9 (8th Cir. 1970); *see also* 2 *The Developing Labor Law* 1639-40

(John E. Higgins, Jr. et al. eds., 5th ed. 2006) ("As used by the Board and the courts, . . . a lockout is most simply and completely defined as the withholding of employment by an employer from its employees for the purpose of either resisting their demands or gaining a concession from them."). The League maintains that by locking out all professional football players, it is "[r]efusing to . . . remain in any relation of employment," and is thus doing one of the acts that cannot be enjoined according to § 4. . . .

The Players respond that § 4(a) does not apply to employer injunctions at all. . . .

. . . The introductory clause of § 4 forbids a court to issue an injunction to prohibit "*any person or persons* participating or interested" in a labor dispute from doing any of the acts set forth below, including those in § 4(a). Employers, of course, are among the persons participating in a labor dispute. The introductory clause thus plainly encompasses employers. If language in a particular subsection is applicable on its face to employees and employers alike (or to employers alone), then there is no need for a specific mention of employers. . . .

The disputed language in § 4(a) — "remain in any relation of employment" — may apply to an employer. Section 3 of the Act makes clear that both employers and employees can be in a "relation of employment." Section 3(b) contemplates that either party to a labor agreement can agree to "withdraw from an employment relation." 29 U.S.C. § 103(b). . . .

Aside from the text and structure of § 4, the Players argue that the policy of the NLGA and the legislative history support their position that § 4(a) offers no protection to employers. To be sure, the policy stated in § 2 is that the individual unorganized worker should be free from the interference, restraint, or coercion of employers in the designation of representatives, self-organization, or other concerted activities. But it does not follow that a prohibition on injunctions against employer lockouts is contrary to the policy of the Act. The Supreme Court has observed that while the Act was designed to protect workingmen, the broader purpose was "to prevent the injunctions of the federal courts from *upsetting the natural interplay of the competing economic forces of labor and capital.*" *Bhd. of R.R. Trainmen v. Chi. River & Ind. R.R. Co.*, 353 U.S. 30, 40 (1957) (emphasis added). An employer's lockout is part of this interplay; it is not the equivalent of a judicial injunction that interferes with the ability of workers to exercise organized economic power. . . .

. . . A one-way interpretation of § 4(a) — prohibiting injunctions against strikes but not against lockouts — would be in tension with the purposes of the Norris-LaGuardia Act to allow free play of economic forces and "to withdraw federal courts from a type of controversy for which many believed they were ill-suited and from participation in which, it was feared, judicial prestige might suffer." *Marine Cooks & Stewards*, 362 U.S. at 369 n. 7. We are not convinced that the policy of the Act counsels against our textual analysis of § 4(a). . . .

[W]e conclude that § 4(a) of the Norris-LaGuardia Act deprives a federal court of power to issue an injunction prohibiting a party to a labor dispute from implementing a lockout of its employees. This conclusion accords with the few decisions that have addressed the specific question. *Clune v. Publishers' Ass'n of N.Y.C.*, 214 F. Supp. 520, 528-29 (S.D.N.Y.), *aff'd*, 314 F.2d 343, 344 (2d Cir. 1963) (per curiam); *Plumbers & Steamfitters Local 598 v. Morris*, 511 F. Supp. 1298, 1311 (E.D. Wash. 1981); *Stone & Webster Eng'g Corp.*, 163 F. Supp. at 896. Because the Norris-LaGuardia Act prohibits the district court from issuing an injunction against the League's lockout of employees, the court's order cannot stand.

B.

Another portion of the injunction is not foreclosed by § 4(a). The district court enjoined not only the League's lockout of employees, *i.e.,* players under contract, but also the League's refusal to deal with non-employees, *i.e.,* free agents and prospective players or "rookies." As to these latter groups of players, § 4(a) does not apply. The refusal of the League and NFL clubs to deal with free agents and rookies is not a refusal "to remain in any relation of employment," for there is no existing employment relationship in which "to remain."

An injunction with respect to the League's actions toward free agents and rookies, however, cannot be issued except in strict conformity with § 7 of the NLGA, 29 U.S.C. § 107, because this is "a case involving or growing out of a labor dispute." *Id.* §§ 101, 107. The present injunction does not conform to § 7. . . .

Section 7 provides that a court has no authority to issue an injunction "except after hearing the testimony of witnesses in open court (with opportunity for cross-examination) in support of the allegations of a complaint made under oath, and testimony in opposition thereto." 29 U.S.C. § 107. Although a hearing is not required where the party enjoined does not contest on appeal that the relevant facts are undisputed, *Kansas City S. Transp. Co. v. Teamsters Local Union No. 41,* 126 F.3d 1059, 1067-68 (8th Cir. 1997), the League does contest the facts in this case, and it is entitled to test the credibility of the Players' evidence by cross-examination. Section 7(c) requires the court to evaluate the relative harms to the parties, and the court's calculus with respect to free agents and rookies undoubtedly was affected by its view that the entire lockout could be enjoined. Whether to enter an injunction requiring the League to deal with free agents and rookies, only to have these players locked out as soon as they enter into any new contract of employment, was not considered. . . . We therefore conclude that the injunction as a whole must be vacated.

IV.

Given our conclusion that the preliminary injunction did not conform to the provisions of the Norris-LaGuardia Act, we need not reach the other points raised by the League on appeal. In particular, we express no view on whether the League's nonstatutory labor exemption from the antitrust laws continues after the union's disclaimer. The parties agree that the Act's restrictions on equitable relief are not necessarily coextensive with the substantive rules of antitrust law, and we reach our decision on that understanding. . . .

BYE, Circuit Judge, dissenting.

. . . Despite the repeated efforts of the legislative branch to come to the rescue of organized labor, today's opinion puts the power of the Act in the service of employers, to be used against non-unionized employees who can no longer avail themselves of protections of labor laws. Because I cannot countenance such interpretation of the Act, I must and hereby dissent. . . .

. . . I must take issue with the majority's conclusion as to this case not representing the outer boundary of the phrase "involving or growing out of a labor dispute." Like the nonstatutory labor exemption, statutory exemption from antitrust liability, which rests in part on the Norris-LaGuardia Act, *Connell Construction Co.,* 421 U.S. at 621-22, lies at the intersection between labor and antitrust laws. . . . "While the Norris-LaGuardia Act's bar of federal-court labor injunctions is not explicitly phrased as an exemption from the antitrust laws, it has been interpreted broadly as a statement of congressional policy that the courts must not use the antitrust laws as a vehicle to interfere in labor disputes." *H.A. Artists & Associates, Inc.*, 451 U.S. at 714. The scope of the two exemptions differs somewhat—"the statutory exemption allows unions to accomplish some restraints by acting unilaterally, [whereas] the nonstatutory exemption offers no similar protection when a union and a nonlabor party agree to restrain competition in a business market," *see Connell Construction Co.*, 421 U.S. at 622,—but there is no place for the application of either at the time labor laws no longer govern and labor policy is no longer implicated.

The Supreme Court recognized as much when it explained that nonstatutory immunity from antitrust review is no longer necessary when "an agreement among employers [is] sufficiently distant in time and in circumstances from the collective-bargaining process that a rule permitting antitrust intervention would not significantly interfere with that process." *Brown*, 518 U.S. at 250. As an example of such endpoint, the Court cited "collapse of the collective-bargaining relationship, as evidenced by decertification of the union." *Id.* (quoting *Brown v. Pro Football, Inc.*, 50 F.3d 1041, 1057 (D.C. Cir. 1995)). With the players having voted to end the NFLPA's status as their collective bargaining representative and the NFLPA likewise having disclaimed its status as the players' representative, this case has reached that endpoint. *See Brady v. NFL*, 640 F.3d 785, 798-99 (8th Cir. 2011) (Bye, J., dissenting) (elaborating on the reasons why the union disclaimer should end the protection against antitrust liability). . . .

NOTES AND QUESTIONS

1. Is the *Brady* majority's opinion consistent with *Brown*'s guidance regarding whether (and when) federal antitrust or labor law should govern professional sports industry labor disputes? Note that the *Brady* majority held only that the Norris-LaGuardia Act barred an injunction against the NFL lockout; it did not rule whether the nonstatutory labor exemption precluded plaintiffs' antitrust claims, resolve the merits of these claims, or consider the issue of whether potential plaintiffs other than players (e.g., consumers, coaches, stadium vendors) have standing to recover damages for antitrust violations arising out of a lockout. How should each of these issues be judicially resolved?

2. The NFL's owners and players agreed to terms on a new CBA in July 2011 and *Brady* was settled before the court addressed one of the NFL's primary contentions: that the NFLPA's disclaimer was a sham initiated to pave the way for the players' antitrust suit and to subvert the collective bargaining process. Just days after the case settled, the NFLPA resumed operations as the players union (following the same strategy it adopted in 1989 in connection with the *Powell* and *McNeil* litigations, *supra*), seemingly lending credence to the sham theory.

   Unions can be dissolved in two ways: (1) by decertification or (2) by a disclaimer of interest (as was done in the *Brady* and *McNeil* cases). Although the two methods are often confused, decertification is a more formal and time-consuming process involving the National Labor Relations Board, which ultimately requires that at least 50 percent of the members of the players association vote to decertify the union in an NLRB-supervised election. See generally Catherine Meeker, *Defining "Ministerial Aid": Union Decertification*

Under the National Labor Relations Act, 66 U. Chi. L. Rev. 999, 1000-1001 (1999). If a majority of the players vote to decertify the union, they cannot vote to re-unionize (and engage in collective bargaining with the league) before the lapse of a 12-month period. 29 U.S.C. §159. In contrast, a disclaimer of interest is an informal procedure pursuant to which the union leadership disclaims authority to represent the players based on at least 50 percent of them indicating they do not desire such representation. *Powell v. NFL*, 764 F. Supp. 1351 (D. Minn. 1991). A majority of the players can reauthorize the union to represent them at any time, creating the possibility of stepping into and out of a collective bargaining relationship as desired based on the circumstances. In light of the differences between decertification and a disclaimer of interest, should the method used to dissolve a union's collective bargaining authority determine whether the dissolution is effective for purposes of the applicability of the Norris-LaGuardia Act's anti-injunction provision or the nonstatutory labor exemption? Relevant to this issue, in *Retail Associates, Inc. and Retail Clerks International Association, Locals Nos. 128 and 633, AFL-CIO*, 120 NLRB 388, 394 (1958), the National Labor Relations Board stated:

> The decision to withdraw must contemplate a sincere abandonment, with relative perma nency, of the multiemployer unit and the embracement of a different course of bargaining on an individual-employer basis. The element of good faith is a necessary requirement in any such decision to withdraw, because of the unstabilizing and disrupting effect on multiemployer collective bargaining which would result if such withdrawal were permitted to be lightly made. The attempted withdrawal cannot be accepted as unequivocal and in good faith where, as here, it is obviously employed only as a measure of momentary expedience, or strategy in bargaining, and to avoid a Board election to test the union majority.

If the *Brady* court had considered the sham disclaimer question, how should it have ruled based on *Retail Associates*?

3. Although the NFL and NFLPA agreed to a new CBA in the *Brady* case's aftermath, their relationship remained contentious. In May 2012, less than a year after agreeing on a new CBA, the NFLPA filed a $4 billion federal lawsuit against the NFL, arguing that the NFL fraudulently induced the NFLPA to settle the *Brady* case and enter the CBA by concealing the existence of a secret salary cap that restrained players' 2010 salaries. *White v. National Football League*, 756 F.3d 585 (8th Cir. 2014). The district court rejected the collusion claim and dismissed the case. On appeal, the Eighth Circuit concluded the NFLPA should have the opportunity to "convince the district court that the dismissal was fraudulently procured," but the Eighth Circuit noted that the NFLPA would bear "a heavy burden in attempting to do so." *Id.* at 569. On remand, the NFLPA was unable to do so and the case was dismissed. *White v. National Football League*, 129 F. Supp. 3d 683 (D. Minn. 2015).

4. For an electronic discussion of the legal and public policy issues raised by the 2011 NFL lockout among a group of sports law professors as it was ongoing, see *A Roundtable Discussion for the Digital Age*, 29 Ent. & Sports Law, 1 (American Bar Association, Summer 2011) (Jeremy Davis, ed.). For an exploration of how the 2011 NFL and NBA lockouts and the legal disputes they spawned will impact collective bargaining and the application of labor

law in professional sports going forward, see Gabriel Feldman, *Antitrust Versus Labor Law in Professional Sports: Balancing the Scales After* Brady v. NFL *and* Anthony v. NBA, 45 U.C. Davis L. Rev. 1221 (2012).

3. *Antitrust Litigation in Player-Management Conflicts*

Despite the broad scope of the nonstatutory labor exemption, there are still some instances in which courts will consider the merits of antitrust challenges to player eligibility rules and other limits on the terms and conditions of professional athletes' employment. As previously discussed, players in team sports can choose not to unionize or may decertify their union, thereby preventing or discontinuing the collective bargaining process and negating the applicability of the nonstatutory labor exemption.

In addition, courts have ruled that the nonstatutory labor exemption does not bar an antitrust challenge by nonparties to collective bargaining agreement terms with anticompetitive effects outside the labor market for players' services. In *Philadelphia World Hockey Club, Inc. v. Philadelphia Hockey Club, Inc.*, 351 F. Supp. 462 (E.D. Pa. 1972), the court held that this exemption does not preclude a rival league's claim that the NHL's reserve clause violates the antitrust laws. The World Hockey Association (WHA) prevailed on its antitrust claim by proving that the reserve clause in the NHL's collective bargaining agreement deprived it from competing for the services of players with the ability to play major league professional hockey. The WHA needed access to such players in order to produce major league professional ice hockey in North America in competition with the NHL.

The nonstatutory labor exemption has not been applied to individual-performer sports, such as tennis, golf, boxing, and others. See, e.g., *Blalock v. Ladies Prof'l Golfers Assn.*, 359 F. Supp. 1260 (N.D. Ga. 1973) (finding that a golfer's one-year suspension imposed by the LPGA with "completely unfettered, subjective discretion" by a group of her competitors violates antitrust law). Professional players in the individual-performer sports generally are not unionized employees who engage in collective bargaining activities. Even if athletes in the sport form a players association and enter into agreements with event promoters or organizers, this generally does not constitute collective bargaining under the federal labor laws or make the nonstatutory labor exemption applicable.

Consequently, there are several instances in which antitrust litigation is not barred by the nonstatutory labor exemption. Thus, there is need to examine the developing framework of antitrust analysis applicable to challenged labor market restraints. Some early cases held that restraints precluding or reducing competition among league clubs for player services are *per se* illegal. See, e.g., *Smith v. Pro-Football Inc.*, 420 F. Supp. 738 (D.D.C. 1976), *aff'd in part and rev'd in part*, 593 F.2d 1173 (D.C. Cir. 1978); *Denver Rockets v. All-Pro Management*, 325 F. Supp. 1049 (C.D. Cal. 1971). Under the *per se* rule, certain agreements among economic competitors such as price fixing of players' wages and some group boycotts are conclusively presumed to be illegal because of their significant anticompetitive effects and are deemed incapable of justification.

On the other hand, the Supreme Court has recognized that the unique features of the sports industry require some uniform rules and agreements among competing teams in order to produce on-field competition that is appealing to consumers, which requires application of the rule of reason. *American Needle*,

Inc. v. NFL, 560 U.S. 183 (2010) ("When 'restraints on competition are essential if the product is to be available at all,' *per se* rules of illegality are inapplicable, and instead the restraint must be judged according to the flexible Rule of Reason"); *National Collegiate Athletic Assn. v. Board of Regents of the Univ. of Okla.*, 468 U.S. 85, 101 (1984) ("refusing to apply *per se* rule to sports industry because some horizontal restraints are necessary 'if product to be available at all'"). Thus, courts generally have applied the more flexible *rule of reason* on a case-by-case basis to determine whether a particular restraint affecting the market for player services violates antitrust law. See, e.g., *Smith v. Pro Football Inc.*, 593 F.2d 1173, 1182 (D.C. Cir. 1978) ("legality of NFL draft should not be governed by *per se* rule . . . legality of player restriction in professional sports should be governed by the rule of reason"); *Mackey v. NFL*, 543 F.2d 606, 619 (8th Cir. 1976) ("unique nature of the business of professional football renders it inappropriate to mechanically apply *per se* illegality rules" to challenged league free agency restrictions). See also *National Hockey League Players' Assn. v. Plymouth Whalers Hockey Club*, 325 F.3d 712 (6th Cir. 2003); *McNeil v. NFL*, 790 F. Supp. 871 (D. Minn. 1992).

Applying the rule of reason to player restraints requires complicated analysis and balancing of several different factors and their economic effects. Considering the validity of the NBA's then-current draft eligibility rules, one court observed:

> The primary disadvantages of the "rule of reason" are that it requires difficult and lengthy factual inquiries and very subjective policy decisions which are in many ways essentially legislative and ill-suited to the judicial process. For instance, in the present case, a complex economic inquiry would be required to determine the economic necessity of action of this type. In addition, the court would be required to determine a standard which could be used to weigh the various public policy goals which might be alleged as justification by the NBA. The court would further be forced to determine whether the boycott was genuinely motivated by the purposes given or by other reasons. Frequently, these motives are closely intertwined.

See *Denver Rockets v. All-Pro Management*, 325 F. Supp. 1049, 1063 (C.D. Cal. 1971).

After the broad judicial characterization of the nonstatutory labor exemption, there are few recent cases in which courts have addressed whether professional sports league labor market restraints violate the federal antitrust laws. Although it is an older case, the Eighth Circuit's application of the rule of reason to the Rozelle Rule in *Mackey* provides an illustration of how courts have applied Sherman Act §1 to labor market restraints and likely would do so today.

MACKEY v. NFL
543 F.2d 606 (8th Cir. 1976)

LAY, Circuit Judge.

. . . ANTITRUST ISSUES

We turn, then, to the question of whether the Rozelle Rule, as implemented, violates § 1 of the Sherman Act, which declares illegal "every contract, combination . . . or conspiracy, in restraint of trade or commerce among the several States." 15 U.S.C. § 1. . . .

RULE OF REASON

The focus of an inquiry under the Rule of Reason is whether the restraint imposed is justified by legitimate business purposes, and is no more restrictive than necessary. . . .

In defining the restraint on competition for players' services, the district court found that the Rozelle Rule significantly deters clubs from negotiating with and signing free agents; that it acts as a substantial deterrent to players playing out their options and becoming free agents; that it significantly decreases players' bargaining power in contract negotiations; that players are thus denied the right to sell their services in a free and open market; that as a result, the salaries paid by each club are lower than if competitive bidding were allowed to prevail; and that absent the Rozelle Rule, there would be increased movement in interstate commerce of players from one club to another.

We find substantial evidence in the record to support these findings. Witnesses for both sides testified that there would be increased player movement absent the Rozelle Rule. . . .

In support of their contention that the restraints effected by the Rozelle Rule are not unreasonable, the defendants asserted a number of justifications. First, they argued that without the Rozelle Rule, star players would flock to cities having natural advantages such as larger economic bases, winning teams, warmer climates, and greater media opportunities; that competitive balance throughout the League would thus be destroyed; and that the destruction of competitive balance would ultimately lead to diminished spectator interest, franchise failures, and perhaps the demise of the NFL, at least as it operates today. Second, the defendants contended that the Rozelle Rule is necessary to protect the clubs' investment in scouting expenses and player development costs. Third, they asserted that players must work together for a substantial period of time in order to function effectively as a team; that elimination of the Rozelle Rule would lead to increased player movement and a concomitant reduction in player continuity; and that the quality of play in the NFL would thus suffer, leading to reduced spectator interest, and financial detriment both to the clubs and the players. Conflicting evidence was adduced at trial by both sides with respect to the validity of these asserted justifications.

The district court held the defendants' asserted justifications unavailing. . . . The court further concluded that elimination of the Rozelle Rule would have no significant disruptive effects, either immediate or long term, on professional football. In conclusion the court held that the Rozelle Rule was unreasonable in that it was overly broad, unlimited in duration, unaccompanied by procedural safeguards, and employed in conjunction with other anticompetitive practices such as the draft, Standard Player Contract, option clause, and the no-tampering rules.

We agree that the asserted need to recoup player development costs cannot justify the restraints of the Rozelle Rule. That expense is an ordinary cost of doing business and is not peculiar to professional football. Moreover, because of its unlimited duration, the Rozelle Rule is far more restrictive than necessary to fulfill that need.

We agree, in view of the evidence adduced at trial with respect to existing players' turnover by way of trades, retirements and new players entering the League, that the club owners' arguments respecting player continuity cannot justify the Rozelle Rule. . . .

In sum, we hold that the Rozelle Rule, as enforced, unreasonably restrains trade in violation of § 1 of the Sherman Act. . . .

NOTES AND QUESTIONS

1. As a threshold matter, an antitrust plaintiff must prove actual or threatened economic loss caused by the anticompetitive effects of the defendant's challenged conduct. This "antitrust injury" requirement is relatively easily satisfied by professional players challenging labor market restraints that reduce their potential income. If an antitrust violation is proved, a player's damages generally are based on the difference between his actual compensation and the value of his services in a free market. See *Smith v. Pro Football, Inc.*, 593 F.2d 1173, 1189-1191 (D.C. Cir. 1979).

2. *Single-Entity Defense.* Most litigation seeking to invalidate player restraints involves claimed violations of §1 of the Sherman Act, which requires concerted anticompetitive conduct. Courts previously rejected the argument that a professional sports league and its member clubs function as a single economic entity whose labor market rules are not subject to challenge under §1, which seems correct given the Supreme Court's rejection of the single entity defense in *American Needle, Inc. v. NFL, supra.*

   In *McNeil v. NFL*, 790 F. Supp. 871 (D. Minn. 1992), the court held that agreements among league clubs to reduce competition for player services are subject to §1. See also *Chicago Professional Sports Ltd. Partnership v. NBA (Bulls IV)*, 95 F.3d 593, 599 (7th Cir. 1996) ("[F]rom the perspective of college basketball players who seek to sell their skills, the teams are distinct, and because the human capital of players is not readily transferable to other sports (as even Michael Jordan learned) the league looks more like a group of firms acting as a monopsony").

3. *Anticompetitive Effects.* Under the rule of reason, a player must prove that the challenged restraint reduces economic competition among the defendants for player services. *National Hockey League Players' Assn. v. Plymouth Whalers*, 419 F.3d 462, 474 (6th Cir. 2005) (dismissing antitrust claims because the mere "diminished quality of athletic competition" is not "an anti-competitive effect within the meaning of the antitrust laws"). For example, agreements among league clubs to fix players' wages, which thereby eliminate individual salary negotiations, have clear anticompetitive effects. *McNeil v. NFL*, 790 F. Supp. 871, 877 (D. Minn. 1992).

   Because their adverse economic effects are not as direct and less clear, other labor market restraints such as player drafts, free agency restrictions, and other forms of allocating players among league clubs may require detailed market analysis to determine their effects on economic competition. In such cases, the plaintiff must prove the relevant market for the services of players and that the defendant league and its clubs have a sufficiently large market share to adversely affect competition. The relevant market has both a product and a geographical component. The product market includes all prospective purchasers of player services that are reasonable substitutes from the players' perspective in terms of earning potential, prestige, and other economic factors. *Smith v. Pro Football, Inc.*, 593 F.2d 1173, 1185 n.48 (D.C. Cir. 1979) (finding that employment in Canadian Football League is not a reasonable substitute for employment with an NFL team). The geographical market is the geographical area "to which players can turn, as a practical matter, for alternate opportunities for employment" as professional athletes. *Fraser v. Major League Soccer, LLC,* 284 F.3d 47, 63 (1st Cir. 2002), *cert. denied,* 537 U.S. 885 (2002) (upholding jury finding of an international market for the services of professional soccer players).

4. *Legitimate Procompetitive Justifications.* Some early cases held that the anticompetitive effects of labor market restraints cannot be justified by procompetitive effects in a different market. As one court explained:

> The draft is "procompetitive," if at all, in a very different sense from that in which it is anticompetitive. The draft is anticompetitive in its effect on the market for players' services, because it virtually eliminates economic competition among buyers for the services of sellers. The draft is allegedly "procompetitive" in its effect on the playing field; but the NFL teams are not economic competitors on the playing field, and the draft, while it may heighten athletic competition and thus improve the entertainment product offered to the public, does not increase competition in the economic sense of encouraging others to enter the market and to offer the product at lower cost. Because the draft's "anticompetitive" and "procompetitive" effects are not comparable, it is impossible to "net them out" in the usual rule-of-reason balancing. The draft's "anticompetitive evils," in other words, cannot be balanced against its "procompetitive virtues," and the draft be upheld if the latter outweigh the former. In strict economic terms, the draft's demonstrated procompetitive effects are nil.

Smith v. Pro Football, Inc., 593 F.2d 1173, 1186 (D.C. Cir. 1979).
More recently, other courts have ruled that procompetitive effects in a closely related market (i.e., those that enhance a professional sports league's ability to more effectively compete with other forms of entertainment) should be balanced against a restraint's anticompetitive effects. *Sullivan v. NFL,* 34 F.3d 1091, 1111-1113 (1st Cir. 1994). In *American Needle, Inc. v. NFL,* 560 U.S. 183, the Supreme Court recognized that a professional sports league's interest in maintaining competitive balance among its member clubs is "legitimate and important," which is "unquestionably an interest that may well justify a variety of collective decisions made by the teams." *American Needle* strongly suggests that a sports league can justify labor market restraints by proving they promote competitive balance and playing field equality among its member clubs, thereby producing better entertainment for consumers, effectively overruling or at least casting substantial doubt on the continuing validity of cases such as *Smith.*

5. *Less Restrictive Alternatives.* Although *Mackey* did not consider this issue, a labor market restraint likely will be invalidated if there is a substantially less restrictive means of achieving the league's procompetitive objective. *Smith v. Pro Football, Inc.,* 593 F.2d 1173, 118 (D.C. Cir. 1979) (holding that the NFL's 16-round draft violated §1 because "significantly less anticompetitive alternatives" exist to maintain competitive balance among NFL clubs). Since *Smith,* there has been a collectively bargained seven-round NFL draft.

6. *Practical Considerations.* Why do major league professional team-sport players generally unionize? Why do the league and its clubs, unlike employers in virtually all other industries, usually prefer that they unionize?

PROBLEM 7-5

Work stoppages and the corresponding legal issues that surround them provide an excellent opportunity to examine labor relations in unionized professional sports and to review the application of labor and antitrust law concepts in disputes between players and their union with the league and its clubs.

Under the existing NBA CBA, the team salary cap amount varies from year to year because it is calculated as a percentage of the league's revenue from the previous season. Because of steadily increasing revenues, the salary cap was $101.9 million for the 2018-19 season. Assume that when the current CBA expires after the 2023-24 season (June 30, 2024), the NBA owners, unhappy with the continually increasing salary cap, vote to lock out the players, demanding that the cap should not increase by more than 2% for the 2024-25 season and for each of the following four seasons.

When voting to end the lockout on December 15, 2024, the NBA club owners mandate that all players under contract for the 2024-25 season report to their respective teams within 72 hours. They unilaterally implement the foregoing salary cap proposal, which the NBPA union had rejected. They also eliminate the "Larry Bird exception" (which allows a team to exceed the salary cap to re-sign and retain the rights to a player whose contract with the team expires and who is eligible for free agency) without any notice to the NBPA after NBA commissioner Adam Silver publicly states it is inconsistent with the "best interests of the game."

During the lockout, some NBA players agreed to lucrative multi-million-dollar contract offers to play for European professional league teams. European league rules generally permit each team to have only two players born in the United States on its roster, so most NBA players were unable to play professional basketball during the lockout. All European teams require their NBA players to give at least two weeks' notice to the team before ending their contract.

Assume that the NBA club owners' collective bargaining representative asserts that economic necessity and the need for certainty in determining each team's labor costs for player salaries justifies their unilateral actions. She claims that notwithstanding increasing league revenues, several NBA team owners, particularly those in smaller markets, lost money during the years in which the previous CBA was in effect because of sharply escalating player salaries attributable to, among other things, the "Larry Bird exception."

The NBPA vigorously objects to this unilateral action and questions whether any club owners actually lost money, particularly because the owners refused to provide the union with any documentation of their claimed losses. The union contends that a combination of increased revenue sharing among NBA teams and a higher luxury tax on teams whose aggregate player salaries exceed the salary cap because of the "Larry Bird exception" is a better solution to the owners' economic concerns. The NBPA proposes that collective luxury tax proceeds be distributed on a pro rata basis to the six NBA teams with the lowest gross revenues to assist them in paying their players' salaries. It also notes that NBA players on European teams cannot meet the 72-hour deadline because of their contractual commitments to their respective clubs.

a.   What labor law remedies, if any, should the NBPA pursue in response to the NBA owners' actions?

b. What must the NBA players do to bring an antitrust challenge to the NBA clubs' unilaterally imposed fixed salary cap increase system and the elimination of the "Larry Bird exception"? Separately analyze whether either of these actions violates §1 of the Sherman Act.

E. DEVELOPING INTERNATIONAL LABOR ISSUES

Professional sports leagues and associations around the globe must grapple with an increasing array of business and legal issues that transcend national borders. Although those issues have so far related in large part to the movement of professional athletes from one country to another, MLB, MLS, the NBA, and the NHL all have at least one club in Canada (the NHL has seven), and it appears that one or more of these major professional leagues may expand outside the United States and Canada, most likely to Europe, in the future. The following case, decided by the European Court of Justice (ECJ), exemplifies some of the legal issues that may arise if this happens. It deserves study not just for the specific issue it addresses under European Union law, but also as an illustration of the complex intersection of the competing interests of players, domestic professional sports clubs, national federations, and international sports governing bodies.

UNION ROYALE BELGE DES SOCIÉTÉS DE FOOTBALL ASSOCIATION, ROYAL CLUB LIÉGOIS, AND UNION DES ASSOCIATIONS EUROPÉENNES DE FOOTBALL (UEFA) v. JEAN-MARC BOSMAN (BOSMAN)

Case C-415/93 (European Court of Justice, 15 December 1995)

* * *

THE RULES GOVERNING THE ORGANIZATION OF FOOTBALL

Association football, commonly known as "football," professional or amateur, is practised as an organized sport in clubs which belong to national associations or federations in each of the Member States.

The national associations are members of the Fédération Internationale de Football Association ("FIFA"), an association governed by Swiss law, which organizes football at world level. FIFA is divided into confederations for each continent, whose regulations require its approval. . . .

TRANSFER RULES

[EDS. FIFA and UEFA regulations, which are incorporated into the rules of the European national associations, govern the movement of football players between clubs. These regulations are applicable to player transfers between clubs in different European Union countries or clubs belonging to the same national association within a European Union country. Pursuant to these regulations, when a player is transferred between clubs, his new club is required to pay his former club a transfer fee to compensate for the former club's development and training of the player. If the two clubs disagree as to the amount of the transfer fee, it is to be determined by a UEFA board of experts based on a predetermined formula. A transfer fee was required to be paid even if the player's contract with his former club had expired. The former club's national association must issue an international clearance certificate before a player is eligible to play for his new club.]

NATIONALITY CLAUSES

[EDS. Many UEFA national football associations have nationality clauses restricting the extent to which foreign players can be recruited or fielded in a match. For the purposes of these clauses, nationality is defined in relation to whether the player can be qualified to play in a country's national or representative team. After collaboration with the European Commission (which is charged with enforcing the European Union's competition laws), UEFA removed the limitations on the number of contracts entered into by each football club with players from other European Union countries and set the number of such players who may participate in any one match at two, this limit not being applicable to players established for over five years in the member country in question. UEFA subsequently adopted the "3 + 2" rule, permitting each national association to limit to three the number of foreign players a club may field in any first division match in their national championships, plus two players who have played in the country of the relevant national association for an uninterrupted period of five years, including three years as a junior. The same limitation also applies to UEFA matches in competitions for club teams.]

REVELANT FACTS AND BOSMAN'S CLAIMS

[EDS. Mr. Bosman, a professional footballer of Belgian nationality, was employed in 1988 by RC Liège, a Belgian first division club, under a contract expiring on June 30, 1990, which assured him an average monthly salary of BFR (Belgian francs) 120,000, including bonuses. On April 21, 1990, RC Liège offered Mr. Bosman a new contract for one season, reducing his pay to BFR 30,000, the minimum permitted by the URBSFA (the Royal Belgian Football Association) federal rules. Mr. Bosman refused to sign and was put on the transfer list. The compensation fee for training was set, in accordance with the said rules, at BFR 11,743,000. Since no club showed an interest in a compulsory transfer, Mr. Bosman made contact with US Dunkerque, a club in the French second division, which led to his being engaged for a monthly salary in the region of BFR 100,000 plus a signing-on bonus of some BFR 900,000. On July 27, 1990, a contract was also concluded between RC Liège and US Dunkerque for the temporary transfer of Mr. Bosman for one year, against payment by US Dunkerque to RC Liège of a compensation fee of BFR 1,200,000 payable on receipt by the Fédération Française de Football (FFF) of the transfer certificate issued by URBSFA. The contract also gave US Dunkerque an irrevocable option for full transfer of the player for BFR 4,800,000. Both contracts between US Dunkerque and RC Liège and between US Dunkerque and Mr. Bosman were, however, subject to the condition that the transfer certificate must be sent by URBSFA to FFF in time for the first match of the season, which was to be held on August 2, 1990. RC Liège, which had doubts as to US Dunkerque's solvency, did not ask URBSFA to send the certificate to FFF. As a result, neither contract took effect. On July 31, 1990, RC Liège also suspended Mr. Bosman, thereby preventing him from playing for the entire season.

In a suit against RC Liège, URBSFA, and UEFA in a Belgian court, Bosman alleged that the transfer rules and nationality clauses were illegal and sought damages for lost earnings caused by the result of the application of the transfer rules. The Cour d'Appel, Liège, a Belgian appellate court, referred the following questions to the European Court of Justice for resolution.]

Are Articles 48, 85 and 86 of the Treaty of Rome of 25 March 1957 to be interpreted as:

(i)   prohibiting a football club from requiring and receiving payment of a sum of money upon the engagement of one of its players who has come to the end of his contract by a new employing club;

(ii) prohibiting the national and international sporting associations or federations from including in their respective regulations provisions restricting access of foreign players from the European Community to the competitions which they organize?

[EDS. The court at length declined to discuss Articles 85 and 86, the European Union competitions laws, relying instead on its interpretations of Article 48's prohibited restrictions on workers' freedom of movement among European Union countries.]

APPLICATION OF ARTICLE 48 TO RULES LAID DOWN
BY SPORTING ASSOCIATIONS

. . . UEFA argued, inter alia, that the Community authorities have always respected the autonomy of sport, that it is extremely difficult to distinguish between the economic and the sporting aspects of football and that a decision of the Court concerning the situation of professional players might call in question the organization of football as a whole. For that reason, even if Article 48 of the Treaty were to apply to professional players, a degree of flexibility would be essential because of the particular nature of the sport.

. . . [I]t is to be remembered that, having regard to the objectives of the Community, sport is subject to Community law only in so far as it constitutes an economic activity within the meaning of Article 2 of the Treaty. . . .

. . . [F]or the purposes of the application of the Community provisions on freedom of movement for workers . . . all that is required is the existence of, or the intention to create, an employment relationship.

Application of Article 48 of the Treaty is not precluded by the fact that the transfer rules govern the business relationships between clubs rather than the employment relationships between clubs and players. The fact that the employing clubs must pay fees on recruiting a player from another club affects the players' opportunities for finding employment and the terms under which such employment is offered.

. . . [T]he freedom of movement of workers guaranteed by Article 48 . . . is a fundamental freedom in the Community system. . . .

WHETHER THE SITUATION ENVISAGED BY THE NATIONAL COURT IS OF A PURELY INTERNAL NATURE

UEFA considers that the disputes pending before the national court concern a purely internal Belgian situation which falls outside the ambit of Article 48 of the Treaty. They concern a Belgian player whose transfer fell through because of the conduct of a Belgian club and a Belgian association.

It is true that . . . the provisions of the Treaty concerning the free movement of workers, and particularly Article 48, cannot be applied to situations which are wholly internal to a Member State. . . . However, it is clear from the findings of fact made by the national court that Mr. Bosman had entered into a contract of employment with a club in another Member State with a view to exercising gainful employment in that State. By so doing, as he has rightly pointed out, he accepted an offer of employment actually made, within the meaning of Article 48(3)(a).

Since the situation in issue in the main proceedings cannot be classified as purely internal, the argument put forward by UEFA must be dismissed.

EXISTENCE OF AN OBSTACLE TO FREEDOM OF MOVEMENT FOR WORKERS

It is thus necessary to consider whether the transfer rules form an obstacle to freedom of movement for workers prohibited by Article 48 of the Treaty. . . .

The Court has also held that the provisions of the Treaty relating to freedom of movement for persons are intended to facilitate the pursuit by Community citizens of occupational activities of all kinds throughout the Community, and preclude measures which might place Community citizens at a disadvantage when they wish to pursue an economic activity in the territory of another Member State. . . .

In that context, nationals of Member States have in particular the right, which they derive directly from the Treaty, to leave their country of origin to enter the territory of another Member State and reside there in order to pursue an economic activity. . . .

Provisions which preclude or deter a national of a Member State from leaving his country of origin in order to exercise his right to freedom of movement therefore constitute an obstacle to that freedom even if they apply without regard to the nationality of the workers concerned. . . .

Since they provide that a professional footballer may not pursue his activity with a new club established in another Member State unless it has paid his former club a transfer fee agreed upon between the two clubs or determined in accordance with the regulations of the sporting associations, the said rules constitute an obstacle to freedom of movement for workers.

EXISTENCE OF JUSTIFICATIONS

First, URBSFA, UEFA and the French and Italian Governments have submitted that the transfer rules are justified by the need to maintain a financial and competitive balance between clubs and to support the search for talent and the training of young players. . . .

As regards the first of those aims, Mr. Bosman has rightly pointed out that the application of the transfer rules is not an adequate means of maintaining financial and competitive balance in the world of football. Those rules neither preclude the richest clubs from securing the services of the best players nor prevent the availability of financial resources from being a decisive factor in competitive sport, thus considerably altering the balance between clubs.

As regards the second aim, it must be accepted that the prospect of receiving transfer, development or training fees is indeed likely to encourage football clubs to seek new talent and train young players.

However, because it is impossible to predict the sporting future of young players with any certainty and because only a limited number of such players go on to play professionally, those fees are by nature contingent and uncertain and are in any event unrelated to the actual cost borne by clubs of training both future professional players and those who will never play professionally. The prospect of receiving such fees cannot, therefore, be either a decisive factor in encouraging recruitment and training of young players or an adequate means of financing such activities, particularly in the case of smaller clubs. Furthermore, as the Advocate General has pointed out, the same aims can be achieved at least as efficiently by other means which do not impede freedom of movement for workers. . . .

Finally, the argument that the rules in question are necessary to compensate clubs for the expenses which they have had to incur in paying fees on recruiting their players cannot be accepted, since it seeks to justify the maintenance of obstacles to freedom of movement for workers simply on the ground that such obstacles were able to exist in the past.

The answer to the first question must therefore be that Article 48 of the Treaty precludes the application of rules laid down by sporting associations, under which a professional footballer who is a national of one Member State may not, on the expiry of his contract with a club, be employed by a club of another Member State unless the latter club has paid to the former club a transfer, training or development fee.

INTERPRETATION OF ARTICLE 48 OF THE TREATY WITH REGARD TO THE NATIONALITY CLAUSES

By its second question, the national court seeks in substance to ascertain whether Article 48 of the Treaty precludes the application of rules laid down by sporting associations, under which, in matches in competitions which they organize, football clubs may field only a limited number of professional players who are nationals of other Member States.

EXISTENCE OF AN OBSTACLE TO FREEDOM OF MOVEMENT FOR WORKERS

As the Court has held . . . above, Article 48 of the Treaty applies to rules laid down by sporting associations which determine the conditions under which professional sports players may engage in gainful employment. It must therefore be considered whether the nationality clauses constitute an obstacle to freedom of movement for workers, prohibited by Article 48.

Article 48(2) expressly provides that freedom of movement for workers entails the abolition of any discrimination based on nationality between workers of the Member States as regards employment, remuneration and conditions of work and employment. . . .

[This] principle applies to clauses contained in the regulations of sporting associations which restrict the right of nationals of other Member States to take part, as professional players, in football matches. . . .

The fact that those clauses concern not the employment of such players, on which there is no restriction, but the extent to which their clubs may field them in official matches is irrelevant. In so far as participation in such matches is the essential purpose of a professional player's activity, a rule which restricts that participation obviously also restricts the chances of employment of the player concerned.

EXISTENCE OF JUSTIFICATIONS

The existence of an obstacle having thus been established, it must be considered whether that obstacle may be justified in the light of Article 48 of the Treaty.

URBSFA, UEFA and the German, French and Italian Governments argued that the nationality clauses are justified on non-economic grounds, concerning only the sport as such. . . .

It must be recalled that in . . . its judgment in *Donà*, the Court held that the Treaty provisions concerning freedom of movement for persons do not prevent the adoption of rules or practices excluding foreign players from certain matches for reasons which are not of an economic nature, which relate to the particular nature and context of such matches and are thus of sporting interest only, such as, for example, matches between national teams from different countries. It stressed, however, that that restriction on the scope of the provisions in question must remain limited to its proper objective.

Here, the nationality clauses do not concern specific matches between teams representing their countries but apply to all official matches between clubs and thus to the essence of the activity of professional players.

In those circumstances, the nationality clauses cannot be deemed to be in accordance with Article 48 of the Treaty, otherwise that article would be deprived of its practical effect and the fundamental right of free access to employment which the Treaty confers individually on each worker in the Community rendered nugatory. . . . None of the arguments put forward by the sporting associations and by the governments which have submitted observations detracts from that conclusion.

It follows . . . that Article 48 of the Treaty precludes the application of rules laid down by sporting associations under which, in matches in competitions which they organize, football clubs may field only a limited number of professional players who are nationals of other Member States. . . .

NOTES AND QUESTIONS

1. *U.S. Leagues in Foreign Countries.* As noted above, U.S. professional sports leagues such as the NHL, NBA, MLB, and MLS have clubs in the United

States and Canada. In addition to cultural differences in business practices and currency valuation, there are many complex legal issues to consider when a professional sports league operates in multiple countries. For example, Canadian labor law is largely provincial rather than national, as it is in the United States. See generally Jo-Annie Charbonneau, *A Comparative Analysis of American and Canadian Antitrust and Labor Laws as Applied to Professional Sports League Lockouts and Potential Solutions to Prevent Their Occurrence*, 26 Marq. Sports L. Rev. 111 (2015).

Considering *Bosman*, how would its labor issues become more complicated if a U.S. professional league established a division or satellite league in two or more countries that are part of the European Union? Note that the ECJ's analysis and application of the EU's workers' freedom of movement law to the challenged player transfer/fee rules and nationality requirements is substantially similar to a U.S. court's application of the rule of reason in a Sherman Act §1 case.

2. *U.S. League Agreements with Foreign Governing Bodies and Professional Leagues.* The NBA and MLB have agreements with foreign leagues and organizations that seek to stabilize the process by which players move from a club in one country to one in another country.

The NBA's agreement with the international governing federation for basketball (FIBA) requires recognition by all concerned parties that an existing player contract will be respected and not interfered with during its term. Note the implications of this agreement in connection with the dispute giving rise to *Boston Celtics v. Shaw, supra.*

A central agreement for MLB is a U.S.-Japanese Player Contract Agreement, although dealings with several other countries, most notably South American countries, Mexico, and Caribbean countries, are important as well. The U.S.-Japanese contract provides, among other things, that American players not under present contractual restrictions in the United States can be contacted by a club in Nippon Professional Baseball (NPB), which is Japan's MLB equivalent, and signed to a contract after clearance by the office of the U.S. commissioner. However, if the player, though not bound by an actual contract, is on the reserve, military, voluntarily retired, restricted, disqualified, suspended, or ineligible list of any club, then approval to sign the player must be obtained through the office of the commissioner.

The issue is more complicated for U.S. clubs wishing to sign a Japanese player. Under a "posting system" agreed to by MLB and NPB in 2013, any NPB club wishing to release a player from his contract must at some point between November 1 and February 1 of the off-season inform MLB's Office of the Commissioner of the amount of money it requires as a "release fee" to allow the player to negotiate with an MLB club. The fee may not exceed $20 million. The Office of the Commissioner then notifies all MLB clubs of the posting, and any interested club willing to pay the release fee then has 30 days to negotiate a contract with the player. Importantly, the release fee buys only the right to negotiate with the player; the monetary terms of the player's negotiated contract are a separate matter altogether. Only the club that successfully negotiates with and signs the player, however, must pay the release fee; those that fail to sign the player are not required to pay. Agents are, of course, heavily involved in the posting process, and NPB players seeking to play in the U.S usually affiliate with an American-based agent to help with the post-posting contract negotiations.

3. *The Risk of Athlete Exploitation.* As sport globalizes and as the potential for athletes and their handlers from all over the world to make large sums of money increases, the potential for exploitation of athletes increases as well. Consider the following description of risks that professional sport's globalization poses to young soccer and baseball players from developing nations:

> One growing concern in the international soccer community . . . is a phenomenon of unscrupulous fraudsters preying on young players from impoverished nations with dreams of international glory. This phenomenon is illustrated perhaps most clearly with West African players.
>
> As European clubs have over the past two decades expanded their recruiting scope and as West African players such as Cameroon national Samuel Eto'o and Ivory Coast national Yaya Toure have found fame and fortune playing in Europe, a seemingly unending pool of young players stand anxious to leave their homes for a chance at what their heroes have achieved. Fraudulent pseudo agents capitalize on this hope.
>
> A European Commission study lays bare the pattern that repeats itself again and again and ensnares these prospects: 1) A pseudo agent sees or otherwise learns of a player interested in playing professionally in Europe; 2) the pseudo agent convinces the player's family that his prospects in Europe are bright and extracts money from the player's family ostensibly in exchange for travel and accommodations in Europe; 3) the pseudo agent arranges for the player to enter Europe on a short-term tourist visa rather than a visa appropriate for an athlete pursuing employment; 4) if the player actually has tryouts with teams, they are with less prestigious teams than promised; 5) if the player is offered a contract, it is generally disadvantageous to the player and advantageous to the pseudo agent; 6) if no contract is offered, the pseudo agent abandons the player; and, 7) the player, unlawfully in the country with few options, turns to illegal activity.
>
> The ever-expanding reach of social media has further exacerbated the problem, with pseudo agents contacting players through Facebook and Twitter. Because FIFA's agent database provides agents' names but not their contact information, an imposter can easily use a false name and his or her own contact information to lure in young players. [While current numbers are unavailable,] as of 2010, an estimated 20,000 young West African soccer players had suffered some version of the above fate and were stranded in Europe.
>
> . . . FIFA guidelines are, by most assessments, ill-equipped to combat this threat and its potential outcome. . . . FIFA regulations aside, due to political instability and in some cases outright corruption, in many of the players' home nations broader immigration controls are often found wanting. Unregistered agents are often able to bribe immigration officials and alter documents. . . .
>
> Like soccer, baseball involves substantial numbers of players leaving their home nations to play abroad, but whereas the destination in soccer is more likely than not Europe, the destination in baseball is more likely than not the United States. Addressing the problem of player abuse in the soccer context, as noted above, is certainly challenging. Doing so, however, in the baseball context, in which hundreds of thousands of young players from Latin America dream of traveling to the United States to play Major League Baseball, is in many ways more complex due the unique position occupied by scouts and coaches who double as informal agents. In the Dominican Republic, which exports far more baseball talent to the United States than any other nation, these quasi agents are known as buscones. Buscon, derived from the Spanish verb buscar, meaning to find, is a broad term used to describe local talent

scouts who act as scout and/or coach and/or agent for baseball prospects in the overwhelmingly poor nation. And although the term buscon is specifically used in the Dominican Republic, similar talent scouts operate in other Latin American nations that supply MLB with players, such as Venezuela, Mexico, and Panama.

Often these buscones discover players when they have barely reached adolescence and work with them for years. Some buscones are largely or entirely beneficent participants in the developmental process . . . [but others] are unabashed opportunists who demand as much as 50% "of an athlete's bonus money as 'compensation' for providing assistance and training prior to signing by a major league club."

In recent years, MLB has attempted to increase the regulation of baseball development in the Dominican Republic and, in particular, of bad-acting buscones, through a number of initiatives. It has adopted guidelines requiring that players receive Spanish-language versions of contracts so that players require no intervention by a buscon or other third-party to read the terms. In addition, to reduce the theft of bonuses or portions of bonuses, MLB provides Dominican prospects tutoring on how to access and protect their money and requires that all bonuses be wired through an established Dominican bank directly to the player. The ultimate efficacy of these reforms remains untold, but it is clear that buscones continue to operate as quasi agents in the Dominican Republic.

See Kenneth L. Shropshire, Timothy Davis, and N. Jeremi Duru, The Business of Sports Agents (3d ed. 2016).

What obligation does the sports industry, which generates huge revenues from athletes' talents and labor, have to protect young athletes from the sorts of exploitation described above? If sports organizations are unable or unwilling to protect these young athletes through regulation, which other regulatory bodies can or should step in?

CHAPTER
8

Regulating Agents

A. INTRODUCTION

As discussed in Chapter 6, the use of agents by professional athletes can be traced back to as early as the mid-1920s, when Charles Pyle negotiated a football contract and endorsement and movie deals for NFL player Harold "Red" Grange. The proliferation in the number and use of agents by athletes occurred in the 1960s and 1970s, as a result of: (1) the demise of reserve and option clauses in standard-form contracts between players and clubs; (2) competition for players between rival leagues (e.g., the National Football League (NFL) and the American Football League (AFL)); (3) the growing strength of labor unions and their positive impact on players' salaries; (4) the increased income of athletes that necessitated advice on matters ranging from taxes to estates; and (5) the increase in players' opportunities to generate outside income through endorsement contracts.

The proliferation in the use of agents also has been accompanied by an expansion in the range of services that they perform. The role of agents extends beyond the commonly held belief that their job is to negotiate a player's contract with his or her club. The functions performed by agents include the following:

> Contract negotiations, tax planning, financial planning, money management, investments, estate planning, income tax preparation, incorporating the client, endorsements, sports medicine consultations, physical health consultations, post-career development, career and personal development counseling, legal consultations and insurance matters.

Walter T. Champion, Jr., *Attorneys Qua Sports Agents: An Ethical Conundrum*, 7 Marq. Sports L.J. 349, 351-52 (1997). Agents also assist athletes in brand building by leveraging endorsements, digital content, and philanthropy.

The range of services that athlete agents perform is indicative of the breadth of substantive expertise required for agents to effectively represent athletes. Few people, however, have the ability or expertise to perform all the tasks identified above. Perhaps out of ignorance or greed, some agents take on more tasks than they can competently handle. Unless they are a part of an agency that employs individuals with diverse professional expertise ready to assist, agents may well overreach and perform at levels approaching negligence. Despite the useful functions provided by agents, inappropriate agent conduct that is detrimental to athletes is a pervasive part of the relationship.

This chapter examines mechanisms that regulate the agent-athlete relationship and seek to enhance the likelihood that agents and athletes fulfill their respective obligations. These mechanisms consist of a web of common law rules, state and federal legislation, and regulations promulgated by players associations. Our examination begins with an analysis of common law principles, derived primarily from the law of agency and contract, which are instrumental in regulating the agent-athlete relationship.

B.   THE NATURE OF THE RELATIONSHIP

1.   Basic Duties

This section examines the legal duties agents owe to their athlete clients and the standard of care adopted by courts to determine if those duties are competently performed. The following excerpt provides the legal framework within which to consider these cases.

THE LEGAL BASIS OF THE RELATIONSHIP[1]

In defending his agent against criticism, former NFL running back Ricky Williams stated. "I'm first and last when it comes to my decisions. . . . I don't work for my agent. My agent works for me."

Williams's statement is instructive for two reasons. First, Williams demonstrates an appreciation for the most fundamental principle of the agent's relationship with his principal: ultimate decision making authority rests with the principal. In addition, Williams's statement illustrates that the relationship between sports agents and the athletes whom they represent are governed by the same core concepts that govern other principal/agent relationships. . . ."

The agency relationship is defined as "the fiduciary relationship which results from the manifestation of consent by one person to another that the other shall act in his behalf and subject to his contract, and consent by the other so to act." The Restatement (Third) of the Law of Agency also provides definitions of agent and principal. The principal is "the one for whom action is to be taken." In the sports context, the athlete is the principal. The agent is "the one who is to act" for the principal. "The essential nature and character of the agency relationship is that the principal authorizes his agent to contract on his behalf with one or more third parties."

These definitions tell us that the agency relationship is consensual—typically expressed in a contract. This is certainly the case in the sports context in which the major sports leagues have developed model contracts for the agent-principal

1. Originally published in Kenneth L. Shropshire, Timothy Davis & Jeremi N. Duru, The Business of Sports Agents (3d ed. 2016). Reprinted with permission of the University of Pennsylvania Press.

relationship. For example, the NFLPA has developed a "Standard Representation Agreement" for mandatory use by agents and their football-player clients. In addition to provisions governing the fees to which an agent is entitled, the NFLPA agreement sets forth general principles including the concept that the "Contract Advisor" shall be required to "act at all times in a fiduciary capacity on behalf of players." The Uniform Athlete Agents Act provides the following definition: "'Agency contract' means an agreement in which a student-athlete authorizes a person to negotiate or solicit on behalf of the student-athlete a professional-sports-services contract or an endorsement contract."

The above definitions relating to agency also inform us that the most basic obligations that agents owe to their principals are defined not only by contract, but also by the fiduciary characteristics of the relationship. A fiduciary is defined as "one who acts primarily for the benefit of another." Consequently, the essence of the principal/agent relationship spawns a fundamental obligation that the "agent owes his principal the fiduciary duty of undivided loyalty and the duty to act in good faith at all times. This fiduciary relationship is imposed by law upon the agent because the very nature of the agency relationship involves the principal entrusting his fortune, reputation, and legal rights and responsibilities to his agent whose actions, for better or worse, vitally affect the economic well-being and reputation of the principal."

Ricky Williams's statement quoted above reflects the basic notion that it is an agent's duty to carry out the desires of the principal. This certainly makes sense, as the agent acts not to carry on its own business affairs, but those of the principal. Thus, it is the agent's duty to act in accordance with his or her principal's instructions even if the agent believes they are unwise. As stated by two commentators, "An agent has the duty to obey all of his principal's lawful instructions no matter how arbitrary or capricious any of those instructions seem to the agent or anyone else. . . . By contrast, if the principal's instructions are illegal, immoral, unethical, or opposed to public policy, as where the principal instructs his agent to bribe another to obtain business for his principal, the agent has no duty to obey." Moreover, by acting on its principal's behalf, the agent assumes a duty that he or she "possesses a degree of skill commensurate with the job to be done and that he will use such skill with diligence." In exercising this duty of reasonable care and skill, it is important to emphasize that the agent does not guarantee or ensure that he or she will achieve the result desired by the client unless the agent has expressly agreed to do so. Rather the agent has fulfilled his or her duty by acting with the care and skill employed by a reasonable person under the same circumstances. . . .

Another basic duty of the agent to the principal seems particularly relevant in the sports context. The agent must account to the principal for all of the principal's funds that come into the agent's possession as a part of the agency relationship. Other basic duties that the agent owes to the principal include the duty to comply with the law, the duty to notify the principal of all matters that may affect the principal's interests, and the duty not to delegate the performance to another without the consent of the principal.

Finally, the agent owes a duty of loyalty and good faith to his or her principal. This duty precludes an agent from acting on behalf of parties adverse to his or her principal. Courts have attempted to incorporate these core concepts into rulings addressing matters ranging from agent malpractice to conflict of interest.

2. *The Standard of Care*

ZINN v. PARRISH

644 F.2d 360 (7th Cir. 1981)

BARTELS, Judge.

This is an appeal in a diversity action by Leo Zinn from a judgment of the District Court for the Northern District of Illinois, Eastern Division, wherein he sought to recover agent fees due him under a personal management contract between him and the defendant Lemar Parrish. . . .

FACTS

For over two decades the appellant Zinn had been engaged in the business of managing professional athletes. He stated that he was a pioneer in bringing to the attention of various pro-football teams the availability of talented players at small black colleges in the South. In the Spring of 1970, Parrish's coach at Lincoln University approached Zinn and informed him that Parrish had been picked by the Cincinnati Bengals in the annual National Football League draft of college seniors, and asked him if he would help Parrish in negotiating the contract. After Zinn contacted Parrish, the latter signed a one-year "Professional Management Contract" with Zinn in the Spring of 1970, pursuant to which Zinn helped Parrish negotiate the terms of his rookie contract with the Bengals, receiving as his commission 10% of Parrish's $16,500 salary. On April 10, 1971 Parrish signed the contract at issue in this case, which differed from the 1970 contract only insofar as it was automatically renewed from year to year unless one of the parties terminated it by 30 days' written notice to the other party. There were no other restrictions placed on the power of either party to terminate the contract.

Under the 1971 contract, Zinn obligated himself to use "reasonable efforts" to procure pro-football employment for Parrish, and, at Parrish's request, to "act" in furtherance of Parrish's interest by: (a) negotiating job contracts; (b) furnishing advice on business investments; (c) securing professional tax advice at no added cost; and (d) obtaining endorsement contracts. It was further provided that Zinn's services would include, "at my request efforts to secure for me gainful off-season employment," for which Zinn would receive no additional compensation, "unless such employment (was) in the line of endorsements, marketing and the like," in which case Zinn would receive a 10% commission on the gross amount. If Parrish failed to pay Zinn amounts due under the contract, Parrish authorized "the club or clubs that are obligated to pay me to pay to you instead all monies and other considerations due me from which you can deduct your 10% and any other monies due you. . . ."

Over the course of Parrish's tenure with the Bengals, Zinn negotiated base salaries for him of $18,500 in 1971; $27,000 in 1972; $35,000 in 1973 (plus a $6,500 signing bonus); and a $250,000 series of contracts covering the four seasons commencing in 1974 (plus a $30,000 signing bonus). The 1974-77 contracts with the Bengals were signed at a time when efforts were being made by the newly-formed World Football League to persuade players in the NFL to "jump" to the WFL to play on one of its teams. By the end of [the] 1973 season

Parrish had become recognized as one of the more valuable players in the NFL. He was twice selected for the Pro Bowl game, and named by Sporting News as one of the best cornerbacks in the league. Towards the end of the 1973 season, the Bengals approached Parrish with an offer of better contract terms than he had earlier been receiving. By way of exploring alternatives in the WFL, Zinn entered into preliminary discussions with the Jacksonville Sharks in early 1974, but decided not to pursue the matter once he ascertained that the Sharks were in a shaky financial position. In retrospect, Zinn's and Parrish's decision to continue negotiating and finally sign with the Bengals was a sound one, for the Sharks and the rest of the WFL with them folded in 1975 due to a lack of funds.

Shortly after signing the 1974 series of contracts, Parrish informed Zinn by telephone that he "no longer needed his services." By letter dated October 16, 1975 Parrish reiterated this position, and added that he had no intention of paying Zinn a 10% commission on those contracts. In view of its disposition of the case, the district court made no specific fact finding as to the amounts Parrish earned during the 1974-77 seasons. Zinn claims that the total was at least $304,500 including bonus and performance clauses. The 1971 contract by its terms entitled Zinn to 10% of the total amount as each installment was paid, and Zinn claims that he has only received $4,300 of the amounts due him. Accordingly, this suit was filed to recover the balance, plus interest at the rate of 5% per annum for vexatious delay in payment, pursuant to Ill.Rev.Stat., ch. 74, § 2.

In addition to negotiating the Bengals contracts, Zinn performed a number of other services at Parrish's request. In 1972 he assisted him in purchasing a residence as well as a four-unit apartment building to be used for rental income; he also helped to manage the apartment building. That same year Zinn negotiated an endorsement contract for Parrish with All-Pro Graphics, Inc., under which Parrish received a percentage from the sales of "Lemar Parrish" t-shirts, sweatshirts, beach towels, key chains, etc. The record shows that Zinn made a number of unsuccessful efforts at obtaining similar endorsement income from stores with which Parrish did business in Ohio. He also tried, unsuccessfully, to obtain an appearance for Parrish on the Mike Douglas Show. Zinn arranged for Parrish's taxes to be prepared each year by H & R Block.[2]

The evidence showed that, despite his efforts, Zinn was unable to obtain off-season employment for Parrish. In this connection, however, it was Zinn's advice to Parrish that he return to school during the off-season months in order to finish his college degree, against the time when he would no longer be able to play football. With respect to Zinn's obligation to provide Parrish with advice on "business investments," he complied first, by assisting in the purchase of the apartment building; and second, by forwarding to Parrish the stock purchase recommendations of certain other individuals, after screening the suggestions himself. There was no evidence that Zinn ever forwarded such recommendations to any of his other clients; he testified that he only did so for Parrish. In summing up Zinn's performance under the contract, Parrish testified as follows:

Did you ever ask Zinn to do anything for you, to your knowledge, that he didn't try to do?

I shall say not, no.

---

2. Once Zinn secured the services of H&R Block for Parrish, his obligation ended. Parrish's contention on appeal that Zinn was at fault for a dispute he later had with the IRS requiring the payment of additional taxes is unfounded.

DISCUSSION

I

We turn, first, to the district court's decision that Zinn's contract was void under the 1940 Act. The Act makes void any contract for investment advice made by an unregistered adviser. 15 U.S.C. § 80b-15(b). . . . [EDS. The court concluded that Zinn had not provided services that brought him within the scope of the act and the contract was not void for his failure to be registered under the act. The court found that Zinn had not held himself out as an investment adviser. Moreover, acts that included Zinn giving Parrish advice regarding a home and an apartment building that Parrish purchased, Zinn engaging in certain managerial tasks at Parrish's request regarding the apartment building, and Parrish sending Zinn $1,500 to invest in Zinn's company did not bring Zinn within the scope of the act. The court concluded that Zinn provided ordinary business advice rather than securities advice. According to the court, "[I]solated transactions with a client as an incident to the main purpose of his management contract to negotiate football contracts do not constitute engaging in the business of advising others on investment securities."]

II

We consider next the district court's judgment that Zinn failed to perform the terms and conditions of his contract. . . . [T]he court concluded that Zinn "was unable to and did not provide the services which he was obligated to provide by the contract under which he sues." We address the findings seriatim.

Employment Procurement

Zinn's obligation under the 1971 Management Contract to procure employment for Parrish as a pro football player was limited to the use of "reasonable efforts." At the time the contract was signed, Parrish was already under contract with the Cincinnati Bengals for the 1970-71 season, with a one-year option clause for the 1971-72 season exercisable by the Bengals. Parrish could not, without being in breach of his Bengals contract, enter into negotiations with other teams for the 1971-72 season. The NFL's own rules prevented one team from negotiating with another team's player who had not yet attained the status of a "free agent." At no time relevant to this litigation did Parrish become a free agent. Thus, unless he decided to contract for future services for the year following the term of the option clause with the Canadian or World Football League, Parrish's only sensible course of action throughout the time Zinn managed him was to negotiate with the Bengals.

Parrish had no objection to Zinn's performance under the professional management contract for the first three years up to 1973, during which time Zinn negotiated football contracts for Parrish. A drastic change, however, took place in 1974 when a four-season contract was negotiated with the Bengals for a total of $250,000 plus a substantial signing bonus. At that time, the new World Football League came into existence and its teams, as well as the teams of the Canadian Football League, were offering good terms to professional football players as an inducement to jump over to their leagues from the NFL. In order to persuade Parrish to remain with the team, the Bengals club itself first initiated the renegotiation of Parrish's contract with an offer of substantially increased compensation. This was not surprising.

Parrish claims, however, that Zinn should have obtained offers from the World Football League that would have placed him in a stronger negotiating position with the Bengals. This is a rather late claim. It was not mentioned in Parrish's letter of termination, and is entirely speculative. Given what Zinn accurately perceived as the unreliability of any offers he might have obtained from the WFL, his representation of Parrish during this period was more than reasonable. As the district court properly noted, prior to the signing of the 1974-77 series of football contracts the needs of the defendant, the services of the plaintiff, and the fees paid by the defendant for those services were all "relatively modest." We conclude that up to that point it is impossible to fault Zinn in the performance of his contract, nor can we find any basis for Parrish to complain of Zinn's efforts in 1974 with respect to procuring employment for him as a pro-football player.

Other Obligations

We focus next on the other obligations, all incidental to the main purpose of the contract. The first of these refers to "negotiating employment contracts with professional athletic organizations and others." Unless this is with respect to a professional football contract, it is difficult to understand to what "professional athletic organizations and others" refers. At all events, there is no claim that there was a failure to negotiate employment contracts with other athletic organizations. And the evidence clearly shows that Zinn performed substantial services in negotiating with the Bengals by letter, telephone, and in person when he and Parrish were flown at the Bengals' expense to Cincinnati for the final stage of negotiations on the 1974-77 series of contracts.

Zinn was further obligated to act in Parrish's professional interest by providing advice on tax and business matters, by "seek[ing] . . . endorsement contracts," and by making "efforts" to obtain for Parrish gainful off-season employment. Each of these obligations was subject to an implied promise to make "good faith" efforts to obtain what he sought. . . . Under Illinois law, such efforts constitute full performance of the obligations. . . . *Id.* Until Parrish terminated the contract, the evidence was clear that Zinn made consistent, good faith efforts to obtain off-season employment and endorsement contracts. Indeed the district court found that Zinn at all times acted in good faith, with a willingness "to provide assistance within his ability." The district court confused success with good faith efforts in concluding that Zinn's failure to obtain in many cases jobs or contracts for Parrish was a failure to perform. Moreover, Zinn did give business advice to Parrish on his real estate purchases, and he did secure tax advice for him.

Parrish fully accepted Zinn's performance for the years 1970, 1971, 1972, and 1973 by remitting the 10% due Zinn under the contract. Parrish was at all times free to discharge Zinn as his agent before a new season began. Instead, he waited until Zinn had negotiated a series of contracts worth a quarter of a million dollars for him before letting Zinn know over the phone that his services were no longer required. That call, coupled with Parrish's failure to make the 10% commission payments as they came due, was a breach of the 1971 contract. [Citation omitted.] The district court was in error in considering Zinn's performance or non-performance during the period following that call, for Parrish by his own breach excused Zinn from any further duties under the contract. . . . Zinn had no obligations thereafter, and Parrish was estopped from asserting Zinn's non-performance as a defense to the suit on the commission fees due him. . . .

Therefore Zinn has a right to recover a 10% commission on all amounts earned by Parrish under the 1974, 1975, 1976, and 1977 Bengals contracts.

We must disagree with the district court's interpretation of the terms of the contract, and Zinn's obligations thereunder, and also with its findings and conclusions concerning Zinn's performance. Insofar as the district court made any findings of fact which are inconsistent with the foregoing, we find them to be clearly erroneous. Consequently, judgment should be entered for Zinn. The decision of the district court is REVERSED, and the case REMANDED for further proceedings consistent with this opinion, including the calculation of damages and interest, if any, due Zinn.

WILLIAMS v. CWI, INC.

777 F. Supp. 1006 (D.D.C. 1991)

SPORKIN, District Judge.

This claim was brought by a young professional basketball player and his wife — Reginald and Kathy Williams — against a financial advisor and his associated companies to recover $50,000 that the Williams had entrusted to the defendant, Waymon Hunt through one of his affiliated companies. Plaintiffs also seek to recover certain costs and expenses that they incurred as a result of Mr. Hunt's actions. Plaintiffs have also prayed for punitive damages. . . .

I.   FINDINGS OF FACT

The facts clearly show that Reginald Williams, a gifted young professional basketball player, and his wife, Kathy, were unsophisticated in matters of finance and business. In the late 1980's, upon his graduation from Georgetown University where he had a distinguished career as a star basketball player, Mr. Williams signed a million-dollar-a-year contract with the Los Angeles Clippers, a National Basketball Association team. As a result of this lucrative contract, Mr. Williams and his wife were looking for opportunities to invest part of Mr. Williams substantial earnings.[1] He was directed to Waymon Hunt, a financial planner, and his company, CWI, Inc., by his wife's parents who had met Mr. Hunt through Clara Neeley who had previously worked in a local bank near Mrs. Williams' parents' home. Ms. Neeley was working for Mr. Hunt by the time the Williams were introduced to him.

---

1. Like many young professional athletes, Mr. Williams was earning a considerable salary but had no experience in making investments or managing his money. He needed reliable expert advice and did not find any readily available. Because Mr. Williams' predicament appears to be a recurring problem for basketball players and other athletes who suddenly receive large disposable incomes, it seems that it would be appropriate for either the NBA, or the players' team, or the players' organization to develop a three-pronged program to assist these young people. First, they could offer at least some rudimentary education in business and finance. Second, they could assemble a package of low-risk blue chip investments for young players that will provide for their futures, as well as a system for referring them to wise and ethical professionals who can advise them on managing money. Third, they might offer a financial incentive for players to place a portion of their funds in a deferred investment program. Perhaps the League and the players' association could even establish their own high-grade, low-risk investment fund. In this way, young athletes would be protected from highly speculative ventures like the one involved in this case.

The Williams first met Mr. Hunt in June of 1988. At that time, they agreed that Mr. Hunt would provide the Williams with financial and tax advice, including preparation of the Williams' tax returns. At approximately that time, Mr. Hunt brought to the Williams' attention an opportunity for investment involving the purchase of a product styled atmospheric reverse refrigeration heating units (hereinafter referred to as "units"). Because of how these units were supposed to perform, they were represented as being capable of producing an investment return and tax benefits.

The Williams agreed to buy $1 million worth of these units through a Hunt affiliated company, Success Through Association ("STA"). In September of 1988, before the Williams decided to make the investment, STA had only $301.50 in its bank account. . . . The Williams did not know this at the time nor were they aware that STA was a Hunt operated and controlled company. The Williams agreed to purchase the reverse refrigeration units under the following terms:

(a)   The Williams would buy $1 million worth of units at a price of $10,000 each.
(b)   The deal would be financed by a $50,000 down payment from the Williams and a loan to be arranged by STA for $950,000.
(c)   STA was to serve as "non-exclusive agent for the purpose of leasing" the units.
(d)   As agent, STA would "arrange for [the Williams] to receive confirmation of the purchase, financing and leases . . . of the units. . . ."
(e)   In the event that the purchase could not be made, STA was to "return [the Williams] deposit in full within one week of [STA's] determination that [the Williams'] criteria cannot be met, but in no event later than December 16, 1988."

Waymon Hunt agreed to arrange for the $950,000 in financing. The Williams signed a purchase agreement and forwarded $50,000 to STA, but no money was ever remitted to the purported manufacturer and seller of the units. Immediately upon STA's receipt of the $50,000, Hunt appropriated the money for his own use. Hunt did not obtain the $950,000 of financing.

Around the time of this transaction, there was an internal battle among the owners of the company that manufactured and sold the units, and the company was placed in receivership. While it later turned out that Mr. Hunt was able to contact a second seller and manufacturer, no purchase of the units ever came to pass. The parties have stipulated that the $50,000 sent to Mr. Hunt's company, STA, was never used to purchase reverse refrigeration units from any entity.

Mr. Hunt has attempted to deviate from the agreement he provided to the Williams, an agreement he drafted, by stating that he was entitled to the $50,000 as a finder's fee for locating financing for the project. He has produced two cashier's checks to show that he spent $68,000 on a fee he paid to a Georgia company, Aslanien Ltd., to obtain financing. He claims he did this on the Williams' behalf, but his testimony is not credible. While this Court cannot deny that Mr. Hunt may have discussed some financing for the purchase of the so-called reverse refrigeration units, it was clear he did not have the Williams in mind when he sent the first check for $34,000 to Aslanien, Ltd. since he wrote that check before the Williams ever signed a contract or purchase order for the units. It is not even clear that they knew about the investment opportunity before Hunt sent the check to Aslanien. Hunt admitted that the second check for $34,000 sent in November of 1988 was sent on behalf of other clients and not the Williams. It is clear that the $50,000 sent to STA by the Williams was to be a down payment on the units. It was not a finder's fee or any other kind of advance fee. Indeed Mr. Hunt conceded in his testimony before the Court that he owes the Williams the $50,000 they sent to him. Although he testified that he does not have the funds to pay the Williams now, he clearly acknowledges that under his agreement with them, he owes them the money.

The Williams are entitled to a judgment against Mr. Hunt on both contract and fraud theories. The contract provided that the money be repaid "if for any reason [STA] cannot fulfill [the Williams] request. . . ." It is also clear that Mr. Hunt's actions with respect to the Williams prove that Mr. Hunt defrauded the Williams. Hunt flat out misappropriated the money given to him. He dissembled when the Williams periodically asked about their investment and its status. He said "things were going fine" when they were not. He never told them that the $50,000 had not been sent to the manufacturer, nor did he inform them that he had not obtained financing. Hunt misrepresented the status of the arrangement when he prepared the Williams' tax returns on which Hunt took certain deductions and credits that could only be taken if a transaction had in fact been consummated. The Williams incurred significant expenses because of Mr. Hunt's violation of the contract and fraudulent conduct. They are entitled to recover the following sums from Hunt:

(a) $50,000, the amount of the down payment that was not returned;
(b) $2,500, the amount paid to Mr. Christopher Moss to prepare amended tax returns for the Williams;
(c) $3,000, the amount paid to Mr. Gary Lu to prepare amended California state tax returns;
(d) $21,000 for the penalties and interest owed to the IRS as a result of the improper tax returns filed by Mr. Hunt;
(e) $4,300 for the penalties and interest owed to the California state government as a result of the improper tax returns prepared by Mr. Hunt;
(f) $3,000 in attorney's fees incurred by the Williams to address the problems created by Mr. Hunt's activities;
(g) $500 for Mr. Moss's expert witness fee; and
(h) $3,000 for the costs of this litigation.

The Williams may not collect tax savings they claim they might have enjoyed had they received legitimate financial advice. It would be too speculative to assume post hoc what investments they might have chosen and what savings they might have received. . . .

Finally, plaintiffs seek punitive damages. The Court finds that they are warranted in this case. Mr. Hunt's egregious behavior was utterly unworthy of someone who calls himself a professional. His fraudulent conduct put the plaintiffs at risk of committing tax fraud. In recognition of these facts, the Court will award $50,000 in punitive damages, an amount that reflects the $50,000 down payment that was misappropriated and that was the basis for the grievous errors made on the Williams tax returns and caused them to incur substantial costs and expenses. . . .

II.   CONCLUSIONS OF LAW

1.   The defendant, Mr. Hunt, breached his contract with the plaintiffs. He should have returned their $50,000 and did not.

2.   The defendant has defrauded the plaintiff in that he
     a)   took money under false pretenses;
     b)   misappropriated the money; and
     c)   prepared improper tax returns. The defendant, Mr. Hunt, is liable to
          the plaintiffs who are entitled to the return of their $50,000.
3.   The preparation of the improper and illegal tax returns was a direct and
     proximate cause of substantial expenses and costs incurred by the Williams
     in the sum of $37,300.
4.   Defendant Hunt's conduct toward the Williams was intentional, willful, and
     egregious therefore the plaintiffs are entitled to punitive damages in the
     amount of $50,000. . . .

Judgment shall be entered for plaintiffs in the amount of $137,300.

NOTES AND QUESTIONS

1.   *Analysis of* Zinn. In *Zinn*, Parrish argued, *inter alia*, that he was not obligated
     to pay his agent because the latter had failed to provide competent services.
     Parrish's position is one commonly asserted by athletes who have been sued
     for fees by their agents. In addition to arguing that agents have provided
     substandard care, athletes assert that agents breached other basic obliga-
     tions owed to them or engaged in some form of illegal conduct.
         In *Zinn*, what standard does the court employ in rejecting Parrish's
     defense? What was the source of the standard adopted by the court? What
     is the role of good faith in determining whether an agent has competently
     performed his or her duties?
2.   *Agent and Athlete Compensation Disputes.* Players have not always prevailed in
     lawsuits against their agents. Agents have argued successfully that they com-
     petently performed the services rendered. Moreover, an agent will argue
     that an athlete's financial plight is the result of the athlete's poor handling
     of his or her financial resources rather than the agent's mishandling. In one
     such case, an agent successfully argued that the athlete's assets had been
     depleted because the athlete "wasted his assets by making exorbitant pur-
     chases, transferring large sums of money to his family members and friends,
     and refusing to save for the future or consider the consequences if he were
     injured or unable to continue playing football." *Clark v. Weisberg*, 1999 WL
     543191, at *2 (N.D. Ill. July 23, 1999).
         Note also that disputes between agents and athletes are now generally
     subject to mandatory arbitration because the standard player-agent con-
     tracts mandated by player association regulations governing agents include
     mandatory arbitration provisions. See *Wichard v. Suggs*, 95 F. Supp. 3d 935
     (E.D. Va. 2015) (applying mandatory arbitration provision of standard
     representation agreement between football player and agent, and hold-
     ing that arbitrator did not act in manifest disregard of the law, award drew
     its essence from the representation agreement, and award did not violate
     public policy); *Wasserman Media Group, Inc. v. Bender*, 2011 WL 1886460
     (S.D.N.Y. May 16, 2011) (confirming arbitration award in favor of agency
     against basketball player); *Adams v. Barnes*, 2010 WL 2484251 (N.D. Tex.
     June 17, 2010) (upholding arbitrator's award granting agent percentage of
     athlete's compensation earned over an eight-year period notwithstanding
     athlete's allegations that arbitrator was biased and engaged in misconduct);

Octagon, Inc. v. Richards, 2010 WL 3932272 (E.D. Va. Oct. 5, 2010) (upholding arbitration award of $279,836.50 in favor of agency against track athlete and rejecting the athlete's attempt to vacate the award).

3. *Analysis of* Williams. *Williams* illustrates that athletes can prevail in suits against agents and the substantive theories to which athletes will resort when suing their agents and/or financial advisors for alleged mismanagement of the athlete's financial affairs. Athletes have sued for breach of contract and negligence. They have also asserted fraud and breach of fiduciary duty claims as a means of potentially recovering punitive damages. See, e.g., *Jones v. Childers,* 18 F.3d 899 (11th Cir. 1994) (court holds that agent committed fraud and Racketeer Influenced and Corrupt Organizations Act ("RICO") violations in relation to an investment scheme in which plaintiff and other investors participated); *Hilliard v. Black,* 125 F. Supp. 2d 1071 (N.D. Fla. 2000) (athletes asserted claims sounding in breach of fiduciary duty, breach of contract, conversion, negligence, and civil conspiracy in contending that Tank Black and his company improperly induced them to invest millions in investment schemes); see also *Gordon v. Vitalis Partners, LLC,* 2010 WL 381119 (N.D. Ill. Jan. 27, 2010) (financial advisor owed fiduciary duty to client, a professional basketball player); *Terrell v. Childers,* 920 F. Supp. 854 (N.D. Ill. 1996) (finding that claims by a former baseball player against his agent for mismanagement of the player's finances and fraud were not subject to summary judgment).

The *Williams* court also identified factors that render athletes particularly vulnerable to unscrupulous agents and financial managers. Do you agree with the court? What additional factors prompt athletes to place what often approaches blind trust in agents and financial managers to manage their financial affairs? A Securities and Exchange Commission (SEC) lawyer involved in the Tank Black matter, discussed in note 4, *infra,* commented, "Professional athletes are prime candidates for financial fraud. Many are unsophisticated in financial matters and suddenly find themselves with a six- or seven-figure salary. They're young, they're trusting, and they've been taken care of most of their lives." L. Jon Wertheim, *Web of Deceit,* Sports Illustrated, May 29, 2000, at 80.

4. *Financial Improprieties.* One of the more notorious cases of financial mismanagement and illegal conduct in the sports industry involved William "Tank" Black, who rose to fame as a successful agent with numerous high-profile NBA and NFL clients. An investigation resulted in allegations that Black not only made under-the-table payments to players, he also fraudulently involved athletes in a pyramid scheme and laundered money. Black and the general counsel of his agency were imprisoned after pleading guilty to federal charges. In a related civil lawsuit, a Florida jury convicted Black of conspiring to commit mail and wire fraud. See Shropshire, Davis & Duru, *supra* at 76-82 (providing recent illustrations of financial improprieties committed by agents and financial advisors).

In some instances, the SEC and federal prosecutors have taken an aggressive stance toward agents and financial advisors. The SEC filed a complaint alleging that financial adviser Donald Lukens "violated federal securities laws by systematically defrauding at least 100 (and perhaps more than 200) clients and brokerage customers collectively of tens of millions of dollars in a series of investment schemes during at least the mid-to-late 1990s." Lukens is said to have represented over 40 athletes at various times. In another case of financial impropriety, Howard J. Golub, the financial manager for athletes, including former professional athletes Lance Parrish and Rich Karlis, was sentenced in 1989 to serve 10 to 12 years in prison and ordered to pay restitution of $163,600 to his clients following Golub's guilty plea to fraud and theft charges. In March 2018, investment adviser Jeremy Joseph Drake entered into a consent decree relating to an SEC complaint alleging he had fraudulently siphoned approximately $1.2 million from the account of an NFL player and his wife. *SEC v. Drake*, 2017 WL 6507766 (C.D. Cal. Dec. 18, 2017). The complaint alleged that the defendant engaged in mail and bank fraud and identity theft in obtaining money and property from the athlete and his wife. In early, 2019, Drake was sentenced to over two years in prison. *Prison Sentence for L.A. Money Advisor who Conned Athlete Out of $1.2 Million*, L.A.Com (Mar. 22, 2019), https://mynewsla.com/crime/2019/03/22/prison-sentence-for-l-a-money-adviser-who-conned-athlete-out-of-1-2-million/.

Former NBA star Tim Duncan fared better than many athletes who are victims of financial improprieties. Duncan entered into a settlement under which he recovered $7.5 million of the $20 million he allegedly lost as a result of the fraudulent conduct of his financial advisor, Charles Banks IV. As a result of his interactions with Duncan, Banks was sentenced to four years in federal prison after having been found guilty of wire fraud. Guillermo Contreras, *Duncan gets back $7.5 million in settlement with ex-advisor*, MySanAntonio.com (Jan. 25, 2018), https://www.mysanantonio.com/news/local/article/Tim-Duncan-gets-back-7-5-million-in-settlement-12526295.php. Banks figured prominently in a lawsuit filed by another former NBA player, Kevin Garnett, who alleged his former accountant worked with Banks in misappropriating $77 million of Garnett's money. Janet Levaux, *Kevin Garnett Sues for Fraud Involving Tim Duncan's Ex-Advisor*, Think Advisor (Sept. 7, 2018); see also *Groves v. Morgan Stanley Smith Barney*, Award: FINRA Office of Dispute Resolution, Case Number 16-02052 (Dec. 19, 2018) (awarding $4.2 million to former NFL player Assante Samuel relating to defendant's negligent supervision of an investment advisor who solicited millions from the athlete for investment in night clubs). Like Banks, Peggy Ann Fulford, who falsely held herself out as a Harvard-educated lawyer and financial advisor in soliciting athlete clients, was held accountable for her actions. She was sentenced to 120 months in prison and ordered to make restitution of over $5.5 million for defrauding professional athletes, including former Heisman Trophy winner and NFL player Ricky Williams, out of millions of dollars. *Self-styled "Financial Advisor" Ordered to Prison after Defrauding Professional Athlete Out of Millions*, Dept. of Justice, U.S. Attorney's Office, S.D. Tex. (Nov. 7, 2018), https://www.justice.gov/usao-sdtx/pr/self-styled-financial-advisor-ordered-prison-after-defrauding-professional-athletes-out; see also *United States v. Adkism*, No. 18CR232 (Apr. 28, 2018) (federal prosecutors filed a 16-count complaint alleging Tonya Adkism, a financial advisor to NFL player Robert Meachem, engaged in mail, wire, and bank fraud and identity theft in misappropriating over $1 million from the athlete).

5. *Financial Advisors Regulations.* In footnote 1 of *Williams*, the district court admonished the NBA to implement reforms to protect athletes such as Mr. Williams. In 2002, the NFLPA became the first professional sports union to attempt to curb the abuse of financial advisors with its promulgation of the NFLPA Regulations and Code of Conduct Governing Registered Player

Financial Advisors. The regulations represent the NFLPA's response to incidents involving mismanagement of players' financial affairs. Those financial advisors who agree to participate, by applying to become registered in the voluntary program, are given "unique information on NFL players, their benefits, and compensation structure." *Introduction*, NFLPA Regulations and Code of Conduct Governing Registered Player Financial Advisors at 1 (2002, as amended 2017). Notwithstanding language indicating that the NFLPA does not endorse the registered financial advisors, participating advisors will be perceived as having received the union's blessing.

In 2006, then current and former NFL players, including Steve Atwater and Ray Crockett, sued the NFLPA alleging it had negligently performed background checks on Kirk Wright, a financial advisor, who defrauded investors, including the athletes, out of more than $100 million. (In May 2008, a federal jury convicted Wright of 467 counts of mail fraud, securities fraud, and money laundering. A few days later, Wright hung himself in his jail cell.) In 2007, a federal district court refused to dismiss the athletes' lawsuit, notwithstanding exculpatory language in the Financial Advisors Regulations, which stated that the NFLPA does not endorse any particular advisor and disclaims responsibility or liability for the acts of financial advisors who participate in its program. In 2010, the Eleventh Circuit Court of Appeals dismissed the former players' contract and tort claims after finding that they were subject to preemption under §301 of the National Labor Relations Act. *Atwater v. National Football League Players Assn.*, 626 F.3d 1170 (11th Cir. 2010); but see *Dent v. National Football League Players Assn.*, 902 F.3d 1109 (9th Cir. 2018) (in a case not involving agents, the court distinguishes *Atwater* in finding that NFL players' class action alleging the NFL negligently hired doctors and failed to warn players of side effects of pain medications was not preempted by the NLRA).

Although the NFLPA prevailed in the lawsuit, it temporarily suspended its financial advisor program, only to reinstate it in 2012 after making changes (*e.g.*, requiring applicants to have eight rather than the previously required five years of licensed experience and increasing the amount of program fees certified advisors must pay). As a result of the case, the NFLPA also strengthened the exculpatory language of its 2011 CBA with the NFL. The language seeks to shield the NFLPA, the NFL, and its clubs from potential liability for fraudulent acts committed against players by NFLPA registered financial advisors. The language provides that "[n]either the NFL, nor any Club, nor the NFLPA shall be responsible for any investment decisions made by players; players and any advisors who they select will bear sole responsibility for any investment or financial decisions that are made." National Football League, *NFL Collective Bargaining Agreement Between the NFL Management Council and the NFL Players Association*, art 51 § 12 (Aug. 4, 2011), https://nfllabor.files .wordpress.com/2010/01/collective-bargaining-agreement-2011-2020. pdf. For a discussion of the NFLPA's Financial Advisor Regulations, see Shropshire, Davis & Duru, *supra*, at 77-82.

6. *An International Perspective.* Internationally, agents perform the broad range of functions that agents perform in the United States. These include contract negotiation; "management and services in matters such as housing, taxes, social security, permits and licenses, financial planning, legal advice, career development and health . . . [;] and organization of sports activities and events." Robert Parrish, *Regulating Players' Agents: A Global Perspective*, in

Players' Agents Worldwide: Legal Aspects (Robert C.R. Siekmann et al. eds., 2007). Similar to the conceptualization of agents in the United States, from an international perspective, the term agent refers to a person who acts as "an intermediary between a sports man or woman and other parties, for example between a football player (employee or potential employee) and a club (employer or potential employer)." *Id.*

Not surprisingly, the problems that have beset the athlete agent industry in the United States arise internationally. Noting the high number of licensed agents in countries such as Spain, Italy, and England, one commentator articulates that regulation of agents is necessary "'to introduce professionalism and morality to the occupation of players' agent in order to protect players whose careers are short.' Rephrased, the absence of player agent regulation will result in a lack of professionalism, immorality and a lack of protection for players." *Id.* at 4.

This author goes on to describe *bungs*, tapping-up, and dual representation as examples of improper agent conduct that demonstrate the need for agent regulation:

> Bungs refer to illegal payments paid by and to agents (and others) in order to facilitate the transfer of a player. . . .
>
> Another FIFA and association rule . . . was the common practice of "tapping-up" which refers to a process, often facilitated by agents, whereby players are offered for sale to other clubs without the knowledge and consent of the club with whom the player is registered. . . . FIFA Players' Agents Regulations state that a licensed players' agent must never "approach a player who is under contract with a club with the aim of persuading him to terminate his contract prematurely or to flout the rights and duties stipulated in the contract. . . ."
>
> The third issue reaching prominence in the UK in the summer of 2006, . . . was the issue of dual representation. This refers to an agent who represents both a club and a player in negotiations. This is prohibited by . . . FIFA Players' Agents Regulations which state that a licensed players' agent is required "to represent only one party when negotiating a transfer."

Id. at 6.

As to the representation of a U.S. athlete wishing to compete abroad, the agent faces a series of challenges. For one, many nations' sports leagues limit the number of foreign players per team, so roster spots with the premier clubs are often scarce. Moreover, while agents are generally not bound by union regulations such as those in the United States, they may find other structural impediments. These impediments may vary among foreign leagues, and learning what they are can be challenging, as obtaining the basic knowledge of business practices in a foreign country can be difficult. Even the question as to whether there is something approaching a standard form contract may not be known. The drafting and negotiation of devices to protect the athlete if things go awry in a foreign country are no simple matter. For example, does an agent really want to have to seek enforcement of contractual obligations in the courts of a foreign country? If not, what are the alternatives? Added to this mix is the need to understand the complexities of the U.S. tax laws and the possible foreign immigration laws. As to immigration, the foreign club may be of assistance. As to tax, the agent advising the athlete is probably on his or her own. See Shropshire, Davis & Duru, *supra* at 177-92 (discussing the role of the agent who advises clients internationally and the challenges such agents face).

PROBLEM 8-1

William Wills, a professional football player, hired Terry Davis as his sports agent. Davis, an attorney, is certified as a contract advisor with the NFLPA. Wills and Davis entered into the NFLPA's standard representation agreement between a player and contract advisor. From 2015 to 2019, with Wills's authorization, Davis received most of Wills's income. Davis gave Wills an allowance for living expenses and occasionally gave Wills advances against his salary when Wills asked for them. In addition to his salary, Wills was paid $20,000 a year to be invested in an annuity on his behalf. Davis was supposed to invest these amounts each year in an annuity for Wills but did not do so. Between 2015 and 2019, Davis used much of Wills's income to cover Davis's business and personal expenses. In 2018, Wills began to suspect that Davis was misappropriating his income and requested an accounting, which Davis said was forthcoming but never provided. Wills became certain that something was wrong when in early 2019 he was informed by the Internal Revenue Service (IRS) that he had not paid his tax deficiencies for years 2016 to 2018. Davis had told Wills that he was paying his taxes at the time he filed Wills's tax returns. The tax returns, which were signed by Wills, were filed by Davis, who had not paid the tax deficiencies. Wills has a tax liability of over $240,000 as a result of the actions taken by Davis. What causes of action may Wills assert in a lawsuit against Davis? See *Willoughby v. Commissioner of Internal Revenue*, 1994 WL 444427 (T.C. Aug. 18, 1994).

3.   *Conflicts of Interest*

One of an agent's fundamental obligations is to not compromise the interests of his or her principal. The requirement that an agent avoid conflicts of interest is derived from the duties of undivided loyalty and good faith that agents owe to their principals. In the sports context, numerous factual scenarios present real or potential conflicts of interest. Historically, the paradigmatic case of a conflict of interest has involved "nondisclosure by an agent of a financial interest that conflicts with that of the athlete client." Shropshire, Davis & Duru, *supra*, at 86. As the following discussion reveals, however, nondisclosure represents only one of the factual scenarios in which conflicts arise in the sports representation business. Nevertheless, we begin our discussion with an example that presents the paradigmatic conflict of interest.

PROBLEM 8-2

Determine whether a conflict of interest exists in the following scenarios and, if so, what mechanisms might be instituted to avoid a conflict.

a.   An agent represents players from different teams in the same sport.
b.   The situation in (a) applies, and the athletes play in the same position.
c.   An agent represents two players on different teams. After a trade, the two players end up on the same team. One player is considerably more valuable than the other player. The league has imposed a salary cap on the total amount of monies that an individual team can allocate to player salaries.

d. An agent encourages an 18-year-old female athlete, who has aspirations to become a sports commentator after her athletic career ends, to accept an offer to pose in a promiscuous photo for a liquor advertisement. The agent is aware that the athlete's parents are opposed to her accepting the offer, that other athletes who have followed this route later regretted having done so and have encountered difficulty moving from sport into television commentary, and that both the agent and athlete will make a great deal of money if she accepts the offer.

e. An agent represents a player and a coach on the same team.

f. A large sports management firm that represents players also enters into a sponsorship sales agreement with a professional league.

g. A large sports management firm represents a superstar professional basketball player while he is a member of the league. After the player retires and becomes co-owner of a team in that league, the sports management firm continues to represent him.

h. A sports management firm that represents baseball players is purchased by a large media conglomerate, which also owns an MLB franchise.

In responding to the preceding scenarios, discuss what additional facts would assist you in determining whether a conflict of interest exists. Also consider the *Argovitz* case and the following: Shropshire, Davis & Duru, *supra*, at 88-94; Joshua Lens, *When a College Coach's Agent Recruits the Coach's Players: Potential Legal and NCAA Ramifications,* 26 Jeffrey S. Moorad Sports L.J. 1 (2019) (discussing conflicts of interest by sports agents); Melissa Neiman, *Fair Game: Ethical Considerations in Negotiation by Sports Agents,* 9 Tex. Rev. Ent. & Sports L. 123 (2007); Jamie E. Brown, *The Battle the Fans Never See: Conflicts of Interest for Sports Lawyers,* 7 Geo. J. Legal Ethics 813, 816 (1994); MLBPA Regulations Governing Player Agents, Section 5(B)(13) (2010, as amended 2018); NFLPA Regulations Governing Contract Advisors, Section 3 (2011, as amended 2016), *infra*; NBPA Regulations Governing Player Agents, Section 3 (1998, as amended 2018), *infra*.

THE DETROIT LIONS, INC. v. ARGOVITZ

580 F. Supp. 542 (D. Mich. 1984)

DeMascio, District Judge.

The plot for this Saturday afternoon serial began when Billy Sims, having signed a contract with the Houston Gamblers on July 1, 1983, signed a second contract with the Detroit Lions on December 16, 1983. On December 18, 1983, the Detroit Lions, Inc. (Lions) and Billy R. Sims filed a complaint in the Oakland County Circuit Court seeking a judicial determination that the July 1, 1983, contract between Sims and the Houston Gamblers, Inc. (Gamblers) is invalid because the defendant Jerry Argovitz (Argovitz) breached his fiduciary duty when negotiating the Gamblers' contract and because the contract was otherwise tainted by fraud and misrepresentation. Defendants promptly removed the action to this court based on our diversity of citizenship jurisdiction. . . .

For the reasons that follow, we have concluded that Argovitz's breach of his fiduciary duty during negotiations for the Gamblers' contract was so pronounced, so egregious, that to deny rescission would be unconscionable.

Sometime in February or March 1983, Argovitz told Sims that he had applied for a Houston franchise in the newly formed United States Football League (USFL). In May 1983, Sims attended a press conference in Houston at which Argovitz announced that his application for a franchise had been approved. The evidence persuades us that Sims did not know the extent of Argovitz's interest in the Gamblers. He did not know the amount of Argovitz's original investment, or that Argovitz was obligated for 29 percent of a $1.5 million letter of credit, or that Argovitz was the president of the Gamblers' Corporation at an annual salary of $275,000 and 5 percent [of] the yearly cash flow. The defendants could not justifiably expect Sims to comprehend the ramifications of Argovitz's interest in the Gamblers or the manner in which that interest would create an untenable conflict of interest, a conflict that would inevitably breach Argovitz's fiduciary duty to Sims. Argovitz knew, or should have known, that he could not act as Sims' agent under any circumstances when dealing with the Gamblers. Even the USFL Constitution itself prohibits a holder of any interest in a member club from acting "as the contracting agent or representative for any player."

Pending the approval of his application for a USFL franchise in Houston, Argovitz continued his negotiations with the Lions on behalf of Sims. On April 5, 1983, Argovitz offered Sims' services to the Lions for $6 million over a four-year period. The offer included a demand for a $1 million interest-free loan to be repaid over 10 years, and for skill and injury guarantees for three years. The Lions quickly responded with a counter offer on April 7, 1983, in the face amount of $1.5 million over a five-year period with additional incentives not relevant here. The negotiating process was working. The Lions were trying to determine what Argovitz really believed the market value for Sims really was. On May 3, 1983, with his Gamblers franchise assured, Argovitz significantly reduced his offer to the Lions. He now offered Sims to the Lions for $3 million over a four-year period, one-half of the amount of his April 5, 1983, offer. Argovitz's May 3rd offer included a demand for $50,000 to permit Sims to purchase an annuity. Argovitz also dropped his previous demand for skill guarantees. The May 10, 1983 offer submitted by the Lions brought the parties much closer.

On May 30, 1983, Argovitz asked for $3.5 million over a five-year period. This offer included an interest-free loan and injury protection insurance but made no demand for skill guarantees. The May 30 offer now requested $400,000 to allow Sims to purchase an annuity. On June 1, 1983, Argovitz and the Lions were only $500,000 apart. We find that the negotiations between the Lions and Argovitz were progressing normally, not laterally as Argovitz represented to Sims. The Lions were not "dragging their feet." Throughout the entire month of June 1983, Mr. Frederick Nash, the Lions' skilled negotiator and a fastidious lawyer, was involved in investigating the possibility of providing an attractive annuity for Sims and at the same time doing his best to avoid the granting of either skill or injury guarantees. The evidence establishes that on June 22, 1983, the Lions and Argovitz were very close to reaching an agreement on the value of Sims' services.

Apparently, in the midst of his negotiations with the Lions and with his Gamblers franchise in hand, Argovitz decided that he would seek an offer from the Gamblers. Mr. Bernard Lerner, one of Argovitz's partners in the Gamblers agreed to negotiate a contract with Sims. Since Lerner admitted that he had no knowledge whatsoever about football, we must infer that Argovitz at the very least told Lerner the amount of money required to sign Sims and further pressed upon Lerner the Gamblers' absolute need to obtain Sims' services. In the Gamblers' organization, only Argovitz knew the value of Sims' services and how critical it was for the Gamblers to obtain Sims. In Argovitz's words, Sims would make the Gamblers' franchise.

On June 29, 1983, at Lerner's behest, Sims and his wife went to Houston to negotiate with a team that was partially owned by his own agent. When Sims arrived in Houston, he believed that the Lions organization was not negotiating in good faith; that it was not really interested in his services. His ego was bruised and his emotional outlook toward the Lions was visible to Burrough and Argovitz. Clearly, virtually all the information that Sims had up to that date came from Argovitz. Sims and the Gamblers did not discuss a future contract on the night of June 29th. The negotiations began on the morning of June 30, 1983, and ended that afternoon. At the morning meeting, Lerner offered Sims a $3.5 million five-year contract, which included three years of skill and injury guarantees. The offer included a $500,000 loan at an interest rate of 1 percent over prime. It was from this loan that Argovitz planned to receive the $100,000 balance of his fee for acting as an agent in negotiating a contract with his own team. Burrough testified that Sims would have accepted that offer on the spot because he was finally receiving the guarantee that he had been requesting from the Lions, guarantees that Argovitz dropped without too much quarrel. Argovitz and Burrough took Sims and his wife into another room to discuss the offer. Argovitz did tell Sims that he thought the Lions would match the Gamblers financial package and asked Sims whether he (Argovitz) should telephone the Lions. But, it is clear from the evidence that neither Sims nor Burrough believed that the Lions would match the offer. We find that Sims told Argovitz not to call the Lions for purely emotional reasons. As we have noted, Sims believed that the Lions' organization was not that interested in him and his pride was wounded. Burrough clearly admitted that he was aware of the emotional basis for Sims' decision not to have Argovitz phone the Lions, and we must conclude from the extremely close relationship between Argovitz and Sims that Argovitz knew it as well. When Sims went back to Lerner's office, he agreed to become a Gambler on the terms offered. At that moment, Argovitz irreparably breached his fiduciary duty. As agent for Sims he had the duty to telephone the Lions, receive its final offer, and present the terms of both offers to Sims. Then and only then could it be said that Sims made an intelligent and knowing decision to accept the Gamblers' offer.

During these negotiations at the Gamblers' office, Mr. Nash of the Lions telephoned Argovitz, but even though Argovitz was at his office, he declined to accept the telephone call. Argovitz tried to return Nash's call after Sims had accepted the Gamblers' offer, but it was after 5 p.m. and Nash had left for the July 4th weekend. When he declined to accept Mr. Nash's call, Argovitz's breach of his fiduciary duty became even more pronounced. Following Nash's example, Argovitz left for his weekend trip, leaving his principal to sign the contracts with the Gamblers the next day, July 1, 1983. The defendants, in their supplemental trial brief, assert that neither Argovitz nor Burrough can be held responsible for following Sims' instruction not to contact the Lions on June 30, 1983. Although it is generally true that an agent is not liable for losses occurring as a result of following his principal's instructions, the rule of law is not applicable when the agent has placed himself in a position adverse to that of his principal.

During the evening of June 30, 1983, Burrough struggled with the fact that they had not presented the Gamblers' offer to the Lions. He knew, as does the court, that Argovitz now had the wedge that he needed to bring finality to the

Lions' negotiations. Burrough was acutely aware of the fact that Sims' actions were emotionally motivated and realized that the responsibility for Sims' future rested with him. We view with some disdain the fact that Argovitz had, in effect, delegated his entire fiduciary responsibility on the eve of his principal's most important career decision. On July 1, 1983, it was Lerner who gave lip service to Argovitz's conspicuous conflict of interest. It was Lerner, not Argovitz, who advised Sims that Argovitz's position with the Gamblers presented a conflict of interest and that Sims could, if he wished, obtain an attorney or another agent. Argovitz, upon whom Sims had relied for the past four years, was not even there. Burrough, conscious of Sims' emotional responses, never advised Sims to wait until he had talked with the Lions before making a final decision. Argovitz's conflict of interest and self dealing put him in the position where he would not even use the wedge he now had to negotiate with the Lions, a wedge that is the dream of every agent. Two expert witnesses testified that an agent should telephone a team that he has been negotiating with once he has an offer in hand. Mr. Woolf, plaintiff's expert, testified that an offer from another team is probably the most important factor in negotiations. Mr. Lustig, defendant's expert, believed that it was prudent for him to telephone the Buffalo Bills and inform that organization of the Gamblers' offer to Jim Kelly, despite the fact that he believed the Bills had already made its best offer to his principal. The evidence here convinces us that Argovitz's negotiations with the Lions were ongoing and it had not made its final offer. Argovitz did not follow the common practice described by both expert witnesses. He did not do this because he knew that the Lions would not leave Sims without a contract and he further knew that if he made that type of call Sims would be lost to the Gamblers, a team he owned.

On November 12, 1983, when Sims was in Houston for the Lions game with the Houston Oilers, Argovitz asked Sims to come to his home and sign certain papers. He represented to Sims that certain papers of his contract had been mistakenly overlooked and now needed to be signed. Included among those papers he asked Sims to sign was a waiver of any claim that Sims might have against Argovitz for his blatant breach of his fiduciary duty brought on by his glaring conflict of interest. Sims did not receive independent advice with regard to the wisdom of signing such a waiver. Despite having sold his agency business in September, Argovitz did not even tell Sims' new agent of his intention to have Sims sign a waiver. Nevertheless, Sims, an unsophisticated young man, signed the waiver. This is another example of the questionable conduct on the part of Argovitz who still had business management obligations to Sims. In spite of his fiduciary relationship he had Sims sign a waiver without advising him to obtain independent counseling.

Argovitz's negotiations with Lustig, Jim Kelly's agent, illustrates the difficulties that develop when an agent negotiates a contract where his personal interests conflict with those of his principal. Lustig, an independent agent, ignored Argovitz's admonishment not to "shop" the Gamblers' offer to Kelly. Lustig called the NFL team that he had been negotiating with because it was the "prudent" thing to do. The Gamblers agreed to pay Kelly, an untested rookie quarterback $3.2 million for five years. His compensation was $60,000 less than Sims', a former Heisman Trophy winner and a proven star in the NFL. Lustig also obtained a number of favorable clauses from Argovitz; the most impressive one being that Kelly was assured of being one of the three top paid quarterbacks in the USFL if he performed as well as expected. If Argovitz had been free from conflicting interests he would have demanded similar benefits for Sims.

Argovitz claimed that the nondisclosure clause in Kelly's contract prevented him from mentioning the Kelly contract to Sims. We view this contention as frivolous. Requesting these benefits for Sims did not require disclosure of Kelly's contract. Moreover, Argovitz's failure to obtain personal guarantees for Sims without adequately warning Sims about the risks and uncertainties of a new league constituted a clear breach of his fiduciary duty.

One cannot help but wonder whether Argovitz took his fiduciary duty seriously. For example, after investing approximately $76,000 of Sims' money, Argovitz, with or without the prior knowledge of his principal, received a finder's fee. Despite the fact that Sims paid Argovitz a 2 percent fee, Argovitz accepted $3,800 from a person with whom he invested Sims' money. In March 1983, Argovitz had all of his veteran players, including Sims, sign a new agency contract with less favorable payment terms for the players even though they already had an ongoing agency agreement with him. He did this after he sold his entire agency business to Career Sports. Finally, Argovitz was prepared to take the remainder of his 5 percent agency fee for negotiating Sims' contract with the Gamblers from monies the Gamblers loaned to Sims at an interest rate of 1 percent over prime. . . . We find this circumstantial evidence useful only insofar as it has aided the court in understanding the manner in which these parties conducted business.

We are mindful that Sims was less than forthright when testifying before the court. However, we agree with plaintiff's counsel that the facts as presented through the testimony of other witnesses are so unappealing that we can disregard Sims' testimony entirely. We remain persuaded that on balance, Argovitz's breach of his fiduciary duty was so egregious that a court of equity cannot permit him to benefit by his own wrongful breach. We conclude that Argovitz's conduct in negotiating Sims' contract with the Gamblers rendered it invalid.

CONCLUSIONS OF LAW . . .

3. The relationship between a principal and agent is fiduciary in nature, and as such imposes a duty of loyalty, good faith, and fair and honest dealing on the agent. . . .
4. A fiduciary relationship arises not only from a formal principal-agent relationship, but also from informal relationships of trust and confidence. . . .
5. In light of the express agency agreement, and the relationship between Sims and Argovitz, Argovitz clearly owed Sims the fiduciary duties of an agent at all times relevant to this lawsuit.
6. An agent's duty of loyalty requires that he not have a personal stake that conflicts with the principal's interest in a transaction in which he represents his principal. As stated in *Burleson v. Earnest*, 153 S.W.2d 869 (Tex. Civ. App. 1941):

> [T]he principal is entitled to the best efforts and unbiased judgment of his agent. . . . [T]he law denies the right of an agent to assume any relationship that is antagonistic to his duty to his principal, and it has many times been held that the agent cannot be both buyer and seller at the same time nor connect his own interests with property involved in his dealings as an agent for another.

Id. at 874.

7. A fiduciary violates the prohibition against self-dealing not only by dealing with himself on his principal's behalf, but also by dealing on his principal's behalf with a third party in which he has an interest, such as a partnership in which he is a member. . . .

8. Where an agent has an interest adverse to that of his principal in a transaction in which he purports to act on behalf of his principal, the transaction is voidable by the principal unless the agent disclosed all material facts within the agent's knowledge that might affect the principal's judgment. *Burleson v. Earnest*, 153 S.W.2d at 874-75.

9. The mere fact that the contract is fair to the principal does not deny the principal the right to rescind the contract when it was negotiated by an agent in violation of the prohibition against self-dealing. As stated in *Burleson*:

> The question, therefore, does not relate to the *mala fides* of the agent nor to whether or not a greater sum might have been procured for the property, nor even to whether or not the vendor received full value therefor. The self-interest of the agent is considered a vice which renders the transaction voidable at the election of the principal without looking into the matter further than to ascertain that the interest of the agent exists.

10. Once it has been shown that an agent had an interest in a transaction involving his principal antagonistic to the principal's interest, fraud on the part of the agent is presumed. The burden of proof then rests upon the agent to show that: his principal had full knowledge, not only of the fact that the agent was interested, but also of every material fact known to the agent that might affect the principal and that, having such knowledge, the principal freely consented to the transaction.

11. It is not sufficient for the agent merely to inform the principal that he has an interest that conflicts with the principal's interest. Rather, he must inform the principal "of all facts that come to his knowledge that are or may be material or which might affect his principal's rights or interests or influence the action he takes." *Anderson v. Griffith*, 501 S.W.2d 695, 700 (Tex. Civ. App. 1973).

12. Argovitz clearly had a personal interest in signing Sims with the Gamblers that was adverse to Sims' interest — he had an ownership interest in the Gamblers and thus would profit if the Gamblers were profitable, and would incur substantial personal liabilities should the Gamblers not be financially successful. Since this showing has been made, fraud on Argovitz's part is presumed, and the Gamblers' contract must be rescinded unless Argovitz has shown by a preponderance of the evidence that he informed Sims of every material fact that might have influenced Sims' decision whether or not to sign the Gamblers' contract.

13. We conclude that Argovitz has failed to show by a preponderance of the evidence either: (1) that he informed Sims of the following facts, or (2) that these facts would not have influenced Sims' decision whether to sign the Gamblers' contract

  a. The relative values of the Gamblers' contract and the Lions' offer that Argovitz knew could be obtained.

  b. That there was significant financial differences between the USFL and the NFL not only in terms of the relative financial stability of the Leagues, but also in terms of the fringe benefits available to Sims.

c.   Argovitz's 29 percent ownership in the Gamblers; Argovitz's $275,000 annual salary with the Gamblers; Argovitz's five percent interest in the cash flow of the Gamblers.

d.   That both Argovitz and Burrough failed to even attempt to obtain for Sims valuable contract clauses which they had given to Kelly on behalf of the Gamblers.

e.   That Sims had great leverage, and Argovitz was not encouraging a bidding war that could have advantageous results for Sims.

14. Under Texas law, a nonbinding prior act cannot be ratified, and the right to seek rescission cannot be waived, unless the party against whom these defenses are asserted had full knowledge of all material facts at the time the acts of ratification or waiver are alleged to have occurred.

15. At no time prior to December 1, 1983, was Sims aware of the material non-disclosures outlined above; accordingly, the defenses of ratification and waiver must be rejected.

16. Defendants asserted defenses of estoppel and latches are also without merit.

17. As a court sitting in equity, we conclude that rescission is the appropriate remedy. We are dismayed by Argovitz's egregious conduct. The careless fashion in which Argovitz went about ascertaining the highest price for Sims' service convinces us of the wisdom of the maxim: no man can faithfully serve two masters whose interests are in conflict.

Judgment will be entered for the plaintiffs rescinding the Gamblers' contract with Sims.

IT IS SO ORDERED.

NOTES AND QUESTIONS

1. *Analysis of* Argovitz. Describe how Argovitz violated his duties of undivided loyalty, good faith, and fair dealing. Will an athlete's knowledge of a conflict or a potential conflict necessarily absolve an agent of liability for a conflict of interest? In *Argovitz* the court concluded that knowledge by Sims of Argovitz's ownership of the Gamblers franchise or approval of the application failed to absolve the agent of responsibility. Why? For another example involving alleged conflicts of interest, see *Mandich v. Watters*, 970 F.2d 462 (8th Cir. 1992) (discussing alleged conflict of interest resulting from a secret side deal negotiated between a player's agent and team that deprived player of post-retirement salaries).

2. Sports Management Network v. Busch. NASCAR driver Kurt Busch alleged, *inter alia*, a conflict of interest resulting in a breach of fiduciary duties by his agent, John Caponigro. Both the sports management agency and the law firm that employed Caponigro also represented entities that employed or had formerly employed Busch. *Sports Management Network v. Busch*, 2019 WL 1057314 (E.D. Mich. Mar. 6, 2019). Concluding that Caponigro's conduct and his firm's conduct gave rise to a conflict of interest that breached Caponigro's duty of loyalty, the court stated:

> There is no doubt that Caponigro acted in violation of Michigan's Rules of Professional Ethics. Caponigro violated MICH. R. PROF'L CONDUCT 1.7(a) by representing a client whose interests are directly adverse to another client, and Rule 1.7(b) by representing a client in a manner that could be materially

limited "by the lawyer's own interests." Caponigro is the CEO and majority stakeholder in SMN [Eds. Sports Management Network]. . . . His representation of Kurt Busch, and Kurt Busch, Inc. is thus inherently limited by his fiduciary loyalty to SMN. . . .

The Sixth Circuit looked at Michigan's Rules of Professional Conduct, Rule 1.7(a), ABA Model Rules, Rule 1.7, and the Restatement 3d of the Laws Governing Lawyers § 122 and held that "providing the client with anything less than full information runs the risk that the client is inadequately informed, thereby making any consent invalid." *Centra*, 538 F.2d at 415. "The Restatement requires that attorneys inform their clients of the nature of the conflict so that the clients are 'aware of the material respects in which the representation could have adverse effects on the interests of that client.'" *Id.* (citing RESTATEMENT § 122 cmt. c(i)).

Caponigro never informed Busch of the nature of his conflicts because Caponigro never believed he had a conflict. He certainly never gave sufficient informed consent so that both parties "underst[ood] the reasons why it may be desirable for each to have independent counsel, with undivided loyalty to the interests of each of them." *Id.* at 415-16 (citing *Unified Sewerage Agency v. Jelco, Inc.*, 646 F.2d 1339, 1345-46 (9th Cir. 1981)).

The conflict between SMN and Busch was exacerbated by SMN's representation of several of the driving teams that employed Busch. SMN provided sponsorship representation for Penske Racing, for whom Busch drove from 2005 to 2011. . . . SMN also represented Busch in several negotiations adverse to Penske, including a buyout from Busch's previous racing team, the terms of his 2010 extension, and the terms of his 2011 separation, which included a waiver of all of his rights under his driver agreement. . . . Caponigro considered Penske and Busch not to be clients but to be "benefactors to this effort that I was putting forth. . . ." He saw himself as one "facilitating a meeting of the minds. . . ." Indeed, Penske Racing paid Caponigro, in the capacity of FCWS [Eds. the law firm for which Caponigro worked], a substantial sum for his "coordination" between Busch and Penske in 2005. . . .

This underscores the unfairness at the heart of Caponigro's conflict of interest. He billed himself as Busch's agent and attorney, but when Busch's interests were adverse to his other clients, the best he could provide was facilitation, not the loyalty that is the lodestone of Rule 1.7. The conflict ran even deeper with Andretti Autosport, with whom SMN negotiated several contracts on Busch's behalf. Andretti Autosport was a client of both FCWS and SMN, and Michael Andretti has been a client of John Caponigro and FCWS since 1990. . . . Regardless of whether Busch can prove injury from these conflicts, they are sufficiently egregious to infect the entire [representation agreement].

Sports Mgmt. Network, 2019 WL 1057314, at 4-5.

PROBLEM 8-3

Agent represents basketball players Williams and Smith, who play for different teams in the same NBA conference. Williams, who is considered by many to be the greatest basketball player of all time, is also the highest-paid athlete (salary and endorsements) in the world. One of Williams's teammates complains about the aggressive play of Smith, who is a solid player but is not a superstar. Williams takes these complaints to Agent, who is currently in the midst of negotiating Smith's contract with his current team, Team A. Team B has also expressed an interest in Smith. Agent rejects Team A's offer of $8.1 million for three years and secures for Smith a $9.6 million deal with Team B, which plays in another conference. Under his contract with Team B, Smith will receive only $6.4 million in his first three years. Agent says that the deal with Team B is better because it will pay Smith $3.2 million ($1.5 million of which is guaranteed) in his fourth year and has less deferred money. Team A's president says that Team A was willing to compromise on the issue of deferred money. What, if any, conflicts or potential conflicts are present here?

4. *Competition for Clients: Conflicts Between Agents*

The underlying source of conflicts between agents is the fierce competition for clients. Factors that contribute to the intense competition that breeds conflict among agents include the significant fees that are potentially available if an agent signs an athlete; the relatively stable pool of potential athlete-clients; the ease with which provisions in standard agent representation agreements allow athletes to terminate their contracts with agents; and the increase in the number of agents over the years.

Despite the swelling ranks of agents, a relatively small number of powerful agents tend to dominate the athlete agent market. In 2018, the New York Times reported that of the approximately 450 NBA certified agents, 9 represented a quarter of NBA players, and 27 represented half of NBA players. Kevin Draper, *Congratulations, You're a Certified N.B.A. Agent. Good Luck Finding a Client,* NY Times (Oct. 17, 2018). The difficulties of obtaining clients is particularly grim for agents attempting to break into the industry. It is estimated that fewer than 10 of the 160 agents certified by the NBPA between 2016 and 2018 represented an NBA player in 2018.

The dynamic is similar in the NFL. At the 2019 NFL draft, two prominent agencies, Creative Artists Agency (CAA) and Legardere, represented 10 of the 32 players selected in the first round. Other first-round drafts picks were largely represented by established agents or agencies. John Aceti & Andrew Levin, *CAA Leads Agencies at NFL Draft with Six Players Taken Thursday,* Sports Business Daily (April 26, 2019).

The 2019 NBA draft differed from the norm, as 16 different agencies represented at least one player drafted in the first round. Andrew Levin, *CAA, Wasserman Lead with Four NBA First-Round Draft Picks,* Print Morning Buzz (June 21, 2019). CAA and Wasserman led the draft with four players each drafted in the first round, followed by BDA Sports Management and Priority Sports & Entertainment with three first round draft picks apiece. *Id.*

Consolidations that proliferated during the 1990s and continue today intensify the competition for clients, particularly challenging smaller firms and individual agents who lack the resources to compete effectively against larger firms. In addition, agents within larger firms often employ aggressive tactics in recruiting athletes; some of these tactics are products of resources that give larger firms a competitive edge. For a discussion of industry consolidation and the demise of large representation firms such as SFX and Assante, and the emergence of new firms, see Shropshire, Davis & Duru, *supra* at 36-50.

A representative example of a termination provision in a standard player-agent contract follows.

NFLPA STANDARD REPRESENTATION AGREEMENT[3]

12.   TERM

The term of this Agreement shall begin on the date hereof and shall remain in effect until such time that it is terminated by either party in which case termination of this Agreement shall be effective five (5) days after written notice of termination is given to the other party. Notice shall be effective for purposes of this paragraph if sent by confirmed email, facsimile or overnight delivery to the appropriate address contained in this Agreement. Notwithstanding the above, if this Standard Representation agreement is being signed by a prospective rookie player (a "rookie" shall be defined as a person who has never signed an NFL Player Contract) prior to the date which is thirty (30) days before the NFL Draft, then this Agreement shall not be terminable by Player until at least 30 days after it has been signed by Player.

If termination pursuant to the above provision occurs prior to the completion of negotiations for an NFL player contract(s) acceptable to Player and signed by Player, Contract Advisor shall be entitled to compensation for the reasonable value of the services performed in the attempted negotiation of such contract(s) provided such services and time spent thereon are adequately documented by Contract Advisor. If termination pursuant to the above provision occurs after Player has signed an NFL player contract negotiated by Contract Advisor, Contract Advisor shall be entitled to fee prescribed in Paragraph 4 above for negotiation of such contract(s). . . .

If the Contract Advisor's Certification is suspended or revoked by the NFLPA or the Contract Advisor is otherwise prohibited by the NFLPA from performing the services he/she has agreed to perform herein, this Agreement shall automatically terminate, effective as of the date of such suspension or termination.

The following case, *Speakers*, illustrates the fierce competition for clients and the standards employed by courts in determining when competition exceeds what is permissible.

SPEAKERS OF SPORT, INC. v. PROSERV, INC.
178 F.3d 862 (7th Cir. 1999)

POSNER, Chief Judge.

The plaintiff, Speakers of Sport, appeals from the grant of summary judgment to the defendant, ProServ, in a diversity suit in which one sports agency has charged another with tortious interference with a business relationship and related violations of Illinois law. The essential facts, construed as favorably to the plaintiff as the record will permit, are as follows. Ivan Rodriguez, a highly successful catcher with the Texas Rangers baseball team, in 1991 signed the first of several one-year contracts making Speakers his agent. ProServ wanted to

---

3. The complete NFLPA Standard Representation Agreement (as amended through March 2016) can be found in Appendix D of NFLPA Regulations Governing Contract Advisors (2016), available at https://nflpaweb.blob.core.windows.net/media/Default/PDFs/Agents/RegulationsAmendedAugust2016.pdf.

expand its representation of baseball players and to this end invited Rodriguez to its office in Washington and there promised that it would get him between $2 and $4 million in endorsements if he signed with ProServ—which he did, terminating his contract (which was terminable at will) with Speakers. This was in 1995. ProServ failed to obtain significant endorsement for Rodriguez and after just one year he switched to another agent who the following year landed him a five-year $42 million contract with the Rangers. Speakers brought this suit a few months later, charging that the promise of endorsements that ProServ had made to Rodriguez was fraudulent and had induced him to terminate his contract with Speakers.

The parties agree that the substantive issues in this diversity suit are governed by Illinois law, and we do not look behind such agreements so long as they are reasonable, . . . as this one is. . . .

Speakers could not sue Rodriguez for breach of contract, because he had not broken their contract, which was, as we said, terminable at will. Nor, therefore, could it accuse ProServ of inducing a breach of contract. . . . But Speakers did have a contract with Rodriguez, and inducing the termination of a contract, even when the termination is not a breach because the contract is terminable at will, can still be actionable under the tort law of Illinois, either as an interference with prospective economic advantage . . . (citations omitted), or as an interference with the contract at will itself. . . . Nothing turns on the difference in characterization.

There is in general nothing wrong with one sports agent trying to take a client from another if this can be done without precipitating a breach of contract. That is the process known as competition, which though painful, fierce, frequently ruthless, sometimes Darwinian in its pitilessness, is the cornerstone of our highly successful economic system. Competition is not a tort, . . . but on the contrary provides a defense (the "competitor's privilege") to the tort of improper interference. . . . It does not privilege inducing a breach of contract, *Soderlund Bros., Inc. v. Carrier Corp., supra*, 215 Ill. Dec. 251, 663 N.E.2d at 8—conduct usefully regarded as a separate tort from interfering with a business relationship without precipitating an actual breach of contract—but it does privilege inducing the lawful termination of a contract that is terminable at will. . . . Restatement, *supra*, [(Second) of Torts,] § 768 comment i. Sellers (including agents, who are sellers of services) do not "own" their customers, at least not without a contract with them that is not terminable at will. . . .

There would be few more effective inhibitors of the competitive process than making it a tort for an agent to promise the client of another agent to do better by him, *Triangle Film Corp. v. Artcraft Pictures Corp.*, 250 F. 981 (2d Cir. 1918) (L. Hand, J.)—which is pretty much what this case comes down to. It is true that Speakers argues only that the competitor may not make a promise that he knows he cannot fulfill, may not, that is, compete by fraud. Because the competitor's privilege does not include a right to get business from a competitor by means of fraud, it is hard to quarrel with this position in the abstract, but the practicalities are different. If the argument were accepted and the new agent made a promise that was not fulfilled, the old agent would have a shot at convincing a jury that the new agent had known from the start that he couldn't deliver on the promise. Once a case gets to the jury, all bets are off. The practical consequence of Speakers' approach, therefore, would be that a sports agent who lured away the client of another agent with a promise to do better by him would be running a grave legal risk.

This threat to the competitive process is blocked by the principle of Illinois law that promissory fraud is not actionable unless it is part of a scheme to defraud, that is, unless it is one element of a pattern of fraudulent acts. . . . By requiring that the plaintiff show a pattern, by thus not letting him rest on proving a single promise, the law reduces the likelihood of a spurious suit; for a series of unfulfilled promises is better (though of course not conclusive) evidence of fraud than a single unfulfilled promise.

Criticized for vagueness, . . . and rejected in most states, . . . the Illinois rule yet makes sense in a case like this, if only as a filter against efforts to use the legal process to stifle competition. Consider in this connection the characterization by Speakers' own chairman of ProServ's promise to Rodriguez as "pure fantasy and gross exaggeration"—in other words, as puffing. Puffing in the usual sense signifies meaningless superlatives that no reasonable person would take seriously, and so it is not actionable as fraud. . . . Rodriguez thus could not have sued ProServ (and has not attempted to) in respect of the promise of $2-$4 million in endorsements. If Rodriguez thus was not wronged, we do not understand on what theory Speakers can complain that ProServ competed with it unfairly.

The promise of endorsements was puffing not in the most common sense of a cascade of extravagant adjectives but in the equally valid sense of a sales pitch that is intended, and that a reasonable person in the position of the "promisee" would understand, to be aspirational rather than enforceable—an expression of hope rather than a commitment. It is not as if ProServ proposed to employ Rodriguez and pay him $2 million a year. That would be the kind of promise that could found an enforceable obligation. ProServ proposed merely to get him endorsements of at least that amount. They would of course be paid by the companies whose products Rodriguez endorsed, rather than by ProServ. ProServ could not force them to pay Rodriguez, and it is not contended that he understood ProServ to be warranting a minimum level of endorsements in the sense that if they were not forthcoming ProServ would be legally obligated to make up the difference to him.

It is possible to make a binding promise of something over which one has no control; such a promise is called a warranty. . . . But it is not plausible that this is what ProServ was doing—that it was guaranteeing Rodriguez a minimum of $2 million a year in outside earnings if he signed with it. The only reasonable meaning to attach to ProServ's so-called promise is that ProServ would try to get as many endorsements as possible for Rodriguez and that it was optimistic that it could get him at least $2 million worth of them. So understood, the "promise" was not a promise at all. But even if it was a promise (or a warranty), it cannot be the basis for a finding of fraud because it was not part of a scheme to defraud evidenced by more than the allegedly fraudulent promise itself.

It can be argued, however, that competition can be tortious even if it does not involve an actionable fraud (which in Illinois would not include a fraudulent promise) or other independently tortious act, such as defamation, or trademark or patent infringement, or a theft of a trade secret; that competitors should not be allowed to use "unfair" tactics; and that a promise known by the promisor when made to be unfulfillable is such a tactic, especially when used on a relatively unsophisticated, albeit very well to do, baseball player. Considerable support for this view can be found in the case law. . . . But the Illinois courts have not as yet embraced the doctrine, and we are not alone in thinking it pernicious. . . . The doctrine's conception of wrongful competition is vague—"wrongful by reason of . . . an established standard of a trade or profession," *Yoakum v. Hartford Fire Ins. Co., supra*, 923 P.2d at 423, or "a violation of recognized ethical rules or established customs or practices in the business community," *RTL Distributing,*

Inc. v. Double S Batteries, Inc., supra, 545 N.W.2d at 591, or "improper because they [the challenged competitive tactics] violate an established standard of a trade or profession, or involve unethical conduct, . . . sharp dealing[, or] over-reaching." *Duggin v. Adams, supra*, 360 S.E.2d at 837. Worse, the established standards of a trade or profession in regard to competition, and its ideas of unethical competitive conduct, are likely to reflect a desire to limit competition for reasons related to the self-interest of the trade or profession rather than to the welfare of its customers or clients. We agree with Professor Perlman that the tort of interference with business relationships should be confined to cases in which the defendant employed unlawful means to stiff a competitor, Harvey S. Perlman, *Interference with Contract and Other Economic Expectancies: A Clash of Tort and Contract Doctrine*, 49 U. CHI. L. REV. 61 (1982), and we are reassured by the conclusion of his careful analysis that the case law is generally consistent with this position as a matter of outcomes as distinct from articulation.

Invoking the concept of "wrongful by reason of . . . an established standard of a trade or profession," Speakers points to a rule of major league baseball forbidding players' agents to compete by means of misrepresentations. The rule is designed to protect the players, rather than their agents, so that even if it established a norm enforceable by law Speakers would not be entitled to invoke it; it is not a rule designed for Speakers' protection. In any event its violation would not be the kind of "wrongful" conduct that should trigger the tort of intentional interference; it would not be a violation of law. . . .

We add that even if Speakers could establish liability under . . . common law of torts . . ., its suit would fail because it cannot possibly establish, as it seeks to do, a damages entitlement (the only relief it seeks) to the agent's fee on Rodriguez's $42 million contract. That contract was negotiated years after he left Speakers, and by another agent. Since Rodriguez had only a year-to-year contract with Speakers—terminable at will, moreover—and since obviously he was dissatisfied with Speakers at least to the extent of switching to ProServ and then when he became disillusioned with ProServ of *not* returning to Speakers' fold, the likelihood that Speakers would have retained him had ProServ not lured him away is too slight to ground an award of such damages. . . . Such an award would be the best example yet of puffing in the pie-in-the-sky sense.

AFFIRMED.

NOTES AND QUESTIONS

1. *Analysis of* Speakers. In affirming the district court's summary judgment on behalf of the defendant, the court in *Speakers* acknowledged the competitive nature of the agent business as reflective of our business system. Consistent with this underlying premise, the court adopts the notion of the competitor's privilege, which validates a broad range of activities in which an agent can engage in attempting to lure clients away from a competitor. Nevertheless, the court circumscribes the parameters of the competitor's privilege. What limitation does the court impose on an agent's permissible conduct in attempting to recruit clients in an established relationship with another agent?

    In *Wright v. Bonds*, 117 F.3d 1427 (9th Cir. 1999) (unpublished opinion), the Ninth Circuit adopted a similar approach. It ruled that in order for MLB player Barry Bonds's former agent to establish interference with prospective economic advantage he had to establish that Bonds's new agent "engaged in some wrongful conduct beyond mere interference." *Id.* Is the range of permissible competitive behavior validated in *Speakers* and *Wright* too broad? One critic of the results reached in these cases argues that although these cases "appear legally accurate, they provide a broad spectrum of competition that borders on interference thereby tolerating unfair and corrupt dealing." Bryan Couch, Comment, *How Agent Competition and Corruption Affects Sports and the Athlete-Agent Relationship and What Can Be Done to Control It*, 10 Seton Hall J. Sport L. 111, 119 (2000). Other discussions of the extreme competitiveness of the agent industry may be found in William Rothstein, *The Business of Sports Representation: Agent Evolution in the "Industry,"* 9 Va. Sports & Ent. L.J. 19 (2009); Timothy Davis, *Regulating the Athlete-Agent Industry: Intended and Unintended Consequences*, 42 Willamette L. Rev. 781 (2006); Zach Schreiber, Note, *Leveling the Playing Field for Sports Agents: How the Two-Hat Theory and the Model Rules of Professional Conduct Collide*, 19 Tex. Rev. Ent. & Sports L. 13 (2018); R. Alexander Payne, *Rebuilding the Prevent Defense: Why Unethical Agents Continue to Score and What Can Be Done to Change the Game*, 13 Vand. J. Ent. & Tech. L. 657 (2011).

For illustrations of the range of issues that arise in disputes between agents see *Núñez Guadalupe v. Lagardere Unlimited*, 2019 WL 2212134 (Tribunal De Apelaciones, Feb. 27, 2019) (In a case decided by a Mexican appellate court, court rejects agent's claims that he was entitled to a commission for assisting another agent to negotiate a NBA player/team contract; the court finds the commission payment was not mentioned in the contract and an alleged consulting contract was not signed by defendant agent); *Champion Pro Consulting Group, Inc. v. Impact Sports Football, LLC*, 845 F.3d 104 (4th Cir. 2016) (affirming lower court rejection of claims alleging that new agents engaged in deception or unfair trade practices in luring players away from their former agents); *Hendrickson v. Octagon, Inc.*, 225 F.Supp.3d 1013 (N.D. Cal. 2016) (discussing validity of fee sharing and non-solicitation provisions in employment contracts of sports agency's former agents); *Indep. Sports & Entm't LLC v. Fegan*, 2017 WL 2598550 (C.D. Cal., May 30, 2017) (state-based claims alleging breach of non-competition provisions asserted by a sports agency against a former agent were not preempted by Section 301 under the Labor Management Relations Act; the claims neither arose from nor were substantially dependent on an analysis of the collective bargaining agreement); *Rosenhaus v. Jackson*, 2016 WL 4592180 (C.D. Cal., Feb. 26, 2016) (vacating arbitration award in favor of agent against athlete who alleged evident partiality by the arbitrator; a new arbitrator ruled in favor of the agent awarding him approximately $950,000 including compensatory damages, attorneys' fees, and court costs); *Luchs v. Pro Tect Management Corp.*, 2009 WL 1364434 (Cal. Ct. App. May 18, 2009) (providing a good description of the dissolution of the business relationship between agents); *Miller v. Walters*, 46 Misc.3d 417 (N.Y. App. Div. 2014) (rejecting agent's tortious interference and unfair competition claims); *Dogra v. CAA Sports, LLC.*, AAA Case No. 01-15-0002-7781 (2016) (Vaughn, Arb.) (an arbitrator relied on contract law principles and the terms of the parties' contract in ruling that CAA's termination of an agent was improper and that the agent was entitled to commissions).

2. *Disparagement.* In the fierce competition for clients, agents try to convince athletes to sign with them by both extolling the virtues of their

organization and disparaging the competition. In *Bauer v. The Interpublic Group of Companies, Inc.*, 255 F. Supp. 2d 1086 (N.D. Cal. 2003), sports agent Frank Bauer alleged that NFL quarterback David Carr's decision to terminate their contractual relationship was based on negative information concerning Bauer that was disseminated by rival agents. In rejecting Bauer's claims, the court stated:

> Bauer's first claim is for intentional interference with contract. "The elements which a plaintiff must plead to state the cause of action for intentional interference with contractual relations are (1) a valid contract between plaintiff and a third party; (2) defendant's knowledge of this contract; (3) defendant's intentional acts designed to induce a breach or disruption of the contractual relationship; (4) actual breach or disruption of the contractual relationship; and (5) resulting damage." *Quelimane Co., Inc. v. Stewart Title Guaranty Co.*, 19 Cal. 4th 26, 55, 77 Cal. Rptr. 2d 709, 726, 960 P.2d 513 (1998). . . .
>
> Bauer has presented no evidence from which a jury could reasonably conclude that any of the defendants committed acts designed to induce a breach or disruption of his contract with Carr. Although there is conflicting evidence as to whether Carr received an anonymous letter containing negative information about Bauer, there is no evidence that defendants sent the letter. Further, the evidence is undisputed that Carr regularly received anonymous letters containing negative information about other agents before he even signed with Bauer. Thus, even if the Court assumes that Carr did receive such a letter about Bauer, as it must in considering defendants' motion for summary judgment, there is no evidence tying that letter to any of the defendants or their agents. There is no evidence that any of the defendants ever made any disparaging comments about Bauer to Carr. There is no evidence that any of the defendants even spoke to Carr during the time he was under contract to Bauer and before he notified Bauer that he was terminating their contract. It would be mere speculation to conclude that the letter must have been sent by the defendants.
>
> In a suit for intentional interference with contract, the plaintiff must show that "the act complained of was the proximate cause of the injury." *Augustine v. Trucco*, 124 Cal. App. 2d 229, 246, 268 P.2d 780 (1954). Bauer has no evidence that any acts by the defendants caused Carr to terminate his contract with Bauer. Carr was the one who initiated contact with the defendants *after* he decided to terminate his contract with Bauer. The National Football League Players Association Regulations Governing Contract Advisors permits agents to speak with players who are under contract with another agent if the player is the one who initiates the communication. The evidence is undisputed that defendants began negotiating with Carr at his request after he had already made his decision to terminate his contract with Bauer. Although there is a dispute of fact as to whether Carr signed a contract with defendants on January 17 or January 22, that dispute is irrelevant because Carr's decision to terminate Bauer occurred before either of those dates.
>
> No reasonable jury could find that defendants induced Carr to terminate his contract with Bauer. Accordingly, summary judgment is granted for defendants on Bauer's claim for intentional interference with contract.

Id. at 1094-95.

3. *Mandatory Arbitration.* A by-product of arbitration provisions in player association regulations governing agents is that disputes between agents are subject to mandatory arbitration. In requiring arbitration of a dispute, courts and arbitrators examine the provisions of the players association regulations

that define the persons and activities that are subject to arbitration. See e.g., *Dye v. Sexton*, 2017 WL 7615571 (N.D. Ga. Dec. 13, 2017) (relying on NFL CBA and NFLPA agent regulations, finds that dispute between agents is subject to arbitration); *Branion v. Wallace*, 2:16-cv-07992-SVW-JC (C.D. Cal. Jan. 18, 2017) (agent's action alleging that another agent and agency intentionally interfered with his contractual relationship with an athlete was subject to NFLPA's mandatory arbitration process, but noting that not all disputes between agents are subject to arbitration); *Mitchell v. Burkhardt*, NFLPA No. 14-CA-4 (Kaplan, Arb.) (finding that claims by a sports agency were not subject to mandatory arbitration because the claimant was not a person upon whom arbitration was imposed, noting there is no provision in NFLPA agent regulations allowing a firm to serve as a contract advisor (agent)).

4. *The Issue of Race and Gender.* Agents of color have risen to prominence in the athlete-agent industry. These include David Mulugheta, the son of Eritrean immigrants who rose from an internship at sports agency, Athletes First, to become an equity partner in the firm. Mulugheta, who represents 31 NFL players, including first-round drafts picks, is known for his talent for negotiating contracts but acknowledges that some still raise questions about "whether that 'young black kid' actually negotiates his players' contracts." Jori Epstein, *NFL agent 'changing the trajectory,'* USA Today (June 26, 2019). In the NBA, Rich Paul, friend of and agent for NBA player LeBron James and creator of the sports agency firm Klutch Sports Group has risen to prominence for his representation of athletes. In 2018, Klutch earned $24.9 million in commissions and landed on Forbes list of the world's top sports agencies. In July 2019, Paul garnered attention when he agreed for Klutch to become the new sports division within United Talent Agency, a leading representation firm that represents Angelina Jolie, Tiffany Haddish, Chris Pratt, and other high-profile actors. The alliance permits Klutch to retain its branding. The alliance better positions United Talent to compete against representation firms, such as CAA, which have sports divisions. Marc Stein, *LeBron James's Agent, Rich Paul, Starts a Sports Division at a Hollywood Firm*, N.Y. Times (Jul 17, 2019). Paul, however, has generated controversy for what some allege is his too close relationship with James and what is perceived as Paul's conflicts of interest in handling his roster of players as well as his inappropriate meddling in the internal affairs of NBA teams. Paul forcefully rejects these claims, pointing out other prominent agents influence team affairs and have close relationships with players. James also has been vocal in attributing some of the criticism to Paul's race as well as to Paul's difference in style and approach to being an agent, particularly as it relates to Paul's relationship with players and the relationships that Paul encourages players to have with each other. S.L. Price, *Against the Rich Paul Machine*, Sports Illus. (Jul. 17, 2019).

In an interesting situation with racial implications, Lamont Smith, a veteran African-American NFL player agent, filed a federal lawsuit against fellow agent Tom Condon. Smith's suit alleged that Condon, who is white, "may have told other current or perspective NFL players . . . that they should not become clients of plaintiff Smith because Smith had alienated general managers of NFL clubs by 'playing the race card.'" Liz Mullen, *Lawsuit Targets IMG Football Chief Condon*, Sports Bus. J. (Sept. 8, 2003). According to Smith, Condon made his statements when they competed to sign clients during the 2001-2003 NFL drafts and with the alleged intent of blackballing him. "It leads a player to think you are not accepted in NFL circles, which could not be further from the truth." *Id.*

Assuming that Condon made the comments asserted in Smith's complaint, would they exceed the bounds of what is considered permissible competition? For discussions of race and sports agents, see Shropshire, Davis & Duru, *supra,* at 60-63; James G. Sammataro, *Business and Brotherhood, Can They Coincide? A Search into Why Black Athletes Do Not Hire Black Agents,* 42 Howard L.J. 535 (1999).

As of 2018, 41 of 830, or 5%, of certified NFL agents were women. Linsay J. Jones, *For Women Rising as NFL Agents, Growing Strength in Numbers Helps Change Landscape,* USA Today (Apr. 19, 2018) (noting a 50% increase since 2010). The low percentage of female agents is due to factors that include coaches steering players away from women and discriminatory treatment emanating from male agents. *Id.* One female agent, Kristian Kuliga, states she was approached at an NFL scouting combine by a male agent who explained, "how she wouldn't be taken seriously." During a meeting at her former agency during a search for a new agent, staff members told Kuliga they "would never [expletive] hire a woman" because "a woman can't be an agent." Nikki Baim, *NFL Agency Is Changing, and It's Because of Women,* Yahoo Sports (May 10, 2019), https://sports.yahoocom/nfl-agency-is-changing-and-its-because-of-women-183049880.html (Nicole Lynn, who in 2019 became the first black woman to represent a top-five NFL Draft pick (Quinnen Williams), explains that race and gender are hurdles to increasing her client base).

Notwithstanding barriers, the number of successful women agents has increased over the last decade as players have begun to focus more on the quality of representation than on what the representation looks like. Liz Mullen, *Women Make Gains in NFL Agent Business,* Sports Business Journal (Oct. 2, 2017), https://www.sportsbusinessdaily.com/Journal/Issues/2017/10/02/Labor-and-Agents/Women-in-NFL.aspx. In 2010, Kelli Masters was the first women to represent a first-round NFL draft pick in third overall pick, Gerald McCoy. Baim, *supra.* Kim Miale of Roc Nation represents several former first-round picks, including Saquon Barkley, Ronnie Stanley, Todd Gurley, and Leonard Fournette. Morgan Moriarty, *How Kim Miale Became a Trailblazing NFL Agent with a Star-Studded Client List,* SBNation (Apr. 10, 2019), https://www.sbnation.com/nfl/2019/4/10/18292317/kim-miale-woman-agent-nfl-draft-saquon-barkley-juju-smith-schuster-bryce-love. In 2018, a record 33 women took the NFLPA agent certification exam. Baim, *supra.*

5. *Consolidation and Conflict.* It is not uncommon for agencies to consolidate or for agents to join larger sports representation agencies. After a few years of working at the new agency, the agent may be terminated or voluntarily depart to establish a competing agency. Similarly, agents, who begin their careers at an agency, will gain experience and later depart to join another agency or establish a new agency. Litigation is often a consequence of these shifting relationships. A paradigmatic example is the dispute between David Dunn and Leigh Steinberg. Dunn, a partner in what was then Steinberg, Moorad & Dunn (a division of Assante), departed to start his own firm. His new firm represented several clients of his previous firm. This led to a lawsuit in which the Steinberg firm alleged that Dunn's new firm conspired to lure clients away from it and that Dunn violated a noncompete covenant.

A Los Angeles jury awarded Steinberg $44.66 million in damages after it decided Dunn had breached his contract, engaged in unfair competition, and had acted with fraud and malice.

In 2005, a California appellate court vacated the $44.66 million jury award. *Steinberg Moorad & Dunn Inc. v. Dunn*, 136 Fed. Appx. 6 (9th Cir. 2005) (unpublished opinion). The court pointed to a state statute that it interpreted as "establishing that non-competition clauses in an employment agreement are unenforceable to the extent that they limit the employee's ability to compete after leaving, whether or not the employee is at-will and whether or not his term of employment has ended." *Id.* at *5.

C.   REGULATIONS AND LEGISLATION

The myriad problems related to the agent industry hasten the call for solutions. The materials in this section explore the efforts that have been and are being made to sanction inappropriate conduct by sports agents. Incidents occurring in 2009 and 2010 underscored the need to regulate the industry, but also revealed that regulatory efforts will not completely solve problems within the industry.

On June 10, 2010, an NCAA investigation and subsequent report revealed that former University of Southern California running back, Reggie Bush, had received impermissible benefits from two men attempting to form a sports agency in conjunction with Bush and his family. According to the NCAA, the improper benefits included cash, merchandise, an automobile, housing, hotel lodging and airline transportation. That same NCAA investigative report revealed that former University of Southern California basketball player O.J. Mayo had also received impermissible benefits from a representative of a sports agency while playing at the school. The violations caused both Bush and Mayo to be permanently disassociated from USC and resulted in Bush voluntarily relinquishing his Heisman Trophy award. Also in 2010, it was found that during the recruitment of eventual Heisman Trophy winning Auburn quarterback Cam Newton, a man said to be representing Newton attempted to secure a six-figure sum in exchange for Newton signing a National Letter of Intent (NLI) to attend Mississippi State University. The investigation resulted in findings of improper dealings on the part of Kenny Rodgers and Cecil Newton, Cam Newton's father. Erick Smith, *NCAA Rules Auburn's Newton Eligible for Now After Rules Violation*, USA Today, Dec. 1, 2010, http://content.usatoday.com/communities/campus-rivalry/post/2010/12/auburn-cam-newton-ncaa-eligible/1.

On October 11, 2010, the NCAA ruled two University of North Carolina football players permanently ineligible for taking improper benefits from agents. The two players, Greg Little and Robert Quinn, were found to have accepted benefits totaling $4,952 and $5,642, respectively. The gifts provided by the agents included travel accommodations to various locations, diamond earrings, and black diamond watches. Erick Smith, *Marvin Austin, Greg Little, Robert Quinn all will not play again for North Carolina*, USA Today (Oct. 11, 2010). A third University of North Carolina football player, Marvin Austin, was dismissed from the team after it was revealed that he had accepted over $10,000 in improper benefits. The fallout from the UNC scandal led to long-time NFL agent, the late Gary Wichard, receiving a nine-month suspension from the NFLPA for having impermissible contact with Austin. *Gary Wichard Suspended 9 Months*, ESPN. com (Dec. 3, 2010), http://sports.espn.go.com/nfl/news/story?id=5880708. See also Timothy G. Nelson, *Flag on the Play: The Ineffectiveness of Athlete-Agent Laws—and How North Carolina Can Take Advantage of a Scandal to Be a Model for Reform*, 90 N.C. L. Rev. 800 (2012) (discussing the evolution of the sports agent's role in American athletics, agent regulations, and how the UNC case presents an opportunity to affect change on a national scale).

The NCAA possesses no authority to regulate sports agents. The NCAA attempts, however, to stymie what it considers inappropriate agent conduct through a set of rules intended to regulate the interaction between student-athletes and agents. For example, NCAA rules prohibit student-athletes from receiving benefits from agents. Therefore, in most instances, a student-athlete who receives money or other benefits from an agent risks losing his or her amateur status and being deemed, by the NCAA, ineligible to participate in intercollegiate competition. See 2018-19 NCAA Division I Manual, Bylaw 12.3.

1. Federal Regulation

a. The Sports Agent Responsibility Trust Act

In September 2004, President George W. Bush signed into law the Sports Agent Responsibility Trust Act (SPARTA), the first federal legislation that specifically regulates sports agents. Sports Agent Responsibility and Trust Act, 15 U.S.C. §§ 7801-7807 (2004). SPARTA is modeled after key provisions of the Uniform Athlete Agents Act (UAAA), which is discussed *infra*. SPARTA does not preempt but rather supplements state requirements imposed by the UAAA. Indeed, SPARTA states that it is the "sense of Congress that States should enact the Uniform Athletes Agents Act . . . to protect student athletes and the integrity of amateur sports from unscrupulous sports agents." *Id.*

Like the UAAA, SPARTA prohibits agents from using improper inducements (e.g., cash payments and gifts) and misleading information to recruit student-athletes. In this regard, SPARTA makes it unlawful for an athlete agent to:

(1) directly or indirectly recruit or solicit a student athlete to enter into an agency contract, by
   (A) giving any false or misleading information or making a false promise or representation; or
   (B) providing anything of value to a student athlete or anyone [including family and friends] associated with the student athlete before the student athlete enters into an agency contract, including any consideration in the form of a loan, or acting in the capacity of a guarantor or co-guarantor for any debt;
(2) enter into an agency contract with a student athlete without providing the student athlete with the disclosure document described in subsection (b); or
(3) predate or postdate an agency contract.

Id. at § 7802

The disclosure document, referred to in (2) above, must conspicuously notify student-athletes, and parents or guardians of athletes under the age of 18, of the potential loss of eligibility to compete as an amateur if he or she signs an agency agreement. Within 72 hours of signing an agency contract or before the next athletic event in which the athlete is eligible to participate, both the student-athlete and agent "by whom you are agreeing to be represented must notify the athletic director of the educational institution at which you are enrolled, or other individual responsible for athletic programs at such educational institution, that you have entered into an agency contract." *Id.* at § 7802. Violations of SPARTA constitute unfair and deceptive acts or practices under the Federal Trade Commission Act and will be enforced by the FTC. Under 15 U.S.C. §§41 et seq., which SPARTA incorporates by reference, such acts are punishable by fines up to $10,000 per incident. 15 U.S.C. §45(l) and (m).

Upon proper notification to the FTC, SPARTA specifically authorizes state attorney generals to bring civil actions in federal court if a:

> "State has reason to believe that an interest of the residents of that State has been or is threatened or adversely affected" by a violation of the SPARTA. States may seek the following relief in these civil actions:
> (A)   enjoin the practice;
> (B)   enforce compliance with this Act; or
> (C)   obtain damages, restitution, or other compensation on behalf of residents of the State.

15 U.S.C. § 7804. If the FTC initiates an action against a defendant, a state may not institute an action against the named defendant during the pendency of the FTC complaint. SPARTA also permits individuals to seek "remedies available under existing Federal or State law or equity." *Id.* at § 7806.

b.   Non-Agent-Specific Federal Legislation

Prior to the enactment of SPARTA, despite calls for it, no federal legislation existed that specifically regulated sports agents. Nevertheless, from time to time, federal criminal laws have been used to address improper conduct by agents. For example, prosecutors employed the RICO and mail fraud statutes in *United States v. Walters*, 997 F.2d 1219 (7th Cir. 1993). Norby Walters, a former nightclub owner, and Lloyd Bloom, who served as his runner, enticed 58 student-athletes, while they had remaining collegiate eligibility, to sign exclusive representation agreements with them. The secret agreements were postdated to be effective after the expiration of the athletes' collegiate athletic eligibility. The athletes submitted false information to their universities regarding any restrictions on their eligibility. Facts providing the predicate for the alleged RICO violation included alleged extortion, mail fraud, and wire fraud. The mail fraud allegedly was committed against the NCAA and occurred when the athletes had their institutions send written documents to the NCAA indicating that the athletes were eligible for intercollegiate competition. The matter became a mail fraud case after prosecutors agreed to dismiss the RICO violations as a part of a plea bargain. A failure of the prosecutors to prove the elements of mail fraud resulted in the Seventh Circuit's dismissal of the claim against Walters. *Walters,* 997 F.2d.

Despite the setback to the U.S. Attorney's office in *Walters*, federal prosecutors have not only relied on RICO and mail fraud laws, but also on SEC regulations and federal laws prohibiting money laundering as grounds for asserting federal criminal charges against agents who have inappropriately handled their athlete-clients' assets. The case involving Tank Black illustrates the use of non-agent-specific federal criminal laws to prosecute agents. This and other cases are discussed *supra*, Section (B)(2). The use of such statutes and the implications of improper payments to student-athletes are also demonstrated in the infamous case of *United States v. Piggie*, 303 F.3d 923 (8th Cir. 2002). Myron Piggie developed a scheme whereby he paid elite high school players to compete for his Amateur Athletic Union (AAU) summer basketball team. "The payments were designed to retain top athletes on his team, gain access to sports agents, obtain profitable sponsorship contracts, and forge ongoing relationships with players to his benefit when the athletes joined the National Basketball Association (NBA)." *Id.* at 924. Between 1995 and 1998, Piggie realized at least $677,760 in income from his scheme. He also anticipated receiving a percentage of the compensation his players would earn after they signed contracts with NBA teams.

The court described the consequences of Piggie's scheme as follows:

After accepting Piggie's payments to play AAU basketball, Jaron Rush, [Corey] Maggette, Kareem Rush, and [Andre] Williams submitted false and fraudulent Student-Athlete Statements to the universities where they were to play intercollegiate basketball. These four athletes falsely certified that they had not previously received payments to play basketball. The athletes delivered through the U.S. Postal Service signed letters of intent asserting their eligibility. Based upon the false assertions that these athletes were eligible amateurs, the University of California, Los Angeles (UCLA); Duke University (Duke); the University of Missouri-Columbia (Missouri); and Oklahoma State University (OSU) (collectively Universities) awarded scholarships to these athletes, enrolled them in classes, and allowed them to play on NCAA basketball teams.

NCAA regulations permit universities to award only thirteen basketball scholarships per year. When Piggie's payments to these players were discovered, the Universities became subject to NCAA penalties. Each school lost the use of one of the thirteen scholarships and lost the value of each player's participation due to the player's NCAA-required suspension. The scholarships were forfeited, and the Universities lost the opportunity to award the scholarships to other top amateur athletes, who had actual eligibility to play intercollegiate basketball. In 1999 and 2000, UCLA lost the benefit of playing Jaron Rush, the $44,862.88 scholarship awarded to him, and also forfeited $42,339 in tournament revenue; Missouri lost the benefit of playing Kareem Rush, and the $9,388.92 scholarship awarded to him; and OSU lost the benefit of playing Williams and the $12,180 scholarship awarded to him. Duke provided Maggette with a $32,696 scholarship for the 1998-1999 season based upon the false assertion that he was an eligible amateur. As a result of the ineligible athlete's participation, the validity of Duke's entire 1998-1999 season was called into question.[4]

NCAA regulations also required each of the four Universities involved to conduct costly internal investigations after Piggie's scheme was discovered. UCLA spent $59,225.36 on the NCAA-mandated investigation of Jaron Rush, Duke spent $12,704.39 on the NCAA-mandated investigation of Maggette, Missouri spent $10,609 on the NCAA-mandated investigation of Kareem Rush, and OSU spent $21,877.24 on the NCAA-mandated investigation of Williams. The total monetary

---

4. Maggette played the full 1998-1999 season for Duke before Piggie's scheme was uncovered.

loss to the Universities was $245,882.79. The scandal following the disclosure of Piggie's scheme caused further intangible harms to the Universities including adverse publicity, diminished alumni support, merchandise sales losses, and other revenue losses.

Pembroke Hill High School (Pembroke), where Jaron and Kareem Rush played high school basketball, sustained a loss of $10,733.89 in investigative costs and forfeiture of property as a result of the conspiracy. Pembroke was placed on probation by the State of Missouri after the violations of Jaron and Kareem Rush were discovered and a mandatory investigation of the matter was concluded. . . .

Id. at 925-26.

Federal prosecutors charged Piggie with violations of non-agent-specific statutes. He pled guilty to conspiracy to commit mail and wire fraud in violation of 18 U.S.C. §371 and failure to file an income tax return in violation of 26 U.S.C. §7203. Thereafter, Piggie received a 37-month prison term and was ordered to pay $324,279.87 in restitution. On appeal, Piggie argued that the court miscalculated the amount of loss to the various institutions in enhancing his base offense levels under federal sentencing guidelines. In rejecting his appeal, the court found that the loss was appropriately calculated given the tangible and intangible harm to both the institutions and athletes who were impacted by Piggie's scheme.

The college basketball scandal discussed in Chapters 3 and 5 *supra*, spawned federal indictments against individuals including coaches, boosters, an Adidas executive, and a runner/aspiring sports agent, Christian Dawkins. Similar to *Piggie*, charges filed against Dawkins included conspiracy to commit wire fraud and wire fraud. Trial Order, *United States v. Dawkins*, 2019 WL 1313711 (S.D.N.Y. Mar. 15, 2019). Dawkins, who received a six-year prison sentence, is appealing his conviction, the resolution of which was pending when this book went to press.

Also similar to *Piggie*, affected schools sought restitution from a defendant; in this case former Adidas executive James Gatto, who was sentenced to a nine-month prison term after being convicted on wire fraud and conspiracy to commit wire fraud charges, Gatto agreed to pay a total of $342,437.75 to the University of Kansas and North Carolina State University. *Gatto to pay back $342K to NC State, Kansas,* ESPN (Apr. 8, 2019), https://www.espn.com/mens-college-basketball/story/_/id/26473901/gatto-pay-back-342k-nc-state-kansas.

2.   *State Regulation: The Uniform Athlete Agents Act*

Two bodies of state law may be available to regulate the agent profession. One level consists of non-agent-specific civil and criminal laws that might be invoked to penalize agents for improprieties. The other level consists of agent-specific legislation. Prior to the year 2000, agent-specific legislation was in effect in 28 states. (The state of Washington had adopted such legislation, but repealed it in 1999.) States achieved a modicum of success in prosecuting agents under these statutes. For example, in 1994, agent Nate Cebrun received 30 days in jail and was fined $2,255 for conduct related to making improper payments to a Florida State University football player and for failing to register in the state as a sports agent. See Shropshire, Davis & Duru, *supra*, at 156-58 (discussing the Cebrun matter and other instances in which states have sanctioned athletes pursuant to agent-specific statutes).

In 2000, the National Conference of Commissioners on Uniform State Laws (now the Uniform Law Commission, hereinafter ULC) completed drafting the Uniform Athlete Agents Act ("UAAA") and presented it to states for adoption. From a regulatory perspective, the primary goal of the UAAA was to protect the interests of student-athletes and academic institutions by regulating the activities of sports agents. The UAAA's other critical goal was to achieve uniformity. Commenting on the need for uniformity, the Prefatory Note to the UAAA states:

> The statutes differ greatly. About two-thirds of the statutes impose registration requirements. There are substantial differences in the registration procedures, disclosure required, and requirements relating to record maintenance, reporting, renewal, notice, warning and security. The term of the registration is one year in thirteen States, two years in four states, and two States do not specify a term. Most States require notification to States or educational institutions and athletes of certain matters, but the matters vary widely. Conscientious agents operating in more than a single State must have nightmares caused by the lack of uniformity in the existing statutes, and the difficulties in compliance and the severity of penalties which may be imposed for violations.

Uniform Athlete Agents Act (2000), at 1.

Critics of the UAAA identified several concerns about its overall effectiveness. The concerns included an increasing lack of uniformity as states adopted variations to the Act, the UAAA's weak deterrence effect arising from under-enforcement and weak penalties, and the belief that the UAAA failed to adequately protect the interests of student-athletes. Responding to such concerns, the Uniform Law Commission formed a committee to expand the UAAA's scope and improve its effectiveness. Rich Cassidy, *Proposed Amendments to Uniform Athlete Agents Act Attract Attention in Chicago*, On Lawyering (Oct. 29, 2013). A statement in support of forming the committee identified reasons for amending the Act.

> [T]he act has received increasing pushback from state regulators. Montana repealed the act in 2007, due to a perceived lack of agents to register; Colorado repealed the registration function of the act in 2010 (a year after the UAAA's initial adoption) for similar reasons. . . . This activity has stemmed in large part from fiscal concerns regarding the cost of implementing and maintaining a registry versus the number of agents who register and the resulting fee revenue, and general burden on regulatory staff. In California and Virginia, bills to enact the UAAA were vetoed in 2010 and 2011, respectively, over similar concerns. The problem is compounded by a culture of disregard for registration laws among unscrupulous agents, and systematic lack of reporting and enforcement on several levels.

Memorandum: Proposed Study Committee on Revisions to the Uniform Athlete Agents Act, NCCUSL (Dec. 7, 2011), https://www.uniformlaws.org/HigherLogic/System/DownloadDocumentFile.ashx?DocumentFileKey=91a63272-9a6f-899e-5de9-0e744a591db7&forceDialog=0.

Prior to its 2015 revision, the UAAA had been adopted in 43 states, territories and Washington, D.C. As of June 2019, the Revised Uniform Athlete Agents Act ("RUAAA"), excerpts from which appear below, had been enacted in 13 states and introduced in 10 states. The revised Act, *infra*, can be found in its entirety at https://www.uniformlaws.org/HigherLogic/System/DownloadDocumentFile.ashx?DocumentFileKey=6a97db74-446e-e102-f517-0bd54fbb7ff4&forceDialog=0.

For informative discussions of state regulation of sports agents see Shropshire, Davis & Duru, *supra*, at 163-74; Seth Myers, *An Intentional Foul: Corruption in*

NCAA Basketball & the Aftermath of the 2017 Scandal, 15 DePaul J. Sports L. 65 (2019) (addressing the 2017 basketball scandal and the impact of the RUAAA and SPARTA on agents); Michael L. Martin, *It's Not a Foul Unless the Ref Blows the Whistle: How to Step Up Enforcement of the UAAA and SPARTA,* 19 Sports Law. J. 209 (2012).

The ULC has formed a committee that has promulgated minor, yet important, amendments to the RUAAA. The amendments grew out of the concerns related to the 2017 college basketball scandal. As a consequence of the scandal, the NCAA revised its regulations to allow basketball student-athletes greater flexibility in deciding when they can become professionals without jeopardizing their collegiate eligibility. The amended NCAA bylaws, adopted on August 8, 2018, permit sports agents to pay student-athletes and their parents for meals and hotel and travel expenses related to agents recruiting student-athletes as clients to the extent permitted under NCAA bylaws. Without the amendments, such payments would violate criminal provisions of both the UAAA and the RUAAA.

PROBLEM 8-4

In 2016, Frank Wilson obtained certification from the NFLPA to serve as a contract advisor. On February 29, 2019, Gerald Robinson, a senior football player at Big-Time University (which is located in a state that has adopted the RUAAA), entered into an NFLPA standard representation agreement authorizing Wilson to serve as his agent. At the time the parties entered into the contract, Wilson was not registered as an athlete agent in the state in which Big-Time is located. Wilson began his solicitation of Robinson at least as early as November 2017, while Robinson was playing his final season of football for Big-Time.

You are the secretary of state of the state in which of Big-Time is located. What charges, if any, would you file against Mr. Wilson? What other consequences may ensue from these facts? In responding, consider the following materials.

REVISED UNIFORM ATHLETE AGENTS ACT (2015)

PREFATORY NOTE. . . .

Some 43 states have enacted the UAAA. However, several states have amended the act to, among other things, deal with a perceived lack of enforcement, broaden the coverage of the act to individuals who do not necessarily recruit or solicit a student athlete to enter into an agency contract, and require notice to educational institutions prior to contact. It became evident that the variations from state to state put uniformity at risk and may have discouraged reputable agents from complying with the act. To deal with these issues, the Uniform Law Commission adopted the Revised Uniform Athlete Agents Act (RUAAA) in July of 2015.

The purposes of the RUAAA include providing enhanced protection for student athletes and educational institutions, creating a uniform body of agent registration information for use by the state agencies registering agents, and simplifying the registration process for agents.

Specifically, the RUAAA:

- Revises the definition of "athlete agent" to include an individual who, for compensation or the anticipation of compensation, serves the athlete in an advisory capacity on a matter related to finances, business pursuits, or career management decisions or manages the business affairs of the athlete by providing assistance with bills, payments, contracts, or taxes, and an individual who gives something of value to a student athlete or another person in anticipation of representing the athlete for a purpose related to the athlete's participation in athletics.
- Contains two alternatives for athlete agent registration. Alternative A includes a true reciprocal registration requirement in that if an individual is issued a certificate of registration by one state, the registration is in good standing and no disciplinary proceedings are pending against the registration, and the law in that state is the same or more restrictive as the law in another state, the other state would be required to register the individual. Alternative B would adopt an interstate compact when the act is enacted by at least five states. The compact would create the Commission on Interstate Regulation of Athlete Agents to provide a single registration site where an individual could register to act as an athlete agent in the states that are members of the compact.
- Adds additional requirements to the signing of an agency contract. . . .
- Requires an agent to notify the educational institution at which a student athlete is enrolled before contacting a student athlete and requires an athlete agent with a preexisting relationship with a student athlete who enrolls at an educational institution and receives an athletic scholarship to notify the institution of the relationship if the agent knows or should have known of the enrollment and the relationship was motivated by the intention of the agent to recruit or solicit the athlete to enter an agency contract or the agent actually recruited or solicited the student athlete to enter a contract.
- Adds criminal penalties for athlete agents who encourage another individual to take on behalf of the agent an action the agent is prohibited from taking and gives student athletes a right of action against an athlete agent in violation of the act.

SECTION 2.   DEFINITIONS. IN THIS [ACT]:

(1)   "Agency contract" means an agreement in which a student athlete authorizes a person to negotiate or solicit on behalf of the athlete a professional-sports-services contract or endorsement contract.

(2)   "Athlete agent":
    (A)   means an individual, whether or not registered under this [act], who:
        (i)   directly or indirectly recruits or solicits a student athlete to enter into an agency contract or, for compensation, procures employment or offers, promises, attempts, or negotiates to obtain employment for a student athlete as a professional athlete or member of a professional sports team or organization;
        (ii)   for compensation or in anticipation of compensation related to a student athlete's participation in athletics:
            (I)   serves the athlete in an advisory capacity on a matter related to finances, business pursuits, or career management decisions,

unless the individual is an employee of an educational institution acting exclusively as an employee of the institution for the benefit of the institution; or

    (II) manages the business affairs of the athlete by providing assistance with bills, payments, contracts, or taxes; or

  (iii) in anticipation of representing a student athlete for a purpose related to the athlete's participation in athletics:

    (I)   gives consideration to the student athlete or another person;

    (II) serves the athlete in an advisory capacity on a matter related to finances, business pursuits, or career management decisions; or

    (III) manages the business affairs of the athlete by providing assistance with bills, payments, contracts, or taxes; but

(B) does not include an individual who:

  (i) acts solely on behalf of a professional sports team or organization; or

  (ii) is a licensed, registered, or certified professional and offers or provides services to a student athlete customarily provided by members of the profession, unless the individual:

    (I)   also recruits or solicits the athlete to enter into an agency contract;

    (II) also, for compensation, procures employment or offers, promises, attempts, or negotiates to obtain employment for the athlete as a professional athlete or member of a professional sports team or organization; or

    (III) receives consideration for providing the services calculated using a different method than for an individual who is not a student athlete.

(3) "Athletic director" means the individual responsible for administering the overall athletic program of an educational institution or, if an educational institution has separately administered athletic programs for male students and female students, the athletic program for males or the athletic program for females, as appropriate. . . .

(6) "Educational institution" includes a public or private elementary school, secondary school, technical or vocational school, community college, college, and university.

(7) "Endorsement contract" means an agreement under which a student athlete is employed or receives consideration to use on behalf of the other party any value that the athlete may have because of publicity, reputation, following, or fame obtained because of athletic ability or performance.

(8) "Enrolled" means registered for courses and attending athletic practice or class. . . .

(9) "Intercollegiate sport" means a sport played at the collegiate level for which eligibility requirements for participation by a student athlete are established by a national association that promotes or regulates collegiate athletics.

(10) "Interscholastic sport" means a sport played between educational institutions that are not community colleges, colleges, or universities.

(11) "Licensed, registered, or certified professional: means an individual licensed, registered, or certified as an attorney, dealer in securities, financial planner, insurance agent, real estate broker or sales agent, tax

consultant, accountant, or member of a profession, other than that of athlete agent, who is licensed, registered, or certified by the state or a nationally recognized organization that licenses, registers, or certifies members
of the profession on the basis of experience, education, or testing.

(12) "Person" means an individual, estate, business or nonprofit entity, public
corporation, government or governmental subdivision, agency, or instrumentality, or other legal entity.

(13) "Professional-sports-services-contract" means an agreement under which
an individual is employed as a professional athlete or agrees to render services as a player on a professional sports team or with a professional sports
organization. . . .

(15) "Recruit or solicit" means attempt to influence the choice of an athlete
agent by a student athlete or, if the athlete is a minor, a parent or guardian
of the athlete. The term does not include giving advice on the selection
of a particular agent in a family, coaching, or social situation unless the
individual giving the advice does so because of the receipt or anticipated
receipt of an economic benefit, directly or indirectly, from the agent.

(16) "Registration" means registration as an athlete agent under this [act].

(17) "Sign" means, with present intent to authenticate or adopt a record. . . .

(19) "Student athlete" means an individual who is eligible to attend an educational institution and engages in, is eligible to engage in, or may be
eligible in the future to engage in, any interscholastic or intercollegiate
sport. The term does not include an individual permanently ineligible to
participate in a particular interscholastic or intercollegiate sport for that
sport. . . .

COMMENT

Only individuals are within the definition of "athlete agent" and therefore
required to register under the act. Corporations and other business entities do
not come within the definition of "athlete agent" and therefore are not required
to register under the act, even though individuals employed by the corporation
or other business entity as athlete agents would be required to register. The definition also includes other individuals or "runners" used by an agent to recruit or
solicit a student athlete to enter into agency contract.

The amendment of the definition of athlete agent . . . expands the definition
to include an individual who:

(1) for compensation, procures or attempts to procure employment for a student athlete as a professional athlete;

(2) for compensation or the anticipation of compensation, represents a student athlete as athlete or advises a student athlete on finances, business
ventures, or career management or manages the business affairs of a student athlete; or

(3) in anticipation of representing a student athlete as athlete, gives consideration to the student athlete or another person. . . .

Recruit or solicit, which is used in the definition of athlete agent, is
defined to mean attempting to influence the choice of an athlete agent by
a student athlete or, if the athlete is a minor, by a parent or guardian of the
athlete. . . .

SECTION 3. [SECRETARY OF STATE] [COMMISSION]; AUTHORITY; PROCEDURE. . . .

ALTERNATIVE A

(a) The [administrative procedure act] applies to this [act]. The [Secretary of State] may adopt rules under the [administrative procedure act] to implement this [act].

ALTERNATIVE B

(a) Except as otherwise provided in this [act], the commission is an agency of the state in which the headquarters of the commission is located and the law of that state, including the law relating to administrative procedure, public records, and public meetings, applies to the commission. The commission may adopt rules under the [administrative procedure act] of the state in which its headquarters is located to implement this [act]. . . .

SECTION 4. ATHLETE AGENT: REGISTRATION REQUIRED; VOID CONTRACT.

(a) Except as otherwise provided in subsection (b), an individual may not act as an athlete agent in this state without holding a certificate of registration under this [act].

(b) Before being issued a certificate of registration under this [act] an individual may act as an athlete agent in this state for all purposes except signing an agency contract, if:
  (1) a student athlete or another person acting on behalf of the athlete initiates communication with the individual; and
  (2) not later than seven days after an initial act that requires the individual to register as an athlete agent, the individual submits an application for registration as an athlete agent in this state.

(c) An agency contract resulting from conduct in violation of this section is void, and the athlete agent shall return any consideration received under the contract. . . .

COMMENT ALTERNATIVE A FOR SECTIONS 5 THROUGH 9

Legislative Note: *There are two alternatives for Sections 5 through 9. Alternative A establishes a registration system in the enacting state which requires the enacting state to register an individual who is registered in another state if the enacting state determines the law of the other state is substantially similar to or more restrictive than the law of the enacting state, the registration in the other state has not been revoked or suspended, and no action involving the agent's conduct as an agent is pending.*

Alternative B creates a central registration agency, the Commission on Interstate Registration of Athlete Agents, and provides that states enacting Alternative B will be entering into an interstate compact with other states that enact it. . . .

SECTION 5. REGISTRATION AS ATHLETE AGENT; APPLICATION; REQUIREMENTS; RECIPROCAL REGISTRATION.

(a) An applicant for registration as an athlete agent shall submit an application for registration to the [Secretary of State] in a form prescribed by the [Secretary of State]. The applicant must be an individual, and the application must be signed by the applicant under penalty of perjury. The application must contain at least the following. . . .

(c) The [Secretary of State] shall issue a certificate of registration to an individual who applies for registration under subsection (b) if the [Secretary of State] determines:

    (1) the application and registration requirements of the other state are substantially similar to or more restrictive than this [act]; and

    (2) the registration has not been revoked or suspended and no action involving the individual's conduct as an athlete agent is pending against the individual or the individual's registration in any state.

(d) For purposes of implementing subsection (c), the [Secretary of State] shall:

    (1) cooperate with national organizations concerned with athlete agent issues and agencies in other states which register athlete agents to develop a common registration form and determine which states have laws that are substantially similar to or more restrictive than this [act]; and

    (2) exchange information, including information related to actions taken against registered athlete agents or their registrations, with those organizations and agencies.

COMMENT

The UAAA required an application for registration as an athlete agent to contain personal and business information about the applicant. RUAAA expands the information required to be contained on the application to require, among other things, disclosure of financial information and, recognizing that communication between an athlete agent and a student athlete may be by electronic means, electronic mail addresses and social media accounts. . . .

Section 5 of the UAAA was not a true reciprocal registration provision in that, while it allowed for submission of the application for registration in one state to another state, the second state was free to require additional information or refuse to issue the registration on various grounds. The amended version is a true reciprocal registration provision in that if an individual registered in one state applies for registration in a second state, the second state is required to grant the registration if it determines the law in the first state is the same or more restrictive than the law in the second state, the registration is in good standing, and no proceeding involving the individual's conduct as athlete agent is pending in any state in which the individual is registered. . . .

SECTION 6. CERTIFICATE OF REGISTRATION; ISSUANCE OR DENIAL; RENEWAL.

(a) Except as otherwise provided in subsection (b), the [Secretary of State] shall issue a certificate of registration to an applicant for registration who complies with Section 5(a).

(b) The [Secretary of State] may refuse to issue a certificate of registration to an applicant for registration under Section 5(a) if the [Secretary of State] determines that the applicant has engaged in conduct that significantly adversely reflects on the applicant's fitness to act as an athlete agent. In making the determination, the [Secretary of State] may consider whether the applicant has:

   (1) pleaded guilty or no contest to, has been convicted of, or has charges pending for, a crime that would involve moral turpitude or be a felony if committed in this state;

   (2) made a materially false, misleading, deceptive, or fraudulent representation in the application or as an athlete agent;

   (3) engaged in conduct that would disqualify the applicant from serving in a fiduciary capacity;

   (4) engaged in conduct prohibited by Section 14;

   (5) had a registration as an athlete agent suspended, revoked, or denied in any state;

   (6) been refused renewal of registration as an athlete agent in any state;

   (7) engaged in conduct resulting in imposition of a sanction, suspension, or declaration of ineligibility to participate in an interscholastic, intercollegiate, or professional athletic event on a student athlete or a sanction on an educational institution; or

   (8) engaged in conduct that adversely reflects on the applicant's credibility, honesty, or integrity.

(c) In making a determination under subsection (b), the [Secretary of State] shall consider:

   (1) how recently the conduct occurred;

   (2) the nature of the conduct and the context in which it occurred; and

   (3) other relevant conduct of the applicant.

(d) An athlete agent registered under subsection (a) may apply to renew the registration by submitting an application for renewal in a form prescribed by the [Secretary of State]. The applicant shall sign the application for renewal under penalty of perjury and include current information on all matters required in an original application for registration.

(e) An athlete agent registered under Section 5'(c) may renew the registration by proceeding under subsection (d) or, if the registration in the other state has been renewed, by submitting to the [Secretary of State] copies of the application for renewal in the other state and the renewed registration from the other state. The [Secretary of State] shall renew the registration if the [Secretary of State] determines:

   (1) the registration requirements of the other state are substantially similar to or more restrictive than this [act]; and

   (2) the renewed registration has not been suspended or revoked and no action involving the individual's conduct as an athlete agent is pending against the individual or the individual's registration in any state.

(f) A certificate of registration or renewal of registration under this [act] is valid for [two] years. . . .

SECTION 7. SUSPENSION, REVOCATION, OR REFUSAL TO RENEW REGISTRATION.

(a) The [Secretary of State] may limit, suspend, revoke, or refuse to renew a registration of an individual registered under Section 6(a) for conduct that would have justified refusal to issue a certificate of registration under Section 6(b). . . .

SECTION 8. TEMPORARY REGISTRATION.

The [Secretary of State] may issue a temporary certificate of registration as an athlete agent while an application for registration or renewal of registration is pending.

SECTION 9. REGISTRATION AND RENEWAL FEES. . . .

COMMENT

The amount of fees is left for each state to determine. Some states with existing acts have set fees in amounts sufficient to recover the cost of administration. . . .

ALTERNATIVE B FOR SECTIONS 5 THROUGH 9. . . .

SECTION 5. COMMISSION ON INTERSTATE REGISTRATION OF ATHLETE AGENTS.

(a)   The Commission on Interstate Registration of Athlete Agents is created. The commission is a body corporate and joint agency of the states that enact an act substantially similar to this [act]. The commission consists of one member from each state that enacts such an act appointed by the Governor of that state. . . . [EDS. The RUAAA discusses the creation and operation of the Commission.]

SECTION 6. REGISTRATION AS ATHLETE AGENT; APPLICATION; REQUIREMENTS.

An applicant for registration as an athlete agent shall submit an application for registration to the commission in a form prescribed by the commission. The applicant must be an individual, and the application must be signed by the applicant under penalty of perjury. The application must contain at least the following:
[EDS. Sections 7-9 are omitted; they parallel Sections 7-9 of Alternative A.]

END OF ALTERNATIVES

SECTION 10. REQUIRED FORM OF AGENCY CONTRACT.

(a)   An agency contract must be in a record signed by the parties.
(b)   An agency contract must contain:
    (1)   a statement that the athlete agent is registered as an athlete agent in this state and a list of any other states in which the agent is registered as an athlete agent;
    (2)   the amount and method of calculating the consideration to be paid by the student athlete for services to be provided by the agent under the contract and any other consideration the agent has received or

received from any other source for entering into the contract or providing the services;

(3) the name of any person not listed in the agent's application for registration or renewal of registration which will be compensated because the athlete signed the contract;

(4) a description of any expenses the athlete agrees to reimburse;

(5) a description of the services to be provided to the athlete;

(6) the duration of the contract; and

(7) the date of execution.

(c) Subject to subsection (g), an agency contract must contain a conspicuous notice in boldface type and in substantially the following form:

WARNING TO STUDENT ATHLETE

IF YOU SIGN THIS CONTRACT:

(1) YOU MAY LOSE YOUR ELIGIBILITY TO COMPETE AS A STUDENT ATHLETE IN YOUR SPORT;

(2) IF YOU HAVE AN ATHLETIC DIRECTOR, WITHIN 72 HOURS AFTER SIGNING THIS CONTRACT OR BEFORE THE NEXT SCHEDULED ATHLETIC EVENT IN WHICH YOU PARTICIPATE, WHICHEVER OCCURS FIRST, BOTH YOU AND YOUR ATHLETE AGENT MUST NOTIFY YOUR ATHLETIC DIRECTOR THAT YOU HAVE ENTERED INTO THIS CONTRACT AND PROVIDE THE NAME AND CONTACT INFORMATION OF THE ATHLETE AGENT; AND

(3) YOU MAY CANCEL THIS CONTRACT WITHIN 14 DAYS AFTER SIGNING IT. CANCELLATION OF THIS CONTRACT MAY NOT REINSTATE YOUR ELIGIBILITY AS A STUDENT ATHLETE IN YOUR SPORT.

(d) An agency contract must be accompanied by a separate record signed by the student athlete or, if the athlete is a minor, the parent or guardian of the athlete acknowledging that signing the contract may result in the loss of the athlete's eligibility to participate in the athlete's sport.

(e) A student athlete or, if the athlete is a minor, the parent or guardian of the athlete may void an agency contract that does not conform to this section. If the contract is voided, any consideration received from the athlete agent under the contract to induce entering into the contract is not required to be returned.

(f) At the time an agency contract is executed, the athlete agent shall give the student athlete or, if the athlete is a minor, the parent or guardian of the athlete a copy in a record of the contract and the separate acknowledgement required by subsection (d).

(g) If a student athlete is a minor, an agency contract must be signed by the parent or guardian of the minor and the notice required by subsection (c) must be revised accordingly.

COMMENT. . . .

A student athlete who opts to void an agency contract under this section because it does not comply with the specified form is not required to return any consideration received to induce the signing of the agency contract because such inducement is prohibited conduct under Section 14. . . .

The compensation referred to in subsection (b)(2) is compensation for services intended to induce the student athlete to sign an agency contract. . . .

SECTION 11. NOTICE TO EDUCATIONAL INSTITUTION.

(a) In this section, "communicating or attempting to communicate" means contacting or attempting to contact by an in-person meeting, a record, or any other method that conveys or attempts to convey a message.

(b) Not later than 72 hours after entering into an agency contract or before the next scheduled athletic event in which the student athlete may participate, whichever occurs first, the athlete agent shall give notice in a record of the existence of the contract to the athletic director of the educational institution at which the athlete is enrolled or at which the agent has reasonable grounds to believe the athlete intends to enroll.

(c) Not later than 72 hours after entering into an agency contract or before the next scheduled athletic event in which the student athlete may participate, whichever occurs first, the athlete shall inform the athletic director of the educational institution at which the athlete is enrolled that the athlete has entered into an agency contract and the name and contact information of the athlete agent.

(d) If an athlete agent enters into an agency contract with a student athlete and the athlete subsequently enrolls at an educational institution, the agent shall notify the athletic director of the institution of the existence of the contract not later than 72 hours after the agent knew or should have known the athlete enrolled.

(e) If an athlete agent has a relationship with a student athlete before the athlete enrolls in an educational institution and receives an athletic scholarship from the institution, the agent shall notify the institution of the relationship not later than 10 days after the enrollment if the agent knows or should have known of the enrollment and:

    (1) the relationship was motivated in whole or part by the intention of the agent to recruit or solicit the athlete to enter an agency contract in the future; or

    (2) the agent directly or indirectly recruited or solicited the athlete to enter an agency contract before the enrollment.

(f) An athlete agent shall give notice in a record to the athletic director of any educational institution at which a student athlete is enrolled before the agent communicates or attempts to communicate with:

    (1) the athlete, or if the athlete is a minor, a parent or guardian of the athlete, to influence the athlete or parent or guardian to enter into an agency contract; or

    (2) another individual to have that individual influence the athlete or, if the athlete is a minor, the parent or guardian of the athlete to enter into an agency contract.

(g) If a communication or attempt to communicate with an athlete agent is initiated by a student athlete or another individual on behalf of the athlete, the agent shall notify in a record the athletic director of any educational institution at which the athlete is enrolled. The notification must be made not later than 10 days after the communication or attempt.

(h) An educational institution that becomes aware of a violation of this [act] by an athlete agent shall notify the [Secretary of State] [commission] and any professional league or players association with which the institution is aware the agent is licensed or registered of the violation. . . .

SECTION 12. STUDENT ATHLETE'S RIGHT TO CANCEL

(a) A student athlete or, if the athlete is a minor, the parent or guardian of the athlete may cancel an agency contract by giving notice in a record of cancellation to the athlete agent not later than 14 days after the contract is signed.

(b) A student athlete or, if the athlete is a minor, the parent or guardian of the athlete may not waive the right to cancel an agency contract.

(c) If a student athlete, parent, or guardian cancels an agency contract, the athlete, parent, or guardian is not required to pay any consideration under the contract or return any consideration received from the athlete agent to influence the athlete to enter into the contract . . .

SECTION 13. REQUIRED RECORDS.

(a) An athlete agent shall create and retain for five years records of the following:
   (1) the name and address of each individual represented by the agent;
   (2) each agency contract entered into by the agent; and
   (3) the direct costs incurred by the agent in the recruitment or solicitation of each student athlete to enter into an agency contract. . . .

SECTION 14. PROHIBITED CONDUCT.

(a) An athlete agent, with the intent to influence a student athlete or, if the athlete is a minor, a parent or guardian of the athlete to enter into an agency contract, may not take any of the following actions or encourage any other individual to take or assist any other individual in taking any of the following actions on behalf of the agent:
   (1) give materially false or misleading information or make a materially false promise or representation;
   (2) furnish anything of value to the athlete before the athlete enters into the contract; or
   (3) furnish anything of value to an individual other than the athlete or another registered athlete agent.

(b) An athlete agent may not intentionally do any of the following or encourage any other individual to do any of the following on behalf of the agent:
   (1) initiate contact, directly or indirectly, with a student athlete or, if the athlete is a minor, a parent or guardian of the athlete, to recruit or solicit the athlete, parent, or guardian to enter an agency contract unless registered under this [act];
   (2) fail to create or retain or to permit inspection of the records required by Section 13;

(3)   fail to register when required by Section 4;
(4)   provide materially false or misleading information in an application for registration or renewal of registration;
(5)   predate or postdate an agency contract; or
(6)   fail to notify a student athlete or, if the athlete is a minor, a parent or guardian of the athlete, before the athlete, parent, or guardian signs an agency contract for a particular sport that the signing may make the athlete ineligible to participate as a student athlete in that sport. . . .

SECTION 15. CRIMINAL PENALTY.

An athlete agent who violates Section 14 is guilty of a [misdemeanor] [felony] and, on conviction, is punishable by [].

Legislative Note: *Each state should determine the penalties to be imposed for a violation of the act. A state may wish to include a suspension or revocation of the registration as a part of the penalty and also may wish to dedicate all or a part of any fine to the enforcement of the act (see, for example, Section 18897.93, California Business and Professionals Code).*

SECTION 16. CIVIL REMEDY.

(a)   An educational institution or student athlete may bring an action for damages against an athlete agent if the institution or athlete is adversely affected by an act or omission of the agent in violation of this [act]. An educational institution or student athlete is adversely affected by an act or omission of the agent only if, because of the act or omission, the institution or an individual who was a student athlete at the time of the act or omission and enrolled in the institution:
    (1)   is suspended or disqualified from participation in an interscholastic or intercollegiate [sports] event by or under the rules of a state or national federation or association that promotes or regulates interscholastic or intercollegiate sports; or
    (2)   suffers financial damage.
(b)   A plaintiff that prevails in an action under this section may recover [actual damages] [treble damages] [,] [punitive damages,] [and] costs [, and reasonable attorney's fees]. An athlete agent found liable under this section forfeits any right of payment for anything of benefit or value provided to the student athlete and shall refund any consideration paid to the agent by or on behalf of the athlete.
[(c)   A violation of this [act] is an [unfair trade or deceptive practice] for purposes of [insert reference to state's unfair trade practices law].] . . . .

SECTION 17. CIVIL PENALTY.

The [Secretary of State] [commission] may assess a civil penalty against an athlete agent not to exceed $[50,000] for a violation of this [act]. . . .

NOTE AND QUESTION

UAAA Prosecutions. In one of the first indictments brought pursuant to the UAAA, on October 13, 2006, a grand jury in Baton Rouge, Louisiana, charged Charles Taplin with two counts of violating Louisiana's version of the UAAA. Taplin allegedly violated the UAAA's registration and notification provisions when he sent text messages to two Louisiana State University football players on behalf of an agent. Taplin was not a registered agent and allegedly failed to notify LSU within seven days of contacting the players. Adrian Angelette, *"Runner" Indicted in Sports Agent Case,* Baton Rouge Advocate (Aug. 15, 2007). While investigating Taplin, information was allegedly uncovered that led to the arrest of Travelle Gaines, a former assistant strength coach at LSU. Gaines was booked on a felony count of engaging in activities prohibited by Louisiana's UAAA—allegedly inviting players to his home where they came into contact with a California-based agent, C.J. Laboy. Adrian Angelette, *La. Law Allows Agent-Athlete Contact Within Rules,* Baton Rouge Advocate, Oct. 26, 2006, at A1. Gaines's attorney denied that his client had done anything illegal.

In October 2008, a Virginia-based and NFLPA-certified contract advisor, Raymond L. Savage, Jr., was indicted for allegedly violating the UAAA. Savage was charged with failing to register under Alabama's UAAA and for initiating contact with a student-athlete. One of Savage's former employee's, Jason Goggins, allegedly contacted Tyrone Prothro, a University of Alabama wide receiver, while the athlete was in the hospital recovering from a broken leg. The indictment of Savage alleged that in 2006 the agent instructed Goggins to visit the player and paid for Goggins's plane fare to Alabama. Goggins's alleged conduct led to his indictment in 2006 for the same alleged violations of Alabama's UAAA. Savage agreed to plead guilty to a misdemeanor, payment of a $2,000 fine, and restrictions on contact with athletes, but was arrested when he failed to appear in court. In Alabama, failure to register under the UAAA is a felony and carries a maximum sentence of ten years in prison and a fine of up to $5,000. Liz Mullen, *State of Alabama Say Agent Ran Afoul of Tough Recruiting Laws,* Sports Bus. J., Nov. 10, 2008, at 13; Peter Dujardin, *Sports Agent Denies He Violated Alabama Law, Will Fight Charges,* Daily Press (Newport News, VA), Oct. 15, 2008, at A11.

The North Carolina Secretary of State's office indicted several individuals who allegedly engaged in conduct that resulted in the imposition of NCAA sanctions against the University of North Carolina at Chapel Hill. (For background information discussing the conduct that violated NCAA rules see NCAA, *University of North Carolina at Chapel Hill, NCAA Public Infractions Report,* March 12, 2012, and discussion in Chapter 3, *supra*). An agent, Terry Watson, was indicted for allegedly providing impermissible benefits to induce athletes to sign an agency contract. Brooke Pryor, *Sports Agent Terry Watson Indicted Related to UNC Athlete-Agent Case,* DailyTarHeel.com, Oct. 10, 2013. Watson pled guilty to 13 counts of athlete-agent inducement and was sentenced to 30 months of probation along with a $5,000 fine and a suspended six-to-eight-month jail sentence. *Ex-NFL Agent Watson Pleads Guilty to Giving Cash to 3 Former UNC Players,* ESPN (Apr. 17, 2017), https://www.espn.com/college-football/story/_/id/19180813/ex-nfl-agent-pleads-guilty-multi-year-north-carolina-tar-heels-sports-agent-probe. Patrick Mitchell Jones, 43, was charged with violating the UAAA by providing an improper inducement of $725 to a former UNC football player. Jones's plea deal required him to acknowledge his improper conduct and to testify against Watson. Aaron Beard, *Ex-agent Pleads Guilty in Multi-Year UNC Sports Agent*

Probe, AP News (April 17, 2017), https://apnews.com/66a89e60415e440791d-1fa7bbe0ee72c. Another of the individuals, Michael Wayne Johnson Jr., was indicted on three felony counts of improper inducements. In 2017, he entered into a plea deal under which the felony charges were reduced to misdemeanors and were to be dismissed if Johnson complied with terms of a 12-month probation. *Ex-NC Central QB Receives Probation in UNC Agents Probe,* USA Today (April 18, 2017), https://www.usatoday.com/story/sports/ncaaf/2017/04/18/ex-nc-central-qb-receives-probation-in-unc-agents-probe/100612502/. Former UNC tutor, Jennifer Thompson, was indicted for allegedly improperly using her relationship with an athlete to induce him to sign a representation agreement with a sports agent. The charges were ultimately dropped. Graham Watson, *Charges Dropped Against Former UNC Tutor Jennifer Wiley Thompson,* Yahoo!Sports, Oct. 2, 2014, http://sports.yahoo.com/blogs/ncaaf-dr-saturday/charges-dropped-against-former-unc-tutor-jennifer-wiley-thompson-203006378.html.

Notwithstanding the foregoing prosecutions, a 2010 study conducted by the Associated Press revealed that over half of the 42 states that have enacted the UAAA had "yet to revoke or suspend a single license, or invoke penalties of any sort." Zagler, *supra.* According to the Associated Press review, "[t]wenty four-states reported taking no disciplinary or criminal actions against sports agents, and were unable to determine if state or local prosecutors had pursued such cases. Others described the laws as being enforced a few times, or rarely, an indication of what a low priority they are." *Id.* Texas was reportedly one of the few states that consistently enforced the UAAA. The review found that between 2008 and 2010 Texas had disciplined 31 agents and levied fines totaling $17,500. *Id.* There is no indication that the number of UAAA prosecutions has increased significantly over the last ten years.

What reasons may underlie the under-enforcement of the UAAA?

PROBLEM 8-5

Bruce Reynolds, a football player, met Mr. Fritz of Complete Sports Management, Inc., when Reynolds played at Allstate University. Fritz is an NFLPA-certified contract advisor. On January 3, 2019, Reynolds met Fritz at the latter's car dealership. To enable Reynolds to purchase a car without paying anything, Fritz advanced Reynolds credit on a "house note." On January 18, 2019, Reynolds signed an undated, standard-form NFLPA representation agreement with Complete. Fritz told Reynolds not to send the agreement to the NFLPA as provided for in the union's regulations. Sometime thereafter, a coach advised Reynolds to sign with another agent, which the athlete did. Reynolds informed Fritz that he had signed with another agent and that he would return the automobile to Fritz. Reynolds also informed Fritz that he would reimburse him for the more than $2,900 in cash and goods that Fritz had extended to Reynolds since January 18. Reynolds was ultimately drafted by the Atlanta Falcons and signed contracts for the years 2019-22 that provided a total compensation of $4.1 million and other incentive bonuses.

Considering the RUAAA and other preceding materials, answer these questions:

a.   Did Fritz violate any rules, regulations, or laws? If so, what are the consequences of any such rules violation?

b.   Is Complete entitled to compensation based on the contracts negotiated by Reynolds's new agent? In responding consider the following:

> In the context of professional sports, the player's breach of an agency agreement does not necessarily entitle the agent to commission. . . . Technically, the agent is only entitled to damages for breach of contract, i.e., the value of the promised performance reduced by any expenses saved. In addition, the agent is entitled to his commission only if he can show that, had he been permitted to continue performance, he would have been able to consummate the contracts upon which he claims commission.

Total Economic Athletic Mgmt of America, Inc. v. Pickens, 898 S.W.2d 98 (Mo. Ct. App. 1995); see also *Marchibroda v. Demoff,* 2013 WL 6638501 (Cal. Ct. App. Dec. 17, 2013) (promise by an agent to pay another agent a percentage of fees earned from representation of athlete is enforceable under neither contract (because promise was made after services were allegedly rendered and lacked consideration) nor quantum meruit where any services performed were not performed at the promisor's request); *Chiapparelli v. Henderson,* 2005 WL 1847221 (Cal. Ct. App. Aug. 5, 2005) (the court found that a plaintiff agent, who failed to obtain a license as required by the applicable state agent regulations, could not collect a percentage of the compensation the defendant had earned from martial arts contests because the representation contract between the agent and defendant was illegal and unenforceable).

3.   Players Associations

a.   Authority to Regulate

As noted in Chapters 6 and 7, in team sports, players associations are unions. These unions represent a principal component of the web of regulation that affects the athlete-agent relationship.

The following excerpt describes the genesis of players associations and how these entities fit into the larger scheme of labor relations law that regulates the representation of employees once they have entered into a collective bargaining agreement with employers.

> In 1983, the NFLPA asserted that it possessed the inherent authority to regulate agents who represented football players in contract negotiations with teams. Pursuant to its asserted authority, the NFLPA mandated that those agents who desired to represent its members be certified by the union. Similarly, in 1986, in response to complaints by players of abuse by agents, the NBPA established a comprehensive system of agent certification. . . . Subsequently, the MLBPA and the NHLPA also established regulatory systems. In varying forms, these unions require sports agents to register with them and to receive "certification" before representing members of their unions.
>
>   The sports unions' power to regulate and certify agents represents a departure from the ways in which employees' unions typically operate. In most industries, unions (pursuant to collective bargaining agreements with employers) negotiate terms and conditions of employment as well as all union member salaries. Professional sports unions, also pursuant to collective bargaining agreements, possess the exclusive authority to negotiate individual player salaries and other terms and conditions of employment such as minimum salaries, pension benefits, health

insurance, playing conditions, travel accommodations, the ability of a player to move from one team to another, medical treatment, and grievance and arbitration procedures. Unlike other unions, however, sports unions have delegated exclusive authority to negotiate individual player salaries. Thus, players are free to select representatives (typically agents and lawyers) to negotiate the individual terms of their contract compensation packages within the framework established by the collective bargaining agreements.

Shropshire, Davis & Duru, *supra*, at 139-40.

In *Collins v. National Basketball Players Ass'n*, 850 F. Supp. 1468 (D. Colo. 1991), the court described the abuses that prompted players unions to legislate the agent-athlete relationship as follows:

> Specifically, players complained that the agents imposed high and non-uniform fees for negotiation services, insisted on execution of open-ended powers of attorney giving the agents broad powers over players' professional and financial decisions, failed to keep players apprised of the status of negotiations with NBA teams, failed to submit itemized bills for fees and services, and, in some cases had conflicts of interest arising out of representing coaches and/or general managers of NBA teams as well as players. Many players believed that they were bound by contract not to dismiss their agents regardless of dissatisfaction with their services and fees, because the agents had insisted on the execution of long-term agreements. Some agents offered money and other inducements to players, their families, and coaches to obtain player clients.

Id. at 1471.

In *Collins*, NBA superstar, Kareem Abdul-Jabbar sued his agent for financial improprieties. Prior to a settlement of the lawsuit, Jabbar's allegations led the NBPA to decertify Collins. Collins then sued the NBPA. Collins lost at the district court level and appealed to the Tenth Circuit, which upheld the district court's recognition of the players union's authority to refuse to recertify an agent. See *Collins v. National Basketball Players Association*, 976 F.2d 740 (10th Cir. 1992) (unpublished). The court reasoned as follows:

> Before the district court, Collins claimed that the NBPA certification process violates the antitrust laws because it amounts to a group boycott. We agree with the district court's analysis of the labor and antitrust statutes and its conclusion that the statutory labor exemption from the Sherman Act permits the NBPA to establish a certification procedure for player agents. Specifically, we hold that the Regulations meet both prongs of the test established in *United States v. Hutcheson*, 312 U.S. 219 (1941), in which the Supreme Court held that labor unions acting in their self-interest and not in combination with nonlabor groups are statutorily exempt from Sherman Act liability.
>
> On appeal, Collins now acknowledges that the NBPA has the statutory authority to establish player agent regulations. [Collins] maintains his attack on the Committee's decision to deny his certification because it was based in part on its finding that he had breached his fiduciary duty as an investment agent and money manager. He argues that his conduct outside of negotiations between players and their teams is not a legitimate interest of the union because it has no bearing on the union's interest in the wage scale and working conditions of its members. . . . The NBPA established the Regulations to deal with agent abuses, including agents' violations of their fiduciary duties as labor negotiators. It was entirely fair for the Committee to conclude that a man who had neglected his fiduciary duties as an investment agent and money manager could not be trusted to fulfill his fiduciary

duties as a negotiator. The integrity of a prospective negotiating agent is well within the NBPA's legitimate interest in maintaining the wage scale and working conditions of its members.

Id. at 2. See also *Dickey v. NFL,* 2018 WL 4623061 (D. Mass. Sept. 26, 2018) (agent's claim that NFLPA's implementation and enforcement of the one-in-three rule (see note 3 *infra*) violated antitrust laws by erecting unreasonable barriers to entry to the disadvantage of less established agent was subject to dismissal pursuant to the statutory labor exemption; the court also held that the plaintiff's antitrust violations premised on the CBA fell within the parameters of the nonstatutory labor exemption).

NOTES AND QUESTIONS

1. *Union Regulatory Authority. Collins* is viewed as standing for the proposition that players associations have the right to regulate agents. The authority of the NFLPA to police agents was impliedly affirmed in *White v. NFL,* 92 F. Supp. 2d 918 (D. Minn. 2000). In a dispute regarding whether agents (who had been dismissed from a case) had to respond to an NFL request for discovery, the court concluded that the CBA and stipulated settlement agreement bound the agents, even though they had not signed those documents. It reasoned that agents give implied consent to be bound by the CBA when they accept the Players Association's permission to negotiate player contracts: "Player agents enjoy significant and ongoing economic benefits" that result directly from the CBA; and:

> [A]gents have expressly agreed to be bound by NFLPA agent regulations which include specific provisions (1) requiring each certified player agent to become familiar with "applicable Collective Bargaining Agreements and other governing documents," and (2) prohibiting certified agents from "negotiating and/or agreeing to any provision in any agreement involving a player which directly or indirectly violates any stated policies or rules established by the NFLPA."

Id. at 924-25.

In *Black v. NFLPA,* 87 F. Supp. 2d 1 (D.D.C. 2000), Tank Black asserted novel theories in attempting to undermine the authority of the NFLPA to revoke his agent certification. Black asserted that three white agents who had been subjected to discipline by the NFLPA had been treated more favorably than he had. Black asserted that by "means of its racially discriminatory and defamatory comments, the NFLPA had tortiously interfered with his existing and prospective contracts." *Id.* at 4. Rejecting Black's contentions, the court found that the NFLPA regulations established arbitration before an NFLPA-selected arbitrator as the mechanism available for Mr. Black to challenge the proposed ruling. *Id.* at 5-6. See Richard T. Karcher, *Fundamental Fairness in Union Regulation of Sports Agents,* 40 Conn. L. Rev. 355 (2007) (discussing the fairness of players association disciplinary processes).

A novel theory was also raised by Daniel Fegan, a well-known sports agent, who sold his sports agency business to Independent Sports & Entertainment ("ISE"). *Independent Sports & Entertainment, LLC v. Fegan,* 2017 WL 2598550 (C.D. Cal. May 30, 2017). The parties' Asset Purchase Agreement ("APA") provided that Fegan would become an employee of ISE and continue to represent his NBA clients. The APA also included a noncompete clause prohibiting Fegan from competing against ISE for a specified period. Alleging that Fegan violated the noncompete, ISE brought arbitration actions against Fegan. ISE also sought injunctive relief in state court precluding Fegan from competing against it pending resolution of the arbitration. After the action was removed to federal court, Fegan argued that ISE's action for injunctive relief was preempted by section 301 of the National Labor Relations Act. Fegan asserted that enforcement of the APA would interfere with his right to act as a player agent under the CBA and NBPA regulations, which in turn would interfere with the NBPA's authority to discipline agents to whom it has delegated authority to represent players.

Recognizing that enforcement of the noncompete might impact Fegan's ability to uphold his obligations to his clients, "a status he derives from the CBA," the court nevertheless rejected his preemption argument. *Id.* at 5. The court found that ISE's action did not concern "a direct challenge to a union's authority to certify and discipline its agents, nor is it a dispute between a union-represented employee or his or her employer." *Id.* at 4. It also concluded that the right on which ISE sued was based on the APA, which is premised on ISE's state contractual claims rather than any right derived from a collective bargaining agreement. In addition, the court held that ISE's claim was not substantially dependent on an analysis of the CBA given that resolution of the dispute could be made without consideration of the CBA.

2. *Suspension and Decertification.* Two of the more severe sanctions that a players association can impose on an agent are suspension and decertification. Section 6 of the NFLPA Regulations Governing Contract Advisors provides that discipline may include one or more of the following:

> (3) Suspension of a Contract Advisor's Certification for a specified period of time during which Contract Advisor shall be prohibited from representing any NFL player in individual contract negotiations with an NFL club or assisting in or advising with respect to such negotiations. During such suspension Contract Advisor shall also be prohibited from engaging either directly or indirectly in any "recruiting activities." The term "recruiting activities" shall be deemed to include recruiting of any NFL players or prospective NFL players on behalf of himself/herself or any representation firm with which the suspended Contract Advisor is associated, and/or recruiting on behalf of any other Contract Advisor or representation firm. During such suspension Contract Advisor may, at the discretion of the Committee on Agent Regulation and Discipline, be prohibited from collecting fees that he/she would otherwise have been entitled to receive pursuant to any Standard Representation Agreement;
>
> (4) Revocation of the Contract Advisor's Certification hereunder. . . .
>
> (6) Imposition of a fine payable within thirty (30) days of the imposition of such fine, with one-half (1/2) of such fine payable to the Players Assistance Trust (PAT).

Section 6 of the NBPA Regulations Governing Player Agents includes similar sanctions. An agent who is suspended may resume work as a certified athlete agent as soon as the suspension ends. An agent who is decertified cannot work as an agent for a minimum of three years and must apply to the union for reinstatement before he or she can resume representing players. NBPA Regulations Governing Player Agents, *supra.*

Agents representing athletes in various sports leagues have engaged in conduct that resulted in suspension or decertification. In 2008, the NBPA suspended agent Calvin Andrews for one year for conduct involving the recruitment of then University of Southern California and later NBA player O.J. Mayo. The NBPA's disciplinary committee found that Andrews, a vice president at Bill Duffy Associates Sports Management, was an intermediary in funneling $30,000 to Mayo. In 2008, the NBPA decertified agent Josh Nochimson for, among other things, stealing approximately $500,000 from clients including Richard Hamilton of the Detroit Pistons.

The NFLPA has also meted out discipline. Its 2010 revocation of Josh Luchs' certification was followed by the 2011 nine-month suspension of the late Gary Wichard, the 2013 six-month suspension of Martin Magid, the three-month suspension of John Rickert, and the 2016 suspension of Ben Dogra. Earlier NFLPA disciplinary action against agents includes the decertification of agent Sean Jones following player Cris Dishman's allegations that Jones had fraudulently induced him to participate in a $1 million loan on which Jones defaulted, the NFLPA's November 2003 decertification of Ajili Hodari for taking "his entire fee out of a signing bonus paid to former client . . . ," Liz Mullen, *NFLPA Decertifies Hodari, Issues Complaints Against 2*, Sports Bus. J., Nov. 17, 2003, at 6, and the 2006 suspension of Carl Poston for "allegedly signing an important contract for a client without fully reading it first." Liz Mullen, *Source: NFLPA Files Complaint Against Arrington's Agent*, Sports Bus. J., Jan. 23, 2006, at 14. See Shropshire, Davis & Duru, *supra*, at 142-43.

3. *NFLPA Amended Regulations.* In attempting to confront problems aggressively in the agent industry, the NFLPA has gone through waves of amendments to its regulations since the early 2000s. In 2002, the NFLPA adopted the one-in-three rule. NFLPA-certified agents are required to negotiate at least one contract during a three-year period in order to retain their certification (see *Dickey*, 2018 WL 4623061, in which the legality of this requirement was upheld). In 2004, the NFLPA amended its regulations to require agents to disclose, in writing, payments they make to runners. In May 2005, the NFLPA amended its regulations to impose a heightened educational requirement. In order to be eligible for certification, prospective agents must have received a postgraduate degree from a college or university or demonstrate sufficient negotiation experience. In 2005, the NLFPA also amended its regulations to require agents to obtain malpractice insurance. In February 2006, the NFLPA decided not to proceed with a proposed amendment that would have reduced the maximum fee that agents can charge from 3 percent to 2 percent. The maximum fee agents can charge for franchise and transition players is, however, reduced under certain circumstances.

In 2007, the NFLPA adopted a new regulation that prohibits suspended agents from directly or indirectly recruiting players during the period of his or her suspension. This amendment responded to agent complaints that agent David Dunn, who was suspended for 18 months in November 2006, recruited clients during his suspension. Responding to complaints by college coaches that agents were jeopardizing the intercollegiate eligibility of student-athletes and encouraging juniors to jump to the NFL before they were ready, the NFLPA in 2007 enacted the "junior rule." This rule prohibited agents from contacting college players prior to mid-January of their third year, or "true" junior year, when players become eligible to declare for the NFL draft. In 2007, the NFLPA also adopted a regulation requiring an agent to disclose to player clients the identity of the coaches, including college coaches, the agent represents. NFLPA, 2007 Amendments to the NFLPA Regulations Governing Contract Advisors (April 4, 2007). On March 17, 2009, the NFLPA Board of Player Representatives voted to modify its "junior rule." The modification allows agents to contact college underclassmen after the latest of either the athlete's last regular season game or conference championship game or after December 1.

In its most recent round of amendments, in 2012 and 2013, the NFLPA incorporated into its regulations a provision requiring mandatory arbitration for disputes between "two or more Contract Advisors with respect to their individual entitlement to fees owed, whether paid or unpaid, by a player-client who was jointly represented by such agents, or represented by a firm with which the agents in question were associated"; language clarifying the meaning of the "sufficient negotiating experience" exception to the educational requirement for certification, to specify that an applicant must have "at least seven years of sufficient negotiating experience"; language clarifying what constitutes an accredited college or university; the requirement of additional disclosures as a part of the application process (i.e., applicants must list unsatisfied liens); and a 30-day window within which applicants who fail the contract advisor exam can notify the NFLPA of their intention to dispute their failing score. NFLPA Legal Dept., *Memorandum from NFLPA Legal Dep't, to Contract Advisors* (April 10, 2012 and May 8, 2013).

In 2014, the NFLPA's Committee on Agent Regulation and Discipline announced it would review all of its regulations governing contract advisors. According to the NFLPA, "players are concerned about the general level of representation being provided, including agents giving bad advice as well as not understanding the collective-bargaining agreement, the salary cap and other key issues." Liz Mullen, *"A Lot of Agent Missteps" Prompt Wholesale NFLPA Review,* Sports Bus. J. (April 21, 2014). Among the matters slated to be addressed by the committee were: the agent exam, the standards for becoming certified, and the numbers of years an agent can retain his or her certification without having a client. In 2019, there was the then burgeoning dispute between the NFLPA and NFL agents as the latter sought higher fees and a larger rule in the NFLPA's upcoming CBA negotiations with owners. Mike Florio, *NFLPA, agents at odds as CBA talks near (and owners love it),* NBC Sports (Mar. 17, 2019), https://profootballtalk.nbcsports.com/2019/03/17/nflpa-agents-at-odds-as-cba-talks-near-and-the-owners-love-it/.

4. *MLBPA and NBPA Regulations.* In 2010, the Major League Baseball Players Association adopted the first major substantive overhaul of its agent regulations since they were initially enacted in 1988. The 2010 regulations include provisions relating to client stealing, solicitation and inducements, runners, and arbitration. See MLBPA Regulations Governing Player Agents, available at http://reg.mlbpaagent.org/Documents/AgentForms/Agent%20Regulations.pdf. For a descriptive overview and a critical analysis of the MLBPA's new agent regulations, see Darren A. Heitner & Jason B. Wolf, *In Baseball's Best Interest? A Discussion of the October 10, 2010 MLBPA Regulations Governing Player Agents,* 10 Va. Sports & Ent. L.J. 249 (2011). In

2013, the MLBPA amended its agent regulations to prohibit agents from lending money to players without first obtaining written approval of the MLBPA. MLBPA, 2013 Amendments to the MLBPA Regulations Governing Player Agents (May 3, 2013), http://reg.mlbpaagent.org/Documents/ AgentForms/Amendments%20to%20the%20MLBPA%20Regulations%20 Governing%20Player%20Agents.pdf.

The MLBPA's regulations were further amended in 2015 to require that agent applicants take a written exam and submit to a background check. Liz Mullen, *MLBPA Announces Agent Certification Now Includes Background Check, Written Exam*, Sports Bus. J. (Jan 13, 2015), http://www.sportsbusinessdaily .com/Daily/Issues/2015/01/13/Labor-and-Agents/MLBPA.aspx.

The NBPA made substantial revisions, effective February 15, 2016, to its agent regulations. Minor revisions became effective February 16, 2018 and June 2019. In articulating the reasons for its first substantial revisions to its regulations since 1991, the NBPA stated:

> Given that nearly thirty (30) years have elapsed since the initial promulgation of these Regulations, the NBPA Executive Committee concluded that the time was ripe to review and analyze the experiences that both they and the Players they represent had in connection with the services provided by their Player Agents. Those experiences demonstrate that amendments to these Regulations were warranted to better reflect the reality of the business between Players and Player Agents, including the role played by recruiters and other employees in assisting Player Agents in soliciting and/or retaining Players as clients and the additional services provided by individuals such as financial advisors invest- ment managers, and tax consultants that [have] become an integral part of Player representation. In conducting this review the NBPA also had the distinct benefit of comparing the regulatory systems that its sister professional sports unions (MLBPA, NFLPA, and NHLPA) had adopted as well as learning from the experiences they had in administering and enforcing them.

NBPA, *NBPA Regulations Governing Player Agents* 10 (as amended June 2019), https://cosmic-s3.imgix.net/fec8eea0-dbdc-11e9-a097-0b637a5431fa- Agent-Regulations–Final–2019.pdf.

Among the changes to the 2016 NBPA's agent regulations are provi- sions: emphasizing the fiduciary character of the player/agent relationship; articulating further the NPBA's authority to adopt and enforce its agent regulations; enhancing the requirements for persons applying for certifica- tion (e.g., applicants must pass a written exam administered by the NBPA and agree to arbitrate any disputes with the NBPA relating to the appli- cant's certification); stating that an agent's certification will automatically expire if he or she, for a five-year period, has no player under contract with an NBA club; making the conduct of individuals, who work with an agent in providing representation services, chargeable against the agent if the conduct violates NBPA agent regulations; requiring that agents dis- close if players are referred to financial advisors; and imposing disclosure requirements on agents who pay third parties to assist the agent in recruit- ing a player. Beginning in 2016-17, annual agent fees were $2,500 for agents who represent 0-9 players, $5,000 for agents who represent 10-19 players, and $7,500 for agents who represent more than 20 players. The NBPA also expanded the range of possible penalties for violations of its agent regu- lations to include fines of up to $100,000, public reprimand, suspension, and decertification. By including fines as a possible penalty, the NBPA joins the NFLPA, MLBPA, and NHLPA, each of which includes fines as a possible penalty for violations of their respective regulations. The NBPA executive committee also announced that it will strictly enforce its prohibition against agents simultaneously representing both players and coaches and management. The NBPA's 2018 revisions were similar to those made by the ULC to the RUAAA, see discussion *infra*, so that the NBPA agent regulations are consistent with changes adopted by the NCAA, which will permit sports agents to pay student-athletes and their parents for meals, lodging, and travel expenses related to agent recruitment of student-athletes. In August of 2019, the NCAA released new requirements for agents seeking to represent college basketball underclassmen who are unsure if they want to enter the NBA draft or remain in college. The rules initially stated that in order for an underclassman to retain his college eligibility if he chooses not to enter the NBA draft, he must sign with an NCAA-approved agent. In order to be NCAA approved, the agent must: (1) possess a bachelor's degree; (2) be certified by the NBPA for at least 3 years; and (3) pass an in-person exam administered at the NCAA's headquarters in Indianapolis. Jeff Borzello, *NCAA Issues Rules for Agents, Lebron Responds*, ESPN (Aug. 7, 2019), https://www.espn.com/mens-college-basketball/story/_/id/27335531/ncaa-issues-rules-agents-lebron-responds. Critics referred to the new requirements as the "Rich Paul Rule," because the requirements would have excluded Rich Paul, the agent for several NBA players including Lebron James, Anthony Davis, and Ben Simmons. Paul has achieved success as a NBPA-certified agent, but he does not have a bachelor's degree. *Id.* The criticism led the NCAA to promptly modify its rules by dropping the college degree requirement. Mark Schlabach, *NCAA Amends 'Rich Paul Rule' Amid Blowback*, ESPN. com (Aug. 12, 2019). The NCAA will continue to require these agents to "have NBPA certification for a minimum of three consecutive years, maintain professional liability insurance, complete the NCAA qualification exam and pay the required fees." *Id.*

5. *An International Perspective.* In the United States, agents are potentially subject to several layers of direct and indirect regulation: state agent regulations, federal regulations, players association regulations, state bar association regulations for agents who are attorneys, and the NCAA (although the NCAA has no authority to regulate agents, agents are indirectly affected by NCAA rules in that players, in order not to violate NCAA rules, avoid engaging in behaviors often encouraged by agents).

Internationally, player agents are also subject to levels of regulations with the degree of regulation largely dictated by the sport and by the country. An agent who seeks to assist a player who plays professional basketball internationally must be certified by the International Basketball Federation (FIBA). FIBA certification is relatively easy to acquire (passing of a test regarded as simple, and the payment of annual dues). To effectively represent players, however, a U.S. athlete representation agency would be wise to establish an international division or partner with a certified agent in the relevant foreign company.

The following excerpt describes FIFA's regulatory scheme and some of the problems that arise with respect to it:

> FIFA's Licensed Players' Agent Regulations require national associations [to] make their own Regulations for Players' Agents based on the guidelines

provided by FIFA, and such guidelines must be approved by the FIFA Players' Status Committee. The FIFA Regulations have received a wide airing . . . and these regulations have in turn been transposed onto national association law. Nevertheless, the pattern of transposition has been varied, and conflicts and inconsistencies remain. For some states, the interventionist nature of state involvement in sport (such as in Greece) can pose problems for national associations obliged to follow national law whilst also being required to pay heed to FIFA regulations. In other cases, some national associations have adopted more detailed and restrictive rules than FIFA requires (as in England), whilst others have simply incorporated the FIFA principles into their registration procedures.

Robert Parrish, *Regulating Players' Agents: A Global Perspective, in* Players' Agents Worldwide: Legal Aspects 12 (Robert C.R. Siekmann et al. eds., 2007); see also Shropshire, Davis and Duru, *supra* at 177-92.

Sport governing body regulations aside, nearly insurmountable obstacles sometimes confront an American agent seeking to represent a player in a foreign country. For instance, in Japan, certification is required in order for an agent to represent a player in Nippon Professional Baseball, Japan's highest-level baseball league, but only Japanese citizens are permitted to acquire the required certification. In addition, the aspiring agent must become licensed as a lawyer in Japan.

b.   Fees

BROWN v. WOOLF
554 F. Supp. 1206 (S.D. Ind. 1983)

STECKLER, District Judge.

This matter comes before the Court on the motions of defendant, Robert G. Woolf, for partial summary judgment and for summary judgment. . . .

The complaint in this diversity action seeks compensatory and punitive damages and the imposition of a trust on a fee defendant allegedly received, all stemming from defendant's alleged constructive fraud and breach of fiduciary duty in the negotiation of a contract for the 1974-75 hockey season for plaintiff who was a professional hockey player. Plaintiff alleges that prior to the 1973-74 season he had engaged the services of defendant, a well-known sports attorney and agent, who represents many professional athletes, has authored a book, and has appeared in the media in connection with such representation, to negotiate a contract for him with the Pittsburgh Penguins of the National Hockey League. Plaintiff had a professionally successful season that year under the contract defendant negotiated for him and accordingly again engaged defendant's services prior to the 1974-75 season. During the negotiations in July 1974, the Penguins offered plaintiff a two-year contract at $80,000.00 per year but plaintiff rejected the offer allegedly because defendant asserted that he could obtain a better, long-term, no-cut contract with a deferred compensation feature with the Indianapolis Racers, which at the time was a new team in a new league. On July 31, 1974, plaintiff signed a five-year contract with the Racers. Thereafter, it is alleged the Racers began having financial difficulties. Plaintiff avers that Woolf continued to represent plaintiff and negotiated two reductions in plaintiff's compensation including the loss of a retirement fund at the same time defendant was attempting to get his own fee payment from the Racers. Ultimately the Racers' assets were seized and the organizers defaulted on their obligations to plaintiff. He avers that he received only $185,000.00 of the total $800,000.00 compensation under the Racer contract but that defendant received his full $40,000.00 fee (5% of the contract) from the Racers.

Plaintiff alleges that defendant made numerous material misrepresentations upon which he relied both during the negotiation of the Racer contract and at the time of the subsequent modifications. Plaintiff further avers that defendant breached his fiduciary duty to plaintiff by failing to conduct any investigation into the financial stability of the Racers, failing to investigate possible consequences of the deferred compensation package in the Racers' contract, failing to obtain guarantees or collateral, and by negotiating reductions in plaintiff's compensation from the Racers while insisting on receiving all of his own. Plaintiff theorizes that such conduct amounts to a prima facie case of constructive fraud for which he should receive compensatory and punitive damages and have a trust impressed on the $40,000.00 fee defendant received from the Racers.

Defendant's motion for partial summary judgment attacks plaintiff's claim for punitive damages, contending that plaintiff has no evidence to support such an award and should not be allowed to rest on the allegations of his complaint. Further, he claims that punitive damages are unavailable as a matter of law in a constructive fraud case because no proof of fraudulent intent is required. By his motion for summary judgment, defendant attacks several aspects of plaintiff's claims against him. He argues (1) that plaintiff cannot recover on a breach of contract theory because Robert G. Woolf, the individual, was acting merely as the agent and employee of Robert Woolf Associates, Inc. (RWA), (2) that defendant's conduct could not amount to constructive fraud because (a) plaintiff alleges only negligent acts, (b) there is no evidence defendant deceived plaintiff or violated a position of trust, (c) there is no showing of harm to the public interest, and (d) there is no evidence that defendant obtained an unconscionable advantage at plaintiff's expense.

The Court concludes that Indiana courts would not adopt a per se rule prohibiting such damages in a constructive fraud action, but would rather consider the facts and circumstances of each case. If elements of recklessness, or oppressive conduct are demonstrated, punitive damages could be awarded. . . .

Indiana cases contain several formulizations of the tort of constructive fraud. Generally it is characterized as acts or a course of conduct from which an unconscionable advantage is or may be derived, . . . or a breach of confidence coupled with an unjust enrichment which shocks the conscience, . . . or a breach of duty, including mistake, duress or undue influence, which the law declares fraudulent because of a tendency to deceive, injure the public interest or violate the public or private confidence. . . . Another formulization found in the cases involves the making of a false statement, by the dominant party in a confidential or fiduciary relationship or by one who holds himself out as an expert, upon which the plaintiff reasonably relies to his detriment. The defendant need not know the statement is false nor make the false statement with fraudulent intent. . . .

The Court believes that both formulizations are rife with questions of fact, *inter alia*, the existence or nonexistence of a confidential or fiduciary relationship . . . and the question of reliance on false representations . . . as well as questions of credibility.

Defendant argues that despite the customary existence of such fact questions in a constructive fraud case, judgment is appropriate in this instance because plaintiff has produced nothing to demonstrate the existence of fact questions. He makes a similar argument in the motion for partial summary judgment on the punitive damages issue. . . .

In this case, defendant has offered affidavits, excerpts of depositions, and photocopies of various documents to support his motions. He contends that such materials demonstrate that reasonable minds could not conclude that defendant did the acts with which the complaint charges him. In response, plaintiff rather belatedly offered portions of plaintiff's depositions as well as arguing that issues such as those raised by a complaint based on constructive fraud are inherently unsuited to resolution on a motion for summary judgment.

Having carefully considered the motions and briefs and having examined the evidentiary materials submitted, the Court concludes that summary judgment would not be appropriate in this action. The Court is not persuaded that there are no fact questions remaining unresolved in this controversy such that defendant is entitled to judgment as a matter of law. As movant for summary judgment, defendant bears the "heavy burden" of clearly demonstrating the absence of any genuine issue of a material fact. . . .

By reason of the foregoing, defendant's motions for partial summary judgment and for summary judgment are hereby DENIED.

NOTES AND QUESTIONS

1. *Fee Maximums.* The matter addressed in *Woolf,* excessive fees charged by agents, is not as troublesome today, given limitations imposed by union regulation of agents. For example, NFLPA agent regulations restrict the maximum amount of fees an agent can charge for negotiating a player contract with a team. An agent can receive a maximum fee of 3 percent of the compensation that a player receives during the playing season covered by the contract the agent negotiates. Compensation is defined broadly to include salaries, signing bonuses, roster bonuses, and other monies earned by a player. (For an example of player association regulations governing agents, see NFLPA Section 4(B), "Contract Advisors Compensation," *infra.*) Note that agents are allowed to charge less than the maximum.

    The NBPA allows an agent to charge a maximum fee of up to 4 percent for the negotiation of a player/team contract; 2 percent is the maximum allowable fee for an agent who negotiates a contract for an NBA player who receives the minimum compensation pursuant to the CBA. Larger representation firms will often waive the fee the NBPA regulations allow in negotiating the first contract between an NBA team and draft picks. Such a firm is willing to forgo the fee as an incentive for the player to sign a representation agreement in anticipation of collecting a larger fee when the player signs a more lucrative contract three or four years later.

    Except for prohibiting an agent from charging a fee for negotiating the contract of a player who makes the league minimum, the MLBPA allows the market to control and sets no maximum on the size of fee an agent can earn for negotiating a player/team contract.

2. *Time of Payment.* At what point in time was the fee paid in *Woolf?* Do the NFLPA regulations effectively resolve when an agent is to be paid his fee?

3. *The Legal Effects of* Brown v. Woolf. The actual legal impact of the case is something of an enigma. The reported opinion only denies summary relief to the defendant. It proffers a theory of constructive fraud, which should serve as a wake-up call to agents, but it does not fully explain the circumstances under which ill-fated reliance on an agent's advice is actionable. The case was settled before it went to trial; thus, the theory is left hanging in a never-never land, evidently not adopted in other jurisdictions and ill-defined in Indiana. Nevertheless, it is important to examine the opinion for what it portends for the theory of constructive fraud and for agents who perhaps overreach in taking fees up front. Though this latter practice has been curtailed in leagues with union regulations restricting the practice, what about other leagues and individual performer sports? What about players performing in foreign countries? Indeed, in some instances, the foreign club pays the agent directly. Is this a conflict of interest?

NFLPA REGULATIONS GOVERNING CONTRACT ADVISORS[5]

(as amended through August 2016)

SECTION 1: SCOPE OF REGULATIONS

A. PERSONS SUBJECT TO REGULATIONS

No person (other than a player representing himself) shall be permitted to conduct individual contract negotiations on behalf of a player and/or assist in or advise with respect to such negotiations with NFL Clubs after the effective date of these Regulations unless he/she is (1) currently certified as a Contract Advisor pursuant to these Regulations; (2) signs a Standard Representation Agreement with the player (See Section 4; Appendix D); and (3) files a fully executed copy of the Standard Representation Agreement with the NFLPA, along with any contract(s) between the player and the Contract Advisor for other services to be provided.

B. ACTIVITIES COVERED

The activities of Contract Advisors which are governed by these Regulations include: the providing of advice, counsel, information or assistance to players with respect to negotiating their individual contracts with Clubs and/or thereafter in enforcing those contracts; the conduct of individual compensation negotiations with the Clubs on behalf of players; and any other activity or conduct which directly bears upon the Contract Advisor's integrity, competence or ability to properly represent individual NFL players and the NFLPA in individual contract negotiations, including the handling of player funds, providing tax counseling and preparation services, and providing financial advice and investment services to individual players. . . .

---

5. The complete NFLPA Regulations Governing Contract Advisors (as amended through August 2016) can be found at https://nflpaweb.blob.core.windows.net/media/Default/PDFs/Agents/RegulationsAmendedAugust2016.pdf.

SECTION 2: CERTIFICATION

After the effective date of these Regulations, any person who wishes to perform the functions of a Contract Advisor as described in Section 1 above must be certified by the NFLPA. . . .

C.   GROUNDS FOR DENIAL OF CERTIFICATION

Grounds for denial of Certification shall include, but not be limited to, the following:

- The applicant has made false or misleading statements of a material nature in his/her application;
- The applicant has misappropriated funds, or engaged in other specific acts such as embezzlement, theft or fraud, which would render him/her unfit to serve in a fiduciary capacity on behalf of players;
- The applicant has engaged in any other conduct that significantly impacts adversely on his/her credibility, integrity or competence to serve in a fiduciary capacity on behalf of players;
- The applicant is unwilling to swear or affirm that he/she will comply with these Regulations and any amendments hereto and/or that he/she will abide by the fee structure contained in the Standard Representation Agreement incorporated into these Regulations;
- The applicant has been denied certification by another professional sports players association;
- The applicant directly or indirectly solicited a player for representation as a Contract Advisor during the period of time between the filing of his/her Application for Certification and Certification by the NFLPA;
- The applicant has not received a degree from an accredited four year college/university and a postgraduate degree from an accredited college/university, unless excepted from this requirement pursuant to Section 2(A). . . .

SECTION 3: STANDARD OF CONDUCT FOR CONTRACT ADVISORS. . . .

A.   GENERAL REQUIREMENTS

A Contract Advisor shall be required to:

(1)   Disclose on his/her Application and thereafter upon request of the NFLPA all information relevant to his/her qualifications to serve as a Contract Advisor, including, but not limited to, background, special training, experience in negotiations, past representation of professional athletes, and relevant business associations or memberships in professional organizations;

(2)   Pay an application fee pursuant to Section 2 above unless waived;

(3)   Pay the annual fee and provide proof of any required insurance documents in a timely manner;

(4)   Attend an NFLPA seminar on individual contract negotiations each year;

(5)   Comply with the maximum fee schedule and all other provisions of these Regulations and any amendments thereto;

(6)   Execute and abide by the printed Standard Representation Agreement with all players represented, and file with the NFLPA a copy of that fully

executed agreement along with any other agreement(s) for additional services that the Contract Advisor has executed with the player. . . ;

(9) Provide on or before May 1 each year, to every player who he/she represents, with a copy to the NFLPA, an itemized statement covering the period beginning March 1 of the prior year through February 28 or 29 of that year, which separately sets forth both the fee charged to the player for, and any expenses incurred in connection with, the performance of the following services:

    (a)   individual player salary negotiations,

    (b)   management of the player's assets,

    (c)   financial, investment, legal, tax and/or other advice to the player, and

    (d)   any other miscellaneous services . . . ;

(14) Fully comply with applicable state and federal laws . . . ;

(16) Disclose in an addendum (in the form attached as Appendix G) attached to the Standard Representation Agreement between the Contract Advisor and player, the names and current positions of any NFL management personnel, NFL coaches, other professional league coaches, or college coaches whom Contract Advisor represents or has represented in matters pertaining to their employment by or association with any NFL club, other professional league club or college;

(17) Act at all times in a fiduciary capacity on behalf of players;

(18) Comply with and abide by all of the stated policies of the NFLPA;

(19) In connection with payments for assistance in recruiting any player:

    (a)   Prepare a SRA Disclosure Form (attached as Appendix E) disclosing any other Contract Advisor(s) to whom the Contract Advisor has paid or has promised to pay money or any other thing of value (excluding any other Contract Advisor(s) whose name appears on the Standard Representation Agreement) in return for recruiting or helping to recruit a player to sign a Standard Representation Agreement;

    (b)   Provide a copy of that SRA Disclosure Form to the player in advance of signing that player to a Standard Representation Agreement so as to allow the player adequate time to consider the information before the player signs the Standard Representation Agreement; [and]

    (c)   Have the player sign that SRA Disclosure Form acknowledging that he is aware of the payments and that he approves of them. . . ;

(20) Educate player-clients as to their benefits, rights and obligations pursuant to the Collective Bargaining Agreement; and to advise and assist those player-clients in taking maximum advantage of those benefits and rights. . . .

B.   PROHIBITED CONDUCT

Contract Advisors are prohibited from:

(1) Representing any player in individual contract negotiations with any Club unless he/she (i) is an NFLPA Certified Contract Advisor; (ii) has signed the Standard Representation Agreement with such player; and (iii) has filed a copy of the Standard Representation Agreement with the NFLPA along with any other contract(s) or agreement(s) between the player and the Contract Advisor;

(2) Providing or offering money or any other thing of value to any player or prospective player to induce or encourage that player to utilize his/her services;

(3)   Providing or offering money or any other thing of value to a member of
        the player's or prospective player's family or any other person for the pur-
        pose of inducing or encouraging that person to recommend the services of
        the Contract Advisor;

(4)   Providing materially false or misleading information to any player or pro-
        spective player in the context of recruiting the player as a client or in the
        course of representing that player as his Contract Advisor;

(5)   Representing or suggesting to any player or prospective player that his/her
        NFLPA Certification is an endorsement or recommendation by the NFLPA
        of the Contract Advisor or the Contract Advisor's qualifications or services;

(6)   Directly or indirectly borrowing money from any player (whether or not the
        player is a client), either by receiving the funds directly from the player or
        by the player providing collateral for or agreeing to guarantee a loan to the
        Contract Advisor by another party;

(7)   Holding or seeking to hold, either directly or indirectly, a financial interest
        in any professional football club or in any other business entity when such
        investment could create an actual conflict of interest or the appearance of a
        conflict of interest in the representation of NFL players;

(8)   Engaging in any other activity which creates an actual or potential conflict
        of interest with the effective representation of NFL players;

(9)   Soliciting or accepting money or anything of value from any NFL Club in a
        way that would create an actual or apparent conflict with the interests of any
        player that the Contract Advisor represents;

(10)   Negotiating and/or agreeing to any provision in a player contract which
        deprives or purports to deprive that player of any benefit contained in any
        collectively bargained agreement between the NFL and the NFLPA or any
        other provision of any applicable documents which protect the working
        conditions of NFL players;

(11)   Negotiating and/or agreeing to any provision in any agreement involving a
        player which directly or indirectly violates any stated policies or rules estab-
        lished by the NFLPA;

(12)   Concealing material facts from any player whom the Contract Advisor is
        representing which relate to the subject of the player's individual contract
        negotiation;

(13)   Failing to advise the player and to report to the NFLPA any known viola-
        tions by an NFL Club of a player's individual contract;

(14)   Engaging in unlawful conduct and/or conduct involving dishonesty, fraud,
        deceit, misrepresentation, or other activity which reflects adversely on his/
        her fitness as a Contract Advisor or jeopardizes his/her effective representa-
        tion of NFL players;

(15)   Failure to comply with the maximum fee provisions contained in Section 4
        of these Regulations;

(16)   Circumventing the maximum fee provisions contained in Section 4 of
        these Regulations by knowingly and intentionally increasing the fees that
        Contract Advisor charges or otherwise would have charged the player for
        other services including, but not limited to, financial consultation, money
        management, and/or negotiating player endorsement agreements . . . ;

(18)   Filing any lawsuit or other proceedings against a player for any matter which
        is subject to the exclusive arbitration provisions contained in Section 5 of
        these Regulations . . . ;

(21)   (a)   Initiating any communication, directly or indirectly, with a player who has entered into a Standard Representation Agreement with another Contract Advisor and such Standard Representation Agreement is on file with the NFLPA if the communication concerns a matter relating to the:
   (i)   Player's current Contract Advisor;
   (ii)   Player's current Standard Representation Agreement;
   (iii) Player's contract status with any NFL Club(s); or
   (iv)   Services to be provided by prospective Contract Advisor either through a Standard Representation Agreement or otherwise.

   (b)   If a player, already a party to a Standard Representation Agreement, initiates communication with a Contract Advisor relating to any of the subject matters listed in Section 3(B)(21)(a) the Contract Advisor may continue communications with the Player regarding any of those matters.

   (c)   Section 3(B)(21) shall not apply to any player who has less than sixty (60) days remaining before his NFL Player Contract expires, and he has not yet signed a new Standard Representation Agreement with a Contract Advisor within the sixty (60) day period.

   (d)   Section 3(B)(21) shall not prohibit a Contract Advisor from sending a player written materials which may be reasonably interpreted as advertising directed at players in general and not targeted at a specific player. . . .

(26)   Directly or indirectly soliciting a prospective rookie player for representation as a Contract Advisor (A "rookie" shall be defined as a person who has never signed an NFL Player Contract) if that player has signed a Standard Representation Agreement prior to a date which is thirty (30) days before the NFL Draft and if thirty (30) days have not elapsed since the Agreement was signed and filed with the NFLPA . . . ;

(31)   Violating any other provision of these Regulations; and/or

(32)   Using, associating with, employing or entering into any business relationship with any individual in the recruitment of prospective player-clients who is not Certified and in good standing as a Contract Advisor pursuant to these Regulations.

A Contract Advisor who engages in any prohibited conduct as defined above shall be subject to discipline in accordance with the procedures of Section 6 of these Regulations. [The sanctions listed in Section 6 include the payment of fines, suspension of certification, and decertification.]

Section 4: Agreements Between Contract Advisors and Players; Maximum Fees. . . .

B.   Contract Advisor's Compensation

(1)   The maximum fee which may be charged or collected by a Contract Advisor shall be three percent (3%) of the "compensation" (as defined within this Section) received by the player in each playing season covered by the contract negotiated by the Contract Advisor, except as follows:

   (a)   The maximum fee which may be charged or collected by a Contract Advisor shall be:

      (i)   Two percent (2%) for a player who signs a one (1) year tender while subject to a Franchise or Transition designation, or as a Restricted Free Agent.

      (ii) One-and-one half-percent (1.5%) for a player who signs a one (1) year tender while subject to a Franchise or Transition designation for the second time he is tagged; and

      (iii) One percent (1%) for player who signs a one (1) year tender while subject to a Franchise or Transition designation for the third time he is tagged.

(2) The Contract Advisor and player may agree to any fee which is less than the maximum fee set forth in (1) above.

(3) As used in this Section 4(B), the term "compensation" shall be deemed to include only salaries, signing bonuses, reporting bonuses, roster bonuses, Practice Squad salary in excess of the minimum Practice Squad salary specified in Article 33 of the Collective Bargaining Agreement, and any performance incentives earned by the player during the term of the contract (including any option year) negotiated by the Contract Advisor. For example, and without limitation, the term compensation shall not include any "honor" incentive bonuses (e.g. ALL PRO, PRO BOWL, Rookie of the Year), or any collectively bargained benefits or other payments provided for in the player's individual contract.

(4) A Contract Advisor is prohibited from receiving any fee for his/her services until and unless the player receives the compensation upon which the fee is based. However, these Regulations recognize that in certain circumstances a player may decide that it is in his best interest to pay his Contract Advisor's fee in advance of the receipt of any deferred compensation from his NFL club. Accordingly, a player may enter into an agreement with a Contract Advisor to pay the Contract Advisor a fee advance on deferred compensation due and payable to the player. Such fee advance may only be collected by the Contract Advisor after the player has performed the services necessary under his contract to entitle him to the deferred compensation. Further, such an agreement between a Contract Advisor and a player must be in writing, with a copy sent by the Contract Advisor to the NFLPA.

    For purposes of determining the fee advance, the compensation shall be determined to be an amount equal to the present value of the deferred player compensation. The rate used to determine the present value of the deferred compensation shall be the rate at which the term "Interest" is defined under Article 1 of the 2011 CBA.

(5) A Contract Advisor who is found to have violated Section 3(B)(2) or (3) of these Regulations shall not be entitled to a fee for services provided to a player who was the subject of an improper inducement under Section 3(B)(2) or (3). In the event that the Contract Advisor collects any fees from the player before a finding of such violation, he/she shall be required to reimburse the player for such fees. . . .

SECTION 6: OVERSIGHT AND COMPLIANCE PROCEDURE. . . .

D.   PROPOSED DISCIPLINARY ACTION

Except in cases where discipline has been imposed prior to the receipt of the answer, CARD [Eds. Committee on Agent Regulation and Discipline] shall, as soon as possible but no later than ninety (90) days after receipt of the answer, inform the Contract Advisor in writing (by confirmed email, facsimile or over-night delivery) of the nature of the discipline, if any, CARD proposes to impose, which discipline may include one or more of the following:

(1)   Issuance by CARD of an informal order of reprimand to be retained in the Contract Advisor's file at the NFLPA's office;

(2)   Issuance by CARD of a formal letter of reprimand which may be made public in NFLPA publications and other media;

(3)   Suspension of a Contract Advisor's Certification for a specified period of time during which Contract Advisor shall be prohibited from repre-senting any NFL player in individual contract negotiations with an NFL club or assisting in or advising with respect to such negotiations. During such suspension Contract Advisor shall also be prohibited from engag-ing either directly or indirectly in any "recruiting activities." The term "recruiting activities" shall be deemed to include recruiting of any NFL players or prospective NFL players on behalf of himself/herself or any representation firm with which the suspended Contract Advisor is associ-ated, and/or recruiting on behalf of any other Contract Advisor or rep-resentation firm. During such suspension Contract Advisor may, at the discretion of CARD, be prohibited from collecting any fees that he/she would otherwise have been entitled to receive pursuant to any Standard Representation Agreement;

(4)   Revocation of the Contract Advisor's Certification hereunder;

(5)   Prohibition of a Contract Advisor from soliciting or representing any new player-clients for a specified period of time. However, Contract Advisor shall retain the right to represent any player-clients signed to a Standard Representation Agreement with Contract Advisor at the time of the sus-pension; and/or

(6)   Imposition of a fine payable within thirty (30) days of the imposition of such fine, with one-half (1/2) of such fine payable to the Players Assistance Trust (PAT).

NBPA REGULATIONS GOVERNING PLAYER AGENTS

(as amended June 2019)[1]

SECTION 3: STANDARD OF CONDUCT FOR PLAYER AGENTS IN PROVIDING SERVICES GOVERNED BY THESE REGULATIONS. . . .

B.   PROHIBITED CONDUCT SUBJECT TO DISCIPLINE

To further effectuate the objectives of these Regulations, Player Agents are pro-hibited from . . . :

(5)   Engaging in conduct which violates any NCAA regulations;

(6)   Holding or seeking to hold, either directly or indirectly, a financial inter-est in any professional basketball team or in any other business venture

---

1. The NBPA Regulations are available at https://cosmic-s3.imgix.net/fec8eea0-dbdc-11e9-a097-0b637a5431fa-Agent-Regulations–Final–2019.pdf.

that would create an actual conflict of interest or the appearance of a conflict of interest between the individual Player and his Player Agent;

(7) Representing the General Manager or coach of any NBA Team (or any other management representative who participates in the team's deliberations or decision concerning what compensation is to be offered individual Players) in matters pertaining to his employment or any other matters in which he has any financial stake in or association with any NBA Team; provided, however, that this provision does not prohibit two individuals within the same agency from separately representing a Player and a coach/GM, provided notice is given to the Player that another agent with the agency represents a coach/GM;

(8) Engaging in any other activity which creates an actual or potential conflict of interest with the effective representation of Players; provided that the representation of two or more Players on any one NBA Team shall not itself be deemed to be prohibited by this provision;

(9) Soliciting or accepting money or anything of value from any NBA Team under circumstances where to do so would create a conflict or an apparent conflict with the interests of any Player he represents . . .;

(12) Concealing material facts from any Player whom the Player Agent is representing which relate to the subject of the individual's contract negotiation . . .;

(20) A Player Agent who engages in any prohibited conduct defined above shall be subject to discipline in accordance with the procedures of Section 6 of these Regulations.

NCAA BYLAW, ARTICLE 12

AUGUST 1, 2019[2]

12.02.1 Agent. [A] An agent is any individual who, directly or indirectly:

(a) Represents or attempts to represent an individual for the purpose of marketing his or her athletics ability or reputation for financial gain; or

(b) Seeks to obtain any type of financial gain or benefit from securing a prospective student-athlete's enrollment at an educational institution or from a student-athlete's potential earnings as a professional athlete.

    12.02.1.1 Application: An agent may include, but is not limited to, a certified contract advisor, financial advisor; marketing representative, brand manager or anyone who is employed or associated with such person.

    12.02.1.2 NCAA Certification Requirement — Men's Basketball. [A] In men's basketball, any individual who solicits a prospective or enrolled student-athlete to enter into an agency contract or attempts to obtain employment for an individual with a professional sports team or organization or as a professional athlete must be certified and maintain active certification per the policies and procedures of the NCAA agent certification program. (See Bylaw 12.3.1.3.) (Adopted: 8/8/18 An NBPA-certified agent

2. The 2019-20 http://www.ncaapublications.com/p-4577-2019-2020-ncaa-division-i-manual-august-version-available-for-presell-now.aspx?CategoryID=0&SectionID=0&ManufacturerID=0&DistributorID=0&GenreID=0&VectorID=0&.

is considered an NCAA-certified agent until the NCAA agent certification program is operational, which will be not later than August 1, 2020.)

12.02.1.2.1 Exception. [A] A family member of a prospective or enrolled student-athlete or an individual acting solely on behalf of a professional sports team or organization is not required to be certified through the NCAA agent certification program. (*Adopted: 8/8/18.*). . . .

* * *

12.3 USE OF AGENTS

12.3.1 General Rule. An individual shall be ineligible for participation in an intercollegiate sport if he or she ever has agreed (orally or in writing) to be represented by an agent for the purpose of marketing his or her athletics ability or reputation in that sport. Further, an agency contract not specifically limited in writing to a sport or particular sports shall be deemed applicable to all sports, and the individual shall be ineligible to participate in any sport. . . .

12.3.1.2 Exception — NCAA-Certified Agents — Men's Basketball. [A] (Adopted: 8/8/18.)

12.3.1.2.1 Elite Senior Prospective Student-Athletes. In men's basketball, on or after July 1 immediately before his senior year in high school, a prospective student-athlete identified as an elite senior in accordance with established policies and procedures may be represented by an NCAA-certified agent (see Bylaw 12.02.1.2). (Adopted: 8/8/18 Applicability to be determined after NBA and NBPA evaluation of, and determination permitting, the eligibility for high school students to enter the NBA draft. Revised: 6/12/19.)

12.3.1.2.2 Enrolled Student-Athletes and Two-Year College Prospective Student-Athletes — After Request for Evaluation From NBA Undergraduate Advisory Committee. [A] In men's basketball, after the conclusion of the playing season, a student-athlete or a two-year college prospective student-athlete who has requested an evaluation from the NBA Undergraduate Advisory Committee may be represented by an NCAA-certified agent (see Bylaw 12.02.1.2). (Adopted: 8/8/18.)

12.3.1.2.3 Expenses From an NCAA-Certified Agent. [A] (Adopted: 8/8/18.)

12.3.1.2.3.1 Expenses Before Agreement. [A] Before signing a written agreement with an NCAA-certified agent, a prospective or enrolled student-athlete (and his family members) who is eligible to be represented by an NCAA-certified agent may receive transportation and meals from an NCAA-certified agent in the locale where the prospective or enrolled student-athlete is located (e.g., locale of home or institution) in conjunction with the process to select an agent. (*Adopted: 8/8/18. For an elite senior high school prospective student-athlete, effective date to be determined after NBA and NBPA evaluation of, and determination permitting, the eligibility for high school students to enter the NBA draft. Expenses permissible after appropriate changes to the Uniform Athlete Agent Act, Revised Uniform Athlete Agent Act and relevant state laws.*)

12.3.1.2.3.2 Expenses After Agreement. [A] After signing a written agreement with an NCAA-certified agent, the agent may provide the prospective or enrolled student-athlete (and his family members) with transportation, lodging and meals associated with meeting with the agent or a professional team. (*Adopted: 8/8/18. For an elite senior high school prospective student-athlete, effective date to be determined after NBA and NBPA evaluation of, and determination permitting, the eligibility for high school students to enter the NBA draft. For an enrolled student-athlete or two-year college prospective student-athlete, effective immediately.*). . . .

12.3.1.2.5 Written Agreement. [A] An agreement between a prospective or enrolled student-athlete and an NCAA-certified agent shall be in writing. An agreement that involves a prospective student-athlete shall be disclosed to the NCAA national office. An agreement that involves an enrolled student-athlete shall be disclosed to his institution. If a high school prospective student-athlete does not sign a contract with a professional team, the agreement must be terminated before full-time enrollment. If an enrolled student-athlete or two-year college prospective student-athlete does not sign a contract with a professional team, the agreement must be terminated before full-time enrollment in the ensuing regular academic term. (*Adopted: 8/8/18.*)

12.3.1.2.6 Compensation for Representation. [A] A prospective or enrolled student-athlete is not required to compensate an NCAA-certified agent for his or her services. (*Adopted: 8/8/18.*) . . .

12.3.1.3 Representation for Future Negotiation. An individual shall be ineligible per Bylaw 12.3.1 if he or she enters into an oral or written agreement with an agent for representation in future professional sports negotiations that are to take place after the individual has completed his or her eligibility in that sport.

12.3.1.4 Benefits from Prospective Agents. An individual shall be ineligible per Bylaw 12.3.1 if he or she (or his or her family members or friends) accepts transportation or other benefits from: (*Revised: 1/14/97, 1/16/19.*)

(a) Any person who represents any individual in the marketing of his or her athletics ability. The receipt of such expenses constitutes compensation based on athletics skill and is an extra benefit not available to the student body in general; or

(b) An agent, even if the agent has indicated that he or she has no interest in representing the student-athlete in the marketing of his or her athletics ability or reputation and does not represent individuals in the student-athlete's sport. . . .

12.3.2 Legal Counsel. Securing advice from a lawyer concerning a proposed professional sports contract shall not be considered contracting for representation by an agent under this rule, unless the lawyer also represents the individual in negotiations for such a contract. . . .

PROBLEM 8-6

For purposes of this question, assume that Wisconsin has adopted the RUAAA in its entirety without any modifications, and that it was in effect during Will Cheatham's dealings with Bill Jammer.

Will Cheatham, an NBPA-certified agent, was licensed to practice law in both Wisconsin and Illinois and maintained his business office in Chicago. He was not registered as an athlete agent with the Wisconsin Secretary of State's office. Through a mutual acquaintance, Cheatham induced Bill Jammer, University of Wisconsin-Madison's (UW) star basketball player, to secretly sign an agent representation agreement on December 1 of Jammer's senior year. This agreement was post-dated to April 15 of the following year, which was after the college basketball season ended.

The day after UW was selected for the NCAA basketball tournament, the NCAA declared Jammer ineligible for NCAA tournament competition after discovering that he had entered into the agent representation agreement with Cheatham the previous December. The NCAA required UW to forfeit 20 games that Jammer played in after signing this agreement, and the university's resulting losing record caused it to be dropped from the NCAA tournament. UW lost $100,000 in revenues it would have received for participating in a first-round NCAA tournament game, and potentially more revenue it could have earned by advancing to subsequent rounds of the tournament.

Although he was a projected second-round pick in this year's NBA draft if he performed well in the NCAA tournament, Jammer was not drafted by any NBA team. Jammer signed as a free agent with the Orlando Magic but did not receive a signing bonus. The last player selected in this year's draft received a $350,000 signing bonus. Jammer signed a contract for the upcoming NBA season, but only received the minimum annual player salary for rookie players of $543,471. Cheatham negotiated Jammer's contract but did not request that the Magic pay Jammer a bonus or a higher salary than the NBA minimum. Cheatham was concerned that the Magic's payment of more money to Jammer would leave the club with less available money under the NBA salary cap to pay Michael Swisher, Cheatham's prized client who was seeking a lucrative free agent deal with the Magic.

a.   Discuss Jammer's potential claims against Cheatham.
b.   Discuss UW's potential claims against Cheatham.
c.   Discuss whether Cheatham has violated the Revised Uniform Athlete Agent Act, and if so, any potential consequences.

D.   ETHICAL ISSUES

Given that attorneys must comply with state-imposed professional codes of conduct, the violation of which may result in disciplinary action, it is not surprising that some attorney agents have claimed that the representation of athlete clients does not involve legal work. Thus, they argue that they should not be subject to professional codes with respect to such services. Attorney agents, attempting to disavow their attorney status in this context, find justification in the fact that nonattorney agents who provide competent services on behalf of their athlete clients are not subject to the same requirements. Most fundamentally, these attorney agents argue that it is unfair to impose standards on them to which nonattorney agents are not bound. As noted by one analyst:

> "Some sports lawyers argue that based on the nature of the representation industry . . . if they enter the industry and hold out themselves as a sports agent, they avoid application of the ethical rules of the legal profession." (citing Robert E. Fraley & F. Russell Harwell, *Ethics and the Sports Lawyer: A Comprehensive Approach*, 13 J. Legal Prof. 9, 19 n.239 (1989).

According to commentators:

> One problem with this argument lies in the nature of the services provided by agents. A principal service provided by the athlete agent is the negotiation of the athlete's contract with his or her team, and 'the general service of negotiation is an area of traditional legal representation.' (citing John C. Weistart & Cym H. Lowell, *The Law of Sports* 53 (1985 Supplement). On the other hand, athlete agents provide services that do not fall within the scope of what is typically considered legal representation. Many of these services relate to the athlete's business affairs for which legal training is not required, such as advice on personal and financial matters.

Shropshire, Davis & Duru, *supra*, at 97. For discussions of the ethical dimensions of the athlete representation industry, see *Id.* at 95-103; Jeffrey Meehan, *Harvard or Hardball? An Examination of Ethical Issues Faced by Lawyer-Agents*, 21 Sports Law J. 45 (2014); David S. Caudill, *Sports and Entertainment Agents and Agent-Attorneys: Discourses and Conventions Concerning Crossing Jurisdictional and Professional Borders*, 43 Akron L. Rev. 697 (2010); Jonathan J. Amoona, *Top Pick: Why a Licensed Attorney Acting as a Sports Agent Is a "Can't Miss" Prospect*, 21 Geo. J. Legal Ethics 599 (2008); Jeremy J. Geisel, Comment, *Disbarring Jerry Maguire: How Broadly Defining "Unauthorized Practice of Law" Could Take the "Lawyer" Out of "Lawyer-Agent" Despite the Current State of Athlete Agent Legislation*, 18 Marq. Sports L. Rev. 225 (2007); Tamara L. Barner, *Show Me the . . . Ethics? The Implications of the Model Rules of Ethics on Attorneys in the Sports Industry*, 16 Geo. J. Legal Ethics 519 (2003); Fraley & Harwell, *supra*.

SPORTS MANAGEMENT NETWORK v. BUSCH

2019 WL 1057314 (E.D. Mich. Mar. 6, 2019)

[Eds. We revisit the dispute between NASCAR driver Kyle Busch and his attorney/agent, discussed *supra*. In the following excerpt, the court states why it rejected the attorney/agent's argument that the state's rules of professional ethics governing attorneys did not apply to him.]

SMN objects to the argument that it provides legal services. John Caponigro denies that SMN practiced law. . . . There is no doubt, however, that John Caponigro practiced law while acting as Busch's agent. Though Caponigro drafted and reviewed contracts in his SMN capacity, he also "exercised [his] legal knowledge for and on Kurt's behalf. . . ." [G]iven the close intermingling of the law firm and the non-law business, and Caponigro's insouciance over the distinction between the two, delineating between legal and non-legal services is impossible. As Caponigro reflected, noting the parties' discussions of attorney "hats" and agents "hats," "I wasn't worried about what hat I was wearing at the time." When asked if he represented Busch as an agent or lawyer in his separation from Penske, Caponigro answered, "I was — I was — I brought every element of my experience, background, and knowledge, legal and otherwise, to him in that instance."

Attorneys serving as sports agents typically have dual functions. Though non-attorneys can of course serve as sports agents, representing an athlete entails many duties that would be considered traditional legal work. See Walter T. Champion, Jr. *Attorneys Qua Sports Agents: An Ethical Conundrum*, 7 MARQ. SPORTS L.J. 349 (Spring 1997). . . . As Caponigro acknowledges, his legal skills have increased his marketability as a sports agent. . . .

Caponigro cannot profit from his law license in good times, but then claim he was only acting as a sports agent when problems arise. Whether or not SMN was engaged in the practice of law is irrelevant; Caponigro held himself out as both an attorney and as an agent of SMN. . . .

ETHICS OPINION

Ala. State Bar Disciplinary Comm'n, Opin. 85-73 (1985)

QUESTION

"A part of my law practice involves sports law, and in addition, I will be teaching the course of Sports Law as an Adjunct Professor of Law at . . . School of Law beginning the fall term of 1985.

My question relates to certain 'agents' who represent athletes and whether or not under the particular fact circumstances set forth in this letter their actions could be construed as the unauthorized practice of law. The fact circumstances consist of the following:

(1) Individuals represent athletes as 'agents' who have graduated from law school with law degrees but are not members of the state bar association or any local bar association in which they are located; and

(2) These individuals state that the reason they have no license to practice law, even though they have a law degree, is that it is unethical for attorneys to solicit business, and in order to obtain athletes as clients, one must solicit.

(3) These agents may belong to or be members of certain organizations involving or relating to sports law. In the biographical section of such organization's or membership's roster, the agents will list immediately following their names or in the biographical sections the following: 'attorney.'

For purposes of this letter, any reference to 'agents' shall include only those individuals who meet the three requirements stated above.

It is obvious that 'agents' have and will be able to continue representing athletes in negotiating contracts for athletes. Furthermore, a person with a law degree does not have to be an attorney and can be an 'agent.' In addition, the listing of these agents' degrees, including law degrees, either publicly or in biographical sections or other matters of writing, is permissible.

The two questions, based on the facts above, for these agents (as defined above) are as follows: (1) Are such agents by listing themselves as 'attorneys' practicing law without a license? (2) Since such agents solicit business, are they violating the Canons of Ethics of the Alabama Bar Association?"

ANSWER

If a law school graduate who is not a member of the Alabama State Bar or of any local bar association describes himself as "attorney" on the membership roster of any organization or any other publication he would "assume to act or hold himself out to the public as a person qualified to practice or carry on the calling of a lawyer" in violation of § 34-3-1, Code of Alabama, 1975, and would be guilty of a misdemeanor as described in the statute.

A law school graduate could not circumvent the statutes prohibiting the unauthorized practice of law by merely failing to become a member of the State Bar or any local bar association nor could he thus circumvent the rules against solicitation, DR 2-103 and DR 2-104. Furthermore, a lawyer shall not permit any person who recommends, employs, or pays him to render legal services for another to direct or regulate his professional judgment in rendering such legal services.

Discussion

Disciplinary Rule 2-103(A)(1) provides:

> (A) A lawyer shall not:
> (1) Solicit his employment or professional engagement or the professional employment or engagement of another whose partner he is, or from whose employment there is an expectation of profit or benefit, directly or indirectly, to himself.

Disciplinary Rule 2-104(A) provides:

> A lawyer shall not recommend employment, as a private practitioner, of himself, his partner, or associate to a non-lawyer who has not sought his advice regarding employment of a lawyer.

Disciplinary Rule 5-107(B) provides:

> A lawyer shall not permit a person who recommends, employs, or pays him to render legal services for another to direct or regulate his professional judgment in rendering such legal services.

An opinion of the Ethics Committee of the Kentucky Bar Association addresses a question closely analogous to that which you pose in your request for opinion.

We adopt as the opinion of the Disciplinary Commission Opinion KBA E-89 of the Ethics Committee of the Kentucky Bar Association and attach the same hereto as Exhibit "A."

ISBA ADVISORY OPINION ON PROFESSIONAL CONDUCT

ISBA Advisory Opinion on Prof'l Conduct, Op. 700 (1980)

Attorney has a "sports law" practice and represents athletes in contract negotiations. The athletes he represents are handled through his law office from which he conducts a private law practice. . . .

The second question presented deals with whether an attorney may handle "player representation" from the same office in which he engages in the general practice of law. It would appear, therefore, that the attorney making this inquiry questions whether the representation of athletes is actually the practice of law in that it may include a wide range of business counseling, as well as contract negotiation. This doubt could be prompted by the fact that nonlawyers frequently engage in these activities.

The committee is of the opinion that, when an attorney engaged in the private practice of law represents a client in contract negotiations and general business counseling, these activities constitute the practice of law and it would be professionally proper to handle them from the same office in which he engages in the general practice of law.

NOTES AND QUESTIONS

1. *Dual Capacity Cases.* In *In re Jackson*, 650 A.2d 675 (D.C. App. 1994), the court held that "a lawyer is held to a high standard of honesty, no matter what role the lawyer is filling: acting as lawyer, testifying as a witness in a proceeding, handling fiduciary responsibilities, or conducting the private affairs of everyday life." In two reported opinions, the courts assumed, without discussion, that lawyers who acted as sports agents were subject to the rules of their respective bar associations. *In re Henley*, 478 S.E.2d 134 (Ga. 1996); *Cuyahoga Cty. Bar Ass'n. v. Glenn*, 649 N.E.2d 1213 (Ohio 1995). The conclusion reached in these cases is consistent with the result courts tend to reach in cases outside the attorney agent context. *In re Dwight*, 573 P.2d 481 (Ariz. 1977), is illustrative of the approach that courts take in these "dual capacity" cases (i.e., instances in which legal and nonlegal advice is provided to a client). In addition to legal services, the attorney therein provided financial advice. The court held that "as long as a lawyer is engaged in the practice of law, he is bound by ethical requirements of that profession, and he may not defend his actions by contending that he was engaged in some other kind of professional activity." *Id.* at 484.

2. *Solicitation.* The Model Rules of Professional Conduct provide in part that an attorney "shall not solicit professional employment by live person-to-person contact when a significant motive for the lawyer's doing so is the lawyer's or law firm's pecuniary gain unless the contact is with a: (1) lawyer; (2) person who has a family, close personal, or prior business or professional relationship with the lawyer or law firm; or (3) person who routinely uses for business purposes the type of legal services offered by the lawyer." MODEL CODE OF PROF'L CONDUCT r. 7.3 (AM. BAR ASS'N 2018). Given this rule, to what extent are attorneys who also act as sports agents allowed to directly solicit the business of athletes? Do the limitations imposed on attorney solicitation of clients place attorney agents at a disadvantage when competing for clients against nonattorney agents? Would strict adherence to the nonsolicitation rule disadvantage some attorney agents more than others? Do the model rules that govern attorneys make it more difficult for attorneys who may be better able to effectively serve athlete clients to gain entry into the agent industry?

PROBLEM 8-7

Robert Williams was admitted to practice and became a licensed member of the bar of North Carolina in 2016. Beginning in 2019, Williams provided services for professional athletes, coaches, and a couple of sports-related entities. With respect to his athlete clients, Williams negotiated player-team contracts, negotiated endorsement deals, and provided a range of other services, such as assisting his athlete clients in managing their financial affairs. He provided similar services to his coach clients. Williams calls himself a sports agent and disavows that he is a practicing attorney, even though he continues to be licensed and notes on his business cards that he is an attorney. Williams is certified as a player representative by both the NFLPA and the NBPA.

Last year, Williams took out several loans on behalf of one of his sports entity clients, the government of St. Timothy. Williams was representing St. Timothy in the island's bid for entry into the Olympic Summer Games. Williams defaulted on the loans procured on behalf of St. Timothy and commingled his assets with those of his governmental client. Following a hearing, the grievance committee of North Carolina disbarred him. Williams filed a court action challenging his disbarment on grounds that he was acting as a sports agent rather than as an attorney.

a.   Assess whether Williams is likely to succeed in having his disbarment set aside on grounds that the services he provided were as an agent and not as an attorney.
b.   Assume that Williams is disbarred because he mismanages monies of one of his athlete clients. Also assume that Williams's only clients are professional athletes. Also assume that over the past five years, Williams has not held himself out as an attorney. He neither identified himself as an attorney on his business cards nor published materials that he usually sends out to prospective athlete clients. What is the likelihood that Williams will be able to set aside his disbarment on grounds that the services he provided were as an agent and not as an attorney?
c.   Assume that Williams is not an attorney. Do the services Williams provides for his athlete clients constitute the unauthorized practice of law?

See *In re Horak*, 647 N.Y.S.2d 20 (1996); *Jackson*, 650 A.2d 675 and the foregoing materials.

CHAPTER

9

Racial Equity Issues in Athletics

A. INTRODUCTION

Race remains a prevalent issue in sport, and one that is increasingly ambiguous and complex. Yet the role of race in sport often is overlooked until a particular event brings it into focus. The event may be a derisive comment made by a television personality in reference to an athlete of color or an event that marks progress toward racial equity, such as an African-American being appointed commissioner of a Power Five athletic conference. Events seemingly unrelated to sports also may inspire discussion of race in sport. Following the election of President Barack Obama on November 4, 2008, for instance, commentators wondered if his achievement might increase access to administrative positions in sports for people of color. They also offered their views on whether the presence of African Americans in leadership positions in sports might have influenced Americans to vote for President Obama.

The goal of this chapter is to introduce you to some of the issues that arise when examining race in the sports context. It attempts to achieve this goal through commentary and leading cases that address race-related issues. The chapter begins with historical perspectives on the role of race in American sport.

B. HISTORICAL PERSPECTIVE

During the early years of professional and collegiate sports, a period extending from after the Civil War to the late 1800s and early 1900s, African Americans participated in organized sports at the amateur and professional levels, including boxing, horse racing, baseball, and cycling. The opportunity to participate during this period was not accompanied by equality of treatment. African Americans were both exploited for their athletic ability and subjected to the indignities that flowed from racial discrimination. To illustrate, African-American athletes suffered the racial epithets of fans and opposing players and the discriminatory acts (e.g., physical attacks) of their own teammates.

The early years of inclusion in amateur and professional sports, albeit limited, were followed by a period during which formal and informal rules excluded blacks from organized professional and collegiate sports. One scholar explains

that the segregation of sports was the result of whites not wanting to associate with African Americans, and whites' belief in the inferiority of African
Americans. Kenneth L. Shropshire, In Black and White: Race and Sports in
America 31 (1996). See generally Arthur Ashe, A Hard Road to Glory (1988)
(discussing the history of African Americans in amateur and professional sports
in America). This period of segregation was followed by what some have coined
the reintegration of sports, which is discussed *infra*.

The following materials illustrate the web of formal and informal rules that
historically prevented African-American athletes from playing for white southern colleges and universities and severely limited their ability to play for northern colleges and universities.

1. Racial Segregation: Intercollegiate Athletics[1]

a. Formal Rules of Exclusion

During the late nineteenth and early twentieth centuries, legally counte-
nanced segregation impacted virtually every aspect of social behavior and interaction, including sport. In college sports, a series of rules and customs limited
black participation to historically black colleges and a few predominantly white
colleges located in the northern United States.

In the South, prohibitions against blacks attending white colleges and universities effectively excluded the black athlete from playing for predominantly
white Southern institutions. Moreover, Jim Crow laws enacted to prohibit whites
and blacks from social interaction extended to bar direct sporting competition
between them. For example, a Texas Penal Code provision, enacted in 1933,
prohibited any "boxing, sparring or wrestling contest or exhibition between any
person of the Caucasian or 'White' race and one of the African or 'Negro' race."
Tex. Art. 614-11(f), Texas Penal Code (1933). Likewise, a 1932 Atlanta city ordi-
nance prohibited amateur baseball clubs of different races from playing within
two blocks of each other.

More broadly written statutes prohibited any form of athletic competition between whites and African Americans. Legislative Act 579 is illustrative.
Enacted by the Louisiana legislature in 1956, the statute prohibited interracial
sports participation. Although similar legislation was defeated in Mississippi,
Mississippi state institutions adopted an "unwritten but ironclad segregation
policy." Thomas E. Foreman, Discrimination Against the Negro in American
Athletics 37 (1957). That such a policy was adopted with respect to sport may
be explained by the fact that Mississippi led former states of the Confederacy
in enacting laws and policies to "ensure effective apartheid." Wendy R. Brown,
*The Convergence of Neutrality and Choice: The Limits of the State's Affirmative Duty to
Provide Equal Educational Opportunity*, 60 Tenn. L. Rev. 63, 74 (1992).

One commentator observed, "What was left for blacks generally was participation of black against black and the formation of Negro leagues. At a less organized level, it meant acceptance of the Jim Crow laws which called for separate
(but almost never equal) playgrounds, public parks, swimming pools, and other

---

1. This section is adapted from Timothy Davis, *Myth of the Superspade: The Persistence of Racism in
College Athletics*, 22 Fordham Urban L.J. 615 (1995).

recreational facilities." John A. Lucas and Ronald A. Smith, Saga of American Sport 275 (1978). Under such a regime, the idea of competition in the South between white and black collegians was out of the question.

b. Informal Rules of Discrimination

During the late nineteenth and early twentieth centuries, blacks played sports for a limited number of northern colleges such as Harvard, Amherst, and Oberlin. Informal rules reinforced by social strictures, however, were as effective as legislation in limiting the opportunities available to black athletes to compete at predominantly white institutions outside the South.

These informal limitations appeared in various guises. In some instances, they were manifested as a virtual prohibition of African Americans from becoming student-athletes. For instance, few black students competed in sports for Catholic universities, because most such institutions excluded African-American students during this period. Often informal Jim Crow laws prohibited blacks from playing sports for the schools that did admit black students.

African-American students' experience at the University of Kansas is illustrative. No formal Jim Crow laws were passed in the state of Kansas. Nevertheless, the official policy of the university attempted to minimize the presence of black students in order to remove them from the mainstream of the school's social and extracurricular activities. One historian notes, "Blacks were denied practically every right except that of attending classes." Raymond Wolters, The New Negro on Campus: Black College Rebellions of the 1920s 316 (1975). The university's denial of African-American students' rights to participate in most extracurricular activities included the right to participate on the university's athletic teams. The head of athletics at the University of Kansas in the 1930s insisted, "[N]o colored man will ever have a chance as long as [I am here]." Loren Miller, *The Unrest Among College Students*, 34 CRISIS 187 (1927). The situation at the University of Kansas illustrates the lack of opportunity for black students to compete for northern universities, which often paralleled those institutions' attitudes and policies toward black students in general.

The environment encountered by black students and student-athletes at the University of Kansas was not unique. Certain athletic conferences, such as the Missouri Athletic Conference (with the exception of Nebraska) systematically excluded black athletes pursuant to so-called "gentlemen's agreements" that prohibited blacks from participating in league contests. These "gentlemen's agreements" constituted a series of written rules or tacit understandings precluding black participation in organized sport.

The reach and impact of "gentlemen's agreements" extended beyond the walls of the institutions that relied on them to exclude black athletes. These agreements severely impacted the few black athletes who were participating for northern universities. Prior to World War II, most northern teams with blacks on their rosters either did not schedule games against southern teams or would leave their African-American players at home when the team traveled south. It has also been suggested that a promise to withdraw voluntarily from games against southern schools was an element of the consideration that some northern institutions extracted from their black athletes.

Illustrations abound of northern schools forcing black players to sit out games against southern teams. For instance, in 1916, Paul Robeson, a member of Rutgers University's football team, was barred from the field of play when Washington and Lee College threatened not to play if he was allowed to participate. Such racially exclusionary practices resulted in black colleges providing the only significant opportunities for the black athlete to compete in college athletics prior to the 1930s.

Northern institutions adopted other informal rules. These rules carried the weight of law and, thus, restricted the ability of black athletes to compete for white colleges and universities. Informal quotas typically restricted the slots open to black athletes to no more than one or two players on a team. In addition to numerical quotas, northern colleges imposed another requirement that limited the number of black student-athletes allowed to compete on their teams. Many of these institutions imposed a "superspade" requirement. In other words, the typical African-American student-athlete playing for a predominantly white college prior to the 1930s tended to be an exceptionally talented starter.

Black student-athletes competing for the few predominantly white colleges willing to admit them were not spared the indignities of racism at their home institutions. Black athletes were excluded from the mainstream of campus social, academic, and athletic life. Black student-athletes were typically not permitted to reside in campus housing or otherwise engage in campus social life. They encountered demeaning comments from coaches, teammates, and other members of the university community, as well as the populace of the local communities in which those colleges were located. This sense of isolation was heightened by an absence of other black students, as well as black faculty, coaches, and administrators.

By the end of World War II, virtually every major collegiate program outside the South had opened its doors to permit at least one African-American player to compete for it. Southern colleges and universities resisted this fundamental change in college sport and continued after World War II to exclude African-American student-athletes. The integration of college sport at predominantly white colleges in the South did not begin until the latter part of the 1960s, but once it did the numbers of African-American players competing for these institutions mushroomed. For discussions of the integration of intercollegiate sport, see Timothy Davis, *Myth of the Superspade: The Persistence of Racism in College Athletics*, 22 Fordham Urban L.J. 615, 633-637 (1995); see also Timothy Davis, *Race and Sports in America: An Historical Overview*, 7 Va. Sports & Ent. L.J. 291 (2008); Forest J. Berghorn, *Racial Participation and Integration in Men's and Women's Intercollegiate Basketball: Continuity and Change, 1958-1985*, 5 Soc. Sport J. 107, 111 (1988).

2. Racial Segregation: Professional Sports

Prior to World War II, the experiences of racial and ethnic minorities in professional sports largely paralleled those of their amateur counterparts. Baseball provides an excellent illustration of the experiences of African Americans in professional sports prior to World War II. It is estimated that approximately 24 blacks played in organized professional baseball during the 1880s. By the 1890s, however, segregation of professional baseball emerged pursuant to a gentleman's agreement that resulted in the total exclusion of black and dark-skinned Latino players from Major League Baseball (MLB). Fair-skinned Latinos were permitted to play, but they were subjected to images that depicted them as "lazy, passive, and inferior," and to other forms of discrimination that continued into the post-World War II era. In addition, fair-skinned Latinos who initially entered American professional baseball systematically received lower-paying contracts than their white counterparts.

Blacks and dark-skinned Latinos developed alternative venues in which to play. Principally, they played in the Negro Leagues and in Latin America, and they barnstormed against white players. (Opportunities for interracial play in a barnstorming capacity were reduced beginning in the 1920s, however, when MLB's first commissioner, Judge Kenesaw Mountain Landis, prohibited major league all-star teams from competing against Negro League teams.)

According to Professor Alfred Mathewson, the term "Negro Leagues" generally has been used somewhat casually to refer to teams that played in the United States from 1880 into the second half of the twentieth century. Alfred D. Mathewson, *Major League Baseball's Monopoly Power and the Negro Leagues*, 35 Am. Bus. L.J. 291, 292 (1998). These leagues consisted primarily of black professional baseball players and black owners. *Id.* He goes on to note that although formal leagues existed, "particularly the Negro American and National Leagues," most Negro League teams were unaffiliated with a formal league and operated independently. *Id.* Professor Mathewson adds that most of these teams traveled throughout the United States engaging in "barnstorming sport" that resulted in them playing both black and white local teams. "Frequently, the games were significant social events in Black communities. Even those teams that were members of formal leagues barnstormed before, during and after joining leagues. The Kansas City Monarchs, who introduced night baseball in 1930, and the Indianapolis Clowns were two of the most successful barnstorming teams." *Id.* at 293.

Segregated baseball also provides insight into the inequity of separate but equal. Black ballplayers' salaries averaged less than half that of white major league ballplayers. While traveling, black players were confronted with inadequate transportation and substandard segregated accommodations. Negro League teams also encountered difficulty finding suitable playing facilities. Some facilities were off limits because of stereotypical fears of blacks. Although some Negro League teams constructed their own facilities, many teams rented major league stadiums at which they often encountered segregated seating restrictions. *Id.* at 294-295.

3.   *The Reintegration of Professional and Amateur Sports*

Baseball would remain segregated until Jackie Robinson joined the Brooklyn Dodgers in 1947. The formal desegregation of baseball would not occur, however, until 1959, when the Boston Red Sox, the last major league baseball team to field an all-white team, promoted Pumpsie Green to the major leagues. The National Football League (NFL) had been integrated from the year of its founding in 1920 until 1934, when a gentlemen's agreement between NFL owners, seeking to remake the league, banned the signing of black players. Daniel Coyle, *Invisible Men*, Sports Illustrated, Dec. 15, 2003, 124. The NFL was reintegrated in 1946 when Kenny Washington, who coincidentally had once roomed with Jackie Robinson at UCLA, joined the Los Angeles Rams. Similar to football, basketball had less of a history of exclusion than baseball. African Americans competed against whites in professional basketball up until World War I. In 1950, a year after the NBA was formed, Chuck Cooper, an African American, was selected in the draft by the Boston Celtics. In 1966, basketball also provided the first African-American coach in a major professional sports league when Bill Russell became coach of the Boston Celtics. See Kenneth L. Shropshire, In Black and White: Race and Sports in America 29-31 (1996).

A confluence of social, political, and economic variables resulted in the integration of professional sports and broader American society. Significant among these variables are (1) expectations for desegregation created by the "democratic idealism spawned by World War II," (2) opportunities created by a shortage of players because of World War II's decimation of the talent pool of white athletes, (3) political activism by blacks and their white allies demanding the desegregation of professionals sports, (4) Supreme Court desegregation decisions, and (5) enactment of federal civil rights legislation. For informative discussions of the integration of major American sports leagues and the factors contributing to the end of segregation, see William C. Rhoden, Forty Million Dollar Slaves: The Rise, Fall, and Redemption of the Black Athlete (2006); Jules Tygiel, Baseball's Great Experiment: Jackie Robinson and His Legacy (1983); Paul Finkleman, *Baseball and the Rule of Law*, 46 Cleve. St. L. Rev. 239 (1998); J. Gordon Hylton, *Essay: American Civil Rights Law and the Legacy of Jackie Robinson*, 8 Marq. Sports L.J. 387 (1998); Shropshire, *supra*.

Additional factors converged to provide incentives for colleges and universities to recruit African-American student-athletes, including political decisions, such as congressional passage of the G.I. Bill (which increased the presence of African Americans on college campuses) and the increased professionalism of college sports following World War II. Historian Adolph Grundman posits that colleges' recruitment of African Americans served a dual purpose: It helped these schools strengthen their athletic programs, while at the same time it promoted the advancement of race relations.

C. RACE AND RACIAL EQUITY IN MODERN SPORTS: AN EVOLVING DEBATE

In the United States, the majority of athletes who play professional basketball and football are African American. During the 2018-2019 season, African Americans accounted for 74.8% of NBA players,[1] and during the 2017 NFL season, African Americans accounted for 69.7% of that league's players.[2] African-American males made up a disproportionate number of student-athletes who played Division I football and basketball in that timeframe as well, at 44.8% and 53.6%, respectively.[3] Their numbers, however, were substantially lower in other

1. See Richard Lapchick, The 2019 Racial and Gender Report Card: National Basketball Association 7 (June 18, 2019).
2. See Richard Lapchick, The 2018 Racial and Gender Report Card: National Football League 4 (January 23, 2019).
3. See Richard Lapchick, The 2018 Racial and Gender Report Card: College Sport 46 (February 27, 2019).

sports. For instance, in baseball, African-American student-athletes comprised just 3.7% of players.[4]

The disproportionate presence of African Americans in basketball and football is misleading to the extent that it suggests race has become a nonissue in American sports.[5] To the contrary, the debate regarding race has merely shifted from the question of distributive justice (e.g., participation opportunities for African Americans in the major sports) to other matters. These issues include: (1) opportunities for minorities in administrative and coaching positions; (2) the underrepresentation of African-American athletes in sports other than football and basketball; (3) stereotype threat; (4) the underrepresentation of Latinos and Asians in intercollegiate athletics; (5) the persistence of racial stereotypes in sports media; and (6) the implications for sport when issues relating to race converge with those relating to gender, globalization, and economic exploitation. Timothy Davis, Foreword, *Losing to Win: Discussions of Race and Intercollegiate Sports*, 2 Wake Forest J L. & Pol'y 1 (2012); see also Kevin Brown & Antonio Williams, *Out of Bounds: A Critical Race Theory Perspective on 'Pay for Play'*, 29 J. Legal Aspects of Sport 30 (2019) (discussing the impact of the disproportionate representation of African-American male basketball and football players and stereotypes of African-American college athletes); Andrew C. Billings, *Talking Around Race: Stereotypes, Media and the Twenty-First Century Collegiate Athlete*, 2 Wake Forest J.L. & Pol'y 199 (2012); Timothy Davis, *Race and Sports in America: An Historical Overview*, 7 Va. Sports & Ent. L.J. 291, 307-311 (2008). The following discussion illustrates the complex and evolving role of race in American sport.

1. Coaching and Administrative Opportunities

a. College Sports

i. Coaching Opportunities

In December 2003, Sylvester Croom became the first African-American head football coach in the history of the Southeastern Conference (SEC) when he was hired to take the reins of Mississippi State University's football team. At the time of his hiring, Croom became the fifth active African-American head football coach among the then 117 schools that made up the NCAA's Division I-A (now Football Bowl Subdivision (FBS)). Shortly after Croom was hired, the University of Georgia hired Damon Evans as its athletic director, making him the first African American to hold such a position in the SEC. The hiring of Croom and Evans were particularly significant given the SEC's history of being one of the last conferences to integrate its universities' athletics programs.

While these hirings represented progress, the celebration around them highlighted the broader problem. Croom and Evans were relative rarities; part of

---

4. *Id.*

5. See N. Jeremi Duru, *Friday Night Lite: How De-Racialization in the Motion Picture* Friday Night Lights *Disserves the Movement to Eradicate Racial Discrimination from American Sport*, 25 Cardozo Arts & Ent. L.J. 485, 487 (2007) (arguing "rather than signaling an end to discrimination in sports, [b]lack visibility in collegiate and professional sports has merely served to mask the racism that pervade[s] the entire sport establishment").

an extremely small group of African Americans in athletics leadership positions at Division I-A institutions. Lack of head coaching diversity in football (in which so many African Americans compete) is particularly troubling, and notwithstanding Croom's hiring and the subsequent appointment of other African Americans as head football coaches, this lack of diversity has prompted numerous initiatives. For instance, in 2003, the now-defunct Black Coaches' Association announced a framework for a report card that annually evaluates Division I institutions' search and hiring processes for head football coaches. Institutions were evaluated based on several factors, including an institution's contact with the BCA during the hiring process, the extent to which institutions made efforts to interview candidates of color, and the diversity of the hiring process. The late Myles Brand, then president of the NCAA, supported the BCA's efforts and also made an institutional commitment to address these concerns, creating an NCAA Diversity and Inclusion Department. Through this department the NCAA developed various programs aimed at addressing the shortage of ethnic minorities in collegiate coaching, including coaching symposia consisting of workshops emphasizing skill development in areas such as communications, booster/alumni relations, fiscal responsibility, moral and ethical considerations, and interview preparation.

Notwithstanding these efforts, five years later there remained a dearth of coaches of color at American colleges and universities. Accompanying the release of its 2008 report card, the BCA called on the NCAA to initiate a college version of the NFL's Rooney Rule, which requires that each NFL team looking for a head coach interview at least one candidate of color before filling the position (the Rooney Rule is discussed in greater detail in section 1.b, below). In addition, the BCA threatened legal action to redress what it characterized as the continued segregation of college football at the head coach position. While the NCAA has taken no such action and the BCA never brought suit, the Division I-A Athletic Directors Association stepped forward in 2008 and created a Rooney Rule-like "best practice" for all head football coaching searches in the FBS.[6] These efforts have proved relatively successful. Between 2008 and 2011, the percentage of FBS collegiate head football coaches of color increased from 6.7% to 12.6% — by far the most substantial increase among college football's four divisions.[7] Stagnation, however, has followed. Indeed, the percentage of FBS collegiate head football coaches of color at the beginning of the 2018-2019 football season was virtually unchanged from 2011.

Ultimately, however, the Rooney Rule concept has been a net positive for equal opportunity in collegiate football coaching. State legislators from around the country, inspired by the Rooney Rule's impact, have expressed interest in requiring their state universities to interview at least one candidate of color when making hires in their athletic departments, and one state, Oregon, has passed legislation to that effect. In July 2009, Oregon passed a law requiring its seven public universities to interview minority candidates before hiring a head coach or athletic director, and in 2015 Oregon passed an additional law requiring that the state's Higher Education Coordinating Commission more closely monitor the universities' compliance with the interview protocols. Rachel

---

6. N. Jeremi Duru, *Call in the Feds: Title VI as a Diversifying Force in the Collegiate Head Football Coaching Ranks*, 2 Wake Forest J.L. & Pol'y 143, 151 (2012).

7. *Id.* at 20.

Bachman, *Kulongoski Signs Minority Coaching Bill*, Oregonian, July 23, 2009, 2009 WLNR 14214680; Oregon House Bill 2561 (2015).

These developments are promising, but head football coaching positions continue to be difficult for minorities to access, and football is not anomalous in this regard. Overall, coaching opportunities for racial minorities in college sports present a bleak picture. For the 2017-2018 season, the racial demographics of combined head coaching positions in all Division I men's sports were as follows: Whites, 86.2%; African Americans, 7.8%; Latinos, 1.9%; Asian Americans, 0.8%; and Native Americans, 0.1%. Similar numbers are present in all Division I head coaching positions for women's sports: Whites, 85.0%; African Americans, 7.3%; Latinos, 2.1%; Asian Americans, 1.7%; and Native Americans, 0.1%.[8] The trend follows for Division II and III head coaching positions, where whites hold 85.6% and 90.9% of positions, respectively. Notably, significant minority hirings in collegiate coaching sometimes spark comments that may be interpreted as racially tinged, and may help explain why representation of minorities among college coaches remains so low. For instance, on January 6, 2014, the University of Texas, which has one of the nation's most storied collegiate football programs, hired Charlie Strong, who is African American, to be its head coach. Strong spent the previous four years as the University of Louisville's head coach where he had tremendous success. He compiled a 37-15 overall record and ended each year with a bowl game, the last of which was an improbable upset victory against the University of Florida in the 2013 Sugar Bowl.

Notwithstanding Strong's track record, within two days of the hire, Red McCombs—a University of Texas booster and one of the richest and most powerful people in the state—attacked it. "I think it was a kick in the face," he stated publicly, "I think the whole thing is a bit sideways . . . I don't have any doubt that Charlie is a fine coach. I think he would make a great position coach, maybe a coordinator. But I don't believe [he belongs at] what should be one of the three most powerful university programs in the world right now at UT-Austin. I don't think it adds up." Max Olson, *Red McCombs bashes Texas hire*, ESPN.com, Jan. 8, 2014, https://www.espn.com/college-football/story/_/id/10257706/ booster-red-mccombs-bashes-texas-longhorns-charlie-strong-hire.

McCombs did not mention race, but might race have impacted McCombs assessment and assertion? See John E. Hoover, *Red McComb calls Texas hiring of Charlie Strong a 'kick in the face,'* TulsaWorld.com, Jan. 7, 2014, http://www .tulsaworld.com/blogs/sports/johnehoover/game-point-red-mccombs-calls- texas-hiring-of-charlie-strong/article_60fae530-77c8-11e3-acb0-0019bb30f31a .html; Jasmine Johnson, *Red McComb's comments on Charlie Strong show racial tension*, DailyTexanOnline.com, Jan. 15, 2014, http://www.dailytexanonline.com/ opinion/2014/01/15/red-mccombs-comments-on-charlie-strong-show-racial- tension-is-alive-and-well-at.

ii.   *Administrative Opportunities*

Coaching is not the only realm of collegiate athletics in which minorities are underrepresented. Minorities are also underrepresented in various

8. *Id.* at 24.

administrative realms of collegiate sport, including athletic directors, conference commissioners, faculty athletics representatives (FAR), and game officials. A detailed discussion of the extent of this underrepresentation, given the breadth of administrative opportunities within intercollegiate athletics, is beyond the scope of this book. Comprehensive information in this regard, however, may be found at the Institute for Diversity and Ethics in Sport, The 2018 Racial and Gender Report Card: College Report (Richard Lapchick, ed.) (Feb. 27, 2019). This report states, for example, that in 2017-2018, whites held 85.3% of FBS FAR positions and 100% of the FBS conference commissioner positions.[9] It bears noting that since the report's publication, the Big Ten became the first FBS conference to appoint an African-American commissioner, Kevin Warren, former Minnesota Vikings Chief Operating Officer. While this is an encouraging development with respect to diversity and inclusion in the administrative ranks of collegiate athletics, it is an anomaly.

b.   Professional Sports

Minorities are beginning to make inroads in coaching and senior-level administrative positions in U.S. professional sports, but progress in the coaching ranks has generally outstripped progress at the senior administrative level. For instance, at the end of the 2018-2019 NBA regular season, people of color held 33.3% of the league's head coaching positions,[10] but only 10.7% of the CEO/president positions.[11]

With respect to both coaching and senior-level administrative diversity, the National Football League has historically lagged behind even the modest gains of the other major American professional sports leagues. This trend continued into the new millennium, prompting the most substantial equal opportunity challenge to an American sports league in recent decades. On September 20, 2003, attorneys Johnnie Cochran and Cyrus Mehri released *Black Coaches in the National Football League: Superior Performance, Inferior Opportunities*, a report concluding that African-American football coaches are victims of discrimination with respect to hiring and firing notwithstanding their superior coaching performance. Following the report's release, Cochran and Mehri threatened to sue the NFL if it failed to take concrete steps to increase the number of African Americans among the league's head coaches. Shortly thereafter, an NFL committee issued guidelines as a part of an effort to foster greater opportunities for African Americans to gain head coaching positions. The guidelines, collectively known as the Rooney Rule, include provisions requiring that at least one person of color be interviewed as a candidate for all head coaching vacancies. And a few years later, the NFL extended the rule to "openings for general manager jobs and equivalent front office positions in addition to head coaching vacancies."

For several years following its adoption, the Rooney Rule was quite successful in increasing the numbers of NFL head coaches and general managers of color. During the twelve years before the Rooney Rule's enactment (1990-2002), the

---

9. See Richard Lapchick, The 2018 Racial and Gender Report Card: College Sport 14-15 (February 27, 2019).

10. See Richard Lapchick, The 2019 Racial and Gender Report Card: National Basketball Association 4 (June 18, 2019).

11. *Id.* at 5.

NFL featured four head coaches of color and one general manager of color, whereas during the twelve years after enactment (2003-2015), the NFL featured 16 head coaches of color and eight general managers of color. Just as notably, those head coaches and general managers of color have generally been successful. During the twelve years before the Rooney Rule's enactment, only one head coach or general manager of color had led a club to the Super Bowl, whereas during the twelve years after enactment, 10 head coaches and general managers of color led their club to the Super Bowl, two of whom did so twice.[12] The diversity gains, however, began tapering considerably in 2012. According to an ESPN study published in July of 2016, whereas 21.2% of head coaches hired between 2007 and 2011 were of color, only 13.9% of those hired between 2012 and 2016 were of color. The numbers for first-time head coaches of color are even worse. Whereas 26.9% of first-time head coaches hired between 2007 and 2011 were of color, only 4.5% of those hired between 2012 and 2016 were of color. Moreover, the study painted a bleak picture of the future, finding that as of 2016 very few of the league's assistant coaches of color held the positions that tended to eventually lead to head coaching positions: offensive coordinator, quarterbacks coach, and offensive line coach. Mike Sando, *Rooney Rule in reverse: Minority coaching hires have stalled*, ESPN.com, July 19, 2016, http://espn.go.com/nfl/story/_/id/17101097/staggering-numbers-show-nfl-minority-coaching-failure-rooney-rule-tony-dungy. Following the 2018 season, those concerns were borne out. Five of the league's eight head coaches of color were fired and, with most clubs intent on hiring offensive head coaches, only one head coach of color (a defensive coach, Brian Flores) was hired, leaving the NFL with only four head coaches of color. In response, equal opportunity advocates have increasingly called for the NFL to strengthen the Rooney Rule by expanding it to offensive coordinator hirings and to establish other equal opportunity initiatives to complement the Rule.

Although the Rooney Rule was initially highly controversial and racially divisive, a 2019 ESPN survey of fans suggests that division is lessening, as 74% of African-American fans and 66% of white fans either "strongly" or "somewhat" approve of the Rule. Jason Reid, *NFL fans and the racial divide*, ESPN.com, Feb. 1, 2019, https://theundefeated.com/features/state-of-the-black-nfl-fan-the-racial-divide-fracturing-the-league/. For a thorough exploration of the Rooney Rule, its origins, and its impact on the NFL and broader society, see N. Jeremi Duru, Advancing the Ball: Race, Reformation, and the Quest for Equal Coaching Opportunity in the NFL (Oxford University Press, 2011).

Overall, across the American professional sporting landscape (even in the NFL where, as noted above, diversity has increased), people of color continue to be underrepresented in administrative positions (e.g., general managers, coaches, team vice presidents) and ownership. For comprehensive information in this regard, see the racial report cards for each major professional sport league generated annually by the Institute for Diversity and Ethics in Sport at the University of Central Florida. For discussions of racial equity relating to coaching and administrative positions in sports see Jonathan Stahler, *Creating an Equitable Playing Field: Vital Protections for Male Athletes in Revenue-Generating*

---

12. See N. Jeremi Duru, *The Rooney Rule's Reach: How the NFL's Equal Opportunity Initiative for Coaches Sponsored Local Government Reform*, Oxford Handbook on Sports Law (Oxford University Press, 2018).

Sports Who Are Predominantly African-American, 3 Ariz. St. U. Sports & Ent. L.J. 231, 233-35 (2014); N. Jeremi Duru, *The Fritz Pollard Alliance, the Rooney Rule, and the Quest to "Level the Playing Field" in the National Football League,* 7 Va. Sports & Ent. L.J. 179 (2008); Jacquelyn Bridgeman, *The Thrill of Victory and the Agony of Defeat: What Sports Tell Us About Achieving Equality in America,* 7 Va. Sports & Ent. L.J. 248 (2008); Robert E. Thomas and Bruce L. Rich, *Under the Radar: The Resistance of Promotion Biases to Market Forces,* 55 Syracuse L. Rev. 301 (2005).

2. Intersections

a. Race and Gender

The racial demographics of women who participate in college sports exemplifies the intersection of race and gender. In 2017-2018, African American women accounted for approximately 43.0% of Division I women basketball players and 23.9% of Division I outdoor track athletes.[13] The profile of women of color participating in Division I athletics overall during the 2017-2018 season was as follows: African-American females comprised 12.4%, Latinas 5.1%, Asians 2.5%, and Native Americans 0.4%; females of two or more races comprised 4.9%.[14]

The data suggests that minority women are not participating in the increased athletic opportunities created by sports such as rowing, golf, lacrosse, and soccer, which many institutions added in order to comply with Title IX. Consequently, women of color appear not to be in a position to derive the same level of benefits from Title IX as white women. Law professors Deborah Brake and Verna Williams explain:

> For the African-American females who decide to pursue athletics, racism and patriarchy in the culture of sport present additional barriers to their continued participation. Consider, for example, that black females frequently are steered into particular sports or positions within sports. Black females are more prevalent in basketball or track. . . [and] the persistence of stereotypes about black women's proper place in sport constrains the athletic opportunities deemed appropriate for them.

Deborah L. Brake and Verna L. Williams, *The Heart of the Game: Putting Race and Educational Equity at the Center of Title IX,* 7 Va. Sports & Ent. L.J. 199, 210-211 (2008). See Alfred D. Mathewson, *Remediating Discrimination Against African American Female Athletes at the Intersection of Title IX and Title IV,* 2 Wake Forest J L. & Pol'y 295 (2012); Lauren Smith, *Black Female Participation Languishes Outside Basketball and Track,* Chron. of Higher Educ. (June 29, 2007).

These barriers to African-American participation in certain sports has prompted litigation. In September of 2017, Nadirah McRae, a female African-American high school field hockey and lacrosse player, filed a federal class action lawsuit against the Philadelphia School District, accusing the School District of derailing African-American girls' athletic ambitions by refusing to let predominantly African-American schools play field hockey and lacrosse against

13. See Richard Lapchick, The 2018 Racial and Gender Report Card: College Sport 47 (February 27, 2019).
14. *Id.* at 18.

predominantly white schools. The lawsuit, which asserts Title VI and Title IX claims, alleges that in an effort to reserve field hockey and lacrosse "for its magnet schools and more privileged high schools, which are not predominately lower-income and African-American," the School District essentially created a Negro League, restricting predominantly African-American schools to games against other such schools and robbing "the [African-American] girls of opportunities to improve their skills and to be seen by college scouts and recruiters." See *McRae v. Sch. Reform Comm'n et al.*, No. 2:17-cv-04054 (E.D. Pa. filed Sept. 12, 2017). At the time of this writing, the case is pending.

b.   Race and Socioeconomic Stratification

Commentators have drawn attention to one possible example of the intersection of race and socioeconomic stratification in examining whether African-American student-athletes, who are disproportionately overrepresented in collegiate revenue-producing sports, are exploited. Professor Rodney Smith, for example, has argued in multiple articles that practices in major college football programs foster the unequal treatment of athletes of color. See Rodney K. Smith, *Head Injuries. Student Welfare, and Saving College Football: A Game Plan for the NCAA*, 41 Pepp. L. Rev. 267, 310 (2014); Rodney K. Smith and Neil Millhiser, *The BCS and Big-Time Intercollegiate Football Receive an "F": Reforming a Failed System*, 2 Wake Forest J.L. & Pol'y 45 (2012); Rodney K. Smith, *When Ignorance Is Not Bliss: In Search of Racial and Gender Equity in Intercollegiate Athletics*, 61 Mo. L. Rev. 329 (1996). Similarly, Professor Goldburn Maynard Jr. argues that the hyper-commercialization of college sports disadvantages African-American athletes economically and academically. Goldburn P. Maynard Jr., *They're Watching You: How the NCAA Infringes on the Freedom of Families*, 2018 Wis. L. Rev. Forward 1, 10 (2018). See also Kevin Brown & Antonio Williams, *supra*, at 30 (discussing the impact of the disproportionate representation of African-American male basketball and football players, and stereotypes of African-American college athletes); Ahmed E. Taha, *Are College Athletes Economically Exploited?*, 2 Wake Forest J.L. & Pol'y 69, 94 (2012) (applying an economic analysis and concluding that the "athletes that generate the most revenue for their colleges are disproportionately black"); Elisia J.P. Gatmen, *Academic Exploitation: The Adverse Impact of College Athletics on the Educational Success of Minority Student-Athletes*, 10 Seattle J. for Soc. Just. 509 (2011) (discussing the exploitation of student-athletes of color).

Another phenomenon at the intersection of race and socio-economic stratification regards access to high school athletics. High schools that serve students from wealthy households often offer more extensive athletic opportunities than those that serve students from under-resourced households. Given that African-American and Latino students hail disproportionately from under-resourced households, their athletic options are disproportionately limited. Four New York City high school students argue that this is the case in their city. In 2018, these students, as part of a class action with help from New York Lawyers for the Public Interest, sued the city for violating its human rights laws through "its unequal handling of the Public School Athletics League." More specifically, the plaintiffs allege that "[t]he city's human rights laws prohibit depriving any public accommodation to a class of citizens, based on race," and that "[t]he Department of Education is in violation of [those laws] by discriminating against black and

Latino students because they provide more sports teams and a greater variety of sports to students of other races." Ben Chapman, *Advocates and students sue city over school sports discrimination*, N.Y. Daily News, June 21, 2018. To support their allegation, the plaintiffs note that:

- The city's Department of Education spends 17% more on sports for white and Asian students than for African-American and Latino students;
- Over 17,000 African-American and Latino students attend high schools offering no sports at all; and
- For those African-American and Latino students who do have sports offered at their high schools, they have on average 10 fewer sports available to them than do white students. See *id.*

At the time of this writing, the case is currently pending. Recall from Chapter 3 that most courts find there exists no constitutional right to participate in interscholastic athletics. Does that weaken these plaintiffs' claims? Why or why not?

c.   Race and Globalization

As is true for many industries, American sport has been impacted by globalization. Illustrations include the worldwide televising of American professional sports, playing American professional sports in overseas venues, international sales of licensed merchandise, programs created to increase the popularity of American professional sports leagues, and the increasing numbers of foreign athletes who play in American professional sports leagues. The dramatic increase in the recruitment of Latin American players by MLB teams raises the issue of the unsavory side of globalization. Commentators allege that MLB teams systematically afford Latin American baseball prospects less favorable treatment than American baseball prospects. See Angela White, Comment, *Curtailing MLB's Recruiting Abuses of Latin American Talent*, 2 Mich. St. Int'l L. Rev. 699 (2017); Timothy Poydenis, *The Unfair Treatment of Dominican-Born Baseball Players: How Major League Baseball Abuses the Current System and Why It Should Implement a Worldwide Draft in 2012*, 18 Sports Law. J. 305 (2011); Adam Wasch, *Children Left Behind: The Effect of Major League Baseball on Education in the Dominican Republic*, 11 Tex. Rev. Ent. & Sports L. 99 (2009). A small proportion of Latin American prospects become MLB stars. The vast majority, however, wash out of baseball before making it to the major leagues, or even the minor leagues, and "[u]nlike players in the U.S., Latin American players are not encouraged to have a backup plan." Instead, pseudo-agents, known as *buscónes*, who work loosely with MLB teams to identify young talent, often "encourage these children to forgo a formal education to focus on baseball full-time." White, *supra*, at 718. Angela White argues in her article, *Curtailing MLB's Recruiting Abuses of Latin American Talent*, that this system, "which is essentially unstructured and unregulated," must be reformed. *Id.*

Another race-related issue on the international stage is athletes being subject to racist behavior while playing. This phenomenon is most prevalent at European soccer matches where racist signs and chants are commonplace. In April 2019, UEFA (Union of European Football Associations) president Aleksander Ceferin acknowledged the magnitude of the problem: "It's 2019. How can that happen? I'm ashamed that here in Europe not a weekend goes by without a discriminatory act taking place in a football stadium, amateur level or professional level. I'm ashamed to see extremist movements use our sport as a vehicle for their messages of hate and intolerance." While UEFA protocol requires that referees stop a match if "racist behavior is of a strong magnitude and intensity," matches are, in fact, rarely stopped, due in part to the subjective standard. English Football Association Chairman Greg Clarke has pushed to strengthen the protocol and eliminate the subjectivity, proclaiming that "there should be no judgement call on whether something is of a strong magnitude. Racism is racism." UEFA, however, has not altered the protocol. Liam Twomey, *UEFA president "ashamed" at number of racist incidents in European football*, ESPN.com, Apr. 2, 2019, https://www.espn.com/soccer/uefa-champions-league/story/3814751/uefa-president-ashamed-at-number-of-racist-incidents-in-european-football. In the absence of European soccer governing bodies taking aggressive action to stamp out racial abuse of players at games, might the European Union step in to protect the players? Although the EU "has no direct authority over sport," legal scholar Michael Ryan argues that Article 13 of the Treaty of Amsterdam "could be interpreted to permit the EU to enact measures to combat spectator racism" and could therefore empower the European Union to address the issue through law. See Michael W. Ryan, *The European Union and Fan Racism in European Soccer Stadiums: The Time Has Come for Action*, 20 Fla. J. Int'l L. 245 (2009).

Currently, however, soccer players of color in Europe are left largely unprotected and to their own devices. While some athletes have understandably shouted back at abusive fans or walked off of the field in protest, others have taken to social media to challenge the racist behavior. For instance, after being serenaded with monkey noises and having bananas thrown at them and other players of color in Spain's First Division during the 2013-2014 season, Neymar and Dani Alves, then playing for FC Barcelona, planned a social media counterattack. They decided that when a banana was next thrown at one of them during a game, he would peel it and eat it on the field in view of the cameras, and Alves did just that on April 27, 2014. Immediately thereafter, Neymar posted a picture on social media sites of him eating a banana, with the note, "We are all monkeys." Before long other athletes, celebrities, and dignitaries around the world—including Brazil's president—posted similar messages in solidarity with the targeted players. Fernando Kallas, *Neymar planned Alves' banana eating anti-racist protest*, AS, April 29, 2014, http://as.com/diarioas/2014/04/29/english/1398770114_882297.html. In addition to raising awareness of racial abuse in soccer, the social media campaign ensured that authorities pursued the perpetrator, and he was ultimately arrested on charges "related to racist provocation." James Rush, *Revealed: How Barcelona players PLANNED banana-eating riposte in advance— as fruit-throwing fan is arrested*, Daily Mail, April 30, 2014.

Yet another issue that demonstrates the confluence of race and internationality involves some leagues' player age eligibility rules. For instance, both the NBA and WNBA have eligibility rules permitting non-U.S. citizens to enter the leagues at a younger age than U.S. citizens. Given that the NBA's and WNBA's domestic player pools are largely African American and that their international player pools are largely non–African American, might these age eligibility rules be viewed as racially discriminatory? See, e.g., N. Jeremi Duru, *This Field Is Our Field: Foreign Players, Domestic Leagues, and the Unlawful Racial Manipulation of American Sport*, 84 Tul. L. Rev. 613 (2010).

NOTES AND QUESTIONS

1. Explanations that have been offered for the dearth of African-American head football college coaches include interference by influential white alumni and fans that hinders the hiring of African-American head football coaches and the refusal of athletic administrators to admit that a problem exists in hiring procedures. In the collegiate ranks, but also in the NFL, some have argued that African-American head football coaches are simply held to a higher standard. At the NFL's 2019 Quarterback Coaching Summit, which is designed to assist aspiring African-American football coaches, NFL Executive Vice President of Football Operations matter-of-factly stated, "We can sell a non-winning white coach, but we struggle to sell a winning black coach." Jim Trotter, *Quarterback Coaching Summit spotlights minority coaches*, ESPN.com, June 25, 2019, http://www.nfl.com/news/story/0ap3000001034559/article/quarterback-coaching-summit-spotlights-minority-coaches. Do you agree or disagree with these various reasons? Are there other reasons for the underrepresentation of racial minorities in coaching and management positions in college and professional sports? Professor Kenneth Shropshire argues that the inability of African Americans to break into leadership is attributable in large part to negative stereotypes. He posits that these stereotypes, in conjunction with the "good old boy" system of hiring, result in lower numbers of blacks in authority positions in sports. Shropshire, *supra*, In Black and White 83-85.

2. *Stacking.* Stacking involves the assignment of certain individuals to specific athletic positions based on race or ethnicity rather than ability. The following account, offered in 2002, describes the history of stacking in the NFL:

> During the 1960s, black NFL players were "stacked" in positions thought by white coaches to require mere raw talent, not talent and brains. Black players were channeled and confined to running back, wide receiver, cornerback, offensive tackle and defensive tackle. The "lily white triangle," the two guards, center and quarterback where the plays and line calls are made, was virtually all white. Of course there were no black quarterbacks. On the defensive side of the ball, virtually no black players played linebacker or safety.
>
> With the coming of the American Football League in 1960, the stereotypes of black football players began to break down. Competing head to head with the NFL, AFL teams were looking for legitimacy and superior football talent. The only issue regarding what position a black football player played in the new league, with the exception of quarterback, was whether or not he could perform.
>
> Ten years ago, there were eight black quarterbacks out of the NFL's 106 quarterbacks and three were starters. In 2002, out of the 104 NFL quarterbacks, 22 are black and nine are starters. Given the chance, black athletes certainly excel as NFL quarterbacks equally as well as their white counterparts.

David Meggyesy, *Let Players Decide Who Coaches Will Be*, Sports Bus. J., Oct. 21-27, 2002.

But are African-American quarterbacks truly given a chance? At the end of the 2018 season, the proportion of African-American quarterbacks in the NFL was almost exactly what it was when Meggyesy wrote the foregoing article in 2002 (roughly 20%) even though more than 70% of the league's overall players were of color. Why does such stacking continue? Might it signal the continued resonance of old stereotypes that African-Americans are not well-suited to playing a cerebral position like quarterback? If so, might a 2015 study indicating that African-American quarterbacks are twice as likely to be benched after a poor performance strengthen that signal? Tom Jacobs, *Black Quarterbacks Are Benched Twice As Often As Whites, Study Finds*, HuffPost.com, Nov. 10, 2015, http://www.huffingtonpost.com/entry/nfl-quarterbacks-race_us_56424242e4b0411d3072c9f9. In what other sports and at what other positions is stacking evident? See Andrew C. Billings, *Talking Around Race: Stereotypes, Media and the Twenty-First Century Collegiate Athlete*, 2 Wake Forest J.L. & Pol'y 199, 210 (2012) (providing examples of stacking in college athletics).

3. The disproportionate number of African-American men in basketball and football gives a false impression that they dominate the world of professional sports. With a couple of exceptions (e.g., baseball and soccer for Latino men), African American and other racial minorities are underrepresented in most other sports. What reasons exist for the absence of racial minorities in most sports other than basketball, football, baseball, and to some extent soccer? Recognizing the need for diversity, sports such as NASCAR have developed programs aimed at increasing minority representation. For example, NASCAR has developed "Drive for Diversity," which seeks to find drivers and mechanics of color. In an effort to reverse the decline of black players, Major League Baseball has instituted programs including "Reviving Baseball in Inner Cities," and "Major League Baseball's Urban Youth Academies," both of which are aimed at developing a pipeline for players of color to eventually compete in the major leagues.

4. Another question that has been the subject of intense debate is whether sports are overemphasized in the African-American community. (Interestingly, the same issue has been raised with respect to young prospective baseball players who live in Latin American countries.) Some commentators argue that far too many young African-American males consider sports their "ticket to upward mobility." The statistics paint a clear picture that very few athletes who compete in high school sports will play at the professional level. The NCAA estimates that the percentage of high school athletes who will play professional basketball is 0.01%. The figure for professional football is 0.024%.

One author notes, however, that the emphasis young African-American males place on athletics is understandable given the historically high profile of blacks in sports. The author notes that each success achieved by African-American athletes raised expectations and resulted in more attention being focused on African-American athletes than on other African-American professionals, such as teachers and accountants. Lori Shontz, *Focus on Sports Hurts Blacks, Some Say*, St. Louis Post-Dispatch, Feb. 22, 2004, at A1. Other reasons offered to explain the focus by young African Americans on sports include the devaluation of African-American males' academic achievement and negative perceptions concerning the likelihood that African-American males will succeed in enterprises outside of sports. *Id.* Whatever reasons may underlie this untoward emphasis on sports, many commentators argue the situation must be turned around. *Id.* See also Kimberly Jade Norwood, *Adult Complicity in the Dis-Education of the Black Male High School Athlete & Societal Failures to Remedy His Plight*, 34 T. Marshall L. Rev. 21 (2008).

D. CASE LAW

The cases that follow address four (among many) contexts in which race has emerged as an issue in sports: (1) the development and promulgation of NCAA initial eligibility rules; (2) employment discrimination claims asserted by minority coaches; (3) the use by American sports teams of Native American mascots, names, and symbols; and (4) racially hostile sports environments. Collectively, these cases provide a glimpse into the complexity of the race-related legal issues that arise in sports.

1. *Academic Racism and Marginalization: NCAA Initial Eligibility Rules*

PROBLEM 9-1

The NCAA is considering a number of proposals designed ostensibly to increase graduation rates of basketball players at the Division I level. The National Association for Coaching Equity and Development, which has stepped into the void left by the BCA, has asked for your advice regarding a couple of the proposals. One proposal is designed to improve graduation rates by creating disincentives for NCAA programs with lower graduation rates. The proposal in question would provide for a reduction of two scholarships for programs with graduation rates that fall below 50% and four scholarships for programs with graduation rates below 25%. A number of coaches fear that the proposals will harm their programs because they take players from weaker high schools, many of which are poorly funded inner-city schools in which a large percentage of the students are racial minorities. The coaches believe that it is more difficult to maintain the higher graduation standards with student-athletes from these poorer schools. As such, they believe that the proposal is questionable on racial equity grounds. A second proposal calls for incentives in the form of additional scholarships for schools with graduation rates above 60% (one new scholarship at 60%, two at 70%, and three at 80% or higher). Once again, many of the coaches believe that this requirement may benefit universities that recruit heavily from wealthier school districts, which include fewer minority students. A few coaches in the association disagree and argue that the graduation incentives and disincentives will ultimately increase the number of minority athletes graduating from universities. Are there legal or ethical problems with the proposals as outlined? What response should the National Association for Coaching Equity and Development offer to such proposals at the legislative level within the NCAA? Consider the following materials.

PRYOR v. NCAA
288 F. 3d 548 (3d Cir. 2002)

MICHEL, Circuit Judge.

In this close and complex appeal, we must decide whether Plaintiffs have stated a claim for purposeful, racial discrimination under Title VI of the Civil

Rights Act of 1964, 42 U.S.C. §2000d *et seq.* (1994) and 42 U.S.C. §1981 (1994), by alleging (among other things) that the National Collegiate Athletic Association adopted certain educational standards because of their adverse impact on black student athletes seeking college scholarships. We hold that they have sufficiently alleged a claim for relief.

As the complaint indicates, the NCAA purportedly tried to improve graduation rates among black student athletes by adopting Proposition 16, a facially neutral rule that establishes scholarship and athletic eligibility criteria for incoming student athletes. As a result of these criteria, Plaintiffs allege, Proposition 16 has caused increased numbers of black student athletes to lose eligibility for receiving athletic scholarships and for participating in intercollegiate athletics during their freshmen year. Plaintiffs further allege that defendant knew of these effects and intended them. And thus, Plaintiffs suggest that the NCAA actually adopted Proposition 16 to "screen out" more black student athletes from ever receiving athletic scholarships in the first place, with the asserted goal of increased graduation rates serving as a mere "pretext."

Because the complaint sufficiently avers that Proposition 16 has adversely impacted the number of black student athletes who qualify for athletic scholarships, and because it alleges the NCAA adopted this otherwise facially neutral policy "because of" this adverse, racial impact, we cannot agree that the Plaintiffs—African-American student athletes who failed to meet the eligibility criteria established by Proposition 16—have failed to state a claim for relief under the liberal notice-pleading requirements of Fed. R. Civ. P. 8(a). . . .

[I]n 1986, the [NCAA's] Division I members adopted Proposition 48, which required incoming high school athletes to have a minimum grade point average of 2.0 and a minimum 700 score on the Scholastic Aptitude Test in order to practice, play and receive an athletic scholarship. As this court has previously stated, the Division I members implemented Proposition 48 to address the perception that its member schools were exploiting athletes "for their talents without concern for whether they graduated." *Cureton v. Nat'l Collegiate Athletic Assoc.*, 198 F.3d 107, 110 (3d Cir.1999). Following the implementation of Proposition 48, graduation rates among athletes, especially among black athletes, increased.

B

In 1992, the Division I schools voluntarily adopted the NCAA's Proposition 16, the provision at issue in this case. Proposition 16 modifies Proposition 48 by increasing the number of core high school courses in which a student athlete must have a minimum GPA, and it determines athletic eligibility based on a formula that combines a student-athlete's GPA and standardized test score. Proposition 16 essentially increases the minimum scores that a high school student athlete must attain to qualify for athletic scholarship aid and eligibility for practicing and competing as a college freshman. For example, if a student athlete had a 2.0 GPA in the core high school courses, he or she must score a 1010 on the SAT. The district court found in a similar case that Proposition 16 puts a greater emphasis on standardized test scores than did its predecessor (Proposition 48).

Cureton I

In 1997, counsel for Plaintiffs in this case sued the NCAA on behalf of different minority student athletes who claimed that Proposition 16 violated the regulations to Title VI of the 1964 Civil Rights Act. *Cureton v. Nat'l Collegiate*

Athletic Assoc., 198 F.3d at 111 (*"Cureton I"*). Specifically, the *Cureton* plaintiffs alleged a Title VI violation based on the theory that Proposition 16 creates a disparate impact on racial minorities. *Id.* . . . [T]he district court concluded that Proposition 16's disparate impact on African-American athletes violated the regulations to Title VI; and so, the court permanently enjoined the continued enforcement of Proposition 16. . . .

This court reversed and remanded with instructions for the entry of judgment for the NCAA. In the court's analysis, the regulations applied only to the specific programs or activities for which an entity uses federal funds, not to the entity at large. *See Cureton I*, 198 F.3d at 114. As a result, the court reasoned, even assuming the NCAA received federal funds, the Title VI regulations did not apply to the NCAA because the NCAA did not exercise "controlling authority" over its member institutions' "ultimate decision" about a student-athlete's eligibility to participate in collegiate athletics. *See id.* at 116-17 (citing and discussing *NCAA v. Tarkanian*, 488 U.S. 179, 197-99, 109 S. Ct. 454, 102 L. Ed. 2d 469 (1988)). Roughly one year after this decision, the Supreme Court held that Title VI creates no claim for disparate impact, contrary to the theory alleged by the plaintiffs in *Cureton I*: "Title VI itself directly reach[es] only instances of intentional discrimination." *Alexander v. Sandoval*, 532 U.S. 275, 281, 121 S. Ct. 1511, 149 L. Ed. 2d 517 (2001). . . .

C

This dispute very much resembles the *Cureton* case, with the variant that Plaintiffs here allege that the NCAA purposefully discriminated against them by adopting Proposition 16. . . .

According to the complaint, Plaintiff Kelly Pryor is an African-American student athlete recruited by San Jose State to play varsity soccer. Pryor has a learning disability. In 1999, as a high school athlete, she signed an agreement, called a National Letter of Intent ("NLI"), to play soccer on a scholarship at San Jose State beginning in the fall of 1999. Plaintiff Warren Spivey is an African-American student athlete who signed an NLI to play football at the University of Connecticut ("UConn"). As with the NLIs signed by all student athletes who receive athletic scholarships, the NLIs signed by Pryor and Spivey contain a condition that would render the agreement void if they failed to meet the eligibility requirements established in Proposition 16.

Neither Pryor nor Spivey met these requirements. Pryor, however, did petition for a waiver based on her learning disability. As a result, she received "partial qualifier" status, meaning she retained her athletic scholarship and could still practice with the San Jose State soccer team; she just could not compete in the team's games. . . .

Spivey himself, meanwhile, did not petition for a waiver; but UConn did so on his behalf, arguing that Spivey's record showed that he was prepared for the academic requirements of college. The NCAA denied this petition, as well as the appeal thereto, meaning Spivey could not receive athletically related financial aid or participate in varsity athletics during his freshman year. According to the complaint, Spivey still attends UConn, but he incurred substantial debt, *i.e.*, student loans, in order to pay his college tuition.

Under Proposition 16, student athletes who fail to meet the eligibility criteria as freshmen may still compete in varsity athletics beginning their sophomore year, provided they meet other minimum academic criteria. Also, Proposition 16 relates only to the award of athletic scholarships; no NCAA policy stops a university from giving a Proposition 16 "casualty" the financial aid that is available to all students. None of the post-freshmen year criteria are at issue in this case.

In February 2000, Pryor and Spivey sued the NCAA and sought to certify a class against it. Pryor alleged that Proposition 16 discriminated against her on account of her learning disability, in violation of the Americans with Disabilities Act and the Rehabilitation Act. . . . In addition, both Pryor and Spivey alleged that, by adopting Proposition 16, the NCAA intentionally discriminated against them on account of their race, in violation of Title VI of the Civil Rights Act and 42 U.S.C. §1981.

As support for their race-discrimination claims, Plaintiffs' complaint cites often to NCAA memoranda and other evidence obtained during the *Cureton* litigation. In particular, the complaint notes that the NCAA responded to an interrogatory about its reasons for adopting Proposition 16 by identifying (as one of its "top ten reasons") the goal that Proposition 16 would promote a higher graduation rate for black athletes and would thereby narrow the "Black/White Gap" between black student-athlete graduation rates and white student-athlete graduation rates. (Pls.' Compl. ¶¶62-63.) Citing statements from the district court's now-vacated decision in *Cureton I*, the complaint asserts that Proposition 16's "explicit race-based goal stands in stark contrast to the characterization of Proposition 16 as a facially neutral rule." (*Id.* ¶64) quoting *Cureton v. NCAA*, 37 F.Supp.2d 687, 705 (E.D. Pa. 1999)). Further, it professes a reliance, in part, on the "serious questions" the *Cureton* court itself had about whether Proposition 16 "function[ed] simply as a proxy for a racial quota." (*Id.* ¶64) (quoting *Cureton, supra.*)

In addition, the complaint identifies a memorandum from the NCAA dated July 1998 asserting that Proposition 48 and Proposition 16 have led to steady increases in the graduation rates for minorities and that no other proposed models would achieve that goal as well as Proposition 16 has. (*Id.* ¶65.) An affidavit from Graham Spanier, a former member of various NCAA committees, similarly avers that Proposition 48—the precursor to Proposition 16—had significantly improved graduation rates of student athletes, with the greatest increase coming among black student athletes. (*Id.* ¶66.) And another memorandum from an NCAA statistician . . . indicates that Proposition 16 projected the highest graduation rate for black and white athletes.

Liberally construed, the complaint maintains that Proposition 16 achieves the NCAA's stated goal of improving graduation rates for black athletes relative to white athletes by simply "screen[ing] out" greater numbers of black athletes from ever becoming eligible in the first place, *i.e.*, from ever receiving athletic eligibility and scholarship aid. (*E.g.*, Pls.' Compl. ¶¶20, 29, 66, 159, 162, 177.) Further, it maintains that although the NCAA knew that Proposition 16 would have a more adverse impact on black student athletes than on white student athletes, the NCAA went ahead and adopted Proposition 16 anyway, based on its "misguided view toward affecting African-American student-athletes' graduation rates by denying [scholarship] eligibility to greater numbers of" black student athletes. (*Id.* ¶¶69, 76.) As support for this assertion, the complaint points to various studies, research and reports by the NCAA showing that Proposition 16 and its precursor (Proposition 48) would disproportionately and negatively impact black student athletes. (*E.g.*, Pls.' Compl. ¶¶71-75.)

Citing these allegations, the complaint also lays out two theories of relief under Title VI and §1981. First, it asserts that because the NCAA adopted

Proposition 16 knowing that it would adversely affect black student athletes, the NCAA thereby acted with "deliberate indifference" to Proposition 16's impact on African-American student athletes. (*Id.* ¶¶164-66, 178.) And that indifference, the theory goes, amounts to the purposeful discrimination proscribed by Title VI and §1981. (*See id.*) Alternatively, the complaint indicates that the evidence of the NCAA's knowledge about Proposition 16's impact as well as other "circumstantial evidence" establishes that the NCAA adopted this policy to intentionally deny athletic eligibility and scholarship aid to a greater number of black athletes. (*See, e.g.*, Pls.' Compl. ¶¶20, 81, 169.) "Any suggestion" that considerations of race did not at least partially motivate the NCAA's adoption of Proposition 16 is "pretextual." (*Id.* ¶¶83, 180.)

In response, the NCAA moved to dismiss Plaintiffs' complaint under Fed. R. Civ. P. 12(b)(6) or, alternatively, for summary judgment.

The District Court Grants the NCAA's Motion to Dismiss

In July 2001, the district judge — the same judge that handled the *Cureton* litigation — granted the NCAA's motion to dismiss. As to Pryor's ADA and Rehabilitation Act claims, the court determined that Pryor lacked standing to effectively remedy her asserted loss of freshman eligibility. . . .

In addition, the court dismissed the two theories that Pryor and Spivey advanced to show purposeful discrimination. . . . [The court's discussion of the district court's rationale for dismissing the Title VI claim is omitted.]

Finally, the district court dismissed Pryor and Spivey's §1981 claim. . . . [The court's discussion of the district court's rationale for dismissing Plaintiffs' §1981 claim is omitted.]

This appeal followed. We have jurisdiction under 28 U.S.C. §1291 (1994) and now affirm in part, reverse in part and remand. . . .

IV

B

As stated, Plaintiffs' complaint and attached exhibits sufficiently allege a claim for purposeful discrimination in the adoption of an otherwise facially neutral policy. In effect, the complaint states that the NCAA purposefully discriminated against black student athletes by adopting a policy with the intent to reduce the number of black athletes who could qualify for athletic scholarship aid. We address this theory first and Plaintiffs' "deliberate indifference" theory thereafter.

1

To recover under Title VI or §1981, Plaintiffs cannot simply assert that Proposition 16 has a disproportionate effect on certain minorities. . . . As the parties agree, Title VI and §1981 provide a private cause of action for intentional discrimination only.

To prove intentional discrimination by a facially neutral policy, a plaintiff must show that the relevant decisionmaker (*e.g.*, a state legislature) adopted the policy at issue "'because of,' not merely 'in spite of,' its adverse effects upon an identifiable group." *Personnel Administrator of Massachusetts v. Feeney*, 442 U.S. 256, 279, 99S. Ct. 2282, 60 L. Ed. 2d 870 (1979); *accord Gen. Bldg. Contractors Assoc.*, 458 U.S. at 391, 102 S. Ct. 3141. A mere awareness of the consequences of an otherwise neutral policy will not suffice. . . .

Once a plaintiff establishes a discriminatory purpose based on race, the decision-maker must come forward and try to show that the policy or rule at issue survives strict scrutiny, *i.e.*, that it had a compelling interest in using a race-based classification and this classification is narrowly tailored to achieve that compelling interest. . . . Racial classifications, well intentioned or not, must survive the burdensome strict scrutiny analysis because " 'absent searching judicial inquiry . . . there is simply no way of determining what classifications are "benign" or "remedial" and what classifications are in fact motivated by illegitimate notions of racial inferiority or simple racial politics.' " This appeal involves only whether the NCAA intended to discriminate against black athletes by adopting Proposition 16, not whether that policy survives strict scrutiny.

"Determining whether invidious discriminatory purpose was a motivating factor [in the adoption of a facially neutral policy] demands a sensitive inquiry into such circumstantial and direct evidence of intent as may be available." *Arlington Heights*, 429 U.S. at 266, 97 S. Ct. 555. Although considering evidence of impact would seem to contradict the principle that no claim for disparate impact lies under Title VI or §1981 . . ., the Supreme Court has more directly stated that the "important starting point" for assessing discriminatory purpose is the "impact of the official action" and "whether it bears more heavily on one race than another." *Arlington Heights*, 429 U.S. at 266, 97 S. Ct. 555. As the Court has explained, the "impact of an official action is often probative of why the action was taken in the first place since people usually intend the natural consequences of their actions." *Bossier Parish School Bd.*, 520 U.S. at 487, 117 S. Ct. 1491.

Other considerations relevant to the purpose inquiry include the "historical background of the . . . decision; [t]he specific sequence of events leading up to the challenged decision; [d]epartures from the normal procedural sequence; and[t]he legislative or administrative history, especially [any] contemporary statements by members of the decisionmaking body." *Id.* . . .

2

In this case, Plaintiffs have stated a claim for purposeful discrimination. As we are reviewing this case at the Rule 12(b)(6) stage, we may affirm the judgment only if "it appears beyond doubt that no set of facts would entitle" Plaintiffs to relief. . . .

Here, it does not appear beyond doubt that Plaintiffs have failed to sufficiently allege facts showing purposeful discrimination by the NCAA. The complaint and attached exhibits make clear that the NCAA considered race as one of its reasons for adopting Proposition 16, with the NCAA stating explicitly that it believed the adoption of this policy would increase the graduation rates of black athletes relative to white athletes. Further, the complaint alleges that the NCAA purposefully discriminated against black student athletes (like Plaintiffs) when it adopted Proposition 16 because the NCAA knew—via various studies and report—that the heightened academic requirements of Proposition 16 would effectively "screen out" or reduce the percentage of black athletes who could qualify for athletic scholarships. In short, the complaint alleges that the NCAA adopted Proposition 16 because it knew that policy would prevent more black athletes from ever receiving athletic scholarship aid in the first place. . . .

[T]his is a case where, based on the face of the complaint and all reasonable inferences thereto, the NCAA at least partially intended to reduce the number of black athletes who could attend college on an athletic scholarship by adopting the heightened academic requirements of Proposition 16. And as the exhibits and complaint allege, the NCAA knew of this impact because of the pre-Proposition 16 studies informing them about this outcome. . . .

[L]iberally construing the allegations, the complaint here conveys that the NCAA adopted Proposition 16 because it allegedly wanted to reduce the number of black athletes who could ever become eligible for athletic scholarships. The complaint further suggests that the NCAA's "stated goal" of wanting to improve graduation rates via Proposition 16 served as a mere "pretext" for its actual goal. . . .

Here . . . the complaint alleges that the NCAA purposefully adopted a policy because that policy would reduce the number of black athletes who could receive athletic scholarships and compete in intercollegiate athletics as freshmen. Further, the complaint indicates that the NCAA knew this policy, Proposition 16, would and has adversely affected black student athletes, not white student athletes, because of the pre-Proposition 16 studies that informed them of this outcome. In other words . . . , the complaint in this case does sufficiently state facts showing intentional, disparate treatment on account of race.

3

The NCAA asserts that both the complaint and the exhibits thereto show only that the NCAA intended to help black athletes by adopting Proposition 16, not harm them. In like vein, it claims that precedent from the Supreme Court, as well as from rulings by other circuit courts, consistently absolve decisionmakers from purposeful-discrimination liability so long as their intent was "benign" or (in the words of Plaintiffs' counsel in *Cureton*) "laudable." For two reasons, however, this argument is unconvincing.

First, as explained above, the complaint adequately alleges that the NCAA sought to achieve its stated goal of improving graduation rates by using a system that would exclude more African-American freshmen who, in the past, might have qualified for scholarships. Further, as the complaint and other exhibits suggest, the NCAA knew that using this approach would also screen out more black student athletes than white student athletes. So again, one could infer that, because the NCAA knew this, it was actually pursuing its stated goal and adopted means as a way to accomplish this sinister purpose while still seeming "laudable" and well intentioned. True, at first glance, some might well consider this theory far fetched. But we are reviewing this case at the pleading stage, not the summary judgment stage. Further, two allegations and the exhibits supporting them support the theory of the complaint: the NCAA openly considered race in formulating Proposition 16; and it had reason to know that the adoption of Proposition 16 would lead to the greater exclusion of black athletes from receiving college athletic scholarships.

Again, one may doubt that the NCAA harbored such ill motives. After all, many NCAA schools have long engaged in fierce recruiting contests to obtain the best high school athletes in the country, many of whom are black. And in today's world of collegiate athletics, better athletes can translate into more revenues and exposure for the schools that sign them. On the other hand, racial discrimination is nearly always irrational and thus, in the words of the Supreme Court, "odious" to our nation's principles of equality. . . . Further, neither our court nor the district court can render "findings" in this case—at least not yet. And findings of fact, of course, turn on evidence, not on one's speculations about the issue. Nothing in our decision today precludes either summary judgment or trial findings that conclude the NCAA did not intend to discriminate on the basis of race.

Second, even assuming the NCAA's assertion that it had only "laudable" goals in adopting Proposition 16 and that it actually wanted only to improve graduation rates among black student athletes, the NCAA has cited no authority holding that a claim for purposeful discrimination may lie only if the accused decision-maker had "bad intentions" or "animus." Quite the contrary. The Court has squarely held that, well-intentioned or not, express or neutral on its face, a law or policy that purposefully discriminates on account of race is presumptively invalid and can survive only if it withstands strict scrutiny review. . . .

Admittedly, this case is not subject to easy categorization. It differs from many Supreme Court precedents in that one could read the complaint and attached exhibits as showing that the NCAA adopted Proposition 16 to benefit the parties now suing for intentional discrimination. . . . And it differs from . . . reverse-discrimination cases in that Plaintiffs here are not, say, white student athletes claiming the NCAA adopted a race-based policy at their expense. Again, putting aside the more sinister theory about the NCAA purposefully using Proposition 16 as a means to discriminate against black athletes, Plaintiffs' complaint can also be read as alleging that (1) the NCAA considered race when it adopted Proposition 16; (2) it did so for the "benign" or "laudable" goal of improving graduation rates among black student athletes; but (3) the policy for achieving that goal—Proposition 16—backfired and has instead worked to the detriment of black athletes. . . .

Plaintiffs also sufficiently allege that the NCAA adopted Proposition 16 for the malevolent purpose of excluding black student athletes from receiving scholarship aid and athletic eligibility. In this regard, we merely reiterate the Supreme Court's established view that a claim for purposeful discrimination may lie even if the decisionmaker adopted the allegedly discriminatory policy or rule at issue for a "beneficial" or "laudable" purpose.

4

As Plaintiffs have sufficiently alleged a claim of purposeful discrimination under the analysis set forth above, they need not establish their alternative theory about the NCAA acting with "deliberate indifference" to the impact of Proposition 16 in order to secure reversal of the total dismissal of the complaint. [EDS. Having stated this, the court rejected plaintiffs' deliberate indifference claim because "Title VI of the Civil Rights Act 'directly reaches only instances of intentional discrimination.'"] . . .

C

Having determined that Plaintiffs have sufficiently alleged a claim for purposeful discrimination, we must also conclude that Plaintiffs have thereby satisfied two of the three elements of the §1981 analysis. To establish a right to relief under §1981, a plaintiff must show (1) that he belongs to a racial minority; (2) "an intent to discriminate on the basis of race by the defendant; and (3) discrimination concerning one or more of the activities enumerated in" §1981, including the right to make and enforce contracts. *Brown v. Philip Morris Inc.*, 250 F.3d at 797. The standard for establishing an "intent to discriminate on the basis of race" is identical in the Title VI and §1981 contexts.

Here, the district court granted the motion to dismiss Plaintiffs' §1981 claim because not only (in the court's view) did Plaintiffs fail to allege facts showing an intent to discriminate; but also because they failed to show that the NCAA had deprived them of their contract rights under the NLI. According to the district court, Plaintiffs agreed to the NLI condition that they satisfy the academic requirements of Proposition 16; and that Plaintiffs therefore received all their rights under their respective NLIs because they had simply failed to meet this condition, meaning the NLIs had by their own force become void.

This analysis is certainly logical. But it fails to account for the argument about the NLI condition resulting from the NCAA's alleged discrimination. . . . In our view, this argument is persuasive. A contract term or condition that violates public policy is void and is thus unenforceable.

In the realm of contract law, the doctrine of public policy reflects principles of law already enumerated by the Constitution and state and federal law. . . . It follows that this doctrine may also void a contract term if that term offends the laws prohibiting racial discrimination. . . .

In this case, we have already determined that Plaintiffs have stated a claim for purposeful discrimination, meaning Plaintiffs have alleged facts sufficient to meet the second prong of §1981 as well. Moreover, as the precedents above show, the NCAA could not avoid §1981 liability here simply because the Proposition 16 condition—an alleged product of purposeful discrimination—was not satisfied. . . . Rather, as Plaintiffs suggest, this condition is void on its face provided Plaintiffs can establish that the NCAA adopted Proposition 16 (and, thus, the condition contained in the Plaintiffs' NLIs) for the purpose of intentionally discriminating on the basis of race. For purposes of the NCAA's Rule 12(b)(6) motion, we hold that Plaintiffs have so established that point. Accordingly, the fact that the condition here was not performed does not serve as a basis for vitiating Plaintiffs' §1981 claim. We therefore reverse and remand Plaintiffs' §1981 claim too.

V. . . .

For the reasons stated above, we affirm the dismissal of Plaintiff Pryor's ADA and Rehabilitation Act claims for want of constitutional standing. But we reverse the Rule 12(b)(6) dismissal of Plaintiffs' Title VI and §1981 claims insofar as they rest on allegations of purposeful discrimination, not deliberate indifference. We remand for additional proceedings consistent with this opinion.

NOTES AND QUESTIONS

1. Identify the NCAA's goals in promulgating Proposition 16. Why did the court reject these goals as a basis for upholding the standardized test component of the NCAA's initial eligibility rules?
2. In 1997, minority student-athletes sued the NCAA claiming that Proposition 16 violated regulations promulgated under Title VI of the 1964 Civil Rights Act because of its disparate impact on African-American athletes. The district court concluded that Proposition 16 had a disparate impact on African-American athletes in violation of the regulations and permanently enjoined enforcement of Proposition 16. It did so even though it accepted the NCAA's stated justification that Proposition 16 was a way to raise all student-athletes' graduation rates. *Cureton v. NCAA*, 37 F. Supp. 2d 687 (E.D. Pa. 1999).

   On appeal, however, the Third Circuit reversed that decision. *Cureton v. NCAA*, 198 F.3d 107 (3d Cir. 1999). The appellate court concluded that the regulations in question applied only to specific programs or activities using federal funds and not to the whole entity. Because the NCAA program allegedly receiving direct funding was not at issue, the regulations could only become applicable if the NCAA had controlling authority over some relevant program receiving federal funding, such as a member school's athletic scholarship program. The court concluded that the NCAA did not exercise controlling authority over member institutions' ultimate decisions about student-athletes' eligibility to participate in athletics, and thus was not subject to the regulations.

For discussions of *Cureton v. NCAA* and the controversy surrounding the standardized test component of the NCAA's initial eligibility rules, see Diane Heckman, *Tracking Challenges to NCAA's Academic Eligibility Requirements Based on Race and Disability*, 222 Ed. L. Rep. 1 (2007); Eli D. Oates, *Cureton v. NCAA: The Recognition of Proposition 16's Misplaced Use of Standardized Tests in the Context of Collegiate Athletics as a Barrier to Educational Opportunity for Minorities*, 35 Wake Forest L. Rev. 445 (2000); Kenneth L. Shropshire, *Colorblind Propositions: Race, the SAT and the NCAA*, 8 Stan. L. & Pol'y Rev. 141 (1997).

3. *The Debate Regarding Initial Eligibility Rules.* What were the ramifications of the *Pryor* court's ruling? Will the ruling have harmful or beneficial effects on student-athletes? How will it affect intercollegiate athletics programs?

Proposition 16 was not the first major NCAA reform related to its initial eligibility requirements. In 1983, NCAA initial eligibility rules known as Proposition 48 were enacted to take effect in 1986. As was true of Proposition 16, critics assailed Proposition 48's requirement as racially biased. They argued that heightened standards would reduce many black student-athletes' access to college, that standardized tests are culturally biased against African Americans, and that standardized tests fail to take into account the often unique circumstances of African-American student-athletes. Proponents of stricter initial eligibility rules argued that such requirements would help to restore academic integrity to colleges and universities that had been undermined by scandals arising within intercollegiate athletics and represented a means of ensuring that student-athletes have a reasonable chance of obtaining a meaningful degree. Informative discussions of the debate surrounding the enactment of NCAA initial eligibility rules can be found in Davis, *supra*, at 664-667; Kenneth L. Shropshire, *Colorblind Propositions: Race, the SAT and the NCAA*, 8 Stan L. & Pol'y Rev. 141 (1997).

As discussed in Chapter 3, in November 2002, the NCAA passed legislation that radically changed its initial eligibility rules. The late NCAA president Myles Brand articulated the following rationale for the revised standard:

> The goal in developing the most recent eligibility models was to maximize graduation rates while minimizing disparate impact. . . . We believe that eliminating the test-score cut will increase access and that the new progress-toward-degree benchmarks — particularly in the student-athlete's first two years — will put athletes on track to graduate at even higher rates than they already do.

Athlete Graduation Rates Continue to Climb, NCAA News, Sept. 1, 2003, at 1, 11. As discussed in Chapter 3(C)(2) supra, in 2011 the NCAA passed legislation imposing more stringent initial eligibility rules that apply to students who entered college after August 1, 2016.

4. *Graduation Success Rates.* In November 2018, the NCAA released the Graduation Success Rates (GSR) for athletes who entered colleges and universities in 2011.[15] The GSR for all Division I athletes was 88%.[16] Division I graduation rates for African-American athletes continued to rise, reaching 79%.[17] Despite the overall improvement, disparities persist when comparing GSRs for Division I African-American and white athletes. The GSRs for all Division I white athletes was 92%,[18] a slight narrowing of the gap from 2017, when the GSRs were 77 and 91% for Division I African-American and white athletes, respectively.[19] Examining specific sports, the GSRs for Division I African-American and white male basketball players were 82 and 93%, respectively.[20] A similar percentage gap is present for African-American and white FBS football players, 75 and 91%, respectively.[21] The GSR gap for African-American and white female Division I athletes is slightly narrower, with African-American females achieving a GSR of 86% and white females achieving a GSR of 95%.[22] The GSRs for African-American and white Division I female basketball players were 89 and 95%, respectively.[23]

2.   *Employment Discrimination: Title VII and Section 1981*

As discussed *supra*, race has been identified as a factor that limits access to coaching and administrative positions and promotion opportunities for African Americans in college and professional sports. In the few instances in which minority coaches have alleged racial discrimination in hiring and promotion in sports, they have resorted to Title VII and Section 1981 of the Civil Rights Act. Title VII prohibits discrimination in employment. Under Title VII, a plaintiff is likely to assert claims premised on disparate treatment (which focuses on intentional racial discrimination) or disparate impact (which focuses on the use of facially neutral employment practices) that unjustifiably discriminate against members of a protected group. Section 1981 is broader in scope in that it applies to the making, performance, and enforcement of all contracts, not just employment contracts. Section 1981 proscribes intentional discrimination.

The *Jackson* case, *infra*, provides a detailed discussion of the proof that plaintiffs must establish in order to prevail in Title VII and Section 1981 actions. *Jackson* also reveals, however, that the proof required in order to establish a cognizable Title VII or Section 1981 claim limits the effectiveness of these traditional antidiscrimination norms for those seeking redress for alleged racial discrimination. See Neil Forester, Comment, *The Elephant in the Locker Room: Does the National Football League Discriminate in the Hiring of Head Coaches?*, 34 McGeorge

15. Michelle Brutlag Hosick, *College Athletes Graduate at Record High Rates*, NCAA News, Nov. 14, 2018, http://www.ncaa.org/about/resources/media-center/news/college-athletes-graduate-record-high-rates.

16. NCAA Research Staff, Trends in Graduation Success Rates and Federal Graduation Rates at NCAA Division I Institutions, NCAA Research 16 (Nov. 2018).

17. *Id.* at 19.

18. *Id.*

19. *Id.*

20. *Id.* at 17.

21. *Id.*

22. *Id.* at 16.

23. *Id.* at 17.

L. Rev. 877 (2003) (outlining the elements of Title VII and Section 1981 claims); Shropshire, *supra* at 65-68 (commenting on how the subjective criteria used by those with hiring authority in sports limits the opportunities available to African-American coaching and general manager candidates, and shields sports organizations from liability for racial discrimination).

JACKSON v. UNIVERSITY OF NEW HAVEN

228 F. Supp. 2d 156 (D. Conn. 2002)

DRONEY, District Judge.

I.   INTRODUCTION

James C. Jackson ("Jackson") brought this action against the University of New Haven ("UNH") and Deborah Chin, the Athletic Director of UNH, alleging racial discrimination in hiring in violation of 42 U.S.C. §1981, 42 U.S.C. §2000d (Title VI), and 42 U.S.C. §2000e-5 (Title VII). . . . Jackson seeks damages as well as equitable relief, costs, and attorney's fees. Pending before the Court is Defendants' Motion for Summary Judgment. . . . For the following reasons, the motion is GRANTED.

II.   FACTS

In February 1999 the head football coach at the University of New Haven ("UNH") left to take a position with the Cleveland Browns of the National Football League. This dispute arises out of the ensuing search for a new head coach at UNH.

Beginning in early February of 1999, UNH posted the head coach position both internally and with the "NCAA market," an online professional publication for university and college athletics. The postings for the head coaching position listed the following requirements:

> A bachelors degree is required, master's degree preferred. *Successful collegiate coaching experience required.* Experience in recruiting, game coaching and knowledge of NCAA rules and regulations is essential.

Further, the duties were listed as follows:

> Implement and manage all aspects of a national caliber Division II football program in accordance with NCAA and university regulations. Areas of responsibility include, but are not limited to coaching, recruiting qualified student athletes, budget management, scheduling, hiring and supervising coaching staff, academically monitoring student-athletes, and promotions and fund-raising.

. . . After receiving 36 applications, UNH's Search Committee, which had been established to select a new head coach, decided to interview six applicants—all of whom had college coaching experience and are Caucasian. Jackson, an African-American, was not among the six applicants interviewed.

Jackson had no college experience, but had been a professional minor league football coach, earned several "coach of the year" honors as such a coach, and was inducted into the minor league football hall of fame. The defendants assert that they decided not to interview Jackson because he lacked the requisite collegiate coaching experience. From the six applicants interviewed, the Search Committee ultimately selected Darren Rizzi, who had been an assistant coach at UNH for four years, to fill the position of head coach.

At the heart of this dispute lies the "collegiate coaching experience" requirement. The parties are in agreement that the posted job qualifications included that requirement and that all of the applicants selected for interviews possessed such experience. However, the parties differ markedly in their characterizations of that prior experience requirement. The defendants maintain that prior NCAA coaching experience was essential to ensure the selection of a candidate sufficiently well-versed in NCAA rules and regulations to both pass the NCAA's annual tests on such regulations and manage the UNH football team successfully. Jackson, however, asserts that the requirement of previous collegiate coaching experience was not necessary to ensure familiarity with NCAA rules and regulations and that it served to exclude otherwise qualified minority applicants, such as himself.

Jackson asserts that the requirement that applicants have prior college coaching experience amounts to discrimination in violation of 42 U.S.C. §1981, 42 U.S.C. §2000d (Title VI), and 42 U.S.C. §2000e-5 (Title VII).[3] Jackson asserts all three of these statutory causes of action against defendant UNH. However, only the §1981 claim is asserted against defendant Chin.

Jackson appears to base his complaint on both the "disparate treatment" and "disparate impact" theories of recovery in that he alleges both that the challenged qualification had a discriminatory effect upon African Americans (disparate impact) and that the defendants intentionally discriminated against him based on his race (disparate treatment). . . .

IV.   Analysis

A.   Disparate Treatment Claim

As mentioned, Jackson alleges that he has been discriminated against in violation of 42 U.S.C. §§1981, 2000d (Title VI), and 2000e-5 (Title VII). To the extent that he claims that he has been discriminated against intentionally, the U.S. Supreme Court has developed a "burden shifting framework" for claims brought under Title VII alleging "disparate treatment." *McDonnell Douglas Corp. v. Green*, 411 U.S. 792, 802, 93 S. Ct. 1817, 36 L. Ed. 2d 668 (1973). Courts have subsequently applied the same burden-shifting framework articulated in *McDonnell Douglas* to disparate treatment claims arising under 42 U.S.C. §§1981 and 2000d (Title VI). . . . Thus, because the test is the same under each of the

3. Title 42 U.S.C. §1981 provides that "[a]ll persons within the jurisdiction of the United States shall have the same right in every State and Territory . . . to the full and equal benefit of all laws." Title 42 U.S.C. §2000d (Title VI) provides that "No person in the United States shall, on the ground of race . . . be excluded from participation in, be denied any benefits of, or be subject to discrimination under any program or activity receiving Federal financial assistance." . . . Finally, Title VII prohibits certain "Unlawful employment practices," which include "fail[ing] or refus[ing] to hire or discharge any individual, or otherwise to discriminate against any individual . . . because of such individual's race. . . ." 42 U.S.C. §2000e-2.

three statutes, this Court will apply the same *McDonnell Douglas* burden-shifting framework to the plaintiff's disparate treatment claim.

Under the burden-shifting framework of *McDonnell Douglas*, a plaintiff alleging disparate treatment based on race and national origin must first establish a prima facie case of discrimination. 411 U.S. at 802, 93 S. Ct. 1817.[5] The burden then shifts to the defendant to offer a legitimate, nondiscriminatory rationale for its actions. *See James v. New York Racing Ass'n*, 233 F.3d 149, 154 (2d Cir. 2000). Finally, if the defendant does offer a non-discriminatory reason for its decision, the burden again shifts to the plaintiff to show that the defendant's stated reason is a mere pretext for discrimination. *See Id.* (citing *St. Mary's Honor Ctr. v. Hicks*, 509 U.S. 502, 506-10, 113 S. Ct. 2742, 125 L. Ed. 2d 407 (1993)). In some circumstances, under *Reeves v. Sanderson Plumbing Products, Inc.*, 530 U.S. 133, 120 S. Ct. 2097, 147 L. Ed. 2d 105, (2000), after the plaintiff offers evidence to show that the defendant's asserted non-discriminatory reason for the hiring is pretextual, the evidence that established the prima facie case will be sufficient to survive a summary judgment motion. . . . Here, the burden-shifting framework does not reach this stage because Jackson has failed to establish a prima facie case.

To establish a prima facie case of discrimination, a plaintiff must show (1) membership in a protected class, (2) qualification for the employment, (3) an adverse employment decision, and (4) circumstances that give rise to an inference of discrimination. *McDonnell Douglas*, 411 U.S. at 802, 93 S. Ct. 1817. . . . Courts have acknowledged this framework is "not inflexible," but that "in establishing a prima facie case the plaintiff must show that [he] applied for an available position for which [he] was qualified, but was rejected under circumstances that give rise to an inference of discrimination." *Brown v. Coach Stores, Inc.*, 163 F.3d 706, 710 (2d Cir. 1998) (citing *Texas Dep't of Cmty. Affairs v. Burdine*, 450 U.S. 248, 253, 101 S. Ct. 1089, 67 L. Ed. 2d 207 (1981)) (internal quotation marks omitted).

The parties do not dispute that Jackson is a member of a protected class. Nor do they dispute that the defendants' decision to hire Rizzi instead of Jackson was adverse to him. However, the parties disagree as to whether Jackson meets the second prong of *McDonnell Douglas*: qualification for the position. In their Motion for Summary Judgment, the defendants assert that Jackson was not qualified because he failed to meet an express condition of the employment, that he did not have prior NCAA coaching experience. Although he maintains that he is qualified, Jackson does not dispute that prior collegiate coaching was an expressly listed qualification for the UNH head coach position, nor does he contend that he had any prior experience coaching in college. However, Jackson's subjective determination that he is qualified for the position is not enough to carry his burden of making out a prima facie case. The Second Circuit, in the context of an age discrimination suit, elaborated on the definition of the "qualification" requirement of the *McDonnell Douglas* prima facie case in *Thornley v. Penton Publ'g*, 104 F.3d 26 (2d Cir. 1997): "As we understand this element, being 'qualified' refers to the criteria the employer has specified for the position." 104 F.3d at 29. The Court further explained that broad deference should be

---

5. The *McDonnell Douglas* burden-shifting framework is only necessary when the plaintiff has failed to offer direct evidence of discriminatory intent. . . . Here, the plaintiff has not offered any evidence of discriminatory intent; thus, the *McDonnell Douglas* inquiry is appropriate.

afforded to employers in selecting hiring criteria: "Absent a showing by the plaintiff that the employer's demands were made in bad faith . . . an employer . . . is not compelled to submit the reasonableness of its employment criteria to the assessment of either judge or jury." *Id.* . . .

Consistent with this understanding, courts have afforded employers considerable latitude in selecting employment qualifications. For example, in *Schaffner v. Glencoe Park Dist.*, 256 F.3d 616 (7th Cir. 2001) the Seventh Circuit considered the "qualification prong" of the *McDonnell Douglas* burden-shifting framework in the context of an ADEA claim. 256 F.3d at 620. There the plaintiff was denied a promotion to the position of "program manager" for park recreational programs—a position that listed as one of its requirements one of several types of bachelor's degrees. The court held that the plaintiff failed to meet the qualification prong of the *McDonnell Douglas* test because she did not possess any of the specified degrees, and was therefore not qualified for the position.

. . . [D]eference must be given the defendants in selecting college coaching experience as a qualification for the position of head coach. Nor is it appropriate for this Court to mandate that the defendants equate Jackson's experience in coaching minor league football with college coaching experience. . . .

There are, however, limits to an employer's latitude in selecting hiring criteria. For example, in *Howley v. Town of Stratford*, 217 F.3d 141 (2d Cir. 2000) the Second Circuit rejected the defendant's argument that the plaintiff, a female firefighter, was "ineligible" for a promotion to assistant-chief because she did not have the required four years of line-officer experience. 217 F.3d at 151. The Court acknowledged that the town was "entitled to set its own criteria" for the position, but held that because the Town had "relaxed" that standard for two male firefighters, the plaintiff's lack of experience should not have resulted in summary judgment for the defendant. *Id.* at 151-52.

Here there is no claim, and Jackson has put forth no evidence, that the defendants failed to apply the prior college coaching experience requirement uniformly to African-Americans and others. Absent any such showing, the defendants are entitled to the deference in selecting hiring criteria recognized in *Thornley*. Moreover, the prior college coaching experience requirement at issue here appears reasonable on its face. There is an obvious and significant nexus between the defendants' need to select a head coach well-versed in NCAA regulations and the requirement that candidates have actual experience in college coaching. Thus, Jackson has failed to make out a prima facie case of disparate treatment in that he has failed to demonstrate that he was qualified for the position of head coach. As Jackson has failed to meet his burden, this Court grants summary judgment as to his disparate treatment claim brought pursuant to 42 U.S.C. §§1981, 2000d (Title VI), and 2000e-5 (Title VII).

B. DISPARATE IMPACT

Unlike disparate treatment, in asserting a claim of disparate impact under Title VII a plaintiff need not allege that the discrimination was intentional. *Griggs v. Duke Power Co.*, 401 U.S. 424, 430-32, 91 S. Ct. 849, 28 L. Ed. 2d 158 (1971) ("[G]ood intent or absence of discriminatory intent does not redeem employment procedures or testing mechanisms that operate as 'built in head winds'"). It is enough that a facially-neutral policy, such as the prior college coaching experience requirement at issue here, be shown to have an adverse impact on a protected group. . . .

However, unlike disparate treatment, the disparate impact theory of recovery is available only for claims brought pursuant to Title VII, and not for claims under 42 U.S.C. §1981 or §2000(d)(Title VI). The U.S. Supreme Court has held that these latter provisions can only be violated by intentional discrimination and that they therefore cannot support a "disparate impact" claim. *See Alexander v. Sandoval*, 532 U.S. 275, 280-85, 121 S.Ct. 1511, 149 L. Ed. 2d 517 (2001) (holding that §2000d (Title VI) proscribes only intentional discrimination and therefore does not support a disparate impact theory of recovery) (citing *Regents of Univ. of Cal. v. Bakke*, 438 U.S. 265, 98 S. Ct. 2733, 57 L.Ed.2d 750 (1978)). . . . *General Bldg. Contractors Ass'n v. Pennsylvania*, 458 U.S. 375, 391, 102 S. Ct. 3141, 73 L. Ed. 2d 835 (1982) (holding that §1981 is only violated by a showing of intentional discrimination). Thus, to the extent that Jackson alleges a disparate impact theory of recovery, his claim is cognizable only under Title VII.

Disparate impact cases, like disparate treatment cases, are governed by a "burden-shifting" framework. The Second Circuit reviewed the disparate impact burden-shifting framework in *NAACP, Inc. v. Town of East Haven*, 70 F.3d 219, 225 (2d Cir. 1995):

> "[A] plaintiff may establish a prima facie case of disparate impact by showing that use of the test causes the selection of applicants . . . in a racial pattern that significantly differs from that of the pool of applicants." Such a showing can be established through the use of statistical evidence which discloses a disparity so great that it cannot reasonably be attributed to chance. To establish a prima facie case, the statistical disparity must be sufficiently substantial to raise an inference of causation. After a prima facie case is established, the employer has the burden of coming forward with evidence to show that the test has "'a manifest relationship to the employment in question.'" If the employer can make such a showing, the plaintiff may nonetheless prevail if he can suggest alternative tests or selection methods that would meet the employer's legitimate needs while reducing the racially disparate impact of the employer's practices. [Citations omitted.]

Id. at 225. . . . As the Court noted in *East Haven*, this framework was statutorily enacted by the Civil Rights Act of 1991. *Id.* at 225 fn. 6. *See also* 42 U.S.C. §2000e-2(k).

Here, as in the disparate treatment context, Jackson has failed to meet his burden of setting forth a prima facie case of disparate treatment. In making out a prima facie case for disparate impact under Title VII, the plaintiff bears the burden of demonstrating that a specific policy or practice of the defendant has had a disproportionately negative impact on the plaintiff's protected class. 42 U.S.C. Section 2000e-2(k)(1)(A) . . . ;[7] *Griggs*, 401 U.S. at 432, 91 S. Ct. 849. "To make this showing, a plaintiff must (1) identify a policy or practice,

---

7. The 1991 Civil Rights Act sets forth the burden of proof required in disparate impact cases at 42 U.S.C. §2000e-2(k), which provides in relevant part:

(k) Burden of proof in disparate impact cases
  (1)(A) An unlawful employment practice based on disparate impact is established under this chapter only if—
    (i) a complaining party demonstrates that a respondent uses a particular employment practice that causes a disparate impact on the basis of race, color, religion, sex, or national origin and the respondent fails to demonstrate that the challenged practice is job related for the position in question and consistent with business necessity; or

(2) demonstrate that a disparity exists, and (3) establish a causal relationship between the two." *Robinson,* 267 F.3d at 160 (citing 42 U.S.C. §2000e-2(k)(1)(A)(I)). *See also Brown v. Coach Stores, Inc.,* 163 F.3d 706, 712 (2d Cir. 1998) ("plaintiff must show that a facially neutral employment policy or practice has a significant disparate impact"). Here, Jackson alleges that the defendants' facially neutral hiring criteria (requiring prior college coaching experience), had a discriminatory impact on African-Americans. Specifically, Jackson asserts that because African-Americans have historically been under-represented in the ranks of NCAA coaches this requirement disproportionately excludes African-Americans from consideration.

Statistics are often an important component of a disparate impact claim. *See Robinson,* 267 F.3d at 160 ("[S]tatistical proof almost always occupies center stage in a prima facie showing of a disparate impact claim"). . . .

The defendants here attack the sufficiency of the plaintiff's statistics. They argue that the plaintiff has not offered any statistical evidence to indicate a causal link between UNH's prior college coaching experience requirement and its negative impact on African-Americans. However, in its memorandum in opposition to the defendants' motion for summary judgment, Jackson does offer statistics suggesting a causal link between the prior experience requirement and its impact on African-Americans, by comparing the pool of applicants to those who were ultimately selected for interviews. Jackson notes that, of the 14 applicants whose race was identified, only 10% of the Caucasians (1 out of 10) did not have college coaching experience, but 50% of the African-American candidates (2 out of 4) did not have college coaching experience. Further, Jackson noted that all six of the applicants selected for interviews were Caucasian. However, this statistical evidence fails to establish a sufficient causal link between the defendants' employment criterion and its impact on African-Americans. The Second Circuit has recognized that exceedingly small sample sizes often result in statistically unreliable evidence. *Lowe v. Commack Union Free*

> (ii) the complaining party makes the demonstration described in subparagraph (C) with respect to an alternative employment practice and the respondent refuses to adopt such alternative employment practice. . . .
> (C) The demonstration referred to by subparagraph (A)(ii) shall be in accordance with the law as it existed on June 4, 1989, with respect to the concept of "alternative employment practice."

. . . Even when the disparate impact case is argued on the basis of 42 U.S.C. 2000e-2(k)(1)(A)(ii), the burden is still on the plaintiff to demonstrate that the challenged employment practice has an adverse impact on a protected group. In *Price v. City of Chicago,* 251 F.3d 656 (7th Cir. 2001), the Title VII plaintiff argued that the 1991 Amendments "eliminated the requirement that the challenged practice has a disparate impact" and that it was enough that "an alternative employment practice with a lesser adverse impact exists and that the employer has failed to adopt it." 251 F.3d at 659. The Seventh Circuit rejected this argument, reasoning that the 1991 Amendments merely provided that "a plaintiff's demonstration shall be in accordance with the law as it existed prior to the Supreme Court's decision in *Wards Cove Packing Co. v. Atonio,* 490 U.S. 642, 109 S. Ct. 2115, 104 L. Ed. 2d 733 (1989)." *Id.* at 660, 109 S.Ct. 2115. Case law prior to *Wards Cove,* the Court continued, "made it clear that an employer has no duty to justify its use of a particular employment practice *unless* the plaintiff establishes that the practice has a disparate impact." *Id.* (emphasis in original).

Sch. Dist., 886 F.2d 1364, 1371-72 (2d Cir. 1989) (holding that the fact that two out of three candidates under age 40 received favorable ratings while only 16 out of 34 candidates over age 40 received such ratings did not support a disparate impact claim in part because of "the unreliability of such a small statistical sample") (superceded by statute on other grounds). The Second Circuit has also indicated that a plaintiff's statistics must meet a certain threshold level of substantiality. . . . Here, the relevant sample size is only 14 (of the 36 applicants, the race of only 14 has been identified), which is too small to yield a statistically significant result.

In *Smith* [*v. Xerox Corp.*, 196 F.3d 358 (2d Cir. 1999)], the Second Circuit cautioned that in assessing whether a statistical disparity is "sufficiently substantial to establish a prima facie case of disparate impact, there is no one test that always answers that question." *Smith*, 196 F.3d at 366. "Instead," the Court reasoned, "the substantiality of a disparity is judged on a case-be-case basis." *Id.* (citing *Watson v. Fort Worth Bank & Trust*, 487 U.S. 977, 996 n. 3, 108 S. Ct. 2777, 101 L. Ed. 2d 827 (1988)). In this case, the plaintiff has failed to provide a sufficiently substantial disparity to survive summary judgment, because the sample is too small.

In addition to the statistics discussed above, the plaintiff has presented an article from the *Sports Business Journal*, which purportedly demonstrates the disparity of college football coaches that are African-American. However, this article—without more—does not present the type of substantial statistical evidence contemplated by the Second Circuit in *Smith*. It is only two pages long, and most of it is an opinion piece rather than a scientific statistical analysis. Even when the author does cite statistics, he does not disclose the basis for them or reveal their methodology. Also, the article fails to set forth the type of statistics that are appropriate in a disparate impact analysis. The only statistics in the article concern the percentages of coaches in the various NCAA divisions that are African-American. However, the essence of a disparate impact analysis is a *comparison*. In *Carter v. Ball*, 33 F.3d 450 (4th Cir. 1994) the plaintiff brought a Title VII discrimination suit against the Secretary of the Navy. The plaintiff in that case attempted to offer statistical evidence "which purportedly demonstrate[d] a statistical imbalance in the Navy's promotional practices." 33 F.3d at 456. The Fourth Circuit upheld the district court's exclusion of the statistical evidence. In so holding, the Court emphasized that "[i]n a case of discrimination in hiring or promoting, the relevant comparison is between the percentage of minority employees and the percentage of potential minority applicants in the qualified labor pool. . . . The mere absence of minority employees in upper-level positions does not suffice to prove a *prima facie* case of discrimination without a comparison to the relevant labor pool." *Id.* . . .[8]

---

8. The statistics offered by the plaintiff in *Carter* were in support of a disparate treatment claim, but the Court held that they would have been inadmissible in a disparate impact case for precisely the same reasons. The Court observed:

the test for a disparate impact claim requires (1) that there is an underrepresentation of the qualified members in a protected class promoted to the positions at issue and (2) that specific elements of the employer's promotion criteria had a significant disparate impact on a protected class. Without any evidence of how many African-Americans were qualified for positions at the level to which [the plaintiff] sought to be promoted, there can be no reliable proof of underrepresentation.

Carter, 33 F.3d at 457 fn. 9. [Citations and internal quotation marks omitted.]

Finally, also in support of his disparate impact claim, the plaintiff asserts that the use of the prior college coaching experience requirement has yielded discriminatory results when applied to other athletic programs at UNH. The plaintiff contends that only one out of 23 coaches hired since 1993, when the plaintiff asserts the prior college coaching experience requirement was adopted for most head coaching positions at UNH, has been African-American. However, even if true, the Supreme Court held in *Wards Cove* that "[t]he percentage of nonwhite workers found in other positions in the employer's labor force is irrelevant to the question of a prima facie statistical case of disparate impact." 490 U.S. at 653, 109 S. Ct. 2115. Thus, the plaintiff has failed to meet his burden of establishing a prima facie case of disparate impact, and this Court also grants summary judgment as to that claim.

For the forgoing reasons, the defendant's Motion for Summary Judgment . . . is GRANTED and the case is DISMISSED.

NOTES AND QUESTIONS

1. *Analyzing* Jackson. The plaintiff based his complaint on "disparate treatment" and "disparate impact" grounds. What is the difference between these arguments as a factual and a legal matter? Which argument do you believe is stronger? What was the court's response to each argument? How much latitude should a university be given in setting coaching experience and related requirements? If you were representing a university involved in such a search, what would you recommend as a legal and practical matter?

2. *Case Law.* The *Jackson* case is not anomalous. Plaintiffs bringing racial discrimination claims in the sports industry have generally encountered difficulty in convincing courts that their employment claims are meritorious. See, e.g., *Wilson v. Lock Haven Univ.*, 2012 WL 1130593 (3d Cir. 2012) (affirming lower court's summary judgment rejection of African-American coach's racial discrimination claim); *Moran v. Selig*, 447 F.3d 748 (9th Cir. 2006) (rejecting retired Caucasian and Latino professional baseball players' claims that Major League Baseball violated Title VII by excluding them from medical and supplemental income plans for former Negro League players, because "providing a remedy for past discrimination only to those who have been discriminated against does not constitute discriminatory conduct"); *Wallace v. Texas Tech Univ.*, 80 F.3d 1042 (5th Cir. 1996) (affirming summary judgment dismissal of Title VII and Section 1981 and 1983 claims brought by a former Texas Tech men's basketball assistant coach who alleged racial discrimination in retaliation for the exercise of his First Amendment right to advise African-American players regarding their eligibility for financial assistance and for having close, personal relationships with players); *Flowers v. Troup County, Ga. School Dist.*, 1 F. Supp. 3d 1363 (N.D. Ga. 2014) (rejecting an African-American football coach's race discrimination claims under Title VII, § 1981, § 1983, and the Equal Protection Clause because the coach did not show the school district's "proffered legitimate, nondiscriminatory reason for his termination was pretext for race discrimination"); *Moberly v. Univ. of Cincinnati Clermont College*, 2010 WL 3489029 (S.D. Ohio 2010) (rejecting racial discrimination and First Amendment claims of African-American coach who alleged he was not reappointed because of his complaints regarding discriminatory treatment of African-American players); *Cowan v. Unified Sch. Dist. 501*, 316 F. Supp. 2d

1061 (D. Kan. 2004) (even though plaintiff established prima facie Title VII claim, defendant presented nondiscriminatory reason for hiring white applicant—the successful applicant's qualifications—that was not pretext for racial discrimination against African-American candidate, given the similarities in the candidates' qualifications; however, inconsistencies in the reasons given by district for selecting candidates for interviews for another coaching position precluded summary judgment on whether reasons were pretext for race discrimination against plaintiff); but see *Banks v. Pocatella Sch. Dist. No. 25*, 429 F. Supp. 2d 1197 (D. Idaho 2006) (African-American coach applicant could proceed on Title VII claim since he presented evidence that school district's asserted reasons for hiring other applicants, plaintiff's alleged poor organizational and communication skills, were pretextual). For a "reverse discrimination" case in which a court found that a white coach's claim that the hiring of a black woman coach instead of him had alleged sufficient facts to establish a violation of Title VII, see *Jacobeit v. Rich Twp. High Sch. Dist. 227*, 673 F. Supp. 2d 653 (N.D. Ill. 2009).

Do the subjective considerations that are relevant in hiring a coach present a virtually insurmountable obstacle to an unsuccessful coaching applicant prevailing in a race discrimination action?

3. *Race-Related Health Complications.* After a 2007 game against the Denver Broncos, Pittsburgh Steelers safety Ryan Clark became life-threateningly ill, resulting in emergency surgery to remove both his gallbladder and spleen. Clark carries the trait for sickle cell anemia, a serious blood disorder that affects people of African descent. While sickle cell trait carriers are generally asymptomatic, in rare cases factors such as extreme athletic exertion and altitude can cause them to become ill. Doctors concluded that these factors (Denver is well above sea level) combined to precipitate Clark's crisis. In 2012, when the Steelers travelled to Denver to face the Broncos in a play-off game, Steelers head coach Mike Tomlin expressed concern about Clark's health and refused to let him play. Clark accepted the decision and had no sickle cell trait–related health problems during the remainder of his career. He acknowledged, though, that after the health crisis his contract negotiations were complicated by his condition. See Chika Duru, *Out for Blood: Employment Discrimination, Sickle Cell Trait, and the NFL*, 9 Hastings Race and Poverty L. J. 265 (2012). In the years since Clark's crisis, other sickle cell trait carrying NFL players have had to make difficult decisions regarding whether to play in games taking place at high elevations. See Mike Tanier, *Football's Silent Killer Forces Players and Teams to Make Tough Choices*, Bleacher Report, July 6, 2017, https://bleacherreport.com/articles/2716677-footballs-silent-killer-forces-players-and-teams-to-make-tough-choices.

If an NFL club developed a policy of disadvantaging sickle cell trait carriers in contract negotiations or completely refusing to hire players with sickle cell trait, might the club be vulnerable to a Title VII disparate impact racial discrimination lawsuit? It bears noting that a crisis like Clark's is extremely rare for a sickle cell trait carrier, and of the dozens of sickle cell trait carriers playing in the NFL, none have ever suffered such an episode. Do these facts change your view?

4. *Intersection of Race and Freedom of Expression.* Are African-American athletes and coaches expected to behave in a way that dilutes their racial identity? For example, African Americans have complained that white coaches and players are afforded much greater latitude to express themselves than their

African-American counterparts. According to this view, African-American athletes and coaches run the risk of incurring costly sanctions if they speak out on racially or politically sensitive issues. See Alfred D. Mathewson, *Grooming Crossovers*, 4 J. Gender Race & Just. 225 (2001) (discussing the role of black athletes in struggling for political, racial, and economic equity in sport). Such allegations lie at the core of two notable lawsuits filed by an African-American coach and player.

Nolan Richardson, an African American, was head coach of the University of Arkansas at Fayetteville's (UAF) men's basketball team from 1985 until he was fired in March 2002. *Richardson v. Sugg*, 325 F. Supp. 2d 919 (E.D. Ark. 2004). Richardson claimed that "he was fired because of his race and because he spoke out on [racial] matters of public concern. . . ." *Id.* at 922. In particular, Richardson alleged that his termination was in retaliation for making comments regarding (1) the difficulties of recruiting African Americans to UAF given Fayetteville's small black population and the social adjustment issues confronting African-American athletes in the Fayetteville community, and (2) the low graduation rates of the overwhelmingly African-American UAF men's basketball team. UAF denied the allegations and asserted that Richardson was fired because of statements he made indicating he had lost interest in the job, such as "[i]f they go ahead and pay me my money, they can take the job tomorrow." *Id.* at 937.

In assessing Richardson's First Amendment claim, the court explained that:

> To prove a violation of her or his First Amendment rights, a public employee must demonstrate that the speech in which he is engaged is protected speech. To establish this, he must show that the speech can be "fairly characterized as constituting a matter of public concern," and not a matter of private interest. Speech is a "matter of public interest or concern" when it touches upon "any matter of political, social or other concern to the community." Opposition to racial discrimination *is* a "matter of inherently public concern." (internal footnotes omitted).

Id. at 941-942.

Applying the foregoing standard, the court rejected Richardson's claim, finding that the comments regarding the social environment at UAF could not be regarded as attempts to raise the social consciousness of the public, or to challenge UAF for anything that it had either done or not done regarding the issue of race as it related to student athletes. Richardson appealed, and the Eight Circuit affirmed the district court's decision.

Free speech considerations lie at the core of the issues raised in *Hodges v. National Basketball Association*, 1998 WL 26183 (N.D. Ill. 1998) as well. There, Craig Hodges alleged that the NBA conspired to keep him out of basketball because he was "an outspoken African-American activist" who commented on political issues, particularly those involving the African-American community. *Id.* at *1. As framed by the court, Hodges asserted that "racial discrimination is at the root of the conspiracy, a conclusion supported by the fact that white players with backgrounds similar to his are free to express themselves politically without suffering any retaliation." *Id.* The court did not have an opportunity to address the merits of Hodges's claims. His suit was dismissed because it was not filed within the applicable two-year statute of limitations period.

A more recent matter that did not spark litigation but did prompt substantial nationwide debate involved a number of NFL and NBA players in the fall of 2014 publicly expressing outrage over the widely publicized deaths of African-American citizens Michael Brown and Eric Garner at the hands of white police officers. Several St. Louis Rams players held their hands up in a "Don't Shoot" pose while walking onto the field before a game in protest of Brown's shooting, and NBA stars including Derrick Rose and LeBron James wore t-shirts reading "I Can't Breathe" in protest of Garner's choking death. Although public opinion was divided, and some (including police groups) called on the Rams, the NFL, and the NBA to discipline the players involved, the club and the leagues did not do so, citing the players' right to express their opinions. Soraya Nadia McDonald, *When it comes to activism, athletes aren't the only ones changing, the leagues that employ them are, too,* Wash. Post, Dec. 9, 2014 /; *No Fines for Rams Players' Salute,* ESPN.com, Dec. 2, 2014, http://espn.go.com/nfl/story/_/id/11963218/the-five-st-louis-rams-players-saluted-slain-teenager-michael-brown-sunday-game-not-fined.

The issue of professional athlete activism exploded in 2016 when NFL quarterback Colin Kaepernick refused to stand for the national anthem before his team's games in protest of the same societal ills Lebron James, Derrick Rose, and others protested against in 2014. As discussed in Chapter 1, other NFL players joined the protest that season, and in 2017, even after Kaepernick was out of the league, many players continued to protest, sparking the ire of President Donald Trump and others who accused the players of being unpatriotic and demanded the players be disciplined. In May 2018, the NFL moved proactively to prevent protest during the 2018 season, enacting a rule requiring players to stand during the playing of the national anthem if they remain on the field; otherwise, the rule required that they stay in the locker room during the anthem or their team would be fined. Trump and Vice President Mike Pence predictably praised the rule, but many commentators skewered the NFL for bending to Trump's will. David Haugh, *NFL's New Anthem Rule Requiring Players to Stand Shows Owners Support Social Activism Only on Their Terms,* ChicagoTribune.com, May 23, 2018. On July 10, 2018, the NFLPA filed a non-injury grievance on behalf of all players against the NFL, arguing that the unilaterally imposed anthem rule is "inconsistent with the collective bargaining agreement and infringes on player rights." Chris Chavez, *NFLPA Files Grievance Over NFL's New National Anthem Policy,* Sports Illustrated, July 10, 2018. In response, the NFL agreed to not fine any team for its players' protests while the league works with the NFLPA on a resolution. Jenna West, *NFL, NFLPA Reach 'Standstill Agreement' Over National Anthem Policy,* SportsIllustrated.com, July 19, 2018, https://www.si.com/nfl/2018/07/19/national-anthem-policy-nfl-nflpa-statement.

Should the clubs and leagues have disciplined the players involved? When players become the subject of criticism, discipline or retaliation regarding racially related expressions that fail to conform to standards deemed acceptable by the majority, what are the acceptable parameters of those standards?

PROBLEM 9-2

Midwestern State University, a Division I-A football power that had fallen on hard times, advertised for a new head football coach. The ad indicated that previous football coaching experience was required. Several applicants applied, including Coach Ross, the head football coach at another college, who was also a friend and former colleague of Midwestern's athletic director, Shoemaker.

Ross, who had over 15 years of collegiate coaching experience, including 8 years as a head coach, applied after being persuaded by Shoemaker to do so. Ross and Shoemaker are both white.

A search committee, chaired by Shoemaker, reviewed numerous applications and invited two applicants for on-campus interviews. One applicant was Ross. The other was an African American, Coach Pegues, who had played college and professional football. Pegues coached at a Division I institution for four years, where he served first as running backs coach and then as wide receivers coach. From there Pegues moved to the NFL, where he coached for seven years for two teams. He served as the quarterbacks coach for the first team for two years. For the past five years, Pegues served as offensive coordinator of a highly regarded NFL team.

During the on-campus interviews, Ross and Pegues met with various constituencies, including football players, the search committee, a faculty committee, and athletic department personnel. Both received favorable responses from the groups with whom they met. However, the faculty, athletes, and athletic personnel stated that they preferred Pegues. During the deliberations of the search committee, Shoemaker stated, "Perhaps I shouldn't say this, but I have to be honest. I feel uneasy with Pegues. How do we know if he'll be outspoken like that Nolan Richardson? I'm also concerned with how the major donors to our football program will react to him. We wouldn't want to lose a major source of financial support by hiring this guy. It wouldn't be worth it." After vigorous debate, the search committee concluded that both candidates were qualified to serve as head football coach. The committee understood, however, that it served in an advisory capacity and the final decision rested with the athletic director, Shoemaker.

Shoemaker extended an offer to Ross, who declined. Shoemaker decided not to extend an offer to Pegues. In explaining why he did not, Shoemaker stated, "Pegues is highly qualified, and I wish him well. I simply don't think he is a good fit for our program."

Pegues has come to your office seeking advice on whether he should pursue an action for employment discrimination on account of race. How would you advise him?

3.   Stereotypes: Racially Stereotyped Mascots — Racism or Pride?

As the following case reveals, the use of Native American names and symbols has spawned considerable controversy and recent litigation.

BLACKHORSE v. PRO-FOOTBALL, INC.
112 F. Supp. 3d 439 (E.D. Va. 2015)

GERALD BRUCE LEE, District Judge.

BACKGROUND

The "Washington Redskins" are a well-known professional football team. The "Redskins" mark was first used by the "Washington Redskins" National Football League ("NFL") franchise in 1933 when then-owner George Preston Marshall selected the name while the team was located in Boston, Massachusetts. "Redskins" was chosen to distinguish the football team from the Boston Braves professional baseball team. . . . The team has used the name ever since. . . . The United States Patent and Trademark Office ("PTO") approved and registered the mark in 1967. . . . Five additional variations of "Redskins" trademarks were approved and registered between 1974 and 1990 (collectively "Redskins Marks"). The registrations of the Redskins Marks have been renewed repeatedly since 1967, with the most recent renewal occurring in 2015. . . . PFI owns, and has always owned, the Redskins Marks.

* * *

The registrability of the Redskins Marks has been litigated for over two decades. In 1992, Susan Harjo and six other Native Americans filed a petition to cancel the registrations of the Redskins Marks under Section 2(a) of the Lanham Act. Seven years later, the TTAB ruled that the Redskins Marks "may disparage" Native Americans when registered and ordered that the registrations of the marks be cancelled. *Harjo v. Pro-Football, Inc.,* 50 U.S.P.Q.2d 1705, 1999 WL 375907 (T.T.A.B. 1999). On appeal, the United States District Court for the District of Columbia reversed the TTAB, holding that (1) the TTAB's finding of disparagement was unsubstantiated, and (2) the doctrine of laches precluded consideration of the case.

The case traversed back and forth between the district court and the D.C. Circuit, with the final outcome being that D.C. Circuit affirmed the district court's ruling that laches barred the claim. *Pro-Football, Inc. v. Harjo,* 565 F.3d 880 (D.C. Cir. 2009). The D.C. Circuit never addressed the TTAB's finding of disparagement on the merits.

On August 11, 2006, while Harjo was pending, Amanda Blackhorse, Marcus Briggs Cloud, Phillip Cover, Jillian Pappan, and Courtney Tsotigh ("Blackhorse Defendants") filed a petition to cancel the same six registrations of the Redskins Marks. The TTAB suspended action in the Blackhorse case until the Harjo litigation concluded in 2009. The parties here have agreed that the entire Harjo record could be entered into evidence in the case before the TTAB. The parties also waived all non-relevance evidentiary objections to that evidence.

On June 18, 2014, the TTAB scheduled the cancellation of the registrations of the Redskins Marks under Section 2(a) of the Lanham Act, 15 U.S.C. § 1052(a), finding that at the time of their registrations the marks consisted of matter that both "may disparage" a substantial composite of Native Americans and bring them into contempt or disrepute. *See Blackhorse v. Pro-Football, Inc.,* 111 U.S.P.Q.2d 1080, 2014 WL 2757516 (T.T.A.B. 2014). This action seeks a de novo review, pursuant to 15 U.S.C. § 1071(b), of the TTAB's decision, based on the TTAB Blackhorse record and the additional evidence the parties have submitted to this Court.

In Count I, PFI seeks a declaration of non-disparagement. In Count II, PFI seeks a declaration of non-contempt or disrepute. . . .

PFI and Blackhorse Defendants filed cross-motions for summary judgment on PFI's Lanham Act . . . claim (Counts I, II . . .) (Docs. 69 & 79). Each motion is now before the Court.

ANALYSIS

* * *

C.   LANHAM ACT CHALLENGES

Section 2(a) of the Lanham Act, 15 U.S.C. § 1052(a), provides that registration should be denied to any mark that "[c]onsists of or comprises immoral, deceptive, or scandalous matter; or matter which may disparage or falsely suggest a connection with persons, living or dead, institutions, beliefs, or national symbols, or bring them into contempt or disrepute. . . ." *Id.* The TTAB has established a two-part test to determine whether a mark contains matter that "may disparage." The parties agree that the test in this case is as follows:

> 1. What is the meaning of the matter in question, as it appears in the marks and as those marks are used in connection with the goods and services identified in the registrations?
> 2. Is the meaning of the marks one that may disparage Native Americans? See *Blackhorse v. Pro-Football, Inc., 111 U.S.P.Q.2d 1080, 2014 WL 2757516, at *4 (T.T.A.B. @ 2014) (citations omitted). . . .*

This inquiry focuses on the registration dates of the marks at issue. *Blackhorse,* 2014 WL 2757516, at *4 (citations omitted). Here, the registration dates are 1967, 1974, 1978, and 1990.

When answering the second question, whether the term "redskins" "may disparage" Native Americans, courts should look to the views of Native Americans, not those of the general public. *Id.* Moreover, Blackhorse Defendants are only required to show that the marks "may disparage" a "substantial composite" of Native Americans. . . .

Courts consider dictionary evidence when determining whether a term "may disparage" a substantial composite of the referenced group. . . . Thus, using a dictionary's usage labels to determine whether a term "may disparage" a substantial composite of Native Americans during the relevant time period is consistent with the Federal Circuit's holding in Boulevard.

However, when dictionaries are not unanimous in their characterization of a term, additional evidence must be adduced to satisfy the PTO's burden. . . .

1.   The Meaning of the Matter in Question is a Reference to Native Americans

The Court finds that the meaning of the matter in question in all six Redskins Marks—the term "redskins" and derivatives thereof—is a reference to Native Americans. PFI admits that "redskins" refers to Native Americans. The team has consistently associated itself with Native American imagery. First, two of the Redskins Marks contain an image of a man in profile that alludes to Native Americans, including one that also has a spear that alludes to Native Americans. . . . Second, the team's football helmets contain an image of a Native American in profile. . . . Third, the team's marching band wore Native American headdresses as part of their uniforms from at least 1967-1990. . . . Fourth . . . the Redskins cheerleaders, the "Redskinettes" also dressed in Native American garb and wore stereotypical black braided-hair wigs. . . . Lastly, Washington Redskins' press guides displayed Native American imagery. . . .

As stated by the TTAB in *Harjo* and confirmed by the D.C. District Court:

> This is not a case where, through usage, the word "redskin(s)" has lost its meaning, in the field of professional football, as a reference to Native Americans in favor of an entirely independent meaning as the name of a professional football team. Rather, when considered in relation to the other matter comprising at least two of the subject marks and as used in connection with respondent's services, "Redskins" clearly both refers to respondent's professional football team and carries the allusion to Native Americans inherent in the original definition of that word.

Pro-Football, Inc. v. Harjo, 284 F. Supp. 2d 96, 127 (D.D.C. 2003) (quoting *Harjo v. Pro-Football, Inc.*, 50 U.S.P.Q.2d 1705, 1999 WL 375907, at *41 (T.T.A.B. 1999)). The Court agrees and finds that because PFI has made continuous efforts to associate its football team with Native Americans during the relevant time period, the meaning of the matter in question is a reference to Native Americans.

2.   *The Redskins Marks "May Disparage" a Substantial Composite of Native Americans During the Relevant Time Period*

The Court finds that the meaning of the marks is one that "may disparage" a substantial composite of Native Americans in the context of the "Washington Redskins" football team. The relevant period for the disparagement inquiry is the time at which the marks were registered. *Blackhorse*, 2014 WL 2757516, at *4 (citations omitted). Here, the Court focuses on the time period between 1967 and 1990. When reviewing whether a mark "may disparage," the PTO does not, and practically cannot, conduct a poll to determine the views of the referenced group. . . .

Furthermore, by using the term "may disparage," Section 2(a) does not require that the mark holder possess an intent to disparage in order to deny or cancel a registration. See *Harjo*, 284 F.Supp.2d at 125; *Blackhorse*, 2014 WL 2757516, at *9-*10 (citing Heeb Media, 2008 WL 5065114, at *8; *Squaw Valley*, 2006 WL 1546500). Also, in order to be cancelled or denied registration, the marks must consist of matter that "may disparage" in the context of the goods and services provided. . . .

a.   Dictionary Evidence

First, the record evidence contains dictionary definitions and accompanying designations of "redskins" that weigh in favor of finding that the Redskins Marks consisted of matter that "may disparage" a substantial composite of Native Americans when each of the six marks was registered. Dictionary evidence is commonly considered when deciding if a term is one that "may disparage." . . .

The record contains several dictionaries defining "redskins" as a term referring to North American Indians and characterizing "redskins" as offensive or contemptuous. [EDS. The court listed eleven dictionaries and their definitions of the term "redskins", including "Webster's Collegiate Dictionary 682 (1898) ("often contemptuous")" and "Collier's Dictionary (1986) ("considered offensive")".]

PFI attempts to rebut Blackhorse Defendants' dictionary evidence by arguing that (1) that the usage label evidence is not relevant because none of the usage labels use the word "disparage"; (2) the modifiers "usually" or "often" make the labels conditional and thus irrelevant under Section 2(a); (3) usage labels are chosen at the dictionary editor-in-chief's discretion with no industry standards for selection; and (4) many dictionaries considered "redskin" a neutral term and only began affixing negative usage labels to it within the last few decades. These arguments fail as they ignore the great weight the Federal Circuit affords to dictionary usage labels.

The Court finds that PFI's argument that dictionary usage labels such as "offensive" and "contemptuous" do not implicate Section 2(a) because they do not label the term "disparaging" is unpersuasive for two reasons. First, the Federal Circuit and the TTAB use "offensive" and "disparage" interchangeably when deciding whether a mark consists of matter that "may disparage. . . ." Furthermore, because the parties conceded that the test for "contempt or disrepute" under Section 2(a) is the same as the "may disparage" test, the distinction between "disparage" and "contemptuous" is one without a difference.

Second, the Court rejects PFI's argument that the modifiers on the usage labels made them conditional and thus irrelevant. In *In re Tinseltown, Inc.*, 212 U.S.P.Q. 863, 1981 WL 40474 (T.T.A.B. 1981), an applicant attempted to register the mark BULLSHIT for personal accessories. The Examiner relied on dictionaries unanimously characterizing the mark as "usu[ally] considered vulgar" to conclude that it consisted of scandalous matter under Section 2(a). . . . The TTAB affirmed the Examiner's decision. . . .

Moreover, the TTAB looks to dictionary definitions and usage labels when determining whether a mark "may disparage" under Section 2(a). See, e.g., *In re Lebanese Arak Corp.*, 94 U.S.P.Q.2d 1215, 2010 WL 766488, at *5 (T.T.A.B. 2010).

Furthermore, Dr. David Barnhart, one of PFI's linguistics experts, said that characterizing "redskins" as "disparaging" from 1967 to 1985 is too strong a term to apply. Criss Decl. Ex. 14 at 181:9-12. However, he did declare that in that same time period, the term "certainly might be offensive." *Id.* This weighs in favor of finding that "redskins" "may disparage" for two reasons. First, Dr. Barnhart stated that "disparage" required intent, Criss Decl. Ex. 14 at 181:13-182:3, and both parties agree that "may disparage," which is the standard posed by Section 2(a)—not does disparage—does not require intent. Second, as explained above, in Section 2(a) "may disparage" cases both the Federal Circuit and the TTAB use "disparage" and derivatives of "offend" interchangeably. . . .

b. Scholarly, Literary, and Media References

Second, the record evidence contains scholarly, literary, and media references that weigh in favor of finding that "redskins" "may disparage" a substantial composite of Native Americans when each of the six Redskins Marks was registered. Scholarly, literary, and media references evidence is often considered when evaluating whether a mark consists of or comprises matter that "may disparage." See *In re Geller*, 751 F.3d 1355, 1358 (Fed. Cir. 2014) (citing articles from the Chicago Tribune and the Courier News to show that associating Islam with terrorism "may disparage" Muslims); *In re Heeb Media*, LLC, 89 U.S.P.Q.2d 1071, 2008 WL 5065114, at *5 (T.T.A.B. 2008) (referencing an article in the New York Observer to demonstrate that "heeb" "may disparage" the Jewish community); *In re Squaw Valley Dev. Co.*, 80 U.S.P.Q.2d 1264, 2006 WL 1546500, at *10-*14 (T.T.A.B. 2006) (holding that the record evidence, including articles from more than ten newspapers and periodicals, sufficiently demonstrated that "squaw" "may disparage" Native Americans).

[EDS. The court cited to and quoted from 27 scholarly, literary, and media references of popular terms for Native Americans, such as Redskins. Two examples are: "Tom Quinn, Redskins/Rednecks, Wash. Daily News, Nov. 5, 1971 ("John Parker, . . . a Choctaw from Oklahoma who works for the Bureau of Indian Affairs, was indignant. 'They should change the name,' he said. 'It lacks dignity, a haphazard slang word that refers to Indians in general but on a lower scale. It is the white people's way of making a mockery, like they used to do to the blacks in the South.'). . . . Irving Lewis Allen, Unkind Words: Ethnic Labeling from Redskin to WASP 3, 18 (1990) (identifying "redskin" as a slur for Native Americans)".]

Here, based on the evidence presented in Geller, *Heeb Media*, and *Squaw Valley*, the Court finds that the scholarly, literary, and media references evidence weighs in favor of finding that the Redskins Marks consisted of matter that "may disparage" a substantial composite of Native Americans between 1967 and 1990. . . .

c. Statements of Individuals or Group Leaders

Third, the record evidence contains statements of Native American individuals or leaders of Native American groups that weigh in favor of finding that the Redskins Marks consisted of matter that "may disparage" a substantial composite of Native Americans during the relevant time period. The TTAB considers statements from individuals in the referenced group and leaders of organizations within that referenced group when it makes its "may disparage" finding. . . .

In support of their argument that prominent Native American organizations and leaders in the Native American community have long opposed the use of the term "redskins" as the name of an NFL football team name, Blackhorse Defendants have submitted several declarations. . . .

[EDS. The court identified numerous statements and declarations of Native American leaders and organizations between 1967 and 1990 affirming that the term "redskins may disparage a substantial composite of Native Americans. These include the following.]

Susan Harjo's declaration is also evidence of the disparaging nature of the "Washington Redskins" team name. Harjo was born in 1945 and is a citizen and enrolled member of the Cheyenne and Arapho Tribes of Oklahoma. . . . Growing up, Harjo and her family members often heard "redskin" being used as a slur. Harjo explained:

> In the 1950s, my brothers, cousins and Cheyenne friends were often called "redskins" by white children at school . . . and sometimes by their parents. On one especially upsetting and painful occasion, an elementary school teacher argued with me about our family history and the Battle of Little Big Horn, and he angrily called me names, including "redskin." He also slandered my great-great-grandfather, Chief Bull Bear, and called him a "redskin" and pushed me into a rosebush. I also remember shopkeepers calling me the epithet "redskin." Altogether, white people probably called me the slur "redskin," or called the group I was with "redskins," at least 100 times.

Id. ¶ 5. . . .

Lastly, Harjo noted that she has always regarded "redskin" as a racial slur and deems it "the most awful slur that can be used to refer to Native American nations, tribes, and persons." *Id.* ¶ 19.

The Court finds that the declarations from these prominent Native American individuals and leaders, replete with the actions of groups concerning the "Washington Redskins" football team and anecdotes of personal experiences with the term "redskin," show that the Redskins Marks consisted of matter that "may disparage" a substantial composite of Native Americans during the relevant time period. . . .

Throughout PFI's briefs it appears to suggest that the evidence of the 1972 meeting with former-PFI president Williams, NCAI's 1993 resolution on the team name, and any other evidence of Native American opposition is immaterial because "mainstream Native Americans" support the team name "Washington Redskins." Respondents in *In re Heeb Media, LLC.*, 89 U.S.P.Q.2d 1071, 2008 WL 5065114 (T.T.A.B. 2008), and *In re Squaw Valley Dev. Co.*, 80 U.S.P.Q.2d 1264, 2006 WL 1546500 (T.T.A.B. 2006), also tried to dismiss the views of those finding a term offensive as out of the mainstream. The TTAB rejected this argument both times. The Court agrees with the TTAB's approach and similarly rejects PFI's attempted characterization of some of Blackhorse Defendants' witnesses and their respective testimony. That a "substantial composite" is not necessarily a majority further compels this result. Assuming the Court accepted PFI's proffered dichotomy of "mainstream" versus "avant-garde" members of a referenced group, as a matter of principle it is indisputable that those with "non-mainstream" views on whether a term is disparaging can certainly constitute a substantial composite of a referenced group. The Court finds that to be the case here.

PFI sought to rebut Blackhorse Defendants' evidence multiple ways. First, PFI relies upon the 1977 All-Indian Half-Time Marching Band and Pageant and Native Americans naming their own sports teams "Redskins" to argue that the term is not disparaging. (Doc. 100 at 37.) Hundreds of Native Americans participated in the half-time program and several-hundred more applied but were ultimately not able to partake in the event. (*Id.*) PFI contends that the "positive tone" of the Native American press reports on the event, among other things, shows that the mark did not consist of matter that "may disparage" a substantial composite Native Americans during the relevant time period. (*Id.*) Additionally, PFI maintains that Native Americans' own extensive use of the term "Redskins" for different nicknames and the names of over twenty local sports teams precludes it from being considered as a term that "may disparage."

The Court finds these arguments unpersuasive because this evidence does not show that a there is not a substantial composite of Native Americans who find the matter was one that "may disparage. . . ."

Accordingly, the Court finds that the record evidence of statements from Native American leaders and groups weighs in favor of finding that between 1967 and 1990, the Redskins Marks consisted of matter that "may disparage" a substantial composite of Native Americans.

Through Section 2(a) of the Lanham Act, 15 U.S.C. § 1052(a), Congress has made a judgment that the federal trademark registration program will not register marks that "may disparage" different groups. A denial or cancellation of registration simply signifies that because a mark does not meet the requirements of the federal trademark registration program, the mark owner will not be able "to call upon the resources of the federal government in order to enforce that mark." In re Fox, 702 F.3d 633, 640 (Fed. Cir. 2012).

The determination of whether a substantial composite of the referenced group believes that a mark consists of a term that "may disparage" is not a mathematical equation requiring the parties to argue over whether the evidence shows that a specific threshold was met. . . . Instead, courts consider (1) dictionary definitions and accompanying editorial designations; (2) scholarly, literary, and media references; and (3) statements of individuals or group leaders of the referenced group on the term.

Here, the Court finds that the record contains evidence in all three categories demonstrating that between 1967 and 1990, the Redskins Marks consisted of matter that "may disparage" a substantial composite of Native Americans. The dictionary evidence included multiple definitions describing the term "redskin" in a negative light, including one from 1898— almost seventy years prior to the registration of the first Redskins Mark—characterizing "redskin" as "often contemptuous." The record evidence also includes references in renowned scholarly journals and books showing that "redskin" was offensive prior to 1967. Encyclopedia Britannica described its poor repute in 1911. The record evidence also shows that in 1972 NCAI, a national Native American organization founded in 1944, sent its president to accompany leaders of other Native American organizations at a meeting with the president of PFI to demand that the team's named be changed. NCAI also passed a resolution which provided that it has always found the term and team name "Redskins" to be derogatory, offensive, and disparaging.

* * *

This remains true even when there is also dictionary evidence that does not characterize the term as offensive, literary references using the term in a non-disparaging fashion, and statements from members of the referenced group demonstrating that they do not think the mark consists of matter that "may disparage." That is because Section 2(a) does not require a finding that every member of the referenced group thinks that the matter "may disparage." Nor does it mandate a showing that a majority of the referenced group considers the mark one that consists of matter that "may disparage." Instead, Section 2(a) allows for the denial or cancellation of a registration of any mark that consists of or comprises matter that "may disparage" a substantial composite of the referenced group.

The Court finds that Blackhorse Defendants have shown by a preponderance of the evidence that there is no genuine issue of material fact as to the "may disparage" claim: the record evidence shows that the term "redskin," in the context of Native Americans and during the relevant time period, was offensive and one that "may disparage" a substantial composite of Native Americans, "no matter what the goods or services with which the mark is used." *In re Squaw Valley Dev. Co.*, 80 U.S.P.Q.2d 1264, 2006 WL 1546500, at *16 (T.T.A.B. 2006). "Redskin" certainly retains this meaning when used in connection with PFI's football team; a team that has always associated itself with Native American imagery, with nothing being more emblematic of this association than the use of a Native American profile on the helmets of each member of the football team.

Accordingly, the Court finds that the Redskins Marks consisted of matter that "may disparage" a substantial composite of Native Americans during the relevant time period, 1967-1990, and must be cancelled. Also, consistent with the parties' concession that Section 2(a)'s "may disparage" and "contempt or disrepute" provisions use the same legal analysis, the Court further finds that the Redskins Marks consisted of matter that bring Native Americans into "contempt or disrepute." Thus, Blackhorse Defendants are entitled to summary judgment on Count[s I and II]. . . .

Also, the standard of review here is different than the standard in *Harjo*. In *Harjo*, the court applied the APA's "substantial evidence" standard: "the Court will reverse the TTAB's findings of fact only if they are 'unsupported by substantial evidence." *Harjo*, 284 F. Supp. 2d at 114 (citing 5 U.S.C. § 706). In *Harjo*, the TTAB made only limited findings of fact in two areas: linguists' testimony and survey evidence. *Harjo*, 284 F. Supp. 2d at 119. Thus, it was only those two areas that were subjected to court scrutiny under the substantial evidence standard. See *id.* Here, the TTAB made 39 findings of fact in two areas: "General Analysis of the Word" and "Native American Objection to Use of the Word Redskins for Football Teams." *Blackhorse*, 2014 WL 2757516, at *25-*28. Moreover, because the TTAB review in this case was brought pursuant to 15 U.S.C. § 1071(b), the Court reviews the entire record de novo—the Court is not restricted to only reviewing the TTAB's findings of fact like the district court in *Harjo*. Even if that was true, the TTAB's findings of fact in Blackhorse were more thorough than the findings of fact in *Harjo*.

NOTES AND QUESTIONS

1. Pro-Football, Inc. appealed the district court's ruling. While the appeal was pending, however, the Supreme Court decided a separate but similar case, *Matal v. Tam*, 137 S.Ct. 1744 (2017), which essentially rendered the *Blackhorse* case moot. The *Tam* case involved a band that sought to trademark

its name— The Slants— but was rejected, as the term "slant" was deemed potentially to disparage Asians. Simon Tam, the band's leader, did not deny that "slant" had traditionally been used as a racial slur, but he said he chose the name to reclaim the word. The Supreme Court determined that the trademark should be allowed, declaring that the Lanham Act provision disallowing terms or phrases that "may disparage" persons of a particular background from receiving federal trademark protection is a First Amendment free speech violation. *Matal v. Tam*, 137 S.Ct. 1744, 1765 (2017). The *Blackhorse* plaintiffs, whose claim relied on that very Lanham Act provision, shortly thereafter abandoned their lawsuit, giving Pro Football Inc. the victory. See Ian Shapiro and Ann E. Marimow, *Washington Redskins win trademark fight over the team's name*, The Washington Post, June 29, 2017. Several months later, in *In re: Brunetti*, the United States Court of Appeals for the Federal Circuit found that the Act's prohibition on trademarks involving "immoral" and "scandalous" terms was, like its prohibition on trademarks involving disparaging terms, "improper content-based restriction on free speech." *In re: Brunetti*, 877 F.3d 1330, 1342 (Fed. Cir. 2017). For more on the *Matal* case, *In re: Brunetti*, and the First Amendment's application to the Lanham Act, see Mark Conrad, *Matal v. Tam— A Victory for the Slants, A Touchdown for the Redskins, But an Ambiguous Journey for the First Amendment and Trademark Law*, 36 Cardozo Arts & Ent. L.J. 83 (2018).

Opponents of the use of Native American names and mascots argue that the symbols are disparaging to Native Americans. Proponents argue that such symbols honor Native Americans. Should it matter that an entity that uses a Native American name or symbol seemingly does so with dignity? What does the *Blackhorse* court say in this regard? For differing perspectives on the *Blackhorse* decision and the use of Native American mascots, see Ingrid Messbauer, *Beyond "Redskins": A Source-Based Framework for Analyzing Disparaging Trademarks and Native American Sports Logos*, 25 Fed. Circuit B.J. 241 (2016); Julie A. Hopkins & Thomas M. Joraanstad, *Challenge-Flag Thrown: The Trademark Trial and Appeal Board's Cancellation of the Redskins' Trademarks and Pro-Football's Chances on Appeal*, 10 J. Bus. & Tech. L. 267 (2015). For earlier discussions of the use of Native American mascots, see Justin P. Grose, *Time to Bury the Tomahawk Chop: An Attempt to Reconcile the Differing Viewpoints of Native Americans and Sports Fans*, 35 Am. Indian L. Rev. 695, 696 (2011); J. Gordon Hylton, *Before the Redskins Were the Redskins: The Use of Native American Team Names in the Formative Era of American Sports, 1857-1933*, 86 N.D. L. Rev. 879 (2010).

2. Does the University of Notre Dame's use of the "Fighting Irish" name and Leprechaun mascot raise the same issues as a school's use of Native Americans as mascots? Why? Why not?

3. *Contrasting Views.* Should it matter if a majority of the members of the general population or of Native Americans find the use of such names and symbols inoffensive?

Consider a 2016 Washington Post survey of Native American attitudes toward the use of Native American mascots. Cox, Clement, and Vargas, *New Poll Finds 9 in 10 Native Americans Aren't Offended by Redskins Name*, Washington Post, May 19, 2016, The survey of 504 Native Americans across the United States found that nine out of ten are not offended by the use of Native American mascots and eight out of ten did not find the term "redskins" to be disrespectful. Notably, some Native Americans and Native American leaders rejected the survey results. *Id.* They questioned the results because of the small sample size—504 Native Americans—and because many of those surveyed are not registered members of tribes and do not live on reservations, suggesting, in the view of these critics, that they are removed from the "true" Native American experience. Assume, *arguendo*, that the survey results do, in fact, accurately reflect the perspectives of the majority of Native Americans. Would that impact your view on the propriety of Native American mascots in high school, college, and professional sports?

4. *Declining Use of Native American Mascots.* Although both the *Blackhorse* case and the *Harjo* case that preceded it were ultimately unsuccessful in court, they—along with other litigation and grassroots efforts over the past several decades—have sparked substantial resistance to the use of Native American names and mascots. Indeed, one report indicates that 1,229 schools had discontinued the use of Native American mascots as of April 2019.[24] And in May 2019, Maine became the first U.S. state to ban the use of Native American mascots in all of its public educational institutions.

Although the NCAA does not prohibit the use of Native American mascots, it does have a policy that "prohibits NCAA colleges and universities from displaying hostile and abusive racial/ethnic/national origin mascots, nicknames or imagery at any of the 88 NCAA championships." Gary T. Brown, *Policy Applies Core Principles to Mascot Issue*, 42 NCAA News, 1, 19, Aug. 15, 2005. This restriction has three components. First, any institution that hosts an NCAA championship competition must cover up any and all offensive references at the site of the competition. Second, institutions can no longer have offensive references on "team mascots, cheerleaders, dance teams, [or] band uniforms" exhibited at NCAA championships. Lastly, institutions with offensive references on their competitive uniforms are prohibited from wearing or displaying them at NCAA-sponsored championships.

The policy allows institutions to appeal the categorization of their school as one "whose mascots are considered hostile or abusive." *Id.* In enacting this exception, the NCAA stated that it would find compelling any evidence that a namesake tribe approved of or supported the institution's use of the name, mascot, and imagery. Several institutions, including Florida State University, Central Michigan University, and the University of Utah, established to the satisfaction of the NCAA's Executive Committee that their use of a Native American name, mascot, or symbol was inoffensive. Others such as the University of North Dakota (UND) had their appeals rejected. In each instance in which the NCAA accepted an appeal, the institution had support from a Native American tribe or tribes, such as the Seminole Tribe of Florida and the Seminole Nation of Oklahoma, which both supported Florida State's appeal. In contrast, two Sioux tribes expressed opposition to UND's use of the name "Fighting Sioux." *Id.*

The NCAA's decision in regard to UND spawned legislative action and litigation. See e.g., *Spirit Lake Tribe of Indians v. NCAA*, 75 F.3d 1089 (2013). In 2012, the citizens of North Dakota overwhelmingly voted to abolish the "Fighting Sioux" mascot. See Levi Rickert, *North Dakotans Vote to Get Rid of "Fighting Sioux" Mascot by a 2 to 1 Margin*, Native News Network, June 13,

24. *Native American Mascots*, MascotDB, https://www.mascotdb.com/reports/blackistone (last visited June 14, 2019).

2012, http://www.nativenewsnetwork.com/north-dakotans-vote-to-get-rid-of-fighting-sioux-mascot-by-2-to-1-margin.html. In June 2016, UND revealed its new logo and name, the Fighting Hawks.

The United States governing body for Lacrosse, a game invented by Native Americans, has taken the strongest stance to date in any major U.S. sport with respect to Native American names and mascots. In 2019, US Lacrosse released a statement reading: "While some people contend these mascots are harmless and are even respectful of indigenous communities, the reality is that they represent the continued dehumanization of Native peoples." The statement went on to announce that it would ban the use of "offensive or stereotypical mascots and logos at events that US Lacrosse controls." Paul Ohanian, *US Lacrosse Position Statement on Native American Mascots*, US Lacrosse, Feb. 7, 2019, https://www.uslacrosse.org/blog/us-lacrosse-position-statement-on-native-american-mascots.None of America's major professional sports leagues has moved to ban or limit the use of Native American mascots, but individual clubs have made the decision to sunset logos and images that depict Native Americans in offensive ways. Most notably, the Cleveland Indians— while maintaining the name of their club— have shelved their "Chief Wahoo" logo, which shows the bright red face of a caricatured figure with a large feather in its hair, an oversized nose, and an exaggerated toothy smile. The club removed the logo from its uniforms as of the 2019 season after pressure from Canadian activists who protested the Indians' use of the logo when playing in Toronto against the Blue Jays and from MLB Commissioner Rob Manfred who deems the logo "no longer appropriate for on-field use." Jordan Bastian, *Indians to stop using Wahoo logo starting in '19*, MLB.com, Jan. 29, 2018; Jacob Bogage, *The Indians' season is over— and so is Chief Wahoo's 71-year run*, Chicago Tribune, Oct. 9, 2018.../../../../AppData/Local/Microsoft/Windows/INetCache/Downloads/, https:/www.chicagotribune.com/sports/ct-spt-indians-chief-wahoo-20181009-story.htmlFor a case implicating the free speech rights of those protesting the use of a Native American mascot on a college campus see, *Crue v. Akin*, 370 F.3d 668 (7th Cir. 2004). For analysis of *Crue*, and the NCAA's mascot policy, see Glenn George, *Playing Cowboy and Indians*, 6 Va. Sports & Ent. L.J. 90 (2006); Timothy M. Keegan, *Harsh Reality: The Prior Restraint Doctrine and the Free Speech Rights of Employees of Public Colleges and Universities*, 33 J.C. & U.L. 625, 627 (2007).

PROBLEM 9-3

In 2015, Donor gave $10 million to University. In 2019, Donor pledged another $50 million to University to be used for the construction of a new state-of-the-art hockey facility for the school and to possibly fund another program. Well into the construction of the facility, controversy erupted concerning whether University should change its nickname, the "Battling Cherokee," and its logo, a majestic Indian head that was designed three years ago by a highly regarded Native American artist. University is one of the country's leading schools in Native American studies and graduates an estimated 25 percent of the Native American doctors in the United States. The controversy arose when a group of white and Native American students and nonstudents protested the nickname and logo. The controversy was only heightened after Donor entered the fray. Donor threatened to halt construction if the school did not retain the name and logo. As legal counsel for University, how would you advise University to proceed? Are there ethical issues to consider?

4. Racially Hostile Environments and Conduct

As noted earlier in this chapter, racial abuse of players by spectators is a frequent occurrence at European soccer matches. Although such abuse is less common than it once was at athletic contests in the United States, it still occurs. Consider the following problem — based loosely on the experience of a former Miami Dolphins football player — as well as the questions and commentary below.

PROBLEM 9-4

A highly paid and very talented African-American NFL running back, Jerome Crawford, had a reputation for being outspoken on what he believed were racial inequities within American society. This resulted in conflicts between Crawford and his teammates and management. During an away game, Crawford was subjected to verbal abuse from fans. Although most of the fans' statements were not racially based, a few were. The latter included threats, such as "we will kill you," and display of a dummy in blackface with Crawford's number on it. The player reacted by directing an obscene gesture toward the fans. Because of his response, the player was fined $10,000 by the NFL for a lack of professionalism. The player refused to play until the league and individual teams implemented measures to protect African-American and other minority football players from racially motivated abuse by fans. You are general counsel for the team on which Crawford plays. What advice should you give to team management as to how it should respond to Crawford's refusal to perform?

Problem 9-4 illustrates what Professor Phoebe Williams characterizes in her seminal article on the topic — *Performing in Racially Hostile Environments* — as the overlooked issue of racially hostile environments created by fans. Phoebe Williams, *Racially Hostile Environments*, 6 Marq. Sports L.J. 287, 289 (1996). Several issues emerge when examining fan-based racial animus against athletes, including the following:

a. In the professional sports setting, to what extent do leagues and teams owe a responsibility to athletes to address racial harassment?
b. With respect to Problem 9-4, assume that the fans' conduct toward Crawford was not overtly racist. Also assume that Crawford was not outspoken on societal matters but was simply having a season in which he had severely underperformed. To what extent might fan criticism of athletes be race-based even though it is not accompanied by obviously racist conduct? Are black athletes, particularly those who are highly paid, subjected to a double standard as it relates to their on-the-field performance? On the other hand, are athletes of color overly sensitive to harsh criticism of fans? Are athletes of color too quick to assume that criticism of them is motivated in part by racial attitudes?

Consider a 2019 incident in which Shane Keisel, a white Utah Jazz basketball fan sitting close to the court at a game in Utah's home arena, told the Oklahoma City Thunder's Russell Westbrook, who is African American, to "get down on [his] knees like [he] used to." Westbrook interpreted the comments as racially motivated (in suggesting African-American subservience) and threatened violence upon Keisel and his wife. Keisel acknowledged heckling Westbrook but denied any racial intent. Within days, the Jazz permanently banned Keisel from its home arena, and the NBA fined Westbrook $25,000 for threatening violence. See Matt Stevens and Kevin Draper, *Russell Westbrook Says Utah Jazz Fan Made 'Racial' Taunt That Led to Confrontation*, N.Y. Times, Mar. 12, 2019. Westbrook's threat was inexcusable, but was his anger reasonable? Might such harassment — even if clearly racially motivated — be justified as a tool calculated to throw off a player's game? Should leagues and sports regulatory bodies view racial taunts differently than despicable nonracial comments made about a player or a player's family member? If so, what reasonable reaction should leagues and teams expect of athletes who are on the receiving end of overtly racial statements and conduct? Professor Williams argues that when confronted with racial hostility "African-American athletes are expected to endure and defer to racially hostile environments without protest." Williams, *supra,* at 308. Professor Williams adds that "standards of professionalism become a metaphor for condoning unlawful racist activity." *Id.* According to Williams, the prevailing attitude is that it becomes the obligation of the athlete as a professional not to lose control. Consequently, professionalism shifts responsibility "for providing an environment free of racial harassment from the employer to the athlete player." *Id.* at 311.

c. Should team owners and league administrators hold fans accountable for racial abuse stemming from activity during a game but expressed through social media outlets such as Twitter or Instagram? During the 2012 NHL playoffs, the Washington Capitals Joel Ward, one of the NHL's few black players, scored a Game 7 overtime goal to propel the Capitals past the Boston Bruins and into the Eastern Conference Semifinals. A "racist tweet storm" followed in which Ward was menacingly threatened and derided by Bruins fans. See Cindy Boren, *Racist Tweet Storm About Joel Ward Prompted by Bruins' Loss to Capitals,* Wash. Post, April 26, 2012. The next day Ted Leonsis, the Capitals' owner, issued the following statement:

> Shame on these folks who decided to take to their keyboards and show their ignorance and their racism and hate. What these people have said and done is unforgivable. I hope they are now publicly identified and pay a huge price for their beliefs. There should be zero tolerance for this kind of hate mongering.

If those who tweeted the racial abuse are publicly identified, should part of the "huge price" Ted Leonsis calls for include league-enforced discipline, such as a prohibition on attending future NHL games?

d. *Youth and High School Context.* Racial abuse of athletes is not limited to the professional, or even collegiate, context. During the fall of 2018 numerous high school football games in various parts of the country were marred by racist taunts. For instance:

(A) In California, a team from a largely Latino school playing an away game was greeted with signs reading "We Love White" and "Build That Wall."

    (B) In Ohio, fans threw bananas at the opposing team, which was composed largely of African-American players, and one fan was dressed as a banana.

    (C) In Georgia, at halftime of a game, one school's marching band spelled out the racial epithet "coon" as a part of its performance.

    (D) In Kentucky, fans taunted the opposing, predominantly African-American, team with a mashed watermelon.

Jason Jordan, *HS football players nationwide respond to racist incidents at games*, USAToday.com, Nov. 13, 2018. The racial targeting of Native Americans in high school sports has been on the rise as well, with Native students hearing comments such as "prairie nigger," "wagon burners," and "dirty Indians." Kalen Goodluck, *Native American athletes and fans face ongoing racism*, High Country News, Apr. 10, 2019, https://www.hcn.org/issues/51.7/tribal-affairs-native-american-athletes-and-fans-face-ongoing-racism. Should the racial abuse of high school athletes be treated differently than such abuse of adult athletes?

How about the racial abuse of elementary school age athletes? In 2018, *The Guardian* published an article on the plight of Juniors FC, a soccer team based in Boise, Idaho, composed of eight- and nine-year-old players, most of whom are of color. The team's coach explained that his players have endured being referenced as "niggers" and "wetbacks" and have taken the field while adults have said things such as "here come the future convicts" and "watch out for your wallets." Tim Froh, *Anonymous letters and threats: How racism came to stalk US youth soccer*, The Guardian, Feb. 15, 2018. How should youth sports governing bodies address such conduct?

The problem is just as profound when the racially hostile sports environment emanates not from fans but from teammates, management, opposing players, or some combination thereof. In *Priester*, a teammate is the source of the racial hostility. Nevertheless, similar issues emerge, including the legal duty of institutions to stymie racially motivated conduct against athletes of color and the adequacy of the law to address racial hostility in sport.

PRIESTER v. LOWNDES COUNTY

354 F.3d 414 (5th Cir. 2004)

STEWART, Circuit Judge.

FACTUAL AND PROCEDURAL BACKGROUND. . . .

On September 14, 1999, Terry, an African-American tenth-grade student at New Hope High School, sustained a serious eye injury during football practice allegedly caused by a white teammate Eli Ward ("Ward"). Leading up to the injury, Ward slapped Terry on the back of the head and derided him in the locker room and during warm-up drills on matters such as his weight and race. On previous occasions, the head football coach Rick Cahalane ("Cahalane") subjected

Terry to numerous racial epithets and derogatory comments concerning his weight.[2] After hearing such comments from Cahalane, Ward used the same derogatory terms toward Terry. The day of the injury, Ward also approached Terry and, without provocation, hit him on the helmet with a rock. Terry was also hit in a similar manner by another fellow player. Cahalane allegedly heard the statements and witnessed the assaults, but he did nothing to protect Terry or take the necessary actions that could stop or prevent the recurrence of the incident. Terry's mother witnessed these events and immediately informed the high school principal, who said he would handle the problem in the morning.

In the midst of a full-contact drill during football practice, the injury occurred subsequent to Terry's successful block of Ward. In response, Cahalane walked over to Ward to "get on to him" about the previous play. While Cahalane and Ward talked, Ward apparently looked at Terry throughout the conversation. Immediately following the conversation, Ward told Terry that he "had something for him." On the next play from scrimmage, Terry alleges that Ward lunged toward him, thrust his hands through his helmet, and gouged his eye. Terry's injury resulted in permanent damage including a torn right lower eyelid, a laceration to his lower punctum and caniliculus (tear duct), chronic tearing, and blurry vision. The school's response was two-fold. First, upon interviewing the coaches and players, New Hope High School principal Mike Halford compiled a report of the incident. In the report, however, no one admitted seeing anyone hit Terry. Second, the school declined to pay Terry's medical bills.

On January 8th, 2001, Eve Priester, individually and as the next friend of her son Terry Priester, pursuant to section 1983, filed suit in federal district court. . . . Priester alleged an agreement between Ward and the coaches to deprive her son of his rights under the Due Process and Equal Protection Clauses of the U.S. Constitution's Fourteenth Amendment.[4] Additionally, she alleged state-law claims of negligence and intentional torts resulting in emotional distress and physical injury.

On February 2, 2001, Priester amended her complaint to include Ward as a defendant, alleging that Ward, motivated by racial animus, subjected Priester to physical and verbal assaults. Ward moved for a Rule 56 summary judgment to dismiss the claim. On August 15, 2001, Ward was dismissed as a defendant by order of the district court because he was not a state actor under Section 1983 and the one-year statute of limitations tolled on September 14, 2000, for the applicable Mississippi tort.

The remaining defendants moved for summary judgment arguing, *inter alia*, that Priester failed to allege any state action to support her section 1983 claim. The district court granted the defendants' motion finding no requisite fair attribution or special relationship between the school and Priester, and thus, an absence of state action to support a section 1983 claim. The district court dismissed the remaining state law claims without prejudice. Priester timely filed a notice of appeal. . . .

---

2. The record shows that Terry Priester was subjected to such derogatory terms as "nigger" and "fat black ass."

4. Although the district court did not construe Eve Priester's complaint as asserting an equal protection claim, she raises this issue on appeal, arguing that New Hope High School did not pay for her son's medical expenses nor did the school respond to their complaints of racial harassment.

DISCUSSION

I.   DISMISSAL OF WARD PURSUANT TO STATE STATUTE OF LIMITATIONS

On appeal, Priester contends that the district court erred in dismissing the former defendant Ward under the one-year statute of limitations for an intentional tort, rather than a theory of negligence. Specifically, Priester argues that the three-year statute of limitations should apply, instead of a one-year statute of limitations, because of both the civil rights nature of this case and the policy of not allowing states to circumvent section 1983 by adopting shorter statute of limitations standards. A close scrutiny of the record, however, reveals that Priester has misconstrued the district court's opinion dismissing the claims stemming from Ward's actions. The district court dismissed Ward as a defendant on two theories; the intentional tort claims were dismissed pursuant to the one-year statute of limitations, while the section 1983 claims were dismissed for lack of state action.

A.   *Intentional Tort Claims*

We find that the district court correctly construed Priester's amended complaint as stating a claim under an intentional tort theory rather than a negligence theory. Priester's complaint states that Ward's alleged actions, "Ward put both of his hands through Priester's helmet and planted his finger in Terry Priester's eye and pulled it as hard as he could," are in the form of an intentional tort rather than negligence. Under the applicable state statute, intentional torts have a one-year statute of limitations period. Thus, the district court correctly found that Priester's claim stated an intentional tort, and that the applicable statute of limitations had run because the amended complaint was filed on February 2, 2001, well over a year from September 14, 1999, the date upon which the alleged injuries occurred during football practice.

B.   *Section 1983 Claims*

To state a cause of action under section 1983 the appellant must allege that the person who deprived him of a federal right was acting under color of law. *Cinel v. Connick*, 15 F.3d 1338, 1342 (5th Cir. 1994). For a private citizen, such as Ward, to be held liable under section 1983, the plaintiff must allege that the citizen conspired with or acted in concert with state actors. *Mylett v. Jeane*, 879 F.2d 1272, 1275 (5th Cir. 1989).

This court has held that a non-state actor may be liable under 1983 if the private citizen was a "willful participant in joint activity with the State or its agents." *Cinel*, 15 F.3d at 1343. The plaintiff must allege: (1) an agreement between the private and public defendants to commit an illegal act and (2) a deprivation of constitutional rights. *Id.* Allegations that are merely conclusory, without reference to specific facts, will not suffice. *Brinkmann v. Johnston*, 793 F.2d 111, 113 (5th Cir. 1986). The district court correctly determined Priester's complaint failed to allege a conspiracy. The complaint alleges that the coaches either ignored or "encouraged and/or allowed" Ward's behavior; however, the complaint does not allege an agreement between Ward and the coaches to commit an illegal act, nor does it allege specific facts to show an agreement. Therefore, we uphold the district court's dismissal of Ward for failure to state a claim under Rule 12(b)(6).

II. DISMISSAL OF SCHOOL DISTRICT OFFICIALS UNDER SECTION 1983

Priester also argues that under section 1983, the district court erred in granting summary judgment to the defendants on two accounts. First, Priester alleges that the school officials' failure to protect Priester from violence during a school activity violates the Due Process clause. Second, Priester contends that the school officials' use of racial epithets and their refusal to both pay for her son's medical expenses and respond to her complaints of racial harassment deprives Priester of his clearly established rights, and thus, violates the Equal Protection clause.

A. Substantive Due Process

Pursuant to the Due Process Clause, Priester argues that the district court erred in summarily dismissing her claim as failing to have the requisite state action. To state a claim under section 1983, a plaintiff must: (1) allege a violation of rights secured by the Constitution of the United States or laws of the United States; and (2) demonstrate that the alleged deprivation was committed by a person acting under color of state law. *McKinney v. Irving Ind. Sch. Dist.*, 309 F.3d 308 (5th Cir. 2002). As for the first prong of *McKinney*, Priester's allegations indicate that her complaint falls under the substantive component of the Due Process Clause. *See Leffall v. Dallas Indep. Sch. Dist.*, 28 F.3d 521, 526 (5th Cir. 1994) (finding a substantive due process claim when the plaintiff alleged that the state had a duty to provide students protection from injury at a school dance). Thus, the district court correctly construed Priester's allegations that the coaches and school officials failed to protect Priester from the attack, as essentially a claim under the substantive component of the Due Process Clause.

As for the second prong of *McKinney*, because the Fourteenth Amendment protects liberty and property interests only against invasion by a state, a section 1983 plaintiff, alleging the deprivation of Due Process under the Fourteenth Amendment, must also show that state action caused his injury. *Bass v. Parkwood Hosp.*, 180 F.3d 234, 241 (5th Cir. 1999). In such cases, the "under color of law" and state action inquiries merge into one. *Id.* This court has consistently held that "the right to be free of state-occasioned damage to a person's bodily integrity is protected by the [F]ourteenth [A]mendment's guarantee of due process." *Doe v. Taylor Ind. Sch. Dist.*, 15 F.3d 443, 450-51 (5th Cir. 1994); *Petta v. Rivera*, 143 F.3d 895 (5th Cir. 1998) (finding that a constitutional right under the Due Process Clause requires more than merely a non-physical harm to give rise to a constitutional tort). Considering that the bodily integrity of Terry was indisputably damaged by Ward's act, he suffered an unquestionable harm to his property. The issue in this case, therefore, is whether the harm to Terry's property was caused by state action.

As a general rule, the state's failure to protect an individual from private violence does not violate the Due Process Clause. . . . This court has clearly held, that absent "certain limited circumstances," substantive due process "does not confer an entitlement to governmental aid as may be necessary to realize the advantages of liberty guaranteed by the Clause." *Walton v. Alexander*, 44 F.3d 1297, 1302 (5th Cir. 1995). Therefore, for Priester to overcome the district court's grant of summary judgment in favor of the defendants, she must show that the alleged harm to her son fits one of those "certain limited circumstances."

i.   Special Relationship Exception

Priester contends that the coaches were effectively state actors because a "special relationship" exists between students and teachers, and thus, the coaches were cloaked with a certain public trust and responsibility to protect her son from harm. We have recognized that when the "special relationship" between the person and the state imposes upon the state a constitutional duty to protect that individual from known threats of harm by private actors, this circumstance constitutes an exception to the general rule that a state has no affirmative duty to protect an individual from private violence. *Walton*, 44 F.3d at 1299. . . .

The special relationship exception, however, has been narrowly construed when applied to school sponsored activities. This court has held that no such special relationship exists between a school district and its students during a school sponsored activity "held outside the time during which students are required to attend school for non-voluntary activities." *Leffall*, 28 F.3d at 529. In *Leffall*, an eighteen-year-old student, named Dameon Steadham, was fatally shot by random gunfire in the parking lot of a public high school after a school dance. *Id.* at 523. The court reasoned that no special relationship existed between the student and the school, because although the student may have been "compelled to attend school during the day, any special relationship that may have existed lapsed when compulsory attendance ended." *Id.* at 530. In other words, "the State does not become the permanent guarantor of an individual's safety by having once offered him shelter." *DeShaney v. Winnebago County Dep't of Soc. Servs.*, 489 U.S. 189, 201 (1989).

In the present case, Priester's claim that lack of supervision during football practice is gross negligence wrongfully rests upon a characterization of the State as a permanent guarantor of a student's safety. It is undisputed that Terry's injuries did not occur during regular school hours, when students are arguably compelled to attend public schools. Rather, Terry's injury occurred after regular school hours during football practice, and thus, at the time his injuries occurred, no special relationship existed between him and the school. Moreover, Priester fails to show that her son was compelled or restrained against his will. High school football practice is a voluntary extra-curricular activity, and thus, Priester cannot claim that her son was in any ways compelled by the school to participate. Priester has cited no relevant case law which supports her special relationship claims. Therefore, because no special relationship exists between a school district and its students during a school-sponsored football practice held outside of the time during which students are required to attend school for non-voluntary activities, the district court did not err in finding no requisite state action under section 1983. . . .

iii.   Fair Attribution Standard

Despite the absence of any exception to the general rule, Priester contends that Ward's actions should be attributed to the school officials because of both: the alleged conspiracy between Cahalane and Ward to gouge her son's eye, and the history of unpunished racial bullying, which she argues was an official endorsement that facilitated Terry's injury. For the purpose of section 1983, private action may be deemed state action when the defendant's conduct is "fairly attributable to the State." *Bass*, 180 F.3d at 241 (5th Cir. 1999). Under the "fair attribution" test, the plaintiff must show: (1) that the deprivation was caused by the exercise of some right or privilege created by the state or by a rule of conduct imposed by the state, or by a person for whom the state is responsible, and (2) that the party charged with the deprivation may fairly be said to be a state actor. *Daniel v. Ferguson*, 839 F.2d 1124, 1130 (5th Cir. 1988). State action will not accrue merely because of government acquiescence or approval of the private entity's actions. *Yeager v. City of McGregor*, 980 F.2d 337, 342 (5th Cir. 1993). A party may fairly be said to be a state actor only when "he has acted with or has obtained significant aid from state officials, or because his conduct is otherwise chargeable to the State." *Daniel*, 839 F.2d at 1130; *Bass*, 180 F.3d at 242 (stating that a "State normally can be held responsible for a private decision only when it has exercised coercive power or has provided such significant encouragement [or] where the government has so far insinuated itself into a position of interdependence . . . that it was a joint participant in the enterprise").

On the facts *sub judice*, Ward's conduct cannot be fairly attributable to the state. Although Priester asserts an alleged conspiracy between Cahalane and Ward, the record shows no evidence of the content of the conversation nor does it highlight any actual agreement. Without knowledge of the content of the conversation or any objective evidence of an agreement, Priester's assertion is nothing more than conclusory. Due to the pleading and proof requirements to present a prima facia case of conspiracy, . . . this evidence is legally insufficient to overcome summary judgment.

Moreover, although the district court did not address Priester's contention that the school officials' failure to adequately respond to either her son's history of racial abuse at the school or Ward's assault on Priester is tantamount to state endorsement, her argument fails to overcome the burden of summary judgment. The record is devoid of any active participation or significant encouragement of the alleged racial abuse by the school officials. Rather than any affirmative act, Priester alleges omissions; the school's inaction and indifference, although morally reprehensible, do not rise to the level of legal action under the fair attribution standard. Nor does the record show any evidence that Ward and the school officials shared the common objective of gouging Terry's eye, as is required to qualify as joint participation. Therefore, Ward's seemingly private conduct may not be charged to the state because the school officials' mere indifference does not arise to the level of fair attribution.

B. Equal Protection

Priester asserts that the school officials use of racial epithets, their inability or unwillingness to respond to complaints of racial mistreatment, and their failure to pay her son's medical expenses violated Priester's equal protection rights. To state a claim of racial discrimination under the Equal Protection Clause and section 1983, the plaintiff "must allege and prove that he received treatment different from that received by similarly situated individuals and that the unequal treatment stemmed from a discriminatory intent." *Taylor v. Johnson*, 257 F.3d 470, 473 (5th Cir. 2001). A discriminatory purpose "implies that the decision maker singled out a particular group for disparate treatment and selected his course of action at least in part for the purpose of causing its adverse effect on an identifiable group." *Id.*

Priester contends that the use of racial epithets, combined with other conduct, deprived her son of his clearly established rights. This court has held that the use of a racial epithet without harassment or other conduct depriving the victim of his established rights does not constitute an equal protection violation. *Williams v. Bramer*, 180 F.3d 699, 706, *clarified*, 186 F.3d 633 (5th Cir. 1999) ("Where

the conduct at issue consists solely of speech, there is no equal protection violation"). Assuming arguendo that Cahalane used racial epithets, Priester must also
demonstrate additional genuine issues of material fact, where school officials
participated in actions that deprived Terry of his constitutional rights.

Priester argues that the additional evidence of racial animus stemmed from
the high school principal's failure to conduct an investigation in regards to
Priester's racial harassment complaints. While the record does not show whether
school officials investigated Priester's twice-weekly complaints of harassment,
the record does indicate that Halford investigated and completed a report
on Terry's injury, resolved a complaint regarding his grades, and investigated
Priester's complaint regarding harassment of her son during a field trip. Thus,
while the school officials may not have adequately responded to all of Priester's
numerous complaints, the record does not show that the officials' inaction
on some of the complaints rises to the level of an equal protection violation.
Moreover, Priester presents no evidence establishing that the alleged racial
harassment went unpunished while other types of misconduct was punished or
that the school did not document the racial harassment in its records. . . .

CONCLUSION

For the foregoing reasons, the judgment of the district court is AFFIRMED. . . .

NOTES AND QUESTIONS

1. *Analysis of* Priester. On what basis did the court affirm the dismissal of
    Defendant Ward on statute of limitations grounds? When an intentional
    tort has its basis in racial animus, should the statute of limitations be tolled
    on public policy grounds (i.e., a racially motivated intentional tort suffi-
    ciently different than other intentional torts to warrant special treatment in
    terms of applying the statute of limitations)? After the decision in the *Priester*
    case, even if you believed that the statute of limitations could not be tolled
    under existing law, would you support legislative action to toll the statute of
    limitations in cases of intentional torts based on racial animus or to extend
    the length of time in which such claims could be brought?

    Neither the coach (Cahalane) nor the player (Ward) was held to be a
    state actor or to have acted under color of state law under Section 1983.
    Why wasn't the coach held to be a state actor or to have acted under the
    color of state law? Isn't he clearly a state actor? Does the fact that prac-
    tices were "voluntary" and held after school render the special relationship
    between a teacher and student different from the relationship that exists
    during school hours? Is this a case in which sport is simply being insulated
    from liability (i.e., the court is being deferential to sport in refusing to find
    that the coach is a state actor)? If the coach were held to be a state actor,
    what would the plaintiff have to plead to link the player's actions to the
    coach and the school? Did the plaintiff in this case simply fail to plead an
    agreement between the coach and the player? What would have to be pled
    in this regard? Would it be sufficient to plead the existence of an implied or
    tacit agreement? In effect, didn't the coach's failure to intervene constitute
    just such an agreement?

The court recognized that a party may assert a violation of substantive due process when the state has a duty to protect students from injury at school. Doesn't a coach have a duty to protect his players in a case like *Priester*? Why did the court refuse to find such a duty to protect the plaintiff from invasion of his bodily integrity? The court notes, "The record is devoid of any active participation or significant encouragement of alleged racial abuse by the school officials." Do you agree with this statement? What about the concerns raised by the student-athlete's mother and the failure of the school to investigate those concerns?

The court also refused to find an equal protection violation in this case. What would the plaintiff have to allege and ultimately prove to be able to prevail on equal protection grounds? The court acknowledges that school officials "may not have adequately responded to all of Priester's numerous complaints," but concludes that "the record does not show that the officials' inaction on some of the complaints rises to the level of an equal protection violation." What would the plaintiff have to prove? Was it enough that the school documented the racial harassment in its records? The court seems to imply that the plaintiff would have to prove that racial harassment was treated differently from other forms of misconduct. Is the court saying that other forms of misconduct also went unpunished or that the plaintiff failed to assert that other forms of misconduct had in fact been treated differently? Given the court's decision, would a school district be advised to take care not to take a hands-off approach to misconduct (i.e., to treat all misconduct equally by failing to punish misconduct generally)?

In *Priester* the court analyzed each issue in seriatim fashion in dispensing with the plaintiff's case. At many points, the court appears to be quite deferential to the school in operating its athletic program. Have they given coaches too much deference in such matters? What are they protecting—the right of participants or the interests of the school to run an unfettered athletic program?

2. *Title VII as a Remedial Option in Cases of Racial Workplace Harassment.* While *Priester* involved amateur athletes, in the professional sports context, Title VII's workplace harassment protections provide a remedy for racially abused athletes. If an employer engages in or encourages harassment or fails to reasonably protect employees from harassment, liability may follow. See 42 U.S.C. § 2000e-2(a).

In November of 2013, Miami Dolphins offensive lineman Richie Incognito was revealed to have harassed and racially abused his teammate, Jonathan Martin, calling him, among other things, a "nigger." See *Slurs in Incognito's Messages*, ESPN.com, Nov. 5, 2013, http://espn.go.com/nfl/story/_/id/9926139/. It was later alleged that a member of the Dolphins coaching staff had, prior to the incident, told Incognito to "toughen up" Martin. See Hank Gola, *Dolphins coaches told Richie Incognito to toughen up Jonathan Martin: report*, N.Y. Daily News.com, Nov. 6, 2013, http://www.nydailynews.com/sports/football/dolphins-coaches-told-incognito-toughen-martin-report-article-1.1508027. Incognito was suspended, and the NFL hired Ted Wells, a partner at the law firm of Paul, Weiss, Rifkind, Wharton, and Garrison, to investigate the matter. In a 144-page report, Wells concluded that Incognito subjected Martin to "'a pattern of harassment' that included racial slurs and vicious sexual taunts . . . ." See *Incognito, others tormented Martin*, ESPN.com, Feb. 15, 2014. Although Martin did not sue, had he chosen to do so, Wells' conclusion would have provided him with the basis of a viable claim under Title VII as well as Florida anti-discrimination law. Brett Snider, *Miami Dolphins Hazing Investigation: What If Jonathan Martin Sues?*, Tarnished Twenty, Nov. 8, 2013, http://blogs.findlaw.com/tarnished_twenty/2013/11/miami-dolphins-hazing-invesigation-what-if-jonathan-martin-sues.html#sthash.KNqa9zB0.dpuf; Lester Munson, *Lawsuit could provide Martin payday*, ESPN.com, http://espn.go.com/nfl/story/_/id/9932264/florida-law-provide-big-payday-jonathan-martin-sue-miami-dolphins-richie-incognito.

3. *Title VI as a Remedial Option in Cases of Fans Abusing Players.* In a case involving alleged opponent-to-opponent racial discrimination, the plaintiffs sought recovery pursuant to Title VI, which prohibits discrimination in programs receiving federal financial assistance. In *Malcolm v. Novato Unified School District*, 2002 WL 31770392 (Cal. App. 1 Dist.) (not selected for official publication), the plaintiffs, two African-American high school basketball players, were subjected to racial harassment by fans of San Marin High School, the opponent home team. About 20 fans attended the game dressed in costumes, which included racial depictions of blacks. Fans also directed racial slurs toward plaintiffs and other African-American players on the visiting team. In asserting their Title VI claim, the plaintiffs alleged that the defendant school district had actual knowledge of the racially hostile environment at San Marin and had failed to take adequate steps to address it. While acknowledging that efforts undertaken by the school district to address racial hostility were not ideal, the court concluded that the district's remedial action was not unreasonable. The court framed the appropriate standard as follows:

> The issue is not whether district officials could have done more or acted more effectively. They could have. Under the current state of the law, however, school districts are not liable for damages because their response to inappropriate behavior is ill advised, ineffective or inept.
>
> . . . The United States Supreme Court has made clear that an action for damages under the federal civil rights legislation invoked here is not [cognizable] unless the school district's role or response is so clearly unreasonable as to reflect deliberate indifference.

Id. at *10. See *Garvey v. Unified School Dist.*, 2005 WL 2548332 (D. Kan. Oct. 12, 2005) (a high school basketball player denied position on boys' basketball team alleged school engaged in racial discrimination in selecting members of team. The court found that the plaintiff could sue for intentional discrimination under Title VI, but the statute allows for neither a disparate impact claim nor the recovery of punitive damages). See *Scott v. State of Hawaii Dept. of Educ.*, 2009 WL 564709 (D. Haw.) (African-American athlete kicked off high school football team failed to present evidence establishing disciplinary rules were applied to him in a discriminatory manner—other students received less harsh punishment for similar violations—and therefore could not sustain a Title VI racial discrimination claim); *Williams v. U.S. Tennis Assn.*, 2009 WL 5088727 (N.D. Cal. Dec. 17, 2009) (tennis player and her mother failed to allege facts sufficient to support their claim that the player was a victim of racial discrimination based on the defendant association's failure to respond to hostile comments made by another player and her mother).

4. *Fans as Victims.* In an interesting twist on the issue of fan harassment, a university was sued on the basis of discrimination in public accommodations when the student manager of its basketball team shouted racial slurs and threats to spectators. *Hawai'i v. Hoshijo,* 102 Haw. 307, 76 P.3d 550 (2003). In holding the university liable, the Hawaii Supreme Court deemed the University of Hawaii to be the owner and operator of a place of public accommodation by virtue of its ownership of a sports facility. It concluded that the student manager was an agent of the university and, at the time, was acting within the scope of his authority. The court held that liability for violation of Hawaii's statute barring discrimination in public accommodations should attach to the university pursuant to *respondeat superior. Id.* at 564. The court also held that the manager's racial slurs did not constitute protected speech under the First Amendment. *Id.* at 564-565.

CHAPTER
10

Gender Equity Issues in Athletics

A.   INTRODUCTION

This chapter explores issues related to sex discrimination and gender equity in athletics. While the focus is largely on developments in the United States, global issues are raised as well. The chapter begins with a brief history, followed by sections focusing on the development of the law over almost five decades. The impact of Title IX on school-based sport programs stretches broadly to address access to participation opportunities, equitable treatment in athletics programs, claims of reverse discrimination, and pregnancy discrimination. Issues of sexual harassment and sexual assault affect athletes of all ages, from youth sport and school-based sport programs to the Olympic and professional levels. Gender-associated issues related to sexual orientation discrimination and transgender and intersex athlete participation are also emerging. Finally, sex discrimination in employment is addressed.

B.   HISTORICAL PERSPECTIVE

While it is often assumed that women are not as competitive as men, ancient artifacts provide evidence that women have been competing in sport just as long as men have competed. Much of the following chronology is based on an informative website titled *History of Women in Sports Timeline,* at http://www.infoplease.com/spot/womeninsportstimeline.html. Women were excluded from the first Olympic Games, which were held in ancient Greece in 776 B.C., but they competed in their own sports contests every four years that were held from approximately 1,000 B.C. to 200 B.C., to honor the Greek goddess Hera who ruled over women and earth. Women were eventually permitted to participate in the ancient Olympics, but they did not receive equal treatment. In 392 B.C., Kyniska, a Spartan princess, won an Olympic chariot race, but she was not permitted to receive her prize in person. Such discrimination continued over time. When the Olympics were revived in 1896, a Greek woman, Melpomene, tried to enter the marathon. She was forbidden from entering the race, but chose to run the course during the event anyway. When she was prohibited from entering the stadium for the final lap, she ran around the outside of the stadium, completing the marathon in about four and a half hours. It was not until 1900 that 16 women were permitted to participate in three exhibition sports — tennis, golf, and croquet — in the modern Olympic Games. A French woman, Alice Milliat, responded to the lack of women's opportunities in the Olympics by founding the Federation Sportive Feminine Internationale, conducting women's only games in multiple sports and events from 1922 through 1934.

In the United States, the first interscholastic athletics activity — gymnastics — occurred at the Latin School for girls in Salem, Massachusetts in 1821. Progress, in terms of participation for women, was slow during the nineteenth century. In 1866, Vassar College formed the first two women's amateur baseball teams; in 1867, the first women's professional baseball team, the Dolly Vardens, was formed, comprised of African American women from Philadelphia. The first athletic games for women in the United States were held in 1882 at the YWCA in Boston. *Physical Education*, a journal published in 1896 by the YMCA, devoted a full issue to women. That same year, the University of California-Berkeley and Stanford University played the first women's intercollegiate basketball game, with Stanford winning 2-1 before 700 fans.

Progress continued slowly in the twentieth century. Some of the cultural opposition to the involvement of women in athletics began to dissipate in the Roaring 20s. In 1920, female swimmers became the first American women to be accorded full Olympic status. There were only three swimming events for women in the 1920 Olympiad, and Ethelda Bleibtrey entered all of them, winning three gold medals. By 1924, Sybil Bauer became the first woman to break an existing men's swimming record with her record-breaking win in the 100-meter backstroke. In the same year, the National Women's Athletic Association was organized. The National Amateur Athletic Federation was founded in 1921, with women being afforded "equal footing [with men] with the same standards, the same program and the same regulations." The Amateur Athletic Union (AAU) added track and field for women in 1922; it also held the first national basketball tournament for women, with six teams participating in 1924. By 1922, 22 percent of U.S. colleges were offering some varsity team sports for women. In 1928, Olympic track and field events were open to women, and American Betty Robinson became the first woman to win a gold medal with her victory in the 100-meter race. Finally, in 1929, Tuskegee Institute in Alabama awarded scholarships to women participating on its track team and hosted a women's track meet.

In 1931, Virne Beatrice "Jackie" Mitchell, a 17-year-old woman pitching for the Chattanooga Lookouts, struck out Babe Ruth and Lou Gehrig in an exhibition game. Baseball commissioner Judge Kenesaw Mountain Landis responded by banning women from professional baseball on the grounds that it was "too strenuous" for them to participate. In 1936, Sally Sterns became the first woman coxswain of a male rowing team at Rollins College. The All American Red Heads women's basketball team was also formed in 1936, and won more than 85 percent of its games against male teams over a 50-year period. Women's gymnastics was added to the Olympic Games in 1936.

After World War II, social norms dictated that women return to more traditional roles and progress for women who wanted to compete in sport remained slow. The All American Girls Professional Baseball League, created in 1943 as a placeholder for baseball while the men served during the war, persisted through

1955. In 1954, the Iowa Girls' High School Athletic Association established a state-wide program that placed girls on equal footing with boys in high school athletics. By 1959, women were permitted to participate in the international cycling championships.

In the 1960s, women made some significant strides in terms of their participation opportunities in competitive athletic events. In 1966, the first intercollegiate women's basketball tournament was played in Pennsylvania, and the Commission on Intercollegiate Athletics for Women (CIAW) was established by the Division for Girl's and Women's Sports in 1967. The CIAW was formed for the purpose of increasing participation by women in competitive sports, which led to the first women's national intercollegiate championship competition in 1969 in the sport of gymnastics.

The 1970s proved to be an historic decade in the evolution of gender equity in athletics for women in the United States. In 1971, the Association for Intercollegiate Athletics for Women (AIAW) was formed, replacing the CIAW and offering seven national championships for women. Through the 1970s, the AIAW was the only major national intercollegiate athletic governing association for women's sports, with membership growing from 278 schools in its inaugural year to more than 800 member institutions by the end of the decade, and national championships growing to 19 sports in three divisions. In 1980, however, the NAIA was the first men's intercollegiate national governing body to offer post-season championships for women, and the NCAA followed suit, offering national championships for women in all three of its divisions by 1982. The AIAW brought an unsuccessful antitrust action against the NCAA in an effort to prevent the NCAA from absorbing women's athletics at the intercollegiate level. See *Association of Intercollegiate Athletics for Women v. National Collegiate Athletic Assn.*, 735 F.2d 577 (D.C. Cir. 1984). Thereafter, the AIAW was soon disbanded.

Sex discrimination was first recognized in 1964 with the passage of the Civil Rights Act. It was another decade before Title IX of the Education Amendments of 1972 (which in 2002 was renamed the Patsy T. Mink Equal Opportunity in Education Act in honor of the Hawaiian congresswoman who was instrumental in its passage) was enacted to require that schools provide equal educational opportunities for both female and male students. Ironically, Title IX was "slipped into a civil-rights law because conservative Southerners thought the idea of granting equal opportunities for women would derail the bill." Welch Suggs, *Title IX at 30*, Chron. Higher Educ., June 21, 2002, at 38. Senators Edith Green of Oregon and Birch Bayh of Indiana, however, guided the bill into law.

The battle for gender equity in sport continues at the national and global (e.g., Olympics) levels. There are bright lights like the performance of women in the 2016 Olympics: "No one is flying home from Rio with more medals than the U.S. women. The full American squad — both men and women — won the most medals overall, 121 . . . [with] the U.S. women [winning] 61, the men [winning] 55, and [with] five in mixed events, including equestrian and mixed-doubles tennis." Greg Myre, *U.S. Women Are the Biggest Winners at the Rio Olympics*, http://www.npr.org/sections/thetorch/2016/08/21/490818961/u-s-women-are-the-biggest-winners-in-rio-olympics.

A new generation of gender related equity issues is also developing. Sexual harassment and sexual assault exist within all levels of sport–scholastic, Olympic, and professional – for athletes and for those who work in the sport industry. The traditional binary classifications of male/ female and masculine/

feminine are being challenged by evidence that gender exists more on a continuum of socially defined masculine and feminine characteristics. People who are uncomfortable with their assigned sex at birth have the option of presenting themselves in a manner more consistent with their perceived sexual identity, utilizing hormone therapy to develop more male or female sex characteristics or completing sex reassignment surgery. Science has also identified individuals with ambiguous genitalia or characteristics of both sexes and hormone levels that do not fit neatly within the average ranges for one sex or the other. All of these situations present interesting challenges within the sport industry and for sport lawyers.

The following materials and problems consider the legal, practical, and policy aspects of gender equity issues primarily in connection with intercollegiate and interscholastic athletics. Title IX litigation encompasses access to participation opportunities, equitable treatment within athletics programs, and reverse discrimination claims. Sexual harassment, sexual orientation discrimination, and retaliation claims under Title IX and other laws have become more frequent in the 2000s.

C. TITLE IX OF THE EDUCATION AMENDMENTS OF 1972

On June 23, 1972, Title IX, 20 U.S.C. §1681, was signed into law by President Richard M. Nixon. The legislation clearly and concisely states: No person in the United States shall, on the basis of sex, be excluded from participation in, be denied the benefits of, or be subjected to discrimination under any education program or activity receiving Federal financial assistance.

The statute does not expressly reference athletics, but the implementing legislation did require the promulgation of regulations to achieve gender equity in all educational opportunities. Title IX gender equity regulations regarding athletics became effective on July 21, 1975 and are codified in 34 C.F.R. §106. The regulations mandate equal access to athletics participation opportunities and equal treatment in those opportunities, including the ability to receive athletics scholarships.

In an effort to limit the scope of Title IX as applied to intercollegiate athletics, two bills were proposed in Congress in 1975 and 1977. In H.R. 8394, Representative O'Hara sought to require that revenues generated by men's sports be used for their funding before being used to support other sports. Senators Tower, Bartlett, and Hruska proposed Senate Bill 2106, which would have excluded revenue-producing sports from Title IX coverage. These legislative efforts, however, were unsuccessful and did not result in any changes to Title IX or its regulations.

For girls who wished to participate in school-based sport programs the legislation and regulations were making an impact: the Department of Health, Education, and Welfare (HEW), the government agency originally responsible for governmental enforcement of Title IX, received almost 100 complaints against more than 50 colleges and universities alleging discrimination in athletics. To provide more guidance on what constitutes compliance with the law, HEW issued a policy interpretation regarding the application of Title IX to athletics. In 1979, *A Policy Interpretation: Title IX and Intercollegiate Athletics,*

45 C.F.R. Part 26, further clarified how to calculate equity in providing athletics scholarships; elaborated on the meaning of equivalent treatment, benefits, and opportunities; and established a new three-part test for schools to measure whether the interests and abilities of all students were effectively accommodated.

In 1980, HEW was reorganized, and the Department of Education (DOE) was formed. The DOE's Office for Civil Rights (OCR) was charged with responsibility for enforcing Title IX. On July 28, 1980, the OCR, in one of its first official acts, issued an interim manual dealing with Title IX and athletics.

Title IX was not vigorously enforced during the 1980s. In *Grove City College v. Bell*, 465 U.S. 555 (1984), the Supreme Court held that Title IX applied only to specific educational programs and activities that directly received federal funding. *Grove City* severely limited OCR's jurisdiction over university athletic programs because college athletics departments (with the exception of United States military academies) do not receive any federal funding. Subsequently, Congress passed the Civil Rights Restoration Act of 1987, which established an institution-wide approach. If the educational institution receives any federal funding, all departments and programs are bound by the requirements of Title IX. Because the vast majority of educational institutions receive some federal funding, virtually all high school and college athletics programs are required to comply with Title IX. Thereafter, the OCR began to enforce Title IX more aggressively.

In *Franklin v. Gwinnett County Public Schools*, 503 U.S. 60 (1992), the Supreme Court unanimously held that prevailing plaintiffs may recover monetary damages and attorney fees for intentional violations of Title IX. The *Gwinnett* decision, coupled with increased enforcement activity on the part of OCR, contributed to a significant rise in the number of Title IX cases in the athletics context. See generally Paul M. Anderson and Barbara Osborne, *A Historical Review of Title IX Litigation*, 18 J. LEGAL ASPECTS OF SPORT 127 (2008).

In 1994 Congress passed the Equity in Athletics Disclosure Act (EADA), 20 U.S.C. §1092, which requires all federally funded institutions of higher education to disclose information regarding their athletics programs, including athletic participation opportunities for men and women. Initial EADA reports were due on October 1, 1996, and the DOE has made this information easily accessible on its website at https://ope.ed.gov/athletics/#/. This data provides information that has increased public awareness and provided a better evidentiary basis for quantifying gender inequities.

On January 16, 1996, the OCR issued *Clarification of Intercollegiate Athletics Policy Guidance: The Three-Part Test*. This test, introduced in the 1979 policy interpretation, provides institutions with three potential ways to show they are providing effective accommodation of the interests and abilities of the underrepresented sex. While the Policy Interpretation has been enforced uniformly by every court that has addressed the equal opportunity issue, significant criticism of the three-part test persists.

As illustrated by the following cases interpreting and applying Title IX to sports, this federal law has dramatically increased the number of interscholastic and intercollegiate athletics participation opportunities for girls as well as facilitated the success of female Olympians and women's national teams. On the other hand, men continue to have significantly greater sports participation opportunities at all levels of competition, and it is clear that the goal of gender equity in athletics has not been fully achieved.

1.   *Equal Athletic Participation Opportunities*

COHEN v. BROWN UNIVERSITY

101 F.3d 155 (1st Cir. 1996), *cert. denied*, 520 U.S. 1186 (1997)

BOWNES, Senior Circuit Judge.

This is a class action lawsuit charging Brown University, its president, and its athletics director (collectively "Brown") with discrimination against women in the operation of its intercollegiate athletics program, in violation of Title IX. . . .

This suit was initiated in response to the demotion in May 1991 of Brown's women's gymnastics and volleyball teams from university-funded varsity status to donor-funded varsity status. Contemporaneously, Brown demoted two men's teams, water polo and golf, from university-funded to donor-funded varsity status. As a consequence of these demotions, all four teams lost, not only their university funding, but most of the support and privileges that accompany university-funded varsity status at Brown. . . .

I

Brown operates a two-tiered intercollegiate athletics program with respect to funding: although Brown provides the financial resources required to maintain its university-funded varsity teams, donor-funded varsity athletes must themselves raise the funds necessary to support their teams through private donations. The district court noted that the four demoted teams were eligible for NCAA competition, provided that they were able to raise the funds necessary to maintain a sufficient level of competitiveness, and provided that they continued to comply with NCAA requirements. The court found, however, that it is difficult for donor-funded varsity athletes to maintain a level of competitiveness commensurate with their abilities and that these athletes operate at a competitive disadvantage in comparison to university-funded varsity athletes. . . .

Brown's decision to demote the women's volleyball and gymnastics teams and the men's water polo and golf teams from university-funded varsity status was apparently made in response to a university-wide cost-cutting directive. . . .

Plaintiffs alleged that, at the time of the demotions, the men students at Brown already enjoyed the benefits of a disproportionately large share of both the university resources allocated to athletics and the intercollegiate participation opportunities afforded to student athletes. Thus, plaintiffs contended, what appeared to be the even-handed demotions of two men's and two women's teams, in fact, perpetuated Brown's discriminatory treatment of women in the administration of its intercollegiate athletics program. . . .

The district court . . . summarized the history of athletics at Brown, finding, . . . that, while nearly all of the men's varsity teams were established before 1927, virtually all of the women's varsity teams were created between 1971 and 1977, after Brown's merger with Pembroke College. The only women's varsity team created after this period was winter track, in 1982.

In the course of the trial on the merits, the district court found that, in 1993-94, there were 897 students participating in intercollegiate varsity athletics, of which 61.87% (555) were men and 38.13% (342) were women. During the same period, Brown's undergraduate enrollment comprised 5,722 students, of which

48.86% (2,796) were men and 51.14% (2,926) were women. The district court found that, in 1993-94, Brown's intercollegiate athletics program consisted of 32 teams, 16 men's teams and 16 women's teams. Of the university-funded teams, 12 were men's teams and 13 were women's teams; of the donor-funded teams, three were women's teams and four were men's teams. At the time of trial, Brown offered 479 university-funded varsity positions for men, as compared to 312 for women; and 76 donor-funded varsity positions for men, as compared to 30 for women. In 1993-94, then, Brown's varsity program — including both university- and donor-funded sports — afforded over 200 more positions for men than for women. Accordingly, the district court found that Brown maintained a 13.01% disparity between female participation in intercollegiate athletics and female student enrollment. . . .

In computing these figures, the district court counted as participants in inter-collegiate athletics for purposes of Title IX analysis those athletes who were members of varsity teams for the majority of the last complete season. . . .

The district court found from extensive testimony that the donor-funded women's gymnastics, women's fencing and women's ski teams, as well as at least one women's club team, the water polo team, had demonstrated the interest and ability to compete at the top varsity level and would benefit from university funding.

The district court did *not* find that full and effective accommodation of the athletics interests and abilities of Brown's female students would disadvantage Brown's male students.

II

Title IX . . . specifies that its prohibition against gender discrimination shall not "be interpreted to require any educational institution to grant prefer-ential or disparate treatment to the members of one sex on account of an imbalance which may exist" between the total number or percentage of per-sons of that sex participating in any federally supported program or activity, and "the total number or percentage of persons of that sex in any com-munity, State, section, or other area." 20 U.S.C.A. §1681(b) (West 1990). Subsection (b) also provides, however, that it "shall not be construed to pre-vent the consideration in any . . . proceeding under this chapter of statistical evidence tending to show that such an imbalance exists with respect to the participation in, or receipt of the benefits of, any such program or activity by the members of one sex."

Applying §1681(b), the prior panel held that Title IX "does not mandate strict numerical equality between the gender balance of a college's athletic pro-gram and the gender balance of its student body." The panel explained that, while evidence of a gender-based disparity in an institution's athletics program is relevant to a determination of noncompliance, "a court assessing Title IX compliance may not find a violation solely because there is a disparity between the gender composition of an educational institution's student constituency, on the one hand, and its athletic programs, on the other hand."

[A 1978 OCR] Policy Interpretation establishes a three-part test, a two-part test, and factors to be considered in determining compliance under 34 C.F.R. §106.41(c)(1) [which provides a non-exhaustive list of ten factors to be consid-ered in determining whether equal athletics are available to both genders]. At issue in this appeal is the proper interpretation of the first of these, the so-called three-part test, which inquires as follows:

(1)   Whether intercollegiate level participation opportunities for male and female students are provided in numbers substantially proportionate to their respective enrollments; or
(2)   Where the members of one sex have been and are underrepresented among intercollegiate athletes, whether the institution can show a history and continuing practice of program expansion which is demonstrably responsive to the developing interests and abilities of the members of that sex; or
(3)   Where the members of one sex are underrepresented among intercollegiate athletes, and the institution cannot show a continuing practice of program expansion such as that cited above, whether it can be demonstrated that the interests and abilities of the members of that sex have been fully and effectively accommodated by the present program.

44 Fed. Reg. at 71, 418.

The district court held that, "because Brown maintains a 13.01% disparity between female participation in intercollegiate athletics and female student enrollment, it cannot gain the protection of prong one." Nor did Brown satisfy prong two. While acknowledging that Brown "has an impressive history of program expansion," the district court found that Brown failed to demonstrate that it has "maintained a continuing practice of intercollegiate program expansion for women, the under-represented sex." . . . [T]he fact that Brown has eliminated or demoted several men's teams does not amount to a continuing practice of program expansion for women. As to prong three, the district court found that Brown had not "fully and effectively accommodated the interest and ability of the under-represented sex" to the extent necessary to provide equal opportunity in the selection of sports and levels of competition available to members of both sexes. . . .

IV

Brown contends that the district court misconstrued and misapplied the three-part test. Specifically, Brown argues that the district court's interpretation and application of the test is irreconcilable with the statute, the regulation, and the agency's interpretation of the law, and effectively renders Title IX an "affirmative action statute" that mandates preferential treatment for women by imposing quotas in excess of women's relative interests and abilities in athletics. Brown asserts, in the alternative, that if the district court properly construed the test, then the test itself violates Title IX and the United States Constitution. . . .

A

Brown's talismanic incantation of "affirmative action" has no legal application to this case and is not helpful to Brown's cause. . . . True affirmative action cases have historically involved a voluntary undertaking to remedy discrimination (as in a program implemented by a governmental body, or by a private employer or institution), by means of specific group-based preferences or numerical goals, and a specific timetable for achieving those goals. . . .

Title IX is not an affirmative action statute; it is an anti-discrimination statute, modeled explicitly after another anti-discrimination statute, Title VI. No aspect of the Title IX regime at issue in this case — inclusive of the statute, the relevant regulation, and the pertinent agency documents — mandates gender-based preferences or quotas, or specific timetables for implementing numerical goals.

Like other anti-discrimination statutory schemes, the Title IX regime permits affirmative action. In addition, Title IX, like other anti-discrimination schemes, permits an inference that a significant gender-based statistical disparity may indicate the existence of discrimination. Consistent with the school desegregation cases, the question of substantial proportionality under the Policy Interpretation's three-part test is merely the starting point for analysis, rather than the conclusion; a rebuttable presumption, rather than an inflexible requirement. In short, the substantial proportionality test is but one aspect of the inquiry into whether an institution's athletics program complies with Title IX. . . .

From the mere fact that a remedy flowing from a judicial determination of discrimination is gender-conscious, it does not follow that the remedy constitutes "affirmative action." Nor does a "reverse discrimination" claim arise every time an anti-discrimination statute is enforced. While some gender-conscious relief may adversely impact one gender — a fact that has not been demonstrated in this case — that alone would not make the relief "affirmative action" or the consequence of that relief "reverse discrimination." To the contrary, race- and gender-conscious remedies are both appropriate and constitutionally permissible under a federal anti-discrimination regime, although such remedial measures are still subject to equal protection review.

B

[In this section the court notes, "*Cohen II* held that the Policy Interpretation is entitled to substantial deference because it is the enforcing agency's 'considered interpretation of the regulation.' "]

F

Brown has contended throughout this litigation that the significant disparity in athletics opportunities for men and women at Brown is the result of a gender-based differential in the level of interest in sports and that the district court's application of the three-part test requires universities to provide athletics opportunities for women to an extent that exceeds their relative interests and abilities in sports. . . .

We view Brown's argument that women are less interested than men in participating in intercollegiate athletics, as well as its conclusion that institutions should be required to accommodate the interests and abilities of its female students only to the extent that it accommodates the interests and abilities of its male students, with great suspicion. To assert that Title IX permits institutions to provide fewer athletics participation opportunities for women than for men, based upon the premise that women are less interested in sports than are men, is (among other things) to ignore the fact that Title IX was enacted in order to remedy discrimination that results from stereotyped notions of women's interests and abilities.

Interest and ability rarely develop in a vacuum; they evolve as a function of opportunity and experience. The Policy Interpretation recognizes that women's lower rate of participation in athletics reflects women's historical lack of opportunities to participate in sports. . . . [T]here exists the danger that, rather than providing a true measure of women's interest in sports, statistical evidence purporting to reflect women's interest instead provides only a measure of the very discrimination that is and has been the basis for women's lack of opportunity to participate in sports. Prong three requires some kind of evidence of interest in athletics, and the Title IX framework permits the use of statistical evidence in assessing the level of interest in sports. Nevertheless, to allow a numbers-based lack-of-interest defense to become the instrument of further discrimination against the under-represented gender would pervert the remedial purpose of Title IX. We conclude that, even if it can be empirically demonstrated that, at a particular time, women have less interest in sports than do men, such evidence, standing alone, cannot justify providing fewer athletics opportunities for women than for men. Furthermore, such evidence is completely irrelevant where, as here, viable and successful women's varsity teams have been demoted or eliminated.

Finally, the tremendous growth in women's participation in sports since Title IX was enacted disproves Brown's argument that women are less interested in sports for reasons unrelated to lack of opportunity. . . .

Brown's relative interests approach is not a reasonable interpretation of the three-part test. This approach contravenes the purpose of the statute and the regulation because it does not permit an institution or a district court to remedy a gender-based disparity in athletics participation opportunities. Instead, this approach freezes that disparity by law, thereby disadvantaging further the under-represented gender. Had Congress intended to entrench, rather than change, the status quo — with its historical emphasis on men's participation opportunities to the detriment of women's opportunities — it need not have gone to all the trouble of enacting Title IX.

VII

Brown may achieve compliance with Title IX in a number of ways: It may eliminate its athletic program altogether, it may elevate or create the requisite number of women's positions, it may demote or eliminate the requisite number of men's positions, or it may implement a combination of these remedies. I leave it entirely to Brown's discretion to decide how it will balance its program to provide equal opportunities for its men and women athletes. I recognize the financial constraints Brown faces; however, its own priorities will necessarily determine the path to compliance it elects to take. . . .

Brown's proposed compliance plan stated its goal as follows: The plan has one goal: to make the gender ratio among University-funded teams at Brown substantially proportionate to the gender ratio of the undergraduate student body. To do so, the University must disregard the expressed athletic interests of one gender while providing advantages for others. The plan focuses only on University-funded sports, ignoring the long history of successful donor-funded student teams. . . .

Brown states that it "seeks to address the issue of proportionality while minimizing additional undue stress on already strained physical and fiscal resources."

The general provisions of the plan may be summarized as follows: (i) Maximum squad sizes for men's teams will be set and enforced. (ii) Head coaches of all teams must field squads that meet minimum size requirements. (iii) No additional discretionary funds will be used for athletics. (iv) Four new women's junior varsity teams — basketball, lacrosse, soccer, and tennis — will be university-funded. (v) Brown will make explicit a de facto junior varsity team for women's field hockey.

The plan sets forth nine steps for its implementation, and concludes that "if the Court determines that this plan is not sufficient to reach proportionality, phase two will be the elimination of one or more men's teams."

The district court found Brown's plan to be "fatally flawed" for two reasons. First, despite the fact that 76 men and 30 women participated on donor-funded varsity teams, Brown's proposed plan disregarded donor-funded varsity teams. Second, Brown's plan "artificially boosts women's varsity numbers by adding junior varsity positions on four women's teams." As to the propriety of Brown's proposal to come into compliance by the addition of junior varsity positions, the district court held:

Positions on distinct junior varsity squads do not qualify as "intercollegiate competition" opportunities under the Policy Interpretation and should not be included in defendants' plan. . . . "[I]ntercollegiate" teams are those that "regularly participate in varsity competition." See 44 Fed. Reg. at 71,413 n.l. Junior varsity squads, by definition, do not meet this criterion. Counting new women's junior varsity positions as equivalent to men's full varsity positions flagrantly violates the spirit and letter of Title IX; in no sense is an institution providing equal opportunity if it affords varsity positions to men but junior varsity positions to women.

The district court found that these two flaws in the proposed plan were sufficient to show that Brown had "not made a good faith effort to comply with this Court's mandate." . . .

The district court ordered Brown to "elevate and maintain women's gymnastics, women's water polo, women's skiing, and women's fencing to university-funded varsity status." . . .

We agree with the district court that Brown's proposed plan fell short of a good faith effort to meet the requirements of Title IX as explicated by this court in *Cohen II* and as applied by the district court on remand. . . .

It is clear, nevertheless, that Brown's proposal to cut men's teams is a permissible means of effectuating compliance with the statute. . . . [A]lthough the district court's remedy is within the statutory margins and constitutional, we think that the district court was wrong to reject out-of-hand Brown's alternative plan to reduce the number of men's varsity teams. After all, the district court itself stated that one of the compliance options available to Brown under Title IX is to "demote or eliminate the requisite number of men's positions." Our respect for academic freedom and reluctance to interject ourselves into the conduct of university affairs counsels that we give universities as much freedom as possible in conducting their operations consonant with constitutional and statutory limits.

Brown therefore should be afforded the opportunity to submit another plan for compliance with Title IX. . . . Accordingly, we remand the case to the district court so that Brown can submit a further plan for its consideration. In all other respects the judgment of the district court is affirmed. . . .

VIII

There can be no doubt that Title IX has changed the face of women's sports as well as our society's interest in and attitude toward women athletes and women's sports. . . . In addition, there is ample evidence that increased athletics participation opportunities for women and young girls, available as a result of Title IX enforcement, have had salutary effects in other areas of societal concern.

One need look no further than the impressive performances of our country's women athletes in the 1996 Olympic Summer Games to see that Title IX has had a dramatic and positive impact on the capabilities of our women athletes, particularly in team sports. These Olympians represent the first full generation of women to grow up under the aegis of Title IX. The unprecedented success of these athletes is due, in no small measure, to Title IX's beneficent effects on women's sports, as the athletes themselves have acknowledged time and again. What stimulated this remarkable change in the quality of women's athletic competition was not a sudden, anomalous upsurge in women's interest in sports, but the enforcement of Title IX's mandate of gender equity in sports.

Affirmed in part, reversed in part, and remanded for further proceedings. . . .

NOTES AND QUESTIONS

1. *Accommodating Interest and Ability.* What factors did the First Circuit consider in determining that Brown University did not fully and effectively accommodate the interests and abilities of the underrepresented sex? Why was the relative interests test, offered by the university to show that women are less interested in sports to justify providing fewer athletics opportunities for women, rejected?

2. *Educational Institution Discretion in the Offering of Sports.* If both sexes' athletic participation interests are not effectively accommodated, *Cohen* illustrates that courts generally give a school some measure of discretion regarding the specific sports to offer. The Office for Civil Rights notes that:

   A college or university is not required to offer particular sports or the same sports for each sex. Also, an institution is not required to offer an equal number of sports for each sex. However, an institution must accommodate to the same degree the athletic interests and abilities of each sex in the selection of sports.

   A college or university may sponsor separate teams for men and women where selection is based on competitive skill or when the activity is a contact sport. Contact sports under the Title IX regulation include boxing, wrestling, rugby, ice hockey, football, basketball and other sports in which the purpose or major activity involves bodily contact.

   Equally effective accommodation also requires a college or university that sponsors a team for only one sex to do so for members of the other sex under certain circumstances. This applies to contact and non-contact sports. For example, a separate team may be required if there is sufficient interest and ability among members of the excluded sex to sustain a team and a reasonable expectation of competition for that team. Also, where an institution sponsors a team in a particular non-contact sport for members of one sex, it must allow athletes of the other sex to try-out for the team if, historically, there have been limited athletic opportunities for members of the other sex.

U.S. Dep't of Educ.: Off. for C.R., Requirements Under Title IX of the Education Amendments of 1972, http://www2.ed.gov/about/offices/list/ocr/docs/interath.html.

3. *Developing a Plan.* Why does the First Circuit provide Brown University with another opportunity to prepare a plan to comply with Title IX? If you were representing Brown University, how would you develop a new compliance plan? In doing so, consider the potential economic and political implications of your recommended compliance plan within the university community. Problem 10-3 provides another opportunity to address these issues.

4. *Title IX Denial of Athletic Participation Opportunities at the High School Level.* In *Ollier v. Sweetwater Union High Sch. Dist.*, 768 F.3d 843 (9th Cir. 2014), the Ninth Circuit affirmed the district court's holding that Sweetwater High School District had not fully and effectively accommodated the interests and abilities of its female athletes when it cut the girls field hockey team. In rejecting the District's argument that it had not retaliated against the coach who raised these issues, the Ninth Circuit panel noted:

> Sweetwater's argument that it fired Coach Martinez because he let an unauthorized parent coach a summer softball team is specious. Not only was Coach Martinez absent when the incident occurred, but he forbade the parent from coaching after learning of his ineligibility to do so. Moreover, the summer softball team in question "was not conducted under the auspices of the high school." Finally, while Coach Martinez did file late paperwork for the Las Vegas tournament, he was not then admonished for it. As with the ineligible player incident, the timing of his termination suggests that Sweetwater's allegedly non-retaliatory reason is merely a *post hoc* rationalization for what was actually an unlawful retaliatory firing. . . . On the record before it, the district court correctly could find that Coach Martinez was fired in retaliation for Plaintiffs' Title IX complaints, not for any of the pretextual, non-retaliatory reasons that Sweetwater has offered.
>
> It appears evident that courts will increasingly be involved in Title IX and gender equity matters at the high school level. Nevertheless, why are so few cases brought at the interscholastic or high school level? What are the challenges faced by a plaintiff? Why were the school district's other reasons for firing Coach Martinez deemed pretextual?

5. *Eleventh Amendment.* Courts have held that the Eleventh Amendment is no bar to private suits brought against states under Title IX of the Education Amendments of 1972. See *Litman v. George Mason Univ.*, 186 F.3d 544 (4th Cir. 1999), *cert. denied*, 528 U.S. 1181 (2000); *Franks v. Kentucky Sch. for the Deaf*, 142 F.3d 360, 363 (6th Cir. 1998); *Doe v. Univ. of Ill.*, 138 F.3d 653, 660 (7th Cir. 1998), vacated and remanded, 119 S. Ct. 2016 (1999), *reinstated in pertinent part*, 200 F.3d 499 (7th Cir. 1999); *Crawford v. Davis*, 109 F.3d 1281, 1283 (8th Cir. 1997).

Much of the earlier litigation under Title IX was focused on providing equal participation opportunities as illustrated in *Cohen v. Brown* supra. The courts and OCR apply the Three-Part test in determining whether or not a school is in compliance. Achieving proportionality to satisfy the first part of the Three-Part Test is difficult for many institutions, and in these situations, schools must rely on the second or third options to show compliance.

BOUCHER v. SYRACUSE UNIVERSITY

1998 WL 167296 (N.D.N.Y. 1998), *vacated in part and appeal dismissed in part,*
164 F.3d 113 (2d Cir. 1999)

SCULLIN, J.

FACTUAL BACKGROUND

The eight named [Plaintiffs] are undergraduate students at Syracuse University, seven of which are, or were, members of the women's club lacrosse team. The other plaintiff is a member of the women's club softball team. . . .

In 1971, Syracuse University ("Syracuse") established a women's intercollegiate athletics program, creating women's varsity basketball, fencing, swimming, tennis and volleyball teams. Field hockey replaced fencing in 1972. Syracuse added women's varsity crew in 1977 and indoor and outdoor track in 1981. In 1982, Syracuse merged its male and female varsity athletic programs into a single all-sport intercollegiate Athletic Department. From 1980 through 1982, the Office for Civil Rights ("OCR") performed a Title IX compliance review and found that Syracuse's intercollegiate program was in compliance with Title IX. In 1996 Syracuse added a women's varsity soccer team, and in 1997 Syracuse added a women's varsity lacrosse team; both of which are receiving the benefits of varsity status, including facilities and scholarships.

With the establishment of these two additional women's sports, Syracuse now offers 21 varsity sports — ten men's varsity sports and eleven women's varsity sports. As stated, Syracuse has also announced its plan to implement women's softball as a varsity sport beginning the 1999-2000 academic year.

All other sport teams are "club" sport teams which are student run and primarily student funded. Any financial assistance Syracuse provides to club sports comes from Recreation Services, an office within the Division of Student affairs. The Athletic Department does not provide any funding for club sports. . . .

I.   TITLE IX

The Department of Education, through its Office for Civil Rights ("OCR") promulgated regulations and a "Policy Interpretation" to clarify the responsibilities of institutions subject to the mandates of Title IX. See 44 Fed.Reg. 71,413-23. This Court has previously found that these regulations are a "reasonable interpretation of the statute, and consequently, affords them controlling weight." The Court further found that it would afford substantial deference to the Policy Interpretation where it "reasonably interprets the regulations." The regulations which are applicable to claims of gender bias in athletics fall within three categories: (1) equality in Athletic Financial Assistance (Scholarships), 34 C.F.R. §106.37(c); (2) Equivalence in Other Athletic Benefits and Opportunities, 34 C.F.R. §106.41(c)(2)-(10); and (3) Effective Accommodation of Student Interests and Abilities, 34 C.F.R. §106.41(c)(1). Presently, Plaintiffs assert that Defendants are in violation of the third category; ineffective accommodation of student interests and abilities.

A.   *Effective Accommodation*

An institution is in violation of Title IX where it does not provide effective accommodation, regardless of whether that institution satisfies the other two categories of compliance. See *Cohen v. Brown University*, 897 F.2d 888, 897 (1st Cir. 1993). An institution cannot satisfy the statute by merely bolstering those programs already in existence or by reducing the opportunities of the over-represented gender.

To survive a motion for summary judgment against an effective accommodation claim, a plaintiff must establish that a question of material fact exists with regard to whether:

(1) intercollegiate level participation opportunities for male and female students are not provided in numbers substantially proportionate to their respective enrollment; and
(2) the interests and abilities of the sex under represented among intercollegiate athletes have not been effectively accommodated by the present program.

Even if Plaintiffs can raise an issue of fact with regard to either of these two elements, Defendants may still succeed on their motion if they can establish, without dispute, that they qualify under any part of Title IX's three-part test, more commonly known as Title IX's "safe harbor" provisions. . . . According to the Policy Interpretation promulgated by the OCR, an institution will be found to be in compliance with Title IX if it falls within any one of the following "safe harbors":

(1) where the institution can show that intercollegiate level participation opportunities for male and female students are provided in numbers substantially proportionate to their respective enrollments; or
(2) where the members of one sex have been and are under represented among intercollegiate athletes, but the institution can show a history and continuing practice of program expansion which is demonstrably responsive to the developing interest and abilities of the members of that sex; or
(3) where the members of one sex are under represented among intercollegiate athletes, and the institution cannot show a continuing practice of program expansion such as that cited above, but the institution can demonstrate that the interests and abilities of the members of that sex have been fully and effectively accommodated by the present program.

In the present case, Defendants argue as an affirmative defense that they fall within the second "safe harbor" provision; that Syracuse has a history and continuing practice of program expansion. Defendants have the burden of demonstrating to this Court that there is no material factual dispute as to whether they qualify for this "safe harbor" immunity.

B.   *Safe Harbor as an Affirmative Defense*

To succeed on their affirmative defense, Defendants must show (1) a history of Program expansion, i.e. that their past actions expanded participation opportunities for the under represented sex in a manner that was demonstrably responsive to their developing interests and abilities; and (2) a continuing practice, i.e. that they continue their practice of program expansion in response to its student bodies abilities and interests.

1.   History of Program Expansion

In January of 1996, the OCR issued a letter entitled, "Clarification of Intercollegiate Athletics Policy Guidance: The Three Part Test" (the "Clarification") which further explained the safe harbor provisions. In doing so it identified three factors that the Court may consider in determining whether an institution has established a history of program expansion:

(1)   the institution's record of adding intercollegiate teams, or upgrading teams to intercollegiate status, for the under represented sex;
(2)   an institution's record of increasing the number of participants in intercollegiate athletics who are members of the under represented sex; and
(3)   an institution's affirmative response to requests by students or others for addition or elevation of sports. OCR Clarification, p. 6.

As set forth in the facts, from 1971 to 1982, Syracuse had a strong history of adding women's sports programs. While it is true that between 1982 and 1995 no new women's teams were added, during this period Syracuse continuously increased the number of women's scholarships and otherwise enhanced its women's programs by providing improved facilities, enhanced coaching staffs, and providing more elaborate support services. Between 1982 and 1995, the number of female participants in varsity sports increased from 148 to 217; an increase of forty-seven percent (47%). During this period, male participation in varsity sports only increased three percent (3%). Since 1995, Syracuse has added two additional women's athletic teams, lacrosse and soccer, and is planning the induction of a third team, softball, by the year 1999. The Court finds as a matter of law that Syracuse has a sufficient history of expanding opportunities for its women student-athletes so to satisfy the first prong of its affirmative defense.

2.   Continuing Practice of Program Expansion

In evaluating whether an institution has complied with the second requirement, that of demonstrating a continuing practice of program expansion, the Court may consider whether there are any formal policies in place which might indicate that the institution is monitoring the pulse of its students' interests in anticipation of expansion. This is particularly relevant where there is no actual expansion currently taking place. However, the best evidence of continued expansion is expansion itself. While Defendants have not established, to the Court' satisfaction, that any formal policy was in place whereby students could voice their interests to the institution, the undisputed testimony of Athletic Director Crouthamel shows that Syracuse did expand its women's athletic program by adding two women's varsity teams with plans of creating a third team by the year 1999. Furthermore, according to Crouthamel's affidavit, these additions were in response to his monitoring of and gathering information regarding club participation at Syracuse; prospective competition with other schools; and the developing interests and abilities at national, regional, and local levels of competition, including information regarding the interest and abilities of the University's feeder schools. Additionally, it is evident from the multiple affidavits submitted by both parties that there are informal means by which self-motivated students bring their interests to Defendants' attention.

The Court does believe that the spirit of Title IX would be better served were the institution to implement a more formal policy by which students could bring their interests and abilities to the attention of the administration.

However, notwithstanding this lack of formal policy, the Court is convinced that taken as a whole, Defendants have continued a practice of program expansion which is responsive to the abilities and interests of its student body. Accordingly, the Court finds that Defendants fall within the second safe harbor provision of Title IX.

C. *Elevation of Club Sports*

Plaintiffs' only remaining claim relates to treatment of female athletes vis-a-vis male athletes in club sports. To date, Plaintiffs have not provided the Court with any evidence that Defendant Syracuse treats men's club teams any different from women's club teams or that Defendant Crouthamel has anything to do with club sports. Nor do Plaintiff's dispute that the club teams are organized, operated and substantially funded by the student body.

[The court granted Defendants' motion for summary judgment and dismissed Plaintiffs' complaint.]

NOTES AND QUESTIONS

1. *Substantial Proportionality.* How did the *Cohen* and *Boucher* courts address the "substantial proportionality" prong of the test? This prong is often very difficult to satisfy, particularly in an era of rising female undergraduate enrollment and if an institution has a football program with a significant number of male participants. See also *Roberts v. Colorado State Bd. of Agric.*, 998 F.2d 824, 830 (10th Cir. 1993), *cert. denied*, 510 U.S. 1004 (1993) ("substantial proportionality entails a fairly close relationship between athletic participation and undergraduate enrollment"; not satisfied by 10.5 percent disparity between enrollment and athletic participation for women); *Brust v. Univ. of Calif.*, 2007 WL 4365521 (E.D. Cal. Dec. 12, 2007) (whether 6 percent disparity between female undergraduate enrollment and intercollegiate athletic participation opportunities satisfies substantial proportionality test is a question of fact); *Miller v. Univ. of Cincinnati*, 2008 WL 203025 (S.D. Ohio Jan. 22, 2008) (1 percent disparity between male undergraduate enrollment and intercollegiate athletic participation opportunities complies with substantial proportionality requirement, observing that the Department of Education permits a multisport athlete to be counted as a participant for each sport).

2. *History and Continuing Practice of Program Expansion. Boucher* illustrates how an educational institution can satisfy part two of the three-part test, which requires an examination of the entire history of the school's women's athletics program to establish a history and continuing practice of adding sports for the underrepresented sex. But see *Mansourian v. Regents of Univ. of Calif.*, 816 F. Supp. 2d 869 (E.D. Cal. 2011) (prong two not satisfied if a significant number of women given opportunity to participate in university's intercollegiate athletics program decline). Why did Brown University fail to prove compliance on this ground? Is the *Cohen* court's requirement that a school "march uninterruptedly in the direction of equal athletic opportunity" difficult to prove? 101 F.3d at 176.

  In the decade after Title IX was adopted, female athletics participation opportunities were regularly added by many institutions. Beginning in the mid-1980s, however, institutions entered what came to be called the "cost containment era" — a time when many schools, particularly public institutions, faced serious budget cuts. As university budgets were cut, it became increasingly difficult for schools to add sports. Thus, there was a hiatus in terms of the addition of women's sports which was exacerbated to some extent by slow economic growth and the rising costs of competitive athletics programs. As one court explained:

> We recognize that in times of economic hardship, few schools will be able to satisfy Title IX's effective accommodation requirement by continuing to expand their women's athletics programs. Nonetheless, the ordinary meaning of the word "expansion" may not be twisted to find compliance under this prong when schools have increased the relative percentages of women participating in athletics by making cuts in both men's and women's sports programs. Financially strapped institutions may still comply with Title IX by cutting athletic programs such that men's and women's athletic participation rates become substantially proportionate to their representation in the undergraduate population.

Roberts v. Colorado State Bd. of Agric., 998 F.2d 824, 830 (10th Cir. 1993), *cert. denied*, 510 U.S. 1004 (1993). What do you think about the suggestion that men's sports be cut? The 2003 *Further Clarification* states the elimination of teams is a disfavored practice because it is contrary to the spirit of Title IX. Department of Education Office for Civil Rights, *Further Clarification of Intercollegiate Athletics Policy Guidance Regarding Title IX Compliance* (July 11, 2003) available at https://www2.ed.gov/about/offices/list/ocr/title9guidanceFinal.html.

3. *Cutting Women's Teams and the Three-Part Test.* Most schools have not achieved substantial proportionality, requiring them to prove a continuing history of program expansion, or that the current program effectively accommodates the interests and abilities of the underrepresented sex. Eliminating a women's sport also eliminates both prong 2 and prong 3 to prove accommodation, yet schools still attempt to cut women's teams. See *Portz v. St. Cloud State Univ.*, 196 F.Supp.3d 963 (D. Minn. 2016). Are there any circumstances that would allow an institution to cut women's teams and be Title IX compliant?

Cohen and *Boucher* make it clear that courts have accepted the three-prong test for evaluating equal athletics participation opportunities in the OCR's 1979 Policy Interpretation. The next case illustrates one institution's attempt to claim compliance using the third part of the three-part test: the current program is fully and effectively accommodating the interests and abilities of the underrepresented sex.

PEDERSON v. LOUISIANA STATE UNIVERSITY
213 F.3d 858 (5th Cir. 2000)

STEWART, Circuit Judge:

We must today determine whether the largest public university in Louisiana has discriminated against women under Title IX in the provision of facilities and teams for intercollegiate athletic competition. . . .

B.   TITLE IX VIOLATION

Appellees argue brazenly that the evidence did not demonstrate sufficient interest and ability in fast-pitch softball at LSU and that, therefore, they cannot be liable under Title IX. The heart of this contention is that an institution with no coach, no facilities, no varsity team, no scholarships, and no recruiting in a given sport must have on campus enough national-caliber athletes to field a competitive varsity team in that sport before a court can find sufficient interest and abilities to exist. It should go without saying that adopting this criteria would eliminate an effective accommodation claim by any plaintiff, at any time. . . . Having reviewed the record, we determine that the district court did not clearly err because there was ample indication of an interest by women in fast-pitch softball. . . .

[T]he student population of LSU is 51% male and 49% female, the population participating in athletics is 71% male and 29% female. Given this breakdown, [appellees] argue that it is improper to consider proportionality, because to do so would be to impose quotas, and that the evidence shows that female students are less interested in participating in sports than male students. The law suggests otherwise. Title IX provides that the district court may consider disproportionality when finding a Title IX violation:

> This subsection shall not be construed to prevent the consideration in any hearing or proceeding under this chapter of statistical evidence tending to show that such an imbalance exists with respect to the participation in or receipt of the benefits of any such program or activity by the members of one sex.

20 U.S.C. §1681(b). LSU's hubris in advancing this argument is remarkable, since of course fewer women participate in sports, given the voluminous evidence that LSU has discriminated against women in refusing to offer them comparable athletic opportunities to those it offers its male students.

Nevertheless, Appellees persist in their argument by suggesting that the district court's reliance on the fact that LSU fields a men's baseball team as evidence of discrimination was improper because there is no requirement that the same sports be offered for both men and women and because LSU offers nine sports for women and only seven for men. We find that it was indeed proper for the district court to consider the fact that LSU fields a men's baseball team while declining to field a comparable team for women despite evidence of interest and ability in fast-pitch softball at LSU.

Appellees finally contest the district court's determination that LSU's decision to add fast-pitch softball and soccer was not for the purpose of encouraging women's athletics. They challenge the district court's finding that LSU did not attempt to determine the interest and ability level of its female student population, contending that there is evidence in the record that shows that LSU does analyze the interest level of its female student athletes. Our review of the record demonstrates no such analysis on the part of LSU. . . . [T]he district court correctly found that LSU did not have a history of expanding women's athletic programs and had not presented credible evidence regarding the interests and abilities of its student body. These findings were not clearly erroneous. . . .

C. Intentional Discrimination

The district court found that LSU had violated and continued to violate the prescriptions of Title IX. The trial judge further concluded that, notwithstanding this threshold finding, a Title IX claimant must additionally prove intentional discrimination on the part of a recipient before she may recover monetary damages. With respect to the claims at issue in this case, the district court considered the question to be a "very close one" but eventually held that LSU did not intentionally violate Title IX. . . . We find that LSU did intentionally violate Title IX, thus we reverse that ruling.

The district court stated that Appellees' actions were not a result of intentional discrimination but rather of "arrogant ignorance, confusion regarding the practical requirements of the law, and a remarkably outdated view of women and athletics which created the byproduct of resistance to change." *Id.* The district court reasoned, inter alia, that, because Athletic Director Dean testified that he believes that his "women's athletics" program is "wonderful" and because he was ignorant of the program's state of compliance with Title IX, Appellees did not intentionally discriminate against women. . . .

If an institution makes a decision not to provide equal athletic opportunities for its female students because of paternalism and stereotypical assumptions about their interests and abilities, that institution intended to treat women differently because of their sex. Moreover, Appellees' ignorance about whether they are violating Title IX does not excuse their intentional decision not to accommodate effectively the interests of their female students by not providing sufficient athletic opportunities.

Apparently, Dean "believed his program to be so wonderful that he invited an investigator from the Department of Education's Office for Civil Rights to visit LSU to evaluate the athletics program's compliance with Title IX." That representative's findings confirmed Dean's ignorance of the actual state of compliance with Title IX by his athletic program but the district court nonetheless reasoned that Dean's testimony was "credible" because "otherwise he would not have invited OCR to LSU to assess the program." This conclusion ignores the fact that, already on notice of potential violations, Dean and others continued to adhere to deprecatory nomenclature when referring to female athletes, refused to authorize additional sports for women, and instead seemed content that the "women's teams fielded [by LSU] during the relevant time frame performed well in competition." This assessment of the athletics program is not merely "arrogance," as the district court concluded, it belies an intent to treat women differently in violation of the law.

It bears noting that the provisions of Title IX and its attendant regulations are not merely hortatory; they exist, as does any law, to sculpt the relevant playing field. Consequently, Appellees' alleged ignorance of the law does not preclude our finding that LSU acted intentionally. Appellees need not have intended to violate Title IX, but need only have intended to treat women differently. . . . Appellees' outdated attitudes about women amply demonstrate this intention to discriminate, and the district court squarely found that LSU's treatment of women athletes was "remarkably outdated," "archaic," and "outmoded." Well-established Supreme Court precedent demonstrates that archaic assumptions such as those firmly held by LSU constitute intentional gender discrimination. [Citations omitted.] We conclude that, because classifications based on "archaic" assumptions are facially discriminatory, actions resulting from an application of these attitudes constitutes intentional discrimination.

In addition to the district court's evaluation of LSU's attitudes as "archaic," our independent evaluation of the record and the evidence adduced at trial supports the conclusion that Appellees persisted in a systematic, intentional, differential treatment of women. For instance, in meetings to discuss the possibility of a varsity women's soccer team, Dean referred to [one female athlete] repeatedly as "honey," "sweetie," and "cutie" and negotiated with her by stating that "I'd love to help a cute little girl like you." Dean also opined that soccer, a "more feminine sport," deserved consideration for varsity status because female soccer players "would look cute running around in their soccer shorts." Dean, charismatically defending LSU's chivalry, later told the coach of the women's club soccer team that he would not voluntarily add more women's sports at LSU but would "if forced to." Among many other examples, [one student] testified that, when she met with representatives of the Sports and Leisure Department to request the implementation of an intramural fast-pitch softball team, she was told that LSU would not sponsor fast-pitch softball because "the women might get hurt."

LSU perpetuated antiquated stereotypes and fashioned a grossly discriminatory athletics system in many other ways. For example, LSU appointed a low-level male athletics department staff member to the position of "Senior Women's Athletic Administrator," which the NCAA defines as the most senior women in an athletic department. LSU consistently approved larger budgets for travel, personnel, and training facilities for men's teams versus women's teams. The university consistently compensated coaches of women's teams at a rate far below that of its male team coaches.

Appellees have not even attempted to offer a legitimate, nondiscriminatory explanation for this blatantly differential treatment of male and female athletes, and men's and women's athletics in general; they merely urge that "archaic" values do not equate to intentional discrimination. . . . Appellees must have been aware that they were discriminating on the basis of sex by not effectively accommodating the interests and abilities of its female student-athletes. . . .

The proper test is not whether [the institution] knew of or is responsible for the actions of others, but is whether Appellees intended to treat women differently on the basis of their sex by providing them unequal athletic opportunity, and, as we noted above, we are convinced that they did. Our review of the record convinces us that an intent to discriminate, albeit one motivated by chauvinist notions as opposed to one fueled by enmity, drove LSU's decisions regarding athletic opportunities for its female students. . . .

NOTES AND QUESTIONS

1. *Offering Practical Counsel.* What arguments did LSU raise in support of its efforts to achieve gender equity in its intercollegiate athletics program, and why did the *Pederson* court reject them? What practical advice would you give to LSU to help bring the school into compliance with Title IX requirements?

    Regarding how to determine women's athletic participation interests, the *Pederson* district court explained:

    > LSU could have obtained this information in a variety of ways, including, *but not limited* to: (1) Requests by students that a sport be added; (2) Requests that an existing club sport be elevated; (3) Participation levels in club or

intramural sports; (4) Interviews with students, admitted students, coaches, administrators or others regarding interest in a particular sport; (5) Results of questionnaires of students and admitted students regarding interest in particular sports; and (6) Participation levels in interscholastic sports by admitted students. Information also could be obtained through discussions with amateur athletic associations or community sports leagues or, perhaps the simplest solution, the inclusion of a "participation and interest" question on the admissions form to the university. However, there was no testimony to support that any credible attempt was made to gather such information.

912 F. Supp. at 915, n.61.

2. *Successful Aftermath.* LSU initially argued that there was a lack of interest on the part of women at LSU in developing a nationally prominent softball program. However, it added women's softball as a varsity sport prior to the final resolution of the *Pederson* case. Ironically, the women's softball team quickly rose to national prominence, winning the Southeastern Conference Championship in May 1999. In 2001, the team tied for third place in the Women's College World Series (WCSC). Their success continues.

3. *Intentional Discrimination.* In *Pederson*, the Fifth Circuit held that LSU had intentionally engaged in gender discrimination in the operation of its intercollegiate athletics program. Sufficient proof of intentional discrimination enables a plaintiff to recover compensatory damages. According to the court, what is the legal standard for proving that an institution intentionally violated Title IX?

The *Pederson* court seemed to be particularly concerned by comments made by LSU athletics personnel to female student-athletes. As legal counsel for an institution, how would you counsel coaches and other athletics personnel to prevent any intentional violations of Title IX?

In *Barrett v. West Chester Univ. of Pennsylvania*, 2003 WL 22803477 at *12 (E.D. Pa. Nov. 12, 2003), the court observed that "[i]n the athletic realm of Title IX, intent is found on the face of most decisions." However, in *Horner v. Kentucky High School Athletic Assn.*, 206 F.3d 685 (6th Cir. 2000), the Sixth Circuit held that a facially neutral policy for determining the sports for which state championships would be sanctioned is not intentional discrimination. The court concluded: "Plaintiffs have simply not established that Defendants had actual knowledge of the discriminatory effect of their facially neutral rule, yet failed to remedy the violation." *Id.* at 697.

In *Portz v. St. Cloud State Univ.*, 297 F. Supp. 3d 929, 939 (U.S.D.C. Minn., 2018), the Eighth Circuit applied the intentional discrimination standard to plaintiffs' claim for damages: "Title IX damage actions which do not involve an institution's official policy require a showing that 'an official who at a minimum has authority to address the alleged discrimination and to institute corrective measures on the recipient's behalf [had] actual knowledge of discrimination in the recipient's programs and fail[ed] to adequately respond.'" Relying on precedent from *Grandson v. Univ. of Minnesota*, 272 F.3d 568, 575-76 (8th Cir. 2001), the court held that athletics programming decisions are not official institutional policy. While the plaintiffs had complained of inequities directly to the athletics director, the Eighth Circuit narrowly determined there was no evidence that SCSU had actual knowledge of the plaintiffs' claimed monetary injuries. The plaintiffs' claims for damages was dismissed. What evidence would be required for a student-athlete to prove the institution was liable for damages under the intentional discrimination standard?

Cohen provided colleges and universities with a clear road map for satisfying the mandate to provide equitable participation opportunities, both in quality and quantity. However, a small percentage of institutions actually satisfy the proportionality prong of the three-part test. The undergraduate population of the average college or university is about 60 percent women and 40 percent men, with the average athletics department participation ratio being approximately 60 percent men and 40 percent women, resulting in the average institution being approximately 20 percent out of proportional compliance. Because of this, institutions have become more creative in providing and counting participation opportunities, as demonstrated in the following case.

BIEDIGER v. QUINNIPIAC UNIVERSITY
691 F.3d 85 (2d Cir. 2012)

RAGGI, Circuit Judge. . . .

Quinnipiac argues that the injunction [issued by the trial court], which prohibits any such future discrimination, should be vacated because it is based on a Title IX ruling infected by errors in counting the varsity athletic participation opportunities afforded Quinnipiac's female students in the 2009-10 school year. Specifically, Quinnipiac faults the district court for excluding from its count of the total athletic participation opportunities afforded female students: (1) 11 roster positions on the women's indoor and outdoor track and field teams, held by members of Quinnipiac's women's cross-country team who were required to join the track teams even though they were unable to compete in 2009-10 because they were injured or "red-shirted"; and (2) all 30 roster positions on Quinnipiac's nascent women's competitive cheerleading team, based on a finding that the team did not afford the athletic participation opportunities of a varsity sport. Quinnipiac further contends that, even if these 41 roster positions should not count as varsity athletic participation opportunities for women, the district court erred in concluding that (3) the resulting 3.62% disparity between the percentage of all participation opportunities in varsity sports afforded female students (58.25%) and the percentage of enrolled female undergraduates (61.87%) established a Title IX violation warranting the challenged injunctive relief. . . .

I. BACKGROUND

A. QUINNIPIAC'S DECISION TO ELIMINATE WOMEN'S VOLLEYBALL PROMPTS THIS TITLE IX ACTION

This lawsuit has its origins in Quinnipiac's March 2009 announcement that in the 2009-10 academic year, it would eliminate its varsity sports teams for women's volleyball, men's golf, and men's outdoor track and field, while simultaneously creating a new varsity sports team for women's competitive cheerleading. Plaintiffs, five Quinnipiac women's volleyball players and their coach, Robin Sparks, filed this action in April 2009, charging the university with violating Title IX by denying women equal varsity athletic participation opportunities, and seeking an injunction that, among other things, prevented Quinnipiac from eliminating its women's volleyball team. After a hearing, the district court preliminarily enjoined Quinnipiac from withdrawing support from its volleyball team, finding that Quinnipiac systematically and artificially increased women's teams' rosters and decreased men's teams' rosters to achieve the appearance of Title IX compliance. . . .

B.   STATUTORY AND REGULATORY BACKGROUND

[The appellate court provides an excellent general summary of the statutory and regulatory background to Title IX, which is followed by a summary of specific materials related to the issue of whether cheer is a sport for Title IX purposes.]

In a 2008 letter, OCR explained that a genuine athletic participation opportunity must take place in the context of a "sport." Letter from Stephanie Monroe, Assistant Sec'y for Civil Rights, OCR, U.S. DOE, to Colleagues, at 1-2 (Sept. 17, 2008) ("2008 OCR Letter"). If a school is a member of a recognized intercollegiate athletic organization, such as the National Collegiate Athletic Association ("NCAA"), that subjects the activity at issue to its organizational requirements, OCR will "presume" that the activity is a sport and that participation can be counted under Title IX. But if that presumption does not apply or has been rebutted, OCR will determine whether the activity qualifies as a sport by reference to several factors relating to "program structure and administration" and "team preparation and competition." . . .

[I]n 2000, OCR had issued two letters stating that cheerleading, whether of the sideline or competitive variety, was presumptively not a sport, and that team members could not be counted as athletes under Title IX. While the letters indicated OCR's willingness to review particular cheerleading programs on a case-by-case basis, the parties stipulated in the district court that, since 2000, OCR has never recognized an intercollegiate varsity cheerleading program to be a sport for Title IX purposes. . . . Nor has Quinnipiac ever sought OCR recognition of its competitive cheerleading program as a sports activity. . . .

Once the numbers of real athletic participation opportunities afforded men and women have been determined in light of these principles, the next step of Title IX effective-accommodation analysis considers whether the numbers are substantially proportionate to each sex's enrollment. . . .

OCR affords schools considerable "flexibility and choice" in deciding how to provide substantially proportionate athletic opportunities to students of both sexes. . . .

C.   THE DISTRICT COURT RULING

At trial, Quinnipiac maintained that it offered athletic participation opportunities to male and female undergraduates substantially proportionate to their respective enrollments. In support, it pointed to evidence showing that, of the 5,686 students enrolled in Quinnipiac's undergraduate programs in the 2009-10 academic year, 3,518 were female and 2,168 were male. Varsity rosters for the first day of team competitions in 2009-10 listed 440 varsity athletes, of whom 274 were female and 166 were male. Thus, Quinnipiac maintained that women represented 61.87% of the total student body and 62.27% of all varsity athletes, while men represented 38.13% of the student body and 37.73% of all varsity athletes. . . .

Plaintiffs challenged Quinnipiac's count of its varsity athletes, arguing that (1) the university manipulated its team rosters to produce artificially undersized men's teams and artificially oversize women's teams; (2) counting the same women's membership on cross-country, indoor track, and outdoor track teams as three distinct athletic participation opportunities was unwarranted because Quinnipiac's indoor and outdoor track teams did not afford cross-country athletes genuine and distinct benefits; and (3) women who participated on the competitive cheerleading team should not be counted at all because the activity had not yet achieved the status of an intercollegiate varsity sport.

After trial, the district court issued a detailed memorandum of decision in favor of plaintiffs . . . reject[ing] plaintiffs' contention that, in setting roster targets for each of its teams, Quinnipiac had manipulated the rosters so as to undercount male participants and overcount female participants, or to set artificially high targets for women's teams that denied women participants genuine athletic opportunities. . . . The district court also decided that none of the 30 roster positions assigned to women's competitive cheerleading should be counted because the activity did not yet afford genuine athletic participation opportunities in a varsity sport. . . .

The district court observed that "in strictly numerical terms," a 3.62% disparity between Quinnipiac's women's 58.25% varsity athletic participation and their 61.87% representation in the undergraduate population reflected only "a borderline case of disproportionate athletic opportunities for women." Id. Nevertheless, the district court concluded that the disparity was significant enough to support judgment in favor of plaintiffs because (1) the disparity was caused by Quinnipiac's own actions and not by natural fluctuations in enrollment; and (2) it was reasonable to expect Quinnipiac to close the gap because the 38 roster positions needed for that purpose would be enough to field a viable women's athletic team, and such a team already existed in the form of the women's volleyball team. . . .

Accordingly, the district court entered a declaratory judgment finding Quinnipiac to have violated Title IX and its implementing regulations by discriminating against women in failing to provide equal athletic participation opportunities to female students, and it permanently enjoined Quinnipiac from continuing to discriminate in this manner. The district court ordered Quinnipiac to submit a plan for complying with the injunction, which plan was to provide for continuation of the women's volleyball team during the 2010-11 athletic season. . . .

II. DISCUSSION

A. QUINNIPIAC'S ARGUMENT AND THE STANDARD OF REVIEW

[The court reviews the award of permanent injunctive relief for abuse of discretion only for clear error and its conclusions of law de novo.]

B. DEFERENCE TO AGENCY INTERPRETATION OF TITLE IX'S IMPLEMENTING REGULATIONS

In addressing Quinnipiac's arguments, we note at the outset that no party challenges the district court's reliance on agency policy statements and letters. . . .

Here, Quinnipiac elected to defend against plaintiffs' discrimination claim only by reference to the first safe harbor created by the three-part test, arguing that its athletics program provided "substantially proportionate" athletic participation opportunities [for women]. In sum, as a matter of Quinnipiac's litigation strategy, resolution of this case effectively turned on whether Quinnipiac's sex based treatment of varsity athletes provided its female students with genuine athletic participation opportunities substantially proportionate to their enrollment. . . .

C.   ATHLETIC PARTICIPATION OPPORTUNITIES FOR WOMEN RUNNERS: DISCOUNTING THE REPORTED NUMBERS FOR INDOOR AND OUTDOOR TRACK

Before the district court, plaintiffs argued that Quinnipiac should not be allowed to count as 54 athletic participation opportunities the cross-country, indoor track, and outdoor track roster positions held by the same 18 women. As the district court recognized, the issue admitted no easy resolution. The 1996 Clarification plainly states that "an athlete who participates in more than one sport will be counted as a participant in each sport in which she participates." 1996 Clarification at 3. But the trial evidence reflected circumstances not addressed in the 1996 Clarification: Quinnipiac's women cross-country runners were not afforded a choice as to whether to participate in more than one sport; they were required to do so. . . . As the district court recognized, these circumstances raise questions as to whether simultaneous participation on the women's cross-country, indoor track, and outdoor track teams at Quinnipiac represented three genuine athletic opportunities, or whether cross-country runners' mandated participation on the indoor and outdoor track teams was simply a form of alternative off-season training for the cross-country runners, one that allowed Quinnipiac to inflate the rosters of its women's indoor and outdoor track teams. . . .

D.   ATHLETIC PARTICIPATION OPPORTUNITIES FOR WOMEN IN COMPETITIVE CHEERLEADING: THE DETERMINATION THAT THE ACTIVITY DOES NOT YET QUALIFY AS A "SPORT"

Competitive cheerleading, which Quinnipiac decided to create as a new women's varsity sport team for 2009-10, is a late twentieth-century outgrowth of traditional sideline cheerleading. Whereas sideline cheerleaders generally strive to entertain audiences or solicit crowd reaction at sport or school functions, a competitive cheerleading team seeks to pit its skills against other teams for the purpose of winning. Thus, to distinguish the two activities, competitive cheerleaders do not attempt to elicit crowd response; generally do not use pom-poms, megaphones, signs, or other props associated with [sideline] cheerleading teams; wear uniforms consisting of shorts and jerseys, much like what women's volleyball players don; and emphasize the more gymnastic elements of sideline cheerleading, such as aerial maneuvers, floor tumbling, and balancing exercises, to the exclusion of those activities intended to rally the watching audience.

The district court nevertheless concluded that the 30 roster positions that Quinnipiac assigned competitive cheerleading for 2009-10 could not be counted under Title IX because the activity did not yet afford the participation opportunities of a varsity "sport."

Preliminary to reaching this conclusion, the district court observed that competitive cheerleading is not yet recognized as a "sport," or even an "emerging sport," by the NCAA, action that would have triggered a presumption in favor of counting its participants under Title IX.

Mindful of these circumstances, the district court proceeded carefully to review the structure, administration, team preparation, and competition of

Quinnipiac's competitive cheerleading program to determine whether it never-theless qualified as a sport whose athletic participation opportunities should be counted for purposes of Title IX. Again, we only briefly summarize the district court's detailed findings, which find ample support in the record evidence. The district court found that in terms of the team's operating budget, benefits, ser-vices, and coaching staff, competitive cheerleading was generally structured and administered by Quinnipiac's athletics department in a manner consistent with the school's other varsity teams. The district court noted two "minor" excep-tions to this conclusion: Quinnipiac did not afford its competitive cheerleading team locker space; and because the NCAA did not recognize competitive cheer-leading as a sport, the team did not receive NCAA catastrophic injury insurance and had to obtain it from a separate provider. With respect to factors relating to the team's preparation and competition, the district court found that the com-petitive cheerleading team's practice time, regimen, and venue were consistent with other varsity sports. Further, as with other varsity sports, the length of the competitive cheerleading season and the minimum number of competitions in which a team would participate were pre-determined by a governing athletic organization, the recently formed National Competitive Stunt and Tumbling Association, of which Quinnipiac was a founding member. Finally, the purpose of the team — to compete athletically at the intercollegiate varsity level — was akin to that of other varsity sports.

At the same time, however, the district court identified a number of circum-stances that sufficiently distinguished Quinnipiac's competitive cheerleading program from traditional varsity sports as to "compel[ ] the decision that, for the 2009-10 season," the program could not "be counted as a varsity sport for purposes of Title IX." First, Quinnipiac did not — and, in 2009-10, could not — conduct any off-campus recruitment for its competitive cheerleading team, in marked contrast not only to the school's other varsity sports teams but also to a typical NCAA Division I sports program. The district court explained the significance of this circumstance: "Although the women on the Quinnipiac competitive cheer team were athletically able, they would have been all the more talented had [Coach] Powers been able to seek out the best competitive cheerleaders around the country, as any other varsity coach would have been able to do."

More important, no uniform set of rules applied to competitive cheerlead-ing competition throughout the 2009-10 season. Indeed, in the ten competi-tions in which the Quinnipiac team participated during the regular season, it was judged according to five different scoring systems. Further, in these competitions, Quinnipiac did not face only varsity intercollegiate competitive cheerleading teams. Rather, it was challenged by "a motley assortment of compet-itors," including collegiate club opponents who did not receive varsity benefits, collegiate sideline cheerleading teams, and all-star opponents unaffiliated with a particular academic institution, some of whom may still have been high-school age. As the district court observed, "application of a uniform set of rules for competition and the restriction of competition to contests against other varsity opponents" are the "touchstones" of a varsity sports program. "Those features ensure that play is fair in each game, that teams' performances can be compared across a season, and that teams can be distinguished in terms of quality."

The concerns raised by these irregularities in season competition were only aggravated by aspects of post-season play. Notably, competitive cheerleading offered no progressive playoff system leading to a championship game. Rather, it provided an open invitational, which neither excluded any team on the basis of its regular season performance nor ranked or seeded participating teams on that basis. Instead, all entrants competed in a single championship round in which the team with the highest score won. That round, moreover, was subject to a new rule of competition that had not applied to Quinnipiac in any of its regular season competitions: a mandatory 45-60 second "spirit" segment in which a team was judged by the intensity of the response it elicited from the crowd and the number of the sponsoring brand's props that it employed, features that Quinnipiac's coach confirmed were more characteristic of sideline rather than competitive cheerleading. Viewing the totality of these circumstances, the district court concluded that the competitive cheerleading team's post-season competition did not conform to expectations for a varsity sport.

Most other varsity sports would have used some system to separate teams and competitors in terms of quality, and would have ranked, seeded, or excluded teams on the basis of their performances during the regular season. Moreover, any other varsity sport would not have imposed new rules of competition in the post-season that teams did not follow during the regular season.

Based on these findings, as well as those pertaining to regular season play, the district court concluded that Quinnipiac's competitive cheerleading team did not compete in circumstances indicative of varsity sports. Thus, it ruled that Quinnipiac's 30 roster positions for competitive cheerleading could not be counted for Title IX purposes because the activity did not yet afford women genuine participation opportunities in a varsity sport.

In challenging this conclusion, Quinnipiac questions the weight the district court assigned the various factors it identified as supporting or undermining recognition of competitive cheerleading as a genuine varsity sport. Quinnipiac argues that this court should decide the question de novo. . . . [E]ven assuming that de novo review were warranted, we conclude for the same reasons stated in detail by the district court and summarized in this opinion that, although there are facts on both sides of the argument, in the end, the balance tips decidedly against finding competitive cheerleading presently to be a "sport" whose participation opportunities should be counted for purposes of Title IX. Like the district court, we acknowledge record evidence showing that competitive cheerleading can be physically challenging, requiring competitors to possess "strength, agility, and grace." Similarly, we do not foreclose the possibility that the activity, with better organization and defined rules, might some day warrant recognition as a varsity sport. But, like the district court, we conclude that the record evidence shows that "that time has not yet arrived."

Accordingly, we conclude that the district court was correct not to count the 30 roster positions assigned to competitive cheerleading in determining the number of genuine varsity athletic participation opportunities that Quinnipiac afforded female students.

E.   FINDING A TITLE IX VIOLATION BASED ON A 3.62% DISPARITY

Having reduced Quinnipiac's claimed athletic participation opportunities for women by 41 — representing 30 competitive cheerleaders and 11 cross-country runners required to join the indoor and outdoor track teams but unable to compete on those teams because of their injuries or red-shirt status — the district court correctly found that the school had a total of 400 varsity athletic participation opportunities, of which 233, or 58.25%, were assigned to women. Because enrollment data established that 61.87% of Quinnipiac's undergraduate population were women, this indicated a 3.62% disparity in the athletic opportunities that Quinnipiac afforded women. See id. The district court concluded that this disparity was sufficient to support a finding that Quinnipiac had failed to afford female students varsity athletic participation opportunities substantially proportionate to their enrollment. See id. at 113.

Quinnipiac argues that a 3.62% disparity is too small to support such a finding. In any event, it submits that the district court erred in holding Quinnipiac responsible for the disparity in light of fluctuations in enrollment and Quinnipiac's good faith reliance on the district court's statement at the time of the preliminary injunction decision that it would likely count all women members of the cross-country, indoor track, outdoor track, and competitive cheerleading teams as athletic participants for purposes of Title IX. Further, Quinnipiac contends that the district court erroneously accorded dispositive weight to the fact that the number of additional female roster spots needed to achieve exact proportionality — 38 — would have been sufficient for Quinnipiac to field an additional varsity team.

Quinnipiac's arguments fail to persuade. First, its emphasis on the relatively small percentage of disparity is unwarranted. The district court itself recognized that "in strictly numerical terms," a 3.62% disparity presents "a borderline case of disproportionate athletic opportunities." . . . While a district court outside this circuit reports finding no case in which a disparity of two percentage points or less has been held to manifest a lack of substantial proportionality, see Equity in Athletics, Inc. v. DOE, 675 F. Supp. 2d 660, 682-83 (W.D. Va. 2009), aff'd, 639 F.3d 91 (4th Cir. 2011), we do not pursue the issue because the disparity in this case is greater than 2%, and we do not, in any event, understand the 1996 Clarification to create a statistical safe harbor at this or any other percentage. Instead, the Clarification instructs that substantial proportionality is properly determined on a "case-by-case basis" after a careful assessment of the school's "specific circumstances," including the causes of the disparity and the reasonableness of requiring the school to add additional athletic opportunities to eliminate the disparity.

Specifically, the district court pointed to record evidence showing that the 3.62% identified disparity was almost entirely attributable to Quinnipiac's own careful control of its athletic rosters. . . .

Accordingly, we reject Quinnipiac's challenge to the district court's finding that the school engaged in sex discrimination in violation of Title IX, and we affirm the order enjoining Quinnipiac from continuing such discrimination.

NOTES AND QUESTIONS

1. *Is Cheerleading a Sport?* Chapter 1 included a discussion on "what is sport"? How did the Second Circuit determine whether cheerleading could be counted as an intercollegiate sport under Title IX?

2. *Adding New Sports.* An increasing number of high school athletic associations now recognize cheer and dance as a competitive sport. A number of states also offer state championships at the high school level in women's flag football (which is becoming very popular and is a significant part of many educational institutions' intramural and club sports programs for women), bowling, rugby, and weightlifting. Texas recognizes women's wrestling. Girls and women have also been successful in their efforts to obtain permission

for them to play tackle football. Sarah Hoye, *Girl, 11, scores in fight against Philadelphia Archdiocese to play football,* http://www.cnn.com/2013/03/14/us/philadelphia-archdiocese-boys-only-football/.

3. *Emerging Sports.* In *Biediger,* the court notes that there is a presumption that a sport qualifies for Title IX purposes if it is recognized by the NCAA, which women's cheer has not been. The NCAA emerging sports for women program is managed by the Committee on Women's athletics to grow opportunities for women student-athletes and add new national championships. The NCAA currently recognizes equestrian, rugby and triathlon in their emerging sports program, with recommendations to add wrestling and acrobatics and tumbling (a version of competitive cheer) in 2020. See *Emerging Sports for Women,* http://www.ncaa.org/about/resources/inclusion/emerging-sports-women. What women's sports should be characterized as "emerging" and why?

4. *Opportunities for Athletes of Color.* In June 2012, a group of concerned African American women gathered at the Schomburg Center for Research in Black Culture in Harlem for a forum in which they argued that Title IX discriminates against black women, raising the issue of whether a disparate number of scholarships are going to white women. *Black Women Say Title IX Discriminates Against Them,* Atlanta Black Star, June 11, 2012, http://atlantablackstar.com/2012/06/11/black-women-say-title-ix-discriminate-against-them/. A recent study reveals that gains for women under Title IX have "not been shared equally by White and African American females. High schools attended by African American females do not offer the same range of sports as those available in schools attended by White females." Moneque Walker Pickett, Marvin P. Dawkins, and Jomills Henry Braddock, *Race and Gender Equity in Sports: Have White and African American Females Benefited Equally from Title IX,* American Behavioral Scientist, http://abs.sagepub.com/content/56/11/1581.abstract. On April 20, 2015, the National Women's Law Center (NWLC) posted the results of an extensive study it had performed as a joint effort with the Poverty and Race Research Action Council. The study presents data "showing that at the national and state levels, girls of color do not receive equal chances to play school sports." The report also examined the "consequences of this inequality for girls of color." Additionally, it offered a number of recommendations for addressing the problem, some of which may be summarized as follows: (1) The federal government should take action against states and districts that fail to provide opportunities for young women, and should accumulate data by gender and race; (2) The state and the federal governments should take steps to provide a stronger base of funding for such equity (e.g., by providing equal funding or greater equity to help fund opportunities in athletics in all districts in a state, regardless of the wealth of the students living in that district); and (3) Each state should assess and monitor participation by young women in athletics in all districts within the state, with particular attention to women of color and poorer women. See Fatima Goss Graves, et al., *Finishing Last,* http://www.nwlc.org/sites/default/files/pdfs/final_nwlc_girlsfinishinglast_report.pdf. When considering new sports, the NCAA has a preference for sports recognized at the interscholastic level. Is this problematic in terms of racial equity? What can be done to address these broader issues of inequity for girls and women of color? See Rodney K. Smith, Lindsay Demery, Erika Torrez, *A Strategy for Strengthening Interscholastic Girls' Football and Starting Intercollegiate Women's Football,* http://asuselj.org/wp-content/uploads/2015/10/Smith-Demery-Torrez-Fall-2014.pdf for an article

arguing that sports like women's football would be more equitable, in terms of gender and race, than the sports typically recommended by the NCAA. Should the NCAA consider racial equity and socioeconomic issues in placing its imprimatur on certain emerging sports? Is women's football the answer to participation opportunity inequities? Alternatively, what other women's sports should be added and why?

2. The Contact Sport Exemption

FORCE v. PIERCE CITY R-VI SCH. DIST.

570 F. Supp. 1020 (W.D. Mo. 1983)

ROBERTS, District Judge.

[EDS. Nichole Force, a 13-year-old female student enrolled in the eighth grade at Pierce City Junior High School in Missouri, sought an injunction that would have allowed her to compete for a place on the school's eighth-grade football team. She had already been involved to a considerable extent in athletics (swimming, diving, organized softball, organized basketball, and elementary school football), and she had grown up with two brothers who excelled at football and who encouraged and helped her in her own athletic endeavors.

Pierce City Junior High School is a public school facility made up of the seventh, eighth, and ninth grades that sponsors an interscholastic athletics program. Boys could participate in football during the fall, basketball during the winter, and track during the spring. The corresponding sports for girls were volleyball, basketball, and track.

The boys' athletics coach for the school said he would let Nichole participate if school administration officials approved. However, school board members expressed concern over the potential precedent involved in granting her request (e.g., the possibility that boys would wish to participate on the girls' volleyball team and that high school girls might wish to play on the high school football team), the potential safety risk to a female competing in a contact sport with males, the administrative difficulties that might ensue (arrangements for locker room facilities, etc.), and that, at least as some board members understood it, the applicable provisions of Title IX and its regulations or Section 1.6 of the Missouri State High School Activities Association (MSHSAA) rules might be violated by permitting coeducational participation in a contact sport. The board voted unanimously to deny the request. While "they all agreed" Nichole would be a good football player and would have no problems playing, if she were permitted to play, the same allowance would have to be made for all other girls as well.

Nichole contended that this refusal to allow her an opportunity to play football was based solely upon the fact that she was a female rather than a male, and that this sex-based determination violated her right to the equal protection of the laws under the Fourteenth Amendment and 42 U.S.C. §1983.]

II. DISCUSSION

The record makes clear, and I find, that defendants' refusal to grant plaintiff's request is the poduct of a gender-based classification. Stated simply, only males are permitted to compete for a place on the Pierce City Junior High School eighth grade football team. Since Nichole is a female, that opportunity is denied to her.

The principles which must govern in this situation are summarized in the opening passages of Section II of the Supreme Court's recent decision in *Mississippi University For Women v. Hogan*, 458 U.S., 102 S. Ct. 3331, 73 L. Ed. 2d 1090 (1982). I can do no better than to quote those passages here:

> Because the challenged policy expressly discriminates among applicants on the basis of gender, it is subject to scrutiny under the Equal Protection Clause of the Fourteenth Amendment. Our decisions also establish that the party seeking to uphold a statute that classifies individuals on the basis of their gender must carry the burden of showing an "exceedingly persuasive justification" for the classification. The burden is met only by showing at least that the classification serves "important governmental objectives and that the discriminatory means employed" are "substantially related to the achievement of those objectives."
>
> Although the test for determining the validity of a gender based classification is straightforward, it must be applied free of fixed notions concerning the roles and abilities of males and females. Care must be taken in ascertaining whether . . . the objective itself reflects archaic and steretypic notions. Thus if the . . . objective is to exclude or "protect" members of one gender because they are presumed to suffer from an inherent handicap or to be innately inferior, the objective itself is illegitimate.
>
> If the State's objective is legitimate and important, we next determine whether the requisite direct, substantial relationship between objective and means is present. The purpose of requiring that close relationship is to assure that the validity of the classification is determined through reasoned analysis rather than through the mechanical application of traditional, often inaccurate, assumptions about the proper roles of men and women. . . .

Defendants do not quarrel with the fact that the present case must be governed by these principles; indeed they candidly acknowledge that fact. They argue, rather, that in the circumstances shown here a gender-based classification fully satisfies those principles. To that end, they identify four "important governmental objectives" which are said to be at stake: (a) maximization of equal athletic educational opportunities for all students, regardless of gender; (b) maintenance of athletic educational programs which are as safe for participants as possible; (c) compliance with Title IX of the Educational Amendments of 1972 and the regulations thereunder; and (d), compliance with the constitution and by-laws of MSHSAA. According to defendants, there is a "substantial relationship" between each of these objectives and a gender based classification which would prevent any female from competing with males for a place on the Pierce City Junior High School eighth grade football team.

Defendants' suggestion with respect to the necessity of compliance with Title IX can, I think, be dealt with in relatively short order. There is in fact nothing whatsoever in Title IX, or in its implementing regulations (34 C.F.R. §106.41(b)), which would mandate the action defendants have taken here.[3] To the contrary,

---

3. 34 C.F.R. §106.41(b) reads as follows: "(b) Separate teams. Notwithstanding the requirements of paragraph (a) of this section, a recipient may operate or sponsor separate teams for members of each sex where selection for such teams is based upon competitive skill or the activity involved is a contact sport. However, where a recipient operates or sponsors a team in a particular sport for members of one sex but operates or sponsors no such team for members of the other sex, and athletic opportunities for members of that sex have previously been limited, members of the excluded sex must be allowed to try-out for the team offered unless the sport involved is a contact sport. For the purposes of this part, contact sports include boxing, wrestling, rugby, ice hockey, football, basketball and other sports the purpose or major activity of which involves bodily contact."

Title IX's regulations leave each school free to choose whether co-educational participation in a contact sport will be permitted. Allowing Nichole Force to compete with males for a place on the Pierce City Junior High School eighth grade football team would no more violate those regulations than would refusing her that opportunity. Title IX simply takes a neutral stand on the subject.

Nor in my judgment can defendants' point regarding compliance with MSHSAA rules withstand scrutiny.[5] A school can hardly validate an otherwise unconstitutional act (assuming for the moment that there is one here) by noting that it has agreed with other schools to commit that act. There can be no doubt, of course, that MSHSAA performs a valuable and needed service for the schools and citizens of this state. But its rules cannot transcend constitutional requirements, and a member school's adherence to those rules cannot make constitutional that which is not.

I accordingly reject defendants' "objectives" (c) and (d) as providing any sort of appropriate predicate for the action taken here. Defendants' first two points, however, have more meat to their bones, and are deserving of more detailed treatment. Each will be examined separately below.

A.   MAXIMIZING PARTICIPATION IN ATHLETICS

One might wonder, at first blush, how denying all females the right to participate in a sport — which is the case here, since Pierce City eighth grade girls are not allowed to compete for a place on the only football team which might be available to them — will result in maximizing the participation of both sexes in athletics. And the short answer is that it probably does not. Defendants' argument in this regard, however, is sufficiently sophisticated to merit more than first blush treatment.

That argument proceeds on three interrelated theories. Defendants suggest, first, that males (as a class) will outperform females (as a class) in most athletic endeavors, given male size, speed and greater ratio of lean body mass. That being so, the argument proceeds, the best way in which to encourage and maximize female participation in athletics is by providing separate male and female teams, where males compete only against males and females only against females, since otherwise males will dominate the competition and ultimately discourage female participation. Pursuant to this idea, defendants have established separate inter-scholastic athletic programs for the two sexes in the Pierce City secondary schools, with the fall season sport being football for males and volleyball for females. But if (second) Nichole Force is permitted to compete for a place on the football team, then other girls must be accorded the same privilege, and boys must be allowed to compete for positions on the volleyball team. When (third) that happens, the girls will lose their best athletes, the boys will come to dominate volleyball, and overall female participation will ultimately wither.

Based upon the expert testimony presented in this case I am willing to accept the proposition that the average male, even at age 13, will to some extent

---

5. Section 1.6 of the MSHSAA by-laws, in pertinent part, reads as follows:

A school, at its own discretion, may allow a student to compete on a team with the opposite sex in baseball, cross country, golf, gymnastics, soccer, softball, swimming, tennis, track or volleyball, provided the school does not offer interscholastic competition for both sexes in that sport.

outperform the average female of that age in most athletic events, although the matter may be open to some dispute. And I note, without being called upon to decide the issue, that a number of courts have held that the establishment of separate male/female teams in a sport is a constitutionally permissible way of dealing with the problem of potential male athletic dominance. . . . Beyond these two points, however, I am unable to accept defendants' argument.

The principal difficulty with the remaining portions of that argument, it seems to me, is that the various hypotheses used to bind it together are just that — hypotheses, and nothing more. There is, for example, no factual indication that the girls' eighth grade volleyball team will be blighted by the defection of its best players to the football field, if Nichole Force is allowed to play football. To the contrary, defendants' own testimony is that Nichole Force is the first and only girl, at any grade level, who has ever made a request to play football. And for that matter, if defendants are correct in their position that females are unable to compete successfully with males in athletics, particularly in contact sports, it is to be expected that such defections would be short-lived in any event, and that the situation would prove to be self-regulating. [Citation omitted.]

Nor is there any factual indication that eighth grade boys at Pierce City Junior High School are waiting eagerly for volleyball to be desegregated. Again to the contrary, there is no indication that any boy has ever expressed a desire to play on the volleyball team. . . . And in any event, it is by no means clear that the District would be constitutionally required to permit boys to participate in girls' volleyball, even if girls were allowed to participate in football. See *Clark v. Arizona Interscholastic Association*, 695 F.2d 1126, 1131-32 (9th Cir. 1982); *Petrie v. Illinois High School Association*, 75 Ill. App. 3d 980, 31 Ill. Dec. 653, 394 N.E.2d 855 (1979) (both holding, on a theory similar to that utilized in *Regents of the University of California v. Bakke*, 438 U.S. 265, 98 S. Ct. 2733, 57 L. Ed. 2d 750 (1978), that the governmental interest in redressing past discrimination against women in athletics is sufficient to justify a regulation which excludes boys from participating on girls' teams, even though girls are allowed to compete on boys' teams).

Finally, even if by some chance defendants' worst case scenario should be realized, there might still be no need for the general breakdown which defendants postulate. For example, if a sufficient number of girls wish to play football, one obvious solution would be to organize a girls' football team; or if so many boys wish to play volleyball that they would dominate the girls' competition in that sport, to form a boys' volleyball team. . . .

There is, however, a further point implicit in defendants' argument on this subject which should be addressed before passing on: the apparent assumption that if, in the interest of maximizing equal athletic opportunities, it is constitutionally permissible to establish separate male and female teams in a given sport and to exclude each sex from the other's team, cases *supra*, then it is equally permissible, in that same interest, to designate separate male and female sports and to exclude each sex from participation in the other's sport. That is a proposition I am unwilling to accept, at least as a general matter. [Citations omitted.]

Each sport has its own relatively unique blend of requirements in terms of skills and necessary physical attributes, and each person, male or female, will for a variety of reasons probably find one or another sport more enjoyable and rewarding than others. In point of fact, volleyball is *not* football; and baseball is *not* hockey; and swimming is *not* tennis. Accordingly, if the idea is to "maximize educational athletic opportunities for all students, regardless of gender," it makes no sense, absent some substantial reason, to deny all persons of one sex the opportunity to test their skills at a particular sport. Of course there may be certain exceptional instances in which there is a "substantial reason" for such an exclusion, as for example where peculiar safety and equipment requirements demand it, see *Lafler v. Athletic Board of Control*, 536 F. Supp. 104 (W.D. Mich. 1982) (boxing), or perhaps where excluding males is necessary to redress past inequality and to foster female participation, see *Clark v. Arizona Interscholastic Association, supra; Petrie v. Illinois High School Association, supra*. But those instances would, I think, be relatively rare, and would need to be factually established. And that is precisely where defendants' present argument fails, as far as the instant case is concerned.

I do not question the idea that maximizing the participation of both sexes in interscholastic athletic events is a worthy, and important, governmental objective. Nor do I question the sincerity of defendants' efforts in that regard. In the circumstances of this case, however, I must and do hold that the gender based classification used by defendants does not bear a sufficiently "substantial" relationship to that objective to withstand a constitutional challenge.

B.   SAFETY

Neither do I question the fact that the "maintenance of athletic educational programs which are as safe for participants as possible" is an "important governmental objective." Indeed, that would seem obvious. Again, however, the facts of this case do not demonstrate a sufficiently "substantial" relationship between that objective and a blanket rule which prohibits all eighth grade females from competing for a place on the Pierce City Junior High School eighth grade football team.

There is no evidence, or even any suggestion, that Nichole Force herself could not safely participate in that football program. And while I do find, from the expert testimony presented, that a "typical" (i.e., average) 13 year old female would in fact, to some degree, have a higher potential for injury in mixed-sex football than would a "typical" (i.e., average) 13 year old male, this does not in my judgment greatly assist the defendants' argument. The problem, of course, is that not all 13 year old females are "typical," any more than all 13 year old males are "typical." Indeed, as defendants' own expert candidly admitted, some 13 year old females could safely play eighth grade football in mixed sex competition, and some 13 year old males could not. And yet I note that the Pierce City R-VI School District permits *any* male to compete in football, regardless of his size, speed, body type, lean body mass, fat body mass, bone structure, "Q" angle measurement or any other factor which might have a bearing on his potential for injury.

In short, the "safety" factor which defendants would utilize to prevent any female from playing eighth grade football — including those who could play safely — is not applied to males at all, even to those who could not play safely. All this tends to suggest the very sort of well-meaning but overly "paternalistic" attitude about females which the Supreme Court has viewed with such concern.[13] See, e.g., *Frontiero v. Richardson*, 411 U.S. 677, 684-87, 93 S. Ct. 1764, 1769-71, 36 L. Ed. 2d 583 (1973). . . .

---

13. The reference here is to governmental attitudes, not parental attitudes. Any parent who feels that his or her child should not play football, or any other interscholastic sport for that matter, remains quite free to withhold consent to that child's participation. The school requires such parental consent before any child is permitted to compete on one of the interscholastic teams.

I reject it here for the simple reason that it is sophistry to suggest a concern with the "administrative burden" of weeding out physically unfit 13 year old females in connection with a football program when there is no concern at all with weeding out physically unfit 13 year old males involved in the same program. In fact, I think, it might be rather difficult to sustain a requirement that females competing for a place on a particular athletic team be subjected to a fitness screening program, when males competing for a place on the same team are subjected to none at all.

I conclude, accordingly, that there is an insufficient relationship between defendants' announced goal of "safety" and a rule which automatically excludes all eighth grade females from competing with eighth grade males for a place on a football team. That holding, I note, is consistent with the result reached by virtually every other court which has considered this same sort of "safety" argument in connection with male/female competition in contact sports. . . .

CONCLUSION

Nichole Force obviously has no legal entitlement to a starting position on the Pierce City Junior High School eighth grade football team, since the extent to which she plays must be governed solely by her abilities, as judged by those who coach her. But she seeks no such entitlement here.

Instead she seeks simply a chance, like her male counterparts, to display those abilities. She asks, in short, only the right to try.

I do not suggest there is any such thing as a constitutional "right to try." But the idea that one should be allowed to try — to succeed or to fail as one's abilities and fortunes may dictate, but in the process at least to profit by those things which are learned in the trying — is a concept deeply engrained in our way of thinking; and it should indeed require a "substantial" justification to deny that privilege to someone simply because she is a female rather than a male. I find no such justification here.

[The court enjoined defendants from refusing to allow Nichole Force to compete for membership on the Pierce City Junior High School eighth-grade interscholastic football team on the same basis that males are allowed to compete.]

Similarly, male athletes have challenged rules prohibiting their ability to compete on all-girls teams when a school does not offer a boys' team in a particular sport.

WILLIAMS v. SCH. DIST. OF BETHLEHEM, PA
998 F.2d 168 (3d Cir. 1993)

SLOVITER, Chief Judge.

Can high school field hockey be considered a contact sport? . . .

I.   FACTS AND PROCEDURAL HISTORY

When John Williams was fourteen years old and in ninth grade, he presented himself for the girls' field hockey team tryouts at Liberty High School, a public school in the School District of Bethlehem, Pennsylvania. He had played intra-mural coed field hockey when he was in eighth grade at a middle school in the School District, but the high school has only a girls' field hockey team. After the tryouts, the coach made tentative position and team assignments based on each player's abilities. John, whose skills were average, would probably have played goalie on the junior varsity team. However, after school officials learned that John and another boy had been issued uniforms, the boys were instructed that they could not play on the girls' field hockey team.

John's parents, plaintiffs Sarah and Wayne Williams, filed this action in October 1990 against the School District of Bethlehem, challenging John's exclusion from the girls' field hockey team. They made claims alleging viola-tions of Title IX . . . ; the Equal Protection and Due Process clauses of the federal Constitution, under 42 U.S.C. §1983; and the Equal Rights Amendment to the Pennsylvania Constitution (E.R.A.), Pa. Const. art. I, §28. . . .

Based on the undisputed facts that the School District limits player partici-pation on the field hockey team to females and that John was not permitted to be a part of the Liberty High School team only because of that policy, the district court granted summary judgment . . . in favor of the plaintiffs, perma-nently enjoining the School District from excluding John from the Liberty High School girls' field hockey team. . . .

II.   DISCUSSION

A.   TITLE IX

1.   *Contact Sport*

Because field hockey is not one of the sports expressly specified in the regu-lation as a contact sport, whether it can be so deemed depends on whether it is a sport "the purpose or major activity of which involves bodily contact." 34 C.F.R. §106.41(b). . . . [P]laintiffs introduced the affidavits of four experts, each of whom concluded that field hockey is not a contact sport. . . .[5] All of these experts relied on the rules of play for field hockey promulgated by the National Federation of State High School Associations, which provide that almost all bodily contact or threatened bodily contact between players is a violation or foul. . . .

[The School District's two experts testified that because of the nature of field hockey, there inevitably will be contact among the players.]

It is not insignificant that the National Federation rules, introduced by the School District, require mouth protectors and shin guards, prohibit spiked shoes, require that artificial limbs be padded, and prohibit wearing jewelry. These rules suggest that bodily contact does in fact occur frequently and is expected to occur during the game. . . .

We hold only that there is sufficient evidence on this record to preclude sum-mary judgment for plaintiffs on that issue.

---

5. Plaintiffs also argue on appeal that field hockey should not be considered a contact sport because it is played coed at the adult level and because there will be no bodily contact with John Williams, who plays goalie. Assuming *arguendo* that John was slated as goalie on the junior varsity team, a matter which is not free from doubt, neither argument is relevant to the threshold ques-tion whether field hockey is a contact sport for purposes of the implementing regulation.

2. *Previously Limited Athletic Opportunities*

If it is determined that field hockey is a contact sport, no other inquiry is necessary because that will be dispositive of the title IX claim. Even if a sport is not a contact sport, and there is no team for the other sex in that sport, the implementing regulation requires that members of the excluded sex be permitted to try out for a single-sex team only if their athletic opportunities have "previously been limited." 34 C.F.R. §106.41(b). In interpreting that language, the district court considered the composition of the athletic program at Liberty High School, which mirrors the team offerings in the School District of Bethlehem overall. The court compared the number of teams for boys and those for girls, noting that as of 1989, each of the two high schools in the School District has had ten boys' teams, ten girls' teams, and two coed teams. The court found that athletic opportunities for girls have surpassed those of boys because girls are permitted to try out for all twenty-two teams whereas boys may try out for only twelve, and it thus concluded that athletic opportunities for boys have "previously been limited."

Plaintiffs argue that even if we find that athletic opportunities for boys at Liberty High School have not been limited, the School District would still be in violation of title IX because it is clear that opportunities for boys in the sport of field hockey have previously been limited. Plaintiffs thus would interpret the regulation's inquiry with respect to prior opportunities as sports-specific, in this case focusing on boys' opportunities in a traditionally female sport. This reading of the regulation language was adopted by the court in *Gomes v. Rhode Island Interscholastic League*, 469 F. Supp. 659, 664 (D.R.I.). . . .

We believe that the contrary interpretation adopted by the New York and New Hampshire courts is more persuasive. In *Mularadelis v. Haldane Central School Board*, 74 A.D.2d 248, 427 N.Y.S.2d 458, 461-64 (1980), the court looked at the phrase at issue in the context of the entire regulation. The court noted that the first clause expressly refers to a "particular sport" ("where a recipient operates or sponsors a team in a particular sport"), and the second clause uses broad and general language, defining the inquiry as whether "athletic opportunities" for members of the excluded sex have previously been limited. *Id.* If Congress had intended the inquiry into "athletic opportunities" to be limited to a "particular sport," it would have so stated, particularly since the phrase "particular sport" was used earlier in the same sentence. *Id.*

This analysis convinced the Superior Court of New Hampshire, which adopted it in *Gil v. New Hampshire Interscholastic Athletic Association*, No. 85-E-646, slip op. at 31-32. We agree. As the School District argues, if the plaintiffs' construction were adopted, there could never be a situation in a non-contact sport in which a team was limited to a single sex without a corresponding team for the other sex because, by definition, the opportunities in that particular sport will be limited for the excluded sex. It would mean that boys will always be able to argue that they had previous limited athletic opportunities just because certain sports have traditionally been considered women's sports, such as field hockey. This would render nugatory the purpose of the phrase in question, which was intended to authorize single-sex teams in certain circumstances.

We believe the district court was correct in implicitly rejecting the plaintiffs' sports-specific interpretation, and in looking instead to the overall athletic opportunities.

We conclude, however, that the district court applied a flawed analysis in holding as a matter of law that athletic opportunities for boys were previously limited at Liberty High School because girls have been able to try out for more teams than boys for almost two decades. The mere opportunity to try out for a team, which the district court found tipped the balance in favor of girls in the School District, is not determinative of the question of "previously limited" athletic opportunities under title IX. "Athletic opportunities" means real opportunities, not illusory ones. If, to satisfy title IX, all that the School District were required to do was to allow girls to try out for the boys' teams, then it need not have made efforts, only achieved in 1989, to equalize the numbers of sports teams offered for boys and girls.

The School District produced evidence that its decision in or about 1975 to allow girls the right to try out for all twenty-two teams did not equalize athletic opportunities between the sexes. . . .

Whether the opportunity for girls to try out for a boys' team is a realistic athletic opportunity with respect to that particular sport may turn on whether there are real and significant physical differences between boys and girls in high school. There was conflicting evidence introduced by the parties on this issue.

Plaintiffs offered evidence to show that the physical differences between boys and girls of high school age are negligible. . . .

It follows that in determining whether boys' athletic opportunities at Liberty have previously been limited, the factfinder must decide whether meaningful physiological differences between boys and girls of high school age negate the significance of allowing girls to try out for boys' teams but not allowing the reverse.

Because the district court erred in finding dispositive the mere opportunity for girls to try out without acknowledging that the School District had created a material issue of fact as to the effect of that opportunity, we will reverse the grant of summary judgment on the plaintiffs' title IX claim and remand for further factual development on the issue whether athletic opportunities for boys have previously been limited. . . .

C. PENNSYLVANIA EQUAL RIGHTS AMENDMENT

The Pennsylvania E.R.A. provides that "[e]quality of rights under the law shall not be denied or abridged in the Commonwealth of Pennsylvania because of the sex of the individual." Pa. Const. art. I, §28. . . .

Although the Supreme Court of Pennsylvania has not addressed the E.R.A. in the context of interscholastic athletics, in a thoughtful opinion the Commonwealth Court made clear that if the classification between boys and girls in connection with team sports is based on impermissible assumptions and stereotypes about the comparative characteristics or abilities of boys and girls, the E.R.A. will be violated. *Commonwealth ex rel. Packel v. Pennsylvania Interscholastic Athletic Ass'n*, 18 Pa. Cmwlth. 45, 334 A.2d 839, 843 (1975) (athletic league provision barring girls from participating in sports with boys violates E.R.A. because it embodies the stereotype that girls are generally weaker and boys generally more skilled at athletics). However, after the Commonwealth Court's decision in *Packel*, the Pennsylvania Supreme Court decided *Fischer v. Department of Public Welfare*, 509 Pa. 293, 502 A.2d 114 (1985), where it accepted the view prevailing among jurisdictions with a state E.R.A. that

> the E.R.A. does not prohibit differential treatment among the sexes when, as here[,] that treatment is reasonably and genuinely based on physical characteristics unique to one sex.

Id. 502 A.2d at 125. [Quotation omitted.]

In defending the E.R.A. claim, the School District argued that because of the undeniable physical differences between girls and boys of high school age, sex was the only classification feasible for accomplishing, *inter alia*, the legitimate and substantial interest of promoting athletic opportunities for girls. As we noted in our discussion of title IX, the parties introduced conflicting evidence on the extent of physical differences between boys and girls at the high school level. . . .

The validity of the School District's policy excluding boys from the field hockey team depends on whether there are "physical characteristics unique to [boys]" which warrant differential treatment. If there are real physical differences between high school boys and high school girls, then the sexes are "not similarly situated as they enter into most athletic endeavors," *Petrie v. Illinois High School Ass'n*, 75 Ill. App. 3d 980, 31 Ill. Dec. 653, 661, 394 N.E.2d 855, 863 (1979), and exclusion based on sex may be justified. . . .

Ultimately, the validity of the classification will depend on the relationship between the classification and the government interest. . . .

We will therefore remand the E.R.A. claim to the district court for factfinding as to whether there are any real physical differences between boys and girls that warrant different treatment, and whether boys are likely to dominate the school's athletic program if admitted to the girls' teams. Only then will it be possible to determine whether the School District's policy of excluding boys from girls' teams is necessary to the School District's recognized interest in preserving meaningful athletic opportunities for girls, . . . and/or whether there is a current need to rectify the admittedly pervasive past discrimination against female high school students with respect to athletic opportunities. . . .

NOTES AND QUESTIONS

1. *Equal Protection.* Why did the *Force* court find that categorically excluding girls from playing high school football violated the Equal Protection Clause? Would it be appropriate for the court to reach this conclusion if boys and girls had proportionately equal athletic participation opportunities on a program-wide basis?

   Because Title IX provides a comprehensive enforcement scheme for gender discrimination in athletics, the *Williams* court refused to consider a male athlete's claim that his exclusion from the girls' field hockey team violated the equal protection clause of the federal constitution. However, other courts have reached a contrary conclusion. See *Cmtys. for Equity v. Mich. High Sch. Athletic Ass'n*, 459 F.3d 676, 690 (6th Cir. 2006), *cert. denied*, 127 S. Ct. 1912 (2007) ("The fact that the Supreme Court implied a private remedy in *Cannon* gives strength to the argument that Congress did not intend for the termination of federal funds — the only remedy explicitly authorized by Title IX — to serve as a comprehensive or exclusive remedy"). In *Fitzgerald v. Barnstable School Committee*, 555 U.S. 246 (2009), the Supreme Court resolved this split among lower courts by holding that Title IX does not preclude a plaintiff from bringing a denial of equal protection claim against a public school to redress gender discrimination under the broader civil rights statute, 42 U.S.C. §1983. The Court explained:

   > A comparison of the substantive rights and protections guaranteed under Title IX and under the Equal Protection Clause lends further support to the conclusion that Congress did not intend Title IX to preclude §1983 constitutional

suits. Title IX's protections are narrower in some respects and broader in others. Because the protections guaranteed by the two sources of law diverge in this way, we cannot agree with the Court of Appeals that "Congress saw Title IX as the sole means of vindicating the constitutional right to be free from gender discrimination perpetrated by educational institutions."

Id. at 256.

Girls and women desiring to play football continue to assert the Equal Protection Clause in the federal or state constitutions with some success. For example, in August 2013, the ACLU of Indiana filed a lawsuit on behalf of a seventh-grade girl who had been refused permission to play on her school football team. The school district quickly settled the matter by simply agreeing to permit the girl to play. Karen Fritz, *Winamac to allow girl on middle school football team,* http://www.pulaskipost.com/index.php?option=com_content&view=article&id=2540%3Awinamac-to-allow-girl-on-middle-school-football-team&catid=4%3Anews&Itemid=1.

Male athletes have successfully argued a violation of equal protection in sport participation opportunities. The issue in *Steele ex rel. J.S. v. Laurel Cty. Bd. Of Educ.,* 2018 WL 5892355 (E.D. Ky. Nov. 9, 2018), was whether a Board of Education rule called "Play up, Stay Up," which prevents students who play sports at the varsity level from later playing at a lower level, violated the Equal Protection clause. The rule specifically stated it does not apply to female basketball, soccer or volleyball players. The Board contended the women's sport exemption was necessary to allow each female team to have enough players to satisfy Title IX. The district court granted summary judgment to the plaintiff, the father of a male basketball player, holding the rule as written facially violated the Equal Protection Clause as the justification was no longer necessary. The Board was ordered to eliminate the rule or revise it to not discriminate based on gender.

Similarly, in *Bao Xiong ex rel. D.M. v. Minn. St. H.S. League,* 917 F.3d 994 (8th Cir. 2019), the appellate court issued a preliminary injunction allowing two eleventh grade males to participate on the high school competitive dance teams. The league had a rule limiting eligibility to participate on high school dance teams to females, but the Eighth Circuit stated the plaintiffs were likely to succeed on their equal protection claim as the justification for the rule, increasing female participation, was no longer necessary because female participation in athletics had been almost exactly proportional to the number of girls enrolled in schools for the past five years.

2. *Title IX.* Title IX's regulations do not require that members of the opposite sex be permitted to try out for unisex contact sports. See *Barnett v. Tex. Wrestling Ass'n.,* 16 F. Supp. 2d 690 (N.D. Tex. 1998) (holding that Title IX was not violated when girls were denied permission to participate against boys at a wrestling tournament). In construing Title IX, what limitation does the *Williams* court impose on the opportunities that boys will have to play on all-girls teams? According to the court, what does Title IX require with regard to athletic participation opportunities offered for boys and girls?

3. *State Constitutional Law.* The *Williams* case illustrates that state constitutional law may provide a basis for remedying gender inequities in interscholastic or intercollegiate athletics. See also *Haffer v. Temple Univ. of Commonwealth Sys. of Higher Educ.,* 678 F. Supp. 517, 536 (E.D. Pa. 1987) ("it is clear that judicial scrutiny of programs challenged under [state] ERA is at least as searching

as that employed in an equal protection analysis"); *Blair v. Washington State Univ.*, 740 P.2d 1379 (1987).

The previous cases both illustrate that opportunities for the underrepresented sex may be limited if a sport offered only for one sex is considered a contact sport. The following case addresses legal requirements for equal opportunity to participate, and equal treatment when an educational institution does allow a student of the opposite sex to participate in a contact sport.

MERCER v. DUKE UNIVERSITY

190 F.3d 643 (4th Cir. 1999)

LUTTIG, Circuit Judge.

Appellee Duke University operates a Division I college football team. . . . Before attending Duke, [Heather Sue] Mercer was an all-state kicker at Yorktown Heights High School in Yorktown Heights, New York. Upon enrolling at Duke in the fall of 1994, Mercer tried out for the Duke football team as a walk-on kicker. Mercer was the first — and to date, only — woman to try out for the team. Mercer did not initially make the team, and instead served as a manager during the 1994 season; however, she regularly attended practices in the fall of 1994 and participated in conditioning drills the following spring.

In April 1995, the seniors on the team selected Mercer to participate in the Blue-White Game, an intrasquad scrimmage played each spring. In that game, Mercer kicked the winning 28-yard field goal, giving the Blue team a 24-22 victory. . . . The kick was subsequently shown on ESPN, the cable television sports network. Soon after the game, [Duke head football coach] Goldsmith told the news media that Mercer was on the Duke football team, and Fred Chatham, the Duke kicking coach, told Mercer herself that she had made the team. . . .

Although Mercer did not play in any games during the 1995 season, she again regularly attended practices in the fall and participated in conditioning drills the following spring. Mercer was also officially listed by Duke as a member of the Duke football team on the team roster filed with the NCAA and was pictured in the Duke football yearbook.

During this latter period, Mercer alleges that she was the subject of discriminatory treatment by Duke. Specifically, she claims that Goldsmith did not permit her to attend summer camp, refused to allow her to dress for games or sit on the sidelines during games, and gave her fewer opportunities to participate in practices than other walk-on kickers. In addition, Mercer claims that Goldsmith made a number of offensive comments to her, including asking her why she was interested in football, wondering why she did not prefer to participate in beauty pageants rather than football, and suggesting that she sit in the stands with her boyfriend rather than on the sidelines.

At the beginning of the 1996 season, Goldsmith informed Mercer that he was dropping her from the team. Mercer alleges that Goldsmith's decision to exclude her from the team was on the basis of her sex because Goldsmith allowed other, less qualified walk-on kickers to remain on the team. Mercer attempted to participate in conditioning drills the following spring, but Goldsmith asked her to leave because the drills were only for members of the team. Goldsmith told Mercer, however, that she could try out for the team again in the fall. . . .

[R]ather than try out for the team again, Mercer filed suit against Duke and Goldsmith, alleging sex discrimination in violation of Title IX. . . .

34 C.F.R. §106.41 . . . reads in relevant part as follows:

ATHLETICS.

(a) General. No person shall, on the basis of sex, be excluded from participation in, be denied the benefits of, be treated differently from another person or otherwise be discriminated against in any interscholastic, intercollegiate, club or intramural athletics offered by a recipient, and no recipient shall provide any such athletics separately on such basis.

(b) Separate teams. Notwithstanding the requirements of paragraph (a) of this section, a recipient may operate or sponsor separate teams for members of each sex where selection for such teams is based upon competitive skill or the activity involved is a contact sport. However, where a recipient operates or sponsors a team in a particular sport for members of one sex but operates or sponsors no such team for members of the other sex, and athletic opportunities for members of that sex have previously been limited, members of the excluded sex must be allowed to try out for the team offered unless the sport involved is a contact sport. For the purposes of this part, contact sports include boxing, wrestling, rugby, ice hockey, football, basketball and other sports the purpose or major activity of which involves bodily contact.

34 C.F.R. §106.41(a)-(b). . . . The district court held, and appellees contend on appeal, that, under this regulation, "contact sports, such as football, are specifically excluded from Title IX coverage." We disagree.

Subsections (a) and (b) of section 106.41 stand in a symbiotic relationship to one another. Subsection (a) establishes a baseline prohibition against sex discrimination in intercollegiate athletics, tracking almost identically the language in the parallel statutory provision prohibiting discrimination by federally funded educational institutions. In addition to generally barring discrimination on the basis of sex in intercollegiate athletics, subsection (a) specifically prohibits any covered institution from "provid[ing] any such athletics separately on such basis."

Standing alone, then, subsection (a) would require covered institutions to integrate all of their sports teams. In order to avoid such a result — which would have radically altered the face of intercollegiate athletics — HEW provided an explicit exception to the rule of subsection (a) in the first sentence of subsection (b), allowing covered institutions to "operate or sponsor separate teams for members of each sex where selection for such teams is based upon competitive skill or the activity involved is a contact sport." By its terms, this sentence permits covered institutions to operate separate teams for men and women in many sports, including contact sports such as football, rather than integrating those teams.

The first sentence of subsection (b), however, leaves unanswered the question of what, if any, restrictions apply to sports in which a covered institution operates a team for one sex, but operates no corresponding team for the other sex. HEW addressed this question in the second sentence of subsection (b).

This second sentence is applicable only when two predicate criteria are met: first, that the institution in question "operates or sponsors a team in a particular sport for members of one sex but operates or sponsors no such team for members of the other sex," and second, that "athletic opportunities for members of that sex have previously been limited." In this case, appellees do not dispute that athletic opportunities for women at Duke have previously been limited, and thus we assume that the second condition has been met. Further, we assume, without deciding, that Duke operated its football team "for members of one sex" — that is, for only men — but did not operate a separate team "for members of the other sex," and therefore that the first condition has also been satisfied. Thus, insofar as the present appeal is concerned, we consider the predicate conditions to application of the sentence to have been met.

Provided that both of the conditions in the protasis of the second sentence of subsection (b) have been met, the apodosis of the sentence requires that "members of the excluded sex must be allowed to try out for the team offered unless the sport involved is a contact sport." The text of this clause, on its face, is incomplete: it affirmatively specifies that members of the excluded sex must be allowed to try out for single-sex teams where no team is provided for their sex except in the case of contact sports, but is silent regarding what requirements, if any, apply to single-sex teams in contact sports. As to contact sports, this clause is susceptible of two interpretations. First, it could be read to mean that "members of the excluded sex must be allowed to try out for the team offered unless the sport involved is a contact sport, *in which case the anti-discrimination provision of subsection (a) does not apply at all.*" Second, it could be interpreted to mean that "members of the excluded sex must be allowed to try out for the team offered unless the sport involved is a contact sport, *in which case members of the excluded sex need not be allowed to try out.*"

Appellees advocate the former reading, arguing that HEW intended through this clause to exempt contact sports entirely from the coverage of Title IX. We believe, however, that the latter reading is the more natural and intended meaning. The second sentence of subsection (b) does not purport in any way to state an exemption, whether for contact sports or for any other subcategory, from the general antidiscrimination rule stated in subsection (a). And HEW certainly knew how to provide for a complete exemption had it wished, Congress itself having provided a number of such exemptions in the very statute implemented by the regulation. Rather, the sentence says, and says only, that covered institutions must allow members of an excluded sex to try out for single-sex teams in non-contact sports. Therefore, the "unless" phrase at the end of the second clause of the sentence cannot (logically or grammatically) do anything more than except contact sports from the tryout requirement that the beginning of the second clause of the sentence imposes on all other sports.

Contrary to appellees' assertion, this reading of the regulation is perfectly consistent with the evident congressional intent not to require the sexual integration of intercollegiate contact sports. If a university chooses not to permit members of the opposite sex to try out for a single-sex contact-sports team, this interpretation respects that choice. At the same time, however, the reading of the regulation we adopt today, unlike the one advanced by appellees, ensures that the likewise indisputable congressional intent to prohibit discrimination in all circumstances where such discrimination is unreasonable — for example, where the university itself has voluntarily opened the team in question to members of both sexes — is not frustrated.

We therefore construe the second sentence of subsection (b) as providing that in non-contact sports, but not in contact sports, covered institutions must allow members of an excluded sex to try out for single-sex teams. Once an institution has allowed a member of one sex to try out for a team operated by the institution for the other sex in a contact sport, subsection (b) is simply no longer applicable, and the institution is subject to the general anti-discrimination provision of subsection (a). To the extent that the Third Circuit intended to hold otherwise in *Williams v. School Dist. of Bethlehem, Pa.*, 998 F.2d 168, 174 (3d Cir. 1993), with its lone unexplained statement that, "[if] it is determined that [a particular sport] is a contact sport, no other inquiry is necessary because that will be dispositive of the title IX claim," we reject such a conclusion as inconsistent with the language of the regulation.

Accordingly, because appellant has alleged that Duke allowed her to try out for its football team (and actually made her a member of the team), then discriminated against her and ultimately excluded her from participation in the sport on the basis of her sex, we conclude that she has stated a claim under the applicable regulation, and therefore under Title IX. We take to heart appellees' cautionary observation that, in so holding, we thereby become "the first Court in United States history to recognize such a cause of action." Br. of Appellees at 20. Where, as here, however, the university invites women into what appellees characterize as the "traditionally all-male bastion of collegiate football," *id.* at 20 n.10, we are convinced that this reading of the regulation is the only one permissible under law.

The district court's order granting appellees' motion to dismiss for failure to state a claim is hereby reversed, and the case remanded for further proceedings.

NOTES AND QUESTIONS

1. *Contact Sport Exemption.* What is the scope of the Title IX contact sport exemption as construed by *Mercer*? From a practical perspective, does the result in *Mercer* represent a victory for women athletes attempting to try out for a single-sex contact sports team? Private universities such as Duke are not state actors subject to federal constitutional rights claims, although state gender discrimination laws may apply to their conduct. For commentary regarding *Mercer*, see Abigail Crouse, Comment, *Equal Athletic Opportunity: An Analysis of* Mercer v. Duke University *and a Proposal to Amend the Contact Sport Exception to Title IX*, 84 Minn. L. Rev. 1655 (2000); Suzanne Sangree, *Title IX and the Contact Sports Exemption: Gender Stereotypes in a Civil Rights Statute*, 32 Conn. L. Rev. 381 (2000).

    After *Mercer*, if you were an athletic director or coach at a public high school or state university, what would you do if a woman asked to try out for football, wrestling, or some other contact sport? How does federal constitutional law equal protection analysis factor into your thinking?

    Is the contact sport exemption good policy? Over 2,000 high school girls participate in football. Women have also participated in NCAA college football games as place kickers; in September 2003, Tonya Butler kicked a field goal for West Alabama University in a Division II Gulf South Conference game against Stillman University. NAIA and NCAA Division II institutions have also awarded football scholarships to women. In 2018, Antoinette "Toni" Harris, a safety, was offered a football scholarship by Bethany College. Morgan Moriarty, *Safety Antoinette "Toni" Harris might have been the 2nd woman ever to earn a college football scholarship* (Jan. 19,

2018), available at https://www.sbnation.com/college-football/2018/1/18/16908018/antoinette-toni-harris-female-safety-scholarship-bethany-college. In 2006, Michaela Hutchinson became the first girl to win a state wrestling championship by defeating a boy in the 103-pound finals of Alaska's large-school wrestling championships; subsequently, at least two other girls have won state championships while competing against boys. For an article advocating the elimination of the contact sport exemption, see Lindsay Demery, Note, *What About the Boys? Sacking the Contact Sports Exemption and Tackling Gender Discrimination in Athletics*, 34 T. Jefferson L. Rev. 373 (2012). Another article argues the contact sports exemption should be changed because refusing to allow females to try out for men's contact sports contributes to the large pay disparities in men's and women's professional sports. Michelle Margaret Smith, Note, *You Play Ball Like a Girl: Cultural Implications of the Contact Sports Exemption and Why it Needs to be Changed*, 66 Clev. St. L. Rev. 677 (2018).

2. *Compensatory Damages Recoverable but Not Punitive Damages.* On remand to the district court, a judgment was rendered in favor of Mercer in the amount of $1 in compensatory damages and $2 million in punitive damages. The Fourth Circuit vacated the punitive damages award and found that punitive damages are unavailable in private actions brought to enforce Title IX. *Mercer v. Duke Univ.*, 50 Fed. Appx. 643 (4th Cir. 2002). The court's holding was premised on the similarity between Title IX and Title VI, and the Supreme Court's ruling in *Barnes v. Gorman*, 536 U.S. 181 (2002) that punitive damages are not recoverable in private actions brought under Title VI. Is this holding in conflict with Supreme Court precedent established in *Franklin v. Gwinnett Co. Pub. Schs.*, 503 U.S. 60 (1992), which stated a "damage remedy is available for an action brought to enforce Title IX" based on the well-established principle that, in the absence of a specific limitation, federal courts may award "all appropriate remedies" to correct violations of federal law? *Id.* at 66, 76. In January 2004, a federal judge awarded Mercer $349,243 in attorney fees. *Mercer v. Duke Univ.*, 301 F. Supp. 2d 454, 470 (M.D. N.C. 2004), *aff'd*, 401 F.3d 199 (4th Cir. 2005), which illustrates the costs and risks of Title IX litigation.

PROBLEM 10-1

Your 14-year-old daughter wants to try out for the boys' wrestling team and is not interested in participating in any other sports. She is an exceptionally talented athlete who has regularly lifted weights for the past two years and is in excellent physical condition. Although she has no prior experience in wrestling, her dream is to one day earn a gold medal as a member of the U.S. Olympic women's wrestling team. No other girls at her high school are interested in wrestling. For the past three years the boys' wrestling team has won the state championship, and several wrestlers have earned college athletic scholarships. The team's coach, whose decision is supported by the school's principal and athletic director, has refused to allow your daughter to try out for the team. Would you allow your daughter to participate in wrestling? Are you willing to file a lawsuit on her behalf to challenge her exclusion? Evaluate the merits of her potential legal claims. See generally Deborah L. Brake, *Wrestling with Gender: Constructing Masculinity by Refusing to Wrestle Women*, 13 NEV. L.J. 486 (2013).

3. *Equal Benefits and Treatment*

While achieving equal athletic participation opportunities is still a work in progress, the following cases illustrate how courts have responded to female athletes' claims that, because of their sex, they have been denied treatment and benefits equivalent to those provided to male athletes.

McCORMICK v. SCH. DIST. OF MAMARONECK

370 F.3d 275 (2d Cir. 2004)

STRAUB, Circuit Judge.

[EDS. Plaintiffs Katherine McCormick and Emily Geldwert assert that the Mamaroneck and Pelham school districts' scheduling of girls' high school soccer in the spring and boys' high school soccer in the fall deprives girls, but not boys, of the opportunity to compete in the New York regional and state championships in soccer, in violation of Title IX. Both are current students and soccer players at these schools.

The New York State Public High School Athletic Association (NYSPHSAA) has approximately 750 members across the state, including the Pelham and Mamaroneck high schools. The NYSPHSAA divides its members into 11 sections and leaves the decision regarding which sports are played in which season to the individual sections. Section I, to which Pelham and Mamaroneck belong, leaves those season scheduling decisions to individual school districts. In New York 714 public schools offer girls' soccer, 649 of which offer it in the fall. The regional and state championships are scheduled at the end of the fall season.

Some girls' soccer teams at Section I schools began playing in the spring 15 years ago because of the popularity of girls' field hockey in the region. The girls' soccer teams in Pelham and Mamaroneck have an opportunity to compete in the Section I spring league championships, in which 19 other schools participate. However, even if they win the sectional championship, they cannot compete at the regional or state championships, as those games are in the fall. Because the school districts schedule boys' soccer in the fall, the boys have a chance to compete in the regional and state championships for boys' soccer which are held at the end of the fall season. Girls' soccer is the only sport at the Pelham and Mamaroneck high schools that is scheduled out of the state championship game season.

Both McCormick and Geldwert qualified in 2003 for the Olympic Development Program (ODP), a program for girls with exceptional ability in soccer. ODP schedules practices and tournaments in the spring based on the assumption that there will be no conflicts with high school soccer, which is typically scheduled in the fall. ODP tryouts are in the fall, but practices do not begin until the winter. Boys in Pelham and Mamaroneck who qualify for ODP do not face the same conflicts between ODP and high school soccer, because they play high school soccer in the fall.

Both McCormick and Geldwert also play soccer for the Eastchester Patriots club team, a private soccer team that competes in various high-level soccer tournaments. Club soccer has practices and tournaments throughout the year. Neither McCormick nor Geldwert planned to play on their high school teams in the spring of 2003 because neither wanted to play high school, club, and

ODP soccer at the same time. In the spring of 2002, Geldwert's participation on the club team caused her to miss some Mamaroneck high school games. McCormick and Geldwert would play for their high school soccer teams if girls' soccer were moved to the fall season and have expressed that they want a chance to compete in the regional and state championships.]

B.   THE REGULATIONS AND THE POLICY INTERPRETATION

[Title IX] regulations state that "[a] recipient which operates or sponsors inter-scholastic, intercollegiate, club or intramural athletics shall provide equal ath-letic opportunity for members of both sexes." *Id.* §106.41(c). In determining whether equal opportunities exist, the Department of Education's Office for Civil Rights ("OCR") considers, among other factors:

(1) Whether the selection of sports and levels of competition effectively accommo-date the interests and abilities of members of both sexes;
(2) The provision of equipment and supplies;
(3) *Scheduling of games and practice time;*
(4) Travel and per diem allowance;
(5) Opportunity to receive coaching and academic tutoring;
(6) Assignment and compensation of coaches and tutors;
(7) Provision of locker rooms, practice and competitive facilities;
(8) Provision of medical and training facilities and services;
(9) Provision of housing and dining facilities and services;
(10) Publicity.

Id. §106.41(c) (emphasis added). Plaintiffs in this case assert that the School Districts do not provide equal opportunities to girls and boys under factor three, "[s]cheduling of games and practice time." . . .

C.   THE DISPARITY IN ATHLETIC OPPORTUNITY

[Under the OCR's 1979] Policy Interpretation, a disparity in one program com-ponent (i.e., scheduling of games and practice time) can alone constitute a Title IX violation if it is substantial enough in and of itself to deny equality of athletic opportunity to students of one sex at a school. Under the Policy Interpretation, a disparity is a difference, on the basis of sex, in benefits, treatment, services, or opportunities that has a negative impact on athletes of one sex when compared with benefits, treatment, services, or opportunities available to athletes of the other sex. A disparity does not mean that benefits, treatment, services, or oppor-tunities are merely different. . . .

[T]he Policy Interpretation makes clear that identical scheduling for boys and girls is not required. Rather, compliance is assessed by first determining whether a difference in scheduling has a negative impact on one sex, and then determining whether that disparity is substantial enough to deny members of that sex equality of athletic opportunity.

Moreover, the Policy Interpretation contemplates that a disparity disadvan-taging one sex in one part of a school's athletics program can be offset by a comparable advantage to that sex in another area. *See* Policy Interpretation, 44 Fed.Reg. at 71,415 ("Institutions will be in compliance if the compared pro-gram components are equivalent, that is, equal or equal in effect. Under this standard, identical benefits, opportunities, or treatment are not required, pro-vided the *overall effect* of any differences is negligible.") (emphasis added). The Policy Interpretation explains also that compliance should not be measured by a "sport-specific comparison" but rather by examining "program-wide benefits and opportunities." *Id.* at 71,422.

Schools thus have considerable flexibility in complying with Title IX. For example, a school that provides better equipment to the men's basketball team than to the women's basketball team would be in compliance with Title IX if it provided comparably better equipment to the women's soccer team than to the men's soccer team. . . .

In the present case, scheduling girls' soccer in the spring clearly creates a disparity — boys can strive to compete in the Regional and State Championships in soccer and girls cannot. Without a doubt, this difference has a negative impact on girls. The School Districts have not pointed to — in their submissions to the District Court or to us — any areas in which female athletes receive comparably better treatment than male athletes at their schools. Thus, the disadvantage that girls face in the scheduling of soccer has not been offset by any advantages given to girls as compared to boys in the Mamaroneck and Pelham athletics programs. Moreover, girls' soccer is the only sport at these schools scheduled in a season that precludes championship game play. Male athletes do not suffer from any comparable disadvantage.

D.   THE SIGNIFICANCE OF THE DISPARITY

Because the School Districts have not come forth with evidence that the disparity in this case has been offset by some comparable advantage to girls or disadvantage to boys, we must determine whether the disparity is "substantial enough" by itself to deny girls at the Mamaroneck and Pelham schools equality of athletic opportunity. We conclude that the disparity meets that threshold.

The School Districts attempt to downplay their denial of opportunity to the girls by arguing that it is unlikely that the girls' teams would even qualify for the championship games. They point out that the Pelham and Mamaroneck teams did not even win their sectional championship in 2002. We are not persuaded by this argument.

First, a team that is bad one year can be a championship contender the next year. Second, even if any of the individual teams in this litigation are less likely than some others to make the State Championships, as counsel for McCormick and Geldwert stated at oral argument, "a girl's reach should exceed her grasp." The greater the potential victory, the greater the motivation to the athletes. Any championship motivates, but a great championship motivates more. . . . Winning the State Championship in New York means being the best team out of 649 teams in the state. Winning the Section I spring soccer championships, which is the best the girls in Pelham and Mamaroneck can hope for, means being the best team out of 19 (or possibly 13) teams. . . . The scheduling of soccer in the spring, therefore, places a ceiling on the possible achievement of the female soccer players that they cannot break through no matter how hard they strive. The boys are subject to no such ceiling. Treating girls differently regarding a matter so fundamental to the experience of sports — the chance to be champions — is inconsistent with Title IX's mandate of equal opportunity for both sexes. Scheduling the girls' soccer season out of the championship game season sends a message to the girls on the teams that they are not expected to succeed and that the school does not value their athletic abilities as much as it values the abilities of the boys.

Nor do we place great weight on the School Districts' argument that these girls are simply not interested in winning. . . .

Moreover, we note that girls and women were historically denied opportunities for athletic competition based on stereotypical views that participating in highly competitive sports was not "feminine" or "ladylike." . . . Despite substantial progress in attitudes about women and sports, the competitive accomplishments of male athletes may continue to be valued more than the achievements of female athletes. The different value that society may place on the competitive success of female athletes as compared to male athletes, however, must not play a role in our assessment of the significance of the denial of opportunity to the female athletes in this case. . . .

E.   JUSTIFICATION FOR DISPARITY

The Policy Interpretation states that "[i]f comparisons of program components reveal that treatment, benefits, or opportunities are not equivalent in kind, quality or availability, a finding of compliance may still be justified if the differences are the result of nondiscriminatory factors." Policy Interpretation, 44 Fed.Reg. at 71,415. The Policy Interpretation lists "[s]ome of the factors that may justify these differences." Although none of the particular factors listed in the Policy Interpretation are relevant in this case, the list does not purport to be exhaustive. However, we conclude that the School Districts have not adequately justified the scheduling of girls' soccer in the spring.

The School Districts offer several reasons for why girls' soccer is scheduled in the spring and why moving it to the fall would be a problem. First, the schools assert that if girls' soccer is moved, there will not be enough field space, they will have to hire another coach, and there might be a shortage of officials. These reasons are not the kind of nondiscriminatory factors that can justify inferior treatment of female athletes. Hiring a new coach and finding more officials may cost money, but the fact that money needs to be spent to comply with Title IX is obviously not a defense to the statute. The schools will have to make some adjustments in order to provide field space to the girls' soccer teams for practices and games. However, the schools have not demonstrated that finding field space for practices will be impossible or will result in significantly shorter or more infrequent practices. In any event, all of these administrative problems could be avoided by moving boys' soccer to the spring. There is no reason that the boys' soccer teams should be entitled to the fields, coaches, and officials in the fall simply because they were in the fall first. The School Districts could comply with Title IX by offering soccer to boys and girls in the fall in alternating years (or every two years) — as long as the girls, who have been thus far denied the fall season, are scheduled in the upcoming 2004 fall season. Because the School Districts could avoid the administrative problems they complain about by alternating boys' and girls' soccer in the fall season, this case does not require us to decide the availability of an "administrative hardship defense," if any, or the threshold that would suffice to justify a significant disparity in equal athletic opportunity on the basis of such a defense.

Second, the School Districts assert that moving soccer to the fall will hurt girls because it will force them to choose between soccer and other fall sports. However, all students athletes must make choices about which sports to play. Currently, the girls at these schools have to choose between soccer and the other sports offered in the spring. If soccer is moved, they will have to pick among fall sports. . . .

Third, the School Districts assert that girls have been playing soccer in the spring for fifteen years because of the "popularity in our region of the girls' field hockey program." The School Districts complain that a "ramification of the ruling below would be the gradual elimination of the girls soccer program because of the lack of participants due to field hockey's allure." . . . The School Districts claim that if soccer is moved, there might not be a sufficient number of athletes to fill out the girls' teams in the fall. However, the School Districts do not offer persuasive data to support this point.

Fourth, the School Districts assert that moving soccer to the fall will result in fewer opportunities for girls to participate in sports in the spring. According to the School Districts, if soccer is moved "a lot of girls may do nothing in the spring." . . . The School Districts have not offered persuasive evidence that the other sports the schools offer in the spring will not be able to accommodate the girls; nor have they claimed an inability to add another spring sport.

Thus, we conclude that none of the reasons offered by the School Districts justify their decisions to schedule girls' soccer in the spring thereby denying the girls' soccer teams the opportunity to compete in the Regional and State Championships. We do not intend to foreclose the possibility that scheduling a sport outside the season of championship game play, may, under certain circumstances, be permissible under Title IX. As mentioned, a school that denied comparable championship opportunities to boys and girls in equal numbers would not be in violation of Title IX. In addition, off-season scheduling that disadvantaged members of only one sex might be permissible if supported by greater justification than that advanced here. We conclude in this case, however, that the School Districts have not adequately justified the unequal provision of competitive opportunities to girls and boys. The denial of equality of athletic opportunity therefore violates Title IX. . . .

G.   COMPLIANCE PLAN

Moving girls' soccer permanently to the fall, the same season as boys' soccer, would seem to be the easiest way for the School Districts to comply with Title IX. However, as discussed, the School Districts would be in compliance with Title IX if they offered soccer to girls and boys on a rational alternating basis — as long as girls are scheduled in the upcoming fall 2004 season. The relevant inquiry is whether girls and boys are given equal opportunities for post-season competition — not whether the sports are scheduled in the same season. We are aware of, and have noted, the problems with the option of alternating the fall season between boys' and girls' soccer. . . .

CONCLUSION

To summarize, we affirm the District Court's holding that the decisions by the School Districts of Mamaroneck and Pelham to schedule girls' high school soccer in the spring and boys' high school soccer in the fall, which deprives girls but not boys of the opportunity to compete in the New York Regional and State Championships in soccer, violates Title IX. . . . However, we modify the District Court's injunction to allow the School Districts to submit a plan that either alternates the fall soccer season between the girls and the boys or moves girls' soccer permanently to the fall. . . .

DANIELS v. SCH. BD. OF BREVARD COUNTY, FLORIDA (DANIELS I)
985 F. Supp. 1458 (M.D. Fla. 1997)

CONWAY, District Judge.

The Plaintiffs in this action are Jessica and Jennifer Daniels, and their father, Daniel Daniels. Jessica and Jennifer are seniors at Merritt Island High School ("MIHS"). They both are members of the girls' varsity softball team.

Plaintiffs have sued the Defendant, School Board of Brevard County, based on disparities between the MIHS girls' softball and boys' baseball programs. They assert claims pursuant to 20 U.S.C. §1681 ("Title IX") and the Florida Educational Equity Act, Fla.Stat. §228.2001 ("the Florida Act"). . . .

IV.   ANALYSIS

A.   SUBSTANTIAL LIKELIHOOD OF SUCCESS ON THE MERITS

Plaintiffs assert that the following inequalities exist at the MIHS softball and baseball facilities, and that these disparities violate Title IX and the Florida Act.

Electronic Scoreboard

It is undisputed that the boys' baseball field has an electronic scoreboard, and that the girls' field has no scoreboard at all. At the preliminary injunction hearing, Defendant's counsel argued that a scoreboard is inessential to varsity softball play. The Court disagrees. A scoreboard is of obvious benefit to players who must keep track of the score, the innings, and the numbers of outs, balls and strikes at any given moment. The prestige factor of a scoreboard is also obvious. As with all the differences the Court addresses in this Order, the fact that the boys have a scoreboard and the girls do not sends a clear message to players, fellow students, teachers and the community at large, that girls' varsity softball is not as worthy as boys' varsity baseball.

Batting Cage

It is also undisputed that the boys' baseball team has a batting cage and the girls' softball team does not. The use of a batting cage sharpens hitting skills. The girls' softball team is technically disadvantaged by the absence of such equipment. At the hearing, Plaintiffs' counsel represented that it would be difficult for the two teams to share one batting cage as a result of differences in the pitching machines each team uses. Accordingly, it appears that sharing the existing batting cage is not feasible.

Bleachers

Photographs submitted by Plaintiffs starkly illustrate that the bleachers on the girls' softball field are in worse condition, and seat significantly fewer spectators, than the bleachers on the boys' field. In fact, at the preliminary injunction hearing, Defendant's counsel admitted that the girls' bleachers are actually "hand-me-downs" that the boys' team passed on to the girls' team after the boys' team received new bleachers. Again, the message this sends the players, spectators and community about the relative worth of the two teams is loud and clear.

Signs

A sign reading "Merritt Island Baseball" is emblazoned in very large letters on the side of a portable structure adjacent to the boys' baseball field. The sign faces MIHS' student parking lot. This sign clearly publicizes only the boys' baseball team. Another sign is located just outside the left field fence of the boys' field. This billboard-type sign reads "Home of the Mustangs;" it faces toward the boys' field. Due to its location, the effect of this second sign is to advertise the boys' baseball team. There are no signs publicizing the girls' softball team.

Bathroom Facilities

There are no restrooms located on the girls' softball field. Restrooms are located on the boys' baseball field. A fence separates the girls' field from the restrooms. There is a dispute concerning whether the coach of the girls' team has been provided with a key to a gate in the fence. Equal access to restroom facilities is such a clearly established right as to merit no further discussion.

Concession Stand/Press Box/Announcer's Booth

A combination concession stand/press box/announcer's booth is located on the boys' baseball field. There is no such structure on the girls' softball field. These facilities affect player and spectator enjoyment of a sport, as well as attendance.

Field Maintenance

The photographs submitted by Plaintiffs facially suggest that the girls' softball field is not as well-maintained as the boys' baseball field. However, at the preliminary injunction hearing, Defendant's counsel stated that the photographs were misleading because MIHS was in the process of reconditioning the girls' field at the time the photographs were taken. Defense counsel maintains that the reconditioning process continues. Accordingly, at this juncture, it is difficult for the Court to evaluate the comparative level of field maintenance.

Lighting

The boys' baseball field is lighted for nighttime play; the girls' softball field is not. Apparently, this single factor was the impetus for this lawsuit.

Nighttime play affects spectator attendance, parental involvement, and player and spectator enjoyment. Nighttime games have a "big league" quality not associated with daytime play. Additionally, lighting affords more flexibility regarding practice scheduling. The absence of lighting on the girls' softball field detrimentally affects the girls' team in all these respects.

After Plaintiffs filed suit, the Brevard County School Board voted to install lighting at MIHS' girls softball field. Plaintiffs contend that they have not received assurance that the lighting will be in place by January 26, 1998, the beginning of the girls' season. . . . Unless the lighting is in place by January 26, 1998, MIHS will be enjoined from using the lights on the boys' baseball field.

The Court determines that the cumulative effect of the inequalities in the two athletic programs is so significant as to give Plaintiffs a substantial likelihood of success on the merits of the Title IX and Florida Act claims. The Defendant has chosen to favor the boys' baseball team with a lighted playing field, a scoreboard, a batting cage, superior bleachers, signs publicizing the team, bathroom facilities, and a concession stand/press box/announcer's booth, but has not seen fit to provide the girls softball team with any of these things. This disparity implicates several of the considerations listed in 34 C.F.R. §106.41. *See* §106.41(2) ("provision of equipment and supplies"), (3) ("[s]cheduling of games and practice times"), (7) ("[p]rovision of . . . practice and competitive facilities"), (8) ("[p]rovision of . . . training facilities"), and (10) ("[p]ublicity"). A balance of the relevant factors favors the Plaintiffs.

The Defendant seeks to avoid liability on the basis that it provides equal funding for the boys' and girls' programs. According to the Defendant, each team has a separate booster club which engages in separate fund-raising activities. The Defendant suggests that it cannot be held responsible if the fund-raising activities of one booster club are more successful than those of another. The Court rejects this argument. It is the Defendant's responsibility to ensure equal athletic opportunities, in accordance with Title IX. This funding system is one to which Defendant has acquiesced; Defendant is responsible for the consequences of that approach.

B.   SUBSTANTIAL THREAT OF IRREPARABLE INJURY

Plaintiffs have also demonstrated a substantial threat of irreparable injury. Each day these inequalities go unredressed, the members of the girls' softball team, prospective members, students, faculty and the community at large, are sent a clear message that girls' high school varsity softball is not as worthy as boys' high school varsity baseball, i.e., that girls are not as important as boys. . . . Further, Jessica and Jennifer are seeking athletic scholarships, many of which, Plaintiffs maintain, are not decided until after the softball season is over. Accordingly, it is critical that the two girls do their best during their final season.

C.   RELATIVE HARM/PUBLIC INTEREST

Since these inequalities should have long ago been rectified, the Court is unsympathetic to Defendant's claims that it will be unduly harmed by the expenditure of funds necessary to level the playing field for girls' softball athletes. For too long, the girls' softball team has been denied athletic opportunity equal to the boys' baseball team. The harm associated with that treatment as second-class athletes is significant. In short, the balance of harms favors Plaintiffs. The players and all others associated with these programs, the school system as a whole, and the public at large, will benefit from a shift to equal treatment.

[The court determined that plaintiffs are entitled to a preliminary injunction to remedy these gender inequities. Because public funds are at stake, the court afforded Defendant an opportunity to submit a plan addressing how it proposes to remedy them.]

DANIELS v. SCH. BD. OF BREVARD COUNTY, FLORIDA (DANIELS II)

995 F. Supp. 1394 (M.D. Fla. 1997)

CONWAY, District Judge.

II.   THE SCHOOL BOARD'S PLAN

[EDS. The school board proposed not to spend any funds to remedy the inequities identified in the prior order because of "financial limitations and tight budgetary constraints under which the School Board was forced to operate. The

Board argued that any monies spent on athletics must obviously be taken from another area of operations which were already lacking in funds."]

The School Board proposes the following remedial measures regarding the specific inequities identified in the prior Order:

Electronic Scoreboard

The School Board says it is not feasible to move the electronic scoreboard on the boys' baseball field back and forth between the baseball field and the girls' softball field. Accordingly, the Board proposes to disallow use of the scoreboard on the boys' field "until such time as the girls' field has a comparable scoreboard."

Batting Cage

The School Board contends that the design and structure of the batting cage on the boys' field precludes moving it back and forth between the two fields. The Board proposes to co-locate the girls' and boys' separate pitching machines so that both teams can use the batting cage on alternate weeks.

Bleachers

The School Board maintains it is not feasible to relocate bleachers from the boys' field to the girls' field. Accordingly, "[u]ntil such time as funds may be raised for the purchase of additional bleachers or bleachers are donated so that the girls' field has bleachers essentially equal in number and quality to the boys' bleachers," the School Board proposes to rope off the boys' bleachers so that "the only area used during games shall be equivalent in size and seating number to those bleachers which presently exist on the girls' softball field."

Signs

The School Board proposes altering the "Merritt Island Baseball" sign facing the student parking lot, to read "Merritt Island Baseball and Softball." Alternatively, the Board proposes to either eliminate all lettering or change the sign to "Merritt Island Athletics." The School Board also proposes to remove the donated "Home of the Mustangs" sign which faces the boys' baseball diamond, and to leave in place a second, gender neutral sign located outside the boys' field.

Bathroom Facilities

The School Board proposes to remove a portion of the fence separating the boys' and girls' fields, so as to permit equal access to the restrooms.

Concession Stand/Press Box/Announcer's Booth

The Board proposes to close down this building until such time as a comparable facility is constructed on the girls' field.

Lighting

The School Board has already approved the installation of lights on the MIHS girls' softball field. The Board anticipates the installation process will be complete by the beginning of the girls' season. If it is not, the Board proposes to disallow use of the lights on the boys' field until the lights on the girls' field are in place.

III.   PLAINTIFFS' RESPONSE TO THE PLAN

Plaintiffs' basic position is that the School Board should be required to remedy the inequities by spending the funds necessary to improve the MIHS girls' softball program, rather than denying the boys' baseball team facilities it already enjoys. . . . Plaintiffs also assert that the School Board's "take it away from the boys" approach is actually designed to generate "backlash" against the girls' softball team. Further, Plaintiffs contend that the Board's plan is inadequate to remedy the perception of inequality because even if the boys are not allowed to use certain facilities — such as the electronic scoreboard, bleachers, lighting and concession stand/press box/announcer's booth — those facilities will remain in place as symbols of inequality. Accordingly, Plaintiffs urge the Court to require the School Board to either completely remove those facilities from the boys' field or provide the girls with equal facilities on their field. Finally, Plaintiffs decry the School Board's claim of "tight budgetary constraints;" they maintain that the Board is slated to receive at least $43 million from the Florida Department of Education for capital improvements.

IV.   ANALYSIS

In giving the School Board the opportunity to submit a plan, the Court had hoped for constructive input, such as a long-range fiscal plan to remedy the inequities identified in the Court's prior Order. Unfortunately, the Board's plan leaves much to be desired; it creates the impression that the Board is not as sensitive as it should be regarding the necessity of compliance with Title IX. The Court is inclined to agree with Plaintiffs that many of the Board's proposals seem more retaliatory than constructive. The Board's approach essentially imposes "separate disadvantage," punishing both the girls and the boys, rather than improving the girls' team to the level the boys' team has enjoyed for years. The Court is sensitive to the financial constraints imposed upon public educational institutions in this day and age; that is yet another reason the Court gave the Board an opportunity to submit a remedial plan, rather than simply entering an injunction decreeing the expenditure of funds by a date certain. However, the fact remains that Plaintiffs have presented substantial evidence that the School Board has violated, and continues to violate, an Act of Congress mandating gender equality in public education.

However, the inquiry does not end here. Before the School Board's response to the Court's November 25 Order was due, Plaintiffs altered the playing field dramatically by filing a separate suit seeking class action status and challenging the Board's treatment of girls' softball on a county-wide basis. . . . On the heels of this filing, a different group of parents and children commenced yet another action claiming gender equity violations with respect to girls' softball programs throughout the county. . . .

As a result of these latest two cases, the Title IX focus has expanded from the softball facilities at one high school to girls' softball programs throughout Brevard County. In the instant suit, two high school girls and a parent sought to force expenditures to improve one softball field. The two subsequent cases presumably seek to force, *inter alia*, the construction of softball fields at three other high schools. These developments dramatically alter the potential financial impact on the School Board.

At this juncture, the Court cannot make a reasoned determination concerning the amount of additional funds the School Board should be required to expend to remedy the inequities present at Plaintiffs' particular high school. The extent to which the Board must further appropriate funds to correct the situation at MIHS must be considered in the context of the two related cases which seek class action treatment and the expenditure of funds on a county-wide basis. Accordingly, with the exception of lighting on the MIHS girls' softball field, which the School Board has already committed to install, for the moment, the Court will impose injunctive measures which do not require additional funding.

V.   PRELIMINARY INJUNCTION

Based on the foregoing, it is ORDERED as follows:

1. Before January 26, 1998, the School Board shall make the following changes at Merritt Island High School:

    a. Remove a portion of the fence separating the boys' baseball field and girls' softball field, so that the restroom facilities are readily accessible to players and spectators at both fields.
    b. Co-locate the girls' and boys' pitching machines so that both teams can use the batting cage, and establish a schedule allowing both teams equal use of the cage.
    c. Change the "Merritt Island Baseball" sign facing the student parking lot, so that it reads "Merritt Island Baseball and Softball," and remove the donated "Home of the Mustangs" sign which faces the boys' baseball diamond.
    d. Install lighting on the girls' softball field.

2. During the pendency of this action and the two related cases, the School Board is not required to deny the boys' baseball team and its spectators use of the electronic scoreboard, existing bleachers and the concession stand/press box/announcer's booth. The Board is also not required to deny the boys' baseball team use of the lights on the baseball field, since the Board is required to install lighting on the girls' softball field by January 26, 1998. Finally, the Board is not required to remove the gender-neutral sign located outside the boys' baseball field.

NOTES AND QUESTIONS

1. *Standing and Mootness.* As a threshold matter, the *McCormick* court held that plaintiffs had standing to bring their Title IX claims although they did not play soccer for their respective schools in 2003. Their claims were not moot because they would have an opportunity to play soccer during their senior year if the sport were played in the fall. 370 F.3d at 284-285. A plaintiff only has standing to assert claims to remedy specific harm that arises out of his or her current or future participation in the school's athletic program. *Boucher v. Syracuse Univ.*, 164 F.3d 113 (2d Cir. 1999); *Cook v. Colgate Univ.*, 992 F.2d 17 (2d Cir. 1993). Without any individualized harm, he or she does not have

standing to generally challenge inequitable treatment or the provision of benefits on the basis of gender in connection with a school's entire athletics program. *Pederson v. Louisiana State Univ.*, 213 F.3d 858, 871-872 (5th Cir. 2000). What is the specific harm that plaintiffs suffered in *McCormick* as a result of being treated unequally? In *Daniels I?*

The women's softball coach at Midland College, TX, filed a Title IX lawsuit claiming discrimination against the women's team for inferior facilities and academic support. The court dismissed the claim for lack of subject matter jurisdiction because Ramos did not have standing to bring claims on behalf of the softball players who were able to file claims themselves. *Ramos v. Midland Coll.*, 2017 WL 10841724 (W.D. Tex. June 29, 2017). What other options does Ramos have to complain about inequities if the College will not act? Is it likely that the players will file a lawsuit? Why or why not?

2. *Disparate Treatment.* Although compliance with Title IX requires a comparison of boys' and girls' sports on a program-wide basis, *McCormick* and *Daniels I* demonstrate that disparate treatment of male and female teams for the same sport may violate this law. What constitutes an illegal disparity for purposes of Title IX?

In *Parker v. Franklin County Community School*, 667 F.3d 910 (7th Cir. 2012), the Court reversed the district court's granting of the school district's summary judgment motion dismissing a group of female athletes' unequal treatment claims by colorfully framing the issue:

> A packed gymnasium, cheerleaders rallying the fans, the crowd on their feet supporting their team, and the pep band playing the school song: these are all things you might expect to see at an Indiana high school basketball game on a Friday night. The crowd becomes part of the game; they provide motivation, support, and encouragement to the players. After all, what would a spectator sport be without the spectators? Unfortunately, this is a question the Franklin County High School girls' basketball teams must answer every season because half their games have been relegated to non-primetime nights (generally Monday through Thursday) to give preference to the boys' Friday and Saturday night games. Non-primetime games result in a loss of audience, conflict with homework, and foster feelings of inferiority. The question we're asked to decide in this appeal is whether such discriminatory scheduling practices are actionable under Title IX. . . . We think the plaintiffs have presented a genuine question of fact that such practices violate the statute, and therefore we vacate the district court's entry of summary judgment in favor of the defendants.

Id. at 913. In October 2012, the parties reached a court-approved agreement that provides for a plan that will improve the scheduling of girls' varsity basketball games through 2017; it requires that more women's games will need to be scheduled at "prime times," which is defined in the Consent Decree as days "when school is not scheduled the next day." See *Parker v. Indiana High School Athletic Association Consent Decree*, http://www.scribd .com/doc/116857761/Parker-v-Franklin-Consent-Decree.

On the other hand, similar to the prevailing judicial approach for correcting unequal participation opportunities, courts are generally reluctant to order a school to take specific action to remedy gender-based unequal treatment that violates Title IX. They prefer for the parties to do this in the form of a negotiated agreement, which can become part of a consent decree. Some courts have encouraged the parties to mutually resolve Title IX litigation by using a professional facilitator with expertise in improving the equality of athletic opportunities for males and females. See *Ridgeway v. Montana High Sch. Assn.*, 858 F.2d 579 (9th Cir. 1988). But see *Portz v. St. Cloud St. Univ.*, 2019 WL 3492457 (D. Minn. Aug. 1, 2019), where the court issued a permanent injunction to require the university to eliminate inferior locker room conditions and to replace women's equipment on the same schedule as men's teams.

3. *Unequal disciplinary treatment.* In *Thomas v. Univ. of Pittsburgh*, 2014 WL 3055361 (W.D. Pa July 7, 2014), a scholarship student-athlete on the women's basketball team was suspended indefinitely following an altercation with a teammate and the basketball coach. The plaintiff alleged that her suspension violated Title IX because it was more severe than sanctions imposed on male athletes who had engaged in more egregious conduct, who were permitted to continue to play and receive the corresponding student-athlete benefits. The court held that "Plaintiff alleges sufficient facts regarding the University's disparate treatment of females and males relating to disciplinary procedures to sustain a Title IX claim." The court also rejected defendants' motions to dismiss plaintiff's punitive damages and equal protection claims.

PROBLEM 10-2

You represent a county school district (District). In 2012, the county started a girl's flag football program in schools within the District. The program has been so successful that in 2016, the state athletics association recognized girl's flag football as a sport for the purposes of statewide and championship competition. Flag football is scheduled during the spring and the girls' teams use the football fields. Each school within the district has locker rooms for the girls, although the lockers are not directly adjacent to the football field, as is the case with the boys' locker room. The girls' locker rooms are not as large as the boy's locker rooms. There are three reasons why the lockers and locker rooms for girls are smaller: (1) fewer girls play flag football; (2) contact-football equipment for boys takes up more space than the equipment used by the girls; and (3) historically girls have used one set of facilities and boys have used the other. Flag football is scheduled for play on Tuesday and Thursday evenings, in part so that the games will not conflict with boys' baseball games is played on Fridays and Saturdays. A group of girls, along with their parents, have insisted that they are being treated unfairly, asserting they are not permitted to play on Fridays and Saturdays, despite the fact that boy's football plays in the fall on Friday evenings. They also argue that the money spent on their uniforms and the quality of the locker rooms are not equal. They have set up a meeting with the Superintendent and have indicated that they will be represented at that meeting by a prominent local lawyer, who happens to be the father of one of the players. You have been asked to be in attendance to represent the district. The Superintendent is concerned with the allegations. She has noted that the last thing she wants is for the District to be found to have treated the girls unfairly during her tenure as Superintendent. What advice will you give the Superintendent? What is the lawyer for the girls likely to argue? How do you suggest this matter be resolved?

4.   *Reverse Discrimination Claims*

Although it is a disfavored practice, many educational institutions have cut men's sports teams or athletics programs in an effort to comply with Title IX. The following case is a gender reverse-discrimination lawsuit in which male college athletes allege that the discontinuance of their sport violates Title IX and their federal equal protection rights.

NEAL v. BOARD OF TRUSTEES OF THE CALIFORNIA STATE UNIVERSITIES

198 F.3d 763 (9th Cir. 1999)

HALL, Circuit Judge:

[This] suit alleged that the decision of California State University, Bakersfield ("CSUB") to reduce the number of spots on its men's wrestling team, undertaken as part of a university-wide program to achieve "substantial proportionality" between each gender's participation in varsity sports and its composition in the campus's student body, violated Title IX and the Equal Protection Clause of the United States Constitution. . . .

Defendant/Appellant CSUB is a large public university where female students outnumbered male students by roughly 64% to 36% in 1996. The composition of CSUB's varsity athletic rosters, however, was quite different. In the 1992-93 academic year, male students took 61% of the university's spots on athletic rosters and received 68% of CSUB's available athletic scholarship money.

This imbalance helped prompt a lawsuit by the California chapter of the National Organization for Women, alleging that the California State University system was violating a state law that is similar to the federal government's Title IX. That lawsuit eventually settled, resulting in a consent decree mandating, *inter alia*, that each Cal State campus have a proportion of female athletes that was within five percentage points of the proportion of female undergraduate students at that school. This portion of the consent decree was patterned after the first part of the three-part Title IX compliance test promulgated by the Department of Education's Office for Civil Rights ("OCR").

When the university agreed to the consent decree, California was slowly emerging from a recession, and state funding for higher education was declining. As a result, CSUB administrators were seriously constrained in what they could spend on athletic programs. The university chose to adopt squad size targets, which would encourage the expansion of the women's teams while limiting the size of the men's teams. In order to comply with the consent decree, CSUB opted for smaller men's teams across the board, rejecting the alternative of eliminating some men's teams entirely. CSUB's plan was designed to bring it into compliance with the consent decree by the 1997-98 academic year, meaning that female students would fill at least 55% of the spaces on the school's athletic teams.[1]

As part of this across-the-board reduction in the number of slots available to men's athletic teams, the size of the men's wrestling team was capped at 27. Although the reduction was protested vigorously by wrestling coach Terry

---

1. This figure assumed 60 percent female enrollment for that year.

Kerr, and team captain Stephen Neal expressed concerns that a smaller squad would prove less competitive, the smaller CSUB team performed exceptionally well, winning the Pac-10 Conference title and finishing third in the nation in 1996. In 1996-97, the men's wrestling roster was capped at 25, and four of these spots went unused. Nevertheless, in response to the rumored elimination of the men's wrestling team, on January 10, 1997, the team filed the instant lawsuit . . .

The district court initially granted a temporary restraining order preventing the reductions, then granted a preliminary injunction to prevent CSUB from reducing the size of the wrestling team. . . .

Appellees recognize that . . . it would be imprudent to argue that Title IX prohibits the use of all gender-conscious remedies. Appellees therefore suggest that gender-conscious remedies are appropriate only when necessary to ensure that schools provide opportunities to males and females in proportion to their relative levels of interest in sports participation. By contrast, Appellants contend that schools may make gender-conscious decisions about sports-funding levels to correct for an imbalance between the composition of the undergraduate student body and the composition of the undergraduate student athletic participants pool. This disagreement has real significance: Men's expressed interest in participating in varsity sports is apparently higher than women's at the present time — although the "interest gap" continues to narrow — so permitting gender-conscious remedies until the proportions of students and athletes are roughly proportional gives universities more remedial freedom than permitting remedies only until expressed interest and varsity roster spots correspond. . . .

In other words, Appellees' interpretation of Title IX would have allowed universities to do little or nothing to equalize men's and women's opportunities if they could point to data showing that women were less interested in sports. But a central aspect of Title IX's purpose was to *encourage* women to participate in sports: The increased number of roster spots and scholarships reserved for women would gradually increase demand among women for those roster spots and scholarships.[4] . . .

Title IX is a dynamic statute, not a static one. It envisions continuing progress toward the goal of equal opportunity for all athletes and recognizes that, where society has conditioned women to expect less than their fair share of the athletic opportunities, women's interest in participating in sports will not rise to a par with men's overnight. The percentage of college athletes who are women rose from 15% in 1972 to 37% in 1998, and Title IX is at least partially responsible for this trend of increased participation by women. . . . Title IX has altered women's preferences, making them more interested in sports, and more likely to become student athletes.

Adopting Appellees' interest-based test for Title IX compliance would hinder, and quite possibly reverse, the steady increases in women's participation and interest in sports that have followed Title IX's enactment.

A number of courts of appeals have addressed another potentially dispositive issue in this appeal — namely, whether Title IX permits a university to diminish athletic opportunities available to men so as to bring them into line with the

---

4. That is, the creation of additional athletic spots for women would prompt universities to recruit more female athletes, in the long run shifting women's demand curve for sports participation. As more women participated, social norms discouraging women's participation in sports presumably would be further eroded, prompting additional increases in women's participation levels. . . .

lower athletic opportunities available to women. Every court, in construing the Policy Interpretation and the text of Title IX, has held that a university may bring itself into Title IX compliance by increasing athletic opportunities for the underrepresented gender (women in this case) *or* by decreasing athletic opportunities for the overrepresented gender (men in this case). [Citations omitted.] An extensive survey of Title IX's legislative history and the regulations promulgated to apply its provisions to college athletics concluded that boosters of male sports argued vociferously before Congress that the proposed regulations would require schools to shift resources from men's programs to women's programs, but that Congress nevertheless sided "with women's advocates" by deciding not to repeal the HEW's athletics-related Title IX regulations. Mary Jo Festle, Playing Nice: Politics and Apologies in Women's Sports 171-76 (1996). Congress thus appears to have believed that Title IX would result in funding reductions to male athletic programs. If a university wishes to comply with Title IX by leveling down programs instead of ratcheting them up, as Appellant has done here, Title IX is not offended.

There is a second reason why a reversal of the district court's order granting injunctive relief on the Title IX claim is warranted. The district court failed to defer properly to the interpretation of Title IX put forward by the administrative agency that is explicitly authorized to enforce its provisions. It is well-established that the federal courts are to defer substantially to an agency's interpretation of its own regulations. . . .

We also note that Appellees' interpretation of Title IX's text has been rejected explicitly by the Seventh Circuit . . . as well as the OCR, and implicitly rejected by the other circuits that have held that a school may cut the number of male athletic slots in order to bring itself into compliance with Title IX. . . .

Finally, the district court below rejected the interpretation of Title IX advocated by the OCR and Appellants on the ground that such a reading of the statute might violate the Constitution. In the court's words, OCR's interpretation would effectively transform Title IX from an anti-discrimination statute to a statute enacted to remedy past discrimination, thus subjecting it to heightened scrutiny. Without speculating whether Title IX would survive such searching constitutional scrutiny, the court notes that it remains unsatisfied with the [*Cohen v. Brown Univ.*, 991 F.2d 888 (1st Cir. 1993)] majority's treatment of these important questions. The court is satisfied that avoiding serious constitutional questions such as an equal protection challenge to a very important Congressional statute is itself ample reason for rejecting the safe harbor idea as part of Title IX.

The district court thus strained to interpret Title IX in a way that ostensibly would avoid these concerns. . . .

The First and Seventh Circuits both have considered at length the constitutionality of the first prong of the OCR's test. In [*Cohen v. Brown Univ.* (*Cohen I*), 991 F.2d 888 (1st Cir. 1993), *Cohen v. Brown Univ.* (*Cohen II*), 101 F.3d 155 (1st Cir. 1996), and *Kelley v. Board of Trustees*, 35 F.3d 265 (7th Cir. 1994)] the courts emphatically rejected the claim that the Policy Interpretation was unconstitutional under the Fourteenth Amendment. The separate reasoning in the two *Cohen* opinions is particularly well-developed. It applied intermediate scrutiny, which we would also do were we addressing the constitutional merits. *See Coalition for Econ. Equity v. Wilson*, 122 F.3d 692, 702 (9th Cir. 1997) ("When the government classifies by gender, it must demonstrate that the classification is substantially related to an important governmental interest, requiring an 'exceedingly persuasive' justification."). *Cohen II* noted that the Policy Interpretation furthered the "clearly important" objectives of "avoid[ing] the use of federal resources to support discriminatory practices, and provid[ing] individual citizens effective protection against those practices." Moreover, it found that " judicial enforcement of federal anti-discrimination statutes is at least an important governmental objective." And *Cohen II* held that the district court's relief, which was essentially identical to what the OCR Policy Interpretation calls for, was "clearly substantially related" to these objectives. . . . Along the same lines, the Seventh Circuit has held that "the remedial scheme established by Title IX and the applicable regulation and policy interpretation are clearly substantially related to" the objective of prohibiting "educational institutions from discriminating on the basis of sex." We adopt the reasoning of *Cohen I, Cohen II,* and *Kelley,* and hold that the constitutional analysis contained therein persuasively disposes of any serious constitutional concerns that might be raised in relation to the OCR Policy Interpretation. The district court's final basis for rejecting the OCR's interpretation of Title IX was therefore erroneous. . . .

This past summer, 90,185 enthusiastic fans crowded into Pasadena's historic Rose Bowl for the finals of the Women's World Cup soccer match. An estimated 40 million television viewers also tuned in to watch a thrilling battle between the American and Chinese teams. The match ended when American defender Brandi Chastain fired the ball past Chinese goalkeeper Gao Hong, breaking a 4-4 shootout tie. . . . The victory sparked a national celebration and a realization by many that women's sports could be just as exciting, competitive, and lucrative as men's sports. And the victorious athletes understood as well as anyone the connection between a 27-year-old statute and tangible progress in women's athletics. . . . Title IX has enhanced, and will continue to enhance, women's opportunities to enjoy the thrill of victory, the agony of defeat, and the many tangible benefits that flow from just being given a chance to participate in intercollegiate athletics. Today we join our sister circuits in holding that Title IX does not bar universities from taking steps to ensure that women are approximately as well represented in sports programs as they are in student bodies.

We REVERSE, and VACATE the preliminary injunction.

NOTES AND QUESTIONS

1. *Capping Team Rosters and Title IX.* In *Neal,* why does the Ninth Circuit reject plaintiffs' claim that capping rosters for men's sports or eliminating men's teams violates Title IX? For purposes of federal equal protection, do you agree with *Neal*'s holding that cutting men's sports (gender-based conduct) is substantially related to an important government interest?

    Almost 20 years ago, Donna Lopiano, a well-known advocate for gender equity and former chief executive officer of the Women's Sports Foundation, cited statistics evidencing that:

    (1) Most schools are adding women's sports without cutting men's sports. (2) The richest schools are the ones that are cutting men's sports. (3) Men's sports participation has continued to increase (not decrease) as women's sports participation grows. At the college level, there are still 30 percent more male than female participants. (4) Some men's and women's sports have been cut from college programs, many simply because of lack of interest.

It's Time for Straight Talk About Title IX, SportsBus. J., April 30-May 6, 2001, at 33. She asserts that some NCAA Division I universities are making a "status decision" to have "a gender equitable program at the highest competitive level with fewer teams, spending more money on each team." She points out the alternatives including moving down to a lower level of competition and continuing to fund all teams, or conducting an athletic program with multiple funding tiers. What are your thoughts regarding her proposal?

2. *Legality of Cutting Sports Teams.* In *Equity in Athletics, Inc. v. U.S. Department of Educ.,* 639 F.3d 91 (4th Cir. 2011), James Madison University announced plans to eliminate seven men's and three women's athletic teams in order to comply with the substantial proportionality prong of OCR's three prong test for Title IX. At the time, women represented 61 percent of the university's undergraduate student population but constituted only 50.7 percent of student-athletes. Opponents challenged the cuts and sought injunctive relief precluding the university from implementing them. In rejecting the plaintiffs' claims, the court held that (1) the use of the substantial proportionality standard does not violate Title IX inasmuch as it neither imposes a mandatory disparate impact requirement nor unlawfully authorizes intentional discrimination; (2) like other courts which have considered the issue, requiring substantial proportionality does not violate the Equal Protection Clause because taking gender into account when decreasing athletic opportunities does not violate the U.S. Constitution; and (3) elimination of the men's teams does not violate due process because generally student-athletes possess no property interest in intercollegiate athletic participation.

Legal scholars have observed:

> [C]ourts have recognized that budget reductions and constraints are a reality at many schools and that Title IX must be interpreted to reflect that reality. While everyone would prefer that schools remedy their past discrimination and reach equity by increasing female opportunities to the level males have long enjoyed (and most schools do so), schools with dwindling budgets cannot always do this. The law allows schools to decide their own level of commitment to athletics and to set their own budgets. As courts have reiterated, Title IX does not dictate these choices and is not the cause of these schools' decision-making; it merely requires that they equitably allocate the opportunities and resources that they have.

Jocelyn Samuels and Kristen Galles, *In Defense of Title IX: Why Current Policies Are Required to Ensure Equality of Opportunity,* 14 Marq. Sports L. Rev. 11, 31 (2003).

A lawsuit by several associations representing men's collegiate wrestling coaches, athletes, and alumni claimed that the three-part test in the OCR's 1979 Policy Interpretation and its 1996 Clarification of Title IX and its regulations is illegal. Plaintiffs sought to enjoin the Department of Education from enforcing Title IX in a manner that allegedly discriminated against male athletes. This lawsuit was dismissed on the grounds that the plaintiffs lacked standing and the federal Administrative Procedure Act barred their claims. *National Wrestling Coaches Assn. v. United States Dept. of Educ.,* 366 F.3d 930 (D.C. Cir. 2004), *cert. denied.,* 545 U.S. 1104 (2005). See also *Cobb v. U.S. Dept. of Educ. Office for Civil Rights,* 487 F. Supp. 2d 1049 (D. Minn. 2007) (no private right to force OCR to withhold federal funds to violator school, but recognizing a private-party claim against OCR if it "assists" violation of Title IX contrary to its legal duty to eliminate discrimination).

The most effective way to avoid the elimination of men's nonrevenue sports likely is to raise private funds to support them. In 2011, for example, the University of California, Berkeley, baseball program was saved from being cut for economic reasons by substantial philanthropic efforts on the part of the supporters of the program. See Benenson, *Baseball Program Will Continue at UC Berkeley* http://news.berkeley.edu/2011/04/08/baseball-to-continue-at-cal/.

3. *Title IX at 40.* A Title IX at 40 Report issued by the National Coalition for Women and Girls in Education made the following findings regarding Title IX and athletics:

> Title IX has increased female participation in sports exponentially. In response to greater opportunities to play, the number of high school girls participating in sports has risen tenfold in the past 40 years, while six times as many women compete in college sports. 2. Huge gains in the number of female athletes demonstrate the key principle underlying the legislation: Women and girls have an equal interest in sports and deserve equal opportunities to participate. 3. Participation in sports confers both immediate and long-term benefits: Female athletes do better in school, are less likely to engage in risky behavior, and are healthier than girls and women who do not participate in sports. 4. Attacks on Title IX often spring from misconceptions about how the law works. Courts have consistently upheld the validity of the law. 5. Despite many gains over the past 40 years, barriers remain to participation in sports for girls and women. Greater enforcement of the law by the federal and state governments, self-policing of compliance by schools, and passage of the High School Athletics Transparency Bills will help bring about greater equity.

National Coalition for Women and Girls in Education, *Title IX at 40: Working to Ensure Gender Equity in Education,* http://www.ncwge.org/PDF/TitleIXat40 .pdf.

4. *Title IX and Economic Policy.* Professor Richard A. Epstein has argued, on legal and economic grounds, that we should "scrap Title IX altogether and rely on schools to allocate their athletic funds as they see fit, spurred by the current powerful social consensus behind the equal-opportunity norm." Richard A. Epstein, *Law and Economics: Just Scrap Title IX,* Nat'l L.J., Oct. 14, 2002. Colleges have two ways to respond to this imbalance: pay to increase the number of women athletes or cut the number of men without charge. With constrained budgets, it's no surprise that colleges slash slots from nonrevenue men's sports, such as wrestling and gymnastics, and use the savings to add far fewer female slots in, say, ice hockey or golf. According to Epstein, the marginal male athlete begs for a chance to clean up the locker room to wrestle without a scholarship; the marginal female athlete receives a large scholarship to induce her to participate. *Id.*

For a contrary view, see Daniel R. Marburger and Nancy Hogshead-Makar, *Is Title IX Really to Blame for the Decline in Intercollegiate Men's Nonrevenue Sports?,* 14 Marq. Sports L. Rev. 65 (2003). Professors Marburger and Hogshead-Makar begin their analysis by distinguishing between the perspectives relied on at the Division I, II, and III levels:

> Inferring the relative emphasis on the consequentialist/utilitarian perspectives, Division I overtly favors promoting intercollegiate athletics as

spectator sports, with the income potential of football and basketball specifically identified in its statement of philosophy. In emphasizing the spectator-orientation of sports, the philosophy specifically notes the goal of a self-financing athletic department. Division II and III members, in contrast, explicitly assert that the primary goal of their athletic programs is to benefit the student-athletes.

Id. at 77.

After examining how the Division I arm's race — the need to provide better facilities and other amenities for revenue-producing football and men's basketball programs to remain competitive in those sports — the authors examine extensive data regarding participation of men and women in intercollegiate athletics at the Division I, II, and III levels. They conclude that placing the blame on Title IX for the decrease in participation opportunities for male athletes may be misplaced:

> As long as football and men's basketball budgets [at the Division I level, in particular] are essentially exempted from budgetary restraints, Title IX proportionality burdens are shifted to nonrevenue sports. This begs the question: is Title IX responsible for a sport's discontinuation, or is it the incentive to favor the growth in the football/men's basketball budget? In answering this question, we should note that the net decrease in men's nonrevenue sports occurred only at the Division I level despite the fact that football and men's basketball are frequently in a position to cross-subsidize the nonrevenue sports. At the Division III level, whether expenditures per participant are substantially more equal between "revenue" and nonrevenue sports, and also between men's and women's sports in general, the net change in the number of men's sports is positive.
>
> If the analysis provided in this study is correct, weakening the proportionality component of Title IX will not spare men's nonrevenue sports at the Division I level. Rather, it will only serve to further accelerate the arms race, with men's and women's nonrevenue sports experiencing equivalent budgetary casualties.

Id. at 93.

Has Title IX been responsible for reducing men's opportunities to participate in intercollegiate athletics, or has the Division I emphasis on marketing and promoting football and men's basketball as spectator and revenue-producing sports in a highly competitive market been the primary cause of such reductions? Is it fair to use revenues produced by Division I football and men's basketball teams to provide athletic participation opportunities for men and women in non-revenue-producing sports? In contrast, at the Division II and III levels of athletic competition, participation is emphasized in competitive sports by many students rather than only elite student-athletes. It is not uncommon for a small university or college to have as many as 30 percent to 40 percent of its students participating in intercollegiate athletics, which provides a significant tool to recruit students to Division II and III educational institutions. What, if anything, can or should be done at the Division I level to address the problems that arise in the gender and racial equity contexts because of the emphasis on a more commercial, revenue-producing, and self-funding model of intercollegiate athletics?

PROBLEM 10-3

You have been retained as legal counsel by a mid-level Division I university with a very successful men's basketball team that generates net revenues of approximately $2.5 million. Three years ago, the men's football team was operating at a loss of over $1 million per year, but it is now losing only $300,000 per year. The women's basketball team produces revenue, but it operates at a net loss of over $100,000 per year. Other men's and women's athletics programs generate very little revenue. The net result is that the athletic program is being run at a deficit of approximately $1 million per year. The president of the university has been pressured by state legislators and is required by mandate from the university's board of trustees to operate the university's athletic program with a balanced budget. The president has communicated this mandate to the athletics director and has made it clear that the athletics budget needs to be balanced within two years.

Currently, 61 percent of the students at the university are women and 39 percent are men. Participation figures in intercollegiate athletics are almost reversed, with 63 percent male and 37 percent female participation in intercollegiate athletics. The football team has 110 participants, including several walk-ons. The school is considering adding women's swimming or women's softball, and its athletics conference recognizes both sports. The university has pool facilities that can easily be converted to use for a women's swimming team, but there is only limited interscholastic competition in swimming in the general geographical area of the university. There is interscholastic competition in softball in the area, but there are no facilities at the university. Building new facilities would involve substantial costs, and the cost of operating the softball team would be slightly higher per student-athlete than operating a swimming program. An interest survey indicates somewhat more interest in participating in softball than swimming on the part of women attending the university.

There has been some talk of dropping the men's track team, which would help some in terms of proportionality, but concerns have been raised in the community that such an act would eliminate a disproportionate number of athletes of color. Men's baseball might also be cut, but it is quite popular with the chairperson of the university's board of trustees, whose son plays on the team.

Based on these facts, what advice would you give? What additional facts would you want to know? What practical problems may arise as you deal with the legal issues raised in this problem?

5.   *Pregnancy and Title IX*

The greatest physiological difference between men and women is that women may bear children. While girls who play sports are less likely than their peers to become pregnant, unexpected pregnancy does occur. Title IX prohibits discrimination based on sex in educational programs or activities at institutions that receive federal funding, and discrimination because of pregnancy is the epitome of sex discrimination. Pregnancy is a temporary medical condition, and equity requires pregnant athletes be treated similarly to any other athlete with a temporary medical condition. Unfortunately, many student-athletes, coaches, and administrators, and school personnel are not familiar with the

Title IX pregnancy regulations, so discriminatory actions frequently occur. The Title IX regulations state:

§106.40 Marital or parental status.

(a) *Status generally.* A recipient shall not apply any rule concerning a student's actual or potential parental, family, or marital status which treats students differently on the basis of sex.

(b) *Pregnancy and related conditions.* (1) A recipient shall not discriminate against any student, or exclude any student from its education program or activity, including any class or extracurricular activity, on the basis of such student's pregnancy, childbirth, false pregnancy, termination of pregnancy or recovery therefrom, unless the student requests voluntarily to participate in a separate portion of the program or activity of the recipient.

(2) A recipient may require such a student to obtain the certification of a physician that the student is physically and emotionally able to continue participation so long as such a certification is required of all students for other physical or emotional conditions requiring the attention of a physician. . . .

(4) A recipient shall treat pregnancy, childbirth, false pregnancy, termination of pregnancy and recovery therefrom in the same manner and under the same policies as any other temporary disability with respect to any medical or hospital benefit, service, plan or policy which such recipient administers, operates, offers, or participates in with respect to students admitted to the recipient's educational program or activity.

(5) In the case of a recipient which does not maintain a leave policy for its students, or in the case of a student who does not otherwise qualify for leave under such a policy, a recipient shall treat pregnancy, childbirth, false pregnancy, termination of pregnancy and recovery therefrom as a justification for a leave of absence for so long a period of time as is deemed medically necessary by the student's physician, at the conclusion of which the student shall be reinstated to the status which she held when the leave began.

Pregnancies for high school and college student-athletes are typically unplanned and create incredible levels of stress. Historically, even throughout the 1980s when Title IX had existed for more than a decade, many schools expelled pregnant students or reassigned them to alternative programs. At the high school level, purported justifications for such exclusion included a fear of contagious pregnancy (the belief that a visibly pregnant student in school would induce other girls to become pregnant), the deterrence theory that the shame of expulsion or mandatory transfer would discourage others from becoming pregnant, fear that a pregnant student would stain the reputation of the institution, and finally, concern for the health risks of a pregnant student attending school and participating in extracurricular activities. Lee Green, *Legal Obligations of Schools to Pregnant and Parenting Student-Athletes,* High School Today (Mar. 14, 2017), available at https://www.nfhs.org/articles/legal-obligations-of-schools-to-pregnant-and-parenting-student-athletes/. Pregnant high school athletes are often removed from athletics immediately, either because of parochial policies that prohibit participation in extracurricular activities or paternalistic beliefs that participation in sport is too dangerous.

While loss of athletics opportunities and/or scholarships can be devastating for a student-athlete, thus far there has been little litigation, although there are exceptions. Tara Brady was a scholarship basketball player at Sacred Heart University, a small Catholic university in Connecticut. In the summer between her freshman and sophomore years, Brady discovered she was pregnant and immediately informed her coach that she was planning to continue the pregnancy to term. The coach told her that she would be a distraction to the team and that she should withdraw from school for her sophomore year because she would not be receiving an athletics scholarship. While Brady wanted to continue her studies as a member of the team, the coach said he would not grant her a medical redshirt because she would be an "insurance liability to the university, a health risk to herself, a distraction to the team, and a risk to [his] job." See *Complaint, Brady v. Sacred Heart University,* No. 3:03 Civ. 514, 8 (D. Conn. March 24, 2003).

Brady later learned she had been treated unfairly, so she contacted the Sacred Heart athletics director and compliance officer. The university readmitted her with a full scholarship for the spring semester of her sophomore year. Brady delivered her baby during the spring semester, and once the basketball season concluded, she contacted the coach about being reinstated on the basketball team. The coach told her they no longer needed her and that she would not receive a scholarship. Brady appealed this decision to the Ad Hoc Financial Aid Review Committee and was reinstated to the basketball team with an athletic scholarship for her junior year. The coach proceeded to exclude Brady for all team events and communicated only through an intermediary. The emotional stress and frustration with the situation became too much to endure, and Brady withdrew from Sacred Heart. Because she could not transfer to another Division I institution without losing a year of eligibility, she enrolled at West Chester University, a Division II institution, where she played for two years receiving a partial scholarship. Brady proceeded to file a lawsuit, which was confidentially settled in March, 2003. *Id.*

Student-athlete pregnancy did not generate much attention until 2007 when ESPN *Outside the Lines* exposed college athletics programs that were requiring female student-athletes to sign contracts acknowledging they would lose their athletics scholarship if they became pregnant and could not compete. The fear of losing their scholarships led to seven student-athletes terminating their pregnancies. Other student-athletes who chose to complete their pregnancies were immediately dismissed from the team and/or scholarships were not renewed at the end of the academic term. *Outside the Lines: Pregnant Pause* (ESPN television broadcast May 13, 2007). Student-athletes who become pregnant may feel trapped in a no-win situation: chose to keep silent and terminate the pregnancy while risking her health by not taking the time to physically recover from the procedure; hide the pregnancy, again risking her health by not receiving prenatal care or proper supervision from an obstetrician; or disclose the pregnancy, be removed from the team, and lose her scholarship.

The ESPN expose prompted the NCAA to develop a *Model Pregnant and Parenting Policy* as well as a *Handbook for Pregnant and Parenting Student-Athletes.* See http://www.ncaa.org/about/resources/inclusion/pregnant-parenting-student-athletes. The Office for Civil Rights also responded by sending a *Dear Colleague Letter* to all colleges and universities receiving federal funding to remind them of the Title IX legal requirements for the nondiscriminatory treatment of student athletes. Dear Colleague Letter from Stephanie Monroe, Office of the

Assistant Sec'y, Office for Civil Rights, Dep't of Educ., June 25, 2007, available at http://www.ed.gov/about/offices/list/ocr/letters/colleague-20070625.html.

Current research on pregnancy and exercise indicates that there is no reason to exclude pregnant athletes from participation until the latter stages of pregnancy, and only then if the sport is a contact sport or puts the athlete at risk of falling. Swimmers, golfers, and runners, for example, can often continue training (and sometimes competing) through the duration of their pregnancy. A competent medical professional, ideally the student-athlete's obstetrician, should make the decision whether to allow the athlete to participate or not, not a coach. Coaches do retain the right to determine whether the student-athlete will compete in games and athletic events, a decision usually based solely on athletics ability.

NOTE AND QUESTIONS

1. *Reverse Discrimination?* In *Butler v. NCAA*, 2006 U.S. Dist. LEXIS 61632 (D. Kan. 2006), a male student-athlete sued the NCAA and the University of Kansas for refusing to extend his athletic eligibility for an additional year because he had fathered a child. Butler claimed gender discrimination under Title IX and the Equal Protection clause and sought injunctive relief to participate in intercollegiate athletics. In failing to find the requisite likelihood of success on the merits for the issuance of an interlocutory injunction, the district court addressed the Title IX claim:

   > Title IX provides in part that "no person in the United States shall, on the basis of sex, be excluded from participation, be denied the benefits of, or be subjected to discrimination under any education program or activity receiving Federal financial assistance." 20 U.S.C. § 1681(a). To state a claim under Title IX, plaintiff must show that he was excluded from a program "on the basis of sex." Plaintiff asserts that he missed an opportunity to participate in football in 2001 when Frazier became pregnant and he decided not to attend NMSU in order to work and later care for his daughter. Plaintiff asserts that if he were a female, he would be able to take advantage of the pregnancy exception, under which an institution can grant a one-year extension of the five-year eligibility "for a female student-athlete for reasons of pregnancy." See Ex. 1, NCAA Bylaws, Art. 14.2.1.3. As defendants point out, the pregnancy exception allows a waiver "for reasons of pregnancy," which appear to be different from reasons of maternity or paternity. See Johnson v. Univ. of Ia., 431 F.3d 325, 332 (8th Cir. 2005) (policy affording biological mothers six weeks of paid leave following birth of child, but not allowing such leave to biological fathers, does not violate Title IX). The Court finds no substantial likelihood of success on the merits of plaintiff's Title IX claim.

   Id at 8-9.

2. *Pregnancy vs. Parenting.* Historically, teen and unmarried pregnancy carried a moral and social stigma. Under Title IX, pregnant student-athletes must be treated like any other athlete with a temporary medical condition — they can't be kicked off the team, prevented from dressing for games, prevented from traveling to games, or any other action unless other athletes who are medically unable to play are treated similarly. While Butler lost his case regarding the NCAA rule, what are the advantages or disadvantages of extending the eligibility clock based on parental status?

The remainder of this chapter addresses gender equity subjects that have significant effects across the sports industry, including youth, high school, college, Olympic, and professional sports. These issues affect male and female athletes as well as men and women in the workplace (e.g., coaches and athletics administrators), with a disproportionately negative impact on women.

D.   SPORT, SEXUAL HARASSMENT, AND SEXUAL VIOLENCE

Sexual harassment is unwanted attention of a sexual nature that creates an uncomfortable environment. It is pervasive in all aspects of our society — in schools, businesses, medicine, law, retail, hospitality, entertainment, and, of course, sport. Sport is often referred to as a microcosm of society (see Chapter 1), and in this context, the hyper-masculinity and violent nature of sport has been referred to as a breeding ground for sexual harassment and sexual assault. See Sarah M. McMahon, *Understanding Community-Specific Rape Myths: Exploring Student Athlete Culture.* 22(4) J. of Women and Social Work 355 (2007).

The Office for Civil Rights provides definitions for discrimination based on sex under Title IX:

> Sexual harassment is unwelcome conduct of a sexual nature. It includes unwelcome sexual advances, requests for sexual favors, and other verbal, nonverbal, or physical conduct of a sexual nature. Sexual violence is a form of sexual harassment. Sexual violence, as OCR uses the term, refers to physical sexual acts perpetrated against a person's will or where a person is incapable of giving consent. A number of different acts fall into the category of sexual violence, including rape, sexual assault, sexual battery, sexual abuse, and sexual coercion.

Office for Civil Rights, Sex-Based Harassment, available at https://www2.ed.gov/about/offices/list/ocr/frontpage/pro-students/issues/sex-issue01.html.

1.   Youth, High School, and Intercollegiate Sport

Recent scandals illuminate the terrible reality that child and adolescent athletes are vulnerable to sexual misconduct by coaches, peers, and others they emulate and trust. Larry Nassar was a team physician with USA Gymnastics and a faculty member and doctor at Michigan State University who used his position to systematically groom and sexually abuse hundreds of athletes over 20 years. He pled guilty to seven counts of child sex abuse and was sentenced for 40 to 175 years in prison after an unprecedented 156 survivors spoke about his abuse at the sentencing hearing. Nassar's victims were as young as six years old and included youth club sport, Olympic, and intercollegiate athletes.

Also disturbing are the number of individuals in positions of authority who were aware of reported incidents and allowed the abuse to persist. The chief executive officer of the United States Olympic Committee, the entire Board of Directors of USA Gymnastics, and the Lou Anna Simon, President of Michigan State University, all resigned for their roles in ignoring complaints about Nassar's "treatments." Subsequently, the president of USA Gymnastics was charged with evidence tampering, Simon was charged with four counts of lying to police, and a criminal investigation into the Twistars gymnastics club, a youth club also affiliated with Nassar, was initiated. See Maya Salam, *How Larry Nassar 'Flouished Unafraid' for So Long*, The New York Times, May 3, 2019, available at https://www.nytimes.com/2019/05/03/sports/larry-nassar-gymnastics-hbo-doc.html. Eventually, the U.S. Department of Education conducted an investigation that revealed incidents of Nassar's abuse reported as early as 1997 and widespread institutional failure to comply with Title IX and the Clery Act, a federal law requiring colleges and universities that receive federal funds to disclose information about crime occurring on and nearby their respective campuses. Paula Lavigne, Dan Murphy, *Federal report cites Michigan State with Systemic 'Serious Violations' of Campus-safety Law* (Jan. 30, 2019), available at https://www.espn.com/espn/story/_/id/25885611/us-department-education-cites-michigan-state-university-clery-act-violations-espn-lines. Civil lawsuits filed against Michigan State University resulted in a $500 million settlement with the 332 plaintiffs. Matt Mencarini, Justin A. Hinkley, *Michigan State and 332 of Larry Nassar's Victims Reach 'Historic' $500 Million Settlement*, Lansing State J. (May 16, 2018), available at https://www.lansingstatejournal.com/story/news/local/2018/05/16/larry-nassar-michigan-state-settlement-lawsuit/614502002/.

Sexual violence committed by coaches has been studied since the 1980s, with numerous situations in which coaches who have unrestricted access to athletes have abused their power. High risk environments include individual training sessions, locker rooms, and travel. Sylvie Parent & Kristine Fortier, *Comprehensive Overview of the Problem of Violence Against Athletes in Sport*, 42(4) J. Sport and Social Issues 227 (2018). Sexual harassment can also occur among peers and between individuals of the opposite sex or same sex. On October 31, 2018, four 15-year-old football players sexually assaulted four freshmen teammates with a broomstick. One of the perpetrators claimed it was a tradition that started generations ago. Elisha Fieldstadt, *Maryland High School Football Players Accused of Sexually Assaulting Teammates with Broom* (Nov. 28, 2018), available at https://www.nbcnews.com/news/us-news/four-maryland-high-school-football-players-accused-raping-teammates-n941126. Harassment by peers is a growing concern, in-person and through social media and electronic communications. Child victims are more likely to struggle with anxiety and depression, experience post-traumatic stress disorder (PTSD), abuse drugs and alcohol, and attempt suicide. Erna Olafson, *Child Sexual Abuse: Demography, Impact, and Interventions*, 4(1) J. of Child & Adolescent Trauma 8 (2011).

a.   Title IX

Under Title IX, sexual harassment and sexual violence are prohibited because these actions are discrimination based on sex that negatively impact a student's ability to fully benefit from the programs or activities offered by the educational institution. Schools are required to be alert to signs of harassment and to take immediate and appropriate action, including investigating, taking effective steps to end the harassment, preventing recurring harassment and retaliation, and remedying the effects of the harassment, if possible. See U.S. Department of Education Office for Civil Rights, *Title IX Resource Guide*

(April 2015) available at https://www2.ed.gov/about/offices/list/ocr/docs/ dcl-title-ix-coordinators-guide-201504.pdf. Title IX provides a cause of action against educational institutions who fail to appropriately investigate and punish acts of harassment and sexual violence, with punitive damages available in cases of intentional discrimination. See *Franklin v. Gwinnett County Public Schools*, 503 U.S. 60, 74 (1992).

Harassment can take many forms, including verbal acts, name calling, graphic gestures, written statements, physical conduct that is threatening, humiliating, or harmful, and physical contact without consent such as sexual assault, sexual battery, and rape. Seemingly smaller acts may accumulate over time to create a hostile environment, but even a single severe act, typically physical conduct, may be enough to negatively impact the student's ability to fully participate in their educational opportunity. Verbal and written forms of harassment are more common in schools than physical harassment. Almost half of all students (56 percent of girls and 40 percent of boys) in grades 7 through 12 experienced sexual harassment during the school year in 2010-11. Girls are more likely than boys to experience unwelcome sexual comments, jokes or gestures or to have sexual rumors spread electronically about them. See Catherine Hill and Holly Kearl, *Crossing the Line: Sexual Harassment at School* (Nov. 2011), available at https:// www.aauw.org/files/2013/02/Crossing-the-Line-Sexual-Harassment-at-School. pdf. Boys are more likely than girls to identify being called homosexual as the most common form of harassment experienced. *Id.* The educational impact of harassment included changing schools (4 percent), staying home from school (12 percent), not wanting to go to school (32 percent), feeling sick (37 percent), difficulty studying or staying focused at school (30 percent), having trouble sleeping (19 percent), and quitting activities and sports (8 percent). *Id.* For all negative outcomes, the impact was greater for girls than for boys.

The Supreme Court first recognized institutional liability for sexual harassment under Title IX in *Gebser v. Lagos Vista Independent School District*, 524 U.S. 274 (1998), for acts of teacher-student sexual harassment. The decision was also instructive relative to damages, explaining that monetary damages were appropriate when "an official of the school district who at a minimum has authority to institute corrective measures on the district's behalf has actual notice of, and is deliberately indifferent to, the teacher's misconduct." *Id.* at 277. The following year, in *Davis v. Monroe County Board of Education*, 526 U.S. 629 (1999), the Supreme Court found that schools could be liable for acts of student to student (peer) harassment and that schools are liable for monetary damages when they have actual knowledge of the conduct and are deliberately indifferent to sexual harassment that is so "severe, pervasive and objectively offensive" that it deprives the victim of educational opportunities and benefits. *Id.* at 650.

Colleges and universities have also been named as defendants in lawsuits when student-athletes have raped other students, both on and off campus. In *Williams v. Board of Regents of the Univ. System of Georgia*, 477 F.3d 1282 (11th Cir. 2007), a female student claimed that a basketball player at the university invited her to his room where they engaged in consensual sex. The basketball player left the room, and a Georgia football player who allegedly was hiding in the closet while the couple had sex then raped the student. During this rape, the basketball player called a teammate who also came to the room and allegedly raped and assaulted the student. Although the men accused of the rapes were not convicted of the criminal charges, the student successfully sued the university under Title IX on the grounds that the coach, athletic director, and university president were all aware that one of the assailants had a history of sexual assault before he was recruited and admitted to the university. The Eleventh Circuit held that given the past history of the recruited student-athlete, the institution had "before the fact notice" and should have made efforts to prevent future harassment from occurring.

In *Simpson v. University of Colorado,* 2007 U.S. App. LEXIS 21478 (10th Cir. Colo. 2007), two women claimed that they were sexually assaulted by University of Colorado football players and recruits at an off-campus party and brought an action against the university under Title IX. The district court granted the university's motion for summary judgment. On appeal, the Tenth Circuit concluded:

> [T]he evidence before the district court would support findings that by the time of the assaults on Plaintiffs, (1) Coach Barnett [the head coach], whose rank in the CU hierarchy was comparable to that of a police chief in a municipal government, had general knowledge of the serious risk of sexual harassment and assault during college-football recruiting efforts; (2) Barnett knew that such assaults had indeed occurred during CU recruiting efforts; (3) Barnett nevertheless maintained an unsupervised player-host program to show high-school recruits "a good time"; and (4) Barnett knew, both because of incidents reported to him and because of his own unsupportive attitude, that there had been no change in the atmosphere since 1997 (when the prior assault occurred) that would make such misconduct less likely in 2001. A jury could infer that "the need for more or different training [of player-hosts] so obvious, and the inadequacy so likely to result in [Title IX violations], that [Coach Barnett could] reasonably be said to have been deliberately indifferent to the need.

Id. at 1184. The football players and recruits in the *Simpson* case were also not convicted of the criminal charges, but the University settled the case for $2.85 million after the Tenth Circuit decision.

The Department of Education Office for Civil Rights issued its first guidance for schools to manage sexual harassment in 1997. See *Sexual Harassment Guidance: Harassment of Students by School Employees, Other Students, or Third Parties,* March 13, 1997. This was followed by a *Revised Sexual Harassment Guidance: Harassment of Students by School Employees, Other Students, or Third Parties* in 2001, which incorporated the precedent established by the Supreme Court in the *Davis* and *Gebser* cases. Following the precedent established in the *Williams* and *Simpson* cases, in 2011 the Department of Education Office for Civil Rights issued a *Dear Colleague Letter* to approximately 7,000 colleges and universities that receive federal funds reminding them of their obligation to students to provide an academic environment free from sexual harassment and sexual violence. The letter also outlined expected processes for the institution to follow to prevent, investigate, address, and remedy sexual harassment and sexual violence utilizing common law precedent and information from experts in sexual harassment and sexual violence.

Hundreds of complaints have been filed with the Office for Civil Rights and in the courts accusing institutions of failing to provide adequate response to complaints of sexual violence. A disproportionate number of these cases accuse student-athletes of being the perpetrators. On average, student-athletes make up approximately 1.7 percent of undergraduate students at Power 5 conference institutions but are involved in 6.3 percent of the Title IX complaints. Paula Levigne, *OTL: College athletes three times more likely to be named in Title IX sexual misconduct complaints* (Nov. 2, 2018), available at https://www.espn.com/espn/otl/story/_/id/25149259/college-athletes-three -s-more-likely-named-title-ix-sexual-misconduct-complaints. Student-athletes are also more likely to be involved in group rape situations — in one plaintiff's complaint against Baylor University, she claimed football recruits who participated in a group rape described it as a bonding experience. *Id.* While this information casts a negative light on big-time college athletics programs, the publicity associated with these complaints may be having a positive effect in increasing awareness of sexual assault on campus and motivating more victims to report their assaults. In the Power 5 conference schools included in the 2018 ESPN Outside the Lines research, almost four times as many sexual misconduct complaints were filed in 2017 than in 2012. Similarly, the Office for Civil Rights had 130 open complaints in 2014 and over 400 open cases in 2017. *Id.*

In an effort to ensure that its member institutions comply with Title IX and to protect their students, the NCAA and its membership began actively developing sexual violence prevention policy in 2010. The process began with a Summit on Violence Prevention in 2011, then engaging with experts in developing the 2014 guide, *Addressing Sexual Assault and Interpersonal Violence,* for the membership and creating an interdisciplinary task force that produced the "Sexual Violence Prevention Toolkit" in 2016. Also in 2016, the NCAA created a Commission to Combat Campus Sexual Violence, which defined the following aspirational culture for members:

> A positive and thriving athletics team culture that revolves around respect and empathy for all, fostering a climate in which all feel that they are respected, valued and contributing members of their teams, athletics programs and institutions; and creating an environment in which students (athletes and nonathletes alike) feel safe and secure, both emotionally and physically, and are free of fears of retaliation or reprisal. The positive culture exuded by a member institution's NCAA teams is the catalyst for a positive culture across an entire campus.

See *NCAA Board of Governors Policy on Campus Sexual Violence,* Aug. 8, 2017.

In 2018, the NCAA Board of Governors updated its Policy on Campus Sexual Violence as follows:

Overarching Principles.
1. Intercollegiate athletics departments should be informed on and integrated in overall campus policies and processes addressing sexual violence prevention and acts of sexual violence, particularly those related to adjudication and resolution of matters related to sexual violence.
2. Intercollegiate athletics departments should review annually the most current Checklist Recommendations of the NCAA Sexual Violence Prevention Toolkit, using it as a guide with resources to conduct ongoing, comprehensive education for student-athletes, coaches and athletics administrators.
3. Intercollegiate athletics programs should utilize their platform to serve as leaders on campus through engagement in and collaboration on efforts to support campus-wide sexual violence prevention initiatives. This includes involving student-athletes in prevention efforts in meaningful ways across the campus, including encouraging use of leadership roles on campus to support such efforts.

Each university chancellor/president, director of athletics and campus Title IX coordinator* must attest annually that:
1. The athletics department is informed on, integrated in, and compliant with institutional policies and processes regarding sexual violence prevention and proper adjudication and resolution of acts of sexual violence.

2. The institutional policies and processes regarding sexual violence prevention and adjudication, and the name and contact information for the campus Title IX coordinator*, are readily available within the department of athletics, and are provided to student-athletes.

3. All student-athletes, coaches and staff have been educated each year on sexual violence prevention, intervention and response, to the extent allowable by state law and collective bargaining agreements.

Further, the athletics department will cooperate with college or university investigations into reports and matters related to sexual violence involving student-athletes and athletics department staff in a manner compliant with institutional policies for all students.

If a school is not able to attest their compliance with the above requirements, it will be prohibited from hosting any NCAA championship competitions for the next applicable academic year.

NCAA Board of Governors Policy on Campus Sexual Violence, updated Aug. 7, 2018.

NOTES AND QUESTIONS

1. *Athletics Culture and Campus Policy.* In 2016, eight women students filed a complaint against the University of Tennessee-Knoxville alleging that the University failed to deal appropriately with a campus climate that condoned or covered up sexual violence on the part of student-athletes, particularly football players. The University settled the matter for $2.48 million, which included attorneys' fees. As part of the settlement, the University also agreed to appoint a special commission to review the handling of sexual violence at all universities that are a part of the Tennessee system. Nate Rau and Anita Wadhwani, *Tennessee Settles Sexual Assault Suit for $2.48 Million,* http://www.tennessean.com/story/news/crime/2016/07/05/tennessee-settles-sexual-assault-suit-248-million/86708442/.

Prior to the *Simpson* case, other football players had been accused of sexual assault at the University of Colorado. Assistant District Attorney Mary Keenan met with CU officials and recommended that "CU adopt a policy of zero tolerance for alcohol and sex in the recruiting program, develop written policies and procedures for supervising recruits, and offer football players annual training by the DA on sexual assault." *Simpson, supra* at 1182. The court reported that Coach Barnett resisted recruiting reform efforts and claimed that "at schools all over the country recruits were shown 'a good time,' met young women, and went to parties, and if such activities weren't allowed at CU, it would be a 'competitive disadvantage' for the football team." *Id.* at 1184.

Would policies like the one suggested by Ms. Keenan have been a strong deterrent to the assaults that provided the basis for the *Simpson* case? Considering that CU paid $2.85 million to settle the *Simpson* case, what would you recommend that the university do to prevent the type of conduct that gave rise to *Simpson*? What impact do you think the NCAA policy will have on changing rape culture in athletics programs?

2. *Title IX Limitations.* Doe was a student at Providence University when she was sexually assaulted by three members of the Brown University football team. Doe filed a lawsuit against Brown claiming it failed to complete the

investigation into the assault and discipline the football players. The First Circuit dismissed the lawsuit as Doe was not a student at Brown University, and the sex discrimination did not occur as part of an educational program or activity. *Doe v. Brown University*, 896 F.3d 127 (1st Cir. 2018). What other legal options might Doe have, assuming she had physical and mental health expenses related to the attack?

3. *Personal Legal Liability and Responsibility.* Individual school officials (such as coaches or athletics administrators) can be held personally liable for their actions regarding acts of harassment by third parties under §1983 for violating a student's civil rights in addition to Title IX claims made against the school. Timothy Davis and Keith E. Smith, *Eradicating Student-Athlete Sexual Assault of Women: Section 1983 and Personal Liability Following* Fitzgerald v. Barnstable, 2009 Mich. St. L. Rev. 629. On August 23, 2013, the Iowa Supreme Court held that the University of Iowa was justified in firing its longtime dean of students for mishandling a student sexual assault case. In a unanimous decision, the court affirmed the lower court's dismissal of the dean of students' claims that he was defamed and wrongfully terminated by UI President Sally Mason. One commentator responded to this decision by noting, "The court's decision is a reminder for practitioners to advise their clients to be proactive in sexual abuse and harassment investigations." Aditi Mukherji, *University of Iowa's Firing Affirmed By Iowa Supreme Court*, http://blogs.findlaw.com/eighth_circuit/2013/08/university-of-iowas-firing-affirmed-by-iowa-supreme-court.html.

4. *Accused's Title IX and Due Process Rights.* The 2011 OCR *Dear Colleague Letter* on sexual violence and the 2014 sexual assault guidance were hailed as model policy by victims' advocates, while others have criticized the policy for requiring a minimum burden of proof — the preponderance of the evidence standard — and inadequate due process for those accused. Since 2011, 256 lawsuits have been filed by accused students against their universities alleging unfair treatment in Title IX sexual misconduct investigations and hearings. About 20 percent of these claims have been made by student-athletes. See Levigne, 2018 *supra*. In September 2017, the Secretary of Education, Betsy deVos, rescinded the 2011 and 2014 sexual assault guidance in favor of a seven-page Q&A document. See *Q&A on Campus Sexual Assault Misconduct* https://www2.ed.gov/about/offices/list/ocr/docs/qa-title-ix-201709.pdf. In November 2018, OCR proposed new sexual harassment regulations that were then open to public comment for 90 days. The proposed regulations increase the burden of proof for victims, require increased due process for those accused, and limits the definition of sexual harassment and institutional liability. A copy of the proposed regulations is available at https://www2.ed.gov/about/offices/list/ocr/docs/background-summary-proposed-ttle-ix-regulation.pdf.

In *Doe v. Columbia University*, No. 15-1536 (2nd Cir. 2016), a male student alleged the investigator, panel, and dean acted with sexual bias in handling a claim of sexual abuse against him by a female student in violation of Title IX. In particular, he asserted that the investigator and panel had: (1) failed to seek out witnesses that might have provided evidence on his behalf and that had been identified as potential sources of evidence supporting his position; (2) failed to act in accordance with established University procedures (due process) designed to protect students accused of abuse; and (3) reached a decision that was contrary to the weight of evidence. Finding the plaintiff's allegations were sufficient to meet the minimal inference of bias necessary under Title IX to defeat a motion to dismiss, the Second Circuit vacated the District Court's dismissal of the plaintiff's action against Columbia University and remanded the case. See *Doe v. Columbia University,* No. 15-1536 (2d Cir. July 29, 2016), http://law.justia.com/cases/federal/appellate-courts/ca2/15-1536/15-1536-2016-07-29.html.

More recently, in *Doe v. Baum,* 903 F.3d 575 (6th Cir. 2018), the accused (Doe) was forced to withdraw from the University of Michigan after the student disciplinary hearing found him likely to have sexually assaulted a female student complainant. Doe asserted federal constitutional due process and Title IX violation claims against the University, alleging the hearing process was biased as his fraternity brother witnesses were not allowed to testify while the female student's sorority sisters were allowed to do so. Additionally, Doe was not allowed to cross examine the female student or her witnesses. The Sixth Circuit reversed the district court's dismissal of Doe's due process and Title IX discrimination claims as differential treatment could be considered sex discrimination.

Not all claims of denial of due process rights by those accused are successful. In *Haidak v. University of Massachusetts-Amherst,* 2019 U.S. App. LEXIS 23482, the First Circuit held that due process could be satisfied by having a neutral party interview the parties in a Title IX disciplinary matter and that cross examination of witnesses by the parties was not required. While Haidak relied upon *Doe v. Baum,* the First Circuit found it unpersuasive, stating:

> We have no reason to believe that questioning of a complaining witness by a neutral party is so fundamentally flawed as to create a categorically unacceptable risk of erroneous deprivation. We also take seriously the admonition that student disciplinary proceedings need not mirror common law trials. . . . If we were to insist on a right to party-conducted cross examination, it would be a short slide to insist on the participation of counsel able to conduct such examination, and at that point the mandated mimicry of a jury-waived trial would be near complete.

Id. at 26-27.

Haidak is significant because its support for university-controlled questioning of the parties in a school-based sexual assault disciplinary hearing conflicts with the newly proposed OCR Title IX regulations, available at https://www2.ed.gov/about/offices/list/ocr/docs/background-summary-proposed-ttle-ix-regulation.pdf.*Doe* and *Haidak* create a conflict among federal appellate courts that may bring the important question of appropriate due process for persons accused of sexual assault and harassment in a school-based disciplinary proceeding to the Supreme Court.

What are the advantages and disadvantages of using preponderance of the evidence from the now withdrawn OCR guidance versus clear and convincing evidence as proposed in the new sexual harassment regulations, as the standard for an institutional disciplinary hearing?

PROBLEM 10-4

As a lawyer and Athletics Director at a major religiously affiliated private university, you have just learned that three student-athletes have been charged with sexual assault. Three young women allege they were assaulted by the student-athletes at an off-campus party after last weekend's victory over the then-top ranked team in the conference. Three of the student-athletes are starters on your highly ranked football team. One of them is a Heisman trophy candidate, and the other is an excellent student who was a member of the prior year's All-Conference Academic team. The third is a student-athlete who was heavily recruited and is sitting out the season (redshirting). When you contact the coach, he assures you that he has "spoken with" the players. He said they admit that there was sexual activity, but no intercourse. They were all adamant that the activity was consensual. The coach expressed his concern and assures you that he and his staff regularly warn team members about such matters in team meetings. The coach, however, notes that, having met with the student-athletes individually and then as a group, he knows and believes the young men. He emphatically added, however, that he is going to sit them for the first half of the game this weekend against a strong conference foe as a message to the team that they are to follow the team policy that clearly provides that they "will not engage in sexual violence." He also added that he regularly warns his players that they need to exercise real care in such matters, stressing that sometimes what seems to be consensual is not. The coaches even had a discussion with the team regarding what consensual means. How do you respond? What needs to be done to satisfy the NCAA Campus Sexual Violence Policy? What are your legal obligations under Title IX? What additional facts will you want to know in order to handle this matter appropriately?

b. Safe Sport

While Title IX provides a cause of action against educational institutions that receive federal funds for students who are harmed by sexual harassment or sexual assault, millions of children and young adults participating in private club and Olympic Development sports had limited protection from harassers and sexual predators despite rampant child abuse. Major sex abuse scandals have plagued virtually all national governing bodies and youth sport organizations. An investigative report of USA Swimming found 590 individuals who allegedly were sexually abused by at least 252 coaches or officials since 1997. Thirty coaches who had been accused of or arrested for child sex abuse or child pornography were allowed to continue working. The youngest reported victim was three years old. Rather than address the abuse, USA Swimming quietly settled complaints to maintain its public image. Alanna Vagianos, *Explosive Report Says USA Swimming Covered Up Hundreds of Sexual Abuse Cases* (Feb. 19, 2018), available at https://www.huffpost.com/entry/usa-swimming-sexual-abuse_n_5a8ad-81fe4b004fc3194c4b2. AAU basketball coach Greg Stephen was sentenced to 180 years in federal prison for sexual exploitation of at least 440 boys from 2005 to 2018. Randy Peterson, *Where's the Outrage from the Greg Stephen Child Sex Abuse Scandal?* DES MOINES REGISTER (May 3, 2019), available at https://www.desmoinesregister.com/story/sports/college/iowa-state/randy-peterson/2019/05/03/greg-stephen-iowa-barnstormers-adidas-aau-basketball-jamie-johnson-child-sex-abuse-federal-prison/1089741001/. ESPN Outside the Lines exposed Conrad Montgomery Avondale Mainwaring, a former Olympic track and field athlete who used his status to groom children who aspired to achieve his level of success. The report identified 41 victims as young as 12 years old in the 1970s through young college-age men in 2016 over a span of 44 years. Similar to Larry Nassar, who disguised his abuse as a medical treatment, Mainwaring claimed his abuse was research, physiotherapy, or mental training. Mike Kessler and Mark Fainaru-Wada, *An Outside the Lines Investigation: 44 Years. 41 Allegations. Now the Past Is Catching Up* (Aug. 1, 2019), available at http://www.espn.com/espn/feature/story/_/id/27244072/44-years-41-allegations-how-caught-former-olympian. These are just a few of hundreds of stories of sexual exploitation and abuse in youth sport.

Congress enacted the Protecting Young Victims from Sexual Abuse and Safe Sport Authorization Act of 2017 (Public Law No: 115-126, Feb. 14, 2018) to protect youth and Olympic athletes from sex abuse and to designate the United States Center for SafeSport as the independent authority to develop training, practices, policies, and procedures to prevent abuse. SafeSport's mission is to "make athlete well-being the centerpiece of our nation's sports culture through abuse prevention, education, and accountability." U.S. Center for SAFESPORT, available at http://safesport.rassmantech.webfactional.com/about/our-work/. The United States Olympic and Paralympic Committee (USOPC) and National Governing Bodies for U.S. Olympic sports (NGBs) are required to adhere to the SafeSport Minor Athlete Abuse Prevention Policies, while other youth sport organizations may utilize these policies, training and education services, and additional resources. The Center provides a confidential online reporting system, investigates complaints, issues a decision, and assigns a sanction. Since March 2017, SafeSport has issued 285 lifetime bans across 50 sports.

PROTECTING YOUNG VICTIMS FROM SEXUAL ABUSE AND SAFE SPORT AUTHORIZATION ACT OF 2017

Public Law No: 115-126, Feb. 14, 2018

TITLE I—PROTECTING YOUNG VICTIMS FROM SEXUAL ABUSE

(Sec. 101) This bill amends the Victims of Child Abuse Act of 1990 to extend the duty to report suspected child abuse, including sexual abuse, to adults who are authorized to interact with minor or amateur athletes at an amateur sports organization facility or at an event sanctioned by a national governing body (NGB) or member of an NGB. An NGB is an amateur sports organization that is recognized by the U.S. Olympic Committee.

An authorized adult who fails to report suspected child abuse within a 24-hour period is subject to criminal penalties.

(Sec. 102) The bill amends the federal criminal code to revise civil remedy provisions for a victim of a human trafficking offense or federal sex offense. Among other things, it changes the civil statute of limitations to 10 years from the date the victim reasonably discovers the violation or injury (currently, 10 years from the date the cause of action arose). The bill also extends the statute of limitations for a minor victim of a human trafficking or federal sex offense to file a civil action to 10 years (currently, 3 years) from the date such individual reaches age 18.

TITLE II—UNITED STATES CENTER FOR SAFE SPORT AUTHORIZATION

(Sec. 201) The bill expands the purposes of the U.S. Olympic Committee to include promoting a safe environment in sports that is free from abuse of amateur athletes.

(Sec. 202) The bill designates the United States Center for Safe Sport to serve as the independent national safe sport organization.

The center has jurisdiction over the U.S. Olympic Committee, NGBs, and Paralympic sports organizations with respect to safeguarding amateur athletes from abuse. It must develop training, practices, policies, and procedures to prevent abuse.

NGBs must implement the policies and procedures to prevent abuse.

(Sec. 203) An amateur sports organization that requests an NGB sanction to host an international amateur athletic competition inside the United States or to sponsor U.S. athletes in an international amateur athletic competition outside the United States must implement and comply with the policies and procedures to prevent abuse.

(Sec. 204) An amateur sports organization that is not subject to the center's policies and procedures to prevent abuse must comply with certain general requirements, including to report suspected child abuse and to limit one-on-one contact between an amateur athlete who is a minor and an adult.

PROBLEM 10-5

You serve on the Board of Directors for a local youth lacrosse organization. As the only attorney on the board, you also provide pro bono legal services. There are more than 5,000 children participating in your organization, ages 5 to 19, with five paid administrators, 16 paid coaches for the elite teams for boys and girls ages 15 to 19, which travel to compete nationally, and over 700 adult volunteers coaching local recreational and state-wide competitive level teams. What policies and procedures is your organization required to follow under the Safe Sport Act? What policies and procedures would you adopt to promote an environment safe for children to participate? What are the pros and cons of educating children about abuse? What process would you recommend for reporting abusive behaviors? Coaches have expressed concerns that parents or players disgruntled about playing time or discipline will make false complaints. Does the SafeSport Response and Resolution Process provide adequate due process for those accused of SafeSport violations?

2.   Professional Sport

On February 15, 2014, NFL running back Ray Rice and his fiancé were arrested and charged with simple assault resulting from a physical altercation in an elevator at the Revel Casino in Atlantic City. Four days later, TMZ released video footage of Rice dragging his fiancé's unconscious body from an elevator. Six weeks later, prosecutors increased Rice's charges to aggravated assault, and the simple assault charges against the fiancé were dropped; police disclosed there was video evidence Rice had knocked her unconscious. Rice and his fiancé were married the next day, on March 28, 2014. Rice pleaded not guilty and applied for a pretrial intervention program for first time offenders. Rice was required to complete a 12-month program and the altercation would be removed from his record. The NFL disciplinary hearing was held on June 16, 2014, with Rice's wife encouraging Commissioner Roger Goodell not to ruin Rice's image and career. On July 14, 2014, the NFL suspended Rice for two games.

The NFL Commissioner announced a new domestic violence policy on August 28, 2014, which includes domestic violence and sexual assault education for all NFL personnel with enhanced training for rookies and new programs for veterans and non-player personnel. Designated team personnel receive training to understand and identify domestic violence and sexual assault risk factors. Those at risk, both potential aggressor or victim, are provided with private, confidential assistance, and information about resources is widely distributed to all players, employees, and families. Under the NFL Personal Conduct Policy, anyone charged with domestic violence or sexual assault is to undergo mandatory evaluation and may be provided with counseling or other services. Those who commit a first offense with physical force and commit assault, battery, domestic violence or sexual assault are to be suspended without pay for six games, with consideration for mitigating factors and increased suspension for aggravating factors. A second offense will result in termination, with an opportunity to petition for reinstatement after one year, but no presumption reinstatement will be granted. Katie Sharp, *NFL Announces New Domestic Violence Policy*, SB NATION, Aug. 28, 2014, available at https://www.sbnation.com/nfl/2014/8/28/6079465/nfl-announces-new-domestic-violence-policy. Twenty-three players have been disciplined since the implementation of the policy.

On August 21, 2015, Major League Baseball became the second professional league to act on a domestic violence, sexual assault and child abuse policy. The agreement holds players accountable through appropriate disciplinary measures while protecting their legal rights and provides resources for the intervention and care of victims, families, and the players as well. Similar to the NFL policy, a strong focus is on training, education, and resources. MLB and MLBPA have a joint policy board for treatment and intervention, comprised of three experts and two representatives from management and the players' association. The MLB Commissioner's Office is responsible for conducting investigations of all allegations and determining sanctions. Players may appeal through arbitration. See Paul Hagen, *MLB, MLBPA Reveal Domestic Violence Policy* (Aug. 21, 2015), available at https://www.mlb.com/news/mlb-mlbpa-agree-on-domestic-violence-policy/c-144508842.

The Joint NBA/NBAPA Policy on Domestic Violence, Sexual Assault and Child Abuse appears as Appendix F in the NBA Collective Bargaining Agreement — 2017. While similar to the MLB policy, significant attention is given to defining domestic violence, sexual assault, and child abuse. It established a Policy Committee comprised of two representatives from the NBA, two representatives from the Players' Association, and three independent experts (one from each subject area) chosen jointly by the appointed representatives, which is responsible for all training and educational programs, selecting a 24-hour confidential hotline service provider, and evaluation and treatment for players who engage in behavior that violates the policy or those who are criminally convicted for a related offense. Players may be placed on administrative leave with pay during an investigation if circumstances warrant. Players who fail to comply are fined $10,000 per day; players who fail to reasonably comply with treatment responsibilities will have additional games added to their suspension. Criminal convictions or pleas are presumed a violation of the policy, while an acquittal also absolves the player of any league disciplinary sanctions. Players found to have engaged in conduct in violation of the policy may be fined, suspended, or dismissed from further association with the League by the Commissioner after a meeting involving all the parties. The Policy also protects whistleblowers from retaliation and strongly encourages victims to report all potential violations on the hotline. The NBA and the NBAPA jointly share the costs of implementing the policy. *NBA Collective Bargaining Agreement — 2017, Appendix F Joint NBA/ NBAPA Policy on Domestic Violence, Sexual Assault, and Child Abuse* (June 30, 2017), available at https://atlhawksfanatic.github.io/NBA-CBA/joint-nbanbapa-policy-on-domestic-vilence-sexual-abuse-and-child-abuse.html.

Neither the NHL nor the WNBA has a formal and separate domestic violence policy, although both leagues have disciplined players for domestic violence. The NHL addresses issues involving domestic violence under the criminal investigation clause in the collective bargaining agreement. Six NHL players have been penalized for domestic violence since 2014, including Los Angeles Kings defenseman Slava Voynov. Voynov was arrested in 2014 and pleaded no contest to a misdemeanor charge of corporal injury to a spouse. The NHL suspended him indefinitely and then terminated his contract while Voynov spent two months in jail before returning to Russia. Jon Garcia, *How the Predators and NHL have handled allegations of domestic violence, sexual assault,* USA Today Network – Tennessee, June 20, 2018. Los Angeles Sparks guard Riquna Williams was suspended by the WNBA for ten games after Williams was arrested and charged with burglary, assault and battery, and aggravated assault with a firearm at the home of an ex-girlfriend. As the WNBA does not have a domestic violence policy, Williams has filed a grievance. Williams, a 2015 All-Star, was re-signed by the Sparks after the incident. Des Bieler, *WNBA Player Suspended 10 Games After Domestic Violence Arrest,* The Washington Post, July 16, 2019.

NOTES AND QUESTIONS

1. *NFL Policy.* More than 20 NFL players were involved in domestic violence or sexual assault situations before the Ray Rice incident that prompted the NFL to become the first major professional league to establish a domestic violence policy. While much ado was made of the expert consultants involved in creating the policy, Deborah Epstein, a law professor and domestic violence expert, and Susan Else, former president of the National Network to End Domestic Violence, resigned their positions on the Commission in May, 2018. Epstein explained: "We wrote a study with concrete implementable recommendations and we gave it to the NFL two years ago. . . . The NFL has not implemented any of those suggestions. They're sitting gathering dust on a shelf somewhere." Al Neal, *Which of the Big 4 has the Best Domestic Violence Policy?* Aug. 24, 2018, available at https://grandstandcentral.com/2018/society/best-domestic-violence-policy-sports/. While NFL players continue to be suspended after domestic violence incidents, what can be done to change the culture?
2. *NBA Policy.* The NBA policy presumes a violation by a player who pleads guilty or is convicted of a domestic violence crime, and it also precludes the player from being disciplined by the league if he is not convicted. What are

the advantages and disadvantages of using the criminal prosecution burden of proof (i.e., beyond a reasonable doubt) to implement an employment policy establishing standards of professional athlete conduct?

3. *MLB Policy.* When the MLB policy was instituted, MLBPA executive director Tony Clark stated: "Players are husbands, fathers, sons and boyfriends. And as such want to set an example that makes clear that there is no place for domestic abuse in our society. We are hopeful that this new comprehensive, collectively-bargained policy will deter future violence, promote victim safety, and serve as a step toward a better understanding of the causes and consequences of domestic violence, sexual assault, and child abuse." See Paul Hagen, *supra.* Thirteen players have been disciplined under the MLB Domestic Violence, Sexual Assault, and Child Abuse policy since 2015, with two players receiving no sanctions and the remainder serving suspensions ranging from 15 to 100 games. Most recently, Dodger's pitcher Julio Urias was investigated for shoving his girlfriend to the ground in a parking lot; no criminal charges were filed, but MLB suspended Urias for 20 games. Does it appear the MLB policy is effectively preventing domestic abuse by MLB players?

E.   SEX-RELATED DISCRIMINATION: SEXUAL ORIENTATION, TRANSGENDER, AND INTERSEX PARTICIPATION

Sociology, psychology, biology, and physiology all indicate that human beings exist more on a continuum of sex and gender than in the binary classification of men and women that U.S. society and the law have constructed. Discriminatory treatment of individuals based on characteristics related to sex, such as sexual orientation, gender identity, and physiological disorders of sex development is an area of evolving legal issues, including those that impact sport.

1.   Sexual Orientation and the Issue of Gender Discrimination

Sexual orientation is a highly ambiguous concept referring to feelings of attraction and behaviors related to attraction. While the majority of people are attracted to the opposite sex, some people are more attracted to characteristics unrelated to biological sex, others' attractions may change throughout their lifetimes, and some are consistently attracted to those with the same biological sex. Within sport, athletes who identify as homosexual, lesbian, gay, or bisexual often kept their identities hidden. Historically, athletes who did publicly acknowledge their sexuality typically did so after retirement. It wasn't until 2014 that MLS player Robbie Rogers became the first active openly gay male athlete in a professional team sport. Jason Collins (NBA) and Michael Sam (NFL) also came out, but they had short professional careers after disclosure. Female athletes, on the other hand, often endured assumptions about their sexuality because of their athletics participation. Ken Reed, *LGBT Athletes Still Facing Harassment and Discrimination*, HuffPost, Aug. 4, 2014.

One of the first lawsuits filed against a coach and university for discriminating against an athlete because of her sexual orientation was filed by Penn State women's basketball player Jennifer Harris against coach Rene Portland, athletics director Tim Curley, and Penn State University. *Jennifer E. Harris v. Maureen ("Rene") Portland, Timothy M. Curley, and the Pennsylvania State University*, Civil Action No. 05-2648 (M.D. Pa. 2005). Portland first mentioned to Harris and her family that she did not recruit lesbians, nor allow them on her team, during a recruiting visit. Harris chose to attend Penn State and had a successful freshman season. However, Portland often criticized Harris's appearance, wanting her to look more feminine, and became suspicious of Harris's growing friendship with a student Portland believed was a lesbian. Portland banned Harris from associating in any way with that student, and when Harris persisted, she was criticized and threatened by the coach, and her playing time was decreased. At the end of the season, Harris was told she was no longer welcome on the team and would not have her scholarship renewed. Harris discussed the situation with the athletics director, who supported Portland's decision. Harris then sued for sexual orientation discrimination under Title IX. This federal law does not directly provide a cause of action for sexual orientation discrimination, but schools have been held responsible for sex discrimination based on a failure to conform to a gender stereotype. The parties agreed to a confidential settlement. Portland was fined $10,000 by the university for failing to comply with the institution's non-discrimination policy and resigned in 2007. See Barbara Osborne, *"No Drinking, No Drugs, No Lesbians"* — *Sexual Orientation Discrimination in Intercollegiate Athletics*, 17 Marq. Sports L. Rev. 481.

More recently, in *Videckis v. Pepperdine Univ.*, 150 F.Supp.3d 1151 (C.D. Cal. 2015), plaintiffs Hayley Videckis and Layana White, members of the Pepperdine University women's basketball team, claimed the head coach and other members of the coaching staff discriminated against them because they were dating. The players were singled out individually and persistently questioned for months about their sexual orientation and the status of their relationship by an academic counselor for the women's basketball team. After the head coach was informed about the academic counselor's questioning, the coach held a team meeting to discuss lesbianism on the team, stating that it was a big issue in women's basketball, it was a reason teams lose, and that it would not be tolerated. The athletes were also questioned by an athletic trainer, and a pattern of false accusations regarding violations of team policies and academic cheating was made against them. Other players on the team were questioned about Videckis and White's sexuality and relationship status. The players believed the coach and staff were concerned their lesbian relationship would have a negative impact on the team and were trying to get them to quit. White was so distraught from the harassment and discrimination she attempted to commit suicide. The court denied Pepperdine's motion to dismiss, finding the plaintiffs had sufficiently alleged sexual orientation discrimination, discrimination based on a failure to conform to gender stereotypes, sex discrimination, and retaliation.

Judge Dean D. Pregerson's decision is instructive in defining the various claims. In recognizing sexual orientation discrimination, he definitively states:

> . . . sexual orientation discrimination is a form of sex or gender discrimination, and that the "actual" orientation of the victim is irrelevant. It is impossible to categorically separate "sexual orientation discrimination" from discrimination on the basis of sex or from gender stereotypes; to do so would result in a false choice. Simply put, to allege discrimination on the basis of sexuality is to state a Title IX claim on the basis of sex or gender.

Id. at 1160.

Regarding gender stereotype discrimination, Judge Pregerson states:

The type of sexual orientation discrimination Plaintiffs allege falls under the broader umbrella of gender stereotype discrimination. Stereotypes about lesbianism, and sexuality in general, stem from a person's views about the proper roles of men and women — and the relationships between them. Discrimination based on a perceived failure to conform to a stereotype constitutes actionable discrimination under Title IX. See <u>Centola</u>, 183 F. Supp. 2d at 410 ("Conceivably, a plaintiff who is perceived by his harassers as stereotypically masculine in every way except for his actual or perceived sexual orientation could maintain a Title VII cause of action alleging sexual harassment because of his sex due to his failure to conform with sexual stereotypes about what 'real' men do or don't do.").

  Here, Plaintiffs allege that they were repeatedly harassed and treated differently from other similarly situated individuals because of their perceived sexual orientation. Coaches, trainers, and support staff repeatedly queried Plaintiffs about their sexual orientation, their private sexual behavior, and their dating lives. Plaintiffs allege that they were told lesbianism would not be tolerated on the women's basketball team. Plaintiffs further allege that they were not cleared to play basketball because of Pepperdine's discriminatory views against lesbianism. If the women's basketball staff in this case had a negative view of lesbians based on lesbians' perceived failure to conform to the staff's views of acceptable female behavior, actions taken on the basis of these negative biases would constitute gender stereotype discrimination. Consequently, Plaintiffs have stated a claim for discrimination because they allege that Pepperdine treated them differently due to their perceived lack of conformity with gender stereotypes, and further that Pepperdine discriminated against them based on stereotypes about lesbianism.

Id. at 1161.

Concerning plaintiff's claims of sex discrimination, he explains:

In addition to stating a claim based on gender stereotyping discrimination, Plaintiffs have stated a claim that they were discriminated against because of their sex. Discrimination on the basis of sex can be defined as treating someone differently simply because that person's sex is different from a similarly situated person of the opposite sex. [Citations omitted.]. . .

  Here, Plaintiffs allege that they were told that "lesbianism" would not be tolerated on the team. If Plaintiffs had been males dating females, instead of females dating females, they would not have been subjected to the alleged different treatment. Plaintiffs have stated a straightforward claim of sex discrimination under Title IX. Cf. Latta v. Otter, 771 F.3d 456, 480 (9th Cir. 2014) (Berzon, J., concurring) (finding same-sex marriage bans were facially discriminatory on the basis of sex because the bans dictated who could marry who based on the sex of the marriage participants).

  This Court's conclusion is in line with a recent Equal Employment Opportunity Commission ("EEOC") decision holding that sexual orientation discrimination is covered under Title VII, and therefore that the EEOC will treat sexual orientation discrimination claims the same as other sex discrimination claims under Title VII. Baldwin v. Anthony Foxx, Sec'y, Dep't of Transp., EEOC Appeal No. 0120133080, 2015 EEOPUB LEXIS 1905, 2015 WL 4397641, at *10, (EEOC July 16, 2015) (holding that "allegations of discrimination on the basis of sexual orientation necessarily state a claim of discrimination on the basis of sex"). The EEOC concluded that "[a]n employee could show that the sexual orientation discrimination he or she experienced was sex discrimination because it involved treatment that would not have occurred but for the individual's sex; because it was based on the sex of the person(s) the individual associates with; and/or because it was premised on the fundamental sex stereotype, norm, or expectation that individuals should be attracted only to those of the opposite sex." Id.

Id. at 1161.

Concerning retaliation, he determines:

Under Title IX, "a plaintiff who lacks direct evidence of retaliation must first make out a prima facie case of retaliation by showing (a) that he or she was engaged in protected activity, (b) that he or she suffered an adverse action, and (c) that there was a causal link between the two." Emeldi, 698 F.3d at 724. In order to make out a prima facie case, a plaintiff "need only make a minimal threshold showing of retaliation." Id.

Here, Plaintiffs have clearly pled a plausible claim for retaliation. Plaintiffs were engaged in protected activity. They complained to the coaching staff and Pepperdine's Title IX coordinator about the harassment they suffered. See Jackson v. Birmingham Bd. of Educ., 544 U.S. 167, 173, 125 S. Ct. 1497, 161 L. Ed. 2d 361 (2005) ("Retaliation against a person because that person has complained of sex discrimination is another form of intentional sex discrimination encompassed by Title IX's private cause of action."). Furthermore, Plaintiffs allege various retaliatory actions they experienced as a result of their complaints. (See, e.g., TAC ¶¶ 34-36, 63-69.) They allege that, ultimately, they were forced off the basketball team and lost their scholarships.

Pepperdine argues that because Plaintiffs tried to hide their relationship status, they therefore never could have made a complaint about discrimination. This argument is without merit. Plaintiffs clearly allege that they complained to the coaching staff and school officials about the intrusive questioning and harassment to which they were subjected. The fact that Plaintiffs may never have explicitly told school officials that they were dating is irrelevant to whether they complained that they were being harassed. Again, requiring that Plaintiffs disclose their sexual orientation or relationship status improperly focuses the inquiry on the status of the victim rather than the bias of the alleged harasser, and imposes a burden that Title IX does not contemplate.

QUESTIONS

1. Is there a clear distinction between sexual orientation, gender stereotyping, and sex discrimination for Title IX (or equal protection) purposes?
2. Coaches have historically had broad control over the behavior and conduct of their teams. Is it acceptable for a coach to impose lifestyle and/or personal beliefs related to sexual orientation or gender conformity on their athletes?

2. Transgender Athletes' Participation Rights

Access to sport participation opportunities is particularly challenging for transgender athletes. In 1975, Richard Raskin underwent gender reassignment surgery and became Renee Richards. Upon winning a tennis tournament in California, Richards was outed as being a transgender person. The U.S. Open responded by implementing the Barr body test, a chromosome test to determine sex, thereby preventing Richards from competing in this event. Richards filed a lawsuit against the U.S. Tennis Association seeking an injunction allowing her to "qualify and/or participate in the United States Open Tennis Tournament, as a woman in the Women's Division." *Richards v. U.S. Tennis Assn.*, 93 Misc. 2d 713, 714 (1977). Richards challenged the use of the Barr body test to determine sex, claiming violations of the Fourteenth Amendment and New York State Human Rights Law. The court agreed that U.S. Tennis instituted the Barr body test specifically to prevent Richards from competing. While U.S. Tennis contended the test was needed for fairness and to keep out imposters, the court sided with the medical evidence that showed Richards's "muscle development, weight, height and physique fit within the female norm." Id. at 721. In granting the preliminary injunction allowing Richards to play, she became the first transgender woman to play professional sport in the United States. She lost in the first round of the U.S. Open to Virginia Wade.

Lawless, a transgender female, sought to apply for LPGA membership to participate in sanctioned events but the LPGA membership application stated that sex was determined at birth. She filed a lawsuit against the LPGA claiming sex discrimination, and on November 30, 2010, the Ladies Professional Golfers Association changed its "female at birth" requirement to allow transgender membership. *Lawless v. LPGA et al.*, Case No. 4:10CV04599 (N.D. Cal. 2010).

At the high school level, state laws and state high school athletics associations dictate whether athletes must participate based on sex at birth or current gender identity. The Transgender Law and Policy Institute encourages all states to allow transgender youth from kindergarten through twelfth grade to participate in their affirmed gender. As of February 2019, 19 states have adopted this permissive policy without requiring transgender participants to undergo hormone therapy or sex-change surgery. Fifteen states require some hormonal modification and then make participation decisions by individual review. Nine states require participants to compete in the sex category assigned on their birth certificate or to complete hormone therapy and surgery. The remaining states have no statewide policy. See *Transathlete High School Policies*, at https://www.transathlete.com/k-12.

In Texas, Mack Beggs, a transgender boy, won the 2017 Texas 6A girls state wrestling championship. Beggs, who had been medically transitioning for over a year, requested to compete as a boy, but the high school athletics association rules classify participants according to the sex indicated on the birth certificate. See Faith Robinson and Nadeem Muaddi, *Transgender boy wins girls' wrestling championship in Texas*, http://www.cnn.com/2017/02/27/us/texas-transgender-wrestler-trnd-hold/index.html. Rather than change the high school athletics association rule, on May 9, 2017, the Texas Senate approved a bill allowing the high school athletics association to disqualify student-athletes taking steroids, including those undergoing hormone replacement therapy. This legislation effectively prevents transgender boys from competing in high school sports in Texas.

At the collegiate level, the NCAA Inclusion of Transgender Student-Athletes handbook, available at https://www.ncaa.org/sites/default/files/Transgender_Handbook_2011_Final.pdf, provides guidance encouraging member institutions to provide opportunities for transgender participants based on current medical and legal standards. A transgender person not undergoing hormone therapy may compete on a men's or women's team based on their sex at birth. A transgender male (FTM) undergoing hormone treatment may compete on a men's team, while a transgender female (MTF) may compete on a women's team after completing one year of hormone treatment. If a transgender female wishes to compete on a women's team during the first year of hormone suppression treatment, the team becomes classified as a mixed team and is counted as a men's team for eligibility purposes.

In 2005, Keelin Godsey was one of the first openly transgender student-athletes to compete in an NCAA Championship. Godsey, who identifies as male, won two national championships in the Division III Women's hammer throw, and earned All-America status in shot put, weight throw, discus throw, and hammer throw. Godsey went on to compete at the 2008 U.S. Olympic Trials, finishing eighth in the hammer throw; he placed fifth in the women's hammer throw at the U.S. Olympic Trials in 2012. Godsey then retired from competition to begin medical transition. Cyd Zeigler, *Trans Hammer Thrower Keelin Godsey Narrowly Misses U.S. Olympic Team,* June 21, 2012, SBNation Outsports.

The IOC updated its "Consensus Meeting on Sex Reassignment and Hyperandrogenism" policy in November 2015. The new policy does not require transgender athletes to complete reassignment surgery. Male transgender athletes (FTM) are immediately eligible to compete, but female transgender athletes (MTF) must maintain below 5 nmol/L for at least 12 months prior to their first competition. Compliance is monitored by testing, with a suspension of 12 months for non-compliance.

On February 22, 2017, the U.S. Department of Education and the U.S. Department of Justice issued a *Dear Colleague Letter* withdrawing the former policy statements issued in a January 7, 2015, letter to Emily Prince from James A. Ferg-Cadina, Acting Deputy Assistant Secretary for Policy, Office for Civil Rights at the Department of Education, and the May 13, 2016, *Dear Colleague Letter on Transgender Students,* which was issued jointly by the Department of Justice and the Department of Education. The remaining guidance is described under *Resources for LGBTQ Students* on the U.S. Department of Education Office for Civil Rights website:

> Every school and every school leader has a responsibility to protect all students and ensure every child is respected and can learn in an accepting environment. Title IX protects all student, including LGBTQ students, from sex discrimination. Title IX encompasses discrimination based on a student's failure to conform to stereotyped notions of masculinity and femininity. Schools should also be aware of their obligation under Title IX and the Family Educational rights and Privacy Act (FERPA) to protect the privacy of their students when maintaining education records.

NOTES AND QUESTIONS

1. *Unfair Competitive Advantage.* An unfair competitive advantage is often raised as a concern for MTF transgender participants. For an article exploring the issue of whether transgender athletes have a competitive advantage, see Steven Petro, *Do Transgender Athletes Have an Unfair Advantage at the Olympics?*, https://www.washingtonpost.com/lifestyle/style/do-transgender-athletes-have-an-unfair-advantage-at-the-olympics/2016/08/05/08169676-5b50-11e6-9aee-8075993d73a2_story.html.

2. *Use of Sex Segregated Facilities.* In *Johnston v. Univ. of Pittsburgh of the Com. Sys. of Higher Educ.,* 97 F.Supp.3d 657 (W.D. Pa. 2015), the court held that the university's policy of requiring students to use sex-segregated bathroom and locker room facilities based on students' natal or birth sex, rather than their

gender identity, does not violate Title IX's prohibition of sex discrimination because the statute does not prohibit discrimination based on transgender status. What are the implications if a transgender student-athlete cannot use the team locker room? What legitimate purpose is served by forcing a self-identified student to use facilities for the opposite sex?

3. *Cisgender Girls Complain About Competing Against Transgender Girls.* Alliance Defending Freedom, an anti-LGBTQ+ law firm filed a complaint with the Department of Education Office for Civil Rights on behalf of three female athletes alleging that the Connecticut Interscholastic Athletic Conference's non-discrimination policy allowing transgender students to compete in the sex they identify with violates Title IX. The complaint was filed after two transgender athletes finished first and second in the 55-meter dash at the state indoor track championships. The complainants claim that allowing boys to compete in girls' events deprives girls of a fair opportunity to win; the transgender girls have responded that they are girls, they should be allowed to compete as girls, and that claims of this sort discount their hard work and training and perpetuate exclusion at school. Samantha Pell, *Girls say Connecticut's transgender athlete policy violates Title IX, file federal complaint,* The Washington Post, June 19, 2019. Is there a solution that is fair to all parties? Would separate categories for transgender and cisgender (gender identity corresponds with birth sex) girls provide equal opportunities?

3.   Intersex Athletes/Disorders of Sex Differentiation

The issue of how gender is determined for purposes of athletic eligibility is becoming a significant issue in the twenty-first century and requires exploration of the corresponding medical, legal, and policy issues. While transgender athletes may undergo hormone therapy and sex reassignment surgery to reconcile their physical presentation with their gender identity, other athletes are born with ambiguous genitalia or disorders of sex differentiation. The controversy surrounding Caster Semenya, South African women's middle-distance runner and 2012 London and 2016 Rio Olympics 800-meter gold medalist, calls into question definitions of gender and sex verification methods and raises significant ethical issues. Sex or gender testing has also been questioned. See Elliott Almond, *Stanford Bioethicist Challenges Controversial Olympics Gender-Testing Policy,* http://www.mercurynews. com/other-sports/ci_20929583/stanford-bioethicist-challenges-controversial-olympics-gender-testing-policy, and Ruth Padawer, *The Humiliating Practice of Sex-Testing Female Athletes,* http://mobile.nytimes.com/2016/07/03/magazine/the-humiliating-practice-of-sex-testing-female-athletes.html.

   In July 2015, the Court of Arbitration for Sport issued an interim award suspending the "IAAF Regulation Governing Eligibility of Females with Hyperandrogenism to Compete in Women's Competition" ("Hyperandrogenism Regulations") for a maximum period of two years in order to give the IAAF, the international governing body for track and field, the opportunity to provide scientific evidence concerning the quantitative relationship between enhanced testosterone levels and improved athletic performance in female hyperandrogenic athletes (i.e., those with high levels of naturally occurring testosterone). Absent such evidence, the CAS panel was unable to conclude that hyperandrogenic female athletes might benefit from such a significant performance advantage that their exclusion from competing as females is justifiable. While the Hyperandrogenism Regulations were suspended, Ms. Dutee Chand, an Indian 200- and 400-meter sprinter, was permitted to compete in both national and international level athletics events. CAS 2014/A/3759, *Dutee Chand v. Athletics Federation of India & International Association of Athletics Federations* (award of July 27, 2015), available at http://plawyered.files.wordpress.com/2015/09/dutee-chand-v-athletics-federatio-of-india-afi-the-international-association-of-athletics-federations-iaaf.pdf.

In March 2018, the IAAF approved new rules specifically for intersex athletes and women with naturally high testosterone levels, requiring these women to lower their testosterone levels to less than 5nmol/L in order to compete internationally at distances from 400 meters to one mile; see *IAAF Eligibility Regulations for the Female Classification*.pdf. The rule has generated significant criticism, as it appears to be targeted toward Caster Semenya, two-time Olympic champion in the 800 meters who has identified as female from birth but was later determined to be intersex, while allowing Dutee Chand, a 100/200 meter sprinter to compete without taking testosterone-suppressing medication. Semenya challenged the IAAF rules in the Court of Arbitration for Sport.

COURT OF ARBITRATION FOR SPORT EXECUTIVE SUMMARY
Semenya v. IAAF, April 30, 2019

INTRODUCTION

1. On 30 April 2019, the Court of Arbitration for Sport ("CAS") delivered an Award with respect to the challenges brought by Caster Semenya and Athletics South Africa ("ASA") to the validity of the IAAF's Eligibility Regulations for the Female Classification (Athletes with Differences of Sex Development) (the "DSD Regulations"). By a majority, the CAS Panel dismissed the requests for arbitration considering that the Claimants could not establish that the DSD Regulation were "invalid." The Panel found that the DSD Regulations are discriminatory but that, on the basis of the evidence submitted by the parties, such discrimination is a necessary, reasonable and proportionate means of achieving the legitimate objective of ensuring fair competition in female athletics in certain events and protecting the "protected class" of female athletes in those events. The Panel also expressed serious concerns about the future practical application of the DSD Regulations. While the evidence has not established that those concerns are justified, or that they negate the conclusion of prima facie proportionality, this may change in the future unless constant attention is paid to the fairness of how the Regulations are implemented.

THE DSD REGULATIONS

2. In 2014 the Indian athlete Dutee Chand brought proceedings before the CAS challenging the IAAF Regulations Governing Eligibility of Females with Hyperandrogenism to Compete in Women's Competition (the "Hyperandrogenism Regulations"). In July 2015, the CAS delivered an

Interim Award partially upholding Ms. Chand's challenge and suspending the Hyperandrogenism Regulations (CAS 2014/A/3759 *Dutee Chand v AFI & IAAF*).

3. In *Chand*, the CAS had determined that the hormone testosterone was the primary cause for the increase in lean body mass in males at puberty and that this provided athletic advantage to male athletes over female athletes. The Panel in that case was not satisfied as to the degree of that advantage and declined to validate the Hyperandrogenism Regulations. The IAAF was given the opportunity to provide further evidence to validate those regulations, which had set the maximum level of testosterone for an athlete in female competition to 10 nmol/L, this being well above the maximum level in the female population and slightly above the minimum level in the male population.

4. In March 2018, the IAAF informed the CAS that it intended to withdraw the Hyperandrogenism Regulations and to replace them with new Regulations. In April 2018, the IAAF enacted the DSD Regulations. In summary, the DSD Regulations establish new requirements governing the eligibility of women with certain differences of sex development ("DSD") to participate in the female classification in eight events (the "Restricted Events") at international athletics competitions ("International Competitions"). The Restricted Events include the 400m, 800m and 1500m races — events in which Ms. Semenya regularly participates at International Competitions.

5. During the course of the proceedings before the CAS, the IAAF explained that, following an amendment to the DSD Regulations, the DSD covered by the Regulations are limited to "46 XY DSD" — i.e., conditions where the affected individual has XY chromosomes. Accordingly, no individuals with XX chromosomes are subjected to any restrictions or eligibility conditions under the DSD Regulations.

6. Athletes with 46 XY DSD have testosterone levels well into the male range. The DSD Regulations require athletes with 46 XY DSD who have a natural testosterone level of above 5 nmol/L, and who experience a "*material androgenizing effect*" from that enhanced testosterone level, to reduce their natural testosterone level to within the normal female range (i.e., to a level below 5 nmol/L) and to maintain that reduced level for a continuous period of at least six months in order to be eligible to compete in a Restricted Event at an International Competition. There is no requirement for, or suggestion of, any surgical intervention to achieve this level.

THE CLAIMANTS' CHALLENGES TO THE VALIDITY OF THE DSD REGULATIONS

7. The DSD Regulations came into force on 1 November 2018. Prior to that date, however, Ms. Semenya and ASA (collectively, the "Claimants") commenced arbitration proceedings before the CAS challenging the validity of the DSD Regulations.

8. The Claimants contended *inter alia* that the DSD Regulations unfairly discriminate against athletes on the basis of sex and/or gender because they only apply (i) to female athletes; and (ii) to female athletes having certain physiological traits. They submitted that the DSD Regulations lack a sound scientific basis; are unnecessary to ensure fair competition within the

female classification; and are likely to cause grave, unjustified and irreparable harm to affected female athletes. Accordingly, the Claimants sought an award from the CAS declaring the DSD Regulations unlawful and preventing them from being brought into force on the basis that the Regulations are unfairly discriminatory, arbitrary and disproportionate and therefore violate the IAAF Constitution, the Olympic Charter, the laws of Monaco, the laws of jurisdictions in which international athletics competitions are held, as well as universally recognised fundamental human rights.

9. In response, the IAAF submitted that the DSD Regulations are based on the best available science; do not discriminate on the basis of any protected characteristic; and are a necessary, reasonable and proportionate means of pursuing the legitimate aim of safeguarding fair competition and protecting the ability of female athletes to compete on a level playing field.

Between 18-22 February 2019, a hearing of the Claimants' challenges was held before the CAS in Lausanne, Switzerland. The CAS Panel comprised the Hon. Dr. Annabelle Bennett AO SC (President); The Hon. Hugh L. Fraser (Arbitrator) and Dr. Hans Nater (Arbitrator). The Panel received detailed written and oral testimony from a large number of factual and expert witnesses. This included experts specialising in gynaecology, andrology and the causes, diagnosis, effects and treatment of DSD; genetics, endocrinology and pharmacology; exercise physiology and sports performance; medical and research ethics; sports regulation and governance; and statistics.

THE AWARD OF THE CAS PANEL

10. After setting out the parties' evidence and submissions, the Panel begins its analysis of the merits by noting that this case involves a complex collision of scientific, ethical and legal conundrums. It also involves incompatible, competing rights. It is not possible to give effect to one set of rights without restricting the other set of rights. Put simply, on one hand is the right of every athlete to compete in sport, to have their legal sex and gender identity respected, and to be free from any form of discrimination. On the other hand, is the right of female athletes, who are relevantly biologically disadvantaged vis-à-vis male athletes, to be able to compete against other female athletes and to achieve the benefits of athletic success. The decision is also constrained by the accepted, necessary, binary division of athletics into male events and female events, when there is no such binary division of athletes. That binary division has not been challenged.

11. The Panel has not found the issues in this case easy to decide. It is clear from the range of expert evidence presented on behalf of the parties that there are many scientific, ethical and regulatory issues on which reasonable and informed minds may legitimately differ. The Panel is mindful that, in considering these issues, it is not acting as a policy maker or regulator. It is neither necessary nor appropriate for the Panel to step into the shoes of the IAAF by deciding how it would have approached issues had it been charged with making policies or enacting rules itself. Instead, its function is a purely judicial one. The Panel must adjudicate the disputed legal issues on the basis of the applicable legal tests and by reference to the arguments and

admissible evidence on the record in these proceedings. While this inevitably requires consideration of arguments and evidence based on an array of policy and scientific matters, the Panel must be mindful of its judicial role and the limits of that role. It is also bound to make its decision based upon the evidence presented to it, taking account of the submissions made by the parties.

DISCRIMINATION

12. The Panel unanimously concludes that the DSD Regulations are prima facie discriminatory since they impose differential treatment based on protected characteristics. In particular, since the DSD Regulations establish restrictions that are targeted at a subset of the female/intersex athlete population, and do not impose any equivalent restrictions on male athletes, it follows that the Regulations are prima facie discriminatory on grounds of legal sex. Similarly, the DSD Regulations create restrictions that are targeted at a group of individuals who have certain immutable biological characteristics (namely a 46 XY DSD coupled with a material androgenising effect arising from that condition), and which do not apply to individuals who do not have those characteristics. It follows that the Regulations are also prima facie discriminatory on grounds of innate biological characteristics.

13. The conclusion that the DSD Regulations are prima facie discriminatory is merely the starting point of the Panel's legal analysis. In particular, it is common ground that a rule that imposes differential treatment on the basis of a particular protected characteristic is valid if it is a necessary, reasonable and proportionate means of attaining a legitimate objective.

NECESSITY

14. The majority of the Panel concludes that the IAAF has succeeded in establishing the necessity requirement.

15. The Panel begins its consideration of this question by observing that once it is recognised that it is legitimate to have separate categories of male and female competition, it inevitably follows that it is necessary to devise an objective, fair and effective means of determining which individuals may, and which may not, participate in those categories.

16. The Panel accepts the IAAF's submission that reference to a person's legal sex alone may not always constitute a fair and effective means of making that determination. This is because the reason for the separation between male and female categories in competitive athletics is ultimately founded on biology rather than legal status. The purpose of having separate categories is to protect a class of individuals who lack certain insuperable performance advantages from having to compete against individuals who possess those insuperable advantages. In this regard, the fact that a person is recognised in law as a woman and identifies as a woman does not necessarily mean that they lack those insuperable performance advantages associated with certain biological traits

that predominate in individuals who are generally (but not always) recognised in law as males and self-identify as males. It is human biology, not legal status or gender identity, that ultimately determines which individuals possess the physical traits which give rise to that insuperable advantage and which do not.

17. Accordingly, the purpose of the male-female divide in competitive athletics is not to protect athletes with a female legal sex from having to compete against athletes with a male legal sex. Nor is it to protect athletes with a female gender identity from having to compete against athletes with a male gender identity. Rather, it is to protect individuals whose bodies have developed in a certain way following puberty from having to compete against individuals who, by virtue of their bodies having developed in a different way following puberty, possess certain physical traits that create such a significant performance advantage that fair competition between the two groups is not possible. In most cases, the former group comprises individuals with a female legal sex and a female gender identity, while the latter group comprises individuals with a male legal sex and male gender identity. However, this is not true of all cases. Natural human biology does not map perfectly onto legal status and gender identity. The imperfect alignment between nature, law and identity is what gives rise to the conundrum at the heart of this case.

The Panel considers that, once it is recognised that the reason for organising competitive athletics into separate male and female categories rests on the need to protect one group of individuals against having to compete against individuals who possess certain insuperable performance advantages derived from biology rather than legal status, it follows that it may be legitimate to regulate the right to participate in the female category by reference to those biological factors rather than legal status alone.

18. It was common ground between the parties that there is a substantial difference in elite sports performance between males and females. It was also common ground that (a) the normal female range of serum testosterone, produced mainly in the ovaries and adrenal glands, is 0.06 to 1.68 nmol/L; and (b) the normal male range of serum testosterone concentration, produced mainly in the testes, is 7.7 to 29.4 nmol/L. On the basis of the scientific evidence presented by the parties, the Panel unanimously finds that endogenous testosterone is the primary driver of the sex difference in sports performance between males and females.

19. The IAAF submitted that all but one of the many different factors that contribute to sport performance — including training, coaching, nutrition and medical support, as well as many genetic variations — are equally available to men and women. The only factor that is available only to men is exposure to adult male testosterone levels. The IAAF submitted that if the purpose of the female category is to prevent athletes who lack that testosterone-derived advantage from having to compete against athletes who possess that testosterone-derived advantage, then it is necessarily "category defeating" to permit any individuals who possess that testosterone-derived advantage to compete in that category. The majority of the Panel accepts the logic of the IAAF's submission.

20. Having carefully considered the expert evidence, the majority of the Panel concludes that androgen sensitive female athletes with 46 XY DSD enjoy a

significant performance advantage over other female athletes without such DSD, and that this advantage is attributable to their exposure to levels of circulating testosterone in the normal adult male range, rather than the normal adult female range. The majority of the Panel observes that the evidence concerning the performances and statistical over-representation of female athletes with 46 XY DSD in certain Relevant Events demonstrates that the elevated testosterone levels that such athletes possess creates a significant and often determinative performance advantage over other female athletes who do not have a 46 XY DSD condition.

21. On this basis, the majority of the Panel accepts that the IAAF has discharged its burden of establishing that regulations governing the ability of female athletes with 46XY DSD to participate in certain events are necessary to maintain fair competition in female athletics by ensuring that female athletes who do not enjoy the significant performance advantage caused by exposure to levels of circulating testosterone in the adult male range do not have to compete against female athletes who do enjoy that performance advantage.

PROPORTIONALITY

The majority of the Panel concludes that, on the evidence adduced, the DSD Regulations are on their face reasonable and proportionate. In reaching this conclusion, the majority notes, amongst other things, that the DSD Regulations do not require any athlete to undergo any surgical intervention, and envisage that affected athletes can control their testosterone levels by using conventional oral contraceptives. The majority has also had regard to the possible side effects of such oral contraceptives, to the nature of the examinations that will be undertaken for the purpose of determining whether an athlete has experienced a "material androgenising effect" from their high testosterone levels, and the risk of individuals' medical confidentiality being compromised.

22. While the majority concludes that the DSD Regulations are not disproportionate on their face, the Panel highlights its serious concerns about aspects of the practical application of the DSD Regulations when they are implemented. In particular, the Panel expresses its concerns about the potential difficulty for an athlete in complying with the requirements under the Regulations (including the possibility that affected athletes may inadvertently, and through no fault of their own, be unable consistently to maintain a natural testosterone level below 5 nmol/L). The Panel also notes the paucity of evidence to justify the inclusion of two events (the 1500m and one-mile events) within the category of Restricted Events. The Panel strongly encourages the IAAF to address the Panel's concerns in its implementation of the DSD Regulations. At the same time, the majority of the Panel observes that it may be that, on implementation and with experience, certain factors, supported by evidence, may be shown to affect the overall proportionality of the DSD Regulations, either by indicating that amendments are required in order to ensure that the Regulations are capable of being applied proportionately, or by providing further support for or against the inclusion of particular events within the category of Restricted Events.

THE PANEL'S EXPRESSION OF GRATITUDE TO MS. SEMENYA

23. In its Award the Panel expressly pays tribute to Ms. Semenya's grace and fortitude throughout this process. The Panel expresses its profound gratitude for her dignified personal participation and the exemplary manner in which she has conducted herself throughout the proceedings.

24. The Panel also stresses that while much of the argument in this proceeding has centered around the "fairness" of permitting Ms. Semenya to compete against other female athletes, there can be no suggestion that Ms. Semenya (or any other female athletes in the same position as Ms. Semenya) has done anything wrong. This is not a case about cheating or wrongdoing of any sort. Ms. Semenya is not accused of breaching any rule. Her participation and success in elite female athletics is entirely beyond reproach and she has done nothing whatsoever to warrant any personal criticism.

NOTES AND QUESTIONS

1. *Appeal of CAS Award.* Semenya and Athletics South Africa appealed the CAS decision to the Swiss Federal Tribunal (SFT), Switzerland's highest court, on the ground that the CAS award upholding the IAAF regulations "violate essential and widely recognised public policy values, including the prohibition against discrimination, the right to physical integrity, the right to economic freedom and respect for human dignity." The SFT initially suspended implementation of the DSD Regulations (which allowed Semenya to compete in some IAAF-sanctioned 800-meters races pending its resolution of their appeal), but soon thereafter reversed its decision, which prevents her from continuing to compete in this event and indicates the appeal is unlikely to be successful.

2. *Mandated Doping?* While the World Anti-doping Code generally prohibits Olympic sport athletes from using banned substances to enhance athletic performance (see Chapter 4.D.4.b), the IAAF DSD Regulations mandate use of hormone suppressing drugs to counteract a female athlete's natural biological advantage in a sport. Is it medically ethical to treat a healthy human being with hormone suppressing drugs that can have debilitating consequences in order to participate in athletics competition? Should it be legally permissible?

3. *Failure to Conform to Gender Stereotypes?* Semenya was designated as a female on her birth certificate, was raised female, and identifies as a female. Complaints that she was "too masculine" by female competitors led to the discovery that Semenya has DSD, disorders of sex differentiation, which results in natural production of higher testosterone levels. Some sports, such as figure skating, favor smaller frames and lower centers of gravity; should male athletes who appear more feminine be tested for appropriate hormone levels? Should other athletes who have natural biological advantages (for example, male athletes such as Jamaican sprinter Usain Bolt and U.S. swimmer Michael Phelps, who each won multiple gold medals in several Olympic Games) be expected to medically correct their advantages?

F.   GENDER-BASED EMPLOYMENT DISCRIMINATION IN ATHLETICS

Gender discrimination affects not only student-athletes; it can also adversely affect coaches and violate Title IX and employment discrimination laws. Since 1977, Vivien Acosta and Linda Jean Carpenter have conducted a longitudinal study, *Women in Intercollegiate Sport* (see http://www.acostacarpenter.org/ 2014%20Status%20of%20Women%20in%20Intercollegiate%20Sport%20-37%20Year%20Update%20-%201977-2014%20.pdf). According to the study, more women are currently employed in administrative and coaching positions in intercollegiate athletics than ever before. However, only 22.3 percent of athletics directors are women, and there are no female administrators at all in 11.3 percent of college athletics programs. Fewer than half (43.4 percent) of women's athletics teams have a female head coach even though the majority (56.8 percent) of paid assistant coaches of women's teams are women. The gender barrier for female coaches is apparent, as fewer than 3 percent of men's teams are coached by a female head coach. Athletics communications appears to mirror the professional sports media, as only 12.1 percent of sports information directors are women. In another recent report, issued by The Institute for Diversity and Ethics in Sport (TIDES) at the University of Central Florida, College Sport received C+ for gender hiring practices by earning 75.1 points, remaining steady from the 2017 CSRGRC. See http://www.tidesport.org/ college-sport.html for reports issued by TIDES grading gender and race in professional and collegiate sports.

Fuhr v. Sch. Dist. of Hazel Park, 364 F.3d 753 (6th Cir. 2004), illustrates the sports cultural bias against hiring female coaches. Geraldine Fuhr had significant experience as the girls' varsity basketball coach at Hazel Park High School for ten years, and concurrently as the assistant boys' varsity basketball coach for eight years. Fuhr applied for the boys' varsity coach position, and only one other candidate, a teacher who had been coaching the boys' freshman basketball team for the past two years, also applied. Both candidates were interviewed, and the Superintendent of Schools informed the search committee that several members of the school board did not want Fuhr as the boys' coach and that they had to honor their wishes. The president of the school board announced that he "was very concerned about a female being the head boys' basketball coach in Hazel Park." *Id.* at 757. Barnett was hired, and Fuhr sued the school district for sex discrimination under Title VII and the Elliot-Larsen Act, a Michigan civil rights act that prohibits discrimination. A jury held in Fuhr's favor, awarding her $455,000 in damages. Subsequently, the district court ordered Hazel Park to hire Fuhr as the boys' varsity basketball coach. Hazel Park appealed, but the Sixth Circuit affirmed, finding that Hazel Park had intentionally discriminated against Fuhr on the basis of sex by not hiring her as the head boys' basketball coach.

In addition to barriers in employing women in college athletics programs, a gender gap also exists in salaries. For an excellent exploration of these disparities and their possible justifications, see Terrence F. Ross, *What Gender Inequality Looks Like in Collegiate Sports*, http://www.theatlantic.com/education/archive/ 2015/03/what-gender-inequality-looks-like-in-collegiate-sports/387985/.   As to the significant salary disparities between men and women coaching at the collegiate level, Ross states, "This income gap is far more nuanced than it seems; and despite how it may appear, it isn't inherently sexist. Men's college sports are, and a federal law — the Equal Pay Act of 1963 — stipulates that the salaries men must be equally tied to the profit their respective programs bring in." *Id.*

The following cases consider potential remedies for gender-based wage discrimination or retaliation by educational institutions against those seeking to ensure compliance with Title IX in the context of athletics.

1.   *Wage Discrimination*

DELI v. UNIVERSITY OF MINNESOTA

863 F. Supp. 958 (D. Minn. 1994)

MAGNUSON, District Judge.

BACKGROUND

Plaintiff Katalin Deli is the former head coach of the University of Minnesota (University) women's gymnastics team. In June 1992, the University terminated her employment. Ms. Deli challenged this dismissal through the University grievance procedure. After review, the University upheld the termination, finding there existed just cause for her termination. . . .

Deli filed the present action against the University, alleging the University improperly paid her less than head coaches of several men's athletic teams. Deli contends that this pay differential, allegedly based on the gender of the athletes she coached, constituted prohibited discrimination on the basis of sex, in violation of Title VII of the Civil Rights Act, 42 U.S.C. §2000e; the Equal Pay Act, 29 U.S.C. §206(d); and Title IX. . . .

Plaintiff contends the Defendant discriminated in the compensation it paid her on the basis of the gender of the athletes she coached. Significantly, Plaintiff does not claim that the University discriminated against her on the basis of Plaintiff's gender, i.e. she does not claim that the University's motivation for paying her less money than the coaches of men's sports was the fact that Plaintiff was a woman and the coaches of men's sports were men. Plaintiff also does not challenge in this action the circumstances, justification or legality of her discharge from employment by the University. . . .

DISCUSSION

I.   TITLE VII CLAIM

Title VII prohibits employers from "discriminating against any individual with respect to his compensation . . . *because of such individual's* race, color, religion, sex or national origin. . . ." 42 U.S.C. §2000e-2(a)(1) (1981). [Emphasis added.] The clear terms of the statute prohibit discrimination in compensation based on the sex of the recipient. The statute does not proscribe salary discrimination based on the sex of other persons over whom the employee has supervision or oversight responsibilities. Even assuming, arguendo, that the University did discriminate in payment of salaries on the basis of the gender of the athletes the Plaintiff coached, such discrimination is not within the scope of Title VII, which prohibits discrimination based on the claimant employee's gender. See *Jackson v. Armstrong School Dist.*, 430 F. Supp. 1050, 1052 (W.D. Pa. 1977) (to be actionable under Title VII, claim must be that claimant was victim of discrimination on basis of claimant's gender, not that of athletes coached by claimant). Plaintiff has failed to state a Title VII claim on which relief can be granted and Defendant is entitled to judgment as a matter of law on Count II of the Complaint.

II.   EQUAL PAY ACT CLAIMS

A.   *"Factor Other Than Sex" Exception*

Plaintiff Deli also claims the Defendant violated the Equal Pay Act because it paid Plaintiff less than the coaches of men's athletics teams, thus discriminating against her on the basis of the gender of the athletes she supervised. Again assuming arguendo that the Defendant did discriminate in the payment of salary based on the gender of athletes supervised, such action would not support this Plaintiff's claim for violation of the Equal Pay Act.

The Equal Pay Act (EPA) prohibits an employer from discriminating between employees on the basis of sex by paying wages to employees . . . at a rate less than the rate at which [the employer] pays wages to employees of the opposite sex . . . for equal work on jobs the performance of which requires equal skill, effort, and responsibility, and which are performed under similar working conditions, except where such payment is made pursuant to . . . (iv) a differential based on any other factor other than sex. 26 U.S.C. §206(d)(1). . . . After review of the admittedly less-than-clear language of the statute and its history, this Court concurs with the reasoning of the Seventh Circuit — the EPA prohibits discrimination based on the gender of the claimant only and does not reach compensation differentials based on the gender of student athletes coached by a claimant. Such compensation differentials are based on a "factor other than sex" and thus are not proscribed by the EPA. Because Plaintiff's Complaint alleges discrimination based on the gender of the athletes she coached, she has failed to state an actionable claim under the Equal Pay Act and Defendant's motion for summary judgment on Plaintiff's EPA claims will be granted.

B.   *Position Not Substantially Equal*

Even if Plaintiff had alleged discrimination in salary based on her own gender, her claim could not withstand summary judgment. . . . [T]he Ninth Circuit recently held that a women's basketball coach who was paid less than a men's basketball coach at the same university failed to show that she would likely prevail on her claims for violation of the Equal Pay Act or Title IX. *Stanley v. University of Southern California*, 13 F.3d 1313 (9th Cir. 1994). The Ninth Circuit affirmed that, consistent with the Equal Pay Act, an employer may pay different salaries to coaches of different genders if the coaching positions are not substantially equal in terms of skill, effort, responsibility, and working conditions. . . . In order to state an Equal Pay Act claim, a Plaintiff must show her position was substantially equal to that of the comparator positions with respect to each of the foregoing attributes.

The comparators Deli has chosen in this suit are the coaches of the men's football, hockey and basketball teams. Defendant has presented evidence to show that all three of those teams are larger than the women's gymnastics team.

The University also proffers evidence that the head coaches in those sports supervise more employees than Deli supervised. Further, Defendant has provided evidence to show that the three teams enjoy significantly greater spectator attendance and generate substantially more revenue for the University than the women's gymnastics team. Finally, the University has alleged and provided evidence to support its contention that the coaches of the three men's athletic teams have greater responsibility for public and media relations than Deli had as the coach of the women's gymnastics team. The foregoing evidence alone, if undisputed, is enough to show the Plaintiff's job and that of the head coaches of men's basketball, football and hockey are not "substantially equal" in terms of responsibility and working conditions. See *Stanley*, 13 F.3d 1313, 1322 (finding substantial difference in responsibility based on essentially same factors as those listed above).

Deli offers no evidence to refute the foregoing. . . .

III.   TITLE IX CLAIMS

Plaintiff's Title IX claims fail on the merits. Courts are to accord the authoritative Department of Education Office for Civil Rights (OCR)'s Policy Interpretation and Title IX Investigator's Manual substantial deference in determining the appropriate application of Title IX. Plaintiff alleges Defendant violated Title IX by compensating her at a lower level than coaches of certain men's sports. According to the OCR Policy Interpretation, differential compensation of coaches violates Title IX "only where compensation or assignment policies or practices deny male and female athletes coaching of equivalent quality, nature or availability" 44 Fed. Reg. at 71416. More generally, according to Title IX implementing regulations, "unequal aggregate expenditures for members of each sex or unequal expenditures for male and female teams [alone] . . . will not constitute noncompliance with [Title IX]" 34 C.F.R. §106.41(c). The Investigator's Manual confirms that the crux of the inquiry is whether differentials in coaches' compensation result in denial of equal athletic opportunity for athletes:

> If availability and assignment of coaches to both programs are equivalent, it is difficult . . . to assert that the lower compensation for coaches in, for example, the women's program, negatively affects female athletes. The intent of [the regulation implementing Title VII] is for equal athletic opportunity to be provided to participants, not coaches.

OCR Title IX Investigator's Manual (1990) at 58.

Plaintiff does not assert in her Complaint or elsewhere that the athletes she supervised received lesser quality coaching as a result of the difference between Plaintiff's salary and salaries paid to coaches of the men's football, hockey and basketball teams. To the contrary, the record shows Plaintiff contends she provided superior coaching and opportunities for the athletes she coached, as evidenced by her coaching honors and the accomplishments of her athletes. . . . Because Plaintiff does not claim or provide any evidence to suggest that due to her receipt of a lower salary than that received by coaches of some men's athletic teams, Plaintiff's coaching services were inferior in "quality, nature or availability" to those provided to the men's teams, she has failed to make out a prima facie claim for violation of Title IX. The Defendant is entitled to summary judgment on Plaintiff's Title IX claims. . . .

NOTES AND QUESTIONS

1. *Unequal Pay Claims.* Why did *Deli* reject the plaintiff's EPA and Title IX claims? What would a plaintiff have to plead and prove to establish successful claims under each of these federal statutes?

   When asserting a Title IX violation because of unequal pay, the plaintiff must assert that the disparity is a result of the gender of the *team* coached, rather than the coach's gender. Under such a theory, the plaintiff coach could be male or female. Cathryn L. Claussen, *Title IX and Employment Discrimination in Coaching Intercollegiate Athletics,* 12 U. Miami Ent. & Sports L. Rev. 149, 150 (1994).

   After the *Stanley* decision relied on by the *Deli* court, the EEOC revised its guidelines to clarify how the EPA should be applied in such cases. The guidelines require that an educational institution provide a non-gender-based reason for paying a male coach more than a female coach. Men and women involved in coaching are to be evaluated based on their duties, not their sports. Should the EEOC adopt further guidelines to address what many female coaches refer to as the "chicken and egg" problem — that is, if they were paid more and given more resources to market their programs, would they be able to overcome social inequities developed over a long period of time and develop programs that would be as successful as men's programs? A pertinent Title IX regulation states:

   > A recipient shall not make or enforce any policy or practice which, on the basis of sex: (a) Makes distinctions in rates of pay or other compensation; (b) Results in the payment of wages to employees of one sex at a rate less than that paid to employees of the opposite sex for equal work on jobs the performance of which requires equal skill, effort, and responsibility, and which are performed under similar working conditions.

   34 C.F.R. §106.54 (2003).

2. *Women Coaching Men's Sports?* Men regularly coach women's teams, but women seldom coach men's teams. Why are there not more objections to this disparity (inequity)? What can or should be done to increase the number of women working in sports? In 2015, the Arizona Cardinals of the National Football League made history when they hired Dr. Jen Welter as a preseason intern with responsibility for coaching inside linebackers. Welter became the first female coach in the NFL's history. She had played rugby in college, but her dream was always to play football. She played pro football as the only woman on the Texas Revolution, a team in the Indoor Football League. See Larry Brown, *Arizona Cardinals Make Jen Welter First Female NFL Coach,* http://www.msn.com/en-us/sports/other/arizona-cardinals-make-jen-welter-first-female-nfl-coach/ar-AAdzlBj?ocid=ansLarryBrownSports11. Becky Hammon, who in 2014 became the first female full-time paid assistant coach in the NBA, has come closer than any other woman to being the head coach of a men's team in a major American sports league, interviewing (unsuccessfully) for an NBA head coach job in 2019. Despite being deeply respected among coaches and players throughout the NBA, it is widely recognized that Hammon faces impediments based strictly on her gender. Greg Popovich, among the greatest head coaches in NBA history and a strong Hammon supporter, explains that for Hammon to get a head coach

position "it's gonna take [a decision-maker] that has some courage and isn't steeped in the old status quo of who can coach and who can't." Greg Moore, *Why isn't Spurs assistant Becky Hammon an NBA head coach yet?*, USAToday. com, Nov. 15, 2018, https://www.usatoday.com/story/sports/nba/spurs/2018/11/15/nba-spurs-assistant-becky-hammon-ready-why-not-head-coach-yet/2013733002/. Why does such a high barrier to entry exist with respect to woman seeking to coach men? Are there legal means of addressing the problem?

PROBLEM 10-6

You represent a Division I-A institution that has a history of being competitive in men's and women's basketball. In fact, your men's basketball team has made the NCAA play-offs six out of the past nine years, and your women's team has made the play-offs eight out of the past nine years. Both programs have been in the revenue-producing category. The women's program currently operates at a slight loss ranging from under $25,000 last year, when the team went to the Sweet Sixteen with a record of 24-6, to just over $100,000 three years ago, when the team was rebuilding and had a record of 14-12. In the past three years, attendance has increased significantly at home games, and the university has just entered into a local television contract for the women's team, including a coach's show, like the one available to the men's coach. The television revenues should make the program profitable if the team remains successful. Indeed, revenues as a percentage have increased more rapidly over the past decade for the women's program than for the men's program.

The women's coach has also been trying to build strong external funding for the program, with increasing but still fairly minimal success in terms of dollars raised for the program. The men's program has operated at a net profit, averaging over $1.5 million each of the past three years. The women's coach received a $10,000 increase in base salary after her successful season and is currently paid $175,000 per year in base salary, with an additional $75,000 per year from other sources of income, including television appearances, camps, apparel contracts, and other activities.

The men's basketball coach left to take a head coaching position in the NBA, and the university is in negotiations with a candidate to replace him. The coach who left for the NBA was paid $1.8 million per year ($600,000 in base salary and $1.2 million from other sources). The new men's coach candidate is demanding a base salary of $800,000 per year with a guarantee of $1.7 million from other sources, for a total of $2.5 million, and average salaries for his assistants of $165,000 per year.

The women's coach has been increasingly vocal about the importance of equal treatment for her program, including equity in salary for herself and her assistant coaches (the average salary for women's assistant coaches was $35,000 last year). The men's football coach is the second-highest-paid coach at the university. He makes $1.2 million in base salary and $750,000 from other sources, for a total of $1.95 million. His assistants average $150,000 per year. The football team has operated at a loss, losing an average of $500,000 per year for the past three years and has made it to a bowl game in only one of those years. The team was 6-5 this year in a rebuilding year, and a strong incoming class has been recruited. The football coach was given a $25,000 raise in base pay.

As general counsel for the university, you have been asked for your advice as to how the university should proceed. If the university meets the new coaching candidate's demands, as the university would like to do (it is getting strong pressure from boosters to hire the coach), do you have a legal or moral obligation to increase salaries for the coaches of the women's team? How would you advise that the university deal with practical problems, for example, with the media and morale in the athletics department?

2.   Wage Discrimination in Women's Professional Sport

Although the above materials primarily address gender-based employment discrimination in collegiate athletics, and although the bulk of the litigation on this score occurs in that context, gender-based employment discrimination disputes come to bear in professional athletics as well. In March 2016, the U.S. Women's National Soccer Team Players Association, on behalf of five national team players, filed an Equal Employment Opportunity Commission (EEOC) wage discrimination claim against the United States Soccer Federation (USSF). The complaint, which is an administrative prerequisite to any eventual suit, revealed that the women's team generated almost $20 million more in revenue in 2015 than the U.S. Men's National Soccer Team but were paid roughly a quarter of what the men earned. See ESPN, *U.S. women's team files wage-discrimination action vs. U.S. Soccer,* http://espn.go.com/espnw/sports/article/15102506/women-national-team-files-wage-discrimination-action-vs-us-soccer-federation. Moreover, the women's team players indicated an interest in potentially striking in advance of the 2016 Summer Olympics if their compensation was not increased.

The USSF did not dispute the players' allegations that they produced more revenue than the men while receiving less compensation, but it brought a lawsuit challenging the players' ability to strike, arguing that the USSF and the union had agreed that neither strikes nor lockouts would be permitted. This "no strike, no lockout" clause appeared in a 2005 collective bargaining agreement (CBA) between the parties. Although both the USSF and the union agreed that the 2005 CBA expired in 2012, they disagreed as to whether their 2013 memorandum of understanding extending the terms of the CBA was necessarily binding with respect to the "no strike, no lockout" clause through the end of 2016. Matt Bonesteel, *Judge rules that U.S. women's soccer team can't go on strike before Olympics,* WashingtonPost.com, June 3, 2016, https://www.washingtonpost.com/news/early-lead/wp/2016/06/03/judge-rules-that-u-s-womens-soccer-team-cant-go-on-strike-before-olympics/. On June 3, 2016, Judge Sharon Johnson Coleman of the U.S. District Court for the Northern District of Illinois sided with the USSF, ruling that the "no strike, no lockout" clause remained in effect and that the United States women's national team could therefore not go on strike. *United States Soccer Federation, Inc. v. United States Women's National Soccer Team Players Association,* 190 F.Supp.3d 777 (N.D. Ill. 2016).

On February 5, 2019, the EEOC issued a letter giving the players the "right to sue" and on March 8, 2019, 28 players associated with the U.S. Women's national team filed a lawsuit against the USSF for violations of the Equal Pay Act and Title VII of the Civil Rights Act. Complaint, *Morgan v. United States Soccer Federation, Inc.,* Case No. 2:19-CV-01717 (U.S.D.C. Central Dist. Cal. Western

Div.); Michael McCann, *Inside USWNT's New Equal Pay Lawsuit vs. U.S. Soccer—and How CBA, EEOC Relate*, SI.com, March 8, 2019, https://www.si.com/soccer/2019/03/08/uswnt-lawsuit-us-soccer-equal-pay-cba-eeoc-gender-discrimination. On July 7, 2019, the women's national team won their fourth FIFA World Cup, and shortly thereafter the plaintiffs and USSF agreed to mediation. The World Cup provided an international stage for pay equity discussions, with four U.S. senators taking up the cause by proposing the Even Playing Field Act, an amendment to the Ted Stevens Olympic and Amateur Sports Act. The bill, if passed, would require NGBs to provide equal pay and investment in national teams regardless of sex. On August 14, 2019, mediation broke down, returning the matter to litigation. A trial date has been set for May 5, 2020. *Women's national soccer team lawsuit gets a May 5 court date in equal pay case*, USAToday.Com, Aug. 20, 2019, https://www.usatoday.com/story/sports/soccer/2019/08/20/womens-national-team-lawsuit-goes-to-trial-may-5/39988433/.

Notwithstanding the revenue and compensation disparities among men's and women's national soccer team players, professional basketball in America seems impacted by an even more deeply-seated and systemic form of gender discrimination. Basketball is the only team sport in America for which there exists a high-profile, long-standing professional league for men as well as one for women. The NBA was founded in 1946, and the WNBA was founded as an NBA subsidiary 50 years later, in 1996. The leagues share administrative staff, marketing schemes, and sponsorships, and some clubs based in the same city share an ownership group, wear the same team colors, and have related names. For instance, Monumental Sports and Entertainment owns both the Washington *Wizards* (NBA) and the Washington *Mystics* (WNBA) and both clubs wear red, white, and blue uniforms. Although the leagues are intertwined and similar in many regards, they differ drastically in one regard that could be the basis for litigation: age eligibility requirements. Men can enter the NBA when they are one year removed from high school, but women cannot enter the WNBA until they are four years removed from high school. Consider the following law review article excerpt exploring the consequences of the different age eligibility thresholds for men and women.

HOOP DREAMS DEFERRED: THE WNBA, THE NBA, AND THE LONG-STANDING GENDER INEQUITY AT THE GAME'S HIGHEST LEVEL

There is nothing subtle about the difference between the NBA's age eligibility rule and the WNBA's age eligibility rule. There are no uncertain terms or buried provisions that suggest trickery or sleight of hand. Rather, the difference is clear and obviously intended: women must be three years older than men to play top-flight professional basketball in the United States. This inequity is not merely an academic matter. Rather, the female player is profoundly disadvantaged in real-world tangible terms. As detailed below, the WNBA's age eligibility rule subjects the female player to an increased likelihood of injury during her college career and a decreased likelihood of financially capitalizing on her athletic talent.

A.   *Risk of Injury*

Injuries are a part of sport, as is the prospect of losing out on riches because of them. However, when an athlete is capable of playing professionally, is prohibited from doing so, and is injured during that period of prohibition, the prohibition requires scrutiny.

In February of the 2012-2013 NCAA basketball season, Nerlens Noel, a freshman center on the University of Kentucky's men's basketball team . . . suffered a gruesome tear of the Anterior Cruciate Ligament (ACL) in his left knee. [Under the NBA age-eligibility rule, Noel was eligible to enter the 2013 NBA draft, while rehabbing his knee] was picked sixth and . . . receive[d] $2,643,600 [in his] rookie contract. . . .

The juxtaposition of Noel's circumstance with those of two former star University of Connecticut women's collegiate basketball players, Caroline Doty and Shea Ralph, illustrates the inequity [in the age-eligibility rules]. Both Doty and Ralph were, like Noel . . . destined for professional stardom, and both, like Noel, tore their ACLs as freshmen. . . .

After rehabilitation, with the WNBA off limits, Doty resumed her career at Connecticut as the team's starting point guard, but she tore her ACL again during the summer before her senior season. Doty again rehabbed her knee, but she could not regain her elite status, and after exhausting her collegiate eligibility in the spring of 2013, professional basketball was not an option.

Ralph, now an assistant coach for the University of Connecticut's women's basketball team, suffered an astounding five ACL tears and subsequent reconstructive surgeries during her collegiate career. She bounced back from her first surgery, and then from her second, to play outstanding basketball, becoming the Big East Player of the Year and an All-American. Eventually, however, as Ralph played out her eligibility at Connecticut, her body broke down. She did not recover as successfully from her third, fourth, and fifth surgeries, and although she was ultimately drafted in the WNBA's third round by the Utah Starzz, her injuries prevented her from ever playing a WNBA game.

Had these women been men, they would have been able to play professional basketball in this country. They were denied the opportunity to enter the WNBA after their freshman years because of their sex, and the subsequent injuries they suffered in college ended their professional aspirations.

B.   Compensation

Even assuming no injuries during the course of a female basketball player's collegiate career, the three additional years she is required to wait before entering the WNBA can represent a loss of hundreds of thousands of dollars.

1.   Domestic Playing Salary

WNBA salaries are relatively low for American professional athletes and they are well below what NBA players make, but they are not insignificant. According to the 2013 WNBA scale set forth in the WNBA CBA, a rookie makes between $37,950 and $48,470 in the first season of her three-year guaranteed contract, with the higher draft picks at the upper end of the range. In each successive season under the contract, the pay increases, and in the third season she will make between $43,197 and $54,384. While these figures may seem modest, it is important to note that the WNBA season and post-season last for only six months, from May through October. So, a highly drafted third-year player will earn the same amount of money over the six-month season as any person in any profession with an annual salary of $108,768 earns over six months, which is roughly four times the average American's individual salary of $28,051. This is real money that the WNBA's age eligibility rule requires women, whose male age-mates are playing in the NBA, to forgo. . . .

2.   *International Playing Salary*

Unfortunately for the women affected, forgoing a WNBA salary is only a small portion of the economic loss they will suffer. Almost uniformly, WNBA players play basketball for teams in European leagues during the WNBA off-season, where they can earn additional money. And generally, the salaries in Europe far outstrip WNBA salaries. Many players earn twice as much in Europe as they earn playing in the WNBA, and some earn four to five times as much. Indeed, because there are few salary restrictions in European leagues, "[m]arquee players can make as much [as] $600,000, including incentives . . . [and] two or three players can reach $1 million." So, combining WNBA and European earnings, most female American professional basketball players earn six figures per year in salary, and some earn seven figures per year.

3.   *Marketing and Endorsements*

Salaries and incentives aside, WNBA players can command substantial sums of money through marketing and endorsement deals. . . . Endorsement compensation figures are difficult to pinpoint, as they are rarely publicly disclosed, but some players, such as the Los Angeles Sparks' Candace Parker and the Minnesota Lynx's Maya Moore reportedly have endorsement deals worth between $3 million and $5 million respectively. Other players have smaller five- and six-figure deals. But all players, once they become professionals, have the potential to sign endorsement contracts; a potential that does not exist while they are collegiate players.

   Taken together, the money a female basketball player can make . . . through her WNBA salary, her European basketball salary, and her endorsement deals can be impressive. . . . With the [age-eligibility] rule in place, she must wait three years to do what the men are able to do immediately.

N. Jeremi Duru, *Hoop Dreams Deferred: The WNBA, the NBA, and the Long-Standing Gender Inequity at the Game's Highest Level,* 3 Utah L. Rev. 559 (2015) (citations omitted).

NOTES AND QUESTIONS

1.   As discussed previously in this chapter and in Chapter 9, Title VII prohibits employers from discriminating against employees and prospective employees based on a number of characteristics, including sex. Do the facts set forth in the above article form the basis of a potentially viable Title VII claim? If so, what entity would be the appropriate defendant? Consider that WNBA players are employed by individual clubs rather than by the WNBA as a whole, but that the age eligibility rule is the WNBA's rule rather than that of any particular club. Further consider that, taken alone, the WNBA age eligibility rule is facially non-discriminatory (it treats all WNBA aspirants alike) and can only be seen as discriminatory when taken together with the NBA's lower age eligibility threshold. In light of these facts and the fact that the WNBA is an NBA subsidiary, might the NBA be the appropriate defendant?
2.   Defendants in Title VII actions can avoid liability by demonstrating that their alleged discriminatory actions or polices are, in fact, legitimate and non-discriminatory. What legitimate purposes might justify the NBA having a lower age eligibility threshold than the WNBA?

3. *Retaliatory Discharge or Punitive Action*

Both male and female coaches have asserted that they have been discharged in retaliation for complaining about gender disparities in institutions' athletic programs. The following case addresses the elements of Title VII and IX retaliatory discharge claims.

LOWREY v. TEXAS A&M UNIVERSITY SYSTEM

11 F. Supp. 2d 895 (S.D. Tex. 1998)

LAKE, Judge.

I. BACKGROUND

Tarleton State University (Tarleton) is a four-year coeducational institution of higher education located in Stephenville, Texas. . . . Tarleton is managed and controlled by the Board of Regents of the Texas A&M University System. . . . Dr. Dennis McCabe is the President of Tarleton. Lonn Reisman is Men's Basketball Coach and Athletics Director. Dr. Lamar Johanson is Dean of the College of Arts and Sciences and Tarleton's Faculty Representative to the NCAA. Jim Johnson is the Men's Athletics Coordinator and the NCAA Compliance Coordinator for Tarleton and a physical education teacher.

A. TWENTY YEARS OF COACHING

Jan Lowrey became Women's Basketball Coach at Tarleton in the fall of 1976. Over the next twenty years Lowrey's teams were very successful. Her teams won twenty or more games in each of her first nine years as coach. They won several conference championships, and in 1992 the team placed second in the Division II national women's basketball tournament.

Lowery's success did not lead to improved conditions for the women's basketball team. For example, the locker room used by the women's team from the early 1980s was the former men's visiting-team dressing room. The room had "a 'gang' shower, four urinals and one toilet, one sink, no dressing tables, no outlets for hair dryers, no storage, and inadequate lockers." Tarleton repeatedly ignored requests from Lowrey for renovations. Lowrey and the team manager ultimately installed shower rods and curtains to divide the showers. Tarleton finally removed the urinals in 1996, but it did not install toilets to replace them.

In 1988 Tarleton hired Lonn Reisman as Men's Basketball Coach. During his first year Reisman's salary was less than Lowrey's. The year before Reisman was hired the men's team won three games and lost twenty-five. In Reisman's first year (1988-89) the men's team improved its record to eighteen wins and eleven losses. The women's team had twenty wins and ten losses that year. Both Lowrey and Reisman received a $1,400 raise in salary as a reward for their winning seasons. In the Spring of 1989 then-Tarleton President Barry Thompson created the position of Assistant Athletics Director and appointed Reisman to the post. Tarleton did not give Lowrey an opportunity to apply for this position. Reisman then held the positions of Assistant Athletics Director, Men's Basketball Coach, and a physical education instructor. By the 1989-90 fiscal year, Reisman's second year at Tarleton and his first year as Assistant Athletics Director, Tarleton was paying Reisman a higher salary than it paid Lowrey, who by then had coached and taught at the university for thirteen years. Tarleton paid Reisman $36,899 and Lowrey $31,137 that year.

On August 27, 1993, Dr. Ron Newsome, Tarleton's Athletics Director, resigned. Although Lowrey was a head coach in the Athletics Department, she learned of Newsome's resignation through the press, not from the university. Over the next few days a Tarleton search committee interviewed three candidates to fill the vacancy: Reisman, Lowrey, and the new football coach, Ronnie Roemisch. On September 1, 1993, McCabe offered the position of Athletics Director to Reisman. Dr. McCabe explained to Lowrey that although she was equally qualified for the position, "he 'was going with Lonn.' "

Lowrey asked Reisman and McCabe to create the position of Associate Athletics Director for her, with a raise in pay commensurate with the duties and responsibilities of such an office. Instead, Reisman offered her the position of Women's Athletics Coordinator. Although this position required Lowrey to assume several new duties, the evidence is unclear whether she received an increase in pay for taking this position.

Earlier that year, on January 28, 1993, McCabe had appointed Lowrey to a special task force to study gender equity at Tarleton. On November 17, 1993, Dr. Janet Schmelzer, an Associate Professor of History at Tarleton, filed a complaint with the Department of Justice's Office for Civil Rights (OCR) alleging sex discrimination at Tarleton in violation of Title IX of the Education Amendments of 1972, 20 U.S.C. §§1681-1688 (1994). Schmelzer's complaint included several allegations of Title IX violations in Tarleton's Athletics Department. In May of 1994, Schmelzer agreed to withdraw her complaint while the parties attempted to mediate the dispute.

Beginning in April of 1994 Reisman began filing several "incident reports" in Lowrey's personnel file, noting among other problems, days when Lowrey was absent from work, arrived late, or left early without notifying Reisman. On September 29, 1994, Reisman conducted a performance review of Lowrey and gave her an average rating of 2.0 on a scale of 1 to 5 (lowest to highest) in nine categories. Reisman sent a copy of the review to Lowrey on October 3, 1994. On October 5, 1994, Reisman recommended that McCabe terminate Lowrey as Women's Athletics Coordinator. Reisman did not notify Lowrey of his recommendation. Reisman reiterated his views in an October 26, 1994, memorandum to McCabe, stating that he "strongly recommended the reassignment of Ms. Jan Lowrey from Women's Athletics Coordinator/ Head Women's Basketball Coach, effective immediately, to Head Women's Basketball Coach."

In an October 28, 1994, letter Schmelzer reminded McCabe of his promise not to allow retaliation against persons who spoke to her regarding matters raised by her OCR complaint and warned him that Title VI would forbid such retaliation regardless of McCabe's promises. On November 4, 1994, President McCabe reassigned Lowrey. She remained Women's Basketball Coach and an instructor in the Physical Education Department, and her salary did not change. Eventually, Lowrey sought employment elsewhere. She resigned from Tarleton on July 15, 1996, and took the head coach's position for the San Jose Lasers, a professional women's basketball team. The Lasers released her from her two-year contract after her first year with the club. . . .

IV.   RETALIATION

Lowrey alleges that defendants are liable are under Title VII, Title IX, and 42 U.S.C. §1983 and the First and Fourteenth Amendments to the Constitution for retaliating against her in response to comments she made criticizing the university and its officials on gender equity issues.

A.   TITLE VII

Title VII prohibits employers from retaliating against employees for filing a discrimination charge or otherwise exercising their rights under Title VII. See 42 U.S.C. §2000e-3 (1994). To establish a prima facie case of retaliation under Title VII a plaintiff must show that:

(1)   she engaged in activity protected by Title VII;
(2)   her employer took an adverse employment action against her; and
(3)   a causal connection exists between the protected activity and the adverse employment action.

See *Mattern v. Eastman Kodak Co.*, 104 F.3d 702, 705 (5th Cir.), cert. denied, 139 L. Ed. 2d 260, 118 S. Ct. 336 (1997). The "adverse employment action" must be an "ultimate employment decision," such as hiring, granting leave, discharging, promoting, or compensating. 104 F.3d at 707; *Dollis v. Rubin*, 77 F.3d 777, 782 (5th Cir. 1995). The only adverse action Lowrey identifies . . . is her removal as Women's Athletics Coordinator.

Tarleton argues that Lowrey cannot make a prima facie case of Title VII retaliation because her removal as Women's Athletics Coordinator was not an adverse employment action. Title VII's antiretaliation provisions address ultimate employment decisions, not "interlocutory or mediate" decisions that might lead to ultimate decisions. *Mattern*, 104 F.3d at 708. Employment actions having only a tangential effect on an ultimate decision are not sufficient to raise a claim of retaliation under Title VII. *Dollis*, 77 F.3d at 781-82. Tarleton argues that because Lowrey's demotion was not one of the five employment actions classified as adverse in *Mattern* (i.e., hiring, granting leave, discharging, promoting, and compensating), it does not constitute an ultimate employment decision.

Demotion is the opposite of promotion. If promotion is an ultimate employment decision, so is demotion. . . . Tarleton does not challenge the remaining elements of Lowrey's prima facie case and has not offered any legitimate, non-discriminatory reasons for Lowrey's demotion. The court will therefore deny summary judgment on her Title VII retaliation claim.

B.   TITLE IX

1.   *Legal Standards*

In *Lakoski v. James*, 66 F.3d 751, 758 (5th Cir. 1995), *cert. denied*, 117 S. Ct. 357 (1996), the court held that Title IX does not imply a cause of action for employment discrimination because Title VII already prohibits such conduct. However, in an appeal from Lowrey's first suit, the Fifth Circuit held that "Title IX affords a right of action for retaliation against employees of federally funded educational institutions." *Lowrey I*, 117 F.3d 242, 249 (5th Cir. 1997) (emphasis added). The *Lowrey I* court examined Department of Education regulations promulgated under Title IX and concluded that they implied a cause of action for retaliation. . . .[62]

While the *Lowrey I* court held that Title IX implies a retaliation claim, the court did not address what substantive legal standards apply to such a claim. Tarleton contends that this court should apply the same rules that courts use for Title VII retaliation claims. After carefully reviewing *Lowrey I* and the treatment of Title IX retaliation claims by other courts, the court generally agrees with Tarleton.

The *Lowrey I* court stated that courts should interpret the antiretaliation provisions of Title IX and 34 C.F.R. §100.7(e) in accordance with the antiretaliation provisions of Title VII and the Age Discrimination in Employment Act (ADEA), 29 U.S.C. §623(e) (1994). . . . Several other circuit and district courts have applied Title VII's burden-shifting scheme and prima facie case requirements to the Title IX retaliation claims before them. [Citations omitted.] The court concludes that Lowrey's Title IX retaliation claim is best analyzed under the standard *Burdine-McDonnell Douglas* burden-shifting scheme for employment discrimination claims. Absent direct evidence of retaliaton, Lowrey has the initial burden of establishing a prima facie case of retaliation in violation of Title IX. If she meets this burden Tarleton may rebut her prima facie case by articulating legitimate, nondiscriminatory reasons for its conduct. If Tarleton meets its burden, the inference of unlawful retaliation dissolves and Lowrey must establish that Tarleton's proffered reasons are pretexts for unlawful behavior. [Citations omitted.]

Tarleton argues that in a Title IX retaliation case the court should require the same three elements of a prima facie case that are required for Title VII retaliation claims. While that test provides a helpful guide for establishing a prima facie case under Title IX, the court must modify it to comply with *Lowrey I* and to conform to the specific activities governed by Title IX.

Because a Title IX retaliation claim only covers conduct protected by Title IX, a plaintiff may only recover under Title IX when the defendant retaliated against her "solely as a consequence of complaints alleging noncompliance with the substantive provisions of Title IX." [Citation omitted.] Therefore Lowrey must first establish as part of her prima facie case that she engaged in activity protected by Title IX, not Title VII.

A Title IX retaliation claim is not limited to actions by an employer against an employee. If Title IX retaliation claims were so limited, students who are not employed by an educational institution would have no protection under Title IX against retaliation by their school. Title IX protects "any individual" who complains about or helps investigate alleged violations of Title IX. [Citations omitted.] In addition, while Title VII protects against employment discrimination, Title IX prohibits gender discrimination in educational programs. [Citation omitted.] *Lakoski v. James*, 66 F.3d 751, 753 (5th Cir. 1995). Retaliation

---

62. 34 C.F.R. §100.7(e)(1997), states:

Intimidatory or retaliatory acts prohibited. No recipient or other person shall intimidate, threaten, coerce, or discriminate against any individual for the purpose of interfering with any right or privilege secured by section 601 of the Act or this part, or because he has made a complaint, testified, assisted, or participated in any manner in any investigation, proceeding or hearing under this part. . . .

claims brought under Title IX protect against a broad array of retaliatory conduct unrelated to employment.

With these distinctions in mind, the court concludes that in order to establish a prima facie case of retaliation under Title IX Lowrey must show that:

(1) she engaged in activities protected by Title IX;
(2) Tarleton took adverse action against her; and
(3) a causal connection exists between her protected activities and Tarleton's adverse action.

2.   Analysis

(a)   Prima Facie Case

Tarleton argues that Lowrey cannot establish a prima facie case of retaliation because

(1) its actions do not constitute an ultimate employment decision; . . .
(2) Lowrey could not articulate any discriminatory actions against her at her deposition; . . . and
(3) there was no causal connection between Tarleton's failure to promote her and her activities protected by Title IX. . . .

Because Tarleton does not deny that Lowrey engaged in activities protected by Title IX, the court's evaluation of Tarleton's arguments must focus on the second and third elements of Lowrey's prima facie case.

(1)   Adverse Action

Tarleton proceeds under the mistaken assumption that Title IX only protects against adverse employment actions that constitute ultimate employment decisions. As explained above, Title IX is not limited to employment decisions; it protects against a broader range of retaliatory conduct.

Lowrey alleges that after she spoke out on Title IX issues Tarleton:

(1) did not promote her to Athletics Director;
(2) limited her authority as Women's Athletics Coordinator;
(3) increased her duties as Women's Athletics Coordinator without a commensurate increase in compensation;
(4) unjustifiably reprimanded her;
(5) isolated and harassed her in the workplace;
(6) withdrew staff support for her;
(7) withdrew support for the women's basketball team; and
(8) demoted her from the position of Women's Athletics Coordinator.

Lowrey fails to explain or support with . . . evidence many of these allegations. She does not explain how Tarleton limited her authority, increased her duties, or isolated and harassed her. Her complaints regarding withdrawn support for her and her team focus on personality conflicts and personal behavior, which are not the type of adverse actions protected by Title IX.

Tarleton admits that it did not promote Lowrey to Athletics Director, and the court has already concluded that Lowrey's alleged demotion was an adverse action. The record also reflects that Lowrey received a reprimand in the fall of 1994 as a result of a secondary violation of NCAA recruiting regulations. Lowrey argues and has submitted evidence that this disciplinary action was more severe than appropriate under the circumstances and was an act of retaliation against her. The court therefore concludes that Lowrey has satisfied the adverse action element of her prima facie case as to three allegedly retaliatory acts:

(1)   Tarleton's failure to promote her to Athletics Director;
(2)   her demotion from the position of Women's Athletics Coordinator; and
(3)   Tarleton's reprimand of Lowery.

(2)   Causal Connection

Lowrey never explains or offers evidence showing how her Title IX activities led to the reprimand she received after the recruiting violation. Although Lowrey attempts to show a causal connection between Tarleton's failure to promote her to Athletics Director, she fails to submit sufficient evidence to raise an issue of fact.

In January of 1993 President McCabe appointed Lowrey to the newly formed Special Task Force to Study Gender Equity. In February of 1993 Lowrey sent a letter to McCabe complaining of continuing gender-equity problems in the Athletics Department. McCabe responded by a February 16, 1993 memorandum, copying Dr. Koy Floyd. Because McCabe sent a copy of his memorandum to Dr. Floyd, a jury could infer that McCabe had also communicated Lowrey's gender-equity complaints to Dr. Floyd. Dr. Floyd was a member of the committee charged with recommending the new Athletics Director. Lowrey thus raises the question whether Dr. Floyd was biased against her because of her advocacy of gender equity issues when the committee met to recommend the new Athletics Director.

This is the only admissible evidence offered by Lowrey that any of the committee members failed to recommend her for Athletics Director because of her gender-equity complaints. . . .

Aside from her allegations regarding Dr. Floyd, who was only one of the four members of the selection committee, Lowrey offers no other admissible evidence that the committee was biased against her, let alone that such bias resulted from her Title IX activities. Lowrey presents no evidence that Dr. Floyd carried his alleged bias into the selection process or that he persuaded the other members of the committee not to recommend her for Athletics Director. The court concludes that Lowrey has failed to establish a causal link between her protected Title IX conduct and Tarleton's failure to promote her to Athletics Director.

Lowrey does offer evidence raising an issue of fact as to the causal link between her Title IX conduct and her demotion. On October 26, 1994, Reisman sent a memorandum to President McCabe recommending Lowrey's reassignment. In this memorandum Reisman complained that "Ms. Lowrey has taken her concerns, complaints, and issues directly to others on campus outside the Athletics Department since the beginning, effectively undermining any viable working relationship we might have had." McCabe acted on Reisman's recommendation and demoted Lowrey. There is thus some evidence that Reisman based his demotion recommendation in part on his displeasure with Lowrey's Title IX conduct.

In summary, Tarleton does not deny that Lowrey engaged in conduct protected by Title IV, and Lowrey has established issues of fact as to whether Tarleton took adverse action against her in the form of her demotion, her reprimand, and Tarleton's failure to promote her to Athletics Director. However, Lowrey has only offered evidence of a causal link between her protected Title IX conduct and her demotion. Lowrey has therefore established a prima facie case only as to her demotion.

(b)   Tarleton's Reasons for Its Action

Under *Burdine* and *McDonnell Douglas*, the burden shifts to Tarleton to articulate legitimate, nondiscriminatory reasons for Lowrey's demotion. Because Tarleton has not attempted to do so the court will deny summary judgment on Lowrey's Title IX retaliatory demotion claim. The court will grant summary judgment as to the remainder of Lowrey's Title IX retaliation claim.[80] . . .

NOTES AND QUESTIONS

1. *Private Right of Action for Retaliation Under Title IX.* A threshold issue is whether there is an implied private right of action under Title IX for retaliation on behalf of employees of educational institutions who raise concerns regarding compliance with the substantive provisions of Title IX. In *Jackson v. Birmingham Board of Education*, 544 U.S. 167 (2005), in a 5-4 decision, the Supreme Court resolved a split in the circuits when it held that Title IX's private right of action encompasses retaliation against an employee who complains about gender-based discrimination.

2. *Retaliation Under Title VII.* Denying the defendant's motion for summary judgment on the plaintiff's retaliation claim under Title VII, the *Lowrey* court states that a demotion should be treated the same as a promotion for Title VII purposes. What else must the plaintiff prove to establish a retaliation claim under Title VII? What proof will be sufficient to prove causality in a retaliation claim?

3. *Retaliation Under Title IX.* How does a Title IX retaliation claim differ, as a matter of legal doctrine, from a Title VII retaliation claim? Why does the *Lowrey* court refuse to require that retaliation claims be limited to employee claims against an employer? If a student prevails in a claim under Title IX, what relief may the student be awarded?

   In *Bryant v. Gardner*, 587 F. Supp. 2d 951 (E.D. Ill. 2008), a coach brought a civil action under Title IX against his high school's principal and the Chicago Board of Education, alleging that his termination as head coach of the men's basketball team was a result of retaliation against him for

---

80. Tarleton has articulated legitimate, nondiscriminatory reasons for its decision not to promote Lowrey to Athletics Director. Tarleton lists the following reasons why McCabe decided to promote Reisman to Athletics Director instead of Lowrey:

(1) the selection committee recommended Reisman;
(2) Reisman had prior administrative experience as Assistant Athletics Director at Tarleton;
(3) Reisman was familiar with different levels of intercollegiate athletics;
(4) Reisman had coached at six different universities, including Tarleton, as well as at the high school level;
(5) Reisman showed fundraising potential; and
(6) Reisman had "cogently and compellingly" articulated an attractive vision for Tarleton athletics.

complaining about the unequal treatment of male and female athletes at his high school. He asserted that female players were allowed to participate in open gym, while male players were prohibited from doing so. The defendants moved for summary judgment, which the court denied, holding that a reasonable jury might find that the board's reasons for terminating the coach were merely a pretext designed to cover a retaliatory motive.

Fresno State University was involved in litigation related to gender discrimination for much of the first decade of this century. First, Diane Milutinovich, an athletics administrator, was dismissed from her position after she complained about inequities in the men's and women's athletics programs. Then, the women's volleyball coach, Lindy Vivas, and women's basketball coach, Stacy Johnson-Klein, were fired after questioning administrators and complaining about inequities in facilities, staffing, and employment between the men's and women's athletics programs. Fresno State settled with Milutinovich for $3.5 million. Juries in separate trials found that the university intentionally discriminated against the coaches and awarded $5.85 million to Vivas and $19.1 million to Johnson-Klein. When Milutinovich retired after 27 years of service, she was honored by the California Senate. See The Associated Press, *Fallout from Fresno State's Multi-Million Dollar Cases,* http://www.titleix.info/resources/Legal-Cases/Fallout-from-Fresno-states-multi-million-dollar-case.aspx.

In May 2017, Jane Meyer, former University of Iowa senior associate athletic director, was awarded $2.3 million in back pay and damages under Title IX for gender and sexual orientation discrimination, retaliation, whistleblower violations, and unequal pay. Soon after the decision, the University paid $1.5 million to settle a long-standing lawsuit filed by Meyer's partner, Tracey Griesbaum, for wrongful termination, gender and sexual orientation discrimination, and retaliation. Additionally, the athletics department paid $2.7 million in legal fees to the law firm representing both Meyer and Griesbaum. See Mark Emmert, *Iowa settles sex discrimination cases for $6.5 million,* HawkCentral.com, May 19, 2017, http://www.hawkcentral.com/story/sports/college/iowa/2017/05/19/tracey-griesbaum-iowa-hawkeye-gary-barta-settlement/333218001/.

CHAPTER
11

Health, Safety, and Risk Management
Issues in Sports

A. INTRODUCTION

This chapter illustrates the health and safety issues, and the corresponding need for careful risk management, which arise in a variety of sports-related contexts. Initially we explore how common law tort principles allocate the risks of injury and establish liability rules for injuries occurring while individuals observe or participate in sporting events. The materials demonstrate judicial recognition that the unique characteristics and features of athletic competition may require modification of general tort principles to further policy objectives. Also, courts have uniquely applied criminal law principles to determine what injury-causing conduct constitutes criminally culpable behavior between participants engaged in sporting activities. In addition to tort and criminal law principles, the chapter examines state and federal statutes (e.g., workers' compensation and disability antidiscrimination statutes) that regulate relationships among sports organizations, clubs, and teams and their respective athletes. Examples include the means of compensating professional athletes for injuries and the participation rights of athletes with a disability who require rules modifications to participate in a sport or potentially pose a health risk to themselves and others.

B. TORT AND CRIMINAL LIABILITY FOR ATHLETICS-RELATED INJURIES

1. *Injury to Spectators*

EDWARD C. v. CITY OF ALBUQUERQUE ET AL.
241 P.3d 1086 (N.M. 2010)

CHÁVEZ, Justice.

The question we must answer is what duty do owner/occupants of commercial baseball stadiums have to protect spectators from projectiles leaving the field of play. The district court applied the most limited duty, which is followed in a minority of jurisdictions, commonly referred to as the "baseball rule." The district court held that the duty was limited to providing screening for the area of the field behind home plate for as many spectators as may reasonably be expected to desire such protection. Because Isotopes Stadium has such screening, the district court granted summary judgment to Defendants.

On appeal, the Court of Appeals reversed summary judgment regarding the City and the Isotopes "on the ground that, under the particular circumstances alleged, there are issues of material fact precluding summary judgment" and rejected application of a limited-duty baseball rule, holding instead that these Defendants owed a duty to exercise ordinary care. *Crespin v. Albuquerque Baseball Club*, LLC, 2009-NMCA-105, ¶¶ 1, 13, 147 N.M. 62, 216 P.3d 827. We granted certiorari to decide whether New Mexico should recognize a limited duty for owner/occupants of commercial baseball stadiums.

Considering the nature of the sport of baseball, which involves spectator participation and a desire to catch balls that leave the field of play, contrary to the Court of Appeals majority opinion, we believe that a limited-duty rule, albeit not the one argued for by Defendants, is warranted by sound policy considerations. Accordingly, we hold that an owner/occupant of a commercial baseball stadium owes a duty that is symmetrical to the duty of the spectator. The spectator must exercise ordinary care to protect himself or herself from the inherent risk of being hit by a projectile that leaves the field of play and the owner/occupant must exercise ordinary care not to increase that inherent risk.

In this case, it is alleged that the injured child was not in an area dedicated solely to viewing the game, but was in the picnic area with tables positioned perpendicular to the field of play. This type of area can be described as a multi-purpose area. It is alleged that, without warning, batting practice commenced when the child was hit by a baseball that left the field of play. Given the scope of duty that we define today and Plaintiffs' allegations, we conclude that, on the record before us, Defendants did not make a prima facie showing entitling them to summary judgment.

I. BACKGROUND

Plaintiffs and their four-year-old son, Emilio, two-year-old daughter, Rachel, and ten-year-old daughter, Cassandra, were attending a Little League party at Isotopes stadium. The City owns the stadium, which is leased by the Isotopes. Plaintiffs were in the stadium's picnic area, located beyond the left field wall in fair ball territory. They "had just sat down with [their] hot dogs and drinks" and had "just begun to eat [their] meals, when without a warning from anyone at the ball park a baseball struck Emilio in the head." During pregame batting practice, New Orleans Zephyrs player Dave Matranga batted a ball out of the park into the picnic area, striking Emilio "in the upper right portion of his head fracturing his skull." The picnic tables in the left field stands are arranged in alignment with the left field foul line, so that seated individuals are not directly facing the field of play, but face perpendicular to the action. Isotopes stadium has a screen or protective netting between home plate and the seats behind home plate, but has no screen or protective netting between home plate and the seats beyond the left field wall. . . .

II.   A LIMITED DUTY FOR OWNER/OCCUPANTS OF BASEBALL STADIUMS IS APPROPRIATE

What duty should owner/occupants of a baseball stadium in New Mexico have to protect spectators from projectiles that leave the field of play? The question of the existence and scope of a defendant's duty of care is a legal question that depends on the nature of the sport or activity in question, the parties' general relationship to the activity, and public policy considerations. . . .

"As a general rule, an individual has no duty to protect another from harm." Grover v. Stechel, 2002-NMCA-049, ¶ 11, 132 N.M. 140, 45 P.3d 80. Certain relationships, such as a possessor of land and a visitor, however, give rise to such a duty. *Id.* The special relationship between Defendants, as owners and occupants of Isotopes stadium, and Plaintiffs, as visitors, places Defendants' duty within the first category. Indeed, Defendants do not dispute that a duty is owed; they simply argue that the scope of that duty should be limited.

New Mexico generally applies a "single standard of reasonable care under the circumstances" to landowners or occupants. *Ford v. Bd. of Cnty. Comm'rs*, 118 N.M. 134, 138, 879 P.2d 766, 770 (1994) (abolishing the distinction between invitees and licensees but not trespassers, because trespassers have "no basis for claiming extended protection" and such "would place an unfair burden on a landowner who has no reason to expect a trespasser's presence" (internal quotation marks and citation omitted)). . . . . .Accordingly, our jury instructions provide that "[a]n [owner] [occupant] owes a visitor the duty to use ordinary care to keep the premises safe for use by the visitor[, whether or not a dangerous condition is obvious]." UJI 13-1309 NMRA. UJI 13-1603 NMRA provides guidance on what constitutes "ordinary care."

> "Ordinary care" is that care which a reasonably prudent person would use in the conduct of the person's own affairs. What constitutes "ordinary care" varies with the nature of what is being done.
>
>   As the risk of danger that should reasonably be foreseen increases, the amount of care required also increases. In deciding whether ordinary care has been used, the conduct in question must be considered in the light of all the surrounding circumstances.

Id.

The Court of Appeals determined that ordinary care was the applicable standard because "Emilio and his injury were [f]oreseeable," and "[c]onsequently, all Defendants owed Emilio a duty to exercise ordinary care for his safety." *Crespin*, 2009-NMCA-105, ¶ 13, 147 N.M. 62, 216 P.3d 827. Foreseeability, however, is but one factor to consider when determining duty and not the principal question. See Restatement (Third) of Torts: Liability for Physical and Emotional Harm § 7 cmt. j (2010) (disapproving the use of foreseeability to limit liability in preference for "articulat[ing] polic[ies] or principle[s] . . . to facilitate more transparent explanations of the reasons for a no-duty [or limited-duty] ruling and to protect the traditional function of the jury as factfinder"). Instead, "duty is a policy question that is answered by reference to legal precedent, statutes, and other principles of law." *Herrera*, 2003-NMSC-018, ¶ 7, 134 N.M. 43, 73 P.3d 181 (internal quotation marks and citation omitted).

In considering the policy implications of adopting the baseball rule, the Court of Appeals determined "that there is no compelling reason to immunize the owners/occupiers of baseball stadiums" because "[c]omparative negligence principles allow the fact finder to take into account the risks that spectators voluntarily accept when they attend baseball games as well as the ability of stadium owners to guard against unreasonable risks that are not essential to the game itself." *Crespin*, 2009-NMCA-105, ¶ 23, 147 N.M. 62, 216 P.3d 827. . . .

To determine whether New Mexico's duty of ordinary care for owners/occupants is appropriate in the context of commercial baseball, we will review baseball spectator injury cases from other jurisdictions for comparison to our owner/occupant duty framework. In doing so, we look for instances where courts have imposed a duty other than the duty to exercise ordinary care that are supported by sound policy consistent with New Mexico's pure comparative fault system and a general interest in promoting safety, welfare, and fairness.

III. THE HISTORY AND DEVELOPMENT OF A BASEBALL RULE

[EDS. After reviewing baseball spectator cases, the court concluded that initially jurisdictions adopted the baseball rule premised on the doctrines of assumption of the risk and contributory negligence. The court found that "in its most limited form, the baseball rule held:

> that where a proprietor of a ball park furnishes screening for the area of the field behind home plate where the danger of being struck by a ball is the greatest and that screening is of sufficient extent to provide adequate protection for as many spectators as may reasonably be expected to desire such seating in the course of an ordinary game, the proprietor fulfills the duty of care imposed by law and, therefore, cannot be liable in negligence.

Akins v. Glens Falls City Sch. Dist., 53 N.Y.2d 325, 441 N.Y.S.2d 644, 424 N.E.2d 531, 534 (1981).

Based on its survey of baseball spectator cases the court concluded that while the *Akins* baseball rule arguably once represented a majority approach across jurisdictions to baseball spectator injury claims, a wide variation in the formulation of the baseball rule now exists, making the *Akins* rule the minority approach. It noted that some jurisdictions impose duties on stadium owners greater than those pronounced in *Akins*, yet less onerous than a general duty of ordinary care.

The court attributed the shift to a move away from the absolute defenses of contributory negligence and assumption of risk, which functioned as complete bars to plaintiff recovery, and to comparative fault tort systems. Aside from shifts in tort law, advances in the game and the business of baseball have also been significant factors contributing to courts' modification of the traditional baseball rule. It concluded that the common theme among contemporary cases modifying the traditional baseball rule is that spectators injured by baseballs are generally allowed to advance their claim when the injury is the result of some circumstance, design, or conduct neither necessary nor inherent in the game. Quoting the New Jersey Supreme Court in *Masionave v. Newark Bears Prof'l Baseball Club, Inc.*, 881 A.2d 700 (N.J. 2005), the court stated, "It would be unfair to hold owners and operators [of baseball stadiums] liable for injuries to spectators in the stands when the potential danger of fly balls is an inherent, expected, and even desired part of the baseball fan's experience." Accordingly, the court applied the *Akins* baseball rule only within the stands—areas "dedicated solely to viewing the game" (*Id.* at 707), where fly balls are inherent, expected, and even desired. "In contrast, multi-purpose areas, such as concourses and playground areas, are outside the scope of the rule" (*Id.* at 707) and are subject to "a duty of reasonable care" (*Id.* at 709). In these multipurpose areas, "[t]he validity of the baseball rule diminishes" because "[f]ans foreseeably and understandably let down their guard when they are in other areas of the stadium" where the fan "is no longer trying to catch foul balls or even necessarily watching the game" (*Id.* at 708), and so fly balls are neither expected nor desired.] . . .

From these seminal and contemporary baseball spectator injury cases, it is clear that the baseball rule, rigid as it may be for injuries arising from necessary and inherent aspects of the game, historically has not been applied to preclude recovery for spectators injured in extraordinary circumstances, where conduct or situations—even stadium design flaws—leading to injury were beyond the norm. Therefore, when a stadium owner or occupant has done something to increase the risks beyond those necessary or inherent to the game, or to impede a fan's ability to protect himself or herself, the courts have generally, and we believe correctly, allowed claims to proceed for a jury to determine whether the duty was breached.

After reviewing the history of baseball spectator injury cases and the rationale and policy choices motivating those decisions, we believe that commercial baseball stadium owners/occupants owe a duty to their fans that is justifiably limited given the unique nature of their relationship, as well as the policy concerns implicated by this relationship. Accordingly, New Mexico's traditional common-law framework for land owners and occupants that would otherwise prescribe a standard duty of ordinary care is inapposite in the limited circumstance of spectator injuries resulting from the play of commercial baseball. At the same time, we reject the baseball rule pronounced in *Akins* because of its extreme and unyielding results. Instead, we modify the duty owed by commercial baseball stadium owners/occupants.

We hold, therefore, that an owner/occupant of a commercial baseball stadium owes a duty that is symmetrical to the duty of the spectator. Spectators must exercise ordinary care to protect themselves from the inherent risk of being hit by a projectile that leaves the field of play and the owner/occupant must exercise ordinary care not to increase that inherent risk. This approach recognizes the impossibility of playing the sport of baseball without projectiles leaving the field of play. This approach also balances the competing interests of spectators who want full protection by requiring screening behind home plate consistent with the *Akins* approach and allowing other spectators to participate in the game by catching souvenirs that leave the field of play. In addition, it balances the practical interest of watching a sport that encourages players to strike a ball beyond the field of play in fair ball territory to score runs with the safety and entertainment interests of the spectators in catching such balls. As long as the owner/occupant exercises ordinary care not to increase the inherent risk of being hit by a projectile leaving the field, he or she need not be concerned about adverse social and economic impacts on the citizens of New Mexico. While not of paramount concern, this approach will bring New Mexico in line with the vast majority of jurisdictions that have considered the issue. . . .

V.   Conclusion

The Court of Appeals rejection of a limited-duty rule is reversed. We adopt a limited-duty rule that applies to owner/occupants of a commercial baseball facility. Under the duty we adopt, an owner/occupant of a commercial baseball stadium owes a duty that is symmetrical to the duty of the spectator. Spectators must exercise ordinary care to protect themselves from the inherent risk of being hit by a projectile that leaves the field of play and the owner/occupant must exercise ordinary care not to increase that inherent risk. Defendants did not make a prima facie case for their entitlement to a summary judgment under the limited duty we announce today, and therefore this matter is remanded to the district court for further proceedings consistent with this Opinion.

IT IS SO ORDERED.

NOTES AND QUESTIONS

1. *General Duty of Reasonable Care to Spectators.* Liability is imposed on a sports facility operator for spectator injury only if there is breach of a legal duty of care. Courts have rejected attempts to hold facility operators strictly liable for spectator injuries by refusing to characterize a sporting event such as a baseball game as an ultrahazardous activity, or considering the sale of a ticket to be the sale of a product subject to strict products liability. *Romeo v. Pittsburgh Assocs.*, 787 A.2d 1027 (Pa. Super. Ct. 2001). Sports event spectators generally are characterized as invitees, meaning they are invited to enter a venue to view a game or event (usually as a paying customer), and "the owner of a [sports] facility has a duty of reasonable care under the circumstances to invitees." *Allred v. Capital Area Soccer League, Inc.*, 669 S.E.2d 777, 779 (N.C. Ct. App. 2008). This duty requires a facility owner or operator to maintain the premises and equipment therein in a reasonably safe condition to prevent spectator injury from normal use of the facility. If this duty is breached and causes harm to a spectator, there is potential liability for negligence. See, e.g., *Pryor v. Iberia Parish Sch. Bd.*, 42 So. 3d 1015, 1021 (La. Ct. App. 2010) (rejecting argument that the defendant should be absolved of liability where the danger to the plaintiff was "open and obvious" [defective bleachers], but the defect was found to present an unreasonable harm).

A facility operator or club also may be liable for failing to use reasonable care in regulating crowd control and fan conduct during sporting events, although it should be noted that the doctrine of sovereign immunity may preclude a negligence suit against a public entity for inadequate crowd control or policing of spectator conduct. See, e.g., *Eneman v. Richter*, 577 N.W.2d 386 (Wis. Ct. App. 1998). Some courts have held that injury caused by fellow spectators while pursuing a ball that goes into the stands as a souvenir is not an inherent risk of attending and observing a game. *Hayden v. Univ. of Notre Dame*, 716 N.E.2d 603 (Ind. Ct. App. 1999). Ruling that a university has a legal duty to protect spectators against a foreseeable risk of such harm, the *Hayden* court explained:

> We find that the totality of the circumstances establishes that Notre Dame should have foreseen that injury would likely result from the actions of a third party in lunging for the football after it landed in the seating area. As a result, it owed a duty to Letitia Hayden to protect her from such injury. The Haydens were seated in Notre Dame's stadium to watch a football game. Notre Dame well understands and benefits from the enthusiasm of the fans of its football team. It is just such enthusiasm that drives some spectators to attempt to retrieve a football to keep as a souvenir. There was evidence that there were

many prior incidents of people being jostled or injured by efforts of fans to retrieve the ball.

716 N.E.2d at 606. However, in *Telega v. Security Bureau, Inc.*, 719 A.2d 372 (Pa. Sup. Ct. 1998), which involved similar facts, the dissenting judge observed: "[t]he risk faced in the case at bar was quite common and customary to the football game and reasonably foreseeable based on past experience. Appellants assumed the risk of being injured by displaced fans pursuing a souvenir football." *Id.* at 378. With which judicial view do you agree?

2. *Application and Evolution of Limited Duty Rule in Baseball Cases.* The general duty of a facility owner or operator to exercise reasonable care to protect invitees does not extend to require protection of spectators from risks inherent to a particular sport. As it relates to the liability of a stadium owner, player, or team to an injured spectator, the majority of courts have adopted what is frequently referred to as the "limited duty" rule. Pursuant to this rule, "there is no legal duty to protect or warn spectators about the 'common, frequent, and expected' inherent risks of observing a sporting event such as being struck by flying objects that go into the stands." *Jones v. Three Rivers Mgmt. Corp.*, 394 A.2d 546, 551 (Pa. 1978).

A rationale frequently articulated in support of the limited duty rule is that spectators assume injury-causing risks that are an inherent part of the activity in question. *S. Shore Baseball, LLC v. DeJesus*, 982 N.E.2d 1076, 1084 (Ind. Ct. App. 2013) ("an operator of a baseball stadium who 'provides screening behind home plate sufficient to meet ordinary demands for protected seating has fulfilled its duty with respect to screening and cannot be subjected to liability for injuries resulting to a spectator by an object leaving the playing field'"); *Wheeler v. Cen. Carolina Scholastic Sports, Inc.*, 798 S.E.2d 438 (N.C. Ct. App. 2017), *aff'd* 370 N.C. 390 (2017) (unpublished) (holding that North Carolina's version of the baseball rule "shields a baseball field operator from liability, even when a patron is struck in an unusual way by a batted ball, so long as the operator provides a screened section"). Proponents of the limited duty rule also argue that not imposing a duty on facility owners for risks inherent in the game promotes allowing owners to construct facilities that enhance consumer choice. Consumers may elect to sit in protected seats or find seats in unprotected areas where their view may be unobstructed and they can become more intimately involved in the particular game.

What policy considerations led the New Mexico Supreme Court in *Edward C.* to reject the liability rule known as the "baseball rule" and to adopt the limited duty rule? For a discussion of the *Edward C.* case, see Christopher McNair, Note & Comment, Edward C. v. City of Albuquerque*: The New Mexico Supreme Court Balks on the Baseball Rule*, 41 N.M. L. Rev. 539 (2011).

Should conceptions of stadium owner liability change in light of what Professor Michael McCann calls the "modern day baseball experience"? McCann writes:

Attending an MLB game in 2017 is a very different experience from attending one 20 years ago. Now-a-days, many, if not most, fans routinely check their phones and go on the Internet while the game is taking place—especially given that some ballparks offer complimentary Wi-Fi. They also take photos of one another and post them on their social media accounts.

Michael McCann, *Yankees Incident Revives an Old Question: How Responsible Are Teams for Foul Ball Injuries?*, SI.com (Sept. 21, 2017). Like McCann, two authors argue for abolition of the baseball rule because of a convergence of factors including: (1) trends in baseball construction that place fans in closer proximity to the field of play; (2) changes in how the game is played, such as the greater velocity at which balls are thrown by pitchers, which decrease a fan's time to react to protect him- or herself; (3) ticket policies that drastically limit fans' ability to choose to sit in protected seats if they desire; (4) the increase in fan distraction from what's occurring on the field resulting from electronic scoreboards, team mascots, teams encouraging fans to use smartphones during games, and other activities; and (5) law and economics policy, which concludes that teams are the low-cost provider and the best risk-avoider for foul-ball-related spectator injuries. The authors urge adoption of a strict liability approach, which would incentivize teams to extend protective netting and enact other safety features at baseball stadiums, given the relatively low cost to MLB teams to add more protective netting. Nathaniel Grow & Zachary Flagel, *The Faulty Law and Economics of the "Baseball Rule,"* 60 Wm. & Mary L. Rev. 59 (2018).

During the 2017 MLB season, injuries requiring hospitalization to a toddler girl at New York's Yankee Stadium and a man at Chicago's Wrigley Field (neither of whom was seated in an area with protective netting) shone light on the duty sports facility operators owe to spectators. MLB had previously recommended (but had not required) that all clubs expand netting to the ends of teams' dugouts; only some clubs followed the recommendations. Following the girl's injury, the Yankees committed to providing greater protection before the start of the 2018 season. All thirty MLB teams have since voluntarily extended protective netting to the end of teams' dugouts.

Events occurring during the 2019 baseball season prompted teams to further examine their policies regarding protected seating. In July 2019, the Chicago White Sox extended protective netting, which now shields fans from line drives, to the foul poles of its stadium. In taking this action, the White Sox joined the Washington Nationals as the only MLB teams to add this extra level of protection. The expanded protection occurred after a string of 2019 incidents, including: a woman being hospitalized after she was struck by a ball hit by a White Sox player; a two-year old girl suffering a fractured skull after she was struck by a line drive at a MLB game in Houston; and a young girl being struck by a foul ball at Dodger Stadium. See Teddy Greenstein, *White Sox become one of the first MLB teams to extend protective netting to the foul poles: "The game is changing,"* Chi. Trib. (July 22, 2019). In August 2019, MLB's Toronto Blue Jays announced that the club would extend protective netting down the baselines of its ballpark before the start of the 2020 baseball season. Ian Harrison, *Blue Jays to Extend Protective Netting for 2020 Season*, ABC News (Aug. 6, 2019) https://abcnews.go.com/Sports/wireStory/blue-jays-extend-protective-netting-2020-season-64807396.

Even if the facility operator or club is not liable for a spectator's initial injury ensuing from being struck by a fly ball or puck, liability may be premised on a defendant's negligent failure to ascertain the nature and extent of a spectator's symptoms after she or he is struck by a foul ball. *Fish v. L.A. Dodgers Baseball Club*, 128 Cal. Rptr. 807 (Cal. Ct. App. 1976).

3. *Distracting Conduct.* Although facility operators and teams generally are not liable for spectator injuries resulting from inherent risks associated with on-field play, they have a legal duty not to increase the inherent risks of

injury from watching a game or athletic event. In *Lowe v. California League of Professional Baseball*, 65 Cal. Rptr. 2d 105 (Cal. Ct. App. 1997), the plaintiff was seated facing forward and watching a baseball game when a team's mascot, a seven-foot-tall caricature of a dinosaur, suddenly began touching the plaintiff from behind with a tail protruding from the mascot's costume. As plaintiff turned to see what was touching him, he was struck in the face by a foul ball and suffered serious injury. The court found that the presence of a team mascot is not an integral part of the game of baseball. It held that the mascot's antics while the game was being played, created a triable issue of fact whether the club increased the inherent risks of watching a baseball game by distracting plaintiff and preventing him from seeing and protecting himself from injury by a batted ball. See also *Gil de Rebollo v. Miami Heat Ass'ns., Inc.*, 137 F.3d 56 (1st Cir. 1998) (club liable for mascot's negligent antics during timeout entertainment routine that caused injury to spectator); *Coomer v. Kan. City Royals*, 437 S.W.3d 184, 203 (Mo. 2014) (eye injury from mascot's hotdog toss is not an inherent risk of watching a baseball game and club may be liable for its mascot's failure "to use reasonable care in conducting Hotdog Launch"); but see *Harting v. Dayton Dragons Prof. Baseball Club*, 870 N.E.2d 766 (Ohio Ct. App. 2007) (spectator assumed risk of injury from foul ball by watching mascot perform rather than game).

Is *Lowe* consistent with cases holding that there is no legal duty to ensure that vendors or other patrons do not obscure the view of the spectators? See *Clapman v. City of New York*, 468 N.E.2d 697 (N.Y. 1984).

4. *Hockey Cases.* In contrast to baseball, courts initially refused to hold that spectators assumed the risk of being hit by hockey pucks that flew into the stands. *Morris v. Cleveland Hockey Club, Inc.*, 98 N.E.2d 49 (Ohio Ct. App. 1951); *Thurman v. Ice Palace*, 97 P.2d 999, 1001 (Cal. Ct. App. 1939) ("It is not common knowledge that pucks used in ice hockey game are liable to be batted into the section occupied by the spectators"). Now "it is undisputed, however, that ice hockey spectators face a known risk of being hit by a flying puck," and a facility operator has no legal duty to eliminate this inherent risk. *Nemarnik v. L.A. Kings Hockey Club, L.P.*, 127 Cal. Rptr. 2d 10, 15 (Cal. Ct. App. 2002). See *Smero v. City of Saratoga Springs*, 75 N.Y.S.3d 120, 122-23 (N.Y. Ct. App. 2018) (court rules that "in the context of hockey rinks, 'the owner's duty owed to spectators is discharged by providing screening around the area behind the hockey goals, where the danger of being struck by a puck is the greatest, as long as the screening is of sufficient extent to provide adequate protection for as many spectators as may reasonably be expected to desire to view the game from behind such screening'"); *Hurst v. East Coast Hockey League*, 637 S.E.2d 560, 562 (S.C. 2006) ("risk of being injured by a foul ball at a baseball game and the risk of being injured by a flying puck at a hockey game are similar risks").

On March 16, 2002, a 13-year-old girl was struck in the head by a deflected hockey puck while watching a National Hockey League (NHL) game between the Columbus Blue Jackets and the Calgary Flames in Columbus, Ohio. Two days later, she died from a blood clot caused when her head violently snapped back when hit by the puck, the first spectator to be fatally injured in the NHL's 85-year history. Phil Taylor, *Death of a Fan*, Sports Illustrated, April 1, 2002 at 58. Her parents received a $1.2 million settlement from the NHL and the arena in which the game was played. Following a common practice in European hockey rinks, the NHL subsequently required its member clubs to install protective netting approximately

30 feet in height and 120 feet in width behind the goals in their playing facilities. Was the NHL legally required to take this action? In *Nemarnik*, the court observed "if we were to impose a duty upon defendants to eliminate all risk of injury from flying pucks, we would force defendants to do either of two things: provide a floor to ceiling protective screen around the rink, thereby reducing the quality of everyone's view; or increase the price of tickets to cover the increased liability costs . . . we find neither alternative to be acceptable." 127 Cal. Rptr. 2d at 17. What other factors may have motivated the NHL's decision?

5. *Establishing Legal Duty of Care by Statute.* Some jurisdictions limit sports facility owner and operator liability by statute. For example, the Illinois Baseball Facility Liability Act requires a spectator injured by a baseball or bat to prove that the screen or backstop behind which he or she was sitting is defective (in a manner other than width or height) because of the facility owner or operator's negligence or that his or her injury was caused by willful or wanton conduct. 745 Ill. Comp. Stat. §38/10 (West 2016). Rejecting a challenge to the constitutionality of the Act, the Illinois court of appeals stated:

> We believe the sport of baseball does have unique characteristics that would reasonably prompt a legislature to enact limited liability legislation. . . . Foul balls traveling at high speeds are common at baseball games. The speed and frequency of foul balls distinguish baseball from most other spectator sports. In this respect, basketball and football spectators, for example, are not similarly situated.

Jasper v. Chi. Nat'l League Ball Club, Inc., 722 N.E.2d 731, 735 (Ill. Ct. App. 1999). See also *Sciarrotta v. Glob. Spectrum*, 944 A.2d 630 (N.J. 2008) (relying in part on the New Jersey Baseball Spectator Safety Act of 2006, the court, in a case involving injuries suffered by a spectator when a hockey puck caromed into the stands, held that the limited duty rule applies to all on-the-field activities, including practice and warm-up periods before a game has begun, and "does not encompass a separate duty to warn of the peril of objects leaving the field of play"). *Id.* at 632.

6. *Liability Waivers.* In *Edward C.*, assume the back of the plaintiffs' ticket contained a printed warning stating, "The holder of this ticket assumes all risk and danger incidental to the game of baseball . . . including specifically (but not exclusively) the danger of being injured by thrown bats, thrown or batted balls . . . and agrees that the participating clubs or their officials, agents and players are not liable for injury related from such causes." Should the court legally recognize and enforce a contractual modification of the defendants' tort duty?

PROBLEM 11-1

Bobby Baron has been baseball's reigning home run king over the past five years. At a game played two nights ago, Baron hit a home run that matched the most home runs ever hit by a major league ballplayer. Over the past week, attendance at baseball games in which Baron's team, the Quest, played has been tremendous given the anticipation that Baron might match and surpass the record.

The Quest home game on July 15 was a sell-out. In the fourth inning, Baron hit his record-shattering home run into the right outfield stands. Jimmy Hands attempted to catch the ball, but it hit him in the face and fell under his seat. As a result of being struck by the ball, Hands required extensive surgery to reconstruct his nose and repair an injury to his eye. To make matters worse for Hands, after the ball fell under his seat, another fan, Harry, violently pushed Hands out of his seat in order to retrieve the ball. As a result of being pushed, Hands suffered a broken arm and lacerations. In the ensuing melee caused by attempts to retrieve the ball, several other fans were injured.

Harry and several other fans who were involved in efforts to retrieve the ball consumed an inordinate amount of alcohol that they had purchased during the game from vendors at Quest Ballpark. The owners of Quest Ballpark had become increasingly concerned with improper fan behavior that stemmed, in part, from the consumption of alcohol. Last year, Quest Ballpark instituted a policy that forbids the sale of alcohol after the seventh inning, but placed no strict limits on the amount of alcohol consumed prior to the seventh inning.

Discuss who, if anyone, may be liable for the injuries suffered by Hands and the other fans. What additional facts might aid you in completing your analysis?

2.   Injury to Athletes

a.   Co-participant Liability

i.   Tort Liability

As you read these cases, consider the following questions: As a matter of policy, should the co-participant liability standard for injuries be the same for all sports? More specifically, should the liability standard be different based on the sport's level of competition (e.g., professional, intercollegiate, interscholastic, or youth sports), degree of organization and governance (e.g., intramural, pickup, or recreational sports), participants (adults or minors), and/or characterization as a contact or noncontact sport? Why or why not?

HACKBART v. CINCINNATI BENGALS, INC. (HACKBART I)
435 F. Supp. 352 (D. Colo. 1977)

MATSCH, Judge

The case arises as a result of an incident which occurred in the course of a professional football game played between the Denver Broncos and the Cincinnati Bengals, in Denver, Colorado, on September 16, 1973. . . .

The incident which gave rise to this lawsuit occurred near the end of the first half of the game at a time when the Denver team was leading by a score of 21 to 3. Dale Hackbart was playing a free safety position on the Broncos' defensive team and Charles Clark was playing fullback on the Bengals' offensive team. The Cincinnati team attempted a forward pass play during which Charles Clark ran into a corner of the north end zone as a prospective receiver. That took him into an area which was the defensive responsibility of Mr. Hackbart. The thrown pass was intercepted near the goal line by a Denver linebacker who then began to run the ball upfield. The interception reversed the offensive and defensive roles of the two teams. As a result of an attempt to block Charles Clark in the end zone, Dale Hackbart fell to the ground. He then turned and, with one knee on the ground and the other leg extended, watched the play continue upfield. Acting out of anger and frustration, but without a specific intent to injure, Charles Clark stepped forward and struck a blow with his right forearm to the back of the kneeling plaintiff's head with sufficient force to cause both players to fall forward to the ground. Both players arose and, without comment, went to their respective teams along the sidelines. They both returned to play during the second half of the game.

Because no official observed it, no foul was called on the disputed play and Dale Hackbart made no report of this incident to his coaches or to anyone else during the game. Mr. Hackbart experienced pain and soreness to the extent that he was unable to play golf as he had planned on the day after the game, he did not seek any medical attention and, although he continued to feel pain, he played on specialty team assignments for the Denver Broncos in games against the Chicago Bears and the San Francisco Forty-Niners on successive Sundays. The Denver Broncos then released Mr. Hackbart on waivers and he was not claimed by any other team. After losing his employment, Mr. Hackbart sought medical assistance, at which time it was discovered that he had a neck injury. When that information was given to the Denver Broncos Football Club, Mr. Hackbart received his full payment for the 1973 season pursuant to an injury clause in his contract.

The claim of the plaintiff in this case must be considered in the context of football as a commercial enterprise. The National Football League (NFL) is an organization formed for the purpose of promoting and fostering the business of its members, the owners of professional football "clubs" with franchises to operate in designated cities. . . .

A collective bargaining contract between that association and the National Football League Player Relations Association, as bargaining agent for the member clubs, was in effect during 1973. . . . There is no provision for disputes between players of different teams. . . .

Football is a contest for territory. . . . The most obvious characteristic of the game is that all of the players engage in violent physical behavior.

The rules of play which govern the method and style by which the NFL teams compete include limitations on the manner in which players may strike or otherwise physically contact opposing players. . . . Players were also subject to expulsion from the game and to monetary penalties imposed by the league commissioner. . . .

The violence of professional football is carefully orchestrated. Both offensive and defensive players must be extremely aggressive in their actions and they must play with a reckless abandonment of self-protective instincts. The coaches make studied and deliberate efforts to build the emotional levels of their players to what some call a "controlled rage."

The large and noisy crowds in attendance at the games contribute to the emotional levels of the players. Quick changes in the fortunes of the teams, the shock of violent collisions and the intensity of the competition make behavioral control extremely difficult, and it is not uncommon for players to "flare up" and begin fighting. The record made at this trial indicates that such incidents as that which gave rise to this action are not so unusual as to be unexpected in any NFL game.

The end product of all of the organization and effort involved in the professional football industry is an exhibition of highly developed individual skills in coordinated team competition for the benefit of large numbers of paying spectators, together with radio and television audiences. It is appropriate to infer that while some of those persons are attracted by the individual skills and precision performances of the teams, the appeal to others is the spectacle of savagery.

While a theory of intentional misconduct is barred by the applicable statute of limitations, the plaintiff contends that Charles Clark's foul was so far outside of the rules of play and accepted practices of professional football that it should be characterized as reckless misconduct. . . .

Alternatively, the plaintiff claims that his injury was at least the result of a negligent act by the defendant. The difference in these contentions is but a difference in degree. Both theories are dependent upon a definition of a duty to the plaintiff and an objective standard of conduct based upon the hypothetical reasonably prudent person. Thus, the question is what would a reasonably prudent professional football player be expected to do under the circumstances confronting Charles Clark in this incident?

Two coaches testified at the trial of this case. Paul Brown has had 40 years of experience at all levels of organized football, with 20 years of coaching professional football. Both Mr. Brown and Mr. Ralston emphasized that the coaching and instructing of professional football players did not include any training with respect to a responsibility or even any regard for the safety of opposing players. They both said that aggressiveness was the primary attribute which they sought in the selection of players. Both emphasized the importance of emotional preparation of the teams. Mr. Brown said that flare-up fighting often occurred, even in practice sessions of his teams.

It is wholly incongruous to talk about a professional football player's duty of care for the safety of opposing players when he has been trained and motivated to be heedless of injury to himself. The character of NFL competition negates any notion that the playing conduct can be circumscribed by any standard of reasonableness.

Both theories of liability are also subject to the recognized defenses of consent and assumption of the risk. Here the question is what would a professional football player in the plaintiff's circumstances reasonably expect to encounter in a professional contest?

All of the witnesses with playing or coaching experience in the NFL agreed that players are urged to avoid penalties. The emphasis, however, is on the unfavorable effects of the loss of yardage, not the safety of the players. It is undisputed that no game is without penalties and that players frequently lose control in surges of emotion.

The conflict in the testimony is the difference in the witnesses' opinions as to whether Mr. Clark's act of striking the plaintiff on the back of the head in reaction to anger and frustration can be considered as "a part of the game." Several former players denounced this incident and said that Mr. Clark's conduct could not be considered customary or acceptable.

It is noteworthy that while this incident was clearly shown on the Denver Broncos' defensive game films, which were routinely reviewed by the defensive players and coaching staff, none of them made it a matter of special attention or concern.

Upon all of the evidence, my finding is that the level of violence and the frequency of emotional outbursts in NFL football games are such that Dale Hackbart must have recognized and accepted the risk that he would be injured by such an act as that committed by the defendant Clark on September 16,

1973. Accordingly, the plaintiff must be held to have assumed the risk of such an occurrence. Therefore, even if the defendant breached a duty which he owed to the plaintiff, there can be no recovery because of assumption of the risk. . . .

While the foregoing findings of fact and conclusions of law are determinative of the claim made by Dale Hackbart against Charles Clark and his employer, this case raises the larger question of whether playing field action in the business of professional football should become a subject for the business of the courts. . . .

To this time professional football has been a self-regulated industry. The only protection which NFL contract players have beyond self-defense and real or threatened retaliation is that which is provided by the league rules and sanctions. It may well be true that what has been provided is inadequate and that these young athletes have been exploited and subjected to risks which should be unacceptable in our social order. . . .

Football has been presumed to be lawful and, indeed, professional football has received the implicit approval of government because these contests take place in arenas owned by local governments and the revenues are subject to taxation. Like coal mining and railroading, professional football is hazardous to the health and welfare of those who are employed as players.

What is the interest of the larger community in limiting the violence of professional football? That question concerns not only the protection of the participants, but also the effects of such violence on those who observe it. Can the courts answer this question? I think not. An ordinary citizen is entitled to protection according to the usages of the society in which he lives, and in the context of common community standards there can be no question but that Mr. Clark's blow here would generate civil liability. It would involve a criminal sanction if the requisite intent were present. The difference here is that this blow was delivered on the field of play during the course of action in a regularly scheduled professional football game. . . .

There is no discernible code of conduct for NFL players. The dictionary definition of a sportsman is one who abides by the rules of a contest and accepts victory or defeat graciously. Webster's Third New International Dictionary, p. 2206 (1971). That is not the prevalent attitude in professional football. There are no Athenian virtues in this form of athletics. The NFL has substituted the morality of the battlefield for that of the playing field, and the "restraints of civilization" have been left on the sidelines.

Mr. Justice Holmes' simple statement of the function of tort law ["The business of the law of torts is to fix the dividing line between those cases in which a man is liable for harm which he has done, and those in which he has not." Justice O.W. Holmes, The Common Law (1881)] and the evidentiary record now before me clearly reveal the density of the thicket in which the courts would become entangled if they undertook the task of allocation of fault in professional football games. The NFL rules of play are so legalistic in their statement and so difficult of application because of the speed and violence of the play that the differences between violations which could fairly be called deliberate, reckless or outrageous and those which are "fair play" would be so small and subjective as to be incapable of articulation. The question of causation would be extremely difficult in view of the frequency of forceful collisions. The volume of such litigation would be enormous and it is reasonable to expect that the court systems of the many states in which NFL games are played would develop differing and conflicting principles of law. It is highly unlikely that the NFL could continue to produce anything like the present games under such

multiple systems of overview by judges and juries. If there is to be any governmental involvement in this industry, it is a matter which can be best considered
by the legislative branch.

My conclusion that the civil courts cannot be expected to control the violence
in professional football is limited by the facts of the case before me. I have considered only a claim for an injury resulting from a blow, without weaponry, delivered emotionally without a specific intent to injure, in the course of regular play
in a league-approved game involving adult, contract players. Football as a commercial enterprise is something quite different from athletics as an extension of
the academic experience and what I have said here may have no applicability in
other areas of physical competition. . . .

HACKBART v. CINCINNATI BENGALS, INC. (HACKBART II)

601 F.2d 516 (10th Cir. 1979)

DOYLE, Circuit Judge.

The question in this case is whether in a regular season professional football game an injury which is inflicted by one professional football player on an
opposing player can give rise to liability in tort where the injury was inflicted by
the intentional striking of a blow during the game. . . .

The evidence at the trial uniformly supported the proposition that the intentional striking of a player in the head from the rear is not an accepted part
of either the playing rules or the general customs of the game of professional
football. . . .

[T]he district court's assumption was that Clark had inflicted an intentional
blow which would ordinarily generate civil liability and which might bring about
a criminal sanction as well, but that since it had occurred in the course of a
football game, it should not be subject to the restraints of the law; that if it were
it would place unreasonable impediments and restraints on the activity. The
judge also pointed out that courts are ill-suited to decide the different social
questions and to administer conflicts on what is much like a battlefield where
the restraints of civilization have been left on the sidelines. . . .

Plaintiff, of course, maintains that tort law applicable to the injury in this
case applies on the football field as well as in other places. On the other hand,
plaintiff does not rely on the theory of negligence being applicable. This is in
recognition of the fact that subjecting another to unreasonable risk of harm,
the essence of negligence, is inherent in the game of football, for admittedly it
is violent. . . .

[T]here are no principles of law which allow a court to rule out certain
tortious conduct by reason of general roughness of the game or difficulty of
administering it.

Indeed, the evidence shows that there are rules of the game which prohibit
the intentional striking of blows. Thus, Article 1, Item 1, Subsection C, provides
that: All players are prohibited from striking on the head, face or neck with the
heel, back or side of the hand, wrist, forearm, elbow or clasped hands.

Thus the very conduct which was present here is expressly prohibited by the
rule which is quoted above.

The general customs of football do not approve the intentional punching or
striking of others. That this is prohibited was supported by the testimony of all of

the witnesses. They testified that the intentional striking of a player in the face or from the rear is prohibited by the playing rules as well as the general customs of the game. Punching or hitting with the arms is prohibited. Undoubtedly these restraints are intended to establish reasonable boundaries so that one football player cannot intentionally inflict a serious injury on another. Therefore, the notion is not correct that all reason has been abandoned, whereby the only possible remedy for the person who has been the victim of an unlawful blow is retaliation. . . .

The Restatement of Torts Second, § 500, distinguishes between reckless and negligent misconduct. Reckless misconduct differs from negligence, according to the authors, in that negligence consists of mere inadvertence, lack of skillfulness or failure to take precautions; reckless misconduct, on the other hand, involves a choice or adoption of a course of action either with knowledge of the danger or with knowledge of facts which would disclose this danger to a reasonable man. Recklessness also differs in that it consists of intentionally doing an act with knowledge not only that it contains a risk of harm to others as does negligence, but that it actually involves a risk substantially greater in magnitude than is necessary in the case of negligence. The authors explain the difference, therefore, in the degree of risk by saying that the difference is so significant as to amount to a difference in kind.

Subsection (f) also distinguishes between reckless misconduct and intentional wrongdoing. To be reckless the *act* must have been intended by the actor. At the same time, the actor does not intend to cause the harm which results from it. It is enough that he realized, or from the facts should have realized, that there was a strong probability that harm would result even though he may hope or expect that this conduct will prove harmless. Nevertheless, existence of probability is different from substantial certainty which is an ingredient of intent to cause the harm which results from the act.

Therefore, recklessness exists where a person knows that the act is harmful but fails to realize that it will produce the extreme harm which it did produce. It is in this respect that recklessness and intentional conduct differ in degree.

In the case at bar the defendant Clark admittedly acted impulsively and in the heat of anger, and even though it could be said from the admitted facts that he intended the act, it could also be said that he did not intend to inflict serious injury which resulted from the blow which he struck.

In ruling that recklessness is the appropriate standard and that assault and battery is not the exclusive one, we are saying that these two liability concepts are not necessarily opposed one to the other. Rather, recklessness under § 500 of the Restatement might be regarded, for the purpose of analysis at least, a lesser included act.

Assault and battery, having originated in a common law writ, is narrower than recklessness in its scope. In essence, two definitions enter into it. The assault is an attempt coupled with the present ability to commit a violent harm against another. Battery is the unprivileged or unlawful touching of another. Assault and battery then call for an intent, as does recklessness. But in recklessness the intent is to do the act, but without an intent to cause the particular harm. It is enough if the actor knows that there is a strong probability that harm will result. Thus, the definition fits perfectly the fact situation here. Surely, then, no reason exists to compel appellant to employ the assault and battery standard which does not comfortably apply fully in preference to the standard which meets this fact situation. . . .

The cause is reversed and remanded for a new trial. . . .

SHIN v. AHN
165 P.3d 581 (Cal. 2007)

CORRIGAN, J.

In *Knight v. Jewett* (1992) 3 Cal. 4th 296, 11 Cal. Rptr. 2d 2, 834 P.2d 696 (*Knight*), we considered the duty of care that should govern the liability of sports participants. We recognized that careless conduct by co-participants is an inherent risk in many sports, and that holding participants liable for resulting injuries would discourage vigorous competition. Accordingly, those involved in a sporting activity do not have a duty to reduce the risk of harm that is inherent in the sport itself. They do, however, have a duty not to increase that inherent risk. Thus, sports participants have a limited duty of care to their co-participants, breached only if they intentionally injure them or "engage[] in conduct that is so reckless as to be totally outside the range of the ordinary activity involved in the sport." (*Knight*, at p. 320, 11 Cal. Rptr. 2d 2, 834 P.2d 696, fn. omitted.) This application of the *primary assumption of risk doctrine* recognizes that by choosing to participate, individuals assume that level of risk inherent in the sport.

This case represents the next generation of our *Knight* jurisprudence. *Knight* involved touch football. We expressly left open the question whether the primary assumption of risk doctrine should apply to noncontact sports, such as golf. We address that question here. We hold that the primary assumption of risk doctrine does apply to golf and that being struck by a carelessly hit ball is an inherent risk of the sport. As we explain, whether defendant breached the limited duty of care he owed other golfers by engaging in conduct that was "so reckless as to be totally outside the range of the ordinary activity involved in [golf]" depends on resolution of disputed material facts. Thus, defendant's summary judgment motion was properly denied. . . .

I.   FACTUAL AND PROCEDURAL BACKGROUND

Plaintiff and defendant were playing golf with Jeffrey Frost at the Rancho Park Golf Course in Los Angeles. Defendant, the first of the threesome to complete the 12th hole, went to the 13th tee box. Plaintiff and Frost then finished putting and followed him. Frost took the cart path to the 13th tee box, which placed him perpendicular to, or slightly behind, defendant and to his right. Plaintiff took a shortcut, which placed him in front of defendant and to his left. Plaintiff stopped there to get a bottle of water out of his golf bag and to check his cell phone for messages. He did so even though he knew (1) that he was in front of the tee box, (2) that defendant was preparing to tee off, and (3) that he should stand behind a player who was teeing off. Defendant inadvertently "pulled" his tee shot to the left, hitting plaintiff in the temple. When struck, plaintiff was 25 to 35 feet from defendant, at a 40- to 45-degree angle from the intended path of the ball. Plaintiff claims his injuries were "disabling, serious, and permanent. . . ."

In his declaration, plaintiff's expert stated that golf etiquette requires that a player ensure that no one is in a position to be struck when he or she hits the ball. (See USGA, The Rules of Golf, *supra,* § 1, Etiquette, p. 1.) If defendant knew plaintiff was in jeopardy, he should have shouted a warning before teeing off. (*Ibid.*)

When plaintiff sued for negligence, defendant sought summary judgment, relying on the primary assumption of risk doctrine. The trial court initially agreed that the doctrine applied, found no triable issue of material fact, and granted summary judgment. However, the trial court later reversed itself, concluding that triable issues remained.

The Court of Appeal affirmed, holding that the primary assumption of risk doctrine did not apply. . . . The Court of Appeal applied general negligence principles and concluded that defendant breached a general duty of care owed to a member of his own playing group by failing to ascertain where he was before teeing off.

We reject the duty analysis of the Court of Appeal and conclude that the primary assumption of risk doctrine regulates the duty a golfer owes both to playing partners and to other golfers on the course. Defendant's summary judgment motion was, however, properly denied. Material questions of fact remain bearing on whether defendant breached his limited duty of care to plaintiff by engaging in conduct that was so reckless as to be totally outside the range of the ordinary activity involved in golf.

II. DISCUSSION

Generally, one owes a duty of ordinary care not to cause an unreasonable risk of harm to others. The existence of a duty is not an immutable fact of nature, but rather an expression of policy considerations providing legal protection. Thus, the existence and scope of a defendant's duty is a question for the court's resolution. When a sports participant is injured, the considerations of policy and duty necessarily become intertwined with the question of whether the injured person can be said to have assumed the risk.

California's abandonment of the doctrine of contributory negligence in favor of comparative negligence led this court to revisit the assumption of risk doctrine in *Knight, supra*, 3 Cal. 4th 296, 11 Cal. Rptr. 2d 2, 834 P.2d 696.

A. KNIGHT AND ITS PROGENY IN THIS COURT

In *Knight, supra*, the plurality noted that there are two types of assumption of risk: primary and secondary. Under the primary assumption of risk doctrine, the defendant owes *no duty* to protect a plaintiff from particular harms arising from ordinary, or simple negligence. In a sports context, the doctrine bars liability because the plaintiff is said to have assumed the particular risks inherent in a sport by choosing to participate. Thus, "a court need not ask what risks a particular plaintiff subjectively knew of and chose to encounter, but instead must evaluate the fundamental nature of the sport and the defendant's role in or relationship to that sport in order to determine whether the defendant owes a duty to protect a plaintiff from the particular risk of harm." ([*Knight, supra*, 3 Cal. 4th] at 313, 315–317.) . . .

The *Knight* court used baseball as an example. In baseball, a batter is not supposed to carelessly throw the bat after getting a hit and starting to run to first base. However, the primary assumption of risk doctrine recognizes that vigorous bat deployment is an integral part of the sport and a risk players assume when they choose to participate. Especially in the heat of competition, and in an effort to get to first base quickly, a batter may be careless in freeing himself or herself from the bat's encumbrance. Thus, under the doctrine, a batter does not have a duty to another player to avoid carelessly throwing the bat after getting a hit.

In *Knight, supra*, 3 Cal. 4th 296, 11 Cal. Rptr. 2d 2, 834 P.2d 696, we stressed the chilling effect that would flow from imposing liability on touch football players for ordinary careless conduct. "[E]ven when a participant's conduct violates a rule of the game and may subject the violator to internal sanctions prescribed by the sport itself, imposition of legal liability for such conduct might well alter fundamentally the nature of the sport by deterring participants from vigorously engaging in activity. . . ." (*Id.* at pp. 318-319, 11 Cal. Rptr. 2d 2, 834 P.2d 696, italics omitted.) Accordingly, we concluded that co-participants' limited duty of care is to refrain from intentionally injuring one another or engaging in conduct that is "so reckless as to be totally outside the range of the ordinary activity involved in the sport." (*Id.* at p. 320, 11 Cal. Rptr. 2d 2, 834 P.2d 696, fn. omitted.)

A majority of this court has since extended *Knight's* application of the primary assumption of risk doctrine to other sports. (Citations omitted.) . . .

Cheong v. Antablin, 946 P.2d 817 (1997) involved skiing. One skier sued another for injuries he suffered when the other skier turned and unintentionally ran into him. We concluded that, "under the applicable common law principles, a skier owes a duty to fellow skiers not to injure them intentionally or to act recklessly, but a skier may not sue another for simple negligence." Because there was no evidence that the defendant acted recklessly or intentionally injured the plaintiff, we concluded that the defendant's motion for summary judgment was properly granted.

Avila v. Citrus Community College Dist., 38 Cal. 4th 148, 41 Cal. Rptr. 3d 299, 131 P.3d 383, involved intercollegiate baseball. A pitcher on the Rio Hondo Community College team (Rio Hondo) hit a batter on the Citrus Community College team (Citrus). The next inning the Citrus pitcher allegedly retaliated by hitting a Rio Hondo batter with a "beanball." The Rio Hondo player sued the Citrus Community College District for negligence. We held the suit was barred by the primary assumption of risk doctrine. It is against the rules of baseball to intentionally throw at a batter. Nevertheless, "being intentionally thrown at is a fundamental part and inherent risk of the sport of baseball. It is not the function of tort law to police such conduct."

B. COURT OF APPEAL CASES APPLYING KNIGHT TO GOLF

In *Knight, supra*, 3 Cal. 4th 296, 11 Cal. Rptr. 2d 2, 834 P.2d 696, we expressly left open the question whether the primary assumption of risk doctrine should be applied to sports like golf. (*Id.* at p. 320, fn. 7, 11 Cal. Rptr. 2d 2, 834 P.2d 696.) . . .

D. SISTER-STATE DECISIONS

The first court to apply the reckless disregard or intentional conduct standard to golf appears to have been the Supreme Court of Ohio in *Thompson v. McNeill* (1990) 53 Ohio St. 3d 102, 559 N.E.2d 705 (*Thompson*). (*Schick v. Ferolito* (2001) 167 N.J. 7, 767 A.2d 962, 966 (*Schick*).) In *Thompson*, at page 706, the defendant "shanked" a shot. The plaintiff, a member of the defendant's foursome, was standing at a 90-degree angle to the intended path of a ball that struck her. The Ohio Supreme Court held that "only injuries caused by intentional conduct, or in some instances reckless misconduct, may give rise to a cause of action [by one golfer against another]." (*Thompson*, at p. 706.)

Applying that standard, the *Thompson* court affirmed a grant of summary judgment in the defendant's favor. "Shanking the ball is a foreseeable and not uncommon occurrence in the game of golf. The same is true of hooking, slicing, pushing, or pulling a golf shot. We would stress that '[i]t is well known that not every shot played by a golfer goes to the point where he intends it to go. If such were the case, every player would be perfect and the whole pleasure of the sport would be lost. It is common knowledge, at least among players, that many bad shots must result although every stroke is delivered with the best possible intention and without any negligence whatsoever.'" *Benjamin v. Nernberg* (1931), 102 Pa.Super. 471, 475-476, 157 A. 10, 11. (*Thompson, supra,* 559 N.E.2d at p. 709.)

In *Schick, supra,* 167 N.J. 7, 767 A.2d 962, the New Jersey Supreme Court followed *Thompson, supra,* 53 Ohio St. 3d 102, 559 N.E.2d 705. In *Schick,* at page 963 the defendant hit a second tee shot, or "mulligan," striking a member of his foursome. The New Jersey Supreme Court applied the reckless or intentional misconduct standard. "We perceive no persuasive reason to apply an artificial distinction between 'contact' and 'noncontact' sports. In fact, only a minority of courts do so. [Citations.]" (*Id.* at p. 968.) The New Jersey Supreme Court went on to hold that the trial court erred in granting the defendant's motion for summary judgment because the facts would have supported a verdict of recklessness. The court pointed to "defendant's own testimony that he perceived plaintiff to be in the 'line of fire' and that he waved plaintiff off in an effort to induce plaintiff to move from his location." (*Id.* at p. 970.) Plaintiff did not move. The defendant did not wait for him to do so and hit his shot anyway. The court held, "[t]hat scenario presents a set of facts that a jury could find constitutes reckless conduct because it may reflect a conscious choice of a course of action with knowledge or reason to know that the action will create serious danger to others." (*Ibid.*) . . .

In *Yoneda v. Tom* (2006) 110 Hawai'i 367, 133 P.3d 796, the plaintiff was struck by a ball hit by a golfer in another group. The plaintiff sued the other golfer as well as the owner and operator of the golf course. The Hawaii Supreme Court concluded that the primary assumption of risk doctrine applied to define the defendant golfer's duty, relying in part on *Knight, supra,* 3 Cal. 4th 296, 11 Cal. Rptr. 2d 2, 834 P.2d 696. . . . Upholding a grant of summary judgment for the defendant golfer, the Hawaii Supreme Court ruled that no one could have reasonably anticipated that a person in the plaintiff's location was in danger of being struck by the defendant's shot. (*Id.* at p. 809.) . . .

E.   APPLICATION OF THE PRIMARY ASSUMPTION OF RISK DOCTRINE

The lesson to be drawn from *Knight* and its progeny, as well as the weight of authority in sister states, is that the primary assumption of risk doctrine should be applied to golf. Thus, we hold that golfers have a limited duty of care to other players, breached only if they intentionally injure them or engage in conduct that is "so reckless as to be totally outside the range of the ordinary activity involved in the sport."

The Court of Appeal relied too heavily on one of golf's rules of etiquette involving safety. Golf's first rule of etiquette provides that "[p]layers should ensure that no one is standing close by or in a position to be hit by the club, the ball or any stones, pebbles, twigs or the like when they make a *stroke* or practice swing." (USGA, The Rules of Golf, *supra,* § 1, Etiquette, p. 1.) The Court of Appeal concluded that "[t]his duty included the duty to ascertain Shin's whereabouts before hitting the ball."

Rules of etiquette govern socially acceptable behavior. The sanction for a violation of a rule of etiquette is social disapproval, not legal liability. This is true, generally, of the violation of the rules of a game. "The cases have recognized that, [in sports like football or baseball], even when a participant's conduct violates a rule of the game and may subject the violator to internal sanctions prescribed by the sport itself, imposition of legal liability for such conduct might well alter fundamentally the nature of the sport by deterring participants from vigorously engaging in activity that falls close to, but on the permissible side of, a prescribed rule. . . ."

G.   DEFENDANT'S SUMMARY JUDGMENT MOTION

Here, summary judgment was properly denied because there are material questions of fact to be adjudicated.

In determining whether defendant acted recklessly, the trier of fact will have to consider both the nature of the game and the totality of circumstances surrounding the shot. In making a golf shot the player focuses on the ball, unlike other sports in which a player's focus is divided between the ball and other players. That is not to say that a golfer may ignore other players before making a shot. Ordinarily, a golfer should not make a shot without checking to see whether others are reasonably likely to be struck. Once having addressed the ball, a golfer is not required to break his or her concentration by checking the field again. Nor must a golfer conduct a headcount of the other players in the group before making a shot.

Many factors will bear on whether a golfer's conduct was reasonable, negligent, or reckless. Relevant circumstances may include the golfer's skill level; whether topographical undulations, trees, or other impediments obscure his view; what steps he took to determine whether anyone was within range; and the distance and angle between a plaintiff and defendant.

Here plaintiff testified at his deposition that he and defendant made eye contact "as I was cutting up the hill." He did not make clear, however, how far he had proceeded up the hill, how far away he was from the defendant, or whether he was stationary when the eye contact occurred. At his deposition, defendant said he looked to see if the area "directly ahead" of him was clear. It is not apparent just how broad or limited that area was. This record is simply too sparse to support a finding, as a matter of law, that defendant did, or did not, act recklessly. This will be a question the jury will ultimately resolve based on a more complete examination of the facts. We do not suggest that cases like this can never be resolved on summary judgment, only that this record is insufficient to do so. . . .

The judgment of the Court of Appeal is affirmed. The case is remanded with directions that litigation should continue under the primary assumption of risk doctrine.

NOTES AND QUESTIONS

1. *Professional Sports.* Is there a sufficient public interest in using the tort system to regulate violence in a "commercial enterprise" such as professional football? Or do you agree with Judge Matsch's view in *Hackbart I* that "[t]he NFL has substituted the morality of the battlefield for that of the playing field, and the 'restraints of civilization' have been left on the sidelines"?

Does an internal disciplinary system administered by the sport's commissioner or governing body combined with the availability of contractual benefits and workers' compensation for injuries eliminate the need to provide tort recovery for player injuries? For professional team sports, would an arbitration process established by the collective bargaining process be a better alternative than judicial resolution? See Benjamin C. Thompson, *Personal Foul . . . 15 Years in Jail: Sports' Problem with Excessive Violence and the Severe Punishment Solution*, 76 UMKC L. Rev. 769, 775 (2008) (providing illustrations of excessive violence in sports).

Consistent with *Hackbart II*, courts generally require professional athletes to prove intentional or reckless conduct by a co-participant in order to recover for playing field injuries. *Falcaro v. Am. Skating Ctr., LLC*, 90 N.Y.S.3d 95 (N.Y. App. Div. 2018); *McKichan v. St. Louis Hockey Club, L.P.*, 967 S.W.2d 209 (Mo. Ct. App. 1998); *Turcotte v. Fell*, 502 N.E.2d 964 (N.Y. 1986). Courts are reluctant to recognize a cause of action for negligence.

> Manifestly a professional athlete is more aware of the dangers of the activity, and presumably more willing to accept them in exchange for a salary, than is an amateur. . . .
>
> Plaintiff does not claim that Fell intentionally or recklessly bumped him, he claims only that as a result of carelessness, Fell failed to control his mount as the horses raced for the lead and a preferred position on the track. While a participant's "consent" to join in a sporting activity is not a waiver of all rules infractions, nonetheless a professional clearly understands the usual incidents of competition resulting from carelessness, particularly those which result from the customarily accepted method of playing the sport, and accepts them. They are within the known, apparent and foreseeable dangers of the sport and not actionable and thus plaintiffs' complaint against Fell was properly dismissed.

Id. at 969-70. See Timothy Davis, *Tort Liability of Coaches for Injuries to Professional Athletes: Overcoming Policy and Doctrinal Barriers*, 76 UMKC L. Rev. 571, 579-80 (2008) (discussing liability of co-participants engaged in professional sports).

2. *General Co-Participant Liability Standard.* Like California, most jurisdictions permit recovery in sports injury cases between co-participants only for intentional or reckless conduct regardless of the level of competition, age or experience of the participants, or organizational structure of the sport. A minority of courts apply a negligence standard that is premised on the duty of reasonable care that one person owes to guard against foreseeable injuries to others. After the Wisconsin Supreme Court in *Lestina v. West Bend Mutual Insurance Co.*, 501 N.W.2d 28, 33 (Wis. 1993), held that "the negligence standard, properly understood and applied is suitable for cases involving recreational team contact sports," the state legislature enacted a statute establishing liability "only if the participant who caused the injury acted recklessly or with intent to cause injury" in a "recreational activity that includes physical contact between persons in a sport involving amateur teams" or "professional teams in a professional league." Wisc. Stat. Ann. §895.525(4m)(a) and (b).

As reflected by *Shin*, the trend is to abandon the contact versus noncontact sport distinction in determining the appropriate co-participant liability standard and to focus on whether the injury-causing risk is inherent to the sporting activity. In *Shin*, the court relied on an Ohio Supreme Court decision wherein the court explained:

> [T]here are different duties and risks appropriate to different sports, but the contact-non-contact distinction does not sufficiently take into account that we are dealing with a spectrum of duties and risks rather than an either-or distinction. Is golf a contact sport? Obviously, a golfer accepts the risk of coming in contact with wayward golf shots on the links, so golf is more dangerous than table tennis, for instance, but certainly not as dangerous as kickboxing. Analyzing liability for injuries inflicted in sports in terms of a continuum along which the standard of care rises as the inherent danger of the sport falls is more useful than distinguishing sports by applying a black-and-white distinction between contact and non-contact sports.

Thompson v. McNeill, 559 N.E.2d 705, 709 (Ohio 1990); see *Karas v. Strevell*, 884 N.E. 2d 122, 134 (Ill. 2008) (without expressly rejecting contact sports distinction, suggesting the focus should be on whether the defendant engaged in conduct "totally outside the range of the ordinary activity involved in the sport"); but see *Ludman v. Davenport Assumption Sch.*, 895 N.W.2d 902, 911 (Iowa 2017) (recognizing the contact-sport exception in cases involving co-participant liability but refusing to extend it to cases involving liability of premises owner); *Allison v. United States*, 927 F. Supp. 2d 550 (C.D. Ill. 2013) (adopting and applying the contact versus noncontact sport distinction). See generally John J. Kircher, *Golf and Torts: An Interesting Twosome*, 12 Marq. Sports L. Rev. 347 (2001) (discussing the applicable standard of care for co-participant liability in golf). Does the recklessness standard provide a sufficient degree of injury protection to participants in non-contact sports such as golf?

3. *Relationship Between Plaintiff's Assumption of Inherent Risks of Injury and Defendant's Legal Duty of Care.* Prior to the widespread adoption of comparative fault principles, the focus was on the plaintiff's subjective awareness of the inherent risks of injury from voluntarily participating in a sporting event, which was an affirmative defense barring a negligence action. In most jurisdictions, as summarized by the *Shin* court, the focus now is on the nature of the defendant's legal duty to protect a co-participant from injury during competition, which is part of the plaintiff's prima facie case. One legal scholar articulates this distinction and explains:

> Primary assumption of the risk focuses not on whether the plaintiff voluntarily assumed a known risk, but on the question of duty. Did the defendant possess a duty to protect the plaintiff from the risk of harm resulting in injury. . . . If the risk causing the injury is an inherent part of the activity, the defendant owed no duty to the plaintiff, and there is no liability.

Timothy Davis, *Avila v. Citrus Community College District: Shaping the Contours of Immunity and Primary Assumption of the Risk*, 17 Marq. Sports L. Rev. 259, 270 (2006).

4. *Application of Co-Participant Liability Standard.* One of the significant differences between the application of the intentional/recklessness and negligence standards is that unreasonably rough play and/or the mere violation of a sport's rules to protect the health and safety of participating athletes (e.g., no touching the face mask in football) without more is insufficient to establish liability under the intentional/recklessness standard, although

such conduct may create a fact question regarding negligence liability. As the Illinois Supreme Court noted:

> [A] majority of courts have concluded that "rules violations are inherent and anticipated aspects of sports contests" and, thus, insufficient to establish sports liability by themselves. [Davis, *supra* at 274]. . . . In games . . ., it is reasonable to assume that the competitive spirit of the participants will result in some rules violations and injuries. That is why there are penalty boxes, foul shots, free kicks, and yellow cards. (citations omitted).
>
> Policy reasons also justify the holding that rules violations, by themselves, are insufficient to impose liability in a contact sport: "Even when a participant's conduct violates a rule of the game and may subject the violator to internal sanctions prescribed by the sport itself, imposition of *legal liability* for such conduct might well alter fundamentally the nature of the sport by deterring participants from vigorously engaging in activity that falls close to but on the permissible side of, a prescribed rule." (Emphasis in original).

Karas v. Strevell, 884 N.E. 2d 122, 133-34 (Ill. 2008).

5. *Premises Liability to Athlete Participants.* In June 2018, a California jury ordered the Los Angeles Rams to pay former NFL running back, Reggie Bush, $12.5 million in damages ($4.95 million in compensatory damages and $7.5 million in punitive damages) for injuries he suffered when he slipped on concrete after he ran out of bounds on a punt return. In his lawsuit, Bush alleged that the Rams permitted a "dangerous condition to exist at the Edward Jones Dome" in St. Louis, the stadium at which the Rams played before relocating the team to Los Angeles. A week before Bush suffered his season-ending injuries, Cleveland Browns quarterback, John McCown, suffered an injury on the same concrete slab. See *DeLong v. R.I. Sports-Center, Inc.*, 182 A.3d 1129, 1134-35 (R.I. 2018) (articulating the following standard for determining if a plaintiff has established a prima facie case of premises liability: (1) the existence of a dangerous or defective condition on the defendants' premises; (2) defendants' notice of that condition for a sufficient period of time; and (3) a causal link between that condition and the plaintiff's injury); *O'Toole ex rel. O'Toole v. Long Island Junior Soccer League, Inc.*, 78 N.Y.S.3d 368, 368 (N.Y. App. Div. 2018) (in holding that primary assumption of risk warranted dismissal of the claim of an experienced youth soccer player injured when his cleat became stuck in a drainage grate that surrounded an athletic field, the court states primary assumption of " 'extends to those risks associated with the construction of the playing field and any open and obvious condition thereon.' ").

PROBLEM 11-2

Consider whether any of the following conduct should give rise to tort liability:

a. A professional boxer bites his opponent's ear during a bout and is disqualified by the referee.
b. An NHL player strikes an opposing player in the head with his fist during a fight and renders him unconscious.
c. A college hockey player breaks an opponent's nose during a fight and is given a three-game suspension for violating league rules prohibiting any fighting.

PROBLEM 11-3

Lisa and Amy were teammates on their college's swim team. During a mandatory weight training session, Lisa was performing steps on a platform when she lost her balance and dropped the weight bar containing two five-kilogram plates. The bar and weights struck Amy's head resulting in serious injury; Amy was three feet away doing pushups when she was struck. Prior to the incident, the swimmers' coach had instructed his athletes to drop weight bars if they were too heavy or caused a swimmer to lose her balance.

Amy has sued Lisa seeking to recover tort damages for the injuries she suffered as a result of being struck in the head by the weights. Is Amy likely to recover against Lisa?

ii.   Criminal Liability

In *People v. Fitzsimmons*, 34 N.Y.S. 1102, 1109 (N.Y. 1895), the court instructed the jury as follows in a case involving the prosecution of a professional boxer for a blow that killed his opponent during a sparring exhibition:

> The public has an interest in the personal safety of its citizens, and is injured where the safety of any individual is threatened, whether by himself or another. A game which involves a physical struggle may be a commendable and manly sport, or it may be an illegal contest. This depends upon whether it is a game which endangers life. Thus, in the prosecution for a death which was caused accidentally in playing the game of football, it was left to the jury to say whether the game was dangerous; for, if so, consent on the part of the players to submit to what the game had in store for them would not protect a player from prosecution.
>
> In other words, gentlemen, nine men, or whatever constitutes a team of football, cannot lawfully engage in a contention upon the green with the idea that the result may terminate in the death or serious injury of one-half of them; but, if the rules of the game and the practices of the game are reasonable, are consented to by all engaged, are not likely to induce serious injury, or to end life, if then, as a result of the game, an accident happens, it is excusable homicide.
>
> No rules or practice of any game whatever can make that lawful which is unlawful by the law of the land, and the law of the land says you shall not do that which is likely to cause the death of another.

The jury acquitted the defendant of manslaughter.

The following cases provide a modern view of criminal liability for injuries that occur on the athletic playing field. Consider whether the law has changed or remained the same since *Fitzsimmons*.

PEOPLE v. SCHACKER

670 N.Y.S.2d 308 (N.Y. Dist. Ct. 1998)

DONOHUE, Judge.

The defendant moved to dismiss the misdemeanor information in the interest of justice pursuant to CPL 170.40. . . .

The defendant is charged with Assault in the Third Degree in violation of Penal Law 120.00.1. The factual portion of the information reads as follows:

> [A]t the Superior Ice Rink . . . the defendant Robert Schacker during an ice hockey game and after a play was over and the whistle had blown, did come up behind Andrew Morenberg who was standing near the goal net and did strike him on the back of the neck and caused him to strike his head on the crossbar of the net, causing him to sustain a concussion, headaches, blurred vision, and memory loss. Injuries had been treated at St. John's Hospital, Smithtown.

Both an X-ray and a CAT scan showed no damage. The final diagnosis was "Contusion Forehead." Thus the medical records show only minor injuries.

Since the defendant had pled "not guilty," the people are required to prove that the defendant possessed the conscious intent to cause physical injury to the complainant. The fact that the act occurred in the course of a sporting event is a defense that tends to deny that the requisite intent was present.

As Chief Judge Benjamin Cardozo said in *Murphy v. Steeplechase Amusement Co.*, 250 N.Y. 479, 482-483, 166 N.E. 173: "One who takes part in such a sport accepts the dangers that inhere in it so far as they are obvious and necessary, just as a fencer accepts the risk of a thrust by his antagonist or a spectator at a ball game the chance of contact with the ball. A different case would be here if the dangers inherent in the sport were obscure or unobserved or so serious as to justify the belief that precautions of some kind must have been taken to avert them." See DeSantis, *Assumption of Risk Doctrine Is Alive and Well*, NYLJ, Dec. 2, 1997, at 1, col. 1. Persons engaged in athletic competition are generally held to have legally assumed the risk of injuries which are known, apparent and reasonably foreseeable consequences of participation. Hockey players assume the risk of injury by voluntarily participating in a hockey game at an ice rink.

This tort rule states a policy "intended to facilitate free and vigorous participation in athletic activities." *Benitez v. New York City Bd. of Educ.*, 73 N.Y.S. 2d 650, 657, 543 N.Y.S.2d 29, 541 N.E.2d 29. This policy would be severely undermined if the usual criminal standards were applied to athletic competition, especially ice hockey. If cross checking, tripping and punching were criminal acts, the game of hockey could not continue in its present form.

The complainant does not assume the risk of reckless or intentional conduct. However, it must be recognized that athletic competition includes intentional conduct that has the appearance of criminal acts. In fact, in many sporting events, physical injuries are caused by contact with other players. However, the players are "legally deemed to have accepted personal responsibility for" the risks inherent in the nature of sport. This includes intentional acts which result in personal injury. Thus, in order to allege a criminal act which occurred in a hockey game, the factual portion of the information must allege acts that show that the intent was to inflict physical injury which was unrelated to the athletic competition. Although play may have terminated, the information herein does not show that the physical contact had no connection with the competition. Furthermore, the injuries must be so severe as to be unacceptable in normal competition, requiring a change in the nature of the game. That type of injury is not present in this case. Firstly, the physical injury resulted from hitting the net, not from direct contact with the defendant. Secondly, the hospital records do not indicate severe trauma to the complainant.

The idea that a hockey player should be prosecuted runs afoul of the policy to encourage free and fierce competition in athletic events. The People argued at the hearing that this was a non-checking hockey league. While the rules of the league may prohibit certain conduct, thereby reducing the potential injuries, nevertheless, the participant continues to assume the risk of a strenuous and competitive athletic endeavor. The normal conduct in a hockey game cannot be the standard for criminal activity under the Penal Law, nor can the Penal Law be imposed on a hockey game without running afoul of the policy of encouraging athletic competition.

For the foregoing reasons, the interest of justice requires a dismissal of this charge pursuant to CPL 170.40.

REGINA v. McSORLEY

2000 British Columbia Provincial Ct. 0116 (Criminal Div. 2000)

KITCHEN, Judge.

[Editors' note: The Vancouver Canucks and the Boston Bruins were both struggling to make the playoffs. Early during the game's first period, Marty McSorley and Donald Brashear engaged in a fight, consisting mainly of clutching and grappling while blows were exchanged. Brashear was much more successful at this than McSorley, delivering several heavy lefts to the side and top of McSorley's head but with surprisingly little effect. The fight ended with Brashear apparently delivering a heavy body blow and wrenching McSorley to the ice surface. McSorley did react to this; it is clear he was in considerable pain at this time. He promptly came to his feet after the linesmen intervened and skated off to the penalty box, showing no adverse effects from the encounter. Brashear, for his part, skated past the Boston bench "dusting off" his hands, suggesting he had made short work of McSorley. This was obviously intended to upset the Boston players.

At the midpoint of the first period, McSorley again attempted to fight with Brashear. McSorley approached Brashear from behind and cross-checked him to the ice. As Brashear was coming to his feet, helmet off, McSorley used his glove to swat Brashear about the head several times. Brashear failed to respond to this and attempted to skate away. The referee gave McSorley three penalties for this—back-to-back two-minute minors for cross-checking and roughing and a ten-minute major for inciting. Shortly afterward, Brashear himself was penalized for interfering with the Boston goalie during play.

From the Brashear penalty in the middle of the first period until the middle of the third period, the game had settled down, and play between the two teams had evened out. During the third period, Brashear was making a play to come from the corner to the front of the Boston net. A Bruin slashed Brashear to prevent this and was given a penalty. During the stoppage in play, Brashear returned to the Vancouver bench, performing what witnesses described as a Hulk Hogan pose for the benefit of the Boston bench. Once again this was an obvious attempt to antagonize the opposing players, and it was effective. Boston complained to the referee, but no action was taken; it was determined that the Boston players had been mocking him at the same time.

With 20 seconds left in the game, which the Canucks were certain to win, McSorley was sent onto the ice by the Bruins coach to regain Boston pride by challenging Brashear to fight again. McSorley unsuccessfully tried to do so. With only three seconds left to play, McSorley, while skating up from behind him, struck Brashear in the head with his stick, bringing it around with his hands together on a horizontal plane like a baseball bat swing. As he was struck on the side of the head, Brashear's helmet was lifted out of position and his shoulder shrugged upward, an apparent reflex reaction to the blow of the stick. The blow was of significant force and caused Brashear to fall to the ice and strike his head. As he collapsed to the ice, he had a grand mal seizure before recovering consciousness. Brashear suffered a grade three concussion and could not continue with physical activity for another month. See https://www.youtube.com/watch?v=eTOfsoJAij4 to view the incident giving rise to Marty McSorley's prosecution.]

This is my decision on the charge against Marty McSorley that he assaulted Donald Brashear with his hockey stick during a hockey game on February 21, 2000. . . .

Some may view the matter as a trial of the game of hockey itself. If that is the expectation, my decision will be a disappointment. My only concern is whether Marty McSorley is guilty of the specific charge alleged against him. . . .

In the context of this case, it is especially important for the public to understand how these proceedings were initiated. The question has been asked, "Why are the courts bringing these proceedings?" The answer of course is that the courts had no part in laying the charge. Judges have little or no control over intake into the justice system. Crown Counsel, in their discretion to prosecute, decide which complaints will result in criminal charges. . . .

There are many groups that claim authority to discipline their members. Some are statutory, such as law societies and judicial councils, and some exist by virtue of private contractual arrangements such as in the case of the National Hockey League. Even where the disciplinary body is statutory, its status is often very controversial. There have been many cases before police discipline tribunals and medical licensing authorities where the public has been suspicious of the process, fearing that those involved are getting special treatment or that the truth is being concealed. In my view, there should be a heavy onus on those purporting to pre-empt the normal criminal process, particularly where it is a private organization such as a group of hockey owners. Statutory bodies must act in the public interest; businessmen have no such obligation. . . .

Obviously, the object of the game is to put the puck in the net—the opposing net. Many of the written rules of the game deal with the legitimate means by which that may be done. Many other written rules deal with the consequences that will follow if the rules are not obeyed. All of these rules are codified in the NHL Official Rules, a copy of which is an exhibit in these proceedings.

But those written rules are only part of the picture. . . . [T]here is an unwritten code of conduct agreed to by the players and the officials. This amalgam of written rules and the unwritten code leads to composite rules, such as the following. It is a legitimate game strategy to slash another player, but if done with sufficient force, and if the referee sees it, then the offender's team plays one player short for two minutes. It is a legitimate game strategy to fight another consenting player, but the offenders are kept off the ice for a period of time determined by the referee. . . .

So the rules of the NHL game of hockey consist of the written rules in the rulebook, a co-existing unwritten code of conduct impliedly agreed to by the players and officials, and guidelines laid down by the officials from game to game. It is within this somewhat indefinite framework that players must play the game. . . .

It is the position of the Crown that this body of evidence permits only two possibilities—that McSorley deliberately struck Brashear to the head without

Brashear's consent, or that he recklessly struck him to the head, not necessarily aiming for the head directly. Recklessness in this case may be likened to willful blindness—ignoring a known risk. . . .

If the blow to the head was intentional, it is common ground that it was an assault. Brashear himself said in evidence that he did not consent to being struck in that manner. The other witnesses agreed that stick blows to the head were not permitted in either the written rules, or the unwritten code . . . players in the NHL would not accept a blow such as that as part of the game. . . .

If the slash was intended for the shoulder, delivered with the intention of starting a fight, my conclusion would be that it was within the common practices and norms of the game. . . .

I conclude that the following occurred.

McSorley had fought Brashear and he had been briefly hurt. He was nevertheless prepared to fight him again, but Brashear frustrated his attempts to do so. Brashear taunted the Boston players and was seen to be responsible for taking the Boston goalie out of the game. This was all fairly routine for McSorley. He was credible when he said he was prepared to let things wind down at the end of the game.

Then Laperriere effectively directed him to get Brashear with about twenty seconds left. This was really too little time to fight but he felt himself pressured to do something. He found himself gliding in from centre ice toward Brashear, sizing him up for possible ways to confront him. Brashear crossed directly in front of him, presenting an easy target. Brashear was the focus of all of McSorley's and Boston's frustrations. McSorley had to do something; he might still be able to start a fight. In the words of McSorley, "It has to be an instantaneous reaction." He had an impulse to strike him in the head. His mindset, always tuned to aggression, permitted that. He slashed for the head. A child, swinging as at a Tee ball, would not miss. A housekeeper swinging a carpetbeater would not miss. An NHL player would never, ever miss. Brashear was struck as intended. Mr. McSorley, I must find you guilty as charged.

PEOPLE v. HALL

999 P.2d 207 (Col. 2000)

BENDER, Justice.

We hold that Nathan Hall must stand trial for the crime of reckless manslaughter. While skiing on Vail mountain, Hall flew off of a knoll and collided with Allen Cobb, who was traversing the slope below Hall. Cobb sustained traumatic brain injuries and died as a result of the collision. The People charged Hall with felony reckless manslaughter. . . .

The charge of reckless manslaughter requires that a person "recklessly cause the death of another person." For his conduct to be reckless, the actor must have consciously disregarded a substantial and unjustifiable risk that death could result from his actions. We hold that, for the purpose of determining whether a person acted recklessly, a particular result does not have to be more likely than not to occur for the risk to be substantial and unjustifiable. A risk must be assessed by reviewing the particular facts of the individual case and weighing the likelihood of harm and the degree of harm that would result if it occurs. Whether an actor consciously disregarded such a risk may be inferred from circumstances such as the actor's knowledge and experience, or from what a similarly situated reasonable person would have understood about the risk under the particular circumstances.

We hold that under the particular circumstances of this case, whether Hall committed the crime of reckless manslaughter must be determined by the trier of fact. Viewed in the light most favorable to the prosecution, Hall's conduct—skiing straight down a steep and bumpy slope, back on his skis, arms out to his sides, off-balance, being thrown from mogul to mogul, out of control for a considerable distance and period of time, and at such a high speed that the force of the impact between his ski and the victim's head fractured the thickest part of the victim's skull—created a substantial and unjustifiable risk of death to another person. A reasonable person could infer that the defendant, a former ski racer trained in skier safety, consciously disregarded that risk. For the limited purposes of a preliminary hearing, the prosecution provided sufficient evidence to show probable cause that the defendant recklessly caused the victim's death. . . .

Like other activities that generally do not involve a substantial risk of death, such as driving a car or installing a heater, "skiing too fast for the conditions" is not widely considered behavior that constitutes a high degree of risk. However, we hold that the specific facts in this case support a reasonable inference that Hall created a substantial and unjustifiable risk that he would cause another's death. . . .

While skiing ordinarily carries a very low risk of death to other skiers, a reasonable person could have concluded that Hall's excessive speed, lack of control, and improper technique for skiing bumps significantly increased both the likelihood that a collision would occur and the extent of the injuries that might result from such a collision, including the possibility of death, in the event that a person like Cobb unwittingly crossed Hall's downhill path. . . . [A] reasonable person could have determined that Hall's conduct was precisely the type of skiing that risked this rare result.

We next ask whether a reasonable person could have concluded that Hall's creation of a substantial risk of death was unjustified. To the extent that Hall's extremely fast and unsafe skiing created a risk of death, Hall was serving no direct interest other than his own enjoyment. Although the sport often involves high speeds and even moments where a skier is temporarily out of control, a reasonable person could determine that the enjoyment of skiing does not justify skiing at the speeds and with the lack of control Hall exhibited. Thus, a reasonable person could have found that Hall's creation of a substantial risk was unjustifiable.

In addition to our conclusion that a reasonable person could have entertained the belief that Hall's conduct created a substantial and unjustifiable risk, we must ask whether Hall's conduct constituted a "gross deviation" from the standard of care that a reasonable law-abiding person (in this case, a reasonable, law-abiding, trained ski racer and resort employee) would have observed in the circumstances. . . .

Having determined that Hall's conduct created a substantial and unjustified risk of death that is a gross deviation from the reasonable standard of care under the circumstances, we next ask whether a reasonably prudent person could have entertained the belief that Hall consciously disregarded that risk. Hall is a trained ski racer who had been coached about skiing in control and skiing safely. Further, he was an employee of a ski area and had a great deal of skiing experience. Hall's knowledge and training could give rise to the reasonable inference that he was aware of the possibility that by skiing so fast and out of control he might collide with and kill another skier unless he regained control and slowed down.

Thus, both Hall's subjective knowledge and the awareness that a reasonable person with Hall's background would have had support the inference that Hall consciously disregarded the risk he created by acting despite his awareness of the risk.

Thus, interpreting the facts presented in the light most favorable to the prosecution, we hold that a reasonably prudent and cautious person could have entertained the belief that Hall consciously disregarded a substantial and unjustifiable risk that by skiing exceptionally fast and out of control he might collide with and kill another person on the slope.

Obviously, this opinion does not address whether Hall is ultimately guilty of any crime. Rather, we hold only that the People presented sufficient evidence to establish probable cause that Hall committed reckless manslaughter, and the court should have bound Hall's case over for trial. . . .

NOTES AND QUESTIONS

1. *Policy Considerations.* When, if ever, is it appropriate to criminally prosecute for player conduct that occurs during competitive sporting events? Can a principled factual or legal distinction be drawn between *Schacker* and *McSorley*? Should the level of competition and age or maturity level of the participants make a difference? What other factors should be considered? Will the possibility of criminal liability have the detrimental effect of chilling vigorous participation and competition in athletic activities? On the other hand, what socially desirable effects may result? See generally *State v. Guidugli*, 811 N.E.2d 567, 574-75 (Ohio Ct. App. 2004) (stating that "given the unique social dynamics involved in sports, criminal prosecution of sports participants for conduct that occurs with the playing of the game is rare"); Jeffrey Standen, *The Manly Sports: The Problematic Use of Criminal Law to Regulate Sports Violence*, 99 J. Crim. L. & Criminology 619, 634 (2009) (discussing *Schacker* and the principles on which courts rely in determining whether to apply criminal sanctions in the athletics context); Jeff Yates & William Gillespie, *The Problem of Sports Violence and the Criminal Prosecution Solution*, 12 Cornell J.L. & Pub. Pol'y 145, 168 (2002) ("Criminal prosecutions can be an effective means by which to send the message that society will not tolerate acts of unnecessary violence by sports participants").

2. *Tort Versus Criminal Liability.* The same playing field conduct may give rise to both tort and criminal liability, although that is not necessarily the case. How do the elements and burdens of proof differ for tort and criminal liability?

    Similar to tort law, physical contact resulting in even severe injury is not criminal if it is "part of the game." Consent is a defense to alleged criminal assault, and it is necessary to determine "whether the conduct of defendant constituted foreseeable behavior in the play of the game" and whether a plaintiff's injury "occurred as a by-product of the game itself." *State v. Shelley*, 929 P.2d 489, 493 (Wash. Ct. App. 1997). Courts have affirmed criminal convictions for injuries caused by intentionally thrown punches during basketball and football games. See e.g., *Shelley*, 929 P.2d at 493 ("There is nothing in the game of basketball, or even rugby or hockey, that would permit consent as a defense to such conduct"); *State v. Floyd*, 466 N.W.2d 919 (Iowa Ct. App. 1990); *People v. Freer*, 86 Misc.2d 280 (N.Y. Dist. Ct. 1976). In 2009, a Canadian high school rugby player was found guilty of manslaughter for an opponent's death, which was caused by fatal injuries resulting from the player's lifting his opponent into the air with his feet facing upward and driving him head first into the ground. The trial judge found that the "defendant intentionally applied force that was outside the rules of the game or any standard by which the game is played." See Bob Mitchell, *Teen Guilty in Rugby Death*, Toronto Star (May 28, 2009).

Another important case was the reckless homicide prosecution of David Stinson, the former head football coach at Pleasure Park High School in Kentucky, for the death of a player from heat stroke during an August 2008 practice. The prosecution of Stinson marked the first time a coach was criminally charged for his on-field conduct. See Zac DesAutels, *Changing the Play: Football and the Criminal Law After the Trial of Jason Stinson*, 8 Willamette Sports L.J. 29, 30 (2010). Stinson was indicted following an incident in which a player collapsed, and later died, after running a series of sprints on a hot Kentucky afternoon. *Id.* at 29. Although Stinson was acquitted on charges of reckless homicide and wanton endangerment, the case marked the first instance in which a court was forced to address the societal issues surrounding assigning criminal liability to athletic coaches.

Should the Stinson trial be viewed as establishing a credible threat of criminal liability for athletic coaches? For perspectives on this question and the societal issues at play in the Stinson trial, see DesAutels, *supra*.

Would criminal liability be appropriate under *Hackbart*'s facts?

3. People v. Hall. This case illustrates the possibility of criminal liability for engaging in dangerous conduct during recreational sports. Would you convict the defendant of reckless manslaughter under the facts in *Hall*? Why or why not?

4. *Appropriate Sentences for Criminal Convictions.* After finding Marty McSorley guilty of assaulting Donald Brashear with a weapon (a hockey stick), Judge Kitchen provided the following explanation for the sentence he imposed:

> The finding of guilt is the real consequence here; the further step of entering a conviction is not necessary. I have concluded that specific deterrence and rehabilitation are served by this. I have concluded that protection of the public is a lesser consideration here. The real concern is that such a sentence may not send the correct message to the community. It must be kept in mind that the consequences to Mr. McSorley are already considerable. He has been without income since the incident, and he has had significant expense in preparing his defence. He has had to endure embarrassing publicity, much more than would be the situation in other assault matters. He will carry the stigma of this with him for the rest of his career; even the rest of his life. If that is not enough to convince anyone that such an offence is to be avoided, there is nothing more a court can do to persuade such a person otherwise.
>
> Before I impose sentence, I have these comments. . . .
>
> Mr. McSorley, you are a man of influence in the game. You were a players' representative. You have had men of high regard in the game stand behind you. You could use your influence to effect changes to the game. The written

rules are not realistic. The penalties do not deter. But please—one way or the other, we need fewer penalties, not more. There is work to be done. The game deserves it.

I grant you a conditional discharge for 18 months. You must keep the peace and be of good behaviour. You are bound by a condition that you will not engage in any sporting event where Donald Brashear is on the opposition.

That is my sentence.

Regina v. McSorley, 2000 B.C.P.C. 0117 (Oct. 6, 2000). By comparison, consider the following sentences for criminal convictions resulting from on-field conduct:

a. In 1988, Minnesota North Star player Dino Ciccarelli was sentenced to one day in jail and fined $1,000 for striking an opposing player several times in the head with his stick during a National Hockey League game.

b. In February 2000, Tony Limon, a Texas high school basketball player, was sentenced to five years in the state penitentiary for deliberately elbowing an opponent (who suffered a concussion and fractured nose as a result) during a game. This conduct was unrelated to any ongoing play, but no foul was called. Limon had previously pled guilty to burglary and was given four years' probation, but he had no prior history of violent behavior.

c. In September 2000, a 16-year-old Illinois high school hockey player was sentenced to two years' probation, ordered not to participate in any contact sports during that time, and required to perform 120 hours of community service after entering an Alford plea (no admission of guilt but acknowledgment that sufficient evidence to convict exists) to a misdemeanor battery charge. The prosecution and sentence resulted from the player's actions as a hockey game was ending: he cross-checked an opposing player from behind, causing the opposing player to crash headfirst into the boards, which permanently paralyzed him from the chest down.

Does the punishment fit the crime in each of these cases? In these examples, what may account for the significant disparities in the sentences imposed? Is there seemingly a different standard for professional athletes as compared to amateur and recreational athletes?

PROBLEM 11-4

During his warm-up between innings, a college pitcher deliberately threw at an opposing team player standing in the on-deck circle 24 feet away from the batter's box. The player was attempting to gauge the speed and time of the pitches, but he did not see the thrown ball in time to avoid it. A high-speed fastball hit him in the face, causing a broken cheekbone and orbital fracture. He now has two permanent blind spots in his left eye. The pitcher's coach told his pitchers to "brush back" any opponents attempting to time their pitches. Although admitting an effort to intimidate his opponent, the pitcher denied he was trying to hit him with the thrown ball.

Would you recommend that the pitcher be criminally prosecuted? As a juror, would you convict him? What would be an appropriate sentence?

C.   LIABILITY OF EDUCATIONAL INSTITUTIONS

1.   High School

a.   Legal Duty of Care

A high school is not an insurer of a student-athlete's safety and is not strictly liable for his or her injuries. To recover for an injury, a high school athlete is required to prove tortious conduct on the part of a school district or its employees. Negligence is the theory traditionally relied on by student-athletes who sue their high schools for sports-related injuries. For example, in *Beckett v. Clinton Prairie School Corp.*, 504 N.E.2d 552, 553 (Ind. 1987), the court held that high school personnel have a duty to exercise ordinary and reasonable care for the safety of student-athletes under their authority. See also *Benitez v. New York City Bd. of Educ.*, 541 N.E.2d 29, 32 (N.Y. 1989) (high school owed student-athlete voluntarily competing in interscholastic football game a duty to protect against injuries arising from unassumed, concealed, or unreasonably increased risks). Absent state law immunity from tort liability, a school may be liable for the negligent conduct of employees such as coaches, trainers, and administrative personnel under vicarious liability principles.

Notwithstanding the foregoing authority, courts increasingly have limited the scope of tort liability for injuries suffered by student-athletes. This is, in part, because of judicial extension of the reckless and intentional conduct standard adopted in co-participant injury cases (see *supra*) to limit the liability of high school coaches and trainers. Similarly, courts' increased willingness to enforce liability waivers against high school student-athletes has limited institutions' tort liability. See, e.g., *Sharon v. City of Newton*, 769 N.E.2d 738 (Mass. 2002). For a general discussion of the liability of high schools to student-athletes, see Timothy Davis, *Avila v. Citrus Community College District: Shaping the Contours of Immunity and Primary Assumption of the Risk*, 17 Marq. Sports L. Rev. 259 (2006); Timothy B. Fitzgerald, *The "Inherent Risk" Doctrine, Amateur Coaching Negligence, and the Goal of Loss Avoidance*, Comment, 99 Nw. U. L. Rev. 889 (2005); Matthew J. Mitten, *Emerging Legal Issues in Sports Medicine: A Synthesis, Summary, and Analysis*, 76 St. John's L. Rev. 5 (2002).

In determining the appropriate liability standard for injuries suffered while participating in interscholastic athletics, the following case illustrates that courts balance the institutional responsibility that arises out of the custodial relationship between schools and their student-athletes (most of whom are minors) with the participants' assumption of the risk of injury inherent in athletic participation. Other relevant policy considerations include the age, skill, and experience levels of those involved in the activity and the extent to which imposing liability may adversely affect the provision of coaching, instruction, and training to develop and enhance athletic performance.

KAHN v. EAST SIDE UNION HIGH SCH. DIST.

75 P.3d 30 (Cal. 2003)

GEORGE, C.J.

This case presents a question concerning the proper application of the doctrine of primary assumption of risk. At the time of her injury, plaintiff was a

14-year-old novice member of defendant school district's junior varsity swim team. She was participating in a competitive swim meet when she executed a practice dive into a shallow racing pool that was located on defendant school district's property and broke her neck. She alleged that the injury was caused in part by the failure of her coach, a district employee, to provide her with any instruction in how to safely dive into a shallow racing pool. She also alleged lack of adequate supervision and further that the coach breached the duty of care owed to her by insisting that she dive at the swim meet despite her objections, her lack of expertise, her fear of diving, and the coach's previous promise to exempt her from diving.

In *Knight v. Jewett* (1992) 3 Cal. 4th 296, 11 Cal. Rptr. 2d 2, 834 P.2d 696 (*Knight*), we considered the proper duty of care that should govern the liability of a sports participant for an injury to a co-participant. We concluded that, in recognition of the circumstance that some risk of injury is inherent in most sports, and in order to avoid the detriment to a sport that would arise from discouraging participants from vigorously engaging in the activity, it is appropriate to hold that a participant breaches a duty of care to a co-participant only if he or she "intentionally injures another player or engages in conduct that is so reckless as to be totally outside the range of the ordinary activity involved in the sport." In the present case, we recognize that the relationship of a sports instructor or coach to a student or athlete is different from the relationship between co-participants in a sport. But because a significant part of an instructor's or coach's role is to challenge or "push" a student or athlete to advance in his or her skill level and to undertake more difficult tasks, and because the fulfilment of such a role could be improperly chilled by too stringent a standard of potential legal liability, we conclude that the same general standard should apply in cases in which an instructor's alleged liability rests primarily on a claim that he or she challenged the player to perform beyond his or her capacity or failed to provide adequate instruction or supervision before directing or permitting a student to perform a particular maneuver that has resulted in injury to the student. A sports instructor may be found to have breached a duty of care to a student or athlete only if the instructor intentionally injures the student or engages in conduct that is reckless in the sense that it is "totally outside the range of the ordinary activity" involved in teaching or coaching the sport.

Applying this standard to the present case, we conclude that, on the basis of the declarations and deposition testimony filed in support of and in opposition to defendants' motion for summary judgment, the Court of Appeal majority erred in determining that the doctrine of primary assumption of risk warranted entry of summary judgment in defendants' favor. We conclude that the totality of the circumstances precludes the grant of defendants' motion for summary judgment. Specifically, we refer to evidence of defendant coach's failure to provide plaintiff with training in shallow-water diving, his awareness of plaintiff's intense fear of diving into shallow water, his conduct in lulling plaintiff into a false sense of security by promising that she would not be required to dive at competitions, his last-minute breach of this promise in the heat of a competition, and his threat to remove her from competition or at least from the meet if she refused to dive. Plaintiff's evidence supports the conclusion that the maneuver of diving into a shallow racing pool, if not done correctly, poses a significant risk of extremely serious injury, and that there is a well-established mode of instruction for teaching a student to perform this maneuver safely. The declarations before the trial court raise a disputed issue of fact as to whether defendant coach provided any instruction at all to plaintiff with regard to the safe performance of such a maneuver, as well as to the existence and nature of the coach's promises and threats. Under these circumstances, the question whether the coach's conduct was reckless in that it fell totally outside the range of ordinary activity involved in teaching or coaching this sport cannot properly be resolved on summary judgment. Accordingly, the judgment of the Court of Appeal is reversed. . . .

The general proposition that a sports instructor or coach owes a duty of due care not to increase the risk of harm inherent in learning an active sport is consistent with a growing line of Court of Appeal opinions that have applied the *Knight* analysis to claims against such defendants. In these cases, the reviewing courts examined the particular circumstances of the sport, its inherent risks, and the relationship of the parties to the sport and to each other. Most also examined the question whether imposing broader liability on coaches and instructors would harm the sport or cause it to be changed or abandoned. In each instance, the Courts of Appeal have agreed that although the coach or athletic instructor did not have a duty to eliminate the risks presented by a sport, he or she did have a duty to the student not to increase the risk inherent in learning, practicing, or performing in the sport.

Subsequent decisions have clarified that the risks associated with *learning* a sport may themselves be inherent risks of the sport, and that an instructor or coach generally does not increase the risk of harm inherent in learning the sport simply by urging the student to strive to excel or to reach a new level of competence. This line of cases analyzes and articulates an important and appropriate limitation on the duty of a sports instructor. The cases point out that instruction in a sport frequently entails challenging or "pushing" a student to attempt new or more difficult feats, and that "liability should not be imposed simply because an instructor asked the student to take action beyond what, with hindsight, is found to have been the student's abilities." (*Bushnell v. Japanese-American Religious & Cultural Center, supra*, 43 Cal. App. 4th at p. 532, 50 Cal. Rptr. 2d 671.) As a general matter, although the nature of the sport and the relationship of the parties to it and to each other remain relevant, a student's inability to meet an instructor's legitimate challenge is a risk that is inherent in learning a sport. To impose a duty to mitigate the inherent risks of learning a sport by refraining from challenging a student, as these cases explain, could have a chilling effect on the enterprise of teaching and learning skills that are necessary to the sport. At a competitive level, especially, this chilling effect is undesirable. . . .

[E]ven keeping in mind the role of the coach or sports instructor, the imposition of a duty to avoid challenging a student to perform beyond his or her current capacity would have a chilling effect on the enterprise of teaching and learning skills that are necessary to the sport . . . a coach or athletic instructor must challenge his or her students, and . . . learning itself can be a risky process, sometimes unavoidably so. . . . [W]hile a student is engaged in the process of learning, he or she frequently is at greater risk than a proficient athlete would be, and a coach does not have a duty to eliminate all the risks presented by inexperience.

We agree that the object to be served by the doctrine of primary assumption of risk in the sports setting is to avoid recognizing a duty of care when to do so would tend to alter the nature of an active sport or chill vigorous participation in the activity. This concern applies to the process of learning to become competent or competitive in such a sport. Novices and children need instruction if they are to participate and compete, and we agree with the many Court of Appeal decisions that have refused to define a duty of care in terms that would inhibit adequate instruction and learning or eventually alter the nature of the sport. Accordingly, we believe that the standard set forth in *Knight* as it applies to co-participants, generally should apply to sports instructors, keeping in mind, of course, that different facts are of significance in each setting. In order to support a cause of action in cases in which it is alleged that a sports instructor has required a student to perform beyond the student's capacity or without providing adequate instruction, it must be alleged and proved that the instructor acted with intent to cause a student's injury or that the instructor acted recklessly in the sense that the instructor's conduct was "totally outside the range of the ordinary activity" involved in teaching or coaching the sport.

Plaintiff's allegations and supporting evidence . . . went far beyond a claim that the coach made an ordinary error of judgment in determining that she was ready to perform the shallow-water dive.

The Red Cross teaching manual submitted by plaintiff acknowledged that the principal danger faced by persons learning to compete in swimming is the shallow-water dive. The risk presented is not simply that the swimmer might suffer bruises or even break an arm; the risk is that the student may sustain serious head and spinal cord injuries by striking the bottom of the pool. Plaintiff presented evidence, both documentary and expert, that a settled progression of instruction in the dive is considered essential to a student's safety. Her own declaration and deposition testimony was that she had not received any instruction at all from her coaches or teammates on the performance of the shallow-water dive. She also claimed that she had expressed a mortal fear of performing the shallow-water dive and that she had been assured by the coach that she would not be required to perform it. Her evidence was that the coach made a last-minute demand that she take a position in the relay race that would require her to dive, threatening that if she did not comply, either she would be dropped from the team or she would not be permitted to compete that day.

With respect to the issue of causation . . . there was a conflict in the evidence on the question whether plaintiff had been instructed not to practice dives on her own. Under the allegations and evidence provided by plaintiff, it was reasonably foreseeable that when the coach told plaintiff she would have to dive (for the first time) at the meet, she would see a need for practice. Under these circumstances and those referred to above, sufficient facts were produced that would support a determination that the absence of prior instruction was the proximate cause of plaintiff's injury.

Applicable California authority establishes that defendants had a duty of supervision that included an obligation to offer plaintiff some protection against her own lack of mature judgment. . . . We do not believe it can be determined as a matter of law that plaintiff's decision to practice shallow-water dives with the help of other students, after the coach unexpectedly told her she was to dive that day, was conduct beyond what the coach should have foreseen and forestalled. . . .

We believe that triable issues of material fact exist regarding the question whether coach McKay breached a duty of care owed to plaintiff, thereby causing her injury, by engaging in conduct that was reckless in that it was totally outside the range of ordinary activity involved in teaching or coaching the sport of competitive swimming. . . .

Concurring Opinion by WERDEGAR, J.

I agree with the majority that an instructor should be liable for a student's injury in the course of learning a sport only if the instructor's conduct is found to have been "'totally outside the range of the ordinary activity' involved in teaching or coaching the sport." Although the majority also adopts *Knight*'s label of such conduct as "reckless," I do not understand our standard, at least in the instructional context, to be equivalent to recklessness as it is sometimes understood, i.e., as the "wilful or wanton misconduct" shown when an actor has "'intentionally done an act of an unreasonable character in disregard of a risk known to him or so obvious that he must be taken to have been aware of it, and so great as to make it highly probable that harm would follow.'" Rather, I believe a coach or instructor departs from the range of ordinary instructional activities, increasing the risks of injury beyond those inherent in teaching a sport, and is therefore subject to liability, when his or her conduct constitutes a gross or extreme departure from the instructional norms. . . .

I believe we must recognize a somewhat greater duty on the part of instructors, especially teachers and coaches of minor students, than the duty participants in a sport owe one another. A school football *coach*, while far from being the insurer of students' safety, is also very differently situated in knowledge, training, experience, and responsibilities from the casual football *player* whose duty we considered in *Knight*. . . . [A] coach or instructor stands somewhat apart from the fray; the coach's role includes observing and directing the competition, and he or she is expected to keep a cooler head than the competitors themselves. When the instructor or coach is a school teacher, moreover, the safety of the minor students will usually be a primary consideration. Society expects—legitimately, in my view—more from instructors and coaches than merely that they will refrain from harming a student intentionally or with wanton disregard for safety. An instructor's gross or extreme lack of care for student safety is not an inherent risk of school athletics programs.

Finally, I believe a standard akin to gross negligence will provide sufficient protection against unfair second-guessing of the instructor's judgment and, therefore, will not unduly chill participation in sports instruction. . . .

Concurring and Dissenting Opinion by KENNARD, J.

I would hold high school coaches to the general standard of ordinary care. . . . I would require the injured plaintiff to establish only negligence, not recklessness. . . .

Thus, defendant coach in this case should be held liable if, in teaching plaintiff the requisite skills of competitive swimming and in supervising her progress, the coach's conduct fell short of that of a *reasonable* coach of student athletes in similar circumstances.

Persons participating in active sports have to expect that a co-participant may play too roughly and thus cause injury. By contrast, coaches of student athletes teach them the skills necessary to perform their sport of choice safely and effectively. Because student athletes, particularly minors, often consider their coach a mentor or role model, they trust the coach not to carelessly and needlessly expose them to injury. The majority's decision puts an end to that trust: Coaches are under no legal obligation to use reasonable care in training their students how best to perform a sport without incurring personal injury.

The concurring opinion agrees with the majority that a coach incurs liability to a student athlete only for conduct "'totally outside the range'" of ordinary coaching activity. But it objects to the majority's labelling such conduct "'reck-less,'" preferring to call it "gross negligence." Whatever one chooses to call it, the standard the majority imposes is dangerously lax; it puts concern for the physical safety of children far down on a secondary school coach's list of priorities. . . .

Because participation in active sports always entails some risk of harm, the traditional negligence standard imposes liability on an athletic coach only for conduct that exposes players to an "*unreasonable* risk" of such harm. . . . Thus, contrary to the majority's view, applying the negligence standard here would leave coaches free to challenge or push their students to advance their skills level as long as they do so without exposing the student athletes to an unreasonable risk of harm. . . .

NOTES AND QUESTIONS

1. *Determining Inherent Risks.* A school is not liable for a player's injury result-ing from the inherent risks of a sport. Determining inherent risks requires a fact-specific analysis of what activities are "part of the game," and which risks of injury are assumed by all participants. An inherent risk is one that is indivisible from the sport. In other words, the inherent risk inquiry focuses on whether the activity at issue constitutes a risk that is among the conse-quences attendant to normal competition in a sport. For example, the risk of being hit by a ball is a consequence of playing baseball. In *Rutherford v. Talisker Canyons Finance, Co., LLC,* 2019 WL 2710230 (Utah June 27, 2019), the Utah Supreme Court adopted an objective standard for determining whether a risk is inherent to a game or recreational activity: "Under a pri-mary assumption of risk analysis, the question is not necessarily whether a skier would 'wish' to encounter a certain risk, but whether a risk is inherent or essential to the sport of skiing and therefore whether the risk is one that a skier reasonably expects to encounter when participating in the sport." *Id.* at *20-21.

   Some risks, however, are divisible from the competition within a sport. Because such risks are not inherent to the sport, they fall outside the scope of primary assumption of the risk. A faulty helmet would be a "divisible risk" because the defect arose from the manufacturing process and not from par-ticipation in an athletic event. Risks generally deemed not to be inherent to sports activities include defective equipment, substandard medical treat-ment, and intentional torts. Marc J. Dobberstein, *"Give Me the Ball, Coach": A Scouting Report on the Liability of High Schools and Coaches for Injuries to High School Pitchers' Arms,* 14 Sports L. J. 49, 53 (2007).

   An athlete does not, however, assume all risks of injury from playing a sport, regardless of how they occur. In this regard, coaches must act neither recklessly nor in a manner that increases risks inherent in an athletic activ-ity. See, e.g., *Koffman v. Garnett,* 574 S.E.2d 258, 261 (Va. 2003) (coach who unexpectedly lifted a 13-year-old football player and slammed him to the ground as part of demonstration on tackling techniques acted imprudently and in "utter disregard" of the student's safety); see also *Patrick v. Great Valley Sch. Dist.,* 296 Fed. App. 258 (3d Cir. 2008) (unpublished) (although coach's conduct in pairing student wrestler with a teammate who was 90 pounds heavier might constitute deliberate indifference to his health and safety, school could not be held liable for violating student's §1983 liberty interest without due process unless facts established that the coach's conduct represented unofficial custom so pervasive as to carry the force of law). *Lemaster v. Grove City Christian Sch.*, 2017 WL 5157610 (Ohio Ct. App., Nov. 7, 2017) (court rules it was for a jury to determine whether a coach acted recklessly in loading 200 pounds of weight to barbell used by a middle-school football player who weighed 97 pounds and was injured while attempting a squat lift).

2. *Inadequate Instruction and Training.* Which of the three liability standards considered in *Kahn* strikes the appropriate balance between enabling coaches to promote interscholastic and youth sports athletic performance and protecting young athletes from increased risks of injury? Should injury resulting from negligent coaching be an inherent risk of playing a sport that is assumed by a young athlete? See Joseph M. Hnylka, *California Drops the Ball: The Lack of a Clear Approach to Recklessness in Sport Injury Litigation,* 11 Va. Sports & Ent. L.J. 77 (2011) (discussing *Kahn, Knight,* and *Shin* and providing comprehensive discussion of California's application of assumption of risk in sport cases).

Relying on the reasoning of the *Kahn* majority, a Maryland appellate court held that a 13-year-old softball player assumed the risk of her injury, a fractured ankle, while attempting to tag an opposing player who slid into her at second base. Plaintiffs claimed that the coach failed to adequately instruct her not to block the base path. The court stated: "Inadequate instruction and training claims have progressed to trial only when a coach provided little or no training before asking the injured athlete to engage in a significantly dangerous play, and compounded that omission by failing to adequately supervise that play." *Kelly v. McCarrick*, 841 A.2d 869, 886-87. (Md. Ct. Spec. App. 2004); *Arnzen v, Temecula Valley Unified Sch. Dist.,* 2017 WL 4942896 (Cal App. Ct. 31, 2017) (stating that while "instructors and coaches owe their students a duty of ordinary care not to direct their students to perform the sport or activity under unsafe conditions, or risks of injury above and beyond the risk inherent in performing the sport *under customary or normal conditions,*" the court concludes that with respect to her negligence claim, a cheerleader failed to demonstrate that she was directed to perform a stunt under unsafe conditions). However, other courts hold that coaches may be held liable for negligence that caused injury. See *Wilson v. O'Gorman High Sch.*, 2008 WL 2571833 at *4 (D.S.D. June 26, 2008) (concluding that "the South Dakota Supreme Court would not adopt the *Kahn* standard, but rather would apply the general negligence standard"); *Sherry v. East Suburban Football League,* 807 N.W.2d 859, 862 (Mich. Ct. App. 2011) (applying negligence standard in a case alleging coach failed to properly train and supervise cheerleaders engaged in "privately sponsored recreational activities").

There also is potential liability for negligently warning students regarding the need for and appropriate use of protective equipment during athletics, which represents an exception to the developing intentional/recklessness standard for improper coaching and instruction. *Henney v. Shelby City Sch. Dist.* 2006 WL 747475, at *3 (Ohio Ct. App. Mar.23, 2006) (coach can be held negligent for failing to supply proper athletic equipment); *Moose v. Mass. Inst. of Tech.*, 683 N.E.2d 706 (Mass. Ct. App. 1997) (adopting negligence standard to determine liability of coach for supplying defective equipment to player); see also *Mone v. Graziadei*, 2017 WL 5076472 (N.J. Super. Ct. App. Div. Oct. 30, 2017) (reasonable jurors could find that coach committed gross negligence in failing to ensure that catcher wore safety equipment during warmups).

Although there is potential institutional liability for supplying athletes with defective sporting equipment, courts have drawn a distinction between accidents resulting from defective equipment and those resulting from sub-optimal playing conditions. *Bukowski v. Clarkson Univ.*, 19 N.Y.3d 353, 357 (N.Y. 2012), is illustrative. Plaintiff, an experienced college baseball player, was struck by a batted ball during a pitching exercise. *Id.* at 355. The court held that the player assumed the inherent risk of being hit by a line drive, despite the absence of a protective L-screen and low lighting in the facility. *Id.* at 356. The court stated that although the lack of adequate lighting and protective screen may be considered "less than optimal for baseball, they still did not constitute risks beyond those assumed by the [player]." *Id.* at 357.

Increasingly, physicians and others warn of the dangers associated with coaches who overtrain young athletes, particularly where an athlete specializes at an early age in one sport. For discussions of this and the potential legal implications, see Phoebe Friesen, et al., *Overuse Injuries in Youth Sports: Legal and Social Responsibility*, 28 J. Legal Aspects Sport 151 (2018) (discussing the increased risk of injuries to athletes in youth sports from overuse, and repetitive and cumulative microtrauma); see also Sam C. Erlich & John T. Holden, *Throwing the Book at Irresponsible Coaches: The Need for Consistent Pitch Limit Laws in Amateur Sports*, 47 Hofstra L. Rev. 527 (2018) (discussing how overwork of pitchers in youth and high school baseball results in athlete injuries and suggesting guidelines).

3. *Aggravation of Existing Injury.* Requiring a high school athlete to continue playing with a known injury may create tort liability for aggravation of the injury. *Morris v. Union High Sch. Dist. A*, 294 P. 998 (Wash. 1931) (finding that "[If] the coach knew that a student in the school was physically unable to play football, or in the exercise of reasonable care should have known it, but nevertheless permitted, persuaded, and coerced such student to play, with the result that he sustained injuries, the district would be liable"). *Id.* at 999. See also *Limones v. Sch. Dist. of Lee Cty.*, 161 So. 3d 384, 394 (Fla. 2015) (recognizing a special relationship between students and schools, the court holds that defendant has a common law duty to supervise the student and to take appropriate post-injury efforts to avoid or mitigate further aggravation of the plaintiff's injury). But see *Christian v. Eagles Landing Christian Acad., Inc.*, 692 S.E.2d 745, 749 (Ga. Ct. App. 2010) (granting summary judgment on behalf of defendant because the coach did not encourage or grant permission to cheerleading squad to perform the stunt that resulted in an injury to a cheerleader).

Permitting an injured athlete to return to play without using reasonable care to determine his or her medical condition also may result in institutional liability. *Jarreau v. Orleans Parish Sch. Bd.*, 600 So. 2d 1389 (La. Ct. App. 1992). See also *Mayall ex rel. H.C. v. USA Water Polo, Inc.*, 909 F.3d 1055 (9th Cir. 2018), discussed *infra* at note 6. However, in *Cerny v. Cedar Bluffs Junior/Senior Public School*, 679 N.W.2d 198 (Neb. 2004), the Nebraska Supreme Court affirmed the lower court's finding that a coach exercised reasonable care by properly evaluating a high school football player for symptoms of a concussion and allowing him to reenter a game. See *Zemke v. Arreola*, 2006 WL 1587101 (Cal. Ct. App. June 12, 2006) (coaches not liable for brain injury caused by second impact syndrome, which was not foreseeable, because student did not appear to have or report symptoms of initial head injury).

4. *Alleged Constitutional Torts.* Increasingly, athletes have asserted claims alleging that injuries or the aggravation of injuries arising from defendants' conduct amount to constitutional torts pursuant to the state-created danger doctrine in violation of the Fourteenth Amendment. Courts have reached different outcomes in these cases. See *Mann v. Palmerton, Area Sch. Dist.*, 33 F.Supp.3d 530 (M.D. Pa. 2014) (finding that a high school football player who sustained a hit during football practice that allegedly left him disoriented and experiencing numbness and his coaches allegedly ordering the player to continue to practice, even though the coach observed the player's disorientation, were sufficient to sustain a cause of action against the municipal defendants), *aff'd*, 872 F.3d 165 (3rd Cir. 2017); *Farrell v. Sch. Dist. of Springfield Twp.*, 2016 WL 4398272 (E.D. Pa. Aug. 17, 2016) (allegations that coach who ran with his elbows extended towards a group of 12-year-olds playing flag football pled facts sufficient to establish second prong of "state-created danger" theory—"the state actor acted with a degree of culpability that shocks the conscience"); *Hickey ex rel. R.B. v. Enterline*, 304 F.Supp.3d 456 (M.D. Pa. 2018) (discussing elements of state-created danger theory); but see *M.U. v. Downingtown High Sch. E.*, 103 F. Supp. 3d 612 (E.D. Pa. 2015) (court finds that that a coach's failure to remove a student from an interscholastic game, after a head injury, did not establish a state-created danger because the coach's decision to allow the plaintiff to continue playing did not shock the conscience and did not amount to the affirmative act required for a plaintiff to sustain a state-created danger theory).

5. *Duty to Provide Emergency Medical Care.* High school personnel have a duty to promptly obtain emergency medical care for an injured athlete. *Mogabgab v. Orleans Parish Sch. Bd.*, 239 So. 2d 456, 460-61 (La. Ct. App. 1970) (noting that because coaches did not seek medical attention for an injured athlete until two hours after his symptoms appeared, they were negligent in causing his death). Although lay athletic personnel are not charged with the knowledge of medical experts, they must recognize a medical emergency and act reasonably under the circumstances. *Kersey v. Harbin*, 531 S.W.2d 76, 80-81 (Mo. Ct. App. 1975). Courts have found coaches liable for improperly providing first aid that worsens an injured athlete's condition. See *Gahan v. Mineola Union Free Sch. Dist.*, 660 N.Y.S.2d 144 (N.Y. App. Div. 1997).

6. *Duty of State High School Athletic Association to Protect Athlete's Health and Safety.* State high school athletic associations often promulgate competition and equipment rules for interscholastic sports played within their respective jurisdictions. Courts have held that these governing bodies have a legal duty to exercise reasonable care when formulating safety rules governing high school athletic competition. See e.g., *Mohr v. St. Paul Fire & Marine Ins. Co.*, 674 N.W.2d 576 (Wis. Ct. App. 2003); *Wissel v. Ohio High Sch. Athletic Ass'n*, 605 N.E.2d 458 (Ohio Ct. App. 1992). As a policy matter, what should a state high school athletic association do to protect the health and safety of those students participating in interscholastic athletics? By comparison, what legal duty, if any, should be imposed on the National Federation of State High School Associations, which promulgates proposed rules for interscholastic

sports but does not have rule-making and enforcement authority? See *Mehr v. FIFA*, 115 F.Supp.3d 1035 (N.D. Cal. 2015) (dismissing negligence claims against worldwide, national, and state soccer governing bodies because "[p]laintiffs have alleged no basis for imputing to any defendant a legal duty to reduce the reduce the risks inherent in the sport of soccer, or to implement any of the 'Consensus Statement' guidelines or concussion management protocols, and have alleged no facts showing that any defendant took any action that increased the risks beyond those inherent in the sport").

Two cases involving youth athletic associations are worth noting. *Mayall ex rel. R.C. v. USA Water Polo, Inc.*, 909 F.3d 1055 (9th Cir. 2018) involved secondary injuries a minor suffered after returning to play following an initial hit. The court holds that the first hit was an inherent risk of water polo but defendant's failure to have a return-to-play policy given knowledge of the dangers of head trauma gave rise to cognizable claims of negligence, voluntary undertaking, and gross negligence against the association. In *Doe v. United States Youth Soccer Assoc.*, 214 Cal.Rptr.3d 552 (Cal. Ct. App. 2017), a minor who was allegedly abused by her soccer coach alleged the abuse was a consequence of the negligence and willful misconduct of youth soccer leagues. In reversing the trial court's sustaining of defendants' demurrers, the court ruled that "defendants had a duty to conduct criminal background checks on all adults who would have contact with children involved in their programs." *Id.* at 559. The court reasoned that liability arose from the special relationship between defendants and the minor given that parents, who entrusted their children with defendants, reasonably expected defendants to protect the children from sexual predators. *Id.* at 565.

b.   Sovereign and Qualified Immunities

PRINCE v. LOUISVILLE MUN. SCH. DIST.

741 So. 2d 207 (Miss. 1999)

WALLER, Justice:

This case arose out of a suit filed by Richard Prince on April 11, 1994, against the Louisville Municipal School District (the District), David Chambiss and Bobby Bowman for injures suffered while Prince was a member of the Nanih Waiya High School football team. . . .

Prince alleged he suffered a heat stroke during football practice at Nanih Waiya High School on August 29, 1991, due to the negligence of football coaches Bowman and Chambliss. Prince further alleged Bowman and Chambliss negligently failed to keep a proper monitor on his health and condition, failed to provide necessary liquids and failed to provide necessary medical care in a timely manner. Prince required hospitalization for his injury and claims to have suffered permanent injuries. . . .

Bowman, Chambliss and the District moved to dismiss Prince's claim [and] . . . claimed (1) Prince's complaint failed to state a claim on which relief could be granted; (2) the defendants were protected by sovereign immunity or qualified sovereign immunity; and (3) based on the pleadings, there was no material issue in dispute and the defendants were entitled to summary judgment. . . .

For the District, the doctrine of sovereign immunity mandates a finding of non-liability.

For Bowman and Chambliss individually, "[p]re-*Pruett* common law mandates a finding of whether the act involved is a discretionary function or a ministerial function. . . . An official will be immune when the act being performed is discretionary."

In *Quinn v. Mississippi State University*, 720 So.2d 843 (Miss. 1998), we were faced with a factual situation comparable to the present case. Bobby Quinn was injured June 22, 1992, while participating in a summer baseball camp at Mississippi State University. An instructor at the camp hit Quinn with a baseball bat during a hitting demonstration. Quinn lost one tooth and suffered permanent damages to four other teeth. Quinn sued the university President, the head baseball coach and an assistant baseball coach, who was also director of the camp.

We affirmed the trial court's granting of summary judgment for the three defendants stating "limited immunity applies to actions by a state agency, an arm of the state or local government and the members thereof, who either for remuneration or as a public service, engage in discretionary functions for which the agency or governmental arm was formed." *Id.* at 849. (citations omitted). The three defendants in *Quinn* were not present at the time of the injury, but they were "engaged in hiring employees, and coordinating, and supervising the baseball program either directly or indirectly. The motion for summary judgment was correctly granted as [the defendants] were engaged in a discretionary activity that served a public interest." *Id.*

In a case even more factually akin to the case at bar, *Lennon v. Petersen*, 624 So. 2d 171 (Ala.1993), the Alabama Supreme Court addressed the effect of qualified immunity on a negligence action brought against a soccer coach and university trainer by an injured soccer player. Patrick Lennon alleged his coach was negligent in not recognizing his injuries and providing the proper treatment. Lennon experienced sharp pain in his hip and groin during soccer practice and received treatment from the University of Alabama at Huntsville athletic trainer, Debbie Lee. Lee diagnosed his injury as "groin strain" and treated him with ice and electricity. Lennon's injury persisted and he sought treatment from a physician after the season ended. Lennon's physician diagnosed his condition as avascular necrosis which had worsened because of the treatment he received during the course of the soccer season from Lee and under the direction of Peterson, his soccer coach. Lennon required surgery to help his problem, but was forced to avoid any activities that could cause a jarring of his hip bones. He also faced the prospect of premature arthritis and a hip joint replacement in the future.

In addressing the negligence claim against Lennon's coach, the Alabama Supreme Court stated:

> Petersen's actions clearly fall into the category of discretionary acts. Petersen had to rely on his own judgment and discretion in making difficult decisions while performing his job. He had to determine what drills his players needed and how long the drills should last. He also had to evaluate his players to determine if they were playing to the best of their ability. He had to make difficult decisions in determining whether a player was injured and should report to the trainer or whether the player was merely faking an injury to avoid practice. He also had to be aware that some players would hide their injuries so that they would be allowed to practice or to play in a game. He was responsible for motivating the players and evaluating their performance. Petersen was acting within his authority in using his discretion in such matters, and he is entitled to discretionary function immunity.

Id. at 174.

Like the defendants in *Quinn*, high school football coaches Bowman and Chambliss were responsible for coordinating and supervising the football program at Nanih Waiya High School. Bowman and Chambliss also faced the same daily coaching decisions as did Coach Peterson in *Lennon*. The Alabama Supreme Court's description of the nature of a coach's job is important to consider. In a typical practice there are strains, sprains and complaints from a coach's players. A coach must consider the good order and discipline of the team when confronted with situational complaints by the players. A coach must use his discretion in judging whether or not an individual player is injured and then, whether the player should report to a trainer or seek other medical aid. There was no evidence presented in the lower court to show that either Bowman or Chambliss did anything beyond exercising ordinary discretion in supervising the Nanih Waiya football practice on August 29, 1991. Prince produced no facts that evidenced any disregard for his health or any other outrageous action on the part of Bowman or Chambliss that might have warranted a departure from our previous holdings. The trial court correctly found the coaches were protected by qualified immunity. . . .

We affirm the trial court's granting of summary judgment in favor of the District because the District was protected by sovereign immunity. Following our prior decision in *Quinn v. Mississippi State University* and the approach of the Alabama Supreme Court in *Lennon v. Petersen*, we affirm the trial court's granting of summary judgment to Bowman and Chambliss based on the protection of qualified immunity. . . .

BANKS, Justice, concurring in part and dissenting in part:

In *Womble v. Singing River Hosp.*, 618 So. 2d 1252 (Miss.1993), this Court removed a then relatively recently discovered blanket immunity for "discretionary" medical decisions. We concluded that medical treatment decisions, however discretionary, were not governmental policy decisions and, therefore, no immunity attached. *Womble* put medical personnel, back on an even footing with all other governmental personnel, where they had always been and where they belonged. Today's decision elevates athletic coaches to the same perch from which we removed medical personnel.

Administrators, commissioners, etc., are immune for policy-making decisions, such as how much money to allocate to particular objectives. Neither they nor other government employees should be immune for breaches of the duty of reasonable care when dealing directly with individuals to whom such a duty is owed. The Alabama Supreme Court construing Alabama law reaches a different result, *Lennon v. Petersen*, 624 So. 2d 171 (Ala.1993), but that simply is not our law.

The majority's reliance upon *Quinn v. Mississippi State University*, 720 So. 2d 843 (Miss.1998), is also misplaced. There we held that the president of the university, the university head baseball coach and the assistant head baseball coach who also directed the baseball camp enjoyed qualified immunity from liability with respect to an injury to a participant in the baseball camp. Neither of these defendants, however, was shown to have had or exercised direct supervisory responsibility for the particular activities out of which the injury arose. These individuals would be counterparts to the hospital administrators and perhaps, chiefs of various medical disciplines as opposed to treating physicians as in the case of *Womble*. No one contends that administrative decisions fall outside the ambit of qualified immunity. The decisions here involved were not administrative.

In my view the football coach and trainer in the instant case owed a duty of reasonable care to the player, the breach of which should incur liability from which there is no immunity. That is not to say that they were, in fact, negligent in breach of their duty. Perhaps what they did was fully in keeping with reasonable care under the circumstances. All I say is that there should be no immunity. . . .

McRae, Justice, concurring in part and dissenting in part:

[T]he coaches were acting in their ministerial capacities, not with discretion. Qualified immunity is not warranted. . . . Coaches Chambliss and Bowman maintained duties to manage their players. Randall Prince suffered harm because his coaches failed to perform their duties such that he suffered heatstroke, and because those same coaches failed to take proper actions afterwards. As coaches directly responsible for serving the general needs of Prince while he is under their power as a football player, the coaches should have more closely monitored Prince's condition. When it became possible that Prince was a candidate for heatstroke, the coaches should have given him rest out of the sun, provided him additional liquids, or simply excused him from practice. There are no means by which to grant qualified immunity. The instant case deals with an extracurricular activity internal to the school, not a promotion of government policy and public good. Accordingly, I dissent to affirming summary judgment for the coaches and the school district.

NOTES AND QUESTIONS

1. *Sovereign Immunity for Public Schools.* As illustrated in *Prince*, under the doctrine of *sovereign immunity*, a public school district, as a subsidiary agency of the state, may be immune from tort liability for negligent acts of its employees causing injury to a high school athlete. See also *Evans v. Oaks Mission Pub. Sch.*, 945 P.2d 492 (Okla. 1997); *Grandalski v. Lyons Township High Sch. Dist. 204*, 711 N.E.2d 372 (Ill. Ct. App. 1999). The scope of this immunity varies on a state-by-state basis.

   Courts generally hold that the operation of an interscholastic athletics program is a governmental function that is covered by sovereign immunity rather than a proprietary function, which is not immune. *Fowler v. Tyler Indep. Sch. Dist.*, 232 S.W.3d 335 (Tex. Ct. App. 2007). In *Lovitt v. Concord Sch. Dist.*, 228 N.W.2d 479 (Mich. Ct. App. 1975), a Michigan court of appeals held that a public high school football program was a physical education activity encompassed within the governmental function of providing education. Finding that the district's athletics program had been operating at a deficit for five years, the court rejected plaintiff's claim that the football program was a proprietary function because an admission fee was charged to games. For discussions of sovereign immunity in the athletic context, see Davis, *Avila v. Citrus College, supra*, at 260-63; Thomas R. Hurst & James N. Knight, *Coaches' Liability for Athletes' Injuries and Deaths*, 13 Seton Hall J. Sport L. 27, 44-47 (2003); Anthony S. McCaskey & Kenneth W. Biedzynski, *A Guide to the Legal Liability of Coaches for a Sports Participant's Injuries*, 6 Seton Hall J. Sport L. 7, 66-77 (1996); see also *Ward v. Mich. State Univ.*, 782 N.W.2d 514 (Mich. Ct. App. 2010) (university's operation of hockey rink constituted a governmental function because it did not operate the rink primarily to generate a profit).

2. *Qualified Immunity for Public School Employees.* The doctrine of *qualified immunity* may protect public school employees such as coaches and athletic

trainers from negligence liability when they are exercising a discretionary act, but not a ministerial act. The disagreement between the majority and dissenting judges in *Prince* relates to whether coaches act in a ministerial or discretionary capacity when supervising a sport and making decisions about medical matters involving athletes. How does one distinguish the performance of a ministerial function from a discretionary function? In *Lennon v. Petersen*, 624 So. 2d 171 (Ala. 1993), the Alabama Supreme Court stated:

> A discretionary function does not include ministerial tasks like the mere filling out of a form, nor does it include acts made 'fraudulently, in bad faith, beyond [the actor's] authority, or . . . under a mistaken interpretation of the law.' . . . Although discretionary functions do not include unauthorized acts, they do include acts that require 'personal deliberation, decision and judgment.'

Id. at 173-74. Accord *Feagins v. Waddy*, 978 So. 2d 712 (Ala. 2007). Considering the underlying policy reasons for qualified immunity, is this the appropriate distinction to be made in the context of high school athletics?

In reaffirming *Prince*, the Mississippi Supreme Court expressed the following concern if the state's tort claims act is not construed to provide immunity to a public school and coaches:

> High school football coaches around the state would lose their ability to control their football teams. Discipline of a football team would become non-existent. If a coach refused a player's request for a water break—to see a trainer—to not have to run any more wind sprints—to not have to do any more one-on-one blocking drills, because of that player's complaint of "feeling weak" or "not feeling good" or simply "not feeling like it," that coach would be very much aware of the fact that he/she would be running the risk of being successfully sued . . . should that player later suffer physical/medical problems related to the coach's failure to cow to the player's every whim and wish. On the other hand, if the coach, in fear of a successful lawsuit, should cow to the player's every whim, wish and demand, then the coach would lose the respect of the players, and discipline and morale would be lost.

Harris ex rel. *Harris v. McCray*, 867 So. 2d 188, 193 (Miss. 2003).

In *Yanero* ex rel. *Yanero v. Davis*, 65 S.W.3d 510 (Ky. 2001), a high school baseball player who was not wearing a batting helmet was injured after being struck in the head by a ball thrown by a classmate. Although the Kentucky Supreme Court adopted the doctrine of qualified immunity, it refused to allow it to shield a coach from negligence related to his failure to supervise the plaintiff so as to require that he wear a batting helmet. "The performance of that duty in this instance was a ministerial, rather than a discretionary, function in that it involved only the enforcement of a known rule requiring that student athletes wear batting helmets during baseball batting practice. The promulgation of such a rule is a discretionary function; the enforcement of it is a ministerial function." *Id.* at 529. See also *Karalyos v. Bd. of Educ. of Lake Forest Cmty. High Sch. Dist.* 115, 788 F. Supp. 2d 727, 731 (N.D. Ill. 2011) (a discretionary act involves an act of discretion and a policy decision); *Clark Cty. Sch. Dist. v. Payo*, 403 P.3d 1270 (Nev. 2017) (discretionary-function immunity applies to school district's decisions to add floor hockey as a part of physical education curriculum and not to provide safety equipment because the decisions were discretionary and policy based; discretionary-function immunity did not extend, however, to decisions related to "negligent administration, instruction, and supervision of the floor hockey class" because such decisions were discretionary but were not policy based); *Elias v. Davis*, 535 S.W.3d 737 (Mo. Ct. App. 2017) (coaches who scrimmaged in full pads with high school football players engaged in a discretionary act within the scope of their official duties and were entitled to qualified immunity in regard to sixteen-year old plaintiff's negligence claim); *Covington Cty. Sch. Dist. v. Magee*, 29 So. 3d 1 (Miss. 2010) (school district was immunized from tort liability relating to the heat-stroke death of a high school football player during practice; a coach's decision to hold practice was considered a discretionary act); but see *Elson ex rel. Elston v. Howland Local Schs.*, 865 N.E.2d 845 (Ohio 2007) (where there was no showing that a coach's position involves policy-making, planning, or enforcement powers, his position did not involve "the exercise of a high degree of official judgment or discretion"; therefore immunity was not an available defense). For commentary regarding institutional liability for heat-related deaths, see David Feingold, *Who Takes the Heat? Criminal Liability for Heat-Related Deaths in High School Athletics*, 17 Cardozo J.L. & Gender 359, 373 (2011).

Courts also recognize exceptions, including gross negligence or reckless conduct, to the availability of qualified immunity as a defense. See e.g., *Swank v. Valley Christian Sch.*, 398 P.3d 1108 (Wash. 2017) (in determining whether coach's conduct precluded him from successfully asserting volunteer immunity as a defense, the court discusses the distinction between simple negligence and gross negligence or recklessness); but see *Barr v. Cunningham*, 89 N.E.3d 315 (Ill. 2017) (rejecting plaintiff's claim to invoke willful and wanton exception to the qualified immunity defense because coach's discretionary act of not requiring an injured athlete to wear safety glasses did not rise to the level of willful and wanton conduct); *Radebaugh v. Wausau Underwriters Ins. Co.*, 909 S.W.2d 210 (Wis. Ct. App. 2018) (unpublished) (rejecting plaintiff's argument that governmental immunity did not protect the school district from tort liability because of the compelling danger exception, but recognizing triable issues of fact as to the reckless conduct exception to the contact sport immunity statute in regard to the individual defendants). For a discussion of the real property exception to the governmental immunity defense, see *Brewington ex rel Brewington v. City of Philadelphia*, 199 A.3d 348 (Pa. 2018) (rejecting governmental immunity defense because of the real property exception, which applies when injury is the result of a negligent failure to maintain property).

3. *Alleged Constitutional Torts.* Courts generally have rejected athletes' efforts to avoid the application of state law sovereign immunity for negligent injury treatment rendered by public school personnel by asserting such claims under the guise of federal constitutional rights violations. In *Burden v. Wilkes-Barre Area School District*, 16 F. Supp. 2d 569 (M.D. Pa. 1998), a federal district court rejected plaintiff's contention that an educational institution's decision not to hire a certified athletic trainer to protect the health and safety of students participating in competitive sports violated an athlete's constitutional right to life and liberty. See also *Davis v. Carter*, 555 F.3d 979 (11th Cir. 2009) (rejecting parents' constitutional claims as a means of circumventing immunity defense in a case in which minor football player died during intense voluntary workout; evidence failed to establish coaches

acted wilfully or maliciously). But see *Roventini v. Pasadena Indep. Sch. Dist.,* 981 F. Supp. 1013 (S.D. Tex. 1997) (holding that allegations of a high school football player's death caused by heat stroke, suffered during a practice in which no certified athletic trainer was present and in which the only persons providing medical assistance were untrained teenage team managers, stated a claim for violation of the decedent's federal constitutional rights), *vacated,* 183 F.R.D. 500 (S.D. Tex. 1998).

PROBLEM 11-5

John, a high school football player, was assaulted by another player, Richard, while the two were walking unsupervised to the locker room from the practice field. The coach stopped the assault but did not otherwise attempt to ascertain the cause of the attack. The following day, John suffered injury resulting from another assault by Richard when the two were left unsupervised in the locker room. The public school district's handbook states that the school possesses a duty to supervise and maintain discipline of students at school. John sued the school district alleging a negligent failure to supervise. Will the school district be successful in asserting sovereign immunity as a defense?

c.   Validity of Liability Waivers

The following materials explore the enforceability of pre-injury contracts pursuant to which a person agrees to release a school district or its employees from liability for negligent failure to use reasonable care to protect the health and safety of students during athletic activities. Differing terminology, including exculpatory clauses, releases, covenants not to sue, and hold harmless agreements, is used to refer to such contracts. Although technical differences exist in specific types of such contracts, what lies at their core is an agreement by one party to accept the risk of harm resulting from another's conduct. If enforceable, these waivers of liability bar a plaintiff's ability to seek recovery from the defendant for harm caused by certain tortious conduct. Determining the validity of liability waivers requires judicial reconciliation of a fundamental tension between contract and tort law.

A basic premise of tort law holds a party responsible for his or her own negligent or intentional misconduct that causes harm to another. An equally fundamental tenet of contract law provides that a competent party has the freedom to construct his or her own bargains and agreements. The Colorado Supreme Court has described a release as standing "at the crossroads of two competing principles: freedom of contract and responsibility for damages caused by one's own negligent acts." Mary A. Connell & Frederick G. Savage, *Releases: Is There Still a Place for Their Use by Colleges and Universities?,* 29 J.C. & U.L. 579, 580 (2003). A helpful discussion of the validity of waivers appears in Elisa Lintemuth, *Parental Rights v. Parens Patriae: Determining the Correct Limitations on the Validity of Pre-Injury Waivers Effectuated by Parents on Behalf of Minor Children,* 2010 Mich. St. L. Rev. 169 (2010).

Some courts have refused to enforce pre-injury waivers on the ground that they violate public policy. In one group of cases, courts rely on public policy grounds to refuse to permit a high school to enforce waivers by a student-athlete or his or her parents or guardian who signed it. In what can be characterized as an intermediate approach, other jurisdictions allow high schools to enforce such waivers against a parent or guardian who signs it, but not against a minor. The third group of jurisdictions have adopted a position that permits parents to sign a release that binds both the parent and minor. The cases that follow, *Wagenblast* and *Sharon*, represent contrasting perspectives on the validity of liability waivers.

WAGENBLAST v. ODESSA SCH. DIST. NO. 105-157-166J
758 P.2d 968 (Wash. 1988)

ANDERSEN, Justice.

Can school districts require public school students and their parents to sign written releases which release the districts from the consequences of all future school district negligence, before the students will be allowed to engage in certain recognized school related activities, here interscholastic athletics?

We hold that the exculpatory releases from any future school district negligence are invalid because they violate public policy.

Probably the best exposition of the test to be applied in determining whether exculpatory agreements violate public policy is that stated by the California Supreme Court. In writing for a unanimous court, the late Justice Tobriner outlined the factors in *Tunkl v. Regents of Univ. of Cal.*, 60 Cal. 2d 92, 383 P.2d 441, 32 Cal. Rptr. 33, 6 A.L.R.3d 693 (1963):

1. *The agreement concerns an endeavor of a type generally thought suitable for public regulation.*

Regulation of governmental entities usually means self-regulation. Thus, the Legislature has by statute granted to each school board the authority to control, supervise, and regulate the conduct of interscholastic athletics. In some situations, a school board is permitted, in turn, to delegate this authority to the Washington Interscholastic Activities Association (WIAA) or to another voluntary nonprofit entity. In the cases before us, both school boards look to the WIAA for regulation of interscholastic sports. The WIAA handbook contains an extensive constitution with rules for such athletic endeavors. . . .

Clearly then, interscholastic sports in Washington are extensively regulated, and are a fit subject for such regulation.

2. *The party seeking exculpation is engaged in performing a service of great importance to the public, which is often a matter of practical necessity for some members of the public.*

This court has held that public school students have no fundamental right to participate in interscholastic athletics. Nonetheless, the court also has observed that the justification advanced for interscholastic athletics is their educational and cultural value. As the testimony of then Seattle School Superintendent Robert Nelson and others amply demonstrate, interscholastic athletics is part and parcel of the overall educational scheme in Washington. The total expenditure of time, effort and money on these endeavors makes this clear. The importance of these programs to the public is substantive; they represent a significant tie of the public at large to our system of public education. Nor can the importance of these programs to certain students be denied; as Superintendent Nelson agreed, some students undoubtedly remain in school and maintain their academic standing only because they can participate in these programs. Given this emphasis on sports by the public and the school system, it would be unrealistic to expect students to view athletics as an activity entirely separate and apart from the remainder of their schooling. . . .

In sum, under any rational view of the subject, interscholastic sports in public schools are a matter of public importance in this jurisdiction.

3. *Such party holds itself out as willing to perform this service for any member of the public who seeks it, or at least for any member coming within certain established standards.*

Implicit in the nature of interscholastic sports is the notion that such programs are open to all students who meet certain skill and eligibility standards. This conclusion finds direct support in the testimony of former Superintendent Nelson and the WIAA eligibility and nondiscrimination policies set forth in the WIAA handbook.

4. *Because of the essential nature of the service, in the economic setting of the transaction, the party invoking exculpation possesses a decisive advantage of bargaining strength against any member of the public who seeks the services.*

Not only have interscholastic sports become of considerable importance to students and the general public alike, but in most instances there exists no alternative program of organized competition. For instance, former Superintendent Nelson knew of no alternative to the Seattle School District's wrestling program. While outside alternatives exist for some activities, they possess little of the inherent allure of interscholastic competition. Many students cannot afford private programs or the private schools where such releases might not be employed. In this regard, school districts have near-monopoly power. And, because such programs have become important to student participants, school districts possess a clear and disparate bargaining strength when they insist that students and their parents sign these releases.

5. *In exercising a superior bargaining power, the party confronts the public with a standardized adhesion contract of exculpation, and makes no provision whereby a purchaser may pay additional reasonable fees and obtain protection against negligence.*

Both school districts admit to an unwavering policy regarding these releases; no student athlete will be allowed to participate in any program without first signing the release form as written by the school district. In both of these cases, students and their parents unsuccessfully attempted to modify the forms by deleting the release language. In both cases, the school district rejected the attempted modifications. Student athletes and their parents or guardians have no alternative but to sign the standard release forms provided to them or have the student barred from the program.

6. *The person or property of members of the public seeking such services must be placed under the control of the furnisher of the services, subject to the risk of carelessness on the part of the furnisher, its employees or agents.*

A school district owes a duty to its students to employ ordinary care and to anticipate reasonably foreseeable dangers so as to take precautions for protecting the children in its custody from such dangers. This duty extends to students engaged in interscholastic sports. As a natural incident to the relationship of a student athlete and his or her coach, the student athlete is usually placed under the coach's considerable degree of control. The student is thus subject to the risk that the school district or its agent will breach this duty of care.

In sum, the attempted releases in the cases before us exhibit all six of the characteristics denominated in [*Tunkl*]. Because of this, and for the aforesaid reasons, we hold that the releases in these consolidated cases are invalid as against public policy. . . .

SHARON v. CITY OF NEWTON

769 N.E.2d 738 (2002)

CORDY, Judge.

In this case, we consider the question of the validity of a release signed by the parent of a minor child for the purpose of permitting her to engage in public school extra-curricular sports activities. The question is one of first impression in the Commonwealth.

A. BACKGROUND

[Editors' note: A 16-year-old student was injured while participating in cheerleading practice at her high school. The injured cheerleader sued, and the City asserted as a defense a waiver of liability the cheerleader and her father had signed.]

The city filed a motion for summary judgment raising the signed release as a defense. . . .

2. SUMMARY JUDGMENT

We conclude that the facts Merav contends are in dispute are not material, enforcement of the release is consistent with our law and public policy, and Newton is entitled to judgment as a matter of law. . . .

b. *Public Policy*

Merav . . . contends that enforcement of the release against her claims would constitute a gross violation of public policy. This argument encompasses at least three separate public policy contentions: first, that it is contrary to public policy to permit schools to require students to sign exculpatory agreements as a prerequisite to participation in extracurricular school sports; second, that public policy prohibits a parent from contracting away a minor child's right to sue for a future harm; and third, that the enforcement of this release would undermine the duty of care that public schools owe their students. . . .

(1) Releases. Massachusetts law favors the enforcement of releases. . . . "There can be no doubt . . . that under the law of Massachusetts . . . in the absence of fraud a person may make a valid contract exempting himself from any liability to another which he may in the future incur as a result of his negligence or that of his agents or employees acting on his behalf." *Schell v. Ford*, 270 F.2d 384, 386 (1st Cir. 1959). Whether such contracts be called releases, covenants not to sue, or indemnification agreements, they represent "a practice our courts have long found acceptable." (citations omitted). . . .

Although Merav has suggested that, if the release at issue here is valid, there is nothing to prevent cities or towns from requiring releases for "simply allowing a child to attend school," such a conclusion does not necessarily follow. We have not had occasion to rule on the validity of releases required in the context of a compelled activity or as a condition for the receipt of essential services (e.g., public education, medical attention, housing, public utilities), and the enforceability of mandatory releases in such circumstances might well offend public policy. . . . In this case, Merav's participation in the city's extracurricular activity of cheerleading was neither compelled nor essential, and we conclude that the public policy of the Commonwealth is not offended by requiring a release as a prerequisite to that participation.

(2) Parent's waiver of a minor's claim. Merav contends that a parent cannot waive, compromise, or release a minor child's cause of action, and that enforcement of such a release against the child would violate public policy.

The purpose of the policy permitting minors to void their contracts is "to afford protection to minors from their own improvidence and want of sound judgment." *Frye v. Yasi*, 327 Mass. 724, 728, 101 N.E.2d 128 (1951). . . . Moreover, our law presumes that fit parents act in furtherance of the welfare and best interests of their children, . . . and with respect to matters relating to their care, custody, and upbringing have a fundamental right to make those decisions for them.

In the instant case, Merav's father signed the release in his capacity as parent because he wanted his child to benefit from participating in cheerleading, as she had done for four previous seasons. He made an important family decision cognizant of the risk of physical injury to his child and the financial risk to the family as a whole. In the circumstance of a voluntary, nonessential activity, we will not disturb this parental judgment. This comports with the fundamental liberty interest of parents in the rearing of their children, and is not inconsistent with the purpose behind our public policy permitting minors to void their contracts.

c.   *The Encouragement of Athletic Activities for Minors.* . . .

To hold that releases of the type in question here are unenforceable would expose public schools, who offer many of the extracurricular sports opportunities available to children, to financial costs and risks that will inevitably lead to the reduction of those programs.[11] It would also create the anomaly of a minor who participates in a program sponsored and managed by a nonprofit organization not having a cause of action for negligence that she would have had had she participated in the same program sponsored as an extracurricular activity by

---

11. The fact that *G.L. c. 258*, § 2, limits the financial exposure of municipalities to $100,000 an occurrence (plus defense costs) does not insulate them from the deleterious impact of inherently unquantifiable financial risk. Consequently, in times of fiscal constraint, those programs are often the targets of budget reductions. A decision exposing school systems to further financial costs and risk for undertaking such programs cannot help but accelerate their curtailment.

the local public school. This distinction seems unwarranted, inevitably destructive to school-sponsored programs, and contrary to public interest.

Merav contends that to enforce the release would convey the message that public school programs can be run negligently, in contravention of the well-established responsibility of schools to protect their students. We disagree. There are many reasons aside from potential tort liability why public schools will continue to take steps to ensure well-run and safe extracurricular programs — not the least of which is their ownership by, and accountability to, the citizens of the cities and towns they serve. Moreover, the Legislature has already made the judgment that the elimination of liability for negligence in nonprofit sports programs is necessary to the encouragement and survival of such programs. . . . The enforcement of the release is consistent with the Commonwealth's policy of encouraging athletic programs for youth and does not contravene the responsibility that schools have to protect their students. . . .

C.   CONCLUSION

For the reasons set forth above, we conclude that Merav's father had the authority to bind his minor child to an exculpatory release that was a proper condition of her voluntary participation in extracurricular sports activities offered by the city. Summary judgment for the city that was entered on the basis of the validity of that release is therefore affirmed. . . .

NOTES AND QUESTIONS

1. *Comparing* Wagenblast *and* Sharon. In *Wagenblast*, the Washington Supreme Court held that requiring a student and his parent or guardian to sign a standard form releasing the school district from liability for negligence in connection with the student's participation in interscholastic athletics violated public policy. Which of the factors articulated in *Tunkl v. University of California* appear most critical as a basis for invalidating waivers in the realm of high school athletics? According to the *Wagenblast* court, is participation in high school sports an important public and practical necessity?

   The *Sharon* court recognized the ability of a minor to avoid a contract. It upheld a waiver, however, because it had been signed by the minor's parent. Which factors most influenced the court's decision? Which court, *Wagenblast* or *Sharon*, most effectively reconciles the competing public policies regarding whether pre-injury liability waivers should be enforced?

   How critical is the inability of minors or their parents to negotiate the terms of a waiver to determining the enforceability of such a provision? Do minors and their parents possess a realistic opportunity to negotiate the terms of waivers of liability for athletic injury?

2. *Developing Law in Other Jurisdictions.* Other courts have exhibited a willingness to enforce liability waivers for negligent injury to minors participating in competitive or recreational sports. *Mohney v. USA Hockey, Inc.*, 5 Fed. Appx. 450 (6th Cir. 2001) (release, signed by minor hockey player and his father, was valid and applied to injuries sustained by the player); *Zivich v. Mentor Soccer Club, Inc.*, 696 N.E.2d 201 (Ohio 1998) (release, signed by mother of injured child, barred child's claim for negligence against volunteers and sponsors of nonprofit sport activities). In *Platzer v. Mammoth Mountain Ski Area*, 128 Cal.

Rptr. 2d 885 (Cal. Ct. App. 2002), a mother who enrolled her eight-year-old son in a ski resort's sports school signed a form assuming the risk of injury associated, among other things, with use of the chairlifts. Her son fell from a lift during a lesson. In upholding the validity of the exculpatory clause, the court rejected plaintiff's argument that public policy precluded enforcement of the release. It noted that California courts have consistently refused to invalidate exculpatory agreements in the recreational sports context. See also *Eriksson v. Nunnink*, 183 Cal. Rptr. 3d 234 (Cal. Ct. App. 2015) (a release signed by minor absolved coach from liability to student injured in equestrian competition unless coach engaged in willful and wanton negligence, but release would not necessarily bar mother's wrongful death claim which was a cause of action distinct from deceased child's; a release of future liability or express assumption of the risk may, however, operate as a defense to the parent's claim); *Pollock v. Highlands Ranch Cmty. Ass'n, Inc.*, 140 P.3d 351 (Colo. Ct. App. 2006) (discussing statute superseding case that had invalidated a release waiving minor child's negligence claim).

Although the foregoing decisions represent an erosion of the rule established in *Wagenblast*, courts in other jurisdictions remain reluctant to enforce waiver clauses. See, *Rutherford v. Talisker Canyons Fin., Co., LLC*, 445 P.3d 474 (Utah 2019) (court holds that: "Absent a relevant, contrary expression of intent from the legislature, . . . a parent cannot release his or her minor child's prospective claims for negligence" because such a release violates public policy); *Miller ex rel. E.M. v. House of Boom Ky.*, 575 S.W.3d 656 (Ky. 2019) (Kentucky Supreme Court holds that a pre-injury waiver signed by parents that released for-profit entities from negligence liability for injuries to child was void as a matter of law); *Galloway v. State*, 790 N.W.2d 252, 258 (Iowa 2010) (holding that public policy precludes the enforceability of pre-injury waiver a parent signs on behalf of child and characterizing *Sharon* as reflective of the minority rule); *Blackwell v. Sky High Sports Nashville Operations, Inc.*, 523 S.W.3d 624 (Tenn. Ct. App. 2017) (rejecting *Sharon* in concluding that Tennessee precedent and public policy invalidated waiver of liability signed by parent on behalf of child who was injured during a dodgeball game at defendant's trampoline park); *Thode ex rel. J.T. v. Monster Mountain, LLC*, 754 F. Supp. 2d 1323, 1327 (M.D. Ala. 2010) (refusing to enforce liability waiver where court approval had not been obtained).

3. *Other Grounds for Invalidating Waivers.* In jurisdictions in which a release of liability for negligence is enforceable, one that attempts to relieve a defendant of liability for its willful misconduct, gross negligence, and intentional torts is invalid. See, e.g., *Eriksson v. Nunnink*, 120 Cal. Rptr. 3d 90 (Cal. Ct. App. 2011) (a finding that an equestrian coach's gross negligence in selecting an unfit horse for the plaintiff would invalidate a liability waiver). Connell & Savage, *supra*, at 603. Courts will also resort to contract interpretation as a mechanism for invalidating waivers that are ambiguous and inconspicuous. Strict interpretation of contracts eases the burden on courts to reconcile the tensions between contract and tort. *Id.* at 605-06.

PROBLEM 11-6

Jerry Abel, who played soccer for a private high school he attended, collapsed during a game following a collision with a player on the opposing team. The opposing player was penalized for the hit, which was hard but typical of hits that frequently occur during soccer matches. Within seconds after Abel collapsed, his coach and the athletic trainer ran onto the soccer field and immediately asked that an assistant coach call an ambulance, which he did. By the time the coach and trainer arrived on the field, Abel had stopped breathing and lost consciousness. The trainer unsuccessfully administered CPR and called for an automated external defibrillator (AED), which was housed in a building at Abel's school. However, it was not brought to the field until 10 minutes after Abel initially collapsed, which was approximately two minutes after Abel died.

It was subsequently determined that Abel suffered from a previously undetected underlying heart condition and that if the AED had been used in a timely manner, Abel most likely would have been revived. It was also determined that prior to the game, Abel's coach noticed during warmups that Abel's breathing seemed slightly labored. When he was questioned by his coach as to how he felt, Abel responded that he was fine and insisted that he be permitted to play. The coach agreed but told Abel to let him know if he started to feel poorly during the game. Prior to the beginning of the soccer season, as a condition to Abel's ability to play sports, both Abel and his parents signed a form that conspicuously absolved the school district and its employees and agents from liability for all negligent conduct arising from Abel's participation in soccer.

Abel's parents have sought your advice regarding the likely success of a tort suit to recover for Abel's death and, if so, against whom. In providing your advice, consider which claims to assert against whom and any potential defenses such parties might assert. If Abel attended a public high school, identify and discuss any other defenses that might be applicable.

2.   College or University

Like the body of law defining a high school's legal duty to protect its students' health and safety, the nature and scope of a university's corresponding legal duty also is rapidly developing. As you read the following cases, consider how the differences between intercollegiate and interscholastic athletics as well as the nature of the relationship between a university and its student-athletes influence the judicial definition of the parameters of this duty. In the context of health and safety, should a distinction be drawn between the duty of care owed by colleges to student-athletes and high schools to their student-athletes?

KLEINKNECHT v. GETTYSBURG COLLEGE
989 F.2d 1360 (3d Cir. 1993)

HUTCHINSON, Circuit Judge.

II.   FACTUAL HISTORY

In September 1988, Drew Kleinknecht was a twenty-year-old sophomore student at [Gettysburg] College, which had recruited him for its Division III intercollegiate lacrosse team. . . .

Lacrosse is a contact sport. In terms of sports-related injuries at the College, it ranked at least fourth behind football, basketball, and wrestling, respectively.

Lacrosse players can typically suffer a variety of injuries, including unconsciousness, wooziness, concussions, being knocked to the ground, and having the wind knocked out of them. Before Drew died, however, no athlete at the College had experienced cardiac arrest while playing lacrosse or any other sport. . . .

Because lacrosse is a spring sport, daily practices were held during the spring semester in order to prepare for competition. Student trainers were assigned to cover both spring practices and games. Fall practice was held only for the players to learn "skills and drills," and to become acquainted with the other team members. No student trainers were assigned to the fall practices.

Drew participated in a fall lacrosse practice on the afternoon of September 16, 1988. Coaches Janczyk and Anderson attended and supervised this practice. It was held on the softball fields outside Musselman Stadium. No trainers or student trainers were present. Neither coach had certification in CPR. Neither coach had a radio on the practice field. The nearest telephone was inside the training room at Musselman Stadium, roughly 200-250 yards away. The shortest route to this telephone required scaling an eight-foot high cyclone fence surrounding the stadium. According to Coach Janczyk, he and Coach Anderson had never discussed how they would handle an emergency during fall lacrosse practice.

The September 16, 1988 practice began at about 3:15 p.m. with jogging and stretching, some drills, and finally a "six on six" drill in which the team split into two groups at opposite ends of the field. Drew was a defenseman and was participating in one of the drills when he suffered a cardiac arrest. According to a teammate observing from the sidelines, Drew simply stepped away from the play and dropped to the ground. Another teammate on the sidelines stated that no person or object struck Drew prior to his collapse.

After Drew fell, his teammates and Coach Janczyk ran to his side. Coach Janczyk and some of the players noticed that Drew was lying so that his head appeared to be in an awkward position. No one knew precisely what had happened at that time, and at least some of those present suspected a spinal injury. . . .

According to the College, Coach Janczyk acted in accordance with the school's emergency plan by first assessing Drew's condition, then dispatching players to get a trainer and call for an ambulance. Coach Janczyk himself then began to run toward Musselman Stadium to summon help. . . .

[T]he team captain, ran toward the stadium, where he knew a training room was located and a student trainer could be found. . . . [He] scaled a chain link fence that surrounded the stadium and ran across the field, encountering student trainer Traci Moore outside the door to the training room. He told her that a lacrosse player was down and needed help. . . . [He] continued into the training room where he told the student trainers there what had happened. One of them phoned Plank Gymnasium and told Head Trainer Donolli about the emergency.

[A]nother team member ran toward . . . the College Union Building. He told the student at the front desk of the emergency on the practice field . . . and she immediately telephoned for an ambulance.

Student trainer Moore was first to reach Drew. . . . Because Drew was breathing, she did not attempt CPR or any other first aid technique, but only monitored his condition, observing no visible bruises or lacerations.

By this time, Coach Janczyk had entered the stadium training room and learned that Donolli had been notified and an ambulance called. Coach Janczyk returned to the practice field at the same time Donolli arrived in a golf cart.

Donolli saw that Drew was not breathing, and turned him on his back to begin CPR with the help of a student band member who was certified as an emergency medical technician and had by chance arrived on the scene. The two of them performed CPR until two ambulances arrived at approximately 4:15 p.m. Drew was defibrillated and drugs were administered to strengthen his heart. He was placed in an ambulance and taken to the hospital, but despite repeated resuscitation efforts, Drew could not be revived. He was pronounced dead at 4:58 p.m.

As the district court observed, the parties vigorously dispute the amount of time that elapsed in connection with the events following Drew's collapse. . . .

The Kleinknechts further maintain, and the College does not dispute, that at least five minutes elapsed from the time that Drew was first observed on the ground until Head Trainer Donolli began administering CPR. Thus, the Kleinknechts contend that evidence exists from which a jury could infer that as long as twelve minutes elapsed before CPR was administered. They also estimate that roughly ten more minutes passed before the first ambulance arrived on the scene.

Prior to his collapse on September 16, 1988, Drew had no medical history of heart problems. The Kleinknechts themselves describe him as "a healthy, physically active and vigorous young man" with no unusual medical history until his death. Brief for Appellants at 3-4. In January 1988, a College physician had examined Drew to determine his fitness to participate in sports and found him to be in excellent health. The Kleinknecht's family physician had also examined Drew in August 1987 and found him healthy and able to participate in physical activity.

Medical evidence indicated Drew died of cardiac arrest after a fatal attack of cardiac arrhythmia. Post-mortem examination could not detect the cause of Drew's fatal cardiac arrhythmia. An autopsy conducted the day after his death revealed no bruises or contusions on his body. This corroborated the statements by Drew's teammates that he was not in play when he suffered his cardiac arrest and dispelled the idea that contact with a ball or stick during the practice might have caused the arrhythmia. . . .

IV.   ANALYSIS

1.   THE DUTY OF CARE ISSUE

Whether a defendant owes a duty of care to a plaintiff is a question of law. . . .

a.   *Special Relationship*

The Kleinknechts argue that . . . a college or university owes a duty to its intercollegiate athletes to provide preventive measures in the event of a medical emergency.

In support of their argument, the Kleinknechts cite the case of *Hanson v. Kynast*, No. CA-828 (Ohio Ct. App. June 3, 1985), *rev'd on other grounds*, 24 Ohio St.3d 171, 494 N.E.2d 1091 (1986). In *Hanson* an intercollegiate, recruited lacrosse player was seriously injured while playing in a lacrosse game against another college. The plaintiff alleged that his university breached its legal duty to have an ambulance present during the lacrosse game. The trial court granted the defendant's motion for summary judgment based on its holding, *inter alia*, that

> There is no duty as a matter of law for the Defendant College or other sponsor of
> athletic events to have ambulances, emergency vehicles, trained help or doctors

> present during the playing of a lacrosse game or other athletic events, and the failure to do so does not constitute negligence as a matter of law.

Id. at 10. The court of appeals reversed, concluding, "[I]t is a question of fact for the jury to determine whether or not appellee University acted reasonably in failing to have an ambulance present at the field or to provide quick access to the field in the event of an emergency." *Id.* at 6. By directing the trial court to submit the case to a jury, the court of appeals implicitly held that the university owed a duty of care to the plaintiff.

Although the *Hanson* court did not specify the theory on which it predicated this duty, we think it reached the correct result, and we predict that the Supreme Court of Pennsylvania would conclude that a similar a duty exists on the facts of this case. Like the lacrosse student in *Hanson*, Drew chose to attend Gettysburg College because he was persuaded it had a good lacrosse program, a sport in which he wanted to participate at the intercollegiate level. Head Trainer Donolli actively recruited Drew to play lacrosse at the College. At the time he was stricken, Drew was not engaged in his own private affairs as a student at Gettysburg College. Instead, he was participating in a scheduled athletic practice for an intercollegiate team sponsored by the College under the supervision of College employees. On these facts we believe that the Supreme Court of Pennsylvania would hold that a special relationship existed between the College and Drew that was sufficient to impose a duty of reasonable care on the College. Other states have similarly concluded that a duty exists based on such a relationship. . . .

Drew was not acting in his capacity as a private student when he collapsed. Indeed, the Kleinknechts concede that if he had been, they would have no recourse against the College. There is a distinction between a student injured while participating as an intercollegiate athlete in a sport for which he was recruited and a student injured at a college while pursuing his private interests, scholastic or otherwise. This distinction serves to limit the class of students to whom a college owes the duty of care that arises here. Had Drew been participating in a fraternity football game, for example, the College might not have owed him the same duty or perhaps any duty at all. There is, however, no need for us to reach or decide the duty question either in that context or in the context of whether a college would owe a duty towards students participating in intramural sports. On the other hand, the fact that Drew's cardiac arrest occurred during an athletic event involving an intercollegiate team of which he was a member does impose a duty of due care on a college that actively sought his participation in that sport. We cannot help but think that the College recruited Drew for its own benefit, probably thinking that his skill at lacrosse would bring favorable attention and so aid the College in attracting other students. . . .

b. Foreseeability

This does not end our inquiry, however. The determination that the College owes a duty of care to its intercollegiate athletes could merely define the class of persons to whom the duty extends, without determining the nature of the duty or demands it makes on the College. . . .

Although the district court correctly determined that the Kleinknechts had presented evidence establishing that the occurrence of severe and life-threatening injuries is not out of the ordinary during contact sports, it held that the College had no duty because the cardiac arrest suffered by Drew, a twenty-year old athlete with no history of any severe medical problems, was not reasonably foreseeable. Its definition of foreseeability is too narrow. Although it is true that a defendant is not required to guard against every possible risk, he must take reasonable steps to guard against hazards which are generally foreseeable. Though the specific risk that a person like Drew would suffer a cardiac arrest may be unforeseeable, the Kleinknechts produced ample evidence that a life-threatening injury occurring during participation in an athletic event like lacrosse was reasonably foreseeable. In addition to the testimony of numerous medical and athletic experts, Coach Janczyk, Head Trainer Donolli, and student trainer Moore all testified that they were aware of instances in which athletes had died during athletic competitions. The foreseeability of a life-threatening injury to Drew was not hidden from the College's view. Therefore, the College did owe Drew a duty to take reasonable precautions against the risk of death while Drew was taking part in the College's intercollegiate lacrosse program.

Having determined that it is foreseeable that a member of the College's inter-scholastic lacrosse team could suffer a serious injury during an athletic event, it becomes evident that the College's failure to protect against such a risk is not reasonable. The magnitude of the foreseeable harm—irreparable injury or death to one of its student athletes as a result of inadequate preventive emergency measures—is indisputable. With regard to the offsetting cost of protecting against such risk, the College prophesied that if this Court accepts that the College owed the asserted duty, then it will be required "to have a CPR certified trainer on site at each and every athletic practice whether in-season or off-season, formal or informal, strenuous or light," and to provide similar cardiac protection to "intramural, club sports and gym class." This "slippery slope" prediction reflects an unwarranted extension of the holding in this case. First, the recognition of a duty here is limited to intercollegiate athletes. No other scenario is presented, so the question whether any of the other broad classes of events and students posited by the College merit similar protection is not subject to resolution. Second, the determination whether the College has breached this duty at all is a question of fact for the jury. This Court recognizes only that under the facts of this case, the College owed a duty to Drew to have measures in place at the lacrosse team's practice on the afternoon of September 16, 1988 in order to provide prompt treatment in the event that he or any other member of the lacrosse team suffered a life-threatening injury. . . .

It may be that the emergency medical measures the College had in place were sufficient to fulfill this duty. It is also possible that the College could not foresee that its failure to provide emergency medical services other than those which it already had in place would substantially contribute to the death of an apparently healthy student. . . .

Our holding is narrow. It predicts only that a court applying Pennsylvania law would conclude that the College had a duty to provide prompt and adequate emergency medical services to Drew, one of its intercollegiate athletes, while he was engaged in a school-sponsored athletic activity for which he had been recruited. Whether the College breached that duty is a question of fact. . . .

NOTE AND QUESTIONS

What is the holding in *Kleinknecht?* What policy reasons justify holding the university liable for the student-athlete's death, particularly since his cardiac arrest was unforeseeable? Does a university sponsoring intercollegiate athletics have a legal duty to have a certified athletic trainer present at all games, practices, and training sessions? See *Kennedy v. Syracuse Univ.*, 1995 WL 548710, at 1-3 (N.D.N.Y. Sept. 12, 1995) (the court dismissed an athlete's claim that the university was negligent for failing to have an athletic trainer present at gymnastics team practices, without considering a university's duty to do so, because there was no proof that inadequate emergency care given by coaches or teammates caused plaintiff's injury).

Consistent with *Kleinknecht*, in *Stineman v. Fontbonne Coll.*, 664 F.2d 1082 (8th Cir. 1981), the Eighth Circuit held that a university has a duty to refer an injured intercollegiate athlete to a physician for medical treatment. The plaintiff was struck in the eye by a ball thrown during softball practice. The team's coaches did not recommend that plaintiff see a physician for treatment of her injury. Because of a delay in obtaining medical treatment, the plaintiff lost the vision in her eye. Without considering the plaintiff's potential contributory negligence, the court awarded her damages of $600,000.

In the summer of 2005, Northwestern University paid $16 million to settle a lawsuit alleging that its employees provided negligent emergency medical treatment to Rashidi Wheeler, a football player with a known asthmatic condition, after he collapsed during a preseason workout, which caused his death. See *Feleccia v. Lackawanna Coll.*, 156 A.3d 1200, 1215 (Pa. Super. Ct. 2017) (relying on *Kleinknecht*, the court holds college owed duty to student-athletes to have "qualified medical personnel available" at a football tryout, "and to provide adequate treatment in the event that an intercollegiate athlete suffered a medical emergency").

Kleinknecht has potentially broad implications regarding the nature and scope of a university's duty to protect the health and safety of its intercollegiate athletes. However, outside the context of emergency medical care, *Orr* and *Searles* illustrate that courts are divided regarding the nature and scope of a university's duty to protect its student-athletes from harm.

ORR v. BRIGHAM YOUNG UNIV.

960 F. Supp. 1522 (D. Utah 1994), *aff'd*, 108 F.3d 1388 (10th Cir. 1997)

Sam, District Judge.

This case raises issues regarding the duty of care owed by a university to one of its football players.

[Eds. Plaintiff Vernon Peter Orr attended Brigham Young University (BYU) from the fall of 1988 until April 1990, and played on the varsity football team for two football seasons. Prior to attending BYU, Orr attended Dixie College in St. George, Utah, and played for two years on the football team. Orr denied having any lower back pain or injury prior to attending BYU. In August 1988, Orr felt pain in his back during a practice drill with a blocking sled during a BYU football practice. He received treatment for his injuries by BYU's athletic trainer while he continued to practice and play in football games during the 1988 season. During the 1989 season, Orr experienced back pain and stiffness but, despite the football coach's directive, did not see the team's athletic trainers for treatment because the pain was not bad and he still felt "pretty much 100%." For the remainder of the 1989 season, Orr had mild episodes of back pain but could not remember if they were reported to the coaching staff or the medical staff.

In the last regular season game of the 1989 season, Orr complained of back pain at halftime and was examined and treated by two orthopedic specialists. Orr returned to play with the instruction that he was to leave the game if the pain increased or changed. Orr played the remainder of the game. After the game, all players who had been injured were instructed to report to the medical clinic in the athletic training room the next day. Orr did not report.

During postseason bowl practice two weeks later, Orr suffered a back injury. He was referred to the medical staff. Examination revealed reticular pain, and he was sent for radiological imaging, which showed three herniated discs. Orr was immediately referred to a neurological surgeon, who performed surgical repair of the herniated discs. At the close of BYU's 1991 winter semester, Orr left BYU to play professional football in Finland. Orr did not return to BYU to complete his education.]

Orr asserts that BYU negligently breached its duty of care owed to him in one or more of the following respects:

a. engendering a win-at-all-cost mentality;
b. excessively pressuring players to perform;
c. using psychological pressure to increase performance at the sacrifice of his health;
d. creating disincentives to report injuries or seek medical attention;
e. conditioning payment for medical services on an athletic trainer's determination of medical need;
f. employing unqualified persons to diagnose and treat football related injuries;
g. allowing unqualified personnel to evaluate his medical fitness to play football;
h. misdiagnosing his injuries;
i. failure of the trainers to refer him to a team physician for diagnosis and treatment;
j. failing to hire a full-time team physician responsible for diagnoses and treatment in lieu of unqualified trainers;
k. approving and encouraging him to play after being injured;
l. using pain killing injections to enable him to continue to play without completely diagnosing his injury;
m. placing greater emphasis on winning football games than on his physical and mental health;
n. losing interest in him and failing to assist him further in his education;
o. failing to act to preserve his health, and to treat his injuries in his long term personal best interest, to see that his educational needs were met; and,
p. engaging in the unauthorized practice of medicine.

BYU argues that "[e]xcept for those duties relating to claims of medical negligence or violations of medical standards of care, the long list of alleged duties owed to Orr and breached by BYU are ones that have never been identified or recognized as duties owed as a matter of law."

Much of Orr's claim of negligence is based upon the breach of purported duties of care created by the special relationship between a university and its student athletes. . . .

Orr, in essence, urges that BYU, having recruited him to play football, assumed the responsibility for his safety and deprived him of the normal opportunity for self protection. . . .

The Utah Supreme Court has not been called upon to rule on the precise issue presented here. However, direction is provided by analogous authority found in several Utah Supreme Court cases, although factually distinguishable. For example, the plaintiff in *Beach v. University of Utah*, 726 P.2d 413 (Utah 1986), alleged breach of a duty of care based upon a special relationship between the university and the student, injured while intoxicated on a field trip sponsored by the university and supervised by a university professor. After examining the relationship of a university and its students, the Utah Supreme Court concluded that the relationship was not custodial in nature and that law and society increasingly recognized the modern college student as an adult and not a child in need of custodial care. The analysis of *Beach* concerning the nature of the parties' relationship is helpful in evaluating Orr's relationship with BYU. . . .

Arguably, Orr, as a collegiate football player, had both demands and advantages distinct from those of the average college student. However, in the court's view, any distinctions are more of a contractual nature than a custodial nature mandating special duties of care and protection beyond those traditionally recognized under a simple negligence theory of liability. BYU, in exchange for a student's promise to play football, agrees to provide the student with such benefits as special consideration in meeting entrance requirements, financial assistance, training table meals, training equipment, medical services, and academic support. Certainly when training and medical services are provided and then negligently performed, liability could result under existing theories of negligence. However, nothing in the facts supports Orr's contentions that, by playing football for BYU, he became in essence a ward of the university without any vestige of free will or independence. At the time Orr began attending BYU he was twenty-two years old, married with one child. The court finds no facts which suggest that Orr's relationship with BYU was custodial in nature.

An athlete's choice to participate in a sport is not coerced. Voluntary association with a collegiate athletic team does not make the student less of "an autonomous adult or the institution more a caretaker." *Beach*, 726 P.2d at 419. n. 5. As noted earlier, the court views any distinctions between a regular student and a student athlete as more contractual in nature than custodial. In short, the court finds no compelling reasons to impose upon colleges and universities additional duties beyond those owed to other students or those presently recognized and available to collegiate athletes under acknowledged legal theories.

Based upon the analysis of the Utah Supreme Court in the analogous case of *Beach v. University of Utah*, the absence of facts supporting a custodial relationship, as well as for sound policy reasons, the court concludes that the supreme court of Utah would reject Orr's claim that duties are owed to him on the basis of a special relationship with the university by virtue of his football player status. . . .

[EDS. The court granted BYU's motion for summary judgment on all of Orr's claims except any arising out of the alleged negligent provision of medical care. BYU conceded it has a duty to conform to the standard of reasonable care when voluntarily providing sports medical care to its student-athletes. The court found that disputed issues of material fact existed as to Orr's claims based on BYU's alleged breach of its duty of care to Orr in diagnosing and treating his medical injuries.]

SEARLES v. TRUSTEES OF ST. JOSEPH'S COLLEGE

695 A.2d 1206 (Me. 1997)

LIPEZ, Justice.

Paul Searles . . . alleged that while playing basketball for St. Joseph's College the negligence of the defendants caused him permanent injuries and that they breached a contract to pay the medical expenses related to his injuries. Because we conclude that genuine issues of material fact exist on Searles's negligence claims, we vacate the judgment in part.

Searles entered St. Joseph's College as a freshman in 1988, having been awarded an athletic scholarship. Searles alleges that while playing basketball he began experiencing pain in his knees during the fall semester of 1988. In January 1989 Searles was diagnosed with patellar tendinitis. He continued to play basketball for the remainder of the school year, and he returned to play for the 1989-1990 season. He stopped playing in 1990 and had surgery on his knees in 1990 and again in 1991.

Searles filed the present action against St. Joseph's College, Rick Simonds, the school's basketball coach, and Peter Wheeler, the athletic trainer, alleging that "[d]espite medical advice and information suggesting that the Plaintiff should not be playing basketball, Defendant Simonds insisted that Paul Searles play. [As a] result, Paul Searles's knees became permanently impaired." . . .

We previously stated that a college has a legal duty to exercise reasonable care towards its students. *Isaacson v. Husson College*, 297 A.2d 98, 103 (Me. 1972). . . . That duty encompasses the duty of college coaches and athletic trainers to exercise reasonable care for the health and safety of student athletes. . . .

Searles alleged that Simonds "knew or should have known Paul Searles should not have been playing basketball in his condition, and should not have played plaintiff." Searles's response to the summary judgment motion included citations to the deposition testimony of Peter Wheeler, St. Joseph's trainer, who stated that he recognized the nature of Searles's problem, was concerned that Searles's continued play would result in greater injury to his knee, and that he discussed Searles's medical problem with Coach Simonds. Searles also alleged that on more than one occasion he advised Simonds that his knees were bothering him, but Simonds "continued to play Plaintiff in games despite knowledge of Plaintiff's condition and general knee soreness as early as January, 1989." The record before the court contains sufficient evidence to raise an issue of material fact as to Simonds's breach of his duty to exercise reasonable care for the health and safety of Searles. . . .

Searles presented medical testimony from Dr. John Herzog that his condition was likely due to "history overuse" and that "the more you play, the longer it's going to hurt and you may have a chronic problem develop." Searles presented evidence that Simonds was aware of his knee injury and continued to play him in games. Searles further alleges that Simonds was so intent on keeping Searles in games that he allowed him to skip basketball practices to preserve his knees for games. Searles himself testified as to the painful injuries he suffered playing basketball. The medical testimony and Searles's own account of his condition create a genuine issue of material fact as to whether he suffered permanent injury as a result of playing basketball at St. Joseph's. . . .

The gravamen of Searles's allegations against Wheeler, set forth in Counts VI and VII of his complaint, involves more than a claim that Wheeler negligently conducted a course of treatment of Searles's injuries that contributed to a worsening of his condition, or that he failed to appreciate the seriousness of Searles's condition. Searles claims that Wheeler "failed to advise Coach Simonds that Paul Searles should not be playing basketball and the condition of Paul Searles's knees was such that continued play before complete healing will likely cause permanent injury." The deposition of Wheeler demonstrates an awareness of the acuteness of Searles's knee problems. Simonds states in his deposition that he was never advised by Wheeler that Searles could be permanently impaired by continued play, and he does not recall the trainer suggesting that Searles should not play. He also asserts that the trainer decided whether an injured player could play basketball, not the coach. To the extent that Searles's claim of negligence against Wheeler involves a failure by Wheeler to communicate to Simonds the nature and extent of Searles's knee problems, or a failure by Wheeler to advise Searles that he should not play basketball in light of Wheeler's knowledge of Searles's medical condition, Searles did not have to provide expert testimony about the standard of care applicable to an athletic trainer. Jurors could apply their common knowledge in determining whether such failures, if they occurred, constituted a breach by Wheeler of his duty to exercise reasonable care for the health and safety of Searles. . . .

[Eds. Searles "[also] alleged that he entered into a contract with St. Joseph's [C]ollege, through its agents, under which the college promised to pay Paul's medical bills if he continued to play for the basketball team." Searles asserted, "Coach Simonds told my parents and me that the school's insurance would pay for all of the medical bills relating to my knee problems." Assuming that Simonds did state to Searles's parents that the school would pay Searles's medical bills, such a statement was deemed insufficient to constitute an offer to enter into a contract. There was no evidence as to the terms of the "offer" purportedly made by Simonds and no evidence that Searles and Simonds had an agreement that Searles had to continue to play basketball in exchange for the payment of his medical expenses. The court found the record did not contain evidence of the existence of a contract and that a judgment had been properly entered in favor of St. Joseph's on the contract claim.]

NOTES AND QUESTIONS

1. *Comparison of* Searles *and* Orr. The *Searles* court ruled that a university has a general legal duty to exercise reasonable care to protect the health and safety of injured student-athletes, whereas *Orr* declines to impose such a broad duty on a university. What reasoning underlies these courts' differing conclusions? According to the *Orr* court, under what limited circumstances might a university be held liable in tort to an injured student-athlete? Consistent with *Searles*, other courts have held that a university has a legal duty not to pressure or permit an injured athlete to return to a game. See *Lamorie v. Warner Pac. Coll.*, 850 P.2d 401 (Or. Ct. App. 1993) (finding that a jury could reasonably find that the player's reinjury of his eye was a foreseeable risk of a coach having directed the player to resume playing basketball, for which the university could be held liable).

2. *University "Special Relationship" with Student-Athletes.* Should there be a legally recognized special relationship between a university and its student-athletes that imposes a duty to protect their health and safety? If so, what should be

the parameters of such a relationship? For commentary regarding whether a special relationship provides the basis for imposing tort liability on universities vis-à-vis their student-athletes, see Brian C. Root, *How the Promises of Riches in Collegiate Athletics Lead to the Compromised Long-Term Health of Student-Athletes: Why and How the NCAA Should Protect Its Student-Athletes' Health,* 19 Health Matrix 279, 295 (2009) (discussing *Kleinknecht* and other cases raising the issue addressed therein); James J. Hefferan, Jr., Note, *Taking One for the Team:* Davidson v. University of North Carolina *and the Duty of Care Owed by Universities to Their Student-Athletes,* 37 Wake Forest L. Rev. 589 (2002); Timothy Davis, *Examining Educational Malpractice Jurisprudence: Should a Cause of Action Be Created for Student-Athletes?,* 69 Denv. U. L. Rev. 57 (1992).

In *Davidson v. Univ. of N.C. at Chapel Hill,* 543 S.E.2d 920 (N.C. Ct. App. 2001), *cert. denied,* 550 S.E.2d 771 (N.C. 2001), a North Carolina appellate court extended *Kleinknecht* by finding a special relationship between the university and a member of a school-sponsored intercollegiate team. Plaintiff, a member of the University of North Carolina's junior varsity cheerleading squad, suffered permanent brain damage and serious bodily injury resulting from a fall that occurred while she was performing a cheerleading stunt called a "two-one-chair" pyramid. The appellate court concluded that a "special relationship" existed between UNC and the plaintiff because of the parties' mutual dependence and the considerable degree of control the university exercised over the plaintiff. In addition, the court found that the "voluntary undertaking" by UNC to "advise and educate its cheerleaders regarding safety," created a duty of care that arose independently of the special relationship between the plaintiff and UNC. *Id.* at 28. But see *Roe v. Saint Louis Univ.,* 2012 WL 6757558 (E.D. Mo. Dec. 31, 2012) at *6, *aff'd on other grounds,* 746 F.3d 874 (8th Cir. 2014) (in rejecting a female student-athlete's claim that she was sexually assaulted because of her university's negligent failure to supervise an off-campus party, the court found that because of the absence of special relationship, the defendant possessed no duty to supervise and ensure plaintiff's safety at the private off-campus party); *McFadyen v. Duke Univ.,* 786 F.Supp.2d 887 (M.D.N.C. 2011) (university was not in a special relationship with members of lacrosse team on the basis of their status as students; the extent of any special relationship that might have arisen between players and university would be limited to the lacrosse team context. Consequently, the university was not the insurer of the safety of team members in other facets of their university experience).

Other courts have focused on the inherent risks of a sport, rather than the existence of a special relationship, when defining the scope of a university's duty to protect its student-athletes' safety. *Bukowski v. Clarkson Univ.,* 971 N.E.2d 849, 851 (N.Y. 2012) (coach and university not liable for injuries sustained by pitcher who was hit by a line drive during indoor practice; the player, who was a knowledgeable and experienced baseball player, assumed the inherent risk of being hit by a line drive); *Geiersbach v. Frieje,* 807 N.E.2d 114, 120 (Ind. Ct. App. 2004) (finding university had a duty only "to avoid reckless or malicious behavior or intentional injury" when conducting sporting events and practices).

A case not involving athletics could expand the circumstances in which a special relationship exists between institutions and their student-athletes so as to require the former to protect athletes from foreseeable harm. In *Regents of the University v. of California v. Rosen,* 413 P.3d 656 (Cal. 2018), a student, who suffered delusions and other mental problems, stabbed a fellow student during a chemistry lab. The injured student sued the university alleging negligence for its failure to "protect her from Thompson's foreseeable violent conduct." *Id.* at 613. The court characterized the salient issue as "whether, and under what circumstances, a college or university owes a duty of care to protect students like Rosen from harm." *Id.* The court concluded that "[c]onsidering the unique feature of the collegiate environment, we hold that universities have a special relationship with their students and a duty to protect them from foreseeable violence during curricular activities." *Id.* The court premised its finding of a special relationship on: (1) college students' dependence on their "college, communities for structure, guidance, and a safe learning environment"; (2) colleges' "superior control over the environment" through rules and restrictions that attempt to maintain a safe environment; (3) colleges' pervasive involvement in students' lives as exemplified by colleges' provision of housing, food, and extracurricular activities; and (4) the ability of colleges to influence students' values and consciousness. *Id.* at 667-69.

3. *University Duty to Protect Opponents' Health and Safety.* Courts have refused to recognize that a special relationship exists between a university and student-athletes at another school or that a university is vicariously liable for its student-athletes' torts; see *Trujillo v. Yeager*, 642 F. Supp. 2d 86, 91 (D. Conn. 2009) ("holding coaches liable in negligence, particularly to players on a different college's team, would unreasonably threaten to chill competitive play"); *Avila v. Citrus Cmty. Coll. Dist.*, 131 P.3d 383 (Cal. 2006) (although university has a legal duty not to increase the risks inherent in an intercollegiate sport, it has no legal duty to prevent its pitcher from intentionally throwing at an opposing team's batter because "being intentionally thrown at is a fundamental part and inherent risk" of baseball); *Kavanagh v. Trs. of Boston Univ.*, 795 N.E.2d 1170, 1178 (Mass. 2003) (university "would have to have specific information about a player suggesting a propensity to engage in violent conduct" to be held directly liable).

4. *NCAA Efforts to Protect Student-Athletes' Health and Safety.* The NCAA publishes a sports medicine handbook available on its website that provides guidelines for protecting the health and safety of student-athletes and for minimizing the risk of significant injury for participants in intercollegiate athletics. These guidelines may be relevant in determining the nature and scope of a university's duty to use reasonable care in connection with sports medicine issues affecting its athletics program. See *Wallace v. Broyles*, 961 S.W.2d 712, 713-16 (Ark. 1998) (asserting that a university may be liable for negligently permitting student-athletes, in violation of NCAA guidelines, to have access to controlled substances in athletic department facilities without prescriptions, labels, instructions, or warnings regarding the dangers or side effects of usage).

Does the NCAA have a legal duty to use reasonable care when promulgating rules to protect athletes' safety? See *Sanchez v. Hillerich & Bradsby Co.*, 128 Cal. Rptr. 2d 529 (Cal. App. 2002) (NCAA may be liable for approving baseball bat if its performance capabilities are proved to increase unreasonably a pitcher's inherent risk of being hit by a batted ball). But see *Lanni v. NCAA*, 42 N.E.3d 542, 553 (Ind. App. 2015) ("We conclude that the NCAA's regulation of the field of play and other rules and policies with respect to safety issues [and] compliance checks . . . do not rise to the level of assuring protection of the student-athletes from injuries that may occur at sporting events. Actual oversight and control cannot be imputed merely from the fact that the NCAA has promulgated rules and regulations and required compliance with those rules and regulations").

In *Bradley v. NCAA*, 249 F.Supp.3d 149, 168 (D. D.C. 2017), the court ruled that the following allegations stated a negligence claim against the NCAA:

> [T]he plaintiff asserts that "[d]efendant NCAA undertook and assumed a duty to protect the physical and mental well-being of all student-athletes participating in intercollegiate sports, including [herself,] . . . [and] a duty to protect student-athletes from brain injuries." The plaintiff then alleges that "[d]efendant NCAA failed in its duties" by, among other things, failing to ensure that the coaches, athletic trainers and graduate assistants were educated about the signs, symptoms[,] and risks of concussions, second-impact syndrome, and post-concussive syndrome; implement appropriate safety procedures and policies regarding care, treatment, and monitoring of student-athletes suffering from concussions, concussion symptoms, and post-concussive symptoms; implement appropriate oversight over its member institutions in their implementation of Concussion Management Plans; provide appropriate guidance to its member institutions on concussion management; [and] safeguard[] its student-athletes from preventable concussion and post-concussion injuries.

The court, however, dismissed the plaintiff's negligence claim against the Patriot League alleging it "assumed the same duties and responsibilities as the NCAA . . . because [its] Policies and Procedures provides that 'Patriot League institutions are expected to abide by all rules and procedures set forth in both the NCAA and Patriot League Materials.'" *Id.* at 175. It reasoned:

> Because considerations of fairness and public policy play a role in a court's analysis of foreseeability in determining duty, the Court agrees with the Patriot League that such public policy considerations provide support for shielding athletic conferences from litigation involving an injury to an athlete based on an athlete's participation in a sporting event sanctioned by the athletic conference, without a showing that the athletic conference took affirmative steps to establish a requisite duty of care.

Id. at 177.

5. *Validity of Liability Waivers.* In the preceding discussion of interscholastic sports, we noted that courts are split on the issue of the validity of liability waivers executed by minors and their parents. Should a different rule apply for waivers executed by adult college student-athletes? See *Roe*, 2012 WL 6757558 at *1 (upholding waiver that releases university of liability for negligence that "may rise by or in connection with [student-athlete's] participation in any activities related to Saint Louis University intercollegiate athletic teams"). But see *UCF Athletic Ass'n v. Plancher*, 121 So. 3d 1097 (Fla. Ct. App. 2013) (exculpatory clause in release did not bar claims because language did not clearly inform athlete that he was contracting away his rights; language suggested clause covered only injuries inherent in the sport); *Feleccia*, 156 A.3d (although liability waivers signed by college student-athletes are generally valid, language of waiver did not indicate that college was being absolved for its own negligence, and trial court improperly failed to consider whether the defendant college's recklessness or gross negligence invalidated the waiver).

6. *Tort Immunity Issues.* Like a public high school system and its employees, a public university and its employees may be immune from liability for negligence in connection with the operation of its athletic program under the doctrines of sovereign and qualified immunity, respectively. *Lennon v. Petersen*, 624 So. 2d 171, 173-75 (Ala. 1993). A university's sovereign immunity from tort liability may be waived to the extent that negligent conduct arising out of a public university's sports program is covered by insurance. *Shriver v. Athletic Council of Kan. State Univ.*, 564 P.2d 451, 455 (Kan. 1977). See also *Wallace*, 961 S.W.2d at 714 (holding that an athletic trainer may be liable for negligence to the extent of his insurance coverage). Tortious conduct more culpable than mere negligence, such as intentional or reckless acts, is not immunized from liability by either sovereign or qualified immunity. See *Wallace*, 961 S.W.2d at 717.

One court has held that sponsoring revenue-generating sports such as intercollegiate football is a proprietary function of a public university that is not protected by sovereign immunity. *Brown v. Wichita State Univ.*, 540 P.2d 66, 86-89 (Kan. 1975). Thus, sovereign immunity would not bar tort suits by athletes injured while participating in these sports. Others have reached a contrary conclusion. *Harris v. Univ. of Mich. Bd. of Regents*, 558 N.W.2d 225, 228 (Mich. Ct. App. 1996) (holding that university sponsorship of intercollegiate athletics is a governmental, not a proprietary, function of a public university, even if some sports generate revenue); *Ward v. Mich. State Univ. (on remand)*, 782 N.W.2d 514, 520 (Mich. Ct. App. 2010) *appeal denied*, 798 N.W.2d 766 (Mich. 2011) (holding the same).

Private universities may be protected from negligence suits by intercollegiate athletes by the doctrine of charitable immunity. Application of this doctrine varies by jurisdiction. See *Gilbert v. Seton Hall Univ.*, 332 F.3d 105 (2d Cir. 2003) (applying conflicts of law principles to determine applicability of charitable immunity doctrine in suit by injured club team player against private university).

PROBLEM 11-7

Amos is a scholarship athlete who is the star wide receiver at Big U, a private NCAA FBS powerhouse whose football program generates approximately $50 million in annual revenues. The week before the game with Large U, Big U's hated rival, Amos suffered a very painful neck injury that prevented him from practicing. Although Big U's team physician recommended that Amos not play, Big U's coach pressured Amos to play because the Large U game would decide the conference championship.

During the game Amos suffered a broken neck, causing permanent paralysis when he was injured in a vicious helmet-to-helmet tackle by Brutus, a Large U defensive back. Large U was penalized 15 yards for Brutus's personal foul, which was characterized by the referees as illegal "spearing."

It is anticipated that Amos will require lifetime care and incur significant medical expenses. During the recruiting process, Big U's head coach told Amos that the university would "take care" of him if he was injured while playing football.

Discuss Amos's potential claims for recovery for his injuries.

D.   SPORTS MEDICINE MALPRACTICE LIABILITY

Professional teams and collegiate educational institutions generally hire a physician or group of physicians to provide medical care to their athletes. Many high schools also select a physician to provide pre-participation physical examinations and emergency medical care to athletes participating in interscholastic athletics.

A "team physician" provides medical services to athletes that are arranged for, or paid for, at least in part, by an institution or entity other than the patient or the patient's parent or guardian. Joseph H. King, Jr., *The Duty and Standard of Care for Team Physicians*, 18 Hous. L. Rev. 657, 658 (1981).

The team physician's primary responsibility is to provide for the physical well-being of athletes. The team physician must provide medical treatment and advice consistent with an individual athlete's best health interests because there is a physician-patient relationship between them. Although one of the team physician's objectives is to avoid the unnecessary restriction of athletic activity, his or her paramount responsibility should be to protect the competitive athlete's health. Matthew J. Mitten, *Team Physicians and Competitive Athletes: Allocating Legal Responsibility for Athletic Injuries*, 55 U. Pitt L. Rev. 129, 140-41 (1993). Team physicians may face extreme pressure from coaches, team management, fans, or the athlete to provide medical clearance to participate or treatment enabling immediate return to play. For scholarly commentary discussing the potential conflicts inherent in the team physician's dual obligations to an athletic team and its athletes, see Dennis Durao, Note, *An Endangered Species: Professional Sports Team Physicians*, 15 Quinnipiac Health L.J. 33 (2012); Steve P. Calandrillo, *Sports Medicine Conflicts: Team Physicians vs. Athlete-Patients*, 50 St. Louis U. L.J. 185 (2005); Scott Polsky, Comment, *Winning Medicine: Professional Sports Team Doctors' Conflicts of Interest*, 14 J. Contemp. Health L. & Pol'y 503 (1998).

As the following case illustrates, the team physician's judgment should be governed only by medical considerations, not the team's need for the services of the player or the athlete's strong desire to play.

KRUEGER v. S.F. FORTY NINERS

234 Cal. Rptr. 579 (Cal. App. 1987) (unpublished)

(In denying review, the California Supreme court ordered that this opinion not be officially published.)

NEWSOM, Associate Justice.

Appellant Charles Krueger began playing professional football with the San Francisco 49'ers (hereafter respondent or the 49'ers) in 1958. He was a defensive lineman for the 49'ers until retiring in 1973, missing only parts of two seasons due to injuries. During his career, however, appellant played despite suffering numerous injuries. He broke his arm and the ring finger on each hand, cracked or broke his nose "innumerable times," suffered multiple dislocations of the fingers and thumbs on both hands, incurred a "blow-out" fracture of the right ocular orbit, developed an eye infection or "pterygium" caused by a foreign substance becoming lodged in the eye, sprained his right knee, and developed hypertension, among other maladies.

[EDS. Injuries and damages to appellant's left knee were the focus of the suit. In October 1963, he ruptured the medial collateral ligament in his left knee. Dr. Taylor, the 49'ers' team physician, performed an operation on the knee, which, Krueger was told, effectuated a "good repair." Dr. Taylor noted in his report of the operation that the anterior cruciate ligament—the function of which is to prevent the tibia from shifting forward on the femur—"appeared to be absent" from appellant's left knee. Such an injury can produce instability in the knee, particularly if combined with other injuries. According to Krueger, he was not told that his left knee evidently lacked the anterior cruciate ligament.

During subsequent seasons Krueger experienced pain and considerable swelling in his left knee. He received treatment from physicians retained by the 49'ers, which consisted of aspiration of bloody fluid from the knee by means of a syringe and contemporaneous injection of Novocain and cortisone, a steroid compound. Appellant testified that he received approximately 50 such "Kepplemann" treatments during 1964, and an average of 14 to 20 per year from 1964 to 1973. He testified that he was never advised by the 49'ers medical staff of the dangers associated with steroid injections in the knee, such as possible rupturing of tendons, weakening of joints and cartilage, and destruction of capillaries and blood vessels. At trial, Krueger offered expert medical testimony that the number of steroid injections appellant claimed to have undergone would have been inappropriate and quite "unusual." X-rays taken between 1964 and 1971 revealed "degenerative post-traumatic changes" in appellant's left knee joint. Appellant's uncontradicted testimony was that he was not told of either of these afflictions by the 49'ers medical staff.

Krueger also testified that he suffered a "hit" on the outside of his knee during a game in 1970 and felt a piece of the knee break off. Notwithstanding the obvious severity of the injury, he was given Empirin codeine and directed to return to the game. For the remainder of the season, he could feel a "considerable piece of substance" dislodged on the outside of his left knee joint; nevertheless, he played the remaining five games of the season. At no time did the team doctors ever advise him that he risked permanent injury by continuing to play without surgery. Krueger testified unequivocally that, had he been advised not to play, he would have followed that advice.

Appellant retired from football following the 1973 season. At the time of his lawsuit, he suffered from traumatic arthritis and a crippling degenerative process in his left knee. He could not stand up for prolonged periods and could not run. He was also unable to walk on stairs without severe pain. His condition was degenerative and irreversible.]

Appellant's action was for fraud or deceit. . . .

The elements of a cause of action for fraud or deceit are as follows: a misrepresentation or suppression of a material fact; knowledge of any falsity; intent to induce reliance; actual and justifiable reliance; and resulting damages. Deceit may be negative as well as affirmative; it may consist in suppression of that which it is one's duty to disclose, as well as in the declaration of that which is false. . . . [T]he intentional concealment of a material fact is actionable fraud only if there is a fiduciary relationship giving rise to a duty to disclose it. The relationship between physician and patient is fiduciary in nature and creates a duty to disclose.

Respondent submits that the record fails to substantiate appellant's claim that material medical information was concealed from him. We disagree. Appellant testified unequivocally that the team's physicians never disclosed to him the adverse effects of steroid injections, or the true nature and extent of the damage to his left knee, particularly the dangers associated with the prolonged violent traumatic impact inherent in professional football. Nor, he testified, was he informed that x-rays taken of his legs revealed the severely degenerated condition of his left knee. . . .

If the case were simply one of conflicting evidence, we would of course affirm the judgment. As to the crucial issue of full disclosure, however, we find the evidence uncontradicted; as will appear, the requisite disclosure was never made. That the team physicians *withheld* no material information from Krueger is not, in our view, the proper focus of inquiry. The critical question is whether full *disclosure* of his medical condition was ever made to Krueger. . . .

In our opinion, the duty of full disclosure within the context of a doctor-patient relationship defines the test for concealment or suppression of facts under Civil Code section 1710, subdivision (3). The failure to make such disclosure constitutes not only negligence, but—where the requisite intent is shown—fraud or concealment as well. A physician cannot avoid responsibility for failure to make full disclosure by simply claiming that information was not withheld.

The testimony that, following his knee surgery in 1963, Krueger was not advised of the adverse effects of steroid injections, or of the risks associated with the continued pursuit of his profession, was uncontradicted. That is, while respondent produced testimony that the physicians treating appellant told him of the general nature of his injury, and did not *conceal* certain information from him, there is no evidence that appellant was ever informed of the continuing risks associated with his injuries. Hence, the requisite disclosure was never made. . . .

[W]e think the record unequivocally demonstrates that, in its desire to keep appellant on the playing field, respondent consciously failed to make full, meaningful disclosure to him respecting the magnitude of the risk he took in continuing to play a violent contact sport with a profoundly damaged left knee. The uncontradicted record shows that Krueger was in acute pain from 1963 on, that he was regularly anesthetized between and during games, and endured repeated, questionable steroid treatments administered by the team physician. X-rays had been taken which fully depicted the extent of his degenerative condition, but he was never so informed. In 1970, part of his knee broke away and yet he was still not given an honest assessment of the seriousness of his condition. Respondent's claim of no concealment cannot be substituted for the professional warnings to which Krueger was at this point so clearly entitled. And it is in this palpable failure to disclose, viewed in the light of the 49'ers compelling obvious interest in prolonging appellant's career, that we find the intent requisite for a finding of fraudulent concealment.

Respecting the element of reliance, appellant's testimony was that he accepted and acted upon the medical advice of the physicians as provided by respondent. No contradictory evidence appears. " '[P]atients are generally persons unlearned in the medical sciences, . . .' " and consequently are entitled to rely upon physicians for full disclosure of material medical information. (*Truman v. Thomas*, supra, 27 Cal. 3d 285, 291, 165 Cal. Rptr. 308, 611 P.2d 902.) Reliance is thus established.

Respondent contends that appellant was or should have been cognizant of the seriousness and permanent nature of the injury to his left knee, but we find no credible evidence supportive of this claim. Certainly, appellant knew that his injury was serious. He was entitled, however, to rely upon respondent's physicians for medical treatment and advice without consulting outside sources or undertaking independent investigation.

Turning to the issues of proximate cause and damages, we note the trial court's finding that appellant's desire to continue playing was so intense that he would have continued even had he been informed of the magnitude of the risk involved. This finding seems to us mere conjecture. Appellant demonstrated throughout his football career a courageous—some might say foolhardy— willingness to endure pain and injuries for the sake of his team and employer, but no credible evidence suggests that he ever assessed and accepted the prospect of permanent disability. On the contrary, he testified that he would have retired had respondent's physicians recommended that course of action, and no contrary evidence was offered by respondent.

Accordingly, we conclude there is no substantial evidence to support the judgment entered by the trial court; and conversely, that appellant established all the elements of a fraudulent concealment case based upon nondisclosure of material medical information. . . .

NOTES AND QUESTIONS

1. *Informed Consent Doctrine.* Why was the team physician found liable in *Krueger?* General informed consent principles apply in the sports medicine context and govern the required disclosure of information by the team physician to a competitive athlete. One commentator has suggested:

> A team physician or consulting specialist should fully disclose to an athlete the material medical risks of playing with an injury, illness or physical abnormality, and the potential health consequences of a given medication or treatment. To enable the athlete to make an informed decision, a physician should clearly warn of all material short and long-term medical risks of continued athletic participation and medical treatment under the circumstances, including any potentially life-threatening or permanently disabling health consequences. . . . To minimize potential legal liability, information concerning the athlete's medical condition, proposed treatment and alternatives, probability of injury or re-injury, severity of harm and potential long-term health effects should be tape recorded when provided verbally and also should be given in writing.

Mitten, *Emerging Legal Issues in Sports Medicine: A Synthesis, Summary, and Analysis, supra* at 26-27 (2002).

To prevail against a team physician for negligent or fraudulent failure to disclose medical information, Krueger holds that an athlete must prove he or she would not have played or undergone the medical treatment that caused the harm if he or she had been properly informed of the material risks. Should this be an objective or subjective standard?

Krueger ultimately was awarded $2.36 million in damages by a trial court, but he settled his claim for between $1 million and $1.5 million. See Jennifer L. Woodlief, *The Trouble with Charlie—Fraudulent Concealment of Medical Information in Professional Football,* 9 Ent. & Sports L. 3 (1991).

In other cases, athletes have been unable to prove that a physician violated the informed consent doctrine. In *Martin v. Casagrande,* 559 N.Y.S.2d

68 (N.Y. App. Div. 1990), a New York appellate court rejected a professional hockey player's claim that a physician intentionally concealed the condition of his knee to induce him to continue playing hockey. Because x-rays and tests performed by the physician did not indicate ligament or meniscal damage to the player's knee, the court held there was no basis for finding that the physician fraudulently withheld this information. The court observed that, at most, the player might have a negligence claim against the physician for failing to properly diagnose the condition of his knee. See also *Jeffers v. D'Allessandro*, 681 S.E.2d 405 (N.C. Ct. App. 2009) (holding a former NFL wide receiver's medical malpractice claim against the team's physician for performing unauthorized procedures beyond the athlete's informed consent was preempted by the NFL's CBA and ordering that the claim go to arbitration).

2. *Physician Standard of Care.* There are few reported cases discussing the appropriate standard of care for malpractice in the sports medicine setting. In malpractice suits involving a medical specialist, the trend is to apply a national standard of care because national specialty certification boards exist to ensure standardized training and certification procedures. Team physicians generally are internists, family practitioners, or orthopedic surgeons with other specialists providing emergency or specialized sports medicine care to athletes. See *Weiss v. Pratt*, 53 So. 3d 395 (Fla. Ct. App. 2011) (holding that pediatric emergency medicine specialist who frequently treats injured football players in hospital emergency room is an expert qualified to testify regarding orthopedic surgeon's negligent treatment of injured football player on field).

Historically, courts ruled that sports medicine is not a separate medical specialty because no national medical specialty board certification or standardized training previously existed. See, e.g., *Fleischmann v. Hanover Ins. Co.*, 470 So. 2d 216, 217 (La. Ct. App. 1985) (refusing to recognize subspecialty in sports medicine). This judicial view, however, is changing as sports medicine becomes a recognized and accepted area of specialization within the medical profession. The American Osteopathic Association has a certification board for sports medicine, and the specialty boards for family practice, internal medicine, emergency medicine, and the American Board of Medical Specialties now recognize sports medicine as a subspecialty of pediatrics. See *Gibson v. Digiglia*, 980 So. 2d 739 (La. Ct. App. 2008) (dismissing athlete's malpractice claim because plaintiff presented "no evidence to establish the standard of care required of a 'team medical director/coordinator' nor have they presented any evidence to support a claim that Dr. Digiglia's actions fell below the standard of care for that alleged sub-specialty of physicians"). If a team physician holds himself out as having special competence in sports medicine, he should be treated as a specialist and held to an awareness of "fundamentals which all practicing specialists in sports medicine should know, based on the types of athletes with whom the physician is involved." Charles V. Russell, *Legal and Ethical Conflicts Arising from the Team Physician's Dual Obligations to the Athlete and Management*, 10 Seton Hall Legis. J. 299, 306-07 (1987).

Sports medicine malpractice cases adopt an "accepted practice" standard of care in determining physician liability. *Mikkelsen v. Haslam*, 764 P.2d 1384, 1386 (Utah Ct. App. 1988) (upholding jury verdict imposing liability on orthopedist on grounds that permitting a patient with a total hip replacement to snow ski was "a departure from orthopedic medical profession standards"); *Classen v. Izquierdo,* 520 N.Y.S.2d 999, 1002 (N.Y. Sup. Ct. 1987) (physician who treats an athlete must "practice in accordance with good and accepted standards of medical care"). Under this standard, acceptable or reasonable medical practices (rather than what has been customary) define the boundaries of a physician's legal duty of care in treating athletes. See generally Mitten, *Emerging Issues in Sports Medicine: A Synthesis, supra,* at 8-30 (providing overview of team physician malpractice liability issues).

Some groups of sports medicine physicians and hospitals are paying professional teams and universities a significant sponsorship fee to treat their players and for the right to advertise themselves as the team's official sports medicine care provider. Do these arrangements create an unethical conflict of interest for physicians?

3. *Out-of-State Physician Malpractice Liability.* Currently, most sports medicine professionals who perform medical services outside their states of licensure are not covered by medical malpractice insurance, which exposes physicians travelling with sports teams to financial risk when they treat players at away games. On June 8, 2016, however, the United States House of Representatives' Energy and Commerce Subcommittee of Health passed the Sports Medicine Licensure Clarity Act (H.R. 921), which became law on Oct. 5, 2018 and clarifies that health care services provided by a sports medicine professional in a state outside the state in which the provider is licensed would be covered by the provider's medical malpractice insurer. See 15 U.S.C. §8601 (2016), https://www.congress.gov/bill/114th-congress/house-bill/921.

4. *Athletic Trainers.* Athletic trainers typically provide a variety of sports medicine services to athletes, such as physical conditioning, injury prevention, emergency medical care, and injury rehabilitation—which may give rise to legal liability if rendered improperly. See, e.g., *Howard v. Mo. Bone & Joint Ctr., Inc.,* 615 F.3d 991 (8th Cir. 2010) (expert testimony establishes athletic trainer's negligence in conducting workout program that caused injury to college athlete); *Ramsey v. Gamber,* 2012 WL 851228 (11th Cir. Mar. 15, 2012) (affirming lower court's determination that former athletic trainer could not be held liable in tort for weight-lifting injury on basis of respondeat superior where plaintiff presented no proof that trainer had the ability to select or terminate employment of weight room assistants); *Bradley v. NCAA,* 249 F. Supp. 3d 149 (DC 2017) (holding that an athletic trainer's decision to run "SCAT2 tests" to assess an athlete's concussion-related symptoms could reasonably qualify as medical services and subject the trainer to the standard of care of a healthcare provider); *Searles,* 695 A.2d at 1210 (an athletic trainer "has the duty to conform to the standard of care required of an ordinary careful trainer" when providing care and treatment to athletes).

5. *Athlete's Contributory Negligence.* An athlete has a legal duty to use reasonable care to protect his own health and safety. For example, he must truthfully disclose his medical history and physical symptoms to the team physician. In *Jarreau,* 600 So. 2d, *supra,* the court, applying contributory negligence principles, found an injured high school football player to be one-third at fault for failing to consult his own physician or requesting that he be referred to a school physician. See *Magee v. Covington Cty. Sch. Dist.,* 96 So. 3d 742 (Miss. Ct.

App. 2012) (absolving nurse practitioner, who conducted pre-participation physical examination of high school student-athlete who later died during practice, from liability where athlete and his mother failed to truthfully disclose the athlete's medical history).

An athlete generally may rely on the recommendations of the team physician or his or her designated consulting specialists regarding when it is appropriate to return to play after an injury without seeking a second medical opinion. His or her reliance on the team physician's recommendations ordinarily is considered reasonable because of the doctor's sports medicine expertise, and the athlete is not required to obtain a confirming medical opinion. *Mikkelsen*, 764 P.2d at 1388; *Krueger*, 234 Cal. Rptr. at 584.

On the other hand, an athlete's failure to follow his or her physician's instructions constitutes contributory or comparative negligence that may reduce or bar his or her recovery. In *Gillespie v. Southern Utah State College*, 669 P.2d 861 (Utah 1983), a college basketball player was found to be solely responsible for aggravating an ankle injury by not following physician instructions concerning proper treatment and rehabilitation. See also *Holtman v. Reese*, 460 S.E.2d 338 (N.C. Ct. App. 1995) (an athlete engaged in high-impact aerobics, snow skiing, and waterskiing contrary to chiropractor's advice). *Starnes v. Caddo Parish Sch. Bd.*, 598 So. 2d 472 (La. Ct. App. 1992) (playing volleyball without wearing knee brace against doctor's advice).

An athlete does not assume the risk of injury from negligent emergency medical care rendered by a physician during a sporting event. In *Classen*, the court denied a summary judgment motion by a ringside physician who allegedly was negligent in allowing a boxer to continue fighting and thereby receive injuries that caused his death. *Classen*, 520 N.Y.S.2d.

PROBLEM 11-8

Midway during the college basketball season, Star Player was diagnosed with a potentially life-threatening heart rhythm disorder. The university's team physician referred him to a prominent cardiologist who medically cleared him to participate with prescribed medication and careful monitoring. The medication made Star Player feel sluggish, and he was unable to play at his previously high level of competition while taking it. This concerned both Star Player, who had aspirations of a future career as a player in the National Basketball Association (NBA), and his college basketball coach, who needed him to perform well during the upcoming NCAA basketball tournament for the team to make the Final Four. After conferring with the university's team physician and head basketball coach, the cardiologist reduced the level of Star Player's medication. Thereafter, he played much better but occasionally was winded and felt light-headed during the first two games of the NCAA tournament. Star Player, who was concentrating on helping his team make the Final Four and impressing NBA scouts, did not tell anyone how he was feeling. While playing a game in the Sweet Sixteen round, Star Player collapsed and died from cardiac arrest.

In a lawsuit by his heirs, consider who may be legally liable for Star Player's death and any defenses that may be raised by defendants.

Comment: Liability for Concussion-Related Injuries[1]

Section E of this chapter will address worker's compensation issues that primarily impact professional athletes. Before turning to that discussion, however, we address an issue that impacts athletes at all levels of participation—concussion-related injuries.

I. INTRODUCTION

Historically, courts generally declined to hold athletics associations, school districts and other defendants liable for concussions. This judicial approach was premised largely on notions related to assumption of risk and informed consent. Risks of injuries, including concussions, were viewed as "known and generally appreciated" within the context of sports given "the reality of contact sports."[2]

Today, courts have adopted a nuanced approach that is more sympathetic to the particular types of injuries suffered by both professional and amateur athletes. This shift is attributable in part to alleged facts that seek to undermine the belief that athletes consent to risks associated with contact sports.[3] Thus, where athletes are not truly informed, the "informed consent" rationale becomes a less effective defense. The rejection of this defense has contributed to the wave of concussion lawsuits that have been filed against the NFL and other sports leagues, as well as on the collegiate, high school, and youth levels.

II. NFL AND NHL CONCUSSION LAWSUITS

In 2011, the first lawsuit regarding concussions suffered by retired NFL players was filed.[4] The complaint alleged numerous causes of action including negligence, fraud, strict liability based on design defect and manufacturing defects, failure to warn, and loss of consortium. Shortly thereafter, a number of other suits were filed, including *Easterling v. NFL*, the first concussion-related class action lawsuit filed against the NFL. In June of 2012, these cases were

---

1. An exhaustive discussion of sports-related concussions and the business, societal, ethical and legal implications thereof is beyond the scope of this comment. Helpful resource materials include: Grant Frazier, *Using Your Head: A Different Approach to Tackling the NFL's Concussion Epidemic*, 10 Harv. J. Sports & Ent. L. 197 (2019); N. Jeremi Duru, *In Search of the Final Head Ball: The Case for Eliminating Heading in Soccer*, 83 Mo. L. Rev. 559 (2018); Taylor Simpson-Wood & Robert H. Wood, *When Popular Culture and the NFL Collide: Fan Responsibility in Ending the Concussion Crisis*, 29 Marq. Sports L. Rev. 13 (2018); Christopher R. Deubert, I. Glenn Cohen & Holly Fernandez Lynch, *Protecting and Promoting the Health of NFL Players: Legal and Ethical Analysis and Recommendations*, 7 Harv. J. Sports & Ent. L. 1 (2016).

2. Dr. Tracey B. Carter, *From Youth Sports to Collegiate Athletics to Professional Leagues: Is There Really "Informed Consent" by Athletes Regarding Sports-Related Concussions?*, 84 UMKC L. Rev. 331, 350 (2015) (citing Heather MacGillivray, *Where is the Awareness in Concussion Awareness: Can Concussed Players Really Assume the Risk in a Concussed State?*, 21 Jeffrey S. Moorad Sports L.J. 529, 529 (2014)).

3. See MacGillivray, *supra* note 2, at 532.

4. *In re Nat'l Football League Players' Concussion Injury Litig.*, 307 F.R.D. 351, 361 (E.D. Pa. 2015), *aff'd*, 821 F.3d 410 (3d Cir. 2016), *as amended* (May 2, 2016).

consolidated and titled *In re National Football League Players' Concussion Injury Litigation.*[5]

The primary question in the consolidated action was whether the NFL should be liable for concussions suffered by NFL players while playing in the league. More specifically, the plaintiffs alleged the NFL was aware of the concussion risks associated with the sport, but intentionally ignored or concealed information pertaining to these risks. Plaintiffs also alleged that the NFL knew or should have known of the increased susceptibility to a variety of medical conditions, including concussions, associated with playing football.[6]

In July of 2013, judicially ordered mediation in *In re National Football League Players' Concussion Injury Litigation* resulted in a settlement, which included $675 million for compensatory claims for players showing neurological symptoms, $75 million for baseline testing, and $10 million for medical education and research.[7] In 2014, the settlement was modified to remove the monetary cap on damages. In April of 2015, a federal district court approved the settlement agreement.[8] Although some class members objected to the terms of the agreement, it was finalized on April 18, 2016 when the Third Circuit Court of Appeals affirmed the trial court's approval of the settlement.[9] Depending on the severity of their condition, former NFL players with dementia can file claims ranging from $1.5 million to $3 million.[10] The settlement does not preclude lawsuits by current players who opted out of the class or players who retired on or after July 7, 2014.[11] As of July 31, 2019, 20,544 NFL players had joined the class, 2,851 claims had been filed, and 954 claims had been approved for payments that have totaled $679,386,317. Total payments are expected to eventually reach at least $1 billion.[12]

The NFL's settlement has spawned additional legal disputes including one between the league and its insurers, in which the NFL has demanded that its insurers fund the $1 billion concussion settlement.[13] Other legal disputes include those involving medical providers, lawyers, and credit card companies that have asserted liens against settlement fund payments intended for former NFL players.[14]

In the wake of the settlement, the NFL also began working to assess "concussion-causing events in the NFL" through a $60 million initiative called "Engineering Roadmap." On November 9, 2017, the league announced that a team of experts

5. Carter, *supra* note 2, *at* 360-01.

6. *In re Nat. Football*, 307 F.R.D. 351, 362.

7. Carter, *supra*, note 2 at 366.

8. *Id.*

9. See *In re Nat'l Football League Players Concussion Injury Litig.*, 821 F.3d at 20.

10. Andy Berg, *Ex-Players Contest Parts of NFL Concussion Settlement*, AthelticBusiness.com (May 2019), https://www.athleticbusiness.com/civil-actions/ex-players-contest-conditions-of-nfl-concussion-settlement.html.

11. See *id.* at 425; see also *Frequently Asked Questions*, NFL Concussion Settlement, https://www.nflconcussionsettlement.com/Docs/posted_faq_set.pdf (last visited Aug. 5, 2019). See *Martin v. Kansas City Chiefs Football Club. LLC.*, 2019 WL 95917 (E.D. Pa. Jan. 3, 2019) (dismissing concussion-related claims of widow of deceased NFL player, because plaintiff had failed to opt out of the class).

12. NFL Concussion Settlement, https://www.nflconcussionsettlement.com/ (last visited July 31, 2019).

13. Jared Shelly, *With $ 1B at Stake, Insurers Pressure NFL to Divulge What it Knew About Concussion Risks*, Risk&Insurance.com (May 17, 2019), https://riskandinsurance.com/nfl-brain-injury-lawsuit-and-insurance/.

14. Brett Murphy & Gus Garcia-Roberts, *NFL's CTE Settlement Payments Stripped Down*, Athletic Business.com (Oct., 2018), https://www.athleticbusiness.com/civil-actions/nfl-s-cte-settlement-payments-stripped-down.html.

studied videos of the nearly 500 concussions reported during the 2015 and 2016 NFL seasons and categorized them by the nature of the incident causing the concussion, the portion of the head involved in the concussion-causing collision, and the position played by the concussed player (cornerbacks were top on the list with almost one-fourth of all concussions). The NFL explained "[t]he data is being shared widely with helmet manufacturers, designers, innovators, entrepreneurs, universities and others to stimulate new ideas and designs for protective equipment." In January 2019, the NFL released records revealing a 23.8% decrease in concussions occurring during games and practices in 2018. This decrease followed the league's implementation of a three-part initiative that included "intervention during early training camp practices, prohibition of underperforming helmet models and a series of rules changes," including those which penalize players for certain types of hits.[15] In an attempt to further reduce concussions, in spring 2019, the NFL requested that teams reduce the use of high-impact practice drills, such as the Oklahoma drill, which pits a blocker, attempting to make room for a running-back, against a defender.[16]

Thus far, the NFL appears to have weathered the bad press associated with concussion-related legal liability, a congressional report detailing how the league sought to influence concussion research,[17] the negative publicity arising from increased public awareness of the neurological risks associated with football, and high-profile incidents in which players diagnosed with CTE engaged in violent acts (e.g., NFL player Aaron Hernandez, who committed suicide after he was found guilty of murder, and Junior Seau, who also committed suicide).[18] Whether this will continue is unclear. New threats to football's sustainability, however, have emerged. These include the reluctance of insurers to provide coverage for football-related head trauma and some parents' fear of allowing their children to play football.

Concussion lawsuits also have been filed against other professional sports leagues, though no group of players has had an outcome that comes close to approximating the NFL settlement. Most notable among other suits is the former NHL players' action against the NHL alleging that the league "concealed what it knew about the long-term effects of repeated head trauma."[19] In July 2018, the players were denied class certification, weakening their chances for a sizable recovery.[20] Thereafter, the NHL and the players reached

---

15. Courtney Cameron, *NFL Releases Results of Concussion-Reduction Strategy,* AthleticBusiness. com (January 2019), https://www.athleticbusiness.com/rules-regulations/nfl-releases-results-of-concussion-reduction-strategy.html.

16. Andy Berg, *NFL Suggests Teams Stop Using High-Impact Drills,* AthleticBusiness.com (May 2019), https://www.athleticbusiness.com/athlete-safety/nfl-suggests-teams-stop-using-high-impact-drills .html.

17. Steve Fainaru & Mark Fainaru-Wada, *Congressional report says NFL waged improper campaign to influence government study,* ESPN.com, May 24, 2016, http://www.espn.com/espn/otl/story/_/id/15667689/congressional-report-finds-nfl-improperly-intervened-brain-research-cost-taxpayers-16-million.

18. Aaron E. Washington-Childs, Note, *The NFL's Problem with Off-Field Violence: How CTE Exposes Athletes to Criminality and CTE's Potential as a Criminal Defense,* 17 V a. Sports & Ent. L.J. 244 (2018).

19. Kevin McGran, *NFL Concussion Settlement could be good news for former NHL players,* thestar.com (Apr. 29, 2015), https://www.thestar.com/sports/hockey/2015/04/29/nfl-concussion-settlement-could-be-good-news-for-former-nhl-players.html.

20. See *In re: National Hockey League Players' Concussion Injury Litigation,* 327 F.R.D. 245 (D. Minn. 2018). For another concussion related case on the professional level see *McCullough v. WWE,* 172 F. Supp. 3d 528, 525 (D. Conn. 2016) (rejecting claims of professional wrestlers who asserted, inter alia, negligence claims contending that the WWE failed to "exercise reasonable care in training, techniques . . . and diagnosing of injuries such as concussions and sub-concussions.").

a $18.9 million settlement. Players who opt into the settlement will each receive payments of $22,000 and up to $75,000 for concussion-related medical expenses. The settlement also provides for neurological testing for players at the league's expense and creates a $2.5 million common good fund for retired players in financial need, including those who do not opt into the litigation.[21]

III.   COLLEGIATE SPORTS CONCUSSION LAWSUITS

Intercollegiate student-athletes have sued the NCAA and their colleges and universities. In September 2011, *Arrington v. NCAA* was the first class action concussion lawsuit asserted against the NCAA. Several subsequent suits were consolidated into *In re Nat'l Collegiate Athletic Ass'n Student-Athlete Concussion Injury Litigation*.[22] Much like the complaints against the NFL and NHL, plaintiffs alleged that the NCAA was negligent in safeguarding student-athletes from the risks of concussions.[23] In July 2014, the parties filed a settlement agreement with the court.[24] Since then, the settlement agreement has undergone several modifications. Notably, in January of 2016, the presiding judge requested that the agreement be altered so that the NCAA would not have complete immunity from future class action concussion litigation.[25]

In August, 2019, the presiding judge granted approval of a settlement agreement in which the NCAA will pay $70 million to set up a 50-year medical monitoring program for college athletes and another $5 million to start a program to research the prevention and treatment of concussions.[26] The settlement's medical monitoring program will allow for medical screenings and evaluations for all current and former NCAA student-athletes, not limited by when they played, what sport they played, how long they played, where they played, or their age. The settlement also imposes requirements on colleges and universities such as requiring that medical personnel trained to diagnose and treat concussions be present at games involving contact sports. The settlement covers over 4 million current and former student-athletes; 1,800 former and current student-athletes elected to opt out of the settlement. Because the settlement does not prohibit individual plaintiffs from bringing concussion-related suits against the NCAA,[27] the NCAA now faces hundreds of them.[28]

One such suit involved Debra Hardin-Ploetz, who filed an action against the NCAA on behalf of her deceased husband, Greg Ploetz. The lawsuit became the first CTE-related case against a sports entity to reach trial.[29] On the trial's third

---

21. See *NHL, retired players reach $19M concussions settlement*, USA Today, Nov. 12, 2018.

22. 2014 WL 7237208, at *1 (N.D. Ill. Dec. 17, 2014); see Carter, *supra* at 365.

23. Paul D. Anderson, *Concussion Litigation Against the NCAA is Gathering Momentum*, NHL Concussion Litigation (Sept. 19, 2012), http://nflconcussionlitigation.com/?p=1137.

24. *Id.*

25. Ben Strauss, *Judge Approves Settlement in Head Injuries Suit Against N.C.A.A.*, N.Y. Times (Jan. 26, 2016).

26. *In re NCAA Student-Athlete Concussion Injury Litigation*, 2019 WL 3776955 (Aug. 12, 2019).

27. See National Collegiate Athletic Association Student-Athlete Concussion Injury Litigation, http://collegeathleteconcussionsettlement.com/.

28. *Wave of concussion lawsuits to test NCAA's liability*, USA Today, Feb. 7, 2019.

29. Michael McCann, *Analyzing* Ploetz v. NCAA, *the First Legal Battle Over CTE to Reach Trial*, SportsIllustrated.com (April 26, 2018), https://www.si.com/college-football/2018/04/26/greg-ploetz-ncaa-cte-concussion-lawsuit.

day, the parties settled for an undisclosed amount.[30] In June 2018, the NCAA announced the formation of a new concussion advisory group that will help "guide the implementation of accepted best practices on campus." The group will be comprised of persons from member institutions and individuals associated with medical and scientific organizations.

Other notable cases involving the NCAA and/or colleges include *Greiber v. NCAA*,[31] in which a female lacrosse player sued the NCAA and Hofstra University for concussion related injuries she allegedly sustained during practice. The plaintiff alleged the NCAA acted negligently in failing to "implement adequate regulations in order to address the detection, treatment, and prevention of head injuries."[32] In finding plaintiff alleged sufficient facts to overcome the NCAA's motion to dismiss, the court emphasized that the source of a duty could arise from the degree of control the NCAA exercises over "rules of play and equipment, and imposed conditions of membership on its member institutions, which included requirements regarding head-injury protocols."[33] In another case, Les Williams, who played defensive end at the University of Alabama, is one of more than one hundred individuals seeking recovery based on allegations that the NCAA and conference failure to warn players of the risk associated with concussions.[34]

The estate of a former Notre Dame football player who died in 2015 and was diagnosed with chronic traumatic encephalopathy (CTE) three years prior to his death received a positive ruling from the Ohio Supreme Court in October 2018 that could have potentially far-reaching effects for similarly-injured plaintiffs in the future.[35] The Ohio Supreme Court became the first appeals court to consider whether CTE is a latent disease, which therefore would extend the time limit for a former player to sue a sports league. Although the court didn't expressly conclude that CTE qualifies as a latent disease, it did not rule that the disease does not qualify. This ruling could help athletes in the future who suffer from the disease and do not realize that they feel the disease's impact from their previous participation in professional sports leagues.

IV.   HIGH SCHOOL AND YOUTH CONCUSSION LAWSUITS

Lawsuits also have been filed by plaintiffs for alleged concussion-related illnesses growing out of their participation in high school and youth sports. Several former athletes have settled lawsuits against their schools. A South Carolina

---

30. Rick Maese, *NCAA concussion case settles three days into trial*, WashPost.com, June 15, 2018, https://www.washingtonpost.com/news/sports/wp/2018/06/15/ncaa-concussion-case-settles-three-days-into-trial/?utm_term=.f9913d5c7994.

31. 2017 WL 6940498 (N.Y. Sup. Ct., Sept. 8, 2017).

32. *Id.* at *4.

33. *Id.* at *5.

34. Jesse Dougherty, *Former Alabama Player Les Williams Is One of More Than 100 Suing NCAA Over Brain Injury,* Wash. Post (July 3, 2018). See also *NCAA Over Parkinson's,* AthleticBusiness.com (Oct., 2018), https://www.athleticbusiness.com/safety-security/former-lineman-files-sues-ncaa-over-parkinson-s.html. See also *Bradley v. NCAA,* 249 F.Supp.3d 149 (D.C. Cir. 2017) (plaintiff alleged the NCAA, athletic conference, and physicians failed to provide her with appropriate medical care after she sustained a head injury); *Rose v. NCAA,* 346 F.Supp.3d 1212 (N.D. Ill. 2018) (denying in part and granting in part NCAA's and Big Ten's motions to dismiss players' concussion-related tort claims).

35. *Schmitz v. NCAA,* 122 N.E.3d 80 (Ohio 2018).

jury awarded $5.87 million in damages to a former athlete, Brett Baker-Goins, who sustained two concussions playing basketball for First Baptist School of Charleston. In addition, a California school district settled a case for $7.1 million involving an athlete who sustained a concussion during a football game at Grossmont Union School District's Monte Vista High School. The athlete, Rashaun Council, alleged that the school's failure to properly treat him after he sustained the concussion led to more serious ailments including brain swelling and permanent brain damage.

In *Mayall v. USA Water Polo, Inc.*,[36] the Ninth Circuit ruled in November 2018 that USA Water Polo was negligent in its failure to implement proper concussion-related protocol for its youth program. A minor was injured during a tournament organized and managed by USA Water Polo when she was hit in the face and suffered a concussion. The athlete's coach returned the athlete to the game, despite failing to have the athlete evaluated by a medical professional. The athlete was subsequently hit in the head several times throughout the game. She suffered from headaches, dizziness, sensitivity to light, and nausea, among other symptoms for months, which resulted in her inability to return to school. The athlete filed suit based on the lack of a USA Water Polo concussion-management policy or return-to-play protocol for its youth water polo teams. The court found the lack of such instruction to be a violation of the duty of care USA Water Polo owed to its participants to create a healthy and safe environment for its competitions. The court also found that USA Water Polo's awareness of the severity of risk that repeat concussions pose to athletes not removed from play, as well as its failure to implement proper policies to combat such risk, amounted to gross negligence under the applicable California law.

In *Swank v. Valley Christian Sch.*, 398 P.3d 1108, 1113 (Wash. 2017) the Washington Supreme Court considered whether a private right of action was implied in a state statute known as the Lystedt Law, which requires schools to develop head injury and concussion protocols. In *Swank*, an athlete died as a result of complications following a hard hit to the head by another player during a football game. The boy's parents alleged that the coach's grossly negligent or reckless actions subsequent to the hit contributed to their son's death. In regard to the parents' common law negligence claim, the court ruled that an implied right of action arose from the Lystedt Law, which encompasses three duties: (1) school districts are required to create and distribute to coaches, youth athletes, and parents a head injury and concussion sheet that must be signed by athletes and their parents; (2) a youth athlete suspected of having suffered a concussion must be immediately removed from play; and (3) a youth athlete who sustains a concussion may not return to play without written clearance by a medical provider. The court also ruled that the Lystadt Law requires coaches to monitor athletes for signs of concussions and to remove athletes from play when those signs are present.[37] Finally, the court found that while a volunteer coach was entitled to limited immunity for negligent conduct, such immunity did not extend to the coach's alleged gross or reckless conduct.[38]

In other cases, however, defendant sports organizations have prevailed by successfully asserting defenses including qualified and governmental immunity. In

---

36. 909 F.3d 1055 (9th Cir. 2018).
37. *Id.* at 1119.
38. *Id.* at 1120.

Hickey v. Enterline,[39] a high school cheerleader fell and struck her head during a cheerleading stunt, causing a concussion and related symptoms. The plaintiff suffered additional injuries following two subsequent practices. Defining a willful tort claim as synonymous with an intentional tort claim under Pennsylvania law, the court rejected plaintiff's argument that the defendant coach was not entitled to qualified immunity because of the willful conduct exception. The court stated that the plaintiff had established facts sufficient to support her Fourteenth Amendment claim that by failing to remove her from practice, the defendant coach had acted with deliberate indifference to the risk resulting from permitting her to continue to practice. The court concluded, however, that the plaintiff's claim could not move forward because the coach was protected by qualified immunity.[40] In *Aspinall v. Murrieta Valley Unified School District*,[41] a high school student suffered a severe concussion while participating in a football practice during a drill in a football physical education class. Plaintiff, who had suffered previous concussions, was not wearing a helmet or pads when he was injured. He asserted negligence and negligent supervision claims. The court, however, found for the school district, rejecting the following theories asserted by the plaintiff: "1) the defendants unreasonably increased the risk of harm to plaintiff by, inter alia, not providing participants in the class with proper equipment including helmets; 2) defendant was negligent in permitting plaintiff to participate given his history of concussions; and 3) defendants acted negligently by not providing plaintiff with proper treatment after his collision with another player."

Like their professional and college counterparts, interscholastic athletic associations and youth sports organizations have adopted measures intended to reduce the risk of concussions. Some states' laws focus on educating principal parties involved in youth sports, including athletes, coaches, trainers, and parents, about adverse effects of concussions.[42] Others limit physical contact, require that athletes be removed from play after a concussion, and require medical clearance before the concussed athlete can return to play.[43] For example, the Illinois High School Association Board of Directors approved a new policy in 2019 that limits football players to two games per week, with a recommendation that players involved in two games only play as one-way players (solely offense or defense), and precludes players from playing games on consecutive days or participating in contact practice the day following games.[44] The significance of these efforts is exemplified by a recent study of sports-related concussions of high school football players in Wisconsin. In a 2019 study, researchers concluded that the "rate of [sports-related concussions] (SRC) sustained in high school football practice decreased by 57% after a rule change limiting the amount and duration of full-contact activities, with no change in competition

---

39. 2018 WL 487846, (M.D. Pa., Jan. 19, 2018).

40. See also *Maselli ex rel. Maselli v. Reg'l Sch. Dist. #10*, 2018 WL 3337053 (Conn. Super. Ct. June 11, 2018) (granting summary judgment in a concussion lawsuit pursuant to immunity).

41. 2018 WL 1163182, (Cal. App. 4th Dist., March 6, 2018),

42. William Wan, *State laws have reduced the concussion risks in high school kids, study finds*, Washington Post, Oct. 19, 2017.

43. *Id.*

44. *IHSA Board Approves Weekly Player Limitations in Football, Classification Changes for 2019*, Illinois High School Association (June 11, 2018), https://www.ihsa.org/NewsMedia/Announcements/tabid/93/ID/1534/IHSA-Board-Approves-Weekly-Player-Limitations-in-Football-Classification-Changes-For-2019.aspx.

concussion rate. Limitation on contract during high school football practice may be one effective measure to reduce the incidence of SRC."[45]

Youth sports governing bodies also have taken action. USA Football has initiated an expansive program entitled "Heads-up Football," which is designed to protect against injuries of all kinds through safety rules and training for coaches.[46] In developing and implementing those rules and training programs, USA Football and the NFL have teamed with the Centers for Disease Control to try to protect the health and safety of participants. Coaches, for example, are given the tools, resources, and certified education to help make youth football better and safer.

E. INJURY COMPENSATION FOR PROFESSIONAL ATHLETES

Like other athletes, professional athletes generally assume the inherent risks of injury while participating in their respective sports. However, league collective bargaining agreements and standard player contracts generally establish a contractual right of professional athletes to receive team-provided or paid medical care and rehabilitation for injuries suffered during training and games. Major league professional athletes also have contractual injury protection guarantees and benefits for career-ending injuries and sport-related disabilities. See, e.g., *Courson v. Bert Bell NFL Player Ret. Plan*, 214 F.3d 136 (3d Cir. 2000) (discussing the disability benefits plan for NFL players). Disputes between a player and team concerning the parties' respective rights and responsibilities under these agreements generally must be submitted to binding arbitration. *Smith v. Houston Oilers, Inc.*, 87 F.3d 717 (5th Cir. 1996); But see *Hendy v. Losse*, 925 F.2d 1470 (9th Cir. 1991) (state tort law claims against club alleging negligent hiring and retention of team physician are actionable because they arose independent of CBA and do not require construction of its terms for resolution); *Horton v. Espindola*, 319 F.Supp. 3d 395 (D.C. Cir. 2018) (in denying team's and coach's motions for summary judgement, court rules that material issues of fact existed as to whether plaintiff's intentional torts claims were preempted by Section 301 of the LMRA); *Brown v. NFL*, 219 F. Supp. 2d 372 (S.D.N.Y. 2002) (former player's claim against NFL for injury caused by referee arises out of common law tort duty, not terms of CBA); *Bentley v. Cleveland Browns Football Co.*, 958 N.E.2d 585 (Ohio Ct. App. 2011) (club's alleged fraudulent and negligent misrepresentations regarding its postoperative rehabilitation facility for players do not require interpretation of NFL CBA and are not required to be submitted to arbitration).

As employees, athletes on professional teams also may be eligible to recover state workers' compensation benefits for injuries or diseases arising from playing a sport. Workers' compensation laws provide a simple and inexpensive

---

45. Adam Y. Pfaller, M. Alison Brooks, Scott Hetzel & Timothy A. McGuine, *Effect of a New Rule Limiting Full Contact Practice on the Incidence of Sports-Related Concussion in High School Football Players*, 47 (10) Am. J. of Sports Medicine 2294 (2019).

46. https://usafootball.com/programs/heads-up-football/?gclid=Cj0KCQjwvo_qBRDQARIsAE-bsH8PctiM3lm5QAyXW80sAlBIrd9kl3cQQJhhFY2kWsEAD_-fg7iUeecaArbaEALw_wcB.

method for employees to obtain compensation and medical expenses for work-related injuries and illnesses. The theory underlying these laws is that businesses should bear the burden of industrial accidents as a component of the cost of production. Thus, workers' compensation is premised on the idea that workplace accidents are a cost of doing business and therefore should be borne by the enterprise that engendered them. In this sense, workers' compensation is a transfer of economic losses from injured workers to industry and, ultimately, to the public.

Under workers' compensation legislation, benefits are available to injured workers without having to prove an employer's common law tort or other statutory liability. Defenses available in common law tort actions, such as contributory negligence, assumption of risk, and the fellow servant rule, are unavailable to employers in workers' compensation actions. The removal of such requirements enables injured employees to avoid the impediments that left many workers uncompensated under the common law.

Employees obtain the security of workers' compensation benefits on a no-fault basis in exchange for relinquishing rights to pursue tort actions against their employers. A worker who accepts workers' compensation benefits or has successfully prosecuted a workers' compensation claim is barred from bringing a common law tort action. Limitations are also imposed on the amount of damages that workers can recover. For example, workers' compensation statutes generally preclude employees from recovering for pain and suffering or punitive damages. Available remedies are typically limited to compensation for disability, medical, death, and burial expenses. Thus, employees waive tort claims against their employers in exchange for a simplified but limited recovery under workers' compensation laws.

State statutes are generally the source of employee rights to workers' compensation benefits. Typically, the right of an employee to receive benefits under workers' compensation laws is dependent on two important criteria: (1) Is the person seeking benefits an "employee" as defined by the relevant state statute? (2) Is the injury for which compensation is sought work-related, or as is commonly stated, did the injury "arise out of" and "in the course of" the claimant's employment? A helpful review and analysis of general workers' compensation principles is provided in Arthur Larson, Lex K. Larson & Thomas A. Robinson, LARSON'S WORKERS' COMPENSATION LAW (2019).

Although professional athletes most often can readily establish the existence of an employee/employer relationship, this characterization sets the stage for the introduction of a myriad of other legal issues that potentially affect injured athletes' entitlement to workers' compensation benefits from their teams. The legal issues related to workers' compensation prevalent in professional sports are too numerous to provide an exhaustive examination in this text. For a general discussion of the law of workers' compensation as it applies to professional athletes, see Gerald Herz, *Professional Athletes and the Law of Workers' Compensation: Rights and Remedies*, in LAW OF PROFESSIONAL AND AMATEUR SPORTS 17-1, 17-3 & 17.4 (Gary A. Uberstine ed., West Group 2002); Matthew Friede, Comment—*Professional Athletes Are "Seeing Stars": How Athletes Are "Knocked-Out" of States' Workers' Compensation Systems*, 38 Hamline L. Rev. 519 (2015); Matthew J. Mitten, *Team Physicians As Co-Employees: A Prescription That Deprives Professional Athletes of an Adequate Remedy for Sports Medicine Malpractice*, 50 St. Louis U. L.J. 211 (2005).

Bodily injury caused by negligent medical treatment is compensable under workers' compensation statutes, see *DePiano v. Montreal Baseball Club, Ltd.*,

663 F. Supp. 116, 117 (W.D. Pa. 1987) but not under tort law. See *Brinkman v. Buffalo Bills Football Club-Div. of Highland Serv., Inc.*, 433 F. Supp. 699, 702 (W.D.N.Y. 1977) (holding that a tort claim for bodily injury from negligent medical treatment was barred by workers' compensation laws). A professional athlete may receive workers' compensation benefits for aggravation of an injury caused by improper treatment by the team's medical personnel. See *Bayless v. Phila. Nat'l League Club*, 472 F. Supp. 625, 629 (E.D. Pa. 1979) ("Once an employer undertakes, through its physicians, to provide proper medical care for any on-the-job illnesses, any harm resulting from the failure to do so is compensable under [state workers' compensation law]"). Aggravation of a player's existing injury caused by a professional team's requirement that the player continue or resume playing is compensable damage under workers' compensation law. See *DePiano*, 663 F. Supp. at 117-18.

The following material provides an introduction to illustrate contemporary issues involving workers' compensation and professional athletics. The principal cases and notes primarily address four issues: (1) the injuries that are compensable under workers' compensation statutes; (2) the constitutionality of workers' compensation statutes that impose limitations on the benefits recoverable by professional athletes; (3) exceptions to the exclusivity of workers' compensation benefits system as the sole state law remedy for player injuries; and (4) the validity of forum selection clauses designating the state in which a player can assert a workers' compensation claim.

PRO-FOOTBALL, INC. v. UHLENHAKE

558 S.E.2d 571 (Va. App. 2002)

BENTON, Judge.

The Workers' Compensation Commission entered an award of permanent partial disability benefits in favor of Jeffrey A. Uhlenhake, a professional football player, for injury to his left foot and denied him an award of benefits for injury to his left knee. Pro-Football, Inc., trading as the Washington Redskins, contends that injuries to a professional football player are not covered by the Act and, alternatively, that the evidence does not support the award of benefits for injury to Uhlenhake's left foot. Uhlenhake contends the evidence proved a compensable injury to his left knee. For the reasons that follow, we affirm the commission's award.

Pro-Football contends that "injuries resulting from voluntary participation in activities where injuries are customary, foreseeable, and expected are not accidental within the meaning of the Virginia Workers' Compensation Act." It argues that "in determining whether an injury is accidental, the relevant focus is upon the predictability of the injury based upon the activity performed."

As a guiding principle, the Workers' Compensation Act provides that "'injury' means only injury by accident arising out of and in the course of employment." Code § 65.2-101. The Act does not . . . specifically define the term "injury by accident." Consequently, the phrase has been the subject of judicial interpretation. . . .

To establish an "injury by accident," a claimant must prove (1) that the injury appeared suddenly at a particular time and place and upon a particular occasion, (2) that it was caused by an identifiable incident or sudden precipitating event, and (3) that it resulted in an obvious mechanical or structural change in the human body. . . .

Pro-Football initially posits that Uhlenhake seeks to recover for "injuries resulting from *voluntary* participation in activities." (Emphasis added.) The evidence proved, however, that Uhlenhake was engaged in an activity required by his employment. He was employed by Pro-Football to train, practice, and play in football games, which is the business of Pro-Football. No evidence proved Uhlenhake undertook a voluntary task when he engaged in the activity, which he alleges caused his injury. This is not a case of an injury "resulting from an employee's voluntary participation in employer-sponsored off-duty recreational activities which are not part of the employee's duties." Code § 65.2-101 (specifying an exclusion from injury by accident). Likewise, this is not a case in which the "injury was the direct result of [an employee] taking a risk of his own choosing, independent of any employment requirements, and one that was not an accepted and normal activity at the place of employment." *Mullins v. Westmoreland Coal Co.*, 10 Va. App. 304, 308, 391 S.E.2d 609, 611 (1990). Uhlenhake was at all relevant times engaged in an activity within the scope of his employment contract.

Pro-Football argues that by engaging in conduct which is physically dangerous and which has a high likelihood of injury, Uhlenhake must "automatically expect to be injured. . . . Pro-Football . . . asserts that "professional football players must accept the risk of injury if they wish to play the game" and argues that "the commission's broadened definition will extend compensability to . . . others who voluntarily participate in employment where injury is either highly probable or certain." It has long been understood, however, that the legislature abolished various common law doctrines, including assumption of the risk, when it adopted the Workers' Compensation Act. . . . In effect, Pro-Football's argument, if accepted, would introduce into the workers' compensation law the concept of assumption of the risk for a hazard that is undisputedly an incident of a worker's occupation.

"To say that football injuries are not accidental because of the probability of injury is, if one looks at it more closely, no more than to say that any activity with a high risk factor should be ruled noncompensable." 2 Larson at § 22.04[1][b]. The commission properly rejected this misguided notion and ruled that "the nature of the employment and the foreseeability of a potential injury does not determine whether an injury sustained in the ordinary course of an employee's duties is an accident." The business of Pro-Football is to engage in the activity of professional football. It employs individuals to constantly perform in a strenuous activity that has risks and hazards. As with coal miners, steel workers, firefighters, and police officers, who are covered by the Act, other classes of employees are regularly exposed to known, actual risks of hazards because "the employment subjects the employee to the particular danger." *Olsten v. Leftwich*, 230 Va. 317, 319, 336 S.E.2d 893, 894 (1985). The commission correctly ruled that professional football players are not exempt from the coverage of the Act when they suffer injuries in the game they are employed to perform.

[EDS. Based on the foregoing standard of review, the court found that credible evidence supported the commission's finding awarding Uhlenhake permanent partial disability benefits for loss of use of his left foot. The court next considered Uhlenhake's challenge of the sufficiency of the evidence to support the commission's finding that his left knee injury resulted from cumulative trauma and, therefore, is not compensable. Noting that the employee bears the burden of proving by a preponderance of the evidence that an injury by accident occurred, the court concluded that credible evidence supported the commission's finding that the "that the [knee] injury was the result of cumulative events" and consequently was not compensable.]

For these reasons, we affirm all aspects of the commission's decision.

NOTES AND QUESTIONS

1. *Covered Injuries.* Describe the team's arguments in support of its contention that Uhlenhake was not entitled to workers' compensation benefits. Is the court's rejection of the team's arguments consistent with the principles and policies that underlie workers' compensation systems? Is a professional hockey player entitled to receive workers' compensation benefits for injuries suffered in a fight with an opposing player during a game, which was ordered by his coach? *Norfolk Admirals v. Jones*, 2005 WL 2847392 (Va. Ct. App. Nov. 1, 2005) (yes). Do you agree? See *Pro-Football, Inc. v. Tupa*, 14 A.3d 678 (Md. Ct. App. 2011) (adopting the approach articulated in *Uhlenhake* on what constitutes an accidental injury for workers' compensation purposes; also invalidating a forum selection clause specifying. the jurisdiction in which injured athlete would be required to file a workers' compensation claim).

2. *Statutory Exclusion.* As noted by the court in *Uhlenhake*, absent a specific exclusion under a particular state's law, injured professional athletes normally are eligible to receive workers' compensation benefits. See *Pro-Football Inc. v. McCants*, 51 A.3d 586, 596 (Md. 2012) (finding professional athlete a "covered employee" for purposes of workers' compensation statute, where athlete "was regularly employed in Maryland while playing football games here, Respondent's presence in other jurisdictions for practice or playing purposes necessarily was merely incidental or occasional"). A few states exclude professional athletes from the definition of employee for workers' compensation purposes or otherwise severely limit the extent to which workers' compensation benefits are available to professional athletes. See, e.g., Fla. Stat. Ann. §440.02(17)(c)(3) (West 2015); Mass. Gen. Laws Ann. Ch. 152, §1(4)(b) (West 2014); Wyo. Stat. Ann. §27-14-102(vii)(F) (West 2018). The Florida and Wyoming statutes provide coverage for professional athletes when their team purchases insurance for the specific purpose of providing workers' compensation benefits for its athletes. What justifies excluding professional athletes from the scope of workers' compensation systems? Do exclusions reflect a bias against athletes? If so, what might underlie such bias?

3. *Notice Requirements.* Finding that Uhlenhake failed to establish a connection between the knee injury and a compensable event, the court upheld the denial of workers' compensation for injury to his left knee. Uhlenhake's ability to recover would have been enhanced if he had provided timely notice of the injury. Generally, an injured employee must provide timely notice to his or her employer and file a claim within the time frame established by the relevant workers' compensation statute. One commentator states that dual purposes underlie the notice requirement: "First, to enable the employer to provide immediate medical diagnosis and treatment with a view to minimizing the seriousness of the injury; and second, to facilitate the earliest possible investigation of the facts surrounding the injury."

Larson, *supra* at §126.01; accord, *Evans v. Ariz. Cardinals Football Club, LLC.*, 262 F.Supp. 3d 935 (N.D. Cal. 2017) (workers' compensation does not bar a claim for relief arising out of an injury aggravated by the employer's fraudulent concealment of the existence of an injury).

To whom should notice be given? Will notice given to a team physician or trainer comply with this procedural requirement? See *Pittsburgh Steelers Sports, Inc. v. Workers' Comp. Appeal Bd.*, 814 A.2d 788 (Pa. Commw. Ct. 2002) (notification of injury given to team trainer is sufficient to meet statutory notice requirements for workers' compensation). A workers' compensation claim must be filed within the relevant statutory time period or it will be barred. *Adams v. N.Y. Giants*, 827 A.2d 299 (N.J. Super. Ct. 2003).

4. *Forum Selection Clauses.* Contracts between players and their teams stipulate the forum in which workers' compensation disputes will be adjudicated. Notwithstanding forum selection clauses, players will often file workers' compensation claims in states, such as California, where workers' compensation laws are considered more employee/player friendly (California allows workers' compensation benefits for injuries caused by cumulative trauma). Professional athletes' filing of workers' compensation claims in California led to a flurry of litigation that ultimately resulted in the enactment of a statute. In *Kansas City Chiefs v. Allen*, 2013 WL 1339820 (W.D. Mo. Mar. 30, 2013), players who sought to file workers' compensation claims in California attempted to overturn an arbitrator's determination that the players desist from pursuing their California workers' compensation claims and file any such claims in Missouri. The plaintiffs' asserted that the arbitrator's decision should be vacated because the choice of law and/or choice of forum provision of the CBA, which provided the basis for the arbitrator's decision, contravened public policy by waiving the right of players to pursue workers' compensation claims in states other than Missouri. In rejecting the players' claims, the court ruled the relevant provision was enforceable because it contravened neither Missouri, the jurisdiction whose law controlled, nor California public policy. See also *Matthews v. NFL Mgmt. Council*, 688 F.3d 1107, 1114 (9th Cir. 2012) (upholding lower court ruling finding player had failed to demonstrate that forum selection clause "violate[d] an explicitly, well-defined and dominant public policy of the state of California"). But see *Pro-Football, Inc. v. Tupa*, 197 Md. App. 463, 466 (Md. Ct. Spec. App. 2011) (invalidating a forum selection clause as contravening Maryland public policy).

In October 2013, California's Governor Jerry Brown signed into law legislation that precludes most professional athletes from filing workers' compensation claims in California. The statute permits professional athletes in the sports of baseball, basketball, football, ice hockey and soccer to pursue cumulative trauma claims in California only if the athlete worked for more than two seasons during the athletes' career for a California-based team and the athlete played for fewer than seven years for a team(s) not based in California. Cumulative trauma injuries include injuries incurred over a period of time such as arthritis and brain injuries such as chronic traumatic encephalopathy. West's Ann. Cal. Labor Code § 3600.5 (2013). For an example of a workers' compensation board ruling applying the California statute, see *Pippen v. W.C.A.B*, 2015 WL 9805479 (Cal. Ct. App. 4th Dist.) (finding that under California § 3600.5, athlete who played only 9% of his games spanning a 17-year career in California failed to establish the substantial connection required in order for the Workers' Compensation Appeals Board to exercise subject matter jurisdiction over the player's cumulative trauma claim).

5. *Off-Season Injuries.* The time of the occurrence of an injury may impact a player's right to workers' compensation benefits. See, e.g., *Dandenault v. Workers' Comp. Appeals Bd.*, 728 A.2d 1001 (Pa. Commw. Ct. 1999) (professional ice hockey player's participation in a summer hockey league to get into shape for the upcoming season was not within the scope of employment when there was no evidence that the player's team either required or encouraged him to engage in that activity); *Robinson v. Dept. of Labor & Indus.*, 326 P.3d 744 (Wash. Ct. App. 2014) (in contrast to club's players who signed a standard NFL player contract that evidenced the parties' mutual consent to an employment relationship, a free agent who injured his knee during an off-season minicamp tryout was not an "employee" entitled to recover workers' compensation benefits). But see *Farren v. Baltimore Ravens*, 720 N.E.2d 590 (Ohio Ct. App. 1998) (summary judgment inappropriate where player, who was injured during the off-season while between contracts, received ambiguous communications and instructions from the team concerning his employment status, thereby creating a question of fact as to his employment status).

LYONS v. WORKERS' COMP. APPEAL BD.
(PITTSBURGH STEELERS SPORTS, INC.)

803 A.2d 857 (Pa. Commw. Ct. 2002)

SMITH-RIBNER, Judge.

Mitchell W. Lyons appeals from an order of the Workers' Compensation Appeal Board (Board) that affirmed the decision of a Workers' Compensation Judge (WCJ) which granted Lyons' claim petition but limited his benefits in accordance with Section 308.1 of the Workers' Compensation Act (Act), Act of June 2, 1915, P.L. 736, *as amended*, added by Section 10 of the Act of July 2, 1993, P.L. 190, 77 P.S. § 565. Lyons is a former professional football player for Pittsburgh Steelers' Sports, Inc. (Steelers), which is a franchise of the National Football League (NFL). Lyons contends that Section 308.1 violates equal protection of the law by imposing an artificially low average weekly wage on certain professional athletes.

[EDS. Before his injury, Lyons played professional football for the Steelers as a tight end and as a special teams player. As a result of a blow to his knee that occurred during a game, Lyons was diagnosed as having sustained a dislocated left knee, with tears of the posterior cruciate ligament, the anterior cruciate ligament, and medial collateral ligament, and possible damage to the meniscus and possible other damage to the interior. As a professional football player, Lyons needed to be able to run; make sudden stops, sharp turns, twists, and quick starts; and be prepared to be tackled when handling the football. Because he could no longer perform those tasks, Lyons was unable to return to his career as a professional football player.]

At the time of his injury, Lyons' actual weekly wage was $8,075.90, and he was paid that wage through February 9, 2000. Since October 31, 2000, Lyons has been gainfully employed by AXA Advisors, a financial planner in Grand Rapids Michigan, with a weekly income of $1,000. Due to the operation of Section 308.1 of the Act, Lyons' partial disability benefit rate is calculated based upon an average weekly wage of $1,176.00 (two times the statewide average weekly wage of $588) rather than Lyons' actual average weekly wage of $8,075.90. The parties stipulated to the facts of Lyons' injury and that, under the Act, Lyons is entitled to partial disability benefits at the rate of $117.33 per week from November 1, 2000 to date and continuing. The $117.33 figure is calculated as two thirds of the difference between Lyons' weekly income of $1,000 and the average weekly wage of $1,176.00 imposed by Section 308.1.

Under the stipulation, Lyons reserved the right to challenge the constitutionality of Section 308.1. . . .

Section 308.1 of the Act limits the amount of partial disability benefits received by professional athletes who are employed by franchises of certain enumerated professional athletic organizations and whose average weekly wage is more than eight times the Statewide average weekly wage. When calculating such benefits, Section 308.1 imposes an artificial average weekly wage equal to two times the Statewide average weekly wage. . . .

Lyons contends that Section 308.1 violates his right to equal protection under the law as guaranteed by the Fourteenth Amendment of the United States Constitution and by Article 1, Section 26 of the Pennsylvania Constitution. The same standards apply when analyzing claims brought under the equal protection provisions of the Pennsylvania Constitution and claims brought under the equal protection provisions of the United States Constitution. *Commonwealth v. Albert*, 563 Pa. 133, 758 A.2d 1149 (2000). The essence of those standards is that the law should treat similarly situated people in similar ways, but the standard allows the legislature to treat people with different needs differently and to classify people for purposes of receiving treatment. *Id.*

The first step in an equal protection analysis is to determine which of three types of scrutiny the reviewing court should apply to the challenged classification: strict scrutiny, intermediate scrutiny or rational basis scrutiny. . . .

Professional athletes are neither a suspect class nor a sensitive classification, and Section 308.1 implicates no fundamental or important right. The right at issue is purely economic, and therefore the rational basis scrutiny applies. . . .

A classification satisfies rational basis scrutiny so long as the legislative distinction has some rational ground that relates to a legitimate state purpose. . . . A law will not be found to violate equal protection under rational basis scrutiny simply because the classifications drawn by the legislature are imperfect or result in some inequality. . . .

Lyons argues that he is being treated disparately because he receives less benefits than a worker earning the same wage in any other line of work. He contends that even among professional athletes the treatment is disparate because Section 308.1 targets only certain athletic organizations; for example, it does not apply to professional athletes who play soccer or to professional athletes who play football but are employed by a start-up league. Lyons further contends that there is no logical reason to distinguish between professional athletes who receive eight times the statewide average weekly wage and those who receive less than that amount, and he suggests that the only purpose served by Section 308.1 is to confer an economic benefit upon the owners of the athletic organizations that the law targets.[2]

---

2. The Steelers correctly note that Section 308.1 affects only professional athletes who have demonstrated an ability to secure post-injury wages with gainful employment. The Section has no effect on an athlete's right to receive total disability benefits or to receive medical treatment.

The District Court of Appeals of Florida considered a similar constitutional challenge to the Florida workers' compensation statute in *Rudolph v. Miami Dolphins, Ltd.*, 447 So. 2d 284 (Fla. Dist. Ct. App. 1983). The statute in question provided that the term employment did not include service performed by a professional athlete, such as a professional football player. Among other things, the claimants in that case argued that the exclusion was unconstitutional in violation of the equal protection clause of the Fourteenth Amendment and the corresponding equal protection guarantee in the state constitution. In upholding the constitutionality of the exclusion, the Florida court provided the following explanation for the basis of the classification:

> The professional athlete exclusion is not a wholly arbitrary one. Professional football players incur serious injuries on a regular, frequent, and repetitive basis. They are generally well paid, and as the NFL contracts in these cases exemplify, they willfully hold themselves out as well-skilled in the sport of their choice. They make a conscious decision to use their skills in an occupation involving a high risk of frequent, repetitive, and serious injury. We cannot say that the legislature's exclusion of this voluntary, though highly dangerous, activity from the worker[s'] compensation act fails to bear some reasonable relationship to a legitimate state purpose and is so completely arbitrary and lacking in equality of application to all persons similarly situated as to violate the cited constitutional provisions.

Id. at 291-292.

The explanation supplied by the Florida court offers a rational basis for treating professional athletes differently that equally supports Section 308.1. The Court agrees that professional athletes wilfully hold themselves out to risk of frequent, repetitive and serious injury in exchange for lucrative compensation. While other occupations are also rewarded for facing risk, professional athletes employed in the major professional sports represent a distinctive blend of risk combined with lucrative compensation. It is also worth observing that professional athletes undergo this risk in order to provide entertainment. While the Court has great respect for professional athletes, the legislature could have rationally placed a different value on those who risk bodily harm to provide entertainment from those, such as police officers and fire fighters, who risk bodily harm to protect society.

Although these characteristics may apply equally to some other occupations, the fact that a classification is imperfect does not render it arbitrary. *McCusker*. Likewise, the legislature could rationally have concluded that professional athletes paid less than eight times the statewide average weekly wage have a greater need for partial disability benefits than athletes who receive greater compensation. The cut-off chosen by the legislature need not be mathematically perfect in order to withstand rational basis scrutiny. *Id.* For the foregoing reasons, the Court affirms the order of the Board.

NOTES AND QUESTIONS

1. *Statutory Limitations on Benefits.* Like the statute upheld in *Lyons*, other statutes impose limitations specifically directed toward professional athletes. To prevent professional athletes from receiving benefits for the same injury from two different sources, some states limit the amount of recoverable workers' compensation benefits. In *Gulf Ins. Co. v. Hennings*, 283 S.W.3d 381

(Tex. App. 2008), a Texas court interpreted several provisions of the Texas workers' compensation act. The court concluded that because the income and medical benefits Hennings received under his contract and collective bargaining agreement were not equal to or in excess of the corresponding workers' compensation benefits, he was not required to elect between the two. Thus, Hennings was entitled to receive both his workers' compensation benefits and his employment-related benefits.

Other states statutorily require that benefits payments from an athlete's team be set off against any workers' compensation benefits awarded to the athlete. In states with such provisions, litigation often arises over what parts of a team's benefits payments should be set off and whether the team is entitled to a dollar-for-dollar or a week-for-week set-off. *Lincoln Hockey, LLC v. D.C. Dept. of Emp't Servs.*, 810 A.2d 862 (D.C. 2002) (limiting the types of payments to be set off under D.C. Code 32-1515(j)); *Smith v. Richardson Sports Ltd.*, 616 S.E.2d 245 (N.C. Ct. App. 2005) (noting complex interaction between North Carolina workers' compensation statute and injury compensation benefits paid by club, pursuant to NFL collective bargaining agreement and injured player's contract, in determining club's credits against player's workers' compensation benefits). Although a team's benefits payments may be deemed advance payments of workers' compensation benefits, those payments may not have the same tax-exempt status as workers' compensation benefits. See *Wallace v. United States*, 139 F.3d 1165 (7th Cir. 1998) (interpreting 26 U.S.C. §104(a)(1) as not exempting a team's benefits payments that had been deemed advanced payments of workers' compensation). The amount to which an athlete is entitled under the workers' compensation statute is often litigated. *Farquhar v. New Orleans Saints*, 16 So. 3d 404 (La. Ct. App. 2009), illustrates the types of computation issues that arise. There the court held that the workers' compensation amount due to the athlete should be based on the amount that he actually earned from playing prior to his injury and not the contract amount. Accord *Hoffman v. New Orleans Saints*, 56 So. 3d 446 (La. Ct. App. 5 Cir. 2011).

2. *Intentional Injury Exception.* Rather than seeking the no-fault fixed benefits provided by workers' compensation, an injured player instead may prefer trying to obtain an uncertain, but potentially much larger, judgment in tort litigation. The exclusive remedy provisions of workers' compensation laws will not bar a tort action against an employer for harm caused by conduct that is intended to injure an employee. If the requisite intent is established, an employee may elect to either receive workers' compensation benefits or bring a tort claim.

Even in jurisdictions that recognize the intentional injury exception to the exclusivity effect of workers' compensation laws, courts generally are not receptive to a professional athlete's claim that his team "intended" his injury, and are rather exacting with regard to the burden imposed on the employee. See, e.g., *DePiano v. Montreal Baseball Club, Ltd.*, 663 F. Supp. 116, 117 (W.D. Pa. 1987) ("In order to constitute an intentional tort, the conduct must be engaged in with the desire to bring about the consequences of the act. A mere knowledge and appreciation of a risk is not the same as the intent to cause injury"); *Brocail v. Detroit Tigers, Inc.* 268 S.W.3d 90, 108 (Tex. App. 2008) ("An employer is deemed to have intended to injure if he had actual knowledge that an injury was certain to occur and wilfully disregarded that knowledge. . . . A plaintiff may establish a corporate employer's actual knowledge by showing that a supervisory or managerial employee had actual knowledge that an injury would follow from what the employer deliberately did or did not do"). See also Timothy Davis, *Tort Liability of Coaches for Injuries to Professional Athletes: Overcoming Policy and Doctrinal Barriers,* 76 UMKC L. Rev. 571, 587-90 (2008) (discussing the intentional conduct exception to the exclusivity of workers' compensation remedies).

3. *Fraudulent Misrepresentation Exception.* Even if a club does not intend to injure a player, in some jurisdictions it may be subject to tort liability for fraudulent concealment of material medical information concerning a player's fitness to play. In *Krueger,* discussed *supra,* the court held that a professional football team fraudulently failed to disclose that a player risked permanent disability by continuing to play with a chronic knee condition. Evidence established that the team "consciously failed" to disclose that the player's knee lacked the anterior cruciate ligament, that steroid injection treatments might have adverse effects, and that he risked permanent injury by continuing to play without surgery. The exclusivity provisions of the California workers' compensation statute were inapplicable because they expressly permitted the recovery of tort damages if the employee's injury was aggravated by the employer's fraudulent concealment of the existence of the injury. Absent a statutory exception to the workers' compensation bar to employee tort claims, however, courts have refused to allow a player to bring a fraud action against a team for misrepresenting or failing to disclose material information about a physical condition that increased the risk of harm from continued play.

In *Gambrell v. Kansas City Chiefs Football Club, Inc.,* 562 S.W.2d 163 (Mo. Ct. App. 1978), a football player alleged that his team and two of its physicians conspired to falsely represent that he was medically fit to play football based on the results of his physical examination. He allegedly was unfit to play because of preexisting back, neck, and spine injuries. After receiving medical clearance to play, the plaintiff severely aggravated an existing injury during a game and was permanently disabled. The court observed that the alleged fraud preceded, and helped to produce, the aggravation of the plaintiff's injury; therefore, the subsequent aggravation merged into the preexisting injury, for which the plaintiff had previously received workers' compensation benefits. Concluding that the player was entitled to only one recovery for his injury, the court found his tort claim barred by the exclusivity provision of the Missouri workers' compensation law.

4. *Workers' Compensation Co-Employee Bar.* In an effort to assert claims for sports medicine malpractice, players have attempted to characterize the team physician as an independent contractor rather than a team employee to avoid the workers' compensation bar to tort against co-employees. Despite earlier authority adopting such a characterization, see *Bryant v. Fox,* 515 N.E.2d 775 (Ill. Ct. App. 1987), more recent case law has rejected it. E.g., *Stringer v. Minn. Vikings Football Club, LLC,* 705 N.W.2d 746 (Minn. 2005) (workers' compensation co-employee doctrine bars tort claim against NFL club's athletic trainers for alleged improper treatment of player who died from heat stroke during preseason practice). See generally Matthew J. Mitten, *Team Physicians as Co-Employees: A Prescription That Deprives Professional Athletes of an Adequate Remedy for Sports Medicine Malpractice,* 50 St. Louis U. L.J. 211 (2006) (critiquing these cases); Dennis Durao, *An Endangered Species: Professional Sports Team Physicians,* 15 Quinnipiac Health L.J. 33, 45 (2012) (examining the liability of team physicians).

F. PARTICIPATION RIGHTS OF ATHLETES WITH PHYSICAL OR MENTAL IMPAIRMENTS

1. Enhanced Risk of Harm to Oneself

In addition to assuming the normal inherent risks of injury, athletes with a physical impairment or abnormality may expose themselves to increased risk or severity of injury by participating in competitive sports. Such athletes—if nevertheless physically capable of playing a sport—sometimes are willing to accept an enhanced risk of injury or potential significant harm to themselves. Although most athletes accept the team physician's medical recommendation not to play competitive sports to avoid exposure to significant health risks, some have resorted to litigation in an effort to continue playing a desired sport.

Beginning in the mid-1970s, athletes with a missing or nonfunctioning paired organ (e.g., an eye or kidney) began asserting a legal right not to be medically excluded from participating in contact sports. In *Neeld v. American Hockey League*, 439 F. Supp. 459 (W.D.N.Y. 1977), the court enjoined enforcement of a professional league bylaw prohibiting one-eyed athletes from playing hockey. The court ruled that this bylaw violated New York's Human Rights Law prohibiting employees from discrimination based on disability unless the characteristic is a bona fide occupational qualification. There was no evidence that blindness in one eye substantially detracted from the plaintiff's ability to play hockey. However, in *Neeld v. NHL*, 594 F.2d 1297 (9th Cir. 1979), the Ninth Circuit rejected the same plaintiff's claim that this bylaw violates the federal antitrust laws. The court concluded that the bylaw's primary purpose of promoting safety outweighed any *de minimis* anticompetitive effect on excluded athletes.

Courts generally have rejected claims by physically impaired athletes that exclusion from athletics violates the federal constitution because they are not a suspect or quasi-suspect class justifying heightened scrutiny of alleged discrimination. *City of Cleburne v. Cleburne Living Ctr., Inc.*, 473 U.S. 432 (1985); *Grube v. Bethlehem Area Sch. Dist.*, 550 F. Supp. 418, 423 (E.D. Pa. 1982) (expressing doubt that excluding handicapped students from high school athletics denies equal protection of the laws); *Neeld v. Am. Hockey League*, 439 F. Supp. 459 (W.D.N.Y. 1977) (professional league's bylaw a product of private conduct, not state action subject to constitutional scrutiny). Even if state action exists, exclusion of physically impaired athletes is legally justifiable if the decision of the governing body, educational institution, or team is rationally related to a legitimate objective. Reliance on the team physician's medical recommendation that an athlete not play rationally furthers the permissible purpose of ensuring the health and safety of its athletes. See generally Matthew J. Mitten, *Amateur Athletes with Handicaps or Physical Abnormalities: Who Makes the Participation Decision?*, 71 Neb. L. Rev. 987, 1004-07 (1992).

The following case considers whether §504(a) of the Rehabilitation Act, 29 U.S.C.A. §§701 et seq., a federal statute that prohibits discrimination against persons with a disability, provides an athlete with a legal right to participate in intercollegiate athletics if medical opinions are divided regarding whether doing so will expose him to an enhanced risk of serious injury or death.

KNAPP v. NORTHWESTERN UNIV.

101 F.3d 473 (7th Cir. 1996), *cert. denied*, 520 U.S. 1274 (1997)

EVANS, Circuit Judge.

Nicholas Knapp wants to play NCAA basketball for Northwestern University—so badly that he is willing to face an increased risk of death to do so. Knapp is a competent, intelligent adult capable of assessing whether playing intercollegiate basketball is worth the risk to his heart and possible death, and to him the risk is acceptable. Usually, competent, intelligent adults are allowed to make such decisions. This is especially true when, as here, the individual's family approves of the decision and the individual and his parents are willing to sign liability waivers regarding the worst-case scenario should it occur.

Northwestern, however, refuses to allow Knapp to play on or even practice with its men's basketball team. Knapp, currently a sophomore at Northwestern, has the basketball skills to play at the intercollegiate level, but he has never taken the court for his team. Although Northwestern does not restrict him from playing pick-up basketball games, using recreational facilities on campus, or exerting himself physically on his own, the university disqualified Knapp from playing on its intercollegiate basketball team. The issue in this case boils down to whether the school—because of § 504 of the Rehabilitation Act of 1973, as amended, 29 U.S.C. § 794—will be forced to let Knapp don a purple uniform and take the floor as a member of Northwestern's basketball team.

[EDS. As a high school senior, Knapp suffered sudden cardiac arrest while playing recreational basketball, which required cardiopulmonary resuscitation and defibrillation to restart his heart. Thereafter, he had an internal defibrillator implanted in his abdomen, which detects heart arrhythmia and delivers a shock to convert heart rhythm back to normal. He subsequently played competitive recreational basketball without any incidents of cardiac arrest and received medical clearance to play college basketball from three cardiologists who examined him.

Northwestern agreed to honor its preexisting commitment to provide Knapp with an athletic scholarship, although he was medically disqualified from playing intercollegiate basketball. Its team physician's recommendation was based on Knapp's medical records and history, the 26th Bethesda Conference guidelines for athletic participation with cardiovascular abnormalities, and opinions of two consulting cardiologists who concluded that Knapp would expose himself to a significant risk of ventricular fibrillation or cardiac arrest during competitive athletics.

All medical experts agreed on the following facts: Knapp had suffered sudden cardiac death because of ventricular fibrillation; even with the internal defibrillator, playing college basketball placed Knapp at a higher risk of sudden cardiac death as compared with other male college basketball players; the internal defibrillator had never been tested under the conditions of intercollegiate basketball; and no person currently played or had ever played college or professional basketball after suffering sudden cardiac death or after having a defibrillator implanted. However, they disagreed regarding whether Knapp should be medically cleared to play intercollegiate basketball. Northwestern's Presidential Directive on Self-Regulation of Intercollegiate Athletics, the Big Ten Conference's Handbook Agreements for Men's Programs, and the NCAA's Constitution and Sports Medicine Handbook all give the team physician sole responsibility to decide whether a student is medically eligible to compete on the basketball team.]

The district court held a hearing solely to determine whether Knapp presently is medically eligible to play intercollegiate basketball. Presented with conflicting evidence, the district court found Knapp medically eligible and Northwestern in violation of the Rehabilitation Act. [It] . . . entered a permanent injunction prohibiting Northwestern from excluding Knapp from playing on its basketball team for any reason related to his cardiac condition. . . .

To prevail on his claim for discrimination under the Act, Knapp must prove that: (1) he is disabled as defined by the Act; (2) he is otherwise qualified for the position sought; (3) he has been excluded from the position solely because of his disability; and (4) the position exists as part of a program or activity receiving federal financial assistance. Northwestern does not dispute that it receives federal financial assistance and that it has excluded Knapp from its intercollegiate basketball program solely because of his cardiac condition, so our focus is on whether Knapp is an "otherwise qualified individual with a disability."

To show that he is disabled under the terms of the Act, Knapp must prove that he (i) has a physical . . . impairment which substantially limits one or more of [his] major life activities, (ii) has a record of such an impairment, or (iii) is regarded as having such an impairment. 29 U.S.C. § 706(8)(B). Knapp satisfies the first element of part (i) of this definition. A cardiovascular problem constitutes a physical impairment under § 706(8)(B). 34 C.F.R. § 104.3(j)(2)(i)(A); 45 C.F.R. § 84.3(j)(2)(i)(A). Northwestern does not dispute this fact, but it instead zeros in on the second element of the disability definition: whether playing intercollegiate basketball is part of a major life activity and, if so, whether its diagnosis of Knapp's cardiac condition substantially limits Knapp in that activity.

In determining whether a particular individual has a disability as defined in the Rehabilitation Act, the regulations promulgated by the Department of Health and Human Services with the oversight and approval of Congress are of significant assistance. Those regulations define "major life activities" as basic functions of life "such as caring for one's self, performing manual tasks, walking, seeing, hearing, speaking, breathing, learning, and working." 34 C.F.R. § 104.3(j)(2)(ii); 45 C.F.R. § 84.3(j)(2)(ii). Regulations regarding equal employment opportunities under the Americans with Disabilities Act, 42 U.S.C. §§ 12101 *et seq.*, adopt the same term and definition and an interpretive note provides a bit more guidance: "'Major life activities' are those basic activities that the average person in the general population can perform with little or no difficulty." 29 C.F.R. pt. 1630, app. § 1630.2. . . .

Knapp contends that playing an intercollegiate sport is an integral part of his major life activity of learning and that his education will be substantially limited if he cannot play on the team. He states that he does not believe he can obtain confidence, dedication, leadership, perseverance, discipline, and teamwork in any better way. The district court agreed with him, determining that *for Knapp,* playing on the Northwestern basketball team was part of the major life activity of learning and that he was substantially limited from such learning by the university. . . .

We do not think that the definition of "major life activity" can be as particularized as Knapp wants it to be. Playing intercollegiate basketball obviously is not in and of itself a major life activity, as it is not a basic function of life on the same level as walking, breathing, and speaking. Not everyone gets to go to college, let alone play intercollegiate sports. We acknowledge that intercollegiate sports can be an important part of the college learning experience for both athletes and many cheering students—especially at a Big Ten school. Knapp has indicated that such is the case for him. But not every student thinks so. Numerous college students graduate each year having neither participated in nor attended an inter-collegiate sporting event. Their sheepskins are no less valuable because of the lack of intercollegiate sports in their lives. Not playing intercollegiate sports does not mean they have not learned. Playing or enjoying intercollegiate sports therefore cannot be held out as a *necessary* part of learning for *all* students.

A few cases, none of them binding on us, have considered school team sports a major life activity in and of themselves. *See Pahulu v. University of Kansas*, 897 F. Supp. 1387 (D. Kan. 1995) (intercollegiate football may be a major life activity); *see also Sandison v. Michigan High School Athletic Assn., Inc.*, 863 F. Supp. 483, 489 (E.D. Mich. 1994) (participation on the cross-country and track teams an important and integral part of education and a major life activity), *rev'd on other grounds*, 64 F.3d 1026 (6th Cir. 1995). . . . Because intercollegiate athletics may be *one part* of the major life activity of learning for *certain* students, the parties here have framed the analysis of what constitutes a major life activity into a choice between a subjective test or an objective test—whether we look at what constitutes learning for Nick Knapp or what constitutes learning in general for the average person. The Rehabilitation Act and the regulations promulgated under it give little guidance regarding whether the determination of what constitutes a major life activity turns on an objective or subjective standard. And while we have previously said that whether a person is disabled is "an individualized inquiry, best suited to a case-by-case determination," we have also indicated that "the definition of 'major life activity' in the regulations 'cannot be interpreted to include working at the specific job of one's choice,'" *Byrne*, 979 F.2d at 565. Other courts have been across the board on whether the test is objective or subjective. *Compare Pahulu*, 897 F. Supp. at 1393 ("for Pahulu, intercollegiate football may be a major life activity, i.e., learning"), and *Sandison*, 863 F. Supp. at 489 (participation on high school teams is "as to them a major life activity") with *Welsh v. City of Tulsa, Okla.*, 977 F.2d 1415, 1417 (10th Cir. 1992) (major life activity of working does not necessarily mean working at the job of one's choice).

We decline to define the major life activity of learning in such a way that the Act applies whenever someone wants to play intercollegiate athletics. A "major life activity," as defined in the regulations, is a basic function of life "such as caring for one's self, performing manual tasks, walking, seeing, hearing, speaking, breathing, learning, and working." 34 C.F.R. § 104.3(j)(2)(ii); 45 C.F.R. § 84.3(j)(2)(ii). These are basic functions, not more specific ones such as being an astronaut, working as a firefighter, driving a race car, or learning by playing Big Ten basketball. . . .

Because learning through playing intercollegiate basketball is only one part of the education available to Knapp at Northwestern, even under a subjective standard, Knapp's ability to learn is not substantially limited. Knapp's scholarship continues, allowing him access to all academic and—except for intercollegiate basketball—all nonacademic services and activities available to other Northwestern students, in addition to all other services available to scholarship athletes. Although perhaps not as great a learning experience as actually playing, it is even possible that Knapp may "learn" through the basketball team in a role other than as a player. Knapp is an intelligent student and athlete, and the inability to play intercollegiate basketball at Northwestern forecloses only a small portion of his collegiate opportunities. . . .

Even if we were inclined to find Knapp disabled under the Rehabilitation Act, he would still come up short because we also hold as a matter of law that he is not, under the statute, "otherwise qualified" to play intercollegiate basketball at Northwestern. . . .

Section 794 does not compel educational institutions to disregard the disabilities of disabled persons. *Southeastern Community College v. Davis*, 442 U.S. 397, 405, 99 S. Ct. 2361, 2366, 60 L. Ed. 2d 980 (1979). It requires only that an "otherwise qualified" disabled person not be excluded from participation in a federally funded program solely because of the disability. *Id.* In other words, although a disability is not a permissible ground for assuming an inability to function in a particular context, the disability is not thrown out when considering if the person is qualified for the position sought. *Id.* at 405-06, 99 S. Ct. at 2366-67. "An otherwise qualified person is one who is able to meet all of a program's requirements in spite of his handicap," see *id.* at 406, 99 S. Ct. at 2367, with reasonable accommodation, *see Arline*, 480 U.S. at 287-88 n. 17, 107 S. Ct. at 1131 n. 17 ("when a handicapped person is not able to perform the essential functions of the job, the court must also consider whether any reasonable accommodation by the employer would enable the handicapped person to perform those functions").

Legitimate physical qualifications may in fact be essential to participation in particular programs. . . .

A significant risk of personal physical injury can disqualify a person from a position if the risk cannot be eliminated. But more than merely an elevated risk of injury is required before disqualification is appropriate. Any physical qualification based on risk of future injury must be examined with special care if the Rehabilitation Act is not to be circumvented, since almost all disabled individuals are at a greater risk of injury. . . .

[EDS. The severity of the potential injury was as high as it could have been—death. In regard to the probability of injury, Knapp's experts testified that playing intercollegiate basketball would expose him to a risk of death between 1 in 34 and 1 in 100. These estimates took into account Knapp's internal defibrillator, apparently the only "accommodation" possible for Knapp's condition. Although these numbers were merely estimates, all of them agreed that the risk to Knapp was higher than to the average male collegiate basketball player. Knapp's experts believed it was an acceptable level of risk. Northwestern's experts agreed with the school's team doctor that although the precise risk could not be quantified, Knapp's participation in competitive Big Ten basketball significantly increased his risk of death to an unacceptable degree.]

The district court judge in this case believed that in the face of conflicting opinion evidence regarding risk, and the fact that no scientific data existed to quantify that risk, the decision on whether Knapp should play falls in the lap of the court. . . .

We disagree with the district court's legal determination that such decisions are to be made by the courts and believe instead that medical determinations of this sort are best left to team doctors and universities as long as they are made with reason and rationality and with full regard to possible and reasonable accommodations. In cases such as ours, where Northwestern has examined both Knapp and his medical records, has considered his medical history and the relation between his prior sudden cardiac death and the possibility of future occurrences, has considered the severity of the potential injury, and has rationally and reasonably reviewed consensus medical opinions or recommendations in the pertinent field—regardless whether conflicting medical opinions exist—the university has the right to determine that an individual is not otherwise medically qualified to play without violating the Rehabilitation Act. The place of the court in such cases is to make sure that the decision-maker has reasonably considered and relied upon sufficient evidence specific to the individual and the potential injury, not to determine on its own which evidence it believes is more persuasive.

Other courts have held the same. In *Pahulu*, for instance, an intercollegiate football player presented testimony of three specialists in an attempt to show that his risk of permanent neurological injury was no greater than any other player's and that the University of Kansas declared him physically ineligible based on misconceptions. The Kansas district court nevertheless found that "the conclusion of the KU physicians, although conservative, is reasonable and rational . . . and is supported by substantial competent evidence for which the court is unwilling to substitute its judgment." *Pahulu*, 897 F. Supp. at 1394. We reject those cases intimating that a school's rational decision has no weight. *See Poole v. South Plainfield Bd. of Educ.*, 490 F. Supp. 948, 954 (D.N.J. 1980) (school board incorrectly "insisted nonetheless in imposing its own rational decision over the rational decision of the Pooles"). . . .

We do not believe that, in cases where medical experts disagree in their assessment of the extent of a real risk of serious harm or death, Congress intended that the courts—neutral arbiters but generally less skilled in medicine than the experts involved—should make the final medical decision. Instead, in the midst of conflicting expert testimony regarding the degree of serious risk of harm or death, the court's place is to ensure that the exclusion or disqualification of an individual was individualized, reasonably made, and based upon competent medical evidence. So long as these factors exist, it will be the rare case regarding participation in athletics where a court may substitute its judgment for that of the school's team physicians. . . .

In closing, we wish to make clear that we are *not* saying Northwestern's decision necessarily is the right decision. We say only that it is not an illegal one under the Rehabilitation Act. On the same facts, another team physician at another university, reviewing the same medical history, physical evaluation, and medical recommendations, might reasonably decide that Knapp met the physical qualifications for playing on an intercollegiate basketball team. Simply put, all universities need not evaluate risk the same way. What we say in this case is that if substantial evidence supports the decision-maker—here Northwestern—that decision must be respected.

Section 794 prohibits authorities from deciding without significant medical support that certain activities are too risky for a disabled person. Decisions of this sort cannot rest on paternalistic concerns. Knapp, who is an adult, is not in need of paternalistic decisions regarding his health, and his parents—more entitled to be paternalistic toward him than Northwestern—approve of his decision. . . . But here, where Northwestern acted rationally and reasonably rather than paternalistically, no Rehabilitation Act violation has occurred. The Rehabilitation Act "is carefully structured to replace . . . reflexive actions to actual or perceived handicaps with actions based on reasoned and medically sound judgments. . . ." *Arline*, 480 U.S. at 284-85, 107 S. Ct. at 1129. . . .

Reversed.

NOTES AND QUESTIONS

1. *Purpose of the Rehabilitation Act.* The Supreme Court has observed that the Rehabilitation Act's objective is to prevent discrimination based on an assumed "inability to function in a particular context." *Southeastern Cmty. Coll. v. Davis*, 442 U.S. 397, 405 (1979). This law is primarily intended to provide handicapped or impaired persons with an opportunity to participate fully in activities in which they have the physical capability and skill to perform. Section 504 of the act is patterned after similar federal statutes prohibiting racial and sexual discrimination. Regulations promulgated under the act by the Department of Education specifically prohibit colleges and high schools from discriminating against qualified handicapped athletes. Qualified handicapped athletes must be given an "equal opportunity for participation" in interscholastic and intercollegiate athletics. 34 C.F.R. §§104.37(c), .47(a); 45 C.F.R. §§84.37(c), .47(a).

2. *Entities Covered by the Rehabilitation Act.* If any part of an educational institution receives federal financial assistance, all of its operations and programs are covered by the Rehabilitation Act. 29 U.S.C.A. §794(b). Thus, virtually all university and high school athletics programs are covered by the act.

3. *Persons Protected by the Rehabilitation Act.* Why did *Knapp* hold that the plaintiff was not entitled to the Act's protection? Would the court's holding be different if Northwestern University refused to honor his athletic scholarship?

4. *"Excluded . . . Solely Because of His Disability."* An educational institution might fear tort liability if it permits an athlete to play a sport contrary to the recommendations of its team physician and the athlete suffers a serious injury or dies while doing so. Is this a valid justification for exclusion given that Nicholas Knapp and his parents were willing to release Northwestern University from any potential liability if a "worst-case scenario" occurred? *Grube v. Bethlehem Area Sch. Dist.*, 550 F. Supp. 418, 424 (E.D. Pa. 1982) (suggesting that fear of contractual liability does not justify excluding impaired athlete willing to waive future tort claims against school for permitting participation). What advice would you give to the university regarding the validity of a tort liability release or waiver?

5. *"Otherwise Qualified" to Participate.* An individual is "otherwise qualified" if "able to meet all of a program's requirements in spite of his handicap." *S.E. Cmty. Coll.*, 442 at 406. For example, an athlete is not "otherwise qualified" if he or she is physically unable to perform or function effectively in a particular sport. How did *Knapp* apply this standard to medical disqualification to play a sport?

Following *Knapp*, in *Class v. Towson Univ.*, 806 F.3d 236, 251 (4th Cir. 2015), the Fourth Circuit upheld a university team physician's medical disqualification of a Towson University football player who suffered exertional heat stroke during practice that caused liver failure necessitating a liver transplant:

> [T]he standard for assessing [the team physician's] judgment not to clear Class for return to football under Towson University's Return-to-Play Policy is not whether we share that judgment or whether she had a better judgment than some other doctor. Rather, the standard is whether her judgment was reasonable—i.e., whether it was individualized to Class, was reasonably made, and was based on competent medical evidence. When applying that standard,

we conclude that [her] decision was supported by legitimate health and safety
concerns, manifested by the medical records, which were not eliminated by
the proposed monitoring system. Therefore, we conclude that her decision
was not unreasonable.

6. *Reasonable Accommodation Requirement.* The Rehabilitation Act requires a
   covered entity to make reasonable accommodations or modifications to its
   program's participation requirements to enable an athlete to play sports.
   Alexander v. Choate, 469 U.S. 287, 300 (1985) ("while a [school] need not
   be required to make 'fundamental' or 'substantial' modifications to accommodate the handicapped, it may be required to make 'reasonable' ones");
   Marshall v. N.Y. State Pub. High Sch. Ass'n, Inc., 290 F.Supp.3d 187 (W.D.N.Y.
   2017) (denying defendant's motion to dismiss on grounds that the
   Rehabilitation Act required reasonable accommodation to a high school
   student who suffered from various health issues); *Grube v. Bethlehem Area
   Sch. Dist.*, 550 F. Supp. 418, 424 (E.D. Pa. 1982) (permitting a high school
   student with one kidney to play football if he wore a protective flak jacket
   was a required reasonable accommodation).
   Do you agree with the Seventh Circuit's holding that the Rehabilitation
   Act did not require the university to allow Knapp to play intercollegiate basketball with an internal defibrillator?

7. *Aftermath of* Knapp. After his unsuccessful litigation against Northwestern,
   Nicholas Knapp transferred to Northeastern Illinois University, which permitted him to play on its basketball team. However, his internal defibrillator
   malfunctioned before a practice three games into the 1997-1998 basketball
   season, and he sat out the rest of the year. Because Northeastern Illinois
   discontinued its intercollegiate basketball program after that season, Knapp
   transferred to Ashland University, where he played for two seasons. Knapp
   quit playing during his third year after his defibrillator again malfunctioned.

8. *Informed Consent Model for Professional Athletes?* In *Mobley v. Madison Square
   Garden LP*, 2013 U.S. Dist. LEXIS 46341 (S.D.N.Y. Mar. 15, 2013), a New York
   federal district court ruled that Cuttino Mobley, a former NBA basketball
   player, may have a valid state law disability discrimination claim against the
   New York Knicks for refusing to allow him to play basketball with hyper-
   trophic cardiomyopathy during the 2008-09 season based on his medical
   disqualification by two cardiologists. In his complaint, Mobley alleged that
   he had been medically cleared to play NBA basketball from 1999-2008 with
   this condition (subject to his signing a liability waiver), and that three other
   cardiologists examined him and concluded there was no material change
   in his heart condition and that he was as fit to play basketball during that
   season as he had been from 1999-2008. The court held that Mobley pled
   sufficient facts to contradict the medical opinions of the two cardiologists
   who had disqualified him and that it was "plausible that he was qualified to
   perform safely the essential functions of a professional basketball player,"
   which he would ultimately have to prove to prevail on his New York disability discrimination law claim against the Knicks. This decision suggests
   that some courts may be willing to adopt an "athlete informed consent
   model for professional athletes, which would enable a professional athlete
   to choose to participate, despite medical disqualification by the team physician, if other competent medical authority clears him to play." Matthew
   J. Mitten, *Enhanced Risk of Harm to One's Self as a Justification for Exclusion from*

Athletics, 8 Marq. Sports L.J. 189, 221-23 (1998). Mobley ultimately dropped the suit in hopes of putting the issue behind him, signing with a different team, and returning to the NBA. Jared Zwerling, *Source: Cuttino Mobley eyes return*, ESPN.com, Aug. 9, 2013, http://espn.go.com/new-york/nba/story/_/id/9554812/cuttino-mobley-drops-lawsuit-try-comeback-source-says.

2. *Enhanced Risk of Harm to Others*

A physically impaired athlete's medical condition may expose other participants to an enhanced risk of harm beyond what is inherent in a particular sport. For example, there have been concerns expressed by some athletes about perceived health risks from playing contact sports with an athlete who has tested positive for human immunodeficiency virus (HIV), which causes the fatal disease acquired immunodeficiency syndrome (AIDS). Despite a consensus among medical experts that the risk of HIV transmission during an athletic event is extremely low, some fear that HIV infection may occur from exposure to an HIV-positive athlete's blood during a game. See Karen Ahearn, *HIV-Positive Athletes*, 7 Sports L.J. 279 (2000); Anthony DiMaggio, *Suffering in Silence: Should They Be Cheered or Feared? (Mandatory HIV Testing of Athletes as a Health and Safety Issue)*, 8 Seton Hall J. Sport L. 663 (1998); John T. Wolohan, *An Ethical and Legal Dilemma: Participation in Sports by HIV Infected Athletes*, 7 Marq. Sports L.J. 373 (1997); Matthew J. Mitten, *AIDS and Athletics*, 3 Seton Hall J. Sport L. 5 (1993).

This issue came to the forefront of public attention with former Los Angeles Lakers superstar player Earvin "Magic" Johnson's November 1991 announcement that he was retiring from the NBA because he tested positive for HIV. Thereafter, Johnson returned to basketball and won the Most Valuable Player award at the 1992 NBA All-Star Game and led the United States men's basketball team to the gold medal in the 1992 Summer Olympics. In September 1992, Johnson announced his decision to rejoin the Lakers, making him the first player to play a professional sport while known to be HIV positive. Prior to the 1992-1993 NBA season, Johnson again retired because of opposing players' concerns that competing against him would expose them to the risk of HIV infection. These fears were exacerbated by a cut on Johnson's arm suffered during a preseason NBA basketball game. In 1996 this issue resurfaced when the Nevada State Athletic Commission suspended professional boxer Tommy Morrison from fighting after he tested positive for HIV.

The following case considers whether it is legal to exclude an athlete known to be HIV positive from participation in competitive sports.

MONTALVO v. RADCLIFFE

167 F.3d 873 (4th Cir.), *cert. denied,* **528 U.S. 813 (1999)**

NIEMEYER, Circuit Judge.

Michael Montalvo, a 12-year old boy with AIDS, was denied admission to a traditional Japanese style martial arts school because of his HIV-positive status. In this action, brought under Title III of the Americans with Disabilities Act (prohibiting discrimination on the basis of disability by places of public accommodation), the district court denied Montalvo relief because his condition posed a significant risk to the health or safety of other students and no reasonable modification could sufficiently reduce this risk without fundamentally altering the nature of the program. We affirm.

Southside Virginia Police Karate Association, Inc. operates a karate school in Colonial Heights, Virginia, known as U.S.A. Bushidokan, which is owned by James P. Radcliffe, II. The school teaches exclusively traditional Japanese, combat-oriented martial arts rather than the more prevalent, family-oriented fitness programs offered by most martial arts schools. Within the first three weeks of lessons at U.S.A. Bushidokan, students learn techniques that involve substantial body contact, and within the first few months they apply these techniques to spar in actual combat situations. Radcliffe testified at trial that the sparring often results in injuries which, while minor, are bloody. . . .

He explained that to progress "through the belt," a level of achievement, a student must "engage in combat activity fighting. You have to do the self-defense. It involves contact, that's what we do." Radcliffe noted that inherent in this form of karate are "consistently scratched skin, scratches, gouges, bloody lips, bloody noses, things of that nature."

In May 1997, Luciano and Judith Montalvo applied to enter their 12-year old son, Michael, into group karate classes at U.S.A. Bushidokan because Michael wanted to learn karate with some friends who had already begun lessons there. Luciano Montalvo signed a "Membership Application and Agreement" form in which he warranted that Michael was "in good health and that [he] suffer[ed] from no illness or condition . . . which would possibly be infectious to others" and that the Montalvos understood that "no member [would] use the facilities with any open cuts, abrasions, open sores, infections, [or] maladies with the potential of harm to others." In fact, however, Michael had AIDS. The Montalvos did not disclose that fact to U.S.A. Bushidokan because they were afraid that U.S.A. Bushidokan would not enroll Michael if it knew of his HIV-positive status, [but U.S.A. Bushidokan] received information [of Michael's HIV status] from an anonymous source. . . .

Title III of the Americans with Disabilities Act ("ADA") was enacted to facilitate disabled individuals' access to places of public accommodation. Consistent with this goal, the Act states broadly:

> No individual shall be discriminated against on the basis of disability in the full and equal enjoyment of the goods, services, facilities, privileges, advantages, or accommodations of any place of public accommodation by any person who owns, leases (or leases to), or operates a place of public accommodation.

42 U.S.C. § 12182(a). The ADA defines "denial of participation" in a program offered by a place of public accommodation to be an act of discrimination. 42 U.S.C. § 12182(b)(1)(A)(i).

Recognizing that the need to protect public health may at times outweigh the rights of disabled individuals, Congress created a narrow exception to this broad prohibition against discrimination based on disability in places of public accommodation. Thus, a place of public accommodation is entitled to exclude a disabled individual from participating in its program "where such individual poses a *direct threat* to the health or safety of others." 42 U.S.C. § 12182(b)(3) (emphasis added). The Act defines "direct threat" as "a significant risk to the health or safety of others that cannot be eliminated by a modification of policies, practices, or procedures or by the provision of auxiliary aids or services." *Id.* When determining whether an individual poses a "direct threat," a place of public accommodation must not base its calculus on stereotypes or generalizations about the effects of a disability but rather must make "an individualized assessment, based on reasonable judgment that relies on current medical knowledge or on the best available objective evidence." 28 C.F.R. § 36.208(c). The relevant factors which the place of public accommodation must weigh and balance are "the nature, duration, and severity of the risk [and] the probability that the potential injury will actually occur." *Id.; see also* 28 C.F.R. Pt. 36, App. B, p. 598 (1998) (noting that the direct threat provision in Title III of the ADA codifies *School Bd. of Nassau County v. Arline*, 480 U.S. 273, 287-88, 107 S. Ct. 1123, 94 L. Ed. 2d 307 (1987) (delineating criteria for determining whether, under § 504 of the Rehabilitation Act, a tubercular teacher posed a significant risk to the school community).

If the place of public accommodation determines that the individual would pose a significant risk to the health and safety of others, it must then ascertain "whether reasonable modifications of policies, practices, or procedures will mitigate the risk," 28 C.F.R. § 36.208(c), to the point of "eliminat[ing]" it as a "significant risk," 42 U.S.C. § 12182(b)(3). . . . Under the ADA, a failure to make a reasonable modification is itself an act of discrimination unless the place of public accommodation can demonstrate that implementing the modification would fundamentally alter the nature of the program. *See* 42 U.S.C. § 12182(b)(2)(A)(ii).

In this case, U.S.A. Bushidokan concedes that its karate school is a place of public accommodation subject to the requirements of Title III and that Michael Montalvo is disabled for purposes of the ADA by virtue of being HIV-positive or having AIDS. U.S.A. Bushidokan also concedes that it denied Michael participation in group karate classes on the basis of his HIV-positive status, the condition that concededly constitutes his disability. But U.S.A. Bushidokan contends that its exclusion of Michael was legally justified because Michael posed a "direct threat" to other members of the karate class. This contention presents two issues: (1) whether Michael's condition posed a significant risk to the health or safety of others and (2) whether reasonable modifications of policies, practices, or procedures were available to eliminate the risk as a significant one.

While the question of whether Michael's HIV-positive status posed a significant risk to the health or safety of others is a "fact intensive determination," the evidence in the record before us is ample to support the district court's conclusion that Michael posed such a risk.

First, both the Montalvos' and U.S.A. Bushidokan's medical experts testified that blood-to-blood contact is a means of HIV transmission, and both experts agreed that AIDS is inevitably fatal. In addition, U.S.A. Bushidokan's expert testified without challenge that it was possible to become infected with the virus from blood splashing into the eyes or onto seemingly intact skin.

Second, the type of activity offered at U.S.A. Bushidokan emphasized sparring, attack drills, and continuous body interaction with the result that the participants frequently sustained bloody injuries, such as nose bleeds, cuts inside the mouth, and external abrasions. Radcliffe testified that blood from those injuries is "extremely likely" to come in contact with other students' skin. Even though U.S.A. Bushidokan had a policy of constantly monitoring for bloody injuries and removing for treatment participants with those injuries, the fast-paced, continuous combat exercises hampered U.S.A. Bushidokan's efforts to eliminate contact when such injury occurred. . . .

The nature, duration, and severity of the risk and probability of transmission—factors outlined by *Arline* and the ADA regulations—indicate that a significant risk to the health and safety of others would exist if Michael were allowed to participate in the group karate classes. The nature of the risk, which *Arline* defines as the mode of transmission of the disease, is blood-to-blood or blood-to-eye contact, according to the testimony of both sides' experts. The duration of the risk, which *Arline* defines as how long the carrier is infectious, is for the length of Michael's life. The severity of the risk is extreme because there is no known cure for AIDS, and, as the Montalvos concede, AIDS is inevitably fatal. And although the exact mathematical probability of transmission is unknown, the mode of transmission is one which is likely to occur in U.S.A. Bushidokan's combat-oriented group karate classes because of the frequency of bloody injuries and body contact. Thus, the nature of the risk, combined with its severity, creates a significant risk to the health and safety of hard-style karate class members.

When balancing the *Arline* factors to determine whether a risk is significant, one need not conclude that each factor is significant on its own. Rather, the gravity of one factor might well compensate for the relative slightness of another. Thus, when the disease at risk of transmission is, like AIDS, severe and inevitably fatal, even a low probability of transmission could still create a significant risk. In this case, therefore, we agree with the district court that Michael's condition posed a significant risk to the health and safety of others. . . .

The experts in this case agreed that HIV can be transmitted through blood-to-blood contact, and the evidence showed that this type of contact occurred frequently in the karate classes at U.S.A. Bushidokan. Thus, the district court's finding that Michael Montalvo posed a significant risk to the health or safety of others is amply supported by the evidence.

Even though Michael Montalvo's condition posed a significant risk to the health or safety of others, U.S.A. Bushidokan would still be required to admit him to group karate classes if a reasonable modification could have eliminated the risk as a significant one. The only modification which was both effective in reducing risk to an insignificant level and in maintaining the fundamental essence of U.S.A. Bushidokan's program was its offer of private karate classes to Michael.

In considering other modifications, U.S.A. Bushidokan was entitled to reject the modification that would soften the teaching style of its program. U.S.A. Bushidokan's unique niche in the martial arts market was its adherence to traditional, "hard-style" Japanese karate, and the contact between participants, which causes the bloody injuries and creates the risk of HIV transmission, was an integral aspect of such a program. To require U.S.A. Bushidokan to make its program a less combat-oriented, interactive, contact intensive version of karate would constitute a fundamental alteration of the nature of its program. The ADA does not require U.S.A. Bushidokan to abandon its essential mission and to offer a fundamentally different program of instruction.

Similarly, U.S.A. Bushidokan was not required to implement further "universal precautions" such as using eye coverings and wearing gloves. The district court found as a fact that these modifications would not accomplish their goal of eliminating or reducing the otherwise significant risk Michael would pose to his classmates. As Radcliffe testified on behalf of U.S.A. Bushidokan, the suddenness of injuries, the tendency of some wounds to splatter blood, the continuing movement and contact, and the inability to detect injuries immediately all would undermine the effectiveness of these precautions, particularly for places not protected by eye coverings, gloves, or other similar coverings. . . .

Accordingly, we conclude that U.S.A. Bushidokan, in excluding Michael Montalvo from participating in its combat-oriented group karate classes, did not violate Title III of the ADA because Michael posed a significant risk to the health and safety of others that could not be eliminated by a reasonable modification.

The judgment of the district court is *AFFIRMED.*

NOTES AND QUESTIONS

1. *Scope of ADA's Coverage.* The Americans with Disabilities Act of 1990 (ADA), 42 U.S.C. §§12101 et seq., is patterned after the Rehabilitation Act, has similar policy objectives, and extends the coverage of federal legal protection of the rights of handicapped and disabled persons. However, the ADA's scope of coverage is broader than that of the Rehabilitation Act because it covers private entities that do not receive federal funding, such as professional sports leagues and their member teams. Courts generally construe the ADA's substantive provisions in a manner consistent with judicial interpretations of the Rehabilitation Act. *Bragdon v. Abbott,* 524 U.S. 624, 631-632 (1998).

   The ADA applies to public entities, 42 U.S.C. §§12131-32, such as public educational institutions as well as employers with 15 or more employees engaged in industries affecting interstate commerce, including professional sports leagues and teams. 42 U.S.C. §12111(5)(A). Persons that own, lease, or operate a place of public accommodation also are subject to the ADA. 42 U.S.C. §12182(a). A place of public accommodation includes "a gymnasium, health spa, bowling alley, golf course, or other place of exercise or recreation." 42 U.S.C. §12181(7)(L). Virtually all public and private grade schools, high schools, colleges, universities, professional teams, and operators of sporting events held in facilities open to the public are subject to the ADA. Under which provision was the *Montalvo* defendant covered by the ADA?

2. *Individuals Protected by ADA.* Although they were both excluded from desired athletic participation, why was Michael Montalvo protected by federal disability discrimination laws, whereas Nicholas Knapp was not? Note that strict judicial application of the "substantially limits a major life activity" requirement can lead to the ironic result that certain physically impaired athletes are covered by the ADA and Rehabilitation Act, but others are not. For example, a blind or deaf athlete is "disabled" because being blind or deaf substantially limits, respectively, the major life activities of seeing or hearing. On the other hand, an athlete with a cardiovascular abnormality or certain other physical impairments may not be able to prove that this medical condition substantially limits a major life activity. Yet blind or deaf athletes are legally entitled to an individualized evaluation of their respective medical conditions, whereas other athletes are not. Is there a principled justification for protecting some physically impaired athletes but not others? Consider that effective January 1, 2009, Congress amended the ADA to provide that "[t]he definition of disability in this Act shall be construed in favor of broad coverage of individuals under this Act, to the maximum extent permitted by the terms of this Act." 42 U.S.C. §12102(4)(A).

3. *Medical Justification for Exclusion.* What is the legal standard for excluding an athlete with an infectious disease from participation in a sport? In *Montalvo,* was the medical evidence of record sufficient to satisfy this standard? See *Bragdon,* 524 U.S. at 626-27 (assessment of risk of HIV transmission "is based on the medical or other objective, scientific evidence available . . . not simply on . . . good-faith belief that a significant risk existed").

Prior to *Montalvo,* two federal district courts held that the exclusion of HIV-positive elementary school students from participation in school-sponsored contact sports does not violate the Rehabilitation Act. *Doe v. Dolton Elementary Sch. Dist. No. 148,* 694 F. Supp. 440, 449 (N.D. Ill. 1988); *Ray v. Sch. Dist. of Desoto Cty.,* 666 F. Supp. 1524, 1537 (M.D. Fla. 1987). These courts, however, failed to cite or rely on any medical evidence finding that there is a significant risk of HIV transmission during contact sports. See also *Anderson v. Little League Baseball, Inc.,* 794 F. Supp. 342 (D. Ariz. 1992) (baseball league's blanket policy prohibiting coaches in wheelchairs from being on the field violates the ADA because there was no individualized assessment of safety risks).

In *Doe v. Woodford County Board of Education,* 213 F.3d 921 (6th Cir. 2000), the Sixth Circuit ruled that placing a member of a high school's junior varsity basketball team who suffered from hepatitis B on "hold" status pending receipt of medical clearance from his physician did not violate the act. The court explained: "It is entirely reasonable for defendants to be concerned and arguably were obligated to be concerned with limiting risk of exposure of any contagion to others as well as limiting any injury that John may suffer." *Id.* at 926. Further, the court observed that "defendants faced potential liability from other students and parents if they allowed John to play on the team and another student accidentally became exposed to John's contagious condition." *Id.* This is a valid concern because courts have held that an athletic event sponsor has a legal duty to use reasonable care to prevent the transmission of contagious diseases during competition. See, e.g., *Joseph E.G. v. E. Irondequoit Cent. Sch. Dist.,* 708 N.Y.S.2d 537 (N.Y. App. Div. 2000) (reversing summary judgment for defendant school district because its affidavits did not address its alleged negligent failure to clean wrestling mats properly after a wrestler sustained a bloody nose); *Silver v. Levittown Union Free Sch. Dist.,* 692 N.Y.S.2d 886 (N.Y. Sup. Ct. 1999) (finding that an athlete may be liable for the negligent transmission of a contagious disease during a wrestling match).

4. *Comparative Law Perspective.* An Australian federal law, the Equal Opportunity Act of 1995, prohibits discrimination against physically impaired persons unless reasonably necessary to protect the health and safety of others. In *Hall v. Victorian Amateur Football Ass'n* EOC ¶92-997 (1999), the Victorian Civil and Administrative Tribunal held that a sports league illegally discriminated against an HIV-positive athlete by excluding him from participating in amateur football, although it had a genuine belief that it was reasonably necessary based on available medical evidence. The tribunal found the risk of HIV transmission "so low" that it is not reasonably necessary to ban him from playing football. It observed that there is no documented case of HIV transmission during sports competition and that neither the Australian Sports Medicine Federation nor the league's infectious disease policy required the player's exclusion. Although medical experts calculated the risk of HIV transmission to be between 1/6,000 and 1/1,250,000

per player per game, the tribunal concluded the "calculated risk is much greater than the real risk." Compliance with the league's blood-borne infectious disease policy would reduce the risk of HIV transmission posed by the plaintiff's participation in the sport. The tribunal noted that even if he were prohibited from playing football, the risk of HIV transmission from other unknown HIV-positive football players would still exist. For an in-depth discussion of the legality of excluding HIV-positive athletes from sports under Australian law, see Roger S. Magnusson & Hayden Opie, *HIV and Hepatitis in Sport: An Australian Legal Framework for Resolving Hard Cases,* 5 Seton Hall J. Sport L. 69 (1995).

PROBLEM 11-9

A local public school board voted to bar a parent from continuing to coach his son's high school football team. The parent is a former paramedic who apparently contracted HIV several years ago while treating an auto accident victim subsequently discovered to be HIV positive. School board members are concerned that the parent could transmit HIV to players while coaching or rendering first aid to injured players. One board member who is a physician does not think it is a good idea for the parent to continue coaching. Does the school board's action violate the ADA or Rehabilitation Act?

3.   *Modification of Rules of the Game*

The essence of sports is competition by all participants in accordance with uniform playing rules and eligibility requirements. In the following case, the Supreme Court considers whether the federal disability discrimination laws require the rules of the game to be modified to enable an athlete with a mental or physical impairment to participate in a sport. Its decision also provides guidance regarding whether eligibility rules must be modified to permit athletes covered by the ADA or Rehabilitation Act to participate in competitive sports, as illustrated by *Cruz v. Pa. Interscholastic Athletic Ass'n Inc.,* 157 F. Supp. 2d 485 (E.D. Pa. 2001), *infra.*

PGA TOUR, INC. v. MARTIN
532 U.S. 661 (2001)

Justice STEVENS delivered the opinion of the Court.

Petitioner PGA TOUR, Inc., a nonprofit entity formed in 1968, sponsors and cosponsors professional golf tournaments conducted on three annual tours. About 200 golfers participate in the PGA TOUR; about 170 in the NIKE TOUR; and about 100 in the SENIOR PGA TOUR. PGA TOUR and NIKE TOUR tournaments typically are 4-day events, played on courses leased and operated by petitioner. . . .

Three sets of rules govern competition in tour events. First, the "Rules of Golf," jointly written by the United States Golf Association (USGA) and the Royal and Ancient Golf Club of Scotland, apply to the game as it is played, not only by millions of amateurs on public courses and in private country clubs throughout the United States and worldwide, but also by the professionals in the tournaments conducted by petitioner, the USGA, the Ladies' Professional Golf Association, and the Senior Women's Golf Association. Those rules do not prohibit the use of golf carts at any time.

Second, the "Conditions of Competition and Local Rules," often described as the "hard card," apply specifically to petitioner's professional tours. The hard cards for the PGA TOUR and NIKE TOUR require players to walk the golf course during tournaments, but not during open qualifying rounds. On the SENIOR PGA TOUR, which is limited to golfers age 50 and older, the contestants may use golf carts. Most seniors, however, prefer to walk.

Third, "Notices to Competitors" are issued for particular tournaments and cover conditions for that specific event. Such a notice may, for example, explain how the Rules of Golf should be applied to a particular water hazard or manmade obstruction. It might also authorize the use of carts to speed up play when there is an unusual distance between one green and the next tee.

The basic Rules of Golf, the hard cards, and the weekly notices apply equally to all players in tour competitions. . . .

Casey Martin is a talented golfer. As an amateur, he won 17 Oregon Golf Association junior events before he was 15, and won the state championship as a high school senior. He played on the Stanford University golf team that won the 1994 National Collegiate Athletic Association (NCAA) championship. As a professional, Martin qualified for the NIKE TOUR in 1998 and 1999, and based on his 1999 performance, qualified for the PGA TOUR in 2000. . . .

Martin is also an individual with a disability as defined in the Americans with Disabilities Act of 1990 (ADA or Act). Since birth he has been afflicted with Klippel-Trenaunay-Weber Syndrome, a degenerative circulatory disorder that obstructs the flow of blood from his right leg back to his heart. The disease is progressive; it causes severe pain and has atrophied his right leg. During the latter part of his college career, because of the progress of the disease, Martin could no longer walk an 18-hole golf course. Walking not only caused him pain, fatigue, and anxiety, but also created a significant risk of hemorrhaging, developing blood clots, and fracturing his tibia so badly that an amputation might be required. For these reasons, Stanford made written requests to the Pacific 10 Conference and the NCAA to waive for Martin their rules requiring players to walk and carry their own clubs. The requests were granted.

When Martin turned pro and entered petitioner's Q-School, the hard card permitted him to use a cart during his successful progress through the first two stages. He made a request, supported by detailed medical records, for permission to use a golf cart during the third stage. Petitioner refused to review those records or to waive its walking rule for the third stage. . . .

At trial, petitioner did not contest the conclusion that Martin has a disability covered by the ADA, or the fact "that his disability prevents him from walking the course during a round of golf." 994 F. Supp. 1242, 1244 (D. Or. 1998). Rather, petitioner asserted that the condition of walking is a substantive rule of competition, and that waiving it as to any individual for any reason would fundamentally alter the nature of the competition. Petitioner's evidence included the testimony of a number of experts, among them some of the greatest golfers in history. Arnold Palmer, Jack Nicklaus, and Ken Venturi explained that fatigue can be a critical factor in a tournament, particularly on the last day when psychological pressure is at a maximum. Their testimony makes it clear that, in their view, permission to use a cart might well give some players a competitive advantage over other players who must walk. They did not, however, express any opinion on whether a cart would give Martin such an advantage.

[T]he District Court . . . judge found that the purpose of the rule was to inject fatigue into the skill of shotmaking, but that the fatigue injected "by walking the course cannot be deemed significant under normal circumstances." *Id.*, at 1250. Furthermore, Martin presented evidence, and the judge found, that even with the use of a cart, Martin must walk over a mile during an 18-hole round,[17] and that the fatigue he suffers from coping with his disability is "undeniably greater" than the fatigue his able-bodied competitors endure from walking the course. *Id.*, at 1251. . . .

As we have noted, 42 U.S.C. § 12182(a) sets forth Title III's general rule prohibiting public accommodations from discriminating against individuals because of their disabilities. The question whether petitioner has violated that rule depends on a proper construction of the term "discrimination," which is defined by Title III to include: "a failure to make reasonable modifications in policies, practices, or procedures, when such modifications are necessary to afford such goods, services, facilities, privileges, advantages, or accommodations to individuals with disabilities, unless the entity can demonstrate that making such modifications would fundamentally alter the nature of such goods, services, facilities, privileges, advantages, or accommodations." § 12182(b)(2)(A)(ii) [Emphasis added.]

Petitioner does not contest that a golf cart is a reasonable modification that is necessary if Martin is to play in its tournaments. Martin's claim thus differs from one that might be asserted by players with less serious afflictions that make walking the course uncomfortable or difficult, but not beyond their capacity. In such cases, an accommodation might be reasonable but not necessary. In this case, however, the narrow dispute is whether allowing Martin to use a golf cart, despite the walking requirement that applies to the PGA TOUR, the NIKE TOUR, and the third stage of the Q-School, is a modification that would "fundamentally alter the nature" of those events.

In theory, a modification of petitioner's golf tournaments might constitute a fundamental alteration in two different ways. It might alter such an essential aspect of the game of golf that it would be unacceptable even if it affected all competitors equally; changing the diameter of the hole from three to six inches might be such a modification. Alternatively, a less significant change that has only a peripheral impact on the game itself might nevertheless give a disabled player, in addition to access to the competition as required by Title III, an advantage over others and, for that reason, fundamentally alter the character of the competition. We are not persuaded that a waiver of the walking rule for Martin would work a fundamental alteration in either sense.

As an initial matter, we observe that the use of carts is not itself inconsistent with the fundamental character of the game of golf. From early on, the essence of the game has been shotmaking—using clubs to cause a ball to progress from the teeing ground to a hole some distance away with as few strokes as possible. . . . There is nothing in the Rules of Golf that either forbids the use of carts

---

17. "In the first place, he does walk while on the course—even with a cart, he must move from cart to shot and back to the cart. In essence, he still must walk approximately 25% of the course. On a course roughly five miles in length, Martin will walk 1 1/4 miles." 994 F. Supp., at 1251.

or penalizes a player for using a cart. That set of rules, as we have observed, is widely accepted in both the amateur and professional golf world as the rules of the game. . . .

Indeed, the walking rule is not an indispensable feature of tournament golf either. As already mentioned, petitioner permits golf carts to be used in the SENIOR PGA TOUR, the open qualifying events for petitioner's tournaments, the first two stages of the Q-School, and, until 1997, the third stage of the Q-School as well. Moreover, petitioner allows the use of carts during certain tournament rounds in both the PGA TOUR and the NIKE TOUR. In addition, although the USGA enforces a walking rule in most of the tournaments that it sponsors, it permits carts in the Senior Amateur and the Senior Women's Amateur championships.

Petitioner, however, distinguishes the game of golf as it is generally played from the game that it sponsors in the PGA TOUR, NIKE TOUR, and (at least recently) the last stage of the Q-School — golf at the "highest level." According to petitioner, "[t]he goal of the highest-level competitive athletics is to assess and compare the performance of different competitors, a task that is meaningful only if the competitors are subject to identical substantive rules." The waiver of any possibly "outcome-affecting" rule for a contestant would violate this principle and therefore, in petitioner's view, fundamentally alter the nature of the highest level athletic event. The walking rule is one such rule, petitioner submits, because its purpose is "to inject the element of fatigue into the skill of shot-making," and thus its effect may be the critical loss of a stroke. As a consequence, the reasonable modification Martin seeks would fundamentally alter the nature of petitioner's highest level tournaments even if he were the only person in the world who has both the talent to compete in those elite events and a disability sufficiently serious that he cannot do so without using a cart.

The force of petitioner's argument is, first of all, mitigated by the fact that golf is a game in which it is impossible to guarantee that all competitors will play under exactly the same conditions or that an individual's ability will be the sole determinant of the outcome. For example, changes in the weather may produce harder greens and more head winds for the tournament leader than for his closest pursuers. A lucky bounce may save a shot or two. Whether such happen-stance events are more or less probable than the likelihood that a golfer afflicted with Klippel-Trenaunay-Weber Syndrome would one day qualify for the NIKE TOUR and PGA TOUR, they at least demonstrate that pure chance may have a greater impact on the outcome of elite golf tournaments than the fatigue resulting from the enforcement of the walking rule.

Further, the factual basis of petitioner's argument is undermined by the District Court's finding that the fatigue from walking during one of petitioner's 4-day tournaments cannot be deemed significant. . . . And even under conditions of severe heat and humidity, the critical factor in fatigue is fluid loss rather than exercise from walking. . . .

Even if we accept the factual predicate for petitioner's argument — that the walking rule is "outcome affecting" because fatigue may adversely affect performance — its legal position is fatally flawed. Petitioner's refusal to consider Martin's personal circumstances in deciding whether to accommodate his disability runs counter to the clear language and purpose of the ADA. . . . An individualized inquiry must be made to determine whether a specific modification for a particular person's disability would be reasonable under the circumstances as well as necessary for that person, and yet at the same time not work a fundamental alteration.

To be sure, the waiver of an essential rule of competition for anyone would fundamentally alter the nature of petitioner's tournaments. As we have demonstrated, however, the walking rule is at best peripheral to the nature of petitioner's athletic events, and thus it might be waived in individual cases without working a fundamental alteration. Therefore, petitioner's claim that all the substantive rules for its "highest-level" competitions are sacrosanct and cannot be modified under any circumstances is effectively a contention that it is exempt from Title III's reasonable modification requirement. But that provision carves out no exemption for elite athletics, and given Title III's coverage not only of places of "exhibition or entertainment" but also of "golf course[s]," 42 U.S.C. §§ 12181(7)(C), (L), its application to petitioner' tournaments cannot be said to be unintended or unexpected, see §§ 12101(a)(1), (5). . . .[51]

Under the ADA's basic requirement that the need of a disabled person be evaluated on an individual basis, we have no doubt that allowing Martin to use a golf cart would not fundamentally alter the nature of petitioner's tournaments. As we have discussed, the purpose of the walking rule is to subject players to fatigue, which in turn may influence the outcome of tournaments. Even if the rule does serve that purpose, it is an uncontested finding of the District Court that Martin "easily endures greater fatigue even with a cart than his able-bodied competitors do by walking." 994 F. Supp., at 1252. The purpose of the walking rule is therefore not compromised in the slightest by allowing Martin to use a cart. A modification that provides an exception to a peripheral tournament rule without impairing its purpose cannot be said to "fundamentally alter" the tournament. What it can be said to do, on the other hand, is to allow Martin the chance to qualify for, and compete in, the athletic events petitioner offers to those members of the public who have the skill and desire to enter. That is exactly what the ADA requires. As a result, Martin's request for a waiver of the walking rule should have been granted.

The ADA admittedly imposes some administrative burdens on the operators of places of public accommodation that could be avoided by strictly adhering to general rules and policies that are entirely fair with respect to the able-bodied but that may indiscriminately preclude access by qualified persons with disabilities. But surely, in a case of this kind, Congress intended that an entity like the PGA not only give individualized attention to the handful of requests that it might receive from talented but disabled athletes for a modification or waiver of a rule to allow them access to the competition, but also carefully weigh the purpose, as well as the letter, of the rule before determining that no accommodation would be tolerable.

The judgment of the Court of Appeals is affirmed.

Justice SCALIA, with whom Justice THOMAS joins, dissenting.

In my view today's opinion exercises a benevolent compassion that the law does not place it within our power to impose. The judgment distorts the text of Title III, the structure of the ADA, and common sense. I respectfully dissent.

---

51. Hence, petitioner's questioning of the ability of courts to apply the reasonable modification requirement to athletic competition is a complaint more properly directed to Congress, which drafted the ADA's coverage broadly, than to us. . . . While Congress expressly exempted "private clubs or establishments" and "religious organizations or entities" from Title III's coverage, 42 U.S.C. § 12187, Congress made no such exception for athletic competitions, much less did it give sports organizations *carte blanche* authority to exempt themselves from the fundamental alteration inquiry by deeming any rule, no matter how peripheral to the competition, to be essential. . . .

Nowhere is it writ that PGA TOUR golf must be classic "essential" golf. Why cannot the PGA TOUR, if it wishes, promote a new game, with distinctive rules (much as the American League promotes a game of baseball in which the pitcher's turn at the plate can be taken by a "designated hitter")? If members of the public do not like the new rules—if they feel that these rules do not truly test the individual's skill at "real golf" (or the team's skill at "real baseball") they can withdraw their patronage. But the rules are the rules. They are (as in all games) entirely arbitrary, and there is no basis on which anyone—not even the Supreme Court of the United States—can pronounce one or another of them to be "nonessential" if the rule-maker (here the PGA TOUR) deems it to be essential. . . .

Is someone riding around a golf course from shot to shot *really* a golfer? The answer, we learn, is yes. The Court ultimately concludes, and it will henceforth be the Law of the Land, that walking is not a "fundamental" aspect of golf.

Either out of humility or out of self-respect (one or the other) the Court should decline to answer this incredibly difficult and incredibly silly question. To say that something is "essential" is ordinarily to say that it is necessary to the achievement of a certain object. But since it is the very nature of a game to have no object except amusement (that is what distinguishes games from productive activity), it is quite impossible to say that any of a game's arbitrary rules is "essential." Eighteen-hole golf courses, 10-foot-high basketball hoops, 90-foot baselines, 100-yard football fields—all are arbitrary and none is essential. The only support for any of them is tradition and (in more modern times) insistence by what has come to be regarded as the ruling body of the sport—both of which factors support the PGA TOUR's position in the present case. (Many, indeed, consider walking to be *the central feature* of the game of golf—hence Mark Twain's classic criticism of the sport: "a good walk spoiled.") . . .

Because step one of the Court's two-part inquiry into whether a requested change in a sport will "fundamentally alter [its] nature," § 12182(b)(2)(A)(ii), consists of an utterly unprincipled ontology of sports (pursuant to which the Court is not even sure whether golf's "essence" requires a 3-inch hole), there is every reason to think that in future cases involving requests for special treatment by would-be athletes the second step of the analysis will be determinative. In resolving that second step—determining whether waiver of the "nonessential" rule will have an impermissible "competitive effect"—by measuring the athletic capacity of the requesting individual, and asking whether the special dispensation would do no more than place him on a par (so to speak) with other competitors, the Court guarantees that future cases of this sort will have to be decided on the basis of individualized factual findings. Which means that future cases of this sort will be numerous, and a rich source of lucrative litigation. One can envision the parents of a Little League player with attention deficit disorder trying to convince a judge that their son's disability makes it at least 25% more difficult to hit a pitched ball. (If they are successful, the only thing that could prevent a court order giving the kid four strikes would be a judicial determination that, in baseball, three strikes are metaphysically necessary, which is quite absurd.)

The statute, of course, provides no basis for this individualized analysis that is the Court's last step on a long and misguided journey. The statute seeks to assure that a disabled person's disability will not deny him *equal access* to (among other things) competitive sporting events—not that his disability will not deny him an *equal chance to win* competitive sporting events. The latter is quite impossible, since the very *nature* of competitive sport is the measurement, by uniform rules, of unevenly distributed excellence. This unequal distribution is precisely what determines the winners and losers—and artificially to "even out" that distribution, by giving one or another player exemption from a rule that emphasizes his particular weakness, is to destroy the game. . . . In the Court's world, there is one set of rules that is "fair with respect to the able-bodied" but "individualized" rules, mandated by the ADA, for "talented but disabled athletes." The ADA mandates no such ridiculous thing. . . .

My belief that today's judgment is clearly in error should not be mistaken for a belief that the PGA TOUR clearly *ought not* allow respondent to use a golf cart. *That* is a close question, on which even those who compete in the PGA TOUR are apparently divided; but it is a *different* question from the one before the Court. Just as it is a different question whether the Little League *ought* to give disabled youngsters a fourth strike, or some other waiver from the rules that makes up for their disabilities. In both cases, whether they *ought* to do so depends upon (1) how central to the game that they have organized (and over whose rules they are the master) they deem the waived provision to be, and (2) how competitive—how strict a test of raw athletic ability in all aspects of the competition—they want their game to be. . . .

And it should not be assumed that today's decent, tolerant, and progressive judgment will, in the long run, accrue to the benefit of sports competitors with disabilities. Now that it is clear courts will review the rules of sports for "fundamentalness," organizations that value their autonomy have every incentive to defend vigorously the necessity of every regulation. They may still be second-guessed in the end as to the Platonic requirements of the sport, but they will *assuredly* lose if they have at all wavered in their enforcement. The lesson the PGA TOUR and other sports organizations should take from this case is to make sure that the same written rules are set forth for all levels of play, and never voluntarily to grant any modifications. The second lesson is to end open tryouts. I doubt that, in the long run, even disabled athletes will be well served by these incentives that the Court has created. . . .

NOTES AND QUESTIONS

1. *Applicability of the ADA.* Because Casey Martin is an independent contractor who qualified for the Professional Golfers' Association (PGA) Tour because of his playing skills rather than being an employee of the PGA, Title I's prohibition against employment discrimination was inapplicable. Because the PGA Tour is not a public entity, Title II did not apply. Therefore, Martin had to fit his disability discrimination claim under Title III, which covers places of public accommodation.

   The PGA initially argued that it is a "private club" exempt from coverage under Title III pursuant to 42 U.S.C. §12187, or alternatively, that the playing area "behind the ropes" that is open only to the competitors is not a "place of public accommodation." Rejecting the first argument, the district court held that the PGA is appropriately characterized as a commercial enterprise operating in the entertainment industry for the economic benefit of its members rather than as a private club. *Martin,* 532 U.S. at 1886. The Ninth Circuit declined to accept the second argument because all members of the public who satisfy certain requirements are eligible to qualify for the PGA Tour and play in its tournaments.

In a vigorous dissent, Justice Scalia argued that in the context of athletics, Title III's coverage is limited to clients and customers of places of public accommodation, not professional athletes seeking to provide entertainment services therein. In response, the majority found that Congress's intent was that the ADA be liberally construed to provide broad protection for all disabled persons and concluded that the PGA, as an operator of a place of public accommodation during its golf tournaments, "may not discriminate against either spectators or competitors on the basis of disability." *Id.* at 681, n.34. With which view do you agree?

2.   *Reasonable Accommodation or Fundamental Alteration of the Sport?* According to the *Martin* majority, when is a sport's governing body required to modify its playing rules to enable an impaired athlete to participate in the sport? Is there a principled judicial basis for distinguishing between "an essential rule of competition" and one that is merely nonessential or has a peripheral impact on the game? Does the majority provide a convincing response to the dissent's assertion that the essence of sport is that everyone plays by the same rules?

The following two cases decided prior to *Martin* illustrate the nature of the individualized inquiry that must be undertaken to determine whether requested rules modifications by impaired athletes would "fundamentally alter" the nature of a particular sport.

In *Shultz v. Hemet Youth Pony League, Inc.*, 943 F. Supp. 1222 (C.D. Cal. 1996), an 11-year-old boy with a medical condition that severely affected the functioning of his leg muscles sought to play baseball in an age division reserved for children younger than him. The sport's governing body refused to modify its rules to permit him to do so. Although the boy was physically able to play baseball with the use of crutches, the governing body was concerned that permitting him to "play down" would create a possible risk of harm to himself and other players, and have adverse ramifications on its liability insurance coverage. The court found that the requested modification had been denied without any consideration of the boy's ability to run or engage in reflexive action or of what significant risks existed because he used crutches to play baseball. It held that the governing body violated the ADA by failing to even attempt to determine whether the game could be modified to accommodate his ability.

In *Elitt v. U.S.A. Hockey*, 922 F. Supp. 217 (E.D. Mo. 1996), the national governing body for amateur hockey denied the request of a youth hockey player with attention deficit disorder that his father or one of his brothers be permitted on the ice with him during practices and scrimmages to help keep him focused on the game. It also denied his request to "play down" to a lower age group. The court held that the denial of the requested modifications did not violate the ADA. Allowing the plaintiff's father or brother to be on the ice during scrimmages would fundamentally alter the nature of the game by disrupting the flow of play and preventing other players from experiencing actual game conditions. Permitting plaintiff to "play down" to the Squirt level was not required because:

> U.S.A. Hockey's age levels are important because they group players who are roughly the same skill and size. . . . Mark has focusing problems and would generally be larger than the average Squirt level player. These two factors would increase the chances of accidental collision as well as the risk of injury to younger and smaller-sized children. In short, Mark's participation in the

lower age group would be too disruptive, thus fundamentally altering the house program.

Id. at 225. See generally Paul M. Anderson, *A Cart That Accommodates: Using Case Law to Understand the ADA, Sports, and Casey Martin,* 1 Va. Sports & Ent. L.J. 211 (2002) (observing that "[t]he cases that have followed Martin have simply refined the analysis that was already there").

In May 2007, the Ladies Professional Golfers Association allowed MacKinzie Kline, a 15-year-old golfer with a congenital heart condition that prevented her from walking long distances without becoming fatigued, to ride in a cart and use an oxygen delivery system when necessary during an LPGA Tour event. LPGA commissioner Carolyn Bivens determined that these accommodations would not provide her with an unfair competitive advantage.

In *Barron v. PGA Tour, Inc.,* 670 F. Supp. 2d 674 (W.D. Tenn. 2009), the court held that the PGA Tour did not violate a professional golfer's rights under the ADA by suspending him for one year for testing positive for exogenous testosterone, a banned substance under its anti-doping program, and refusing to grant him a therapeutic use exemption. Plaintiff alleged he suffers from abnormally low testosterone, which causes him to have a reduced sex drive, experience fatigue, and have a compromised immune system, and that by refusing to allow him to take medically prescribed exogenous testosterone and suspending him for using it, the PGA Tour discriminated against him in violation of the ADA. The court concluded that he had not shown a likelihood of success on his claim:

> Barron has not shown that the "reasonable accommodation" he has requested (allowing him to continue taking exogenous Testosterone) is necessary in order for him to continue playing golf in PGA Tour events. His complaint and post-hearing brief, at most, claim that he needs these Testosterone shots to address specific medical concerns relating to a reduced sex drive, fatigue, and a compromised immune system-not to play golf. While Barron's abnormally low Testosterone may in some way cause him to be a less competitive golfer than he would be if he were permitted to take the Testosterone injections, [the ADA] simply does not provide a remedy under those circumstances.

Id. at 685-86. After his suspension ended, the PGA Tour granted Barron a therapeutic use exemption to use testosterone while attempting to qualify for the 2011 PGA Tour, which was based on new medical information he submitted. See generally Travis Tygart & Anthony R. Ten Haagen, *The Americans With Disabilities Act, The United States Anti-Doping Agency, and the Effort Toward Equal Opportunity: A Case Study of the* United States Anti-Doping Agency v. George Hartman *Matter,* 2 Harv. J. Sports & Ent. L. 199 (2011) (discussing ADA's reasonable accommodation requirement as applied to athlete's therapeutic use of synthetic testosterone).

3. *Alternative qualification times for disabled runners.* In *Holzmueller ex rel. A.H. v. Ill. High Sch. Ass'n,* 263 F.Supp. 3d 705 (N.D. Ill. 2017), *aff'd* 881 F.3d 587 (7th Cir. 2018), Aaron Holzmueller, a high school runner with cerebral palsy from Illinois, sued the Illinois High School Association ("IHSA"), which operates the state's high school track and field championships, under the ADA and the Rehabilitation Act. During the regular season, Holzmueller competed as a part of the Evanston Township High School track team, but

time qualification thresholds prevented his participation in the state championships. The principle thrust of his suit was a demand for an accommodation that would lower the qualification time threshold for para-ambulatory runners.. The district court granted summary judgment for the IHSA, finding that, as a matter of law, the requested accommodations were not reasonable. The court noted that it does not matter "whether a disabled runner like Holzmueller has a realistic chance to qualify for the finals; [the question] turns on whether Holzmueller would have a realistic shot at qualifying *if he were not disabled.*" *Id.* at *10. The court found no evidence in the record that Holzmueller could qualify were he not disabled and reasoned that because 90% of the state's able-bodied runners similarly could not qualify, the qualification thresholds have no "particular exclusionary effect on the handicapped," including Holzmueller. *Id.* In sum, in granting IHSA summary judgment, the court found that Holzmueller's "request is inconsistent with the Supreme Court's teaching in *Martin* and [Holzmueller] has identified no authority that requires IHSA to provide disabled athletes an equivalent opportunity for athletic success by lower qualifying standards for participation . . . in championship events." *Id.* at *12.

4.   *Competition Between Able-Bodied and Disabled Athletes.* South African Oscar Pistorius had both legs amputated below the knee when he was 11 months old, because he was born without the fibula in his lower legs and had other defects in his feet. Running with "Cheetah" prosthetic legs—a pair of J-shaped carbon fiber blades that touch only a few inches of ground and that attach to his knees—he easily won the 100- and 200-meter sprints at the 2007 Paralympic World Cup. In addition, he has set world records for disabled athletes in the 100-, 200-, and 400-meter dashes. Currently, there are limited biomechanical studies of amputee runners, and his speed on prosthetic legs cannot be precisely compared with what his speed would be on natural legs.

In 2008, the Court of Arbitration for Sport ruled that Pistorius was eligible to run in International Association of Athletics Federations sanctioned track events with his prosthetic legs. *Pistorius v. IAAF,* CAS 2008/A/1480, award of 16 May 2008. An IAAF rule prohibited the use of "any technical device that incorporates springs, wheels or any other element that provides the user with an advantage over another athlete not using such a device." However, the CAS panel rejected the IAAF's argument that the use of a technical device providing an athlete "with any *advantage,* however small, in any part of a competition . . . must render that athlete ineligible to compete regardless of any compensating disadvantages." It concluded that the use of a passive device such as the "Cheetah" prosthetic legs does not violate this rule "without convincing scientific proof that it provides him with *an overall net advantage* over other athletes." The panel concluded that because scientific evidence did not prove that Pistorius obtained a metabolic or biomechanical advantage from using the "Cheetah" prosthetic legs, his exclusion would not further the rule's purpose of ensuring fair competition among athletes. Pistorius was unable to qualify for the 2008 Beijing Olympics, but four years later he qualified for the 2012 London Olympics, representing South Africa in both the 400-meter individual race and the 4×400-meter relay.

Are the federal disability laws violated if a U.S. athletic governing body refuses to allow Pistorius to compete in track events against able-bodied male runners? See *McFadden v. Grasmick,* 485 F. Supp. 2d 642 (D. Md.

2007) (court previously granted injunctive relief allowing "world class" Olympic wheelchair racer to compete alongside footed athletes in races within school district, but denies preliminary injunction seeking to require state high school athletic association to allow her to earn points in separate wheelchair racing events that count in determining team track and field state champion); *Badgett v. Ala. High Sch. Athletic Assn.*, 2007 WL 2461928 (N.D. Ala.) (refusing to grant preliminary injunction to enable wheelchair athlete to compete against able-bodied runners in state track and field championship, because doing so would raise legitimate competitive fairness and safety concerns).

In response to a June 2010 United States Government Accountability Office report finding that public elementary and secondary school students with disabilities do not have an equal opportunity to participate in extracurricular sports, the Department of Education's Office for Civil Rights (OCR), which is responsible for enforcing Section 504 of the Rehabilitation Act and Title II of the ADA, issued on January 25, 2013, written guidance regarding the obligations of covered elementary, secondary, and postsecondary educational institutions to provide students with disabilities the opportunity to participate in interscholastic, intercollegiate, club, and intramural athletics. Department of Education, Office for Civil Rights, January 25, 2013, Directive. The directive states that educational institutions must provide "qualified students with disabilities an equal opportunity for participation in extracurricular athletics in an integrated manner to the maximum extent appropriate to the needs of the student." *Id.* at 7. An educational institution is required to create additional athletic participation opportunities (e.g., wheelchair basketball or tennis) for students with disabilities who are unable to participate in its existing extracurricular athletics program even with reasonable modifications thereto.

5. *Disabled Spectator Protections.* Disabled spectators have experienced mixed success in bringing ADA or Rehabilitation Act discrimination claims against professional leagues or operators of sports venues. See, e.g., *Miller v. Cal. Speedway Corp.*, 536 F.3d 1020 (9th Cir. 2008) (holding race track operator responsible under the ADA to provide their handicapped spectators with a line of sight comparable to members of the general public); *Paralyzed Veterans of Am, v. D.C. Arena L.P.*, 117 F.3d 579 (D.C. Cir. 1997) (violation not to provide line of sight over standing spectators for those in wheelchairs); *Stoutenborough v. NFL*, 59 F.3d 580 (6th Cir. 1995) (NFL television "blackout" rule does not discriminate against hearing-impaired persons); *Feldman v. Pro Football, Inc.*, 579 F. Supp. 2d 697, 709 (D. Md. 2008) (ADA requires NFL club and stadium operator to provide equal access to aural information broadcast over FedExField public address system, including "music with lyrics, play information, advertisements, referee calls, safety/emergency information, and other announcements"); *Access Now Inc. v. S. Fla. Stadium Corp.*, 161 F. Supp. 2d 1357 (S.D. Fla. 2001) (stadium has reasonable number of wheelchair seating spaces; no evidence that plaintiff's proposed facility modifications would actually make stadium more accessible to disabled); *Cortez v. NBA*, 960 F. Supp. 113 (W.D. Tex. 1997) (rejecting hearing-impaired patron's demand for captioning and interpretative services while attending NBA games). See also *Celano v. Marriott Int'l, Inc.*, 2008 WL 239306 (N.D. Cal.) (failure to provide "accessible" or "single-rider" carts to enable disabled persons to play golf at defendant's courses violates ADA).

PROBLEM 11-10

Able is a paraplegic and a nationally ranked player in wheelchair racquetball competitions. He wants to play in an A-level open tournament with footed players, but he asks that he be permitted two bounces to hit the ball. The Official Rules of Racquetball require the ball to be returned on one bounce in a game between footed players, but they allow for two bounces if both participants are playing in wheelchairs.

The general manager of the Metropolis Athletic Club, which is organizing the tournament, has refused to grant Able's request. However, she will allow him to play in a novice league with footed players and be given only one bounce or to set up a wheelchair league if there are a sufficient number of other wheelchair players. Some footed players have expressed concern about whether it would be safe to play against Able in tournament competition. Able rejected these proposed alternatives and insists on being placed in the A League and given two bounces.

Does Able have a valid disability discrimination claim against the Metropolis Athletic Club for refusing to allow him to participate in its A League tournament with his requested rules modification?

4. Modification of Eligibility Requirements

Students with mental impairments sometimes take longer to complete their schooling than students without such impairments and therefore find themselves too old to participate in interscholastic athletics as juniors or seniors in high school. Consider Eric Dompierre, a Michigan high school athlete with Down syndrome. Dompierre played sports throughout his childhood in Ishpeming, Michigan. When he entered Ishpeming High School as a freshman, Dompierre joined the football and basketball teams. Because of his Down syndrome, however, Dompierre progressed through his academic career more slowly than his non-mentally impaired mates of the same age, and by January 2012—the second semester of his junior year—he was already 19 years old. This made him ineligible under a Michigan High School Athletic Association rule prohibiting any student who turns 19 before September 1 of his or her senior year from participating in interscholastic athletics. See Tim Rohan, *Age Is Obstacle for Athlete with Down Syndrome*, N.Y. Times, April 12, 2012, at B13. In response to a national outcry spurred by an Internet and social media campaign to "Let Eric Play!" the MHSAA member schools voted in May 2012 to enact a waiver provision to permit age-ineligible athletes to participate if:

> 1) [The applicant's educational progress] was delayed prior to initial enrollment in the ninth grade solely because of a medically documented disability under the federal Americans with Disabilities Act or Michigan's Persons With Disabilities Civil Rights Act; and
> 2) At the time of the waiver request, [the] student [has] a defined disability documented to diminish both physical and either intellectual or emotional capabilities, does not create a health or safety risk to participants, and does not create a competitive advantage for the team.

See MHSAA Regulation 1 §2(B) (2011-2012). Although Dompierre's athletic eligibility status was resolved without litigation, the following case provides guidance regarding how a court may have decided an ADA or Rehabilitation Act claim by Dompierre against the MHSAA.

CRUZ v. PENNSYLVANIA INTERSCHOLASTIC ATHLETIC ASS'N, INC.

157 F. Supp. 2d 485 (E.D. Pa. 2001)

BUCKWALTER, District Judge.

[EDS. Luis Cruz was a 19-year-old public school special education student who was educable mentally retarded in his fourth year at Ridley High School, a recipient of federal funding. He had played several sports in his first three years at Ridley High School, including football, wrestling, and track. Because he was a student with a disability, Luis Cruz was educated in accordance with an individualized education program (IEP), pursuant to the federal Individuals with Disabilities Education Act (IDEA). As a "non-graded" student, Luis Cruz was not enrolled in a particular numerical grade. His window of opportunity to participate in high school instruction and sports at an earlier age was limited and he did not have comparable opportunities as non-special education children, since due to his intellectual limitations he entered elementary school between ages eleven and twelve, rather than at the customary younger age, and then stayed an additional two years over the regular education students.

The defendant was the Pennsylvania Interscholastic Athletic Association, Inc. (P.I.A.A.), a Pennsylvania nonprofit membership corporation composed of most public and many private high schools in Pennsylvania, for a total of approximately 1,350 schools. A purpose of P.I.A.A. is to develop and apply rules regulating interscholastic athletic competition among its members. The P.I.A.A.'s "Age Rule" provided that "[a] pupil shall be ineligible for interscholastic athletic competition upon attaining the age of nineteen years, with the following exception: If the age of 19 is attained on or after July 1, the pupil shall be eligible, age-wise, to compete through that school year."

A school was required to forfeit a contest for using an ineligible coach or contestant. P.I.A.A. rules permitted students to participate in eight semesters of interscholastic sports; however, Cruz was only been permitted to participate in six semesters. The Director of Special Education Services observed that he still needed the remaining two semesters of interscholastic sports activities to interact with peers and adults, familiarize himself with demands and responsibilities, and develop interpersonal skills that would help him maintain employment after high school. Participation in these activities was vitally important to the development of his self-esteem and self-confidence. Although there was a provision for waiving either the eight-semester or transfer rules, with the key issue usually being "athletic intent," there was no waiver provision for the age rule. This was only the second time the P.I.A.A. had received a request for a waiver of this rule by a student with an IEP.]

The purposes of [the age rule] are: (1) to protect high school athletes of customary age from the dangers and unfairness of participation with those who are older and thus perhaps physically larger, stronger, and more mature and experienced; (2) to limit the possibility that the team with the over-age student will gain an unfair competitive advantage over opponents; (3) to have available the maximum number of team positions for high school athletes who are of customary age for students in high school; and (4) to maintain uniformity of standards with regard to the age of participants. . . .

[According to Bradley Cashman, the P.I.A.A.'s executive director, the age rule did not provide for any waivers because it would be an overly burdensome task to evaluate competitive advantage in individual cases.] An assessment of whether the student would "skew the overall competitiveness of the particular activity" or whether the student would constitute a competitive advantage would have to be looked at not only sport by sport, but individual by individual. Such an assessment would involve examining the individual in comparison with members of his or her own team, and in comparison with members of opposing teams. Such an assessment would involve projecting future athletic performance, at a time in the student's life when athletic ability is changing. This would be a very difficult, complex, and burdensome assessment involving many variables, including both objective and subjective elements, according to Mr. Cashman. . . .

P.I.A.A. estimates that it would have to significantly increase the size of its staff, doubling or tripling it, in order to perform assessments of whether a student would "skew the overall competitiveness of the particular activity" or whether the student would constitute a competitive advantage.

Luis Cruz is not a "star" player in any of his interscholastic sports. Luis Cruz has been included in the football program for an inclusive experience. He is a marginal player and appeared in football games on a very limited basis such as a few kickoffs where the performance apparently was not critical. At the same time, the non-special education students of Ridley High School are attempting to be inclusive. They have rallied around him, as he is a "great team player."

Luis Cruz is not more experienced than other players. In fact, he is less experienced and therefore has played football only on a very limited basis. Further, he is five foot three inches tall and weighs 130 pounds, which is by no means greater than the average height and weight of other, even younger, participants. It is thus readily apparent that there is no safety threat to others or competitive advantage in the situation presented here. Also, again, there is no "cut" policy on the football squad, so Luis Cruz is not replacing any other student who would otherwise have an opportunity to play.

Luis Cruz has "good basic skills" in wrestling, but there are "a lot of better wrestlers than him." He is not a safety risk factor, but he may have a competitive advantage based on his outstanding dual meet record.

In track, where there is also a no-cut policy, Luis Cruz is not a fast runner, does not displace other students, has no competitive advantage and represents no safety risk. He runs a minute behind qualifying time in the mile. He has been unable to earn points in dual meets and would only place by default.

The plaintiffs claim that defendant has violated . . . Section 504 of the Rehabilitation Act of 1973, 29 U.S.C. § 794, *et seq.* [and] the Americans with Disabilities Act (ADA), 42 U.S.C. § 12101, *et seq.* . . .

With respect to the Rehabilitation Act, 29 U.S.C. § 794(a) provides in part that no individual with a disability shall be subjected to discrimination under any program or activity receiving federal financial assistance. There is no evidence that the defendant receives federal financial assistance. . . .

The only remaining claim of plaintiff is under the ADA. The P.I.A.A. is, in my opinion, a public entity under Title II of that Act and plaintiff's claim should be viewed according to its provisions. . . .

[T]his court was waiting for the decision in *PGA Tour, Inc. v. Casey Martin*, 531 U.S. 1049, 121 S. Ct. 1879, 149 L. Ed. 2d 904 (2001), decided by the Supreme Court on May 29, 2001. The opinion is not directly on point with this case. First, it concerns Title III of the ADA, and second, the causal connection between the disability and the exclusion from an activity is more direct in the

Martin case. But in *Martin*, the Supreme Court made clear that a basic requirement of the ADA is the evaluation of a disabled person on an individual basis. According to *Martin*, three inquiries are contemplated by ADA: (1) whether the requested modification is reasonable; (2) whether it is necessary for the disabled individual; and (3) whether it would fundamentally alter the nature of the competition. The case presently before this court, it seems to me, requires the same analysis.

It is clear from the findings of fact that Luis Cruz would not fundamentally alter the nature of the competition in football and track and that the modification of the age rule is necessary for him to be able to play in interscholastic competition in those two sports. What is more difficult to assess is whether the modification is reasonable. Initially, that involves a determination as to whether the age rule is essential to the P.I.A.A. sports program. . . .

It now seems clear that a rule is essential to a program unless it can be shown that the waiver of it would not fundamentally alter the nature of the program.

This determination must be made on an individual basis. The court has looked at the specific facts applicable to Luis Cruz in reaching its conclusion stated earlier in this opinion. In doing so in this case, it is clear that Luis Cruz playing on the football team and track team would not fundamentally alter the nature of P.I.A.A. interscholastic competition.

There is another consideration regarding reasonable modification and that is the burden that would be placed upon the P.I.A.A. to administer a waiver rule in connection with age. P.I.A.A. claims that a procedure by which Cruz would be granted a waiver of the age rule would be an undue burden on it. Specifically, the P.I.A.A. argues that requiring it to develop a waiver system which would assess whether an over-age student would have a competitive advantage over opponents in a given sport would be unreasonable as it would require complex fact-finding as well as extremely difficult judgments about leadership skills, motivational abilities, physical maturity, benefits of experience, quickness, agility, strength, and sport-specific abilities which are extremely difficult to measure. . . .

In light of the other waivers which the P.I.A.A., through district committees, routinely considers, namely transfer and 8 term waivers (some of which require the determination of athletic intent), and in view of the apparent ability of the P.I.A.A. to make what must be very difficult decisions in those waiver cases, I do not believe that an age waiver rule would put an undue burden on the P.I.A.A. The statistics to date suggest that there may not be many occasions for the age waiver to be requested. On the present record, it does not appear that a waiver process would place an unreasonable burden on the P.I.A.A. Indeed, the waiver process proposed by plaintiffs would require initially that the student seeking the waiver have an IEP which requires participation in interscholastic sports. Again, on this record, the P.I.A.A. should not be unreasonably burdened by such a process. . . .

[EDS. The court issued the following order: "(1) Defendant is restrained and prohibited from application and enforcement of its by-law as to age ineligibility with respect to Luis Cruz, unless done so pursuant to a waiver rule which provides for an individual evaluation of him. (2) Thus, as to any interscholastic sports in which Luis Cruz wishes to participate, the defendant must entertain an application for waiver of its by-laws as to age ineligibility rules pursuant to procedures that it establishes. (3) Failure to adopt such waiver procedures in a timely manner as to Luis Cruz will result under this opinion in his being eligible to participate in interscholastic football and track for the 2001-2002 school year."]

NOTES AND QUESTIONS

1. *Application of ADA and Rehabilitation Act to Amateur Athletics Governing Bodies.* *Cruz* held that the Pennsylvania Interscholastic Athletic Association is not covered by the Rehabilitation Act because it does not receive federal funding, but it is covered as a public entity under Title II of the ADA. Other courts have found that a state high school athletic association is covered by Title II, *Washington v. Ind. High Sch. Athletic Assn., Inc.*, 181 F.3d 840 (7th Cir. 1999), or else have assumed such coverage. *Sandison v. Mich. High Sch. Athletic Assn., Inc.*, 64 F.3d 1026 (6th Cir. 1995). This conclusion was strengthened by the Supreme Court's holding that a state high school athletic association may be a state actor exercising public governance over interscholastic sports. *Brentwood Acad. v. Tenn. Secondary Sch. Athletic Ass'n*, 531 U.S. 288 (2001). Moreover, state disability discrimination laws may apply and provide a similar measure of protection to disabled athletes. *Baisden v. W,V. Secondary Schs. Activities Comm'n*, 568 S.E.2d 32 (W. Va. 2002).

   Although the NCAA is not subject to the Rehabilitation Act unless it receives federal financial assistance, *NCAA v. Smith*, 525 U.S. 459 (1999), courts have found coverage under Title III of the ADA based on its control of its members' athletic programs through its student-athlete eligibility requirements. See e.g., *Matthews v. NCAA*, 179 F. Supp. 2d 1209 (E.D. Wash. 2001); *Bowers v. NCAA*, 118 F. Supp. 2d 494 (D.N.J. 2000); *Tatum v. NCAA*, 992 F. Supp. 1114 (E.D. Mo. 1998). The United States Olympic Committee is subject to the Rehabilitation Act if it receives funding from Congress or other federal agencies. *Shepherd v. USOC*, 94 F. Supp. 2d 1136 (D. Colo. 2000), *aff'd on other grounds*, 513 F.3d 1191 (10th Cir. 2008).

2. *When Are Modifications to Athlete Eligibility Rules Required?* Prior to *Martin*, courts were divided on whether a student-athlete's compliance with a maximum age limit is an essential eligibility requirement. See, e.g., *Washington v. Ind. High Sch. Athletic Ass'n, Inc.*, 181 F.3d 840 (7th Cir. 1999) (no); *Sandison v. Mich. High Sch. Athletic Ass'n, Inc.*, 64 F.3d 1026 (6th Cir. 1995) (yes); *Pottgen v. Mo. State High Sch. Activities Ass'n*, 40 F.3d 926 (8th Cir. 1994) (yes). How does the *Cruz* court apply *Martin* to athlete eligibility standards?

   Starego v. N.J. State Interscholastic Athletic Assn, 970 F. Supp. 2d 303 (D.N.J. 2013), also involved a high school athlete, Anthony Starego, who, like Eric Dompierre and Luis Cruz, had developmental disabilities and sought extra high school eligibility. After four years on the Brick Township High School football team, Anthony, who is autistic and was by that time nineteen years old, requested a waiver of a New Jersey State Interscholastic Athletic Association rule that would have prevented a fifth year of eligibility due to his age. The Association denied the waiver request and Anthony, together with his parents, sued under the ADA. The Court noted that "the very essence of the ADA" requires that "Anthony was provided with [the same] access and opportunity to play football afforded to every other student without a disability" and concluded that Anthony, in those first four years, was provided that access. *Id.* at 317. As such, it found that Anthony failed to show that the Association's decision violated the ADA. *Id.* Within weeks of the decision, however—whether to avoid an appeal (which Starego's parents promised to file) or out of compassion—the Association reversed course and granted Starego a fifth year of eligibility. See Scott Stump, *NJSIAA Reverses Ruling*,

Grants Eligibility to Brick Kicker with Autism, ShoreSportsNetwork.com, Sept. 27, 2013, http://shoresportsnetwork.com/njsiaa-reverses-ruling-grants-eligibility-to-brick-kicker-with-autism/.

Could uniform athletic eligibility rules applied without any exceptions be construed as effectively per se illegal under the federal disability discrimination laws? What are valid legal justifications for refusing to grant a waiver in an individual case? What practical advice would you give to an athletic governing body's management regarding how to ensure compliance with the ADA and Rehabilitation Act?

It is important to note that student-athletes with the same disability may not be entitled to the same scope of protection under the federal disability discrimination laws. For example, in determining whether granting a waiver would fundamentally alter the nature of a sport by providing a competitive advantage or would adversely affect other participants' safety, an athlete's individual size, skills, and athletic prowess will be the dispositive factors. *Cruz* illustrates that this is a fact-specific inquiry and that the outcome will vary based on the individual athlete and subject sport.

In *Baisden v. West Virginia Secondary Schools Activities Commission,* 568 S.E.2d 32, 44 (W. Va. 2002), the West Virginia Supreme Court explained:

> While we decide, through this opinion, that individualized assessments are required in cases of this nature and that reasonable accommodations may be made through waiver of the age nineteen rule under certain circumstances, we do not believe that the facts of this case justify waiver as an accommodation. Mr. Baisden turned nineteen on July 27, 2001. He is six feet four inches tall and weighs 280 pounds. He runs the forty-yard-dash in 5.3 seconds. His participation in high school football would permit him to compete in this contact sport against students approximately five years younger. The safety of younger, smaller, more inexperienced students would be unreasonably compromised. In our view, this would fundamentally alter the structure of the interscholastic athletic program, a result which is not required by reasonable accommodation standards in anti-discrimination law.

3.   *Legal Challenges to NCAA Academic Eligibility Standards.* Over the years there have been several ADA challenges to the NCAA's initial academic eligibility requirements based on a sliding scale consisting of a student-athlete's grade point average in designated high school core courses and standardized test scores. See, e.g., *Cole v. NCAA,* 120 F. Supp. 2d 1060 (N.D. Ga. 2000); *Tatum v. NCAA,* 992 F. Supp. 1114 (E.D. Mo. 1998); *Bowers v. NCAA,* 974 F. Supp. 459 (D.N.J. 1997); *Ganden v. NCAA,* 1996 WL 680000 (N.D. Ill. 1996). See also *Matthews v. NCAA,* 179 F. Supp. 2d 1209 (E.D. Wash. 2001) (challenging NCAA's 75/25 rule, designed to ensure student-athletes maintain a course load equivalent to the general student body during the normal school year). See generally Maureen A. Weston, *Academic Standards or Discriminatory Hoops? Learning-Disabled Student-Athletes and the NCAA Initial Academic Eligibility Requirements,* 66 Tenn. L. Rev. 1049 (1999).

As the *Cole* court explained:

> Defendant NCAA's minimum academic scores, which are set by representatives of member institutions, are an essential eligibility requirement. See e.g., Ganden, 1996 WL 680000 at 15 (finding "little doubt" that the eligibility

requirements "serve important interests of the NCAA athletics"). The criteria are designed to ensure that an entering student-athlete is academically prepared, in light of the rigors of intercollegiate athletic competition, to succeed in his or her educational endeavors. The initial-eligibility requirement is also integral to the NCAA's mission of maintaining amateurism in intercollegiate sports. The purpose of the NCAA's academic eligibility requirements is to ensure that students are not merely admitted to universities to participate in intercollegiate sports, but also are admitted to promote and develop educational leadership and scholarship.

120 F. Supp. 2d at 1071. The court held that "[a]bandoning the eligibility requirements altogether for this or any athlete is unreasonable as a matter of law and is not required by the ADA." *Id.* However, the ADA requires the NCAA to make reasonable modifications for student-athletes with learning disabilities on an individualized basis. For scholarly commentary on the interaction between the ADA and the NCAA's academic eligibility standards see Yuri Nicholas Walker, *Playing the Game of Academic Integrity vs. Athletic Success: The Americans with Disabilities Act (ADA) and Intercollegiate Student-Athletes with Learning Disabilities,* 15 Marq. Sports L. Rev. 601 (2005); Susan M. Denbo, *Disability Lessons in Higher Education: Accommodating Learning-Disabled Students and Student-Athletes Under the Rehabilitation Act and the Americans with Disabilities Act,* 41 Am. Bus. L.J. 145, 146 (2003).

On May 27, 1998, the NCAA and Department of Justice entered into a consent decree regarding the application of NCAA initial eligibility bylaws to learning-disabled student-athletes. It provides that mere designation as a remedial or special education course does not preclude it from satisfying an NCAA core course requirement (depending on its content, certain remedial courses may be substituted for core courses); the waiver committee will include experts in learning disabilities and consider certain factors in individual circumstances; and student-athletes who did not satisfy initial academic eligibility requirements are permitted to regain a fourth season of athletic eligibility by satisfactory college academic performance. See U.S. Department of Justice, *NCAA Consent Decree re: Initial-eligibility requirements for students with learning disabilities,* https://www.ada.gov/ncaa.htm#anchor3691.

CHAPTER

12

Intellectual Property Issues in Sports

A. INTRODUCTION

The licensing and sale of sports-related intellectual property rights, such as trademarks, service marks, and copyrights generate billions of dollars in annual revenues for professional leagues and clubs, the United States Olympic Committee (USOC), the National Collegiate Athletic Association (NCAA), university and high school athletics programs, and other sports organizations such as the National Association for Stock Car Auto Racing (NASCAR) and the Professional Golfers Association (PGA). These revenues are derived from various sources, including: the sale of television, radio, and Internet broadcasting rights for sports events; trademark and team logo licensing agreements; and league, team, or event sponsorship deals with advertisers. In addition, popular athletes and coaches license various aspects of their identity, such as their name or image, to others for commercial purposes, thereby earning a substantial amount of money for endorsing various products and services. At the outset, consider how intellectual property differs from personal and real property as well as why intellectual property rights may be substantially more valuable.

Sports event broadcasting rights are a multibillion-dollar source of revenue, which now exceeds aggregate revenues from fan attendance at game and athletic events. The NFL's television contracts with Fox, CBS, and NBC, effective after the 2013 football season, will pay the NFL an average of $3.1 billion a year in rights fees over the life of these nine-year deals through 2022. Major League Baseball's television contracts with three media entities, Fox, Turner Sports (specifically TBS), and ESPN will generate approximately $12.4 billion through 2021. In April 2010, the NCAA entered into an agreement with CBS and Turner Sports pursuant to which they will pay almost $11 billion for the television rights to the "Final Four" men's basketball tournament for 14 years.

The licensing and merchandising of sports brands (i.e., trademarks and logos) also generate billions of dollars in aggregate revenues for professional and amateur sports leagues and other entities. PricewaterhouseCoopers estimates that the value of licensed sports merchandise sales will be approximately $14.5 billion in 2019. Sports sponsorship revenues, which include naming rights and sponsorship of professional, Olympic, and intercollegiate teams, sports events, and organizations, and professional leagues and their member clubs, are estimated to be $18.3 billion for 2019.

Well-known athletes and coaches have entered into lucrative deals to promote and endorse a variety of products and services. For the most popular athletes, income earned from the licensing of their identities to sell products and services may be greater than that derived from his or her athletic ability or success. For example, Michael Jordan signed his first Nike endorsement contract in 1985 for $2.5 million, and he has earned more money from endorsement deals than from playing NBA basketball. Before ever playing in an NBA game, LeBron James signed a five-year, $5 million endorsement deal with Upper Deck trading cards and a seven-year shoe endorsement deal with Nike worth more than $90 million. According to Forbes, the one hundred highest-paid athlete endorsers, the majority of whom are basketball and football players, earned $4 billion in endorsement income from June 2018 to June 2019. Soccer star Lionel Messi, the world's highest-paid athlete endorser, earned $127 million. Tennis player Serena Williams earned $25 million as the highest-paid female athlete endorser.

One commentator notes: "Every traditional area of intellectual property has a basis for application in the sporting arena," and advises "those wishing to seriously consider venturing into the nebulous world of 'sports law' to acquaint themselves with these nexus of intellectual property and sport." Darryl C. Wilson, *The Legal Ramifications of Saving Face: An Integrated Analysis of Intellectual Property and Sport*, 4 Vill. Sports & Ent. L.J. 227, 275-276 (1997). At a 2001 National Sports Law Institute conference held at Marquette University Law School, NFL executive vice president and league counsel Jeff Pash remarked: "Professional sports league general counsels used to focus on antitrust and labor issues, now their focus is on intellectual property issues."

This chapter addresses intellectual property rights recognized and protected by federal laws (e.g., Lanham Act, Copyright Act of 1976, Patent Act, Ted Stevens Olympic & Amateur Sports Act) as well as by state laws (e.g., misappropriation, contract, defamation, right of privacy, right of publicity). It is important to understand that intellectual property laws provide an economic incentive to create and identify products and services, which benefits consumers, and limit the scope of intellectual property rights necessary to avoid conferring an overbroad legal monopoly that harms consumers. The mere creation of a popular sports competition with substantial commercial value does not necessarily establish exclusive intellectual property rights. Third parties have the legal right to use commercially valuable ideas and information arising out of the production of sports events that are in the "public domain" to create collateral products and services desired by consumers, such as sports-related media accounts, books, and artistic or expressive works, and any others (e.g., fantasy games).

It initially considers how trademark and unfair competition law protect the owners of sports-related trademarks, logos, and other identifying insignia from infringement and economic harm to their rights. Next, the nature and scope of legal protection for game accounts and broadcasting of sporting events under federal copyright law, as well as state misappropriation and unfair competition laws, is addressed. Finally, an athlete's protected interests in his or her privacy, reputation, and identity is considered. Overriding First Amendment limits on federal and state law protection of the intellectual property of sports organizations and athletes are considered as each of these topics is covered.

B.   TRADEMARKS, LOGOS, AND OTHER IDENTIFYING INSIGNIA

1.   *Trademark Infringement*

Common law trademark and service mark rights are acquired by first usage of a name, logo, or other symbol to identify one's products or services, to distinguish them from those of others, and to denote a consistent level of quality of the product or service identified by the mark. In *White v. Board of Regents of University of Nebraska*, 614 N.W.2d 330 (Neb. 2000), the court determined that a university acquired rights in "Husker Authentics" by virtue of its first use of this mark in connection with the advertising and sale of products to season ticket holders, alumni, and boosters. Professor Thomas McCarthy observes that "the exclusive 'property' right of a trademark is defined by consumer perception." 1 J. Thomas McCarthy, McCarthy on Trademarks and Unfair Competition (5th ed.), §2:10 (West June 2019 Update). In other words, the nature and scope of one's property interest in a trademark generally is only the right to prevent consumer confusion. As the Seventh Circuit explained: "the trademark laws exist not to 'protect' trademarks, but . . . to protect the consuming public from confusion, concomitantly protecting the trademark owner's right to a non-confused public." *James Burrough, Ltd. v. Sign of the Beefeater, Inc.*, 540 F.2d 266, 276 (7th Cir. 1976).

A sports team's name functions as a trademark or a service mark by virtue of public association of that name with a particular team. Sports team names generally are either inherently distinctive or have acquired "secondary meaning," therefore entitling them to trademark protection. An inherently distinctive mark is one that is coined or arbitrary in relation to the goods or services it identifies, such as "Miami Dolphins" for an NFL club, or suggestive of the club's desired characteristics, such as "Tennessee Titans." See *In re WNBA Enterprises LLC*, 70 U.S.P.Q.2d 1153 (T.T.A.B. 2003) (finding "Orlando Miracle" to be an inherently distinctive mark for Women's National Basketball Association club in Orlando). As one court explained: "Secondary meaning is the consuming public's understanding that the mark, when used in context, refers, not to what the descriptive word ordinarily describes, but to the particular business that the mark is meant to identify." *Maryland Stadium Authority v. Becker*, 806 F. Supp. 1236, 1241 (D. Md. 1992) (finding that the public identifies "Camden Yards" with a Baltimore baseball stadium). A term or phrase may become associated with a sports team (e.g., "Evil Empire" for the New York Yankees) through public usage or fans' recognition, thereby conferring trademark rights on the club. *New York Yankees Partnership v. Evil Enterprises, Inc.*, 2013 WL 1305332 (T.T.A.B.). In addition to sports team names and other identifiers, logos such as the Oakland Raiders' pirate and The Ohio State University's "Brutus Buckeye" function as trademarks that identify particular teams. Distinctive helmet and uniform designs and colors also can function as trademarks. See, e.g., *Board of Supervisors of the La. State Univ. v. Smack Apparel Co.*, 550 F.3d 465 (5th Cir. 2008) (finding that well-known and long-used color schemes, logos, and designs identify university's sports teams); *Dallas Cowboys Cheerleaders, Inc. v. Pussycat Cinema, Ltd.*, 604 F.2d 200, 204 n.5 (2d Cir. 1979) (finding trademark rights in a uniform "universally recognized as the symbol of the Dallas Cowboys Cheerleaders").

Trademark rights exist indefinitely as long as the mark continues to be used and serves as an indication of the source of the seller's goods or services. *Boston Prof'l Hockey Assn. v. Dallas Cap & Emblem Mfg., Inc.*, 510 F.2d 1004, 1011 (5th Cir. 1975) ("[T]here is no reason why trademarks should ever pass into the public domain by the mere passage of time"). However, such rights are lost if usage of the mark to identify, advertise, or promote the seller's goods or services is discontinued.

The Lanham Act, 15 U.S.C. §1051, et seq., provides nationwide legal protection for federally registered trademarks and remedies for their infringement by unauthorized usage that creates a likelihood of consumer confusion. Federal registration provides *prima facie* evidence of the registrant's ownership and exclusive right to use of the mark for the subject goods or services as well as the validity of the registration. The Act permits the filing of an "intent to use application" for a mark, which "shall constitute constructive use of the mark, conferring a right of priority, nationwide in effect, on or in connection with the goods or services specified in the registration" if it is subsequently federally registered. 15 U.S.C. §1057(c). The applicant generally must adopt and use the mark in connection with the described goods or services within two years after filing of the application.

a.   As Name of Sports Team or Event

While reading the following case, consider whether you agree with the court's view regarding the scope of the plaintiffs' exclusive rights in the "Colts" mark and whether the evidence establishes infringement of their trademark rights by the defendant.

INDIANAPOLIS COLTS, INC. v. METROPOLITAN BALTIMORE FOOTBALL CLUB LIMITED PARTNERSHIP

34 F.3d 410 (7th Cir. 1994)

POSNER, Chief Judge.

The Indianapolis Colts and the National Football League, to which the Colts belong, brought suit for trademark infringement (15 U.S.C. §§ 1051 *et seq.*) against the Canadian Football League's new team in Baltimore, which wants to call itself the "Baltimore CFL Colts." . . .

A bit of history is necessary to frame the dispute. In 1952, the National Football League permitted one of its teams, the Dallas Texans, which was bankrupt, to move to Baltimore, where it was renamed the "Baltimore Colts." Under that name it became one of the most illustrious teams in the history of professional football. In 1984, the team's owner, with the permission of the NFL, moved the team to Indianapolis, and it was renamed the "Indianapolis Colts." The move, sudden and secretive, outraged the citizens of Baltimore. The city instituted litigation in a futile effort to get the team back—even tried, unsuccessfully, to get the team back by condemnation under the city's power of eminent domain—and the Colts brought a countersuit that also failed.

Nine years later, the Canadian Football League granted a franchise for a Baltimore team. Baltimoreans clamored for naming the new team the "Baltimore Colts." And so it was named—until the NFL got wind of the name and threatened legal action. The name was then changed to "Baltimore CFL Colts" and publicity launched, merchandise licensed, and other steps taken in preparation for the commencement of play this summer. . . . [S]ince the Canadian Football League is not well known in the United States—and "CFL" has none of the instant recognition value of "NFL"—the inclusion of the acronym in the team's name might have little impact on potential buyers even if prominently displayed. Those who know football well know that the new "Baltimore Colts" are a new CFL team wholly unrelated to the old Baltimore Colts; know also that the rules of Canadian football are different from those of American football and that teams don't move from the NFL to the CFL as they might from one conference within the NFL to the other. But those who do *not* know these things—and we shall come shortly to the question whether there are many of these football illiterates—will not be warned off by the letters "CFL." The acronym is a red herring, and the real issue is whether the new Baltimore team can appropriate the name "Baltimore Colts." . . .

No one questions the validity of "Indianapolis Colts" as the trademark of the NFL team that plays out of Indianapolis and was formerly known as the Baltimore Colts. If "Baltimore CFL Colts" is confusingly similar to "Indianapolis Colts" by virtue of the history of the Indianapolis team and the overlapping product and geographical markets served by it and by the new Baltimore team, the latter's use of the abandoned mark would infringe the Indianapolis Colts' new mark. The Colts' abandonment of a mark confusingly similar to their new mark neither broke the continuity of the team in its different locations—it was the same team, merely having a different home base and therefore a different geographical component in its name—nor entitled a third party to pick it up and use it to confuse Colts fans, and other actual or potential consumers of products and services marketed by the Colts or by other National Football League teams, with regard to the identity, sponsorship, or league affiliation of the third party, that is, the new Baltimore team. . . .

A professional sports team is like Heraclitus's river: always changing, yet always the same. When Mr. Irsay transported his team, the Baltimore Colts, from Baltimore to Indianapolis in one night in 1984, the team remained, for a time anyway, completely intact: same players, same coaches, same front-office personnel. With the passage of time, of course, the team changed. Players retired or were traded, and were replaced. Coaches and other nonplaying personnel came and went. But as far as the record discloses there is as much institutional continuity between the Baltimore Colts of 1984 and the Indianapolis Colts of 1994 as there was between the Baltimore Colts of 1974 and the Baltimore Colts of 1984. . . . The Colts were Irsay's team; it was moved intact; there is no evidence it has changed more since the move than it had in the years before. There is, in contrast, no continuity, no links contractual or otherwise, nothing but a geographical site in common, between the Baltimore Colts and the Canadian Football League team that would like to use its name. Any suggestion that there is such continuity is false and potentially misleading.

Potentially, for if everyone *knows* there is no contractual or institutional continuity, no pedigree or line of descent, linking the Baltimore-Indianapolis Colts and the new CFL team that wants to call itself the "Baltimore Colts" (or, grudgingly, the "Baltimore CFL Colts"), then there is no harm, at least no harm for which the Lanham Act provides a remedy, in the new Baltimore team's appropriating the name "Baltimore Colts" to play under and sell merchandise under. If not everyone knows, there is harm. . . .

Shubh ✗

The legal standard under the Act has been formulated variously, but the various formulations come down to whether it is likely that the challenged mark if permitted to be used by the defendant would cause the plaintiff to lose a substantial number of consumers. Pertinent to this determination is the similarity of the marks and of the parties' products, the knowledge of the average consumer of the product, the overlap in the parties' geographical markets, and the other factors that the cases consider. The aim is to strike a balance between, on the one hand, the interest of the seller of the new product, and of the consuming public, in an arresting, attractive, and informative name that will enable the new product to compete effectively against existing ones, and, on the other hand, the interest of existing sellers, and again of the consuming public, in consumers being able to know exactly what they are buying without having to incur substantial costs of investigation or inquiry.

To help judges strike the balance, the parties to trademark disputes frequently as here hire professionals in marketing or applied statistics to conduct surveys of consumers. . . .

The plaintiffs' study, conducted by Jacob Jacoby, was far more substantial and the district judge found it on the whole credible. The 28-page report with its numerous appendices has all the trappings of social scientific rigor. Interviewers showed several hundred consumers in 24 malls scattered around the country, shirts and hats licensed by the defendants for sale to consumers. The shirts and hats have "Baltimore CFL Colts" stamped on them. The consumers were asked whether they were football fans, whether they watched football games on television, and whether they ever bought merchandise with a team name on it. Then they were asked, with reference to the "Baltimore CFL Colts" merchandise that they were shown, such questions as whether they knew what sport the team played, what teams it played against, what league the team was in, and whether the team or league needed someone's permission to use this name, and if so whose. . . . [A]nother group of mallgoers was asked the identical questions about a hypothetical team unappetizingly named the "Baltimore Horses." The idea was by comparing the answers of the two groups to see whether the source of confusion was the name "Baltimore Colts" or just the name "Baltimore," in which event the injunction would do no good since no one suggests that the new Baltimore team should be forbidden to use "Baltimore" in its name, provided the name does not also include "Colts." . . .

Jacoby's survey of consumers' reactions to the "Baltimore CFL Colts" merchandise found rather astonishing levels of confusion not plausibly attributable to the presence of the name "Baltimore" alone, since "Baltimore Horses" engendered much less. . . . Among self-identified football fans, 64 percent thought that the "Baltimore CFL Colts" was either the old (NFL) Baltimore Colts or the Indianapolis Colts. But perhaps this result is not so astonishing. Although most American football fans have heard of Canadian football, many probably are unfamiliar with the acronym "CFL," and as we remarked earlier it is not a very conspicuous part of the team logo stamped on the merchandise. Among fans who watch football on television, 59 percent displayed the same confusion; and even among those who watch football on cable television, which attracts a more educated audience on average and actually carries CFL games, 58 percent were confused when shown the merchandise. Among the minority not confused about who the "Baltimore CFL Colts" are, a substantial minority, ranging from 21 to 34 percent depending on the precise subsample, thought the team somehow sponsored or authorized by the Indianapolis Colts or the National Football League. . . .

[W]e cannot say that the district judge committed a clear error in crediting the major findings of the Jacoby study and inferring from it and the other evidence in the record that the defendants' use of the name "Baltimore CFL Colts" whether for the team or on merchandise was likely to confuse a substantial number of consumers. . . .

AFFIRMED.

NOTES AND QUESTIONS

1. *Analysis of* Indianapolis Colts. Why did the NFL and its Indianapolis club have the right to prevent unauthorized use of "Baltimore Colts" by a Canadian Football League club even after the NFL club left Baltimore? How did they prove that the Baltimore CFL Colts team violated its trademark rights?

    The use of the same trademark or service mark by different teams or sports organizations, even in connection with the same sport, does not inevitably create a likelihood of consumer confusion. Rather, a fact-specific analysis must be done on a case-by-case basis. In *Harlem Wizards Em't. Basketball, Inc. v. NBA Props., Inc.*, 952 F. Supp. 1084 (D.N.J. 1997), the court held that an NBA club's proposed name change to the "Washington Wizards" would not infringe a "show basketball" team's prior use of "Harlem Wizards." Unlike the Washington NBA club, the Harlem club is not a competitive sports team that plays in a professional league. The Harlem Wizards combine trick and comedic basketball in a form of entertainment similar to that of the world-famous Harlem Globetrotters. Although the Harlem club has the right to use "Wizards" for its entertainment services, the court concluded that the NBA club's concurrent use of the same mark will not create a likelihood of confusion among basketball fans. The teams do not compete with each other for fan patronage. The Harlem club markets its games to event organizers at high schools, colleges, and charitable organizations through direct mail, trade shows, and trade magazines, whereas the NBA club advertises its games directly to fans. Survey results evidenced that consumer familiarity with the Harlem Wizards team "is almost nonexistent." *Id.* at 1098. There is a significant disparity between the parties' respective ticket prices, and the court found "it unlikely that consumers will attend a Harlem Wizards' game expecting to see NBA basketball or purchase NBA tickets expecting to see the Harlem Wizards perform show basketball." *Id.* By contrast, in *Champions Golf Club, Inc. v. Champions Golf Club, Inc.*, 78 F.3d 1111 (6th Cir. 1996), the court found a likelihood of consumer confusion regarding the (nonexistent) affiliation between two independently owned and operated golf courses located in Nicholasville, Kentucky, and Houston, Texas, which were using the "Champions" mark.

2. *Effects of Club's Relocation on Trademark Rights.* Consistent with *Indianapolis Colts*, the Seventh Circuit held that the NFL's Los Angeles Rams club retained its rights to continue using "Rams" to identify the team name even though it relocated to St. Louis (then moved back to LA in 2016). *Johnny Blastoff, Inc. v. L.A. Rams Football, Co.*, 188 F.3d 427 (7th Cir. 1999). Observing that the franchise was founded in 1937 as the Cleveland Rams, moved to become the Los Angeles Rams in 1946, and was again moving to become the St. Louis Rams in 1995, the court concluded, "[T]he Rams organization and the NFL had a long-established priority over the use of the 'Rams' name in

connection with the same professional football team, regardless of urban affiliation." *Id.* at 435. (The Rams moved back to Los Angeles in 2011.)

However, other courts have expressed a narrow view regarding the scope of a club's protectable rights in its name after it relocates. In *Major League Baseball Properties, Inc. v. Sed Non Olet Denarius, Ltd.*, 817 F. Supp. 1103 (S.D.N.Y. 1993), *vacated pursuant to settlement*, 859 F. Supp. 80 (S.D.N.Y. 1994), the court held that discontinued use of the "Brooklyn Dodgers" trademark after the club relocated to Los Angeles in 1958 constituted an abandonment of rights in this composite mark and that a Brooklyn restaurant may use the name "The Brooklyn Dodger." The court found that "[i]n Brooklyn, the 'Los Angeles Dodgers' and the 'Brooklyn Dodgers' are seen as two separate entities which have been wholly unrelated for more than 30 years." *Id.* at 1125. The court concluded that "Brooklyn is more than a geographic designation or appendage to the word 'Dodgers.' The 'Brooklyn Dodgers' was a non-transportable cultural institution separate from the 'Los Angeles Dodgers' or the 'Dodgers' who play in Los Angeles." *Id.* at 1128.

Legal considerations aside, business reasons may justify treating the favorable goodwill developed by a popular local sports franchise over the years as "a non-transportable cultural institution." For example, the NFL decided to leave the "Browns" identity in Cleveland when the franchise relocated to Baltimore in 1996. The franchise formerly named the "Cleveland Browns" established a new identity as the "Baltimore Ravens." The NFL expansion club that began playing in Cleveland in 1999 is named the "Cleveland Browns." See *Hawaii-Pacific Apparel Group, Inc. v. Cleveland Browns Football Co. LLC*, 418 F. Supp. 2d 501 (S.D.N.Y. 2006) (holding that, by enforcing its claimed trademark rights during the four-year period in which Browns franchise did not play in Cleveland, the NFL retained rights in the DAWG POUND mark).

b.   Affixation of Sports-Related Mark to Merchandise

The following materials consider the nature and scope of legal protection provided to owners of sports team names, logos, and other identifying insignia and whether unauthorized usage by others in connection with the advertising and sale of collateral or promotional merchandise (e.g., wearing apparel) constitutes trademark infringement or violates other legally protected rights.

North American consumers annually purchase billions of dollars' worth of merchandise bearing the names and logos of their favorite teams. Do consumers do so because of their desire to identify with the team, to purchase goods produced or licensed by the team, or for other reasons?

In *National Football League Properties, Inc. v. Consumer Enterprises, Inc.*, 327 N.E.2d 242, 246 (Ill. App. 1975), the court observed that the NFL's "trademarks are associated with highly successful football teams that enjoy tremendous notoriety. Through the extensive licensing arrangements developed and perpetuated by [the NFL] and its licensees, the buying public has come to associate the trademark with the sponsorship of the NFL or the particular member team involved." It concluded "that the trademarks of the teams copied by defendant indicate sponsorship or origin in addition to their ornamental value." See also *University Bookstore v. Board of Regents of the Univ. of Wis. Sys.*, 33 U.S.P.Q.2d 1385, 1405 (T.T.A.B. 1994) ("[T]he mark of a university on clothing can signify that the university endorses and licenses the sale of such wearing apparel by the manufacturer. . . . It is a question of fact as to whether consumers view such indicia as 'merely ornamental' or as symbols that identify a secondary source of sponsorship").

However, "[m]any trademark law scholars oppose expanding the traditional scope of trademark law protection, which is limited to preventing a likelihood of consumer confusion regarding the source or origin of a product or service, simply to prevent 'free riding' (that is, misappropriation of the goodwill associated with a trademark and perceived unjust enrichment from its unauthorized use on collateral or promotional products unrelated to the mark owner's primary business activities). Doing so creates inappropriately broad property rights in trademarks, with resulting trademark monopolies and reduced market competition that increases consumer prices for collateral products." Matthew J. Mitten, *From Dallas Cap to American Needle and Beyond: Antitrust Law's Limited Capacity to Stitch Consumer Harm from Professional Sports Club Trademark Monopolies*, 86 Tul. L. Rev. 901, 914-915 (2012). See also J. Gordon Hylton, *The Over-Protection of Intellectual Property Rights in Sport in the United States and Elsewhere*, 21 J. Legal Aspects Sport 43, 49-50 (2011) ("Permitting fans to purchase unlicensed clothing bearing the name or logo of their favorite team would make it easier for less economically well-off fans to express their support for their teams. Teams would still be able to market their own merchandise . . . but they would not be able to exercise monopoly control over their names and symbols"). Nevertheless, "[r]egardless of scholarly concerns over whether merchandising rights are in accordance with the purpose of trademark law, trademark merchandising has long represented a 'fait accompli' in trademark practice." Irene Calboli, *The Case for a Limited Protection of Trademark Merchandising*, 2011 U. Ill. L. Rev. 865, 890.

To avoid weakening valuable trademark rights that may be licensed and generate substantial revenues, professional teams and educational institutions must carefully monitor unauthorized third-party use of their trademarks and take timely, necessary steps to prevent infringement of their marks. The affirmative defense of laches may bar or limit monetary recovery for infringement if a mark owner's delay in asserting its trademark rights prejudices an infringer that detrimentally relied on such inaction. *University of Pittsburgh v. Champion Prods. Inc.*, 686 F.2d 1040 (3d Cir. 1982), *cert. denied*, 495 U.S. 1087 (1982) (university's 36-year delay in objecting to unauthorized sale of clothing and novelty items bearing its name and panther mascot bars an accounting for past infringement, but not an injunction against future unauthorized use).

Regarding the requisite "likelihood of confusion" that must be shown to prove trademark infringement under the Lanham Act or similar state trademark infringement laws, in *Bd. of Governors of the Univ, of North Carolina v. Helpingstine*, 714 F. Supp. 167, 172 (M.D.N.C. 1989), the court observed:

> While cases have indicated at one extreme that an alleged infringer's use of a mark with the knowledge that the public will be aware of the mark's origin is enough to establish likelihood of confusion, . . . and at the other that likelihood of confusion occurs only where there would be confusion as to the origin of the goods themselves, . . . the majority of courts have taken the middle ground on this issue. This middle position, which both parties recognize in this case, is that the requisite likelihood of confusion will exist where there is likelihood of confusion as to source, sponsorship or endorsement of the goods.

The following case illustrates how courts apply a multifactor test to determine whether the unauthorized usage of a sports team mark on collateral or promotional merchandise creates a likelihood of consumer confusion.

NATIONAL FOOTBALL LEAGUE PROPERTIES, INC. v. NEW JERSEY GIANTS, INC.

637 F. Supp. 507 (D.N.J. 1986)

BARRY, District Judge.

[EDS. Plaintiff, the New York Football Giants, Inc., owned and operated the New York Giants, an NFL team that had played all of its home games at Giants' Stadium in East Rutherford, New Jersey, since 1976. In what was then the New York Football Giants' 60-year history, home games had been played at several locations in the New York metropolitan area, including in Connecticut and New Jersey. To maintain continuity of tradition, the club always had used the name "New York Giants," which along with "Giants" is a federally registered trademark under the Lanham Act and under New Jersey and New York state law.

Plaintiff National Football League Properties, Inc. (NFLP), is the marketing arm of the NFL's member clubs, and is licensed by the clubs to use their trademarks and is authorized to protect them from infringement. NFLP licensed selected companies to use the "Giants" and "New York Giants" marks on a wide variety of merchandise, including T-shirts, sweatshirts, caps, jackets, and other wearing apparel. NFLP had a quality control program in which it supervised and approved the conception, design, color combinations, production, and distribution of all merchandise licensed to bear the marks of the Giants and other NFL clubs.

Defendant, the New Jersey Giants, Inc., in an effort to exploit the anomaly of a team bearing the name of one state while playing in another, began to sell various items of inferior quality sports-related apparel bearing the words "New Jersey GIANTS" without authorization from NFLP or the New York Giants club.]

Defendant's "New Jersey GIANTS" merchandise competes directly with licensed NFL merchandise bearing the New York Football Giants' marks, because NFLP has licensed the same types of merchandise sold by defendant. Moreover, defendant's "New Jersey GIANTS" merchandise is likely to confuse consumers into believing that it is part of the wide array of licensed merchandise sponsored and approved by the New York Football Giants and available to the public through NFLP's licensing program.

But the Giants and NFLP have no control over defendant's business activities or over the nature and clearly inferior quality of the merchandise sold by defendant and, indeed, the quality of that merchandise does not satisfy the quality control standards imposed by NFLP on its licensees. The sale of inferior quality merchandise bearing the NFL marks, or colorable imitations thereof, will adversely affect NFLP's business including the poor impression of the NFL and its Member Clubs that will be held by the consumer.

Because the demand for merchandise bearing the NFL marks is finite, any sales of unlicensed merchandise bearing those marks will cause direct economic harm to NFLP's licensees thus reducing the royalties payable by licensees to NFLP and reducing the size of the fund available for NFL Charities. Defendant's activities in the sale of its "New Jersey GIANTS" merchandise will interfere, as well, with NFLP's business and cause harm to its reputation and goodwill with licensees and retailers actively promoting the products of NFLP's licensees. If NFLP is unable to abide by its agreement to protect licensees from companies that use the NFL marks without authorization, licensees will lose confidence in the NFLP's licensing program and the value of a license will be impaired thus harming the business of NFLP.

Defendant's use of its trade name and the solicitation and sale of "New Jersey GIANTS" merchandise is also likely to confuse the public into believing that the New York Football Giants has changed the team's name to the New Jersey Giants or does not object to being referred to by that name. Neither is true, of course, and while one may wonder why the New York Giants resist a new name and may wish, perhaps, that it were otherwise, the fact remains that the Giants have the right to retain the long-standing goodwill and reputation they have developed in the name "New York Giants" and efforts in that regard will be undermined were defendant's conduct permitted to continue. . . .

In a case for service mark or trademark infringement and unfair competition, a plaintiff is entitled to a permanent injunction against a defendant by showing that that defendant's activities are likely to confuse consumers as to the source or sponsorship of the goods. In order to be confused, a consumer need not believe that a plaintiff actually produced a defendant's merchandise and placed it on the market. Rather, a consumer's belief that a plaintiff sponsored or otherwise approved the use of the mark satisfies the confusion requirement.

In a suit, as here, involving competing goods, the relevant factors to be considered in a determination as to whether a likelihood of confusion exists are:

(1) The degree of similarity between the owner's mark and the alleged infringing mark;
(2) The strength of the owner's mark;
(3) The price of the goods and other factors indicative of the care and attention expected of consumers when making a purchase;
(4) The length of time the defendant has used the mark without evidence of actual confusion;
(5) The intent of the defendant in adopting the mark;
(6) The evidence of actual confusion.

Defendant's mark "New Jersey GIANTS" is similar to the Giants' registered marks "New York Giants" and "Giants" and the dominant element of the mark—" Giants"—is identical, rendering those marks particularly confusing. . . .

The second . . . factor is similarly satisfied. Through extensive media coverage and commercial use, the NFL marks, including those of the Giants, are extremely strong, and, accordingly, are entitled to a wide range of protection.

With reference to the third . . . factor, the likelihood of confusion in this case is enhanced because both NFLP's licensed apparel bearing the Giants' marks and defendant's apparel, which is the same type of apparel, are low to moderately priced and purchasers will not exercise a high degree of care in determining whether the merchandise has been sponsored or approved by the NFL and the Giants.

Defendant, which only began selling its merchandise in 1982 and had total sales of less than $5000.00 at the time its activities were halted by the restraining order, used the mark without evidence of actual confusion. In establishing the existence of a likelihood of confusion in actions such as this, however, there is no requirement that incidents of actual confusion be shown and such evidence is unnecessary where other factors so strongly suggest the likelihood of confusion.

However, the consumer survey conducted by Dr. Jacoby and Guideline Research demonstrated substantial actual confusion and a substantial potential for further actual confusion. The results of the survey, which found that over 57% of respondents were actually and likely confused and that football fans were confused in even higher percentages (67%), is extremely strong evidence of likely confusion, and far in excess of the evidence relied upon by courts for this purpose. . . .

Defendant's intentional, willful, and admitted adoption of a mark closely similar to the existing marks "Giants" and "New York Giants" manifested . . . an intent to confuse. . . .

Defendant's use of the Giants' marks is likely to cause confusion or mistake or deceive purchasers of such merchandise as to the source, sponsorship or approval by the NFL and the Giants. . . .

[The court concluded defendant's conduct constituted unfair competition in violation of federal and New Jersey law as well as tortious misappropriation of plaintiffs' goodwill and interference with their business relationships.]

NOTES AND QUESTIONS

1. *Application of Likelihood of Confusion Standard to Trademark Infringement and Counterfeiting.* The *New Jersey Giants* case identifies several factors relevant to whether defendant's unauthorized usage of a sports team mark creates a likelihood of confusion. Why was the defendant's use of "New Jersey Giants" on apparel found to infringe the New York Giants marks for "entertainment services in the form of professional football games and exhibitions"?

    Whether the requisite likelihood of confusion exists is a question of fact decided on a case-by-case basis. Examples of infringement include *Boston Athletic Assn. v. Sullivan*, 867 F.2d 22 (1st Cir. 1989) (unauthorized use of "Boston Marathon" to sell T-shirts); *Univ. of Ga. Athletic Assn. v. Laite*, 756 F.2d 1535 (11th Cir. 1985) (unauthorized use of University of Georgia bulldog mark and logo portraying an English bulldog for "Battlin' Bulldog Beer"); *Ohio State Univ. v. Thomas*, 738 F. Supp. 2d 743 (S.D. Ohio 2010) (unauthorized use of Ohio State trademarks, including university colors, in connection with website and electronic magazines covering university sports teams); *Bd. of Trustees of Univ. of Arkansas v. Professional Therapy Services, Inc.*, 873 F. Supp. 1280 (W.D. Ark. 1995) (unauthorized use of "Razorbacks" and hog's head logo by sports and physical therapy clinic).

    Intentional and unauthorized use of a mark that is known to be "identical with, or substantially indistinguishable from" a federally registered mark (15 U.S.C. § 1127) in connection with the sale or advertising of goods or services and creates a likelihood of confusion also constitutes trademark counterfeiting (15 U.S.C. § 1114), which may enable the mark owner to recover statutory damages and attorneys' fees under the Lanham Act. See, e.g., *Ohio State University v. Skreened, Ltd.*, 16 F. Supp. 3d 905 (S.D. Ohio 2014) (defendant's unauthorized sale of shirts bearing marks identical to or substantially indistinguishable from university's federally registered marks sold by its licensees constitutes counterfeiting as well as trademark infringement and unfair competition).

2. *Anticybersquatting Consumer Protection Act of 1999.* The significant expansion and use of the Internet in recent years has given rise to "cybersquatting," which is the registration of well-known trademarks (including those of sports teams and events) as domain names (i.e., website addresses) by those who are not the trademark owners. Their objectives usually are to sell rights to the domain names back to the trademark owners at a profit or to attract Internet users to their websites, which offer services such as online sports gambling. Cybersquatting (e.g., using newjerseygiants.com to advertise and sell New Jersey Giants merchandise without NFLP's authorization) that creates a likelihood of consumer confusion constitutes trademark infringement and unfair competition. See, e.g., *March Madness Athletic Assn. v. Netfire, Inc.*, 310 F. Supp. 2d 786 (N.D. Tex. 2003) (www.marchmadness.com infringes NCAA's federally registered March Madness mark for basketball tournament); *Quokka Sports, Inc. v. Cup Int'l Internet Ventures*, 99 F. Supp. 2d 1105 (N.D. Cal. 1999) (defendants' www.americascup.com website, "masquerading as an official site associated with the America's Cup event," infringes registered mark "America's Cup"). It also may violate the Anticybersquatting Consumer Protection Act (ACPA) of 1999, a provision of the Lanham Act, which provides a trademark owner with a cause of action against a defendant for bad-faith registration or use of a domain name that is (1) identical to or confusingly similar to a distinctive mark or (2) identical to or confusingly similar to, or dilutes, a famous mark. 15 U.S.C. §1125 (d)(1)(A). See *March Madness Athletic Assn. v. Netfire, Inc.*, 310 F. Supp. 2d 786 (N.D. Tex. 2003) (defendants' registration and use of www.marchmadness.com violates the ACPA, entitling the NCAA to injunctive relief). The ACPA also authorizes an action against the domain name itself for forfeiture or transfer to the trademark owner if the domain name registrant cannot be located or is not subject to personal jurisdiction by an American court. 15 U.S.C. §1125(d)(2)(A).

3. *Collective Licensing of League Clubs' Trademarks.* Major professional sports leagues such as the NFL, NBA, NHL, and MLB currently market, license, and enforce their clubs' trademark rights collectively through a central league-operated entity. To maximize the revenues from its national sponsorship agreements, which generally are distributed pro rata to its member clubs, a sports league may have exclusive agreements with its official sponsors and corresponding limits on its member clubs' individual sponsorships with other companies. A club that violates league restrictions on its local sponsorship agreements may be liable for breach of contract and fiduciary duty, tortious interference with contractual relationships, and trademark infringement. See *NFL Properties, Inc. v. Dallas Cowboys Football Club, Ltd.*, 922 F. Supp. 849 (S.D.N.Y. 1996). See Chapter 6 for a discussion of antitrust law challenges to a professional league's exclusive control and licensing of its member clubs' trademarks.

4. *Primacy of the First Amendment.* In *Univ. of Alabama Bd. of Trustees v. New Life, Inc.*, 683 F.3d 1266 (11th Cir. 2012), the University of Alabama alleged that an artist's paintings, prints, and calendars infringed its trademarks because his unauthorized inclusion of the university's crimson and white uniforms and helmets therein created a likelihood of consumer confusion that it sponsored or endorsed these products. Characterizing the paintings, prints,

and calendars as expressive speech protected by the First Amendment, the Eleventh Circuit held it "should construe the Lanham Act narrowly when deciding whether an artistically expressive work infringes a trademark." *Id.* at 1278. Such usage does not violate the Lanham Act "unless the use of the mark has no artistic relevance to the underlying work whatsoever, or, if it has some artistic relevance, unless it explicitly misleads as to the source or the content of the work." *Id.* at 1278. Applying this standard, the court concluded:

> The depiction of the University's uniforms in the content of these items is artistically relevant to the expressive underlying works because the uniforms' colors and designs are needed for a realistic portrayal of famous scenes from Alabama football history. Also there is no evidence that Moore ever marketed an unlicensed item as "endorsed" or "sponsored" by the University, or otherwise explicitly stated that such items were affiliated with the University. . . . Even if "some members of the public would draw the incorrect inference that [the University] had some involvement with [Moore's paintings, prints, and calendars,] . . . that risk of misunderstanding, not engendered by any overt [or in this case even implicit] claim . . . is so outweighed by the interest in artistic expression as to preclude" any violation of the Lanham Act.

Id. at 1278-1279. See also *Brown v Electronic Arts, Inc.*, 724 F.3d 1235 (9th Cir. 2013) (rejecting former NFL player's claim that unauthorized use of his likeness in *Madden NFL* football video games violated §43(a) of the Lanham Act because its use is "artistically relevant" and does not explicitly mislead consumers into believing he endorses or is involved with the game's production).

5. *Fair Use or Parody of a Trademark.* In *WCVB-TV v. Boston Athletic Association*, 926 F.2d 42, 46 (1st Cir. 1991), the First Circuit explained: "In technical trademark jargon, the use of words for descriptive purposes is called a 'fair use,' and the law usually permits it even if the words themselves also constitute a trademark." The court held that a television station's use of "Boston Marathon" to describe its unlicensed broadcast of the event is not trademark infringement, although another local television station was exclusively authorized to broadcast this event. This was judicially characterized as fair use of the Boston Marathon mark merely to describe the event defendant was broadcasting that did not create any viewer confusion. See also *Dream Team Collectibles, Inc. v. NBA Props., Inc.*, 958 F. Supp. 1401, 1421 (E.D. Mo. 1997) (use of NBA team name on framed collage of trading cards depicting players in team uniforms "not likely to cause confusion, but is a simply a way to identify a particular NBA team").

Would a state lottery based on the unauthorized use of regular season NFL game scores constitute trademark infringement or fair use? See *NFL v. Governor of Del.*, 435 F. Supp. 1372, 1380 (D. Del. 1977) (legally permissible to truthfully describe services offered, but creating a false public impression that the mark owner authorizes or approves such services is prohibited). This case gained significance after *Murphy v. NCAA*, 138 S. Ct. 1461 (2018), in which the U.S. Supreme Court ruled that the Professional and Amateur Sports Act of 1992, 28 U.S.C. §3701 et seq., which generally prohibited states from permitting sports betting, violates the U.S. Constitution's anti-commandeering doctrine that "withhold[s] from Congress the power to issue orders directly to the States." Soon thereafter, several states enacted laws permitting regulated sports betting, and many others are considering legislation to legalize it.

For the same reason that underlies the fair use defense, the parody of a trademark is not infringing. In *Cardtoons, L.C. v. Major League Baseball Players Assn.*, 95 F.3d 959 (10th Cir. 1996), the Tenth Court held that parody trading cards with caricatures of baseball players and critical commentary does not create public confusion regarding the source of the cards. The court explained that "as with all successful parodies, the effect of the cards is to amuse rather than confuse." *Id.* at 967. In *Ohio State University v. Skreened, Ltd.*, 16 F. Supp. 3d 905 (S.D. Ohio 2014), the court observed: "[A]n allegation of parody is but one consideration to be considered in the larger context of possible infringement. The evidence here does not . . . suggest that Defendants are seeking to be ironic commentators on academia or college athletic culture [simply by selling shirts bearing a university's trademarks without authorization]; the only evidence before this Court is that Defendants are trying to make a buck by appropriating marks for commercial use."

2. *Trademark Dilution*

The Trademark Dilution Revision Act of 2006 (TDRA), which is part of the Lanham Act, protects the owner of a "famous mark" from unauthorized use of its mark or a similar mark that is likely to cause dilution of the mark's distinctiveness. 15 U.S.C. §1125(c). Proof that the defendant's unauthorized usage creates actual or likely confusion or actual economic injury is not required. The statute provides a remedy for tarnishing the goodwill associated with a famous mark by using it in a disparaging manner outside the context of permissible parody, or a blurring of the mark's distinctiveness because it is used to identify a wide range of unrelated goods and services.

To be "famous," the mark must be "widely recognized by the general consuming public of the United States as a designation of source of the goods or services of the mark's owner." 15 U.S.C. §1125(c)(2)(A). Examples of sports trademarks that are famous because of their extensive national and/or international promotion and recognition are the Indianapolis 500 auto race, the Kentucky Derby horse race, and the Masters golf tournament, as well as the marks of major league professional teams, national sports governing bodies (e.g., USOC, NCAA, NASCAR) and many universities with prominent, successful football and basketball teams.

In *Dallas Cowboys Football Club, Ltd. v. America's Team Properties*, 616 F. Supp. 2d 622 (N.D. Tex. 2009), the court ruled that the unauthorized use of "America's Team" on apparel "blurs the uniqueness" of the mark and tarnishes it because it is used in connection with the defendant's inferior goods. Similarly, in *New York City Triathlon LLC v. NYC Triathlon Club Inc.*, 95 U.S.P.Q.2d 1451 (S.D.N.Y. 2010), another court held that defendant's unauthorized usage of the "New York City Triathlon" marks as the name of its athletic club blurred and tarnished their distinctiveness in violation of the dilution statute by creating a negative association because of defendant's reputation for poor customer service.

The following cases, which were decided prior to enactment of the TDRA, provide graphic examples of usages that tarnish sports marks. In *NBA Properties v. Untertainment Records LLC*, 1999 WL 335147 (S.D.N.Y. 1999), a federal district court held that the unauthorized use of an altered NBA logo showing a silhou-etted basketball player dribbling a basketball with a handgun in his other hand to advertise a rap album violates the federal dilution statute. Because "linking the NBA Logo with violence and drugs will adversely color the public's impres-sions of the NBA," the court concluded that "[a]ny suggestion that the NBAP or the NBA endorses violence, gunplay or drug use, or that they have chosen to associate themselves with those who do, will likely tarnish their reputation with their corporate customers and partners, as well as the public at large." *Id.* at *9. Similarly, in *Dallas Cowboys Cheerleaders, Inc. v. Pussycat Cinema, Ltd.*, 604 F.2d 200, 205 (2d Cir. 1979), the Second Circuit ruled that the unauthorized use of female actors wearing well-known Dallas Cowboys' Cheerleaders' uniforms in a "sexually depraved film . . . has 'tendency to impugn (plaintiff's services) and injure plaintiff's business reputation.'"

3. *Ted Stevens Olympic and Amateur Sports Act: Olympic Marks*

The United States Olympic and Paralympic Committee (USOPC) owns the exclusive right to use and license the Olympic marks within the United States. *USOC v. Intelicense Corp., S.A.*, 737 F.2d 263 (2d Cir. 1984), *cert. denied*, 469 U.S. 982 (1984). The Ted Stevens Olympic and Amateur Sports Act (ASA) prohibits the unauthorized usage of the Olympic name and marks, including the five-ring Olympic symbol, "for the purpose of trade, to induce the sale of any goods or services, or to promote any theatrical exhibition, athletic performance, or competition." 36 U.S.C. §220506(c). The ASA extended the USOC's exclusive property rights to include the "Pan-American" and "Paralympiad" marks, which are now protected to the same extent as the Olympic marks. *USOC v. Toy Truck Lines, Inc.*, 237 F.3d 1331 (Fed. Cir. 2001).

The Olympic marks have a broader scope of protection under federal law beyond that generally provided to other trademarks and service marks. In *San Francisco Arts & Athletics, Inc. v. USOC*, 483 U.S. 522 (1987), the Supreme Court held that the ASA's language and legislative intent evidenced Congress's intent to grant the USOC exclusive rights to control use of the Olympic marks regard-less of whether their unauthorized usage creates a likelihood of confusion. The Court explained:

> One reason for Congress to grant the USOC exclusive control of the word "Olympic," as with other trademarks, is to ensure that the USOC receives the benefit of its own efforts so that the USOC will have an incentive to continue to produce a "quality product," that, in turn, benefits the public. See 1 J. McCarthy, Trademarks and Unfair Competition § 2:1, pp. 44-47 (1984). But in the special circumstance of the USOC, Congress has a broader public interest in promot-ing, through the activities of the USOC, the participation of amateur athletes from the United States in "the great four-yearly sport festival, the Olympic Games." . . . The USOC's goal under the Olympic Charter, Rule 24(B), is to fur-ther the Olympic movement, that has as its aims: "to promote the development of those physical and moral qualities which are the basis of sport"; "to educate young people through sport in a spirit of better understanding between each other and of friendship, thereby helping to build a better and more peaceful world"; and "to spread the Olympic principles throughout the world, thereby creating international goodwill." Congress' interests in promoting the USOC's

activities include these purposes as well as those specifically enumerated in the USOC's charter. Section 110 directly advances these governmental interests by supplying the USOC with the means to raise money to support the Olympics and encourages the USOC's activities by ensuring that it will receive the benefits of its efforts.

Id. at 537-538. Defendant's unauthorized use of "Gay Olympic Games" for an athletics competition in San Francisco was found to be infringing regardless of whether it tends to cause any confusion. See also *USOC v. Tobyhanna Camp Corp.*, 2010 WL 4617429 (M.D. Pa.) (use of "Camp Olympik" and non-interlocked five-ring Olympic symbol for children's summer camp infringing); *USOC v. Xclusive Leisure & Hospitality Ltd.*, 2008 WL 3971120 (N.D. Cal.) (enjoining unauthorized usage of Olympic marks in United States to advertise and sell tickets and hospitality packages to the Beijing Olympics).

The ASA "grandfathers" the rights of those who lawfully used the Olympic marks prior to 1950 (the year in which the ASA's predecessor statute was enacted) to advertise and sell their goods or services. However, such users may not expand the scope of their goods or services sold under the Olympic mark or adopt new marks with the word "Olympic" therein. In *O-M Bread, Inc. v. USOC*, 65 F.3d 933 (Fed. Cir. 1995), the Federal Circuit held that the proposed use of "Olympic Kids" for bakery products is not a permitted extension of a prior user's grandfathered right to use the Olympic mark for bakery products. The court found these "different marks present a different commercial impression and are not legal equivalents." *Id.* at 938. It concluded that "commercial growth into new 'Olympic'-based marks is outside the letter of the statute, as well as outside its spirit.

The ASA does not prohibit all unauthorized uses of the Olympic marks. As one court observed, "because the [ASA] grants the USOC rights over and above both the common law and [the Lanham Act], the language and scope of the Act must be strictly construed." *USOC v. American Media, Inc.*, 156 F. Supp. 2d 1200, 1209 (D. Colo. 2001). For example, the media may report about Olympic sports competitions, which would include use of the word "Olympic" and competition photographs containing Olympic marks in news reporting. In *American Media*, the court ruled that the mere publication of an Olympic preview magazine titled "Olympics USA" is noncommercial speech that does not infringe the USOC's rights under the ASA. However, the publisher's usage of the Olympic marks in a manner falsely suggesting that the USOC officially endorses or authorizes its magazine would violate the Lanham Act.

Unless a likelihood of public confusion as to origin, sponsorship, or affiliation is created, the Olympic mark may be used for purely expressive purposes. In *Stop the Olympic Prison v. USOC*, 489 F. Supp. 1112 (S.D.N.Y. 1980), the court found that publication and distribution of a poster with the words "Stop the Olympic Prison" to marshal public opposition to the planned conversion of the Lake Placid Olympic Village into a prison after the 1980 Olympics does not violate the Stevens Act. The publisher was not using the Olympic mark to make a profit; its only purpose was to disseminate its political views in an effort to change future plans for the Olympic Village. The court found that the poster was not likely to be viewed as a commercial advertisement for the sale of any goods or services, and it was not used to promote any theatrical exhibition or athletic competition.

PROBLEM 12-1

a. Does the University of Michigan have a legal right to prevent the NCAA Division I-AA Delaware University Blue Hens from using its well-known blue and gold "winged tips" helmet design as part of its football team uniform? Would it be able to prevent a Wisconsin high school football team from doing so?

b. Can the NFL prevent a women's professional football league from identifying itself as the "National Women's Football League" and calling its championship game the SupHer Bowl?

c. In 1994 Marquette University, whose school colors are blue and gold, changed the name of its athletic teams from the "Warriors" to the "Golden Eagles" to discontinue using a potentially disparaging characterization of Native Americans. (See Chapter 9 for an in-depth discussion of this issue.) Does Marquette have the right to prohibit an off-campus bookstore from selling blue and gold Marquette Warriors T-shirts?

d. A nutrition supplement manufacturer includes the statement "This product does not contain any substances banned by the National Collegiate Athletic Association" on the label of its product. Does this violate the Lanham Act?

e. Analyze whether The Ohio State University is likely to obtain a federally registration for the word "THE" to advertise, identify, and sell clothing bearing this claimed trademark.

f. Consider whether any of the following unauthorized usages violates the USOC's rights in the Olympic marks:

   i.   An Iowa farmer prunes his cornfield into the shape of the interlocking Olympic rings during the summer before the upcoming Olympic Games. Does your determination depend on whether he charges a fee to enter his cornfield and view the Olympic rings?

   ii. To stimulate local interest in a student science project, a high school district dubs a series of races by mice through an obstacle course the "Rat Olympics."

   iii. The "Redneck Olympics" features the cigarette flip, bobbing for pigs' feet, mud pit belly flop, toilet seat throwing, big hair contest, and seed spitting.

   f. Does the new NHL Las Vegas club's adoption and usage of "Golden Knights" as its team name infringe the trademark rights of the U.S. Army's Parachute Team, which has been known for over 50 years as the "Golden Knights"?

4. Ambush Marketing

Ambush marketing is a creative advertising practice by a business other than an official sponsor that seeks to create an association with a sports event without using the event's name, trademarks, or logos. It encompasses "intentional efforts to weaken [a] competitor's official association with a sport organization, which has been acquired through the payment of sponsorship fees" as well as seeking "to capitalize on the goodwill, reputation and popularity of a particular sport or event by creating an association without the authorization or consent of the necessary parties." Steve McKelvey and John Grady, *Ambush Marketing: The Legal Battleground for Sports Marketers,* 21 Ent. & Sports Law 8, 9 (2004).

Official event sponsors claim that ambush marketing dilutes the value of their sponsorships. Ambush marketing may harm event organizers, which need sponsorship money to fund production of a sporting event. When ambush marketers receive commercial benefits by free-riding on an event's popularity or goodwill, the value of an official sponsorship may be significantly reduced. This creates an economic disincentive to be an official event sponsor, with a corresponding incentive to engage in ambush marketing instead. This in turn reduces the value of official sponsorships and causes sporting event organizers to lose sponsorship revenues. See *USOC v. American Media, Inc.*, 156 F. Supp. 2d 1200, 1204 (D. Colo. 2001) (alleging that defendant's ambush marketing will encourage other companies to do so, which will adversely affect USOC's ability to fund the United States' participation in the Olympic Games). Successful ambush marketing campaigns also may harm consumers of sporting events. A decrease in sponsorship revenues could force event organizers to find new revenue sources (e.g., cable or pay-per-view television broadcasts rather than free-to-air telecasts), or possibly result in the discontinuance of sporting events that lack adequate commercial sponsorship support.

Despite ambush marketing's potential adverse economic effects on the official sponsorship of sporting events, one commentator has observed:

> Sports organizations, however, remain reluctant to challenge ambush marketing campaigns legally for several reasons: limited case law exists regarding ambush marketing; corporations have successfully defended ambush marketing claims with claims of commercial free speech or fair use; most ambush campaigns are short-lived; an adverse court decision could create an onslaught of ambush campaigns; and courts support of the use of disclaimers, thus allowing ambush companies to make limited use of a registered trademark so long as they avoid creating consumer confusion.

Lori Bean, Note, *Ambush Marketing: Sports Sponsorship Confusion and the Lanham Act*, 75 B.U. L. Rev. 1099, 1101-1102 (1995). Another observes, "While many people complain that [ambush marketing] involves a question of business ethics, others say it is aggressive advertising. Thus, smart lawyers can devise strategies for corporate clients that stay on the legal side." Robert N. Davis, *Ambushing the Olympic Games*, 3 Vill. Sports & Ent. L.J. 423, 430 (1996).

Under current U.S. law, ambush marketing is illegal only if it creates a likelihood of consumer confusion. In *Federation Internationale De Football v. Nike, Inc.*, 285 F. Supp. 2d 64 (D.D.C. 2003), the court refused to preliminarily enjoin Nike's use of "USA 03" to advertise and sell various products in connection with its sponsorship of the U.S. Women's National Soccer Team. Plaintiff Federation Internationale De Football (FIFA) used "USA 2003" in connection with its 2003 women's soccer World Cup held in the United States. Nike was not a World Cup sponsor and was not authorized to use FIFA's marks. Although Nike did not use FIFA's name or refer to the World Cup, FIFA alleged that Nike's usage of "USA 03" was infringing and illegally interfered with its official sponsorship contracts.

Holding that FIFA had not shown a substantial likelihood of success on the merits of its claims, the court observed:

> Nike argues that its use of "USA 03" (or "United States 2003") is innocent, given the company's sponsorship of the Women's National Team. After all, the team that Nike is backing is the United States team for the year 2003, and therefore, "USA 03" is an appropriate and understandable way for Nike to associate itself with that

group of players. The Court agrees that Nike's preexisting and entirely legitimate relationship with the Women's World Cup provides an important context for its use of the disputed marks. For there can be little doubt, in light of the success that the U.S. women enjoyed in the 1999 World Cup, that the team and the event are already linked in the public mind. As such, Nike's careful use of a mark that might be affiliated with both is not necessarily an indication of bad faith, but instead of savvy marketing. Whenever that team plays in this country, it is to be expected that the sponsors of both the team and the event would want to use trademarks that reflect the United States and that emphasize this year's date. Nike's doing so here thus may not indicate a deliberate attempt to deceive the buying public.

Id. at 73-74.

Even if there currently are only limited legal remedies for combating ambush marketing, a sporting event organizer can minimize its successful use and any resulting detrimental effects by developing a comprehensive anti-ambush marketing plan. For example, it can contractually prohibit broadcasters from selling commercial time to the competitors of official sponsors. Nonsponsor advertisements and signage in connection with a sporting event should be carefully monitored to ensure that the event's name, marks, and logos are not included therein. See generally Anne M. Wall, *The Game Behind the Games*, 12 Marq. Sports L. Rev. 557 (2002) (detailing Olympic governing bodies' defensive strategies to deter ambush marketing and protect exclusive contractual rights of official sponsors).

Courts will enforce contract rights to prevent unfair competition that causes a likelihood of consumer confusion. In *Mastercard International, Inc. v. Sprint Communications Co.*, 1994 WL 97097 (S.D.N.Y.), *aff'd*, 23 F.2d 397 (2d Cir. 1994), an international soccer federation granted exclusive rights to Mastercard to use the 1994 World Cup Soccer Tournament trademarks on "all card-based payment and account access devices." The court held that Mastercard's contract rights precluded the United States Local Organizing Committee from authorizing Sprint Communications to use and imprint those marks on phone cards. Finding that Sprint's conduct violated the Lanham Act, the court concluded, "Sprint wishes to use the World Cup marks to convey to the world the false impression that its use of the marks on calling cards is officially sanctioned by the World Cup organization. Clearly, that is not the case, and Mastercard, which has the exclusive right to use the mark for such purposes, is entitled to enjoin this deceptive use." *Id.* at *4.

PROBLEM 12-2

a. Zeebok paid a $40 million sponsorship fee to the International Olympic Committee (IOC) for the exclusive right to use the IOC's trademarks to advertise, promote, and sell athletic footwear and to be designated as the official sneaker of the upcoming Olympic Games, which will be held in the United States. One week before the Olympic Games begin, Badidas, a rival athletic footwear company, begins airing a series of commercials incorporating television broadcasts from prior Olympic Games showing gold medal-winning track athletes wearing Badidas sneakers with the five multi-colored Olympic rings prominently displayed in the background of the stadium in which these events were held. The television broadcasts were posted on YouTube.com without the permission of the IOC and its contractually authorized U.S. television broadcaster of the 2016 Rio Olympic

Games. Discuss whether Badidas' commercials violate any rights of Zeebok, the IOC, or these Olympic athletes (none of whom approved or received any compensation for Badidas' commercials) and identify any additional information needed to analyze the legal issues raised by these facts.

b.   Koors Brewing Company provides free NCAA men's basketball "Final Four" tickets as grand prizes to winners of its "Koors Light Tourney Time Sweepstakes" beer promotion held during the month of March. The back of each ticket states, "Unless specifically authorized in advance by the NCAA, this ticket may not be offered in a commercial promotion or as a prize in a sweepstakes or contest." The NCAA permits only official sponsors of its "Final Four" men's basketball tournament to do so, and it refuses to allow any manufacturers of alcoholic beverages to become official sponsors. Is Koors' conduct legal?

C.   REAL-TIME GAME ACCOUNTS AND BROADCASTING RIGHTS

1.   *Historical Background*

Historically, producers of sporting events sought to protect their claimed property right in live game accounts and play-by-play descriptions under state misappropriation, unfair competition, and contract laws. The then-current federal copyright laws did not provide any legal protection for sporting events or simultaneously recorded broadcasts. Relying primarily on the misappropriation doctrine established by the Supreme Court in *International News Service v. Associated Press*, 248 U.S. 215 (1918), courts broadly held that the creator of a game or athletic event has an exclusive property right in its commercial value while it is occurring. Recognizing that the production of athletic events requires the expenditure of substantial time, effort, and money, these courts prohibited observers and listeners—whether inside or outside the facility in which the event occurred—from unauthorized transmission of live game accounts to the public for commercial benefit. See, e.g., *National Exhibition Co. v. Fass*, 143 N.Y.S.2d 767 (N.Y. Sup. Ct. 1955); *Pittsburgh Athletic Co. v. KQV Broad. Co.*, 24 F. Supp. 490 (W.D. Pa. 1938); *Twentieth Century Sporting Club v. Transradio Press Service, Inc.*, 300 N.Y.S. 159 (N.Y. Sup. Ct. 1937). See generally Bruce P. Keller, *Condemned to Repeat the Past: The Reemergence of Misappropriation and Other Common Law Theories of Protection for Intellectual Property*, 11 Harv. J.L. & Tech. 401 (1998) (tracing historical reliance on state misappropriation law to protect sports-related intellectual property rights).

In *Pittsburgh Athletic Co. v. KQV Broadcasting Co.*, the court held: "the Pittsburgh Athletic Company [owner of the Pittsburgh Pirates professional baseball club], by reason of its creation of the game, its control of the park, and its restriction of the dissemination of news therefrom, has a property right in such news, and the right to control the use thereof for a reasonable time following the games." 24 F. Supp. at 492. The Pittsburgh Athletic Company sold the exclusive rights to broadcast Pirates games played at Forbes Field by radio to General Mills, Inc. The defendant broadcast by radio play-by-play accounts of Pirates games described by observers outside Forbes Field who were able to see them being played. Finding that the defendant's conduct violated the baseball club's property rights, the court ruled that its unauthorized broadcast of Pirates games constitutes misappropriation, unfair competition, and tortious interference with contract rights in violation of Pennsylvania laws.

2. *Nature and Scope of Copyright Law Protection*

After 1976 (when Congress amended federal copyright law), producers of sporting events sought to protect their claimed exclusive rights to commercially exploit the economic value of games and other athletic competitions as well as related collateral products such as broadcasts, real-time accounts and scores, and statistics under federal copyright law.

To encourage creative expression, such as books, movies, music, media broadcasts, and other entertainment products, the Copyright Act of 1976 protects "original works of authorship fixed in any tangible medium of expression." 17 U.S.C. §102(a). The Copyright Act grants copyright owners the exclusive right to use and authorize others to use the copyrighted work in five statutorily defined ways, including the right to copy or duplicate a copyrighted broadcast of a sports event and to "publicly perform" it. 17 U.S.C. §106. The act provides that anyone who violates any of these exclusive rights engages in copyright infringement. 17 U.S.C. §501(a). The owner of a copyright has a variety of available remedies for infringement, including injunctive relief and the recovery of actual or statutory damages, the infringer's profits, and attorney fees. 17 U.S.C. §§502-505.

It is important to understand that copyright law does not protect ideas, procedures, systems, or methods of operation, "regardless of the form in which it is described, explained, illustrated, or embodied," 17 U.S.C. §102(b), which are considered to be in the public domain. Neither the underlying idea for a type of athletic event nor a system or method of playing a sport is copyrightable. In *Hoopla Sports and Entertainment, Inc. v. Nike, Inc.*, 947 F. Supp. 347 (N.D. Ill. 1996), the court held that the concept of an international high school all-star basketball game is not copyrightable, and plaintiff cannot prevent defendant from using its idea to conduct a similar event. The court observed that "the methods or rules of playing basketball games are not generally copyrightable." *Id.* at 354. See also *Seltzer v. Sunbrock*, 22 F. Supp. 621, 630 (S.D. Cal. 1938) (rejecting plaintiff's claim that his idea of a system for staging a transcontinental roller-skating race is protected by copyright law; "[a] system, as such, can never be copyrighted. If it finds any protection, it must come from the patent laws").[1]

The following case considers the scope of protection that federal copyright law provides to the producer of a sports event.

---

1. To be a patentable invention under the federal Patent Act, a sport or game must be useful, non-obvious, and novel, which are difficult statutory requirements to satisfy. 35 U.S.C. §100, et seq. For example, the Patent Office issued U.S. Patent No. 4,911,433 to the Arena Football League for its unique system for playing indoor professional football. See generally Carl A. Kukkonen, III, *Be a Good Sport and Refrain from Using My Patented Putt: Intellectual Property Protection for Sports Related Movements*, 80 J. Pat. & Trademark Off. Soc'y 808 (Nov. 1998). See also *ProBatter Sports, LLC v. Sports Tutor, Inc.*, 680 Fed.Appx. 972 (Fed. Cir. 2017) (affirming validity of patented designs for pitching machine that simulates pitches by analyzing a video projection of an actual pitcher).

NBA v. MOTOROLA, INC.
105 F.3d 841 (2d Cir. 1997)

WINTER, Circuit Judge.

The facts are largely undisputed. Motorola manufactures and markets the SportsTrax paging device while STATS supplies the game information that is transmitted to the pagers. The product became available to the public in January 1996, at a retail price of about $200. SportsTrax's pager has an inch-and-a-half by inch-and-a-half screen and operates in four basic modes: "current," "statistics," "final scores" and "demonstration." It is the "current" mode that gives rise to the present dispute. In that mode, SportsTrax displays the following information on NBA games in progress: (i) the teams playing; (ii) score changes; (iii) the team in possession of the ball; (iv) whether the team is in the free-throw bonus; (v) the quarter of the game; and (vi) time remaining in the quarter. The information is updated every two to three minutes, with more frequent updates near the end of the first half and the end of the game. There is a lag of approximately two or three minutes between events in the game itself and when the information appears on the pager screen.

SportsTrax's operation relies on a "data feed" supplied by STATS reporters who watch the games on television or listen to them on the radio. The reporters key into a personal computer changes in the score and other information such as successful and missed shots, fouls, and clock updates. The information is relayed by modem to STATS's host computer, which compiles, analyzes, and formats the data for retransmission. The information is then sent to a common carrier, which then sends it via satellite to various local FM radio networks that in turn emit the signal received by the individual SportsTrax pagers. . . .

COPYRIGHTS IN EVENTS OR BROADCASTS OF EVENTS

The NBA asserted copyright infringement claims with regard both to the underlying games and to their broadcasts. . . .

INFRINGEMENT OF A COPYRIGHT IN THE UNDERLYING GAMES

In our view, the underlying basketball games do not fall within the subject matter of federal copyright protection because they do not constitute "original works of authorship" under 17 U.S.C. § 102(a). Section 102(a) lists eight categories of "works of authorship" covered by the act, including such categories as "literary works," "musical works," and "dramatic works." The list does not include athletic events, and, although the list is concededly non-exclusive, such events are neither similar nor analogous to any of the listed categories.

Sports events are not "authored" in any common sense of the word. There is, of course, at least at the professional level, considerable preparation for a game. However, the preparation is as much an expression of hope or faith as a determination of what will actually happen. Unlike movies, plays, television programs, or operas, athletic events are competitive and have no underlying script. Preparation may even cause mistakes to succeed, like the broken play in football that gains yard-age because the opposition could not expect it. Athletic events may also result in wholly unanticipated occurrences, the most notable recent event being in a championship baseball game in which interference with a fly ball caused an umpire to signal erroneously a home run.

What "authorship" there is in a sports event, moreover, must be open to copying by competitors if fans are to be attracted. If the inventor of the T-formation in football had been able to copyright it, the sport might have come to an end instead of prospering. Even where athletic preparation most resembles authorship—figure skating, gymnastics, and, some would uncharitably say, professional wrestling—a performer who conceives and executes a particularly graceful and difficult—or, in the case of wrestling, seemingly painful—acrobatic feat cannot copyright it without impairing the underlying competition in the future. A claim of being the only athlete to perform a feat doesn't mean much if no one else is allowed to try.

For many of these reasons, *Nimmer on Copyright* concludes that the "[f]ar more reasonable" position is that athletic events are not copyrightable. 1 M. Nimmer & D. Nimmer, *Nimmer on Copyright* § 2.09[F] at 2-170.1 (1996). *Nimmer* notes that, among other problems, the number of joint copyright owners would arguably include the league, the teams, the athletes, umpires, stadium workers and even fans, who all contribute to the "work."

Concededly, caselaw is scarce on the issue of whether organized events themselves are copyrightable, but what there is indicates that they are not. In claiming a copyright in the underlying games, the NBA relied in part on a footnote in *Baltimore Orioles, Inc. v. Major League Baseball Players Assn.*, 805 F. 2d 663, 669 n. 7 (7th Cir.1986), *cert. denied*, 480 U.S. 941, 107 S. Ct. 1593, 94 L. Ed.2d 782 (1987), which stated that the "[p]layers' performances" contain the "modest creativity required for copyright ability." However, the court went on to state, "Moreover, even if the [p]layers' performances were not sufficiently creative, the [p]layers agree that the cameramen and director contribute creative labor to the telecasts." *Id.* This last sentence indicates that the court was considering the copyright ability of telecasts—not the underlying games, which obviously can be played without cameras.

We believe that the lack of caselaw is attributable to a general understanding that athletic events were, and are, uncopyrightable. . . .

INFRINGEMENT OF A COPYRIGHT IN THE BROADCASTS OF NBA GAMES

As noted, recorded broadcasts of NBA games—as opposed to the games themselves—are now entitled to copyright protection. The Copyright Act was amended in 1976 specifically to insure that simultaneously-recorded transmissions of live performances and sporting events would meet the Act's requirement that the original work of authorship be "fixed in any tangible medium of expression." 17 U.S.C. § 102(a). . . . Congress specifically had sporting events in mind: [T]he bill seeks to resolve, through the definition of "fixation" in section 101, the status of live broadcasts—sports, news coverage, live performances of music, etc.—that are reaching the public in unfixed form but that are simultaneously being recorded. H.R. No. 94-1476 at 52, *reprinted in* 1976 U.S.C.C.A.N. at 5665. The House Report also makes clear that it is the broadcast, not the underlying game, that is the subject of copyright protection. . . .

Although the broadcasts are protected under copyright law, the district court correctly held that Motorola and STATS did not infringe NBA's copyright because they reproduced only facts from the broadcasts, not the expression or description of the game that constitutes the broadcast. The "fact/expression dichotomy" is a bedrock principle of copyright law that "limits severely the scope of protection in fact-based works." *Feist Publications, Inc. v. Rural Tel. Service Co.*, 499 U.S. 340, 350, 111 S. Ct. 1282, 1290, 113 L. Ed. 2d 358 (1991). "'No author may copyright facts or ideas. The copyright is limited to those aspects of the work—termed "expression"—that display the stamp of the author's originality.'" *Id.* (quoting *Harper & Row, Publishers, Inc. v. Nation Enter.*, 471 U.S. 539, 547, 105 S. Ct. 2218, 2224, 85 L. Ed. 2d 588 (1985)).

We agree with the district court that the "[d]efendants provide purely factual information which any patron of an NBA game could acquire from the arena without any involvement from the director, cameramen, or others who contribute to the originality of a broadcast." Because the SportsTrax device and AOL site reproduce only factual information culled from the broadcasts and none of the copyrightable expression of the games, appellants did not infringe the copyright of the broadcasts. . . .

NOTES AND QUESTIONS

1. *Sports Events and Performances.* Why did the *Motorola* court hold that a sports event or performance is not subject to protection under federal copyright law? Considering that elite athletic performance on either an individual or team basis normally involves significant creative activity and generally has substantial commercial value, was the *Motorola* court's conclusion correct? See *National Assn. of Broadcasters v. Copyright Royalty Tribunal*, 675 F.2d 367, 377 and n.16 (D.C. Cir. 1982) (noting apparent understanding of Congress during hearings on Copyright Act of 1976 that "the mere performance of a sport or game could not be copyrighted at common law"). As one noted commentator observes:

   > Although the commercial value of professional sports cannot be doubted, and although judges should not determine copyrightability [sic] according to their subjective evaluation of an artistic work, nonetheless copyright extends only to "works of authorship," not to every commercially valuable activity. Failure to appreciate that distinction would result in according copyright protection not only to athletic events, but also to a heart surgeon's operation on diseased tissue or the twisting of knobs in the control center of a nuclear power plant—both important and commercially valuable activities, to be sure, but neither remotely capable of copyright protection.

   1-2 M. Nimmer and D. Nimmer, *Nimmer on Copyright* §2.09[F][2] (2015).

2. *Sports Broadcasts.* The *Motorola* court ruled that the Copyright Act of 1976 protects the broadcast of a sporting event, even though it does not protect the underlying event itself. Is there a principled basis for drawing this distinction? Why didn't the *Motorola* defendants' conduct constitute infringement of the copyright in the broadcast of NBA games?

3. *Ownership of Sports Broadcast Copyright.* A threshold issue is who owns the copyright to the broadcast of a sporting event—the clubs playing the particular game, the league, the broadcaster of the game, or the players participating in the game? In general, ownership of a copyright initially vests in the author(s) of the work. 17 U.S.C. §201(a). The Copyright Act recognizes that a work may be jointly authored and its copyright co-owned. 17 U.S.C.

§201(a). *In re National Football League Sunday Ticket Antitrust Litigation*, 2019 WL 3788253 (9th Cir.) at *10 ("[]n the absence of an agreement otherwise, the person or company that creates the telecast is the 'author' of the telecast for the purposes of copyright law. . . . Assuming that this rule applies in the league sports setting, the team or network that creates the telecasts would be the sole owner of the copyright in the telecasts, absent some agreement to the contrary."). A broadcaster's camera angles, types of shots, use of instant replays, split screens, special effects, and commentary supplies the creativity necessary for "authorship" of a broadcast sports event for purposes of copyright law. *Baltimore Orioles, Inc. v. Major League Baseball Players Assn.*, 805 F.2d 663, 668-669 (7th Cir. 1986); *National Assn. of Broadcasters v. Copyright Royalty Tribunal*, 675 F.2d 367, 377-379 (D.C. Cir. 1982). Whether the copyright for broadcast games is owned by a sports league or its member clubs that produce the game generally is determined by contract. *Chi. Prof'l Sports Ltd. Partnership v. NBA*, 874 F. Supp. 844, 850-851 (N.D. Ill. 1995), *reversed on other grounds*, 95 F.3d 593 (7th Cir. 1996). Ownership of the copyright for a sports broadcast vis-à-vis the league and its clubs or the broadcaster generally also is contractually determined. See, e.g., *NFL v. Insight Telecomm. Corp.*, 158 F. Supp. 2d 124, 128 (D. Mass. 2001) ("The NFL owns the copyright in all regular season and post-season NFL game telecasts, as confirmed by the League's contracts with the networks").

Players generally do not own the copyright to a sports broadcast. In *Baltimore Orioles, Inc. v. Major League Baseball Players Assn.*, 805 F.2d 663, 670 (7th Cir. 1986), the Seventh Circuit held:

> Because the Players are employees and their performances before broadcast audiences are within the scope of their employment, the telecasts of major league baseball games, which consist of the Players' performances, are works made for hire within the meaning of § 201(b). . . . Thus, in the absence of an agreement to the contrary, the Clubs are presumed to own all of the rights encompassed in the telecasts of the games. The district court found that there was no written agreement that the Clubs would not own the copyright to the telecasts, and, therefore, that the copyright was owned by the Clubs.

See also *Big Fights Inc. v. Ficara*, 40 U.S.P.Q.2d 1377, 1378 (S.D.N.Y. 1996) (the promoter of a professional boxing match, not the boxers, owns the copyright in film of the match).

4. *Sports Scores and Statistics.* Although mere facts such as game scores and statistics are not copyrightable, their original and creative compilation is a form of expression that is protected under federal copyright law. In *Feist Publications, Inc. v. Rural Telephone Service Co., Inc.*, 499 U.S. 340 (1991), the Supreme Court explained:

> "No one may claim originality as to facts." [Citation omitted.] This is because facts do not owe their origin to an act of authorship. The distinction is one between creation and discovery: The first person to find and report a particular fact has not created the fact; he or she has merely discovered its existence. . . . Factual compilations, on the other hand, may possess the requisite originality. The compilation author typically chooses which facts to include, in what order to place them, and how to arrange the collected data so that they may be used effectively by readers. These choices as to selection and arrangement, so long as they are made independently by the compiler and

entail a minimal degree of creativity, are sufficiently original that Congress may protect such compilations through the copyright laws.

Id. at 347-348. See, e.g., *Nat'l Football Scouting, Inc. v Rang*, 912 F. Supp. 2d 985, 990 (W.D. Wash. 2012) (prospective NFL player grades are "compilations of data chosen and weighed with creativity and judgment," which constitute a copyrightable "numeric expression of a professional opinion").

5. *Cheerleadering Uniforms.* In *Star Athletica LLC v. Varsity Brands Inc.,* 137 S. Ct. 1002, 1012 (2017), the Supreme Court ruled that designs on a cheerleading uniform, a form of creative expression, are copyrightable if "when identified and imagined apart from the useful article [i.e., the uniform itself], it would qualify as a pictorial, graphic, or sculptural work either on its own or when fixed in some other tangible medium." But the scope of copyright protection is limited. "To be clear, the only feature of the cheerleading uniform eligible for a copyright in this case is the two-dimensional work of art fixed in the tangible medium of the uniform fabric. . . . [There is] no right to prohibit any person from manufacturing a cheerleading uniform of identical shape, cut, and dimensions to the ones on which the decorations in this case appear." *Id.* at 1013.

3. Infringement of a Sports Broadcast

In *NFL v. McBee & Bruno's, Inc.,* 792 F.2d 726 (8th Cir. 1986), the Eighth Circuit ruled that a sports bar's unauthorized interception of the broadcast of a sports event through the use of satellite dish antennae and its showing to patrons, which occurred in the mid-1980s, constitutes copyright infringement. It explained:

> The Copyright Act protects "original works of authorship fixed in any tangible medium," 17 U.S.C. § 102(a), including "motion pictures and other audiovisual works," 17 U.S.C. § 102(a)(6). As for live broadcasts, such as the football games at issue here, the Act states that "[a] work consisting of sounds, images, or both, that are being transmitted, is 'fixed' . . . if a fixation of the work is being made simultaneously with its transmission," 17 U.S.C. § 101; "[t]o 'transmit' is defined as 'to communicate . . . by any device or process whereby images or sounds are received beyond the place from which they are sent.'"

Id. at 731-732. This is an unauthorized "public performance" of a copyrighted sports broadcast, which the Copyright Act defines as a display "at a place open to the public or at any place where a substantial number of persons outside of a normal circle of a family and its social acquaintances is gathered." 17 U.S.C. §101. The court rejected the defendant's argument that its display of blacked-out NFL games is non-infringing conduct under § 110(5) of the Copyright Act, which precludes copyright liability for "communication of a transmission embodying a performance . . . by the public reception of the transmission on a single receiving apparatus of a kind commonly used in private homes[,]" because residential satellite dish antennae were relatively uncommon in the United States at that time. See also *NFL v. PrimeTime 24 Joint Venture,* 211 F.3d 10, 13 (2d Cir. 2000), *cert. denied,* 532 U.S. 941 (2001) ("PrimeTime's uplink transmission of signals captured in the United States is a step in the process by which NFL's protected work wends its way to a public audience [in Canada] . . .

and [b]ecause PrimeTime did not have authorization to make such a public performance, PrimeTime infringed the NFL's copyright").

The following case illustrates that the Internet provides a modern means for infringing copyrighted sports event broadcasts and enables unauthorized web-casts to occur throughout the world—conduct that clearly violates U.S. law, but possibly not foreign laws.

NFL v. TVRADIONOW CORP.

53t U.S.P.Q.2d 1831 (W.D. Pa. 2000)

ZIEGLER, J.

This is a civil action for money damages and equitable relief, filed by the National Football League ("NFL"), National Basketball Association ("NBA"), and NBA Properties, Inc. ("NBA Properties") (collectively "the Sports Leagues") . . . contending that defendants violated the Copyright Act, 17 U.S.C. Section 106. . . .

The gravamen of this dispute concerns the public performance of plaintiffs' copyrighted programming from Toronto, Canada, to computer users in the United States since November 30, 1999, over the Internet. Specifically, defendants have streamed copyrighted professional football and basketball games as well as copyrighted programs such as "60 Minutes," "Ally McBeal," and "Star Trek Voyager," framed with advertisements obtained by defendants. Plaintiffs allege that defendants have captured United States programming from television stations in Buffalo, New York and elsewhere, converted these television signals into computerized data and streamed them over the Internet from a website called iCraveTV.com. According to plaintiffs, any Internet user may access iCraveTV.com by simply entering three digits of any Canadian area code, one of which is provided to the user on the site itself, and by clicking two other buttons. Further, Internet users from the United States and elsewhere easily may revisit the site because iCraveTV causes a small file, or cookie, to be deposited in a user's computer during his or her initial visit so that the user can automatically bypass defendants' screening process. . . . [T]he Court is mindful of the long-standing precept that the United States copyright laws do not have extraterritorial operation. *See Allarcom Pay Television, Ltd. v. General Instrument Corp.*, 69 F.3d 381 [36 U.S.P.Q.2d 1654] (9th Cir. 1995).

Defendants argue that their website is for Canadian viewers only and it is not intended for citizens of the United States and elsewhere. Thus, the argument continues, the alleged improper acts are limited to Canada.

Plaintiffs have presented testimony, sworn affidavits and declarations establishing that Pennsylvania residents have accessed defendants' website and viewed the programs which were streamed thereon. Further, defendants posted an article on the Website by a United States citizen noting that access to defendants' website could be obtained by any United States citizen with little or no difficulty.

Accordingly, when an allegedly infringing act occurring without the United States is publicly performed within the United States, the Copyright Act is implicated and a district court possesses jurisdiction. [Citations omitted.] Subject matter jurisdiction exists because, although the streaming of the plaintiffs' programming originated in Canada, acts of infringement were committed within the United States when United States citizens received and viewed defendants' streaming of the copyrighted materials. These constitute, at a minimum, public performances in the United States. . . .

The plaintiffs have established without rejoinder from the defendants that they have copyright . . . ownership of several items, including, among others, the Super Bowl, the NBA Finals, and the NFL playoff games and regular League games. . . .

Defendants do not deny that they have copied these items, represented themselves as the authors and that they have publicly performed them over the Internet. Rather, defendants argue that there is no desire on the part of defendants for any United States residents to access iCraveTV. Notwithstanding defendants' intentions, the Court finds that plaintiffs have presented sufficient facts to establish their claims of copyright . . . infringement. . . .

A January 25, 2000 breakdown of "impressions" and "clicks" onto the iCraveTV website, generated by a private ad serving system (DART) utilized by Cox, reported 1.6 million impressions (page views) from United States visitors on the iCraveTV website. This figure was second only to the figure for Canada, which was 2.0 million.

Defendants also use a "Real Video" server to stream video programming through their website. This server maintains "logs" of the Internet Protocol addresses of computers that contact defendants' server to obtain access to video programming. An analysis of the Real Video server logs shows that substantial numbers of persons in the United States received the streaming of programming, including programming in which plaintiffs own copyrights. [E]vidence in the record shows that plaintiffs are likely to succeed in showing that defendants are unlawfully publicly performing plaintiffs' copyrighted works in the United States. Defendants do so by transmitting (through use of "streaming" technology) performances of the works to the public by means of the telephone lines and computers that make up the Internet. 17 U.S.C. Section 101. This activity violates plaintiffs' rights to perform their works publicly and to authorize others to do so. 17 U.S.C. Sections 106, 501(a). . . .

Defendants have submitted a declaration of a Canadian law professor, Michael Geist, which argues that defendants' activities are permissible under Canadian law. However, because plaintiffs seek relief under U.S. law for infringements of the U.S. Copyright Act, there is no need for this Court to address any issue of Canadian law. . . .

[The court preliminarily and permanently enjoined defendants from infringing plaintiffs' copyrighted works through streaming or otherwise into the United States via the iCraveTV.com site or any other Internet site or online facility without plaintiffs' prior consent.]

NOTES AND QUESTIONS

1. *Copyright Infringement of a Live Sports Broadcast.* Why does the *TVRadionow Corp.* defendants' conduct constitute copyright infringement even if it was lawful in Canada? See also *Live Nation Motor Sports, Inc. v. Davis,* 2006 WL 3616983 (N.D. Tex. 2006) (providing unauthorized access to a motorcycle racing producer's live webcasts through defendant's website is copyright infringement). See generally Michael J. Mellis, *Internet Piracy of Live Sports Telecasts,* 18 Marq. Sports L. Rev. 259 (2008).

The Internet enables unauthorized webcasts to occur throughout the world, but currently there exists no uniform global scope of copyright law protection for sports broadcasts. In *TVRadionow Corp.*, defendants claimed their conduct was permissible under Canadian law, an issue the court found unnecessary to resolve because plaintiffs only sought relief under U.S. copyright law. In 2008, an Israeli court refused to grant the English Football Association Premier League's request for an injunction against unauthorized Internet broadcasting of its games because of judicial uncertainty as to whether such conduct violates Israel's copyright law. *Football Association Premier League Ltd v. Netvision 013 Barack Ltd.*, MCA 011646/08 (Dist. Ct. Tel Aviv, July 16, 2008) (unofficial English translation) ("[W]hat interests the TV viewers is the game itself, and there is almost no importance in the 'original work,' i.e. photography angles and replays. . . . It seems artificial to grant copyright to TV photography. In actual fact, there is nothing original in the photography, it is just a documentation of the game itself to which, as all agree, copyright does not apply.").

As illustrated by *Aereo* and *Fox Broadcasting*, the complexities of modern technology make it difficult to determine what constitutes infringement of a sports broadcast.

Effectively characterizing it as an unauthorized form of Internet streaming, in *American Broadcasting Companies, Inc. v. Aereo, Inc.*, 134 S. Ct. 2498 (2014), the Supreme Court ruled that a system combining the functionality of a standard TV antenna, a DVR, and a Slingbox-like device, which enabled users to watch live television programs broadcast over the public airwaves, including sports events, over the Internet in real-time constitutes copyright infringement. The Court held that this technologically complex system of retransmitted television broadcasts is analogous to a cable television system, which publicly performs the copyrighted programs it broadcasts to its subscribers. The Copyright Act permits a cable television system to do so without infringement liability pursuant to a compulsory license requiring payment of statutorily determined fees, which are distributed to owners of the copyrighted broadcasts. On remand, the district court determined that the Supreme Court "did not imply, much less hold, that simply because an entity performs publicly in much the same way as a CATV system, it is necessarily a cable system entitled to a § 111 compulsory license." The court issued a preliminary injunction "barring Aereo from retransmitting programs to its subscribers while the programs are still being broadcast." *American Broadcasting Companies, Inc. v. Aereo, Inc.*, 112 U.S.P.Q.2d 1582 (S.D.N.Y. 2014).

In comparison, *Fox Broadcasting Co., Inc. v. Dish Network LLC*, 114 U.S.P.Q.2d 1100 (C.D. Cal. 2015), held that a satellite television provider's Dish Anywhere service (which includes a DVR and built-in Sling device), which enables its subscribers to view copyrighted television programming such as sports events on their personal computers and mobile devices, does not violate copyright law. Distinguishing *Aereo*, the court concluded that subscribers' use of this service to access their individual live or recorded programming and transfer it to these Internet-connected devices does not result in a public performance of copyrighted programming because the provider has a license for initial retransmission of this programming to its subscribers.

2. *Copyright Infringement of a Taped Sports Broadcasts.* Tape recording of televised sports broadcasts for solely in-home, personal use is not copyright

infringement. *Sony Corp. of Am. v. Universal City Studios, Inc.*, 464 U.S. 417, 449 (1984) (characterizing this activity as "time-shifting for private home use" that is noninfringing fair use of copyrighted broadcast pursuant to §107 of Copyright Act). But, the unauthorized public performance of taped broadcasts of sports events (which would include posting on YouTube) constitutes copyright infringement. In *New Boston Television, Inc. v. Entertainment Sports Programming Network, Inc.*, 215 U.S.P.Q. 755 (D. Mass. 1981), ESPN contended that its rebroadcast of taped sports event highlights is permissible fair use. Rejecting this alleged defense and finding copyright infringement, the court stated:

> While protection of the public right of access to [newsworthy] information is a primary justification for the fair use defense, this right is sufficiently protected merely by enabling defendants to report the underlying facts which the plaintiff's videotapes record. It does not however permit defendants to appropriate the plaintiff's expression of that information by copying the plaintiff's films themselves.

Id. at 756.

In *Viacom Int'l v. YouTube, Inc.*, 718 F. Supp. 2d 514 (S.D.N.Y. 2010), *aff'd and reversed and remanded on other grounds*, 676 F.3d 19 (2d Cir. 2012), a federal district court held that the Digital Millenium Copyright Act does not require YouTube to self-police its website for infringing content posted by third parties such as copyrighted broadcast and webcast sports events. YouTube is required to remove copyrighted material in accordance with this federal law only when it has actual knowledge that a specific posting contains copyrighted material that has been posted without the copyright owner's authorization.

4. Misappropriation of Real-Time Game Accounts and Scores

In *NBA v. Motorola, Inc., supra*, the Second Circuit ruled that federal copyright law preempted (i.e., barred or precluded) the NBA's state law commercial misappropriation claim because the defendants' collection and dissemination of "strictly factual information about the games" was obtained from NBA games broadcast on television and radio, which was information already in the public domain. The court explained:

> When Congress amended the Copyright Act in 1976, it provided for the preemption of state law claims that are interrelated with copyright claims in certain ways. Under 17 U.S.C. § 301, a state law claim is preempted when: (i) the state law claim seeks to vindicate "legal or equitable rights that are equivalent" to one of the bundle of exclusive rights already protected by copyright law under 17 U.S.C. § 106—styled the "general scope requirement"; and (ii) the particular work to which the state law claim is being applied falls within the type of works protected by the Copyright Act under Sections 102 and 103—styled the "subject matter requirement."
>
> The district court concluded that the NBA's misappropriation claim was not preempted because, with respect to the underlying games, as opposed to the broadcasts, the subject matter requirement was not met. . . . We hold that where the challenged copying or misappropriation relates in part to the copyrighted broadcasts of the games, the subject matter requirement is met as to both the broadcasts and the games. . . .

Although game broadcasts are copyrightable while the underlying games are not, the Copyright Act should not be read to distinguish between the two when analyzing the preemption of a misappropriation claim based on copying or taking from the copyrightable work. . . .

Copyrightable material often contains uncopyrightable elements within it, but Section 301 preemption bars state law misappropriation claims with respect to uncopyrightable as well as copyrightable elements. . . .

It is often difficult or impossible to separate the fixed copyrightable work from the underlying uncopyrightable events or facts. Moreover, Congress, in extending copyright protection only to the broadcasts and not to the underlying events, intended that the latter be in the public domain. . . .

105 F.3d at 848-849.

The *Motorola* court held that a state law "hot-news" misappropriation claim was not preempted. It determined all elements, however, were not satisfied because the defendants' collection and dissemination of only real-time factual information did not have an adverse economic effect on the production or broadcasting of NBA games:

We therefore find the extra elements—those in addition to the elements of copyright infringement—that allow a "hot-news" claim to survive preemption are: (i) the time-sensitive value of factual information, (ii) the free-riding by a defendant, and (iii) the threat to the very existence of the product or service provided by the plaintiff.

We conclude that Motorola and STATS have not engaged in unlawful misappropriation under the "hot-news" test set out above. To be sure, some of the elements of a "hot-news" *INS* claim are met. The information transmitted to SportsTrax is not precisely contemporaneous, but it is nevertheless time-sensitive. Also, the NBA does provide, or will shortly do so, information like that available through SportsTrax. . . .

However, there are critical elements missing in the NBA's attempt to assert a "hot-news" *INS*-type claim. As framed by the NBA, their claim compresses and confuses three different informational products. The first product is generating the information by playing the games; the second product is transmitting live, full descriptions of those games; and the third product is collecting and retransmitting strictly factual information about the games. The first and second products are the NBA's primary business: producing basketball games for live attendance and licensing copyrighted broadcasts of those games. The collection and retransmission of strictly factual material about the games is a different product: e.g., box-scores in newspapers, summaries of statistics on television sports news, and real-time facts to be transmitted to pagers. In our view, the NBA has failed to show any competitive effect whatsoever from SportsTrax on the first and second products and a lack of any free-riding by SportsTrax on the third.

With regard to the NBA's primary products—producing basketball games with live attendance and licensing copyrighted broadcasts of those games—there is no evidence that anyone regards SportsTrax or the AOL site as a substitute for attending NBA games or watching them on television. In fact, Motorola markets SportsTrax as being designed "for those times when you cannot be at the arena, watch the game on TV, or listen to the radio. . . ."

The NBA argues that the pager market is also relevant to a "hot-news" *INS*-type claim and that SportsTrax's future competition with Gamestats satisfies any missing element. We agree that there is a separate market for the real-time transmission of factual information to pagers or similar devices, such as STATS's AOL site. However, we disagree that SportsTrax is in any sense free-riding off Gamestats.

An indispensable element of an *INS* "hot-news" claim is free riding by a defendant on a plaintiff's product, enabling the defendant to produce a directly competitive product for less money because it has lower costs. SportsTrax is not such a product. The use of pagers to transmit real-time information about NBA games requires: (i) the collecting of facts about the games; (ii) the transmission of these facts on a network; (iii) the assembling of them by the particular service; and (iv) the transmission of them to pagers or an on-line computer site. Appellants are in no way free-riding on Gamestats. Motorola and STATS expend their own resources to collect purely factual information generated in NBA games to transmit to SportsTrax pagers. They have their own network and assemble and transmit data themselves.

105 F.3d at 853-854.

If athletic events and factual accounts of games are not copyrightable, why does §301 of the Copyright Act preempt some state law remedies for their unauthorized commercial appropriation? Although it found a separate commercial market for the real-time transmission of game accounts, why did the court hold that defendants' conduct does not infringe the NBA's state law rights?

Consistent with *Motorola*, even if there are no issues of preemption because the data is obtained from sources other than a copyrighted broadcast of an athletic event, courts have held that unauthorized commercial use of sports statistics in the public domain does not violate state misappropriation law. In *National Football League v. Governor of the State of Delaware*, 435 F. Supp. 1372 (D. Del. 1977), the NFL sought to enjoin the unauthorized use of its game schedules and scores as the basis for a Delaware state football lottery. Although defendants profited from public popularity generated by NFL games, the court found no misappropriation of the league's property:

> The only tangible product of plaintiffs' labor which defendants utilize in the Delaware Lottery are the schedule of NFL games and the scores. These are obtained from public sources and are utilized only after plaintiffs have disseminated them at large and no longer have any expectation of generating revenue from further dissemination.

Id. at 1377. It is impermissible, however, to advertise or sell a product or service incorporating public domain sports statistics in a manner creating a likelihood of consumer confusion regarding its authorization, affiliation, or endorsement by the sports entity or athletic event, which would constitute trademark infringement and/or unfair competition.

The following case illustrates that the producer of a sports event may limit access to real-time scores and game information by contract (for example, by allowing admission only if ticket holders or members of the media agree to comply with certain conditions).

MORRIS COMMUNICATIONS CORP. v. PGA TOUR, INC.

235 F. Supp. 2d 1269 (M.D. Fla. 2002), *aff'd,* **364 F.3d 1288 (11th Cir.),** *cert. denied,*
543 U.S. 919 (2004)

Schlesinger, District Judge.

At issue in this case is the extent to which the PGA Tour may be allowed to limit the access of Morris [Communications Corporation ("Morris")] and other media entities to its own private golf tournaments. Specifically, the Court must resolve whether the PGA Tour may legally condition access to its tournaments on Morris's agreement not to syndicate "real-time" golf scores obtained from an on-site media center. . . .

The parties' dispute in this case concerns the on-line publication of "real-time" golf scores [which] are scores that are transmitted electronically nearly contemporaneously to their actual occurrence on the golf course. In this way, Internet users are able to track during a golf tournament each participating player's progress on a hole-by-hole basis. In order to improve its scoring capabilities for its tournaments, including transmission of real-time golf scores over the Internet, the PGA Tour has designed and implemented an elaborate electronic relay known as the Real-Time Scoring System ("RTSS").

RTSS works as follows: During a given golf tournament, volunteer workers called "hole reporters" follow each group of golfers on the golf course and tabulate the scores of each player at the end of each hole. The scores are then collected by other volunteers located at each of the eighteen greens on the golf course, who, with the aid of hand-held wireless radios, relay the scoring information to a remote production truck staffed by personnel employed by the PGA Tour. The scores of all participating golfers are then processed at the remote production truck and transmitted by the PGA Tour to its Internet web-site, pga-tour.com. The PGA Tour claims that it takes "about five minutes" for the information to be routed from the production truck to pgatour.com. At the same time, real-time scores are also transmitted to an on-site media center where accredited members of the media are able to access the scores. The same information is also transmitted to various electronic "leaderboards" located throughout the golf course for public viewing by spectators. The leaderboards do not simultaneously show the real time scores of all participating golfers. Rather, they typically show only the top ten or fifteen scores.

Due to the nature and size of golf courses, which may span as much as 150 acres, comprehensive real-time scores—that is, up-to-the-minute scores of every competitor—can only be compiled using a relay system such as RTSS. During a golf tournament, different groups of players compete contemporaneously at different holes such that any one spectator can only view a limited number of players at any one of the eighteen holes. Thus, in order to generate real-time scores, it is necessary to have individuals stationed at each hole as the tournament progresses so that the entire golf course can be monitored simultaneously. Acknowledging that some kind of relay system is needed to generate the type of real-time scoring information it wishes to syndicate, Morris submits that it is unable to implement such a system itself due to the PGA Tour rules prohibiting unauthorized use of wireless communication devices on the golf course at its tournaments. . . .

[Morris' federal and state antitrust claims] alleged that the PGA Tour possesses monopoly power over access to its golf tournaments and has unfairly used that power by attempting to stifle competition in the separate market for syndicated real-time golf scores. In response, the PGA Tour argued that it enjoys a property right in RTSS and that its regulations restricting the syndication of real-time golf scoring information gathered and generated by RTSS constitute a reasonable safeguard against would-be free riders seeking to unfairly capitalize on its product. . . .

Morris asks the Court to force the PGA Tour to provide Morris with the compilation of scores, for which the PGA Tour spends considerable money and time creating, at no cost to Morris. . . .

Morris contends that it is not free-riding . . . [In *NBA. v. Motorola, Inc.*, 105 F.3d 841 (2d Cir. 1997)] the court found that Motorola did not free-ride when it created a network that disseminated scores from NBA basketball games. Three distinctions between *Motorola* and the instant case make Morris's claim untenable. First, the *Motorola* court used a very high standard for free-riding that is applicable only in cases with the hot-news exception. . . . More importantly, the information that Motorola used to create its product was in the public domain, having been broadcast on television or radio. Specifically, Motorola-paid reporters, who had heard the radio or television broadcast scores, reported the information to a central location and merely relayed what had been known to the world. Golf, unlike basketball, precludes a single person gathering all the information occurring on all 18 holes. So when television and radio cover a basketball game, the score is presented to the public through those media outlets, allowing Motorola to obtain the information and republish it. If Morris were able to gather scores from all 18 holes through a television or radio broadcast, Morris could then republish that information, absent a hot-news exception. However, golf's atypical format prevents any single television or radio broadcast from providing results from all 18 holes live. The PGA Tour does publish the scores in the media center,[18] but the media cannot disseminate that information except as the PGA Tour's press credentials allow them to do.[19] As a result, the scores, which are not protected by copyright, remain outside the public domain and within the PGA Tour's control, because the PGA Tour provides access with certain restrictions.[20] Finally, Motorola benefited from the NBA's costs in producing and marketing the games and from the radio and television stations who paid for broadcast rights: that is Motorola capitalized on the NBA's positive externalities. However, the NBA and the broadcast stations had already reaped the profits of their investment, and the information was in the public domain at the moment of broadcasting. Additionally, once in the public domain, Motorola "expend[ed] their own resources to collect purely factual information generated in NBA games." *Id.* at 854. While here, Morris does not expend its own resources in gathering information, which is not in the public domain, but instead free-rides on the PGA Tour's compilation of scores. . . .

The PGA Tour claims that the restrictions have a valid business justification, because they are necessary to protect a property right in the scores that it compiled by use of RTSS. Morris argues that the PGA Tour lacks a property right in the score, thus negating the claimed business justification. For the following reasons, the Court finds that the PGA Tour does have a property right in the scores compiled by the use of RTSS, but that property right vanishes when the scores are in the public domain.

The PGA Tour's property right does not come from copyright law, as copyright law does not protect factual information, like golf scores. *See Feist Publications v. Rural Tel. Serv. Co.*, 499 U.S. 340, 348, 111 S. Ct. 1282, 113 L. Ed. 2d 358 (1991).

---

18. The PGA Tour also publishes the scores of the top players to the spectators, who are present under a license from the PGA Tour which prevents their dissemination of the scores off the course.

19. Currently, the PGA Tour allows Morris to publish the scores as quickly as it can re-key them from the media center, but the PGA Tour does not allow Morris to sell or syndicate that information. Also, a compiler of information can limit the dissemination of that information through contracts, including contracts found on tickets. *See ProCD v. Zeidenberg*, 86 F.3d 1447, 1451 (7th Cir. 1996).

20. Even if the information were in the public domain, the PGA Tour would have the ability to limit the use of the information it provides to Morris under contract law. [Citation omitted.]

However, the PGA Tour controls the right of access to that information and can place restrictions on those attending the private event, giving the PGA Tour a property right that the Court will protect. . . . [T]he instant case deals with facts that are not subject to copyright protection. The compiler of the information . . . collects information, which it created, at a cost. Also the events occur on private property to which the general public does not have unfettered access, and the creator of the event can place restrictions upon those who enter the private property. The vastly increased speed that the Internet makes available does not change the calculus or the underlying property right. Accordingly, the PGA Tour . . . has a property right in the compilation of scores, but that property right disappears when the underlying information is in the public domain.

Whether the PGA Tour has a separate right to license or sell broadcast rights on the Internet, like sports and entertainment producers currently enjoy in dealing with television and radio, is a novel question. . . .

Both parties would certainly agree that the Internet provides an opportunity to profit from a product by selling advertisement. Television, radio, and print media operate on a similar, if not identical, principle: the selling of advertisement to viewers, listeners, or readers of entertainment, be it sports, entertainment, or news. Therefore, the Court finds that the PGA Tour has a right to sell or license its product, championship golf, and its derivative product, golf scores, on the Internet in the same way the PGA Tour currently sells its rights to television broadcasting stations. . . .

Accordingly, the Court finds that the PGA Tour is justified in its restrictions because (1) Morris free-rides on the PGA Tour's efforts, (2) the PGA Tour has a property right in the scores before they are in the public domain, and (3) the PGA Tour has the right to license or sell broadcasting rights of its products over the Internet. . . .

[I]n this case, Morris is seeking access to the media center and the scoring system at no cost, putting it at a competitive advantage to the PGA Tour. The PGA Tour offers access to the scores through a license as evidenced by its contract with USA Today, and Morris is free to negotiate for the purchase of a license which would put it on a competitive plane with the PGA Tour. . . .

[The court granted the PGA Tour's summary judgment motion and dismissed Morris's antitrust claims.]

NOTES AND QUESTIONS

1. Why does the PGA Tour have a state law property right in its real-time golf scores, and how long does this right last? Is *Morris Communications* consistent with *Motorola's* holding that the NBA did not have a protectable property interest in its real-time game scores?

    In *Morris Communications Corp. v. PGA Tour, Inc,* 364 F.3d 1288, 1298 (11th Cir. 2004), the Eleventh Circuit affirmed that the PGA Tour's property right in compiled real-time golf scores enables it to prevent their unauthorized commercial usage:

    > The district court correctly found that a company—even a monopolist company—that expends time and money to create a valuable product does not violate the antitrust laws when it declines to provide that product to its competitors for free. PGA has accommodated Morris at every step along the way,

has agreed to sell its product to Morris, and has acted appropriately to protect its economic interests and investments. Yet Morris demands that it be given access to the product of PGA's proprietary RTSS, without compensating PGA, so that Morris can then sell that product to others for a fee. That is the classic example of "free-riding."

2. In *Wisconsin Interscholastic Athletic Assn. v. Gannett Co., Inc.*, 658 F.3d 614 (7th Cir. 2011), the Seventh Circuit held that a high school athletic association, which the parties stipulated is a state actor, has a property right in its tournament games and that its exclusive contract to stream games over the Internet does not violate the First Amendment. Relying on *Zacchini v. Scripps-Howard Broadcasting Co.*, 433 U.S. 562 (1977), the court ruled that the "WIAA has the right to package and distribute its performance; nothing in the First Amendment confers on the media an affirmative right to broadcast entire performances." *Id.* at 622. It explained:

> The idea that reporting and streaming are synonymous is also at odds with experience in the private sector. There, everyone understands that there is a difference between a description of an event like the Super Bowl, Women's World Cup, or the College World Series and the right both to videotape that entertainment and then to publish it as one sees fit. In each of these situations the producer of the entertainment — the NFL, FIFA, or the NCAA — normally signs a lucrative contract for exclusive, or semi-exclusive, broadcast rights for the performance. Meanwhile, all media report on the events. *Cf. Home Box Office*, 587 F.2d at 1253 ("Contracts conferring the exclusive right to broadcast sporting events and artistic or theatrical performances are commonplace."). Gannett's argument boils down to an assertion that a government actor cannot, under any circumstances, act like the NFL, FIFA or NCAA. But the First Amendment does not require such a draconian rule. . . . WIAA is not prohibiting the media from reporting on its events, nor is it imposing outrageous fee for media members to have access to games. It does not require the media to submit stories or blog post to its editors before they are published. Any of these actions would make this a significantly different case.

Id. at 628-629.

3. *Drafting Exercise.* The *Morris Communications* district court observes that contract law may be used to limit event spectators' use of scores and accounts of live sporting events. On behalf of a sports team, draft appropriate language for spectator admission tickets and event signage to prohibit unauthorized use of such information, including a description of any action that may be taken to enforce and to minimize noncompliance with its terms.

PROBLEM 12-3

a. Since 1914, several private rooftop clubs overlooking Wrigley Field have sold tickets for fans to watch Chicago Cubs home baseball games, live or on television, and have used the federally registered "Cubs" and "Wrigley Field" marks in their advertising. Cubs home games generally are sold out, and all games are televised. These rooftop clubs have business licenses issued by the City of Chicago. All of them have spectator capacities of at least 30 persons, and some charge patrons as much as $150 per game. Consider the likely success of the Cubs' lawsuit alleging that the rooftop clubs' conduct constitutes copyright and trademark infringement, unfair competition, and misappropriation of the club's property. Also consider the Cubs' potential nonlegal remedies and how this dispute might be amicably resolved from the perspective of all parties. See *Detroit Baseball Club v. Deppert*, 27 N.W. 856 (Mich. 1886); Ronnie Bitman, Note, *Rocking Wrigley: The Chicago Cubs' Off-Field Struggle to Compete for Ticket Sales with Its Rooftop Neighbors*, 56 Fed. Comm. L.J. 377 (2004).

b.   MLB Advanced Media, Major League Baseball's Internet subsidiary, claims ownership of all real-time data used by sports websites to provide live graphical simulations of baseball games over the Internet. However, some webcasters operate sites providing very detailed game accounts, including the location of each pitch, that are updated every 30 to 90 seconds. Some webcasters obtain this information from employees who are present at MLB games; whereas others get their data from employees who are watching televised games or listening to radio broadcasts. Only one webcaster has paid for and is licensed to use the real-time data from MLB games, but no others are willing to pay the fee for obtaining licensing rights. Evaluate whether this manner of unauthorized Internet description of a baseball game infringes MLB's intellectual property rights.

D.   ATHLETE'S LANHAM ACT AND STATE LAW PRIVACY, REPUTATION, AND PUBLICITY RIGHTS

Today's professional athlete is a celebrity and probably attains that status, at least locally, much earlier than the onset of his or her professional career. The best-known athletes have entered into lucrative deals to promote and endorse a wide variety of products and services. Income earned from the licensing of a player's identity to sell products and services may be greater than that derived from his or her athletic earnings. For example, the most elite and widely recognized male and female athletes, such as LeBron James, Lionel Messi, and Serena Williams, earn millions annually, far surpassing their income from purely athletic accomplishments. All of them have multiple endorsement deals carefully crafted by their representatives. The evolution of the various laws protecting an athlete's personality rights requires consideration of trademark and unfair competition under the federal Lanham Act, which was previously considered in this chapter, as well as state defamation, privacy, and publicity laws as well.

1.   *Lanham Act*

The unauthorized misappropriation of an athlete's name, likeness, or other aspects of his or her identity violates §43(a) of the Lanham Act, 15 U.S.C. §1125(a), if it causes consumer confusion regarding whether he or she has endorsed or sponsored particular products and services. This federal statutory claim provides a consumer protection-based cause of action, and state trademark and unfair competition laws establish a similar standard. As the Ninth Circuit has observed: "Many people may assume that when a celebrity's name is used in a television commercial, the celebrity endorses the product advertised. Likelihood of confusion as to endorsement is therefore a question for the jury." *Abdul-Jabbar v. General Motors Corp.*, 85 F.3d 407, 413 (9th Cir. 1996).

In *Hillerich & Bradsby v. Christian Brothers*, 943 F. Supp. 1136 (D. Minn. 1996), defendant sold its Pro-Rite hockey blades with the name "Messier" clearly affixed on the blade and product label without the permission of Mark Messier, who led the Edmonton Oilers and the New York Rangers to a total of six Stanley Cup championships and was twice voted the most valuable player in the National Hockey League. The court ruled that this unauthorized commercial use of Messier's name created the false impression that he endorsed defendant's hockey blades in violation of §43(a) and enjoined defendant from using Messier's name on its products or in connection with their advertising and sale without his express permission.

An athlete may use his or her name or other unique identifying characteristics (e.g., former Heisman trophy winner Tim Tebow's practice of "Tebowing," which depicts him in the Christian-athlete practice of dropping to one knee in prayer) as a trademark or service mark, and it may be federally registered under the Lanham Act after acquiring secondary meaning as the source or origin of goods or services (i.e., it functions as a brand name that the public associates with an identifiable athlete). For example, the name "Tiger Woods" has been federally registered as a trademark for art prints, calendars, mounted photographs, notebooks, pencils, pens, posters, trading cards, and unmounted photographs. Unauthorized usage of an athlete's federally registered name that creates a likelihood of consumer confusion regarding the source or sponsorship of goods or services constitutes trademark infringement and unfair competition in violation of the Lanham Act and virtually all state laws.

Courts require that a person's photo, image, likeness, or distinguishing characteristic actually function as a trademark to be protected by the Lanham Act's provisions prohibiting trademark infringement. In *ETW Corp. v. Jireh Publishing, Inc.*, 332 F.3d 915, 922 (6th Cir. 2003), the Sixth Circuit observed:

> Here, ETW claims protection under the Lanham Act for any and all images of Tiger Woods. This is an untenable claim. ETW asks us, in effect, to constitute Woods himself as a walking, talking trademark. Images and likenesses of Woods are not protectable as a trademark because they do not perform the trademark function of designation. They do not distinguish and identify the source of goods. They cannot function as a trademark because there are undoubtedly thousands of images and likenesses of Woods taken by countless photographers, and drawn, sketched, or painted by numerous artists, which have been published in many forms of media, and sold and distributed throughout the world. No reasonable person could believe image, they all originated with Woods.

See also *Pirone v. Macmillan, Inc.*, 894 F.2d 579, 583 (2d Cir. 1990) ("[u]nder some circumstances, a photograph of a person may be a valid trademark—if, for example, a particular photograph was consistently used on specific goods").

2. State Laws

In the United States, various state laws protect the reputation, privacy, and publicity rights of celebrities, including athletes. The First Amendment of the U.S. Constitution, which protects freedom of speech and expression, as well as state constitutional provisions, provides a significant limit on the ability of state law to recognize and protect reputation, privacy, and publicity rights and must always be considered.

a.   Defamation

The tort of defamation includes both oral (slander) and written (libel) statements. The scope of its legal protection is not limited to celebrities, but defamation assumes special significance in this context. Professional athletes are written about regularly in various forms of broadcast, print, and Internet media. Their lives, both professionally and personally, are scrutinized, at times to excruciating degrees, with statements that may harm their personal or professional reputations.

Although there are variations in state law definitions and approaches to defamation, a general definition of defamation is set forth in the Restatement (Second) of Torts, §558 (1977), which provides, "To create liability for defamation, there must be: (a) a false and defamatory statement concerning another; (b) an unprivileged communication to a third party; (c) fault amounting at least to negligence on the part of the publisher; and (d) either actionability of the statement irrespective of special harm or the existence of special harm caused by the publication."

Several observations can be made about this definition regarding the world of sports. Statements must be both false and defamatory, meaning they tend to damage the reputation of the person identified by the statement in the minds of others. Not included in the definition, but generally accepted as a part thereof, is that the false statement (its truth is an absolute defense) must be one of fact, not merely opinion. Most of what is written about the professional performance of athletes is opinion, which is not legally actionable even if it harms his or her reputation. See, e.g., *Time, Inc. v. Johnston*, 448 F.2d 378, 380 (4th Cir. 1971) ("as a paid performer," a professional athlete "assumed the risk of publicity, good or bad, . . . so far as it concerned his public performance"); *Washington v. Smith*, 893 F. Supp. 60 (D.D.C. 1995), *aff'd*, 80 F.3d 555 (D.C. Cir. 1996) (a statement in a newspaper article that a coach "usually finds a way to screw things up" and "[t]his season will be no different" is a nonactionable opinion regarding the team's potential for an upcoming season and the coach's ability).

On the other hand, asserting that an athlete "fixed" a boxing match and used cocaine with his opponent thereafter, or knowingly used "loaded" gloves are statements of fact that harm one's professional reputation and may cause resulting economic loss. *Cobb v. Time, Inc.*, 278 F.3d 629 (6th Cir. 2002); *Dempsey v. Time Inc.*, 252 N.Y.S.2d 186 (N.Y. Sup. Ct. 1964). See also *Faigin v. Kelly*, 978 F. Supp. 420 (D.N.H. 1997), *aff'd*, 184 F.3d 67 (1st Cir. 1999) (a pro football player's charge that a former agent engaged in untrustworthy conduct in handling his business affairs). False factual statements about an athlete's personal life such as alleged criminal conduct also are defamatory.

Since *New York Times v. Sullivan*, 376 U.S. 254 (1964), the traditional state law elements of defamation effectively have been modified by federal constitutional law; therefore, First Amendment issues must also be considered. In addition to state law elements of defamation, a prominent athlete is considered to be a "public figure" who must prove by clear and convincing evidence that a defamatory statement was made with "actual malice," meaning the defendant had knowledge of its falsity or a reckless disregard regarding whether or not it was true. See, e.g., *Cobb v. Time, Inc.*, 278 F.3d 629 (6th Cir. 2002); *Cepeda v. Cowles Magazines and Broadcasting*, 392 F.2d 417 (9th Cir. 1968).

b.   Right of Privacy

The right of privacy, as a distinct concept of legal protection, was first enunciated in a famous law review article by Samuel Warren and Louis Brandeis that was published in the *Harvard Law Review* in 1890. Warren and Brandeis argued that a separate tort protecting a person's right to privacy existed at common law and should be recognized:

> Later, there came a recognition of man's spiritual nature, of his feelings and his intellect. Gradually, the scope of these legal rights broadened; and now the right to life has come to mean the right to enjoy life, the right to be let alone; the right to liberty secures the exercise of extensive civil privileges; and the term "property" has grown to comprise every form of possession—intangible, as well as tangible.

Samuel D. Warren and Louis D. Brandeis, *The Right to Privacy*, 4 Harv. L. Rev. 193, 193 (1890).

A further impetus to the development of the right of privacy occurred many years later through the scholarship of Professor William Prosser. He identified four separate categories that he advocated should be subsumed under a general concept of privacy: (1) protection against intrusion into one's private affairs; (2) avoidance of disclosure of one's embarrassing private facts; (3) protection against publicity placing one in a false light in the public eye; and (4) remedies for appropriation, usually for commercial advantage, of one's name or likeness. William Prosser, *Privacy*, 48 Cal. L. Rev. 383 (1960). These four categories of torts have been adopted in most states, though there is no unanimity as to the nature and scope of their common law development by courts. In some states, statutes have codified these torts.

The first three torts concern intrusions into one's private life and affairs, and athletes have relied on one or more of these legal theories in asserting various invasion of privacy claims. See, e.g., *Spahn v. Julian Messner, Inc.*, 286 N.Y.S.2d 832 (N.Y. 1967) (publication of unauthorized fictionalized biography of well-known baseball player violates statutory privacy law); *Terry Gene Bollea v. Gawker Media LLC* (Fla. Cir. Ct. 2016) (jury verdict for former professional wrestler Hulk Hogan against the website Gawker Media for publishing an unauthorized videotape of him having sex; subsequently settled for $31 million plus part of the proceeds from website's bankruptcy sale); *Erin Andrews v. Marriott International Inc.* (Tenn. Cir. Ct. 2016) (Nashville jury awards sports broadcaster Erin Andrews $55 million in damages arising out of a 2008 peeping Tom incident and posting of a video of her naked on the internet); *Jason Pierre-Paul v. ESPN Inc.* 2016 WL 4530884 at *1 (S.D. Fla. Aug. 29, 2016) (refusing to dismiss NFL player's invasion of privacy claim because improperly obtained medical records concerning amputation of his right index finger after hand injury in a fireworks accident are "not publicly available" and "generally considered private").

The fourth privacy tort is readily distinguishable from the others because of its recognition of the commercial value in one's name or likeness. Today, it is the basis for a separate tort known as the "right of publicity," which is recognized in a majority of states by common law or statute.

c.   Right of Publicity

Courts initially refused to characterize celebrity names and likenesses as protectable property rights. In *Hanna Mfg. Co. v. Hillerich & Bradsby Co.*, 78 F.2d 763, 766 (5th Cir. 1935), the Fifth Circuit held that "fame is not merchandise." It concluded that an athlete has a valid claim for unauthorized commercial use of his name only if such usage falsely suggests that he uses or endorses the product, thereby constituting unfair competition.

In 1953, a U.S. court recognized the right of publicity for the first time. *Haelan Laboratories, Inc. v. Topps Chewing Gum, Inc.*, 202 F.2d 866 (2d Cir. 1953), *cert. denied*, 346 U.S. 816 (1953). The case involved a dispute over the rights to use baseball players' images on bubblegum trading cards. One company had been assigned these rights by the players; however, the defendant produced its own cards without the players' permission. One of the central issues was whether the players' rights, if any, were assignable — or if they were strictly personal to the player. The Second Circuit held that New York law recognized a common law right of publicity, which is a freely transferable property right, not just a personal right. The court explained "in addition to and independent of the right of privacy . . . a man has a right in the publicity value of his photograph, i.e., the right to grant the exclusive privilege of publishing his picture." *Id.* at 868. See generally J. Gordon Hylton, *Baseball Cards and the Birth of the Right of Publicity: The Curious Case of* Haelan Laboratories v. Topps Chewing Gum, 12 Marq. Sports L. Rev. 273 (2001).

The common law development of the right of publicity since *Haelan Laboratories* has not been uniform nationwide. In many states, the right of publicity has been created and defined by statute. By common law or statute, a majority of states (but not all) now recognize a right of publicity claim for unauthorized commercial use of an athlete's identity. See generally 1 J. Thomas McCarthy, *Rights of Publicity and Privacy* (2d ed.), §§6:2-6:6 (Westlaw 2019). In some jurisdictions, a common law right of publicity may have been recognized initially by a federal court in an effort to predict the nature and scope of its protection by its state courts. These federal cases may be subject to effective reversal by state courts as happened when the New York Court of Appeals (the state's highest court) rejected *Haelan*'s creation of a common law right of publicity under New York law. Today, New York recognizes only a statutory right of publicity.

As one court observed, "a celebrity has a legitimate proprietary interest in his public personality. A celebrity must be considered to have invested his years of practice and competition in a public personality which eventually may reach marketable status. . . . A name is commercially valuable as an endorsement of a product or for use for financial gain only because the public recognizes it and attributes good will and feats of skill or accomplishments of one sort or another to that personality." *Uhlaender v. Henricksen*, 316 F. Supp. 1277, 1282-1283 (D. Minn. 1970). Is this a convincing rationale for recognizing this legal right?

A well-known sports journalist has observed:

> As sports passed from Jackie Robinson to Curt Flood to free agency, athletes were branded less by team than by their own personhood. They had become, in the parlance of marketers and agencies, their own brands. Social media — Twitter in particular — allowed them to bypass magazines and television entirely and speak directly to their "followers," while "monetizing" their various "platforms."

Steve Rushin, *There and Back*, Sports Illustrated, August 11, 2014, http://www .si.com/vault/2014/08/11/106623799/there-and-back.

In some states, the right of publicity is a property right that may be transferred and is descendible. By contrast, defamation and privacy rights generally are personal in nature, cannot be assigned, and expire when the person dies.

i. Elements of a Right of Publicity Claim

NEWCOMBE v. ADOLF COORS CO.

157 F.3d 686 (9th Cir. 1998)

HUG, Chief Judge.

[Don] Newcombe is a former major league baseball all-star who pitched for the Brooklyn Dodgers and other teams from 1949 until 1960. He had previously starred in the so-called Negro leagues and was one of the first African-American players to play in the major leagues after Jackie Robinson broke the color barrier in 1947. Newcombe is the only player in major league history to have won the Most Valuable Player Award, the Cy Young Award, and the Rookie of the Year Award. . . .

Newcombe's baseball career was cut short due to his service in the Army and a personal battle with alcohol. He is a recovering alcoholic and he has devoted a substantial amount of time using his fame to advocate the dangers of alcohol. . . .

Killian's Irish Red Beer, owned by Coors Brewing Co., published an advertisement in the February 1994 *Sports Illustrated* "swimsuit edition" that featured a drawing of an old-time baseball game. The drawing was on the left half of the full-page advertisement while the right half was filled with text and a picture of a glass of beer. The baseball scene focused on a pitcher in the windup position and the background included a single infielder and an old-fashioned outfield fence. The players' uniforms did not depict an actual team, and the background did not depict an actual stadium. However, Newcombe, along with family, friends and former teammates, immediately recognized the pitcher featured in the advertisement as Newcombe in his playing days.

Newcombe filed suit . . . alleging [, *inter alia*,] that his identity had been misappropriated in violation of California statutory and common law, that the advertisement was defamatory because it portrayed him—a recovering alcoholic—as endorsing beer. He sought to enjoin the advertisement from future publication, and he asked for $100,000,000 in damages. . . .

While denying that the pitcher in the advertisement was a "likeness" of Newcombe, Coors admitted that the drawing in the color advertisement was based on a newspaper photograph of Newcombe pitching in the 1949 World Series. The drawing and the newspaper photograph are virtually identical, as though the black and white newspaper photo had been traced and colored in. The only major differences between the newspaper photograph of Newcombe and the drawing of him are that the pitcher's uniform number has been changed from "36" to "39," and the bill of the hat in the drawing is a different color from the rest of the hat. Otherwise, the drawing in the advertisement appears to be an exact replica of the newspaper photograph of Newcombe. . . .

CAL. CIV. CODE § 3344 AND COMMON LAW MISAPPROPRIATION

Newcombe contends that the defendants violated his right of privacy and used his likeness and identity to their commercial advantage in violation of his statutory rights under Cal. Civ. Code § 3344 and common law right of privacy. California has long recognized a common law right of privacy for the protection of a person's name and likeness against appropriation by others for their advantage. *Eastwood v. Superior Court of Los Angeles County*, 149 Cal. App. 3d 409, 416, 198 Cal. Rptr. 342 (1983). This California common law cause of action has been complemented by the enactment of Cal. Civ. Code § 3344. That section neither replaces nor codifies the common law cause of action. Section 3344(g) specifically provides that the statutory remedies of the section are cumulative and in addition to any others provided by law.

To sustain a common law cause of action for commercial misappropriation, a plaintiff must prove: "(1) the defendant's use of the plaintiff's identity; (2) the appropriation of plaintiff's name or likeness to defendant's advantage, commercially or otherwise; (3) lack of consent; and (4) resulting injury." *Eastwood*, 149 Cal. App. 3d at 417, 198 Cal. Rptr. 342.

Cal. Civ. Code § 3344 provides in relevant part, "Any person who knowingly uses another's name, voice, signature, photograph, or likeness, in any manner . . . for purposes of advertising . . . without such person's prior consent . . . shall be liable for any damages sustained by the person." Cal. Civ. Code § 3344(a). Section 3344, unlike a common law claim, thus requires a plaintiff to establish: (1) a "knowing" use; (2) for purposes of advertising, and (3) a direct connection between the use and the commercial purpose.

[W]e must first decide whether Newcombe's likeness was actually used. Necessarily, we must address how identifiable an image must be to constitute a likeness under the common law and section 3344. Neither the common law nor section 3344 indicate to whom or to what degree the plaintiff must be identifiable from the alleged likeness.

We find a useful definition in section 3344 itself. Section 3344(b) states that a photograph must be "readily identifiable" as the plaintiff in order for the plaintiff to prevail. A person is deemed to be readily identifiable from a photograph "when one who views the photograph with the naked eye can reasonably determine that the person depicted in the photograph is the same person who is complaining of its unauthorized use." Cal. Civ. Code § 3344(b)(1). Because a likeness and a photograph are so similar—a photograph is a visual image that is obtained by using a camera while a likeness is a visual image of a person other than a photograph—we find application of this standard appropriate to likenesses as well as photographs. Therefore, we hold that in order to constitute Newcombe's likeness, the pitcher depicted in the advertisement must be readily identifiable as Newcombe.

Having viewed the advertisement, we hold that a triable issue of fact has been raised as to whether Newcombe is readily identifiable as the pitcher in the advertisement. Initially, we note that the drawing in the advertisement and the newspaper photograph of Newcombe upon which the drawing was based are virtually identical. The pitcher's stance, proportions and shape are identical to the newspaper photograph of Newcombe; even the styling of the uniform is identical, right down to the wrinkles in the pants. The defendants maintain that stance alone cannot suffice to render a person readily identifiable, and that even if it could, the drawing of the pitcher in the advertisement was essentially generic and could have been any one of thousands of people who have taken to the pitcher's mound to throw a baseball. We disagree.

It may be the case that Newcombe's stance is essentially generic, but based on the record before us, Newcombe is the only one who has such a stance. The record contains pictures of other pitchers in the windup position but none of these pitchers has a stance similar to Newcombe's, thus giving us no basis to reach the conclusion proposed by the defendants that the pitcher in the advertisement is "generic." . . . [T]here is a genuine issue of material fact as to whether Newcombe's stance was so distinctive that the defendants used his likeness by using a picture of Newcombe's stance.

In addition to the identifiability of the pitcher in the advertisement as Newcombe based on the pitcher's stance, the pitcher's skin is moderately dark, which is quite similar to Newcombe's skin color. A jury could rationally find from this that Newcombe was readily identifiable, even though his facial features were not entirely visible.

Furthermore, while the drawing in the advertisement was slightly altered from the newspaper photograph, that does not alter our conclusion that there is a genuine issue of material fact as to whether the advertisement made use of Newcombe's likeness. For example, the uniform number in the advertisement ("39") is only slightly different than Newcombe's number ("36")—the first number is the same and the second number is simply inverted and the advertisement utilized the same block style numbers that were used on Newcombe's jersey—and it is arguable that the similarity in numbers could either consciously or subconsciously conjure up images of Newcombe. *See Motschenbacher v. R.J. Reynolds Tobacco Co.*, 498 F.2d 821, 822 & 827 (9th Cir. 1974) (plaintiff's identity had been used despite fact that number on the plaintiff's car had also been changed from "11" to "71"). Also, we do not find persuasive the fact that the coloring of the bill of the hat in the advertisement is different, in light of the fact that the rest of the uniform is identical to the uniform in the newspaper photograph of Newcombe. *See id.* (plaintiff's identity had been used even though exterior of the car had been altered). . . .

As to the remaining factors for a common law misappropriation claim, the second prong of the *Eastwood* test has been met in that Newcombe's likeness was certainly used to Coors' and Belding's commercial advantage as the drawing which resembled Newcombe was a central figure in the advertisement and the purpose of the advertisement was to attract attention. *See Eastwood*, 149 Cal. App. 3d at 420, 198 Cal. Rptr. 342 ("one of the primary purposes of advertising is to motivate a decision to purchase a particular product or service. The first step toward selling a product or service is to attract the consumers' attention"). . . .

The third and fourth prongs of the *Eastwood* test were satisfied with respect to Coors . . . because Newcombe did not consent to the use of his likeness, and he was injured because he was not compensated for the use of his likeness. As a result, we hold that summary judgment was improper as to Coors and Belding on Newcombe's common law misappropriation claim.

With regard to Newcombe's statutory claim, the district court alternatively held that summary judgment was appropriate because Newcombe had failed to establish a direct connection between the use of his likeness and defendants' commercial purpose. Section 3344(e) states that not all uses of likeness are a "use" that requires consent; only those uses where the "likeness was so directly connected with the commercial sponsorship" constitute a "use" under § 3344(a). However, whether such a connection is present "shall be a question of fact." Cal. Civ. Code § 3344(e). Despite the express command that the connection between defendants' use of Newcombe's likeness and the commercial sponsorship of Killian's Red Beer is a matter of fact, the district court concluded that summary judgment in favor of defendants was appropriate as "it is beyond dispute that defendants were not trying to use plaintiff's identity to sell beer." We disagree. It would not be unreasonable for a jury to conclude that there was a direct connection between Newcombe, as the central feature of the advertisement, and the commercial sponsorship of Killian's Red. . . .

[EDS. The Ninth Circuit reversed the trial court's grant of summary judgment in favor of defendant Coors and the advertisement's creator on Newcombe's common law and statutory right of publicity claims. However, it affirmed the granting of summary judgment on his defamation and false light claims. Consider why the court likely did so, and if its ruling is correct.]

NOTES AND QUESTIONS

1. *Which State's Law Applies?* In our modern technological age, a right of publicity claim may potentially exist in many jurisdictions. An advertisement that inappropriately uses the likeness of an athlete may be published nationwide, not just in one state. Conflict of laws principles generally provide that the state law of the plaintiff's domicile governs.

2. *Scope of Protectable Publicity Rights.* As illustrated by *Newcombe*, California recognizes both a common law and statutory right of publicity, but each has differing elements. How do they differ? What aspects of Don Newcombe's identity were used in the subject advertisement, and how would you prove he is readily identifiable as the pitcher in the advertisement? Courts have broadly defined the protected aspects of an athlete's identity to encompass more than merely his or her name or photo. See, e.g., *Abdul-Jabbar v. Gen. Motors Corp.*, 85 F.3d 407 (9th Cir. 1996) (birth name of Lew Alcindor not abandoned as indicia of identity despite name change to Kareem Abdul-Jabbar after conversion to Islam); *Ventura v. Titan Sports, Inc.*, 65 F.3d 725 (8th Cir. 1995) (athlete's distinctive voice); *Ali v. Playgirl, Inc.*, 447 F. Supp. 723 (S.D.N.Y. 1978) (facial features and moniker "The Greatest"); *Hirsch v. S.C. Johnson & Son, Inc.*, 280 N.W.2d 129 (Wis. 1979) ("Crazy Legs" nickname). A state statutory or common law right of publicity also may protect an athletic performance. *Zacchini v. Scripps-Howard Broadcasting Co.*, 433 U.S. 562 (1977).

3. *Unauthorized Commercial Use of an Athlete's Identity or for Purposes of Advertising or Trade.* *Newcombe* demonstrates that infringement of an athlete's right of publicity occurs if an aspect of one's identity is used to advertise and sell a product or service without permission. Examples of infringing commercial usage include incorporating an athlete's photo into a product such as sports trading cards, drinking glasses, or clothing. *Haelan Labs., Inc. v. Topps Chewing Gum*, 202 F.2d 866 (2d Cir. 1953); *Vinci v. American Can Co.*, 459 N.E.2d 507 (Ohio 1984); *Shamsky v. Garan, Inc.*, 632 N.Y.S.2d 930 (N.Y. Sup. Ct. 1995).

Courts generally refuse to characterize the use of a famous athlete's name or identity in connection with the sale of a product as legally permissible incidental or informational use. Rather, such usage is unauthorized commercial appropriation of the athlete's persona. In *Abdul-Jabbar v. Gen. Motors*

Corp., 85 F.3d 407 (9th Cir. 1996), the Ninth Circuit held that, although such information is newsworthy, an auto manufacturer's use of Lew Alcindor's name and college basketball records in a television advertisement is commercial usage. The auto manufacturer gained a commercial advantage from the advertisement, which attracted the attention of television viewers of the 1993 NCAA men's basketball tournament. See also *Town & Country Properties, Inc. v. Riggins*, 457 S.E.2d 356 (Va. 1995) (use of former NFL player's name in flyer to sell his former home violates his publicity rights). But see *Jordan v. Jewel Food Stores, Inc.*, 83 F. Supp. 3d 761, 767 (N.D. Ill. 2015) (Jewel-Osco grocery store ad in magazine's commemorative issue congratulating former Chicago Bulls player Michael Jordan on his induction into pro basketball hall of fame does not necessarily satisfy the "commercial purpose" element of the Illinois Right of Publicity Act as a matter of law, which defines it as "the public use or holding out of an individual's identity (i) on or in connection with the offering for sale or sale of a product, merchandise, goods, or services; (ii) for purposes of advertising or promoting products, merchandise, goods, or services; or (iii) for the purpose of fundraising").

Unauthorized use of a person's identity is a necessary element of a claim for infringement of publicity rights. An athlete's consent to the use of his or her identity for commercial purposes may be either express or implied under the circumstances. The scope of such consent is necessarily determined on a case-by-case basis and requires careful contract drafting to delineate which rights are conferred or licensed either exclusively or non-exclusively. See, e.g., *Cepeda v. Swift & Co.*, 415 F.2d 1205 (8th Cir. 1969); *O'Brien v. Pabst Sales Co.*, 124 F.2d 167 (5th Cir. 1941); *Sharman v. C. Schmidt & Sons, Inc.*, 216 F. Supp. 401 (E.D. Pa. 1963); *Andretti v. Rolex Watch U.S.A., Inc.*, 437 N.E.2d 264 (N.Y. 1982).

4. *"First-Sale Doctrine."* Courts have applied the "first-sale doctrine" to the right of publicity. The doctrine enables the purchaser of authorized sports trading cards or other products bearing an athlete's likeness to resell them or incorporate them into other sports memorabilia, such as framed displays. *Allison v. Vintage Sports Plaques*, 136 F.3d 1443 (11th Cir. 1998); *Upper Deck Authenticated, Ltd. v. CPG Direct*, 971 F. Supp. 1337 (S.D. Cal. 1997); *Major League Baseball Players Assn. v. Dad's Kid Corp.*, 806 F. Supp. 458 (S.D.N.Y. 1992).

5. *Remedies for Infringement.* As requested in *Newcombe*, available remedies for violation of one's publicity rights are damages and injunctive relief. See generally Laura L. Stapleton and Matt McMurphy, *The Professional Athlete's Right of Publicity*, 10 Marq. Sports L. Rev. 23, 53-62 (1999). In 2015, a Chicago jury awarded Michael Jordan $8.9 million in damages for violation of his right of publicity by Dominick's, a Chicago grocery store chain that included a coupon for discounts on steaks in its congratulatory ad in a Sports Illustrated commemorative issue recognizing his induction into the pro basketball hall of fame. In 2016, current and former Division I college football and former men's basketball players began receiving checks ranging from less than $100 to $9300 from a $60 million fund settling their right of publicity litigation against Electronic Arts, Inc. and the NCAA arising out of the unauthorized use of their images in college video games, which is discussed *infra*.

6. *Governing Body Rules to Maintain College and High School Athletes' "Amateur" Status.* Although college and high school athletes may have legally protectable publicity rights in the respective states in which they are domiciled,

the NCAA and state high school athletics governing bodies have rules prohibiting their commercial exploitation to maintain their amateur eligibility to participate in intercollegiate or interscholastic sports competition. See generally Sean Hanlon and Ray Yasser, *"J.J. Morrison" and His Right of Publicity Lawsuit Against the NCAA*, 15 Vill. Sports & Ent. L.J. 241 (2008). For example, to retain his eligibility to play football for the University of Colorado, the NCAA prohibited U.S. Olympic moguls skier Jeremy Bloom from earning future endorsement and modeling contract income needed to finance his training. See *Bloom v. NCAA*, 93 P.3d 621 (Colo. App. 2004) (upholding NCAA bylaws prohibiting student-athletes from being paid for advertisements and product endorsements). In 2003, the Ohio High School Athletic Association (OHSAA) declared LeBron James ineligible to continue playing high school basketball for violating its rule prohibiting "capitalizing on athletic fame by receiving money or gifts of monetary value." James had accepted two "throwback" jerseys worth a combined $845 from an Akron sporting goods store for posing for photos to be displayed on its walls. Although an Ohio trial court ultimately enjoined the OHSAA from enforcing its rule, James was required to serve a two-game suspension for his conduct.

ii.   First Amendment Limitations

The First Amendment of the U.S. Constitution limits the permissible scope of protection of publicity rights under state law. In *Titan Sports, Inc. v. Comics World Corp.*, 870 F.2d 85, 88 (2d Cir. 1989), the Second Circuit noted the "inherent tension between the protection of an individual's right to control the use of his likeness and the constitutional guarantee of free dissemination of ideas, images, and newsworthy matter in whatever form it takes." Lower courts have struggled to draw the line between unauthorized commercial use of one's identity that may be prohibited by state law and communicative or expressive use protected by the First Amendment, which has not been clearly defined by the U.S. Supreme Court.

In *Zacchini v. Scripps-Howard Broadcasting, Inc.*, 433 U.S. 562 (1977), the Supreme Court held that the media's right to report newsworthy events does not permit the unauthorized broadcast of a performer's entire act, which threatens harm to its economic value. A local Ohio television station sent a news crew to film the act of Hugo Zacchini, the "human cannonball," who was performing at a county fair. This was done despite Zacchini's request that his performance not be filmed. His entire 15-second performance was shown on the evening news. In a 5-4 decision, the Court ruled that showing his entire act is not permitted by the First Amendment's protection of news reporting. Under the majority's view, the television station's broadcast is not protected by the United States Constitution, because it substantially reduced the commercial value of Zacchini's entertainment product and corresponding economic incentive to produce his performance. However, the dissenting justices concluded that the First Amendment broadly protects the media from a right of publicity or commercial appropriation claim "absent a strong showing . . . that the news broadcast was a subterfuge or cover for private or commercial exploitation." *Id.* at 581.

The *Zacchini* case is notable, not for the clarity of its line-drawing, but for its clear demonstration that such line-drawing regarding the scope of First

Amendment protections is one that is often difficult and likely to be criticized, whatever the result reached. When the usage of an athlete's identity moves from the purely commercial, as is most likely the case in the advertising or sale of a product or service, to more of a mixed medium—such as films, television, radio, newspapers and other literary works as well as artistic expression—the more likely that First Amendment issues will arise.

The First Amendment broadly immunizes the media from state law liability for infringement of publicity rights, even though media publications and broadcasts usually are for-profit commercial activity. The media may use a celebrity's name, photograph, and other aspects of his or her identity in connection with truthful news reporting. Courts have broadly extended constitutional protection to media republications of news coverage of sporting events and athletic accomplishments even if used for advertising purposes. For example, in *Montana v. San Jose Mercury News, Inc.*, 34 Cal. App. 4th 790 (Cal. Ct. App. 1995), the court held that a newspaper may contemporaneously reproduce a full-page account of the San Francisco Forty-Niners four Super Bowl victories in the 1990s in poster form for public sale without violating the publicity rights of Joe Montana, the team's quarterback. Even though his name and likeness appeared on the posters, they were depictions of newsworthy events in which Montana had played a prominent role. See also *Namath v. Sports Illustrated*, 371 N.Y.S.2d 10 (App. Div. 1975), *aff'd*, 352 N.E.2d 584 (N.Y. 1976) (dismissing athlete's right of publicity claim against magazine for using his photograph in advertisements to promote subscriptions).

On the other hand, the use of news coverage of an athletic event incorporating an athlete's name or likeness to advertise or sell unrelated products is not constitutionally protected. In *Pooley v. National Hole-in-One Association*, 89 F. Supp. 1108 (D. Ariz. 2000), the defendant made a videotape of a professional golfer's hole-in-one and used his name to promote its hole-in-one fundraising competitions. Denying defendant's motion to dismiss plaintiff's right of publicity claim, the court ruled:

> [W]hile Plaintiff's hole-in-one at the Bay Hill Classic was open to national observation and public videotaping, its *subsequent* unauthorized reproduction was not automatically privileged simply because the hole-in-one continued to be a "newsworthy" event. Defendant did not create the videotape in connection with a news account. Defendant did not include Plaintiff's name and videotape footage simply to communicate an idea. It capitalized on Plaintiff's name, reputation, and prestige in the context of an advertisement. The promotional videotape went one step further and implied a false connection between the Plaintiff and its business. The Court finds that the use of Plaintiff's identity was strictly commercial and not protected by the First Amendment.

Id. at 1114 (emphasis original).

The First Amendment has been judicially construed to permit the limited usage of historical accounts of player records and accomplishments as well as video depictions of their athletic performances. In *Gionfriddo v. Major League Baseball*, 94 Cal. App. 4th 400 (Cal. Ct. App. 2001), a group of retired professional baseball players claimed the unauthorized use of their names and likenesses in for-profit print and video publications providing historical information about MLB players violated their right of publicity. The court found that "[t]he public has an enduring fascination in the records set by former players and in memorable moments from previous games, . . . [which] are the standards by which the public measures the performance of today's players." *Id.* at 415. Affirming summary judgment for defendants, it concluded: "Balancing plaintiffs' negligible economic interests against the public's enduring fascination with baseball's past, we conclude that the public interest favoring the free dissemination of information regarding baseball's history far outweighs any proprietary interests at stake." *Id.*

Similarly, in *C.B.C. Distribution and Marketing, Inc. v. Major League Baseball Advanced Media*, 505 F.3d 818 (8th Cir. 2007), the Eighth Circuit ruled that the unauthorized use of MLB players' names and statistics in online fantasy baseball games is protected by the First Amendment. The court explained that "the information used in CBC's fantasy baseball games is all readily available in the public domain, and it would be strange law that a person would not have a first amendment right to use information that is available to everyone." The court found the *Gionfriddo* court's views "persuasive[,]" stating that "recitation and discussion of factual data concerning the athletic performance of [players on MLB's website] command a substantial public interest, and, therefore, is a form of public expression due substantial constitutional protection." *Id.* at 823-24. Courts generally have followed *C.B.C. Distribution.* See, e.g., *CBS Interactive Inc. v. National Football League Players Assn., Inc.*, 259 F.R.D. 398 (D. Minn. 2009) (fantasy football game's unauthorized use of NFL players' names, player profiles, up-to-date statistics, injury reports, participant blogs, pictures, images, and biographical information does not violate their publicity rights); *Daniels v. FanDuel, Inc.*, 109 N.E.3d 390, 396-397 (Ind. 2018) (unauthorized commercial use of former college football players' names and likenesses in online fantasy sports contests, which "bears resemblance to the publication of the same information in newspapers and websites," is within Indiana right of publicity statute's "newsworthiness" or "public interest" exceptions, while observing "it would be difficult to draw the conclusion that the athletes are endorsing any particular product such that there has been a violation of the right of publicity").

In *Cardtoons, L.C. v. Major League Baseball Players Assn.*, 95 F.3d 959 (10th Cir. 1996), the Tenth Circuit recognized a parody defense based on the First Amendment to a right of publicity claim. Cardtoons produced a series of baseball cards that lampooned MLB players and allowed identification of the individual players. The court explained:

> Cardtoons' parody trading cards receive full protection under the First Amendment. The cards provide social commentary on public figures, major league baseball players, who are involved in a significant commercial enterprise, major league baseball. While not core political speech (the cards do not, for example, adopt a position on the Ken Griffey, Jr., for President campaign), this type of commentary on an important social institution constitutes protected expression.

Id. at 969.

In *ETW v. Jireh Publishing, Inc.*, 332 F.3d 915 (6th Cir. 2003), the Sixth Circuit held that the First Amendment protects a sports artist's freedom of expression to include the likenesses of famous professional athletes (e.g., Tiger Woods and other legendary professional golfers) in a painting commemorating Woods's historic victory in the 1997 Masters Tournament, reprints of which were sold to the public. The court explained that the First Amendment protects expressive materials "including music, pictures, films, photographs, paintings, drawings, engravings, prints, and sculptures," which is not limited even if it is sold.

Observing that famous athletes, "through their pervasive presence in the media . . . have come to symbolize certain ideas and values in our society and have become a valuable means of expression in our culture," the court concluded: "While the right of publicity allows celebrities like Woods to enjoy the fruits of their labors, here Rush [the sports artist] has added a significant creative component of his own to Woods's identity. Permitting Woods's right of publicity to trump Rush's right of freedom of expression would extinguish Rush's right to profit from his creative enterprise." *Id.* at 938. But see *Doe a/k/a Tony Twist v. TCI Cablevision*, 110 S.W.3d 363, 374 (Mo. 2003), *cert. denied*, 540 U.S. 1106 (2004) (unauthorized metaphorical reference to Tony Twist, an ex-NHL player known as an on-ice "enforcer," in a comic book with a fictional Mafia don with a long list of evil deeds "has very little literary value compared to its commercial value" and "free speech must give way to the right of publicity").

As you read the following case, consider whether courts are applying a consistent legal principle that appropriately balances an athlete's economic interest in preventing unauthorized use of his identity for commercial purposes with the First Amendment's protection of freedom of expression.

IN RE NCAA STUDENT-ATHLETE NAME & LIKENESS LITIGATION
724 F.3d 1268 (9th Cir. 2013), *cert. denied*, 135 S. Ct. 42 (2014)

BYBEE, Circuit Judge:

Video games are entitled to the full protections of the First Amendment, because "[l]ike the protected books, plays, and movies that preceded them, video games communicate ideas—and even social messages—through many familiar literary devices (such as characters, dialogue, plot, and music) and through features distinctive to the medium (such as the player's interaction with the virtual world)." *Brown v. Entm't Merchs. Ass'n*, ___ U.S. ___, 131 S. Ct. 2729, 2733, 180 L. Ed. 2d 708 (2011). Such rights are not absolute, and states may recognize the right of publicity to a degree consistent with the First Amendment. *Zacchini v. Scripps-Howard Broad. Co.*, 433 U.S. 562, 574-75, 97 S. Ct. 2849, 53 L. Ed. 2d 965 (1977). In this case, we must balance the right of publicity of a former college football player against the asserted First Amendment right of a video game developer to use his likeness in its expressive works.

The district court concluded that the game developer, Electronic Arts ("EA"), had no First Amendment defense against the right-of-publicity claims of the football player, Samuel Keller. We affirm. Under the "transformative use" test developed by the California Supreme Court, EA's use does not qualify for First Amendment protection as a matter of law because it literally recreates Keller in the very setting in which he has achieved renown. The other First Amendment defenses asserted by EA do not defeat Keller's claims either.

I

Samuel Keller was the starting quarterback for Arizona State University in 2005 before he transferred to the University of Nebraska, where he played during the 2007 season. EA is the producer of the *NCAA Football* series of video games, which allow users to control avatars representing college football players as those avatars participate in simulated games. In *NCAA Football,* EA seeks to replicate each school's entire team as accurately as possible. Every real football player on each team included in the game has a corresponding avatar in the game with the player's actual jersey number and virtually identical height, weight, build, skin tone, hair color, and home state. EA attempts to match any unique, highly identifiable playing behaviors by sending detailed questionnaires to team equipment managers. Additionally, EA creates realistic virtual versions of actual stadiums; populates them with the virtual athletes, coaches, cheerleaders, and fans realistically rendered by EA's graphic artists; and incorporates realistic sounds such as the crunch of the players' pads and the roar of the crowd.

EA's game differs from reality in that EA omits the players' names on their jerseys and assigns each player a home town that is different from the actual player's home town. However, users of the video game may upload rosters of names obtained from third parties so that the names do appear on the jerseys. In such cases, EA allows images from the game containing athletes' real names to be posted on its website by users. . . .

In the 2005 edition of the game, the virtual starting quarterback for Arizona State wears number 9, as did Keller, and has the same height, weight, skin tone, hair color, hair style, handedness, home state, play style (pocket passer), visor preference, facial features, and school year as Keller. In the 2008 edition, the virtual quarterback for Nebraska has these same characteristics, though the jersey number does not match, presumably because Keller changed his number right before the season started.

Objecting to this use of his likeness, Keller [and nine other former NCAA football or men's basketball players, including Ed O'Bannon] filed a putative class-action complaint in the Northern District of California asserting, as relevant on appeal, that EA violated his right of publicity under California Civil Code § 3344 and California common law. . . .

A

The California Supreme Court formulated the transformative use defense in *Comedy III Productions, Inc. v. Gary Saderup, Inc.,* 25 Cal. 4th 387, 106 Cal. Rptr. 2d 126, 21 P.3d 797 (2001). The defense is "a balancing test between the First Amendment and the right of publicity based on whether the work in question adds significant creative elements so as to be transformed into something more than a mere celebrity likeness or imitation." The California Supreme Court explained that "when a work contains significant transformative elements, it is not only especially worthy of First Amendment protection, but it is also less likely to interfere with the economic interest protected by the right of publicity." The court rejected the wholesale importation of the copyright "fair use" defense into right-of-publicity claims, but recognized that some aspects of that defense are "particularly pertinent." . . .

Comedy III gives us at least five factors to consider in determining whether a work is sufficiently transformative to obtain First Amendment protection. *See* J. Thomas McCarthy, *The Rights of Publicity and Privacy* § 8:72 (2d ed. 2012). First, if "the celebrity likeness is one of the 'raw materials' from which an original work is synthesized," it is more likely to be transformative than if "the depiction or imitation of the celebrity is the very sum and substance of the work in question." Second, the work is protected if it is "primarily the defendant's own expression"—as long as that expression is "something other than the likeness of the celebrity." *Id.* This factor requires an examination of whether a likely purchaser's primary motivation is to buy a reproduction of the celebrity, or to buy the expressive work of that artist. Third, to avoid making judgments concerning "the quality of the artistic contribution," a court should conduct an inquiry "more quantitative than qualitative" and ask "whether the literal and imitative or the creative elements predominate in the work." Fourth, the California Supreme Court indicated that "a subsidiary inquiry" would be useful in close cases: whether "the marketability and economic value of the challenged work derive primarily from the fame of the celebrity depicted." Lastly, the court indicated that "when an artist's skill and talent is manifestly subordinated to the overall goal of creating a conventional portrait of a celebrity so as to commercially exploit his or her fame," the work is not transformative. . . .

California courts have applied the transformative use test in relevant situations in four cases. First, in *Comedy III* itself, the California Supreme Court applied the test to T-shirts and lithographs bearing a likeness of The Three Stooges and concluded that it could "discern no significant transformative or creative contribution." The court reasoned that the artist's "undeniable skill is manifestly subordinated to the overall goal of creating literal, conventional depictions of The Three Stooges so as to exploit their fame." *Id.* "[W]ere we to decide that [the artist's] depictions were protected by the First Amendment," the court continued, "we cannot perceive how the right of publicity would remain a viable right other than in cases of falsified celebrity endorsements."

Second, in *Winter v. DC Comics,* the California Supreme Court applied the test to comic books containing characters Johnny and Edgar Autumn, "depicted as villainous half-worm, half-human offspring" but evoking two famous brothers, rockers Johnny and Edgar Winter. 30 Cal. 4th 881, 134 Cal. Rptr. 2d 634, 69 P.3d 473, 476 (2003). The court held that "the comic books are transformative and entitled to First Amendment protection." It reasoned that the comic books "are not just conventional depictions of plaintiffs but contain significant expressive content other than plaintiffs' mere likenesses." . . .

Third, in *Kirby v. Sega of America, Inc.,* the California Court of Appeal applied the transformative use test to a video game in which the user controls the dancing of "Ulala," a reporter from outer space allegedly based on singer Kierin Kirby, whose "'signature' lyrical expression . . . is 'ooh la la.'" The court held that "Ulala is more than a mere likeness or literal depiction of Kirby," pointing to Ulala's "extremely tall, slender computer-generated physique," her "hairstyle and primary costume," her dance moves, and her role as "a space-age reporter in the 25th century," all of which were "unlike any public depiction of Kirby." "As in *Winter,* Ulala is a 'fanciful, creative character' who exists in the context of a unique and expressive video game."

Finally, in *No Doubt v. Activision Publishing, Inc.,* the California Court of Appeal addressed Activision's *Band Hero* video game. 192 Cal. App. 4th 1018, 122 Cal. Rptr. 3d 397, 400 (2011), *petition for review denied,* 2011 Cal. LEXIS 6100 (Cal. June 8, 2011) (No. B223996). In *Band Hero,* users simulate performing in a rock band in time with popular songs. Users choose from a number of avatars, some of which represent actual rock stars, including the members of the rock band No Doubt. Activision licensed No Doubt's likeness, but allegedly exceeded the scope of the license by permitting users to manipulate the No Doubt avatars to play any song in the game, solo or with members of other bands, and even to alter the avatars' voices. The court held that No Doubt's right of publicity prevailed despite Activision's First Amendment defense because the game was not "transformative" under the *Comedy III* test. It reasoned that the video game characters were "literal recreations of the band members," doing "the same activity by which the band achieved and maintains its fame." According to the court, the fact "that the avatars appear in the context of a videogame that contains many other creative elements[ ] does not transform the avatars into anything other than exact depictions of No Doubt's members doing exactly what they do as celebrities." The court concluded that "the expressive elements of the game remain manifestly subordinated to the overall goal of creating a conventional portrait of No Doubt so as to commercially exploit its fame." . . .

With these cases in mind as guidance, we conclude that EA's use of Keller's likeness does not contain significant transformative elements such that EA is entitled to the defense as a matter of law. The facts of *No Doubt* are very similar to those here. EA is alleged to have replicated Keller's physical characteristics in *NCAA Football*, just as the members of No Doubt are realistically portrayed in *Band Hero*. Here, as in *Band Hero*, users manipulate the characters in the performance of the same activity for which they are known in real life—playing football in this case, and performing in a rock band in *Band Hero*. The context in which the activity occurs is also similarly realistic—real venues in *Band Hero* and realistic depictions of actual football stadiums in *NCAA Football*. As the district court found, Keller is represented as "what he was: the starting quarterback for Arizona State" and Nebraska, and "the game's setting is identical to where the public found [Keller] during his collegiate career: on the football field."

The Third Circuit came to the same conclusion in *Hart v. Electronic Arts, Inc.*, 717 F.3d 141 (3d Cir. 2013). In *Hart*, EA faced a materially identical challenge under New Jersey right-of-publicity law, brought by former Rutgers quarterback Ryan Hart. ("*Keller* is simply [*Hart*] incarnated in California."). Though the Third Circuit was tasked with interpreting New Jersey law, the court looked to the transformative use test developed in California. *See id.* at 158 n. 23 (noting that the right-of-publicity laws are "strikingly similar . . . and protect similar interests" in New Jersey and California, and that "consequently [there is] no issue in applying balancing tests developed in California to New Jersey"); *see also id.* at 165 (holding that "the Transformative Use Test is the proper analytical framework to apply to cases such as the one at bar"). Applying the test, the court held that "the *NCAA Football* . . . games at issue . . . do not sufficiently transform [Hart]'s identity to escape the right of publicity claim," reversing the district court's grant of summary judgment to EA.

As we have, the Third Circuit considered the potentially transformative nature of the game as a whole, and the user's ability to alter avatar characteristics. Asserting that "the lack of transformative context is even more pronounced here than in *No Doubt*," and that "the ability to modify the avatar counts for little where the appeal of the game lies in users' ability to play as, or alongside [,] their preferred players or team," the Third Circuit agreed with us that these changes do not render the *NCAA Football* games sufficiently transformative to defeat a right-of-publicity claim. . . .

Given that *NCAA Football* realistically portrays college football players in the context of college football games, the district court was correct in concluding that EA cannot prevail as a matter of law based on the transformative use defense. . . .

AFFIRMED.

THOMAS, Circuit Judge, dissenting:

Because the creative and transformative elements of Electronic Arts' *NCAA Football* video game series predominate over the commercial use of the athletes' likenesses, the First Amendment protects EA from liability. Therefore, I respectfully dissent.

I

The First Amendment affords additional protection to *NCAA Football* because it involves a subject of substantial public interest: collegiate football. *Moore v. Univ. of Notre Dame*, 968 F. Supp. 1330, 1337 (N.D. Ind. 1997). Because football is a matter of public interest, the use of the images of athletes is entitled to constitutional protection, even if profits are involved. . . .

The majority confines its inquiry to how a single athlete's likeness is represented in the video game, rather than examining the transformative and creative elements in the video game as a whole. . . .

When EA's *NCAA Football* video game series is examined carefully, and put in proper context, I conclude that the creative and transformative elements of the games predominate over the commercial use of the likenesses of the athletes within the games. . . .

The college teams that are supplied in the game do replicate the actual college teams for that season, including virtual athletes who bear the statistical and physical dimensions of the actual college athletes. But, unlike their professional football counterparts in the *Madden NFL* series, the NCAA football players in these games are not identified.

The gamers can also change their abilities, appearances, and physical characteristics at will. Keller's impressive physical likeness can be morphed by the gamer into an overweight and slow virtual athlete, with anemic passing ability. And the gamer can create new virtual players out of whole cloth. Players can change teams. The gamer could pit Sam Keller against himself, or a stronger or weaker version of himself, on a different team. Or the gamer could play the game endlessly without ever encountering Keller's avatar. In the simulated games, the gamer controls not only the conduct of the game, but the weather, crowd noise, mascots, and other environmental factors. Of course, one may play the game leaving the players unaltered, pitting team against team. But, in this context as well, the work is one of historic fiction. The gamer controls the teams, players, and games.

Applying the *Comedy III* considerations to *NCAA Football* in proper holistic context, the considerations favor First Amendment protection. The athletic likenesses are but one of the raw materials from which the broader game is constructed. The work, considered as a whole, is primarily one of EA's own expression. The creative and transformative elements predominate over the commercial use of likenesses. The marketability and economic value of the game comes from the creative elements within, not from the pure commercial exploitation of a celebrity image. The game is not a conventional portrait of a celebrity, but a work consisting of many creative and transformative elements. . . .

Unlike the majority, I would not punish EA for the realism of its games and for the skill of the artists who created realistic settings for the football games. That the lifelike roar of the crowd and the crunch of pads contribute to the gamer's experience demonstrates how little of *NCAA Football* is driven by the particular likeness of Sam Keller, or any of the other plaintiffs, rather than by the game's artistic elements.

In short, considering the creative elements alone in this case satisfies the transformative use test in favor of First Amendment protection. . . .

NOTES AND QUESTIONS

1. *Analysis of* NCAA Student-Athlete Name & Likeness Litigation. Do you agree with the majority or dissent's decision and reasoning regarding the appropriate balance between creative expression protected by the First Amendment and non-protected unauthorized usage that may be actionable under state publicity rights laws? What are the policy and practical implications of their respective rulings? Which view is most consistent with *Zacchini, supra*?

2. C.B.C. Distribution and Marketing *Distinguished.* The Ninth Circuit majority opinion states:

> We similarly reject Judge Thomas's argument that Keller's right-of-publicity claim should give way to the First Amendment in light of the fact that "the essence of *NCAA Football* is founded on publicly available data." Judge Thomas compares *NCAA Football* to the fantasy baseball products that the Eighth Circuit deemed protected by the First Amendment in the face of a right-of-publicity claim in *C.B.C. Distribution and Marketing,* 505 F.3d at 823-24. But there is a big difference between a video game like *NCAA Football* and fantasy baseball products like those at issue in *C.B.C.* Those products merely "incorporate[d] the names along with performance and biographical data of actual major league baseball players." *NCAA Football,* on the other hand, uses virtual likenesses of actual college football players. It is seemingly true that each likeness is generated largely from publicly available data—though, as Judge Thomas acknowledges, EA solicits certain information directly from schools—but finding this fact dispositive would neuter the right of publicity in our digital world. Computer programmers with the appropriate expertise can create a realistic likeness of any celebrity using only publicly available data. If EA creates a virtual likeness of Tom Brady using only publicly available data—public images and videos of Brady—does EA have free reign to use that likeness in commercials without violating Brady's right of publicity? We think not, and thus must reject Judge Thomas's point about the public availability of much of the data used given that EA produced and used actual likenesses of the athletes involved.

724 F.3d at 1283, n. 2. Is the majority's reasoning convincing? See also *Electronic Arts v. Davis,* 775 F.3d 1172 (9th Cir. 2013), *cert. denied,* 136 S. Ct. 1448 (2016) ("historic teams" featured in Madden NFL games, which allows gamers to control avatars resembling retired NFL players, is not an "incidental use" protected by the First Amendment because their likenesses are "central to the creation of an accurate virtual simulation of an NFL game").

3. *Does the Broadcast of a Game or Sports Event Without Athletes' Consent Violate Their Right of Publicity?* In *In re NCAA Student–Athlete Name & Likeness Licensing Litigation,* 990 F. Supp. 2d 996 (N.D. Cal. 2013), the court held that a right of publicity claim by college football and basketball players arising out of the unauthorized use of their images in televised games is not preempted by the First Amendment or Copyright Act and may be recognized in some jurisdictions, although such a claim is not viable under California's statutory right of publicity law. In another case, the Sixth Circuit subsequently affirmed the dismissal of a claim that "college players have a 'right of publicity' in their

names and images as they might appear in television broadcasts of football or basketball games in which the plaintiffs participate," characterizing it as "a legal fantasy" under Tennessee law. *Marshall v. ESPN, Inc.,* 111 F. Supp. 3d 815 (M.D. Tenn. 2015), *aff'd,* 668 Fed. Appx. 155 (6th Cir. 2016).

Most courts have ruled that the Copyright Act preempts athletes' claims that unauthorized telecasts of games or athletic competitions in which they participated violates their publicity rights. See e.g., *Dryer v NFL,* 814 F.3d 938 (8th Cir. 2016); *Ray v. ESPN, Inc.,* 783 F.3d 1140 (8th Cir. 2015); *Baltimore Orioles, Inc. v. Major League Baseball Players Assn.,* 805 F.2d 663 (7th Cir. 1986); *Somerson v. McMahon,* 956 F. Supp. 2d 1345 (N.D. Ga. 2012). See also *Baiul v. NBC Sports,* 118 USPQ2d 1641 (S.D.N.Y. 2016) (figure skater's state law accounting, unjust enrichment, and conversion claims based on allegation that she has been deprived of royalties to which she is entitled based on television broadcaster's use and exploitation of motion picture recordings of her performance are preempted by the Copyright Act).

In *Baltimore Orioles,* the Seventh Circuit explained:

> [I]f a baseball game were not broadcast or were telecast without being recorded, the Players' performances similarly would not be fixed in tangible form and their rights of publicity would not be subject to preemption. By virtue of being videotaped, however, the Players' performances are fixed in tangible form, and any rights of publicity in their performances that are equivalent to the rights contained in the copyright of the telecast are preempted.

805 F.2d at 675.

4. *Unauthorized Sale of Photographs of Athletes Does Not Infringe Their Right of Publicity.* In *Maloney v. T3Media, Inc.,* 94 F. Supp. 3d. 1128 (C.D. Cal. 2015), *aff'd,* 853 F.3d 1004 (9th Cir. 2017), the court ruled that federal copyright law preempts the right of publicity claims of Catholic University men's basketball team members that won the 2001 NCAA Division III championship arising out of the unauthorized sale of their copyrighted photographs owned by the NCAA. Observing that there was no use of their likenesses "not wholly contained within the photographs" or "independent of the mere sale of the pictures," the court concluded: "Thus their right-of-publicity claims involve the same subject matter, i.e. the photographs, and the same rights, i.e. the display, reproduction, and distribution, encompassed by the Copyright Act. Consequently, these claims are preempted." 94 F. Supp. 3d at 1138-1140. In affirming, the Ninth Circuit cited and relied on *Ray* and *Dryer, supra,* to support its conclusion that "the right of publicity should be construed in accordance with the Restatement [Third] of Unfair Competition [§47], 'which limits liability to misappropriation for the purposes of trade' [that] almost perfectly distinguish[es] between the cases finding preemption and those permitting publicity-right claims to proceed." 853 F.3d at 1018. It explained that "the crucial distinction is not between categories of copyrightable works, but how those copyrighted works are used." *Id.*

5. *Unauthorized Copying and Inclusion of Athletes' Tattoos in Video Games.* In *Solid Oak Sketches, LLC v. 2K Games, Inc.,* 2018 WL 1626145 (S.D.N.Y.), the owner of copyright registrations for five tattoos realistically depicted on NBA players Eric Bledsoe, LeBron James, and Kenyon Martin in an NBA basketball simulation video game alleged that the game's developer and marketer infringed its rights. The court denied defendants' motion for judgment on

the pleadings, rejecting their fair use and de minimus copying defenses. Because of the inherent difficulties of conducting a side-by-side comparison of the video game and the tattoos, it concluded that extrinsic evidence is necessary to resolve the necessarily fact-intensive issues raised by these defenses.

PROBLEM 12-4

Consider whether the following use of player names and identities without authorization from the player, players association, or league violate any legally protected rights:

a. A minor league baseball league affixes the names and photos of members of its all-star team to merchandise such as T-shirts, mugs, and other souvenirs that are sold in the venue hosting its all-star game without their prior written authorization.

b. A company makes and sells bobblehead dolls depicting famous professional athletes and identifies them by name in the product's packaging.

c. A car dealer's giveaway of a football autographed by the starting quarterback of the local NFL team, who is paid to endorse another local dealer's vehicles, is advertised on the radio. The dealer was the successful bidder for the football at a local charity's fund raiser. All prospective customers who visit its showroom are eligible to win this prize.

d. A nationally circulated sports magazine does a feature story on the rigorous off-season workout program of an All-Pro NFL linebacker, which includes a sentence stating that he takes daily protein supplements. Next to the story, there is a paid advertisement for Brand X protein supplements. The player uses Brand Y protein supplements, but he is not an endorser of any brand of protein supplements.

e. In 2015, Pierre Garcon filed a class action suit on behalf of current NFL players against FanDuel, alleging misappropriation of their publicity rights, violation of §43 of the Lanham Act, and unjust enrichment by unauthorized usage of their names and playing statistics in its daily fantasy sports games. Which, if any, of these claims are likely to be successful?

f. Muhammad Ali Enterprises, LLC asserts that a video aired by Fox prior to Super Bowl LI, which featured images of famous NFL athletes and referred to them as "the greatest," along with images of the late Muhammad Ali, the deceased boxer widely known as "the greatest," violates his right of publicity. Is this claim likely to be successful?

g. A Pennsylvania artist makes and sells "Greek Freak" T-shirts with his painting, based on publicly available photographs, of the face of Milwaukee Bucks player Giannis Antetokounmpo, who is widely known as the "Greek Freak" and who won the 2019 NBA Most Valuable Player award. Antetokounmpo owns a federally registered trademark for "Greek Freak," which he licenses to be used in connection with the advertising and sale of a variety of merchandise, including hats and shirts. The Pennsylvania artist's T-shirts are sold online on his website as well as on his Facebook and Instagram pages without Antetokounmpo's authorization. Has the artist violated any of Antetokounmpo's legal rights?

TABLE OF CASES

Principal cases are indicated by italics.

INDEX